Krause – Minkus

STANDARD CATALOG OF®

U.S. STAMPS

2004 EDITION • LISTINGS 1845 – DATE

Steven R. Unkrich – Editor

Special Contributors

Herman Axelrod • Mike Bush • David A. Clark • Leroy P. Collins III • Francis J. Crown, Jr.
Tony L. Crumbley • James W. Crumpacker • John L. DuBois • David Eeles • Joel Hawkins • Peter Hoffman
Patricia A. Kaufmann • Joann Lenz • Ron Maifeld • Jerry Palazolo • Michael Perry
Peter W.W. Powell • Francis C. Pogue • Michael Rogers • Terry Scott • Richard Spielberg
Richard Stambaugh • Vernon Stoupe Jr. • Scott Templin • Marios Thedossiou • Dan Undersander

A fully illustrated collector's catalog for the postage stamps of the United States
with stories of the men, women, places and events that have shaped America's history.

© 2004 by Krause Publications

Published by

krause publications
An imprint of F+W Publications, Inc.

700 East State Street • Iola, WI 54990-0001
715-445-2214 • 888-457-2873
www.krause.com

Our toll-free number to place an order or obtain a free catalog is 800-258-0929.

Library of Congress Catalog Number: 2004093617
ISBN: 0-87349-706-6

Edited by Steven R. Unkrich
Designed by Patsy Howell

Printed in the United States of America

Contents

A note from the editor

Greetings and thank you for choosing the Krause-Minkus 7th Edition Standard Catalogue of U.S. Stamps. While the Krause-Minkus catalogues have been around for some time, this is my first edition as editor. The experience has been rewarding.

My involvement with philately over the last 15 years has been enlightening. Not satisfied with simply collecting, I organized programs, invited speakers and functioned as show chairman for my local stamp club for several years. I am involved with the APS mentor program and have occasionally helped out with their annual "stamp camp" held during the summer. A few of you might recognize my name from some of the articles which I've submitted to *Stamp Collector* over the last few years. I hold a membership in a variety of philatelic organizations, including the APS and USSS, plus other smaller philatelic groups.

But enough about me. Let's talk about the catalogue. As with the previous catalogue, features such as Decoding the Catalogue, a comprehensive Subject Index, and useful philatelic information for each stamp issue, have been updated. The introduction has been updated in the section dealing with Luminescence. Much of the print is in bold and has a larger font for easier reading. These features, among others, make this catalogue one of the easiest to understand and use.

This year's catalogue has several completely new features. Previously, there was a listing of Plate Number Coil Strips following the regular issues section. Known plate numbers and prices in Strips of 5, Strips of 3, and Used Singles were the only information listed. That listing has been replaced with a spreadsheet format which not only includes the plate numbers and prices, but also roll sizes, plate number interval, back number interval, tagging varieties, and prices for imperforate strips. For easy referencing, self-adhesive and gum-activated lists have been combined and sorted by denomination. I think our readers will find this new feature comprehensive and convenient.

Mint Bureau precancel prices have been added to individual listings. Rare city precancels and precancel varieties are priced. We have added prices for mint singles and plate blocks for sheet stamps, plus singles, pairs and line pairs for coils. Information is still needed on some early mint precancels.

The sections for Test Stamps and Test Booklets have been improved. No other catalogue provides such a comprehensive listing of US test material. New finds have been added along with a number of price changes. These sections will continue to improve thanks to the dedication of several individuals in the test/dummy study group.

Canal Zone Envelopes and Wrappers has been improved. Previous listings were not always helpful in describing the correct images. The proper information has been added to make this section easy to understand.

Many sections of the catalogue have been improved in this manner and will continue to improve. However, we need your feedback. New contributors are encouraged and appreciated. Comments and suggestions can be sent to me through Krause or by my personal email at Sunkrich@cinci.rr.com.

Finally, I would like to thank all of the contributors who helped me on this edition of the catalogue as well as those employees at Krause whose assistance was invaluable. Thank you.

Catalog Introduction

While such factors as age, quantity issued, scarcity and especially demand all have a bearing on the value of a given stamp or cover, the fundamental determinants of value for any given stamp are its grade and its condition. In general, the scarcer and more valuable the basic stamp, the greater the importance of grade or centering in determining its market value.

Grade is a rough measure of the relationship between the printed design of the stamp and its edges or margins, a characteristic that also is often referred to as a stamp's *centering*.

Generally speaking, the more nearly equal in width all margins of a stamp are, and the farther those equal margins are from the printed design, the more desirable the stamp will be to collectors. A stamp with unusually broad margins of identical width on all sides may sell for as much as 100 times the price of an otherwise identical stamp with unbalanced margins and perforations or, in the case of imperforate stamps, a copy with a straightedge cutting the printed design.

Condition refers to the overall appearance and quality of the stamp — the state of its health, so to speak — which can enhance or detract from the desirability (and hence the demand and value) of a stamp.

Stamp Grade

Values shown in this catalog reflect the prices that you may expect to pay for a listed stamp in a grade between **fine** (visibly off-center on two sides, with margins or perforations either just touching or barely clear of the printed design on one side) and **very fine** (barely off-center on one side, with all margins or perforations almost equally distant and well clear of the printed stamp design).

This intermediate grade, which has been the predominant grade in which stamps have been collected for more than a century, is referred to as **fine-to-very fine**, often abbreviated as "**f-vf.**" To define the term more explicitly, fine-to-very-fine stamps may be perceptibly off-center to one side, or very slightly off-center on two sides, with the stamp design printed clear of all sides and untouched by any of the margins. (Imperforate stamps graded f-vf will have at least two and usually three margins clear of the printed design.)

Stamps of grades lower than fine-to-very-fine (such as **very good** and **fine**) will usually sell for less than the f-vf copies that are priced here, whereas stamps of grades higher than fine-to-very fine (including **very fine** and the elusive **extremely fine** or **superb**) will sell for more than the stamps that are priced here.

Stamp Condition

Values shown in this catalog reflect the prices that you may expect to pay for a listed stamp in fault-free condition, clear of any detectable defects.

Defects of condition on stamps include (but are not necessarily limited to) tears, scrapes, thins (places where some of the paper is missing from the back of a stamp, often due to inept removal of a hinge), stains, foxing (a yellowish-brown staining) and so-called tropical toning (brown spots on the gum or perforation tips), absence of original gum, the presence of substantial hinge remnants, inclusions (pieces of foreign matter accidentally embedded in the stamp paper during manufacture), heavy, smeared or otherwise disfiguring cancellations or postal markings, pulled, torn or clipped perforations, creases, pinholes, missing corners, and faded, bleached or oxidated pigments and other color changelings (wherein the color of the stamp has changed after it was produced). Extremely defective stamps, with pieces missing, the design unrecognizable due to stains or postmarks and other serious shortcomings, may be virtually uncollectible and unsalable at any price, even if sound, well-centered examples of the same stamp have a high catalog value. The actual, nominal value of stamps in such poor condition has no relationship whatsoever to the values listed in this or any other catalog.

Stamps that have been repaired or altered (with filled thins, regumming, reperforation, repaired tears, bleaching to remove soiling or lighten a cancel, handprinted notes on the back of the stamp) also are generally regarded as defective and valued accordingly. Repaired stamps may be quite presentable and collectible, but they will generally have only a fraction of the value of a comparable, sound example of the same stamp. Knowingly attempting to represent and sell a repaired copy of a damaged stamp as a sound copy in original condition is fraud.

Just as defects and other undesirable traits detract from a stamp's condition, thereby diminishing its value, exceptionally desirable aspects of a stamp's condition can enhance that value, sometimes substantially.

Positive attributes to a stamp's condition can include unusually wide margins on all sides, exceptionally fresh-looking paper and ink color and sharpness of the printing, unusually crisp, sharp and regular perforations (especially on older stamps), the presence of margin selvage (especially with a plate number or other marginal printing of significance) and, on 19th-century stamps, most or all of the original gum.

Minkus Catalog Values

Values in the price columns for early stamps reflect either unused, original-gum fine-very fine stamps (UnFVF) or canceled fine-very fine stamps (UseFVF). For stamps issued since 1940, the price grades reflect mint never-hinged very fine (MNHVF) and canceled very fine (UseVF) stamps. Most unused stamps since 1940 are collected in mint, never-hinged condition, with full, undisturbed and unblemished original gum on the back.

Where a stamp or other catalog-listed item is seldom sold publicly, values appear in italics. Where adequate pricing information for a specific item has proven to be currently unobtainable (as in the case of a recently discovered error or, more prosaically, a common plate block in used condition) in the place of a value a line appears (—).

Every reasonable effort has been made to make the values in this catalog as accurate, realistic and up-to-date as possible. Sources for pricing information may include (but are not necessarily limited to) dealers' published retail price lists and advertisements, auction catalogs with published prices realized, and prices solicited from selected dealers, individuals and collector organizations. This information may have been reviewed for accuracy and consistency by individual specialist-collectors and specialist-dealers.

The minimum stamp value in this catalog (20¢) represents the cost to a retail stamp dealer to maintain in inventory and supply to a collector on demand a single copy of even the most common stamp in fault-free condition and a grade of fine-to-very-fine. The comparable minimum for a first day cover is $1. These figures more accurately reflect a dealer's cost of doing business than the scarcity of a given stamp or FDC.

Values in this catalog do not reflect the generally much lower cost of stamps acquired in mixtures, collections, bulk lots or other large-quantity purchases, nor stamps sold at unusually advantageous prices to attract additional business or offered as approvals, premiums, and so forth. In addition, some stamps can be acquired at lower prices through public auctions and mail-bid sales in which the collector may sometimes secure a lot at an uncontested minimum bid or reserve price.

The publishers of this catalog neither buy nor sell stamps.

Minkus Catalog Listings

Shown here is a typical listing from the catalog, displaying most of the kinds of information that this catalog can provide.

A. Year of Issue

B. Title of Issue, often as assigned by the U.S. Post Office Department or the U.S. Postal Service.

1995. LOVE CHERUB BOOKLET ISSUE *Self-adhesive booklet, offset and intaglio by Banknote Corporation of America, imperforate (die cut).*

 CM1695 *Love Cherub, short design*

CM1695		MNHVF	UseVF
(32¢)	**multicolored** phosphored paper	.50	.20
	FDC *(Feb. 1, 1995)*	1.90	
	n. Pane of 20, plus label (convertible booklet)	16.00	
	vn. Pane of 20, intaglio red (inscriptions) omitted	1,000.00	

C. Description of Issue, a brief synopsis of the person, place or thing depicted on or commemorated by the issue, with information on any special characteristics or significance and any series of which it is a part.

D. Printing details of the type of printing, printer(s) and gauge of the perforations or rouletting.

E. Minkus Catalog Number appears adjacent to the image of the stamp and also at the beginning of the corresponding price listing for stamps in a grade of fine-to-very-fine. Collectors can use the Minkus catalog numbers to organize their collections, and to identify stamps when buying, selling or exchanging stamps for their collections. Minkus catalog numbers also are used in Minkus stamp albums and supplements.

Each Minkus catalog number refers to a specific stamp. Varieties of that stamp are identified by suffixes appended to the basic catalog number (see item M). Where stamps that are similar in appearance are regarded as distinct issues, collectors are referred to the other issue or issues in a footnote (see item N).

With few exceptions, and unlike other catalogs, Minkus catalog numbers are assigned in strict chronological sequence, and definitive issues (stamps that may go back to press for additional printings at any time to furnish new stocks) are listed separately from commemorative issues (typically printed in a single, much smaller run than their definitive counterparts). Definitive series that extend over many years are identified by series name, but are listed in the order and at the intervals at which they were released by the U.S. Post Office Department or U.S. Postal Service. This avoids the confusing situation of clumps of stamps from an ongoing series being listed at random and arbitrary intervals throughout the catalog, and the necessity of introducing additional subnumbers (e.g., 123B, 123C, 123D) due to a miscalculation of the number of stamps in a given set or series. The stamps are organized into their natural sets in Minkus stamp albums and supplements.

Minkus catalog numbers consist of numerals only for regular definitive issues (e.g., Minkus 123, which refers to the Continental Bank Note Co. 5¢ Prussian blue Zachary Taylor definitive released in 1875). Other types of postage and revenue stamps listed in this catalog are indicated by a prefix. "CM" indicates commemorative stamps (e.g. Minkus CM123, which refers to the 3¢ blue Byrd Antarctic Expedition 11 commemorative of 1933), "A" indicates airmail stamps (e.g. Minkus A123, which refers to the 45¢ multicolored Hypersonic Airliner stamp in the se-tenant block of four from the Future Mail Transportation issue of 1989), and so on.

F. Description of Image, sometimes but not invariably the same as item B, is intended to represent the design title by which collectors refer to the individual stamp. In practice, many stamps are readily recognized both ways. For example, Minkus CM24 is well-known to stamp collectors both as the $1 denomination from the Trans-Mississippi commemoratives of 1898 (the title of the issue) and as the $1 black Western Cattle in Storm commemorative (the description of the image).

G. Denomination is the numeric value of the stamp (or, in the case of a lettered value issue or an un-valued issue, the equated value at time of issue).

H. Color. When a single color or up to three distinct colors are used they are listed, else the term "multicolor" is used.

I. Tagging. Where relevant, on selected U.S. stamps beginning in the 1960s, the term refers to the presence of a special ink on the face of the stamp visible only under ultraviolet light, used to position the envelope on which the stamp is affixed correctly so that the cancellation will be applied in automated facing-canceling equipment.

J. Quantity Printed is recorded, where available, typically for U.S. commemorative and airmail issues. For U.S. definitives, which may go back to press many times in the course of their working life, accurate figures are rarely available. Quantities include accurate counts and approximate estimates made by the U.S. Post Office Department and Postal Service, counts of quantities shipped but not including stamps returned, unused or destroyed when the issue was taken off sale and, in some cases, accurate counts of copies sold.

K. Catalog Values are expressed in U.S. dollars for unused stamps (UnFVF) and used stamps (UseFVF) in fine-to-very-fine condition for issues prior to 1940, and for mint never-hinged (MNHVF) and used (UseVF) for post 1940 releases. Unused stamps refer to those that have not been canceled with most of their original gum (for 19th century issues) or full original gum, lightly hinged (for early 20th century stamps). Stamps issued without gum are identified in the listings. Used stamps refer to those that have been canceled correctly in the course of performing their intended function.

L. Date of Issue is displayed, in most cases on the same line as that used for the basic first day cover listing.

M. Additional Varieties include (where relevant) plate blocks, se-tenant configurations, paper type, gum type, tagging presence and type, perforation varieties, major errors, plate flaws and varieties.

N. Footnotes convey additional important information about the stamp and related varieties or issues.

Introduction to Stamps

The ability to accurately identify a stamp is indispensible to your full enjoyment of and participation in the stamp hobby. Differences in printing, gum, paper, watermark, ink, perforation, luminescence and design variations that may be slight — but which are readily apparent to the trained eye — can be the key to getting the most out of the time you spend with your collection. They also can be the difference between a common stamp worth a handful of pennies and a rarity valued at thousands of dollars.

There is no substitute for the knowledge that you can gain from the experience of closely examining and working with stamps, not only those in your own collection, but also those that you can read about in philatelic literature and see on display at stamp shows and, if you are fortunate, in the albums of friends at the local stamp club.

The following text is intended to familiarize you with the basic considerations of collecting stamps and the terminology and jargon of the stamp hobby. Inquiries, suggestions and requests for additional clarifications may be addressed to Editor, Krause Minkus Stamp Catalog, Krause Publications, 700 E. State St., Iola WI 54990-0001. (www.krause.com)

Stamp Printing

All stamps may be characterized by the technique or techniques by which they are printed. Although others exist, a few primary printing technologies have been used, alone or in combination, on virtually all United States postal paper: intaglio; lithography; gravure; letterpress; and embossing. (Since 1989, holography also has been used to print the special foil patches that have served as stamp images on several U.S. stamped envelopes and stamps.)

Intaglio (also known as Line-Engraving, Engraving, Etching)

The first step in the intaglio process is creating a **master die**, a small, flat block of soft steel upon which the stamp design is recessed engraved in reverse. The original art intended for use on the stamp is photographically reduced to the appropriate size to serve as a tracing guide for the initial outline of the design on steel.

The highly skilled and detailed work of creating the master die is done by an engraver, who lightly traces the design on the steel, then slowly develops the fully detailed engraving, using gravers, burins and other small chisel-like tools to carve a fine pattern of precisely positioned grooves that collectively form the finished image.

At various points during the engraving process, the engraver hand-inks the dies and makes impressions to check his progress, thereby creating incomplete images of what will become the finished design, known as **progressive die proofs**.

After the engraving is complete, the soft steel of the master die is hardened greatly through various processes so that it will be able to withstand the stress and pressure of the subsequent operations needed to convert it into an intaglio printing plate.

Next, a **transfer roll** is prepared, consisting of a roll of soft steel mounted on a mandrel, which, as the term "transfer roll" implies, is used to transfer the engraved subject from the master die to the intaglio printing plate, a blank roll of soft steel, mounted at the center of a mandrel, which is a metal axle of lesser diameter. The mandrel is placed in a transfer press, in which it rotates freely, and the highly polished soft steel of the transfer roll is brought into contact with the hardened master die in the bed of the press.

The bed of the transfer press is slowly rocked back and forth under increasing pressure, forcing or "rocking in" the soft steel of the transfer roll in every finely engraved line of the hard master die, and eventually transferring the complete engraved image. The resulting design on the transfer roll, now positive in appearance (with its design components as they are intended to appear on the printed stamp), is referred to as a **relief transfer**, because the lines of engraving that were carved into the master die stand out on the completed roll. The soft steel of the transfer roll is hardened, as was the master die before it, after the number of relief transfers that are required have been created.

Because the relief is what is used to create the intaglio printing plate, any imperfections during the creation of the relief transfer may result in flaws that will appear on the finished stamps. A small fleck of foreign material present during the rocking-in process may leave a mark on the relief transfer. Similarly, imperfections in the steel of the transfer roll may cause the loss of part of the design from the master die. These flaws are known as **relief breaks**, which appear as small, uninked areas on the finished stamp. Reliefs also may be deliberately modified to minimize or rectify such flaws, resulting in what is referred to as an **altered relief**, the characteristics of which again will be expressed on the finished stamp.

When the transfer roll has been completed and hardened, it is used to rock in the design to a large plate of polished, soft steel, where it again appears in reversed form as on the original master die. Layout lines or position dots are placed to precisely locate the transfer roll over the plate, and may sometimes later appear on stamps if they are not burnished away during final plate preparation.

It is during this process that double transfers, shifted transfers and dropped transfers occur.

A **shifted transfer** on a plate is one that shows doubling of part of or all the design (typically one edge or corner of the design), usually because the relief transfer shifted slightly while the design was being rocked into the printing plate.

A similar effect also can be achieved on the plate when a defective transfer is incompletely removed, and a second transfer is rocked in over it. Any place where the engraving of the original

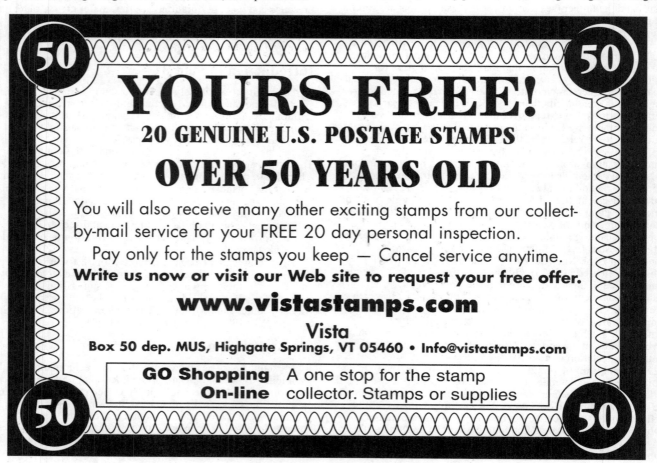

transfer remains and is not covered by the second transfer is likely to appear on the printed stamp as a **double transfer** (or, in cases where traces of two previous transfers exist, a **triple transfer**). Sometimes the printers need to delete the original transfer from a plate and enter it from scratch again. Should this completed transfer show some traces of the original impression, it is referred to as a **partial double transfer**.

A **dropped transfer** is one that is made normally but is misaligned with respect to the other designs on the plate. A stamp printed from such a dropped transfer will be noticably out of alignment with the stamps around it in the final sheet.

Failure to center the transfer roll correctly on the plate will result in the failure of the relief transfer to completely record all portions of the master die, resulting in the loss of the edge of the engraved design on the finished stamp. This is known as a **short transfer**.

The impressions of the transfer roll on the plate often are referred to as **subjects**, and as many of these subjects are transferred as are required for the final plate (typically 200 or 400 subjects on most plates up to the 1950s and 1960s).

When all the subjects have been put in place, all position dots, layout lines and any minor scratches, burrs or imperfections are removed from the printing surface. With the addition of marginal and other sheet markings including guide lines, arrows and plate numbers, a **plate proof** is printed to confirm that the plate is ready to produce stamps. (**Trial color proofs** may also be printed in a variety of colors other than those eventually selected for the finished stamps, to test the clarity and appearance of the finished print in different hues.) When these impressions are approved, the **printing plate** is machined for fitting onto a press, hardened and sent off to the plate vault, ready to be used.

On the press, the intaglio plate is inked, and its smooth surface is wiped clean, leaving ink only in the lines created by the relief transfer. Paper is then forced under pressure into the engraved recessed lines, the ink of which is transferred to the surface of the stamp paper. When dry, the lines of ink on the intaglio stamp remain slightly raised, giving such stamps their characteristic crisply ridged feel, and slight depressions (known as debossing) on the back of the stamp show where these inked lines appear on the front.

For the first century or so of U.S. intaglio stamp production, prior to the advent of modern, high-speed presses, paper used in intaglio stamp production often was moistened to facilitate the transfer of the ink, known as a **wet printing**. However, this sometimes led to uneven shrinkage by the time the stamps were perforated, resulting in improperly perforated stamps, or misperfs. More modern presses that supplanted early models do not require the use of moistened paper, thus giving rise to stamps that exist in both **wet print** and **dry print** versions.

Until 1915, only **flat press plates** were used to print engraved United States stamps. **Rotary press** printing was introduced in that year and slowly spread to account for an ever larger share of U.S. stamp production. Older **rotary press plates** require additional machining and are curved under pressure to fit the press cylinder. The stretching of the plate during the curving process distorts the subjects on it, with the result that stamps printed from rotary press plates usually are longer or wider than the same stamps printed from flat plate presses. The two basic versions of the Harding Memorial Issue (Minkus CM60 and CM62) provide a good example of this frequently encountered phenomenon. With the exception of the 1919 coil waste issues (Minkus 410-12), all rotary press issues up to 1953 have between one and four **gum breaker ridges** per stamp, impressed on the gum to break its even surface across the back of the stamp during manufacture to inhibit the natural tendency of rotary press-printed stamps to curl.

In the early days of intaglio flat-plate printing, heavily worn plates were sometimes spruced up to give additional service by re-entering their designs, reapplying the transfer roll to the old plate to sharpen worn-down designs. However, if the registration between the transfer roll and the engraving on the worn plate is not exact, or if the original transfer is not completely burnished flat before the design is rocked in again, the result is often a **re-entry**.

In a **re-entry**, another kind of **double transfer** can be created, which will appear on stamps printed from such a subject as a design with portions of the previous, worn design still visible.

If the alignment is exact and the placement of the transfer roll is true, a skillful re-entry may be all but undetectable.

Other, slightly less radical techniques of rendering a worn plate fit for continued use usually require that the plate be softened by having its temper drawn (generally by the precise application of heat and cooling) for retooling by hand, Among the techniques involved are **retouching** (the deepening or modification of lines by etching), and **recutting** (the deepening or alteration of lines with an engraving tool). If the resulting inked impression varies slightly from the original, it is referred to as a **re-engraved** stamp.

The intricate line patterns of intaglio printing are an excellent safeguard against would-be counterfeiters, but additional techniques also have been used to make intaglio stamps even more difficult to forge. One of these that was especially popular in the early days of U.S. stamp production was the incorporation of **lathework** and other **engine-turned designs** into the backgrounds and frames of various issues — complicated and precisely repeated designs produced on a mechanical device called an engraving engine. Examples of such patterns can clearly be seen in the frame and spandrels of the 1851 3¢ Washington stamps (Minkus 10-11) and the complex frame of the 1860 24¢ Washington (40).

Bicolored engraved stamps, such as the high values of the 1869 Pictorial issue (92-96), the 1901 PanAmerican commemoratives (CM26-31) and the 24¢ Jenny airmail stamp of 1918 (A3), are created by passing the printing sheet through a flat-bed press two times, once with a plate to print the frame, and a second time, with a second plate inked in a different color, to print the vignette at the center of the design. Performing either of these operations with the sheet incorrectly oriented would result in one part of the stamp being printed upside-down in relation to the rest of the design, creating the category of major error referred to as inverted-center (or inverted-frame) errors, or **inverts**, in common parlance.

Except for such bicolored issues, all other engraved U.S. stamps for more than a century were single-color designs until the advent of the **Giori Press** at the Bureau of Engraving and Printing in 1957. The Giori Press, capable of intaglio printing in two or three colors simultaneously, made its philatelic debut with the 4¢ 48-Star Flag commemorative (CM406) on July 4, 1957, and soon made a distinctive mark on U.S. postage stamps, including the multicolored high values of the Champions of Liberty series, the Conservation series and the American Credo series.

Another innovation in intaglio printing was the **Huck Multicolor Press**, first used in 1969 to print the 6¢ Angel Gabriel stamp from the 1969 Christmas issue (649), starting June 19, 1968, according to BEP data. The Huck Press not only printed in as many as nine colors and applied phosphorescent taggant to stamps, but it also gummed and perforated them all at the same time.

Lithography (also Photolithography, Offset Lithography, Stone Lithography, Dilitho, Planography, Collotype)

To produce a printed design, lithography uses the principle that oil and water do not mix. The design is produced from original artwork and transferred in an oily or greasy ink onto the printing surface, originally a prepared surface of stone (from which lithography takes its name) but now more frequently a metal surface. This greasy design can attract and hold the ink for transfer onto the surface to be printed, while the rest of the plate is moistened with an acidic fluid that repels such ink, corresponding to the uninked portions of the design. To create a plate, special transfer paper is used to make duplicates of the desired design from the original lithographic stone or plate, which are in turn assembled to create the final lithographic printing plate.

In a well-crafted lithographic stamp, the design may have fine and sharply printed lines as in an intaglio stamp, but its design also will have distinct, solidly inked areas that are not to be seen either on intaglio or on gravure issues. Also, unlike either intaglio printing (where lines of ink are raised on the surface of the stamp) or letterpress printing (where the inked areas are impressed into the paper, leaving a debossed surface on the back of the stamp), both sides of a stamp printed by lithography are completely flat.

Offset Lithography, also known as offset printing, refers to a refinement of the basic lithographic technique, whereby a greasy ink impression on a rubber blanket transfers the lithographic image from the printing surface to the paper. The first use of offset lithography on regular United States postage stamps took place with the Washington-Franklin definitives of 1918-20 (Minkus 403-09), when the technique was introduced due to manpower and material restrictions on intaglio printing caused by World War I. Offset lithography and intaglio were used together in printing the 5¢ Homemakers commemorative of 1964 (CM538) and the 1976 Bicentennial souvenir sheets (CM839-42), which showcased the ability of lithography to convey subtle textures, tints and tones.

Because of its greater ease of use and range of applications, offset lithography has largely replaced lithography today, and is now frequently referred to as simply "offset."

Gravure (including such variants as Photogravure, Rotogravure, Heliogravure)

The preparation of stamps for printing by gravure begins with the photographing of the intended design through a fine mesh, referred to as a dot-matrix screen, which renders it onto a metal plate as a pattern of tiny dots. A chemical process etches this fine dot or halftone pattern onto the plate, where it is converted into a multitude of shallow pits or depressions, known as **cells**, which hold the ink during the printing process.

In the gravure printing process, the paper pressed against the gravure plate lifts the ink out of the cells to produce the intended design. Deeper, larger cells produce the more heavily inked and frequently darker portions of the printed design. Shallow, small cells produce more lightly inked and often lightly colored areas on the stamp.

The chief use of gravure is in producing multicolored stamps. Using only the primary colors red, yellow and cyan (blue), along with black, gravure's dot pattern can be combined and recombined to furnish almost any color that might be required. These overlapping patterns of dots, clearly visible under magnification, are the key characteristic by which gravure stamps may be easily identified.

The first gravure U.S. stamps were printed by private firms: the 1967 5¢ Thomas Eakins commemorative (Minkus CM585), printed by Photogravure & Color Co. of Moonachie, N.J.; and the 1968 6¢ Walt Disney issue (CM602), printed by the Achrovure Division of Union-Camp Corp. in Englewood, N.J. In 1970, Guilford Gravure Inc. of Guilford, Conn., produced both the setenant Anti-Pollution issue (CM643-46) and all of the

Christmas stamps (655-59) for the Bureau of Engraving and Printing.

The following year, the BEP acquired the multicolor Andreotti Press, and began printing its own gravure stamps, the first of these being the 8¢ Missouri Statehood issue (CM654).

Letterpress (also known as Typography, Surface Printing, Flexography, Dry Offset, High Etch)

Essentially the opposite of intaglio printing, in letterpress printing it is the raised rather than the incised areas of the printing plate that are inked to print the finished design. In fact, the process of creating the printing plate is an inversion of the intaglio process as well, with an additional step in which the design is transferred to another surface before the creation of the transfer roll. This results in the transfer roll's having a recessed rather than a relief design, which means that the final plate will have the areas that are to be inked raised above rather than carved into the surface, similar to a rubber handstamp.

Reproducing a letterpress transfer electromechanically is referred to as **electrotype** or **stereotype** production, and these are then gathered together in the desired configuration to form the plate from which stamps are produced. A plate for letterpress printing, made using the assembled electrotypes, is referred to as an **electroplate**.

The first postage stamps for nationwide use to make use of letterpress printing were the first newspaper and periodical issues of 1865 (Minkus N1-4), which were printed by the National Bank Note Co. in combination with embossing and an engine-turned engraved design to create an almost forgery-proof set. The American Bank Note Co. also combined offset vignettes showing the flags with engraved frames in 1943-44 to produce the Overrun Countries series (CM251-63). More typically (and less dramatically), letterpress was used to create the Molly Pitcher and Hawaii Sesquicentennial overprints of 1928 (CM79-81), the Kansas-Nebraska overprints of 1929 (495-516) and the many different Bureau precancels used over the years.

As with a piece of paper printed using a handstamp or a typewriter, paper printed by letterpress will show a slight depression (debossing) in the printed portion of the printed side of the paper, and a slight elevation (embossing) on the reverse side of the paper. This is characteristic of letterpress.

Embossing (also Colorless Embossing, Blind Embossing, Relief Printing)

Not truly a printing technique (since, technically, ink need not be involved), embossing is, however, an important security technique used on U.S. postal paper (chiefly stamped envelopes). In embossing, a design is carved into a die, which is reproduced to yield a shallow, three-dimensional sculpture from which additional embossing dies are made. A similar back plate, or platen, mirroring the design is created, and the two sides are pressed together to create the embossed image (often with ink on the inside of the die in front, producing the inscribed, denominated printed collar around the embossed portrait or image).

Embossing also has been used on some U.S. stamps, including the first issue newspaper and periodical stamps of 1865.

Holography

The United States produced its first hologram stamps in 2000, 12 years after Austria issued the first one in the world, on Oct. 18, 1988. Brazil followed with a hologram sheetlet of three stamps on Oct. 14, 1989. Fernando Catta-Preta, now president of Trace Holographic Art & Design, Inc., was responsible for the production of both the Brazilian and American hologram stamps.

The United States also has issued four hologram envelopes, three of which used the same hologram scene, a Space Station and Shuttle. The vignette, on foil, was positioned inside the envelope and visible through a die-cut window at the upper right.

The denomination was printed to the left of the window on the envelope, first 25¢ on Dec. 3, 1989 (Minkus EN917), and then 29¢ on Jan. 21, 1992 (Minkus EN925) and 32¢ on Sept. 22, 1995 (Minkus EN945). The other U.S. envelope hologram design was

The first U.S. hologram stamp.

the 25¢ Football Issue (Minkus EN918) of Sept. 9, 1990, which had the same configuration but featured a hologram of a football scene and the National Football League Lombardi Trophy.

Holographic reproduction is technically printing, but ink is not used. Instead, a captured light wave interference pattern that emanated from a three-dimensional object is reproduced on thin foil through microscopic embossing. The resulting ghostly image is visible through reflected ambient light, not an ink laid on paper.

The holographer has three basic starting points — the use of flat images or pictures on different planes, much as a shadowbox; the use of a small three-dimensional model, which might be wafer-thin; and the use of computer-generated images to simulate an actual model.

First, an "H1" image of the model, lit by pure light from a laser, is made in an extremely high-resolution light-sensitive emulsion on a glass plate. A wave of light is essentially flat, but when it reflects off an object, it acquires the shape of that object. When this "deformed" object beam of light crosses an undistorted reference beam at the plate surface, an interference pattern is recorded in the film's emulsion. This pattern is similar to the expanding circular waves you'd see on the smooth surface of a lake if you were to throw two rocks into it. The interference pattern is like a "fingerprint" — an accurate representation of the two beams that created it. When the reference beam is reproduced by shining a light onto it, it "sculpts" this beam and reflects it exactly in the shape (the wavefront) of the other beam, the object beam that illuminated the object.

The H1 image is lined up with the model, and an "H2" image is made of it on another glass plate – a hologram of a hologram. This H2 plate is then silvered and electroplated, producing a thin sheet of nickel with a surface of silver. This coated plate then serves, again in the electroforming part of the process, to generate several copies, or shims as they are known in the industry. These are affixed to the printing cylinders, and embossed with heat and pressure into a polyester film.

Printing of the hologram portions of stamps takes place on a rotary embossing machine whose printing roll is extremely smooth, at the sub-micron level. Heating elements allow the polyester film to deform microscopically and therefore diffract white light into its chromatic components.

Finally, adhesive is applied to the holograms' backs, and they are die cut to shape and applied to the stamp sheet, which has been separately printed through traditional methods.

Under the right light conditions, the viewer sees a true three-dimensional "wavefront" sculpted, as it were, from the very light that illuminates it. Looking at an object and looking at a hologram are essentially the same. In both cases, the same wavefronts reach the viewer's eyes, but in the case of the hologram the object is not physically present.

Stamp Components and Characteristics

If a stamp's image is derived in large measure from its printing (and the techniques used), the rest of the characteristics that define it have to do with the materials used in the stamp's creation — ink, gum, paper and separation technique — and some of the key observable characteristics of these materials, including the watermark, the method of stamp separation and the gauge of its perforations or rouletting, as well as the presence or absence of luminescence.

Examples may be found of otherwise identical stamps that differ in only one or two subtle respects, creating, at the least, two interesting varieties to seek out for your album and, at the most, an opportunity for the observant stamp collector to pick out a gem amid a pile of perfectly common postage. Few of us may ever have such an experience, to be sure, but fortune favors those who have prepared. Contrarily, collectors who are unaware that a rarity exists will never find it.

Ink and Color

Ink is the basic stuff of printing, typically consisting of a finely powdered admixture or suspension of mineral, natural organic or synthetic organic pigment in a liquid solvent or base.

Ink is directly related to color. Many of the inks used in printing 19th-century stamps were mixed by hand to the closely guarded specifications of the private printing firms that did the work, and the color often varied perceptibly from batch to batch. This gave rise to at least some of the many collectible shades and hues found on a number of classic U.S. issues, such as the 24¢ Washington definitives (Minkus 54-56) of 1861-63.

This wealth of color varieties continued briefly even after the Bureau of Engraving and Printing assumed responsibility for printing virtually all U.S. stamps in 1894, best reflected in the many shades of the 2¢ issues of 1894 (170-74) and 1895-98 (189-92). Thereafter, inks became considerably more standardized and the number and variety of color varieties decreased markedly. Still, there are some highly collectible exceptions to this rule, such as the 1922 11¢ Hayes definitive (430).

One consequence of the arrival of single-press-run multicolor printing in the 1950s and 1960s was that minor variations in the individual colors on a stamp became harder to clearly discern, and in time came to be largely ignored, except on monochrome engraved stamps where such varieties remained easy to see. At the same time, however, there slowly developed a considerable increase in the number of color-omitted errors — errors that could never have taken place on monochrome intaglio stamps.

An important transition in inks took place in the 1970s under federal health regulations, when solvent-based inks used at the BEP were screened for potential toxicity and adverse health and environmental effects, and replaced with new, safer water-based inks of similar color. As a result, different shades can be seen on the versions of some values of the Prominent Americans and Americana definitives printed both before and after this period.

In fact, ink is not the only variable that determines the color of a stamp. The quantity of ink, the pressure with which it is applied, the type of paper and its moisture content at the time that the printing takes place and the type of base that carries the pigment in the ink all can affect the apparent color.

Of special concern to collectors are stamps printed in **fugitive ink**, which is soluble and tends to run or dissolve when the stamp is immersed in such otherwise innocuous liquids as water or watermark fluid. Fugitive inks include synthetic organic pigments produced as derivatives of nitrobenzene (aniline inks) and some photogravure stamps as well. Some modern U.S. commemoratives printed in purple can suffer ink damage when immersed in watermark fluid, including the 1963 5¢ Eleanor Roosevelt (CM522), 1964 5¢ Amateur Radio (CM541) and the 1980 15¢ Edith Wharton (CM953).

Stamps that have had their color altered after they were printed, intentionally or accidentally, are referred to as **color changelings**.

Generally such changelings occur as the result of a photochemical reaction (such as prolonged exposure to sunlight or artificial light) or chemical activity (such as the use of a cleaning agent or solvent to remove soiling or lighten a heavy cancel).

One especially notorious kind of accidental color changeling is often seen on 19th-century and early 20th-century yellow, orange and red U.S. stamps in which the oxidation of sulfur compounds in the pigment turns the image a deep brown shade, occasionally approaching black. The immersion of one of these affected stamps in a mild solution of hydrogen peroxide frequently will reverse the effects of such oxidation, though it may not return the stamp precisely to its original color.

While many collectors retain color changelings as curios, they are in fact nothing more than stamps in which the ink has been irreversibly damaged (much as the paper or perforations might be damaged). Color changelings have no place in an authentic collection of the production varieties of U.S. stamps.

Gum

Stamp gum is known in a wide range of textures, shades and degrees of reflectivity. In addition, the gum arabic used on many 19th-century and early 20th century U.S. stamps was applied to the stamps in two formulations — a harder mixture intended to remain dry in storage even during months of relatively high seasonal heat and humidity (summer gum), and a softer gum that was used on stamps produced for use in the drier, cooler months (winter gum). Most stamp gums today use dextrine or polyvinyl alcohol as a base.

Shiny and matte or dull-finish gum varieties are cataloged separately in those instances where both are known to be found on the same U.S. definitive stamps, even though such stamps may not be distinguishable in used condition or used on cover.

The gum on unused stamps encountered by collectors exists in a variety of conditions, which are listed, abbreviated and defined here in decreasing order of desirability:

Mint Never Hinged (MNH) stamps have pristine gum just as originally acquired from the post office, without a blemish, fingerprint or mark of any kind. Mint prices in this catalog for stamps issued since 1940 refer to stamps in this condition.

Lightly Hinged (LH) stamps have 50 percent to 100 percent of their original gum, but show a minor disturbance on the back, such as traces where a stamp hinge was previously located, so-called disturbed gum or a fingerprint. Prices in this catalog for unused stamps issued prior to 1940 are for stamps in this condition. Many earlier 19th-century stamps are less likely to have much of their original gum still intact.

Heavily Hinged (HH) stamps have less than 50 percent of their original gum and/or remnants of older non-peelable paper hinges still affixed to the back of the stamp.

All three of the preceding types of unused stamps are sometimes referred to as **original gum** stamps, their desirability and value increasing according to the the quantity and quality of the gum. However, not all unused stamps have original gum.

No Gum (NG) stamps are stamps from which the original gum has been removed. For purposes of saving the stamp, it may sometimes be advisable to soak off an especially heavy hinge remnant, which may otherwise cause a stamp to warp, buckle or even tear internally. Stamps issued without gum, such as the 1935 Farley issues (CM 142-61) and the Continental Bank Note Co. special printing of the 1875 newspaper and periodical stamps (SPN5-28), are for all practical purposes regarded as mint, never-hinged in that state.

Regummed (R, RG or RE) stamps are stamps from which the original gum has been removed and other gum has been added later. When it is clearly identified as such, there is nothing objectionable about a regummed stamp, and auction catalog realizations often seem to suggest that collectors are willing to pay a bit more for an expertly regummed stamp than for its NG counterpart.

However, it is fraud to knowingly represent and sell regummed stamps as original-gum copies, which is often attempted to obtain the considerably higher price that such OG stamps typically command. Similarly, it is fraudulent to chemically or otherwise remove a light cancellation from a stamp and offer it as unused. Both regumming and removal of cancellations have some skilled practitioners, which is why expertization is recommended for valuable mint stamps.

Paper

Paper, the medium for all printing, consists of dried sheets of processed vegetable fiber laid down on a fine screen from a water suspension. The two basic broad classifications of paper are **laid paper** in which the lines left by the screen during the papermaking process are still visible in transmitted light, and **wove paper**, which has no such visible grain or lines. Papers also may be categorized as thin or thick, soft or hard, and according to their naturally occurring color (as in the listings for some U.S. stamped envelopes).

A very thin, hard translucent paper known as **pelure** also has occasionally been used for U.S. stamps, including the 1847 5¢ and 10¢ St. Louis postmaster provisionals (Minkus PM28-29). **India paper** refers both to a softer, thin translucent paper used for pulling intaglio die and plate proofs and to a tougher, opaque, thin paper, rarely but occasionally used in U.S. stamp printing, including varieties of the 1851 3¢ and 12¢ Washington (10p, 17p).

In addition, **colored paper** has been deliberately selected for use in specific issues, as in the orange paper of the 1956 3¢ Nassau Hall issue (CM395), the light Venetian red paper used for the 1965 5¢ Dante issue (CM549) and the tan paper of the 1976 Telephone Centennial commemorative (CM836).

Ribbed paper, which has actual ridges on the front or back side of the stamp, or both, was used for some of the Continental Bank Note Co. issues of 1873 (119-30). The ribs are parallel and typically run horizontally across the stamp, although vertical ribbed paper is known as well on stamps including the CBNC 15¢ Daniel Webster (128).

Double paper has two-very different meanings. On the previously mentioned 1873 CBNC issues (119-30), it refers to a security paper patented by Charles F. Steel, in which a thin, weak surface paper and a thicker, stronger backing paper were bonded before printing. This produced a two-layer stamp, the printed design of which would be ruined if any attempt were made to clean a cancel after the stamp had been used.

The second meaning of double paper is in reference to the rotary presses that began producing U.S. stamps in 1915. Rotary presses print stamps on a continuous roll of paper, and when one roll of paper ends, the beginning of a new roll is spliced to the end of it so that production will not be interrupted. Stamps printed on the splice, where paper of the old and new rolls overlaps, are typically marked, cut out and discarded when the stamps are separated into sheets and panes. However, stamps printed across the splice do occasionally escape detection and survive to reach collectors, and these are known as **rotary press double paper** varieties.

Paper with silk fibers also was used in printing 1873 CNBC issues (119-30). As the name implies, this is paper with one or several long, colored silk threads embedded in it. In this it differs from some early U.S. revenue stamps printed on so-called "silk paper," in which more numerous short, colored fibers are impressed during the papermaking process. Although it has rarely been used on U.S. stamps, a third silk-related paper is **granite paper** of the sort found on the 1967 5¢ Lions International issue (CM576), in which the grayish paper is shot through with short red and blue silk fibers, mimicking the veins in the rock for which it is named.

In an effort to better control uneven paper shrinkage during stamp manufacturing, in 1909 the Bureau of Engraving and Printing tried using high rag-content paper in place of the wood fiber paper then chiefly used to print stamps. This experimental stock, used for some 1¢ to 15¢ definitives and a small part of the printing of the 1909 2¢ Lincoln Memorial commemorative (CM42), is referred to as **bluish paper**, although many people describe it as actually more gray in color, best seen in comparing the back of the stamp to others of the same period. See the note preceding Minkus 263-72. Unscrupulous fakers have sometimes attempted to simulate these pricey varieties of otherwise relatively inexpensive stamps by tinting them, so competent expertizing is recommended.

A very small number of the definitives of this same period were printed on a grayish, thick, hard stock known as China Clay paper, said to have mineral content of 5 percent to 20 percent rather than the 2 percent that was the standard at the time (although recent research conducted on paper from long-authenticated copies of these stamps failed to confirm the presence of such clay). These **China Clay paper** varieties, which appear even darker than the bluish paper varieties and also are known on the 1¢ to 15¢ definitives, are cataloged here as subvarieties of the 1908-09 definitives (237p-46p).

For information about Hi-Brite paper, fluorescent papers, phosphor-tagged and pre-phosphored papers, and other papers characterized by their response to ultraviolet light, please refer to the luminescence section of this introduction.

Watermarks

A watermark is a pattern laid down on paper during manufacturing. Shallow designs in metal, called bits, are woven into the screen on which the pulp is formed and drained. When the paper is dry and light is transmitted through it, the impression of the designs of these bits shows as a bright pattern in the paper, which is slightly thinner where the bits were positioned.

On most stamps, watermarks may best be seen by immersing them in **watermark fluid**, a nonaqueous fluid that will not moisten the gum on mint stamps. The fluid increases the transparency of the paper, to make watermarks show more clearly as dark patterns when the stamp is placed face-down in the fluid. (Look under Ink for fugitive inks, which notes U.S. stamps printed with inks that are soluble in watermark fluid.)

Single line USPS watermark

Double line USPS watermark

The widest range of U.S. watermarks on postal paper consists of those on U.S. postal stationery, including 1873-75 postal cards (PC 1-3), Official Mail envelopes of 1991 (PDEN82-83) and a wide range of watermarks on stamped envelopes of 1853-1968 (EN 1-855).

U.S. postage stamps are known with three watermarks: the double-line watermark "USPS" (for "U.S. Postage Stamp") used on the definitives of 1895-98 (187-210) and the single-line "USPS" watermark used on paper for the 1910-15 Washington-Franklin definitives (273-347); and the double-line watermark "USIR" (for "U.S. Internal Revenue") intended for use on U.S. revenue stamps but used in error for the 1895 6¢ Garfield (198w) and 8¢ Sherman (200w) and a 1951 printing of the $1 Woodrow Wilson stamp from the 1938 Presidential definitive series (553w).

Separation Methods

The makers of the earliest stamps apparently gave little concern to how their users would remove the stamps from the sheets or panes to affix them to mailing pieces. Simply tearing them off or using scissors was time-consuming and messy. The most popular method for separation chosen soon became so universally used that it provided the term for these original stamps – imperforate. After some experimentation, the size and number of holes in lines of perforations were generally standardized for stamp paper to allow the most efficient removal of stamps.

Mostly, perforations consist of round holes punched or g round into the paper, but other methods also have been used, such as hyphen-hole perforations (tiny, rectangular holes) and rouletting (slits, which may be straight or take other shapes). These last two are common on some revenue stamps.

In recent years, the growing popularity of self-adhesive stamps that require no application of moisture to adhere has led to the use of razor-sharp knives that pierce the stamps to allow their removal from a backing paper. This so-called die cutting can consist of straight cuts delineating a traditional rectangular stamp, irregular cuts around an odd-shaped stamp, and (the method preferred by the U.S. Postal Service) cuts that simulate the familiar perforations, usually called a **serpentine die cut**.

The technology of perforation and die cutting could be the subject of a long discourse. For most collectors, however, it is sufficient to know only a few terms and techniques.

Mainly, it is important to know how to gauge the perforations because their size may be the main difference between two catalog listings. A tool called a **perforation gauge** is used to measure the teeth of paper left around a stamp when it is torn along its perforations. If, for example, 10 teeth are found along two centimeters on the side of a stamp, it is said to measure "perf

Vertically Pair, Imperforate Between

Vertical Pair, Imperforate Horizontally

Vertical Pair, Imperforate

Horizontal Pair, Imperforate Between

Horizontal Pair, Imperforate Vertically

Horizontal Pair, Imperforate

peak —→

valley —→

Left: serpentine die-cut

Right: Straight die-cut

10." In defining a stamp's perforation measurement, the top horizontal side is given first, followed by the right side.

Looking at a single common U.S. stamp design, the Mother's Day issue of 1934, will provide illustration of how stamps that may look the same to the naked eye are actually different. The flat press version of this stamp (CM128) is perforated 11, meaning that its perforations measure 11 all around. However, the perforations on the rotary press version (CM127) measure 11x10∫, meaning that it is perf 11 on the top and 10 ∫ (or slightly fewer teeth) on the right side. In addition, a third version of the stamp (CM144) is imperforate.

The same perforation measurement applies to other methods of separation, including rouletting and serpentine-shaped die cutting.

Specialists refer to the protruding paper teeth of serpentine due-cut stamps as "peaks" that surround the indented "valleys." In some cases, coil stamps might have a different number of peaks on each side of the stamp. In these cases the number of peaks is used to distinguish the varieties. A stamp with 10 peaks on the left and 11 on the right would be designated as 10x11, for example. The designation does not correlate to the stamp's perforation gauge measurement.

The size of the holes (fine or coarse) and their quality (rough or clean cut) are also used in classifying stamps.

In addition to plate manufacturing errors, which include double impressions in the engraving, and printing errors, which include missing or inverted colors, and folding of the paper in the press, the widest variety of errors occurs in the perforation process. To aid with the explanation of these errors, we have the illustrations on the left and on page XVII. However, none of these errors occur on the stamp illustrated.

Especially in the case where an imperforate version of a same-design stamp has a value considerably more than the perforated version, unscrupulous people may trim the perforations off and purport it to be imperforate. It is always wise to collect imperforate stamps in multiples of at least two and to obtain a certificate of authenticity from a recognized philatelic authority.

Luminescence

Luminescence is the broad general term used to describe all facets of collecting using an ultraviolet light. Luminescence and its characteristics can be used both as an expertizing tool and as a form of collecting specialty. The term breaks down into two main subcategories, fluorescence and phosphorescence.

Fluorescent stamps glow while exposed to UV light, but not after the light source is removed. Phosphorescent stamps glow even after the source of light is removed. This glow can last for only a fraction of a second to close to a minute in some cases. The easiest way to tell the difference, however, is by the type of illumination used.

All luminescent stamps glow under shortwave UV light, but fluorescent stamps also glow under longwave UV light. Phosphorescent stamps do not. Different characteristics of the same stamp can be seen when both light sources are used.

To fully understand luminescence and its significance to stamp collectors it is important to know a bit of background on why stamps glow.

Fluorescence

As previously mentioned, fluorescence simply means that a stamp or piece of postal stationery exhibits some form of glow

when illuminated by longwave UV light. Longwave ultraviolet light is the same type of popular black light that is found in poster shops and roller skating rinks. It has no harmful effects to the eyes.

A number of different factors come into play to make a fluorescent stamp glow. Both organic and inorganic substances (either native to the paper or introduced) can react to light, including optical brighteners, ink components, certain pigments and a host of others.

Therefore, as a result of any of these factors, different printings of the same stamp can react differently to UV light, causing collectible varieties to occur. Some of these varieties include the so-called Hi-Brite papers (caused by optical brighteners), fluorescent ink types (caused by ink components) and fluorescent overprintings to aid mail processing. Some of these varieties are intentional, but many are not. They are a result of technological changes in stamp production. Most are highly collectible and some are even rare.

One note of caution, however: Fluorescent varieties on used stamps can be faked, so they are generally bought, sold and traded either as mint examples or on cover. As a result, listings are scarce for fluorescent varieties, and they are valued only as unused examples. Phosphorescent tagging (or the lack thereof) cannot be effectively faked, so listings for these items are more plentiful in both mint and used condition.

As an expertizing tool, the UV light can aid in uncovering many types of fakery, including filled thins, regumming, removed cancellations, altered designs and other repairs. The main principle behind this detection technique is that any paper exhibits some form of fluorescent reaction. None turns completely black under UV light.

Regardless of origin or technological mastery, every batch of paper has different characteristics and a specific weave. Any alteration to this unique pattern (or addition of other fibers) can easily be detected with fluorescent light.

Phosphorescence

Phosphorescent stamps are used by several countries, including the United States and Great Britain. Phosphorescent varieties can be seen only under shortwave UV light. Unlike longwave UV light, shortwave can cause temporary (but painful) eye damage if used improperly. Virtually any pair of prescription glasses provides adequate protection for most collecting activities. Even off-the-shelf reading glasses are usually adequate because they contain UV filters.

Unlike many fluorescent varieties, most stamps with phosphorescent characteristics were intentionally created as such. This is completely true with United States stamps.

After World War II, the U.S. Post Office Departmental faced with a huge challenge. Never before had there been such a high literacy rate among the population, with so much mail traveling through the system. Adding to this burden was the rapidly increasing volume of commercial mail. As a result, mail sorting and processing, which had always been a manual task, could no longer be accomplished in that manner.

By the late 1950s, the USPOD began to seriously explore ideas that had been kicked around since the late 1930s. These ideas ranged from magnetics to color recognition systems.

During the late 1950s, a contract was let to the Pitney-Bowes Corp. (of postage meter fame) to begin experimenting with fluorescence and phosphorescence, and the firm created a number of different stamp and postal stationery essays to test the viability of such systems for automated mail sorting and processing. In 1960 Pitney-Bowes felt satisfied their research was complete and on August 2 presented a formal proposal to the post office. This document outlined what tagging would accomplish to facilitate the separating, canceling, and sorting of mail. Fluorescence ultimately was dropped in favor of phosphorescence, and the actual tagging program on live U.S. stamps was piloted by National Cash Register Co. of Dayton, Ohio. Dayton was chosen not only because of the NCR

A specially tagged label (top) was issued Aug. 1, 1963, for use on airmail letters that did not bear the newly tagged stamp (left).

At right, misregistered tagging results in two stamps (second row) with no tagging

connection, but also because it had a large enough volume of mail to warrant such testing. These tests were to last several years, and the early tagged stamps could be found only in the Dayton area and at the Philatelic Division in Washington, D.C.

Although the first tagged stamp was released Aug. 1, 1963, in Dayton, Ohio, it was not the stamp that was being honored! There was no first-day cancel. The cancel simply read "FIRST DAY OF USE LUMINESCENT TAGGING." That stamp, a phosphorescent-coated version of the 8¢ Jet Over Capitol airmail stamp, Minkus A64z, was coated with a calcium silicate suspension that made the stamps glow a bright orange-red.

A special tagged airmail label also was released the same day and was used on many covers. The sole purpose of this early form of U.S. tagging was to separate airmail letters from standard mail. The tests were a success.

Within a few months, the purpose of experimental phosphorescent tagging was expanded to include the automatic facing and canceling of mail. In addition to separating air mail from other classes, mail no longer had to be presorted by hand so that the stamps were all in the same corner before they could be canceled. The new equipment could detect the stamp's location, determine that it was genuine, cancel it with one of four canceling heads, and send it to one of four trays (each of which could be faced in the same direction and ready for sorting). If a genuine stamp was not detected in a proper location, the mail would be sent to a fifth tray for a clerk's individual attention. A new form of taggant was introduced for this purpose. It was a suspension of zinc orthosilicate, which glows a bright greenish yellow under shortwave UV light. Thus airmail and standard mail could still be separated (by the color of the glow) and all letters could be faced and canceled.

Since both types of taggant were mineralogical derivatives, they could not be dissolved to form a solution; they had to be a suspension. A transparent lacquer was chosen as the carrier. Also, as mineralogical derivatives, the two compounds were highly abrasive. This came into play later, with different forms of tagging created to avoid such wear.

This tagged lacquer was applied by a color station on the printing press (sometimes as a separate press run) after all other colors were printed.

On Oct. 26, 1963, the first full printing run of tagged stamps was produced. It was the 5¢ City Mail Delivery commemorative, Minkus CM524. As a result, the first untagged errors also were produced, where no tagging was applied to some stamps. Even though the taggant itself is invisible under standard light, its absence as an untagged error is classified as a form of color-omitted error.

Tagging continued to be an experimental application for several years. Most issues that were released with tagging also exist as issued varieties without tagging, and some of the tagged varieties have become scarce.

By January 1967, stamp production was converted to printing all stamps (except those intended to be precanceled) as phosphorescent tagged issues. By 1969, most post offices had the special facing and canceling equipment designed for use with tagged stamps. By 1973, even the high-value Prominent Americans series stamps had been released as tagged stamps.

There now are numerous types of applications of taggant, each a separate and collectible type, and some stamps exist with more than one type.

The earliest tagged stamps featured overall tagging. This simply means that when a single stamp is viewed under UV light, the entire surface is coated. Several types of this overall tagging were used and are distinguished and collected by specialists.

One major variety of this type of tagging occurs on several issues, most notably the 5¢ National Park Service issue, Minkus CM565z. The basic stamp was untagged, but tagging could be applied at two different stages of production.

Normally **overall tagging** was applied to the stamps after printing, but before perforating. The second, and scarcer, type was tagged after perforating (TAP). This allowed tagging to seep through the perforation holes and leave some tagging on the gum side. Also, some markings and tagging flaws can be seen on the face-side of the stamp where perforation hole paper (chad) affected the application. Both types are listed by Minkus and are collected by specialists.

There are three major types of overall tagging.

Type I tagging. Initially, taggant was applied with four rubber mats that, as a unit, covered most of the same area as the printing plates. Since each mat covered less than 25 percent of the printing area, untagged borders remained around each side of the panes. On stamps, the tagging is heavy and often visible in normal light; under UV it is clear and bright.

Type II tagging. To improve coverage, a continuous silicone roller was designed that only left untagged areas along with two parallel outer web margins. Improper setting of this roller, however, could also leave significant untagged areas along the pane edges, so a wider roll (Type IIa) was developed that left little, if any, untagged area. Both Type II and IIa tagging is bright but often grainy.

Type III tagging. Tagging was also applied using a pair of curved steel plates like those used for printing stamps. Depending on how well these plates were registered with the printing plates, there can be either no blank margins are quite wide ones (similar to Type II). If the plates were not well registered with the printing plates cross-web joint lines appear the stamps either as a bright hot line or a dark line. The tagging compound is usually heavy and often visible in normal light; under UV it is dull and blurred.

As a direct result of the abrasive nature of taggant on perforating and processing equipment, production shifted to other forms of tagging, the most common being block-over-vignette tagging (**block tagging** for short). This is where most of the surface of a stamp is coated with taggant, but is in the form of a block that does not extend over the perforations. Various sizes of tagging blocks have been used over the years.

Another form of tagging related to block tagging is **cut-to-shape tagging**. This type is one of the more visually stunning of the many that have been tried. With cut-to-shape tagging, the tagging rollers or mats are cut to match a specific area on a stamp design. Recent examples of this form of tagging are the 1999 American Glass or the bugs (CM2072-75), and Insects & Spiders stamps (CM2098), where the taggant covers only the bottles on each stamp.

Some stamps, such as the 1973 Mail Order commemorative, feature a form of **bar tagging** that extends across the center portion of the stamp as a horizontal bar.

The advantages of these two forms of tagging are that a portion of the stamp design is not covered by taggant, which allows cancellation ink to penetrate the surface of the paper. Remember that taggant is suspended in lacquer, which creates an effective barrier between cancel and paper.

A less-frequently used form of tagging involves including the tagging ink in one of the pigmented printing inks. This was most frequently used on U.S. postal cards, but was tried on several stamps as early as 1968, with the release of the 6¢ Leif Erickson issue (CM606).

Although such an inclusion saves a production step and is effective, any pigment affects the visible characteristics of the tagging. Dark colors can so overpower the taggant that it does not give off a strong enough signal to trigger automated equipment.

Beginning with an experimental test stamp in 1987, Minkus 876, the U.S. Postal Service began using paper with the taggant already applied before printing. That stamp, a major variety of the then-current 22¢ Flag over Capitol coil, incorporated a "T" at the bottom of each stamp to designate "Test."

Although that particular form of coated, tagged paper (from England) proved to be too costly to utilize for most issues, the USPS was convinced it wanted to move forward on this form of tagging. Simultaneously, stamp production was reverting from block tagging to overall tagging on many issues, since the abrasive nature of taggant was not as much of a consideration on modern, high-speed equipment. As a result, numerous definitive stamps (particularly the Great Americans series) exist with more than one type of tagging.

By 1989, when the 25¢ Flag over Yosemite definitive, Minkus 891, was released, the USPS was ready to roll out production of stamps printed on phosphored papers. Several different types of these papers exist (both coated and uncoated), and specialists still don't fully agree on correct terminology. But each of these is a collectible type, and at least one stamp (the engraved 25¢ Flag over Mount Rushmore) was printed on both.

In some cases, where the stamp design is particularly dark, stamps printed on phosphored papers have been block tagged over the printing as well to ensure a strong enough signal.

All this means there's a whole new world of beautiful collectible stamps available by simply turning on your UV lamp. Just take the time to get to know the stamps and the listings… and keep us posted on your findings. There are more discoveries to be made!

In addition to all the basic types of tagging, there are a number of tagging freaks and errors available.

Besides untagged errors, which exist for most tagged stamps, there also are stamps that were never intended to be tagged but are. This is primarily because they've been accidentally printed on tagged paper. Recently this occurred with the 10¢ Eagle and Shield self-adhesive, (Minkus 1205).

Another form of tagging error (affecting only two stamps so far) is the wrong taggant. The 26¢ Rushmore airmail and 13¢ Letters airmail (booklet) both exist with the zinc-orthosilicate (greenish-yellow) taggant, rather than the calcium silicate (orange-red) taggant intended for them. These stamps, which can't be distinguished under normal light, are truly rare.

The most common form of tagging freak is misregistered tagging, which occurs when the tagging mats are out of alignment with the printing plates. Because these stamps look normal under standard light and give off an adequate tagging signal, they were rarely caught and destroyed by the Bureau of Engraving and Printing. Many of these items are quite visually stunning.

Tagging also can be used as an effective tool for identifying stamps. Different types of stamps printed by different presses are usually easily distinguished by their tagging types. For example, the 14¢ Ice Boat stamp of the Transportation coil series, Minkus 827 and 827A, are easily distinguished without having to pull out a millimeter gauge to measure design width. The original (wider) version printed from the Cottrell presses has overall tagging. The later B-press printings (narrower) has block tagging. There are many other examples as well.

All in all, tagging on U.S. stamps forms a fascinating and colorful collecting specialty that can be as inexpensive or as expensive as you want it to be. There's also the constant thrill of the chase involved because there's always a chance of making a new discovery.

Postmasters' Provisionals

Although the first government-issued adhesive stamps did not appear until 1847, the postmaster at New York City began using his own adhesives in July 1845, immediately after the Congressional act establishing the new postal rates. A number of postmasters in other cities also used either hand-stamps or adhesives of their own design. They are listed here in alphabetical order.

1846. ALEXANDRIA, VA. ISSUE Postmaster Daniel Bryan issued *typeset, imperforate* stamps without gum. Known copies of stamps are cut to shape. The circle of the 5¢ black-on-buff is found with 39 (Type I) or 40 asterisks (Type II).

PM1-PM2

		UnFVF	UseFVF
PM1			
5¢	**black,** on buff paper, Type I	78,000.00	—
	v. Type II		
PM2		UnFVF	UseFVF
5¢	**black,** on blue paper, Type II	—	—

1846. ANNAPOLIS, MD. ISSUE Postmaster Martin E. Revell issued red stamps printed onto the upper right corner of white envelopes. Envelopes with circular design and figure "2" hand-stamped are known and believed to be locals. Blue circular designs without numeral or "PAID" were used as postmarks.

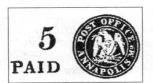

PM3

		UnFVF	UseFVF
PM3			
5¢	**carmine red**		225,000.00

1845. BALTIMORE, MD. ISSUE Envelopes in various shades of paper with the signature of the postmaster, James M. Buchanan, printed in black, blue or red. Colors listed below are those of the "PAID" numeral, and oval.

PM4-PM5

		UnFVF	UseFVF
PM4		UnFVF	UseFVF
5¢	blue	—	7,000.00
PM5		UnFVF	UseFVF
5¢	red	—	10,000.00
PM6		UnFVF	UseFVF
5¢	black	—	18,000.00
PM7		UnFVF	UseFVF
5¢	blue +5¢ blue	—	—
PM8		UnFVF	UseFVF
10¢	red	—	20,000.00
PM9		UnFVF	UseFVF
10¢	blue	—	17,000.00
PM10		UnFVF	UseFVF
10¢	black	—	—

1846. ADHESIVE STAMP ISSUE Adhesive stamps *printed by intaglio on white or bluish papers, and imperforate.* Eleven varieties of the 5¢ and five varieties of the 10¢ stamps are known.

PM11

		UnFVF	UseFVF
PM11		UnFVF	UseFVF
5¢	**black,** on white paper	—	7,500.00
	p. Bluish paper	65,000.00	7,500.00
PM12		UnFVF	UseFVF
10¢	**black,** on white paper	—	55,000.00
	p. Bluish paper	—	60,000.00

1846. BOSCAWEN, N.H. ISSUE Postmaster Worcester Webster issued a *typeset, imperforate* stamp of which only one copy is known.

PM13

		UnFVF	UseFVF
PM13		UnFVF	UseFVF
5¢	**dull blue**	—225,000.00	

1846. BRATTLEBORO, VT. ISSUE Postmaster Frederick N. Palmer issued *intaglio, imperforate* stamps printed from plates of 10 separately engraved subjects. The imprint "Eng'd by Thos. Chubbuck, Bratto," appears below the middle stamp of the bottom row. Eleven varieties are known.

PM14

		UnFVF	UseFVF
PM14		UnFVF	UseFVF
5¢	**black,** on buff paper	—	10,000.00
	On cover	—	35,000.00

1846. LOCKPORT, N.Y. ISSUE Postmaster Hezekiah W. Scovell issued adhesive labels with double-lined oval hand-stamped in red, "PAID" in black, and a hand-written "5." One copy and other fragments are known.

PM 15

		UnFVF	UseFVF
PM15		UnFVF	UseFVF
5¢	**red,** on buff paper, on cover	—225,000.00	

1846. MILLBURY, MASS. ISSUE Postmaster Asa H. Waters issued *imperforate stamps printed singly from a woodcut on a hand press.*

PM16 *George Washington*

		UnFVF	UseFVF
PM16		UnFVF	UseFVF
5¢	**black,** on bluish paper	135,000.00	25,000.00
	On cover	—	90,000.00

1846. NEW HAVEN, CONN. ISSUE Postmaster Edward A. Mitchell used a brass hand-stamp to impress envelopes with his provisional stamp as the envelopes were brought to the post office. The postmaster's signature was added to prevent forgery. Reprints are known having been made at various times between 1871 and 1932.

PM17-18

PM17
		UnFVF	UseFVF
5¢	red	—	75,000.00

PM18
		UnFVF	UseFVF
5¢	blue, on buff paper	—	110,000.00

1845. NEW YORK, N.Y., GEORGE WASHINGTON ISSUE Robert H.
Morris was the first postmaster to issue adhesive stamps as early as
July 15, 1845. They featured George Washington's portrait, adapted
from the then-current banknotes. The New York provisionals were
also used by postmasters at Albany, Boston, Philadelphia,
Washington, and probably other cities with a view of testing the
practical usage of adhesive stamps. Reprints in black, blue, green,
red, and brown were struck from a new plate.

The original stamps were *printed by intaglio* from plates of 40 by
Rawdon, Wright & Hatch. They were *imperforate* and usually initialed
"A.C.M." (Alonzo Castle Monson, a clerk in the post office) before
sale.

PM19 *George Washington*

PM19
		UnFVF	UseFVF
5¢	black, on bluish paper	1,300.00	500.00
	On cover	—	650.00
	Pair	5,250.00	1,300.00
a.	Signed "R.H.M."	12,500.00	3,000.00
b.	without signature	3,200.00	750.00
p.	blue paper	6,500.00	3,500.00
p1.	gray paper	5,250.00	2,000.00

1846. PROVIDENCE, R.I. ISSUE Postmaster Welcome B. Sayles
issued *intaglio-printed, imperforate* stamps produced from copper
plates containing 12 subjects. The stamps were engraved directly
onto the plate.

PM20
		UnFVF	UseFVF
5¢	black	375.00	1,750.00

PM21
		UnFVF	UseFVF
10¢	black	1,200.00	15,000.00
	Pair, 1 each 5¢ & 10¢	1,850.00	—

Reprints with initials on the back were made in 1898.

1845-46. ST. LOUIS, MO. ISSUE Postmaster John M. Wimer
issued *imperforate* stamps printed from copper plates of six subjects.
Varieties of each stamp are known. *Wove paper.*

PM22-PM29
Missouri coat of arms

PM22
		UnFVF	UseFVF
5¢	black, on greenish paper	6,500.00	4,250.00

PM23
		UnFVF	UseFVF
10¢	black, on greenish paper	6,500.00	3,750.00

PM24
		UnFVF	UseFVF
20¢	black, on greenish paper	—	30,000.00

1846. ST. LOUIS, MO. ISSUE Previous stamps in new paper color.
Varieties exist.

PM25
		UnFVF	UseFVF
5¢	black, on gray lilac paper	—	5,000.00

PM26
		UnFVF	UseFVF
10¢	black, on gray lilac paper	5,000.00	2,500.00

PM27
		UnFVF	UseFVF
20¢	black, on gray lilac paper	—	22,500.00

1847. ST. LOUIS, MO. ISSUE Previous stamp designs on pelure
paper.

PM28
		UnFVF	UseFVF
5¢	black, on bluish paper	—	6,500.00

PM29
		UnFVF	UseFVF
10¢	black, on bluish paper	—	6,500.00

Regular Postal Issues

The First Government stamps were put into use early in July 1847. They superseded Postmasters' Provisionals and other stamps which were thereafter not tolerated by the Postmaster General. The 5¢ stamp paid for carrying an ordinary letter up to 300 miles, and the 10¢ value was used for letters requiring higher postage.

Rawdon, Wright, Hatch & Edson of New York engraved the stamps and printed them in sheets of 200, which were cut into panes of 100 before distribution to the post offices. *The stamps were printed on thin, bluish wove paper. They were unwatermarked and imperforate, intaglio.*

1847. BENJAMIN FRANKLIN ISSUE

1 Benjamin Franklin, first postmaster general, after painting by James B. Longacre

1		UnFVF	UseFVF
5¢	**red brown**	6,000.00	525.00
	orange brown	6,000.00	525.00
	black brown	6,000.00	525.00
	bright orange brown	7,500.00	850.00
	bright reddish brown	—	—
	brown orange	—	1,400.00
	dark brown	6,500.00	625.00
	dark brown orange	—	—
	dark olive brown	—	—
	gray brown	7,000.00	650.00
	orange	—	—
	reddish brown	—	—
	On cover, numeral *5* cancel	—	600.00
	Mark in "S" at upper right	5,000.00	550.00
	Double impression	—	—
	Double transfer, top frame line	—	750.00
	Double transfer, top and bottom frame lines	—	750.00
	Double transfer, bottom and lower part of left frame line	—	3,000.00
	Double transfer, top, bottom, left frame lines	—	3,000.00
	Double transfer. "U," "POST OFFICE," and left numeral	—	1,500.00
	Double transfer, top and upper part of side frame lines, "U" "POST OFFICE"	—	—
	FDC *(July 1, 1847)*		
	Earliest known usage: *July 7, 1847*		

1875. BENJAMIN FRANKLIN SPECIAL PRINTING ISSUE Special Printing of the 1847 Regular Issue. New dies were engraved, and the stamps were printed by the Bureau of Engraving and Printing on *gray-blue paper. They are imperforate, without gum and both taller and narrower than the originals.* Intaglio. Reproductions on laid paper are known. Not valid for postage.

1 Original (1847): The top edge of Franklin's shirt touches the frame on a level with the top of the "F" of "FIVE."

SP1 Reproduction (1875): The top of the shirt is on a level with the top of the figure "5."

SP1		UnFVF	UseFVF
5¢	**red brown** (4,779 copies sold)	700.00	
	brown	700.00	
	dark brown	700.00	

1847. GEORGE WASHINGTON ISSUE

2 George Washington, first president of the United States, after painting by Gilbert Stuart, Boston Museum of Fine Arts

2		UnFVF	UseFVF
10¢	**black**	27,500.00	1,200.00
	gray black	27,500.00	1,200.00
	greenish black	—	1,750.00
	On cover		1,800.00
	Mark across lips	—	1,800.00
	Mark in necktie	—	1,800.00
	Short transfer at top	18,000.00	1,250.00
	Vertical line through second "F" of "OFFICE"	—	1,400.00
	Double transfer, left and bottom frame line	—	2,000.00
	Double transfer, "POST OFFICE"	—	2,500.00
	Double transfer, "X" at lower right	—	2,000.00
	v. Diagonal bisect on cover		13,000.00
	v1. Horizontal bisect on cover		—
	v2. Vertical bisect on cover		35,000.00

Government imitations of the 5¢ (in blue) and 10¢ (in Venetian red) were printed in 1947 and are listed as CM290 in the commemorative stamp section.

Note: The earliest known use of any U.S. stamp is a pen-canceled pair of No. 2 with a New York City postmark of "July 2," 1847, sent to Indianapolis, Ind.

1875. GEORGE WASHINGTON SPECIAL PRINTING ISSUE

2 Original (1847): The left and right vertical outlines of the coat point at the "T" of "TEN" and between the "T" and "S" of "CENTS," respectively.

SP2 Reproduction (1875): Above lines point to the right edge of "X" and to the center of the "S" of "CENTS."

SP2		UnFVF	UseFVF
10¢	**black** (3,883 copies sold)	900.00	
	gray black	900.00	

1851. BENJAMIN FRANKLIN ISSUE The 1851-57 Regular Issue consisted of 1¢, 3¢, 5¢, 10¢, and 12¢ denominations, issued to cover the needs of a rapidly expanding postal service.

While the production methods of the day were excellent, they were not of uniform consistency. As a result, more than one type of some of the stamps are recognized by collectors. It will add to your pleasure to determine the correct types of your stamps through the use of illustrations in this catalog.

Toppan, Carpenter, Casilear & Co. printed the stamps on unwatermarked paper. Intaglio, imperforate.

3, 18 Benjamin Franklin, after bust by Jean Antoine Houdon. For detailed descriptions of Types I-V, see Nos. 3-9 and 18-24.

DECODING THE CATALOG

Although the United States had adhesive postages stamps as early as 1842, our first general-issue adhesives — a 5¢ stamp picturing Benjamin Franklin and a 10¢ stamp depicting George Washington —were released July 1, 1847.

The designs, featuring our nation's first postmaster general and first president, were appropriate selections for our first stamps. These issues, Minkus Nos. 1 and 2, were immediately popular. The firm Rawdon, Wright, Hatch and Edson printed them. The 5¢ stamp paid the half-ounce single-letter rate for distances less than 300 miles; the 10¢ paid the same rate for letters traveling more than 300 miles.

Although there is no real problem with identification, our first stamps were reproduced in 1875 as a part of the great centennial celebration for 1876. These new stamps, Minkus SP1 and SP2, are designated as special printings.

The U.S. Post Office Dept. wanted all existing U.S. stamps reprinted for sale to collectors (but not as valid postage), but the original dies for these stamps were no longer available, so the Bureau of Engraving and Printing had to create entirely new dies. The results were predictable, of course: The resulting stamps have numerous differences from the originals.

Most notably, the 1875 versions were printed on an ungummed, slightly bluish paper. Since the 1875 stamps were not valid for postage, most are unused (although some bear cancels). Also, the design size is different. The originals measure 18 millimeters by 23 1/2 mm, while the 1875 versions are taller and shorter (18 1/2 mm by 23 1/2 mm).

Numerous differences are easily spotted in the engravings. These include (on the 5¢) a very differently shaped shirt lace and a more rounded eye on the re-engraved. On the 10¢, there are many mouth and eye differences. The left edge of the coat is straighter on the 1847 version. The initials are more clearly seen on both originals.

3 *Type I is the most complete design of the various types of this stamp. It shows the full scroll work at the top and bottom of the design. The ornaments in the upper right corner are "doubled."*

3

		UnFVF	UseFVF
1¢	**blue** Type I	175,000.00	57,500.00
	dark blue	—	—
	pale blue	—	—
	On cover		52,000.00
	Pair, one each Type I and Type II		70,000.00
	FDC *(July 1, 1851)*		

1857. BENJAMIN FRANKLIN TYPE IA REGULAR ISSUE

4, 19 *Type Ia has the design complete at the bottom but incomplete at the top.*

4

		UnFVF	UseFVF
1¢	**blue** Type Ia	35,000.00	9,500.00
	On cover		14,000.00
	Curl on "C"	37,500.00	11,000.00
	Curl on shoulder	37,500.00	11,000.00
	Earliest documented cover: *April 19, 1857*		

1851. BENJAMIN FRANKLIN TYPE IB ISSUE

5 *Type Ib has the design at the top complete and the design at the bottom nearly complete. Type Ib is often mistaken for Type I.*

Type Ic has bottom right ornaments incomplete.

5

		UnFVF	UseFVF
1¢	**blue** Type Ib	14,000.00	6,500.00
	dark blue	14,000.00	6,500.00
	pale blue	14,000.00	6,500.00
	On cover		6,500.00
	FDC *(July 1, 1851)*		130,000.00
	Type 1c	6,000.00	1,400.00

Catalog prices for the above stamp are for nice examples of the type. Stamps with a slightly less complete design at the bottom are worth about one-fourth of the above prices.

1857. BENJAMIN FRANKLIN TYPE II ISSUE

6, 20 *Type II has the top line always complete, the top ornaments complete or partially cut away. The bottom line is always complete, while the little balls of the bottom scrolls and the bottom of the lower plume ornaments are missing.*

6

		UnFVF	UseFVF
1¢	**blue** (Plate 1) Type II	1,100.00	140.00
	dark blue	1,100.00	140.00
	pale blue	1,100.00	150.00
	On cover		190.00
	Double transfer	1,150.00	170.00
	Plate 2 *(Dec. 5, 1855)*	1,100.00	150.00
	Cracked plate	1,300.00	375.00
	Double transfer	1,200.00	200.00
	Triple transfer	1,500.00	375.00
	Plate 3 *(May 6, 1856)*	—	400.00
	Double transfer	—	450.00
	Plate 4 *(April 19, 1857)*	3,400.00	1,100.00
	Curl in hair	—	1,200.00
	FDC *(July 1, 1851)*		17,500.00

1851. BENJAMIN FRANKLIN TYPE III ISSUE

7, 21 *Type III has both the top and bottom lines broken. It should be noted particularly that the side ornaments are complete. If they are not, the stamp has been cut out of a perforated stamp of Type V (No. 24.) The finest examples of No. 7 are found in position 99R2, which is why that item is listed separately.*

7

		UnFVF	UseFVF
1¢	**blue** Type III	11,500.00	2,500.00
	On cover		3,200.00
	Position 99R2	15,000.00	4,500.00

1851. BENJAMIN FRANKLIN TYPE IIIA ISSUE

8, 22 *Type IIIa has the outer line broken at the top or bottom of the stamp but both lines are not broken on the same stamp.*

8

		UnFVF	UseFVF
1¢	**blue** (Plate 1E) Type IIIa	4,250.00	875.00
	dark blue	4,250.00	875.00
	pale blue	4,250.00	875.00
	On cover		1,100.00
	Double transfer, 1 inverted (blue)	5,000.00	1,250.00
	Double transfer, 1 inverted (dark blue)	5,000.00	1,250.00
	Double transfer, 1 inverted (pale blue)	5,000.00	1,250.00
	Plate 2	—	—
	Plate 4	4,250.00	1,100.00
	FDC *(July 1, 1851)*		
	Earliest known usage: (Plate 1E: *July 5, 1851;* Plate 4: *April 8, 1857)*		

1852. BENJAMIN FRANKLIN TYPE IV ISSUE Imperforate.

9, 23 *Type IV, similar to Type II, but with the outer lines recut in several different ways.*

9

		UnFVF	UseFVF
1¢	**blue** Type IV (recut Type IV) (recut once at top & once at bottom)	750.00	110.00
	On cover		145.00
	Plate block of 8, w/imprint	—	
	Bottom frame line broken	—	275.00
	Cracked plate	900.00	175.00
	Double transfer	825.00	130.00
	Triple transfer, 1 inverted	900.00	175.00
	t. Recut once at top	725.00	125.00
	t1. Recut once at top and twice at bottom	750.00	125.00
	t2. Recut twice at bottom	825.00	145.00
	t3. Recut once at bottom	850.00	155.00
	t4. Recut once at bottom & twice at top	875.00	160.00
	t5. Recut twice at top & twice at bottom	900.00	220.00
	t6. Printed both sides	—	—
	t7. Double impression	—	—
	v. Perforated 12 1/2 (unofficial)	—	3,000.00
	v1. Diagonal bisect on cover		—
	v2. Vertical bisect on cover		—
	Earliest documented cover: *June 5, 1852*		

1851. GEORGE WASHINGTON ISSUE Imperforate.

10, 11, 25 George Washington after bust by Jean-Antoine Houdon, Mount Vernon, Va. Type I with outer frame lines at top and bottom. For descriptions of Types II and III, see Nos. 26 and 27.

10

		UnFVF	UseFVF
3¢	**orange brown** Type I	3,000.00	85.00
	deep orange brown	3,200.00	140.00
	copper brown	3,500.00	200.00
	On cover		—
	Mark on lower right diamond	—	150.00
	Nick on shoulder	—	100.00
	Double transfer	—	125.00
	Triple transfer	—	350.00
	p. Thin, India-like paper	—	500.00
	t. Printed both sides	—	—
	FDC *(July 1, 1851)*		12,000.00

1851. GEORGE WASHINGTON ISSUE Imperforate.

11

		UnFVF	UseFVF
3¢	**Venetian red** Type I	240.00	10.00
	claret	290.00	15.00
	bright brown carmine	280.00	18.50
	brown carmine	235.00	10.50
	dark brown carmine	235.00	10.50
	dark violet	235.00	10.50
	dull brown carmine	260.00	12.00
	dull carmine red	275.00	20.00
	dull orange red	220.00	9.00
	dull rose carmine	220.00	9.00
	Plate block of 8	3,750.00	
	Mark on lower right diamond	325.00	25.00
	Nick on shoulder	265.00	10.50
	Cracked plate	775.00	160.00
	Worn plate	240.00	10.00
	Double transfer in "CENTS"	375.00	50.00
	Double transfer in "THREE CENTS"	275.00	12.00
	Double transfer in "THREE CENTS" & rosettes double	390.00	65.00
	Triple transfer	375.00	50.00
	t. Double impression	—	5,000.00
	v. Perforated 12 1/2 (unofficial)	—	6,000.00
	Earliest documented cover: *Oct. 4, 1851*		

1856. THOMAS JEFFERSON ISSUE Imperforate.

12, 28-30 Thomas Jefferson, after painting by Gilbert Stuart. Type I, with full projections at top and bottom as well as the sides. Copies that do not have these complete projections at top and bottom are trimmed from perforated varieties issued at a later date. For a description of Type II see Nos. 31 and 32.

12

		UnFVF	UseFVF
5¢	**red brown** Type I	17,500.00	750.00
	dark red brown	17,500.00	750.00
	Double transfer	—	1,350.00
	Earliest documented cover: *March 24, 1856*		

1855. GEORGE WASHINGTON TYPE I ISSUE

13, 33 George Washington, after painting by Gilbert Stuart. Type I. For description of Types II-IV, see Nos. 14-16 and 34-37.

13, 33 Type I has the "shells" at the lower corners almost complete. The line below "TEN CENTS" is very nearly complete. The outer lines above the middle of the stamp and over the "X" in each upper corner are broken. There are three small circles on each side opposite the words "TEN CENTS."

13

		UnFVF	UseFVF
10¢	**green** Type I	14,000.00	675.00
	dark green	14,000.00	675.00
	yellow green	14,000.00	675.00
	On cover		900.00
	Curl in left "X"	14,500.00	900.00
	Double transfer	14,500.00	900.00
	FDC *(May 1855)*		

1855. GEORGE WASHINGTON TYPE II ISSUE Imperforate.

14, 34 Type II has the outer line at the bottom broken in the middle, the "shells" are partially cut away, and the design is complete at the top. There are three small circles on each side.

14

		UnFVF	UseFVF
10¢	**green** Type II	4,000.00	175.00
	dark green	4,000.00	175.00
	yellow green	4,000.00	175.00
	On cover		290.00
	Curl opposite left "X"	4,500.00	325.00
	Double transfer	4,500.00	300.00
	Earliest documented cover: *May 12, 1855*		

DECODING THE CATALOG

The United States 3¢ 1851 issue has been the single most-studied stamp of the United States and, as a result, there are significant bodies of work to help the collector. The stamp comes in only two formats and three design types. The formats are imperforate and perforated 15 1/2. The imperforate stamps were released in 1851; the perforated ones in 1857. The design types of the 3¢ stamp are all related to the frame lines surrounding the design.

All stamps of the 1851 and 1857 series were demonetized in 1861, after the southern states seceded during the early part of the Civil War.

Type I (left)

Of the three design types found on the 3¢ value, Type I is the only one found both on imperforate and perforated stamps. Since the perforated Type I stamps are worth considerably more than the imperforate ones, there is no incentive to fake imperforates by trimming perforations. The distinguishing feature of Type I is a frame line on all four sides of the design.

There are two main varieties of the Type I imperforate, Minkus 10 and 11. No. 10 is an orange brown stamp, produced from the early 3¢ plates. As a result, the impressions of these stamps are strong and clear, with fine design lines clearly visible.

No. 11 comes in a number of different shades (the most common of these is dull red) from plates used from late 1851 on. Impressions on these stamps range from crisp and clear to blurry and worn.

In 1857, stamps printed from the 1851 plates were perforated, but with what was considered unsatisfactory results. Since the stamp images were laid in on the plates with no idea of later perforating, they appear very close together. As a result, perforating between these stamps was very difficult without cutting into the design.

Type II (left)

Type II is found only on perforated stamps.

After some Type I stamps had been perforated, it was decided that the top and bottom frame lines should be removed from future plates to allow for horizontal perforating without cutting the design. The distance between columns of stamps on the plates was considered acceptable with the frame lines, so new plates were prepared using continuous vertical frame lines. This variety, Minkus 26, is the most common type of the 3¢ stamp.

Type III (left)

Type III is a major variety, Minkus 27.

Although similar to Type II, Type III has had a slight design change. The side frame lines extend only to the top and bottom of the stamp design. There are no top or bottom frame lines. Because Type III stamps are considerably more valuable than their Type II counterparts, it is important to be able to tell the type for sure. The most easily mistaken examples are those Type II stamps from the top or bottom of the pane, where the side frame lines stop at the top or bottom of the stamp design. To be sure that your stamp is indeed a Type III example, you should be able to see a frame line break at both the top and the bottom of the stamp design. If one is obscured, then it is best to assume it is a margin copy Type II example.

1855. GEORGE WASHINGTON TYPE III ISSUE

15, 35 Type III has outer lines broken above the top label that contains words "U.S. POSTAGE" and the lines are broken above the "X" numerals. The shells and outer line at the bottom are partially cut away. There are three small circles on each side.

15

		UnFVF	UseFVF
10¢	**green** Type III	4,000.00	175.00
	dark green	4,000.00	175.00
	yellow green	4,000.00	175.00
	On cover		290.00
	Curl on forehead	4,500.00	325.00
	Curl to right of left "X"	4,500.00	325.00
	Double transfer at top and bottom	—	—
	Earliest documented cover: *May 19, 1855*		

1856. GEORGE WASHINGTON TYPE IV ISSUE

16, 36 Type IV has had the outer lines at the top or bottom of the stamp, or at both places, recut. There are three small circles on each side.

16

		UnFVF	UseFVF
10¢	**green** Type IV (outer line recut at top only)	25,000.00	1,375.00
	dark green	25,000.00	1,375.00
	yellow green	25,000.00	1,375.00
	On cover		1,900.00
	t. Outer line recut at bottom only	26,000.00	1,700.00
	t1. Outer line recut at top and bottom	29,000.00	2,000.00
	Earliest documented cover: *July 10, 1855*		

All four types of the 10¢ stamp occur on the same sheet, so that pairs and blocks showing combination of these types exist.

1851. GEORGE WASHINGTON TYPE I ISSUE

17, 38 George Washington, Type I, with complete frame lines. For Type II see No. 39.

17

		UnFVF	UseFVF
12¢	**black** Type I	5,000.00	275.00
	deep black	5,000.00	275.00
	gray black	5,000.00	275.00
	On cover		1,500.00
	Double transfer	5,250.00	350.00
	Recut in lower left corner	5,250.00	400.00
	Triple transfer	5,500.00	475.00
	p. Thin, India-like paper	—	850.00
	t. Printed on both sides	—	10,000.00
	y. Diagonal bisect on cover		2,500.00
	On "Via Nicaragua" cover		5,750.00
	y1. Vertical bisect on cover		8,500.00
	y2. Quarter on cover		—
	FDC *(July 1, 1851)*; EKU *(Aug. 4, 1851)*		

1861. BENJAMIN FRANKLIN TYPE I ISSUE Regular Issue, printed by Toppan, Carpenter & Co., had the same designs and types as the preceding issue, with some further types and values being noted. Three new values, the 24¢, 30¢, and 90¢ stamps, were added to this issue.

This issue marked a great milestone in postal service progress. Due to a pressing need for a faster stamp dispensing method, the stamps were machine perforated and easily and quickly separated, instead of having to be cut apart by scissors. *Intaglio, perforated 15.*

While No. 18 has the complete design like the imperforate stamp No. 3, it does not have the "doubled" ornaments in the upper right corners.

18

		UnFVF	UseFVF
1¢	**blue** Type I	1,800.00	500.00
	On cover		750.00
	Cracked plate	—	850.00
	Double transfer	1,950.00	650.00
	Earliest documented cover: *Jan. 15, 1861*		

The normal setting of the perforating machine was such that perforations cut the design on almost every stamp. Prices quoted are for such copies. Where the perforations do not cut the design No. 18 stamps command very high premiums.

1857. BENJAMIN FRANKLIN TYPE IA ISSUE

19

		UnFVF	UseFVF
1¢	**blue** Type Ia	21,000.00	6,500.00
	On cover		7,500.00
	Curl on shoulder	22,500.00	6,500.00
	Earliest documented cover: *Nov. 2, 1857*		

1857. BENJAMIN FRANKLIN TYPE II ISSUE

20

		UnFVF	UseFVF
1¢	**blue** (Plate 2) Type II	1,000.00	250.00
	On cover		290.00
	Cracked plate	1,250.00	525.00
	Double transfer	1,050.00	290.00
	Plate 4	3,000.00	850.00
	Curl in hair	—	1,000.00
	Double transfer	3,250.00	1,450.00
	Plate 11	1,150.00	325.00
	Double transfer	—	—
	Plate 12	950.00	250.00
	Earliest documented cover: *July 25, 1857*		

1857. BENJAMIN FRANKLIN TYPE III ISSUE

21

		UnFVF	UseFVF
1¢	**blue** Type III	12,000.00	2,700.00
	On cover		2,500.00
	Position 99R2	—	10,000.00
	Earliest documented cover: *Sept. 19, 1857*		

The finest examples of No. 21 are found in position 99R2, which is why that item is listed separately.

1857. BENJAMIN FRANKLIN TYPE IIIA ISSUE

22

		UnFVF	UseFVF
1¢	**blue** (Plate 4) Type IIIa	1,900.00	425.00
	On cover		525.00
	Double transfer	2,100.00	525.00
	v. Horizontal pair, imperforate between	—	5,000.00
	Plate 11	2,000.00	500.00
	Double transfer	2,100.00	525.00
	Triple transfer	—	—
	Plate 12	2,000.00	500.00
	Earliest documented cover: *July 26, 1857*		

1857. BENJAMIN FRANKLIN TYPE IV ISSUE

23

		UnFVF	UseFVF
1¢	**blue** Type IV recut top and once at bottom	8,000.00	625.00
	Cracked plate	8,250.00	825.00
	On cover	—	900.00
	Double transfer	8,250.00	750.00
	Triple transfer, 1 inverted	8,750.00	900.00
	t. Recut once at top	7,350.00	660.00
	t1. Recut once at top and twice at bottom	7,500.00	675.00
	t2. Recut twice at bottom	7,750.00	700.00
	t3. Recut once at bottom	8,000.00	725.00
	t4. Recut once at bottom and twice at top	8,250.00	750.00
	t5. Recut twice at top and twice at bottom	8,500.00	800.00
	Earliest documented cover: *July 25, 1857*		

1857. BENJAMIN FRANKLIN TYPE V ISSUE

24 Type V occurs only on the perforated stamps. The top and bottom lines are broken and the sides of the design have been partially cut away. Trimmed copies of this stamp

often are offered as Type III imperforate. They easily can be detected since Type III, and all other types that come imperforate, have the complete design at the sides.

24		UnFVF	UseFVF
1¢	**blue** Type V	170.00	35.00
	On cover		45.00
	Plate block of 8, w/imprint	3,500.00	
	Curl in hair	240.00	57.50
	Curl on shoulder	240.00	67.50
	Curl over "C" of "CENT"	250.00	67.00
	Curl over "E" of "CENT"	275.00	82.50
	Horizontal dash in hair	350.00	85.00
	"Ring" below ear	350.00	95.00
	Double curl in hair	290.00	75.00
	Double transfer, at bottom	295.00	95.00
	Double transfer, at top	240.00	85.00
	Plate 5	495.00	125.00
	Curl in "O" of "ONE"	—	—
	Curl on shoulder	—	—
	p. Laid paper	—	—
	v. Vertical strip of 5, imperforate horizontally	—	—
	Earliest documented cover: *Nov. 17, 1857*		

1857. GEORGE WASHINGTON TYPE I ISSUE

25		UnFVF	UseFVF
3¢	**rose** Type I	2,250.00	90.00
	brownish carmine	2,250.00	90.00
	dull red	2,250.00	85.00
	On cover		100.00
	Gash on shoulder	2,400.00	90.00
	Cracked plate	3,350.00	550.00
	Double transfer	2,500.00	115.00
	Double transfer, "GENTS"	—	650.00
	Triple transfer	—	600.00
	Worn plate	2,250.00	85.00
	v. Horizontal pair, imperforate vertically	—	—
	v1. Vertical pair, imperforate horizontally	—	10,000.00
	Earliest documented cover: *Feb. 28, 1857*		

Fakes are known of the horizontal pair, imperforate vertically.

1857. GEORGE WASHINGTON TYPE II ISSUE

26 Type II has the outer frame removed at the top and bottom of the design. The side frame lines were recut to form continuous lines from the top to the bottom of the plate so they extend beyond the design of the stamp.

26		UnFVF	UseFVF
3¢	**Venetian red** Type II	75.00	6.50
	bright carmine	—	—
	brown carmine	140.00	17.00
	dull red	75.00	7.00
	dull rose brown	75.00	7.00
	orange brown	—	—
	On cover		8.00
	Cracked plate	725.00	220.00
	Double transfer	110.00	17.00
	Double transfer in rosettes, line through "POSTAGE"	—	350.00
	Left frame line double	110.00	17.00
	Right frame line double	110.00	17.00
	Transfer damage above lower left rosette	85.00	9.00
	Transfer damage, retouched	105.00	10.00
	Transfer damage, retouched w/2 vertical lines	120.00	11.00
	Worn plate	85.00	7.50
	t. Double impression	—	2,500.00
	v. Horizontal pair, imperforate between	—	—
	v1. Horizontal pair, imperforate vertically	4,000.00	
	v2. Vertical pair, imperforate horizontally	—	10,000.00
	Earliest documented cover: *Sept. 14, 1857*		

1857. GEORGE WASHINGTON TYPE III ISSUE

27 Type III has the outer frame lines removed at the top and bottom of the design. The side frame lines extend only to the top and bottom of the stamp design.

27		UnFVF	UseFVF
3¢	**Venetian red** Type III	225.00	65.00
	brownish carmine	225.00	65.00
	dull red	225.00	65.00
	claret	250.00	65.00
	On cover		90.00
	Damaged transfer, above lower left rosette	260.00	80.00
	Damaged transfer, retouched	250.00	72.50
	Double transfer	325.00	125.00
	Double transfer, bottom part of stamp & rosettes	—	200.00
	Triple transfer	—	400.00
	Worn plate	225.00	55.00
	Earliest documented cover: *June 11, 1857*		

1857. THOMAS JEFFERSON TYPE I ISSUE has full projections at top and bottom.

28, 28A, 29, 30 *Type I Thomas Jefferson*

28		UnFVF	UseFVF
5¢	**red brown** Type I	4,500.00	760.00
	bright red brown	4,750.00	950.00
	pale red brown	3,000.00	760.00
	Earliest documented cover: *Aug. 23, 1857*		

28A		UnFVF	UseFVF
5¢	**henna brown (Indian red)**	30,000.00	2,600.00
	On cover		4,500.00
	Earliest documented cover: *March 31, 1858*		

1858. THOMAS JEFFERSON TYPE I ISSUE

29		UnFVF	UseFVF
5¢	**brick red** Type I	25,000.00	1,300.00
	On cover		1,750.00
	Earliest documented cover: *Oct. 6, 1858*		

L1859. THOMAS JEFFERSON TYPE I ISSUE

30		UnFVF	UseFVF
5¢	**brown** Type I	2,250.00	325.00
	dark brown	2,250.00	325.00
	pale brown	2,250.00	325.00
	yellow brown	2,250.00	350.00
	On cover		475.00
	Earliest documented cover: *March 21, 1859*		

1860. THOMAS JEFFERSON TYPE II ISSUE 31, 32 *Type II does not have full projections at the top and bottom. These projections have been partially or completely cut away.*

31, 32 *Type II Thomas Jefferson*

31		UnFVF	UseFVF
5¢	**brown** Type II	1,900.00	240.00
	dark brown	1,900.00	240.00

yellow brown	1,900.00	240.00
On cover		325.00
Cracked plate	—	
Printed on both sides	4,400.00	4,600.00
Earliest documented cover: *May 4, 1860*		

1861. THOMAS JEFFERSON TYPE II ISSUE

32

		UnFVF	UseFVF
5¢	**orange brown** Type II	1,000.00	1,000.00
	dark orange brown	1,150.00	1,100.00
	On cover		2,300.00
	Earliest documented cover: *May 8, 1861*		

1857. GEORGE WASHINGTON TYPE I ISSUE

33

		UnFVF	UseFVF
10¢	**green** Type I	16,500.00	750.00
	bluish green	16,500.00	750.00
	dark green	16,500.00	750.00
	yellowish green	16,500.00	850.00
	On cover		1,200.00
	Curl in left "X"	18,000.00	950.00
	Double transfer	18,000.00	950.00
	Vertical pair, imperforate horizontally	—	—
	Earliest documented cover: *Sept. 21, 1857*		

1857. GEORGE WASHINGTON TYPE II ISSUE

34

		UnFVF	UseFVF
10¢	**green** Type II	5,000.00	250.00
	bluish green	5,000.00	250.00
	dark green	5,000.00	250.00
	yellowish green	5,000.00	250.00
	On cover		325.00
	Curl opposite left "X"	—	350.00
	Double transfer	5,250.00	300.00
	Earliest known usage: *July 27, 1857*		

1857. GEORGE WASHINGTON TYPE III ISSUE

35

		UnFVF	UseFVF
10¢	**green** Type III	5,000.00	250.00
	bluish green	5,000.00	250.00
	dark green	5,000.00	250.00
	yellowish green	5,000.00	250.00
	On cover		325.00
	Curl in left "X"	—	350.00
	Curl on forehead	—	350.00
	Double transfer	—	—
	Earliest documented cover: *July 25, 1857*		

1857. GEORGE WASHINGTON TYPE IV ISSUE

36

		UnFVF	UseFVF
10¢	**green** Type IV, recut at top	32,500.00	2,000.00
	bluish green	32,500.00	2,000.00
	dark green	32,500.00	2,000.00
	yellowish green	32,500.00	2,000.00
	On cover		2,650.00
	t. Recut once at bottom	33,500.00	2,300.00
	t1. Recut at top and bottom	35,000.00	2,350.00
	t2. Recut once at top	32,500.00	2,250.00
	Earliest documented cover: *July 25, 1857*		

1859. GEORGE WASHINGTON TYPE V ISSUE

37 *Type V had the side ornaments partially cut away. In no case do three small circles remain on each side of the stamp. There usually is one small circle at each side, but some copies show two or three small circles on the right side. The outer lines at the top are complete except over the right "X." Trimmed copies of this stamp are offered as imperforates. If an imperforate does not have three circles at each side it is a trimmed fake.*

37

		UnFVF	UseFVF
10¢	**green** Type V	240.00	55.00
	bluish green	240.00	55.00
	dark green	240.00	55.00
	yellowish green	240.00	55.00
	On cover		77.00
	Plate block of 8, w/imprint	17,500.00	—
	Curl in "E" of "CENTS"	350.00	90.00
	Curl in "T" of "CENT"	350.00	90.00
	Curl (small) on forehead	325.00	77.00

Double transfer at bottom	350.00	90.00
Cracked plate	—	—
Earliest documented cover: *April 29, 1859*		

1857. GEORGE WASHINGTON TYPE I ISSUE

38

		UnFVF	UseFVF
12¢	**black** Type I	1,300.00	250.00
	gray black	1,300.00	250.00
	On cover		585.00
	Double transfer	1,480.00	275.00
	Triple transfer	1,600.00	—
	v. Diagonal bisect on cover		17,500.00
	v1. Horizontal pair, imperforate between	12,500.00	—
	Earliest documented cover: *July 30, 1857*		

1859. GEORGE WASHINGTON TYPE II ISSUE

39 *Type II has the frame line broken or missing on one or both sides.*

39

		UnFVF	UseFVF
12¢	**black** Type II	750.00	170.00
	deep black	750.00	170.00
	On cover		625.00
	Double transfer, frame line at left	800.00	200.00
	Double transfer, frame line at right	800.00	200.00
	Vertical line through rosette	925.00	260.00
	Earliest documented cover: *June 1, 1860,* or *Dec. 9, 1859*		

1860. GEORGE WASHINGTON ISSUE

40 *George Washington*

40

		UnFVF	UseFVF
24¢	**gray lilac**	1,600.00	300.00
	gray	1,600.00	300.00
	lilac	1,600.00	300.00
	On cover		1,000.00
	Plate block of 12, w/imprint	32,000.00	
	v. Imperforate single (not regularly issued)	—	
	v1. Pair, imperforate	—	
	Earliest documented cover: *July 7, 1860*		

1860. BENJAMIN FRANKLIN ISSUE

41 *Benjamin Franklin*

41

		UnFVF	UseFVF
30¢	**orange**	1,850.00	400.00
	reddish orange	1,850.00	425.00
	yellow orange	1,850.00	425.00
	On cover		1,250.00
	Cracked plate	—	—
	Double transfer	2,000.00	525.00
	Recut at bottom	2,100.00	575.00
	v. Imperforate single (not regularly issued)	—	
	v1. Pair, imperforate	—	—
	Earliest documented cover: *Aug. 8, 1860*		

1860. GEORGE WASHINGTON ISSUE

42 *Gen. George Washington, after a painting by John Trumbull, Yale University*

42

		UnFVF	UseFVF
90¢	**deep blue**	2,600.00	5,750.00
	blue	2,600.00	5,750.00
	On cover		225,000.00
	Double transfer at bottom	2,900.00	—
	Double transfer at top	2,900.00	—
	Short transfer at bottom, left and right	2,900.00	—
	v. Imperforate single (not regularly issued)		—
	v1. Pair, imperforate	—	—
	Earliest documented cover: *Sept. 11, 1860*		

Many fake cancellations exist on this stamp.

1875. BENJAMIN FRANKLIN SPECIAL PRINTING ISSUE

Special Printing of the 1857-61 Regular Issue. The original dies were intact, but new plates were made of the 1¢, 3¢, 10¢ and 12¢ values. Since these were perforated 12, while the originals were 15, they are quite easy to distinguish from the originals. The issue is very bright in color, *printed on white paper, issued without gum. Printed intaglio by the Continental Bank Note Co.* Not valid for postal use.

SP3

		UnFVF	UseFVF
1¢	**brilliant blue** (3,846 copies sold)	625.00	
	Cracked plate	775.00	
	Double transfer	775.00	

1875. GEORGE WASHINGTON SPECIAL PRINTING ISSUE

SP4

		UnFVF	UseFVF
3¢	**bright vermilion** (479 copies)	3,750.00	

1875. THOMAS JEFFERSON SPECIAL PRINTING ISSUE

SP5

		UnFVF	UseFVF
5¢	**bright orange brown** (878 copies)	1,350.00	
	Margin strip of 4, w/plate number	11,000.00	

1875. GEORGE WASHINGTON SPECIAL PRINTING ISSUE

SP6

		UnFVF	UseFVF
10¢	**bluish green** (516 copies)	3,500.00	

1875. GEORGE WASHINGTON SPECIAL PRINTING ISSUE

SP7

		UnFVF	UseFVF
12¢	**greenish black** (489 copies)	4,000.00	

1875. GEORGE WASHINGTON SPECIAL PRINTING ISSUE

SP8

		UnFVF	UseFVF
24¢	**dark violet black** (479 copies)	4,000.00	

1875. BENJAMIN FRANKLIN SPECIAL PRINTING ISSUE

SP9

		UnFVF	UseFVF
30¢	**yellow orange** (480 copies)	4,000.00	

1875. GEORGE WASHINGTON SPECIAL PRINTING ISSUE

SP10

		UnFVF	UseFVF
90¢	**indigo** (454 copies)	4,500.00	

This set is known imperforate.

1861. BENJAMIN FRANKLIN ISSUE

Upon the outbreak of the War between the States in 1861, the postal authorities in Washington demonetized all U.S. postage stamps issued up to that time to prevent possible use in the Confederate States and place financial pressure on them. (It is interesting to note that due to the scarcity of metal coins during this period, stamps encased in small containers often were pressed into use as small change.)

The National Bank Note Co. obtained the engraving and printing contract and prepared a set of eight essay designs in the form of finished 1¢, 3¢, 5¢, 10¢, 12¢, 24¢, 30¢ and 90¢ stamps with numerical denominations, and evidently submitted them for approval prior to Aug. 1. At least six of these miscalled "August" designs were not approved. Beginning Aug. 17, postage stamps were issued from new plates of 1¢, 3¢, 5¢, 10¢, 12¢ and 90¢ made from altered designs. The set was com-

pleted by regular printings from the 24¢ and 90¢ essay plates after possible alterations on them. A second printing from the 10¢ essay plate was issued and was known to be used in September 1861.

The second set of designs, regularly issued, are listed here, as well as two denominations, 2¢ and 15¢, added in 1863 and 1866 respectively. The essays as well as the issued stamps are on *unwatermarked paper, intaglio and perforated 12.*

43, 65, 70, 76, SP11 *Benjamin Franklin, after bust by Jean Caffert, Pennsylvania Academy of Fine Arts*

Unissued design: There is no dash under the tip of the ornaments at the right of the numeral in the upper left corner.

43 *A dash has been added under the tip of the ornament at the right of the numeral in the upper left corner.*

43

		UnFVF	UseFVF
1¢	**blue**	310.00	30.00
	bright blue	310.00	30.00
	pale blue	310.00	30.00
	ultramarine	750.00	275.00
	dark blue	550.00	90.00
	indigo	550.00	90.00
	On cover		40.00
	Plate block of 8, w/imprint	6,000.00	
	Dot on "U"	350.00	37.50
	Double transfer	—	45.00
	t. Printed on both sides	—	2,500.00
	p. Laid paper	—	—
	v. Vertical pair, imperforate horizontally	—	—
	Earliest known usage: *Aug. 17, 1861;* Earliest documented cover: *Aug. 21, 1861*		

1863. ANDREW JACKSON ISSUE

44 *Andrew Jackson, after miniature by John Wood Dodge*

44

		UnFVF	UseFVF
2¢	**black**	350.00	45.00
	deep black	350.00	45.00
	gray black	350.00	45.00
	On cover		75.00
	Plate block of 8, w/imprint	14,000.00	
	Cracked plate	—	—
	Double transfer	400.00	55.00
	Double transfer of top left corner & "POSTAGE" ("Atherton shift")	—	12,500.00
	Double transfer of right side ("Preston shift")	—	—
	Short transfer	375.00	55.00
	Triple transfer	—	—
	p. Laid paper	—	—
	t. Printed on both sides	—	5,000.00

y. Diagonal bisect on cover		1,250.00
y1. Horizontal bisect on cover		3,500.00
y2. Vertical bisect on cover		1,250.00
Earliest documented cover: *July 6, 1863*		

1861. GEORGE WASHINGTON ISSUE

45 *George Washington, after bust by J.A. Houdon*

Unissued Design: The ornaments forming the corners of the design are plain.

45 *A ball has been added to each corner of the design and the ornaments have been enlarged.*

45		UnFVF	UseFVF
3¢	**pink**	7,500.00	700.00
	On cover		850.00
	FDC *(Aug. 17, 1861)*		25,000.00
	a. rose pink	550.00	150.00
	On cover		180.00
	av. Vertical pair, imperforate horizontally	2,500.00	750.00
	b. pigeon blood pink	17,500.00	3,500.00
	On cover		4,250.00

It is almost impossible to describe a "pink" in words, but it should be kept in mind that the inking on a "pink" is rather heavy, and the lines of the design do not stand out as sharply as on the other shades. The color, while not as outstanding as a dull pink ribbon, is nevertheless on that order. It is not any of the shades of brown, dull red, rose red, or brown red so often mistaken for the real pink.

1861. GEORGE WASHINGTON ISSUE

46		UnFVF	UseFVF
3¢	**brown carmine**	150.00	2.50
	dull brown red	150.00	2.50
	dull red	130.00	2.50
	pale carmine red	130.00	2.50
	dark brown red	275.00	2.50
	On cover		3.50
	Plate block of 8, w/imprint	4,250.00	
	Cracked plate	—	—
	Double impression		6,000.00
	Double transfer	150.00	550.00
	p. Laid paper	—	—
	t. Printed on both sides	3,250.00	2,750.00
	v. Vertical pair, imperforate horizontally	3,500.00	750.00

1861. THOMAS JEFFERSON ISSUE

47 *Thomas Jefferson. Unissued Design (left): No leaflets project from the corner ornaments. Issued design (right): A leaflet projects from each corner ornament.*

47		UnFVF	UseFVF
5¢	**buff**	20,000.00	800.00
	brown yellow	20,000.00	850.00
	olive yellow	—	1,000.00
	On cover		1,100.00
	Earliest documented cover: *Aug. 18, 1861*		

1862. THOMAS JEFFERSON ISSUE

48		UnFVF	UseFVF
5¢	**red brown**	4,500.00	450.00
	dark red brown	4,500.00	450.00

On cover			675.00
Double transfer		4,750.00	500.00
Earliest documented cover: *Jan. 2, 1862*			

1863. THOMAS JEFFERSON ISSUE

49		UnFVF	UseFVF
5¢	**brown**	1,200.00	110.00
	dark brown	1,200.00	110.00
	pale brown	1,200.00	110.00
	black brown	1,350.00	160.00
	On cover		160.00
	Double transfer, bottom frame line	1,300.00	125.00
	Double transfer, bottom & top frame lines	1,350.00	140.00
	Double transfer, top frame line	1,300.00	125.00
	p. Laid paper	—	—
	Earliest documented cover: *Feb. 3, 1863*		

1861. GEORGE WASHINGTON TYPE I ISSUE

50, 51 *George Washington*

50 *Type I does not have a heavy curved line cut below the stars, and the ornament directly over the center star at the top has only one outer line. This stamp is found only on thin, semi-transparent paper.*

50		UnFVF	UseFVF
10¢	**green** Type I	6,750.00	950.00
	dark yellow green	6,750.00	950.00
	On cover		1,300.00
	Double transfer	—	—
	FDC *(Sept. 17, 1861)*		

1861. GEORGE WASHINGTON TYPE II ISSUE

51 *Type II has a heavy curved line cut below the stars. The ornament directly over the center star at the top has a double outer line.*

51		UnFVF	UseFVF
10¢	**green** Type II	750.00	45.00
	dark green	800.00	55.00
	yellow green	750.00	50.00
	blue green	800.00	55.00
	On cover		67.00
	Plate block of 8, w/imprint	8,000.00	
	Double transfer	825.00	55.00
	v. Vertical pair, imperforate horizontally	—	3,500.00
	Earliest known usage: *Aug. 20, 1861*	—	—

1861. GEORGE WASHINGTON ISSUE

52 *George Washington*

Unissued Design. The four corners of the design are rounded.

52 The four corners of the design have had ovals and scrolls added to form "square corners."

52		UnFVF	UseFVF
12¢	**black**	1,250.00	90.00
	gray black	1,250.00	100.00
	On cover		130.00
	Double transfer of bottom frame line	1,350.00	120.00
	Double transfer of top frame line	1,350.00	120.00
	Double transfer of top & bottom frame lines	1,400.00	125.00
	FDC *(Aug. 17, 1861)*; EKU *(Aug. 30, 1861)*		

1866. ABRAHAM LINCOLN ISSUE was released on the anniversary of his assassination at Ford's Theatre.

53 Abraham Lincoln

53		UnFVF	UseFVF
15¢	**black**	1,750.00	150.00
	On cover		225.00
	Plate block of 8, w/imprint	—	
	Cracked plate	1,850.00	160.00
	Double transfer	1,200.00	120.00
	Earliest documented cover: *April 14, 1866*		

1861. GEORGE WASHINGTON ISSUE

54-56 George Washington (distinguished primarily by minute color differences)

54		UnFVF	UseFVF
24¢	**violet**	9,500.00	1,250.00
	gray violet	3,250.00	1,250.00
	Earliest documented cover: *Aug. 20, 1861*		

No. 54 is found only on thin, semi-transparent paper, while Nos. 55 and 56 are on a thicker and more opaque paper.

1861. GEORGE WASHINGTON ISSUE

55		UnFVF	UseFVF
24¢	**red lilac**	2,000.00	180.00
	brown lilac	1,600.00	130.00
	steel blue	8,000.00	650.00
	blackish violet	800.00	80.00
	violet, on thin paper *(Aug. 17, 1861)*	—	—
	grayish lilac, on thin paper	—	—
	On cover		225.00
	Scratch under "A" of "POSTAGE"	—	—
	Earliest documented cover: *Sept. 21, 1861*		

1862. GEORGE WASHINGTON ISSUE

56		UnFVF	UseFVF
24¢	**lilac**	1,200.00	100.00
	gray lilac	1,200.00	100.00
	gray	1,200.00	100.00
	dark lilac	30,000.00	2,250.00
	On cover		175.00
	Scratch under "A" of "POSTAGE"	—	—
	p. Printed on both sides	—	3,500.00
	v. Pair, imperforate	—	—
	Earliest documented cover: *Oct. 23, 1862*		

1861. BENJAMIN FRANKLIN ISSUE

57 Benjamin Franklin

57		UnFVF	UseFVF
30¢	**orange**	1,600.00	160.00
	deep orange	1,600.00	160.00
	On cover		375.00
	p. Printed on both sides	—	—
	FDC *(Aug. 17, 1861)*; EKU *(Aug. 20, 1861)*		

1861. GEORGE WASHINGTON ISSUE

58 George Washington

Unissued design. There is no spot of color in the apex of the lower line of the angle at the top of the design. No row of dashes appear between the lines of the angle, and the lines in the leaf at the left of the "U" at the lower left of the design run at an angle.

58 There is a spot of color in the apex of the lower line of the angle at the top of the design. A row of small dashes appear between the lines of the angle, and the lines in the leaf at the lower left corner of the stamp are nearly vertical.

58		UnFVF	UseFVF
90¢	**blue**	2,750.00	425.00
	dark blue	3,000.00	525.00
	pale blue	2,500.00	425.00
	dull blue	2,750.00	425.00
	On cover		17,500.00
	FDC *(Aug. 17, 1861)*; EKU *(Nov. 27, 1861)*		

1875. BENJAMIN FRANKLIN SPECIAL PRINTING ISSUE Again the dies were available and new plates were made of the 1¢, 2¢, 10¢ and 12¢ values. Printed on hard, extremely white paper, absolutely white gum and without grill. They can be distinguished by their color shades, which are very deep and clear, and the white paper (compared to the slightly yellowish of the originals). *Intaglio by the National Bank Note Co., perforated 12.* Used copies are seldom found.

SP11		UnFVF	UseFVF
1¢	**dark ultramarine** *(3,195 copies)*	775.00	900.00

1875. ANDREW JACKSON SPECIAL PRINTING ISSUE

SP12		UnFVF	UseFVF
2¢	**jet black** *(979 copies)*	3,500.00	8,500.00

1875. GEORGE WASHINGTON SPECIAL PRINTING ISSUE

SP13		UnFVF	UseFVF
3¢	**brown red** *(465 copies)*	4,000.00	6,500.00

1875. THOMAS JEFFERSON SPECIAL PRINTING ISSUE

SP14		UnFVF	UseFVF
5¢	**light yellow brown** *(672 copies)*	4,000.00	2,500.00

1875. GEORGE WASHINGTON SPECIAL PRINTING ISSUE

SP15		UnFVF	UseFVF
10¢	**bluish green** *(451 copies)*	3,250.00	12,000.00

1875. GEORGE WASHINGTON SPECIAL PRINTING ISSUE

		UnFVF	UseFVF
SP16			
12¢	deep black *(389 copies)*	4,750.00	8,000.00

1875. ABRAHAM LINCOLN SPECIAL PRINTING ISSUE

		UnFVF	UseFVF
SP17			
15¢	deep black *(397 copies)*	5,250.00	10,000.00

1875. GEORGE WASHINGTON SPECIAL PRINTING ISSUE

		UnFVF	UseFVF
SP18			
24¢	deep brown violet *(346 copies)*	5,500.00	11,000.00

1875. BENJAMIN FRANKLIN SPECIAL PRINTING ISSUE

		UnFVF	UseFVF
SP19			
30¢	brown orange *(346 copies)*	4,250.00	12,500.00

1875. GEORGE WASHINGTON SPECIAL PRINTING ISSUE

		UnFVF	UseFVF
SP20			
90¢	dark blue *(317 copies)*	5,750.00	60,000.00

1867. GEORGE WASHINGTON w/GRILL ISSUE Stamps of 1861-66, impressed with grills of various sizes. The grills were adopted in order to prevent the removal of cancellation ink for the illegal reuse of stamps. They were impressed into the stamps in the form of small pyramids arranged in parallel rows as noted for each type of grill listed.

Grills with points projecting upward from face of the stamp.

Grill A. *Grill covers the entire stamp and appears as small mounds that have small breaks in their tops. The overall grill was found to weaken the stamps, which tended to tear when being removed from their panes. An essay grill is similar, but paper breaks appear on only a few, if any, of each of the individual mounds that make up the entire grill.*

		UnFVF	UseFVF
59			
3¢	rose grill A	5,000.00	1,500.00
	On cover		1,600.00
	a. Printed on both sides	—	—
	v. Pair, imperforate	—	
	Earliest documented cover: *Aug. 13, 1867*		

1867. THOMAS JEFFERSON GRILL A ISSUE

		UnFVF	UseFVF
60			
5¢	brown grill A	—	130,000.00
	dark brown	—	130,000.00

1867. BENJAMIN FRANKLIN GRILL A ISSUE

		UnFVF	UseFVF
61			
30¢	orange grill A	—	20,000.00

1868. GEORGE WASHINGTON GRILL B ISSUE *This grill, about 18 x 15mm in size, containing 22 x 18 rows of points projecting upward from the face of the stamp, exists on only four copies of the 3¢ rose. The grill points differ from any other issued grill. A variety of Grill C, No. 62, often is mistaken for this item.*

		UnFVF	UseFVF
61A			
3¢	rose grill B	—	175,000.00
	Earliest documented cover: *Feb. 1868*		

1867. GEORGE WASHINGTON GRILL C ISSUE

Grill C. *The grill was produced by the same grill roller as Grill A, after the roller had been machined to "erase" portions of the grill so that it now formed groups of grill points on each stamp rather than grilling all over the stamps. This grill is about 13 x 16mm with 16 to 17 by 18 to 21 points projecting upward from the face of the stamp.*

		UnFVF	UseFVF
62			
3¢	rose grill C	5,000.00	850.00
	On cover		1,150.00
	Double grill	6,250.00	2,250.00
	Grill with points down	5,750.00	1,200.00
	v. Pair, imperforate	—	
	Earliest documented cover: *Nov. 19, 1867*		

No. 62 shows rows of grill points, not as heavily impressed as the normal grill, forming a grill whose total area is about 18 x 15mm. Caused by a failure to cut deeply enough into the grill roller when it was being machined, which left a few areas on the roller only "partially erased."

1868. ANDREW JACKSON w/GRILL D ISSUE Grill with points projecting downward. *The tips of the grill points form vertical ridges. This grill is about 12 x 14mm, always has 15 points in each horizontal row, with 17 to 18 points in each vertical row.*

Detail of grill D

		UnFVF	UseFVF
63			
2¢	black grill D	15,000.00	3,000.00
	On cover		3,500.00
	Double transfer	—	—
	Split grill	—	3,250.00
	Earliest documented cover: *Feb. 15, 1868*		

1868. GEORGE WASHINGTON GRILL D ISSUE

		UnFVF	UseFVF
64			
3¢	rose grill D	6,000.00	850.00
	On cover		1,100.00
	Double grill	—	—
	Split grill	—	1,050.00
	Earliest documented cover: *Feb. 2, 1868*		

1868. BENJAMIN FRANKLIN Z GRILL ISSUE only two used copies of No. 65 are known. One is the New York Public Library collection. The other sold at auction in 1998 for the price listed. One reason for the 1¢ Z grill's rarity is that 1¢ stamps were chiefly used on printed circulars and commercial wrappers — the junk mail of the post-Civil War era. Most covers with these stamps were promptly discarded at a time when stamp collecting was just getting under way.

The Z grill itself was not identified as a grill pattern until 1915 — 47 years after the stamp was issued — at which time the first 1¢ Z grill was identified. The second used copy of this rarity was identified the following year.

Grill Z: *When originally discovered by William L. Stevenson, this then-unknown grill was given the algebraic "unknown" symbol of "Z" and it has thus remained. It is very easy to distinguish from other pyramid grills as the tip of the pyramids are horizontal ridges, all through the entire area of the grill, while on the D, E and F grills these ridges are vertical. The grill is about 11 x 14mm, with 13 to 14 by 17 to 18 points.*

 65   *Detail of grill Z*

		UnFVF	UseFVF
65			
1¢	blue grill Z	—	935,000.00

1868. ANDREW JACKSON GRILL Z ISSUE

		UnFVF	UseFVF
66			
2¢	black grill Z	7,000.00	1,150.00
	On cover		1,250.00
	Double grill	—	—
	Double transfer	7,500.00	1,150.00
	Earliest documented cover: *Feb. 11, 1868*		

1868. GEORGE WASHINGTON GRILL Z ISSUE

		UnFVF	UseFVF
67			
3¢	rose grill Z	12,500.00	3,000.00
	On cover		3,750.00
	Double grill	14,000.00	—
	Earliest documented cover: *Feb. 12, 1868*		

1868. GEORGE WASHINGTON GRILL Z ISSUE

68		UnFVF	UseFVF
10¢	**green** grill Z	125,000.00	—

1868. GEORGE WASHINGTON GRILL Z ISSUE

69		UnFVF	UseFVF
12¢	**black** grill Z	11,000.00	1,400.00
	Double transfer of top frame line	—	1,600.00
	On cover		2,000.00
	Earliest documented cover: *Feb. 15, 1868*		

1868. ABRAHAM LINCOLN GRILL Z ISSUE

69A		UnFVF	UseFVF
15¢	**black** grill Z	220,000.00	—

1868. BENJAMIN FRANKLIN GRILL E ISSUE This grill was created by filing some points from the "D" grill. *It is about 11 x 13mm and has 14 by 15 to 17 points.*

Detail of grill E

70		UnFVF	UseFVF
1¢	**blue** grill E	2,750.00	425.00
	dull blue	2,750.00	425.00
	On cover		550.00
	Split grill	2,850.00	500.00
	Double grill	—	575.00
	Earliest documented cover: *March 9, 1868*		

1868. ANDREW JACKSON GRILL E ISSUE

71		UnFVF	UseFVF
2¢	**black** grill E	1,400.00	140.00
	gray black	1,400.00	140.00
	intense black	1,500.00	180.00
	On cover		250.00
	Grill with points up	—	—
	Split grill	1,550.00	160.00
	Double grill	—	—
	Double transfer	1,500.00	155.00
	Triple grill	—	—
	v. Diagonal or Vertical Bisect on cover		2,000.00
	Earliest documented cover: *March 11, 1868*		

1868. GEORGE WASHINGTON GRILL E ISSUE

72		UnFVF	UseFVF
3¢	**rose** grill E	800.00	20.00
	pale red	800.00	20.00
	pale rose	800.00	20.00
	lake red	875.00	25.00
	On cover		27.50
	Split grill	875.00	27.50
	Double grill	—	—
	Triple grill	—	—
	p. Very thin paper	825.00	25.00
	Earliest documented cover: *Feb. 19, 1868*		

1868. GEORGE WASHINGTON GRILL E ISSUE

73		UnFVF	UseFVF
10¢	**green** grill E	5,000.00	250.00
	blue green	5,000.00	250.00
	dark green	5,000.00	250.00
	On cover		400.00
	Double transfer	—	325.00
	Split grill	5,250.00	325.00
	Double grill	6,400.00	500.00
	p. Very thin paper	5,250.00	325.00
	Earliest documented cover: *Feb. 21, 1868*		

1868. GEORGE WASHINGTON GRILL E ISSUE

74		UnFVF	UseFVF
12¢	**black** grill E	4,500.00	300.00
	gray black	4,500.00	300.00
	On cover		500.00
	Double transfer of bottom frame line	4,750.00	375.00
	Double transfer of top frame line	4,750.00	375.00

	Double transfer of top & bottom frame line	4,900.00	425.00
	Split grill	4,750.00	375.00
	Earliest documented cover: *Feb. 29, 1868*		

1868. ABRAHAM LINCOLN GRILL E ISSUE

75		UnFVF	UseFVF
15¢	**black** grill E	8,750.00	550.00
	gray black	8,750.00	550.00
	On cover		850.00
	Split grill	—	675.00
	Double grill	—	950.00
	Earliest documented cover: *May 2, 1868*		

1868. BENJAMIN FRANKLIN GRILL F ISSUE This grill was created by again filing points from the "E" grill. *It is about 9 x 13mm and has 11 to 12 by 15 to 17 points.*

76		UnFVF	UseFVF
1¢	**blue** grill F	1,000.00	200.00
	dark blue	1,000.00	200.00
	pale blue	1,000.00	200.00
	On cover		240.00
	Split grill	1,050.00	230.00
	Double grill	—	370.00
	Double transfer	1,050.00	240.00
	p. Very thin paper	1,050.00	220.00
	Earliest documented cover: *March 19, 1868*		

1868. ANDREW JACKSON GRILL F ISSUE

77		UnFVF	UseFVF
2¢	**black** grill F	475.00	50.00
	gray black	475.00	50.00
	On cover		62.50
	Plate block of 8, w/imprint	—	
	Split grill	525.00	55.00
	Double grill	—	180.00
	Double transfer	525.00	55.00
	v. Bisect (any) on cover		1,250.00
	Earliest documented cover: *March 27, 1868*		

1868. GEORGE WASHINGTON GRILL F ISSUE

78		UnFVF	UseFVF
3¢	**rose** grill F	360.00	7.50
	a. rose red	360.00	7.50
	On cover		9.00
	Plate block of 8, w/imprint	6,600.00	
	Double transfer	410.00	10.00
	Grill with points up		
	Split grill	390.00	8.00
	Quadruple split grill	650.00	130.00
	Double grill	—	
	Triple grill	—	160.00
	p. Very thin paper	360.00	7.00
	t. Printed on both sides	2,250.00	—
	v. Pair, imperforate	—	—
	v1. Vertical pair, imperforate horizontally	1,100.00	
	Earliest documented cover: *March 26, 1868*		

1868. THOMAS JEFFERSON GRILL F ISSUE

79		UnFVF	UseFVF
5¢	**brown** grill F	3,000.00	700.00
	black brown	3,150.00	850.00
	On cover		800.00
	Double transfer of top frame line	—	—
	Split grill	3,500.00	725.00
	Double grill	—	—
	p. Very thin paper	3,250.00	725.00
	Earliest documented cover: *Aug. 19, 1868*		

1868. GEORGE WASHINGTON GRILL F ISSUE

80		UnFVF	UseFVF
10¢	**yellow green** grill F	2,500.00	175.00
	blue green	2,500.00	175.00
	dark green	2,500.00	175.00
	green	2,500.00	175.00
	On cover		250.00
	Double transfer	—	—
	Split grill	2,600.00	225.00
	Quadruple split grill	—	625.00
	Double grill	—	350.00
	p. Very thin paper	2,600.00	225.00
	Earliest documented cover: *May 28, 1868*		

1868. GEORGE WASHINGTON GRILL F ISSUE

81

		UnFVF	UseFVF
12¢	**black** grill F	2,800.00	190.00
	gray black	2,800.00	190.00
	On cover		275.00
	Split grill	3,100.00	250.00
	Double grill	—	425.00
	Double transfer of bottom frame line	3,100.00	240.00
	Double transfer of top frame line	3,100.00	240.00
	Double transfer of top & bottom frame lines	—	275.00
	Triple grill	—	—
	p. Very thin paper	3,100.00	250.00

Earliest documented cover: *May 27, 1868*

1868. ABRAHAM LINCOLN GRILL F ISSUE

82

		UnFVF	UseFVF
15¢	**black** grill F	3,250.00	250.00
	gray black	3,250.00	250.00
	On cover		350.00
	Plate block of 8, w/imprint	35,000.00	
	Double transfer of upper right corner	—	—
	Split grill	3,500.00	325.00
	Quadruple split grill	4,000.00	625.00
	Double grill	—	450.00
	p. Very thin paper	3,500.00	300.00

Earliest documented cover: *May 4, 1868*

1869. GEORGE WASHINGTON GRILL F ISSUE

83

		UnFVF	UseFVF
24¢	**gray lilac** grill F	5,500.00	900.00
	gray	5,500.00	900.00
	On cover		1,300.00
	Plate block of 8, w/imprint	57,500.00	
	Scratch under "A" in "POSTAGE"	—	—
	Split grill	5,750.00	900.00
	Double grill	6,800.00	1,750.00

Earliest documented cover: *Nov. 28, 1868*

1868. BENJAMIN FRANKLIN GRILL F ISSUE

84

		UnFVF	UseFVF
30¢	**orange** grill F	5,500.00	700.00
	deep orange	5,500.00	700.00
	On cover		1,500.00
	Split grill	5,700.00	750.00
	Double grill	7,250.00	1,500.00
	Double grill, one split	—	—

Earliest documented cover: *Nov. 10, 1868*

1869. GEORGE WASHINGTON GRILL F ISSUE

85

		UnFVF	UseFVF
90¢	**blue** grill F	10,000.00	1,400.00
	dark blue	10,000.00	1,400.00
	On cover		55,000.00
	Split grill	10,500.00	1,450.00
	Double grill	14,000.00	—

Earliest documented cover: *May 8, 1869*

Most of the stamps that bear grills can be found with double grills, triple grills, split grills and quadruple split grills. Double grills are two impressions of the grill on the same stamp, triple grills are three impressions of the grill on the same stamp, split grills are those with about half of a normal grill on each end or on each side of the stamp and quadruple split grills are those that show just a small portion of the grill on each corner of the stamp. The split grill varieties were caused by misplacing the stamps under the grill roller so that the grills were not properly placed on the stamps. Fake grills exist.

1869. National Bank Note Co. Pictorial Series
This series of stamps was printed by the National Bank Note Co. The stamps are square in design. For some reason, now difficult to understand, this series was not popular and was replaced with a new series in about a year. The stamps were grilled with a new size of grill, Grill G, 9 1/2 x 9 1/2mm in size. The stamps were *printed in intaglio on hard wove paper, unwatermarked and were perforated 12.* The series includes the first U.S. bicolored postage stamps. (But see the Documentary R3.)

Three denominations of these stamps are known with inverted centers and are extremely scarce. This was the first time an error of this type was issued and was due to carelessness when printing the bi-colored stamps.

1869. BENJAMIN FRANKLIN ISSUE

86 Benjamin Franklin

Detail of grill G

86

		UnFVF	UseFVF
1¢	**buff**	750.00	160.00
	brown orange	750.00	160.00
	dark brown orange	750.00	160.00
	On cover		300.00
	Plate block of 10, w/imprint	—	
	Margin block of 4, w/arrow	5,800.00	
	Double transfer	—	—
	Split grill	825.00	200.00
	Double grill	1,175.00	340.00
	Double grill, 1 split	—	—
	Grill omitted, original gum	4,250.00	

Earliest documented cover: *April 1, 1869*

1869. PONY EXPRESS ISSUE

87 Pony Express

87

		UnFVF	UseFVF
2¢	**brown**	700.00	80.00
	dark brown	700.00	80.00
	pale brown	700.00	80.00
	yellow brown	700.00	75.00
	On cover		125.00
	Plate block of 10, w/imprint	—	
	Margin block of 4, w/arrow	3,500.00	
	Double transfer	—	95.00
	Split grill	850.00	100.00
	Quadruple split grill	—	425.00
	Double grill	—	300.00
	Grill omitted, original gum	2,250.00	
	p. Printed on both sides	—	9,000.00
	v. Bisect (any) on cover		3,000.00

Earliest documented cover: *March 20, 1869*

1869. EARLY LOCOMOTIVE ISSUE

88 Early Locomotive

88

		UnFVF	UseFVF
3¢	**ultramarine**	280.00	17.00
	blue	575.00	100.00
	dark ultramarine	300.00	20.00
	pale ultramarine	300.00	20.00
	On cover		30.00
	Plate block of 10, w/imprint	7,500.00	
	Margin block of 4, w/arrow	1,650.00	
	Double transfer	375.00	35.00
	Split grill	350.00	40.00
	Quadruple split grill	650.00	150.00
	Double grill	600.00	110.00
	Triple grill	—	—
	Grill omitted	1,100.00	—
	t. Double impression	—	—

Earliest documented cover: *March 27, 1869*

1869. GEORGE WASHINGTON ISSUE

89 *George Washington*

89		UnFVF	UseFVF
6¢	**ultramarine**	2,750.00	180.00
	pale ultramarine	2,750.00	180.00
	On cover		425.00
	Margin block of 4, w/arrow	14,000.00	
	Double transfer	—	260.00
	Split grill	3,000.00	300.00
	Quadruple split grill	—	825.00
	Double grill	—	650.00
	v. Vertical bisect on cover		—

Earliest documented cover: *April 26, 1869*

1869. SHIELD AND EAGLE ISSUE

90 *Shield and Eagle*

90		UnFVF	UseFVF
10¢	**yellow**	2,000.00	120.00
	yellowish orange	2,000.00	120.00
	On cover		375.00
	Margin block of 4, w/arrow	11,250.00	
	Split grill	2,150.00	150.00
	Double grill	—	425.00

Earliest documented cover: *April 1, 1869*

1869. STEAMSHIP ADRIATIC ISSUE

91 *Steamship Adriatic*

91		UnFVF	UseFVF
12¢	**green**	3,200.00	130.00
	bluish green	3,200.00	130.00
	dark green	3,200.00	130.00
	yellowish green	3,200.00	130.00
	On cover		425.00
	Margin block of 4, w/arrow	11,500.00	
	Split grill	2,700.00	165.00
	Double grill	—	425.00

Earliest documented cover: *April 1, 1869*

1869. LANDING OF COLUMBUS TYPE I ISSUE

92 *Landing of Columbus. Type I has a white area coming to an apex under the "T" of "POSTAGE." It is also known as the "unframed picture."*

92		UnFVF	UseFVF
15¢	**brown & blue** Type I	7,000.00	575.00
	dark brown & blue	7,000.00	575.00
	pale brown & blue	7,000.00	575.00
	On cover		1,850.00

Split grill		8,000.00	700.00
Double grill		—	850.00
Grill omitted		10,000.00	—

Earliest documented cover: *April 2, 1869; March 31, 1869,* cancel on off-cover stamp

1869. LANDING OF COLUMBUS TYPE II ISSUE

 93v. *Inverted center*

93 *Landing of Columbus. Type II has a diamond ornament under the "T" of "POSTAGE," a line has been drawn around the circumference of the central design so that the picture appears to be framed. Some diagonal shading lines have been drawn around the base of the picture.*

93		UnFVF	UseFVF
15¢	**brown & blue** Type II	3,250.00	220.00
	dark brown & blue	3,250.00	220.00
	On cover		875.00
	Plate block of 8, w/imprint	40,000.00	
	Double transfer	—	—
	Split grill	3,500.00	325.00
	Double grill	5,700.00	500.00
	v. Center inverted	275,000.00	18,000.00
	v1. Center doubled, 1 inverted	—	35,000.00
	v2. Imperforate, horizontally	2,750.00	

Earliest documented cover: *April 5, 1869*

1869. SIGNING OF THE DECLARATION OF INDEPENDENCE ISSUE

94 The Declaration of Independence *from a painting by John Trumbell (1756-1843) in the U.S. Capitol*

94v. *Inverted Center*

94		UnFVF	UseFVF
24¢	**green & violet**	6,500.00	675.00
	bluish green & violet	6,500.00	675.00
	On cover		15,000.00
	Split grill	7,250.00	875.00
	Double grill	—	2,250.00
	Grill omitted	9,500.00	—
	v. Center inverted (83 known)	275,000.00	19,000.00
	On cover		100,000.00

Earliest documented cover: *April 7, 1869*

1869. SHIELD, EAGLE AND FLAGS ISSUE

95v *Flags Inverted*

95 *Shield, Eagle and Flags*

95		UnFVF	UseFVF
30¢	**blue & carmine**	7,000.00	500.00
	dull blue & dark carmine	7,000.00	500.00
	On cover		22,500.00
	Split grill	7,500.00	600.00
	Double grill	—	1,100.00
	Grill omitted	8,250.00	—
	Double paper, grill omitted	7,750.00	—
	v. Flags inverted (46 known)	210,000.00	65,000.00

Earliest documented cover: *May 22, 1869*

1869. ABRAHAM LINCOLN ISSUE

96 *Abraham Lincoln*

96		UnFVF	UseFVF
90¢	carmine & black	9,250.00	2,200.00
	carmine rose & black	9,250.00	2,200.00
	On cover	—	—
	Split grill	—	—
	Grill omitted	15,000.00	—
	Earliest documented cover: *May 10, 1869*		

1875. BENJAMIN FRANKLIN SPECIAL PRINTING PICTORIAL ISSUE

Again the dies were available, and a new plate was made for the 1¢ and for the frame of the 15¢. The frame is similar to the Type I of the 1869 issue except that it is without the fringe of brown shading lines around the central vignette. *Printed by the National Bank Note Co., without grill, intaglio on hard white paper, with white crackly gum, perforated 12.*

SP21		UnFVF	UseFVF
1¢	buff (approx. 2,750 copies sold)	625.00	325.00

1875. PONY EXPRESS SPECIAL PRINTING PICTORIAL ISSUE

SP22		UnFVF	UseFVF
2¢	brown *(4,755 copies)*	750.00	558.00

1875. EARLY LOCOMOTIVE SPECIAL PRINTING PICTORIAL ISSUE

SP23		UnFVF	UseFVF
3¢	ultramarine *(1,406 copies)*	6,000.00	4,500.00

1875. GEORGE WASHINGTON SPECIAL PICTORIAL ISSUE

SP24		UnFVF	UseFVF
6¢	ultramarine *(2,226 copies)*	1,900.00	2,000.00

1875. SHIELD AND EAGLE SPECIAL PRINTING PICTORIAL ISSUE

SP25		UnFVF	UseFVF
10¢	yellow *(1,947 copies)*	2,000.00	1,700.00

1875. STEAMSHIP ADRIATIC SPECIAL PRINTING PICTORIAL ISSUE

SP26		UnFVF	UseFVF
12¢	bright green *(1,584 copies)*	3,000.00	3,250.00

1875. LANDING OF COLUMBUS SPECIAL PRINTING PICTORIAL ISSUE

SP27		UnFVF	UseFVF
15¢	brown & blue Type III *(1,981 copies)*	1,900.00	1,050.00
	a. Imperforate horizontally (single stamp)	3,500.00	7,000.00

1875. DECLARATION OF INDEPENDENCE SPECIAL PRINTING PICTORIAL ISSUE

SP28		UnFVF	UseFVF
24¢	deep green & violet *(2,091 copies)*	2,500.00	1,600.00

1875. SHIELD, EAGLE AND FLAGS SPECIAL PRINTING PICTORIAL ISSUE

SP29		UnFVF	UseFVF
30¢	bright blue & carmine *(1,356 copies)*	3,500.00	2,750.00

1875. ABRAHAM LINCOLN SPECIAL PRINTING PICTORIAL ISSUE

SP30		UnFVF	UseFVF
90¢	carmine & black *(1,356 copies)*	5,400.00	5,500.00

1880. BENJAMIN FRANKLIN SPECIAL PRINTING PICTORIAL ISSUE

on soft porous paper, without grill. Perforated 12. Printed by the American Bank Note Co.

SP31		UnFVF	UseFVF
1¢	buff without gum *(approx. 2,500 copies)*	325.00	200.00
	Plate block of 10, w/imprint	18,000.00	
	brown orange, without gum (approx 3,000 copies)	325.00	200.00

1870. National Bank Note Co. Portrait Series

The short-lived pictorial issue of 1869 was replaced by a series of new portraits, known as the Large Bank Notes. The first issues were produced by the National Bank Note Co. The new stamps were issued both with and without grills, a pattern of indentations in the paper designed to foil reuse of the

stamps. The grilled stamps are listed as Nos. 97-107, and the ungrilled stamps are Nos. 108-118. The grills are of two sizes, *Grill H*, about 10 x 12mm with sharp tips on the grill points, and *Grill I*, about 8 1/2 x 10mm having rather blunt tips on the grill points. Grill H was used on all values while Grill I was used only on the 1¢ through 7¢ values. *Intaglio on thin to medium thick white wove paper, unwatermarked and perforated 12.*

1870. BENJAMIN FRANKLIN ISSUE

97, 108 *Benjamin Franklin after bust by Rubricht. The pearl at the left of the numeral "1" is clear.*

Detail of grill H

Detail of grill I

97		UnFVF	UseFVF
1¢	ultramarine grill H	2,000.00	125.00
	dark ultramarine	2,000.00	125.00
	dull ultramarine	2,000.00	125.00
	On cover		175.00
	Double transfer	2,250.00	155.00
	Split grill	2,300.00	155.00
	Quadruple split grill	—	475.00
	Double grill	—	275.00
	v. Grill I	—	—
	Earliest documented cover: *April 9, 1870*		

1870. ANDREW JACKSON ISSUE

98, 109 *Andrew Jackson after bust by Hiram Powers*

In the notch formed underneath the semi-circular ornament to the left of the "S" of "U.S." the lines forming the notch do not quite join at the apex of the notch. This stamp is always of a red brown shade.

98		UnFVF	UseFVF
2¢	red brown grill H	1,200.00	60.00
	dark red brown	1,200.00	60.00
	dull red brown	1,200.00	60.00
	On cover		95.00
	Split grill	1,250.00	85.00
	Quadruple split grill	2,400.00	225.00
	Double grill	1,575.00	140.00
	v. Diagonal bisect on cover	—	—
	v1. Grill I	—	—
	Earliest documented cover: *July 14, 1870*		

1870. GEORGE WASHINGTON ISSUE

99, 110 *George Washington. Under the word "THREE," the long tail of the ribbon is lightly shaded along its lower edge.*

99		UnFVF	UseFVF
3¢	green grill H	725.00	20.00
	deep green	725.00	20.00

pale green	725.00	20.00
yellow green	725.00	19.00
On cover		27.50
Plate block of 10, w/imprint	7,750.00	
Plate block of 12, w/imprint	9,000.00	
Cracked plate	—	90.00
Double transfer	—	22.50
Split grill	775.00	25.00
Quadruple split grill	—	140.00
Double grill	1,000.00	75.00
v. Grill I	—	—
v1. Printed on both sides	—	—
v2. Pair, imperforate	1,250.00	

Earliest documented cover: *March 24, 1870*

1870. ABRAHAM LINCOLN ISSUE

100, 111 *Abraham Lincoln after bust by Leonard Volk. The first four vertical lines of the shading in the lower part of the left ribbon, to the left and downward from the "S" of "SIX," are of normal strength.*

100			UnFVF	UseFVF
6¢	**carmine** grill H		4,250.00	450.00
	carmine rose		4,250.00	450.00
	dull carmine		4,250.00	450.00
	On cover			750.00
	Split grill		4,500.00	550.00
	Quadruple split grill		—	950.00
	Double grill		—	900.00
	v. Grill I		—	—

Earliest documented cover: *Aug. 1870*

DECODING THE CATALOG

Most of the varieties of the United States 3¢ Large Bank Note issue are inexpensive, and all are fairly easy to distinguish, with practice.

As a group, the Large Bank Note issues were in use from 1870-89. The stamps were produced by the National Bank Note Co., the Continental Bank Note Co. and the American Bank Note Co., chronologically in that order. Of these, stamps printed by ABN are on thicker, softer paper than the other two, which are thinner, harder and more translucent. Excluding special printings (which the average collector rarely encounters), the 3¢ divides into six basic different stamps, with three design types.

Type I (left)

The first of these is Type I, produced by NBN, which can be found on Minkus 99 and 110. The biggest distinguishing factor of Type I is the tail of the ribbon in the lower-left area of the stamp, under the word "Three." There is no shading under the ribbon, giving it the appearance of having a white outline. Minkus 99 is grilled; 110 is not. The grills on No. 99 appear very faintly at times. This is normal for these stamps.

Type II (left)

There are two basic stamps of Type II. These are Minkus 122 and 134. These were produced by CBN and ABN, respectively. Type II is characterized by heavy shading under the ribbon ends below "Three." The CBN printing (Minkus 122) is on hard, translucent paper, while the ABN printing (Minkus 134) is on thicker, softer opaque paper.

Type II, re-engraved (left)

The characteristics of Type II, re-engraved, are basically the same as Type II, except that the shading surrounding the vignette oval is about half the previous width, and a horizontal line has been added under the word "Cents."

Two stamps, both printed on ABN soft, opaque paper, exist. The first, Minkus 146, is green. The second, Minkus 135, is vermillion, leaving no confusion as to types.

1871. EDWIN STANTON ISSUE

101, 112 *Edwin M. Stanton, Attorney General under Buchanan and Secretary of War under Lincoln and Johnson, actively opposed the latter's Reconstruction policies. An attempt to dismiss him served as the pretext for Johnson's impeachment in 1868. Appointed to the Supreme Court in 1869, Stanton died before he could take office.*

There are no semi-circles around the ends of the lines forming the ball in the lower right corner.

101

		UnFVF	UseFVF
7¢	**vermilion** grill H	3,000.00	350.00
	On cover		600.00
	Split grill	3,250.00	450.00
	Quadruple split grill	—	775.00

	UnFVF	UseFVF
Double grill	—	725.00
v. Grill I	—	—

Earliest documented cover: *Feb. 12, 1871*

1871. THOMAS JEFFERSON ISSUE

102, 113, 138 *Thomas Jefferson after bust by Hiram Powers. The scroll ornament at the right end of the upper label, below the letter "E" of "POSTAGE," is clear.*

102

		UnFVF	UseFVF
10¢	**brown**	4,750.00	650.00
	dark brown	4,750.00	650.00
	yellow brown	4,750.00	650.00
	On cover		950.00
	Split grill	5,000.00	700.00
	Double grill	—	1,200.00

Earliest documented cover: *June 2, 1870*

DECODING THE CATALOG

The United States 6¢ Large Bank Note issue of 1870-89 is one of the easiest to identify of all the Large Bank Note series stamps. It features not only design differences but distinguishable colors as well. All you need is to learn how to decode the catalog listings. All are fairly easy to distinguish once you know what to look for. As is most often the case, the task gets easier with practice.

As a group, the Large Bank Note issues were in use from 1870-89. The stamps were produced by the National Bank Note Co., the Continental Bank Note Co. and the American Bank Note Co., chronologically in that order. Of these, stamps printed by ABN are on thicker, softer paper than the other two, which are thinner, harder and more translucent.

Excluding special printings (which the average collector rarely encounters), the 6¢ divides into five different basic stamps, with three design types.

Type I (left)

The first of these is Type I, produced by NBN, which can be found on Minkus 100 and 111. Both of these stamps are carmine colored (with shades). The biggest distinguishing design factor of Type I is the ribbon end in the lower left (beneath the word "SIX"). Type I examples feature fine, well delineated engraving lines with no shadow in the curl.

Minkus 100 is grilled; 111 is not. The grills on No. 100, as with all in the series, appear very faintly at times. This is normal for these stamps, and all should be expertized due to their value.

Type II (left)

There are two basic stamps of Type II. These are Minkus 124 and 137. These were produced by CBN and ABN, respectively. The basic colors (and respective shades) are dull pink or venetian red, and pink.

Further, the CBN printing (Minkus 124) is on hard, translucent paper, while the ABN printing (Minkus 137) is on thicker, softer opaque paper.

Type II is distinguishable by again looking at the lower-left ribbon curl, which has had shading lines added to the design (the so-called secret mark).

Type II, re-engraved (left)

The general characteristics of Type II, re-engraved, Minkus 147, are the same as the basic Type II, except that identifying it gets even easier. First, the color usually is more of a rose to brown-red color. Again, these shades are unique to these printings.

Unlike either Type I or Type II, the re-engraved version features only three vertical lines to the left of the vignette frame. Previous printings have four (upper right). This is an absolute determiner.

Of all printings, the grilled NBN and re-engraved versions are the most costly and worth looking for.

1872. HENRY CLAY ISSUE

103, 114 *Henry Clay after bust by Joel T. Hart. Clay was the first prominent Speaker of the House and "The Great Pacificator" of the Senate, where he effected compromises between slavery and anti-slavery forces. Twice a candidate for President, in 1824 he threw his electoral votes to John Quincy Adams, defeating Jackson, and served as Adams' Secretary of State.*

The "2" in the figure "12" has balls nearly round in shape at the upper and lower portion of the figure.

		UnFVF	UseFVF
103			
12¢	**pale violet**	21,000.00	2,600.00
	On cover		6,250.00
	Split grill	—	3,250.00

Earliest documented cover: *Feb. 10, 1872*

DECODING THE CATALOG

The Large Bank Note issues (1¢-90¢ values) were in use from 1870-89. The stamps were produced by the National Bank Note Co., the Continental Bank Note Co. and the American Bank Note Co., chronologically in that order. Of these, stamps printed by ABN are on thicker, softer paper than the other two, which are thinner, harder and more translucent.

Excluding special printings (which the average collector rarely encounters), the 10¢ issue divides into six basic different stamps, with three design types. The regularly issued stamp types are found here.

Type I (left)

Design Type I of the 10¢ large Bank Note is easily distinguished. There are three basic stamps. To the left of the portrait oval are five complete vertical lines. This characteristic also is present on Type II. To the upper-right of the portrait (beneath the "E" in "POSTAGE") is a small oval curl. It features strong curled shading lines beneath it and a double diagonal line above it. There are no markings in the curl.

Minkus 102 is printed on white, wove paper and bears a grill. The grill sometimes is quite faint. Minkus 113 also is on wove paper but has no grill. Minkus 138 is on softer, thicker paper. It has no grill, and the back, opaque side looks creamy.

Type II (left)

Type II stamps are quite easily distinguished from Type I. As in Type I, five vertical lines are found to the left of the portrait oval. Unlike Type I, a secret mark has been added to the design. It is a curved line that appears in the curl beneath the "E" of "POSTAGE." In most cases, this is a very pronounced line.

Minkus 126 is on thin, hard translucent paper.
Minkus 139 is printed on thicker, soft opaque paper.

Type III (bottom left)

When the American Bank Note Co. produced the reengraved Type III in 1882, it made several changes to the design, including removing the secret mark. As a result of these changes, Type III is the easiest to distinguish at a glance. The entire stamp has a different appearance to it, including a much darker outline and more definition to Jefferson's facial features.

Type III stamps have only four full vertical lines to the left of the portrait oval; the others have five.

Even though the so-called secret mark is no longer present in the upper-right curl, the appearance is quite different. Instead of two curved shading lines there now are cross-hatched straight lines forming the shading. Also, the horizontal shading lines all around the design have been darkened considerably.

There is only one kind of Type III stamp, Minkus 148. However, a black-brown shade of the stamp (recognized as a minor variety) is worth between 5 and 10 times more than the many other shades of the same stamp. It pays to decode the catalog.

1870. DANIEL WEBSTER PORTRAIT ISSUE

104, 115 *Daniel Webster after bust by S.V. Clevenger. (For Webster's biography, see CM115.) The thin lines shading the triangles, and below the letters "U.S. POSTAGE" are fine but of normal color and strength.*

104		UnFVF	UseFVF
15¢	**orange**	5,500.00	1,000.00
	bright orange	5,500.00	1,200.00
	dark orange	5,500.00	1,200.00
	On cover		1,900.00
	Split grill	5,750.00	1,250.00
	Double grill	—	—
	Earliest documented cover: *June 2, 1870*		

1870. GEN. WINFIELD SCOTT ISSUE

105, 116, 129 *Gen. Winfield Scott after bust by Coffee. A hero of the War of 1812, Scott (1786-1866) is considered the greatest American general between George Washington and Robert E. Lee. (For further biography, see CM173.)*

105		UnFVF	UseFVF
24¢	**purple**	—	5,500.00
	dull purple	—	5,500.00
	On cover		—
	Split grill	—	—
	Earliest documented cover: *July 11, 1872*		

1870. ALEXANDER HAMILTON ISSUE

106, 117 *Alexander Hamilton was Washington's aide and secretary during the Revolution and commanded troops at Yorktown. One of the drafters of the Constitution, he advocated an extremely strong central government. As first Secretary of the Treasury, "the Hamiltonian system" established the fiscal policy, strengthened federal government and the public credit, promoted industrialization as opposed to Jefferson's concept of an agricultural economy, and aroused factionalism, which led to the development of political parties in America. Thwarting Aaron Burr's election as President in 1800 and as governor of New York in 1804, he was killed by the latter in a pistol duel.*

106		UnFVF	UseFVF
30¢	**black**	14,000.00	2,200.00
	deep black	14,000.00	2,200.00
	On cover		3,500.00
	Double grill	—	—
	Earliest documented cover: *Aug. 23, 1870*		

1870. OLIVER PERRY ISSUE

107 *At the age of 28, Commodore Oliver Hazard Perry (1785-1819) forced a British surrender in the vicious battle of Lake Erie, Sept. 10, 1813, and reported, "We have met the enemy, and they are ours." It was the first time in history that an entire British squadron was defeated and every ship captured.*

107		UnFVF	UseFVF
90¢	**carmine**	13,500.00	1,500.00
	dark carmine	13,500.00	1,500.00
	On cover		—
	Double grill	—	
	Split grill		1,650.00
	FDC *(April 12, 1870)*		

1870. BENJAMIN FRANKLIN ISSUE

108		UnFVF	UseFVF
1¢	**ultramarine**	500.00	15.00
	dark ultramarine	500.00	15.00
	gray blue	500.00	15.00
	pale ultramarine	500.00	15.00
	On cover		18.00
	Double transfer	—	20.00
	Worn plate	475.00	15.00
	Earliest documented cover: *May 7, 1870*		

1870. ANDREW JACKSON ISSUE

109		UnFVF	UseFVF
2¢	**red brown**	325.00	8.00
	dark red brown	325.00	8.00
	orange brown	325.00	10.00
	pale red brown	325.00	9.00
	On cover		11.00
	Bisect (any) on cover		700.00
	Double transfer	—	12.00
	v. Double impression	—	—
	Earliest documented cover: *June 11, 1870*		

1870. GEORGE WASHINGTON ISSUE

110		UnFVF	UseFVF
3¢	**green**	225.00	1.50
	dark green	225.00	1.50
	pale green	225.00	1.50
	yellow green	325.00	1.60
	On cover		2.10
	Plate block of 10, w/imprint	3,500.00	
	Double transfer	—	12.00
	Cracked plate	—	55.00
	Worn plate	300.00	1.50
	v. Double impression	—	1,250.00
	v1. Printed both sides	—	1,750.00
	Earliest documented cover: *March 1, 1870*		

1870. ABRAHAM LINCOLN ISSUE

111		UnFVF	UseFVF
6¢	**carmine**	750.00	21.00
	brown carmine	750.00	21.00
	dark carmine	750.00	21.00
	rose	750.00	21.00
	violet carmine	700.00	30.00
	On cover		42.50
	Vertical bisect on cover		—
	Double paper	—	—
	Double transfer	—	—
	v. Double impression	—	1,500.00
	Earliest documented cover: *March 28, 1870*		

1871. EDWIN STANTON ISSUE

112		UnFVF	UseFVF
7¢	**vermilion**	1,150.00	80.00
	deep vermilion	1,150.00	80.00
	On cover		160.00
	Cracked plate	—	—
	Double transfer	—	
	Earliest documented cover: *May 11, 1871*		

1870. THOMAS JEFFERSON ISSUE

113		UnFVF	UseFVF
10¢	**brown**	975.00	17.00
	dark brown	975.00	17.00
	yellow brown	975.00	17.00
	On cover		37.50
	Double transfer	—	75.00
	Earliest documented cover: *May 25, 1870*		

1870. HENRY CLAY ISSUE

114		UnFVF	UseFVF
12¢	**pale violet**	1,750.00	150.00
	dark violet	1,750.00	150.00
	violet	1,750.00	150.00
	On cover		425.00
	Earliest documented cover: *July 9, 1870*		

1870. DANIEL WEBSTER ISSUE

115		UnFVF	UseFVF
15¢	**orange**	1,900.00	165.00
	deep orange	1,900.00	165.00
	On cover		310.00

			UnFVF	UseFVF
	v. Double impression		—	1,650.00
	Earliest documented cover: *June 24, 1870*			

1870. GEN. WINFIELD SCOTT ISSUE

116			UnFVF	UseFVF
24¢	**purple**		1,500.00	120.00
	bright purple		1,500.00	120.00
	dark purple		1,500.00	120.00
	dull purple		1,500.00	120.00
	On cover			1,500.00
	Double paper		—	
	Earliest documented cover: *Nov. 18, 1870*			

1871. ALEXANDER HAMILTON ISSUE

117			UnFVF	UseFVF
30¢	**black**		5,000.00	180.00
	On cover			775.00
	Earliest documented cover: *July 13, 1870*			

1872. OLIVER PERRY ISSUE

118			UnFVF	UseFVF
90¢	**carmine**		4,000.00	275.00
	dark carmine		4,000.00	275.00
	On cover			—
	Earliest documented cover: *Sept. 1, 1872*			

1873. Continental Bank Note Co. Portrait Series

The Continental Bank Note Co. was awarded the printing contract for the Large Bank Note Issues for the period of May 1, 1873, through April 30, 1877. This contract later was extended until this company was consolidated with the American Bank Note Co. on Feb. 4, 1879. When Continental took over the printing contract, it took over some of the plates and the dies used by National in the production of the stamps of 1870-71. While the designs of the stamps printed by Continental are similar or identical to those printed by National, the 1¢ through 12¢ easily may be identified because the Continental stamps had so-called "secret marks." The 15¢ can be distinguished by plate wear and some shade variation, and the 30¢ and 90¢ can be distinguished by slight shade differences. The stamps were printed on hard, white wove paper, varying from thin to thick, that generally is difficult or impossible to differentiate from the paper used by National. *The paper is unwatermarked and the stamps are printed by intaglio, perforated 12.*

Grill J about 7x9mm, with blunt tips, was used on all values except the 24¢ and 90¢.

1873. BENJAMIN FRANKLIN ISSUE

 119, 132 *Benjamin Franklin. In the pearl at the left of the numeral "1" there is a small dash of color.*

 Detail of grill J

119			UnFVF	UseFVF
1¢	**ultramarine**		225.00	4.00
	blue		225.00	4.00
	dark ultramarine		240.00	4.00
	dull ultramarine		225.00	4.00
	gray blue		225.00	4.25
	On cover			5.00
	Plate block of 12, w/imprint		6,000.00	
	"Cogwheel" punch cut in paper		375.00	
	Cracked plate		—	—
	Double paper		375.00	
	Double transfer		290.00	7.50
	p. Paper with silk fibers		—	25.00
	p1. Ribbed paper		240.00	5.25
	v. With grill		2,000.00	
	v1. Pair, imperforate		—	550.00
	Earliest documented cover: *Aug. 22, 1873*			

1873. ANDREW JACKSON ISSUE

 120, 121, 133 *Andrew Jackson. In the notch formed underneath the semi-circular ornament immediately to the left of the "S" of "U.S.," the lines forming the apex of the notch join in a small point of color.*

120			UnFVF	UseFVF
2¢	**brown**		375.00	16.00
	dark brown		375.00	16.00
	dark red brown		375.00	16.00
	yellow brown		375.00	17.50
	On cover			22.50
	Vertical bisect on cover			—
	Cracked plate		—	—
	Double paper		500.00	35.00
	Double transfer		—	22.50
	W/secret mark		410.00	19.00
	p. Ribbed paper		400.00	19.00
	v. Double impression		—	—
	v1. With grill		1,850.00	750.00
	Earliest documented cover: *July 12, 1873*			

1875. ANDREW JACKSON ISSUE

121			UnFVF	UseFVF
2¢	**vermilion**		350.00	8.00
	On cover			12.50
	Plate block of 12, w/imprint		—	
	Double paper		—	—
	Double transfer		—	—
	p. Paper with silk fibers		450.00	15.00
	p1. Ribbed paper		—	—
	p2. With grill		750.00	
	v. Pair, imperforate		—	—
	Earliest documented cover: *July 15, 1875*			

1873. GEORGE WASHINGTON ISSUE

 122, 134 *George Washington. Under the word "THREE," the long tail of the ribbon is heavily shaded along its lower edge.*

122			UnFVF	UseFVF
3¢	**green**		130.00	1.25
	bluish green		130.00	1.25
	dark green		130.00	1.25
	yellow green		130.00	1.25
	dark yellow green		130.00	1.25
	olive green		130.00	1.25
	On cover			2.00
	Plate block of 10, w/imprint		2,600.00	
	Plate block of 12, w/imprint		3,500.00	
	Plate strip of 5, w/imprint		775.00	
	Plate strip of 6, w/imprint		900.00	
	"Cogwheel" punch cut in paper		275.00	225.00
	Cracked plate		—	32.50
	Double transfer		—	5.75
	Double paper		190.00	8.00
	Short transfer		—	15.00
	p. Ribbed paper		150.00	2.10
	p1. Paper with silk fibers		—	5.00
	p2. With grill		500.00	
	v. Double impression		—	1,250.00
	v1. Printed on both sides		—	
	v2. Pair, imperforate		850.00	
	v3. Horizontal pair, imperforate between			1,300.00
	v4. Horizontal pair, imperforate vertically		—	—
	Earliest documented cover: *July 17, 1873*			

1875. ZACHARY TAYLOR ISSUE

123, 136 *Zachary Taylor. This is a historically interesting stamp for it marked the inauguration of the Universal Postal Union, setting a 5¢ rate for mail abroad and the blue color, which was generally adhered to after 1898. Also unusual in a changing world, the 5¢ rate for a letter to Europe stood for 78 years, until Nov. 1, 1953, when the rate was changed to 8¢.*

123 5¢		UnFVF	UseFVF
	Prussian blue	575.00	17.00
	bright blue	575.00	17.00
	dark blue	575.00	17.00
	greenish blue	575.00	25.00
	pale blue	550.00	20.00
	On cover		32.50
	Cracked plate	—	170.00
	Double paper	625.00	—
	Double transfer	—	32.50
	p. Paper with silk fibers	—	32.50
	p1. Ribbed paper	—	—
	p2. With grill	3,000.00	
	Earliest documented cover: *July 10, 1875*		

1873. ABRAHAM LINCOLN ISSUE

124, 137 *Abraham Lincoln. The first four vertical lines of the shading in the lower part of the left ribbon, to the left and downward from the "S" in "SIX," have been made heavier.*

124 6¢		UnFVF	UseFVF
	dull Venetian red	400.00	15.00
	brown rose	400.00	15.00
	rose	400.00	15.00
	On cover		45.00
	Plate block of 12, w/imprint	16,000.00	
	Double paper	—	
	p. Paper with silk fibers	—	40.00
	p1. Ribbed paper	—	19.00
	p2. With grill	1,800.00	
	Earliest documented cover: *June 8, 1873*		

1873. EDWIN STANTON ISSUE

125 *Edwin Stanton. A small semi-circle has been drawn around each end of the two lines that outline the ball in the lower right corner.*

125 7¢		UnFVF	UseFVF
	vermilion	1,100.00	60.00
	dark vermilion	1,100.00	60.00
	On cover		175.00
	Plate block of 12, w/imprint	—	
	Double paper	—	—
	Double transfer of "SEVEN CENTS"	—	200.00
	Double transfer in lower left corner	—	95.00
	p. Paper with silk fibers	—	130.00
	p1. Ribbed paper	—	95.00
	p2. With grill	3,250.00	
	Earliest documented cover: *Sept. 10, 1873*		

> Please read the introduction to this catalog carefully. It contains much valuable information for all stamp collectors, and also makes the catalog easier to use.

1873. THOMAS JEFFERSON ISSUE

126, 139 *Thomas Jefferson. The scroll ornament at the right end of the upper label, below the letter "E" of "POSTAGE," has a small crescent of color within it.*

126 10¢		UnFVF	UseFVF
	brown	950.00	17.00
	dark brown	950.00	17.00
	yellow brown	950.00	17.00
	On cover		32.50
	Plate block of 10, w/imprint	10,500.00	
	Plate block of 12, w/imprint	13,000.00	
	Double paper	800.00	
	Double transfer	—	
	p. Paper with silk fibers	—	31.00
	p1. Ribbed paper	—	28.00
	p2. With grill	3,500.00	
	v. Pair, imperforate	—	2,750.00
	v1. Horizontal pair, imperforate between	—	2,500.00
	Earliest documented cover: *Aug. 2, 1873*		

1874. HENRY CLAY ISSUE

127 *Henry Clay. The balls of the figure "2" are crescent shaped instead of nearly round.*

127 12¢		UnFVF	UseFVF
	blackish violet	1,800.00	75.00
	On cover		325.00
	p. Ribbed paper	—	100.00
	p1. With grill	5,250.00	
	Earliest documented cover: *Jan. 3, 1874*		

1873. DANIEL WEBSTER ISSUE

128, 140 *Daniel Webster. The thin lines shading the triangles and below the letters "U.S. POSTAGE" are worn. These areas show less color and therefore appear more white than the 15¢ National printing.*

128 15¢		UnFVF	UseFVF
	yellow orange	2,100.00	120.00
	dull orange	2,100.00	120.00
	red orange	2,100.00	120.00
	On cover		300.00
	Double paper	—	
	p. Paper with silk fibers	2,200.00	135.00
	p1. Paper with vertical ribs	2,150.00	125.00
	p2. With grill	5,250.00	
	Earliest documented cover: *July 22, 1873*		

1874. GEN. WINFIELD SCOTT ISSUE

The 24¢ Continental has been the subject of much controversy. It is known that 365,000 copies of this stamp were printed and delivered to the Stamp Agent, but there is no documentation that any of them were issued to post offices. In 1885, 364,950 copies of the 24¢ stamps were destroyed, for they were no longer needed to make up the then-existing postage rates. It is not known whether these were all Continentals. Some experts think that unused examples can be distinguished by their gum, with the Continentals bearing a thinner and lighter-colored gum than the Nationals. Another possible means of identification lies in the paper. The Continental 24¢ was printed from the same plate as the National 24¢, so they are identical in design. The Philatelic Foundation issued a certificate of genuineness to a used 24¢ on vertically ribbed paper; experts believe that only Continental used such paper. The listing below is based on that single item.

129		UnFVF	UseFVF
24¢	light purple		—400,000.00

1874. ALEXANDER HAMILTON ISSUE

130		UnFVF	UseFVF
30¢	gray black	2,500.00	90.00
	greenish black	2,500.00	90.00
	On cover		725.00
	Double paper	—	—
	Double transfer	—	130.00
	p. Paper with silk fibers	—	
	p1.Ribbed paper	2,600.00	115.00
	p2.With grill	22,500.00	
	Earliest documented cover: *Oct. 14, 1874*		

The 30¢ Continental and 30¢ National are identical except in shade.

1874. OLIVER PERRY ISSUE

131		UnFVF	UseFVF
90¢	rose carmine	2,750.00	220.00
	dull rose carmine	2,750.00	220.00
	On cover		7,500.00

The 90¢ Continental and the 90¢ National are identical except in shade.

1875. BENJAMIN FRANKLIN SPECIAL PRINTING OF THE 1873 PICTORIAL ISSUE which was still in use. For some reason, these stamps usually were cut apart with scissors so that the perforations generally are mutilated. The special printing can be identified by the color shades and by the very white paper (instead of the yellowish of the original issue). Numbers sold are not known. Some estimate can be made by studying the table that follows SP57. *Printed by the Continental Bank Note Co., intaglio on hard white wove paper, perforated 12, and issued without gum.*

SP32		UnFVF	UseFVF
1¢	bright ultramarine	15,000.00	

1875. ANDREW JACKSON SPECIAL PRINTING PICTORIAL ISSUE

SP33		UnFVF	UseFVF
2¢	blackish brown	7,500.00	

1875. ANDREW JACKSON SPECIAL PRINTING PICTORIAL ISSUE

SP34		UnFVF	UseFVF
2¢	carmine vermilion	33,000.00	

1875. GEORGE WASHINGTON SPECIAL PRINTING PICTORIAL ISSUE

SP35		UnFVF	UseFVF
3¢	bluish green	20,000.00	

1875. ZACHARY TAYLOR SPECIAL PRINTING PICTORIAL ISSUE

SP36		UnFVF	UseFVF
5¢	bright blue	90,000.00	

1875. ABRAHAM LINCOLN SPECIAL PRINTING PICTORIAL ISSUE

SP37		UnFVF	UseFVF
6¢	pale rose	17,500.00	

1875. EDWIN STANTON SPECIAL PRINTING PICTORIAL ISSUE

SP38		UnFVF	UseFVF
7¢	scarlet vermilion	5,100.00	

1875. THOMAS JEFFERSON SPECIAL PRINTING PICTORIAL ISSUE

SP39		UnFVF	UseFVF
10¢	yellow brown	13,000.00	

1875. HENRY CLAY SPECIAL PRINTING PICTORIAL ISSUE

SP40		UnFVF	UseFVF
12¢	black violet	5,000.00	

1875. DANIEL WEBSTER SPECIAL PRINTING PICTORIAL ISSUE

SP41		UnFVF	UseFVF
15¢	bright orange	17,000.00	

1875. WINFIELD SCOTT SPECIAL PRINTING PICTORIAL ISSUE

SP42		UnFVF	UseFVF
24¢	dull purple	4,200.00	

1875. ALEXANDER HAMILTON SPECIAL PRINTING PICTORIAL ISSUE

SP43		UnFVF	UseFVF
30¢	greenish black	13,000.00	

1875. OLIVER PERRY SPECIAL PRINTING PICTORIAL ISSUE

SP44		UnFVF	UseFVF
90¢	violet carmine	13,000.00	

1879. American Bank Note Co. Portrait Series The American Bank Note Co. absorbed the Continental Bank Note Co. on Feb. 4, 1879, and continued to print postage, department and newspaper stamps. American used many of the plates bearing the Continental imprints, so the imprint does not always accurately indicate the producing firm. The American Bank Note Co. printed stamps on unwatermarked, soft, porous paper instead of the hard paper used by National and Continental. With the exception of one type of the 10¢, all the stamps from 1¢ through the 12¢ carry the same "secret marks" as the Continentals. With the exception of the color changes on the 3¢, 30¢ and 90¢ that were issued later, these stamps were issued in 1879. *All were printed by intaglio and perforated 12.*

1879. BENJAMIN FRANKLIN ISSUE

132		UnFVF	UseFVF
1¢	dark ultramarine	300.00	3.50
	blue	300.00	3.50
	gray blue	300.00	3.50
	On cover		4.00
	Plate block of 10, w/imprint	4,500.00	
	Double transfer	—	9.50
	Earliest documented cover: *Jan. 3, 1879*		

1879. ANDREW JACKSON ISSUE

133		UnFVF	UseFVF
2¢	vermilion	130.00	3.00
	orange vermilion	130.00	3.00
	On cover		3.50
	Plate block of 10, w/imprint	1,750.00	
	Plate block of 12, w/imprint	2,250.00	
	Double transfer	—	
	Double impression	—	400.00
	Earliest documented cover: *Dec. 18, 1878*		500.00

1879. GEORGE WASHINGTON ISSUE

134		UnFVF	UseFVF
3¢	green	90.00	.80
	dark green	90.00	.80
	dull green	90.00	.80
	On cover		1.00
	Plate block of 10, w/imprint	1,250.00	
	Plate block of 12, w/imprint	1,500.00	
	Plate block of 14, w/imprint	1,800.00	
	Double transfer	—	—
	Short transfer	—	6.00
	Double impression	—	
	v. Pair, imperforate	550.00	
	Earliest documented cover: *Aug. 3, 1878*		

1887. GEORGE WASHINGTON ISSUE

135		UnFVF	UseFVF
3¢	vermilion	65.00	45.00
	On cover		105.00
	Plate block of 10, w/imprint	1,400.00	
	Plate block of 12, w/imprint	1,600.00	
	Plate strip of 5, w/imprint	475.00	
	Plate strip of 6, w/imprint	550.00	
	Earliest documented cover: *Oct. 18, 1887*		

1879. ZACHARY TAYLOR ISSUE

136		UnFVF	UseFVF
5¢	blue	450.00	10.00
	bright blue	450.00	10.00
	dark blue	450.00	10.00
	dull blue	450.00	10.00
	On cover		22.50
	Plate block of 12, w/imprint	11,500.00	
	Earliest documented cover: *Feb. 26, 1879*		

1879. ABRAHAM LINCOLN ISSUE

137		UnFVF	UseFVF
6¢	dull pink	900.00	17.00
	brown pink	900.00	17.00
	pink	900.00	17.00
	On cover		40.00
	Earliest documented cover: *July 1, 1879*		

1879. THOMAS JEFFERSON ISSUE

138		UnFVF	UseFVF
10¢	brown like No. 102, but no secret mark	2,250.00	22.00
	yellow brown	2,250.00	22.00
	On cover		47.50
	Double transfer	—	45.00
	Earliest documented cover: *Sept. 5, 1879*		

1879. THOMAS JEFFERSON ISSUE

139

		UnFVF	UseFVF
10¢	**brown** like No. 126, with secret mark	1,750.00	22.00
	black brown	1,900.00	37.50
	yellow brown	1,750.00	25.00
	On cover		40.00
	Cracked plate	—	—
	Double transfer	—	45.00
	Pair, 1 each Nos. 138, 139	4,850.00	275.00
	v. Vertical pair, imperforate between		
	Earliest documented cover: Oct. 5, 1878		

1879. DANIEL WEBSTER ISSUE

140

		UnFVF	UseFVF
15¢	**orange**	300.00	22.00
	red orange	300.00	22.00
	yellow orange	300.00	22.00
	On cover		85.00
	Plate block of 12, w/imprint	6,750.00	
	Earliest documented cover: May 29, 1879		

1882. ALEXANDER HAMILTON ISSUE

141

		UnFVF	UseFVF
30¢	**black**	850.00	45.00
	greenish black	850.00	45.00
	On cover		425.00
	Plate block of 10, w/imprint	15,000.00	
	Earliest documented cover: Aug. 8, 1881		

1888. ALEXANDER HAMILTON ISSUE

142

		UnFVF	UseFVF
30¢	**orange brown**	375.00	85.00
	dark orange brown	375.00	85.00
	On cover		1,400.00
	Plate block of 10, w/imprint	7,000.00	
	Plate block of 12, w/imprint	—	
	Plate strip of 5, w/imprint	2,650.00	
	Earliest documented cover: Sept. 7, 1888		

1880. OLIVER PERRY ISSUE

143

		UnFVF	UseFVF
90¢	**carmine**	2,250.00	225.00
	carmine rose	2,250.00	225.00
	rose	2,250.00	225.00
	On cover		5,000.00
	Double paper	—	—
	Earliest documented cover: June 24, 1882		

1880. OLIVER PERRY ISSUE

144

		UnFVF	UseFVF
90¢	**dark red violet**	1,100.00	225.00
	bright purple	1,100.00	225.00
	On cover		10,000.00
	Plate block of 10, w/imprint	25,000.00	
	Plate block of 12, w/imprint	—	
	Plate strip of 5, w/imprint	7,500.00	
	v. Pair, imperforate	2,500.00	
	Earliest documented cover: Oct. 29, 1888		

1880. SPECIAL PRINTING OF THE 1879 ISSUE
By the American Bank Note Co. Designs on soft porous paper, intaglio, perforated 12.

SP45

		UnFVF	UseFVF
1¢	**deep ultramarine**	32,000.00	

SP46

		UnFVF	UseFVF
2¢	**blackish brown**	15,000.00	

SP47

		UnFVF	UseFVF
2¢	**scarlet vermilion**	57,000.00	

SP48

		UnFVF	UseFVF
3¢	**bluish green**	65,000.00	

SP49

		UnFVF	UseFVF
5¢	**deep blue**	75,000.00	

SP50

		UnFVF	UseFVF
6¢	**pale rose**	28,000.00	

SP51

		UnFVF	UseFVF
7¢	**scarlet vermilion**	6,000.00	

SP52

		UnFVF	UseFVF
10¢	**deep brown**	30,000.00	

SP53

		UnFVF	UseFVF
12¢	**black purple**	9,000.00	

SP54

		UnFVF	UseFVF
15¢	**orange**	25,000.00	

SP55

		UnFVF	UseFVF
24¢	**blackish violet**	6,200.00	

SP56

		UnFVF	UseFVF
30¢	**greenish black**	18,000.00	

SP57

		UnFVF	UseFVF
90¢	**pale carmine**	20,000.00	

The Post Office Department kept no separate records of the sales of the 1875 and 1880 Special Printings but did list the combined sales which we show here. The 1880 printing is the more rare of the two.

1¢	SP32, SP45	388	10¢	SP39, SP52	180
2¢	SP33, SP46	416	12¢	SP40, SP53	282
2¢	SP34, SP47	917	15¢	SP41, SP54	169
3¢	SP35, SP48	267	24¢	SP42, SP55	286
5¢	SP36, SP49	317	30¢	SP43, SP56	179
6¢	SP37, SP50	185	90¢	SP44, SP57	170
7¢	SP38, SP51	473			

1881-82. RE-ENGRAVED DESIGNS OF 1873 ISSUE
for the 1¢, 3¢, 6¢, and 10¢ denominations. They were *printed by the American Bank Note Co. by intaglio on soft, porous, unwatermarked paper and were perforated 12.*

132 *1879 Design*

145 *1881 Design, re-engraved:* The vertical lines forming the background in the upper part of the stamp have been made much heavier and the background now appears to be almost solid. Lines of shading also have been added to the curving ornaments in the upper corners of the stamps.

145

		UnFVF	UseFVF
1¢	**ultramarine**	75.00	1.20
	bright ultramarine	75.00	1.20
	dull blue	75.00	1.20
	gray blue	75.00	1.20
	On cover		1.40
	Plate block of 10, w/imprint	1,600.00	
	Plate block of 12, w/imprint	1,800.00	
	Plate strip of 5, w/imprint	475.00	
	Plate strip of 6, w/imprint	575.00	
	"Cogwheel" punch cut in paper	190.00	
	Double transfer	105.00	6.00
	Earliest documented cover: Nov. 2, 1881		

1881. GEORGE WASHINGTON ISSUE

134 *1879 Design*

146 *1881 Design, re-engraved:* The shading at the sides of the large central oval is only about half the previous thickness. A short horizontal dash has been added just below the "TS" of "CENTS."

146

		UnFVF	UseFVF
3¢	**blue green**	75.00	.80
	green	75.00	.80
	yellow green	75.00	.80

On cover			1.00
Plate block of 10, w/imprint	1,600.00		
Plate strip of 5, w/imprint	500.00		
Cracked plate	—		
Double transfer	—	12.00	
Punched w/8 small holes in a circle	210.00		
v1. Plate block of 10, w/imprint	3,000.00		
v2. Double impression	—	—	
Earliest documented cover: *Aug. 7, 1881*			

1882. ABRAHAM LINCOLN ISSUE

147 There are only three vertical lines from the outside of the panel to the outside of the stamps. The preceding issue had four lines.

147		UnFVF	UseFVF
6¢	**rose**	525.00	65.00
	dull rose	525.00	65.00
	brown red	475.00	110.00
	On cover		160.00
	On cover (brown red)		230.00
	Double transfer	650.00	100.00
	Block of 4	2,500.00	700.00
	Earliest documented cover: *June 1, 1882*		

1882. THOMAS JEFFERSON ISSUE

148 There are only four vertical lines between the left side of the oval and the edge of the shield. The preceding issues had five lines. The lines of the background have been made heavier so that these stamps appear much more heavily inked than their predecessors.

148		UnFVF	UseFVF
10¢	**brown**	160.00	6.00
	olive brown	175.00	6.00
	orange brown	160.00	6.00
	purple brown	175.00	6.00
	yellow brown	160.00	6.00
	black brown	800.00	47.50
	On cover		11.00
	Plate block of 10 w/imprint	3,250.00	
	Plate block of 12, w/imprint	4,000.00	
	Plate strip of 5, w/imprint	1,100.00	
	Plate strip of 6, w/imprint	1,300.00	
	v. Double impression	—	
	Earliest documented cover: *May 4, 1882*		

1882-88. American Bank Note Co. Portrait Series

New designs. *Intaglio, unwatermarked soft, porous paper, perforated 12.*

1887. BENJAMIN FRANKLIN ISSUE

149 Benjamin Franklin

149		UnFVF	UseFVF
1¢	**ultramarine**	100.00	2.25
	bright ultramarine	100.00	2.25
	On cover		2.50
	Plate block of 10, w/imprint	1,550.00	
	Plate block of 12, w/imprint	1,850.00	
	Plate strip of 5, w/imprint	625.00	
	Plate strip of 6, w/imprint	750.00	
	Double transfer	—	
	v. Pair, imperforate	1,000.00	525.00
	Earliest documented cover: *July 15, 1887*		

1883. GEORGE WASHINGTON ISSUE

150, 151 George Washington. This stamp was issued to pay the reduced rate for First Class letters as provided by an Act of Congress approved March 3, 1883, and effective Oct. 1, 1883.

150		UnFVF	UseFVF
2¢	**red brown**	40.00	.80
	dark red brown	40.00	.80
	orange brown	40.00	.80
	On cover		1.00
	Plate block of 10, w/imprint	1,100.00	
	Plate block of 12, w/imprint	1,300.00	
	Plate strip of 5, w/imprint	290.00	
	Plate strip of 6, w/imprint	360.00	
	Double transfer	55.00	2.25
	v. Pair, imperforate	—	
	v1. Horizontal pair, imperforate between	2,000.00	—
	FDC *(Oct. 1, 1883)*		2,000.00

1887. GEORGE WASHINGTON ISSUE

151		UnFVF	UseFVF
2¢	**green**	45.00	.80
	bright green	45.00	.80
	dark green	45.00	.80
	On cover		1.00
	Plate block of 10, w/imprint	1,000.00	
	Plate block of 12, w/imprint	1,200.00	
	Plate strip of 5, w/imprint	300.00	
	Plate strip of 6, w/imprint	375.00	
	Double transfer	—	3.25
	v. Printed on both sides	—	
	Pair, imperforate	1,000.00	1,000.00
	Earliest documented cover: *Sept. 21, 1887*; EKU *(Sept. 20, 1887)*		

1883. ANDREW JACKSON ISSUE

152, 153 Andrew Jackson. This denomination was issued to pay the rate on First Class letters of double weight.

152		UnFVF	UseFVF
4¢	**deep bluish green**	275.00	15.00
	blue green	275.00	15.00
	On cover		47.50
	Plate block of 10, w/imprint	4,250.00	
	Plate block of 12, w/imprint	5,000.00	
	Plate block of 6, w/imprint	1,200.00	
	Cracked plate	—	
	Double transfer	—	
	v. Pair, imperforate	—	
	v1. Horizontal pair, imperforate between	—	
	FDC *(Oct. 1, 1883)*		40,000.00

1883. SPECIAL PRINTING ISSUE of the 2¢ and 4¢ stamps of 1883. *Printed by the American Bank Note Co., intaglio on soft, porous paper, the 2¢ with gum and the 4¢ without gum, both perforated 12.* Quantities are not known.

SP59		UnFVF	UseFVF
2¢	**red brown**	400.00	
	v. Horizontal pair, imperforate between	2,000.00	

1883. SPECIAL PRINTING ISSUE

SP60		UnFVF	UseFVF
4¢	**blue green**	27,500.00	

1889. ANDREW JACKSON ISSUE

153		UnFVF	UseFVF
4¢	**carmine**	190.00	18.00
	dull rose	190.00	18.00
	rose carmine	190.00	18.00
	On cover		45.00

Plate block of 10, w/imprint	4,500.00	
Plate block of 12, w/imprint	5,250.00	
Plate strip of 5, w/imprint	1,400.00	
Plate strip of 6, w/imprint	1,700.00	
Double transfer	—	
Earliest documented cover: *Jan. 18, 1889*		

1882. JAMES GARFIELD ISSUE

154 *James Garfield. This design was issued to honor the late President, who was shot on July 2, 1881, after only 200 days in office, by a disgruntled office-seeker, and died Sept. 19 after 11 weeks of botched medical care.*

154

5¢		UnFVF	UseFVF
	olive brown	275.00	7.50
	brown	275.00	7.50
	gray brown	275.00	7.50
	On cover		16.00
	Plate block of 10 w/imprint	5,000.00	
	Plate block of 12, w/imprint	5,500.00	
	Plate strip of 5, w/imprint	1,650.00	
	Plate strip of 6, w/imprint	1,900.00	
	FDC *(April 10, 1882)*		

1882. JAMES GARFIELD SPECIAL PRINTING ISSUE

Special printing of the 5¢ Garfield stamp of 1882 is very difficult to distinguish from the regular printing of the same year. *American Bank Note Co., intaglio on soft, porous paper without gum, perforated 12.*

SP58

5¢		UnFVF	UseFVF
	light brownish gray (2,463 sold)	28,500.00	

1888. JAMES GARFIELD ISSUE

155

5¢		UnFVF	UseFVF
	indigo	225.00	14.00
	dark blue	225.00	14.00
	blue	225.00	14.00
	On cover		22.50
	Plate block of 10, w/imprint	6,500.00	
	Plate block of 12, w/imprint	8,000.00	
	Plate strip of 5, w/imprint	1,500.00	
	Plate strip of 6, w/imprint	1,800.00	
	v. Pair, imperforate	1,200.00	
	Earliest documented cover: *March 15, 1888*		

1890. American Bank Note Co. Small Size Portrait Series

The American Bank Note Company produced this series in a smaller size than had been used previously. All stamps in this series are *intaglio on unwatermarked soft, porous paper, perforated 12.*

1890. BENJAMIN FRANKLIN ISSUE

156 *Benjamin Franklin*

156

1¢		UnFVF	UseFVF
	dull blue	22.00	.80
	blue	22.00	.80
	dark blue	22.00	.80
	ultramarine	22.00	.80
	On cover		1.00
	Plate block of 10, w/imprint	750.00	
	Plate block of 12, w/imprint	925.00	
	Plate block of 14, w/imprint	1,200.00	
	Plate strip of 5, w/imprint	160.00	
	Plate strip of 6, w/imprint	190.00	
	Plate strip of 7, w/imprint	220.00	
	Double transfer	—	—
	v. Pair, imperforate	150.00	
	FDC *(Feb. 27, 1890)*		

1890. GEORGE WASHINGTON ISSUE

157, 158 *George Washington*

158v *Cap on left "2"*

158v2 *Cap on right "2"*

157

2¢		UnFVF	UseFVF
	lake	200.00	1.25
	bright lilac carmine	200.00	1.25
	lilac carmine	250.00	1.00
	On cover		1.75
	Plate block of 10, w/imprint	4,000.00	
	Plate strip of 5, w/imprint	1,350.00	
	Double transfer	—	—
	v. Pair, imperforate	100.00	
	FDC *(Feb. 22, 1890)*		17,500.00

158

2¢		UnFVF	UseFVF
	carmine	36.00	.65
	carmine rose	36.00	.65
	dark carmine	36.00	.65
	On cover		1.00
	Plate block of 10, w/imprint	550.00	
	Plate block of 12, w/imprint	675.00	
	Plate block of 14, w/imprint	850.00	
	Plate strip of 5, w/imprint	150.00	
	Plate strip of 6, w/imprint	180.00	
	Plate strip of 7, w/imprint	210.00	
	Double transfer	—	3.25
	v. Cap on left "2"	100.00	2.50
	Plate block of 12, w/imprint	1,250.00	
	v1. Pair, 1 w/cap, 1 without		—
	v2. Cap on both "2's"	475.00	20.00
	v3. Pair, 1 w/cap on 1 "2"		
	1 w/cap on both "2's"	—	—
	v4. Pair, imperforate	125.00	
	Earliest documented cover: *April 29, 1890* (No. 158); *Oct. 1, 1892* (158v); *Sept. 15, 1892* (No. 158v3)		

1890. ANDREW JACKSON ISSUE

159 *Andrew Jackson*

159

3¢		UnFVF	UseFVF
	dark lilac	65.00	6.50
	bright lilac	65.00	6.50
	lilac	65.00	6.50
	On cover		16.00
	Plate block of 10, w/imprint	2,750.00	
	Plate strip of 5, w/imprint	500.00	
	v. Pair, imperforate	165.00	
	FDC *(Feb. 28, 1890)*		

1890. ABRAHAM LINCOLN ISSUE

160 *Abraham Lincoln*

160

4¢		UnFVF	UseFVF
	dark brown	75.00	2.25
	black brown	75.00	2.25
	On cover		14.00
	Plate block of 10, w/imprint	3,000.00	
	Plate strip of 5, w/imprint	550.00	
	Double transfer	105.00	
	v. Pair, imperforate	165.00	
	Earliest documented cover: *July 16, 1890*		

1890. ULYSSES S. GRANT ISSUE

161 *Ulysses S. Grant*

161

5¢		UnFVF	UseFVF
	chocolate	65.00	2.50
	yellow brown	80.00	2.75
	On cover		13.00
	Plate block of 10, w/imprint	2,800.00	
	Plate strip of 5, w/imprint	475.00	
	Double transfer	100.00	3.25
	v. Pair, imperforate	165.00	
	Earliest documented cover: *June 14, 1890*		

1890. JAMES GARFIELD ISSUE

162 *James Garfield*

162

6¢		UnFVF	UseFVF
	brown red	75.00	17.00
	dark brown red	75.00	17.00
	On cover		35.00
	Plate block of 10, w/imprint	2,900.00	
	Plate strip of 5, w/imprint	500.00	
	v. Pair, imperforate	175.00	
	FDC *(Feb. 22, 1890);* Earliest documented cover: *May 30, 1890*		

1890. W.T. SHERMAN ISSUE

163 *W.T. Sherman, from an 1888 photograph by Napoleon B. Sarony.*

163

8¢		UnFVF	UseFVF
	purple brown	50.00	11.00
	gray lilac	50.00	11.00
	magenta	50.00	11.00
	On cover		29.00
	Plate block of 10, w/imprint	1,800.00	
	Plate strip of 5, w/imprint	340.00	
	v. Pair, imperforate	1,250.00	
	Earliest documented cover: *May 21, 1893*		

1890. DANIEL WEBSTER ISSUE

164 *Daniel Webster*

164

10¢		UnFVF	UseFVF
	deep bluish green	250.00	20.00
	dark green	175.00	3.50
	green	175.00	3.50
	On cover		10.00
	Plate block of 10, w/imprint	4,000.00	
	Plate strip of 5, w/imprint	950.00	
	Double transfer	—	—
	v. Pair, imperforate	175.00	
	FDC *(Feb. 22, 1890);* Earliest documented cover: *April 7, 1890*		

1890. HENRY CLAY ISSUE

165 *Henry Clay*

165

15¢		UnFVF	UseFVF
	indigo	200.00	17.00
	dark indigo	200.00	17.00
	On cover		65.00
	Plate block of 10, w/imprint	8,500.00	
	Plate strip of 5, w/imprint	1,500.00	
	Double transfer	—	—
	Triple transfer	—	—
	v. Pair, imperforate	500.00	
	FDC *(Feb. 22, 1890);* Earliest documented cover: *May 27, 1890*		

DECODING THE CATALOG

Between 1890 and 1898, a sequence of similar series of United States definitive stamps were released. These are known as the Small Bank Notes (1890-93) and the First Bureau Issue (1894-98). These stamps had values ranging between 1¢ and 90¢.

The Small Bank Note stamps, produced by the American Bank Note Co. in 1890-93, are easy to distinguish, since they had no triangles in the upper corners. Beginning in 1894, stamp production was taken over by the Bureau of Engraving and Printing in Washington, D.C. During 1894-98, three basic groups of similar-appearing stamps of this First Bureau Issue were released. These stamps, classed as the 1894, 1895 and 1898 issues, are not difficult to distinguish if you know what you are looking for.

All varieties of the 8¢ value of the series, picturing William Tecumseh Sherman, are perf 12. The first version of the 8¢ Sherman, printed by ABNC in 1893 (Krause-Minkus 163), has no upper corner triangles, making it easy to tell from the Bureau issues that follow. It is known in shades of lilac, gray lilac, magenta and purple brown.

The subsequent Bureau issues were printed in violet brown or purple brown. The first of these was printed on paper without a watermark (Krause-Minkus 179). The perforations for the most part on these stamps are quite crude, making identification fairly simple.

The second 8¢ issue (Minkus 200) was printed on paper bearing a double-line USPS watermark. Any single stamp from this subset should show at least a partial capital "U," "S," "P" or "S" (for "U.S. Postage Stamp"). The watermarked paper was placed into use to help deter the counterfeiting of stamps, which had been a problem.

A small quantity of the 8¢ Shermans was printed on paper intended for use in printing revenue stamps, watermarked "USIR" (for "U.S. Internal Revenue"). This watermark error (Krause-Minkus 200w) is scarce and valuable. A similar error also exists on the 6¢ Garfield definitive of the same series.

Other values from the First Bureau Issue of definitives were reissued in changed colors in 1897-98 to conform to newly introduced Universal Postal Union regulations regarding stamp color, intended to make mail simple to sort and recognize internationally. However, there was no special niche for an 8¢ stamp under the new scheme, so it was not reissued in a new color.

1890. THOMAS JEFFERSON ISSUE

166 *Thomas Jefferson*

166		UnFVF	UseFVF
30¢	black	350.00	25.00
	gray black	350.00	25.00
	full black	350.00	25.00
	On cover		600.00
	Plate block of 10, w/imprint	12,500.00	
	Plate strip of 5, w/imprint	2,250.00	
	Double transfer	—	—
	v. Pair, imperforate	750.00	

FDC *(Feb. 22, 1890)*; Earliest
documented cover: *April 14, 1890*

1890. OLIVER HAZARD PERRY ISSUE

167 *Oliver Hazard Perry*

167		UnFVF	UseFVF
90¢	orange	525.00	110.00
	red orange	525.00	110.00
	yellow orange	525.00	110.00
	On cover		—
	Plate block of 10, w/imprint	25,000.00	
	Plate strip of 5, w/imprint	3,250.00	
	Short transfer at bottom	—	—

v. Pair, imperforate			1,000.00

FDC *(Feb. 22, 1890)*; Earliest
documented cover: *Feb. 7, 1892*

Stamps of all values of the 1890 issue exist imperforate. They are considered finished proofs.

1894. Bureau of Engraving and Printing Portrait Series
Issues from this point through the 1980s were printed by the Bureau of Engraving and Printing, except where otherwise noted.

The first issue of stamps by the Bureau was very similar in design to the issue of 1890, but triangles were added to the upper corners of the stamps and there were some differences in the denominations issued. The stamps were *printed by intaglio on unwatermarked paper, perforated 12. All of the perforation varieties listed here are believed to have been issued legitimately. Other perforation and imperforate varieties exist on some values, but they were not released through regular postal methods.*

1894. BENJAMIN FRANKLIN ISSUE

168, 169, 187, 188 *Benjamin Franklin*

168		UnFVF	UseFVF
1¢	ultramarine	30.00	4.00
	bright ultramarine	30.00	4.00
	dark ultramarine	30.00	4.00
	On cover		12.50
	Plate block of 6, w/imprint	400.00	
	Plate strip of 3, w/imprint	135.00	
	Double transfer	40.00	5.50
	Earliest documented cover: *Oct. 18, 1894*		

DECODING THE CATALOG

Between 1890-98, two similar United States definitive series of stamps with denominations ranging between 1¢ and 90¢ were released. These are known as the Small Bank Notes and the First Bureau Issue. The Small Bank Note stamps, produced in a smaller size than previously by the American Bank Note Co. in 1890, are easy to distinguish, since they had no triangles in the upper corners.

Beginning in 1894, stamp production was taken over by the Bureau of Engraving and Printing. From 1894-98, three basic groups of similar-appearing stamps of this series were released.

These stamps, classed as the 1894, 1895 and 1898 issues, are not difficult to distinguish if you know what you are looking for.

All varieties of the 1¢ value of the series are perforated 12.

The first 1¢ issue (Krause-Minkus 168-169) was printed on unwatermarked paper. The perforations for the most part on these stamps are quite crude, making identification fairly

simple. Minkus 168 is ultramarine. Minkus 169 is blue.

The second 1¢ issue (Minkus 187) also is blue but printed on paper bearing a double-line USPS watermark. Any single stamp from this subset should show at least a partial letter U, S or P.

The watermarked paper was placed into use to help stem the counterfeiting of stamps, which had been a problem with the 2¢ value.

Any single stamp from double-line watermark subset should show at least a partial letter U, S or P, probably not so clear as those shown here.

The third 1¢ issue, (Minkus 188) also was printed on watermarked paper but is easiest to distinguish by its color. It is green and was changed to conform to then-current Universal Postal Union regulations regarding stamp colors.

169

1¢		UnFVF	UseFVF
	blue	60.00	2.50
	bright blue	60.00	2.50
	dark blue	60.00	2.50
	On cover		16.00
	Plate block of 6, w/imprint	800.00	
	Plate strip of 3, w/imprint	275.00	
	Double transfer	—	3.75
	Earliest documented cover: *Nov. 11, 1894*		

1894. GEORGE WASHINGTON ISSUE

170-174, 189-192 *George Washington*

I   II   III

170-172, 189 *Type I. The horizontal lines of background are of same thickness.*

173, 190 *Type II. The horizontal lines are thin within the triangle.*

174, 191, 192 *Type III. The horizontal lines are interrupted by the frame of the triangle and are thin within the triangle.*

170

2¢		UnFVF	UseFVF
	pink triangle I	24.00	3.25
	dull pink	24.00	3.25
	On cover		11.00
	Plate block of 6, w/imprint	275.00	
	Plate strip of 3, w/imprint	110.00	
	Double transfer	—	—
	v. Vertical pair, imperforate horizontally	2,250.00	
	Earliest documented cover: *Oct. 16, 1894*		

171

2¢		UnFVF	UseFVF
	carmine lake triangle I	125.00	2.75
	dark carmine lake	125.00	2.75
	On cover		9.00
	Plate block of 6, w/imprint	1,750.00	
	Plate strip of 3, w/imprint	575.00	
	Double transfer	—	3.50
	Earliest documented cover: *Oct. 11, 1894*		

172

2¢		UnFVF	UseFVF
	carmine triangle I	25.00	1.50
	dark carmine	25.00	2.25
	dull scarlet	25.00	2.25
	scarlet	25.00	.45
	On cover		2.00
	Plate block of 6, w/imprint	350.00	
	Plate strip of 3, w/imprint	120.00	
	Double transfer	—	3.25
	v. Vertical pair, imperforate horizontally	3,000.00	
	v1. Horizontal pair, imperforate between	2,000.00	
	Earliest documented cover: *Oct. 13, 1894*		

173

2¢		UnFVF	UseFVF
	carmine triangle II	275.00	5.00
	dark carmine	275.00	5.00
	On cover		15.00
	Plate block of 6, w/imprint	3,000.00	
	Plate strip of 3, w/imprint	1,100.00	
	Earliest documented cover: *Feb. 16, 1895*		

174

2¢		UnFVF	UseFVF
	carmine triangle III	105.00	5.00
	dull carmine	105.00	5.00
	On cover		15.00
	Plate block of 6, w/imprint	1,650.00	
	Plate strip of 3, w/imprint	475.00	
	Dot in "S" of "Cents"	140.00	5.75
	v. Horizontal pair, imperforate between	1,750.00	
	v1. Horizontal pair, imperforate vertically	1,500.00	
	Earliest documented cover: *April 2, 1895*		

1894. ANDREW JACKSON ISSUE

175, 193 *Andrew Jackson*

175

3¢		UnFVF	UseFVF
	dark lilac	95.00	7.25
	lilac	95.00	7.25
	On cover		25.00
	Plate block of 6, w/imprint	1,250.00	
	Plate strip of 3, w/imprint	425.00	
	Margin block of 4, w/arrow	475.00	
	v. Pair, imperforate	200.00	
	Earliest known usage: *Oct. 20, 1894*		

1894. ABRAHAM LINCOLN ISSUE

176, 194, 195 *Abraham Lincoln*

176

4¢		UnFVF	UseFVF
	dark brown	120.00	4.00
	brown	120.00	4.00
	On cover		18.00
	Plate block of 6, w/imprint	1,750.00	
	Plate strip of 3, w/imprint	525.00	
	Margin block of 4, w/arrow	600.00	
	v. Pair, imperforate	—	
	Earliest known usage: *Oct. 16, 1894*		

1894. ULYSSES S. GRANT ISSUE

177, 196, 197 *Ulysses S. Grant*

177

5¢		UnFVF	UseFVF
	chocolate	115.00	5.00
	dark chocolate	115.00	5.00
	yellow brown	115.00	5.00
	On cover		20.00
	Plate block of 6, w/imprint	1,150.00	
	Plate strip of 3, w/imprint	425.00	
	Margin block of 4, w/arrow	450.00	
	Diagonal lines omitted in oval background (worn plate)	100.00	4.50
	Double transfer	125.00	6.50
	v. Pair, imperforate	250.00	
	v1. Vertical pair, imperforate horizontally	2,250.00	
	Earliest documented cover: *Oct. 23, 1894*		

1894. JAMES GARFIELD ISSUE

178, 198, 199 *James Garfield*

178

6¢		UnFVF	UseFVF
	red brown	135.00	19.00
	On cover		45.00
	Plate block of 6, w/imprint	2,650.00	
	Plate strip of 3, w/imprint	625.00	
	Margin block of 4, w/arrow	650.00	
	v. Vertical pair, imperforate horizontally	1,500.00	
	Earliest documented cover: *Aug. 11, 1894*		

1894. WILLIAM T. SHERMAN ISSUE

179, 200 *W.T. Sherman*

179

8¢		UnFVF	UseFVF
	purple brown	120.00	13.00
	dark purple brown	120.00	13.00
	On cover		45.00
	Plate block of 6, w/imprint	1,750.00	
	Plate strip of 3, w/imprint	575.00	
	Margin block of 4, w/arrow	625.00	
	Earliest documented cover: *May 8, 1895*		

1894. DANIEL WEBSTER ISSUE

180, 201-203 *Daniel Webster*

180

10¢		UnFVF	UseFVF
	blue green	225.00	9.00
	dark green	225.00	9.00
	dull green	225.00	9.00
	On cover		32.50
	Plate block of 6, w/imprint	2,850.00	
	Plate strip of 3, w/imprint	1,000.00	
	Double transfer	290.00	12.50
	v. Pair, imperforate	500.00	
	Earliest documented cover: *Nov. 19, 1894*		

1894. HENRY CLAY ISSUE

181, 204, 205 *Henry Clay*

181

15¢		UnFVF	UseFVF
	indigo	270.00	45.00
	dark blue	270.00	45.00
	On cover		110.00
	Plate block of 6, w/imprint	4,500.00	
	Plate strip of 3, w/imprint	1,375.00	
	Margin block of 4, w/arrow	1,300.00	
	Earliest documented cover: *Dec. 6, 1894*		

1894. THOMAS JEFFERSON ISSUE

182, 206 *Thomas Jefferson*

182

50¢		UnFVF	UseFVF
	orange	450.00	100.00
	dark orange	450.00	100.00
	On cover		1,000.00
	Plate block of 6, w/imprint	9,000.00	
	Plate strip of 3, w/imprint	2,100.00	
	Margin block of 4, w/arrow	2,100.00	
	Earliest known usage: *Dec. 12, 1894*		

DECODING THE CATALOG

Between 1890-98, there were two similar United States definitive series of stamps released. These are known as the Small Bank Notes and the First Bureau Issue. These stamps had denominations ranging between 1¢ and 90¢. The Small Bank note stamps, produced by the American Bank Note Co. in 1890, are easy to distinguish, since they had no triangles in the upper-left and upper-right-hand corners.

Beginning in 1894, stamp production was taken over by the Bureau of Engraving and Printing. From 1894-98, three basic groups of similar-appearing stamps were released. These stamps, classed as the 1894, 1895 and 1898 issues, are not difficult to distinguish if you know what you are looking for.

The first 10¢ issue of the series (Minkus 180) was green and printed on unwatermarked paper. The perforations for the most part were quite crude, making identification of these stamps fairly simple. The second 10¢ issue (Minkus 201) also was green, but was printed on paper bearing a double-line USPS watermark. Any single stamp from this subset should show at least a partial letter of U, S, P or S. The watermarked paper was placed into use to help avoid the counterfeiting of stamps. The third 10¢ issue is brown and is broken down into Types I and II (Minkus 202 and 203). The color was changed from green to conform to Universal Postal Union rules.

Type I

Type I (Minkus 202) is the same as all previous First Bureau 10¢ issues. The tips of the ornamentation surrounding the denomination at both left and right are clear of the white portrait frame line oval.

Type II

Type II (Minkus 202-203), a red-brown stamp, is different. The ornamentation on both the right and left sides intrudes into the white portrait frame line oval.

1894. OLIVER HAZARD PERRY ISSUE was the first regular issue dollar-value stamp.

183, 184,
207, 208
*Commodore
Oliver
Hazard Perry*

183, 184, 207 *Type I.*
Circles enclosing "$1" are broken.

184, 208 *Type II.*
Circles are complete.

183		UnFVF	UseFVF
$1	**black** Type I	800.00	300.00
	gray black	800.00	300.00
	On cover		2,250.00
	Plate block of 6, w/imprint	17,000.00	
	Plate strip of 3, w/imprint	4,250.00	
	Margin block of 4, w/arrow	4,750.00	
	Earliest documented cover: *Aug. 1895;*		
	EKU: *Jan. 18, 1895*		

184		UnFVF	UseFVF
$1	**black** Type II	2,300.00	575.00
	On cover		3,850.00
	Plate block of 6, w/imprint (including 2 of No. 183)	26,500.00	
	Plate strip of 3, w/imprint (including 1 of No. 183)	6,250.00	
	Block of 4, 2 each No. 183, 184	9,000.00	
	Pair, 1 each Type I and II	4,000.00	
	Margin block of 4, w/arrow	9,750.00	
	Earliest documented cover: *March 22, 1895*		

1894. JAMES MADISON ISSUE

185, 209 *James Madison*

185		UnFVF	UseFVF
$2	**dark blue**	3,100.00	1,050.00
	bright blue	3,100.00	1,050.00
	On cover		4,000.00
	Plate block of 6, w/imprint	40,000.00	
	Plate strip of 3, w/imprint	13,500.00	
	Margin block of 4, w/arrow	14,500.00	
	Earliest documented cover: *July 18, 1895*		

1894. JOHN MARSHALL ISSUE

186, 210 *John Marshall, after painting by Henry Inman, the first great Chief Justice of the United States, was appointed to the office by John Adams in 1801. In 34 brilliant and forceful years' service, he firmly established the Constitution as the supreme law of the land, and the Court as its final arbiter. In the case of Marbury vs. Madison in 1803, he created a precedent in setting aside an act of Congress as unconstitutional.*

186		UnFVF	UseFVF
$5	**dark green**	4,500.00	2,250.00
	On cover		—
	Plate strip of 3, w/imprint	21,000.00	
	Margin block of 4, w/arrow	21,000.00	
	EKU: *July 6, 1896*		

1895-1898. BUREAU OF ENGRAVING AND PRINTING PORTRAIT DESIGNS ON WATERMARKED PAPER ISSUE Although in the planning stages for some time, the issuance of U.S. postage stamps on watermarked paper coincided with the discovery of a counterfeit of the 2¢ denomination. It was believed that the new paper would add a measure of protection. The paper is watermarked with the letters "USPS," for "United States Postage Stamp," in double-lined capital letters, each letter 1/2-inch wide and 11/16-inch (16mm) high. The letters are arranged all over the stamp paper, one letter per square inch, so that each pane of 100 stamps has 90 letters. The watermarks appear both horizontally and vertically on the stamps. Seldom does a stamp show a complete letter of the watermark. More commonly, a single stamp will have a portion of one to even four letters.

Denomination portraits remained the same as on the previous series. The color changes of 1898 are integrated with this sequence of stamps. *Intaglio, perforated 12.*

187 *Double-line USPS watermark*

187		UnFVF	UseFVF
1¢	**deep blue**	5.75	.65
	dark blue	5.75	.65
	indigo	5.75	.65
	pale blue	5.75	.65
	On cover		1.10
	Plate block of 6, w/imprint	210.00	
	Plate strip of 3, w/imprint	26.00	
	Double transfer	—	.85
	Earliest documented cover: *May 16, 1895*		

188		UnFVF	UseFVF
1¢	**deep green**	7.50	.40
	dark green	7.50	.40
	dark yellow green	7.50	.40
	yellow green	7.50	.40
	On cover		.50
	Plate block of 6, w/imprint	175.00	
	Plate strip of 3, w/imprint	37.50	
	Double transfer	12.00	.90
	v. Pair, imperforate	150.00	
	v1. Horizontal pair, imperforate vertically	—	
	FDC (*Jan. 31, 1898*)		700.00

189		UnFVF	UseFVF
2¢	**carmine** Type I	25.00	1.50
	dark carmine	25.00	1.50
	dull carmine	25.00	1.50
	On cover		3.50
	Plate block of 6, w/imprint	375.00	
	Plate strip of 3, w/imprint	120.00	
	Double transfer	45.00	5.00
	FDC (*July 7, 1895*); Earliest known usage: *May 2, 1895*		

190		UnFVF	UseFVF
2¢	**carmine** Type II	25.00	3.25
	dark carmine	25.00	3.25
	dull carmine	25.00	3.25
	On cover		6.75
	Plate block of 6, w/imprint	410.00	
	Plate strip of 3, w/imprint	120.00	
	Horizontal pair, No. 189, 190	70.00	15.00
	Earliest documented cover: *May 27, 1895*		

191		UnFVF	UseFVF
2¢	**carmine** Type III	4.75	.40
	dark carmine	4.75	.40
	dull carmine	4.75	.40
	On cover		.50
	Plate block of 6, w/imprint	175.00	
	Plate strip of 3, w/imprint	22.50	
	Double transfer	16.50	1.25
	Triple transfer	—	
	Shading omitted in right upper triangle (worn plate)	—	
	v. Pair, imperforate	175.00	
	Earliest documented cover: *May 31, 1895*		

192
2¢

	UnFVF	UseFVF
red Type IV	7.00	.40
deep red	13.50	.40
orange red	10.00	.60
rose carmine	250.00	100.00
On cover		.50
Plate block of 6, w/imprint	200.00	
Plate strip of 3, w/imprint	37.50	
Double transfer	18.00	.65
n. Booklet pane of 6 (April 18, 1900; EKU: May 4, 1900)	425.00	

Earliest documented cover: *Nov. 27, 1897*

193
3¢

	UnFVF	UseFVF
dark red violet	32.00	1.50
dark purple	32.00	1.50
dull purple	32.00	1.50
On cover		7.50
Plate block of 6, w/imprint	650.00	
Plate strip of 3, w/imprint	150.00	
Margin block of 4, w/arrow	175.00	
Double transfer	45.00	3.00
v. Pair, imperforate	200.00	

Earliest documented cover: *Feb. 18, 1896*

194
4¢

	UnFVF	UseFVF
dark brown	32.00	2.00
black brown	32.00	2.00
dark yellow brown	32.00	2.00
On cover		7.50
Plate block of 6, w/imprint	450.00	
Plate strip of 3, w/imprint	125.00	
Margin block of 4, w/arrow	150.00	
Double transfer	35.00	2.50
v. Pair, imperforate	200.00	

Earliest documented cover: *Oct. 12, 1895*

195
4¢

	UnFVF	UseFVF
chocolate	25.00	1.10
brownish claret	25.00	1.10
dark orange brown	25.00	1.10
lilac brown	25.00	1.10
orange brown	25.00	1.10
rose brown	25.00	2.00
On cover		8.00
Plate block of 6, w/imprint	450.00	
Plate strip of 3, w/imprint	100.00	
Margin block of 4, w/arrow	120.00	
Double transfer	.30	1.25
Extra frame line at top	45.00	3.50

FDC *(Oct. 7, 1898)*

196
5¢

	UnFVF	UseFVF
dark orange brown	32.00	2.25
brown	32.00	2.25
dark red brown	32.00	2.25
reddish brown	32.00	2.25
On cover		6.00
Plate block of 6, w/imprint	400.00	
Plate strip of 3, w/imprint	120.00	
Diagonal lines omitted in oval background (worn plate)	32.50	2.25
Double transfer	35.00	3.00
Margin block of 4, w/arrow	130.00	
v. Pair, imperforate	200.00	

Earliest documented cover: *Sept. 14, 1895*

197
5¢

	UnFVF	UseFVF
dark blue	27.00	.90
blue	27.00	.90
bright blue	27.00	.90
dull blue	27.00	.90
On cover		8.00
Plate block of 6, w/imprint	450.00	
Plate strip of 3, w/imprint	120.00	
Diagonal lines omitted in oval background (worn plate)	35.00	.75
Double transfer	40.00	1.50
Margin block of 4, w/arrow	140.00	

FDC *(March 8, 1898)*

198
6¢

	UnFVF	UseFVF
red brown	75.00	4.50
dull brown	75.00	4.50
On cover		22.50
Plate block of 6, w/imprint	1,100.00	
Plate strip of 3, w/imprint	250.00	
Margin block of 4, w/arrow	395.00	

	UnFVF	UseFVF
p. Thin paper	80.00	4.00
w. Watermarked "USIR"	2,000.00	325.00
v. Pair, imperforate	200.00	

Earliest documented cover: *Sept. 14, 1895*

199
6¢

	UnFVF	UseFVF
lake	35.00	2.25
claret	35.00	2.25
lilac carmine	35.00	2.25
purple lake	42.50	3.00
On cover		14.00
Plate block of 6, w/imprint	700.00	
Plate strip of 3, w/imprint	150.00	
Double transfer	52.50	3.00
Margin block of 4, w/arrow	150.00	
v. Pair, imperforate	200.00	

FDC *(Dec. 31, 1898)*

200
8¢

	UnFVF	UseFVF
purple brown	55.00	1.75
dark lilac brown	55.00	1.75
lilac brown	40.00	1.25
On cover		12.00
Plate block of 6, w/imprint	650.00	
Plate strip of 3, w/imprint	200.00	
Double transfer	70.50	2.25
Margin block of 4, w/arrow	220.00	
w. Watermarked "USIR"	1,550.00	100.00
v. Pair, imperforate	300.00	

Earliest documented cover: *Dec. 24, 1895*

201, 202 *Type I. Oval below "TEN CENTS" is intact.*

203 *Type II. Oval below "TEN CENTS" is broken by lines.*

201
10¢

	UnFVF	UseFVF
dark green Type I	75.00	1.50
green	75.00	1.50
On cover		12.50
Plate block of 6, w/imprint	750.00	
Plate strip of 3, w/imprint	275.00	
Double transfer	80.00	3.25
v. Pair, imperforate	225.00	

Earliest documented cover: *Feb. 16, 1896*

202
10¢

	UnFVF	UseFVF
brown Type I	160.00	2.50
dark brown	160.00	2.50
On cover		12.50
Plate block of 6, w/imprint	700.00	
Plate strip of 3, w/imprint	650.00	
Double transfer	150.00	4.00
Pair, 1 each (202, 203)	13,000.00	

FDC *(Nov. 11, 1898)*

203
10¢

	UnFVF	UseFVF
orange brown Type II	85.00	2.00
brown	85.00	2.00
yellow brown	85.00	2.00
On cover		14.00
Plate block of 6, w/imprint	950.00	
Plate strip of 3, w/imprint	400.00	
Margin block of 4, w/arrow	425.00	

FDC *(Nov. 11, 1898)*

204
15¢

	UnFVF	UseFVF
indigo	185.00	8.00
blackish blue	185.00	8.00
On cover		50.00
Plate block of 6, w/imprint	2,100.00	
Plate strip of 3, w/imprint	700.00	
Margin block of 4, w/arrow	725.00	
v. Pair, imperforate	625.00	

Earliest documented cover: *Feb. 27, 1897*

205		UnFVF	UseFVF
15¢	**olive green**	130.00	7.50
	dark olive green	130.00	7.50
	On cover		27.50
	Plate block of 6, w/imprint	1,500.00	
	Plate strip of 3, w/imprint	500.00	
	Margin block of 4, w/arrow	625.00	
	FDC (Nov. 30, 1898)		

206		UnFVF	UseFVF
50¢	**orange**	235.00	19.00
	dark red orange	235.00	19.00
	dull red orange	235.00	19.00
	red orange	235.00	19.00
	On cover		325.00
	Plate block of 6, w/imprint	3,750.00	
	Plate strip of 3, w/imprint	850.00	
	Margin block of 4, w/arrow	900.00	
	v. Pair, imperforate	675.00	
	Earliest documented cover: Feb. 27, 1897		

207		UnFVF	UseFVF
$1	**black** Type I	525.00	65.00
	greenish black	525.00	65.00
	On cover		2,000.00
	Plate block of 6, w/imprint	3,000.00	
	Plate strip of 3, w/imprint	2,100.00	
	Margin block of 4, w/arrow	2,200.00	
	Earliest documented cover: Sept. 5, 1898		

208		UnFVF	UseFVF
$1	**black** Type II	1,050.00	140.00
	greenish black	1,050.00	140.00
	On cover		3,350.00
	Plate block of 6, w/imprint (4 Type II, 2 Type I)	19,500.00	
	Plate strip of 3, w/imprint (2 Type II, 1 Type I)	3,750.00	
	Margin block of 4, w/arrow	4,750.00	
	Pair, 1 each Nos. 207, 208	1,950.00	
	v. Pair, imperforate	1,250.00	
	Earliest documented cover: April 6, 1896		

209		UnFVF	UseFVF
$2	**dark blue**	875.00	275.00
	bright blue	875.00	275.00
	On cover		3,200.00
	Plate block of 6, w/imprint	14,000.00	
	Plate strip of 3, w/imprint	3,500.00	
	Margin block of 4, w/arrow	4,000.00	
	v. Pair, imperforate	2,250.00	
	Earliest documented cover: July 16, 1895		

210		UnFVF	UseFVF
$5	**dark green**	2,100.00	425.00
	On cover		10,000.00
	Plate block of 6, w/imprint	60,000.00	
	Plate strip of 3, w/imprint	7,250.00	
	Margin block of 4, w/arrow	8,500.00	
	v. Pair, imperforate	2,250.00	
	Earliest documented cover: Nov. 3, 1896		

1902-03. REGULAR ISSUE had only two of its 14 values actually released in 1902, the balance being issued during 1903. All of these stamps were *perforated, with the 1¢, 4¢, and 5¢ being issued imperforate as well,* although the 4¢ imperforate now exists only with the large slots of the Schermack coil cut into the sides. The 1¢ and 5¢ also were issued in coil form. Finally, the 1¢ and 2¢ stamps were issued as booklet panes, six stamps to a pane. *Intaglio, double-line watermark USPS, perforated 12.*

211, 225, 228, 230, B13 *Benjamin Franklin*

211		UnFVF	UseFVF
1¢	**deep bluish green**	9.00	.20
	dark green	9.00	.20
	gray green	9.00	.20
	green	9.00	.20
	yellow green	9.00	.20
	On cover		.50

	UnFVF	UseFVF
Plate block of 6, w/imprint	145.00	
Plate strip of 3, w/imprint	27.50	
Cracked plate	8.00	.60
Double transfer	11.00	.75
Worn plate	8.00	.60
n. Booklet pane of 6 (March 6, 1907)	425.00	
n1. Pane w/plate number 3472 over left stamp	—	
v. Arrow block w/"color ball"	—	
EKU (Feb. 8, 1903)		

212, B14, B15, B16 *George Washington*

212		UnFVF	UseFVF
2¢	**carmine**	12.00	.20
	bright carmine	12.00	.20
	dark carmine	12.00	.20
	carmine rose	12.00	.20
	On cover		.50
	Plate block of 6, w/imprint	150.00	
	Plate strip of 3, w/imprint	40.00	
	Cracked plate	—	.75
	Double transfer	17.50	.75
	n. Booklet pane of 6 (Jan. 24, 1903)	400.00	
	EKU (Jan. 17, 1903)		

213 *Andrew Jackson after engraving by A. Sealey*

213		UnFVF	UseFVF
3¢	**dark red violet**	52.50	2.25
	bright violet	52.50	2.25
	violet	52.50	2.25
	Plate block of 6, w/imprint	600.00	
	Plate strip of 3, w/imprint	175.00	
	Cracked plate	—	
	Double transfer	65.00	3.50
	On cover		8.00
	v. Arrow block w/"color ball"	—	
	EKU (March 21, 1903)		

214, 226 *U.S. Grant*

214		UnFVF	UseFVF
4¢	**brown**	57.50	1.00
	dark brown	57.50	1.00
	dark yellow brown	57.50	1.00
	orange brown	57.50	1.00
	reddish brown	57.50	1.00
	yellow brown	57.50	1.00
	On cover		10.00
	Plate block of 6, w/imprint	600.00	
	Plate strip of 3, w/imprint	175.00	
	Double transfer	60.00	2.25
	EKU (March 13, 1903)		

215, 227, 229 *Abraham Lincoln*

215

5¢		UnFVF	UseFVF
	deep blue	57.50	1.15
	blue	57.50	1.15
	dark blue	57.50	1.15
	dull blue	57.50	1.15
	On cover		7.00
	Plate block of 6, w/imprint	600.00	
	Plate strip of 3, w/imprint	175.00	
	Cracked plate	55.00	4.00
	Double transfer	65.00	3.00
	EKU *(Feb. 10, 1903)*		

216 *James Garfield*

216

6¢		UnFVF	UseFVF
	brown red	70.00	2.00
	claret	70.00	2.00
	deep claret	70.00	2.00
	dull brown red	70.00	2.00
	On cover		10.00
	Plate block of 6, w/imprint	700.00	
	Plate strip of 3, w/imprint	200.00	
	Double transfer	62.50	3.00
	EKU *(May 8, 1903)*		

217 *Martha Washington*

217

8¢		UnFVF	UseFVF
	violet black	42.50	1.60
	black	42.50	1.60
	blue black	42.50	1.60
	blue lilac	42.50	1.60
	blue violet	42.50	1.60
	On cover		7.50
	Plate block of 6, w/imprint	550.00	
	Plate strip of 3, w/imprint	120.00	
	Double transfer	37.50	2.00
	EKU *(Dec. 27, 1902)*		

218 *Daniel Webster*

218

10¢		UnFVF	UseFVF
	pale red brown	60.00	1.15
	dark red brown	60.00	1.15
	red brown	60.00	1.15
	On cover		7.00
	Plate block of 6, w/imprint	750.00	
	Plate strip of 3, w/imprint	150.00	
	Double transfer	60.00	8.00
	EKU *(March 12, 1903)*		

219 *Benjamin Harrison died March 13, 1901, and this stamp with his likeness was issued a year later. It was the first U.S. stamp with a 13¢ denomination, the first stamp issued in the 1902 Regular Issue Series. A first-day cover found Nov. 18, 1999, constitutes the first FDC of the 20th century.*

219

13¢		UnFVF	UseFVF
	black brown	42.50	6.50
	purple black	42.50	6.50
	On cover		32.50
	Plate block of 6, w/imprint	500.00	

		UnFVF	UseFVF
	Plate strip of 3, w/imprint	125.00	
	FDC *(Nov. 18, 1902)*		

220 *Henry Clay*

220

15¢		UnFVF	UseFVF
	olive green	150.00	4.50
	dark olive green	150.00	4.50
	On cover		70.00
	Plate block of 6, w/imprint	1,950.00	
	Plate strip of 3, w/imprint	500.00	
	Double transfer	160.00	8.00
	Margin block of 4, w/arrow	550.00	
	EKU *(Sept. 24, 1903)*		

221 *Thomas Jefferson*

221

50¢		UnFVF	UseFVF
	orange	425.00	20.00
	deep orange	425.00	20.00
	On cover		600.00
	Plate block of 6, w/imprint	5,250.00	
	Plate strip of 3, w/imprint	1,250.00	
	Margin block of 4, w/arrow	1,500.00	
	EKU *(Feb. 17, 1904)*		

222 *David Farragut (1801-70), known as the Hero of New Orleans and Mobile Boy because of his success in stopping blockade-running in the Civil War. Became the first American Navy admiral in 1866.*

222

$1		UnFVF	UseFVF
	black	750.00	45.00
	gray black	750.00	45.00
	On cover		1,250.00
	Plate block of 6, w/imprint	10,500.00	
	Plate strip of 3, w/imprint	1,950.00	
	Margin block of 4, w/arrow	2,250.00	
	EKU *(Jan. 23, 1904)*		

223, 365 *James Madison*

223

$2		UnFVF	UseFVF
	dark blue	1,075.00	140.00
	blue	1,075.00	140.00
	On cover		2,100.00
	Plate block of 6, w/imprint	22,000.00	
	Plate strip of 3, w/imprint	3,200.00	
	Margin block of 4, w/arrow	4,000.00	
	EKU *(Feb. 17, 1904)*		

224, 366 *John Marshall (1755-1835) 4th Chief Justice of the U.S. (1801-35)*

224

$5		UnFVF	UseFVF
	dark green	2,800.00	525.00

On cover			4,250.00
Plate block of 6, w/imprint		42,000.00	
Plate strip of 3, w/imprint		8,000.00	
Margin block of 4, w/arrow		10,000.00	
EKU *(Feb. 17, 1904)*			

1906-08. REGULAR ISSUES OF 1902-03 *Imperforate.*

225		UnFVF	UseFVF
1¢	**deep bluish green**	20.00	17.50
	dark green	20.00	17.50
	green	20.00	17.50
	On cover		17.50
	Plate block of 6, w/imprint	165.00	
	Margin block of 4, w/arrow	80.00	60.00
	Center line block	120.00	80.00
	Double transfer	30.00	15.00
	EKU *(Feb. 1, 1907)*		

226 Four Cent, imperforate, with slots at sides. These slots aided in the vending of coil stamps by the machines of the Schermack Co.

226		UnFVF	UseFVF
4¢	**brown**	30,000.00	25,000.00
	On cover		120,000.00
	Pair	70,000.00	
	Line pair	175,000.00	
	EKU *(May 27, 1908)*		

227		UnFVF	UseFVF
5¢	**blue**	375.00	475.00
	On cover		—
	Plate block of 6, w/imprint	2,800.00	
	Center line block	2,800.00	
	Margin block of 4, w/arrow	1,800.00	
	EKU *(Sept. 15, 1908)*		

Please exercise caution in buying singles of this stamp, particularly used copies. Certification by respected authorities recommended.

1908. COIL STAMP 1902-03 SERIES ISSUE were the first coils issued. They have been faked extensively by fraudulently perforating the imperforates in the case of the 1¢ stamps and also by trimming off perforations on both the 1¢ and 5¢ stamps. It is recommended that these stamps be collected in pairs. *Perforated 12 horizontally.*

228		UnFVF	UseFVF
1¢	**blue green** pair	68,500.00	—
	Line pair	110,000.00	
	EKU *(none known)*		

229		UnFVF	UseFVF
5¢	**blue** pair	9,000.00	—
	Line pair	19,500.00	
	EKU *(Sept. 18, 1908)*		

Perforated 12 vertically.

230		UnFVF	UseFVF
1¢	**blue green** pair	6,000.00	—
	Line pair	11,000.00	
	Double transfer		—
	EKU *(none known)*		

1903. TWO-CENT SHIELD ISSUE was issued because of public dislike for the 2¢ "Flag" design of the 1902-03 series. The "Shield" stamp comes in a wide range of shades. It was issued perforated, imperforate, in booklet panes, and also in coil form, so that a considerable display can be made of this single denomination. *The stamps were flat-plate printed, double-line watermark USPS, Type I, perforated 12.*

231-236, B17, B18, B19, B20 *George Washington*

Type I: The leaf next to the "2" at left penetrates the border.

Type II: Border to the left of the leaf is formed by a strong line. Lower left inside curve line enlarged.

231		UnFVF	UseFVF
2¢	**carmine** Type I	4.00	.20
	bright carmine	4.00	.20
	red	4.00	.20
	carmine rose	4.50	.20
	scarlet	4.00	.20
	On cover		.50
	Plate block of 6, w/imprint	75.00	
	Plate strip of 3 w/imprint	16.00	
	Double transfer	8.00	1.50
	n. Booklet pane of 6	100.00	
	v. Vertical pair, rouletted between	800.00	
	v1. Vertical pair, imperforate horizontally	2,500.00	
	v2. Vertical pair, imperforate between	1,000.00	
	EKU *(Nov. 19, 1903)*		

232		UnFVF	UseFVF
2¢	**lake** Type II	7.50	.50
	carmine	7.50	.50
	carmine lake	7.50	.50
	scarlet	7.50	.50
	Plate block of 6	150.00	
	n. Booklet pane of 6	150.00	
	EKU *(June 5, 1903)*		

1903. TWO-CENT SHIELD COIL ISSUE *Imperforate.*

233		UnFVF	UseFVF
2¢	**carmine** Type II	20.00	15.00
	carmine rose	20.00	15.00
	scarlet	20.00	15.00
	On cover		15.00
	Plate block of 6, w/imprint	200.00	
	Center line block	140.00	175.00
	Double transfer	22.50	12.50
	Margin block of 4, w/arrow	80.00	85.00
	EKU *(Oct. 26, 1906)*		

234		UnFVF	UseFVF
2¢	**lake** Type II	50.00	40.00
	scarlet	50.00	40.00
	On cover		70.00
	Plate block of 6, w/imprint	700.00	
	Center line block	400.00	
	Margin block of 4, w/arrow	180.00	

1903. TWO-CENT SHIELD COIL ISSUE *Coil stamp, perforated 12 horizontally.*

235		UnFVF	UseFVF
2¢	**carmine** Type I pair	95,000.00	100,000.00
	Line pair	—	
	EKU *(Oct. 2, 1908)*		

Perforated 12 vertically.

236		UnFVF	UseFVF
2¢	**scarlet** Type II pair	7,000.00	4,250.00
	Double transfer	7,750.00	
	Line pair	—	
	EKU *(none known)*		

1908-09 WASHINGTON & FRANKLIN ISSUE consisted of 12 stamps, ranging from 1¢ to $1. The 1¢ stamp has a portrait of Franklin in the central medallion with the words "ONE CENT" at the base of the stamp. The 2¢ stamp, with Washington in the medallion, is inscribed "TWO CENTS." The 3¢ stamp to $1 stamps have Washington in the medallion with numerals of value in each of the lower corners.

As an experiment to counteract the shrinking caused by printing on wet paper, some rows of stamps were separated by 3mm spacing instead of the usual 2mm. Intermediate-size spacings exist and command the lower of the two prices listed for different spacings. *Flat plate printing, watermarked double-line USPS (187), and perforated 12.*

A very few of this series, up through the 15¢ value, were printed on a grayish, hard, thick paper known as *China Clay*. The paper had up to 10 times the mineral content of normal stamp paper of the time.

237, B21, B22 *Benjamin Franklin*

237		UnFVF	UseFVF
1¢	**green**	6.00	.20

Washington-Franklin Identifier

PERF.	WMK.	1¢ Text	2c Text	1¢ Numeral	2¢ Numeral	Washington Numeral	Franklin Numeral
12	Double	237, 263	238, 264			239-248, 265-272	313-314
	Single	273	274	297	298	275-282	305-312
Coil 12	Double	254, 258	255, 259			256-257, 260-262	
	Single	285, 287	286, 288			289	
Imperforate	Double	249	250			251-253	
	Single	283	284	299	300, 342		
	Unwmk.			367, **406**	368, **407-407D**	369-370, **408**	
Coil 8 1/2	Single	290, 292	291, 293	301, 303	302, 304	294-296	
10	Double						331
	Single			315	316	317-321	322-330
	Unwmk.			348, 414	349	350-355	356-364
Coil 10	Single			333, 335, 340, 343	334, 336, 341, 344	337-339, 345-347	
	Unwmk.			371, 374	372, 375	373, 376-378	379
11	Double		399				
	Single				332		
	Unwmk.			380, **403**, 415, 416	381, **404-404D**, 417	382-387, **405-405A**	388-398
12x10, 10x12	Single			315v, 315v1	316v	319v	
12 1/2	Unwmk.			**409**			
11x10, 10x11	Unwmk.			410, 413	411-411A	412	

237 -- Numbers in normal type designate stamps printed by intaglio on a flat-bed press. The design is about 18 1/2-19mm wide and 22mm high

340 -- Numbers in italic designate stamps printed by intaglio on a rotary press.

407 -- Numbers in bold designate stamps printed by offset. These stamps are characterized by the smoothness of the printed surface and by the blurred appearance of the image.

bright green		6.00	.20
dark green		6.00	.20
yellow green		6.00	.20
On cover			.50
Plate block of 6, w/imprint		45.00	
Plate block of 6, w/imprint & open star		50.00	
Plate block of 6, w/small solid star		75.00	
Block of 4, 2mm spacing		25.00	1.25
Block of 4, 3mm spacing		27.50	1.50
Cracked plate		—	
Double transfer		8.00	.60
v. Horizontal pair, imperforate between		1,000.00	
n. Booklet pane of 6 (Dec. 2, 1908)		140.00	120.00
FDC (Dec. 14, 1908)			20,000.00
p. China Clay paper		800.00	

238 *George Washington, value in words.*

238		**UnFVF**	**UseFVF**
2¢	**carmine**	6.00	.20
	dark carmine	6.00	.20
	pale carmine	6.00	.20
	On cover		.50
	Plate block of 6, w/imprint	45.00	
	Plate block of 6, w/imprint & open star	50.00	
	Plate block of 6, w/small solid star	70.00	
	Block of 4, 2mm spacing	22.50	.60
	Block of 4, 3mm spacing	25.00	.75
	Cracked plate	—	
	Double transfer	10.00	
	Double transfer (1¢ design of No. 237)	1,250.00	
	n. Booklet pane of 6 (Nov. 16, 1908)	125.00	110.00
	FDC (Dec. 1, 1908)		35,000.00
	p. China Clay paper	1,000.00	

1908. GEORGE WASHINGTON TYPE I ISSUE Details of Type I:

1. The top line of the toga from the front of the neck to the top of the button is very weak, as are the upper parts of the fine lines of shading that join this top line. The top part of the fifth of these shading lines is missing.

2. Two shading lines under the point of the chin are heavy.

3. The line between the lips is thin. This usually is an easy checking point for this type.

4. The lock of hair behind the ear is formed at the bottom by two lines of shading, the lower line being considerably shorter than the upper.

5. The hair lines above and a little to the right of the ear form an "arrowhead."

6. The outline of the inner oval forms a solid line at the bottom.

239 *George Washington. Type I: All stamps of this design and perforated 12 are Type I. While the description of the type is given here in detail, the areas noted by the small figures "1" and "3" in the drawing will almost always prove sufficient as checking areas.*

239		**UnFVF**	**UseFVF**
3¢	**violet** Type I	27.50	2.50
	dark violet	27.50	2.50
	pale violet	27.50	2.50
	On cover		7.50
	Plate block of 6, w/imprint	200.00	

Plate block of 6, w/imprint & star	300.00	
Block of 4, 2mm spacing	110.00	15.00
Block of 4, 3mm spacing	120.00	17.50
Double transfer	37.50	4.00
p. China Clay paper	800.00	
FDC (Dec. 26, 1908)		

240		**UnFVF**	**UseFVF**
4¢	**orange brown**	30.00	1.00
	brown	30.00	1.00
	dark orange brown	30.00	1.00
	dull orange brown	30.00	1.00
	On cover		5.00
	Plate block of 6, w/imprint	300.00	
	Plate block of 6, w/imprint & star	475.00	
	Block of 4, 2mm spacing	140.00	7.50
	Block of 4, 3mm spacing	150.00	9.00
	Double transfer	45.00	
	p. China Clay paper	1,000.00	
	FDC (Dec. 26, 1908)		

241		**UnFVF**	**UseFVF**
5¢	**blue**	40.00	2.00
	bright blue	40.00	2.00
	dark blue	40.00	2.00
	On cover		8.00
	Plate block of 6, w/imprint	400.00	
	Plate block of 6, w/imprint & star	600.00	
	Block of 4, 2mm spacing	175.00	12.50
	Block of 4, 3mm spacing	185.00	10.00
	Double transfer	45.00	
	p. China Clay paper	800.00	
	FDC (Dec. 21, 1908)		

242		**UnFVF**	**UseFVF**
6¢	**red orange**	47.50	5.00
	dull orange	47.50	5.00
	orange	47.50	5.00
	On cover		17.50
	Plate block of 6, w/imprint	600.00	
	p. China Clay paper	625.00	
	FDC (Dec. 31, 1908)		

243		**UnFVF**	**UseFVF**
8¢	**olive green**	37.50	2.50
	dark olive green	37.50	2.50
	On cover		16.00
	Plate block of 6, w/imprint	400.00	
	Double transfer	47.50	
	p. China Clay paper	800.00	
	FDC (Dec. 18, 1908)		

244		**UnFVF**	**UseFVF**
10¢	**yellow**	55.00	1.50
	On cover		8.00
	Plate block of 6, w/imprint	650.00	
	Double transfer	—	
	p. China Clay paper	800.00	
	p1. Very thin paper	—	
	FDC (Jan. 7, 1909)		

245		**UnFVF**	**UseFVF**
13¢	**blue green**	37.50	20.00
	dark blue green	37.50	20.00
	On cover		90.00
	Plate block of 6, w/imprint	400.00	
	p. China Clay paper	800.00	
	FDC (Jan. 11, 1909); EKU (March 5, 1909)		

246		**UnFVF**	**UseFVF**
15¢	**gray blue**	50.00	6.00
	dull gray blue	50.00	6.00
	On cover		110.00
	Plate block of 6, w/imprint	525.00	
	p. China Clay paper	800.00	
	FDC (Jan. 18, 1909)		

247		**UnFVF**	**UseFVF**
50¢	**gray lilac**	250.00	17.50
	dull gray lilac	250.00	17.50
	On cover		4,500.00
	Plate block of 6, w/imprint	6,000.00	
	Margin block of 4, w/arrow	1,100.00	
	FDC (Jan. 13, 1909)		

248		**UnFVF**	**UseFVF**
$1	**violet brown**	375.00	75.00
	dull violet brown	375.00	75.00
	On cover		5,250.00
	Plate block of 6, w/imprint	11,500.00	

Margin block of 4, w/arrow	1,900.00	
Double transfer	—	
FDC *(Jan. 29, 1909)*		

1908. WASHINGTON & FRANKLIN TYPE I ISSUE *Imperforate.*

249

1¢	UnFVF	UseFVF
green	6.00	4.00
bright green	6.00	4.00
dark green	6.00	4.00
yellow green	6.00	4.00
On cover		8.00
Plate block of 6, w/imprint	55.00	
Plate block of 6, w/imprint & open star	60.00	
Plate block of 6, w/small solid star	600.00	
Block of 4, 2mm spacing	25.00	
Block of 4, 3mm spacing	25.00	
Center line block	35.00	
Margin block of 4, 2 or 3mm spacing, w/arrow	30.00	
Double transfer	—	
FDC *(Dec. 23, 1908)*		

250

2¢	UnFVF	UseFVF
carmine	7.50	3.00
dark carmine	7.50	3.00
pale carmine	7.50	3.00
On cover		4.50
Plate block of 6, w/imprint	75.00	
Plate block of 6, w/imprint & star	80.00	
Block of 4, 2 or 3mm spacing	30.00	
Center line block	40.00	
Double transfer	12.50	3.50
Double transfer (1¢ design of No. 237)	1,000.00	
Margin block of 4, 2 or 3mm spacing, w/arrow	35.00	
FDC *(Dec. 14, 1908)*		

251

3¢	UnFVF	UseFVF
violet Type I	17.50	20.00
On cover		40.00
Plate block of 6, w/imprint	175.00	
Center line block	75.00	80.00
Double transfer	20.00	
Margin block of 4, w/arrow	60.00	80.00
FDC *(March 3, 1909)*		

252

4¢	UnFVF	UseFVF
brown	27.50	22.50
orange brown	27.50	22.50
dark orange brown	27.50	22.50
dull orange brown	27.50	22.50
On cover		70.00
Plate block of 6 w/imprint	200.00	
Plate block of 6, w/imprint & star	225.00	
Block of 4, 2 or 3mm spacing	95.00	
Center line block	125.00	
Double transfer	40.00	
Margin block of 4, 2 or 3mm spacing, w/arrow	100.00	
FDC *(Feb. 25, 1909)*; EKU *(March 13, 1909)*		

253

5¢	UnFVF	UseFVF
blue	42.50	30.00
On cover		90.00
Plate block of 6, w/imprint	350.00	
Center line block	220.00	200.00
Cracked plate	—	
Margin block of 4, w/arrow	200.00	160.00
FDC *(Feb. 27, 1909)*		

1908-10. WASHINGTON & FRANKLIN COIL ISSUE *Flat plate printing, double-line USPS watermark, and perforated 12 either on the sides or at the top and bottom of the stamp. Perforated 12 horizontally.*

254

1¢	UnFVF	UseFVF
green	22.50	12.50
dark green	22.50	12.50
On cover		35.00
Pair	60.00	65.00
Line pair	150.00	275.00
FDC *(Dec. 29, 1908)*		

255

2¢	UnFVF	UseFVF
carmine	37.50	8.00
dark carmine	37.50	8.00
On cover		25.00
Pair	65.00	30.00

Line pair	275.00	135.00
Double transfer (1¢ design of No. 237)	—	1,350.00
FDC *(Jan. 2, 1909)*		

256

4¢	UnFVF	UseFVF
brown	85.00	70.00
On cover		150.00
Pair	225.00	300.00
Line pair	650.00	550.00
FDC *(Aug. 15, 1910)*		

257

5¢	UnFVF	UseFVF
blue	100.00	85.00
dark blue	100.00	85.00
On cover		165.00
Pair	275.00	300.00
Line pair	750.00	550.00
FDC *(Jan. 2, 1909)*; EKU *(Sept. 21, 1909)*		

1908-10. WASHINGTON & FRANKLIN COIL ISSUE *Perforated 12 vertically.*

258

1¢	UnFVF	UseFVF
green	50.00	30.00
On cover		60.00
Pair, 2mm spacing	135.00	105.00
Pair, 3mm spacing	120.00	95.00
Line pair	350.00	200.00
Double transfer	—	
FDC *(Jan. 2, 1909)*		

259

2¢	UnFVF	UseFVF
carmine	47.50	7.50
On cover		20.00
Pair, 2mm spacing	125.00	30.00
Pair, 3mm spacing	115.00	25.00
Line pair	350.00	125.00
FDC *(Jan. 12, 1909)*		

260

4¢	UnFVF	UseFVF
brown	115.00	55.00
On cover		90.00
Pair, 2mm spacing	325.00	250.00
Pair, 3mm spacing	340.00	270.00
Line pair	850.00	400.00
FDC *(Feb. 23, 1909)*		

261

5¢	UnFVF	UseFVF
blue	125.00	75.00
dark blue	125.00	75.00
On cover		150.00
Pair	350.00	325.00
Line pair	900.00	550.00
FDC *(Feb. 23, 1909)*		

262

10¢	UnFVF	UseFVF
yellow	1,750.00	850.00
On cover		8,500.00
Pair	4,200.00	3,800.00
Line pair	7,500.00	6,850.00
FDC *(Feb. 23, 1909)*		

1909. WASHINGTON & FRANKLIN ISSUE *Stamps of 1908-09 on bluish gray paper.* The paper used in this experimental printing was made with a 30% rag stock instead of all wood pulp. Here is a quote from the Report of the Third Assistant Postmaster General for the fiscal year ending June 30, 1909: "The intaglio process by which our postage stamps are printed necessitates a preliminary wetting down of the paper, which is bleached chemical wood stock. This wetting down causes a varying shrinkage, which has resulted in heavy waste from the cutting of the perforations into the stamp design. The Bureau of Engraving and Printing experimented with a paper made of about 30% rag stock, in the hope that it would show less shrinkage, but this paper did not overcome the difficulty as it was found to shrink very unevenly. Some of the stamps printed on this paper, which was of a slightly bluish tinge, were issued to the Postmaster at Washington, D.C., and to others." Actually, the paper is of a color distinctly different from the normal paper, but this shows up better by comparison than it does by the examination of just a single copy of either the normal or the bluish gray paper. We have noted the presence of tiny black specks on much of the blue paper, sometimes only a few to a stamp and best seen with the aid of a magnifying glass. These stamps were *flat plate printed, watermarked double-line USPS, and perforated 12.*

263

1¢	UnFVF	UseFVF
green	85.00	85.00
On cover		185.00
Plate block of 6, w/imprint	900.00	

		UnFVF	UseFVF
	Plate block of 6, w/imprint & star	2,500.00	
	Block of 4, 2mm spacing	350.00	375.00
	Block of 4, 3mm spacing	675.00	
	FDC *(Feb. 16, 1909)*		
	Earliest documented cover: *Feb. 22, 1909*		

264
2¢ **carmine** — UnFVF 75.00 — UseFVF 70.00
On cover — 150.00
Plate block of 6, w/imprint — 900.00
Plate block of 6, w/imprint & star — 1,150.00
Block of 4, 2mm spacing — 340.00 — 400.00
Block of 4, 3mm spacing — 380.00
Double transfer — —
FDC *(Feb. 16, 1909)*
Earliest documented cover: *Feb. 23, 1909*

265
3¢ **deep violet** Type I — UnFVF 1,600.00 — UseFVF 1,600.00
On cover — —
Plate block of 6, w/imprint — 15,000.00
Earliest documented cover: *Dec. 27, 1910*

266
4¢ **orange brown** — UnFVF 15,000.00 — UseFVF —
Plate block of 6, w/imprint — 115,000.00
Plate strip of 3, w/imprint — —

267
5¢ **blue** — UnFVF 3,500.00 — UseFVF 3,750.00
On cover — 5,250.00
Plate block of 6, w/imprint — 30,000.00

268
6¢ **red orange** — UnFVF 1,150.00 — UseFVF 1,000.00
On cover — 11,000.00
Plate block of 6, w/imprint — 12,500.00
Earliest documented cover: *Sept. 14, 1911*

269
8¢ **olive green** — UnFVF 16,000.00 — UseFVF —
Plate block of 6, w/imprint — 120,000.00
Plate strip of 3 w/imprint — —

270
10¢ **yellow** — UnFVF 1,400.00 — UseFVF 1,150.00
On cover — —
Plate block of 6, w/imprint — 15,000.00
Earliest documented cover: *Feb. 3, 1910*

271
13¢ **blue green** — UnFVF 2,350.00 — UseFVF 1,450.00
On cover — —
Plate block of 6, w/imprint — 17,500.00

272
15¢ **pale ultramarine** — UnFVF 1,150.00 — UseFVF 1,000.00
On cover — —
Plate block of 6, w/imprint — 7,500.00

1910-14. WASHINGTON & FRANKLIN ISSUE This issue was identical with the 1908-09 series in design, but a 7¢ stamp was added while the 50¢ and $1 stamps were discontinued. The stamps were printed on paper with a new watermark, single-line USPS, intended to make the paper stronger and more uniform. For this new watermark, the letters "USPS," for "United States Postage Stamps," are only 5/16 of an inch high, compared with the 9/16-inch height of the double-line watermark previously used on Bureau of Engraving and Printing paper. The letters were arranged in diagonal rows. About 77 letters appear on a pane of 100 stamps, so sometimes stamps will have portions of two or three letters. The letters can be right-side-up or upside-down on sheet stamps; booklet stamps have single-line watermarks sideways. *Flat plate printing. Perforated 12.*

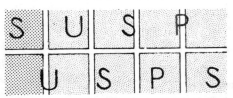
273, B30 *Single-line USPS watermark*

273
1¢ **green** — UnFVF 6.00 — UseFVF .20
dark green — 6.00 — .20
pale green — 6.00 — .20
yellowish green — 6.00 — .20
On cover — .50

	Plate block of 6, w/imprint & "A"	60.00	
	Plate block of 6, w/imprint & star	70.00	
	Block of 4, 2mm spacing	22.50	2.75
	Block of 4, 3mm spacing	22.50	2.75
	Cracked plate	—	
	Double transfer	10.00	
n.	Booklet pane of 6	125.00	100.00

Earliest documented cover: *Nov. 21, 1911*
FDC *(Nov. 23, 1910)*

274
2¢ **carmine** (B31, B32, B33) — UnFVF 5.75 — UseFVF .20
dull carmine — 5.75 — .20
lake — 200.00 — —
On cover — .50
Plate block of 6, w/imprint & "A" — 60.00
Plate block of 6, w/imprint & star — 65.00
Block of 4, 2mm spacing — 22.50 — 1.00
Block of 4, 3mm spacing — 21.00 — .80
Cracked plate — —
Double transfer — 9.00 — —
Double transfer (1¢ design of No. 273) — — — 850.00
n. Booklet pane of 6 — 100.00
Earliest documented cover: *June 1, 1911*
FDC *(Nov. 23, 1910)*
FDC booklet *(Nov. 30, 1910)*

275 *George Washington*

275
3¢ **violet** Type I — UnFVF 15.00 — UseFVF 1.50
deep violet — 15.00 — 1.50
lilac — 17.50 — 1.50
On cover — 7.00
Plate block of 6 — 125.00
Plate block of 6, w/imprint & star — 165.00
Block of 4, 2mm spacing — 65.00 — 8.00
Block of 4, 3mm spacing — 67.50 — 8.00
FDC *(Jan. 16, 1911)*
Earliest documented cover: *June 19, 1911*

1911. GEORGE WASHINGTON ISSUE

276 *George Washington*

276
4¢ **brown** — UnFVF 22.50 — UseFVF .75
dark brown — 22.50 — .75
orange brown — 22.50 — .75
On cover — 7.00
Plate block of 6 — 240.00
Plate block of 6, w/imprint & star — 200.00
Block of 4, 2mm spacing — 100.00
Block of 4, 3mm spacing — 95.00
FDC *(Jan. 20, 1911)*

277 *George Washington*

277
5¢ **blue** — UnFVF 22.50 — UseFVF .75
dark blue — 22.50 — .75
pale blue — 22.50 — .75

On cover		4.50	
Plate block of 6	200.00		
Plate block of 6 w/imprint	180.00		
Plate block of 6, w/imprint & "A"	200.00		
Plate block of 6, w/imprint & star	175.00		
Block of 4, 2mm spacing	100.00	5.00	
Block of 4, 3mm spacing	95.00	4.50	
Double transfer	—		
FDC (Jan. 25, 1911)			
Earliest documented cover: March 28, 1911			

278 *George Washington*

278		UnFVF	UseFVF
6¢	**red orange**	30.00	.85
	dull red orange	30.00	.85
	On cover		.40
	Plate block of 6, w/imprint	300.00	
	Plate block of 6, w/imprint & star	275.00	
	Block of 4, 2mm spacing	125.00	8.00
	Block of 4, 3mm spacing	120.00	7.50
	FDC (Jan. 25, 1911); EKU (May 25, 1911)		

279		UnFVF	UseFVF
7¢	**black**	70.00	8.50
	deep black	70.00	8.50
	gray black	70.00	8.50
	On cover		50.00
	Plate block of 6	850.00	
	Earliest documented cover: May 1, 1914		

280 *George Washington*

280		UnFVF	UseFVF
8¢	**light olive green**	95.00	12.50
	dark olive green	95.00	12.50
	On cover		50.00
	Plate block of 6, w/imprint	900.00	
	Plate block of 6, w/imprint & star	1,100.00	
	Block of 4, 2 or 3mm spacing	400.00	65.00
	FDC (Feb. 8, 1911)		

281		UnFVF	UseFVF
10¢	**yellow**	85.00	4.00
	On cover		15.00
	Plate block of 6, w/imprint	900.00	
	Plate block of 6, w/imprint & star	850.00	
	Block of 4, 2 or 3mm spacing	375.00	25.00
	Earliest documented cover: Feb. 17, 1911		
	FDC (Jan. 24, 1911)		

282		UnFVF	UseFVF
15¢	**pale ultramarine**	225.00	15.00
	On cover		85.00
	Plate block of 6	2,000.00	
	FDC (March 1, 1911)		
	Earliest documented cover: Aug. 31, 1912		

1910. GEORGE WASHINGTON ISSUE *Imperforate.*

283		UnFVF	UseFVF
1¢	**green**	3.00	2.75
	dark green	3.00	2.75
	pale green	3.00	2.75
	yellowish green	3.00	2.75
	On cover		4.00
	Plate block of 6 w/imprint & "A"	40.00	
	Plate block of 6, w/imprint & star	65.00	
	Block of 4, 2 or 3mm spacing	9.50	11.00
	Center line block	20.00	15.00
	Double transfer	6.00	
	Margin block of 4, w/arrow	10.00	11.00

Earliest documented cover: March 1, 1911			
FDC (Dec. 1910)			

284		UnFVF	UseFVF
2¢	**carmine**	5.50	3.00
	On cover		3.00
	Plate block of 6, w/imprint & "A"	115.00	
	Plate block of 6, w/imprint & star	150.00	
	Block of 4, 2 or 3mm spacing	20.00	12.50
	Margin block of 4, w/arrow	25.00	17.50
	Center line block	42.50	40.00
	Cracked plate	—	
	Double transfer	7.50	
	Double transfer (1¢ design of No. 283)	1,200.00	
	Earliest documented cover: Dec. 15, 1910		
	FDC (Dec. 1910)		

1910. WASHINGTON & FRANKLIN COIL ISSUE *This stamp is relatively common in singles and vertical pairs. Perforated 12 horizontally.*

285		UnFVF	UseFVF
1¢	**green**	22.50	12.50
	dark green	22.50	12.50
	On cover		35.00
	Pair	50.00	35.00
	Line pair	250.00	225.00
	FDC (Nov. 1, 1910)		

286		UnFVF	UseFVF
2¢	**carmine**	37.50	17.50
	dark carmine	37.50	17.50
	pale carmine	37.50	17.50
	On cover		40.00
	Pair	135.00	75.00
	Line pair	425.00	
	FDC (Nov. 1, 1910)		

1910. WASHINGTON & FRANKLIN COIL ISSUE *Perforated 12 vertically.*

287		UnFVF	UseFVF
1¢	**green**	85.00	37.50
	dark green	85.00	37.50
	On cover		60.00
	Pair, 2mm spacing	200.00	90.00
	Pair, 3mm spacing	220.00	100.00
	Line pair	325.00	260.00
	FDC (Nov. 1, 1910)		

288		UnFVF	UseFVF
2¢	**carmine**	575.00	250.00
	dark carmine	575.00	250.00
	pale carmine	575.00	250.00
	On cover		600.00
	Pair, 2 or 3mm spacing	1,950.00	
	Line pair	4,000.00	3,150.00
	FDC (Nov. 1, 1910)		

1910. GEORGE WASHINGTON ORANGEBURG COIL ISSUE Known as the "Orangeburg Coil" (because it is only known used from Orangeburg, N.Y.). No. 289 is the rarest of all U.S. coil stamps. One coil of 500 stamps was made, and only about a dozen unused copies are known. The stamps were used by Bell and Co., Inc., manufacturing chemists, of Orangeburg to mail samples of products and used copies bear a wavy-line cancellation used at Orangeburg, N.Y., at the time. *Perforated 12 vertically.*

289 *George Washington*

289		UnFVF	UseFVF
3¢	**deep violet** Type I	28,500.00	7,000.00
	On cover		15,500.00
	Pair	78,500.00	
	EKU (March 8, 1911)		

1910. WASHINGTON & FRANKLIN COIL ISSUE *Perforated 8 1/2 horizontally.*

290		UnFVF	UseFVF
1¢	**green**	4.50	5.00
	dark green	4.50	5.00
	On cover		7.50

Pair		8.00	16.50
Line pair		25.00	40.00
FDC *(Dec. 12, 1910)*			

291			**UnFVF**	**UseFVF**
2¢	**carmine**		30.00	12.50
	dark carmine		30.00	12.50
	pale carmine		30.00	12.50
	On cover			20.00
	Pair		75.00	32.50
	Line pair		150.00	125.00
	FDC *(Dec. 23, 1910)*			

1910. WASHINGTON & FRANKLIN COIL ISSUE *Perforated 8 1/2 vertically.*

292		**UnFVF**	**UseFVF**
1¢	**green**	20.00	20.00
	dark green	20.00	20.00
	On cover		50.00
	Double transfer	—	
	Pair	55.00	65.00
	Line pair	115.00	135.00
	FDC *(Dec. 12, 1910)*		

293		**UnFVF**	**UseFVF**
2¢	**carmine**	40.00	10.00
	dark carmine	40.00	10.00
	pale carmine	40.00	10.00
	On cover		20.00
	Pair	85.00	22.50
	Line pair	165.00	80.00
	FDC *(Dec. 16, 1910)*		

294		**UnFVF**	**UseFVF**
3¢	**violet** Type I	50.00	50.00
	deep violet	50.00	50.00
	red violet	50.00	50.00
	On cover		100.00
	Pair, 2 or 3mm spacing	110.00	125.00
	Line pair	250.00	275.00
	FDC *(Sept. 18, 1911)*		

295		**UnFVF**	**UseFVF**
4¢	**brown**	50.00	50.00
	dark brown	50.00	50.00
	On cover		100.00
	Pair, 2 or 3mm spacing	110.00	125.00
	Line pair	250.00	250.00
	FDC *(April 15, 1912)*		

296		**UnFVF**	**UseFVF**
5¢	**blue**	50.00	50.00
	dark blue	50.00	50.00
	On cover		100.00
	Pair	110.00	105.00
	Line pair	250.00	300.00
	FDC *(March 1913)*		

1912. MODIFIED GEORGE WASHINGTON ISSUE *1¢ and 2¢ stamps with numerals instead of words for denomination. Flat press printing, single-line USPS watermark (wmk 273), perforated 12.*

297, B34, B35, B36, B43 *George Washington*

297		**UnFVF**	**UseFVF**
1¢	**green**	5.00	.20
	dark green	5.00	.20
	pale green	5.00	.20
	yellow green	5.00	.20
	On cover		.25
	Plate block of 6	55.00	
	Plate block of 6, w/"A"	60.00	
	Plate block of 6, w/"A" & imprint	65.00	
	Cracked plate	11.00	
	Double transfer	5.00	
	n. Booklet pane of 6 *(Feb. 10, 1912)*	65.00	
	v. Vertical pair, imperforate horizontally	700.00	
	FDC *(Feb. 13, 1912)*		

298, B37, B38, B39, B40, B41, B42, B43 *George Washington Type I. The following detailed description is provided, although any 2¢ that fits Point 1 is a Type I.* 1. The line from the front of the neck to and over the top of the button is very weak. The shading lines that run into this line (top of toga) are thin in the area above the cross hatching lines. 2. One shading line in the first (upper) curve of the ribbon above the left numeral and one line in the second (middle) curve above the right numeral. 3. There is a white dash below the ear. 4. The shading lines of the face terminate in front of the ear and are not joined with each other. 5. The lock of hair behind the ear is formed at the bottom by two lines of shading, the lower one being considerably shorter than the other. 6. The hair lines above the ear and slightly to the right form an arrowhead. 7. The shading lines just to the left of the ear form a fairly solid color.

298		**UnFVF**	**UseFVF**
2¢	**carmine** Type I	4.50	.20
	dark carmine	4.50	.20
	lilac carmine	4.50	.20
	On cover		.25
	Plate block of 6	70.00	
	Plate block of 6, w/"A"	85.00	
	Double transfer	6.25	
	n. Booklet pane of 6	65.00	
	v. Double impression	—	
	Earliest documented cover: *June 6, 1912*		
	FDC *(Feb. 14, 1912)*		

1912. MODIFIED GEORGE WASHINGTON ISSUE *Imperforate.*

299		**UnFVF**	**UseFVF**
1¢	**green**	1.25	.60
	dark green	1.25	.60
	pale green	1.25	.60
	yellow green	1.25	.60
	On cover		1.00
	Plate block of 6	17.50	
	Plate block of 6, w/"A"	25.00	
	Plate block of 6, w/"A" & imprint	42.50	
	Center line block	8.00	8.00
	Cracked plate	—	
	Double transfer	2.25	.75
	Margin block of 4, w/arrow	4.50	2.75
	FDC *(March 9, 1912)*		

300		**UnFVF**	**UseFVF**
2¢	**carmine** Type I	1.30	.60
	dark carmine	1.30	.60
	scarlet red	1.30	.60
	On cover		1.00
	Plate block of 6	30.00	
	Plate block of 6, w/"A"	40.00	
	Plate block of 6, w/"A" & imprint	45.00	
	Center line block	9.00	8.00
	Cracked plate	—	
	Margin block of 4, w/arrow	5.50	
	FDC *(Feb. 23, 1912)*		

1912. GEORGE WASHINGTON MODIFIED DESIGN COIL ISSUE *Perforated 8 1/2 horizontally.*

301		**UnFVF**	**UseFVF**
1¢	**green**	5.50	4.50
	dark green	5.50	4.50
	On cover		7.25
	Pair	12.50	8.00
	Line pair	27.50	20.00
	Double transfer	—	
	FDC *(March 18, 1912)*		

302

		UnFVF	UseFVF
2¢	**carmine** Type I	7.50	4.50
	dark carmine	7.50	4.50
	On cover		10.00
	Pair	20.00	9.00
	Line pair	35.00	25.00
	Double transfer	10.00	
	FDC *(March 18, 1912)*		

1912. GEORGE WASHINGTON MODIFIED DESIGN COIL ISSUE
Perforated 8 1/2 vertically.

303

		UnFVF	UseFVF
1¢	**green**	22.50	6.25
	On cover		12.50
	Pair	45.00	12.50
	Line pair	75.00	40.00
	FDC *(May 18, 1912)*		

304

		UnFVF	UseFVF
2¢	**carmine** Type I	35.00	1.25
	dark carmine	35.00	1.25
	On cover		7.00
	Pair	75.00	7.00
	Line pair	150.00	20.00
	Double transfer	35.00	
	FDC *(March 21, 1912)*		

1912-14. BENJAMIN FRANKLIN REDESIGNED ISSUE values from 8¢ through 50¢. *Flat plate printing, single-line USPS watermark (wmk 273), perforated 12.*

305-314 *Benjamin Franklin*

305

		UnFVF	UseFVF
8¢	**pale olive green**	30.00	1.25
	olive green	30.00	1.25
	On cover		12.50
	Plate block of 6, w/imprint & "A"	400.00	
	FDC *(Feb. 14, 1912)*		

306

		UnFVF	UseFVF
9¢	**salmon pink**	45.00	12.50
	rose red	45.00	12.50
	On cover		40.00
	Plate block of 6	550.00	
	Earliest documented cover: *May 1, 1914*		
	FDC *(April 1914)*		

307

		UnFVF	UseFVF
10¢	**orange yellow**	32.50	.50
	brown yellow	300.00	5.00
	yellow	32.50	.50
	On cover		2.25
	Plate block of 6, w/"A"	370.00	
	Plate block of 6, w/"A" & imprint	420.00	
	Double transfer	—	
	FDC *(Jan. 20, 1912)*		

308

		UnFVF	UseFVF
12¢	**chocolate**	40.00	4.25
	deep chocolate	40.00	4.25
	On cover		22.50
	Plate block of 6	450.00	
	Double transfer	47.50	
	Triple transfer	65.00	
	Earliest documented cover: *June 2, 1914*		
	FDC *(April 1914)*		

309

		UnFVF	UseFVF
15¢	**gray black**	65.00	4.00
	gray	65.00	4.00
	On cover		15.00
	Plate block of 6	650.00	
	Plate block of 6, w/"A"	625.00	
	Plate block of 6, w/"A" & imprint	600.00	
	Double transfer	—	
	FDC *(Feb. 14, 1912)*		

310

		UnFVF	UseFVF
20¢	**gray blue**	150.00	17.50
	ultramarine	150.00	17.50
	On cover		125.00
	Plate block of 6	1,650.00	

Earliest documented cover: *May 1, 1914*
FDC *(April 1914)*

311

		UnFVF	UseFVF
30¢	**orange red**	115.00	17.50
	dark orange red	115.00	17.50
	On cover		225.00
	Plate block of 6	1,250.00	
	Earliest documented cover: *May 1, 1914*		
	FDC *(April 1914)*		

312

		UnFVF	UseFVF
50¢	**violet**	350.00	20.00
	pale violet	350.00	20.00
	On cover		1,750.00
	Plate block of 6	8,250.00	
	Earliest documented cover: *May 1, 1914*		
	FDC *(April 1914)*		

1912-14. BENJAMIN FRANKLIN REDESIGNED ISSUE *Double-line USPS watermark (wmk 187).*

313

		UnFVF	UseFVF
50¢	**violet**	225.00	20.00
	On cover		1,750.00
	Plate block of 6, w/"A" & imprint	4,000.00	
	Margin block of 4, w/arrow	950.00	
	FDC *(Feb. 14, 1912)*		

314

		UnFVF	UseFVF
$1	**violet brown**	425.00	65.00
	On cover		6,250.00
	Plate block of 6, w/"A" & imprint	9,100.00	
	Double transfer	475.00	
	Margin block of 4, w/arrow	1,950.00	
	FDC *(Feb. 14, 1912)*		

1914-15. WASHINGTON & FRANKLIN ISSUE with *perforation 10.* *Flat plate printing, single-line USPS watermark (wmk 273).*

315-321, B44, B45, B49 *George Washington*

315

		UnFVF	UseFVF
1¢	**green**	2.75	.20
	bright green	2.75	.20
	dark green	2.75	.20
	yellow green	2.75	.20
	On cover		.25
	Plate block of 6	35.00	
	Plate block of 10, w/"COIL STAMPS"	120.00	
	Cracked plate	—	
	Double transfer	4.00	
	n. Booklet pane of 6	3.75	1.25
	n1v. Booklet pane of 6, ungummed, imperforate	1,000.00	
	v. Perforated 12x10	750.00	650.00
	v1. Perforated 10x12	—	300.00
	v2. Vertical pair, imperforate horizontally	425.00	—
	v3. Vertical pair, imperforate between	8,000.00	
	Earliest documented cover: *Dec. 20, 1913*		
	FDC *(Sept. 5, 1914)*		

316

		UnFVF	UseFVF
2¢	**rose red** Type I (B46, B47, B48, B49)	2.25	.20
	dark carmine	2.25	.20
	dark rose	2.25	.20
	scarlet	2.25	.20
	red	2.25	.20
	rose	2.25	.20
	On cover		.25
	Plate block of 6	25.00	
	Plate block of 10, w/"COIL STAMPS"	125.00	
	Cracked plate	8.00	
	Double transfer	—	
	n. Booklet pane of 6	22.50	4.50
	v. Perforated 12x10	—	750.00
	Earliest documented cover: *Jan. 6, 1914*		
	FDC *(Sept. 5, 1914)*		

317

		UnFVF	UseFVF
3¢	**violet** Type I	12.50	2.00
	bright violet	12.50	2.00
	dark violet	12.50	2.00

reddish violet		12.50	2.00
On cover			3.00
Plate block of 6		160.00	
FDC *(Sept. 18, 1914)*			

318			
4¢	**brown**	**UnFVF**	**UseFVF**
		30.00	.75
dark brown		30.00	.75
orange brown		30.00	.75
yellow brown		30.00	.75
On cover			475.00
Plate block of 6		450.00	
FDC *(Sept. 7, 1914)*			

319			
5¢	**blue**	**UnFVF**	**UseFVF**
		27.50	.70
bright blue		27.50	.70
dark blue		27.50	.70
indigo blue		27.50	.70
On cover			2.50
Plate block of 6		375.00	
v. Perforated 12x10		—	2,000.00
Earliest documented cover: *April 14, 1915*			
FDC *(Sept. 14, 1914)*			

320			
6¢	**red orange**	**UnFVF**	**UseFVF**
		45.00	2.00
dark red orange		45.00	2.00
pale red orange		45.00	2.00
On cover			7.50
Plate block of 6		475.00	
Plate block of 6, w/imprint & star		375.00	
Block of 4, 2 or 3mm spacing		170.00	12.50
FDC *(Sept. 28, 1914)*			

321			
7¢	**black**	**UnFVF**	**UseFVF**
		75.00	5.00
deep black		75.00	5.00
gray black		75.00	5.00
On cover			32.50
Plate block of 6		800.00	
FDC *(Sept. 10, 1914)*			

322-331 *Benjamin Franklin*

322			
8¢	**yellow olive**	**UnFVF**	**UseFVF**
		30.00	1.25
dull yellow olive		30.00	1.25
On cover			7.00
Plate block of 6, w/"A"		475.00	
Plate block of 6, w/"A" & imprint		425.00	
Double transfer		—	
v. Double impression		—	
FDC *(Sept. 26, 1914)*			

323			
9¢	**salmon**	**UnFVF**	**UseFVF**
		35.00	2.00
dark salmon		35.00	2.00
On cover			22.50
Plate block of 6		550.00	
FDC *(Oct. 6, 1914)*			

324			
10¢	**orange yellow**	**UnFVF**	**UseFVF**
		40.00	.40
golden yellow		40.00	.40
yellow		40.00	.40
On cover			6.50
Plate block of 6		775.00	
Plate block of 6, w/"A"		850.00	
Plate block of 6, w/"A" & imprint		600.00	
FDC *(Sept. 9, 1914)*			

325			
11¢	**deep bluish green**	**UnFVF**	**UseFVF**
		20.00	9.00
dark green		20.00	9.00
green		20.00	9.00
On cover			22.50
Plate block of 6		225.00	
FDC *(Aug. 12, 1915)*			

326			
12¢	**maroon**	**UnFVF**	**UseFVF**
		23.00	4.25
dark maroon		23.00	4.25

copper red		25.00	4.50
On cover			17.50
Plate block of 6		275.00	
Double transfer		25.00	
Triple transfer		30.00	
FDC *(Sept. 10, 1914)*			

So-called vertical pair, imperforate between, really have at least one perforation hole between the stamps.

327			
15¢	**gray black**	**UnFVF**	**UseFVF**
		110.00	8.50
gray		110.00	8.50
On cover			47.50
Plate block of 6		900.00	
Plate block of 6, w/"A"		925.00	
Plate block of 6, w/"A" & imprint		900.00	
FDC *(Sept. 16, 1914)*			

328			
20¢	**pale ultramarine**	**UnFVF**	**UseFVF**
		175.00	4.50
ultramarine		175.00	4.50
On cover			130.00
Plate block of 6		2,850.00	
FDC *(Sept. 19, 1914)*			

329			
30¢	**orange red**	**UnFVF**	**UseFVF**
		225.00	20.00
dark orange red		225.00	20.00
On cover			225.00
Plate block of 6		3,250.00	
FDC *(Sept. 19, 1914)*			

330			
50¢	**violet**	**UnFVF**	**UseFVF**
		600.00	22.50
On cover			1,500.00
Plate block of 6		11,500.00	
FDC *(Dec. 13, 1915)*			

1914-15. BENJAMIN FRANKLIN ISSUE This is the only value of the 1914-15 issues, *perforated 10, printed on old paper with the double-line USPS watermark (wmk 187).*

331			
$1	**violet black**	**UnFVF**	**UseFVF**
		725.00	85.00
On cover			9,500.00
Plate block of 6, w/"A" & imprint		10,500.00	
Margin block of 4, w/arrow		3,000.00	
Double transfer		750.00	
FDC *(Feb. 8, 1915)*			

1915. GEORGE WASHINGTON ISSUE As an experiment toward finding a more satisfactory perforation, 190,000 Type I 2¢ stamps were perforated 11 and sold through the Washington post offices, mostly to large users who were asked to report concerning the perforations. *Single-line watermark USPS (wmk 273), perforated 11.*

332			
2¢	**rose red** Type I	**UnFVF**	**UseFVF**
		100.00	225.00
On cover			900.00
Plate block of 6		950.00	
Earliest documented cover: *July 19, 1915*			

1914. GEORGE WASHINGTON COIL ISSUE *Coil stamps, perforated 10 horizontally.*

333			
1¢	**green**	**UnFVF**	**UseFVF**
		1.25	1.25
dark green		1.25	1.25
On cover			2.00
Pair		2.75	3.50
Line pair		6.50	6.00
FDC *(Nov. 14, 1914)*			

334			
2¢	**carmine** Type I	**UnFVF**	**UseFVF**
		8.50	8.00
dark carmine		8.50	8.00
On cover			12.50
Pair		17.50	17.50
Line pair		45.00	60.00
FDC *(July 22, 1914)*			

1914. GEORGE WASHINGTON COIL ISSUE *Coil stamps, perforated 10 vertically.*

335			
1¢	**green**	**UnFVF**	**UseFVF**
		22.50	7.50
dark green		22.50	7.50
On cover			12.50
Pair		60.00	15.00
Line pair		125.00	55.00
FDC *(May 29, 1914)*			

336

		UnFVF	UseFVF
2¢	**carmine** Type I	32.50	1.75
	dark carmine	32.50	1.75
	red	32.50	1.75
	On cover		10.00
	Pair	80.00	5.00
	Line pair	175.00	17.50
	FDC *(April 25, 1914)*		

337

		UnFVF	UseFVF
3¢	**violet** Type I	225.00	125.00
	dark violet	225.00	125.00
	On cover		200.00
	Pair	475.00	280.00
	Line pair	900.00	775.00
	FDC *(Dec. 18, 1914)*		

338

		UnFVF	UseFVF
4¢	**brown**	120.00	47.50
	On cover		100.00
	Pair	275.00	220.00
	Line pair	600.00	550.00
	FDC *(Oct. 2, 1914)*		

339

		UnFVF	UseFVF
5¢	**blue**	47.50	32.50
	On cover		52.50
	Pair	90.00	175.00
	Line pair	200.00	425.00
	FDC *(July 30, 1914)*		

1914-16. WASHINGTON & FRANKLIN ROTARY PRESS COIL ISSUE
    The rotary press was first used in production of the following coil stamps. The press plates are curved into a half circle. Two plates are fitted around a cylinder and when the cylinder is rotated it prints on the paper being passed beneath it. An increase in printing speed and efficiency results as the paper is a continuous roll.
    When plates are curved to fit the cylinder, there is a slight increase in the size of each stamp design in the direction the plate is curved. Designs on the flat plate presses run about 18 1/2 to 19mm wide by 22mm high. They stretch to 19 1/2 to 22mm wide on the rotary plates that are curved sidewise to the design, and to 22 1/2 to 23mm high when the plates are curved lengthwise to the design. A line of ink is deposited on the paper between stamp designs, where the two plates are joined on the cylinder.
Designs 18 1/2 to 19mm wide by 22 1/2mm high, single-line USPS watermark (wmk 273), perforated 10 horizontally.

The designs of rotary press stamps are larger in one dimension than those of flat press stamps. The illustration here shows to the left the rotary press coil No. 340 being taller than the flat press No. 333.

The other illustration shows the rotary press coil No. 343 being wider than a flat press version No. 335.

340

		UnFVF	UseFVF
1¢	**green**	6.50	4.25
	pale green	6.50	4.25
	On cover		8.00
	Pair	15.00	9.00
	Line pair	40.00	27.50
	FDC *(Dec. 12, 1915)*		

341 Type III. Same as Type II except two lines of shading in the curves of the ribbons.

341

		UnFVF	UseFVF
2¢	**carmine** Type III	10.00	4.25
	carmine rose	10.00	4.25
	red	10.00	4.25
	On cover		9.00
	Pair	25.00	10.00
	Line pair	55.00	22.50
	v. carmine, Type I	2,000.00	325.00
	Earliest documented cover: *Dec. 21, 1915*		

1914. WASHINGTON ROTARY PRESS SIDEWISE COIL ISSUE
Imperforate, sidewise coil. Design 19 1/2 to 20mm wide by 22mm high.

342

		UnFVF	UseFVF
2¢	**carmine** Type I	375.00	750.00
	On cover		—
	Pair	675.00	2,250.00
	Line pair	1,250.00	8,500.00
	FDC *(June 30, 1914)*		

1914-16. WASHINGTON ISSUE *Perforated 10 vertically. Designs 19 1/2 to 20mm wide by 22mm high.*

343

		UnFVF	UseFVF
1¢	**green**	10.00	2.50
	On cover		4.00
	Pair	25.00	2,250.00
	Line pair	65.00	12.50
	Earliest documented cover: *March 22, 1915*		
	FDC *(Nov. 11, 1914)*		

344v Type II. Shading lines in ribbons same as Type I. The top line of toga rope is heavy, and the rope is heavily shaded. The shading lines on the face, in front of the ear, are joined by a heavy vertical curved line.

344

		UnFVF	UseFVF
2¢	**carmine** Type III	10.00	1.15
	carmine rose	10.00	1.15
	On cover		2.25
	Pair	22.50	2.75
	Line pair	55.00	7.25
	v. carmine, Type II *(June 1915)*	85.00	10.50
	v1. carmine, Type I *(June 30, 1914)*	110.00	4.25
	FDC *(Dec. 1915)*		

345

		UnFVF	UseFVF
3¢	**violet** Type I	225.00	115.00
	dark violet	225.00	115.00
	red violet	225.00	115.00
	On cover		180.00
	Pair	550.00	300.00
	Line pair	1,100.00	700.00
	FDC *(Feb. 2, 1916)*		

346

		UnFVF	UseFVF
4¢	**yellow brown**	27.50	20.00
	brown	27.50	20.00
	On cover		45.00
	Cracked plate	35.00	
	Pair	60.00	50.00
	Line pair	150.00	100.00
	FDC *(Nov. 5, 1915)*		

347

		UnFVF	UseFVF
5¢	**blue**	32.50	17.50
	On cover		42.50
	Pair	75.00	50.00
	Line pair	180.00	100.00
	Double transfer	—	
	FDC *(March 9, 1916)*		

1916-17. WASHINGTON & FRANKLIN ISSUE *Flat plate printing, unwatermarked, perforated 10.*

348

		UnFVF	UseFVF
1¢	**green** (B50, B51, B53)	6.00	.50
	blue green	6.00	.50
	dark green	6.00	.50
	dull green	6.00	.50

		UnFVF	UseFVF
On cover			.50
Plate block of 6		150.00	
Booklet pane of 6 *(Oct. 15, 1916)*		10.00	
x. Experimental Bureau precancel New Orleans, La.			7.50
x1. Experimental Bureau precancel Augusta, Maine			17.50
x2. Experimental Bureau precancel Springfield, Mass.			8.00
FDC *(Sept. 27, 1916)*			

349
2¢

	UnFVF	UseFVF
carmine Type I (B52, B53, B54, B55)	4.00	.35
dark carmine	4.00	.35
rose red	4.00	.35
On cover		.50
Double transfer	6.00	
Plate block of 6	130.00	
Booklet pane of 6 *(Oct. 8, 1916)*	85.00	
x. Experimental Bureau precancel New Orleans, La.		500.00
x1. Experimental Bureau precancel Springfield, Mass.		22.50
FDC *(Sept. 25, 1916)*		

350
3¢

	UnFVF	UseFVF
violet Type I	65.00	15.00
dark violet	65.00	15.00
On cover		40.00
Plate block of 6	1,400.00	
Double transfer in "CENTS"	90.00	
x. Experimental Bureau precancel New Orleans, La.		1,000.00
x1. Experimental Bureau precancel Springfield, Mass.		200.00
FDC *(Nov. 11, 1916)*		

351
4¢

	UnFVF	UseFVF
yellow brown	42.50	2.25
dark brown	42.50	2.25
On cover		12.50
Double transfer	—	
Plate block of 6	675.00	
x. Experimental Bureau precancel Springfield, Mass.		175.00
FDC *(Oct. 7, 1916)*		

352
5¢

	UnFVF	UseFVF
blue	65.00	2.25
dark blue	65.00	2.25
dull blue	65.00	2.25
On cover		12.50
Plate block of 6	900.00	
x. Experimental Bureau precancel Springfield, Mass.		175.00
FDC *(Oct. 17, 1916)*		

353 *The "Five Cent Red Error" was caused by mistakenly using a 5¢ transfer roll in re-entering three positions on plate 7942, a plate of the 2¢ stamps. Of the 400 positions on the plate, 397 copies were 2¢ and three copies were 5¢. The error was not discovered until a considerable number of sheets were in the post offices, and many of them were picked up by collectors. The errors exist perforated 10 (No. 353), perforated 11 (No. 385), and imperforate (No. 370). The shade actually is carmine, but the stamp commonly is called the "Red Error."*

353
5¢

	UnFVF	UseFVF
carmine	550.00	700.00
On cover		1,950.00
Block of 9, one 5¢ error in middle of block of 2¢ stamps	750.00	

	UnFVF	UseFVF
Block of 12, two 5¢ errors (2 middle stamps) w/ten 2¢ stamps	1,500.00	
Earliest documented cover: *May 25, 1917*		

354
6¢

	UnFVF	UseFVF
red orange	80.00	7.50
orange	80.00	7.50
On cover		40.00
Double transfer	—	
Plate block of 6	1,400.00	
x. Experimental Bureau precancel New Orleans, La.		2,500.00
x1. Experimental Bureau precancel Springfield, Mass.		175.00
FDC *(Oct. 10, 1916)*		

355
7¢

	UnFVF	UseFVF
black	100.00	12.50
deep black	100.00	12.50
gray black	100.00	12.50
On cover		45.00
Plate block of 6	1,400.00	
x. Experimental Bureau precancel Springfield, Mass.		175.00
FDC *(Nov. 10, 1916)*		

356
8¢

	UnFVF	UseFVF
yellow olive	55.00	6.50
dark yellow olive	55.00	6.50
On cover		30.00
Plate block of 6, w/"A"	625.00	
Plate block of 6, w/"A" & imprint	575.00	
x. Experimental Bureau precancel Springfield, Mass.		150.00
FDC *(Nov. 13, 1916)*		

357
9¢

	UnFVF	UseFVF
salmon	50.00	15.00
On cover		40.00
Plate block of 6	775.00	
x. Experimental Bureau precancel Springfield, Mass.		150.00
FDC *(Nov. 16, 1916)*		

358
10¢

	UnFVF	UseFVF
orange yellow	95.00	1.25
On cover		8.00
Plate block of 6	1,400.00	
x. Experimental Bureau precancel Springfield, Mass.		150.00
FDC *(Oct. 17, 1916)*		

359
11¢

	UnFVF	UseFVF
deep bluish green	35.00	22.50
On cover		45.00
Plate block of 6	375.00	
x. Experimental Bureau precancel Springfield, Mass.		500.00
FDC *(Nov. 16, 1916)*		

360
12¢

	UnFVF	UseFVF
chocolate	45.00	5.50
On cover		22.50
Plate block of 6	650.00	
Double transfer	60.00	6.00
Triple transfer	70.00	9.00
x. Experimental Bureau precancel Springfield, Mass.		200.00
FDC *(Oct. 10, 1916)*		

361
15¢

	UnFVF	UseFVF
gray black	165.00	12.50
gray	165.00	12.50
On cover		85.00
Plate block of 6	2,900.00	
Plate block of 6, w/"A" & imprint	—	
x. Experimental Bureau precancel Springfield, Mass.		150.00
FDC *(Nov. 16, 1916)*		

362
20¢

	UnFVF	UseFVF
pale blue	225.00	12.50
blue	225.00	12.50
On cover		725.00
Plate block of 6	3,750.00	
x. Experimental Bureau precancel Springfield, Mass.		125.00
FDC *(Dec. 5, 1916)*		

362A		UnFVF	UseFVF
30¢	**orange red**	4,500.00	—
	Plate block of 6	—	

No. 362A Two sheets of 100 stamps of the 30¢ denomination were discovered without any trace of watermark, as authenticated by The Philatelic Foundation's expert committee.

363		UnFVF	UseFVF
50¢	**light violet**	950.00	65.00
	On cover		2,250.00
	Plate block of 6	42,500.00	
	FDC *(March 2, 1917)*	—	

364		UnFVF	UseFVF
$1	**violet black**	625.00	20.00
	On cover		3,000.00
	Block of 6, w/"A" & imprint	14,000.00	
	Margin block of 4, w/arrow	3,250.00	
	Double transfer	850.00	22.50
	FDC *(Dec. 22, 1916)*		

1917. JAMES MADISON ISSUE

365 *James Madison*

365		UnFVF	UseFVF
$2	**dark blue**	325.00	45.00
	On cover		1,750.00
	Plate block of 6	5,000.00	
	Margin block of 4, w/arrow	1,450.00	
	Double transfer	—	
	EKU *(April 10, 1917)*		

1917. JOHN MARSHALL ISSUE

366 *John Marshall*

366		UnFVF	UseFVF
$5	**light green**	250.00	50.00
	On cover	1,750.00	
	Plate block of 6	4,000.00	
	Margin block of 4, w/arrow	1,150.00	
	EKU *(April 10, 1917)*		

1916-1917. GEORGE WASHINGTON ISSUE *Imperforate.*

367		UnFVF	UseFVF
1¢	**green**	1.15	1.00
	bluish green	1.15	1.00
	dark green	1.15	1.00
	On cover		1.50
	Plate block of 6	12.50	
	Center line block	8.50	6.25
	Margin block of 4, w/arrow	4.50	3.25
	Double transfer	2.50	1.25
	FDC *(Dec. 8, 1916)*		

368		UnFVF	UseFVF
2¢	**carmine** Type I	1.40	1.30
	carmine rose	1.40	1.30
	dark carmine	1.40	1.30
	dark rose	1.40	1.30
	On cover		2.50
	Plate block of 6	22.50	
	Plate block of 6, from plate No. 7942	175.00	
	Center line block	8.50	7.00
	Cracked plate	—	
	Margin block of 4, w/arrow	6.50	5.75
	FDC *(Dec. 8, 1916)*		

368A		UnFVF	UseFVF
2¢	**deep rose**, Type Ia		15,000.00
	On cover		22,500.00
	Pair (one example known)		105,000.00
	EKU *(Feb. 17, 1920)*		

Type Ia is similar to Type I, but lines of the design are stronger. This is particularly noticeable on the toga button, toga rope and rope shading lines, which are heavy. Lines in the ribbons are similar to Type I.

369 *On Type II the top line of the toga rope is heavy and the rope shading lines are also heavy and complete. The line between the lips is heavy.*

369		UnFVF	UseFVF
3¢	**violet** Type I	15.00	8.50
	dull violet	15.00	8.50
	On cover		17.50
	Plate block of 6	125.00	
	Center line block	70.00	70.00
	Double transfer	17.50	
	Margin block of 4, w/arrow	60.00	35.00
	Triple transfer	—	
	v. violet, Type II	12.50	5.50
	dark violet	12.50	5.50
	On cover		11.50
	Plate block of 6	100.00	
	Center line block	60.00	60.00
	Margin block of 4, w/arrow	47.50	30.00
	Double transfer	12.50	
	Earliest documented cover: *April 30, 1918*		
	FDC *(Oct. 13, 1917)*		

370		UnFVF	UseFVF
5¢	**carmine**	12,500.00	
	On cover		—
	Block of 9, one 5¢ error in middle of block of 2¢ stamps	15,000.00	
	Block of 12, two 5¢ errors (two middle stamps) w/ten 2¢ stamps	30,800.00	
	FDC *(March 1917)*		

This stamp commonly is called the "Red Error," but really is carmine. See note with No. 353.

1916-22. WASHINGTON ROTARY PRESS COIL ISSUE
Unwatermarked, perforated 10 horizontally. Stamp designs 18 1/2 to 19mm wide by 22 1/2mm high.

371		UnFVF	UseFVF
1¢	**green**	.75	.20
	yellowish green	.75	.20
	On cover		.50
	Pair	2.00	.65
	Line pair	4.00	.75
	Cracked plate	—	
	Double transfer	2.25	
	FDC *(Jan. 10, 1918)*		

372		UnFVF	UseFVF
2¢	**carmine** Type III	3.00	1.75
	On cover		3.50
	Pair	5.75	4.00
	Line pair	20.00	
	Cracked plate	12.00	7.50
	v. carmine, Type II *(Nov. 15, 1916)*	14.50	4.75
	On cover		10.00
	Pair	32.50	7.50
	Line pair	125.00	
	Cracked plate	—	
	FDC *(1919)*		

373		UnFVF	UseFVF
3¢	**violet** Type I	4.50	1.50
	bluish violet	4.50	1.50
	dull violet	4.50	1.50
	On cover		2.50
	Pair	11.00	4.00
	Line pair	27.50	10.00
	FDC *(Oct. 10, 1917)*		

1916-22. WASHINGTON ISSUE *Perforated 10 vertically. Stamp designs 19 1/2 to 20mm wide by 22mm high.*

374

		UnFVF	UseFVF
1¢	**green**	.60	.20
	yellowish green	.60	.20
	On cover		.50
	Pair	1.25	.65
	Line pair	4.00	1.25
	Cracked plate	7.50	
	Double transfer	—	
	Rosette crack on head	50.00	
	FDC (Nov. 17, 1916)		

375

		UnFVF	UseFVF
2¢	**carmine** Type III	8.50	.20
	carmine rose	8.50	.20
	On cover		.50
	Pair	21.00	.65
	Line pair	50.00	3.50
	Cracked plate	—	
	Double transfer	—	
	v. carmine, Type II (Nov. 17, 1916)	1,650.00	800.00
	On cover		850.00
	Pair	4,000.00	17.50
	Line pair	9,000.00	5,000.00
	FDC (Nov. 17, 1916)		

376

		UnFVF	UseFVF
3¢	**violet** Type II	11.50	1.25
	dull violet	11.50	1.25
	gray violet	11.50	1.25
	On cover		1.00
	Pair	24.00	2.25
	Line pair	60.00	2.75
	v1. violet, Type I (July 23, 1917)	17.50	3.25
	reddish violet	17.50	3.25
	On cover		7.00
	Pair	35.00	8.00
	Line pair	125.00	45.00
	FDC (Feb. 4, 1918)		

377

		UnFVF	UseFVF
4¢	**yellow brown**	10.50	4.00
	On cover		8.50
	Pair	24.00	10.00
	Line pair	65.00	17.50
	Cracked plate	—	
	FDC (Oct. 19, 1917)		

378

		UnFVF	UseFVF
5¢	**blue**	3.50	1.25
	On cover		1.75
	Pair	8.00	2.25
	Line pair	25.00	7.00
	FDC (Jan. 15, 1919)		

379

		UnFVF	UseFVF
10¢	**orange yellow**	19.00	12.50
	On cover		17.50
	Pair	47.50	27.50
	Line pair	125.00	50.00
	FDC (Jan. 31, 1922)		5,300.00

1917-19 WASHINGTON & FRANKLIN ISSUE *Flat press printing, unwatermarked paper, perforated 11.*

380

		UnFVF	UseFVF
1¢	**green** (B56, B57, B58, B59, B66, B67, B76)	.55	.20
	dark green	.55	.20
	pale green	.55	.20
	yellowish green	.55	.20
	On cover		.35
	Plate block of 6	17.50	
	Cracked plate	7.50	
	Double transfer	5.50	2.00
	n. Booklet pane of 6	2.75	.35
	n1. Booklet pane of 30	1,100.00	
	v. Double impression	175.00	
	v1. Horizontal pair, imperforate between	200.00	
	v2. Perforated 10 at top	675.00	
	v3. Perforated 10 at bottom	675.00	
	v4. Vertical pair, imperforate between	500.00	
	v5. Vertical pair, imperforate horizontally	150.00	
	Earliest documented cover: Sept. 10, 1917		
	FDC (March 23, 1917)		

381

		UnFVF	UseFVF
2¢	**rose red** Type I (B60, B61, B62, B63, B64, B65, B66, B68)	.50	.20
	dark rose	.50	.20
	rose carmine	.50	.20
	On cover		.35
	Plate block of 6	18.00	
	Cracked plate	—	
	Double transfer	6.00	
	Retouch in hair	—	
	Double impression	160.00	
	n. Booklet pane of 6 (March 31, 1917)	4.50	
	n1. Booklet pane of 30	27,500.00	
	v. Horizontal pair, imperforate vertically	200.00	125.00
	v1. Vertical pair, imperforate between	500.00	250.00
	v2. Vertical pair, imperforate horizontally	150.00	
	a. deep rose, Type Ia	225.00	175.00
	dark rose	225.00	175.00
	On cover		325.00
	Plate block of 6	1,800.00	
	Plate block of 6, two stamps Type I	7,500.00	
	Pair, 1 each Type I & Ia	1,000.00	
	Earliest documented cover: Aug. 12, 1917		
	FDC (March 23, 1917)		

382

		UnFVF	UseFVF
3¢	**violet** Type I (B69, B70)	12.50	.20
	dark violet	12.50	.20
	dull violet	12.50	.20
	reddish violet	12.50	.20
	On cover		.35
	Plate block of 6	100.00	
	n. Booklet pane of 6 (Oct. 17, 1917)	60.00	17.50
	v. Double impression	200.00	
	v1. Vertical pair, imperforate horizontally	400.00	
	FDC (March 23, 1917)		

382A

		UnFVF	UseFVF
3¢	**violet** Type II	15.00	.40
	dark violet	15.00	.40
	On cover		.65
	Plate block of 6	150.00	
	n. Booklet pane of 6	50.00	
	v. Double impression	200.00	
	v1. Perforated 10 at top	8,000.00	5,500.00
	v2. Perforated 10 at bottom	8,000.00	5,500.00
	v3. Vertical pair, imperforate horizontally	250.00	150.00
	Earliest documented cover: June 18, 1918		
	FDC (Feb. 25, 1918)		

383

		UnFVF	UseFVF
4¢	**yellow brown**	11.50	.30
	brown	11.50	.30
	dark brown	11.50	.30
	orange brown	11.50	.30
	On cover		2.00
	Plate block of 6	140.00	
	Double transfer	15.00	
	v. Double impression	—	
	FDC (March 23, 1917)		

384

		UnFVF	UseFVF
5¢	**blue**	8.50	.25
	dark blue	8.50	.25
	dull blue	8.50	.25
	On cover		.35
	Plate block of 6	125.00	
	Double transfer	10.50	
	v. Horizontal pair, imperforate between	2,250.00	
	FDC (March 23, 1917)		

385

		UnFVF	UseFVF
5¢	**carmine**	400.00	500.00
	On cover		1,500.00
	Strip of 3 (Nos. 381-385-381)	500.00	
	Block of 9, one 5¢ error in middle of 2¢ block	600.00	
	Block of 12, two 5¢ errors (2 middle stamps) within ten 2¢ stamps	1,000.00	
	Earliest documented cover: March 27, 1917		

This stamp commonly is called the "Red Error" but really is carmine. See note with No. 353.

386

		UnFVF	UseFVF
6¢	**red orange**	12.50	.40
	orange	12.50	.40
	On cover		2.50
	Plate block of 6	145.00	
	Double transfer	—	
	v. Perforated 10 at bottom	3,000.00	2,500.00

		UnFVF	UseFVF
	v1. Perforated 10 at top	3,000.00	2,500.00
	FDC *(March 23, 1917)*		

387
7¢

		UnFVF	UseFVF
	black	25.00	1.25
	deep black	25.00	1.25
	gray black	25.00	1.25
	On cover		8.00
	Plate block of 6	220.00	
	Double transfer	—	
	FDC *(March 24, 1917)*		

388
8¢

		UnFVF	UseFVF
	yellow olive	12.50	1.00
	dark olive green	12.50	1.00
	olive green	12.50	1.00
	On cover		300.00
	Plate block of 6	125.00	
	Plate block of 6, w/"A"	150.00	
	Plate block of 6, w/"A" & imprint	200.00	
	v. Perforated 10 at bottom		3,250.00
	v1. Perforated 10 at top		3,250.00
	v2. Vertical pair, imperforate between	—	
	FDC *(March 24, 1917)*		

389
9¢

		UnFVF	UseFVF
	salmon	14.00	2.50
	On cover		15.00
	Plate block of 6	125.00	
	Double transfer	20.00	5.00
	v. Perforated 10 at bottom	4,000.00	5,500.00
	v1. Perforated 10 at top	4,000.00	5,500.00
	FDC *(March 12, 1917)*		

390
10¢

		UnFVF	UseFVF
	orange yellow	17.50	.25
	On cover		2.00
	Plate block of 6	165.00	
	Plate block of 6, w/"A"	300.00	
	FDC *(March 24, 1917)*		

391
11¢

		UnFVF	UseFVF
	deep bluish green	9.00	3.00
	dull green	9.00	3.00
	green	9.00	3.00
	On cover		8.50
	Plate block of 6	115.00	
	Double transfer	12.50	3.25
	v. Perforated 10 at bottom	3,750.00	2,000.00
	v1. Perforated 10 at top	3,750.00	2,000.00
	FDC *(May 19, 1917)*		

392
12¢

		UnFVF	UseFVF
	brown purple	9.00	.65
	a. brown carmine	9.00	.65
	On cover		4.00
	Plate block of 6	115.00	
	Double transfer	12.50	
	Triple transfer	20.00	
	v. Perforated 10 at bottom	—	3,000.00
	v1. Perforated 10 at top	—	3,000.00
	FDC *(May 12, 1917)*		

393
13¢

		UnFVF	UseFVF
	apple green	10.50	6.50
	dark apple green	10.50	6.50
	pale apple green	10.50	6.50
	On cover		20.00
	Plate block of 6	125.00	
	FDC *(Jan. 11, 1919)*		

394
15¢

		UnFVF	UseFVF
	gray black	37.50	1.25
	gray	37.50	1.25
	On cover		22.50
	Plate block of 6	450.00	
	Double transfer	—	
	FDC *(May 21, 1917)*		

395
20¢

		UnFVF	UseFVF
	pale blue	47.50	.50
	dark blue	47.50	.50
	gray blue	47.50	.50
	On cover		.75
	Plate block of 6	500.00	
	Double transfer	—	
	v. Double impression	1,250.00	
	v1. Perforated 10 at bottom	—	8,000.00
	v2. Perforated 10 at top	—	8,000.00
	v3. Vertical pair, imperforate between	425.00	
	FDC *(May 12, 1917)*		

396
30¢

		UnFVF	UseFVF
	orange red	37.50	1.25
	dark orange red	37.50	1.25
	On cover		150.00
	Plate block of 6	500.00	
	Double transfer	—	
	v. Double impression	—	
	v1. Perforated 10 at bottom	4,000.00	4,750.00
	v2. Perforated 10 at top	4,000.00	4,750.00
	FDC *(May 12, 1917)*		

397
50¢

		UnFVF	UseFVF
	reddish violet	65.00	.90
	pale violet	65.00	.90
	red violet	65.00	.90
	On cover		400.00
	Plate block of 6	1,650.00	
	Double transfer	100.00	1.50
	v. Perforated 10 at bottom	—	8,000.00
	v1. Perforated 10 at top	—	8,000.00
	v2. Vertical pair, imperforate between	1,800.00	1,000.00
	FDC *(May 19, 1917)*		

398
$1

		UnFVF	UseFVF
	black purple	55.00	1.75
	brown purple	55.00	1.75
	blackish brown	1,100.00	750.00
	On cover		550.00
	Plate block of 6, w/"A" & imprint	1,350.00	
	Double transfer	75.00	2.00
	Margin block of 4, w/arrow	250.00	
	FDC *(May 19, 1917)*		

1917. GEORGE WASHINGTON ISSUE The 2¢ carmine stamp of 1908-09 issues existed in 1917 in the imperforate form at the New York Post Office. The old stock was returned to the Bureau of Engraving and Printing and was perforated with the then-current perforation. It is identical to No. 238 except for the perforation and is listed here according to the year of its release. *Flat plate printing, double-line USPS watermark (wmk 187), perforated 11.*

399
2¢

		UnFVF	UseFVF
	carmine	275.00	450.00
	On cover		2,000.00
	Plate block of 6, w/imprint	2,250.00	
	Earliest documented cover: *Oct. 10, 1917*		

1918-20. BENJAMIN FRANKLIN ISSUE New, horizontal designs. *Flat plate printing, unwatermarked, perforated 11.*

400, 401 *Benjamin Franklin*

400
$2

		UnFVF	UseFVF
	orange & black	650.00	225.00
	On cover		1,850.00
	Center line block	3,000.00	
	Margin block of 4, w/arrow	2,800.00	
	Plate block of 8, w/arrow	13,500.00	
	FDC *(Aug. 23, 1918)*		

401
$2

		UnFVF	UseFVF
	carmine & black	190.00	40.00
	lilac carmine & black	190.00	40.00
	Plate block of 8, w/arrow	—	
	Center line block	—	
	Margin block of 4, w/arrow	—	
	On cover		—
	FDC *(Nov. 1, 1920)*		

402 *Benjamin Franklin*

402
$5

		UnFVF	UseFVF
	deep green & black	225.00	35.00
	On cover		1,500.00
	Center line block	1,050.00	

Margin block of 4, w/arrow   1,000.00
Plate block of 8, w/arrow   3,850.00
FDC *(Aug. 23, 1918)*

1918-20. GEORGE WASHINGTON ISSUE Offset Printing. This is
the first time the Post Office Department did not use engraved plates.
It was a direct result of World War I. During this period the Bureau of
Engraving and Printing was hard pressed by the demands for stamps
and government printing of all types. Printing inks for postage stamps
used barites as a base, and as the war went on this basic material
grew inferior in quality and contained a gritty substance that wore out
the engraved plates more quickly; high quality steel was difficult to
obtain, so all conditions combined resulted in the unsatisfactory
experiment of offset printing. These stamps can easily be identified by
the smoothness of the printed surface when contrasted with any of the
earlier stamps, all of which were engraved. This can be told apart by
actual touch, as the engraved stamps have a "rough" feeling, and the
offsets a "soapy" feeling. If you hold an engraved stamp at a flat angle
against a light and observe it through a magnifying glass, the actual
ridges of the ink may be observed, while on the offsets there is no fine
detail, and the stamps have a blurred appearance. The offsets are
smaller than the engraved, usually about 1/2mm narrower in width
(with the exception of the Type IV 3¢) and from 1/2mm to 1mm less in
length. The offsets run from 21 to 21 1/2mm high. Three
denominations were made in this style of printing, 1¢, 2¢, and 3¢,
each value being *perforated 11* and *imperforate,* and the 1¢ also
came *perforated 12 1/2. Unwatermarked, perforated 11.*

Exact dates of issue are not known; dates listed are approximate.

403 *George Washington*

Type IV: *Top line of toga
rope is broken. Lines
inside toga button read
"D (reversed) ID." The
line of color in the left "2"
is very thin and is usually
broken.*

Type V: *Top line of the
toga is complete. Five
vertical shading lines in
toga button. Line of color
in left "2" is very thin and
usually broken. Shading
dots on nose form a
triangle with six dots in
third row from bottom.*

Type Va: *Same as Type
V except on the shading
dots on the nose, in
which the third row from
the bottom has only four
dots instead of six.*

Type VI: *Same as Type
V but there is a heavy
line of color in the left "2."*

Type VII: *The line of color
in the left "2" is clear and
unbroken, heavier than
on Type V or Va, but not
as heavy as on Type VI.
An extra vertical row of
dots has been added on
the lip, making four rows
of three dots instead of
two dots. Additional dots
have been added to the
hair on top of the head.*

403		UnFVF	UseFVF
1¢	**dull green**	2.00	.75
	a. dark green	2.25	.75
	emerald	2.00	.75
	On cover		1.50
	Plate block of 6	16.50	
	"Flat nose" (nose appears so)	—	
	v. Double impression	25.00	
	v1. Horizontal pair, imperforate between	95.00	
	FDC *(Dec. 24, 1918)*		

404-404D *George Washington. There are five types
of the 2¢ offset stamps, each of which appears only
on the offset stamps.*

404		UnFVF	UseFVF
2¢	**rose red** Type VII	17.50	.35
	On cover		.40
	Plate block of 6	135.00	
	Retouch on cheek	375.00	
	v. Double impression	65.00	
	Earliest documented cover: *Nov. 10, 1920*		

404A		UnFVF	UseFVF
2¢	**rose red** Type V	15.00	1.00
	bright carmine	15.00	1.00
	rose carmine	15.00	1.00
	On cover		2.50
	Plate block of 6	125.00	
	Line through "2" & "EN"	30.00	
	v. Double impression	55.00	8.50
	v1. Horizontal pair, imperforate vertically	—	
	v2. Vertical pair, imperforate horizontally	850.00	
	Earliest documented cover: *April 20, 1920*		

404B		UnFVF	UseFVF
2¢	**rose red** Type Va	8.00	.35
	On cover		65.00
	Plate block of 6	75.00	
	Plate block of 6, w/monogram over number	90.00	
	"CRNTS" rather than "CENTS"		
	Retouch of "P" in "POSTAGE"	50.00	
	Retouch on toga	—	
	v. Double impression	25.00	
	v1. Vertical pair, imperforate between	1,250.00	
	Earliest documented cover: *July 16, 1920*		

404C		UnFVF	UseFVF
2¢	**rose red** Type VI	45.00	1.50
	bright carmine	45.00	1.50
	On cover		3.75
	Plate block of 6	350.00	
	Plate block of 6, w/monogram over number	450.00	
	v. Double impression	150.00	
	v1. Vertical pair, imperforate between	—	
	v2. Vertical pair, imperforate horizontally	—	
	Earliest documented cover: *July 30, 1920*		

404D		UnFVF	UseFVF
2¢	**rose red** Type IV	25.00	4.25
	carmine	25.00	4.25
	On cover		10.00

Plate block of 6		185.00	
Misformed "2" at left		35.00	
Scar on forehead		45.00	
FDC *(March 15, 1920)*			825.00

1918. GEORGE WASHINGTON ISSUE

405 *George Washington. There are two types of the 3¢ offset stamps, each of which appears only on the offset stamps.*

Type III: *Top line of toga is strong but the fifth shading line is missing. The center shading line of the toga button consists of two vertical dashes with a dot between them. The "P" and "O" of "POSTAGE" have a line of color between them.*

Type IV: *The "P" and "O" of "POSTAGE" are joined with no line of color between them. The center shading line runs right through the dot in the toga button.*

405			UnFVF	UseFVF
3¢	**purple** Type III		3.00	.40
	dark purple		3.00	.40
	dull purple		3.00	.40
	On cover			.50
	Plate block of 6		40.00	
	v. Double impression		35.00	
	v1. Printed on both sides		425.00	
	FDC *(March 23, 1918)*			

405A			UnFVF	UseFVF
3¢	**purple** Type IV		1.25	.20
	dull purple		1.25	.20
	violet		1.25	.20
	On cover			.25
	Plate block of 6		15.00	
	"Blister" under "U.S."		4.25	
	Retouch under "U.S."		4.25	
	v. Double impression		17.50	6.00
	v1. Printed on both sides		225.00	
	Earliest documented cover: *June 30, 1918*			

1919-20. GEORGE WASHINGTON ISSUE *Imperforate offset stamps.*

406			UnFVF	UseFVF
1¢	**dull green**		10.00	8.50
	green		10.00	8.50
	On cover			15.00
	Plate block of 6		75.00	
	Center line block		55.00	45.00
	Margin block of 4, w/arrow		40.00	36.00
	FDC *(Jan. 21, 1919)*			

407			UnFVF	UseFVF
2¢	**rose red** Type IV		35.00	30.00
	On cover			65.00
	Plate block of 6		285.00	
	Center line block		200.00	
	Margin block of 4, w/arrow		175.00	
	Earliest documented cover: *April 30, 1920*			

407A			UnFVF	UseFVF
2¢	**rose red** Type V		190.00	85.00
	On cover			200.00
	Plate block of 6		1,750.00	

Center line block		900.00	450.00	
Margin block of 4, w/arrow		800.00		
Earliest documented cover: *June 30, 1920*				

407B			UnFVF	UseFVF
2¢	**rose red** Type Va		12.50	8.50
	carmine		12.50	8.50
	On cover			14.00
	Plate block of 6		85.00	
	Plate block of 6, w/monograph over number		200.00	
	Center line block		50.00	60.00
	Margin block of 4, w/arrow		50.00	40.00
	Earliest documented cover: *July 3, 1920*			

407C			UnFVF	UseFVF
2¢	**rose red** Type VI		35.00	22.50
	On cover			35.00
	Plate block of 6		300.00	
	Center line block		190.00	175.00
	Margin block of 4, w/arrow		165.00	
	Earliest documented cover: *Sept. 7, 1920*			

407D			UnFVF	UseFVF
2¢	**rose red** Type VII		1,500.00	575.00
	On cover			1,050.00
	Plate block of 6		12,500.00	
	Center line block		7,700.00	
	Margin block of 4, w/arrow		5,500.00	
	Earliest documented cover: *Nov. 3, 1920*			

408			UnFVF	UseFVF
3¢	**violet** Type IV		8.75	6.00
	On cover			11.00
	Plate block of 6		50.00	
	Center line block		45.00	45.00
	Margin block of 4, w/arrow		40.00	30.00
	v. Double impression		100.00	
	Earliest documented cover: *Oct. 5, 1918*			

1919. GEORGE WASHINGTON ISSUE

The 1¢ offset was issued with a trial perforation 12 1/2 made by the Rossbach perforating machine, a two-way rotary perforator that perforated a single sheet one direction, and then the other. The machine proved unsatisfactory as nearly half of the sheets that were perforated had to be destroyed. Of the 6,641 sheets of 400 images that were perforated by this machine, only 3,466 were good enough to send to the post offices. These were cut into panes of 100 before they were issued. Even the sheets that were released consisted, for the most part, of very badly centered stamps. *Perforated 12 1/2.*

409			UnFVF	UseFVF
1¢	**dull green**		14.00	16.50
	On cover			50.00
	Plate block of 6		140.00	
	v. Horizontal pair, imperforate vertically		450.00	
	FDC *(Aug. 15, 1919)*			

The Rotary Press Issues that follow form the final group of issues that bear the Washington design of 1914-15. Here is how rotary press intaglio stamps can be distinguished from stamps of similar designs printed by flat press intaglio or offset:

1. Rotary press stamps are always wider or taller than flat press or offset stamps. This measurement concerns the printed design only.

2. The back of a rotary press stamp is almost always free of color, while flat press stamps often have small bits of color on the back.

3. With the exception of stamps printed from coil waste, the perforated rotary press stamps will show one or more ridges extending across the back of the stamp. These ridges were forced into the paper in an effort to keep the stamps from curling. This is easily apparent on unused stamps, but much more difficult to detect on used stamps. Most flat press stamps do not have these ridges.

1919. GEORGE WASHINGTON ISSUE *Designs 19 1/2 to 20mm wide by 22mm high. Printed from coil waste sheets, no "breaker bar" ridges on back of stamps, unwatermarked, perforated 11x10.*

410 *George Washington*

410

		UnFVF	UseFVF
1¢	**green**	8.00	8.00
	bluish green	8.00	8.00
	yellowish green	8.00	8.00
	On cover		20.00
	Plate block of 4	75.00	
	Plate block of 4, w/star	90.00	
	Plate block of 4, w/"S 30"	100.00	
	Double transfer	15.00	
	v. Vertical pair, imperforate horizontally		50.00
	v1. Block of 4, imperforate horizontally	100.00	
	v2. Plate block of 6, imperforate horizontally	750.00	
	FDC (June 14, 1919)		

411 *George Washington*

411

		UnFVF	UseFVF
2¢	**carmine red** Type II	2,500.00	3,200.00
	Plate block of 4	10,500.00	
	Plate block of 4, w/"S 20"	17,500.00	

411A

		UnFVF	UseFVF
2¢	**carmine red** Type III	10.00	9.00
	On cover		22.50
	Plate block of 4	.75	
	Plate block of 4, w/star	125.00	
	Plate block of 4, w/"S 30"	75.00	
	Plate block of 4, w/inverted "S 30"	400.00	
	Double transfer	17.50	
	v. Horizontal pair, imperforate vertically	750.00	
	v1. Vertical pair, imperforate horizontally	50.00	50.00
	v2. Block of 4, imperforate horizontally	100.00	
	FDC (June 14, 1919)		

412 *George Washington*

412

		UnFVF	UseFVF
3¢	**gray lilac** Type II	32.50	35.00
	On cover		85.00
	Plate block of 4	250.00	
	FDC (June 14, 1919)		

1920. GEORGE WASHINGTON ISSUE *Rotary press, stamp designs 18 1/2 to 19mm wide by 22 1/2mm high, unwatermarked, perforated 10x11, breaker bar ridges on stamps.*

413

		UnFVF	UseFVF
1¢	**green**	10.00	1.00
	bluish green	10.00	1.00
	On cover		5.50
	Plate block of 6 (vertical), w/plate number opposite center horizontal row	135.00	
	FDC (May 26, 1920)		2,000.00

1921. GEORGE WASHINGTON ISSUE *Rotary press, stamp designs 18 1/2 to 19mm wide by 22 1/2mm high, unwatermarked, perforated 10, breaker bar ridges on stamps.*

414

		UnFVF	UseFVF
1¢	**green**	.55	.20
	dark green	.55	.20
	On cover		.35
	Plate block of 6 (vertical), number opposite center horizontal row	27.50	
	Plate block of 4	12.50	
	Double transfer	—	
	Triple transfer	—	
	v. Horizontal pair, imperforate between	975.00	
	FDC (May 26, 1921)		

1922. GEORGE WASHINGTON ISSUE chronologically, the last of the Washington-Franklin stamps, apparently produced to use up waste sheets. *Rotary press, stamp design 19mm wide by 22 1/2mm high, unwatermarked, perforated 11, breaker bar ridges on stamps.*

415

		UnFVF	UseFVF
1¢	**green**	15,000.00	3,200.00
	On cover		3,500.00
	Earliest documented cover: *Dec. 21, 1922*		

1921. GEORGE WASHINGTON ISSUE *Rotary press, stamp design 19 1/2 to 20mm wide by 22mm high, unwatermarked, perforated 11, no breaker bar ridges.*

416 *George Washington*

416

		UnFVF	UseFVF
1¢	**green**	120.00	130.00
	On cover		1,800.00
	Plate block of 4	900.00	
	Plate block of 4, w/star	950.00	
	Plate block of 4, w/"S 30"	850.00	
	Earliest documented cover: *June 25, 1921*		

417 *George Washington*

417

		UnFVF	UseFVF
2¢	**carmine** Type III	85.00	115.00
	On cover		700.00
	Plate block of 4	700.00	
	Plate block of 4, w/star	725.00	
	Plate block of 4, w/"S 30"	675.00	
	Recut in hair	120.00	
	v. Perforated 10 on left side	—	
	Earliest documented cover: *May 5, 1921*		

1922-34. Regular Issue Series Featured famous people and scenes within two similar frames. Some of the denominations were produced, in part, with what are known as "Star Plates." On these particular plates, the vertical rows are spaced 3mm apart instead of 2 3/4mm in an effort to improve the perforating. The plates are identified with a large 5-point or 6-point star placed with the plate number. *Flat plate printing, unwatermarked, perforated 11.*

1925. NATHAN HALE ISSUE in the Regular Issue Series of 1922-34 was the first fractional-value postage stamp issued by the United States. Honored Hale, a school teacher and a 21-year-old captain in the Continental Army, who in 1776 volunteered for spy duty behind the British lines on Long Island. Captured by the British on Sept. 21, he was hanged the next morning and his body left hanging for several days. His last words were: "I only regret that I have but one life to lose for my country."

418, 473 *Nathan Hale from a statue by Bela Lyon Pratt, Yale Campus.*

418

		UnFVF	UseFVF
1/2¢	**olive brown**	.30	.20
	dark olive brown	.25	.20
	dull olive brown	.25	.20
	Plate block of 6	4.50	
	Plate flaw on fraction bar	.75	.20
	FDC (April 4, 1925) (Washington, D.C.)		18.00
	FDC (New Haven)		25.00

1923. BENJAMIN FRANKLIN ISSUE in the Regular Issue Series of 1922-34.

419, 443, 446, 448, 449A, 450, 461, 469, 474, 495, 506, B71, B72, B77 *Benjamin Franklin*

419		UnFVF	UseFVF
1¢	**green**	1.50	.20
	dark green	1.50	.20
	dull green	1.50	.20
	Plate block of 6	17.50	
	Double transfer	3.50	
	n. Booklet pane of 6	7.00	
	Earliest documented cover: *Jan. 10, 1924*		
	FDC *(Jan. 17, 1923)* FDC *(Washington, D.C.)*		30.00
	FDC *(Philadelphia)*		47.50

1925. WARREN HARDING ISSUE in the Regular Issue Series of 1922-34. Honored the 29th president, who had died suddenly on a trip to San Francisco, Calif., two years earlier. Harding (1865-1923), an Ohio native, was a newspaper publisher and politician whose administration was rife with corruption.

420, 444, 451, 462, 470, 472, 475, 496, 507 *Warren Harding*

420		UnFVF	UseFVF
1 1/2¢	**yellow brown**	2.50	.25
	brown	2.50	.25
	dull yellow brown	2.50	.25
	Plate block of 6	25.00	
	Double transfer	—	
	FDC *(March 19, 1925)*		30.00

See also CM60-63, a 2¢ black Harding of the same design as 420. Some include it with the 1922-34 Regular Issue Series.

1923. GEORGE WASHINGTON TYPE I ISSUE in the Regular Issue Series of 1922-34.

421, 445, 447, 449, 452, 463, 471, 476, 476A, 497, 508, B73, B74, B75, B76, B77 *George Washington. Type I has thin hair lines at top center of head.*

421		UnFVF	UseFVF
2¢	**carmine** Type I	1.25	.20
	Plate block of 6	17.50	
	Plate block of 6, w/small 5-point star (top only)	450.00	
	Plate block of 6, w/large 5-point star (top only)	550.00	
	Plate block of 6, w/large 5-point star (side only)	60.00	
	Plate block of 6, w/large 6-point star (top only)	700.00	
	Plate block of 6, w/large 6-point star (side only)	850.00	
	Double transfer	2.50	.75
	n. Booklet pane of 6	8.50	1.00
	v. Horizontal pair, imperforate vertically	200.00	
	v1. Vertical pair, imperforate horizontally	500.00	
	v2. Perforated 10 at bottom	3,500.00	
	v3. Perforated 10 at top	3,500.00	
	FDC *(Jan. 15, 1923)*		42.50

1923. ABRAHAM LINCOLN ISSUE in the Regular Issue Series of 1922-34.

422, 453, 464, 477, 498, 509 *Abraham Lincoln*

422		UnFVF	UseFVF
3¢	**reddish violet**	18.00	.65
	bright violet	18.00	.65
	dark violet	18.00	.65
	violet	18.00	.65
	Plate block of 6	125.00	
	FDC *(Feb. 12, 1923) (Washington, D.C.)*		35.00
	FDC *(Hodgeville, Ky.)*		300.00

1923. MARTHA WASHINGTON ISSUE in the Regular Issue Series of 1922-34.

423, 454, 465, 478, 499, 510 *Martha Washington*

423		UnFVF	UseFVF
4¢	**yellow brown**	20.00	.20
	brown	20.00	.20
	Plate block of 6	130.00	
	Double transfer	—	
	v. Perforated 10 at bottom	420.00	
	v1. Perforated 10 at top	420.00	
	v2. Horizontal pair, imperforate between	—	
	v3. Vertical pair, imperforate horizontally	—	
	FDC *(Jan. 15, 1923)*		70.00

1922. THEODORE ROOSEVELT ISSUE in the Regular Issue Series of 1922-34. Honored the 26th president, who took office at the age of 43, upon the assassination of William McKinley. A New York native, Roosevelt (1858-1919), known for his love of nature and conservation, championed the strenuous life in his personal habits and through the force of his personality greatly broadened the use of executive power.

424, 455, 466, 479, 500, 511 *Theodore Roosevelt*

424		UnFVF	UseFVF
5¢	**Prussian blue**	20.00	.20
	Plate block of 6	145.00	
	Double transfer	—	
	v. Horizontal pair, imperforate vertically	1,500.00	
	v1. Pair, imperforate	1,600.00	
	v2. Perforated 10 at bottom	—	450.00
	v3. Perforated 10 at top	—	450.00
	FDC *(Oct. 27, 1922) (Washington, D.C.)*		150.00
	FDC *(N.Y.)*		200.00
	FDC *(Oyster Bay)*		1,350.00

1922. JAMES GARFIELD ISSUE in the Regular Issue Series of 1922-34.

425, 456, 467, 480, 501, 512 *James Garfield*

DECODING THE CATALOG

Despite some confusion about the 2¢ value of the 1922 series, it really is not too difficult a stamp to figure out. There are 10 major stamps (and several overprints), but each has its own notable characterisitics.

The 2¢ 1922 issue.

There is only one design type for the flat-plate issues and two types for the rotary press. Beyond that, differentiating the stamps is just a matter of knowing the characteristics of each and their printing types.

During the time the 2¢ value was being produced, the Bureau of Engraving and Printing was switching production from flat-plate presses to rotary presses. Rotary presses, no longer in the experimental stage by then, were far more efficient for rapid stamp production. Flat-plate presses use flat printing plates that leave their inked impressions on single sheets of paper. A rotary press, on the other hand, utitlizes a printing cylinder that prints on a continuous roll of paper.

To create these cylinders, it was necessary to bend two flat printing plates and join them to form a full cylinder. By bending these printing plates, the stamp image became slightly distorted in length or width, depending upon which direction the plate was bent, and the resulting stamp designs were either slightly taller or wider than their flat-plate counterparts.

FLAT-PLATE ISSUES

The 2¢ value was first released on Jan. 15, 1923, as a flat-plate issue with perforations that measure 11 on a standard gauge. This stamp is cataloged as Minkus 421.

One additional flat-plate version of this stamp was released, an imperforate variety, Minkus 445. The basic design dimensions of these stamps are 19 1/4 millimeters by 22 1/4 mm.

Most flat-plate stamps are easy to identify because of light "setoff" on the reverse side; flecks of ink where wet sheets of freshly printed stamps were stacked atop one another, leaving a minor impression.

The icanthus scroll area on both sides of the stamp is another simple distinguishable difference between Type I (left) and II (right). Note the heavy line at the top of the scroll and the nicely engraved details in the leaf of Type II.

ROTARY PRESS TYPE I ISSUES

The rotary press stamps give collectors the most trouble. There are six basic types of this stamp but only two different design-size measurements. The remaining differences are determined by format and

perforation measurements. This group also contains the scarcest varieties of this stamp.

The design on stamps printed from plates that were curved vertically measures 19 1/4 mm by 22 1/2 mm. This is slightly taller than other 2¢ issues. They are:

• Minkus 452, a sheet stamp with perforations that measure 10 on all four sides.

• Minkus 471, a vertical (or endwise) coil, with perforations that measure 10 at top and bottom. There are straight edges on left and right sides.

• Minkus 476, the most common 2¢ issue. It is a sheet stamp with perforations that measure 11 by 10 1/2.

The design on rotary press-printed stamps printed from plates that were curved horizontally, measures 19 3/4 mm by 22 1/4 mm. This is slightly wider than the other 2¢ issues. They are:

• Minkus 463, the intended stamp from this format. It is a horizontal (or sidewise) coil with perforations that measure 10 on both sides.

• Minkus 447 and Minkus 449, sheet stamps created from coil waste. They are the scarcest of the 2∫¢ issues and sell for about $100 and $300, respectively, mint or used. In fact, both are worth more used with a demonstrable contemporaneous cancel. Minkus 447 has perfo-

Type I (left) is not as clearly engraved as Type II (right). Type II features greatly strengthened hair lines, eye shadowing and numerous other design differences.

rations that measure 11 at top and bottom and 10 on the left and right sides. Minkus 449 has perforations that measure 11 on all four sides.

ROTARY PRESS TYPE II ISSUES

The Type II rotary press stamp was created from a new die. Distinguishing the popular and somewhat scarce Type II stamps is very easy, even on a heavily canceled used stamp, because there are several die differences.

Without going into great detail, Die II was created from a transfer of a Die I image. Once the new die was created, there was some touching up done, presumably to strengthen the image. These touch-ups are what create the differences between Types I and II.

The quickest and best way to determine a Type II stamp is by the heavily reinforced lines in the hair. But there are more than 10 other differences to be found. A few are illustrated here.

The Type II stamps are Minkus 463v, a horizontal coil sometimes found in pairs with Minkus 463, a Type I stamp; and 476A, a sheet stamp perforated 11 by 10 1/2.

The corner circles are slightly finer and more distinct on Type II examples (right) than on Type 1 (left).

DECODING THE CATALOG

Although it may lack something of the intimidating complexity of the Washington-Franklin series that preceded it, the United States definitive series of 1922-32 nonetheless includes a number of significant catalog-listed varieties of considerable interest to U.S. stamp specialists. The 7¢ McKinley definitive from that series, printed in black as if in belated mourning for the assassinated president, was first issued as a flat-plate-printed stamp on unwatermarked paper on May 1, 1923 (Minkus 426). This first version of the stamp was perforated 11. This perf 11 7¢ stamp is known printed in gray black as well as black, although neither version commands a premium.

A rotary-press-printed version of the 7¢ McKinley, in which the design measures 19 1/4 millimeters by 22 1/2 mm, was issued three years later, on May 29, 1926 (Minkus 457). It is perforated 10.

A third version of the stamp, also printed on the rotary press, was released on July 27, 1927 (Minkus 481). Stamps from this printing, perforated 11 by 10 1/2, are the most common of the three basic versions of the stamp.

Although the design dimensions are identical to those of the earlier rotary press stamp, mint copies of the 1927 stamps have breaker bar ridges in the gum on the back of the stamp, added during production to minimize gum curl.

There are no such breaker bars on the gum of the 1926 rotary press 7¢ McKinleys.

The same is true of the final two collectible versions of this stamp, the Kansas-Nebraska overprints. In 1929, these overprints were added to the 1¢ through 10¢ definitives in an experiment to limit the ability of thieves to sell stamps stolen from post offices by identifying the states in which they were located. (The theory was that the criminals would peddle such large quantities of stamps far from where they had been stolen, but would find no buyers for their purloined postage if it was all overprinted to show its source as a distant state.) Both these overprints were added exclusively to the perf 11 by 10 1/2 McKinleys. Any "Kans." and "Nebr." overprints found on perf 10 or perf 11 7¢ McKinleys are forgeries.

425

6¢		UnFVF	UseFVF
	red orange	35.00	.55
	dull red orange	35.00	.55
	Plate block of 6	300.00	
	Double transfer	50.00	1.75
	Double transfer, recut	50.00	1.75
	FDC *(Nov. 20, 1922)*		250.00

1923. WILLIAM MCKINLEY ISSUE in the Regular Issue Series of 1922-34.

426, 457, 481, 502, 513 *William McKinley*

426

7¢		UnFVF	UseFVF
	black	9.00	.35
	gray black	9.00	.35
	Plate block of 6	55.00	
	Double transfer	—	
	FDC *(May 21, 1923)* *(Washington, D.C.)*		175.00
	FDC *(Niles, Ohio)*		250.00

1923. ULYSSES S. GRANT ISSUE in the Regular Issue Series of 1922-34.

427, 458, 482, 503, 514 *Ulysses S. Grant*

427

8¢		UnFVF	UseFVF
	yellow olive	50.00	.85
	dull yellow olive	50.00	.85
	Plate block of 6	550.00	
	Double transfer	—	
	FDC *(May 1, 1923)*		210.00

1923. THOMAS JEFFERSON ISSUE in the Regular Issue Series of 1922-34.

428, 459, 483, 504, 515 *Thomas Jefferson*

428

9¢		UnFVF	UseFVF
	carmine rose	15.00	.75
	dull carmine rose	15.00	.75
	Plate block of 6	150.00	
	Double transfer	—	
	FDC *(Jan. 15, 1923)*		210.00

1923. JAMES MONROE ISSUE in the Regular Issue Series of 1922-34.

429, 460, 468, 484, 505, 516 *James Monroe*

429

10¢		UnFVF	UseFVF
	orange yellow	19.00	.25
	dull orange yellow	19.00	.25
	Plate block of 6	150.00	
	v. Pair, imperforate	1,350.00	
	v1. Vertical pair, imperforate horizontally	750.00	
	v2. Perforated 10 at bottom	—	750.00
	v3. Perforated 10 at top	—	750.00
	FDC *(Jan. 15, 1923)*		190.00

1922. RUTHERFORD B. HAYES ISSUE in the Regular Issue Series of 1922-34. Honored the 19th president, who gained office by one electoral vote. Hayes (1822-1893), born in Ohio and wounded in the Civil War, brought honesty and moderate reform to the office after a contentious campaign in 1876, in which he actually lost the popular vote.

430, 485 *Rutherford B. Hayes*

430

		UnFVF	UseFVF
11¢	**turquoise blue**	2.50	.30
	dull bluish green	2.50	.30
	dull yellowish green	2.50	.30
	greenish blue	2.50	.30
	Plate block of 6	24.00	
	v. Pair, imperforate	—	
	FDC *(Oct. 4, 1922) (Washington, D.C.)*		650.00
	FDC *(Freemont, Ohio)*		2,000.00

No. 430 is known in a wide range of color shades between yellow green and light blue.

1923. GROVER CLEVELAND ISSUE in the Regular Issue Series of 1922-34. Honored the 22nd and 24th president, the only president to be married in the White House and the first to have a child born in the White House — popularly known as "Baby Ruth" — and the only president who served two non-consecutive terms. Cleveland (1837-1885) was born and died in New Jersey but achieved political prominence in New York.

431, 486 *Grover Cleveland*

431

		UnFVF	UseFVF
12¢	**maroon**	6.25	.20
	deep maroon	6.25	.20
	Plate block of 6	80.00	
	Plate block of 6, w/large 5-point star (side only)	125.00	
	Plate block of 6, w/large 6-point star (side only)	250.00	
	Double transfer	12.50	1.00
	v. Horizontal pair, imperforate vertically	1,000.00	
	v1. Pair, imperforate	—	
	FDC *(March 20, 1923) (Washington, D.C.)*		210.00
	FDC *(Boston, Mass.)*		210.00
	FDC *(Caldwell, N.J.)*		240.00

1926. BENJAMIN HARRISON ISSUE in the Regular Issue Series of 1922-34.

432, 487 *Benjamin Harrison*

432

		UnFVF	UseFVF
13¢	**green**	10.00	.30
	dull green	10.00	.30
	Plate block of 6	130.00	
	Plate block of 6, w/large 5-point star	1,950.00	
	FDC *(Jan. 11, 1926) (Washington, D.C.)*		25.00
	FDC *(Indianapolis, Ind.)*		35.00
	FDC *(North Bend, Ind.)*		175.00

1923. AMERICAN INDIAN ISSUE in the Regular Issue Series of 1922-34.

433, 488 *American Indian from a photograph of Chief Hollow Horn Bear of the Brule Sioux tribe, taken on his visit to Washington, D.C., for the inauguration of Theodore Roosevelt.*

433

		UnFVF	UseFVF
14¢	**blue**	4.75	.50
	Plate block of 6	130.00	
	Double transfer	—	
	FDC *(May 1, 1923) (Washington, D.C.)*		450.00
	FDC *(Muskogee, Okla.)*		1,800.00

1922. STATUE OF LIBERTY ISSUE in the Regular Issue Series of 1922-34.

434, 489 *Statue of Liberty*

434

		UnFVF	UseFVF
15¢	**gray black**	25.00	.20
	light gray black	22.50	.20
	Plate block of 6	225.00	
	Plate block of 6, w/large 5-point star (side only)	450.00	
	FDC *(Nov. 11, 1922)*		600.00

1925. WOODROW WILSON ISSUE in the Regular Issue Series of 1922-34. Honored the 28th president, who was a child in Georgia during the Civil War, fought in World War I to make the world "Safe for Democracy" and failed to convince Congress of the virtue of a League of Nations. Wilson (1856-1924) was president of Princeton University before launching his political career.

435, 490 *Woodrow Wilson*

435

		UnFVF	UseFVF
17¢	**black**	12.00	.20
	gray black	12.00	.20
	Plate block of 6	170.00	
	FDC *(Dec. 28, 1925) (w/o cachet)*		30.00
	FDC *(w/cachet)*		275.00

1923. GOLDEN GATE ISSUE in the Regular Issue Series of 1922-34 featured the same view as that on the 5¢ value in the Panama-Pacific Exposition commemorative (CM49, CM54) but with different craft on the water.

436, 491 *Golden Gate*

436

		UnFVF	UseFVF
20¢	**carmine red**	22.50	.20
	dark carmine red	22.50	.20
	Plate block of 6	220.00	
	Plate block of 6, w/large 5-point star (side only)	425.00	
	v. Horizontal pair, imperforate vertically	2,250.00	
	FDC *(May 1, 1923) (Washington, D.C.)*		550.00
	FDC *(San Francisco, Calif.)*		3,500.00
	FDC *(Oakland, Calif.)*		7,250.00

1922. NIAGARA FALLS ISSUE in the Regular Issue Series of 1922-34 featured a view of the American Falls at the popular honeymoon site, over which 20% of the world's freshwater supply is reputed to flow.

437, 492 *Niagara Falls*

437

		UnFVF	UseFVF
25¢	**green**	19.00	.50
	yellow green	19.00	.50
	Plate block of 6	175.00	
	Double transfer	—	

v. Perforated 10 at bottom	—	
v1. Perforated 10 at top	—	
v2. Vertical pair, imperforate horizontally	1,000.00	
FDC *(Nov. 11, 1922)*		700.00

1923. Bison Issue was the only one in the Regular Issue Series of 1922-34 without a descriptive ribbon under the vignette.

438, 493 *Bison*

438		UnFVF	UseFVF
30¢	olive brown	35.00	.50
	Plate block of 6	220.00	
	Double transfer	50.00	2.00
	FDC *(March 20, 1923)*		900.00

1922. Arlington Issue in the Regular Issue Series of 1922-34 featured the amphitheatre at Arlington (Va.) National Cemetery where the unknown soldier of World War I was buried in 1921, in the cenotaph in the foreground.

439, 494 *Arlington*

439		UnFVF	UseFVF
50¢	gray lilac	57.00	.20
	dull gray lilac	57.00	.20
	Plate block of 6	625.00	
	FDC *(Nov. 11, 1922)*		1,500.00

1923. Lincoln Memorial Issue in the Regular Issue Series of 1922-34 featured the newly constructed memorial to the slain Civil War president in Washington, D.C.

440 *Lincoln Memorial*

440		UnFVF	UseFVF
$1	purple brown	47.00	.50
	purple black	47.00	.50
	Plate block of 6	350.00	
	Double transfer	85.00	1.00
	Margin block of 4, w/arrow	175.00	
	FDC *(Feb. 12, 1923) (Washington, D.C.)*		6,000.00
	FDC *(Springfield, Ill.)*		6,500.00

1923. U.S. Capitol Issue in the Regular Issue Series of 1922-34 featured the home of the House of Representatives (foreground) and the Senate in Washington, D.C.

441 *U.S. Capitol*

441		UnFVF	UseFVF
$2	blue	100.00	6.00
	Plate block of 6	800.00	
	Margin block of 4, w/arrow	400.00	
	FDC *(March 20, 1923)*		17,500.00

1923. Head of Freedom Issue The only bicolor in the Regular Issue Series of 1922-34 featured the head of the statue atop the U.S. Capitol building in Washington, D.C.

442 *Head of* Armed Freedom

442		UnFVF	UseFVF
$5	carmine & blue	200.00	13.50
	lilac carmine & dark blue	200.00	13.50
	Plate block of 8, w/arrow & two plate numbers	2,150.00	
	Center line block	850.00	
	Margin block of 4, w/arrow	825.00	
	FDC *(March 20, 1923)*		32,500.00

1923. Issue in the Regular Issue Series of 1922-34. *Imperforate.*

443		UnFVF	UseFVF
1¢	green	7.50	3.00
	dark green		3.00
	dull green	7.50	3.00
	Plate block of 6	70.00	
	Center line block	40.00	
	Margin block of 4, w/arrow	35.00	
	FDC *(March 16, 1923)*		

444		UnFVF	UseFVF
1 1/2¢	yellow brown	1.50	1.00
	brown	1.50	1.00
	Plate block of 6	17.50	
	Center line block	10.50	
	Margin block of 4, w/arrow	7.00	
	Double transfer	—	
	FDC *(April 4, 1925)*		50.00

No. 444 exists in a rotary press printing, No. 472.

445		UnFVF	UseFVF
2¢	carmine	1.50	1.00
	dark carmine	1.50	1.00
	dull carmine	1.50	1.00
	Plate block of 6	25.00	
	Plate block of 6, w/large 5-point star	70.00	
	Center line block	12.50	
	Margin block of 4, w/arrow	7.50	
	FDC *(March 20, 1923)*		

1923-24. Rotary Press Printings in the Regular Issue Series of 1922-34. *From coil waste, no breaker bar ridges on back of stamps, designs 19 1/2 to 20mm wide by 22mm high, unwatermarked, perforated 11x10.*

446		UnFVF	UseFVF
1¢	green	90.00	90.00
	Plate block of 4, w/star	700.00	
	Earliest documented cover: *March 26, 1924*		

447		UnFVF	UseFVF
2¢	carmine	75.00	85.00
	dark carmine	75.00	85.00
	Plate block of 4, w/star	375.00	
	Recut in eye	90.00	125.00
	Earliest documented cover: *Feb. 20, 1923*		

1923-24. Rotary Press Printing Issue in the Regular Issue Series of 1922-34. *Perforated 11.*

448		UnFVF	UseFVF
1¢	green	18,000.00	6,000.00
	dark green	18,000.00	6,000.00
	dull green	18,000.00	6,000.00
	Earliest documented cover: *March 25, 1924*		

449		UnFVF	UseFVF
2¢	carmine	300.00	320.00
	Plate block of 4, w/star	2,000.00	
	Recut in eye	—	
	Earliest documented cover: *June 29, 1923*		

Nos. 448 and 449 were made from coil waste. Design 18 1/2 to 19mm wide by 22 1/2mm high.

449A		UnFVF	UseFVF
1¢	green	—	120,000.00
	x. Bureau precancel Kansas City, Mo.		100,000.00

Note: Only 13 copies known, most with Bureau precancel.

Identifier of the 1922-34 Regular Issues

Frame	Perf. 11	Perf. 11 x 10	Perf. 10	Coil 10	Perf. 11 x 10 1/2 or 10 1/2 x 11	Imperf.
	418-434, 448-449	446-447	450-460	461-471, 520, 522	473-489 495-517, 519	443-445 472
	435-442				490-494	

1923-26. ROTARY PRESS PRINTING ISSUE in the Regular Issue
Series of 1922-34. *Breaker bar ridges on backs of stamps, designs 18 1/2 to 19mm wide by 22 1/2mm high, unwatermarked, perforated 10.*

450

		UnFVF	UseFVF
1¢	**green**	7.50	1.00
	light green	7.50	1.00
	yellow green	7.50	1.00
	Plate block of 4	75.00	
	x. Bureau precancel (MNH / 64 diff.)	2.00	
	Plate block of 4	—	
	FDC *(Oct. 17, 1923)*		700.00

451

		UnFVF	UseFVF
1 1/2¢	**yellow brown**	3.75	1.00
	dark brown	3.75	1.00
	Plate block of 4	30.00	
	Pair, horizontal or vertical gutter between	150.00	
	x. Bureau precancel (MNH / 76 diff.)	2.25	
	Plate block of 4	—	
	FDC *(March 19, 1925)*		45.00

452

		UnFVF	UseFVF
2¢	**carmine** (B78, B79, B80)	2.00	.35
	Plate block of 4	17.50	
	n. Booklet pane of 6 *(Aug. 27, 1926)*	75.00	
	x. Bureau precancel (MNH / 58 diff.)	2.50	
	Plate block of 4	—	
	FDC *(April 1924)*		1,400.00

453

		UnFVF	UseFVF
3¢	**reddish violet**	20.00	2.50
	Plate block of 4	170.00	
	x. Bureau precancel (MNH / 41 diff.)	4.00	
	Plate block of 4	—	
	FDC *(Aug. 1, 1925)*		60.00

454

		UnFVF	UseFVF
4¢	**yellow brown**	14.00	.80
	dark yellow brown	14.00	.80
	Plate block of 4	125.00	
	x. Bureau precancel (MNH / 36 diff.)	3.00	
	Plate block of 4	—	
	FDC *(April 4, 1925)*		60.00

455

		UnFVF	UseFVF
5¢	**blue**	14.00	.80
	deep blue	14.00	.80
	Plate block of 4	120.00	
	Double transfer	—	
	v. Horizontal pair, imperforate vertically	—	
	x. Bureau precancel (MNH / 38 diff.)	3.00	
	Plate block of 4	—	
	FDC *(April 4, 1925)*		65.00

456

		UnFVF	UseFVF
6¢	**orange**	6.25	.75
	dull orange	6.25	.75

	Plate block of 4	60.00	
	x. Bureau precancel (MNH / 36 diff.)	3.00	
	Plate block of 4	—	
	FDC *(April 4, 1925)*		65.00

457

		UnFVF	UseFVF
7¢	**black**	9.00	6.50
	Plate block of 4	65.00	
	x. Bureau precancel (MNH / 18 diff.)	—	
	Plate block of 4	—	
	FDC *(May 29, 1926)*		70.00

458

		UnFVF	UseFVF
8¢	**yellow olive**	20.00	4.00
	pale yellow olive	20.00	4.00
	Plate block of 4	150.00	
	x. Bureau precancel (MNH / 18 diff.)	—	
	Plate block of 4	—	
	FDC *(May 29, 1926)*		80.00

459

		UnFVF	UseFVF
9¢	**red**	4.25	2.50
	Plate block of 4	32.50	
	x. Bureau precancel (MNH / 13 diff.)	—	
	Plate block of 4	—	
	FDC *(May 29, 1926)*		80.00

460

		UnFVF	UseFVF
10¢	**orange yellow**	50.00	.45
	Plate block of 4	325.00	
	x. Bureau precancel (MNH / 39 diff.)	—	
	Plate block of 4	—	
	FDC *(June 8, 1925)*		100.00

1923-26. ROTARY PRESS COIL ISSUE in the Regular Issue Series of 1922-34. *Designs 19 1/2 to 20mm wide by 22 1/4mm high, perforated 10 vertically.*

461

		UnFVF	UseFVF
1¢	**yellow green**	.35	.20
	green	.35	.20
	Pair	.75	.20
	Line pair	2.00	.25
	Double transfer	2.50	.75
	Gripper cracks	2.50	.75
	x. Bureau precancel (MNH / 92 diff.)	.25	
	Line pair	1.25	
	FDC *(July 18, 1923)*		550.00

462

		UnFVF	UseFVF
1 1/2¢	**yellow brown**	.75	.20
	dark brown	.75	.20
	Pair	2.00	.25
	Line pair	6.00	.50
	x. Bureau precancel (MNH / 107 diff.)	.50	
	Line pair	3.00	
	FDC *(March 19, 1925)*		55.00

463 *George Washington: Type I (left) and Type II*

463 *Type II. There are three heavy hair lines at the top center of the head.*

463		UnFVF	UseFVF
2¢	carmine Type I	.45	.20
	dark carmine	.45	.20
	Pair	.75	.20
	Line pair	2.00	.25
	Line pair, 1 each Type I & Type II	625.00	
	Double transfer	1.75	.50
	Gripper cracks	2.00	1.75
	x. Bureau precancel (MNH / 55 diff.)	.35	
	Line pair	2.50	
	FDC (Jan. 10, 1923)		2,000.00

463A		UnFVF	UseFVF
2¢	carmine Type II	115.00	12.50
	dark carmine	115.00	12.50
	Pair	—	
	Line pair	525.00	
	x. Bureau precancel (2 diff.)	—	
	Line pair	—	

Note: Known to exist in MNH condition.

464		UnFVF	UseFVF
3¢	reddish violet	5.50	.30
	dark violet	5.50	.30
	Pair	12.50	.50
	Line pair	30.00	1.00
	Cracked plate	—	
	x. Bureau precancel (MNH / 42 diff.)	2.00	
	Line pair	—	
	FDC (May 10, 1924)		125.00

465		UnFVF	UseFVF
4¢	yellow brown	3.75	.50
	brown	3.75	.50
	Pair	9.00	1.00
	Line pair	35.00	2.75
	x. Bureau precancel (MNH / 23 diff.)	2.00	
	Line pair	—	

466		UnFVF	UseFVF
5¢	blue	1.75	.20
	Pair	3.50	.40
	Line pair	12.50	.60
	x. Bureau precancel (MNH / 28 diff.)	2.50	
	Line pair	—	
	FDC (March 5, 1924)		100.00

467		UnFVF	UseFVF
6¢	orange	9.50	.35
	Pair	22.50	.50
	Line pair	50.00	2.50
	x. Bureau precancel (MNH / 5 diff.)	—	
	Line pair	—	
	FDC (Aug. 18, 1932)		

468		UnFVF	UseFVF
10¢	orange yellow	3.50	.20
	Pair	7.50	.25
	Line pair	22.50	1.00
	x. Bureau precancel (MNH / 25 diff.)	3.50	
	Line pair	—	
	FDC (Dec. 1, 1924)		110.00

1924. ROTARY PRESS COIL ISSUE in the Regular Issue Series of 1922-34. *Designs 18 1/2 to 19mm wide by 22 1/2mm high, perforated 10 horizontally.*

469		UnFVF	UseFVF
1¢	yellow green	.35	.20
	green	.35	.20
	Pair	.75	.25
	Line pair	3.00	.50
	FDC (July 19, 1924)		90.00

470		UnFVF	UseFVF
1 1/2¢	yellow brown	.35	.20
	brown	.35	.20
	Pair	.75	.25
	Line pair	3.00	.50
	FDC (May 9, 1925)		75.00

471		UnFVF	UseFVF
2¢	carmine	.35	.20
	Pair	.75	.25
	Line pair	2.00	
	Cracked plate	5.00	2.00
	FDC (Dec. 31, 1923)		125.00

1926. ROTARY PRESS ISSUE in the Regular Issue Series of 1922-34. *Imperforate, design 18 1/2 to 19mm wide by 22 1/2mm high. Most of these stamps show the breaker bars on the back, but there was a printing of this stamp that did not have them. The stamp was issued in sheets of 400, with both vertical and horizontal gutters.*

472		UnFVF	UseFVF
1 1/2¢	yellow brown	2.25	2.00
	brown	2.25	2.00
	Plate block of 4	55.00	
	Center block w/crossed gutters & dashes	20.00	22.50
	Block of 4, gutter between	8.50	9.50
	Margin block, w/dash	9.50	13.50
	Without gum breaker ridges	80.00	
	Pair, horizontal or vertical gutter between	200.00	
	FDC (Aug. 27, 1926)		50.00

1926-34. ROTARY PRESS ISSUE in the Regular Issue Series of 1922-34. *Designs 18 1/2 to 19mm wide by 22 1/2mm high, breaker bar ridges on back of stamps, unwatermarked, perforated 11x10 1/2.*

473		UnFVF	UseFVF
1/2¢	olive brown	.25	.20
	Plate block of 4	1.50	
	Damaged plate	1.35	
	Pair, gutter between	125.00	
	Retouched plate	1.35	
	x. Bureau precancel (MNH / 99 diff.)	.50	
	Plate block of 4	3.00	
	FDC (May 25, 1929)		30.00

474		UnFVF	UseFVF
1¢	green (B81, B82, B83, B89, B90, B91)	.25	.20
	yellow green	.25	.20
	Plate block of 4	2.00	
	FDC (June 10, 1927)		3,500.00
	Cracked plate	—	
	Pair, gutter between	135.00	
	x. Bureau precancel (MNH / 237 diff.)	.35	
	Plate block of 4	1.25	
	n. Booklet pane of 6 (Nov. 2, 1927)	5.50	
	FDC (Nov. 2, 1927) Booklet pane		3,500.00
	v. Horizontal pair, imperforate between	—	
	v1. Vertical pair, imperforate between	2,650.00	—
	Earliest documented cover: May 24, 1927		

475		UnFVF	UseFVF
1 1/2¢	yellow brown	2.00	.20
	dark brown	2.00	.20
	Plate block of 4	70.00	
	x. Bureau precancel (MNH / 74 diff.)	1.00	
	Plate block of 4	—	
	FDC (May 17, 1927)		45.00

476		UnFVF	UseFVF
2¢	carmine red Type I	.25	.20
	lilac carmine	.25	.20
	Plate (corner) block of 4	2.00	
	Plate block (vertical) of 10, w/number opposite 3rd horizontal row, (experimental electric eye plates)	4.50	
	Margin block of 4, w/electric eye marking	.35	.25
	Pair, gutter between	180.00	
	x. Bureau precancel (65 diff.)	.50	

Plate block of 4		2.50	
n. Booklet pane of 6		2.00	
FDC *(Dec. 10, 1926)*			45.00
p. Thin (experimental) paper		—	
v. Horizontal pair, imperforate between		2,250.00	
v1. Vertical pair, imperforate between		—	
FDC *(March 28, 1935)* w/electric eye marking			1,300.00

476A		UnFVF	UseFVF
2¢	**carmine red** Type II	300.00	15.00
	Plate block of 4	1,800.00	
	x. Bureau precancel (MNH / 4 diff.)	—	
	Plate block of 4	—	
	Pair, horizontal or vertical gutter between	1,000.00	
	Earliest documented cover: *Dec. 19, 1928*		

Note: Not known to exist in MNH condition.

477		UnFVF	UseFVF
3¢	**reddish violet**	.55	.20
	Plate block of 4	8.00	
	x. Bureau precancel (MNH / 57 diff.)	1.25	
	Plate block of 4	—	
	v. red violet (re-issue) *(Feb. 7, 1934)*	.25	.20
	Plate block of 4	4.75	
	Gripper cracks	3.00	
	FDC *(Feb. 3, 1927)*		47.50

478		UnFVF	UseFVF
4¢	**yellow brown**	2.75	.20
	dark brown	2.75	.20
	Plate block of 4	70.00	
	x. Bureau precancel (MNH / 34 diff.)	1.35	
	Plate block of 4	—	
	Pair, gutter between	200.00	
	FDC *(May 17, 1927)*		55.00

479		UnFVF	UseFVF
5¢	**blue**	2.25	.20
	Plate block of 4	15.00	
	x. Bureau precancel (MNH / 56 diff.)	1.35	
	Plate block of 4	—	
	Pair, gutter between	275.00	
	Double transfer	—	
	FDC *(March 24, 1927)*		55.00

480		UnFVF	UseFVF
6¢	**orange**	2.25	.20
	dull orange	2.25	.20
	Plate block of 4	15.00	
	x. Bureau precancel (MNH / 48 diff.)	1.75	
	Plate block of 4	—	
	Pair, horizontal or vertical gutter between	200.00	
	FDC *(July 27, 1927)*		65.00

481		UnFVF	UseFVF
7¢	**black**	2.25	.20
	Plate block of 4	15.00	
	x. Bureau precancel (MNH / 45 diff.)	1.75	
	Plate block of 4	—	
	v. Vertical pair, imperforate between	125.00	75.00
	v1. Block of 4, imperforate between	250.00	
	FDC *(March 24, 1927)*		60.00

482		UnFVF	UseFVF
8¢	**yellow olive**	2.25	.20
	pale yellow olive	2.25	.20
	Plate block of 4	15.00	
	x. Bureau precancel (MNH / 54 diff.)	1.75	
	Plate block of 4	—	
	FDC *(June 10, 1927)*		65.00

483		UnFVF	UseFVF
9¢	**red**	2.00	.20
	orange red	2.00	.20
	salmon	2.00	.20
	Plate block of 4	15.00	
	x. Bureau precancel (MNH / 43 diff.)	1.50	
	Plate block of 4	—	
	Pair, gutter between	—	
	v. rose *(May 17, 1927)*	2.00	.20
	FDC *(1931)*		65.00

484		UnFVF	UseFVF
10¢	**orange yellow**	4.00	.20
	Plate block of 4	25.00	
	x. Bureau precancel (MNH / 57 diff.)	2.50	
	Plate block of 4	—	
	Double transfer	—	
	FDC *(Feb. 3, 1927)*		90.00

485		UnFVF	UseFVF
11¢	**turquoise green**	2.75	.20
	Plate block of 4	12.50	
	x. Bureau precancel (MNH / 33 diff.)	10.00	
	Plate block of 4	—	
	Retouch on forehead	6.50	.75
	FDC *(Sept. 4, 1931)*		125.00

486		UnFVF	UseFVF
12¢	**brown purple**	6.00	.20
	purple brown	6.00	.20
	Plate block of 4	27.50	
	x. Bureau precancel (MNH / 33 diff.)	4.00	
	Plate block of 4	—	
	FDC *(Aug. 25, 1931)*		125.00

487		UnFVF	UseFVF
13¢	**yellow green**	2.25	.20
	blue green	2.25	.20
	pale yellow green	2.25	.20
	Plate block of 4	14.00	
	x. Bureau precancel (MNH / 28 diff.)	5.00	
	Plate block of 4	—	
	Pair, gutter between	1.50	
	FDC *(Sept. 4, 1931)*		125.00

488		UnFVF	UseFVF
14¢	**blue**	4.00	.50
	Plate block of 4	20.00	
	x. Bureau precancel (MNH / 27 diff.)	4.00	
	Plate block of 4	—	
	FDC *(Sept. 8, 1931)*		125.00

489		UnFVF	UseFVF
15¢	**gray black**	8.00	.20
	gray	8.00	.20
	Plate block of 4	35.00	
	x. Bureau precancel (MNH / 33 diff.)	6.00	
	Plate block of 4	—	
	FDC *(Aug. 27, 1931)*		140.00

1931. ROTARY PRESS ISSUE in the Regular Issue Series of 1922-34. *The designs of the following stamps are horizontal rather than vertical, so perforation measurements are 10 1/2x11.*

490		UnFVF	UseFVF
17¢	**black**	5.50	.20
	Plate block of 4	25.00	
	x. Bureau precancel (MNH / 29 diff.)	7.50	
	Plate block of 4	—	
	FDC *(Brooklyn, N.Y.)*		3,000.00
	FDC *(July 25, 1931)* *(Washington, D.C.)*		450.00

491		UnFVF	UseFVF
20¢	**carmine rose**	9.50	.20
	Plate block of 4	50.00	
	x. Bureau precancel (MNH / 37 diff.)	9.00	
	Plate block of 4	—	
	Double transfer	20.00	
	FDC *(Sept. 8, 1931)*		325.00

492		UnFVF	UseFVF
25¢	**green**	11.00	.20
	Plate block of 4	50.00	
	x. Bureau precancel (MNH / 29 diff.)	10.00	
	Plate block of 4	—	
	FDC *(Brooklyn, N.Y.)*		2,500.00
	FDC *(July 25, 1931)* *(Washington, D.C.)*		450.00

493		UnFVF	UseFVF
30¢	**olive brown**	17.50	.20
	Plate block of 4	85.00	
	x. Bureau precancel (MNH / 31 diff.)	10.00	
	Plate block of 4	—	
	Cracked plate	27.50	.75
	Retouch in head	27.50	.75
	FDC *(Sept. 8, 1931)*		325.00

494		UnFVF	UseFVF
50¢	**lilac**	42.50	.20
	red lilac	42.50	.20
	Plate block of 4	200.00	
	x. Bureau precancel (MNH / 28 diff.)	20.00	
	Plate block of 4	—	
	FDC *(Sept. 4, 1931)*		450.00

1929. KANSAS AND NEBRASKA OVERPRINTS ISSUE in the Regular Issue Series of 1922-34 were issued to help prevent loss by post office burglaries. It was thought that stolen stamps in those two states could be traced more easily if they were overprinted. Approximately one year's supply was printed and delivered to the post offices in Kansas and Nebraska for use starting May 1, 1929, but no further printings were made. The overprinting was done on the regular 1¢ to 10¢ stamps of the 1922-34 designs. *Rotary press printing, unwatermarked, perforated 11x10 1/2.* All denominations were issued.

"Wide spacing pairs" noted below designate vertical pairs on which the overprints are 32mm apart rather than 22mm.

495, 499, 502, 503, 504 *Kansas overprint*

Kans.

495		UnFVF	UseFVF
1¢	**green**	2.00	1.50
	Plate block of 4	30.00	
	Wide spacing pair	30.00	
	v. Vertical pair, 1 w/out overprint	300.00	
	FDC (Washington, D.C.)		50.00
	FDC (Newton, Kans.)		450.00

496		UnFVF	UseFVF
1 1/2¢	**yellow brown**	3.00	2.25
	Plate block of 4	40.00	
	Wide spacing pair	60.00	
	v. Vertical pair, 1 w/out overprint	325.00	
	FDC		60.00

497		UnFVF	UseFVF
2¢	**carmine red**	3.00	1.00
	Plate block of 4	35.00	
	Wide spacing pair	45.00	
	FDC		60.00

498		UnFVF	UseFVF
3¢	**reddish violet**	15.00	11.00
	Plate block of 4	145.00	
	v. Vertical pair, 1 w/out overprint	400.00	
	FDC		75.00

499		UnFVF	UseFVF
4¢	**yellow brown**	15.00	8.50
	Plate block of 4	145.00	
	v. Vertical pair, 1 w/out overprint	400.00	
	FDC		100.00

500		UnFVF	UseFVF
5¢	**blue**	12.50	9.00
	Plate block of 4	120.00	
	FDC		100.00

501		UnFVF	UseFVF
6¢	**orange**	25.00	15.00
	Plate block of 4	325.00	
	FDC (Washington, D.C.)		125.00
	FDC (Newton, Kans.)		650.00

502		UnFVF	UseFVF
7¢	**black**	25.00	20.00
	Plate block of 4	375.00	
	v. Vertical pair, 1 w/out overprint	400.00	
	FDC		150.00

503		UnFVF	UseFVF
8¢	**yellow olive**	70.00	60.00
	Plate block of 4	675.00	
	FDC (Washington, D.C.)		150.00
	FDC (Newton, Kans.)		650.00

504		UnFVF	UseFVF
9¢	**salmon**	12.50	10.00
	Plate block of 4	150.00	
	FDC		150.00

505		UnFVF	UseFVF
10¢	**orange yellow**	20.00	12.50
	Plate block of 4	275.00	
	Pair, gutter between	—	
	FDC		200.00

506, 510, 511, 512, 514, 516 *Nebraska overprint*

Nebr.

506		UnFVF	UseFVF
1¢	**green**	2.25	2.00
	Plate block of 4	30.00	
	v1. Period omitted after "Nebr"	40.00	
	Wide spacing pair	35.00	
	v. Vertical pair, 1 w/out overprint	275.00	
	FDC (Washington, D.C.)		50.00
	FDC (Beatrice, Nebr.)		400.00

507		UnFVF	UseFVF
1 1/2¢	**yellow brown**	2.25	2.00
	Plate block of 4	40.00	
	Wide spacing pair	35.00	
	FDC (Washington, D.C.)		60.00
	FDC (Hartington, Nebr.)		350.00

508		UnFVF	UseFVF
2¢	**carmine red**	2.25	1.00
	Plate block of 4	25.00	
	Wide spacing pair	50.00	
	FDC (Washington, D.C.)		60.00
	FDC (Auburn, Beatrice or Hartington, Nebr.)		350.00
	EKU (April 15, 1929)		

509		UnFVF	UseFVF
3¢	**reddish violet**	11.00	8.00
	Plate block of 4	120.00	
	Wide spacing pair	70.00	
	v. Vertical pair, 1 w/out overprint	400.00	
	v1. Period omitted after "Nebr"	—	—
	FDC (Washington, D.C.)		75.00
	FDC (Beatrice or Hartington, Nebr.)		350.00

510		UnFVF	UseFVF
4¢	**yellow brown**	15.00	10.00
	Plate block of 4	175.00	
	Wide spacing pair	110.00	
	FDC (Washington, D.C.)		100.00
	FDC (Beatrice or Hartington, Nebr.)		350.00

511		UnFVF	UseFVF
5¢	**blue**	12.50	11.50
	Plate block of 4	175.00	
	FDC (Washington, D.C.)		100.00
	FDC (Beatrice or Hartington, Nebr.)		375.00

512		UnFVF	UseFVF
6¢	**orange**	35.00	17.50
	Plate block of 4	350.00	
	FDC		125.00

513		UnFVF	UseFVF
7¢	**black**	18.50	12.50
	Plate block of 4	225.00	
	FDC		150.00

514		UnFVF	UseFVF
8¢	**yellow olive**	25.00	17.50
	Plate block of 4	325.00	
	Wide spacing pair	160.00	
	FDC		150.00

515		UnFVF	UseFVF
9¢	**salmon**	30.00	22.50
	Plate block of 4	350.00	
	Wide spacing pair	140.00	
	v. Vertical pair, 1 w/out overprint	600.00	
	FDC		150.00

516		UnFVF	UseFVF
10¢	**orange yellow**	85.00	17.50
	Plate block of 4	775.00	
	FDC		200.00

1930-32. WARREN G. HARDING NEW DESIGN ISSUE in the Regular Issue Series of 1922-34. *Rotary press printing, unwatermarked, perforated 11x10 1/2.*

517, 520 *Warren G. Harding*

517		UnFVF	UseFVF
1 1/2¢	**yellow brown**	.25	.20
	dull brown	.25	.20
	Plate block of 4	2.25	

x. Bureau precancel (MNH / 96 diff.)	.25		
Plate block of 4	1.50		
Pair, horizontal or vertical gutter between	175.00		
FDC w/o cachet *(Dec. 1, 1930)*		4.50	
FDC w/cachet		45.00	

1930-32. GEORGE WASHINGTON ISSUE used the design of the 2¢ carmine red stamp issued five months earlier as part of the Washington Bicentennial Issue (CM101) in a new color and denomination.

518, 521, 523, B92, B93 *George Washington*

518		UnFVF	UseFVF
3¢	**reddish violet**	.25	.20
	pale reddish violet	.25	.20
	Plate block of 4	1.25	
	x. Bureau precancel (MNH / 64 diff.)	.40	
	Plate block of 4	2.50	
	Double transfer	1.00	.25
	Gripper cracks	1.10	.30
	Recut on nose	1.75	.60
	Pair, gutter between	2.00	
	n. Booklet pane of 6 *(July 25, 1932)*	37.50	
	v. Vertical pair, imperforate between	300.00	
	FDC w/o cachet *(June 16, 1932)*		7.50
	FDC w/cachet		40.00
	FDC Booklet Pane		200.00

1930-32 WILLIAM H. TAFT ISSUE in the Regular Issue Series of 1922-34 honored the 27th president, who was later appointed Chief Justice of the Supreme Court, a position he embraced more than president. Taft (1857-1930), of Cincinnati, Ohio, had the White House stables converted to a garage for the first presidential automobiles, ordered in 1909.

519, 522 *William H. Taft*

519		UnFVF	UseFVF
4¢	**yellow brown**	.90	.20
	dark brown	.90	.20
	Plate block of 4	11.50	
	x. Bureau precancel (MNH / 46 diff.)	2.50	
	Plate block of 4	—	
	Gouge on right "4"	2.00	.60
	Recut on right "4"	2.00	.60
	Pair, gutter between	—	
	FDC w/o cachet *(June 4, 1930)*		6.00
	FDC w/cachet		60.00

1930-32. WARREN G. HARDING NEW DESIGN COIL ISSUE in the Regular Issue Series of 1922-34. *Perforated 10 vertically.*

520 *Line Pair*

520		UnFVF	UseFVF
1 1/2¢	**yellow brown**	1.50	.20
	Pair	3.50	.20
	Line pair	7.50	.50
	x. Bureau precancel (MNH / 101 diff.)	1.00	
	Line pair	3.50	
	FDC w/o cachet *(Dec. 1, 1930)*		5.00
	FDC w/cachet		60.00

1930-32. GEORGE WASHINGTON COIL ISSUE *Perforated 10 vertically.*

521		UnFVF	UseFVF
3¢	**reddish violet**	1.75	.20
	pale violet	1.75	.20
	Pair	4.25	.50
	Line pair	5.50	.60
	x. Bureau precancel (MNH / 46 diff.)	2.50	
	Line pair	—	
	Gripper cracks	—	
	Recut on nose	—	
	Recut around eyes	—	
	FDC w/o cachet *(June 24, 1932)*		25.00
	FDC w/cachet		95.00

1930-32. WILLIAM H. TAFT COIL ISSUE in the Regular Issue Series of 1922-34. *Perforated 10 vertically.*

522		UnFVF	UseFVF
4¢	**yellow brown**	2.75	.75
	Pair	6.00	.85
	Line pair	17.50	1.50
	x. Bureau precancel (MNH / 23 diff.)	3.00	
	Line pair	—	
	FDC w/o cachet *(Sept. 18, 1930)*		15.00
	FDC w/cachet		50.00

1930-32. GEORGE WASHINGTON COIL ISSUE *Perforated 10 horizontally.*

523		UnFVF	UseFVF
3¢	**reddish violet**	1.00	.75
	pale violet	1.00	.75
	Pair	3.00	.80
	Line pair	4.00	1.50
	FDC w/o cachet *(Oct. 12, 1932)*		15.00
	FDC w/cachet		50.00

1938-43. Presidential Series The first regular issues in almost six years are known as the Presidential Series because all but three of its 32 designs feature the portraits of former presidents of the United States. Sixteen years would pass before the "Prexies" began to be supplemented with another definitive series. *The values from 1/2¢ through 50¢, including coils, are printed by rotary press intaglio and are perforated 11x10 1/2. The $1, $2 and $5 values are printed by flat press intaglio, perforated 11.*

1938. BENJAMIN FRANKLIN ISSUE in the Presidential Series.

524 *Benjamin Franklin (1706-1790), first Postmaster General appointed by the Continental Congress, began his career as a printer and editor in Philadelphia, where he founded the first circulating library in America, the American Philosophical Society, and the nucleus for the University of Pennsylvania; he invented the Franklin stove, and made important experiments identifying lightning with electricity. He was deputy postmaster at Philadelphia 1737-53 and then (with William Hunter) postmaster general for the colonies until 1774, greatly expanding and improving postal service. An active patriot, both here and in England, for 20 years before the Revolution, he served in the 2nd Continental Congress, was appointed postmaster general, and aided in drafting the Declaration of Independence, of which he was a signer. Sent to France as a diplomat in 1776, he was enormously popular and successful there. With John Jay and John Adams, he negotiated the peace treaty with Great Britain in 1783. An important member of the Constitutional Convention in 1787, he signed the Constitution without entirely approving it. His last public act was in signing a petition to Congress for the abolition of slavery.*

524		UnFVF	UseFVF
1/2¢	**red orange**	.25	.20
	Plate block of 4	.50	
	x. Bureau precancel (MNH / 199 diff.)	.35	
	Plate block of 4	1.75	
	FDC *(May 19, 1938)*	—	

1938. GEORGE WASHINGTON ISSUE in the Presidential Series.

525, 556, 565, B94, B95, B96, B98, B101, B102, B109, B110 *George Washington, unanimously elected first president, mainly supported the federalist and industrialist policies of Alexander Hamilton (see No. 106) against the states' rights and agrarian theories of Thomas Jefferson (see No. 47). He was criticized for "aristocratic tendencies," for the 1794 Jay's Treaty with Great Britain, and for the excise tax that led to the Whiskey Rebellion of 1794; he brought the nation power and prestige, put down severe Indian troubles, and effected treaties opening the Mississippi to navigation.*

525

1¢		UnFVF	UseFVF
	green	.25	.20
	pale green	.25	.20
	Plate block of 4	.50	
	x. Bureau precancel (MNH / 701 diff.)	.20	
	Plate block of 4	1.00	
	FDC *(April 25, 1938)*	3.00	
	Pair, gutter between	—	
	n. Booklet pane of 6	2.00	
	FDC Booklet Pane		15.00

1938. MARTHA WASHINGTON ISSUE in the Presidential Series.

526, 557, 566 *Martha Washington, wife of the first president, was known as "the prettiest and richest widow in Virginia" when Washington met her in 1758. Married to him in January 1759, she managed his plantations during the Revolution, visited him at Valley Forge and Newburgh, and was a gracious and popular First Lady.*

526

1 1/2¢		UnFVF	UseFVF
	yellow brown	.25	.20
	ocher	.25	.20
	Plate block of 4	.50	
	Pair, horizontal or vertical gutter between	175.00	
	x. Bureau precancel (MNH / 404 diff.)	.25	
	Plate block of 4	1.25	
	v. Horizontal pair, imperforate between	175.00	
	vx. Bureau precancel (MNH) St. Louis	20.00	
	z. Tagged	—	
	FDC *(May 5, 1938)*	—	

No. 526z was produced circa 1955 as a result of experiments conducted by Pitney-Bowes for the Post Office Department. A single copy is known in collectors' hands.

1938. JOHN ADAMS ISSUE in the Presidential Series.

527, 558, 567, B97, B98, B103, B104, B105, B106, B107, B108, B109, B110 *John Adams, second president (1797-1801), attacked the Stamp Act in 1765, served in the first and second Continental Congress, nominated George Washington to command the American forces, helped to draft the Declaration of Independence, and (according to Jefferson) was "the pillar of its support on the floor of Congress." He served as commissioner to France 1777-79, went with John Jay and Benjamin Franklin to England to negotiate the peace treaty, and the first American envoy to the Court of St. James. Serving as vice president in both of Washington's terms, he was elected president in 1796. He was opposed by the Jefferson faction for the Alien and Sedition Acts, for which he was directly responsible, and by the Hamilton faction for his conciliatory policy toward France, which averted war. Defeated by Jefferson in the election of 1800, he retired to private life in Massachusetts.*

527

2¢		UnFVF	UseFVF
	rose	.25	.20
	rose pink	.25	.20
	Plate block of 4	.50	

Plate block of 10 (vertical), with number opposite 3rd horizontal row	7.50	
x. Bureau precancel (MNH / 161 diff.)	.50	
Plate block of 4	2.50	
Pair, horizontal or vertical gutter between	—	
Recut at top of head	2.50	1.25
n. Booklet pane of 6	6.00	
p. Thin, translucent paper	—	
FDC *(June 3, 1938)*		3.00
FDC Booklet Pane		15.00

1938. THOMAS JEFFERSON ISSUE in the Presidential Series.

528, 559, 568, B99, B100, B111, B112 *Thomas Jefferson, third president (1801-09), was the chief author of the Declaration of Independence and one of its signers. As a wartime legislator and governor in Virginia, he worked to abolish a landed aristocracy, separate church from state, and establish public schools. Returning to Congress in 1783, he headed the committee debating the peace treaty, devised the American monetary system and laid the basis for later organization of western territories. He was minister to France 1785-89, became first secretary of state, and was elected vice president under John Adams. Strongly opposed to Alexander Hamilton, whose policies he felt led toward monarchy, he championed individual liberties, states' rights and an agrarian economy. Tied with Burr for electoral votes in 1800, he was supported by Hamilton and chosen president by the House of Representatives. In his two terms he authorized the Louisiana Purchase (CM32-CM36), warred against the Tripolitan pirates (CM178), dispatched the Lewis and Clark and Pike expeditions, and obtained a Congressional act abolishing the importation of slaves. A distinguished scholar, philosopher and patron of the arts, he founded the University of Virginia and greatly influenced the revival of classical architecture in America.*

528

3¢		UnFVF	UseFVF
	violet	.25	.20
	Plate block of 4	.50	
	Plate block of 10 (vertical), with number opposite 3rd horizontal row	.25	
	x. Bureau precancel (MNH / 87 diff.)	1.00	
	Plate block of 4	5.00	
	Pair, horizontal or vertical gutter between	175.00	
	n. Booklet pane of 6	8.50	
	v. Horizontal pair, imperforate between	1,100.00	
	v1. Pair, imperforate	2,750.00	
	FDC *(June 16, 1938)*		3.00
	FDC Booklet Pane		15.00

1938. JAMES MADISON ISSUE in the Presidential Series.

529, 560 *James Madison, fourth president (1809-17), is known as "the Father of the Constitution." A Virginian identified with Jefferson's liberal reforms there, he joined with Hamilton in proposing the Constitutional Convention, acted as recorder of the proceedings, took a large part in framing the Constitution, greatly aided its ratification and proposed the first 10 amendments: The Bill of Rights. Criticized as inept in his leadership in the War of 1812, he successfully advocated a protective tariff, a strong military organization and a national system of roads and canals.*

529

4¢		UnFVF	UseFVF
	bright purple	1.15	.20
	rose lilac	1.15	.20
	Plate block of 4	4.50	
	x. Bureau precancel (MNH / 30 diff.)	2.50	
	Plate block of 4	15.00	
	FDC *(July 1, 1938)*		3.00

1938. WHITE HOUSE ISSUE in the Presidential Series.

530, 561 *The White House*

530		UnFVF	UseFVF
4 1/2¢	**gray**	.25	.20
	dark gray	.25	.20
	Plate block of 4	1.25	
	x. Bureau precancel (MNH / 27 diff.)	1.50	
	Plate block of 4	10.00	
	FDC *(July 11, 1938)*		3.00

1938. JAMES MONROE ISSUE in the Presidential Series.

531, 562 *James Monroe, fifth president (1817-25), fought in the 3rd Virginia Regiment at Harlem Heights, White Plains, Trenton (where he was wounded), Brandywine, Germantown and Monmouth. He studied law under Jefferson, served in the Continental Congress, 1783-86, and fought the Constitution because he believed it made the federal government too powerful. As a senator, he bitterly opposed Washington and Hamilton. As minister to France, he was recalled for over-sympathizing with the French Revolution and failing to follow Washington's instructions. Four times governor of Virginia, he was sent back to France in 1803 to aid in negotiating the Louisiana Purchase (CM34). Secretary of State and of War under Madison, he was elected president in 1816, ushering in the "Era of Good Feeling," and re-elected in 1820 with all but one vote, which was given to John Quincy Adams so that only Washington might have the honor of unanimous election. Monroe acquired Florida from Spain, supported the Missouri Compromise, settled the Canadian border and eliminated its forts and proclaimed the Monroe Doctrine prohibiting further European colonization or interference in the Americas.*

531		UnFVF	UseFVF
5¢	**light blue**	.25	.20
	pale blue	.25	.20
	Plate block of 4	1.25	
	x. Bureau precancel (MNH / 44 diff.)	.75	
	Plate block of 4	—	
	Pair, gutter between	—	
	FDC *(July 21, 1938)*		3.00

1938. JOHN QUINCY ADAMS ISSUE in the Presidential Series.

532, 563 *John Quincy Adams, sixth president (1825-29), was the son of John Adams (No. 527). When appointed secretary of state by Monroe, he already had seen diplomatic service in France, the Netherlands, Prussia, Russia and England; spent 5 years in the Senate; taught rhetoric at Harvard; and headed the peace commission that negotiated the Treaty of Ghent in 1814. He obtained the cession of Florida from Spain and shared credit with Monroe in formulating the Monroe Doctrine. Running second to Andrew Jackson in the popular vote in 1824, he was elected president by the House of Representatives through the support of Henry Clay (No. 103). As president, he expanded the executive powers, favored internal improvements and refused to build a personal political machine. Defeated by Jackson in 1828, he was elected to the House of Representatives in 1831 and served there until his death 17 years later.*

532		UnFVF	UseFVF
6¢	**orange**	.35	.20
	Plate block of 4	1.50	
	x. Bureau precancel (MNH / 45 diff.)	.75	
	Plate block of 4	—	
	FDC *(July 28, 1938)*		3.00

1938. ANDREW JACKSON ISSUE in the Presidential Series.

533 *Andrew Jackson, seventh president (1829-37), symbolized the common people's rise in power. A frontiersman, military hero (CM173) and senator from Tennessee, he received the largest popular vote in 1824, but was defeated in the House of Representatives when Henry Clay threw his own electoral votes to John Quincy Adams. Elected by a landslide in 1828, Jackson instituted national political conventions and the "spoils system," expanded the president's power, checked federal spending on internal improvements, paid off the national debt and destroyed the privileged Bank of the United States. Opposed to the states'-rights theories of John Calhoun, he countered South Carolina's refusal to collect protective-tariff duties by sending troops and naval forces to Charleston.*

533		UnFVF	UseFVF
7¢	**sepia**	.45	.20
	lilac brown	.45	.20
	Plate block of 4	2.00	
	x. Bureau precancel (MNH / 44 diff.)	1.00	
	Plate block of 4	—	
	FDC *(Aug. 4, 1938)*		3.00

1938. MARTIN VAN BUREN ISSUE in the Presidential Series.

534 *Martin Van Buren, eighth president (1837-41), was a senator, governor of New York, and secretary of state and vice president under Jackson, whose policies he attempted to follow as president. He inaugurated the independent treasury, opposed federal spending for internal improvements and advocated tariffs for revenue only. Alienating the North by his appeasement of the British in a Canadian border incident, and the South by his opposition to the annexation of Texas, he was defeated by William Henry Harrison in the 1840 election, failed to win the Democratic nomination in 1844 and was defeated by Zachary Taylor in 1848.*

534		UnFVF	UseFVF
8¢	**olive green**	.45	.20
	light olive green	.45	.20
	olive	.45	.20
	Plate block of 4	2.20	
	x. Bureau precancel (MNH / 44 diff.)	.75	
	Plate block of 4	—	
	FDC *(Aug. 11, 1938)*		3.00

1938. WILLIAM HENRY HARRISON ISSUE in the Presidential Series.

535 *William Henry Harrison, ninth president (1841), fought in the Battle of Fallen Timbers (CM89), served as secretary of the Northwest Territory and as its delegate to Congress, was first governor of the Indiana Territory (CM338), defeated the Indians under Tecumseh at Tippecanoe, defeated the British and Indians in the Battle of the Thames, was a member of both houses of Congress and served briefly as minister to Colombia. After his overwhelming victory in the 1840 election, he died of pneumonia a month after taking office.*

535		UnFVF	UseFVF
9¢	**rose pink**	.50	.20
	pink	.50	.20
	Plate block of 4	2.25	
	x. Bureau precancel (MNH / 38 diff.)	1.25	
	Plate block of 4	—	
	Pair, gutter between	—	
	FDC *(Aug. 18, 1938)*		3.00

1938. John Tyler Issue in the Presidential Series.

536, 564 *John Tyler, 10th president (1841-45), had served as governor of Virginia and as a member of both houses of Congress before his election as vice president in 1840. As president after Harrison's death, he differed with the Whig Party on constitutional principles and lost his party's support. He signed the Preemption Act enabling settlers to get government land, reorganized the Navy, annexed Texas and settled the boundary between Maine and Canada. Later, in 1861, he was chairman of the unsuccessful peace conference at Washington and remained loyal to Virginia when it seceded.*

536		UnFVF	UseFVF
10¢	**Venetian red**	.45	.20
	dull Venetian red	.45	.20
	Plate block of 4	2.00	
	x. Bureau precancel (MNH / 43 diff.)	1.25	
	Plate block of 4	—	
	FDC *(Sept. 2, 1938)*		3.00

1938. James Knox Polk Issue in the Presidential Series.

537 *James Knox Polk, 11th president (1845-49), served as speaker of the House and as governor of Tennessee before his highly successful term as president. He fought the spoils system, settled the Oregon boundary dispute by accepting the 49th parallel and giving Vancouver to the British, reduced the tariff, restored the independent treasury system abolished under Tyler and won a war with Mexico. An expansionist but not an imperialist, he approved the acquisition of Texas, New Mexico and California, but opposed retaining Mexico by force.*

537		UnFVF	UseFVF
11¢	**cobalt**	.75	.20
	Plate block of 4	4.25	
	x. Bureau precancel (MNH / 41 diff.)	4.00	
	Plate block of 4	—	
	FDC *(Sept. 8, 1938)*		5.00

1938. Zachary Taylor Issue in the Presidential Series.

538 *Zachary Taylor, 12th president (1849-50), came to the White House after a distinguished 40-year Army career in which he gained the nickname "Old Rough and Ready." He fought in the War of 1812, the Black Hawk and Seminole Wars and the Mexican War, which he ended by defeating Santa Anna at Buena Vista in 1847. In his 16 months as president, he resumed the spoils system. A former slave-holder, he worked for California's admission as a free state. He died of typhus in 1850.*

538		UnFVF	UseFVF
12¢	**light reddish violet**	1.40	.20
	Plate block of 4	6.00	
	x. Bureau precancel (MNH / 33 diff.)	5.00	
	Plate block of 4	—	
	FDC *(Sept. 14, 1938)*		5.00

1938. Millard Fillmore Issue in the Presidential Series.

539 *Millard Fillmore, 13th president (1850-53), spent four terms in the House of Representatives before his election as vice president under Taylor. As president he favored the compromise policy in the slavery issue, signed the Fugitive Slave Act, approved the negotiations leading to the opening of trade with Japan (CM363), and maintained neutrality in foreign wars.*

539		UnFVF	UseFVF
13¢	**blue green**	2.25	.20
	dark blue green	2.25	.20
	Plate block of 4	9.50	
	x. Bureau precancel (MNH / 28 diff.)	8.50	

	Plate block of 4	—	
	FDC *(Sept. 22, 1938)*		5.00

1938. Franklin Pierce Issue in the Presidential Series.

540 *Franklin Pierce, 14th president (1853-57), congressman, senator and brigadier general in the Mexican War, won the Democratic nomination in 1852 on the 49th ballot. As president, he effected the Gadsden Purchase (CM370), sent Matthew Perry to open trade with Japan (CM363), attempted to secure a base in Santo Domingo and annex Cuba, Hawaii and Alaska, and signed the Kansas-Nebraska Bill leaving slavery in those territories to popular vote. Attempting impartiality in domestic policy and imperialism in foreign policy, he generally failed at both and retired to obscurity.*

540		UnFVF	UseFVF
14¢	**blue**	1.15	.20
	Plate block of 4	6.00	
	x. Bureau precancel (MNH / 23 diff.)	5.00	
	Plate block of 4	—	
	FDC *(Oct. 6, 1938)*		5.00

1938. James Buchanan Issue in the Presidential Series.

541 *James Buchanan, 15th president (1857-61), had served successively as congressman, minister to Russia, senator, secretary of state under Polk and minister to Great Britain. A conservative and ineffective president, he expressed moral opposition to slavery and secession, but furthered one and condoned the other. His administration saw the growth of the new Republican Party, the Lincoln-Douglas debates and the abolitionist John Brown's raid on the federal armory at Harper's Ferry, Virginia, for which Brown was hanged. Failing to meet the challenge of South Carolina's secession and her firing on Fort Sumter, Buchanan left the office on the brink of the Civil War.*

541		UnFVF	UseFVF
15¢	**slate**	.65	.20
	Plate block of 4	3.00	
	x. Bureau precancel (MNH / 38 diff.)	1.50	
	Plate block of 4	—	
	FDC *(Oct. 13, 1938)*		5.00

1938. Abraham Lincoln Issue in the Presidential Series.

542 *Abraham Lincoln, 16th president (1861-65), worked as a rail-splitter, surveyor and postmaster of Salem, Ill.; served a term in Congress; and became an outstanding jury lawyer before attaining national prominence through a series of debates with Stephen A. Douglas, against whom he was running for the Senate in 1858. Nominated as the Republican presidential candidate in 1860 because of his conservative views on slavery, his election signaled the secession of seven Southern states. Given almost dictatorial powers in the Civil War, he followed a middle course between the radicals and defeatists, ably commanding the Union war effort and diplomatically handling his cabinet and his generals. Although he had hoped for a gradual, compensated abolition of slavery, in 1863 he issued the Emancipation Proclamation freeing all slaves in rebel territory. The same year marked his Gettysburg Address (CM320). Re-elected in the dark days of 1864, he made his great Second Inaugural Address: "With malice toward none, with charity for all...let us strive on to finish the work we are in; to bind up the nation's wounds...to do all which may achieve a just and lasting peace." His compassionate program for conciliation and reconstruction was never achieved. Ten days later, five days after Lee's surrender at Appomattox, he was assassinated by a Southern fanatic while attending a theater play.*

542		UnFVF	UseFVF
16¢	**black**	1.25	.60

Plate block of 4	6.00	
x. Bureau precancel (MNH / 6 diff.)	—	
Plate block of 4	—	
FDC (Oct. 20, 1938)		6.00

1938. ANDREW JOHNSON ISSUE in the Presidential Series.

543 *Andrew Johnson, 17th president (1865-69), a self-educated tailor, was a congressman, governor of Tennessee and the only Southern senator to support the Union in the Civil War. His success as military governor of Tennessee led to his election as vice president. As president after Lincoln's death, he attempted to carry out Lincoln's conciliatory policies of Reconstruction, but was thwarted by the radical Republicans in Congress. His removal of War Secretary Edwin M. Stanton (No. 101) for conspiracy led to his impeachment, which fell one vote short of the two-thirds majority needed to remove him from the White House. Elected to the Senate again in 1875, he died the same year.*

543		UnFVF	UseFVF
17¢	**rose red**	1.25	.20
	Plate block of 4	6.00	
	x. Bureau precancel (MNH / 27 diff.)	—	
	Plate block of 4	—	
	FDC (Oct. 27, 1938)		6.00

1938. ULYSSES S. GRANT ISSUE in the Presidential Series.

544 *Ulysses S. Grant, 18th president (1869-77), led the Union forces to victory in the Civil War (CM174). As president, he authorized harsh Reconstruction policies that kept sectional hatreds alive, and, although he was personally honest, his administration was involved in grave scandals. His achievements included civil service reform and the funding of the national debt. Left penniless by the collapse of a banking house in 1884, he was persuaded by Mark Twain (CM205) to write his "Personal Memoirs," which he finished four days before his death in 1885. They realized almost $450,000.*

544		UnFVF	UseFVF
18¢	**brown carmine**	2.25	.25
	rose brown	2.25	.25
	Plate block of 4	10.00	
	x. Bureau precancel (MNH / 5 diff.)	—	
	Plate block of 4	—	
	FDC (Nov. 3, 1938)		6.00

1938. RUTHERFORD B. HAYES ISSUE in the Presidential Series.

545 *Rutherford B. Hayes, 19th president (1877-81), former congressman and governor of Ohio, ran second to Samuel J. Tilden in the 1876 election, but was chosen president by a partisan electoral commission by a vote of 185-184. His administration returned local government to the South, ending the Reconstruction, and made ineffective attempts at civil service reform.*

545		UnFVF	UseFVF
19¢	**light reddish violet**	2.00	.60
	Plate block of 4	9.50	
	x. Bureau precancel (MNH / 8 diff.)	—	
	Plate block of 4	—	
	FDC (Nov. 10, 1938)		6.00

1938. JAMES A. GARFIELD ISSUE in the Presidential Series.

546 *James A. Garfield, 20th president (1881), Republican leader of the House, was a senator-elect when chosen president in 1880. Four months after his inauguration, he was fatally shot by a man who had been turned down in a bid to become ambassador to France.*

546		UnFVF	UseFVF
20¢	**blue green**	1.25	.20

bright blue green	1.25	.20
Plate block of 4	5.00	
x. Bureau precancel (MNH / 39 diff.)	3.50	
Plate block of 4	—	
FDC (Nov. 10, 1938)		6.00

1938. CHESTER A. ARTHUR ISSUE in the Presidential Series.

547 *Chester A. Arthur, 21st president (1881-85), who succeeded to the office after Garfield's assassination, was an able and honest administrator. He supported civil service reform, arranged a canal treaty (unratified) with Nicaragua, vetoed a Chinese-exclusion bill and began the rebuilding of the Navy.*

547		UnFVF	UseFVF
21¢	**slate blue**	2.25	.20
	Plate block of 4	10.00	
	x. Bureau precancel (MNH / 5 diff.)	—	
	Plate block of 4	—	
	FDC (Nov. 22, 1938)		7.00

1938. GROVER CLEVELAND ISSUE in the Presidential Series.

548 *Grover Cleveland, 22nd and 24th president (1885-89 and 1893-97), reform governor of New York, was an honest and independent president. In his first term he enlarged the civil service, followed a conciliatory policy toward the South, avoided the spoils system, opposed pork-barrel pension bills, and vetoed more than two-thirds of the congressional acts presented to him. Defeated by Benjamin Harrison in 1888, he ran again and was re-elected in 1892. His second term was marked by a severe depression, a fight against inflation, an income tax law (declared unconstitutional), the use of troops to end the mail stoppage in the Pullman strike, and a firm stand against the British use of force in a boundary dispute with Venezuela.*

548		UnFVF	UseFVF
22¢	**vermilion**	1.50	.75
	Plate block of 4	12.50	
	x. Bureau precancel (MNH / 4 diff.)	—	
	Plate block of 4	—	
	FDC (Nov. 22, 1938)		7.00

1938. BENJAMIN HARRISON ISSUE in the Presidential Series.

549 *Benjamin Harrison, 23rd president (1889-93), was a grandson of William Henry Harrison, ninth president. A Union regimental commander in the Civil War and senator for one term, as president he greatly expanded the pension list, signed the McKinley high-tariff bill and the Sherman silver purchase act, followed imperialistic policies in the Pacific, convened the first Pan-American Conference in 1889 and aided the admission to the Union of the Dakotas, Montana and Washington in 1889 and Idaho and Wyoming in 1900.*

549		UnFVF	UseFVF
24¢	**gray green**	4.25	.35
	Plate block of 4	20.00	
	x. Bureau precancel (MNH / 8 diff.)	—	
	Plate block of 4	—	
	FDC (Dec. 2, 1938)		8.00

1938. WILLIAM McKINLEY ISSUE in the Presidential Series.

550 *William McKinley, 25th president (1897-1901), former Congressman and governor of Ohio, was elected on a platform of high tariff and maintenance of the gold standard; raised the tariff to the highest level in American history and signed the Gold Standard Act of 1900. After the sinking of the Maine at Havana, public opinion forced his intervention in the Cuban rebellion; the resulting Spanish-American War ended in a temporary American protectorate over Cuba, the purchase of the Philippine Islands, the annexation of Puerto Rico and Guam and the*

establishment of the United States as a world power. His administration also marked the annexation of Hawaii, intervention in China and agitation for a Panama Canal. Re-elected on the "full dinner pail" platform, he was fatally shot by an anarchist the following September while visiting the Pan-American Exposition (CM26-31).

550

25¢		UnFVF	UseFVF
	claret	1.20	.20
	rose lilac	1.20	.20
	Plate block of 4	5.00	
	x. Bureau precancel (MNH / 23 diff.)	7.50	
	Plate block of 4	—	
	FDC *(Dec. 2, 1938)*		8.00

1938. THEODORE ROOSEVELT ISSUE in the Presidential Series.

551 *Theodore Roosevelt, 26th president (1901-09), achieved early fame as assistant secretary of the Navy under McKinley, as organizer of the Rough Riders (CM315) in the Spanish-American War and as a crusading governor of New York. Given the Republican vice presidential nomination, "to get him out of the way," upon McKinley's death he became, at 43, America's youngest president. He fought government corruption by big business, recognized Panama when it revolted from Colombia, began the construction of the Panama Canal (CM48 and CM198), won the Nobel Peace Prize for his successful mediation of the Russo-Japanese War, organized conservation of national resources and instituted the Pure Food and Drugs Act. Virtually bequeathing the presidency to William Howard Taft, he became dissatisfied with Taft's conservative policies and ran against him in 1912, splitting the Republican ticket so that both lost to Woodrow Wilson. He also was noted as a naturalist, explorer and writer.*

551

30¢		UnFVF	UseFVF
	deep ultramarine	5.00	.20
	ultramarine	5.00	.20
	blue	15.00	
	deep blue	110.00	
	Plate block of 4	22.50	
	x. Bureau precancel (MNH / 27 diff.)	9.50	
	Plate block of 4	—	
	FDC *(Dec. 8, 1938)*		10.00

1938. WILLIAM HOWARD TAFT ISSUE in the Presidential Series.

552 *William Howard Taft, 27th president (1909-13), had distinguished careers before and after his presidency. He was a federal judge, solicitor general under Benjamin Harrison, dean of the University of Cincinnati Law School, president of the Philippines Commission, first civil governor of the Philippines, secretary of war and provisional governor of Cuba.*
His administration dissolved the Standard Oil and American Tobacco Co. trusts, set up the Department of Labor and drafted the 16th and 17th Amendments (authorizing the income tax and the direct election of senators). Defeated in 1912, he became a lecturer and Yale law professor. Appointed chief justice of the United States in 1919, he served until his death in 1930.

552

50¢		UnFVF	UseFVF
	light red violet	8.50	.20
	Plate block of 4	40.00	
	x. Bureau precancel (MNH / 24 diff.)	20.00	
	Plate block of 4	—	
	FDC *(Dec. 8, 1938)*		15.00

Flat plate printing, perforated 11.

1938. WOODROW WILSON ISSUE in the Presidential Series.

553 *Woodrow Wilson, 28th president (1913-21), was president of Princeton University and a reform governor of New Jersey before his election in 1912. His first administration instituted the Federal Reserve Act, Farm Loan Act, Federal Trade Commission, Clayton Anti-Trust Act and Adamson Eight-House Law. (His entire tenure saw three Constitutional*

Amendments: direct election of Senators, prohibition and women's suffrage.) In foreign affairs, in his first term he had difficulties with some Latin American countries, sent the Pershing Expedition into Mexico, established partial protectorates in Santo Domingo, Haiti and Nicaragua, and maintained neutrality in World War I despite foreign pressures and the infringement of American rights. Re-elected with the slogan, "He kept us out of war," within a month of his inauguration he was forced by German sinking of American ships to ask for a declaration of war. An apostle of international cooperation, he went to Paris to negotiate the peace treaty, in which he said the League of Nations was the "most essential part." When the Senate rejected both the treaty and the league, he toured the country for public support, suffered a stroke and became an invalid. He won the Nobel Peace Prize in 1919 and died in 1924.

553

$1		UnFVF	UseFVF
	dark purple and black	10.00	.20
	Plate block of 4	45.00	
	Center line block	30.00	
	Margin block of 4, w/arrow	27.50	
	FDC *(Aug. 19, 1938)*		60.00
	w. Watermarked "USIR"	300.00	70.00
	w. Plate block of 4	1,800.00	
	FDC *(dry print 1954)*		30.00
	v. Vertical pair, imperforate between	2,750.00	
	v1. Vertical pair, imperforate horizontally	1,500.00	
	a. red violet and black *(Aug. 31, 1954)*	9.00	.20
	(dry print)		
	Plate block of 4	40.00	
	av. Vertical pair, imperforate between	7,500.00	
	av1. Vertical pair, imperforate horizontally	1,000.00	

No. 553a is printed on pre-gummed, whiter and thicker paper. It was printed on "dry" paper; No. 553 was printed on pre-dampened paper.

1938. WARREN G. HARDING ISSUE in the Presidential Series.

554 *Warren G. Harding, 29th president (1921-23), was an Ohio newspaperman and senator who supported prohibition, anti-strike legislation, women's suffrage and high tariffs; opposed the League of Nations as a threat to national sovereignty. Overwhelmingly elected in 1920 on a "return to normalcy" platform, he worked to repeal excess profits and high income taxes and to revise the tariff. In 1921 he called the Washington Conference to limit naval armaments. Returning from a visit to Alaska in 1923, he died unexpectedly at San Francisco.*

554

$2		UnFVF	UseFVF
	green and black	27.50	4.75
	yellow green and black	27.50	4.75
	Plate block of 4	135.00	
	Center line block	85.00	35.00
	Margin block of 4, w/arrow	85.00	
	FDC *(Sept. 29, 1938)*		125.00

1938. CALVIN COOLIDGE ISSUE in the Presidential Series.

555 *Calvin Coolidge, 30th president (1923-29), attained prominence in 1919, when, as governor of Massachusetts, he suppressed the Boston police strike on the grounds that "there is no right to strike against the public safety." Elected vice president, he succeeded to the presidency upon Harding's death. In a period of prosperity, his administration was cautious and passive in domestic affairs and isolationist toward Europe. He opposed the League of Nations, approved the World Court, vetoed the Soldiers' Bonus Act, twice vetoed the Farm Relief Bill, refused to intervene in the coal strike of 1927 and reduced the national debt by $2 billion in three years. He declined to run for a third term.*

555

$5		UnFVF	UseFVF
	carmine and black	115.00	4.50
	red brown and black	3,000.00	1,000.00
	Plate block of 4	500.00	
	Center line block	—	12.50
	Margin block of 4, w/arrow	400.00	
	FDC *(Nov. 17, 1938)*		210.00

1939. PRESIDENTIAL COIL ISSUE in the Presidential Series. Used the same designs as the sheet stamps. *Rotary press, perforated 10 vertically.*

556		UnFVF	UseFVF
1¢	**green**	.25	.20
	light green	.25	.20
	Pair	.50	
	Line pair	1.50	
	x. Bureau precancel (MNH / 269 diff.)	.25	
	Line pair	1.00	
	FDC *(Jan. 10, 1939)*		5.00

557		UnFVF	UseFVF
1 1/2¢	**yellow brown**	.25	.20
	ocher	.25	.20
	Pair	.50	
	Line pair	1.50	
	x. Bureau precancel (MNH / 179 diff.)	.25	
	Line pair	1.25	
	FDC *(Jan. 20, 1939)*		5.00

558		UnFVF	UseFVF
2¢	**rose**	.25	.20
	Pair	.50	
	Line pair	1.50	
	x. Bureau precancel (MNH / 101 diff.)	.50	
	Line pair	2.50	
	FDC *(Jan. 20, 1939)*		5.00

559		UnFVF	UseFVF
3¢	**violet**	.25	.20
	Pair	.50	
	Line pair	1.50	
	x. Bureau precancel (MNH / 46 diff.)	5.00	
	Line pair	—	
	Gripper cracks	—	
	p. Thin, translucent paper	—	
	FDC *(Jan. 20, 1939)*		5.00

560		UnFVF	UseFVF
4¢	**bright purple**	7.50	.75
	Pair	17.50	
	Line pair	32.50	
	x. Bureau precancel (MNH / 13 diff.)	—	
	Line pair	—	
	FDC *(Jan. 20, 1939)*		5.00

561		UnFVF	UseFVF
4 1/2¢	**gray**	.75	.50
	Pair	1.50	
	Line pair	5.50	
	x. Bureau precancel (MNH / 3 diff.)	15.00	
	Line pair	—	
	FDC *(Jan. 20, 1939)*		5.00

562		UnFVF	UseFVF
5¢	**bright blue**	6.00	.50
	Pair	12.50	
	Line pair	27.50	
	x. Bureau precancel (MNH / 6 diff.)	—	
	Line pair	—	
	FDC *(Jan. 20, 1939)*		5.00

563		UnFVF	UseFVF
6¢	**orange**	1.25	.50
	Pair	2.00	
	Line pair	7.50	
	x. Bureau precancel (MNH / 8 diff.)	—	
	Line pair	—	
	FDC *(Jan. 20, 1939)*		7.00

564		UnFVF	UseFVF
10¢	**Venetian red**	12.50	1.25
	Pair	22.50	
	Line pair	50.00	
	x. Bureau precancel (MNH / 4 diff.)	—	
	Line pair	—	
	FDC *(Jan. 20, 1939)*		10.00

1939. PRESIDENTIAL COIL ISSUE in the Presidential Series. *Rotary press, perforated 10 horizontally.*

565		UnFVF	UseFVF
1¢	**green**	.75	.25
	Pair	1.25	
	Line pair	2.25	
	FDC *(Jan. 27, 1939)*		6.00

566		UnFVF	UseFVF
1 1/2¢	**yellow brown**	1.50	.75
	Pair	4.50	

			UnFVF	UseFVF
	Line pair	2.75		
	FDC *(Jan. 27, 1939)*			6.00

567		UnFVF	UseFVF
2¢	**rose**	2.50	.75
	Pair	6.00	
	Line pair	4.00	
	FDC *(Jan. 27, 1939)*		6.00

568		UnFVF	UseFVF
3¢	**violet**	2.25	.75
	Pair	6.00	
	Line pair	4.00	
	FDC *(Jan. 28, 1939)*		6.00

1954-73. Liberty Series

The series takes its name from the Statue of Liberty, which was used as the design of the first stamp issued, the 8¢ value, as well as a similar 8¢ value, a 3¢ value and an 11¢ value. The design of the 3¢ and first 8¢ stamp were also used on an imperforate souvenir sheet (CM388) for the Fifth International Philatelic Exhibition. Because of the various printing methods and formats, it is a challenging series for collectors.

1955. BENJAMIN FRANKLIN ISSUE in the Liberty Series. *Rotary press, perforated 11x10 1/2.*

569 *Benjamin Franklin*

569		MNHVF	UseVF
1/2¢	**vermilion** wet print	.25	.20
	Plate block of 4	.50	
	x. Bureau precancel (6 diff.)	4.00	
	Plate block of 4	—	
	FDC *(Oct. 20, 1955)*		1.75
	p. Dry print *(May 1958)*	.25	.20
	Plate block of 4	.50	
	px. Bureau precancel (35 diff.)	.40	
	Plate block of 4	4.00	

Note: Bureau precancels for 569 without regard to printing types 37 different.

1954. GEORGE WASHINGTON ISSUE in the Liberty Series. *Rotary press, perforated 11x10 1/2.*

570, 587 *George Washington*

570		MNHVF	UseVF
1¢	**dull green** wet print	.25	.20
	Plate block of 4	.50	
	x. Bureau precancel (78 diff.)	3.00	
	Plate block of 4	—	
	Pair, gutter between	—	
	FDC *(Aug. 26, 1954)*		1.75
	p. Dry print *(March 1956)*	.25	.20
	Plate block of 4	.50	
	px. Bureau precancel (79 diff.)	.35	
	Plate block of 4	4.00	
	p1. Hi-Brite paper	—	
	Plate block of 4	—	

Note: Bureau precancels for 570 without regard to printing types 113 different.

1956. MOUNT VERNON ISSUE in the Liberty Series. *Rotary press, perforated 10 1/2x11.*

571 *Mount Vernon, home of George Washington, on the south bank of the Potomac, 16 miles below Washington, D.C. Land was part of the Royal Grant to Lord Culpepper, who in 1674 granted 5,000 acres to Nicolas Spencer and John Washington,*

great-grandfather of George. Since 1858 preserved and restored by Mount Vernon Ladies Association.

571		MNHVF	UseVF
1 1/2¢	**brown carmine** dry print	.25	.20
	Plate block of 4	.50	
	x. Bureau precancel (45 diff.)	1.50	
	Plate block of 4	8.50	
	FDC (Feb. 22, 1956)		1.75

1954. THOMAS JEFFERSON ISSUE in the Liberty Series. *Rotary press, perforated 11x10 1/2.*

572, 588 *Thomas Jefferson*

572		MNHVF	UseVF
2¢	**rose** dry print	.25	.20
	Plate block of 4	.50	
	x. Bureau precancel (86 diff.)	1.25	
	Plate block of 4	8.50	
	Pair, gutter between	—	
	FDC (Sept. 15, 1954)		1.75
	p. Silkote paper (Dec. 1954)	1,250.00	
	Plate block of 4	—	

Note: Silkote paper was used for only 50,000 stamps. Silkote varieties need expertization.

1954. STATUE OF LIBERTY ISSUE in the Liberty Series. *Rotary press, perforated 11x10 1/2.*

573, 589, B113, B114, B115, B116 *Statue of Liberty*

573		MNHVF	UseVF
3¢	**violet** wet print	.25	.20
	Plate block of 4	.50	
	x. Bureau precancel (30 diff.)	4.50	
	Plate block of 4	—	
	Pair, gutter between	150.00	
	n. Booklet pane of 6 (June 30, 1954)	4.50	
	nv. Booklet pane of 6, imperforate	—	
	between vertically		
	p. Dry print (Sept. 1956)	.25	.20
	Plate block of 4	.50	
	px. Bureau precancel (103 diff.)	.40	
	Plate block of 4	7.00	
	pn. Booklet pane of 6	4.50	
	pz. Tagged, Type II (July 6, 1966)	.35	.25
	Plate block of 4	5.00	
	pz1. Tagged, Type IIa	—	
	Plate block of 4	—	
	pz2. Tagged, Type III	—	
	Plate block of 4	—	
	p1. Hi-Brite paper	—	
	Plate block of 4	—	
	v. Horizontal pair, imperforate between	2,000.00	
	v1. Pair, imperforate (18 3/4x22 1/2mm)	2,250.00	
	FDC (June 24, 1954)		1.75
	FDC Booklet pane		5.00
	FDC tagged		30.00

Type I tagging: mat tagging. The four separate mats used did not cover the entire sheet of 400 stamps and certain untagged areas help to identify this variety. See expanded definition in the catalog introduction.

Type II tagging: roll tagging. Continuously surfaced rolls replaced the previously used tagging mats. Only the plate number selvage margin is partially tagged, and the plate number blocks have one untagged margin.

Type III tagging: curved metal plate tagging. Sheet margins are almost fully tagged but a "hot line" of intense phosphor-tagging or untagged narrow gap, 1mm or less in width, can appear on stamps from any position in the pane.

Note: Bureau precancels for 573 without regard to printing types 106 different.

1954. ABRAHAM LINCOLN ISSUE in the Liberty Series. *Rotary press, perforated 11x10 1/2.*

574, 590, B117, B118, B119, B120 *Abraham Lincoln*

574		MNHVF	UseVF
4¢	**magenta** wet print	.25	.20
	Plate block of 4	.50	
	x. Bureau precancel (11 diff.)	15.00	
	Plate block of 4	—	
	Pair, gutter between	—	
	n. Booklet pane of 6 (July 31, 1958)	2.75	
	nv. Booklet pane of 6, imperforate	—	
	between horizontally		
	p. Dry print (July 1956)	.25	.20
	Plate block of 4	.50	
	px. Bureau precancel (94 diff.)	.50	
	Plate block of 4	7.50	
	Pair, gutter between	—	
	pn. Booklet pane of 6	2.75	
	pz. Tagged, Type II (Nov. 2, 1963)	.50	
	Plate block of 4	.50	
	p1. Hi-Brite paper	—	
	Plate block of 4	—	
	v. Horizontal pair, imperforate between	3,600.00	
	FDC (Nov. 19, 1954)		1.75
	FDC Booklet pane		4.00
	FDC tagged		100.00

Note: Bureau precancels for 574 without regard to printing types 95 different.

1954. JAMES MONROE ISSUE in the Liberty Series. *Rotary press, perforated 11x10 1/2.*

575 *James Monroe*

575		MNHVF	UseVF
5¢	**blue** dry print	.25	.20
	Plate block of 4	.65	
	x. Bureau precancel (20 diff.)	5.00	
	Plate block of 4	—	
	Pair, gutter between	—	
	FDC (Dec. 2, 1954)		1.75

1955. THEODORE ROOSEVELT ISSUE in the Liberty Series. *Rotary press, perforated 11x10 1/2.*

576 *Theodore Roosevelt*

576		MNHVF	UseVF
6¢	**rose red** wet print	.25	.20
	Plate block of 4	1.75	
	x. Bureau precancel (6 diff.)	—	
	Plate block of 4	—	
	p. Dry print (March 1957)	.40	.25

Plate block of 4		1.70	
px. Bureau precancel (22 diff.)		4.00	
Plate block of 4		—	
v. Block of 4 imperforate (one known)		23,000.00	
FDC *(Nov. 18, 1955)*			1.75

Note: Bureau precancels for 576 without regard to printing types 23 different.

1956. WOODROW WILSON ISSUE in the Liberty Series. *Rotary press, perforated 11x10 1/2.*

577 *Woodrow Wilson*

577		MNHVF	UseVF
7¢	**carmine red** dry print	.25	.20
	Plate block of 4	1.25	
	x. Bureau precancel (16 diff.)	15.00	
	Plate block of 4	—	
	FDC *(Jan. 10, 1956)*		1.75
	p. Hi-Brite paper	—	
	Plate block of 4	—	

1954. STATUE OF LIBERTY ISSUE in the Liberty Series. *Rotary and flat plate press, perforated 11 (also see 591). The torch extends between "U.S." and "Postage" to the top of the design.*

578, 578A *Statue of Liberty*

578		MNHVF	UseVF
8¢	**deep blue & carmine**	.25	.20
	Plate block of 4, both red & blue numbers	2.00	
	x. Bureau precancel (12 diff.)	6.50	
	Plate block of 4	—	
	Plate block (corner) of 4, blue number only	—	
	Plate block (corner) of 4, red number only	—	
	v. Double impression, carmine	650.00	
	FDC *(April 9, 1954)*		1.75

Flat plate printing, 22.7mm high. See also 591 for Type II.

1954. STATUE OF LIBERTY ISSUE in the Liberty Series. *Rotary press, perforated 11x10 1/2.*

578A		MNHVF	UseVF
8¢	**deep blue and carmine**	.40	.20
	Plate block of 4, both red and blue numbers	3.00	—
	FDC *(April 9, 1954)*		

Rotary press printing, 22.9mm high, slightly taller than No. 578.

1956. THE ALAMO ISSUE in the Liberty Series. *Rotary press, perforated 10 1/2x11.*

579 *The Alamo, called the "Cradle of Texas Liberty," founded in 1718 as Mission de San Antonio de Valero, beseiged in 1836 by Gen. Santa Anna and 1,000 Mexicans; the 184 Texan defenders under Col. William Barrett Travis, including Davy Crockett and James Bowie, fought to the last man. Site is now a historic shrine and museum.*

579		MNHVF	UseVF
9¢	**rose lilac** dry print	.25	.20
	Plate block of 4	1.25	
	a. deep rose lilac	—	
	Plate block of 4	—	
	x. Bureau precancel (15 diff.)	20.00	
	Plate block of 4	—	
	FDC *(June 14, 1956)*		2.00

1956. INDEPENDENCE HALL ISSUE in the Liberty Series. *Rotary press, perforated 10 1/2x11.*

580 *Independence Hall, where the Declaration of Independence was adopted and which for many years housed the Liberty Bell.*

580		MNHVF	UseVF
10¢	**brown purple** dry print	.25	.20
	Plate block of 4	1.00	
	a. deep brown purple	—	
	Plate block of 4	—	
	x. Bureau precancel (16 diff.)	2.00	
	Plate block of 4	—	
	p. Hi-Brite paper	—	
	Plate block of 4	—	
	z. Tagged, Type II *(July 6, 1966)*	2.50	1.50
	Plate block of 4	60.00	
	z1. Tagged, Type IIa	—	
	Plate block of 4	—	
	z2. Tagged, Type III	—	
	Plate block of 4	—	
	FDC *(July 4, 1956)*		2.00
	FDC tagged		30.00

1956. MONTICELLO ISSUE in the Liberty Series. *Rotary press, perforated 10 1/2x11.*

581 *Monticello, Thomas Jefferson's estate in Virginia*

581		MNHVF	UseVF
20¢	**bright blue** dry print	.50	.20
	Plate block of 4	1.75	
	a. deep blue	—	
	Plate block of 4	—	
	x. Bureau precancel (20 diff.)	3.50	
	Plate block of 4	—	
	p. Hi-Brite paper	—	
	Plate block of 4	—	
	FDC *(April 13, 1956)*		2.50

1955. ROBERT E. LEE ISSUE in the Liberty Series. *Rotary press, perforated 11x10 1/2.*

582 *Robert E. Lee*

582		MNHVF	UseVF
30¢	**black** wet print	1.50	.25
	Plate block of 4	6.00	
	x. Bureau precancel (14 diff.)	—	
	Plate block of 4	—	
	p. Dry print *(June 1957)*	1.00	.20
	Plate block of 4	5.50	
	px. Bureau precancel (17 diff.)	30.00	
	Plate block of 4	—	
	FDC *(Sept. 21, 1955)*		2.50

Note: Bureau precancels for 582 without regard to printing types 17 different.

1955. JOHN MARSHALL ISSUE in the Liberty Series. *Rotary press, perforated 11x10 1/2.*

583 *John Marshall*

583		MNHVF	UseVF
40¢	**brown carmine** wet print	2.75	.25
	Plate block of 4	13.00	
	x. Bureau precancel (3 diff.)	—	
	Plate block of 4	—	
	p. Dry print *(April 1958)*	2.00	.20
	Plate block of 4	8.00	
	px. Bureau precancel (10 diff.)	90.00	
	Plate block of 4	—	
	FDC *(Sept. 24, 1955)*		4.00

Note: Bureau precancels for 583 without regard to printing types 10 different.

1955. SUSAN B. ANTHONY ISSUE in the Liberty Series. *Rotary press, perforated 11x10 1/2.*

584 *Susan B. Anthony*

584		MNHVF	UseVF
50¢	**red violet** wet print	2.00	.20
	Plate block of 4	13.00	
	x. Bureau precancel (17 diff.)	—	
	Plate block of 4	—	
	Cracked plate (No. 25231, upper left)	—	
	p. Dry print *(April 1958)*	1.50	.20
	Plate block of 4	7.00	
	px. Bureau precancel (17 diff.)	35.00	
	Plate block of 4	—	
	FDC *(Aug. 25, 1955)*		6.00

Note: Bureau precancels for 584 without regard to printing types 19 different.

1955. PATRICK HENRY ISSUE in the Liberty Series honored the patriot who, in 1775, uttered the famous phrase, "As for me, give me liberty, or give me death." Henry (1736-99) served five one year terms as governor of Virginia and worked hard to secure passage of the Bill of Rights. *Rotary press, perforated 11x10 1/2.*

585 *Patrick Henry*

585		MNHVF	UseVF
$1	**dark lilac** wet print	7.00	.20
	Plate block of 4	25.00	
	x. Bureau precancel Los Angeles	—	
	Plate block of 4	—	
	p. Dry print *(Oct. 1958)*	5.00	.20
	Plate block of 4	22.50	
	px. Bureau precancel (5 diff.)	40.00	
	Plate block of 4	175.00	
	FDC *(Oct. 7, 1955)*		10.00

Note: Bureau precancels for 585 without regard to printing types 5 different.

1956. ALEXANDER HAMILTON ISSUE in the Liberty Series. *Flat plate, perforated 11.*

586 *Alexander Hamilton*

586		MNHVF	UseVF
$5	**black** dry print	70.00	6.50
	Plate block of 4	300.00	
	FDC *(March 19, 1956)*		65.00

1954. GEORGE WASHINGTON ISSUE in the Liberty Series. *Horizontal coil, rotary press, perforated 10 vertically.*

587		MNHVF	UseVF
1¢	**dull green** wet print	.45	.25
	Pair	.75	
	Line pair	1.50	
	x. Bureau precancel (86 diff.)	3.00	
	Pair	6.50	
	Line pair	75.00	
	p. Dry print, large holes *(Aug. 1957)*	.50	.20
	Pair	.35	
	Line pair	.75	
	px. Bureau precancel (30 diff.)	4.00	
	Pair	9.00	
	Line pair	90.00	
	ps. Dry print, small holes, *(Feb. 1960)*	.50	.20
	Pair	.75	
	Line pair	1.00	
	psx. Bureau precancel New Orleans	—	
	Pair	—	
	Line pair	—	
	v. Pair, imperforate	2,250.00	
	FDC *(Oct. 8, 1954)*		1.75

Note: Bureau precancels for 587 without regard to printing types 118 diff.

1954. THOMAS JEFFERSON ISSUE in the Liberty Series. *Horizontal coil, rotary press, perforated 10.*

588		MNHVF	UseVF
2¢	**rose** wet print	.25	.20
	Pair	.35	
	Line pair	.75	
	x. Bureau precancel (109 diff.)	3.50	
	Pair	8.00	
	Line pair	85.00	
	p. Dry print, large holes *(May 1957)*	.25	.20
	Pair	.35	.25
	Line pair	.75	.30
	px. Bureau precancel (32 diff.)	4.00	
	Pair	10.00	
	Line pair	100.00	
	pss. Dry print, small holes, shiny gum *(Aug. 1961)*	.25	.20
	Pair	.35	.25
	Line pair	1.00	.40
	pssx. Bureau precancel (56 diff.)	1.00	
	Pair	2.50	
	Line pair	18.50	
	pssxv. Pair, imperforate	500.00	
	Line pair	—	
	pssz. Tagged, Type II *(May 6, 1968)*	.25	.20
	Pair	.35	.25
	Line pair	.75	.30
	psszv. Pair, imperforate	600.00	
	Line pair, imperforate	1,200.00	
	psmz. Dry print, small holes, matte gum, tagged	.25	.20
	Pair	.70	
	Line pair	2.00	
	psmv. Pair imperforate, dry print, matte gum, untagged	575.00	
	Line pair, imperforate	—	
	FDC *(Oct. 22, 1954)*		1.75
	FDC tagged		20.00

The imperforate pair, untagged, listed above (588psmv) is known with a Bureau precancel of Riverdale, Md.

Note: Bureau precancels for 588 without regard to printing types 191 diff.

1954. STATUE OF LIBERTY ISSUE in the Liberty Series. *Horizontal coil, rotary press, perforated 10.*

589		MNHVF	UseVF
3¢	**purple** wet print, large holes	.25	.20
	Pair	.50	.25
	Line pair	1.00	.45
	a. Wet print, small holes	—	—
	Pair	—	—
	Line pair	300.00	
	x. Bureau precancel (75 diff.)	1.00	
	Pair	2.50	

Line pair		17.00	
p. Dry print, large holes *(May 1957)*		.75	.20
Pair		1.00	
Line pair		1.50	
Gripper cracks		—	
px. Bureau precancel (38 diff.)		—	
Pair		—	
Line pair		—	
ps. Dry print, small holes *(July 31, 1958)*		.30	.20
Pair		.50	.25
Line pair		.60	.45
psx. Bureau precancel (55 diff.)		1.25	
Pair		3.00	
Line pair		20.00	
pv. Pair, imperforate, (19 1/2x22mm)		1,500.00	850.00
Line pair, imperforate		—	
psz. Tagged *Look* Magazine printing Type II *(Dec. 1966)*		6.00	3.00
Pair		12.00	
Line pair		150.00	
psz1. Tagged, Type III philatelic printing *(June 26, 1967)*		2.50	.75
Pair		5.00	
Line pair		25.00	
FDC *(July 20, 1954)*			1.75
FDC tagged			50.00

No. 589psz1, the so-called "Look Coil," was prepared for Look *magazine in coil rolls of 3,000 subjects. All but 99,000 of this issue were affixed to outgoing mail and return addressed envelopes on an automatic labeling machine at Des Moines, Iowa. The earliest known use was Dec. 29, 1966. The common usage was in combination with a 2¢ Jefferson coil (No. 588). The paper on which the stamps were printed is plain, without fluorescent content, and tagging is uniform and brilliant. A special printing was issued, in coils of 500 subjects, to satisfy collector demands (No. 589psz1). The original printing had a sharper, more well-defined design. The reprint has a more intense shade of purple ink. The philatelic examples were on slightly fluorescent paper, the tagging was less intense and on some coils a tagging plate flaw repeats every 24th stamp, both as a "Hot" line and/ or as an untagged line.*

Note: Bureau precancels for 589 without regard to printing types 142 different.

1958. ABRAHAM LINCOLN ISSUE in the Liberty Series. *Horizontal coil, rotary press, perforated 10.*

590

		MNHVF	UseVF
4¢	**bright purple** wet print (Bureau precancel only)	29.00	1.00
	Pair	50.00	2.50
	Line pair	425.00	40.00
	x. Bureau precancel only (17 diff.)	12.50	
	Pair	25.00	
	Line pair	150.00	
	p. Dry print, large holes *(June 1958)*	.75	.20
	Pair	1.00	.25
	Line pair	2.00	.45
	px. Bureau precancel (6 diff.)	—	
	Pair	—	
	Line pair	—	
	ps. Dry print, small holes *(July 31, 1958)*	.75	.20
	Pair	1.00	.25
	Line pair	2.00	.45
	psx. Bureau precancel (65 diff.)	3.00	
	Pair	7.50	
	Line pair	35.00	
	psxv. Pair, imperforate (precanceled - Seattle, Wash.)	—	
	psv. Pair, imperforate	125.00	75.00
	Line pair, imperforate	250.00	
	p1. Hi-Brite paper	—	
	Pair	—	
	Line pair	—	
	FDC *(July 31, 1958)*	.75	.20

Note: Bureau precancels for 590 without regard to printing types 83 different.

1958. STATUE OF LIBERTY ISSUE in the Liberty Series. *Giori press, perforated 11. The torch and flame do not break through the wording*

"U.S. POSTAGE," *the Statue of Liberty is larger than on 578 and the word "LIBERTY" is smaller and lower.*

591 *Statue of Liberty*

578

591

591

		MNHVF	UseVF
8¢	**deep blue & carmine**	.25	.20
	Plate block of 4	1.00	
	x. Bureau precancel (12 diff.)	6.50	
	Plate block of 4	—	
	FDC *(March 22, 1958)*		1.75

1958. JOHN JAY ISSUE in the Liberty Series. *Rotary press, perforated 11x10 1/2.*

592 *John Jay (1745-1829), statesman, first Chief Justice of the Supreme Court (1789-94) and governor of New York (1795-1801). He was a delegate and, in 1778, president of the Continental Congress. Aided Franklin in negotiating peace with Great Britain.*

592

		MNHVF	UseVF
15¢	**brown purple** dry print	.75	.20
	Plate block of 4	2.75	
	x. Bureau precancel (12 diff.)	25.00	
	Plate block of 4	—	
	p1. Hi-Brite paper	—	
	Plate block of 4	—	
	p1z. Tagged, Type II *(July 6, 1966)*	1.25	.50
	Plate block of 4	9.00	
	p1z1. Tagged, Type IIa	—	
	Plate block of 4	—	
	p1z2. Tagged, Type III	—	
	Plate block of 4	—	
	FDC *(Dec. 12, 1958)*		2.50
	FDC tagged		35.00

1958. PAUL REVERE ISSUE in the Liberty Series. *Rotary press, perforated 11x10 1/2.*

593, 614 *Paul Revere (1735-1818), silversmith, copper engraver, and one of three patriots made famous by Longfellow for his ride from Charleston to Lexington, April 18, 1775, to warn of British march. He designed and printed the first issue of continental currency and first official seal for colonies.*

593

		MNHVF	UseVF
25¢	**deep blue green**	1.50	.20
	Plate block of 4	5.00	
	x. Bureau precancel (11 diff.)	40.00	
	Plate block of 4	—	
	p1. Hi-Brite paper	—	
	Plate block of 4	—	
	FDC *(April 18, 1958)*		2.50

1959. BUNKER HILL MONUMENT ISSUE in the Liberty Series. *Rotary press, perforated 11x10 1/2.*

594, 598 *Bunker Hill Monument (220 feet high) erected in 1843 on the site (then called Breed's Hill) of the first major battle of the Revolutionary War (June 17, 1775). Gen. Joseph Warren, commander of U.S. forces at this battle, issued the now-famous order, "Don't shoot until you see the whites of their eyes." Outnumbered four-to-one, the colonists lost the battle but inflicted very heavy casualties on the British troops. This moral victory gave the colonists new inspiration. Background of the stamp shows the Pine Tree flag adopted by the Commonwealth of Massachusetts at the beginning of the Revolutionary War.*

594

		MNHVF	UseVF
2 1/2¢	**slate blue** dry print	.25	.20
	Plate block of 4	.65	
	x. Bureau precancel (123 diff.)	1.25	
	Plate block of 4	6.50	
	FDC *(June 17, 1959)*		1.75

1959. HERMITAGE ISSUE in the Liberty Series. *Rotary press, perforated 10 1/2x11.*

595, 597 *Hermitage, home of Andrew Jackson*

595

		MNHVF	UseVF
4 1/2¢	**blue green** dry print	.25	.20
	Plate block of 4	.75	
	x. Bureau precancel (23 diff.)	2.00	
	Plate block of 4	—	
	FDC *(March 16, 1959)*		1.75

1959. BENJAMIN HARRISON ISSUE in the Liberty Series. *Rotary press, perforated 11x10 1/2.*

596 *Benjamin Harrison (see No. 549)*

596

		MNHVF	UseVF
12¢	**carmine red** dry print	.30	.20
	Plate block of 4	1.50	
	x. Bureau precancel (6 diff.)	35.00	
	Plate block of 4	—	
	FDC *(June 6, 1959)*		2.00
	Plate block of 4	4.00	
	FDC *(May 6, 1968)*, tagged		12.00
	z. Tagged, Type IIa *(May 6, 1968)*	.35	.20
	FDC tagged		30.00

Type IIa tagging: wide roll tagging. All margins are fully tagged.

1959. HERMITAGE COIL ISSUE in the Liberty Series. *Coil, perforated 10 horizontally.*

597

		MNHVF	UseVF
4 1/2¢	**blue green** large holes	2.00	1.25
	Pair	3.00	2.50
	Line pair	15.00	5.00
	x. Bureau precancel (21 diff.)	50.00	
	Pair	100.00	
	Line pair	400.00	
	s. Small holes *(April 1961)*	20.00	2.00
	Pair	30.00	5.00
	Line pair	425.00	60.00
	sx. Bureau precancel (4 diff.)	200.00	
	Pair	500.00	
	Line pair	3,000.00	
	FDC *(May 1, 1959)*		1.75

Note: Bureau precancels for 597 without regard to printing types 23 different.

1959. BUNKER HILL MONUMENT COIL ISSUE in the Liberty Series. *Rotary press, perforated 10 vertically.*

598

		MNHVF	UseVF
2 1/2¢	**slate blue** large holes	.25	.20
	Pair	.50	.40
	Line pair	3.50	1.25
	x. Bureau precancel (93 diff.)	4.00	
	Pair	10.00	
	Line pair	95.00	
	s. Small holes (Bureau precancel) *(Jan. 1961)*	—	—
	Pair	—	
	Line pair	—	
	sx. Bureau precancel only (40 diff.)	150.00	
	Pair	350.00	
	Line pair	3,000.00	
	FDC *(Sept. 9, 1959)*		2.00

Note: Bureau precancels for 598 without regard to printing types 94 different.

1960. PALACE OF THE GOVERNORS in the Liberty Series. *Rotary press, perforated 10 1/2x11.*

599, 600 *Palace of the Governors, Santa Fe, N. Mex., was built in 1610. It is now a historical shrine and memorial to early Spanish life and culture in this country, and reflects the contributions made to the progress and development of the southwestern United States.*

599

		MNHVF	UseVF
1 1/4¢	**turquoise blue**	.25	.20
	Plate block of 4	.50	
	x. Bureau precancel (142 diff.)	.20	
	Plate block of 4	1.00	
	FDC *(June 17, 1960)*		2.00

Note: Bureau precancels for 599 without regard to printing types 105 diff.

1960. PALACE OF THE GOVERNORS COIL ISSUE in the Liberty Series. *Rotary press, perforated 10 horizontally.*

600

		MNHVF	UseVF
1 1/4¢	**turquoise blue** large holes	15.00	.25
	Pair	25.00	5.00
	Line pair	225.00	50.00
	x. Bureau precancel (91 diff.)	3.00	
	Pair	6.50	
	Line pair	40.00	
	s. Small holes *(May 1960)*	.20	.20
	Pair	.25	.25
	Line pair	2.25	1.00
	sx. Bureau precancel (79 diff.)	.50	
	Pair	1.00	
	Line pair	12.00	
	FDC *(June 17, 1960)*		1.75

1961. STATUE OF LIBERTY ISSUE in the Liberty Series. *Giori press, perforated 11.*

601 *Statue of Liberty*

601

		MNHVF	UseVF
11¢	**carmine red & blue**	.30	.20
	Plate block of 4	1.25	
	z. Tagged, Type OP *(Jan. 11, 1967)*	2.25	1.75
	Plate block of 4	35.00	
	FDC *(June 15, 1961)*		2.50
	FDC tagged		30.00
	x. Bureau precancel New York	—	
	Plate block of 4	—	

Type OP tagging: Stamps printed on a Giori press then had tagging overprinted on the sheets by an offset press.

Tagging was not done on the sheet-fed Giori press. Instead, the printed sheets were transferred to an offset press where the taggant was added. This process required the use of a gripper mechanism that left one margin of each sheet untagged. This usually occurred on the left margin and it was trimmed off before the panes where shipped to the post offices. Occasionally, the gripper was used on the right margin. This left the untagged space on the righthand margin and it remained on the finished panes. The tagging itself is heavy and often visible in normal light; under UV it is bright and uniform.

1961. JOHN J. PERSHING ISSUE in the Liberty Series. *Rotary press, perforated 11x10 1/2*

602 *John J. Pershing (1860-1948) commanded the American Expeditionary Forces in Europe during World War I. A leader of vision and courage, Pershing was honored by Congress in 1917 with the title "General of the Armies."*

602		MNHVF	UseVF
8¢	**brown**	.25	.20
	Plate block of 4	1.00	
	x. Bureau precancel (16 diff.)	4.50	
	Plate block of 4	—	
	FDC *(Nov. 17, 1961)*		2.25

There is disagreement concerning whether No. 602 is actually part of the Liberty Series. Although printed within the same period, it does not match the design characteristics of other stamps in the series.

1962. EVERGREEN WREATH AND BURNING CANDLES ISSUE The first Christmas stamp issued by the United States, was intended for use on greeting cards and also to remind the public to shop and mail early. *Giori press, perforated 11.*

603 *Evergreen wreath and burning candles*

603		MNHVF	UseVF
4¢	**green & red**	.25	.20
	Plate block of 4	.75	
	FDC *(Nov. 1, 1962)*		2.00

1962. GEORGE WASHINGTON ISSUE *Rotary press, perforated 11x10 1/2. Issued to meet increased postal rates, effective Jan. 7, 1963.*

604, 605 *George Washington from bust by Houdon*

604		MNHVF	UseVF
5¢	**gray blue**	.25	.20
	Plate block of 4	.45	
	x. Bureau precancel (18 diff.)	3.00	
	Plate block of 4	—	
	Pair, gutter between	—	
	v. Horizonal pair, imperforate between	12.50	
	p1. Hi-Brite paper	—	—
	Plate block of 4	—	—
	z. Tagged, Type I *(Oct. 28, 1963)*	—	.20
	Plate block of 4	—	—
	z1. Tagged, Type II *(April 1964)*	—	—
	Plate block of 4	—	—
	z2. Tagged, Type IIa	—	—
	Plate block of 4	—	—
	z3. Tagged, Type III	—	—
	Plate block of 4	—	—
	n1. Booklet pane of 5 with label slogan 1 ("Your Mailman...") Tagged Type I	8.00	3.00
	FDC pane *(Nov. 23, 1962)*		3.00
	n2. Booklet pane of 5 with label slogan 2 ("...Use Zone Number...")	20.00	3.50
	n2p. Hi-Brite paper	30.00	
	n2z. Booklet pane of 5, tagged, with label slogan 2	80.00	7.50
	FDC pane *(Oct. 28, 1963)*	—	—
	n3. Booklet pane of 5 with label slogan 3 ("...Always Use ZIP Code")	4.00	1.50
	n3p. Hi-Brite paper	7.00	10.00
	n3z. Booklet pane of 5, tagged, with label slogan 3	2.50	1.50
	FDC *(Nov. 23, 1962)*		1.75
	FDC tagged single		25.00
	FDC tagged booklet pane *(Dayton, Ohio)*		100.00
	FDC tagged booklet pane *(Washington, D.C.)*		125.00

1962. GEORGE WASHINGTON COIL ISSUE *rotary press, perforated 10 vertically.*

605		MNHVF	UseVF
5¢	**gray blue**	.25	.20
	Pair	2.00	
	Line pair	4.00	
	pv. Pair, imperforate	375.00	
	Line pair, imperforate	750.00	
	p1. Hi-Brite paper	—	
	Pair	—	
	Line pair	—	
	x. Bureau precancel (14 diff.)	5.00	
	Line pair	75.00	
	z. Tagged, Type I *(Oct. 28, 1963)*	1.25	.30
	Pair	2.50	
	Line pair	5.00	
	z1. Tagged, Type II	—	
	Pair	—	
	Line pair	—	
	FDC *(Dayton, Ohio)* *(Nov. 23, 1962)*		1.75
	FDC tagged *(Washington, D.C.)*		30.00

1963. U.S. FLAG AND WHITE HOUSE ISSUE *Giori press, perforated 11.*

606 *U.S. Flag and White House*

606		MNHVF	UseVF
5¢	**blue & red**	.25	.20
	Plate block of 4	.75	
	Pair, gutter between	—	
	z. Tagged, Type OP *(Aug. 25, 1966)*	.25	.20
	Plate block of 4	2.00	
	zv. Horizontal pair, imperforate	1,250.00	
	FDC *(Jan. 9, 1963)*		1.75
	FDC tagged		25.00

1963. ANDREW JACKSON ISSUE *issued to accommodate the 1¢ increase in First Class rates, effective Jan. 7, 1963. Rotary press, perforated 11x10 1/2.*

607, 608 *Andrew Jackson*

607		MNHVF	UseVF
1¢	**green**	.25	.20
	Plate block of 4	.75	
	x. Bureau precancel (10 diff.)	3.00	
	Plate block of 4	—	
	Pair, gutter between	—	
	p1. Hi-Brite paper	—	
	Plate block of 4	—	
	z. Tagged, Type II *(July 6, 1966)*	.25	.20
	Plate block of 4	.75	
	z1. Tagged, Type IIa	—	—
	Plate block of 4	—	
	z2. Tagged, Type III	—	—
	Plate block of 4	—	
	FDC *(March 22, 1963)*		1.75
	FDC tagged		25.00

1963. ANDREW JACKSON COIL ISSUE *rotary press, perforated 10 vertically.*

608		MNHVF	UseVF
1¢	**green**	.25	.20

Pair	.25		
Line pair	2.00		
x. Bureau precancel (5 diff.)	12.50		
Line pair	—		
z. Tagged, Type II *(July 6, 1966)*	.25	.20	
Pair	.25		
Line pair	.75		
FDC *(May 31, 1963)*		1.75	
FDC tagged		25.00	

1963. CHRISTMAS TREE AND WHITE HOUSE This second
Christmas stamp was based on an on-the-spot painting made by artist
Lily Spandorf of President Kennedy lighting the National Christmas
tree. *Giori press, perforated 11.*

609 *Christmas Tree and White House*

609		MNHVF	UseVF
5¢	**dark blue, indigo & red**	.25	.20
	Plate block of 4	.50	
	Pair, gutter between	—	
	FDC *(Nov. 1, 1963)*		2.00
	z. Tagged, Type OP *(Nov. 2, 1963)*	.65	.50
	Plate block of 4	4.50	
	FDC tagged		60.00

1964. HOLIDAY EVERGREENS ISSUE The third Christmas issue
also was a U.S. postal first, featuring four different stamp designs in a
regular-size pane of 100 stamps. *Giori press, perforated 11 (carmine,
green and black).*

610 *Holly*

611 *Mistletoe*

612 *Poinsettia*

613 *Conifer sprig*

610		MNHVF	UseVF
5¢	**Holly**	.25	.20
611		**MNHVF**	**UseVF**
5¢	**Mistletoe**	.25	.20
612		**MNHVF**	**UseVF**
5¢	**Poinsettia**	.25	.20
613		**MNHVF**	**UseVF**
5¢	**Conifer sprig**	.25	.20
	y. Se-tenant block of 4	1.00	1.00
	Plate block of 4	1.25	
	FDC *(Nov. 9, 1964)* any single		2.50
	FDC, block		4.00
	z. Tagged, Type OP (any single) *(Nov. 10, 1964)*	1.75	.50
	zy. Se-tenant block of 4	3.50	
	Plate block of 4	6.00	
	FDC tagged any single *(Dayton, Ohio)*		20.00
	FDC tagged block *(Washington, D.C.)*		60.00

1965. PAUL REVERE COIL ISSUE in the Liberty Series. *Rotary
press, perforated 10 vertically.*

614		MNHVF	UseVF
25¢	**deep blue green** small holes	.45	.25
	Pair	1.00	
	Line pair	2.25	
	v. Pair, imperforate	45.00	
	Line pair, imperforate	90.00	

zss. Tagged, shiny gum *(April 3, 1973)*	.45	.25	
Pair	1.25		
Line pair	3.00		
zsm. Tagged, matte gum *(1980)*	.50	.25	
Pair	1.50		
Line pair	3.50		
FDC *(Feb. 25, 1965)*		2.50	
FDC tagged		25.00	

1965. ANGEL GABRIEL ISSUE the design is based on a watercolor
by Lucille Gloria Chabot. *Giori press printing, perforated 11.*

615 *Angel Gabriel blowing his horn*

615		MNHVF	UseVF
5¢	**red, green & yellow**	.25	.20
	Plate block of 4	.55	
	Pair, gutter between	—	
	FDC *(Nov. 2, 1965)*		1.75
	z. Tagged, Type OP *(Nov. 15, 1965)*	.75	.20
	Plate block of 4	5.50	
	FDC tagged		50.00

1965-78. Prominent Americans Series The series
included a few presidents but generally honored men and women who
had gained prominence in many walks of life. There was no unifying
design theme in the series.

1968. THOMAS JEFFERSON ISSUE in the Prominent Americans
Series, from a portrait by Rembrandt Peale. *Perforated 11x10 1/2.*

616, 634, B127, B129, B130, B132, B134 *Thomas
Jefferson*

616		MNHVF	UseVF
1¢	**green** tagged Type II	.25	.20
	Plate block of 4	.25	
	z. Tagged, Type III	.25	.20
	Plate block of 4	.25	
	FDC *(Jan. 12, 1968)*		2.00
	n. Booklet pane of 8	1.00	.25
	FDC *(Jan. 12, 1968)*		2.00
	nm. Booklet pane of 8, matte gum	90.00	1.25
	FDC *(March 1, 1971)*		90.00
	n1. Booklet pane of 4	1.00	
	FDC *(May 10, 1971)*		15.00
	zo. Tagging omitted (error)		
	Plate block of 4	—	
	Plate block of 4, half untagged	—	
	zx. Untagged & Bureau precancel (19 diff.)	3.00	.20
	Plate block of 4	—	

1967. ALBERT GALLATIN ISSUE in the Prominent Americans
Series. As treasury secretary under Jefferson, Gallatin (1761-1849)
reshaped U.S. financial policy. He was a member of Congress,
1795-1801. *Rotary press, perforated 11x10 1/2.*

617 *Albert Gallatin, statesman*

617		MNHVF	UseVF
1 1/4¢	**light green**	.25	.20
	Plate block of 4	7.50	
	x. Bureau precancel (14 diff.)	5.50	
	Plate block of 4	—	
	FDC *(Jan. 30, 1967)*		1.75

1966. FRANK LLOYD WRIGHT ISSUE in the Prominent Americans Series. Wright (1869-1959) developed a "prairie" style of architecture with horizontal lines and projecting eaves and introduced open planning in houses (see CM1071 and CM1967). New York City's Guggenheim Museum, also on the stamp, was a notable design success. *Rotary press, perforated 11x10 1/2.*

618, B128, B131, BA24 *Frank Lloyd Wright, architect*

618		MNHVF	UseVF
2¢	**blue** tagged Type II	.25	.20
	Plate block of 4	.50	
	Pair, gutter between	—	
	zo. Tagging omitted (error)	—	
	Plate block of 4	—	
	z1. Tagged, Type IIa	.25	.20
	Plate block of 4	.50	
	z2. Tagged, Type III	.25	.20
	Plate block of 4	.50	
	FDC *(June 8, 1966)*		1.75
	n. Booklet pane of 6, shiny gum	1.00	
	FDC *(May 7, 1971)* booklet pane of 6, shiny gum		15.00
	nm. Booklet pane of 6, dull gum	1.00	
	FDC *(Oct. 31, 1975)* booklet pane of 6, dull gum		100.00
	n1. Booklet pane of 5 plus Slogan 4 label ("Mail Early"), shiny gum	1.25	
	FDC *(Jan. 8, 1968)* booklet pane of 5		4.00
	n2. Booklet pane of 5 plus Slogan 5 label ("Use Zip Code"), shiny gum	1.25	
	FDC *(Jan. 8, 1968)* booklet pane of 5		3.00
	zx. Untagged & Bureau precancel (41 diff.)	1.00	
	Plate block of 4	7.50	
	zxo. Tagged with Bureau precancel (error)	—	

1967. FRANCIS PARKMAN ISSUE in the Prominent Americans Series. After travel and study in the American West, Parkman (1823-93) wrote *The Oregon Trail* (see CM1549) and other works. *Rotary press, perforated 10 1/2x11.*

619, 693 *Francis Parkman, historian*

619		MNHVF	UseVF
3¢	**purple** tagged Type II	.25	.20
	Plate block of 4	.30	
	FDC *(Sept. 16, 1967)*		1.75
	zo. Tagging omitted (error)	—	
	Plate block of 4	—	
	zx. Untagged & Bureau precancel (11 diff.)	1.50	—
	Plate block of 4	—	

1965. ABRAHAM LINCOLN ISSUE in the Prominent Americans Series, from a photograph by Mathew Brady. *Rotary press, perforated 11x10 1/2.*

620, 635 *Abraham Lincoln*

620		MNHVF	UseVF
4¢	**black**	.25	.20
	Plate block of 4	.40	
	x. Bureau precancel (49 diff.)	2.00	
	Plate block of 4	—	

Pair, gutter between		—	
FDC *(Nov. 19, 1965) (New York, N.Y.)*			1.75
z. Tagged, Type II *(Dec. 1, 1965)*		.25	.20
Plate block of 4		.55	
z1. Tagged, Type IIa		.25	—
Plate block of 4		.55	
z2. Tagged, Type III		.25	.20
Plate block of 4		.55	
FDC tagged *(Dayton, Ohio)*			40.00
FDC tagged *(Washington, D.C.)*			45.00

1965. GEORGE WASHINGTON ISSUE in the Prominent Americans Series. The design from a portrait by Rembrandt Peale portrayed the Father of our Country with a creased and pock-marked face and drew strong criticism from the public. The Post Office Department responded by issuing a redesigned stamp (No. 646) with a smoother-appearing face. *Rotary press, perforated 11x10 1/2.*

621, 636 *George Washington*

621		MNHVF	UseVF
5¢	**deep blue**	.25	.20
	Plate block of 4	.60	
	x. Bureau precancel (7 diff.)	—	
	Plate block of 4	—	
	Pair, gutter between	—	
	FDC *(Feb. 22, 1966)*		1.75
	z. Tagged, Type II *(Feb. 23, 1966)*	.25	.20
	Plate block of 4	.60	
	z1. Tagged, Type IIa		
	Plate block of 4	.60	
	z2. Tagged, Type III		
	Plate block of 4	.60	
	FDC tagged *(Dayton, Ohio)*		100.00
	FDC tagged *(Washington, D.C.)*		27.50

1966. FRANKLIN D. ROOSEVELT ISSUE in the Prominent Americans Series. This was the first stamp to honor the beloved 32nd president since his memorial series, CM271-274, the first of which was issued June 27, 1945, just two months after his sudden death. *Rotary press, perforated 10 1/2x11.*

622, B127, B128 *Franklin D. Roosevelt*

622		MNHVF	UseVF
6¢	**black brown**	.25	.20
	Plate block of 4	.65	
	x. Bureau precancel (35 diff.)	1.50	
	Plate block of 4	—	
	Pair, gutter between	150.00	
	FDC *(Jan. 29, 1966)*		1.75
	z. Tagged, Type II	.25	.20
	Plate block of 4	1.00	
	z1. Tagged Type IIa	—	—
	Plate block of 4	—	—
	FDC *(Dec. 29, 1966)*		40.00
	nz. Booklet pane of 8	1.50	
	FDC *(Dec. 28, 1967)* booklet pane of 8		2.50
	n1z. Booklet pane of 5 plus Slogan 4 label ("Mail Early")	1.50	
	FDC *(Jan. 9, 1968)* booklet pane of 5		125.00
	n2z. Booklet pane of 5 plus Slogan 5 label ("Use Zip Code")	1.50	
	FDC *(Jan. 9, 1968)* booklet pane of 5		150.00
	zo. Tagging omitted (error)	—	

1966. ALBERT EINSTEIN ISSUE in the Prominent Americans Series. The German-born theoretical physicist (1879-1955) won the Nobel Prize in 1921 and became the living symbol of a scientist to generations of Americans who could not grasp his work (see CM908). *Rotary press, perforated 11x10 1/2.*

623 *Albert Einstein, physicist*

623		MNHVF	UseVF
8¢	**violet**	.25	.20
	Plate block of 4	1.00	
	x. Bureau precancel (18 diff.)	2.00	
	Plate block of 4	—	
	FDC *(March 14, 1966)*		4.50
	z. Tagged, Type II	.25	.20
	Plate block of 4	1.00	
	z1. Tagged, Type IIa	—	—
	Plate block of 4	—	
	z2. Tagged, Type III	—	—
	Plate block of 4	—	
	FDC tagged *(July 6, 1966)*		40.00

1967. ANDREW JACKSON ISSUE in the Prominent Americans Series, honored the seventh president and hero of the war of 1812. *Rotary press, perforated 11x10 1/2.*

624 *Andrew Jackson*

624		MNHVF	UseVF
10¢	**lavender** tagged Type II or III	.25	.20
	Plate block of 4	1.00	
	FDC *(March 15, 1967)*		1.75
	zo. Tagging omitted (error)	—	
	Plate block of 4	—	
	zx. Untagged & Bureau precancel (12 diff.)	15.00	.20
	Plate block of 4	—	

1968. HENRY FORD ISSUE in the Prominent Americans Series. The industrialist (1863-1947) grasped the concept of mass production to make him the world's largest maker of inexpensive, standardized cars. *Rotary press, perforated 10 1/2x11.*

624A *Henry Ford, auto manufacturer*

624A		MNHVF	UseVF
12¢	**black** tagged Type II	.25	.20
	Plate block of 4	1.20	
	FDC *(July 30, 1968)*		3.00
	zo. Tagging omitted (error)	—	
	Plate block of 4	—	
	zx. Untagged & Bureau precancel (3 diff.)	2.00	.25
	Plate block of 4	—	

1967. JOHN F. KENNEDY ISSUE in the Prominent Americans Series. Kennedy (1917-63), the 35th U.S. president, was the first Catholic and youngest man in the office. He won a Pulitzer Prize in 1956 for *Profiles in Courage*. He was assassinated during a parade in Dallas. *Rotary press, perforated 11x10 1/2.*

625 *John F. Kennedy*

625		MNHVF	UseVF
13¢	**brown** tagged Type II	.25	.20

Plate block of 4		1.35	
z. Tagged, Type III		.25	.20
Plate block of 4		1.35	
FDC *(May 29, 1967)*			2.50
zo. Tagging omitted (error)		—	
zx. Untagged & Bureau precancel (3 diff.)		3.00	
Plate block of 4		—	

1968. OLIVER WENDELL HOLMES ISSUE in the Prominent Americans Series. As associate justice of the Supreme Court, Holmes (1841-1935) became known as the Great Dissenter who respected human rights and property rights. *Rotary press, perforated 11x10 1/2.*

626, 721, 721A, B146 *Oliver Wendell Holmes*

626		MNHVF	UseVF
15¢	**maroon** design Type I, tagged Type III	.25	.20
	Plate block of 4	1.50	
	FDC *(March 8, 1968)*		1.75
	zx. Untagged & Bureau precancel lines only	.75	.30
	Plate block of 4	7.50	
	zx1. Untagged & Bureau precancel cities (8 diff.)	30.00	—
	Plate block of 4	—	

Type I: crosshatching on tie complete and strong; bottom of necktie just touches coat. Type II: crosshatching on tie (lines running upper left to lower right) very faint; necktie does not touch coat. Type III: (only known on booklet pane) overall design smaller and "15¢" closer to head.

626A		MNHVF	UseVF
15¢	**maroon** design Type II, tagged	.50	.20
	Plate block of 4	8.50	
	Pair, gutter between		
	zo. Tagging omitted (error)	—	
	Plate block of 4	—	

626B		MNHVF	UseVF
15¢	**maroon** design Type III perforated 10	.25	.20
	n. Booklet pane of 8, Type III *(June 14, 1978)*	2.50	1.25
	FDC, single from booklet pane		1.75
	FDC, booklet pane		3.50
	v. Pair, imperforate between	—	
	nv. Booklet pane of 8, vertically imperforate between	—	

1967. GEORGE C. MARSHALL ISSUE in the Prominent Americans Series. As Army Chief of Staff, Marshall (1880-1959) played a major role in World War II, was secretary of state in 1947-49, and directed the Marshall Plan for European recovery, for which he was given the Nobel Prize in 1953. *Rotary press, perforated 11x10 1/2.*

627 *George C. Marshall, diplomat and general*

627		MNHVF	UseVF
20¢	**olive brown**	.35	.20
	Plate block of 4	1.75	
	x. Bureau precancel lines only	.65	
	Plate block of 4	5.00	
	x1. Bureau precancel cities (13 diff.)	2.50	
	Plate block of 4	—	
	FDC *(Oct. 24, 1967)*		2.00
	z. Tagged	.40	.20
	Plate block of 4	2.00	
	m. Matte gum	.40	
	FDC tagged, *(April 3, 1973)*		40.00

1967. FREDERICK DOUGLASS ISSUE in the Prominent Americans Series paid tribute to the black abolitionist and statesman (1817-1895), son of a slave, who escaped and established the *North Star* newspaper to fight slavery. *Rotary press, perforated 11x10 1/2.*

 628 *Frederick Douglass, abolitionist and statesman*

628		MNHVF	UseVF
25¢	**maroon**	.50	.20
	Plate block	2.00	
	x. Bureau precancel (9 diff.)	17.50	
	Plate block of 4	—	
	FDC *(Feb. 14, 1967)*		4.50
	a. lilac carmine	20.00	
	Plate block of 4	—	
	z. Tagged	.40	.20
	Plate block of 4	2.00	

FDC tagged *(April 3, 1973)*			45.00
m. Matte gum		.45	

1968. JOHN DEWEY ISSUE in the Prominent Americans Series honored an educator and philosopher (1859-1952), who argued truth was evolutionary and fought authoritarian methods in education. *Rotary press, perforated 10 1/2x11.*

 629 *John Dewey, philosopher and educator*

629		MNHVF	UseVF
30¢	**purple**	.65	.25
	Plate block of 4	2.75	
	x. Bureau precancel (14 diff.)	3.00	
	Plate block of 4	—	
	FDC *(Oct. 21, 1968)*		2.50
	z. Tagged	.45	.25
	Plate block of 4	2.25	
	FDC tagged *(April 3, 1973)*		45.00

DECODING THE CATALOG

As a result of printing technology advances and the ever-changing needs of the stamp-using public, there frequently are changes made to definitive stamps during their lifetimes that create collectible (and sometimes scarce) varieties. Most of these varieties aren't noticed by the average user, and certainly weren't noted by the United States Post Office Department, but to collectors, each is a different stamp.

Such changes, which affect perforation, printing and design, frequently occurred throughout the 19th and early part of the 20th centuries, and have become less common as stamp designs and series are replaced more frequently.

Among the more recent stamps to be affected by design type differences is the 15¢ Oliver Wendell Holmes stamp of the Prominent Americans series. Although none of the varieties is particularly scarce, it is important to know how to decode the catalog and be able to differentiate the three types that collectively make up five different stamps.

Type I

First released March 8, 1968, as a sheet stamp, the Holmes issue had a life span of more than 12 years. When the first-class postage rate rose to 15¢ in 1978, it became the workhorse stamp of the U.S. Postal Service. Booklet and coil versions of the stamp were quickly released June 14, 1978, to meet the increased need of the new rate. Later, without notice, re-engraved versions of both the sheet and coil versions were released. These new types had significant differences from the originals, and it did not take collectors long to find them.

Although several design differences exist among these stamps, it's simplest to focus on the denomination and the necktie areas.

Type I

Type I of the 15¢ Holmes stamp occurs on both sheet and coil versions, Minkus 626 and 721. The top line of the cents sign points to the left of the "E" in "POSTAGE." Also, the tip of Holmes' tie touches the edge of his robe, and there is a consistent cross-hatch pattern throughout the lower part of the tie.

Type II

Like Type I, Type II occurs on both the sheet and coil versions of the stamp, and is quite simple to distinguish. These stamps include Minkus 626A and 721A. On Type II examples, the top line of the cents sign lines up almost squarely with the "E" in "POSTAGE." There is a slight space between the bottom of the tie and the robe, and the crosshatched area on the right side of the tie has an interruption that leaves a small white spot. The engraving on Type II stamps generally looks crisper and cleaner than on Type I.

Type II

Type III

Type III

Type III of the Holmes stamp is not only the most easily spotted, but also occurs only on the perf 10 booklet stamps. In this version, Minkus 626B, the entire design has been redrawn and shortened. The top of the cents sign points to the "G" of "POSTAGE," and the length of the tie has been cut nearly in half.

1968. THOMAS PAINE ISSUE in the Prominent Americans Series honored the American patriot and essayist (1737-1809), who hastened the Declaration of Independence with *Common Sense*. He was prosecuted in England and France for later writings there and alienated many in the United States with his *Letter to Washington* after the war. *Rotary press, perforated 11x10 1/2.*

630 *Thomas Paine, essayist*

630		MNHVF	UseVF
40¢	**dark blue**	.75	.25
	Plate block of 4	3.30	
	x. Bureau precancel (7 diff.)	35.00	
	Plate block of 4	—	
	FDC *(Jan. 29, 1968)*		3.00
	z. Tagged	.75	.25
	Plate block of 4	2.25	
	zm. Matte gum	.75	
	Plate block of 4	3.00	
	FDC tagged *(April 3, 1973)*		45.00

1968. LUCY STONE ISSUE in the Prominent Americans Series honored the woman suffragist and anti-slavery lecturer (1818-93) who achieved notariety by keeping her own name after marriage. *Rotary press, perforated 11x10 1/2.*

631 *Lucy Stone, suffragist and reformer*

631		MNHVF	UseVF
50¢	**maroon**	1.00	.25
	Plate block of 4	4.50	
	x. Bureau precancel (14 diff.)	7.50	
	Plate block of 4	—	
	FDC *(Aug. 13, 1968)*		4.00
	Pair, gutter between	—	
	z. Tagged	1.00	.25
	Plate block of 4	3.00	
	FDC tagged *(April 3, 1973)*		50.00

1967. EUGENE O'NEILL ISSUE in the Prominent Americans Series honored the prolific writer (1888-1953) of plays regarded among the best in American history, including *Mourning Becomes Electra, The Iceman Cometh,* and *Long Day's Journey into Night. Rotary press, perforated 11x10 1/2.*

632, 672 *Eugene O'Neill, playwright*

632		MNHVF	UseVF
$1	**dark purple**	2.25	.30
	blackish violet	—	—
	Plate block of 4	10.00	
	x. Bureau precancel (8 diff.)	35.00	
	Plate block of 4	—	
	FDC *(Oct. 16, 1967)*		7.50
	z. Tagged	1.75	.50
	Plate block of 4	7.00	
	FDC tagged *(April 3, 1973)*		65.00

1966. JOHN BASSETT MOORE ISSUE in the Prominent Americans Series. Moore (1860-1947) was an authority on international law and assistant secretary of state in 1898. High values of this series were tagged for use with automated equipment for postmarking large envelopes. *Rotary press, perforated 11x10 1/2.*

633 *John Bassett Moore, jurist*

633		MNHVF	UseVF
$5	**dark gray**	10.00	3.00
	Plate block of 4	40.00	
	FDC *(Dec. 3, 1966)*		40.00
	z. Tagged	8.00	3.00
	Plate block of 4	30.00	
	FDC tagged *(April 3, 1973)*		125.00

1968. THOMAS JEFFERSON COIL ISSUE in the Prominent Americans Series. *Rotary press, perforated 10 vertically.*

634		MNHVF	UseVF
1¢	**green** tagged	.25	.20
	Pair	.25	
	Line pair	.25	
	FDC *(June 12, 1968)*		1.75
	v. Pair, imperforate	30.00	
	Line pair, imperforate	60.00	
	zx. Untagged & Bureau precancel (5 diff.)	2.50	
	Pair	.25	
	Line pair	50.00	

1966. ABRAHAM LINCOLN COIL ISSUE in the Prominent Americans Series. *Rotary press, perforated 10 vertically.*

635		MNHVF	UseVF
4¢	**black** tagged Type II	.25	.20
	Pair	.25	
	Line pair	.75	
	FDC *(May 29, 1966)*		1.75
	v. Pair, imperforate	850.00	
	Line pair, imperforate	1,500.00	
	v1. Pair, imperforate between	—	
	zo. Tagging omitted (error)	—	
	Pair	—	
	Line pair	—	
	zx. Untagged & Bureau precancel (35 diff.)	4.00	
	Pair	10.00	
	Line pair	85.00	

1966. GEORGE WASHINGTON COIL ISSUE in the Prominent Americans Series. *Rotary press, perforated 10 vertically.*

636		MNHVF	UseVF
5¢	**deep blue** tagged Type II	.25	.20
	Pair	.25	
	Line pair	.40	
	FDC *(Sept. 8, 1966)*		1.75
	v. Pair, imperforate	200.00	
	Line pair, imperforate	350.00	
	zo. Tagging omitted (error)	—	
	Pair	—	
	Line pair	—	
	zx. Untagged & Bureau precancel (45 diff.)	4.00	
	Pair	10.00	
	Line pair	75.00	
	zxv. Pair, imperforate untagged (precanceled - *Mount Pleasant, Iowa*)	350.00	
	Line pair, imperforate untagged (precanceled)	1,000.00	
	zxv1. Pair, imperforate (precanceled - *Chicago, Ill.*)	1,500.00	
	m. Matte gum	.25	
	Pair	1.25	
	Line pair	6.00	

1968. FRANKLIN D. ROOSEVELT COIL ISSUE in the Prominent Americans Series. *Rotary press, perforated 10 vertically.*

637, 638 *Franklin D. Roosevelt*

637		MNHVF	UseVF
6¢	**black brown** tagged	.25	.20

		MNHVF	UseVF
Pair		.20	
Line pair		.55	
FDC (Feb. 28, 1968)			1.75
v. Pair, imperforate		2,250.00	
Line pair, imperforate		—	
zo. Tagging omitted		—	
Pair		—	
Line pair		—	
zx. Untagged & Bureau precancel (30 diff.)		8.00	
Pair		17.50	
Line pair		175.00	

1967. FRANKLIN D. ROOSEVELT COIL ISSUE in the Prominent Americans Series. *Rotary press, perforated 10 horizontally.*

638

		MNHVF	UseVF
6¢	**black brown** tagged	.25	.20
	Pair	.25	
	Line pair	1.25	
	FDC (Dec. 28, 1967)		1.75
	v. Pair, imperforate	70.00	
	Line pair, imperforate	125.00	
	zo. Tagging omitted (error)	—	
	Pair	—	
	Line pair	—	

Nos. 639-643 are not assigned.

1966. TRADITIONAL CHRISTMAS ISSUE featured a design showing a portion of Hans Memling's 15th century painting *Madonna and Child with Angels. Giori press printing and offset, perforated 11.*

644 *Madonna and Child*

644

		MNHVF	UseVF
5¢	**multicolored**	.25	.20
	Plate block of 4	.75	
	FDC (Nov. 1, 1966)		1.75
	z. Tagged, Type OP	.30	.20
	Plate block of 4	1.75	
	FDC tagged (Nov. 2, 1966 - Dayton, Ohio & Washington, D.C.)		50.00

1967. TRADITIONAL CHRISTMAS ISSUE design was the same as the 1966 issue, but printed in much larger size. *Giori press printing and offset, perforated 11.*

645 *Madonna and Child*

645

		MNHVF	UseVF
5¢	**multicolored**	.25	.20
	Plate block of 4	.65	
	FDC (Nov. 6, 1967)		2.00
	zo. Tagging omitted (error)	—	
	Plate block of 4	—	

1967. GEORGE WASHINGTON ISSUE in the Prominent Americans Series was a redesigned version of the original stamp (No. 621) with a so-called "clean shaven" portrait. *Giori press printing and offset, perforated 11.*

646, 747A *Redesigned George Washington*

621 *Original (1965)*

646

		MNHVF	UseVF
5¢	**deep blue** tagged, shiny gum	.25	.20
	Plate block of 4	.75	
	FDC (Nov. 17, 1967)		1.75
	zo. Tagging omitted shiny gum (error)	—	
	Plate block of 4	—	
	m. Matte gum	.25	.20
	Plate block of 4	1.50	
	mzo. Tagging omitted, matte gum (error)	—	
	Plate block of 4	—	
	zx. Untagged & Bureau precancel (29 diff.)	4.50	.20
	Plate block of 4	—	

1968. FLAG OVER WHITE HOUSE ISSUE continued the "Flag Over..." theme begun with the 5¢ stamp, No. 606. *Giori press printing, perforated 11, overall tagging.*

647, 650, 654 *Flag Over White House*

647

		MNHVF	UseVF
6¢	**dark blue, green & red** tagged Type OP	.25	.20
	Plate block of 4	.50	
	FDC (Jan. 24, 1968)	—	1.75
	v. Vertical pair, imperforate between	500.00	
	v1. Vertical pair, imperforate horizontally	500.00	
	zo. Tagging omitted (error)	—	
	Plate block of 4	—	
	FDC		200.00

1968. SERVICEMAN'S AIRLIFT ISSUE was intended for airlift of parcels to service members overseas in Alaska, Hawaii and Puerto Rico. The design was a late 19th century woodcarving of a flying eagle. *Giori press printing and offset, perforated 11.*

648 *Flying Eagle*

648

		MNHVF	UseVF
$1	**multicolored**	3.00	2.00
	Plate block of 4	12.75	
	Pair, gutter between	—	
	FDC (April 4, 1968)		7.50

1968. TRADITIONAL CHRISTMAS ISSUE featured a design showing a portion of *The Annunciation* by the 15th century Flemish artist Jan van Eyck. This was the first stamp printed on the multicolor *Huck press. Intaglio, perforated 11.*

649 *Angel Gabriel*

649

		MNHVF	UseVF
6¢	**multicolored** tagged Type B	.25	.20
	Plate block of 10	2.00	
	v. light yellow omitted	55.00	
	FDC (Nov. 1, 1968)		2.00
	v1. Pair, imperforate	250.00	
	zx. Untagged (Nov. 2, 1968)	.30	.20
	Plate block of 10	3.00	
	zxv. Pair, imperforate	300.00	

Type B tagging: Billet or bar-like shapes designed to register within the limits of a single stamp. Untagged areas surround the design and were intended to register with the perforations.

1969. FLAG OVER WHITE HOUSE COIL STAMP ISSUE
was the first multicolored postage stamp produced in coil form. Same design as No. 647. *Coil, Huck press, intaglio, perforated 10 vertically, block tagged.*

650

		MNHVF	UseVF
6¢	**dark blue, green & red** tagged	.25	.20
	Pair	.50	.30
	FDC *(May 30, 1969)*		1.75
	v. Pair, imperforate	550.00	
	zo. Tagging omitted (error)	5.00	

1969. CONTEMPORARY CHRISTMAS ISSUE
featured a 19th century painting, *Winter Sunday in Norway, Maine*, by an unknown artist from the collection of the New York State Historical Association, Cooperstown, N.Y. *Intaglio, perforated 11x10 1/2.*

651 *Winter Sunday in Norway, Maine*

651

		MNHVF	UseVF
6¢	**multicolored** tagged	.25	.20
	Plate block of 10	1.95	
	FDC *(Nov. 3, 1969)*		2.00
	Experimental precancel	.35	.25
	FDC all 4 cities singles		2.75
	Plate block of 10	85.00	
	v. light green omitted	25.00	1.75
	v1. light green, red, and yellow omitted	950.00	
	v2. yellow omitted	2,500.00	
	v3. yellow and red omitted	2,850.00	
	v4. Pair, imperforate	1,100.00	
	zo. Tagging omitted (error)	4.00	
	Plate strip of 10	—	

Experimental precanceled stamps were sold for use by the public, imprinted, "ATLANTA, GA," "BALTIMORE, MD," "MEMPHIS, TN," and "NEW HAVEN, CT."

1970. DWIGHT D. EISENHOWER ISSUE
in the Prominent Americans Series bore the portrait of the 34th president of the United States (1890-1969). *Rotary press, perforated 11x10 1/2.*

652, 653, B129, B130, B131, B132 *Dwight D. Eisenhower*

652

		MNHVF	UseVF
6¢	**blue** tagged Type II, shiny gum	.25	.20
	Plate block of 4	1.00	
	FDC *(Aug. 6, 1970)*		1.75
	n. Booklet pane of 8	1.50	
	FDC booklet pane of 8		3.00
	n1. Booklet pane of 5 plus Slogan 4 label ("Mail Early")	1.50	
	FDC booklet pane of 5		75.00
	n2. Booklet pane of 5 plus Slogan 5 label ("Use Zip Code")	1.50	
	FDC booklet pane of 5		25.00
	m. Experimental dull-finish gum	.25	
	Plate block of 4	1.00	
	nm. Booklet pane of 8, dull-finish gum	2.00	
	FDC booklet pane of 8, dull-finish gum		—
	zo. Tagging omitted (error)	—	
	zx. Untagged & Bureau precancel (6 diff.)	5.00	
	Plate block of 4	—	

1970. DWIGHT D. EISENHOWER COIL ISSUE
in the Prominent Americans Series. *Rotary press, perforated 10 vertically.*

653

		MNHVF	UseVF
6¢	**blue** tagged, shiny gum	.25	.20
	Pair	.25	
	Line pair	.50	
	FDC *(Aug. 6, 1970)*		
	m. Matte gum	.25	.20
	Pair	.60	
	Line pair	1.50	
	v. Pair, imperforate	1,500.00	
	Line pair, imperforate	—	
	zo. Tagging omitted (error)	8.50	
	zx. Untagged & Bureau Precancel (4 diff.)	7.00	.20
	Line pair	150.00	

1970. FLAG OVER WHITE HOUSE ISSUE
Same design as No. 647 *(Giori press)* and No. 650 *(Huck press)*. Huck press printings are 0.05 inches smaller than Giori printings. *Huck press, perforated 11x10 1/2.*

654

		MNHVF	UseVF
6¢	**dark blue, green & red** tagged Type B	.25	.20
	Margin block of 20	3.25	
	FDC *(Aug. 7, 1970)*		1.75
	v. Horizontal pair, imperforate between	175.00	
	zo. Tagging omitted (error)	3.00	
	Margin block of 20	—	

1970. CONTEMPORARY CHRISTMAS ISSUE
consisted of four different designs of toys, *printed se-tenant, gravure at Guilford Gravure, Inc., perforated 11x10 1/2.*

655 *Antique toy locomotive*

656 *Toy wheeled horse*

657 *Mechanical tricycle toy*

658 *Doll carriage toy*

655

		MNHVF	UseVF
6¢	**multicolored** tagged	.25	.20

656

		MNHVF	UseVF
6¢	**multicolored** tagged	.25	.20
	v1. Pair, imperforate (No. 656, 658)	—	

657

		MNHVF	UseVF
6¢	**multicolored** tagged	.25	.20

658

		MNHVF	UseVF
6¢	**multicolored** tagged	.25	.20
	FDC *(Nov. 5, 1970)* (any single)		2.50
	FDC se-tenant block		6.00
	y. Se-tenant block of 4	1.50	2.50
	Plate block of 8	3.50	
	v. black omitted, any single	2,500.00	
	black omitted, block of 4	—	
	x. Precanceled, any single	.75	.20
	FDC of precanceled single		15.00
	xy. Se-tenant block of 4, precanceled	1.50	
	FDC precanceled block of 4		20.00

1970. TRADITIONAL CHRISTMAS ISSUE
Gravure at Guilford Gravure, Inc., perforated 10 1/2x11.

659 The Nativity *by Lorenzo Lotto*

659

		MNHVF	UseVF
6¢	**multicolored** tagged design Type I	.25	.20
	Plate block of 8	3.50	
	FDC *(Nov. 5, 1970)*		1.75
	v. black omitted	575.00	.20
	x. Precanceled	.25	.20

	Plate block of 8	3.50	
xv.	Precanceled, blue omitted	1,200.00	
a.	Type II	.25	.20
	Plate block of 8	3.50	
ax.	Type II, precanceled	.25	.20
	Plate block of 8	3.50	
	FDC, Type II		3.00

Type I has a slightly blurry impression and no gum breaker ridges. Type II has a shiny surfaced paper, sharper impression, and both horizontal and vertical gum breaker ridges. Type I precancel is gray black; Type II precancel is intense black.

1971. ERNIE PYLE ISSUE in the Prominent Americans Series honored the World War II correspondent and newsman who died by enemy gunfire on April 18, 1945. He won the Pulitzer Prize in 1943. *Cottrell press printing, perforated 11x10 1/2.*

 660 *Ernie Pyle*

660		MNHVF	UseVF
16¢	**brown** tagged	.30	.20
	Plate block of 4	1.30	
	FDC *(May 7, 1971)*		2.50
zo.	Tagging omitted (error)	—	
	Plate block of 4	—	
zx.	Untagged & Bureau precancel (4 diff.)	15.00	.40
	Plate block of 4	—	

1971. FLAG OVER WHITE HOUSE ISSUE was similar to No. 647, but with the new first-class denomination. *Intaglio, Huck press, perforated 11x10 1/2.*

 661, 662 *Flag Over White House*

661		MNHVF	UseVF
8¢	**dark blue, red & slate green** tagged Type B	.25	.20
	Margin block of 20	3.75	
	FDC *(May 10, 1971)*		1.75
v.	green omitted	500.00	
v1.	Horizontal pair, imperforate between	55.00	
v2.	Vertical pair, imperforate	55.00	
zo.	Tagging omitted (error)	3.00	

1971. FLAG OVER WHITE HOUSE COIL ISSUE Huck press, perforated 10 vertically.

662		MNHVF	UseVF
8¢	**dark blue, red & slate green** tagged Type B	.20	.20
	Pair	1.75	
	FDC *(May 10, 1971)*		1.75
v.	Pair, imperforate	50.00	
zo.	Tagging omitted (error)	—	
	Pair	—	

1971. DWIGHT D. EISENHOWER ISSUE in the Prominent Americans Series used the same basic design as Nos. 652 and 653, but with an 8¢ denomination, new colors; and no dot is between "Eisenhower" and "USA" on No. 663. *Giori press printing, perforated 11.*

 663 *Dwight D. Eisenhower*

663		MNHVF	UseVF
8¢	**black, blue gray & red** tagged Type OP	.25	.20
	Plate block of 4	.75	
x.	Bureau precancel (24 diff.)	2.00	
	Plate block of 4	—	
	Pair, gutter between	350.00	
p.	Hi-Brite paper	—	
	Plate block of 4	—	
zo.	Tagging omitted (error)	3.00	
	Plate block of 4	—	
	FDC *(May 10, 1971)*		1.75

1971. DWIGHT D. EISENHOWER BOOKLET ISSUE in the Prominent Americans Series had a dot between "Eisenhower" and "USA." *Intaglio, rotary press, perforated 11x10 1/2.*

 663A, B133, B134, B135 *Dwight D. Eisenhower*

663A		MNHVF	UseVF
8¢	**reddish brown,** tagged, in booklet form only	.25	.20
	FDC single *(May 10, 1971)*		2.00
n.	Booklet pane of 8, shiny gum	2.00	
	FDC *(May 10, 1971)* booklet pane of 8		2.50
n1.	Booklet pane of 7 plus Slogan 4 label ("Mail Early"), dull-finish gum	2.00	
	FDC *(Jan. 28, 1972)* booklet pane of 7		2.00
n2.	Booklet pane of 7 plus Slogan 5 label ("Use Zip Code"), dull-finish gum	2.00	
	FDC *(Jan. 28, 1972)* booklet pane of 7		2.00
n3.	Booklet pane of 4 plus two labels (Slogans 5 and 4), dull-finish gum	1.50	
	FDC *(Jan. 28, 1972)* booklet pane of 4		2.00
n4.	Booklet pane of 6, shiny gum	1.00	.75
	FDC *(May 10, 1971)* booklet pane of 6		2.50

All these booklet stamps have 1 or 2 straight edges.

1971. DWIGHT D. EISENHOWER COIL ISSUE in the Prominent Americans Series. *Coil, intaglio, perforated 10 vertically.*

664		MNHVF	UseVF
8¢	**reddish brown** tagged	.25	.20
	Pair	.30	
	Line pair	.60	
v.	Pair, imperforate	45.00	
	Line pair, imperforate	75.00	
v1.	Pair, imperforate between	6,250.00	
zx.	Untagged & Bureau precancel (34 diff.)	4.00	.25
	Line pair	75.00	
	FDC *(May 10, 1971)*		1.75

1971. U.S. POSTAL SERVICE ISSUE marked the transition from the U.S. Post Office Department to the U.S. Postal Service under the direction of Postmaster General Winton M. Blount. It featured the new logo for the agency, and 16.3 million first-day cancels were applied — nearly double the previous record. *Gravure, perforated 11x10 1/2.*

 665 *USPS emblem*

665		MNHVF	UseVF
8¢	**multicolored** tagged	.25	.20
	Plate block of 12	2.00	
	FDC *(July 1, 1971)*		1.75

1971. CONTEMPORARY CHRISTMAS ISSUE Gravure, perforated 10 1/2x11.

666 *A partridge in a pear tree*

666		MNHVF	UseVF
8¢	**multicolored** tagged	.25	.20
	Plate block of 12	3.00	
	FDC *(Nov. 10, 1971)*		2.00
	zo. Tagging omitted (error)	—	

1971. TRADITIONAL CHRISTMAS ISSUE Gravure, perforated 10 1/2x11.

667 Adoration of the Shepherds, *by Giorgione*

667		MNHVF	UseVF
8¢	**multicolored** tagged	.25	.20
	Plate block of 12	3.00	
	FDC *(Nov. 10, 1971)*		2.00
	v. gold omitted	600.00	

1972. FIORELLO H. LAGUARDIA ISSUE in the Prominent Americans Series paid tribute to a politician who served his country as a congressman and as mayor of New York City. *Intaglio, perforated 11x10 1/2.*

668 *Fiorello H. LaGuardia*

668		MNHVF	UseVF
14¢	**dark brown** tagged	.25	.20
	Plate block of 4	1.25	
	FDC *(April 24, 1972)*		1.75
	zx. Untagged & Bureau precancel (3 diff.)	45.00	.25
	Plate block of 4	—	

1972. BENJAMIN FRANKLIN ISSUE in the Prominent Americans Series honored the printer, writer, postmaster general and statesman with a stamp intended primarily to pay postage for educational materials. *Intaglio, perforated 10 1/2x11.*

669 *Benjamin Franklin*

669		MNHVF	UseVF
7¢	**light blue** shiny gum, tagged	.25	.20
	Plate block of 4	.75	
	m. Matte gum	.25	
	Plate block of 4	1.35	
	FDC *(Oct. 20, 1972)*		1.75

		MNHVF	UseVF
	zo. Tagging omitted (error)	—	
	Plate block of 4	—	
	zx. Untagged & Bureau precancel (13 diff.)	2.00	.20
	Plate block of 4	—	

1972. CONTEMPORARY CHRISTMAS ISSUE *Photogravure, perforated 10 1/2x11.*

670 *Santa Claus*

670		MNHVF	UseVF
8¢	**multicolored** tagged	.25	.20
	Plate block of 12	3.00	
	FDC *(Nov. 9, 1972)*		1.75

1972. TRADITIONAL CHRISTMAS ISSUE Gravure, perforated 10 1/2x11.

671 *Angels from painting* Mary, Queen of Heaven, *in the National Gallery of Art*

671		MNHVF	UseVF
8¢	**multicolored** tagged	.25	.20
	Plate block of 12	3.00	
	FDC *(Nov. 9, 1972)*		1.75
	v. black omitted	4,500.00	
	v1. pink omitted	175.00	

1973. EUGENE O'NEILL COIL ISSUE see design for No. 632. This was the first dollar-value stamp issued in tagged form. *Intaglio and perforated 10 vertically.*

672		MNHVF	UseVF
$1	**dark purple** tagged, shiny gum	2.00	.45
	Pair	3.50	.90
	Line pair	5.00	1.40
	FDC *(Jan. 12, 1973)*		4.00
	m. Matte gum	2.00	
	Pair	4.00	
	Line pair	6.00	
	v. Pair, imperforate	2,250.00	
	Line pair, imperforate	4,250.00	

1973. AMADEO P. GIANNINI ISSUE in the Prominent Americans Series honored the American banker who rose from humble origins to originate consumer bank loans and develop what was the world's largest private bank, the Bank of America. *Intaglio and perforated 11x10 1/2.*

673 *Amadeo P. Giannini*

673		MNHVF	UseVF
21¢	**banknote green** tagged	.40	.25
	Plate block of 4	1.60	
	FDC *(June 27, 1973)*		2.25

1973. TRADITIONAL CHRISTMAS ISSUE Gravure, Andreotti press.

674 Madonna and Child *by Raphael*

674		MNHVF	UseVF
8¢	**multicolored** tagged	.25	.20
	Plate block of 12	3.00	
	Pair, gutter between	—	
	FDC *(Nov. 7, 1973)*		1.75

1973. CONTEMPORARY CHRISTMAS ISSUE Gravure, perforated 10 1/2x11.

675 *Christmas Tree needlepoint by Dolli Tingle*

675		MNHVF	UseVF
8¢	**multicolored** tagged	.25	.20
	Plate block of 12	3.00	
	Vertical pair, gutter between	—	
	FDC *(Nov. 7, 1973)*		1.75
	v. Vertical pair, imperforate between	325.00	

1973. CROSSED FLAGS ISSUE was made available in anticipation of higher postal rates. Use of the 13-star flag in the design was in tribute to the American Revolution Bicentennial. *Intaglio, Huck press, perforated 11x10 1/2.*

676, 677 *50-star and 13-star flags*

676		MNHVF	UseVF
10¢	**red & blue** tagged	.25	.20
	Plate block of 20	4.00	
	FDC *(Dec. 8, 1973)*		1.75
	v. blue omitted	175.00	
	v1. Horizontal pair, imperforate between	60.00	
	v2. Horizontal pair, imperforate vertically	—	
	v3. Vertical pair, imperforate horizontally	1,150.00	
	v4. Vertical pair, imperforate	950.00	
	zo. Tagging omitted (error)	6.00	

1973. CROSSED FLAGS COIL ISSUE Intaglio, Huck press, perforated 10 vertically.

677		MNHVF	UseVF
10¢	**red & blue** tagged	.40	.25
	Pair	1.00	
	Line pair	1.50	
	FDC *(Dec. 8, 1973)*		1.75
	v. Pair, imperforate	37.50	
	Line pair, imperforate	10.00	
	zo. Tagging omitted (error)	7.50	
	Pair	20.00	

Note: The lines on this issue, which can occur every 4 stamps, are usually incomplete. Full, complete lines sell for a premium.

1973. JEFFERSON MEMORIAL ISSUE met the new 10¢ postal rates for first-class mail. *Intaglio, rotary press, perforated 11x10 1/2.*

678, 679, B137, B138 *Jefferson Memorial*

678		MNHVF	UseVF
10¢	**blue** tagged, Type II or III	.25	.20
	Plate block of 4	.85	
	FDC *(Dec. 14, 1973)*		1.75
	n. Booklet pane of 5 plus label	1.50	
	FDC *(Dec. 14, 1973)*		2.25
	n1. Booklet pane of 6	5.75	
	FDC *(Aug. 5, 1974)*		5.25
	n2. Booklet pane of 8	1.75	
	FDC *(Dec. 14, 1973)*		2.50
	n2zo. Booklet pane of 8, tagging omitted (error)	—	
	v. Vertical pair, imperforate between	800.00	
	v1. Vertical pair, imperforate horizontally	500.00	
	zo. Tagging omitted (error)	—	
	zx. Untagged & Bureau precancel (10 diff.)	2.00	—
	Plate block of 4	—	

1973. JEFFERSON MEMORIAL COIL ISSUE Rotary press, perforated 10 vertically.

679		MNHVF	UseVF
10¢	**blue** tagged	.25	.20
	Pair	.40	
	Line pair	.75	
	FDC *(Dec. 14, 1973)*		1.75
	v. Pair, imperforate	—	
	Pair, imperforate	40.00	
	Line pair, imperforate	75.00	
	zx. Untagged & Bureau precancel (14 diff.)	3.00	.25
	Line pair	65.00	

1974. ZIP CODE ISSUE Another new 10¢ stamp underlined the importance of moving mail rapidly. *Gravure, perforated 11x10 1/2.*

680 *ZIP moves mail rapidly*

680		MNHVF	UseVF
10¢	**multicolored** tagged with small rectangle in center of stamp	.25	.20
	Plate block of 8	1.75	
	Pair, gutter between	—	
	FDC *(Jan. 4, 1974)*		1.75
	v. yellow omitted	50.00	

1974. ELIZABETH BLACKWELL ISSUE in the Prominent Americans Series honored the first woman medical doctor of modern time. *Intaglio, perforated 11x10 1/2.*

681 *Dr. Elizabeth Blackwell*

681		MNHVF	UseVF
18¢	**purple** tagged	.30	.25
	Plate block of 4	1.25	
	FDC *(Jan. 23, 1974)*		2.00

1974. SWINGING BELL COIL ISSUE paid bulk rate. *Intaglio, perforated 10 vertically.*

682 *Swinging bell*

682
6.3¢

		MNHVF	UseVF
brick red tagged		.25	.20
Pair		.40	
Line pair		.75	
FDC *(Oct. 1, 1974)*			1.75
v. Pair, imperforate		200.00	
Line pair, imperforate		600.00	
zx. Untagged & Bureau precancel (129 diff.)		.25	
Pair		.90	
Line pair		1.00	
zxv. Pair, imperforate (precanceled Washington, D.C.)		60.00	
Line pair, imperforate		150.00	
zxv1. Pair, imperforate (precanceled Columbus, Ohio)		550.00	
zxv2. Pair, imperforate (precanceled Garden City, N.J.)		850.00	

1974. CONTEMPORARY CHRISTMAS ISSUE *Gravure, perforated 11x10 1/2.*

683 The Road - Winter, *from Currier and Ives print*

683
10¢

		MNHVF	UseVF
multicolored tagged		.25	.20
Plate block of 12		2.25	
FDC *(Oct. 23, 1974)*			1.75
v. buff omitted, pane of 50		600.00	

1974. DOVE OF PEACE ISSUE the first self-adhesive stamp, used glue that was very unstable and has caused most, if not all, stamps to discolor. *Gravure, imperforate, straight die cut, self-adhesive with backing.*

684 *Dove of Peace weather vane atop Mount Vernon*

684
10¢

		MNHVF	UseVF
multicolored self-adhesive		.25	.20
Plate block of 20		2.25	
FDC *(Nov. 15, 1974)*			3.00

Two types of rouletting were used on backing paper.

1974. TRADITIONAL CHRISTMAS ISSUE *Gravure, perforated 10 1/2x11.*

685 The Perussis Altarpiece, *15th century French artist unknown, Metropolitan Museum of Art, New York City*

685
10¢

		MNHVF	UseVF
multicolored tagged		.25	.20

Plate block of 10		2.25	
FDC *(Oct. 23, 1974)*			1.75

1975. CONTEMPORARY CHRISTMAS ISSUE featured stamps that for the first time in U.S. postal history were issued without a printed denomination. The stamps were valid for the first-class rate at the time of issue, 10¢. *Gravure, perforated 11 1/4.*

686, 686A, 686B *Louis Prang Christmas Card*

686
(10¢)

		MNHVF	UseVF
multicolored tagged		.30	.20
Plate block of 12		3.75	
FDC *(Oct. 14, 1975)*			1.75
v. Pair, imperforate		120.00	

1975. CONTEMPORARY CHRISTMAS ISSUE Gravure, perforated 11.

686A
(10¢)

		MNHVF	UseVF
multicolored tagged		.30	.20
Plate block of 12		5.00	
FDC *(Oct. 14, 1975)*			1.75

1975. CONTEMPORARY CHRISTMAS ISSUE Gravure, perforated 10 1/2x11.

686B
(10¢)

		MNHVF	UseVF
multicolored tagged		.60	.20
Plate block of 12		15.00	
FDC *(Oct. 14, 1975)*			1.75

1975. TRADITIONAL CHRISTMAS ISSUE Gravure, perforated 11.

687 *Domenico Ghirlandaio* Madonna and Child

687
10¢

		MNHVF	UseVF
multicolored tagged		.30	.20
Plate block of 12		3.75	
Damaged "d" (plate flaw)		5.00	
FDC *(Oct. 14, 1975)*			1.75
v. Pair, imperforate		120.00	

1975-81. Americana Series Consisted mainly of symbols of America's principles and goals. When arranged in "blocks" of four by consecutive denomination, phrases on each stamp form a unifying rounded frame.

1975. CAPITOL DOME ISSUE in the Americana Series showed the dome of the U.S. Capitol, home of the Senate and House of Representatives. *Intaglio, rotary press, perforated 11x10 1/2.*

688, 697, 702, 702A *Capitol Dome*

688
9¢

		MNHVF	UseVF
green on gray paper, tagged		.25	.20
Plate block of 4		.75	

DECODING THE CATALOG

The 9¢ United States Americana series definitive stamp, originally released Nov. 24, 1975, exists in four basic major types. It is one of the easiest of all U.S. stamps to positively determine all major varieties available. Only one of these four types is significantly valued above the rest. The following information will help you to identify each.

Type I

There are two major Type I Capitol stamps. Both are printed on gray paper and feature a design that measures 18 1/2 by 22 1/2 millimeters. The first, Minkus 688, is a sheet version with perforations measuring 11 by 10 1/2. It was the first type of this stamp. The second variety is Minkus 697, which was released March 5, 1976. It is a coil version (straight edges top and bottom) that has vertical perforations measuring 10.

Type II

The two varieties of the Type II Capitol stamp, released simultaneously on March 11, 1977, were printed on white paper and are told apart by their perforation measurements. Both are from booklets (se-tenant with the 13¢ Flag Over Capitol). There was only one 9¢ stamp in each pane, with a straight edge always at left. The design of the Type II stamps is slightly smaller than that of Type I (17 1/2 by 20 1/2 mm). Minkus 702 has perforations that measure 11 by 10 1/2. Minkus 702A measures 10 on all three sides. The perf 10 variety sells for more than $30 mint, many times the price of its more common cousins.

		1.75
FDC *(Nov. 24, 1975)*		
m. Matte gum	1.00	.20
Plate block of 4	5.25	
zo. Tagging omitted (error)	—	
zx. Untagged & Bureau precancel lines only	1.00	.20
Plate block of 4	7.50	
zx1. Untagged & Bureau precancel cities (3 diff.)	10.00	
Plate block of 4	—	—

1975. COLONIAL PRINTING PRESS ISSUE in the Americana Series (see CM199). *Intaglio, perforated 11x10 1/2.*

689 *Early printing press*

689		MNHVF	UseVF
11¢	**orange** on gray paper, tagged	.25	.20
	Plate block of 4	1.00	
	Pair, gutter between	—	
	FDC *(Nov. 13, 1975)*		1.75
	zo. Tagging omitted (error)	3.00	

1975. FLAG OVER INDEPENDENCE HALL ISSUE Huck press, perforated 11x10 1/2, textured gum with breakers.

690, 694, 782 *Flag over Independence Hall*

690		MNHVF	UseVF
13¢	**dark blue & red** large-block tagged	.25	.20
	Plate block of 20	5.50	
	FDC *(Nov. 15, 1975)*		1.75
	v. Horizontal pair, imperforate between	50.00	
	v1. Vertical pair, imperforate	1,000.00	

1975. EAGLE AND SHIELD ISSUE in the Americana Series. *Gravure, perforated 11 1/4.*

691 *Eagle and shield*

691		MNHVF	UseVF
13¢	**multicolored** tagged with eagle-shape untagged area	.25	.20
	Plate block of 12	3.50	
	x. Untagged & Bureau precancel lines only	.90	
	Plate block of 12	12.00	
	x1. Untagged & Bureau precancel cities (4 diff.)	2.00	
	Plate block of 12	—	
	Pair, gutter between	150.00	
	FDC *(Dec. 1, 1975)*		1.75
	v. yellow omitted	200.00	
	v1. Pair, imperforate	50.00	

691A		MNHVF	UseVF
13¢	**multicolored** perforated 11 (L-perforation)	40.00	15.00
	Plate block of 12	400.00	
	EKU *(March 31, 1976)*		—

1975. OLD NORTH CHURCH ISSUE in the Americana Series pictured the church from whose steeple the patriots were signaled of the advance of the British in the Revolutionary War. *Intaglio, perforated 11x10 1/2.*

692 *Old North Church, Boston*

692 24¢		MNHVF	UseVF
	red on blue paper, tagged	.50	.25
	Plate block of 4	2.00	
	FDC *(Nov. 14, 1975)*		1.75
	zo. Tagging omitted (error)	5.00	
	Plate block of 4	20.00	

1975. FRANCIS PARKMAN COIL ISSUE in the Prominent Americans Series (see No. 619). *Coil, intaglio, perforated 10 horizontally.*

693 *Francis Parkman*

693 3¢		MNHVF	UseVF
	purple tagged, shiny gum	.25	.20
	Pair	.30	.20
	Line pair	.35	.20
	FDC *(Nov. 4, 1975)*		1.75
	m. Matte gum	.25	
	Pair	.30	
	Line pair	.50	
	v. Pair, imperforate	27.50	
	Line pair, imperforate	45.00	
	zx. Untagged & Bureau precancel lines only	2.00	.25
	Pair	5.00	.30
	Line pair	20.00	.35
	zx1. Untagged & Bureau precancel cities (7 diff.)	3.50	
	Line pair	60.00	
	zxm. Untagged & Bureau precancel nonprofit	.25	
	Line pair	2.50	
	zxmv. Pair, imperforate	6.50	
	Line pair, imperforate	20.00	

1975. FLAG OVER INDEPENDENCE HALL COIL ISSUE (see 690, 782). *Coil, intaglio, Combination Press, perforated 10 vertically.*

694 *Flag over Independence Hall*

694 13¢		MNHVF	UseVF
	dark blue & red tagged, textured gum	.25	.20
	Pair	.50	
	Line pair	.45	
	FDC *(Nov. 15, 1975)*		1.75
	v. Pair, imperforate	25.00	
	Line pair, imperforate	50.00	
	zo. Tagging omitted (error)	—	
	s. smooth gum	.30	
	Pair	1.30	
	vs. Pair, imperforate, smooth gum	25.00	

1975. LIBERTY BELL ISSUE in the Americana Series pictured the bell in Independence Hall, Philadelphia, rung in July 1776 to proclaim the signing of the Declaration of Independence. It cracked in 1835. *Booklet panes, intaglio, perforated 11x10 1/2, matte gum.*

695, 696, B139, B140, B141 *Liberty Bell*

695 13¢		MNHVF	UseVF
	brown from booklet panes only, tagged	.25	.20
	FDC *(Oct. 31, 1975)*		1.75
	n. Booklet pane of 6	2.00	1.00
	FDC pane *(Oct. 31, 1975)*		2.25
	n1. Booklet pane of 7 plus label	1.75	.50
	FDC pane *(Oct. 31, 1975)*		2.50
	n1zo. Booklet pane of 7 plus label, tagging omitted (error)	—	
	n2. Booklet pane of 8	2.00	.75
	FDC pane *(Oct. 31, 1975)*		2.75
	n2zo. Booklet pane of 8, tagging omitted (error)	—	
	n3. Booklet pane of 5 plus label	1.50	.50
	FDC single *(April 2, 1976)*		1.75
	FDC pane *(April 2, 1976)*		2.25
	v. Vertical pair, imperforate between	525.00	

1975. LIBERTY BELL COIL ISSUE in the Americana Series. *Coil, intaglio, perforated 10 vertically.*

696 13¢		MNHVF	UseVF
	brown shiny gum, tagged	.25	.20
	Pair	.50	
	Line pair	.80	
	FDC *(Nov. 25, 1975)*		1.75
	m. Matte gum	.30	
	Pair	.60	
	Line pair	2.00	
	v. Pair, imperforate	25.00	
	Line pair, imperforate	60.00	
	v1. Pair, imperforate between	1,400.00	
	zo. Tagging omitted (error)		—
	zx. Untagged & Bureau precancel lines only	3.50	.50
	Pair	10.00	1.00
	Line pair	50.00	6.50
	zx1. Untagged & Bureau precancel cities (9 diff.), matte gum	5.00	
	Pair	20.00	—
	Line pair	100.00	
	zxm. Untagged & Bureau precancel lines only	—	
	Line pair	—	
	xzm1. Untagged & Bureau precancel presorted 2mm spacing	1.00	
	Line pair	10.00	
	zxm2. Untagged & Bureau precancel presorted 0.5mm spacing		15.00
	Pair	—	—

1976. CAPITOL DOME COIL ISSUE in the Americana Series (see 688). *Coil, perforated 10 vertically.*

697 *Capitol Dome*

697 9¢		MNHVF	UseVF
	green on gray paper, shiny gum, tagged	.25	.20
	Pair	.40	
	Line pair	1.00	
	FDC *(March 5, 1976)*		1.75
	v. Pair, imperforate	160.00	
	v1. Line pair, imperforate	375.00	
	zx. Untagged & Bureau precancel lines only	.60	.35
	Pair	1.20	
	Line pair	25.00	
	zx1. Untagged & Bureau precancel cities (4 diff.)	5.00	
	Pair	10.00	
	Line pair	90.00	
	zx1v. Pair, imperforate (precanceled - *Pleasantville, N.Y.*)	600.00	
	Line pair	2,000.00	
	zxm. Untagged & Bureau precancel presorted 2mm spacing, matte finish gum	.40	

Pair	.80	
Line pair	10.00	
zxm1. Untagged & Bureau precancel	20.00	
presorted 0.5mm spacing		
Pair	40.00	
Line pair	150.00	

1976. AMERICAN EAGLE ON DRUM COIL ISSUE in the Americana Series was the first of several to show musical instruments. *Coil, perforated 10 vertically.*

698 *American eagle on drum*

698		MNHVF	UseVF
7.9¢	**red** on canary paper, shiny gum, tagged	.25	.20
	Pair	.50	
	Line pair	.75	
	FDC *(April 23, 1976)*		1.75
	m. Matte gum	.35	
	Pair	.50	
	Line pair	1.50	
	v. Pair, imperforate	575.00	
	v1. Line pair, imperforate	—	
	zx. Untagged & Bureau precancel cities (108 diff.)	.25	
	Pair	—	
	Line pair	1.50	
	zxm. Untagged & Bureau precancel car-rt sort, matte finish gum	.20	
	Line pair	1.50	

1976. CONTEMPORARY CHRISTMAS ISSUE was based on Nathaniel Currier's *Winter Pastime* lithograph from 1855. Two presses were used in its production — a gravure press and a new multicolor press. The gravure press has all-over tagging, and the lettering at the base is black; the multicolor press printing (70 percent of the issue) has block tagging and grey-black lettering at the base. *Gravure, perforated 11.*

699, 699A *Winter Pastime*

699		MNHVF	UseVF
13¢	**multicolored** overall tagged	.40	.25
	Plate block of 10	4.00	
	FDC *(Oct. 27, 1976)*		1.75
	v. Pair, imperforate	100.00	

699A		MNHVF	UseVF
13¢	**multicolored** block tagged	.40	.25
	Plate block of 20	7.75	
	FDC *(Oct. 27, 1976)*		2.00
	v. Pair, imperforate	120.00	
	v1. Vertical pair, imperforate between	—	
	v2. red omitted	—	
	v3. yellow omitted	—	
	zo. Tagging omitted (error)	12.50	

1976. TRADITIONAL CHRISTMAS ISSUE The religious theme featured John Singleton Copley's *Nativity* (1776). *Gravure, perforated 11.*

700 *Nativity*

700		MNHVF	UseVF
13¢	**multicolored** tagged	.40	.25

Plate block of 12	4.75		
FDC *(Oct. 27, 1976)*			1.75
v. Pair, imperforate	95.00		

1976. SAXHORNS COIL ISSUE in the Americana Series showed another musical instrument. *Coil, intaglio, perforated 10 vertically.*

701 *Saxhorns*

701		MNHVF	UseVF
7.7¢	**brown** on canary paper, tagged	.25	.20
	Pair	.50	
	Line pair	1.00	
	FDC *(Nov. 20, 1976)*		1.75
	zx. Untagged & Bureau precancel precancel (160 diff.)	.25	.40
	Pair	.50	
	Line pair	1.75	
	zxv. Pair, imperforate (2 diff.)	1,750.00	
	Line pair, imperforate	4,500.00	

1977. CAPITOL DOME BOOKLET ISSUE in the Americana Series consisted of seven 13¢ stamps and one 9¢ stamp in a single vending machine booklet pane on white paper. *Intaglio, produced with two different perforations.*

702, 703; 702A, 703A *Capitol dome and flag over Capitol*

702		MNHVF	UseVF
9¢	**green** tagged, perforated 11x10 1/2	1.00	.20
	FDC *(March 11, 1977)*		10.00

1977. CAPITOL DOME BOOKLET ISSUE in the Americana Series. *Perforated 10.*

702A		MNHVF	UseVF
9¢	**green** tagged	35.00	22.50
	FDC *(March 11, 1977)*		15.00

1977. FLAG OVER CAPITOL BOOKLET ISSUE *Perforated 11x10 1/2.*

703		MNHVF	UseVF
13¢	**red & blue** tagged (B143, B144)	.25	.20
	FDC *(March 11, 1977)*		2.50
	n. Booklet pane of 8 (7 No. 703 and 1 No. 702)	2.75	
	FDC pane		25.00
	y. Se-tenant pair, No. 702, 703	1.00	1.00

1977. FLAG OVER CAPITOL ISSUE in the Americana Series. *Perforated 10.*

703A		MNHVF	UseVF
13¢	**red & blue** tagged	.75	.50

FDC *(March 11, 1977)*		2.00
n. Booklet pane of 8 (7 No. 703A and 1 No. 702A)	40.00	25.00
FDC pane		15.00
y. Se-tenant pair, No. 702A, 703A	35.00	24.00

1977. RURAL MAIL BOX ISSUE Gravure, perforated 11.

704 *Rural mail box*

704		MNHVF	UseVF
13¢	**multicolored** tagged	.40	.20
	Plate block of 10	4.00	
	FDC *(Oct. 21, 1977)*		1.75
	v. Pair, imperforate	300.00	
	zv. Overall tagging (error)	—	
	Vertical pair, gutter between	—	

1977. WASHINGTON KNEELING AT PRAYER ISSUE was based on a painting by J.C. Leyendecker. *Gravure, Combination Press, perforated 11.*

705 *Gen. Washington kneeling at prayer*

705		MNHVF	UseVF
13¢	**multicolored** tagged	.40	.20
	Plate strip of 20	8.00	
	FDC *(Oct. 21, 1977)*		1.75
	v. Pair, imperforate	70.00	
	zv. Overall tagging (error)	—	

Note: The multicolor Combination Press issue (No. 705) has "floating" plate numbers, a set of five numbers sandwiched between two or three blanks, so that on a plate strip of 20 there are five numbers and five blanks, six numbers and four blanks, seven numbers and three blanks or eight numbers and two blanks. There are no ZIP or Mail Early slogans.

Nos. 706-707 are not assigned.

1977. CONTEMPLATION OF JUSTICE ISSUE in the Americana Series. *Intaglio, rotary press, perforated 11x10 1/2.*

708, 709 *Contemplation of Justice*

708		MNHVF	UseVF
10¢	**purple** on gray paper, shiny gum, tagged	.25	.20
	Plate block of 4	.70	
	FDC *(Nov. 17, 1977)*		1.75
	m. Matte gum	.25	
	Plate block of 4	1.00	
	zo. Tagging omitted (error)	—	
	zx. Untagged & Bureau precancel *Chicago*, shiny gum	10.00	—
	Plate block of 4	—	

1977. CONTEMPLATION OF JUSTICE COIL ISSUE in the Americana Series. *Coil, intaglio, perforated 10 vertically.*

709		MNHVF	UseVF
10¢	**purple** on gray paper, tagged	.25	.20
	Pair	.40	
	Line pair	1.00	
	FDC *(Nov. 4, 1977)*		1.75
	v. Pair, imperforate	70.00	

Line pair, imperforate	125.00	
m. Matte gum	.50	
Pair	.75	
Line pair	2.50	
mv. Pair, imperforate	70.00	
Line pair, imperforate	120.00	
zx. Untagged & Bureau precancel cities (2 diff.), shiny gum	25.00	2.00
Pair	50.00	
Line pair	—	
zxm. Untagged & Bureau precancel lines only	.75	
Line pair	20.00	

1977. QUILL PEN AND INKWELL ISSUE in the Americana Series highlighted one of four roots of democracy — the ability to write. *Intaglio, rotary press, perforated 11x10 1/2.*

710, 742 *Quill pen and inkwell*

710		MNHVF	UseVF
1¢	**blue** on green paper, tagged	.25	.20
	Plate block of 4	.25	
	FDC *(Dec. 8, 1977)*		1.75
	m. Matte gum	.25	.20
	Plate block of 4	.25	
	Horizontal pair, gutter between	—	
	zo. Tagging omitted (error)	—	
	zx. Untagged & Bureau precancel (3 diff.)	1.50	
	Plate block of 4	20.00	
	p. White paper, dull finish gum	—	
	Plate block of 4	—	

1977. SYMBOLS OF SPEECH ISSUE in the Americana Series highlighted the freedom to speak out — a root of democracy. *Intaglio, rotary press, perforated 11x10 1/2.*

711, 711A *Symbols of speech*

711		MNHVF	UseVF
2¢	**brown** on green paper, shiny gum, tagged	.25	.20
	Plate block of 4	.50	
	FDC *(Dec. 8, 1977)*		1.75
	m. Matte gum	.25	
	Plate block of 4	2.25	
	zo. Tagging omitted (error)	—	
	zx. Untagged & Bureau precancel (2 diff.)	1.50	
	Plate block of 4	20.00	

1981. SYMBOLS OF SPEECH ISSUE in the Americana Series.

711A		MNHVF	UseVF
2¢	**brown** on cream paper, matte gum, tagged	.25	.20
	Plate block of 4	.30	
	FDC *(Nov. 7, 1981)*		1.00

1977. BALLOT BOX ISSUE in the Americana Series highlighted another root of democracy — the right to vote. *Intaglio, rotary press, perforated 11x10 1/2.*

712 *Ballot box*

712		MNHVF	UseVF
3¢	**olive** on green paper, shiny gum, tagged	.25	.20

Plate block of 4	.30	
Horizontal pair, gutter between	—	
FDC *(Dec. 8, 1977)*		1.75
m. Matte gum	.25	.20
Plate block of 4	.50	
zo. Tagging omitted (error)	—	
zx. Untagged & Bureau precancel lines only	1.00	
Plate block of 4	5.00	
zx1. Untagged & Bureau precancel cities (5 diff.)	25.00	
Plate block of 4	—	

1977. READING AND LEARNING ISSUE in the Americana Series highlighted the importance of reading as a root of democracy. *Intaglio, rotary press, perforated 11x10 1/2.*

713 *Reading and learning*

713		**MNHVF**	**UseVF**
4¢	**maroon** on cream paper, tagged	.25	.20
	Plate block of 4	.50	
	FDC *(Dec. 8, 1977)*		1.75
	m. Matte gum	.25	
	Plate block of 4	1.25	
	zo. Tagging omitted (error)	—	
	zx. Untagged & Bureau precancel lines only	1.25	
	Plate block of 4	6.50	
	zx1. Untagged & Bureau precancel *Chicago*	75.00	
	Plate block of 4	—	

1978. INDIAN HEAD PENNY ISSUE For the first time, a U.S. definitive was specially designed in a smaller size so that 150 stamps could be produced in place of the usual 100 stamp pane. *Intaglio, perforated 11.*

714 *Indian Head penny*

714		**MNHVF**	**UseVF**
13¢	**brown & blue** on tan paper, tagged	.25	.20
	Plate block of 4	1.75	
	Vertical pair, gutter between	—	
	FDC *(Jan. 11, 1978)*		1.75
	v. Horizontal pair, imperforate vertically	275.00	
	zo. Tagging omitted (error)	—	

1978. STATUE OF LIBERTY ISSUE in the Americana Series featured a stark close-up of the head of the famed symbol of America in New York Harbor. *Intaglio, perforated 11x10 1/2.*

715, 716 *Statue of Liberty*

715		**MNHVF**	**UseVF**
16¢	**blue** tagged	.30	.20
	Plate block of 4	1.50	
	FDC *(March 31, 1978)*		1.75

1978. STATUE OF LIBERTY COIL ISSUE in the Americana Series. *Coil, intaglio, perforated 10 vertically.*

716		**MNHVF**	**UseVF**
16¢	**blue** overall tagged	.35	.20
	Pair	.70	
	Line pair	1.50	
	FDC *(March 31, 1978)*		1.75

z. Block tagging	.50	.20
Pair	1.00	.25

716A		**MNHVF**	**UseVF**
16¢	**multicolored** block tagged, B Press (design slightly narrower than 716, no joint line)	—	
	Pair	—	

1978. SANDY HOOK LIGHTHOUSE ISSUE in the Americana Series showed a lighthouse in New Jersey. *Intaglio, rotary press, perforated 11x10 1/2.*

717 *Sandy Hook lighthouse*

717		**MNHVF**	**UseVF**
29¢	**blue** on blue paper, shiny gum, tagged	.50	.65
	Plate block of 4	2.75	
	FDC *(April 14, 1978)*		1.75
	m. Matte gum	2.00	.25
	Plate block of 4	15.25	

1978. "A" STAMP ISSUE Non-Denominated "A" Stamp Issue marked the new First Class postage rate (15 cents) which went into effect May 29. The stamps were printed in 1975 and 1976 and had been stored for use in this contingency. *Gravure, two perforation sizes.*

718-720 *"A" left of stylized eagle*

718		**MNHVF**	**UseVF**
15¢	**orange** perforated 11, tagged	.30	.25
	Plate block of 4	1.50	
	FDC *(May 22, 1978)*		1.75
	v. Pair, imperforate	100.00	
	v1. Vertical pair, imperforate horizontally	750.00	

1978. "A" STAMP ISSUE

718A		**MNHVF**	**UseVF**
15¢	**orange** perforated 11 1/4, tagged	.30	.25
	Plate block of 4	1.50	
	FDC *(May 22, 1978)*		1.75

1978. "A" BOOKLET STAMP ISSUE *Booklet stamps, intaglio, perforated 11x10 1/2.*

719		**MNHVF**	**UseVF**
15¢	**orange** tagged	.25	.20
	FDC *(May 22, 1978)*		1.75
	n. Booklet pane of 8	2.25	.50
	FDC, pane		3.00
	v. Vertical pair, imperforate between	1,750.00	

1978. "A" STAMP COIL ISSUE *Coil, intaglio, perforated 10 vertically.*

720		**MNHVF**	**UseVF**
15¢	**orange** tagged	.25	.15
	Pair	.50	
	Line pair	.75	
	FDC *(May 22, 1978)*		1.75
	v. Pair, imperforate	95.00	
	Line pair, imperforate	195.00	

1978. OLIVER WENDELL HOLMES COIL ISSUE in the Prominent Americans Series used the same design as No. 626 to meet the new postal rate. *Intaglio, coil, perforated 10 vertically.*

721		**MNHVF**	**UseVF**
15¢	**maroon,** shiny gum, Type I, tagged	.25	.20
	Pair	.50	
	Line pair	1.25	
	FDC *(June 14, 1978)*		1.75
	m. Matte gum, Type I	.50	

		MNHVF	UseVF
Pair		1.25	
Line pair		2.00	
zx. Untagged & Bureau precancel		20.00	.30
Chicago			
Pair		50.00	
Line pair		500.00	
v. Pair, imperforate, shiny gum		30.00	
Line pair, imperforate, shiny gum		75.00	
mv. Pair, imperforate, matte gum		50.00	
v1. Pair, imperforate between		225.00	
Line pair, imperforate between		600.00	

1978. OLIVER WENDELL HOLMES ISSUE in the Prominent Americans Series.

721A

		MNHVF	UseVF
15¢	**maroon** Type II matte gum, tagged	.25	.20
	Pair	.50	
	Line pair	2.50	
	mv. Pair, imperforate	90.00	
	Line pair, imperforate	300.00	

For booklet pane issued the same date see No. 626B.

1978. AMERICAN FLAG ISSUE in the Americana Series featured the 15-star Fort McHenry flag, which in 1814 inspired Francis Scott Key to compose *The Star Spangled Banner. Intaglio, Combination Press.*

722, 722A, 723 *American flag*

722

		MNHVF	UseVF
15¢	**red, blue & gray** perforated 11, tagged	.30	.20
	Plate block of 20	7.00	
	FDC *(June 30, 1978)*		1.75
	v. gray omitted	600.00	
	v1. Vertical pair, imperforate	25.00	
	zo. Tagging omitted (error)	3.00	

1978. AMERICAN FLAG BOOKLET ISSUE in the Americana Series.

722A

		MNHVF	UseVF
15¢	**red, blue & gray** booklet stamp, perforated 11x10 1/2, tagged	.35	.20
	FDC *(June 30, 1978)*		1.75
	n. Booklet pane of 8	3.50	2.00
	FDC pane		2.75

1978. AMERICAN FLAG COIL ISSUE in the Americana Series. *Coil, intaglio, perforated 10 vertically.*

723

		MNHVF	UseVF
15¢	**red, blue & gray**	.40	.20
	Pair	1.00	
	FDC *(June 30, 1978)*		1.75
	v. Pair, imperforate	25.00	
	v1. Pair, imperforate between	165.00	
	v2. gray omitted	35.00	
	zo. Tagging omitted (error)	5.00	

1978. AMERICAN ROSES BOOKLET ISSUE Intaglio, perforated 10.

724, B148 *Two roses: Red Masterpiece (1974 Rose of the Year) and Medallion (winner of two high honors)*

724

		MNHVF	UseVF
15¢	**orange, red & green** tagged	.25	.20
	FDC *(July 11, 1978)*		1.75
	n. Booklet pane of 8	2.25	3.00
	FDC, pane		3.75
	nv. Pane of 8, imperforate	—	
	nv1. Pair, imperforate	400.00	
	nzo. Pane of 8, tagging omitted (error)	25.00	

1978. STEINWAY GRAND PIANO COIL ISSUE in the Americana Series of musical instruments. Met the bulk rate. *Intaglio, perforated 10 vertically.*

725 *Steinway grand piano*

725

		MNHVF	UseVF
8.4¢	**blue** on canary paper, shiny gum, tagged	.25	.20
	Pair	.40	
	Line pair	3.75	
	FDC *(July 13, 1978)*		1.75
	zx. Untagged & Bureau precancel cities (144 diff.)	.25	
	Line pair	1.75	
	zxv. Pair, imperforate (precanceled - Newark, N.J.)	20.00	
	Line pair	60.00	
	zxv1. Pair, imperforate (precanceled - Washington, D.C.)	750.00	
	zxv2. Pair, imperforate (precanceled - Brownstown, Ind.)	1,000.00	
	zxv3. Pair, imperforate (precanceled - Oklahoma City, Okla.)	1,500.00	
	zxmv. Pair, imperforate	12.00	
	Line pair, imperforate	25.00	
	zxmv1. Pair, imperforate between	35.00	
	Line pair, imperforate between	100.00	
	zxm. Untagged & Bureau precancel lines only, matte gum, untagged	.20	
	Pair	—	
	Line pair	1.50	

1978. BLOCKHOUSE ISSUE in the Americana Series showed the reconstructed blockhouse at Fort Nisqually, Washington. *Intaglio, perforated 11x10 1/2.*

726 *Blockhouse*

726

		MNHVF	UseVF
28¢	**brown** on blue paper, tagged, shiny gum	.50	.20
	Plate block of 4	2.40	
	FDC *(Aug. 11, 1978)*		1.75
	m. Matte gum	1.25	
	Plate block of 4	10.00	

1978. CONTEMPORARY CHRISTMAS ISSUE Gravure, *perforated 11.*

727 *Child astride a hobby horse, by Dolli Tingle*

727

		MNHVF	UseVF
15¢	**multicolored** tagged	.40	.20
	Plate block of 12	5.50	
	Pair, gutter between	—	
	FDC *(Oct, 18, 1978)*		1.75
	v. Pair, imperforate	95.00	
	v1. Vertical pair, imperforate horizontally	2,250.00	

1978. MADONNA AND CHILD WITH CHERUBIM ISSUE featured a terra cotta sculpture in the National Gallery of Art. *Gravure, perforated 11.*

728 Madonna and Child with Cherubim, *sculpture by Andrea della Robbia*

728		MNHVF	UseVF
15¢	**multicolored** tagged	.40	.20
	Plate block of 12	5.50	
	FDC *(Oct. 18, 1978)*		1.75
	v. Pair, imperforate	90.00	
	v1. Vertical pair, imperforate between	22.50	
	v2. Vertical pair, imperforate horizontally		725.00

1978. KEROSENE TABLE LAMP ISSUE in the Americana Series was the first of four high-value issues that featured early lamps. *Intaglio and offset, perforated 11.*

729 *Kerosene table lamp*

729		MNHVF	UseVF
$2	**multicolored** tagged	3.50	1.00
	Plate block of 4	14.50	
	FDC *(Nov. 16, 1978)*		7.00

1979. RUSH LAMP AND CANDLE HOLDER ISSUE in the Americana Series. *Intaglio and offset, perforated 11.*

730 *Rush lamp and candle holder*

730v *"CIA Invert"*

730		MNHVF	UseVF
$1	**multicolored** tagged	2.00	.25
	Plate block of 4	9.50	
	FDC *(July 2, 1979)*		3.50
	v. brown inverted	15,000.00	
	v1. brown omitted	275.00	
	v2. orange, tan and yellow omitted	350.00	
	zo. Tagging omitted (error)	10.00	
	zx. Untagged & Bureau precancel lines only (2 diff. line widths)	1.75	
	Plate block of 4	7.50	

Note: On March 27, 1986, a mail room employee of the United States Central Intelligence Agency, after buying stamps at a shopping mall postal sub-station in the Washington, D.C., suburb of McLean, Va., for agency use, discovered he had bought 95 copies of the $1 Rush Lamp and Candle Holder stamp — nearly a full pane of 100 — with an inverted design. He and fellow workers had removed 10 more stamps from the pane to prepare for a mailing before they noticed the disjointed printing.

The Americana Series stamp was printed first in offset for the tan background, the yellow candle and flame and the red halo behind it, and then in intaglio for the engraved candle holder and lettering in dark brown. In this case one sheet of 400 stamps was fed into the intaglio press upside-down so that the two elements did not line up correctly — the brown was inverted.

The finder and eight fellow workers each held one copy for themselves, replaced the stamps, and disposed of the remaining error stamps to a dealer. Because of the supersecret nature of the agency's affairs and the fact that the employee used agency money to buy the stamps, controversy erupted over the ownership of the errors. Three employees quit their jobs rather than turn in the stamps they had kept. It has become known as the CIA Invert.

1979. RAILROAD CONDUCTOR'S LANTERN ISSUE in the Americana Series. *Intaglio and offset, perforated 11.*

731 *Railroad conductor's lantern*

731		MNHVF	UseVF
$5	**multicolored** tagged	8.50	2.25
	Plate block of 4	33.00	
	FDC *(Aug. 23, 1979)*		13.50

1979. COUNTRY SCHOOLHOUSE ISSUE in the Americana Series. *Intaglio, perforated 11x10 1/2.*

732 *Country schoolhouse, Morris Township School No. 2, Devils Lake, N.D.*

732		MNHVF	UseVF
30¢	**green** on blue paper, tagged	1.00	.30
	Plate block of 4	2.50	
	FDC *(Aug. 27, 1979)*		1.75
	zo. Tagging omitted (error)	—	
	zx. Untagged & Bureau precancel lines only	1.00	
	Plate block of 4	6.50	

1979. IRON "BETTY" LAMP ISSUE in the Americana Series. *Intaglio and offset, perforated 11.*

733 *Iron "Betty" lamp from the Plymouth Colony*

733		MNHVF	UseVF
50¢	**black, orange & tan** tagged	1.00	.20
	Plate block of 4	3.50	
	FDC *(Sept. 11, 1979)*		2.00
	v. black omitted	300.00	
	v1. Vertical pair, imperforate horizontally	1,750.00	
	zo. Tagging omitted (error)	—	
	zx. Untagged & Bureau precancel lines only (2 diff. line widths)	1.50	
	Plate block of 4	7.00	

1979. SANTA CLAUS CHRISTMAS TREE ORNAMENT ISSUE Gravure, perforated 11.

734 *Santa Claus Christmas tree ornament*

734		MNHVF	UseVF
15¢	**multicolored** tagged	.40	.20
	Plate block of 12	5.50	
	FDC *(Oct. 18, 1979)*		1.75
	v. green & yellow omitted	575.00	
	v1. green, yellow & tan omitted	650.00	

1979. TRADITIONAL CHRISTMAS ISSUE *Black is misaligned on all color-omitted copies. Gravure, perforated 11.*

735 *Madonna and Child from the Gerard David painting* The Rest on the Flight into Egypt. *National Gallery of Art, Washington, D.C.*

735		MNHVF	UseVF
15¢	**multicolored** tagged	.40	.20
	Plate block of 12	5.50	
	FDC *(Oct. 18, 1979)*		1.75
	v. Pair, imperforate	90.00	
	v1. Vertical pair, imperforate between	2,250.00	
	v2. Vertical pair, imperforate horizontally	750.00	

1979. STANDARD SIX-STRING GUITAR COIL ISSUE in the Americana Series met the non-profit mailing rate. *Intaglio, perforated 10 vertically.*

296 Standard six-string guitar

736		MNHVF	UseVF
3.1¢	**brown** on canary paper, tagged	.25	.20
	Pair	.35	
	Line pair	1.50	
	FDC *(Oct. 25, 1979)*		1.75
	v. Pair, imperforate	1,375.00	
	Line pair, imperforate	3,750.00	
	zx. Untagged & Bureau precancel	.20	
	Pair	.50	
	Line pair	2.00	

Bureau precancel: lines only and found on three different paper color shades.

1980. HISTORIC WINDMILLS ISSUE   Intaglio, perforated 11.

737 *Robertso Windmill, Williamsburg, Va.;* 738 *Replica of The Old Windmill, Portsmouth, R.I.;* 739 *Cape Cod Windmill, Eastham, Mass.;* 740 *Dutch Mill at Fabyan Park Forest Preserve near Batavia, Ill.;* 741 *A Southwestern Windmill, Texas* B149

737		MNHVF	UseVF
15¢	**Virginia, brown** on yellow paper, tagged	.30	.20

738		MNHVF	UseVF
15¢	**Rhode Island, brown** on yellow paper, tagged	.30	.20

739		MNHVF	UseVF
15¢	**Massachusetts, brown** on yellow paper, tagged	.30	.20

740		MNHVF	UseVF
15¢	**Illinois, brown** on yellow paper, tagged	.30	.20

741		MNHVF	UseVF
15¢	**Texas, brown** on yellow paper, tagged	.30	.20
	FDC *(Feb. 7, 1980)* any single		2.00
	y. Se-tenant strip of 5	1.50	1.00
	FDC, strip		6.00
	n. Booklet pane of 10 (2 each Nos. 737-41)	3.50	4.50
	FDC, pane		5.00

1980. QUILL PEN AND INKWELL COIL ISSUE in the Americana Series. *Coil, intaglio, perforated 10 vertically.*

742		MNHVF	UseVF
1¢	**blue** on green paper, shiny gum, tagged	.25	.20
	Pair	.25	
	Line pair	.50	
	FDC *(March 6, 1980)*		1.75
	m. Matte gum	.25	
	Pair	.25	
	Line pair	.50	
	mv. Pair, imperforate	175.00	
	Line pair, imperforate	275.00	
	zo. Tagging omitted (error)	—	

1980. DOLLEY MADISON ISSUE honored the wife (1768-1849) of President James Madison, who influenced Washington, D.C., society

and politics with two presidents. The stamp was produced in the mini-stamp format identical in size to the 1978 Indian Head Penny stamp (No. 714). *Intaglio, perforated 11.*

743 *Dolley Madison, pencil sketch from Gilbert Stuart painting*

743		MNHVF	UseVF
15¢	**red brown & sepia** tagged	.40	.20
	Plate block of 4	2.00	
	FDC *(May 20, 1980)*		1.75

1980. WEAVER MANUFACTURED VIOLINS COIL ISSUE in the musical instruments set of the Americana Series met the non-profit organization rate. *Intaglio, perforated 10 vertically.*

744 *Weaver manufactured violins*

744		MNHVF	UseVF
3.5¢	**purple** on yellow paper, tagged	.25	.20
	Pair	.25	
	Line pair	1.00	
	FDC *(June 23, 1980)*		1.75
	v. Pair, imperforate	225.00	
	Line pair, imperforate	400.00	
	zx. Untagged & Bureau precancel lines only	.20	
	Pair	.50	
	Line pair	1.25	
	zxv. Pair, imperforate	—	

1980. CONTEMPORARY CHRISTMAS ISSUE *Gravure, perforated 11.*

745 *Season's Greetings, toys on a window sill*

745		MNHVF	UseVF
15¢	**multicolored** tagged	.50	.20
	Plate block of 20	10.00	
	v. light brown omitted	25.00	
	v1. Pair, imperforate	80.00	
	v2. Vertical pair, imperforate horizontally	—	
	v3. Plate block of 20, imperforate	850.00	
	v4. Horizontal pair, imperforate between	3,400.00	
	zo. Tagging omitted (error)	—	
	FDC *(Oct. 31, 1980)*		1.75

1980. TRADITIONAL CHRISTMAS ISSUE *Gravure, perforated 11.*

746 *Vignette of Madonna and Child from the Epiphany Window, Bethlehem Chapel at Washington Cathedral*

746

		MNHVF	UseVF
15¢	**multicolored** tagged	.50	.20
	Plate block of 12	5.50	
	Pair, gutter between	—	
	FDC *(Oct. 31, 1980)*		1.75
	v. Pair, imperforate	80.00	
	v1. Plate block of 12, imperforate	650.00	

1980-99. Great Americans Series The series featured
Americans from many walks of life who had distinguished themselves.

1980. SEQUOYAH ISSUE the first in the Great Americans Series, honored the unschooled Cherokee Indian scholar (c.1770-1843) who devised a written alphabet for his tribe. *Intaglio, perforated 11x10 1/2.*

747 *Sketch from portrait of Sequoyah by Charles Banks Wilson*

747

		MNHVF	UseVF
19¢	**brown** overall tagged	.30	.20
	Plate block of 4	2.25	
	FDC *(Dec. 27, 1980)*		1.75

1980. WASHINGTON COIL ISSUE in the Prominent Americans Series. (See No. 646.)

747A *"Shaved" Washington coil*

747A

		MNHVF	UseVF
5¢	**deep blue** tagged	.25	.20
	Pair	.30	.20
	Line pair	1.25	—
	FDC *(March 31, 1981)*		25.00
	v. Pair, imperforate	1,000.00	

1981. NON-DENOMINATED "B" STAMP ISSUE marked the change of the First Class domestic postage rate to 18¢ which went into effect March 22, 1981. The design was identical to the "A" stamp except for the background color and the letter. *Gravure, perforated 11x10 1/2.*

748-750, B150 *"B" to left of stylized eagle*

748

		MNHVF	UseVF
18¢	**purple** tagged	.30	.20
	Plate block of 4	1.40	
	Horizontal pair, gutter between	—	
	FDC *(March 15, 1981)*		2.00

1981. NON-DENOMINATED "B" BOOKLET ISSUE *Booklet pane, intaglio, perforated 10.*

749

		MNHVF	UseVF
18¢	**purple** tagged	.30	.20
	FDC *(March 15, 1981)*, single		1.75
	n. Booklet pane of 8	3.50	1.50
	FDC pane		4.00

1981. NON-DENOMINATED "B" COIL ISSUE *Coil, intaglio, perforated 10 vertically.*

750

		MNHVF	UseVF
18¢	**purple** tagged	.40	.20
	Pair	.80	
	Line pair	1.65	
	FDC *(March 15, 1981)*		1.75
	v. Pair, imperforate	120.00	
	Line pair, imperforate	200.00	

1981. FREEDOM OF CONSCIENCE ISSUE in the Americana Series highlighted Freedom of Conscience — an American Right with the torch in the upraised hand of the Statue of Liberty. *Intaglio, rotary press, perforated 11x10 1/2.*

751, 752 *Torch of the Statue of Liberty*

751

		MNHVF	UseVF
12¢	**red brown** on beige paper, tagged	.25	.20
	Plate block of 4	1.15	
	FDC *(April 8, 1981)*		1.75
	zo. Tagging omitted (error)	5.00	

U.S. Postal Service Plate-Numbering Change

In response to collector complaints that its plate-numbering system resulted in many inconvenient and costly blocks of 10, 12 and 20 stamps, the USPS in January 1981 instituted a new plate number arrangement. Under the new system, most sheets were to contain a single plate number consisting of one (for monocolor stamps) to six digits, each digit representing a given printing plate and color. Thus, under this system, most plate blocks returned to blocks of four.

Booklet panes hereafter also contain a plate number in the selvage.

In coils, a plate number was incorporated into some stamps in the roll, at various intervals between stamps, depending on press used.

1981. FREEDOM OF CONSCIENCE COIL ISSUE in the Americana Series. *Coil, intaglio, perforated 10 vertically.*

752

		MNHVF	UseVF
12¢	**red brown** on beige paper, tagged	.25	.20
	Pair	.50	.25
	Line pair	1.50	
	FDC *(April 8, 1981)*		1.75
	v. Pair, imperforate	200.00	
	Line pair, imperforate	400.00	
	zx. Untagged & Bureau precancel presorted	5.00	.25
	Pair	150.00	
	Line pair	500.00	
	zx1. Untagged & Bureau precancel lines only	.75	
	Line pair	20.00	
	azx. Carmine on beige paper, untagged & Bureau precancel presorted only	1.00	.25
	Pair	2.00	
	Line pair	20.00	

1981. AMERICA THE BEAUTIFUL ISSUE featured an American flag above a landscape and a phrase from the song *America the Beautiful*, written by Katherine Lee Bates (1859-1929) of Falmouth, Mass., in 1893, inspired by the view from Pike's Peak in Colorado. *Intaglio, perforated 11.*

753 *"...for amber waves of grain"*

753

		MNHVF	UseVF
18¢	**multicolored** tagged	.30	.20
	Plate block of 20	8.50	
	FDC *(April 24, 1981)*		1.75
	v. Pair, imperforate	100.00	
	v1. Vertical pair, imperforate horizontally	1,000.00	

1981. AMERICA THE BEAUTIFUL COIL ISSUE featured an American flag over the coastline below South Portland Head Lighthouse of Portland, Maine, and a phrase from the song, *America the Beautiful*. It was the first coil stamp with a plate number as part of the design. *Coil, intaglio, perforated 10 vertically. Plate number every 52 stamps.*

754 *"...from sea to shining sea"*

754

		MNHVF	UseVF
18¢	**multicolored** tagged	.30	.20
	Pair	.60	.20
	v. Pair, imperforate	18.00	
	v1. Pair, imperforate between	—	
	zo. Tagging omitted (error)	—	
	FDC *(April 24, 1981)*		1.75

> *Listings and prices for plate number coil strips and singles appear at the end of this definitives section of the Krause-Minkus catalog.*

1981. AMERICA THE BEAUTIFUL COMBINATION BOOKLET

consisting of two 6¢ and six 18¢ stamps. *Intaglio, perforated 11.*

755 *Circle of Stars*

756 *"...for purple mountain majesties"* B151

755

		MNHVF	UseVF
6¢	**blue** tagged	.55	.25
	FDC *(April 24, 1981)*		2.00

756

		MNHVF	UseVF
18¢	**multicolored** tagged	.30	.20
	FDC *(April 24, 1981)*		1.75
	y. Se-tenant pair, No. 755, 756	.90	
	n. Booklet pane of 8 (2 No. 755, 6 No. 756)	3.00	
	nv. Booklet pane, vertically imperforate between	75.00	
	FDC pane		5.00

1981. GEORGE MASON ISSUE

in the Great Americans Series honored an early leader (1725-92) of pre-Revolutionary Virginia patriots, whose draft of a Bill of Rights formed the basis for the first 10 Amendments to the Constitution. *Intaglio, perforated 11x10 1/2.*

757 *George Mason*

757

		MNHVF	UseVF
18¢	**blue** overall tagged	.30	.20
	Plate block of 4	2.50	
	FDC *(May 7, 1981)*		1.75
	zo. Tagging omitted (error)	4.50	

1981. WILDLIFE BOOKLET ISSUE

featured 10 wild animals native to the United States. *Intaglio, perforated 11.*

758 *Bighorn sheep*

759 *Puma*

760 *Harbor seal*

761 *Bison*

762 *Brown bear*

763 *Polar bear*

764 *Elk (Wapiti)*

765 *Moose*

766 *White-tailed deer*

767 *Pronghorn antelope*

B152

758

		MNHVF	UseVF
18¢	**Bighorn sheep, brown,** tagged	.50	.20

759

		MNHVF	UseVF
18¢	**Puma, brown,** tagged	.50	.20

760

		MNHVF	UseVF
18¢	**Harbor seal, brown,** tagged	.50	.20

761

		MNHVF	UseVF
18¢	**Bison, brown,** tagged	.50	.20

762

		MNHVF	UseVF
18¢	**Brown bear, brown,** tagged	.50	.20

763

		MNHVF	UseVF
18¢	**Polar bear, brown,** tagged	.50	.20

764

		MNHVF	UseVF
18¢	**Elk (Wapiti), brown,** tagged	.50	.20

765

		MNHVF	UseVF
18¢	**Moose, brown,** tagged	.50	.20

766

		MNHVF	UseVF
18¢	**White-tailed deer, brown,** tagged	.50	.20

767

		MNHVF	UseVF
18¢	**Pronghorn antelope, brown,** tagged	.50	.20
	FDC, any single *(May 14, 1981)*		1.75
	n. Booklet pane of 10 (Nos. 758-67)	8.50	4.00
	nzo. Booklet pane of 10, untagged pane (3 known)	750.00	
	nv. Booklet pane, vertically imperforate between	1,500.00	
	FDC, pane		6.00

1981-95. Transportation Series

featured a wide spectrum of means of moving people or goods. Some — as the initial 18¢ stamp in the series — were famous in history or literature; others had a touch of whimsy.

1981. SURREY COIL ISSUE

in the Transportation Series showed a vehicle with four wheels and two bench seats. *Coil, intaglio, perforated 10 vertically. Plate number every 24 stamps.*

768 *Surrey with the fringe on top*

Great Americans Series Identifier

Entries are in denomination order. All stamps listed provide basic data: denomination, person honored, and catalog number. Information is entered in the columns for perforation, gum and tagging only when such information better identifies the different varieties of the stamp. The Great American series apparently ended in 1999, but if further varieties are found, this listing will be updated and modified in future editions.

Denomination/Name	Cat. No.	Perf.	Gum	Tagging	Without Tagging
1¢ Dorothea Dix	807	11 1/4 H			
1¢ Dorothea Dix	807A	10 3/4 L		Block (small)	
1¢ Dorothea Dix	807Abz	10 3/4 L		Block (large)	
1¢ Margaret Mitchell	857				Error (857zo)
2¢ Igor Stravinsky	798				Error (798zo)
2¢ Mary Lyon	872				Error (872zo)
2¢ Mary Lyon	872zx				Intentional
3¢ Henry Clay	804				Error (804zo)
3¢ Paul Dudley White, MD	861		Matte		Error (861zo)
3¢ Paul Dudley White, MD	861zxm		Matte		Intentional
3¢ Paul Dudley White, MD	861zxs		Shiny		Intentional
4¢ Carl Schurz	801				Error (801zo)
4¢ Father Flanagan	858				
4¢ Father Flanagan	858zx				Intentional (light gray violet)
4¢ Father Flanagan	858zx1				Intentional (slate violet)
5¢ Pearl Buck	803				
5¢ Hugo L. Black	854				Error (854zo)
5¢ Luis Muñoz Martin	927				Error (927zo)
5¢ Luis Muñoz Martin	927zx				Intentional
6¢ Walter Lippmann	848				
7¢ Abraham Baldwin	819				
8¢ Henry Knox	847				
9¢ Sylvanus Thayer	842				
10¢ Richard Russell	815			Block (small)	
10¢ Richard Russell	815bz			Block (large)	
10¢ Red Cloud	877		Matte	Block (large)	Error (877zo)
10¢ Red Cloud	877pzm		Matte	Phosphored paper	
10¢ Red Cloud	877pzs		Shiny	Phosphored paper	
10¢ Red Cloud	877pzs1		Shiny	Carmine, phosphored paper	
10¢ Red Cloud	877z		Matte	Overall	
11¢ Alden Partridge	823				Error (823zo)
13¢ Crazy Horse	785				Error (785zo)
14¢ Sinclair Lewis	826			Block (small)	
14¢ Sinclair Lewis	826bz			Block (large)	
14¢ Julia Ward Howe	871				
15¢ Buffalo Bill Cody	894			Block (large)	
15¢ Buffalo Bill Cody	894z			Overall	
15¢ Buffalo Bill Cody	894pz			Phosphored paper	Error (894zo)
17¢ Rachel Carson	769				Error (769zo)
17¢ Belva Ann Lockwood	856				Error (856zo)
18¢ George Mason	757				Error (757zo)
19¢ Sequoyah	747				
20¢ Ralph Bunch	784				Error (784zo)
20¢ Thomas H. Gallaudet	802				Error (802zo)
20¢ Harry S. Truman	811	11 L		Block (small)	
20¢ Harry S. Truman	904	11 1/4 H		Block (large)	Error (904zo)*
20¢ Harry S. Truman	904z	11 1/4 H		Overall	Error (904zo)*
20¢ Harry S. Truman	904pz			Phosphored paper	
20¢ Virginia Apgar	1052				
21¢ Chester Carlson	911				Error (911zo)
22¢ John J. Audubon	839	11 L		Block (small)	Error (839zo)
22¢ John J. Audubon	839bz	11 L		Block (large)	Error (83920)
22¢ John J. Audubon	839A	11 1/4 H			
23¢ Mary Cassatt	915			Block (large)	

Denomination/Name	Cat. No.	Perf.	Gum	Tagging	Without Tagging
23¢ Mary Cassatt	915z			Overall	Error (915zo)
23¢ Mary Cassatt	915pzm		Matte	Phosphored paper	
23¢ Mary Cassatt	915pzs		Shiny	Phosphored paper	
25¢ Jack London (sheet)	853	11 H			Error (853zo)
25¢ Jack London (booklet)	888	11 L			Error (888zo)
25¢ Jack London (booklet)	889	10 H			Error (889zo)
28¢ Sitting Bull	919				
29¢ Earl Warren	983				
29¢ Thomas Jefferson	1009				
30¢ Frank C. Laubach	816	11 L		Block (small)	
30¢ Frank C. Laubach	816A	11 1/4 H		Block (large)	
30¢ Frank C. Laubach	816Az	11 1/4 H		Overall	
32¢ Milton S. Hershey	1096				
32¢ Cal Farley	1124				
32¢ Henry R. Luce	1168				
32¢ Lila & DeWitt Wallace	1171				
35¢ Charles R. Drew, MD	770				Error (770zo)
35¢ Dennis Chavez	946				
37¢ Robert Millikan	786				Error (786zo)
39¢ Grenville Clark	825	11 L		Block (small)	
39¢ Grenville Clark	825bz	11 L		Block (large)	
39¢ Grenville Clark	825A	11 1/4 H		Block (large)	
40¢ Lillian M. Gilbreth	813	11 L		Block (small)	
40¢ Lillian M. Gilbreth	813A	11 1/4 H		Block (large)	
40¢ Claire Chennault	932			Overall	
40¢ Claire Chennault	932pzm		Matte	Phosphored paper	
40¢ Claire Chennault	932pzs		Shiny	Phosphored paper	
40¢ Claire Chennault	932pzsg		Low-gloss	Phosphored paper	
45¢ Harvey Cushing, MD	895			Block (large)	Error (895zo)
45¢ Harvey Cushing, MD	895z			Overall	
46¢ Ruth Benedict	1114				
50¢ Chester W. Nimitz	824	11 L	Shiny	Overall	Error (824zo)
50¢ Chester W. Nimitz	824A	11 1/4 H	Matte	Block (large)	Error (824Azo)
50¢ Chester W. Nimitz	824Apz	11 1/4 H	Shiny	Phosphored paper	
50¢ Chester W. Nimitz	824Az1	11 1/4 H	Matte	Overall	
52¢ Hubert H. Humphrey	957		Matte	Phosphored paper	
52¢ Hubert H. Humphrey	957pz		Shiny	Phosphored paper	
55¢ Alice Hamilton, MD	1093				
55¢ Justin S. Morrill	1228				
56¢ John Harvard	860				
65¢ H.H. "Hap" Arnold	916				Error (916zo)
75¢ Wendell Wilkie	981		Matte	Phosphored paper	
75¢ Wendell Wilkie	981pz		Shiny	Phosphored paper	
77¢ Mary Breckinridge	1200				
78¢ Alice Paul	1095				
$1 Bernard Revel	862				
$1 Johns Hopkins	918		Matte	Block (large)	
$1 Johns Hopkins	918z		Matte	Overall	Error (918zo)
$1 Johns Hopkins	918pzm		Matte	Phosphored paper	
$1 Johns Hopkins	918pzs		Shiny	Phosphored paper (Mottled)	
$1 Johns Hopkins	918pzsg		Low-gloss	Phosphored paper (grainy)	
$2 William Jennings Bryan	855				Error (855zo)
$5 Bret Harte	878			Block	Error (878zo)
$5 Bret Harte	878pz			Block (large)	

Symbols: (in Perf. column) H = Harrow (perfect corners); L = L perforator

Footnotes

* Impossible to tell if "tagging omitted" version is from block- or overall-tagging version.

768		MNHVF	UseVF
18¢	**brown** overall tagged	.35	.20
	Pair	.60	
	v. Pair, imperforate	125.00	
	FDC *(May 18, 1981)*		2.00

1981. RACHEL CARSON ISSUE in the Great Americans Series honored the scientist and author (1907-1964) of *Silent Spring.* When published, the book touched off an international controversy over pesticides. From March 22, 1981, to April 2, 1988, 17¢ was the additional 1-ounce rate (12-ounce maximum). *Intaglio, perforated 11x10 1/2.*

769 *Rachel Carson*

769		MNHVF	UseVF
17¢	**green** overall tagged	.30	.20
	Plate block of 4	1.50	
	FDC *(May 28, 1981)*		1.75
	zo. Tagging omitted (error)	—	

1981. CHARLES R. DREW ISSUE in the Great Americans Series honored the scientist and surgeon (1904-1950) who discovered and developed methods to preserve blood plasma in large quantities. He was the first black surgeon selected for membership on the American Board of Surgery. *Intaglio, perforated 11x10 1/2.*

770 *Charles R. Drew, MD*

770		MNHVF	UseVF
35¢	**gray** overall tagged	.50	.25
	Plate block of 4	3.50	
	FDC *(June 3, 1981)*		2.50
	zo. Tagging omitted (error)	—	

Note: Plate blocks from plates 3 & 4 carry a premium.

1981. ELECTRIC AUTO COIL ISSUE in the Transportation Series showed an electrically powered coupe. From March 22, 1981, to April 2, 1988, 17¢ was the additional-ounce rate (12-ounce maximum). *Coil, intaglio, perforated 10 vertically. Plate number every 24 stamps.*

771 *Electric auto, 1917*

771		MNHVF	UseVF
17¢	**blue** overall tagged	.35	.20
	Pair	.60	
	FDC *(June 25, 1981)*		2.00
	v. Pair, imperforate	—	
	zo. Tagging omitted (error)	—	
	zx1. Untagged (Bureau precancel, Type 1: "PRESORTED" 11 1/2mm)	.35	.35
	zx2. Untagged (Bureau precancel, Type II: "PRESORTED" 12 1/2mm)	.75	.60
	zx3. Untagged (Bureau precancel, Type III: "PRESORTED" 13 1/2mm)	1.00	.50
	zv. Pair, imperforate	650.00	

1981. NON-DENOMINATED "C" ISSUE marked the new First Class postage rate of 20¢, which went into effect Nov. 1, 1981. The stamp was intended for domestic use only. Design same as the "A" and "B" issues, except for letter and background color. *Gravure, perforated 11x10 1/2, design size 19x22mm.*

772-774 *"C" to left of stylized eagle*

772		MNHVF	UseVF
(20¢)	**brown** tagged	.35	.20
	Plate block of 4	1.50	
	FDC *(Oct. 11, 1981)*		1.75
	zo. Tagging omitted (error)	9.00	

1981. NON-DENOMINATED "C" BOOKLET PANE ISSUE *Booklet panes, intaglio, perforated 11x10 1/2 design size 15x18mm.*

773		MNHVF	UseVF
(20¢)	**brown** tagged	.50	.20
	FDC *(Oct. 11, 1981)* any single		1.75
	n. Booklet pane of 10	5.00	5.00
	FDC (pane)		5.50

1981. NON-DENOMINATED "C" COIL ISSUE *Intaglio, perforated 10 vertically, design size 19x22mm.*

774		MNHVF	UseVF
(20¢)	**brown** tagged	.60	.20
	Pair	1.20	
	Line pair	1.50	
	FDC *(Oct. 11, 1981)*	1.75	
	v. Pair, imperforate	2,000.00	
	Line pair, imperforate		

1981. CHRISTMAS ISSUE consisted of two stamps. A contemporary design depicting a teddy bear on a sleigh and a traditional design of Madonna and Child by Botticelli. *Gravure, perforated 11.*

775 *Teddy bear on a sleigh*

775		MNHVF	UseVF
20¢	**multicolored** tagged	.50	.20
	Plate block of 4	2.50	
	FDC *(Oct. 28, 1981)*		1.75
	v. Pair, imperforate	250.00	
	v1. Vertical pair, imperforate horizontally	—	

776 Madonna and Child, *detail by Sandro Botticelli, in the collection of The Art Institute of Chicago*

776		MNHVF	UseVF
20¢	**multicolored** tagged	.50	.20
	Plate block of 4	2.50	
	FDC *(Oct. 28, 1981)*		1.75
	v. Pair, imperforate	110.00	
	v1. Vertical pair, imperforate horizontally	1,550.00	

1981. FIRE PUMPER COIL ISSUE in the Transportation Series depicted an Amoskeag fire pumper. It carried a steam-producing boiler that operated an engine to pump water from available sources. *Coil, intaglio, perforated 10 vertically. Plate number every 24 stamps.*

777 *Fire pumper, 1860s*

777		MNHVF	UseVF
20¢	**red** overall tagged	.40	.20
	Pair	.80	
	FDC *(Dec. 10, 1981)*		2.00
	v. Pair, imperforate	1,000.00	

1981. MAIL WAGON COIL ISSUE in the Transportation Series showed a vehicle typical of wagons used in early rural free delivery (RFD) service. Bulk rate. *Coil, printed by intaglio, perforated 10 vertically. Plate number every 24 stamps.*

778 *Mail wagon, 1880s*

778		MNHVF	UseVF
9.3¢	**dark red** overall tagged	.25	.20
	Pair	.25	
	FDC *(Dec. 15, 1981)*		2.00
	zv. Pair, imperforate	115.00	
	zx. Untagged (Bureau precancel)	.25	.25
	FDC Bureau precancel		300.00

1981. FLAG OVER SUPREME COURT ISSUE *Intaglio, perforated 11.*

779-781, B154, B155, B156 *Flag Over Supreme Court Building; in the foreground is statue* Contemplation of Justice *by noted American James Earle Fraser*

779		MNHVF	UseVF
20¢	**black, dark blue & red** perforated 11, tagged	.35	.20
	Plate block of 20	9.00	
	FDC *(Dec. 17, 1981)*		1.75
	v. Vertical pair, imperforate	35.00	
	v1. Vertical pair, imperforate horizontally	500.00	
	v2. Block of 4, imperforate	75.00	
	v3. black omitted	300.00	
	v4. dark blue omitted	85.00	
779A		MNHVF	UseVF
20¢	**black, dark blue & red** perforated 11 1/4, tagged	.35	.20
	Plate block of 20	9.00	

1981. FLAG OVER SUPREME COURT COIL ISSUE *Coil, intaglio, perforated 10 vertically. Plate number every 52 or 48 stamps.*

780		MNHVF	UseVF
20¢	**black, dark blue & red** block tagged	.35	.20
	Pair	.70	
	FDC *(Dec. 17, 1981)*		1.75
	a. slate blue, dark blue and red	—	
	b. black, dark blue and brick red	—	
	v. black omitted	50.00	
	v1. dark blue omitted	1,500.00	
	v2. Pair, imperforate	10.00	
	v3. Pair, imperforate between	1,200.00	
	zx. Untagged (Bureau precancel)	.50	.20
	Pair	1.00	.50
	zo. Tagging omitted (error)		

1981. FLAG OVER SUPREME COURT ISSUE *Intaglio, perforated 11.*

781		MNHVF	UseVF
20¢	**black, dark red & blue** tagged	.35	.20
	FDC *(Dec. 17, 1981)*		1.75
	n. Booklet pane of 6	2.50	3.00
	FDC pane		6.00
	n1. Booklet pane of 10	4.50	4.75
	FDC pane *(June 1, 1982)*		10.00

1981. FLAG OVER INDEPENDENCE HALL ISSUE *Intaglio, Combination Press, perforated 11, smooth gum. (See 690, 694.)*

782 *Flag Over Independence Hall*

782		MNHVF	UseVF
13¢	**dark blue & red** small-block tagged	.60	.25

Plate block of 20	70.00	
Plate block of 6	17.50	
v. Vertical pair, imperforate	150.00	
v1. Horizontal pair, imperforate vertically	—	
zo. Tagging omitted (error)	3.00	

1982. BIGHORN SHEEP BOOKLET ISSUE featured the Bighorn sheep used in the 1981 Wildlife booklet (No. 758). *Booklet pane, intaglio, perforated 11.*

783, B157 *Bighorn sheep*

783		MNHVF	UseVF
20¢	**blue** Type I, overall tagged, 18 3/4mm wide	.50	.20
	FDC *(Jan. 8, 1982),* single		1.75
	n. Booklet pane of 10	5.00	5.00
	nv. Booklet pane, imperforate between vertically	110.00	
	zo. Tagging omitted (error)	100.00	
	nzo. Booklet pane of 10, untagged	30.00	
783A		MNHVF	UseVF
20¢	**blue** Type II, block tagged, 18 1/2mm wide	.50	.20
	n. Booklet pane of 10	15.00	.50

Type I is 18 3/4mm wide, Type II is 18 1/2mm wide.

1982. RALPH BUNCHE ISSUE in the Great Americans Series honored the first black Nobel Peace Prize winner. Bunche (1904-1971), a United Nations official, was awarded the prize in 1950 for negotiating an armistice between the Palestinian Arabs and the Israelis in 1949. *Intaglio.*

784 *Ralph Bunche*

784		MNHVF	UseVF
20¢	**maroon** overall tagged	.35	.20
	Plate block of 4	2.75	
	FDC *(Jan. 12, 1982)*		2.00
	zo. Tagging omitted (error)	—	

1982. CRAZY HORSE ISSUE in the Great Americans Series honored the Oglala Sioux Indian leader (c.1842-77) who, joining Sitting Bull and other Sioux on the Little Big Horn River, was prominent in the defeat of Gen. George A. Custer and the Seventh Cavalry there on June 25, 1876. *Intaglio, perforated 11x10 1/2.*

785 *Crazy Horse*

785		MNHVF	UseVF
13¢	**light maroon** overall tagged	.35	.20
	Plate block of 4	1.50	
	FDC *(Jan. 15, 1982)*		1.75
	zo. Tagging omitted (error)	—	

1982. ROBERT MILLIKAN ISSUE in the Great Americans Series honored the Nobel Prize-winning physicist, educator, humanitarian, and key figure in the development of the California Institute of Technology (1868-1953). *Intaglio, perforated 11x10 1/2.*

786 *Robert Millikan*

786		MNHVF	UseVF
37¢	**blue** overall tagged	.60	.20
	Plate block of 4	3.50	
	FDC *(Jan. 26, 1982)*		1.75
	zo. Tagging omitted (error)	—	

1982. HIGH WHEELER BICYCLE COIL ISSUE in the Transportation Series. Intended for bulk mailings by non-profit organizations. *Coil, intaglio, perforated 10 vertically. Plate number every 24 stamps.*

787 *High wheeler bicycle, 1870s*

787		MNHVF	UseVF
5.9¢	**blue** overall tagged	.25	.20
	Pair	.30	
	FDC *(Feb. 17, 1982)*		2.00
	zx. Untagged (Bureau precancel)	.25	.20
	Pair	.30	
	FDC (Bureau precancel)		200.00
	zv. Pair, imperforate	150.00	
	Line pair, imperforate	—	

1982. HANSOM CAB COIL ISSUE in the Transportation Series pictured a one-horse, two-wheeled vehicle designed by Joseph Hansom. It paid bulk rate. *Coil, intaglio, perforated 10 vertically. Plate number every 24 stamps.*

788 *Hansom cab, 1890s*

788		MNHVF	UseVF
10.9¢	**purple** overall tagged	.25	.20
	Pair	.50	
	FDC		2.00
	zx. Untagged (Bureau precancel)	.30	.25
	FDC *(March 26, 1982)* (Bureau precancel)		300.00
	zv. Pair, imperforate	160.00	
	Line pair, imperforate	—	

1982. CONSUMER EDUCATION COIL ISSUE served to bring attention to consumer education issues by educators, government agencies, consumer organizations, business, labor organizations, and media. *Coil, intaglio, perforated 10 vertically. Plate number every 24 stamps.*

789 *Consumer education, wise shoppers stretch dollars*

789		MNHVF	UseVF
20¢	**blue** overall tagged	.50	.20
	Pair	.75	
	FDC *(April 27, 1982)*		1.75
	v. Pair, imperforate	95.00	
	Line pair, imperforate	—	
	zo. Tagging omitted (error)	4.00	

Minkus albums cover the globe. See your
stamp dealer or hobby shop for a selection.

1982. LOCOMOTIVE COIL ISSUE in the Transportation Series pictured a steam engine representative of those used in the 1860s and '70s. *Coil, intaglio, perforated 10 vertically. Plate number every 24 stamps.*

790 *Locomotive, 1870s*

790		MNHVF	UseVF
2¢	**black** overall tagged	.25	.20
	Pair	.30	
	FDC *(May 20, 1982)*		2.00
	v. Pair, imperforate	50.00	
	Line pair, imperforate	—	
	zo. Tagging omitted Plate #8	—	

(For similar design with "2 USA" see No. 873.)

1982. STAGECOACH COIL ISSUE in the Transportation Series showed a stagecoach made by Abbott & Downing of Concord, N.H. The precanceled version met the Third Class, non-profit, five-digit-sort bulk rate. "Stagecoach 1890s" measures 19 1/2mm long. *Coil, intaglio, perforated 10 vertically. Plate number every 24 stamps.*

791 *Stagecoach, 1890s*

791		MNHVF	UseVF
4¢	**brown** overall tagged	.25	.20
	Pair	.30	
	FDC *(Aug. 19, 1982)*		2.00
	v. Pair, imperforate	850.00	
	zo. Tagging omitted (error)	—	
	zx. Untagged (Bureau precancel: "Nonprofit Org")	.25	.20
	zxv. Pair, imperforate, untagged (precanceled)	750.00	

(For similar design with "Stagecoach 1890s" measuring 17mm long, see No. 868.)

Listings and prices for plate number coil strips and singles appear at the end of this definitives section of the Krause-Minkus catalog.

1982. CHRISTMAS ISSUE consisted of a single traditional design and a block of four contemporary designs. The contemporary design features a block of four children and snow scenes designed by Dolli Tingle. *Gravure, perforated 11.*

792-795

792		MNHVF	UseVF
20¢	Sledding, **multicolored,** tagged	.35	.20

793		MNHVF	UseVF
20¢	Building snowman, **multicolored,** tagged	.35	.20

794		MNHVF	UseVF
20¢	Skating, **multicolored,** tagged	.35	.20

795		MNHVF	UseVF
20¢	Decorating tree, **multicolored,** tagged	.35	.20
	FDC *(Oct. 28, 1982)* any single		2.00
	y. Se-tenant block of 4	1.50	

Plate block of 4	3.50	
FDC block of 4		4.00
v. Block of 4, imperforate	3,250.00	
v1. Block of 4, imperforate horizontally	900.00	

1982. TRADITIONAL CHRISTMAS ISSUE depicted a Madonna and Child by Giovanni Battista Tiepolo, an 18th century painter. *Gravure, perforated 11.*

796 Madonna and Child, *by Giovanní Battista Tiepolo, National Gallery of Art*

796 20¢		MNHVF	UseVF
	multicolored tagged	.35	.20
	Plate block of 20	13.75	
	FDC (Oct. 28, 1982)		1.75
	v. Horizontal pair, imperforate vertically	—	
	v1. Vertical pair, imperforate horizontally	—	
	v2. Pair, imperforate	—	

1982. KITTEN AND PUPPY ISSUE was a postcard-rate stamp issued to satisify demand for those who sent a holiday postcard. *Gravure, perforated 11.*

797 *Kitten and puppy playing in snow*

797 13¢		MNHVF	UseVF
	multicolored tagged	.35	.20
	Plate block of 4	2.00	
	FDC (Nov. 3, 1982)		2.00
	v. Pair, imperforate	650.00	

1982. IGOR STRAVINSKY ISSUE in the Great Americans Series marked the 100th anniversary of the birth of the Russian-born composer (1882-1971) of operas and ballets. He became a U.S. citizen in 1945. *Intaglio.*

798 *Igor Stravinsky*

798 2¢		MNHVF	UseVF
	brown overall tagged	.25	.20
	Plate block of 4	.30	
	Pair, gutter between	7.50	
	FDC (Nov. 18, 1982)		1.75
	zo. Tagging omitted (error)	—	

1983. SLEIGH COIL ISSUE in the Transportation Series showed an antique sleigh typical of the 1880s. It was for use by authorized non-profit organizations. *Coil, intaglio, perforated 10 vertically. Plate number every 24 stamps.*

799 *Sleigh, 1880s*

799 5.2¢		MNHVF	UseVF
	red overall tagged	.25	.20
	Pair	.30	
	FDC (March 21, 1983)		2.00
	zx. Untagged (Bureau precancel)	.25	
	FDC (Bureau precancel)		150.00

1983. HANDCAR COIL ISSUE in the Transportation Series showed a manually-operated railroad handcar made in Bucyrus, Ohio. *Coil, intaglio, perforated 10 vertically. Plate number every 24 stamps.*

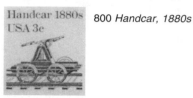

800 *Handcar, 1880s*

800 3¢		MNHVF	UseVF
	green overall tagged	.25	.20
	Pair	.30	
	FDC (March 25, 1983)		2.00

> *Listings and prices for plate number coil strips and singles appear at the end of this definitives section of the Krause-Minkus catalog.*

1983. CARL SCHURZ ISSUE in the Great Americans Series honored the German-born American reformer, public official, and journalist (1829-1906). *Intaglio, perforated 11x10 1/2.*

801 *Carl Schurz*

801 4¢		MNHVF	UseVF
	purple overall tagged	.20	.20
	Plate block of 4	.60	
	FDC (June 3, 1983)		1.75
	zo. Tagging omitted (error)	4.00	

1983. THOMAS H. GALLAUDET ISSUE in the Great Americans Series honored the pioneer educator (1787-1851) who devoted his life to the education of the speaking- and hearing-impaired. *Intaglio, perforated 11x10 1/2.*

802 *Thomas H. Gallaudet*

802 20¢		MNHVF	UseVF
	green overall tagged	.40	.20
	Plate block of 4	4.00	
	Plate Nos. 5 & 6 carry a premium	—	
	Plate Nos. 8 & 9 carry a large premium	—	
	FDC (June 10, 1983)		2.00
	zo. Tagging omitted (error)	4.00	

1983. PEARL BUCK ISSUE in the Great Americans Series honored the author, humanitarian, and winner of both the Pulitzer and Nobel Prizes (1892-1973). *Intaglio, perforated 11x10 1/2.*

803 *Pearl Buck*

803

		MNHVF	UseVF
5¢	**red brown** overall tagged	.20	.20
	Plate block of 4	.80	
	FDC *(June 25, 1983)*		1.75

1983. HENRY CLAY ISSUE in the Great Americans Series honored the American statesman (1777-1852) known as "The Great Compromiser." *Intaglio, perforated 11x10 1/2.*

804 *Henry Clay*

804

		MNHVF	UseVF
3¢	**olive** overall tagged	.20	.20
	Plate block of 4	.60	
	zo. Tagging omitted (error)	4.00	
	FDC *(July 13, 1983)*		1.75

1983. EXPRESS MAIL BOOKLET ISSUE although not labeled as such nor restricted to that class of mail, was released principally for Express Mail Next Day Service use. *Booklet pane, gravure, perforated 10 vertically.*

805, B159 *Eagle and moon*

805

		MNHVF	UseVF
$9.35	**multicolored** tagged	25.00	20.00
	FDC *(Aug. 12, 1983)*		60.00
	n. Booklet pane of 3	60.00	
	FDC, booklet pane		175.00

1983. OMNIBUS COIL ISSUE in the Transportation Series featured a type of transportation popular in the second half of the 19th century. *Coil, intaglio, perforated 10 vertically. Plate number every 24 stamps.*

806 *Omnibus, 1880s*

806

		MNHVF	UseVF
1¢	**purple** overall tagged	.20	.20
	Pair	.20	.20
	FDC *(Aug. 19, 1983)*		2.00
	v. Pair, imperforate	675.00	

(For similar design with "1 USA," see No. 867.)

1983. DOROTHEA DIX ISSUE in the Great Americans Series honored the 19th century crusader for the poor and mentally impaired (1802-87). *Intaglio, perforated 11 1/4 or 10 3/4.*

807 *Dorothea Dix*

807

		MNHVF	UseVF
1¢	**black** tagged (small block) perforated 11 1/4	.20	.20

	Plate block of 20	2.00	
	FDC *(Sept. 23, 1983)*		1.75
	v. Pair, imperforate	450.00	
	v1. Vertical pair, imperforate between	3,000.00	

807A

		MNHVF	UseVF
1¢	**black** tagged (small block) perforated 10 3/4	.20	.20
	Plate block of 20	2.00	
	v. Vertical pair, imperforate horizontally	—	
	bz. Large block tagged *(1985)*	.20	.20
	Plate block of 20	2.00	

1983. MOTORCYCLE COIL ISSUE in the Transportation Series was often used as a change-maker in vending machines. The 5¢ denomination met no specific postal value. *Coil, intaglio, perforated 10 vertically. Plate number every 24 stamps.*

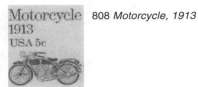

808 *Motorcycle, 1913*

808

		MNHVF	UseVF
5¢	**dark green** overall tagged	.25	.20
	Pair	.30	
	FDC *(Oct. 10, 1983)*		2.00
	v. Pair, imperforate	2,750.00	
	zo. Tagging omitted (error)	—	

Listings and prices for plate number coil strips and singles appear at the end of this definitives section of the Krause-Minkus catalog.

1983. CHRISTMAS ISSUE consisted of a Santa Claus design and a Madonna and Child by Raphael. *Gravure, perforated 11.*

809 *Santa Claus*

809

		MNHVF	UseVF
20¢	**multicolored** tagged	.35	.20
	Plate block of 20	12.50	
	FDC *(Oct. 28, 1983)*		2.00
	v. Pair, imperforate	175.00	

810 Madonna and Child, *by Raphael, National Gallery of Art*

810

		MNHVF	UseVF
20¢	**multicolored** tagged	.35	.20
	Plate block of 4	2.50	
	FDC *(Oct. 28, 1983)*		1.75

1984. HARRY S. TRUMAN ISSUE in the Great Americans Series honored the 33rd president of the United States, on the centennial of his birth. Truman (1884-1972) came to office upon the death of Franklin D. Roosevelt and made the decision to use the atomic bomb to help end World War II. *Intaglio, perforated 11.*

Transportation Series Identifier

As with the Great Americans Identifier, entries here are by denomination, in order of issue of that denomination. All stamps listed provide basic data: denomination, form of transportation depicted, and catalog number. There is information in the gum, tagging and without tagging columns only when such information will assist in properly identifying a stamp.

Denomination/Name	Cat.	Gum	Tagging	Without Tagging
1¢ Omnibus (USA 1)	806			
1¢ Omnibus (1 USA)	867pz		Prephosphored	
1¢ Omnibus	867zxm	Matte		
1¢ Omnibus	867zxs	Shiny		
2¢ Locomotive (USA 2¢)	790			
2¢ Locomotive (2¢ USA)	873			
2¢ Locomotive	873zx			Intentional
3¢ Handcar	800			
3¢ Conestoga Wagon	883			
3¢ Conestoga Wagon	883zxm	Matte		Intentional
3¢ Conestoga Wagon	883zxs	Shiny		Intentional
3.4¢ School Bus	843			
3.4¢ School Bus	843zx			Bureau precancel
4¢ Stagecoach (19 1/2mm long)	791			Error (791zo)
4¢ Stagecoach	791zx			Bureau precancel
4¢ Stagecoach (17mm long)	868	Block		
4¢ Stagecoach	868z	Overall		
4¢ Steam Carriage	943			
4¢ Steam Carriage	943zx			Intentional
4.9¢ Buckboard	846			
4.9¢ Buckboard	846zx			Bureau precancel
5¢ Motorcycle	808			Error (808zo)
5¢ Milk Wagon	879			
5¢ Circus Wagon (05 USA, intaglio)	931			
5¢ Circus Wagon	931z			Intentional
5¢ Circus Wagon (05 USA, gravure)	1007	No		Intentional
5¢ Circus Wagon (USA 5¢)	1077	No		Intentional
5¢ Canoe (brown)	955	No		Bureau service indicator
5¢ Canoe (red)	979	No		Bureau service indicator
5.2¢ Sleigh	799			
5.2¢ Sleigh	799zx			Bureau precancel
5.3¢ Elevator	906			Bureau service indicator
5.5¢ Star Route Truck	865			
5.5¢ Star Route Truck	865zx			Bureau service indicator
5.9¢ Bicycle	787			
5.9¢ Bicycle	787zx			Bureau precancel
6¢ Tricycle	841			
6¢ Tricycle	841zx			Bureau precancel
7.1¢ Tractor	870			
7.1¢ Tractor	870zx			Bureau service indicator ("Nonprofit Org")
7.1¢ Tractor	870zx1			Bureau service indicator ("Nonprofit 5-Digit ZIP+4)
7.4¢ Baby Buggy	814			
7.4¢ Baby Buggy	814zx			Bureau precancel
7.6¢ Carreta	903	No		Bureau service indicator
8.3¢ Ambulance (18 1/2 mm long)	845			
8.3¢ Ambulance	845zx			Bureau precancel
8.3¢ Ambulance (18mm long)	845A	No		Bureau precancel
8.4¢ Wheel Chair	901	No		Bureau service indicator
8.5¢ Tow Truck	869			
8.5¢ Tow Truck	869zx			Bureau service indicator
9.3¢ Mail Wagon	778			
9.3¢ Mail Wagon	778zx			Bureau precancel

Denomination/Name	Cat.	Gum	Tagging	Without Tagging
10¢ Canal Boat	874	Matte	Block	
10¢ Canal Boat	874pz	Shiny	Pre-phosphored	
10¢ Canal Boat	874zm	Matte	Overall	
10¢ Canal Boat	874zs	Shiny	Overall	
10¢ Tractor Trailer	954		No	Bureau service indicator, gray
10¢ Tractor Trailer	1042			Bureau service indicator, black
10.1¢ Oil Wagon	837			
10.1¢ Oil Wagon	837zx			Bureau precancel, black
10.1¢ Oil Wagon	837zx1			Bureau precancel, red
10.9¢ Hansom Cab	788			
10.9¢ Hansom Cab	788zx			Bureau precancel
11¢ Caboose	812			
11¢ Caboose	812zx			Bureau precancel
11¢ Caboose	812zx1			Intentional
11¢ Stutz Bearcat	844			
12¢ Stanley Steamer (18mm long)	831		Block	Error (831zo)
12¢ Stanley Steamer	831p		Hi-Brite Paper	
12¢ Stanley Steamer	831xz		No	Bureau precancel
12¢ Stanley Steamer	831A		No	Bureau precancel
12.5¢ Pushcart	838			
12.5¢ Pushcart	838zx		No	Bureau precancel
13¢ Police Patrol Wagon	914		No	Bureau service indicator
13.2¢ Coal Car	900		No	Bureau service indicator
14¢ Iceboat (17 1/2mm long)	827		Overall	Error (827zo)
14¢ Iceboat (17 1/4mm long)	827A		Block	
15¢ Tugboat	899		Block	Error (899zo)
15¢ Tugboat	899z		Overall	
16.7¢ Popcorn Wagon	898		No	Bureau service indicator
17¢ Electric Auto	771			Error (771zo)
17¢ Electric Auto	771zx1			Bureau precancel 11 1/2mm
17¢ Electric Auto	771zx2			Bureau precancel 12 1/2mm
17¢ Electric Auto	771zx3			Bureau precancel 13 1/2mm
17¢ Dog Sled	859			
17.5¢ Racing Car	880			
17.5¢ Racing Car	880zx			Bureau service indicator
18¢ Surrey	768			
20¢ Fire Pumper	777			
20¢ Cable Car	913		Block	
20¢ Cable Car	913z		Overall	
20¢ Cog Railway	1086			
20.5¢ Fire Engine	907		No	Bureau service indicator
21¢ Railroad Mail Car	902		No	Bureau service indicator
23¢ Lunch Wagon	949	Matte	Overall*	
23¢ Lunch Wagon	949ps	Shiny	Prephosphored*	
24.1¢ Tandem Bicycle	912	No		Bureau service indicator
25¢ Bread Wagon	866			Error (866zo)
32¢ Ferryboat	1085			
$1 Seaplane	928	Matte	Overall	
$1 Seaplane	928pz	Shiny	Prephosphored **	
$1 Seaplane	928pzg	Dull	Prephosphored ***	

* Tagging is solid, smooth-appearing
**Tagging is mottled
*** Tagging is grainy

811 *Harry S. Truman*

811

20¢	black tagged (small block)	MNHVF .35	UseVF .20
	Plate block of 20	12.00	
	FDC *(Jan. 26, 1984)*		2.00

(See also No. 904.)

1984. RAILROAD CABOOSE COIL ISSUE in the Transportation Series. The untagged version was issued to meet the bulk rate. The tagged version met no postal rate; it was issued for collectors. *Coil, intaglio, perforated 10 vertically. Plate number every 52 stamps for Plate 1 and 48 stamps for Plate 2.*

812 *Railroad caboose, 1890s*

812

11¢	red block tagged	MNHVF .25	UseVF .20
	Pair	.35	
	FDC *(Feb. 3, 1984)*		2.00
	zx. Untagged (Bureau precancel)	.25	.20
	zx1. deep red, untagged (unprecanceled) *(Sept. 25, 1991)*	—	

> *Listings and prices for plate number coil strips and singles appear at the end of this definitives section of the Krause-Minkus catalog.*

1984. LILLIAN GILBRETH ISSUE in the Great Americans Series honored the pioneering American engineer (1878-1972) who searched for efficient working methods in industry and the home. Together with her husband, she laid the foundation for the field of industrial engineering. *Intaglio, perforated 11 or 11 1/4.*

813, 813A *Lillian Gilbreth*

813

40¢	green, tagged (small block) perforated 11	MNHVF .60	UseVF .20
	Plate block of 20	10.00	
	FDC *(Feb. 24, 1984)*		2.00

813A

40¢	green tagged (large block) perforated 11 1/4 *(1987)*	MNHVF .60	UseVF .20
	Plate block of 4	2.00	

1984. BABY BUGGY COIL ISSUE in the Transportation Series. The untagged version was issued to meet the rate for carrier-route presorted bulk mailings. The tagged stamp was a "collector" issue, meeting no specific postal rate. *Coil, intaglio, perforated 10 vertically. Plate number every 52 stamps.*

814 *Baby buggy, 1880s*

814

7.4¢	brown block tagged	MNHVF .25	UseVF .20
	Pair	.35	
	FDC *(April 7, 1984)*		2.00
	zx. Untagged (Bureau precancel: "Blk. Rt. CAR-RT SORT")	.25	.20
	FDC		300.00

1984. RICHARD RUSSELL ISSUE in the Great Americans Series honored the former U.S. Senator and his 50 years of public service. Two years after becoming, at age 33, the youngest governor in Georgia's history, Russell (1897-1971) was elected to fill the unexpired term of one of the state's U.S. Senators. He was subsequently re-elected six times to the U.S. Senate. *Intaglio, perforated 11.*

815 *Richard Russell*

815

10¢	blue tagged (small block)	MNHVF .25	UseVF .20
	Plate block of 20	7.00	
	FDC *(May 31, 1984)*		1.75
	bz. Large block tagged	.25	.20
	Plate block of 20	7.00	
	v. Horizontal pair, imperforate between	2,000.00	
	v1. Vertical pair, imperforate between	—	
	v2. Vertical pair, imperforate horizontally	—	
	v3. Pair, imperforate	1,250.00	

Imperforate printer's waste is known to exist, and in one case was used as postage.

1984. FRANK C. LAUBACH ISSUE in the Great Americans Series honored the literacy advocate and educator (1884-1970) who developed methods to educate the illiterate and created alphabets and written languages where none previously existed. *Intaglio, perforated 11 or 11 1/4.*

816, 816A *Frank C. Laubach*

816

30¢	green tagged (small block) perforated 11	MNHVF .75	UseVF .20
	Plate block of 20	18.00	
	FDC *(Sept. 2, 1984)*		1.75

816A

30¢	green tagged (large block) perforated 11 1/4	MNHVF .75	UseVF .20
	Plate block of 4	2.25	
	FDC *(June 25, 1988)*		1.75
	z. Overall tagging *(1990)*	1.00	
	Plate block of 4	25.00	

1984. CHRISTMAS ISSUE consisted of a child's drawing of Santa Claus and a Madonna and Child by Lippi. *Gravure, perforated 11.*

817 Santa Claus, *by Danny La Boccetta, winner of a stamp design project*

817

20¢	multicolored tagged	MNHVF .25	UseVF .20

		MNHVF	UseVF
Plate block of 4		1.50	
FDC *(Oct. 30, 1984)*			1.75
v. Horizontal pair, imperforate vertically		975.00	

818 Madonna and Child, *by Fra Filippo Lippi, National Gallery of Art*

818		MNHVF	UseVF
20¢	**multicolored** tagged	.25	.20
	Plate block of 4	1.50	
	FDC *(Oct. 30, 1984)*		1.75

1985. ABRAHAM BALDWIN ISSUE in the Great Americans Series honored the man (1754-1807) who wrote the charter for Franklin College, now the University of Georgia, the first state university in the United States. *Intaglio, perforated 11.*

819 *Abraham Baldwin*

819		MNHVF	UseVF
7¢	**red** tagged (small block)	.25	.20
	Plate block of 20	4.00	
	FDC *(Jan. 25, 1985)*		1.75

1985. NON-DENOMINATED "D" ISSUE marked the new First Class postage rate of 22¢, which went into effect Feb. 17, 1985. The issue was for domestic use only. Issued in sheet, coil, and booklet form. *Gravure, perforated 11. Plate number every 38 stamps.*

820-822, B160 *"D" and stylized eagle*

820		MNHVF	UseVF
(22¢)	**green** tagged	.45	.20
	Plate block of 20	25.00	
	FDC *(Feb. 1, 1985)*		1.75
	v. Vertical pair, imperforate	50.00	
	v1. Vertical pair, imperforate horizontally	1,300.00	
	zo. Untagged (error)	—	

1985. NON-DENOMINATED "D" COIL ISSUE

821		MNHVF	UseVF
(22¢)	**green** block tagged perforated 10	.60	.20
	Pair	1.20	
	FDC *(Feb. 1, 1985)*		1.75
	v. Pair, imperforate	45.00	
	vzo. Pair, imperforate, tagging omitted (error)	85.00	

> *Listings and prices for plate number coil strips and singles appear at the end of this definitives section of the Krause-Minkus catalog.*

1985. NON-DENOMINATED "D" RATE BOOKLET ISSUE

822		MNHVF	UseVF
(22¢)	**green** tagged	.40	.20
	FDC *(Feb. 1, 1985)* single		1.75
	n. Booklet pane of 10	8.50	

		MNHVF	UseVF
nv. Booklet pane of 10, imperforate between horizontally		—	
FDC (Booklet pane)			7.50

1985. ALDEN PARTRIDGE ISSUE in the Great Americans Series honored the military educator (1785-1854) on his 200th birthday. After a career at the U.S. Military Academy at West Point, N.Y., Partridge was superintendent there from 1814-17, but refused to step down when Sylvanus Thayer (Minkus No. 842) was named to succeed him. A court martial found Partridge guilty of insubordination, and he resigned from the Army. As a civilian, he founded a school in Vermont that combined academics with military training, and he became known as the Father of the Reserve Officer Training Corps. *Intaglio, perforated 11.*

823 *Alden Partridge*

823		MNHVF	UseVF
11¢	**blue** overall tagged	.25	.20
	Plate block of 4	1.20	
	FDC *(Feb. 12, 1985)*		2.00
	zo. Tagging omitted (error)	.85	

1985. CHESTER W. NIMITZ ISSUE in the Great Americans Series honored the fleet admiral, whose leadership during World War II brought about key naval victories. Nimitz (1885-1966) was acknowledged as one of the Navy's foremost administrators and strategists. *Gravure, perforated 11 or 11 1/4.*

824, 824A *Chester W. Nimitz*

824		MNHVF	UseVF
50¢	**brown** overall tagged, perforated 11, shiny gum	.90	.20
	Plate block of 4	8.00	
	FDC *(Feb. 22, 1985)*		3.00
	zo. Tagging omitted (error)	7.00	

824A		MNHVF	UseVF
50¢	**brown** tagged (large block) perforated 11 1/4, matte gum	.90	.20
	Plate block of 4	6.50	
	zo. Tagging omitted (error)	7.00	
	z1. Overall tagging	.90	
	Plate block of 4	6.50	
	pz. Prephosphored paper, mottled tagging, shiny gum *(1992)*	.90	
	Plate block of 4	7.00	

1985. GRENVILLE CLARK ISSUE in the Great Americans Series honored a leading advocate (1882-1967) of civil liberties and peace through world federalism. *Intaglio, perforated 11 or 11 1/4.*

825, 825A *Grenville Clark*

825		MNHVF	UseVF
39¢	**purple** tagged (small block) perforated 11	.75	.20
	Plate block of 20	24.00	
	FDC *(March 20, 1985)*		2.00
	bz. Large block tagged	.75	.20
	Plate block of 20	24.00	
	v. Vertical pair, imperforate between	2,000.00	
	v1. Vertical pair, imperforate horizontally	575.00	

825A		MNHVF	UseVF
39¢	**purple** tagged (large block), perforated 11 1/4	.75	.20
	Plate block of 4	4.00	

1985. SINCLAIR LEWIS ISSUE in the Great Americans Series honored the novelist and short story writer (1885-1951) on the centennial of his birth. In 1930, Lewis became the first American to win a Nobel Prize for Literature. *Intaglio, perforated 11.*

826 *Sinclair Lewis*

826		MNHVF	UseVF
14¢	**gray** tagged (small block)	.25	.20
	Plate block of 20	9.00	
	FDC *(March 21, 1985)*		1.75
	bz. Large block tagged	.25	.20
	Plate block of 20	9.00	
	v. Horizontal pair, imperforate between	10.00	
	v1. Vertical pair, imperforate between	2,000.00	
	v2. Vertical pair, imperforate horizontally	125.00	

1985. ICEBOAT COIL ISSUE in the Transportation Series issued to meet the First Class rate for postcards, beginning Feb. 17, 1985. *Coil, intaglio, perforated 10 vertically. Plate number every 24 stamps (Cottrell, 827) and every 52 stamps (B-Press, 827A).*

827, 827A *Iceboat, 1880s*

827		MNHVF	UseVF
14¢	**blue** Type I, overall tagged	.25	.20
	Pair	.35	
	FDC *(March 23, 1985)*		1.75
	v. Pair, imperforate	100.00	
	zo. Tagging omitted (error)	—	

827A		MNHVF	UseVF
14¢	**blue** Type II, block tagged	.25	.20
	Pair	.35	

Type I is 17 1/2mm wide with overall tagging. Type II is 17 1/4mm wide with block tagging.

1985. FLAG OVER THE CAPITOL ISSUE consisted of sheet and coil versions, and a booklet stamp the width of two normal definitive stamps. *Coil, intaglio, perforated 11. Plate number every 52 or 48 stamps on coil issues.*

828, 829, 876 *Flag Over the U.S. Capitol*

828		MNHVF	UseVF
22¢	**black, blue & red** block tagged	.35	.20
	Plate block of 4	3.00	
	Pair, gutter between	—	
	FDC *(March 29, 1985)*		1.75

1985. FLAG OVER THE U.S. CAPITOL COIL ISSUE *Coil, intaglio. Perforated 10 vertically.*

829		MNHVF	UseVF
22¢	**black, blue & red** block tagged	.40	.20
	Pair	1.00	
	FDC *(March 29, 1985)*		1.75
	a. black stars in flag (rather than blue)	1.00	
	b. slate blue, blue, and red	—	

	v. Pair, imperforate	15.00	
	zo. Tagging omitted (error)	3.00	

(For similar design with "T" at bottom, see No. 876.)

> **Listings and prices for plate number coil strips and singles appear at the end of this definitives section of the Krause-Minkus catalog.**

1985. FLAG OVER THE CAPITOL BOOKLET ISSUE This was the first U.S. booklet pane in the format of a single row of five stamps. *Booklet pane, intaglio, perforated 10 horizontally.*

830, B161, B162 *Flag Over the U.S. Capitol*

830		MNHVF	UseVF
22¢	**black, blue & red** tagged	.40	.20
	FDC *(March 29, 1985)*		1.75
	n. Booklet pane of 5	3.00	2.50
	FDC booklet pane		3.50

Issued for use in vending machines, and was available with one or two panes.

1985. STANLEY STEAMER COIL ISSUE in the Transportation Series featured the first successfully operated steam automobile in New England. *Coil, intaglio, perforated 10 vertically. Plate number every 24 stamps (Cottrell, 831) and every 52 stamps (B-Press, 831A).*

831, 831A *Stanley steamer, 1909*

831		MNHVF	UseVF
12¢	**blue** Type I, overall tagged	.25	.20
	Pair	.30	
	FDC *(April 2, 1985)*		1.75
	p. Hi-Brite paper	—	
	zx. Untagged (Bureau precancel: "PRESORTED FIRST-CLASS")	.25	.20
	Pair	—	
	zo. Tagging omitted (error)	—	

831A		MNHVF	UseVF
12¢	**blue** Type II, untagged (Bureau precancel: "PRESORTED FIRST-CLASS")	.25	.20
	Pair	.30	
	FDC *(Sept. 3, 1987)*		60.00

Type I: "Stanley Steamer 1909" is 18mm long;
Type II: "Stanley Steamer 1909" is 17 1/2mm long.

1985. SEASHELL BOOKLET ISSUE

Frilled Dogwinkle

Reticulated Helmet

New England Neptune

Calico Scallop

Lightning Whelk

832 *Frilled dogwinkle*

833 *Reticulated helmet*

834 *New England neptune*

835 *Calico scallop*

836 *Lightning whelk*

B163, B164

832		MNHVF	UseVF
22¢	Frilled dogwinkle, **black & brown** tagged	.35	.20

833		MNHVF	UseVF
22¢	Reticulated helmet, **black & multicolored** tagged	.35	.20

834		MNHVF	UseVF
22¢	New England neptune, **black & brown** tagged	.35	.20

835		MNHVF	UseVF
22¢	Calico scallop, **black & purple** tagged	.35	.20

836		MNHVF	UseVF
22¢	Lightning whelk, **multicolored** tagged	.35	.20
	FDC *(April 4, 1985)* any single		2.00
	y. Se-tenant strip of 5	3.00	
	n. Booklet pane of 10 (2 each Nos. 832-36)	4.00	
	FDC booklet pane		7.50
	nv. purple omitted, horizontal pair of 835, pane	700.00	
	nv1. Booklet pane of 10, imperforate between vertically	650.00	
	nv2. Booklet pane, imperforate	—	
	zo. Tagging omitted (error)	—	
	nzo. Booklet pane of 10, untagged	—	

Note: Mis-registered tagging is common on this issue.

1985. OIL WAGON COIL ISSUE in the Transportation Series. The 10.1¢ untagged denomination first was issued to meet the rate for bulk Third Class mail presorted to the 5-digit ZIP code. The tagged stamp was issued for collectors. *Coil, intaglio, perforated 10 vertically. Plate number every 52 stamps.*

837 *Oil wagon, 1890s*

837		MNHVF	UseVF
10.1¢	**blue** block tagged	.25	.20
	Pair	.35	
	FDC *(April 18, 1985)*		1.75
	zx. Untagged (Bureau precancel in black: "Bulk Rate")	.25	.20
	FDC *(April 18, 1985)*		2.50
	zxv. Pair, imperforate	85.00	
	zx1. Untagged (Bureau precancel in red: "Bulk Rate/Carrier Route Sort")	.25	.20
	FDC *(June 27, 1988)*		1.75
	zx1v. Pair, imperforate	1.00	

1985. PUSHCART COIL ISSUE in the Transportation Series. The 12.5¢ untagged denomination was issued as the basic rate for bulk Third Class mail. The tagged version originally had no rate use. Covers from a *Reader's Digest* mailing in 1989 used pairs of the 12.5¢ to meet the First Class letter rate. *Perforated 10 vertically. Plate number every 52 stamps.*

838 *Pushcart, 1880s*

838		MNHVF	UseVF
12.5¢	**olive** block tagged	.25	.20
	Pair	.35	
	FDC *(April 18, 1985)*		1.75
	zx. Untagged (Bureau precancel: "Bulk Rate")	.25	
	zxv. Pair, imperforate	50.00	

> *Listings and prices for plate number coil strips and singles appear at the end of this definitives section of the Krause-Minkus catalog.*

1985. JOHN J. AUDUBON ISSUE in the Great Americans Series celebrated the 200th birthday of the artist-naturalist (1785-1851). *Intaglio, perforated 11 or 11 1/4.*

839, 839A *John J. Audubon*

839		MNHVF	UseVF
22¢	**blue** tagged (small block) perforated 11	.40	.20
	Plate block of 20	16.00	
	FDC *(April 23, 1985)*		2.00
	bz. Large block tagged	.40	.20
	Plate block of 20	16.00	
	v. Horizontal pair, imperforate between	2,750.00	
	v1. Vertical pair, imperforate between	—	
	v2. Vertical pair, imperforate horizontally	2,500.00	
	zo. Tagging omitted (error)	4.00	

839A		MNHVF	UseVF
22¢	**blue** tagged (large block) perforated 11 1/4	.40	.20
	Plate block of 4	1.50	

1985. EXPRESS MAIL ISSUE Although valid for use on other classes of mail, was intended for use in four types of Express Mail Service: 1) Same Day Airport Service, 2) Custom Designed Service, 3) Next Day

Service, and 4) International Service. *Booklet pane, gravure, perforated 10 vertically.*

840, B165, B166 *Eagle and moon*

840		MNHVF	UseVF
$10.75	**multicolored** Type I	15.00	9.00
	FDC *(April 29, 1985)*		50.00
	n. Booklet pane of 3	52.00	
	FDC		150.00
	a. Type II *(June 19, 1989)*	17.00	12.00
	FDC		250.00
	an. Booklet pane of 3	52.00	
	FDC		700.00

Type I: Overall dull appearance, "$10.75" appears grainy. Type II: More intense colors, "$10.75" smoother, much less grainy.

1985. TRICYCLE COIL ISSUE in the Transportation Series met the basic rate for Third Class bulk mailings by non-profit organizations. The tagged version met no specific domestic postal rate. However, it could be added to a U.S. 15¢ post card when rates to Canada were raised to 21¢ in 1988. *Coil, intaglio, perforated 10 vertically. Plate number every 52 stamps.*

841 *Tricycle, 1880s*

841		MNHVF	UseVF
6¢	**brown** block tagged	.25	.20
	Pair	.30	
	FDC *(May 6, 1985)*		1.75
	zx. Untagged (Bureau precancel: "Nonprofit Org.")	.25	.20
	Pair	.30	
	zxv. Pair, imperforate	225.00	

1985. SYLVANUS THAYER ISSUE in the Great Americans Series honored the former commandant of the U.S. Military Academy at West Point, N.Y. (1785-1872). *Intaglio, perforated 11.*

842 *Sylvanus Thayer*

842		MNHVF	UseVF
9¢	**green** tagged (small block)	.25	.20
	Plate block of 20	4.25	
	FDC *(June 7, 1985)*		2.00

1985. SCHOOL BUS COIL ISSUE in the Transportation Series. The untagged version was issued for basic rate for carrier-route presort Third Class bulk mailings by non-profit organizations. The tagged version was issued for collectors. *Coil, intaglio, perforated 10 vertically. Plate number every 24 stamps.*

843 *School bus, 1920s*

843		MNHVF	UseVF
3.4¢	**green** overall tagged	.20	.20
	Pair	.30	
	FDC *(June 8, 1985)*		1.75
	zx. Untagged (Bureau precancel: "Nonprofit Org. CAR-RT SORT")	.25	.20
	FDC		250.00

1985. STUTZ BEARCAT COIL ISSUE in the Transportation Series showed a 1933 Super Bearcat designed by the H.C.S. Motor Car Co. The 11¢ denomination met no single rate; however, a pair met the first-ounce, First Class letter rate. *Coil, intaglio, perforated 10 vertically. Plate number every 24 stamps.*

844 *Stutz Bearcat, 1933*

844		MNHVF	UseVF
11¢	**green** overall tagged	.25	.20
	Pair	.30	
	FDC *(June 11, 1985)*		1.75

1985. AMBULANCE COIL ISSUE in the Transportation Series. The untagged 8.3¢ denomination was issued for Third Class mail presorted by carrier route. The tagged version was issued as a "collector" item; it met no postal rate. *Coil, intaglio, perforated 10 vertically. Plate number every 24 stamps (Cottrell, 845) and every 52 stamps (B-Press, 845A).*

845, 845A *Ambulance, 1860s*

845		MNHVF	UseVF
8.3¢	**green** Type I, tagged	.20	.20
	Pair	.30	
	FDC *(June 21, 1985)*		1.75
	zx. Untagged (Bureau precancel: "Blk. Rt. CAR-RT SORT")	.25	.20
	Pair	.30	
	FDC		250.00

845A		MNHVF	UseVF
8.3¢	**green** Type II, untagged (Bureau precancel: "Blk. Rt./CAR-RT/SORT")	.20	.20
	Pair	.30	
	FDC *(Aug. 29, 1986)*		250.00

Type I: "Ambulance 1860s" is 18 1/2mm long. Type II: "Ambulance 1860s" is 18mm long.

1985. BUCKBOARD COIL ISSUE in the Transportation Series. The 4.9¢ untagged denomination was issued for non-profit Third Class mail presorted to the 5-digit ZIP code. The tagged version met no postal rate and was issued basically for collectors. *Plate number every 24 stamps.*

846 *Buckboard, 1880s*

846		MNHVF	UseVF
4.9¢	**brown** overall tagged	.25	.20
	pair	.30	
	FDC *(June 21, 1985)*		1.75
	zx. Untagged (Bureau precancel: "Nonprofit Org.")	.35	.20
	FDC		2.50

1985. HENRY KNOX ISSUE in the Great Americans Series honored the first U.S. Secretary of War (1750-1806) during the 200th anniversary year of his appointment. Fort Knox, in Kentucky, where the bulk of the nation's gold bullion is stored, is named for him. *Intaglio, perforated 11.*

847 *Henry Knox*

847		MNHVF	UseVF
8¢	**olive** overall tagged	.25	.20
	Plate block of 4	.40	
	FDC *(July 25, 1985)*		1.75

1985. WALTER LIPPMANN ISSUE in the Great Americans Series honored the newsman, political analyst, and author (1889-1974). Among many other awards and prizes, Lippmann earned two Pulitzer Prizes and a Peabody award. *Intaglio, perforated 11.*

848 *Walter Lippmann*

848		MNHVF	UseVF
6¢	**orange** tagged (large block)	.25	.20
	Plate block of 20	2.90	
	FDC *(Sept. 9, 1985)*		1.75
	v. Vertical pair, imperforate between	2,450.00	

1985. ENVELOPE STAMP COIL ISSUE prepaid First Class rate for mailers using ZIP + 4. *Coil, gravure, perforated 10 vertically. Plate number every 24 stamps.*

849 *Letters*

849		MNHVF	UseVF
21.1¢	**multicolored** block tagged	.35	.20
	Pair	.50	
	FDC *(Oct. 22, 1985)*		1.75
	zx. Untagged, Bureau-printed service indicator: "ZIP+4"	.35	.20
	Pair	.50	

Some precanceled stamps are known with light tagging.

1985. CONTEMPORARY CHRISTMAS ISSUE was a painting of poinsettias by James Dean of Annandale, Va. *Gravure, perforated 11.*

850 *Poinsettia plants*

850		MNHVF	UseVF
22¢	**multicolored** tagged	.35	.20
	Plate block of 4	1.40	
	FDC *(Oct. 30, 1985)*		1.75
	v. Pair, imperforate	125.00	

1985. TRADITIONAL CHRISTMAS ISSUE depicted one of four versions of *The Genoa Madonna,* an enameled terra-cotta Madonna and Child by Luca della Robbia. *Gravure, perforated 11.*

851 *Sculpture by Luca della Robbia, Detroit Institute of Arts*

851		MNHVF	UseVF
22¢	**multicolored** tagged	.35	.20
	Plate block of 4	1.50	
	FDC *(Oct. 30, 1985)*		1.75
	v. Pair, imperforate	100.00	

1985. GEORGE WASHINGTON & MONUMENT COIL ISSUE met the basic presort rate for First Class letter mail. *Coil, intaglio, perforated 10 vertically. Plate number every 24 stamps.*

852 *George Washington and the Washington Monument*

852		MNHVF	UseVF
18¢	**multicolored** block tagged, shiny gum	.35	.20
	Pair	.70	
	FDC *(Nov. 6, 1985)*		1.75
	v. Pair, imperforate	975.00	
	zx. Untagged (Bureau-printed service indicator: "PRESORTED FIRST-CLASS")	.35	.20
	zo. Tagging omitted (error)	2.00	1.75
	vzo. Pair	4.00	3.50
	zm. Matte gum	.35	
	Pair	.70	
	zxv. Pair, imperforate, precanceled	800.00	

Some precanceled stamps are known with light tagging.

1986. JACK LONDON ISSUE in the Great Americans Series honored the author (1875-1916) of 50 books including *The Call of the Wild, White Fang,* and *The Sea-Wolf. Intaglio, perforated 11.*

853, 888, 889 *Jack London*

853		MNHVF	UseVF
25¢	**blue** tagged (large block) perforated 11	.45	.20
	Plate block of 4	1.50	
	FDC *(Jan. 11, 1986)*		2.00
	zo. Tagging omitted (error)	—	

For booklet panes of 10 and 6, see Nos. 888-889.

1986. HUGO L. BLACK ISSUE in the Great Americans Series honored the Supreme Court justice (1886-1971) on his 100th birthday. *Intaglio, perforated 11.*

854 *Hugo L. Black*

854		MNHVF	UseVF
5¢	**deep olive green** tagged (large block)	.25	.20
	Plate block of 4	.90	

FDC *(Feb. 27, 1986)*   1.75
zo. Tagging omitted (error)   —

1986. WILLIAM JENNINGS BRYAN ISSUE in the Great Americans
Series honored the famed orator and legislator (1860-1925). *Intaglio, perforated 11.*

855 *William Jennings Bryan*

855		MNHVF	UseVF
$2	**purple** tagged (large block)	3.25	.75
	Plate block of 4	20.00	
	FDC *(March 19, 1986)*		7.00
	zo. Tagging omitted (error)	10.00	

1986. BELVA ANN LOCKWOOD ISSUE in the Great Americans
Series honored the first woman candidate for president and the first woman admitted to practice before the U.S. Supreme Court (1830-1917). *Intaglio, perforated 11.*

856 *Belva Ann Lockwood*

856		MNHVF	UseVF
17¢	**blue green** tagged (large block)	.35	.20
	Plate block of 4	1.75	
	FDC *(June 18, 1986)*		1.75
	zo. Tagging omitted (error)	5.00	

1986. MARGARET MITCHELL ISSUE in the Great Americans Series
honored the Pulitzer Prize winning author (1900-49) of *Gone With the Wind. Intaglio, perforated 11.*

857 *Margaret Mitchell*

857		MNHVF	UseVF
1¢	**brown** tagged (large block)	.25	.20
	Plate block of 4	.30	
	FDC *(June 30, 1986)*		2.50
	zo. Tagging omitted (error)	3.00	

1986. FATHER FLANAGAN ISSUE in the Great Americans Series
released on the centennial of his birth, honored Rev. Edward Joseph Flanagan (1886-1948), the founder of Boys Town. The center protects and educates abused and underprivileged youth. *Intaglio, perforated 11.*

858 *Father Flanagan*

858		MNHVF	UseVF
4¢	**purple** tagged (large block)	.25	.20
	Plate block of 4	.40	
	FDC *(July 14, 1986)*		1.75
	zx. Untagged, light gray violet *(1991)*	.25	.20
	Plate block of 4	.40	
	zx1. Untagged, slate violet *(1993)*	.25	.20
	Plate block of 4	.40	

1986. DOG SLED COIL ISSUE in the Transportation Series. The 17¢
denomination represents the rate for the second ounce of First Class

mail. *Coil, intaglio, perforated 10 vertically. Plate number every 52 stamps.*

859 *Dog sled, 1920s*

859		MNHVF	UseVF
17¢	**blue** block tagged	.30	.20
	Pair	.50	
	FDC *(Aug. 20, 1986)*		1.75
	v. Pair, imperforate	475.00	

> *Listings and prices for plate number coil strips and singles appear at the end of this definitives section of the Krause-Minkus catalog.*

1986. JOHN HARVARD ISSUE in the Great Americans Series
honored the 17th century American colonist and philanthropist (1607-1638), coinciding with the 350th anniversary of Harvard University, the oldest institution of higher learning in the United States. *Intaglio, perforated 11.*

860 *John Harvard*

860		MNHVF	UseVF
56¢	**crimson** tagged (large block)	1.10	.20
	Plate block of 4	5.25	
	FDC *(Sept. 3, 1986)*		2.00

1986. PAUL DUDLEY WHITE ISSUE in the Great Americans Series
honored the authority on cardiovascular disease and a pioneer in its diagnosis, treatment, and prevention (1886-1973). *Intaglio, perforated 11.*

861 *Dr. Paul Dudley White*

861		MNHVF	UseVF
3¢	**blue** tagged (large block), matte gum	.25	.20
	Plate block of 4	.35	
	FDC *(Sept. 15, 1986)*		1.75
	zo. Tagging omitted (error) (Plate No. 2 or 3)	—	
	zxm. Untagged (intentional), matte gum *(1994)*	.25	.20
	Plate block of 4	.35	
	zxs. Untagged (intentional) shiny gum	.25	
	Plate block of 4	.35	

1986. BERNARD REVEL ISSUE in the Great Americans Series
honored the scholar and educator (1885-1940) in conjunction with the centennial of Yeshiva University, the nation's oldest and largest Jewish institution of higher learning. A six-pointed Star of David is hidden in the engraving for the beard. *Intaglio, perforated 11.*

862 *Dr. Bernard Revel*

862		MNHVF	UseVF
$1	**blue** tagged (large block)	2.00	.25
	Plate block of 4	13.00	
	FDC *(Sept. 23, 1986)*		4.00

1986. CHRISTMAS ISSUE The contemporary stamp featured a winter village scene, which was designed by Dolli Tingle of Westport, Conn. The traditional stamp depicts the oil-on-wood painting *Perugino Madonna*, by Il Perugino. *Gravure, perforated 11.*

 863 *Village scene*

863		MNHVF	UseVF
22¢	**multicolored** tagged	.50	.20
	Plate block of 4	2.75	
	FDC *(Oct. 24, 1986)*		2.00

 864 *Perugino Madonna*

864		MNHVF	UseVF
22¢	**multicolored** tagged	.50	.20
	Plate block of 4	2.75	
	FDC *(Oct. 24, 1986)*		2.00

1986. STAR ROUTE TRUCK COIL ISSUE in the Transportation Series showed a truck used to carry mail under contract with the Post Office Dept. The 5.5¢ rate was for nonprofit Third Class mail presorted to the carrier route. The tagged version was a "collector" issue meeting no specific postal rate. *Coil, intaglio, perforated 10 vertically. Plate number every 52 stamps.*

 865 *Star Route truck, 1910s*

865		MNHVF	UseVF
5.5¢	**maroon** block tagged	.25	.20
	Pair	.35	
	FDC *(Nov. 1, 1986)*		1.75
	zx. Untagged (Bureau-printed service indicator: "Nonprofit Org. CAR-RT SORT")	.25	.20
	FDC		5.00

1986. BREAD WAGON COIL ISSUE in the Transportation Series. *Coil, intaglio, perforated 10 vertically. Plate number every 52 or 48 stamps.*

 866 *Bread wagon, 1880s*

866		MNHVF	UseVF
25¢	**orange brown** block tagged, plates 2, 3, 4	.40	.20
	brown, plates 1, 5	.40	.20
	Pair	1.00	
	FDC *(Nov. 22, 1986)*		1.75
	v. Pair, imperforate	10.00	
	v1. Pair, imperforate between	500.00	
	zo. Tagging omitted (error)	—	

1986. OMNIBUS COIL ISSUE in the Transportation Series. Type of No. 806, redesigned, ("1 USA" instead of "USA 1"). *Coil, intaglio, perforated 10 vertically. Plate number every 52 stamps for plate 1 and 2. Plate number every 48 stamps for plate 3.*

 867 *Omnibus, 1880s*

867		MNHVF	UseVF
1¢	**violet** block tagged	.25	.20
	Pair	.30	
	FDC *(Nov. 26, 1986)*		1.75
	v. Pair, imperforate	2,400.00	
	pz. Prephosphored paper	.25	.20
	Pair	.30	
	zxm. Untagged, matte gum	.25	.20
	Pair	.30	
	zxs. Untagged, shiny gum	.25	.20
	Pair	.30	

For similar design with "USA 1¢" see No. 806.

1986. STAGECOACH ISSUE in the Transportation Series. Type of No. 791, re-engraved. "Stagecoach 1890s" is 17mm long. *Coil, intaglio, perforated 10 vertically. Plate number every 52 stamps.*

 868 *Stagecoach, 1890s*

868		MNHVF	UseVF
4¢	**red brown** block tagged	.25	.20
	Pair	.30	
	FDC *(Aug. 1986)*		1.75
	v. Pair, imperforate	600.00	
	z. Overall tagging *(1990)*	.50	.20
	Pair	.75	

1987. TOW TRUCK COIL ISSUE in the Transportation Series. The 8.5¢ rate was for nonprofit, Third Class mail. *Coil, intaglio, perforated 10 vertically. Plate number every 52 stamps.*

 869 *Tow truck, 1920s*

869		MNHVF	UseVF
8.5¢	**dark gray** block tagged	.50	.20
	Pair	.50	.20
	FDC *(Jan. 24, 1987)*		1.75
	zx. Untagged (Bureau-printed red service indicator: "Nonprofit Org.")	.25	.20
	Pair	—	
	FDC		5.00

1987. TRACTOR COIL ISSUE in the Transportation Series. The 7.1¢ value was issued for Third Class non-profit mail presorted by ZIP code. *Coil, intaglio, perforated 10. Plate number every 52 stamps.*

870 *Tractor, 1920s*

870		MNHVF	UseVF
7.1¢	**dark red** block tagged	.25	.20

Pair .50
FDC *(Feb. 6, 1987)* 1.75
zx. Untagged, Bureau-printed service .25 .20
   indicator: "Nonprofit Org."
Pair .50
FDC *(Feb. 6, 1987)* 5.00
zx1. Untagged (Bureau-printed service .25 .20
   indicator: "Nonprofit 5-Digit Zip+4")
Pair .50
FDC *(May 26, 1989)* 1.75

1987. JULIA WARD HOWE ISSUE in the Great Americans Series
honored the social reformer and author of *The Battle Hymn of the
Republic.* Well known for her abolitionist sentiment, Howe (1819-
1910) also was a champion of the rights of women and the less
fortunate. *Intaglio, perforated 11.*

871 *Julia Ward Howe*

871		MNHVF	UseVF
14¢	**red** tagged (large block)	.25	.20
	Plate block of 4	.75	
	FDC *(Feb. 12, 1987)*		1.75

1987. MARY LYON ISSUE in the Great Americans Series honored a
pioneer of higher education for women. Lyon (1797-1849) organized
Wheaton College in 1834 and founded Mount Holyoke College in
1837. *Intaglio, perforated 11.*

872 *Mary Lyon*

872		MNHVF	UseVF
2¢	**blue** tagged (large block)	.25	.20
	Plate block of 4	.30	
	FDC *(Feb. 28, 1987)*		1.75
	zo. Tagging omitted (error) (Plate No. 1)	—	
	zx. Untagged (intentional) (Plate No. 2)	.25	
	Plate block of 4	.30	

1987. LOCOMOTIVE COIL ISSUE in the Transportation Series. Type
of No. 790, redesigned. *Coil, intaglio, perforated 11. Plate number
every 52 stamps for plate 1 and every 48 stamps for plate 2.*

873 *Locomotive, 1870s*

873		MNHVF	UseVF
2¢	**black** block tagged	.25	.20
	Pair	.30	
	FDC *(March 6, 1987)*		2.00
	zxm. Untagged, matte gum	.25	.20
	zxs. Untagged, shiny gum	.25	.20

For similar design with "USA 2¢" see No. 790.

> *Listings and prices for plate number coil strips
> and singles appear at the end of this
> definitives section of the Krause-Minkus catalog.*

1987. CANAL BOAT ISSUE in the Transportation Series. *Coil,
intaglio, perforated 10. Plate number every 52 stamps.*

874 *Canal boat, 1880s*

874		MNHVF	UseVF
10¢	**sky blue** block tagged matte gum	.25	.20
	Pair	.40	.20
	FDC *(April 11, 1987)*		1.75
	v. Pair, imperforate	—	—
	pz. Prephosphored paper, shiny gum	.25	.20
	pzm. Prephosphored paper, matte gum	—	—
	zm. Overall tagged, matte gum *(1993)*	.25	.20
	zo. Tagging omitted	—	—
	zs. Overall tagged, shiny gum *(1994)*	.25	.20

1987. FLAG WITH FIREWORKS ISSUE This stamp replaced the Flag
Over Historic Buildings issues. *Gravure, perforated 11.*

875, B172 *Flag with fireworks*

875		MNHVF	UseVF
22¢	**multicolored** tagged	.35	.20
	Plate block of 4	1.75	
	FDC *(May 9, 1987)* single		1.75
	n. Booklet pane of 20	8.50	
	FDC, booklet pane *(Nov. 30, 1987)*		12.00

1987. FLAG OVER CAPITOL COIL ISSUE This stamp was issued to
test prephosphored paper, which is tagged before printing. Every
stamp has an imprinted "T" in the lower margin. *Coil, intaglio,
perforated 10 vertically. Plate number every 48 stamps.*

876		MNHVF	UseVF
22¢	**black, blue & red** with "T" at bottom	.40	.20
	Pair	.75	
	FDC *(May 23, 1987)*		2.50

1987. RED CLOUD ISSUE in the Great Americans Series honored
the chief (1822-1909) of the Oglala Sioux. *Intaglio, perforated 11.*

877 *Red Cloud*

877		MNHVF	UseVF
10¢	**carmine red** tagged (large block)	.25	.20
	Plate block of 4	.75	
	FDC *(Aug. 15, 1987)*		2.00
	z. Overall tagged (1990)	.25	.20
	Plate block of 4	.75	
	zo. Tagging omitted (error)	—	
	pzm. Phosphored paper, solid tagging,	.25	.20
	matte gum		
	Plate block of 4	.75	
	pzs. Phosphored paper, mottled tagging,	.25	.20
	shiny gum		
	Plate block of 4	.75	
	pzs1. carmine phosphored paper, mottled	.25	
	tagging (1995)		
	Plate block of 4	.75	

1987. BRET HARTE ISSUE in the Great Americans Series honored
the author and poet (1836-1902) famous for stories and poems of the
American West. *Intaglio, perforated 11.*

878 *Bret Harte*

878		MNHVF	UseVF
$5	**Venetian red** tagged (large block)	8.00	2.00
	Plate block of 4	40.00	
	y. Pane of 20	120.00	
	FDC *(Aug. 25, 1987)*		20.00
	zo. Tagging omitted (error)		
	pz. Phosphored paper, solid tagging *(March 1992)*	8.00	2.00
	Plate block of 4	35.00	
	pzy. Pane of 20	120.00	

1987. MILK WAGON COIL ISSUE in the Transportation Series met no specific postal rate; it was used as a changemaker in postal vending machines. *Coil, intaglio, perforated 10 vertically. Plate number every 52 stamps.*

 879 *Milk wagon, 1900s*

879		MNHVF	UseVF
5¢	**charcoal** block tagged	.25	.20
	Pair	.30	
	FDC *(Sept. 25, 1987)*		1.75

1987. RACING CAR COIL ISSUE in the Transportation Series. The Marmon Wasp, shown here, won the first Indianapolis 500-mile auto race in 1911. Denomination covered the rate for ZIP+4 presorted mail. *Coil, intaglio, perforated 10 vertically. Plate number every 52 stamps.*

 880 *Racing car, 1911*

880		MNHVF	UseVF
17.5¢	**blue violet** block tagged	.30	.20
	Pair	.50	
	FDC *(Sept. 25, 1987)*		1.75
	v. Pair, imperforate	2,250.00	
	zx. Untagged (Bureau-printed red service indicator: "ZIP+4 Pre-sort")	.30	.20
	Pair	.50	

1987. CHRISTMAS ISSUE The contemporary design consisted of tree ornaments; the traditional design displays a portion of Giovanni Battista Moroni's painting *A Gentleman in Adoration before the Madonna. Gravure, perforated 11.*

 881 *Madonna and Child*

881		MNHVF	UseVF
22¢	**multicolored** tagged	.50	.20
	Plate block of 4	2.75	
	FDC *(Oct. 23, 1987)*		2.00

 882 *Tree ornament*

882		MNHVF	UseVF
22¢	**multicolored** tagged	.50	.20
	Plate block of 4	2.75	
	Pair, gutter between	—	
	FDC *(Oct. 23, 1987)*		2.00

1988. CONESTOGA WAGON COIL ISSUE in the Transportation Series. The wagon was invented by Pennsylvania Dutch to transport produce to markets. *Intaglio, perforated 10 vertically. Plate number every 52 stamps for plate 1 and 48 stamps for all other plate numbers.*

 883 *Conestoga wagon, 1800s*

883		MNHVF	UseVF
3¢	**dark lilac purple** block tagged	.25	.20
	Pair	.30	
	FDC *(Feb. 29, 1988)*		1.75
	zxm. Untagged, matte gum *(1992)*	.25	.30
	zxs. Untagged, shiny gum *(1995)*	.30	.30
	zxs1. Untagged, low gloss gum	.30	.30

1988. NON-DENOMINATED "E" ISSUE consisted of three versions: sheet, coil, and booklet. The stamps were released to meet the new 25¢ First Class rate. In a departure from previous letter-denominated stamps, this showed a picture of the Earth, as in a child's spelling primer. *Gravure, perforated 11.*

 884-886, B173 *"E" and Earth*

884		MNHVF	UseVF
(25¢)	**multicolored** block tagged	.50	.20
	Plate block of 4	2.00	
	FDC *(March 22, 1988)*		1.75
	zo. Tagging omitted (error)	—	

1988. NON-DENOMINATED "E" COIL ISSUE Intaglio, perforated 10 vertically. Plate number every 24 stamps.

885		MNHVF	UseVF
(25¢)	**multicolored** block tagged	.50	.20
	Pair	.75	
	FDC *(March 22, 1988)*		1.75
	v. Pair, imperforate	100.00	

Listings and prices for plate number coil strips and singles appear at the end of this definitives section of the Krause-Minkus catalog.

1988. NON-DENOMINATED "E" BOOKLET ISSUE Booklet, perforated 10.

886		MNHVF	UseVF
(25¢)	**multicolored** block tagged	.50	.20
	FDC *(March 22, 1988)*		1.75
	n. Booklet pane of 10	6.50	
	FDC, booklet pane		7.50

1988. PHEASANT BOOKLET ISSUE designed for sale in vending machines as well as over the counter, this booklet was the first in the Flora and Fauna Series and the first produced for the U.S. Postal Service by the American Bank Note Co. *Gravure, 10x11.*

 887, B174, B175 *Pheasant*

887		MNHVF	UseVF
25¢	**multicolored** tagged	.50	.20
	FDC *(April 29, 1988)* single		1.75
	n. Booklet pane of 10	6.00	
	a. red removed from background sky	6.00	.50

an. Booklet pane of 10	75.00	
nv. Booklet pane of 10, horizontally imperforate between	2,250.00	
FDC, booklet pane		8.00

Fully imperforate panes were cut from printer's waste.

1988. JACK LONDON BOOKLET ISSUE in the Great Americans Series was of the same design as No. 853. *Intaglio, by Bureau of Engraving and Printing, perforated 11 or 10.*

888

	MNHVF	UseVF
25¢ blue tagged (large block) perforated 11 (B176, B177, B178)	.45	.20
FDC single *(May 3, 1988)*		2.00
n. Booklet pane of 10	4.50	5.00
FDC booklet pane		8.00
zo. Tagging omitted (error)	7.00	
nzo. Booklet pane of 10, tagging omitted	100.00	

889

	MNHVF	UseVF
25¢ blue tagged (large block) perforated 10	.50	.20
FDC single *(May 3, 1988)*		1.75
n. Booklet pane of 6	2.75	
FDC, booklet pane		4.00
zo. Tagging omitted (error)	3.00	
nzo. Booklet pane of 6, tagging omitted	55.00	

1988. FLAGS WITH CLOUDS ISSUE Gravure, perforated 11.

890, 890A, B180 *Flag with clouds*

890

	MNHVF	UseVF
25¢ multicolored tagged	.35	.20
Plate block of 4	3.25	
Pair, gutter between	—	
FDC *(May 6, 1988)*		1.75

1988. FLAGS WITH CLOUDS BOOKLET ISSUE Gravure, perforated 11.

890A

	MNHVF	UseVF
25¢ multicolored tagged	.50	.20
FDC *(May 6, 1988)* single		1.75
n. Booklet pane of 6	2.75	3.00
FDC, booklet pane		4.50

1988. FLAG OVER YOSEMITE COIL ISSUE showed the U.S. flag billowing over Half Dome, Yosemite's most striking example of glacier-carved granite. *Coil, intaglio, perforated 10 vertically. Plate number every 52 or 48 stamps.*

891 *Flag over Yosemite*

891

	MNHVF	UseVF
25¢ multicolored block tagged	.40	.20
Pair	.75	
FDC *(May 20, 1988)*		1.75
v. Pair, imperforate	35.00	
pz. Prephosphored paper, mottled tagging	.40	.20
Pair	.75	
FDC *(Feb. 14, 1989)*		1.75
pzv. Pair, imperforate, prephosphored paper	20.00	
v1. Pair, imperforate between	450.00	
a. black trees	150.00	
zo. Tagging omitted (error)	3.00	

1988. OWL AND GROSBEAK ISSUE in the Flora and Fauna Series depicted two colorful birds in a booklet format. *Gravure, perforated 10.*

892, B179 *Saw-whet owl*

892

	MNHVF	UseVF
25¢ multicolored tagged	.40	.20
FDC *(May 28, 1988)*		1.75

893 *Rose-breasted grosbeak*

893

	MNHVF	UseVF
25¢ multicolored tagged	.40	.20
y. Se-tenant pair, No. 892-93	1.00	.50
FDC *(May 28, 1988)*		1.75
n. Booklet pane of 10 (5 No. 893y)	4.50	6.00
yzo. Tagging omitted (error), se-tenant pair	7.50	
nzo. Booklet pane of 10, tagging omitted	—	

1988. BUFFALO BILL CODY ISSUE in the Great Americans Series honored the military scout, showman, and raconteur (1846-1917) of the Wild West. *Intaglio, perforated 11.*

894 *Buffalo Bill Cody*

894

	MNHVF	UseVF
15¢ maroon tagged (large block)	.30	.20
Plate block of 4	3.50	
FDC *(June 6, 1988)*		2.00
z. Overall tagged *(1990)*	.30	.20
Plate block of 4	2.00	
pz. Phosphored paper (solid tagging)	.30	.20
Plate block of 4	2.00	
zo. Tagging omitted (error)	10.00	

1988. HARVEY CUSHING ISSUE in the Great Americans Series honored the "father of neurosurgery" (1869-1939). He is credited with laying the foundation for the field of brain surgery. *Intaglio, perforated 11.*

895 *Harvey Cushing*

895

	MNHVF	UseVF
45¢ blue tagged (large block)	1.00	.20
Plate block of 4	4.00	
FDC *(June 17, 1988)*		2.00
z. Overall tagged *(1990)*	1.50	.50
Plate block of 4	11.00	
zo. Tagging omitted (error)	7.00	

Nos. 896 and 897 are not assigned.

1988. POPCORN WAGON COIL ISSUE in the Transportation Series featured the 1902 model of the C. Cretors and Co. No. 1 Wagon. The first completely self-contained model, which could go wherever needed, was introduced in 1893. The value represented the prepaid base bulk mail rate. *Coil, intaglio, perforated 10 vertically. Plate number every 52 stamps.*

898 *Popcorn wagon, 1902*

898 16.7¢		MNHVF	UseVF
	dark rose (Bureau-printed service indicator "Bulk Rate")	.35	.20
	Pair	.50	
	FDC *(July 7, 1988)*		1.75
	v. Pair, imperforate	175.00	

1988. TUGBOAT COIL ISSUE in the Transportation Series showed a tugboat representative of the type used in the first decade of the 20th century. *Coil, intaglio, perforated 10 vertically. Plate number every 52 stamps.*

 899 *Tugboat, 1900s*

899 15¢		MNHVF	UseVF
	purple block tagged	.30	.20
	Pair	.50	
	FDC *(July 12, 1988)*		1.75
	zo. Tagging omitted (error)	—	
	z. Overall tagged *(July 1990)*	.30	.20
	zy. Pair, overall tagged	.50	
	v. Pair imperforate	—	

1988. COAL CAR COIL ISSUE in the Transportation Series issued to pay a single Third Class bulk mail item presorted to 5-digit ZIP codes. *Coil, intaglio, perforated 10 vertically. Plate number every 52 stamps.*

 900 *Coal car, 1870s*

900 13.2¢		MNHVF	UseVF
	dark green (Bureau-printed red service indicator "Bulk Rate")	.30	.20
	Pair	.50	
	FDC *(July 19, 1988)*		1.75
	v. Pair, imperforate	100.00	

1988. WHEEL CHAIR COIL ISSUE in the Transportation Series depicted a 1928 wicker wheelchair produced by the Invacare Corp. of Elyria, Ohio. Issued to pay postage for non-profit bulk rate mail. *Coil, intaglio, perforated 10 vertically. Plate number every 52 stamps for plate 1 and every 48 stamps for plates 2 and 3.*

 901 *Wheel chair, 1920s*

901 8.4¢		MNHVF	UseVF
	dark violet (Bureau-printed red service indicator: "Non-profit")	.30	.20
	Pair	.50	
	FDC *(Aug. 12, 1988)*		1.75
	v. Pair, imperforate	650.00	

Listings and prices for plate number coil strips and singles appear at the end of this definitives section of the Krause-Minkus catalog.

1988. RAILROAD MAIL CAR COIL ISSUE in the Transportation Series issued to meet the single-piece rate for presorted First Class mail to either the 3 or 5 digit ZIP code. *Coil, intaglio, perforated 10 vertically. Plate number every 52 stamps for plate 1 and 48 for plate 2.*

 902 *Railroad mail car, 1920s*

902 21¢		MNHVF	UseVF
	green (Bureau-printed red service indicator "Presorted 1st Class")	.35	.20
	Pair	.75	
	FDC *(Aug. 16, 1988)*		1.75
	v. Pair, imperforate	65.00	

1988. CARRETA COIL ISSUE in the Transportation Series showed a cart used by settlers in Spanish California. Issued to pay the rate for non-profit bulk mailers. *Coil, gravure, perforated 10 vertically. Plate number every 52 stamps.*

 903 *Carreta, 1770s*

903 7.6¢		MNHVF	UseVF
	brown Bureau-printed red service indicator: "Nonprofit"	.25	.20
	Pair	.30	
	FDC *(Aug. 30, 1988)*		1.75

1988. HARRY S. TRUMAN ISSUE in the Great Americans Series. A new version. *Perforated 11 1/4.*

904 20¢		MNHVF	UseVF
	black tagged (large block), matte gum	.35	.20
	Plate block of 4	3.50	
	FDC *(Sept. 1, 1988)*		—
	z. Overall tagged *(1990)*	.35	.20
	Plate block of 4	4.00	
	pz. Phosphored paper, mottled tagging, shiny gum *(1993)*	.40	.20
	Plate block of 4, shiny gum	2.50	
	zo. Tagging omitted (error)	10.00	

(See also No. 811.)

1988. HONEYBEE COIL ISSUE in the Flora and Fauna Series. *Coil, intaglio, perforated 10. Plate number every 48 stamps.*

 905 *Honeybee*

905 25¢		MNHVF	UseVF
	multicolored block tagged	.40	.20
	Pair	.75	
	FDC *(Sept. 2, 1988)*		1.75
	v. black (intaglio) omitted	65.00	
	v1. black (offset) omitted	550.00	
	v2. yellow (offset) omitted	—	
	v3. Pair, imperforate	55.00	
	v4. Pair, imperforate between	1,000.00	
	zo. Tagging omitted (error)	7.00	

1988. ELEVATOR COIL ISSUE in the Transportation Series issued to pay the nonprofit Third Class rate for mail presorted to the carrier route. *Coil, intaglio, perforated 10 vertically. Plate number every 52 stamps.*

906 *Elevator, 1900s*

906		MNHVF	UseVF
5.3¢	**black** (Bureau-printed red service indicator: "Nonprofit/Carrier Route Sort")	.25	.20
	Pair	.30	
	FDC (Sept. 16, 1988)		1.75

1988. FIRE ENGINE COIL ISSUE in the Transportation Series issued to prepay the First Class mail rate presorted by ZIP+4. *Coil, intaglio, perforated 10 vertically. Plate number every 52 stamps.*

907 *Fire engine, 1900s*

907		MNHVF	UseVF
20.5¢	**red** (Bureau-printed black service indicator: "ZIP+4 Presort")	.35	.20
	Pair	.30	
	FDC (Sept. 28, 1988)		2.00

> *Listings and prices for plate number coil strips and singles appear at the end of this definitives section of the Krause-Minkus catalog.*

1988. EAGLE AND MOON ISSUE was designed to meet the increased rate for Express Mail. Although intended for that use, it also was valid for postage classes where a high value was needed. *Offset and intaglio, perforated 11.*

908 *Eagle and Moon*

908		MNHVF	UseVF
$8.75	**multicolored** tagged	25.00	8.00
	Plate block of 4	110.00	
	FDC (Oct. 4, 1988)		30.00

1988. CHRISTMAS ISSUE The contemporary issue depicted a snowy scene and was released at Berlin, N.H., to honor Irving Berlin and his song *White Christmas. Gravure, perforated 11 1/2.*

909 *Snowy village scene*

909		MNHVF	UseVF
25¢	**multicolored,** tagged	.35	.20
	Plate block of 4	1.50	
	FDC (Oct. 20, 1988)		2.00
	Pair, gutter between	—	

1988. MADONNA AND CHILD BY BOTTICELLI ISSUE The traditional issue is based on the painting *Madonna and Child* by Italian master Sandro Botticelli. *Intaglio and offset, perforated 11 1/2.*

910 Madonna and Child *by Botticelli*

910		MNHVF	UseVF
25¢	**multicolored** tagged	.35	.20
	Plate block of 4	1.50	
	FDC (Oct. 20, 1988)		2.00
	v. gold omitted	30.00	

1988. CHESTER CARLSON ISSUE in the Great Americans Series honored the man (1906-1968) who invented xerography and began an office copying revolution. *Intaglio, perforated 11.*

911 *Chester Carlson*

911		MNHVF	UseVF
21¢	**blue violet** tagged (large block)	.35	.20
	Plate block of 4	2.25	
	FDC (Oct. 21, 1988)		1.75
	zo. Tagging omitted (error)	—	

1988. TANDEM BICYCLE COIL ISSUE in the Transportation Series issued to meet the rate for unpresorted ZIP+4 mail, of particular use to mid-size businesses. *Coil, intaglio, perforated 10 vertically. Plate number every 52 stamps.*

912 *Tandem bicycle, 1890s*

912		MNHVF	UseVF
24.1¢	**deep blue violet** (Bureau-printed red service indicator: "ZIP+4")	.35	.20
	Pair	.75	
	FDC (Oct. 26, 1988)		1.75

1988. CABLE CAR COIL ISSUE in the Transportation Series featured a conveyance used in many cities in the very late 1900s and still a common sight in San Francisco. Issued to prepay the rate for the second ounce of First Class mail. *Coil, intaglio, perforated 10 vertically. Plate number every 48 stamps.*

913 *Cable car, 1880s*

913		MNHVF	UseVF
20¢	**dark violet,** block tagged	.35	.20
	Pair	.75	
	FDC (Oct. 28, 1988)		1.75
	v. Pair, imperforate	75.00	
	z. Overall tagged (1990)	.35	.20
	Pair	.75	

1988. POLICE PATROL WAGON COIL ISSUE in the Transportation Series issued to meet the single-piece rate for presorted First Class mailings of postcards. *Coil, intaglio, perforated 10 vertically. Plate number every 52 stamps.*

914 *Police patrol wagon, 1880s*

914		MNHVF	UseVF
13¢	**black** (Bureau-printed red service indicator: "Presorted First Class")	.25	.20
	Pair	.50	
	FDC *(Oct. 29, 1988)*		1.75

1988. MARY CASSATT ISSUE in the Great Americans Series honored the American painter and etcher (1845-1926) who spent most of her life in France. *Intaglio, perforated 11.*

915 *Mary Cassatt*

915		MNHVF	UseVF
23¢	**purple** tagged (large block)	.45	.20
	Plate block of 4	2.25	
	FDC *(Nov. 4, 1988)*		1.75
	z. Overall tagged *(1990)*	.60	.20
	Plate block of 4	3.00	
	pzm. Phosphored paper (solid tagging) matte gum	.60	.20
	Plate block of 4	3.00	
	pzs. Phosphored paper (mottled tagging) shiny gum	.60	.20
	Plate block of 4	3.25	
	zo. Tagging omitted (error)	7.00	

1988. H.H. "HAP" ARNOLD ISSUE in the Great Americans Series honored the "father of the modern air force" (1886-1950). The stamp met the rate for a 3-ounce First Class letter. *Intaglio, perforated 11.*

916 *H.H. "Hap" Arnold*

916		MNHVF	UseVF
65¢	**dark blue** tagged (large block)	1.25	.20
	Plate block of 4	5.00	
	FDC *(Nov. 5, 1988)*		2.50
	zo. Tagging omitted (error)	7.50	

No. 917 is not assigned.

1989. JOHNS HOPKINS ISSUE in the Great Americans Series honored the founder of the hospital and university that bears his name. Hopkins (1795-1873) dedicated his fortune to the relief of suffering and advancement of knowledge. *Intaglio, perforated 11.*

918 *Johns Hopkins*

918		MNHVF	UseVF
$1	**blackish blue** tagged (large block) matte gum	2.00	.30
	Plate block of 4	7.00	
	y. Pane of 20	35.00	
	FDC *(June 7, 1989)*		5.00
	z. Overall tagged *(1990)*	1.75	.30
	Plate block of 4	7.00	
	zy. Pane of 20	35.00	
	zo. Tagging omitted (error)	10.00	

	pzm. Phosphored paper (solid tagging) matte gum *(1992)*	1.75	.30
	Plate block of 4	7.50	
	pzmy. Pane of 20	40.00	
	pzs. Phosphored paper (mottled tagging) shiny gum *(1993)*	2.00	.30
	Plate block of 4	8.00	
	pzsy. Pane of 20	40.00	
	pzsg. Phosphored paper (grainy tagging) semi-gloss gum	2.00	.30
	Plate block of 4	8.00	
	pzsgy. Pane of 20	35.00	

1989. SITTING BULL ISSUE in the Great Americans Series honored the chief, spiritual and political leader of the Hunkpapa Sioux (c.1831-90). Issued to meet the rate for postcards sent via surface mail from the United States to all foreign destinations other than Canada and Mexico. *Intaglio, perforated 11.*

919 *Sitting Bull*

919		MNHVF	UseVF
28¢	**green** tagged (large block)	.50	.20
	Plate block of 4	3.00	
	FDC *(Sept. 14, 1989)*		2.25

1989. SLEIGH WITH GIFTS ISSUE Both the traditional and contemporary stamps were available in both sheet and booklet versions. The two versions of the sleigh contemporary design are noticeably different. The booklet version is printed in five colors, the sheet stamp in four. Sleigh runners of the booklet version are decidedly thicker than on the sheet version. The package to the rear of the sleigh has a bow the same color as the package on the booklet stamp, whereas the bow is of a different color on the sheet version. Finally, the board running under the sleigh is pink on the booklet version and the same color as the sleigh on the sheet version. The two versions of the traditional are identical, other than the booklet stamp having perforations on only two or three sides. *Gravure, perforated 11.*

920, 921, B185 *Sleigh with gifts*

920		MNHVF	UseVF
25¢	**multicolored** tagged	.40	.20
	Plate block of 4	1.75	
	FDC *(Oct. 19, 1989)*		1.75
	v. Vertical pair, imperforate horizontally	750.00	

1989. SLEIGH WITH GIFTS BOOKLET ISSUE

921		MNHVF	UseVF
25¢	**multicolored** booklet stamp, tagged	.40	.20
	FDC *(Oct. 19, 1989)* single		1.75
	n. Booklet pane of 10	3.00	
	FDC booklet pane	—	8.00
	nv. Booklet pane of 10, red omitted	7,150.00	
	nv1. Booklet pane of 10, horizontally imperforate between	—	

1989. THE DREAM OF ST. ALEXANDRIA ISSUE *Intaglio, perforated 11 1/2.*

922, B184 The Dream of St. Alexandria *by Lucovico Carracci*

922

25¢	multicolored tagged	BBMNHVF	UseVF
		.40	.20
	Plate block of 4	1.75	
	FDC *(Oct. 19, 1989)* single		1.75
	n. Booklet pane of 10	3.00	
	FDC booklet pane	—	8.00
	nv. Booklet pane of 10, offset red omitted	750.00	
	nv1. Booklet pane of 10, imperforate	—	

No. 923 is not assigned.

1989. EAGLE AND SHIELD SELF-ADHESIVE ISSUE was available in a do-it-yourself booklet format that permitted the purchaser to fold the pane of 18 die-cut stamps into a more convenient pocket-sized package. The stamps also were available in strips of 18 with the stamps spaced apart for use in affixing machines. *Gravure, die cut between.*

924 *Eagle and shield*

924

25¢	multicolored tagged	MNHVF	UseVF
		.40	.20
	n. Booklet pane of 18	12.00	
	FDC *(Nov. 10, 1989)* single		1.75
	v. Vertical pair, no die cutting between	850.00	
	v1. Pair, no die cutting	—	

No. 925 is not assigned.

1990. BEACH UMBRELLA ISSUE was a vacation-themed stamp meeting the postcard rate. *Booklet stamp, gravure, perforated 11 1/2.*

926, B187 *Beach umbrella*

926

15¢	multicolored booklet stamp, tagged	MNHVF	UseVF
		.30	.20
	n. Booklet pane of 10	4.25	
	FDC *(Feb. 3, 1990)*		1.75
	v. blue omitted	225.00	
	nv. Booklet pane of 10, blue omitted	1,650.00	

1990. LUIS MUÑOZ MARIN ISSUE in the Great Americans Series honored the first popularly elected governor of Puerto Rico (1898-1980). This is a major design change for the Great American series in which a zero precedes denominations of less than 10¢, and information about the subject ("Governor, Puerto Rico") is part of the design. *Intaglio, perforated 11.*

927 *Luis Muñoz Marin*

927

5¢	dark rose, overall tagged	MNHVF	UseVF
		.25	.20
	Plate block of 4	.30	
	FDC *(Feb. 18, 1990)*		1.75
	zo. Tagging omitted (error)	.65	
	Plate block of 4 (Plate No. 1)	2.75	
	zx. Untagged (intentional) *(1991)*	.25	.20
	Plate block of 4 (Plate No. 2)	.65	

1990. SEAPLANE COIL ISSUE in the Transportation Series was the first design in the series to feature aircraft. *Coil, intaglio. Perforated 10 vertically. Plate number every 52 stamps for plate 1 and 48 stamps for plate 2.*

928 *Seaplane, 1914*

928

$1	dark blue & red overall tagged, matte gum	MNHVF	UseVF
		1.75	.50
	Pair	3.50	1.00
	FDC *(April 20, 1990)*		3.00
	v. Pair, imperforate	2,500.00	—
	pz. Phosphored paper, mottled tagging, shiny gum *(1993)*	1.75	.50
	Pair	3.50	1.00
	pzg. Phosphored paper, grainy tagging, dull gum *(1998)*	1.75	.50
	Pair	3.50	1.00

1990. FLAG ISSUE FOR AUTOMATIC TELLER MACHINES The USPS tested dispensing of stamps through bank ATM equipment. Available in panes of 12 the same size as a dollar bill and *printed on polyester film by gravure.* This issue was available as a test through 22 machines in the Seattle, Wash., area. *Self-adhesive, straight-line die cut.*

929 *U.S. flag*

929

25¢	red & dark blue tagged	MNHVF	UseVF
		.50	.50
	n. Pane of 12	6.00	
	FDC single *(May 18, 1990)*		1.75

1990. BOBCAT ISSUE in the Flora and Fauna Series was the first high-value stamp. Printed in panes of 20, with four plate numbers, copyright notice and descriptive information on the selvage. *Intaglio and offset, perforated 11.*

930 *Bobcat*

930

$2	multicolored tagged	MNHVF	UseVF
		4.00	1.25
	Plate block of 4	18.00	
	FDC *(June 1, 1990)*		7.00
	v. Intaglio black omitted	350.00	
	zo. Tagging omitted (error)	10.50	7.00

1990. CIRCUS WAGON COIL ISSUE in the Transportation Series pictured a wagon that could transport live animals from city to city. The wagons could also be loaded on flatbed train cars and were also designed to carry gear or personnel. *Coil, intaglio, Bureau of Engraving and Printing, perforated 10 vertically. Plate number every 52 stamps.*

931 *Circus wagon, 1900s*

931

5¢	carmine red overall tagged	MNHVF	UseVF
		.25	.20
	Pair	.30	
	FDC *(Aug. 31, 1990)*		1.75
	z. Untagged, matte gum	.25	.20
	z1. Untagged low gloss gum	.25	.20

Pair	.30	
v. Pair, imperforate	875.00	

For stamps of this design inscribed "USA 5¢" see No. 1007 (gravure) or No. 1077 (intaglio).

1990. CLAIRE LEE CHENNAULT ISSUE in the Great Americans Series honored the pioneer air power tactician (1890-1958) who formed and led the Flying Tigers in China in World War II. *Intaglio, perforated 11.*

932 *Claire Lee Chennault*

932		**MNHVF**	**UseVF**
40¢	**dark blue** overall tagged, matte gum	.75	.20
	Plate block of 4	3.75	
	FDC *(Sept. 6, 1990)*		2.00
	pzm. Phosphored paper (solid tagging) matte gum	.75	
	Plate block of 4	3.75	
	pzs. Phosphored paper (mottled tagging) shiny gum	.75	.20
	Plate block of 4	4.00	
	pzsg. Phosphored paper (grainy tagging) low-gloss gum	.75	
	Plate block of 4	4.00	

1990. CONTEMPORARY CHRISTMAS ISSUE featured a cut-paper Christmas tree. There are noticeable design and color differences between the sheet and booklet versions of this stamp. *Gravure, perforated 11 or 11 1/2 x 11.*

933, 934, B190 *Christmas tree*

Perforated 11

933		**MNHVF**	**UseVF**
25¢	*Perforated 11* **multicolored** tagged	.40	.20
	Plate block of 4	1.75	
	FDC *(Oct. 18, 1990)*		2.00
	v. Vertical pair, imperforate horizontally	1,100.00	

Perforated 11 1/2 x 11

934		**MNHVF**	**UseVF**
25¢	**multicolored** booklet stamp, tagged	.40	.20
	FDC *(Oct. 18, 1990)* single		2.00
	n. Booklet pane of 10	5.00	3.50
	FDC booklet pane		6.00

1990. MADONNA AND CHILD ISSUE *Offset and intaglio, perforated 11 1/2.*

935, 936, B191 Madonna and Child *by Antonello da Messina*

935		**MNHVF**	**UseVF**
25¢	**multicolored** tagged	.40	.20
	Plate block of 4	1.75	
	FDC *(Oct. 18, 1990)*		2.00

936		**MNHVF**	**UseVF**
25¢	**multicolored** booklet stamp, tagged	.40	.20
	FDC *(Oct. 18, 1990)* single		2.00

n. Booklet pane of 10	5.00	
FDC booklet pane		6.50

The booklet version has a much heavier shading in the Madonna's veil where it meets the right frame line.

1991. "F" (FLOWER) NON-DENOMINATED ISSUE came in sheet, coil, and two different booklet types with "F" and "Flower" on the face to continue the "alphabet primer" theme. Its face value was 29¢, the new First Class mail rate. *Gravure, perforated 13.*

937-940, B192, B193, B194 *"F" and tulip*

937		**MNHVF**	**UseVF**
(29¢)	**multicolored** tagged	.50	.20
	Plate block of 4	2.25	
	FDC *(Jan. 22, 1991)*		1.75
	v. Vertical pair, imperforate	700.00	
	v1. Horizontal pair, imperforate vertically	1,200.00	

1991. "F" (FLOWER) NON-DENOMINATED BOOKLET ISSUE Dark green leaf. *Bureau of Engraving and Printing, perforated 11 1/4.*

938		**MNHVF**	**UseVF**
(29¢)	**multicolored** booklet stamp, tagged	.50	.20
	FDC *(Jan. 22, 1991)*		1.75
	n. Booklet pane of 10	6.00	
	FDC booklet pane		7.50

1991. "F" (FLOWER) NON-DENOMINATED BOOKLET ISSUE Bright green leaf, pale yellow less pronounced, black dies in leaf. *KCS Industries, perforated 11.*

939		**MNHVF**	**UseVF**
(29¢)	**multicolored** booklet stamp, printed by KCS Industries, tagged	.50	.20
	FDC *(Jan. 22, 1991)* single		1.75
	n. Booklet pane of 10	25.00	
	FDC, booklet pane		7.50
	v. Pair, imperforate horizontally	—	

1991. "F" (FLOWER) NON-DENOMINATED COIL ISSUE Coil, perforated 10 vertically. Plate number every 24 stamps.

940		**MNHVF**	**UseVF**
(29¢)	**multicolored** tagged	.60	.20
	Pair	.75	
	FDC *(Jan. 22, 1991)*		1.75
	v. Pair, imperforate	35.00	

1991. NON-DENOMINATED 4¢ MAKE UP ISSUE has a value of 4¢, to be used with a 25¢ stamp to meet the new 29¢ First Class rate. *Offset, perforated 11.*

941 *Text explaining how to use stamp*

941		**MNHVF**	**UseVF**
(4¢)	**bister & carmine**	.25	.20
	Plate block of 4	.30	
	FDC *(Jan. 22, 1991)*		1.75
	v. Vertical pair, imperforate horizontally	125.00	

1991. "F" NON-DENOMINATED ATM FLAG ISSUE was identical in design and material to No. 929, with the denomination replaced by an "F" and the inclusion of "For U.S. Addresses Only." *Gravure, straight-line die cut.*

942 *"F" and U.S. flag*

942
(29¢)

		MNHVF	UseVF
black, dark blue & red tagged		.50	.20
n. Pane of 12		7.00	
FDC *(Jan. 22, 1991)* single			1.75
FDC (pane of 12)			10.00

1991. STEAM CARRIAGE COIL ISSUE in the Transportation Series depicted the "Richard Dudgeon," which is now in the Museum of American History of the Smithsonian Institution. *Coil, intaglio, perforated 10 vertically. Plate number every 52 stamps.*

943 *Steam carriage, 1866*

943
4¢

		MNHVF	UseVF
maroon overall tagged		.25	.20
Pair		.30	
FDC *(Jan. 25, 1991)*			1.75
v. Pair, imperforate		625.00	
zx. Untagged (intentional)		.25	
Pair		.30	

> *Listings and prices for plate number coil strips and singles appear at the end of this definitives section of the Krause-Minkus catalog.*

1991. FAWN ISSUE in the Flora and Fauna Series met the rate for postcards. *Gravure, perforated 11.*

944 *Fawn*

944
19¢

		MNHVF	UseVF
multicolored tagged		.35	.20
Plate block of 4		1.50	
FDC *(March 11, 1991)*			1.75
v. red omitted		850.00	
zo. Tagging omitted (error)		8.50	

1991. FLAG OVER MOUNT RUSHMORE COIL ISSUE marked the 50th anniversary of the South Dakota monument that features the carved images of Presidents Washington, Jefferson, T. Roosevelt, and Lincoln. *Coil, intaglio, perforated 10 vertically. Plate number every 48 stamps.*

945, 945A *Flag over Mount Rushmore; "29" and "USA" outlined in white*

945
29¢

		MNHVF	UseVF
red, blue & maroon mottled tagging		.50	.20
Pair		1.00	.20
FDC *(March 29, 1991)*			1.75
v. Pair, imperforate		25.00	
p. Phosphor-coated "Lenz" paper		5.00	.50

945A
29¢

		MNHVF	UseVF
red, blue & brown color change "Toledo brown" (error), tagged		5.00	—
Pair		10.00	
FDC			1.75

For gravure version of this design, see No. 963.

1991. DENNIS CHAVEZ ISSUE in the Great Americans Series honored the first U.S. born Hispanic (1888-1962) elected to the U.S. Senate. *Intaglio, by Stamp Venturers, perforated 11.*

946 *Dennis Chavez*

946
35¢

		MNHVF	UseVF
black phosphored paper, mottled tagging		.75	.20
Plate block of 4		3.50	
FDC *(April 3, 1991)*			2.00

1991. FLOWER ISSUE is a "denominated" version of the "F" stamp, initially released in sheet and booklet types. *Gravure, perforated 11.*

947, 947A, 948, 982, B195, B195A *Tulip*

947
29¢

		MNHVF	UseVF
multicolored tagged, perforated 11		.40	.20
Plate block of 4		1.75	
FDC *(April 5, 1991)*			1.75

1991. FLOWER ISSUE Perforated 13x12 3/4.

947A
29¢

		MNHVF	UseVF
multicolored tagged, perforated 12 1/2x13		.40	.20
Plate block of 4		1.75	

1991. FLOWER BOOKLET ISSUE

948
29¢

		MNHVF	UseVF
multicolored booklet stamp, tagged, perforated 11		.40	.20
FDC *(April 5, 1991)* single			1.75
n. Booklet pane of 10		8.00	
nv. Pane of 10, vertically imperforate between		1,900.00	
FDC booklet pane			7.50
nv1. Pane of 10, imperforate horizontally		2,800.00	
v. Horizontal pair, imperforate vertically		250.00	
z. Phosphored paper *(1993)*		.50	.20
nz. Booklet pane of 10		25.00	
g. Low gloss gum *(August 1993)*		.50	
ng. Booklet pane of 10, low-gloss gum		8.00	

For coil version of the Flower Issue, see Nos. 966 and 982.

1991. LUNCH WAGON COIL ISSUE in the Transportation Series met the new second-ounce First Class mail rate. *Coil, intaglio, perforated 10 vertically. Plate number every 48 stamps.*

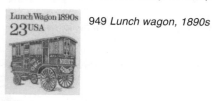

949 *Lunch wagon, 1890s*

949
23¢

		MNHVF	UseVF
blue overall tagged, matte gum		.50	.20
Pair		.75	
FDC *(April 12, 1991)*			1.75
ps. Phosphored paper (mottled tagging) shiny gum *(1993)*		.50	.20
Pair		.75	
pm. Phosphored paper (mottled tagging) matte gum *(1993)*		.50	.20
Pair		.75	
v. Pair, imperforate		150.00	

1991. WOOD DUCK ISSUE in the Flora and Fauna Series *produced by the Bureau of Engraving and Printing with lettering and numbers in black and by KCS Industries with the lettering and numbers in red. Gravure, perforated 10.*

950, 951, B196, B196a, B197, B198 *Wood duck*

950		MNHVF	UseVF
29¢	**multicolored** booklet stamp, black inscription (Bureau of Engraving and Printing), tagged	.75	.20
	FDC *(April 12, 1991)*		1.75
	n. Booklet pane of 10	8.00	
	FDC booklet pane		9.00
	v. Vertical pair, imperforate horizontally	200.00	
	nv. Pane of 10, horizontally imperforate between	1,000.00	
	z. Phosphored paper	.75	.20
	nz. Pane of 10, phosphored paper	8.00	

1991. WOOD DUCK ISSUE in the Flora and Fauna Series. *Perforated 11.*

951		MNHVF	UseVF
29¢	**multicolored** booklet stamp, red inscription (KCS Industries), tagged	1.00	.20
	FDC *(April 12, 1991)*		1.75
	n. Booklet pane of 10	8.75	
	FDC booklet pane		9.00
	v. Vertical pair, imperforate between	—	
	v1. Pair, imperforate	3,960.00	

1991. U.S. FLAG WITH OLYMPIC RINGS BOOKLET ISSUE was a booklet version with a flag motif. *Gravure, perforated 11.*

952, B199, B200, B201 *U.S. flag with Olympic rings*

952		MNHVF	UseVF
29¢	**multicolored** booklet stamp, tagged	.75	.20
	FDC *(April 21, 1991)*		1.75
	n. Booklet pane of 10	8.00	
	FDC booklet pane		7.50
	v. Vertical pair, imperforate between	—	
	nv. Pane of 10, horizontally imperforate between	—	

1991. HOT AIR BALLOON BOOKLET ISSUE met the postcard rate for First Class mail and was available in booklet form. *Gravure, perforated 10.*

953, B203 *Hot air balloon*

953		MNHVF	UseVF
19¢	**multicolored** booklet stamp, tagged	.30	.20
	FDC *(May 17, 1991)*		1.75
	n. Booklet pane of 10	4.50	
	FDC booklet pane	—	7.50

1991. TRACTOR TRAILER COIL ISSUE in the Transportation Series was for use by bulk business mailers. Since there was no service endorsement on the stamp, mass mailers were required to endorse each piece of mail franked with this stamp. *Coil, intaglio, Bureau of Engraving and Printing, perforated 10 vertically. Plate number every 48 stamps.*

954 *Tractor trailer, 1930s*

954		MNHVF	UseVF
10¢	**green** (Bureau-printed gray service indicator: "Additional Presort Postage Paid")	.25	.20
	Pair	.30	
	FDC *(May 25, 1991)*		1.75
	v. Pair, imperforate	150.00	

For version with service indicator in black, see No. 1042.

1991. CANOE COIL ISSUE in the Transportation Series was for use by nonprofit mailers. *Coil, intaglio, Bureau of Engraving and Printing, perforated 10 vertically. Plate number every 48 stamps.*

955 *Canoe, 1800s*

955		MNHVF	UseVF
5¢	**brown** (printed gray service indicator: "Additional Nonprofit Postage Paid")	.25	.20
	Pair	.30	
	FDC *(May 25, 1991)*		1.75
	v. Pair, imperforate	325.00	

For gravure version of No. 955 in red, see No. 979.

1991. FLAGS ON PARADE ISSUE celebrated the 125th anniversary of Memorial Day. *Gravure, perforated 11.*

956 *Flags on parade*

956		MNHVF	UseVF
29¢	**multicolored** overall tagged	.50	.20
	Plate block of 4	2.00	
	FDC *(May 30, 1991)*		1.75
	pz. Phosphor-coated paper	1.00	

1991. HUBERT H. HUMPHREY ISSUE in the Great Americans Series honored the former vice president, Minnesota senator and mayor of Minneapolis (1911-1978). A date error in the selvage inscription, showing the wrong dates of his tenure as vice president, was corrected with a re-release of the stamp in 1993. *Intaglio, perforated 11.*

957 *Hubert H. Humphrey*

957		MNHVF	UseVF
52¢	**purple** phosphored paper (solid tagging) matte gum	1.50	.20
	Plate block of 4	6.00	
	FDC *(June 3, 1991)*		2.00
	pz. Phosphored paper (mottled tagging) shiny gum *(1993)*	1.00	.20
	Plate block of 4	5.00	

1991. EAGLE AND OLYMPIC RINGS ISSUE met 8-ounce Express Mail rate. The stamp was valid for other mail as well. *Intaglio and offset, perforated 11.*

958 *Eagle and Olympic rings*

958

$9.95	**multicolored** tagged	MNHVF	UseVF
		15.00	7.50
	Plate block of 4	100.00	
	FDC *(June 6, 1991)*		25.00

1991. AMERICAN KESTREL ISSUE in the Flora and Fauna Series was the first U.S. stamp issued without a cents sign in the denomination and a "0" preceding the single digit value. *Offset by American Bank Note Co. in shiny-gummed panes of 100, perforated 11.*

959 *American kestrel*

959

1¢	**multicolored**	MNHVF	UseVF
		.25	.20
	Plate block of 4	.30	
	FDC *(June 22, 1991)*		1.75

For versions inscribed "USA 1¢," see No. 1079 (sheet) and No. 1115 (coil).

1991. BLUEBIRD ISSUE in the Flora and Fauna Series. *Offset, perforated 11.*

960 *Eastern bluebird*

960

3¢	Eastern bluebird	MNHVF	UseVF
		.25	.20
	Plate block of 4	.30	
	FDC *(June 22, 1991)*		1.75

For version inscribed "USA 3¢" see No. 1123.

1991. CARDINAL ISSUE in the Flora and Fauna Series met the postcard rate to Canada and Mexico. *Gravure, perforated 11 1/2x11.*

961 *Cardinal*

961

30¢	**multicolored** on phosphored paper	MNHVF	UseVF
		.45	.20
	Plate block of 4	2.00	
	FDC *(June 22, 1991)*		1.75
	v. red omitted	850.00	
	zo. Tagging omitted (error)	8.50	

1991. STATUE OF LIBERTY TORCH ISSUE was designed for sale through ATM machines. This issue provided 18 stamps on a backing sheet the same size as a dollar bill. Unlike its predecessors (Nos. 929 and 942), this issue was printed on paper. *Gravure, die cut, imperforate.*

962 *Liberty torch*

962

29¢	**black, gold & green** tagged, die cut	MNHVF	UseVF
		.60	.30
	FDC *(June 25, 1991)*		1.75
	n. Pane of 18, plain paper back	12.00	
	FDC *(pane of 18)*		14.00
	nv. Pane of 18, printed backing paper	12.50	
	v. Pair, die cut omitted	3,750.00	

1991. FLAG OVER MOUNT RUSHMORE COIL ISSUE similar to No. 945. *Coil, gravure, American Bank Note Co., perforated 10 vertically. Plate number every 24 stamps.*

963 *Flag over Mount Rushmore; "29" and "USA" not outlined in white*

963

29¢	**blue, red & brown** tagged	MNHVF	UseVF
		.50	.25
	Pair	1.00	
	FDC *(July 4, 1991)*		1.75

For intaglio version of the same design, see No. 945.

> *Listings and prices for plate number coil strips and singles appear at the end of this definitives section of the Krause-Minkus catalog.*

1991. EAGLE AND OLYMPIC RINGS ISSUE met the Priority Mail rate for second-day delivery of up to 2 pounds. *Intaglio and offset, perforated 11.*

964 *Eagle and Olympic rings*

964

$2.90	**multicolored** tagged	MNHVF	UseVF
		5.00	2.75
	Plate block of 4	25.00	
	FDC *(July 7, 1991)*		9.00
	v. Intaglio black omitted	3,500.00	
	v1. Vertical pair, imperforate horizontally	—	

1991. FISHING BOAT COIL ISSUE met the First Class rate for domestic postcards. *Coil, gravure, American Bank Note Co., perforated 10 vertically. Plate number every 36 stamps.*

965 *Fishing boat, two rope loops on mooring*

965

		MNHVF	UseVF
19¢	**multicolored** Type I, tagged	.40	.20
	Pair	.75	
	FDC *(Aug. 8, 1991)*		1.75
	a. Type II (lighter colors, sharper print) *(1992)*	.40	.20
	Pair	.75	
	zo. Tagging omitted (error, wrong paper used) *(1993)*	1.00	.30
	Pair	2.00	.75

Imperforates in this design came from printer's waste. For version with one loop of rope tying boat to piling, see No. 1044.

1991. FLOWER COIL ISSUE "Roulettes," a series of slits, rather than "perforations," or cut holes, facilitate separation. *Coil, gravure, Stamp Venturers, rouletted 10 vertically. Plate number every 33 stamps.*

966 *Tulip*

966

		MNHVF	UseVF
29¢	**multicolored** tagged	.75	.20
	Pair	1.25	
	FDC *(Aug. 16, 1991)*		1.75

1991. EAGLE OVER COASTLINE, OLYMPIC RINGS ISSUE met the rate for international Express Mail pieces weighing up to 8 ounces to 109 countries. *Intaglio and offset, perforated 11.*

967 *Eagle over coastline, Olympic rings*

967

		MNHVF	UseVF
$14	**multicolored** tagged	30.00	17.50
	Plate block of 4	130.00	
	FDC *(Aug. 31, 1991)*		32.50
	v. Intaglio red omitted (value and rings)	—	

No. 968 is not assigned.

1991. U.S. FLAG COIL ISSUE included a service indicator and met the First Class presort rate. *Coil, gravure, American Bank Note Co., perforated 10 vertically. Plate number every 24 stamps.*

969 *U.S. flag*

969

		MNHVF	UseVF
23¢	**red & blue** printed service indicator: "Presorted First Class"	.65	.20
	Pair	1.00	
	FDC *(Sept. 27, 1991)*		1.75

1991. USPS OLYMPIC SPONSOR ISSUE was released to promote the USPS sponsorship of the Olympic Games in Barcelona, Spain. *Gravure, perforated 11.*

970 *Eagle and Olympic rings*

970

		MNHVF	UseVF
$1	**multicolored** tagged	2.75	.75
	Plate block of 4	12.00	
	FDC *(Sept. 20, 1991)*		3.00

1991. SANTA DESCENDING A CHIMNEY ISSUE

971, 972, 972A *Santa descending a chimney*

971

		MNHVF	UseVF
29¢	**multicolored** tagged	.45	.20
	Plate block of 4	2.00	
	FDC *(Oct. 17, 1991)*		1.75
	v. Vertical pair, imperforate horizontally	500.00	
	v1. Horizontal pair, imperforate vertically	325.00	

1991. SANTA BOOKLET ISSUE Of these six designs, four are totally different and two are modifications of the sheet stamp design. *Perforated 11, gravure.*

972

		MNHVF	UseVF
29¢	**multicolored** booklet stamp, Type I, tagged	.45	.20
	FDC *(Oct. 17, 1991)* single		2.00

972A

		MNHVF	UseVF
29¢	**multicolored** booklet stamp, Type II, tagged	.45	.20
	FDC single		2.00
	y. Se-tenant pair, Nos. 972, 972A	.90	
	n. Booklet pane, 2 each 4 Nos. 972, 972A	2.00	
	FDC booklet pane	—	4.00
	nv. Booklet pane imperforate	—	

Type I has an extra vertical line of brick in the top row of bricks at left; Type II is missing that vertical line of brick.

973, B208 *Santa checking his list*

973

		MNHVF	UseVF
29¢	**multicolored** booklet stamp, tagged	.45	.20
	FDC *(Oct. 17, 1991)* single		2.00
	n. Booklet pane of 4	1.50	
	FDC booklet pane	—	4.00

974 *Santa leaving gifts*

974

		MNHVF	UseVF
29¢	**multicolored** booklet stamp, tagged	.45	.20
	FDC single		2.00
	n. Booklet pane of 4	1.50	
	FDC booklet pane		4.00
	v. Booklet pane imperforate	—	

975 *Santa ascending chimney*

975

		MNHVF	UseVF
29¢	**multicolored** booklet stamp, tagged	.45	.20
	FDC single		2.00
	n. Booklet pane of 4	1.50	
	FDC booklet pane		4.00
	v. Booklet pane imperforate	—	

976 *Santa departing in sleigh*

976

		MNHVF	UseVF
29¢	**multicolored** booklet stamp, tagged	.45	.20
	FDC single		2.00
	n. Booklet pane of 4	1.50	
	FDC booklet pane		4.00
	v. Booklet pane imperforate	—	

1991. TRADITIONAL CHRISTMAS ISSUE Intaglio and offset, perforated 11.

977, B209 *From* Madonna and Child with Donor *by Antoniazzo Romano*

977

		MNHVF	UseVF
29¢	**multicolored** tagged	.45	.20
	Plate block of 4	2.00	
	FDC *(Oct. 17, 1991)* single		1.75
	n. Booklet pane of 10	8.00	
	FDC booklet pane		8.00
	v. Booklet single, red & black (intaglio) omitted	3,750.00	

No. 978 is not assigned.

1991. CANOE COIL ISSUE in the Transportation Series. *Coil, gravure, Stamp Venturers, perforated 10 vertically. Plate number every 33 stamps.*

979 *Canoe, 1800s*

979

		MNHVF	UseVF
5¢	**red** (printed service indicator: "Additional Nonprofit Postage Paid")	.25	.20
	Pair	.30	
	FDC *(Oct. 22, 1991)*		1.75
	g. Low-gloss gum	.50	—
	Pair	1.00	—

For intaglio version in brown, see No. 955.

1991. EAGLE AND SHIELD NON-DENOMINATED COIL ISSUE met the needs of permit mailers on presorted bulk mail pieces. The value of the stamp is 10¢, with additional postage paid by mailers at the time of mailing. *Coil, gravure, American Bank Note Co. (plate numbers beginning with "A" every 24 stamps), perforated 10 vertically.*

980 *Eagle and shield*

980

		MNHVF	UseVF
(10¢)	**multicolored** (printed service indicator: "Bulk Rate")	.25	.20
	Pair	.30	
	FDC *(Dec. 13, 1991)*		1.75
	v. Pair, imperforate	—	

See Nos. 1011, 1012, 1129, 1204 and 1205 for similar stamps printed by the Bureau of Engraving and Printing and Stamp Venturers.

> *Listings and prices for plate number coil strips and singles appear at the end of this definitives section of the Krause-Minkus catalog.*

1992. WENDELL L. WILLKIE ISSUE in the Great Americans Series honored the man (1892-1944) who lost in the 1940 presidential election and then served the Roosevelt administration on a diplomatic mission. *Intaglio, perforated 11.*

981 *Wendell L. Willkie*

981

		MNHVF	UseVF
75¢	**maroon** phosphored paper (solid tagging) matte gum	1.25	.50
	Plate block of 4	5.50	
	FDC *(Feb. 16, 1992)*		3.00
	pz. Phosphored paper (mottled tagging) shiny gum	1.25	.50
	Plate block of 4	5.50	

1992. FLOWER PERFORATED COIL ISSUE Gravure, perforated 10 vertically. Plate number every 33 stamps.

982 *Tulip*

982

		MNHVF	UseVF
29¢	**multicolored** tagged	.75	.20
	Pair	1.25	
	FDC *(March 3, 1992)*		1.75

1992. EARL WARREN ISSUE in the Great Americans Series honored the former Chief Justice of the United States. Warren (1891-1974) was the driving force in the landmark case Brown vs. Board of Education that outlawed racial segregation in public schools. *Intaglio, perforated 11.*

983 *Earl Warren*

983

		MNHVF	UseVF
29¢	**blue** phosphored paper (mottled tagging)	.50	.20
	Plate block of 4	2.75	
	FDC *(March 9, 1992)*		2.00

1992. Flag Over White House Coil Issue honored the 200th anniversary of the home and office of the president of the United States. *Intaglio, perforated 10 vertically. Plate number every 48 stamps.*

984 *U.S. flag, White House*

984		MNHVF	UseVF
29¢	**blue & red** tagged, phosphored paper	.50	.20
	Pair	1.00	2.00
	FDC *(April 23, 1992)*		
	a. indigo & red	—	
	Pair	—	
	v. Pair, imperforate	20.00	

1992. USA Coil Issue was for presorted First-Class mailings. The background is a graduated blue; "First-Class" is 9 1/2mm long, and "23" is 6mm long. *Coil, gravure, American Bank Note Co., perforated 10 vertically (plate numbers start with "A" every 24 stamps).*

985 *Chromed "USA"*

985		MNHVF	UseVF
23¢	**multicolored** (printed service indicator: "Presorted First-Class")	.50	.20
	Pair	.75	
	FDC *(July 21, 1992)*		1.75

See Nos. 994 and 1010 for similar stamps printed by the Bureau of Engraving and Printing and by Stamp Venturers.

1992. Postage and Mailing Center Coil Issue tested postage and mail center equipment that weighed items for mailing, determined the postage necessary for the desired level of service, and printed stamps with the appropriate amount of postage. *Coil, intaglio by Bureau of Engraving and Printing, and denomination printed in black, phosphored paper, perforated 9 3/4 horizontally. Plate number every 48 stamps.*

986 *Shield & bunting*

986		MNHVF	UseVF
(variable rate)	**red & blue** variable rate, denomination 1¢ to $99.99, solid tagging, matte gum	.50	.50
	FDC *(Aug. 20, 1992)*		7.50
	pz. denomination 19¢-$99.99, mottled tagging, shiny gum	1.50	.50

See also Nos. 1040, 1053 and 1117. Also located in On Demand Postage Section see Nos. OD3, OD4, OD5 and OD6.

1992. Pledge of Allegiance Issue honored the centennial of the pledge, first recited by school children for the 400th anniversary of Columbus' voyage of discovery. *Gravure, perforated 10.*

987, 1008, B211, B212, B213, B214, B215 *Flag, "I pledge allegiance..."*

987		MNHVF	UseVF
29¢	**multicolored** black inscription, booklet stamp, tagged	.75	.20
	FDC *(Sept. 8, 1992)* single		1.75
	n. Booklet pane of 10	7.50	
	FDC booklet pane		7.00
	a. Perforated 11x10 on 2 or 3 sides	1.25	.50
	an. Booklet pane of 10	12.00	
	av. Pair, imperforate	900.00	—

For version with red inscription see No. 1008.

1992. Eagle and Shield Self-Adhesive Issue was produced by three different contractors, each is identifiable through the color of the inscription "(USA 29)": red for Stamp Venturers of Fairfax, Va.; green for Dittler Brothers, Inc., of Oakwood, Ga.; and brown for Banknote Corporation of America, Inc., of Suffern, N.Y. These stamps were issued in panes of 17 plus a label on flexible backing paper, suitable for folding into a booklet. The stamps also were available in strips of 17 with the stamps spaced apart for use in affixing machines. *Straightline die cut, gravure.*

988, 990, 992 *Eagle and shield*

988		MNHVF	UseVF
29¢	**multicolored** red inscription, tagged	.45	.30
	FDC *(Sept. 25, 1992)* single		2.00
	n. Pane of 17, plus label	12.00	
	FDC booklet pane		12.00

No. 989 is not assigned.

990		MNHVF	UseVF
29¢	**multicolored** green inscription, tagged	.45	.30
	FDC *(Sept. 25, 1992)* single		2.00
	n. Pane of 17, plus label	15.00	
	FDC booklet pane		12.00

No. 991 is not assigned.

992		MNHVF	UseVF
29¢	**multicolored** brown inscription, tagged	.45	.30
	FDC *(Sept 25, 1992)*		2.00
	n. Pane of 17, plus label	14.50	
	FDC pane of 17		12.00
	v. Pair, imperforate	175.00	
	v1. brown omitted	450.00	

No. 993 is not assigned.

1992. "USA" Coil Issue for presorted First-Class mailings was reformatted in larger coils. The background is solid blue; "First-Class" is 9mm long, and "23" is 6 1/2mm long. *Coil, gravure, Bureau of Engraving and Printing (plate number beginning with a numeral rather than a letter), perforated 10 vertically. Plate number every 24 stamps.*

994 *"USA"*

994		MNHVF	UseVF
23¢	**multicolored** printed service indicator: "Presorted First-Class," shiny gum	.50	.20
	Pair	.75	
	FDC *(Oct. 9, 1992)*		1.75
	z. Tagged (error)	—	65.00
	m. Matte gum	.50	.20
	Pair	.75	
	v. Pair, imperforate	125.00	
	v1. Imperforate stamp with plate No. 1111	250.00	

In this version, "23" is 7mm long. See Nos. 985 and 1010 for versions printed by the American Bank Note Co. or by Stamp Venturers.

1992. Contemporary Christmas Issue consisted of a se-tenant block of four stamps in both sheet and booklet formats with design differences ("Greetings" is 27mm long on the sheet version and 25mm long on the booklet version) and a self-adhesive stamp with essentially the same basic design ("Greetings" is only 21 1/2mm long). Offset, perforated 11 1/2x11. Microprinting "Copyright 1992" was used for the first time on a U.S. stamp.

995, 999, 1005 *Locomotive*

996, 1000 *Pony & rider*

997, 1001 *Fire engine*

998, 1002 *Steamship*

B217

995		MNHVF	UseVF
29¢	Locomotive **multicolored,** tagged	.45	.20
996		MNHVF	UseVF
29¢	Pony & rider **multicolored,** tagged	.45	.20
997		MNHVF	UseVF
29¢	Fire engine **multicolored,** tagged	.45	.20
998		MNHVF	UseVF
29¢	Steamship **multicolored,** tagged	.45	.20
	FDC *(Oct. 22, 1992)* any single		2.50
	y. Se-tenant block of 4	3.50	
	Plate block of 4	4.50	
	FDC block of 4		4.00

1992. CONTEMPORARY BOOKLET ISSUE Gravure, Multi-Color Corporation, perforated 11.

999		MNHVF	UseVF
29¢	Locomotive **multicolored,** booklet single	.45	.20
1000		MNHVF	UseVF
29¢	Pony & rider **multicolored,** booklet single	.45	.20
1001		MNHVF	UseVF
29¢	Fire engine **multicolored,** booklet single	.45	.20
1002		MNHVF	UseVF
29¢	Steamship **multicolored,** booklet single	.45	.20
	FDC *(Oct. 22, 1992)* any single		2.50
	n. Booklet pane of 4 (Nos. 999-1002)	3.50	
	FDC booklet pane		4.00
	nv. Booklet pane of 4, imperforate	—	
	nv1. Booklet pane of 4, imperforate horizontally	—	

1992. TRADITIONAL CHRISTMAS ISSUE *Intaglio and offset, perforated 11 1/2x11.*

1003, B218 Madonna and Child *by Bellini*

1003		MNHVF	UseVF
29¢	**multicolored** tagged	.45	.20
	Plate block of 4	3.00	
	FDC *(Oct. 22, 1992)* single		1.75
	n. Booklet pane of 10	8.00	
	FDC booklet pane		8.00

No. 1004 is not assigned.

1992. CONTEMPORARY CHRISTMAS SELF-ADHESIVE ATM ISSUE featured the toy locomotive design with "Greetings" measuring only 21 1/2mm. *Gravure, die cut, self-adhesive.*

1005 *Toy locomotive*

1005		MNHVF	UseVF
29¢	**multicolored** tagged	.75	.20
	FDC *(Oct. 22, 1992)*		1.75
	n. Pane of 18	12.00	
	FDC pane of 18		14.00

1992. PUMPKINSEED SUNFISH ISSUE in the Flora and Fauna Series met the second 1/2-ounce rate for international mail and the 1-ounce rate to Mexico. *Intaglio and offset, perforated 11 1/2x11.*

1006 *Pumpkinseed sunfish*

1006		MNHVF	UseVF
45¢	**multicolored** tagged	1.00	.20
	Plate block of 4	5.50	
	FDC *(Dec. 2, 1992)*		2.00
	v. Intaglio black omitted	600.00	

1992. CIRCUS WAGON COIL ISSUE in the Transportation Series was a redesigned version of the stamp of 1990 (No. 931). *Coil, gravure, American Bank Note Co., perforated 10 vertically. Plate number every 24 stamps.*

1007		MNHVF	UseVF
5¢	**red** untagged	.25	.20
	Pair	.30	
	FDC *(Dec. 8, 1992)*		1.75

For intaglio stamps of this design see No. 931 ("05 USA") and No. 1077 ("USA 5¢").

1993. PLEDGE OF ALLEGIANCE ISSUE new version with red "USA" and denomination, printed by Stamp Venturers. The booklets in which the stamps are found were assembled by KCS Industries, a division of Banta Corp. Gravure, perforated 10.

1008		MNHVF	UseVF
29¢	**multicolored** red inscription, tagged	.75	.20
	FDC *(March 1993)* single		1.75
	n. Booklet pane of 10	7.50	
	FDC booklet pane		7.00
	v. Pair, imperforate	900.00	

For similar stamp with black inscription, see No. 987.

1993. THOMAS JEFFERSON ISSUE in the Great Americans Series honored the third president of the United States (1743-1826) on the 250th anniversary of his birth. *Intaglio, Stamp Venturers, perforated 11 1/2x11.*

1009 *Thomas Jefferson*

1009		MNHVF	UseVF
29¢	**indigo** phosphored paper (solid tagging)	.50	.30
	Plate block of 4	2.50	
	Plate block of 8, w/position diagram	5.50	
	FDC *(April 13, 1993)*		2.00

1993. USA ISSUE for presorted First-Class mailings. The background is violet blue; "First-Class" is 8 1/2mm long, and "23" is 6 1/2mm long. *Coil, gravure, Stamp Venturers (plate numbers beginning with an "S"), perforated 10 vertically. Plate number every 33 stamps.*

1010		MNHVF	UseVF
23¢	**multicolored** printed service indicator: "Presorted First-Class"	.75	.20
	Pair	1.00	
	FDC *(May 14, 1993)*		1.75
	v. Pair, imperforate	—	

In this version, "23" is 8 1/2mm long. See No. 985 and No. 994 for versions printed by the American Bank Note Co. and by the Bureau of Engraving and Printing.

1993. EAGLE AND SHIELD NON-DENOMINATED COIL ISSUE met the needs of permit mailers on presorted Bulk Mail pieces. Similar to earlier version, No. 980. Design differences include reversal of "USA" and "BULK RATE" and colors reversed to "USA" in blue and "BULK RATE" in red. The stamp's face value is 10¢, with additional postage paid by mailers at the time of mailing. *Coil, printed by gravure by the Bureau of Engraving and Printing (plate numbers beginning with numeral rather than letter) and Stamp Venturers (plate numbers beginning with "S"), perforated 10 vertically. The Stamp Venturers version has the eagle in metallic gold, the Bureau of Engraving and Printing version in orange yellow. Plate number every 24 stamps.*

1011, 1012 *"USA" before "Bulk Rate"*

1011		MNHVF	UseVF
(10¢)	**multicolored** (Bureau of Engraving and Printing) shiny gum	.30	.20
	Pair	.60	
	FDC *(May 29, 1993)*		1.75
	v. Pair, imperforate	15.00	
	z. Tagged (error), shiny gum	2.00	1.50
	zv. Tagged (error), pair imperforate	—	—
	g. Low gloss gum	.30	.20
	Pair	.60	

1012		MNHVF	UseVF
(10¢)	**multicolored** (Stamp Venturers) shiny gum	.30	.20
	Pair	.60	
	g. Low gloss gum	.30	.20
	Pair	.60	
	FDC *(May 29, 1993)*		1.75

See No. 980, 1129, 1204 and 1205 for similar design printed by the American Bank Note Co.

> **Listings and prices for plate number coil strips and singles appear at the end of this definitives section of the Krause-Minkus catalog.**

1993. FUTURISTIC SPACE SHUTTLE ISSUE prepaid the Priority Mail rate. *Offset and intaglio, perforated 11.*

1013 *Futuristic Space Shuttle*

1013		MNHVF	UseVF
$2.90	**multicolored**	6.50	2.50
	Plate block of 4	27.50	
	FDC *(June 23, 1993)*		7.50

1993. RED SQUIRREL ISSUE in the Flora and Fauna Series. *Self-adhesive First Class letter-rate stamp. Gravure, Dittler Brothers, Inc., die cut.*

1014 *Red squirrel*

1014		MNHVF	UseVF
29¢	**multicolored** from booklet or coil, tagged	.50	.20
	FDC *(June 25, 1993)* single		1.75
	n. Pane of 18	12.00	

	FDC pane of 18		14.00
	Coil strip of 18	12.00	

No. 1015 is not assigned.

1993. RED ROSE ISSUE *self-adhesive stamp in the Flora and Fauna Series. Gravure by Stamp Venturers, die cut.*

1016 *Red Rose*

1016		MNHVF	UseVF
29¢	**multicolored** from booklet or coil, tagged	.50	.20
	FDC *(Aug. 19, 1993)* single		1.75
	n. Pane of 18	12.00	
	FDC pane of 18		14.00
	Coil strip of 18	12.00	

No. 1017 is not assigned.

1993. AFRICAN VIOLET BOOKLET ISSUE in the Flora and Fauna Series. *Gravure by KCS Industries, perforated 10x11.*

1018, B224, B225 *African violet*

1018		MNHVF	UseVF
29¢	**multicolored** from booklet, tagged	.75	.20
	FDC *(Oct. 8, 1993)* single		1.75
	n. Booklet pane of 10	5.50	
	FDC booklet pane		8.00

1993. CONTEMPORARY CHRISTMAS ISSUE consisted of four contemporary designs available in gummed panes (18x25mm, perforated 11 1/2) and booklets (18x21mm, perforated 11x10) and self-adhesive panes. The Snowman design of the Contemporary issues was available self-adhesive both with the other three designs and by itself in panes available through ATM machines. *Printed by gravure by the Bureau of Engraving and Printing (sheets and booklets), and Avery Dennison (self-adhesive); perforated 11.*

1019, 1023, 1029 *Jack-in-the-box*

1020, 1024, 1030 *Reindeer*

1021, 1025, 1031 *Snowman*

1022, 1026, 1032 *Toy soldier*

B226

1019		MNHVF	UseVF
29¢	Jack-in-the-box, tagged	.50	.20

1020		MNHVF	UseVF
29¢	Reindeer, tagged	.50	.20

1021		MNHVF	UseVF
29¢	Snowman, tagged	.50	.20

1022		MNHVF	UseVF
29¢	Toy soldier, tagged	.50	.20
	FDC *(Oct. 21, 1993)* any single		1.75
	y. Se-tenant block of 4	2.00	.80
	Plate block of 4	3.00	
	FDC block of 4		4.00

1023		MNHVF	UseVF
29¢	Jack-in-the-box, tagged	.50	.20

1024		MNHVF	UseVF
29¢	Reindeer, tagged	.50	.20

1025		MNHVF	UseVF
29¢	Snowman, tagged	.50	.20

1026		MNHVF	UseVF
29¢	Toy soldier, tagged	.50	.20
y.	Se-tenant block of 4	2.00	.80
	FDC *(Oct. 21, 1993)* any single		2.50
n.	Booklet pane of 10 (three each Nos. 1023, 1024; two each Nos. 1025, 1026)	6.50	
n1.	Booklet pane of 10 (two each Nos. 1023, 1024; three each Nos. 1025, 1026)	6.50	
	FDC booklet pane		4.00

1993. TRADITIONAL CHRISTMAS ISSUE was available in sheet and booklet form. *The booklet version is larger than the sheet version (booklet overall stamp 28.95x22.09mm; sheet overall stamp 23.1x30.2mm). There are design differences between the two items, also. Perforated 11 (No. 1027) or 11 1/2x11 (No. 1028).*

1027, 1028, B227 Madonna and Child in a Landscape, *by Giovanni Battista Cima (1497)* from North Carolina Museum of Art

1027		MNHVF	UseVF
29¢	multicolored tagged	.50	.20
	Plate block of 4	3.50	
	FDC *(Oct. 21, 1993)*		1.75

1028		MNHVF	UseVF
29¢	multicolored booklet single, tagged	.50	.20
	FDC *(Oct. 21, 1993)* single		1.75
n.	Booklet pane of 4	4.00	
	FDC booklet pane		4.00
nv.	Booklet pane of 4, imperforate	—	

1993. CONTEMPORARY CHRISTMAS SELF-ADHESIVE ISSUE Printed by Avery Dennison, straight die cut. Plate number every 24 stamps for coil version.

1029		MNHVF	UseVF
29¢	Jack-in-the-box, tagged	.50	.20

1030		MNHVF	UseVF
29¢	Reindeer, tagged	.50	.20

1031		MNHVF	UseVF
29¢	Snowman, tagged	.50	.20
v.	With plate No. (from coil) VIIIIIII single	3.50	3.50

1032		MNHVF	UseVF
29¢	Toy soldier, tagged	.50	.20
	FDC *(Oct. 28, 1993)* any single		2.25
n.	Pane of 12 (3 of each design)	10.00	
	FDC pane of 12		10.00
y.	Se-tenant block of 4	2.00	1.50
y1.	Se-tenant coil strip of 4	2.00	—

Nos. 1033-1036 are not assigned.

1993. SNOWMAN ATM PANE ISSUE Die-cut (self-adhesive).

1037 *Snowman*

1037		MNHVF	UseVF
29¢	multicolored tagged	.75	.25
	FDC *(Oct. 28, 1993)* single		1.75
n.	Pane of 18	12.00	
	FDC pane of 18		14.00

Although the placement is different, the Snowmen depicted on Nos. 1021 and 1031 have three buttons and seven snowflakes beneath the nose. No. 1025 has two buttons and five snowflakes beneath the nose.

1993. PINE CONE ISSUE *Self-adhesive stamp* in the Flora and Fauna Series. *Gravure by the Banknote Corporation of America, die cut. Plate number every 22 stamps for coil issue.*

1038 *Pine cone*

1038		MNHVF	UseVF
29¢	multicolored from booklet or coil, tagged	.50	.20
	FDC *(Nov. 5, 1993)* single		1.75
n.	Pane of 18	14.00	
	FDC pane of 18		14.00
	Coil strip of 18	14.00	

1994. EAGLE ISSUE Self-adhesive, gravure by National Label Co. for 3M, die cut. Plate number every 18 stamps for coil version.

1039 *Eagle*

1039		MNHVF	UseVF
29¢	red, cream & blue from booklet or coil, tagged	.50	.20
	FDC *(Feb. 4, 1994)* single		1.75
n.	Pane of 18	15.00	
	FDC pane of 18		12.50
	Coil strip of 18	15.00	

1994. POSTAGE AND MAILING CENTER (PMC) COIL ISSUE by Unisys, similar to No. 986, but oriented vertically. *Gravure by Guilford Gravure for American Bank Note Co., perforated 9 3/4 vertically. Plate number every 24 stamps.*

1040 *Shield & bunting*

1040		MNHVF	UseVF
(variable rate)	red and blue, denomination 19¢-$99.99 printed in black, phosphored paper	.50	.50
	FDC *(Feb. 19, 1994)*		7.50

See also Nos. 986, 1053 and 1117. Also located in On Demand Postage Section see Nos. OD3, OD4, OD5, and OD6.

1994. SURRENDER OF BURGOYNE AT SARATOGA ISSUE Design of this stamp was taken from an engraving originally prepared to be part of the 1869 definitive series, the first U.S. pictorial postage stamps. John Trumbull's painting *The Surrender of Gen. Burgoyne at Saratoga* is the basis for the stamp design. *Intaglio by Stamp Venturers in panes of 20, perforated 11 1/2.*

1041 The Surrender of Gen. Burgoyne at Saratoga *from a painting by John Trumbull in the U.S. Capitol*

1041		MNHVF	UseVF
$1	dark blue tagged	2.00	.75
	Plate block of 4	9.00	
	FDC *(May 5, 1994)*		2.50

1994. TRACTOR TRAILER COIL ISSUE in the Transportation Series. Reprint of No. 954, showing a 1930s tractor trailer, issued for use by permit mailers. *Coil, gravure, Bureau of Engraving and Printing., perforated 10 vertically. Plate number every 24 stamps.*

 1042 *Tractor trailer*

1042		MNHVF	UseVF
10¢	**green** Bureau-printed service indicator (in gray): "Additional Presort Postage Paid"	.25	.20
	Pair	.30	
	FDC *(May 25, 1994)*		1.75
	v. Pair, imperforate	—	

See also No. 954.

1994. STATUE OF LIBERTY ISSUE Self-adhesive pane. Die cut. Plate number every 36 stamps for coil version.

 1043 *Statue of Liberty*

1043		MNHVF	UseVF
29¢	**multicolored** from booklet or coil, tagged	.50	.20
	FDC *(June 24, 1994)* single		1.75
	n. Pane of 18 (convertible booklets)	12.00	
	FDC pane of 18		12.50
	Coil strip of 18	12.00	

1994. FISHING BOAT COIL ISSUE Originally issued in 1991 (No. 965), this design was reprinted in 1992 in lighter colors (No. 965z1). This 1994 version easily is identifiable by counting the "loops" of rope on the mooring. The original and initial two reprintings had two loops, this version has a single loop. *Coil, gravure by Stamp Venturers, perforated 10 vertically. Plate number every 33 stamps.*

 1044 *Boat, single loop on mooring*

1044		MNHVF	UseVF
19¢	**multicolored** tagged	.50	.20
	Pair	1.00	
	FDC *(June 25, 1994)*		1.75

See also No. 965.

1994. MOON LANDING ISSUE Celebrated the 25th anniversary of the moon landing with an Express Mail denomination. *Offset and intaglio, perforated 10 1/2x11.*

 1045 *Moon landing, 25th anniversary*

1045		MNHVF	UseVF
$9.95	**multicolored** tagged	25.00	10.00
	Plate block of 4	100.00	
	FDC *(July 20, 1994)*		25.00

1994. WASHINGTON AND JACKSON ISSUE was a design submitted by a firm seeking to win the contract for the 1869 issue. *Intaglio by Stamp Venturers in panes of 20, perforated 11 1/2.*

1046 *Washington and Jackson*

1046		MNHVF	UseVF
$5	**dark green** tagged	10.00	3.75
	Plate block of 4	50.00	
	FDC *(Aug. 19, 1994)*		13.50

1994. CONTEMPORARY CHRISTMAS ISSUE consisted of two designs. The Santa Claus stamp was issued only as a self-adhesive. The Holiday Stocking design was issued both in sheet form and in booklets of 20 stamps. *Printed by gravure by Avery Dennison* (Santa self-adhesive), *by Ashton-Potter USA Ltd.* (Holiday Stocking). *Perforated 11* (No. 1047).

 1047, B232 *Christmas stocking*

1047		MNHVF	UseVF
29¢	**multicolored** from sheet or booklet, tagged	.50	.20
	Plate block of 4	3.50	
	FDC *(Oct. 20, 1994)*		1.75
	v. Pair, imperforate	—	
	n. Booklet pane of 20	8.50	
	FDC booklet pane		15.50
	nv. Booklet pane, imperforate horizontally	—	

1994. TRADITIONAL CHRISTMAS ISSUE was issued both in sheet and booklet form, with the total size of the booklet version 0.05mm more horizontally and 0.03mm less vertically than the sheet version. Printed by offset and intaglio by the Bureau of Engraving and Printing, perforated 11 (No. 1048), 10x11 (No. 1049).

 1048, 1049, B233 Madonna and Child, *by Elizabetta Sirani*

1048		MNHVF	UseVF
29¢	**multicolored** shiny gum, tagged	.50	.20
	Plate block of 4	3.50	
	g. low gloss gum	.50	.20
	Plate block of 4	3.50	
	FDC *(Oct. 20, 1994)*		1.75

1049		MNHVF	UseVF
29¢	**multicolored** from booklet, tagged	.50	.20
	FDC *(Oct. 20, 1994)* single		1.75
	n. Booklet pane of 10	5.50	
	FDC booklet pane		4.50
	v. Pair, imperforate	—	
	nv1. Booklet pane, imperforate	600.00	

1994. CONTEMPORARY SANTA CLAUS BOOKLET ISSUE Gravure, die cut. Plate number every 36 stamps for coil version.

1050 *Santa Claus*

1050		MNHVF	UseVF
29¢	**multicolored** from booklet or coil, tagged	.50	.20
	FDC *(Oct. 20, 1994)* single		1.75
	n. Pane of 12 (convertible booklet)	10.50	
	FDC pane of 12		10.00
	Coil strip of 12	10.50	
	v. With plate No. from coil	3.50	

1994. CARDINAL IN SNOW ATM ISSUE this is a self-adhesive stamp in panes of 18 for automated teller machines (ATM). The stamp released at the same time as the Christmas issues, with the design having a decidedly winter holiday motif. *Gravure by Avery Dennison, die cut.*

1051 *Cardinal in snow*

1051		MNHVF	UseVF
29¢	**multicolored** tagged	.50	.20
	FDC *(Oct. 20, 1994)* single		1.75
	n. Pane of 18	14.50	
	FDC pane of 18		15.00

1994. VIRGINIA APGAR ISSUE in the Great Americans Series honored a medical researcher (1909-1974) whose simple assessment method allows doctors and nurses in the delivery room to make an immediate evaluation of a newborn baby's general condition. This process aids in the identification of those infants who need immediate medical attention. *Intaglio by the Banknote Corporation of America, perforated 11.*

1052 *Virginia Apgar*

1052		MNHVF	UseVF
20¢	**brown** phosphored paper grainy tagging	.50	.20
	a. orange brown	.50	.20
	Plate block of 4	2.50	
	FDC *(Oct. 24, 1994)*		1.75

1994. POSTAGE AND MAILING CENTER (PMC) COIL ISSUE another ECA Gard stamp with variable denomination (20¢-$99.99), similar to No. 986, with different type font. Initial release was in Detroit, Mich. *Coil, phosphored paper, perforated 9 3/4 vertically. Plate number every 48 stamps.*

1053 *Shield & bunting*

1053		MNHVF	UseVF
(variable rate)	**red & blue,** denomination (1¢-$9.99)	.50	.50
	printed in black, mottled tagging, shiny gum		
	FDC *(Nov. 9, 1994)*		7.50
	pz. solid tagging, matte gum	—	—

See Nos. 986, 1040, 1117. Also located in On Demand Postage Section. See Nos. OD3, OD4, OD5, and OD6.

Non-denominated Service-Inscribed Series

1994. BLACK "G" SHEET ISSUE the first in the Non-denominated Service-Inscribed Series was the most prolific of the rate-change issues. It pictured "Old Glory" and the letter "G." A total of 16 items were released, including specific items for First Class letter rate, First Class presort, postal card rate, coils and booklets, and two types of self-adhesives. Sheet stamps, overall dimensions 0.84x0.99 inches. *Gravure, printed by Bureau of Engraving and Printing, black "G," perforated 11 1/4x11.*

1054, 1055-1063, B235, B236, B237, B238 *Old Glory for U.S. addresses only*

1054		MNHVF	UseVF
(32¢)	**red, blue, gray & black** tagged	.50	.20
	Plate block of 4	50.00	
	FDC *(Dec. 13, 1994)*		2.00
	n. Booklet pane of 10	6.00	
	FDC booklet pane		8.50

1994. RED "G" SHEET ISSUE in the Non-denominated Service-Inscribed Series. *Printed by Stamp Venturers, red "G," perforated 11.*

1055		MNHVF	UseVF
(32¢)	**red, blue, gray & black** tagged	.75	.20
	Plate block of 4	4.00	
	FDC *(Dec. 13, 1994)*		1.90

1994. BLACK "G" BOOKLET ISSUE in the Non-denominated Service-Inscribed Series. *Printed by Bureau of Engraving and Printing, black "G," perforated 10.*

1056		MNHVF	UseVF
(32¢)	**red, blue, gray & black** tagged	.50	.20
	FDC single *(Dec. 13, 1994)*		1.90
	n. Booklet pane of 10	6.00	
	FDC booklet pane		8.50

1994. BLUE "G" BOOKLET ISSUE in the Non-denominated Service-Inscribed Series. *Printed by American Bank Note Co., blue "G," perforated 11.*

1057		MNHVF	UseVF
(32¢)	**red, blue, gray & black** tagged	.50	.20
	FDC single *(Dec. 13, 1994)*		1.90
	n. Booklet pane of 10	9.00	
	FDC booklet pane		8.50
	v. Pair, imperforate	—	
	nv. Booklet pane imperforate	—	

1994. RED "G" BOOKLET ISSUE in the Non-denominated Service-Inscribed Series. *Printed by KCS Industries, red "G," perforated 11.*

1058		MNHVF	UseVF
(32¢)	**red, blue, gray & black** tagged	.50	.20
	FDC single *(Dec. 13, 1994)*		1.90
	n. Booklet pane of 10	6.00	
	FDC booklet pane		8.50
	v. Horizontal pair imperforate between	500.00	
	v1. Horizontal pair imperforate vertically	—	
	nv. Booklet pane of 10, imperforate	—	

1994. BLACK "G" COIL ISSUE in the Non-denominated Service-Inscribed Series. *Printed by Bureau of Engraving and Printing, black "G," by gravure, perforated 10 vertically. Plate number every 24 stamps.*

1059		MNHVF	UseVF
(32¢)	**red, blue, gray & black** tagged	.50	.20
	Pair	1.00	.30
	FDC *(Dec. 13, 1994)*		1.90
	v. Pair, imperforate	275.00	
	v1. Pair, imperforate between	—	

1994. BLUE "G" COIL ISSUE in the Non-denominated Service-Inscribed Series. *Printed by American Bank Note Co., blue "G," perforated 10 vertically. Plate number every 24 stamps.*

1060		MNHVF	UseVF
(32¢)	red, blue, gray & black tagged	.50	.20
	Pair	1.25	.30
	FDC *(Dec. 13, 1994)*		1.90

1994. RED "G" COIL ISSUE in the Non-denominated Service-Inscribed Series. *Printed by Stamp Venturers, red "G," perforated 10 vertically. Plate number every 33 stamps.*

1061		MNHVF	UseVF
(32¢)	red, blue, gray & black tagged	.50	.20
	Pair	1.25	.30
	FDC *(Dec. 13, 1994)*		1.90

1994. RED "G" COIL ISSUE in the Non-denominated Service-Inscribed Series. *Printed by Stamp Venturers, red "G," rouletted 10 vertically. Plate number every 33 stamps.*

1061A		MNHVF	UseVF
(32¢)	red, blue, gray & black tagged	.50	.20
	Pair	1.25	.30
	FDC *(Dec. 13, 1994)*		1.90

Listings and prices for plate number coil strips and singles appear at the end of this definitives section of the Krause-Minkus catalog.

1994. "G" SELF-ADHESIVE ISSUE in the Non-denominated Service-Inscribed Series. *Gravure by Avery Dennison, black "G," imperforate and die cut. Plate number every 36 stamps for coil version.*

1062 *Old Glory for U.S. addresses only*

1062		MNHVF	UseVF
(32¢)	red, dark blue, light blue, gray & black,	1.00	.35
	from booklet or coil, tagged		
	FDC single *(Dec. 13, 1994)*		1.90
	n. Pane of 18	17.50	
	FDC pane of 18		15.00
	Coil strip of 18	17.50	

1994. "G" SELF-ADHESIVE ATM ISSUE in the Non-denominated Service-Inscribed Series. *Dispensed sheetlet, self-adhesive, printed by gravure by Avery Dennison, black "G," imperforate and die cut.*

1063		MNHVF	UseVF
(32¢)	red, blue & black tagged	1.00	.35
	FDC single *(Dec. 13, 1994)*		1.90
	n. Pane of 18	17.50	
	FDC pane of 18		15.00

Non-denominated Service-Inscribed Series

1994. "G" FIRST-CLASS PRESORT RATE COIL ISSUE in the Non-denominated Service-Inscribed Series. *Gravure by Stamp Venturers, black "G," blue background, coil stamp, perforated 10 vertically. Plate number every 33 stamps.*

1064 *Old Glory First-Class Presort*

1064		MNHVF	UseVF
(25¢)	red, dark blue, gray, black & light blue	.50	.50
	Pair	1.00	1.00
	FDC *(Dec. 13, 1994)*		1.90

1994. BLACK "G" POSTCARD RATE ISSUE in the Non-denominated Service-Inscribed Series. *Printed by Bureau of Engraving and Printing, black "G," yellow background. Gravure, perforated 11.*

1065 *Old Glory Postcard Rate*

1065		MNHVF	UseVF
(20¢)	red, blue, gray, yellow & black tagged	.50	.20
	Plate block of 4	5.00	
	FDC *(Dec. 13, 1994)*		1.90
	v. Pair, imperforate	—	

1994. RED "G" POSTCARD RATE ISSUE in the Non-denominated Service-Inscribed Series. *Gravure by Stamp Venturers, red "G," perforated 11.*

1066		MNHVF	UseVF
(20¢)	red, blue, gray, yellow & black, tagged	.50	.20
	Plate block of 4	3.00	
	FDC *(Dec. 13, 1994)*		1.95

1994. NON-DENOMINATED "MAKE-UP" RATE ISSUE in the Non-denominated Service-Inscribed Series, had a value of 3¢, to be used with a 29¢ stamp to meet the new First Class rate. *Offset, perforated 11, printed by American Bank Note Co., bright blue with thin lettering.*

1067, 1068 *Dove*

1067		MNHVF	UseVF
(3¢)	red, bright blue & tan	.20	.20
	Plate block of 4	.50	
	FDC *(Dec. 13, 1994)*		1.90
	v. Pair, imperforate	175.00	
	v1. Plate block, imperforate	—	
	v2. Pair, imperforate, bright blue omitted	—	
	(printer's waste)		

1994. NON-DENOMINATED "MAKE-UP" RATE in the Non-denominated Service-Inscribed Series. *Offset by Stamp Venturers, darker blue with thick lettering, perforated 11.*

1068		MNHVF	UseVF
(3¢)	red, dark blue & tan	.20	.20
	Plate block of 4	.50	
	FDC *(Dec. 13, 1994)*		1.90

1995. "G" NONPROFIT PRESORT COIL ISSUE in the Non-denominated Service-Inscribed Series. *Coil, gravure by American Bank Note Co., black "G," green background, perforated 10 vertically. Plate number every 24 stamps.*

1069 *Old Glory "Nonprofit Presort"*

1069		MNHVF	UseVF
(5¢)	green & multicolored untagged	.25	.20
	Pair	.30	.25
	FDC *(Jan. 12, 1995)*		1.90

First-day covers received a Dec. 13, 1994 cancellation although these stamps were not yet available on that date.

1995. BUTTE AND "NONPROFIT ORGANIZATION" COIL ISSUE in the Non-denominated Service-Inscribed Series. Beginning early in 1995, the USPS introduced several series of coils for use by various mass mailers that showed the service but no denomination. The additional cost of the mail service was prepaid directly by the mailer at the post office where the mailing took place. *Gravure. Printed by J.W. Fergusson & Sons for Stamp Venturers, perforated 10 vertically. Plate number every 14 stamps. Back number every 10 stamps.*

1070, 1130 *Butte and "Nonprofit Org."*

1070

(5¢)		MNHVF	UseVF
	yellow, blue & red untagged	.25	.20
	Pair	.30	.25
	v. Pair, imperforate	675.00	
	FDC *(March 10, 1995)*		1.90

American Culture Series

1995. CAR HOOD AND "BULK RATE" COIL ISSUE in the American Culture Series. *J.W. Fergusson & Sons for Stamp Venturers, perforated 10 vertically. Plate number every 14 stamps. Back number every 10 stamps.*

1071, 1132 *Car hood and "Bulk Rate"*

1071

(10¢)		MNHVF	UseVF
	black, brown & red brown untagged	.30	.20
	Pair	.35	.25
	FDC *(March 17, 1995)*		1.90

1995. TAIL FIN PRESORTED FIRST-CLASS COIL ISSUE in the American Culture Series. *Printed by Bureau of Engraving and Printing, perforated 10 vertically. Plate number every 24 stamps.*

1072, 1073, 1133 *Tail fin and "Presorted First-Class Card"*

1072

(15¢)		MNHVF	UseVF
	yellow orange & multicolored untagged	.40	.30
	Pair	.50	.35
	FDC *(March 17, 1995)*		2.25

1995. TAIL FIN PRESORTED FIRST-CLASS COIL ISSUE in the American Culture Series. *J.W. Fergusson & Sons for Stamp Venturers, perforated 10 vertically. Plate number every 14 stamps. Back numbers every 10 stamps.*

1073

(15¢)		MNHVF	UseVF
	buff & multicolored untagged	.40	.30
	Pair	.50	.35
	FDC *(March 17, 1995)*		2.25

1995. JUKE BOX PRESORTED FIRST-CLASS COIL ISSUE in the American Culture Series. *Printed by Bureau of Engraving and Printing, perforated 10 vertically. Plate number every 24 stamps.*

1074, 1075, 1134, 1153, 1161 *Juke Box and "Presorted First-Class"*

1074

(25¢)		MNHVF	UseVF
	dark red, yellow green & multicolored, untagged	.65	.40
	Pair	.75	.50
	FDC *(March 17, 1995)*		1.90

1995. JUKE BOX "PRESORTED FIRST CLASS" COIL ISSUE in the American Culture Series. *J.W. Fergusson & Sons for Stamp Venturers, perforated 10 vertically. Plate number every 14 stamps. Back number every 10 stamps.*

1075

(25¢)		MNHVF	UseVF
	orange red, bright yellow green & multicolored untagged	.65	.40
	Pair	.75	.50
	FDC *(March 17, 1995)*		1.90

1995. FLAG OVER FIELD ATM ISSUE Avery Dennison, self-adhesive, die cut.

1076 *Flag over field*

1076

32¢		MNHVF	UseVF
	multicolored tagged	1.00	.30
	FDC *(March 17, 1995)*		1.90
	n. Pane of 18	14.50	
	FDC pane of 18		14.50

1995. CIRCUS WAGON COIL ISSUE in the Transportation Series was a redesigned gravure version of the earlier coil issued in intaglio (No. 931) and gravure (No. 1007). *Coil, intaglio by Stamp Venturers, perforated 9 3/4 vertically. Plate number every 14 stamps. Back number every 10 stamps.*

1077 *Circus wagon, 1900s*

1077

5¢		MNHVF	UseVF
	red untagged	.25	.20
	Pair	.30	
	FDC *(March 20, 1995)*		1.90

For intaglio & gravure versions of this design inscribed "05 USA," see Nos. 931 & 1007.

1995. FLAG OVER PORCH SELF-ADHESIVE BOOKLET ISSUE Gravure by Avery Dennison, serpentine die cut 8 3/4. Plate number every 40 stamps for coil version.

1078, 1080, 1081, 1082, 1083, 1116, 1125-28, 1150, B239, B240, B241 (SA), B244, B245, B246 (WAG) *Flag over porch*

1078

32¢		MNHVF	UseVF
	multicolored from booklet or coil, phosphored paper, large "1995"	.50	.20
	FDC single *(April 19, 1995)*		2.00
	n. Pane of 20 plus label (convertible booklet)	17.50	
	FDC pane of 20		15.50
	n1. Pane of 15 plus label (various layouts)	9.00	
	n2. Booklet pane of 16 but one stamp removed from upper left or lower right position	—	
	a. Small "1995"	4.50	.20
	an. Pane of 20 plus label (convertible booklet)	90.00	
	FDC small "1995"		2.00
	FDC pane of 20		45.00
	Coil strip of 20	20.00	

1078n2 cannot be made from 1078n1 because the label is die cut and, if removed, leaves an impression of the die cutting.

1995. AMERICAN KESTREL ISSUE in the Flora and Fauna Series. Redesigned denomination. *Offset by Bureau of Engraving and Printing, in panes of 100, perforated 11 1/4x11.*

1079, 1115 *American Kestrel*

1079		MNHVF	UseVF
1¢	**multicolored** tagged	.25	.20
	g. low gloss gum	.25	.20
	Plate block of 4	.30	
	FDC *(May 10, 1995)*		1.75

For version inscribed "USA 01," see No. 959. For coil, see No. 1115.

1995. FLAG OVER PORCH ISSUE Gravure by J.W. Fergusson & Sons for Stamp Venturers, blue "1995." Perforated 10 1/4x10 1/2.

1080		MNHVF	UseVF
32¢	**multicolored** tagged	.60	.20
	Plate block of 4	2.50	
	FDC *(May 19, 1995)*		2.00
	v. Pair, imperforate (vertical preferred)	75.00	

1995. FLAG OVER PORCH BOOKLET ISSUE Perforated 10 3/4x9 3/4.

1081		MNHVF	UseVF
32¢	**multicolored** tagged	.80	.20
	FDC *(May 19, 1995)* single		2.00
	n. Booklet pane of 10	6.25	
	FDC booklet pane		8.50
	nv. Booklet pane of 10, imperforate	—	

1995. FLAG OVER PORCH COIL ISSUE Gravure by Bureau of Engraving and Printing, perforated 9 3/4 vertically. Plate number every 24 stamps.

1082		MNHVF	UseVF
32¢	**multicolored** tagged, shiny gum, matte gum, red "1995"	.50	.20
	Pair	1.00	
	FDC *(May 19, 1995)*		2.00
	v. Pair, imperforate	35.00	

1995. FLAG OVER PORCH COIL ISSUE Gravure by J.W. Fergusson & Sons for Stamp Venturers, perforated 9 3/4 vertically. Plate number every 14 stamps. Back number every 10 stamps.

1083		MNHVF	UseVF
32¢	**multicolored** tagged, blue "1995"	.75	.20
	Pair	1.00	
	FDC *(May 19, 1995)*		2.00

1995. PINK ROSE ISSUE in the Flora and Fauna Series offered a new color, denomination and die-cut format to simulate perforations in an updated self-adhesive booklet or coil for use in the 32¢ rate period. *Gravure by J.W. Fergusson & Sons for Stamp Venturers, serpentine die cut 11 1/4x11 3/4. Plate number every 22 stamps for coil version.*

1084, B247, B248, B249, B250, B251, B252 *Pink rose*

1084		MNHVF	UseVF
32¢	**pink, green & black** phosphored paper	.70	.20
	FDC *(June 2, 1995)* single		1.90
	n. Pane of 20 plus label (convertible booklet)	12.00	
	FDC booklet pane		15.50
	n1. Pane of 15 plus label, various layouts *(1996)*	20.00	
	n2. Pane of 14, no label	22.50	
	n3. Pane of 16, no label	22.50	
	n4. Booklet pane of 16 with one stamp removed, no label, various layouts	22.50	—
	v. Horizontal pair imperforate between (no die cut)	—	
	v1. black omitted	1,000.00	

Note: 1084n4 cannot be made from 1084n3 because the label is die cut and, if removed, leaves an impression of the die cutting.

1995. PINK ROSE COIL ISSUE in the Flora and Fauna Series.

1084A		MNHVF	UseVF
32¢	**pink, green & black** pair	1.00	—

1995. FERRYBOAT COIL ISSUE in the Transportation Series. New York City steam ferryboat. *Coil, intaglio, perforated 9 3/4 vertically. Plate number every 48 stamps.*

1085 *Ferryboat, 1900s*

1085		MNHVF	UseVF
32¢	**deep blue** phosphored paper, shiny gum	.65	.20
	Pair	1.25	
	FDC *(June 2, 1995)*		1.90
	vs. Pair, imperforate, shiny gum	—	
	g. low gloss gum	.60	
	vg. Pair imperforate, low gloss gum	—	
	a. Bronx (bright) blue	6.00	5.00
	Pair	12.00	10.00

1995. COG RAILWAY COIL ISSUE in the Transportation Series. The cog railway is used for steep inclines and prevents slippage. *Coil, intaglio, perforated 9 3/4 vertically. Plate number every 48 stamps.*

1086 *Cog Railway, 1870s*

1086		MNHVF	UseVF
20¢	**green** phosphored paper	.40	.20
	Pair	.75	
	FDC *(June 9, 1995)*		1.90
	v. Pair, imperforate	.75	

1995. BLUE JAY ISSUE in the Flora and Fauna Series. Produced in booklet form to pay the First Class domestic postcard rate. *Gravure by Stamp Venturers, perforated 11x10.*

1087, 1135-36, B253 *Blue Jay*

1087		MNHVF	UseVF
20¢	**multicolored** phosphored paper	.45	.20
	FDC *(June 15, 1995)* single		1.90
	n. Booklet pane of 10	4.25	
	FDC booklet pane		8.50

1995. SPACE SHUTTLE CHALLENGER ISSUE prepaid the Priority Mail rate. *Offset and intaglio (panes of 20) by Ashton-Potter (USA) Ltd., perforated 11. (See No. 1119.)*

1088 *Space Shuttle* Challenger

1088		MNHVF	UseVF
$3	**multicolored** phosphored paper	6.00	3.00
	Plate block of 4	25.00	
	FDC *(June 22, 1995)*		7.75
	v. Horizontal pair, imperforate between	—	

1995. PEACHES AND PEAR ISSUE in the Flora and Fauna Series. *Gravure, perforated 11x9 3/4.*

1089, 1091, 1091A *Peaches*

1090, 1092, 1092A *Pear*

B255

1089		MNHVF	UseVF
32¢	**multicolored** phosphored paper	.75	.20
	FDC *(July 8, 1995)*		1.90

1090		MNHVF	UseVF
32¢	**multicolored** phosphored paper	.75	.20
	FDC *(July 8, 1995)* single		1.90
	Se-tenant pair, No. 1089-90	1.50	1.20
	n. Booklet pane of 10 (5 No. 1090y)	6.25	
	FDC booklet pane		8.50

1995. PEACHES AND PEAR SELF-ADHESIVE ISSUE (Peaches) in the Flora and Fauna Series. *Gravure by Avery Dennison, self-adhesive, serpentine die cut 8 3/4.*

1091		MNHVF	UseVF
32¢	**multicolored** phosphored paper	.75	.30
	FDC *(July 8, 1995)*		1.90

1995. PEACHES AND PEAR SELF-ADHESIVE COIL ISSUE (Peaches) in the Flora and Fauna Series. *Gravure by Avery Dennison, serpentine die cut 8 3/4 vertically. Plate number every 40 stamps.*

1091A		MNHVF	UseVF
32¢	**multicolored**	.75	.30
	FDC *(July 8, 1995)*		1.90
	Se-tenant pair	1.50	

1995. PEACHES AND PEAR SELF-ADHESIVE ISSUE (Pear) in the Flora and Fauna Series. *Gravure by Avery Dennison, self-adhesive, serpentine die cut 8 3/4.*

1092		MNHVF	UseVF
32¢	**multicolored** phosphored paper	.85	.30
	FDC *(July 8, 1995)* single		1.90
	n. Pane of 20 (10 each Nos. 1091-92 plus label) (convertible booklet)	16.00	
	FDC Pane of 20		15.50

1995. PEACHES AND PEAR SELF-ADHESIVE COIL ISSUE (Pear) in the Flora and Fauna Series. *Gravure by Avery Dennison, serpentine die cut 8 3/4 vertically. Plate number every 40 stamps.*

1092A		MNHVF	UseVF
32¢	**multicolored**	.85	.30
	FDC *(July 8, 1995)*		1.90
	Se-tenant pair (1091A and 1092A)	1.50	
	FDC, pair (1091A and 1092A)		2.50

1995. ALICE HAMILTON ISSUE in the Great Americans Series paid tribute to a pioneer in industrial medicine, the first woman on the faculty of Harvard University and a socially committed physician (1869-1970) who played a key role in documenting and taking steps to prevent lead poisoning in the workplace. Issued to pay 2-ounce First Class letter rate. *Intaglio by Banknote Corp. of America, perforated 11 1/4x11.*

1093 *Alice Hamilton*

1093		MNHVF	UseVF
55¢	**green** phosphored paper, grainy tagging	1.10	.20
	Plate block of 4	5.50	
	FDC *(July 11, 1995)*		2.25

1995. SPACE SHUTTLE ENDEAVOUR ISSUE Prepaid the basic Express Mail rate. *Offset and intaglio (panes of 20) by Ashton-Potter (USA) Ltd., perforated 11.*

1094 *Space Shuttle* Endeavour

1094		MNHVF	UseVF
$10.75	**multicolored** phosphored paper	21.00	8.00
	Plate block of 4	92.50	
	FDC *(Aug. 4, 1995)*		25.00

1995. ALICE PAUL ISSUE in the Great Americans Series recognized a leader in the U.S. movement to extend the right to vote to women (honored about the same time on a commemorative, CM1745) and one of the earliest proponents of the Equal Rights Amendment (1885-1997). Issue to pay 3-ounce First Class letter rate. *Intaglio by Banknote Corporation of America, perforated 11 1/4x11.*

1095 *Alice Paul*

1095		MNHVF	UseVF
78¢	**purple** phosphored paper solid tagging	1.75	.25
	Plate block of 4	8.00	
	FDC *(Aug. 18, 1995)*		2.25
	a. Dark violet grainy tagging *(April 1996)*	1.75	—
	Plate block of 4	8.00	

1995. MILTON S. HERSHEY ISSUE in the Great Americans Series celebrated the chocolate manufacturer and philanthropist (1857-1945) whose orphans' home, established in 1909, has provided a home and education for generations of disadvantaged boys and girls. Issued to pay basic First Class letter rate. *Intaglio by Banknote Corporation of America, perforated 11 1/4x11.*

1096 *Milton S. Hershey*

1096		MNHVF	UseVF
32¢	**chocolate brown** phosphored paper solid tagging	.65	.20
	Plate block of 4	3.75	
	FDC *(Sept. 13, 1995)*		1.50

Pioneers of Aviation Series

1995. EDDIE RICKENBACKER ISSUE in the Pioneers of Aviation Series honored the racing car driver and automotive and aviation manufacturer (1890-1973) who earned his greatest recognition as a flying ace during World War I, in which he shot down 22 enemy aircraft and four observation balloons. Issued to pay the 1/2-ounce rate for letters to foreign nations other than Canada and Mexico — mail typically carried by air, in keeping with the subject of the stamp, but without the "airmail" designation — no longer needed on such mail, all of which is now typically carried by air. *Gravure by Bureau of Engraving and Printing, perforated 11 1/4. (See No. 1250.)*

1097 *Eddie Rickenbacker*

1097		MNHVF	UseVF
60¢	**multicolored** phosphored paper	.75	.20
	Plate block of 4	6.00	
	FDC *(Sept. 25, 1995)*		1.75

1995. CONTEMPORARY CHRISTMAS ISSUE consisted of four Victorian-era designs — two depicting Santa Claus and two portraying children with toys — *produced in sheet, booklet and self-adhesive booklet and coil form. Offset by Sterling Sommer for Ashton-Potter (USA) Ltd., perforated 11 1/2.*

1098, 1102, 1106 *Santa on rooftop*

1099, 1103, 1107 *Child and jumping jack*

1100, 1104, 1108 *Child and tree*

1101, 1105, 1109 *Santa in workshop*

B257

1098		MNHVF	UseVF
32¢	Santa on rooftop, phosphored paper	.60	.20

1099		MNHVF	UseVF
32¢	Child and jumping jack, phosphored paper	.60	.20

1100		MNHVF	UseVF
32¢	Child and tree, phosphored paper	.60	.20

1101		MNHVF	UseVF
32¢	Santa in workshop, phosphored paper	.60	.20
	FDC *(Sept. 30, 1995)* any single		2.25
	y. Se-tenant block or strip of 4 Nos. 1098-1101	3.00	
	Plate block of 4	3.50	
	FDC booklet pane		5.00
	n. Booklet pane of 10 (3 of Nos. 1098-99 & 2 of Nos. 1100-01)	6.50	
	n1. Booklet pane of 10 (2 of Nos. 1098-99 & 3 of Nos. 1100-01)	6.50	
	v. Block or strip of 4, imperforate	—	

1995. CONTEMPORARY CHRISTMAS COIL ISSUE Constituted the first U.S. coil issue with multiple se-tenant designs. *Gravure for Avery Dennison, serpentine die cut 11 1/4 vertically. Plate number every 20 stamps.*

1102		MNHVF	UseVF
32¢	Santa on rooftop, phosphored paper	.60	.20

1103		MNHVF	UseVF
32¢	Child and jumping jack, phosphored paper	.60	.20

1104		MNHVF	UseVF
32¢	Child and tree, phosphored paper	.60	.20

1105		MNHVF	UseVF
32¢	Santa in workshop, phosphored paper	.60	.20
	FDC *(Sept. 30, 1995)* any single		2.25
	y. Coil strip of 4 (1 each of Nos. 1102-1105)	3.00	
	FDC coil strip of 4		5.00
	Coil strip of 20	20.00	

1995. CONTEMPORARY CHRISTMAS BOOKLET ISSUE Gravure for Avery Dennison, serpentine die cut 11 1/4.

1106		MNHVF	UseVF
32¢	**multicolored** phosphored paper	.60	.20

1107		MNHVF	UseVF
32¢	**multicolored** phosphored paper	.60	.20

1108		MNHVF	UseVF
32¢	**multicolored** phosphored paper	.60	.20

1109		MNHVF	UseVF
32¢	**multicolored** phosphored paper	.60	.20
	FDC *(Sept. 30, 1995)* any single		2.25

	n. Pane of 20 (5 each of 1106-09 plus label) (convertible booklet)	12.00	
	FDC pane of 20		15.50

1995. MIDNIGHT ANGEL CHRISTMAS BOOKLET ISSUE Offset by Banknote Corporation of America, serpentine die cut 11 1/2.

1110, 1110A, B259, B260, B261, B262 *Midnight Angel*

1110		MNHVF	UseVF
32¢	**multicolored** phosphored paper	.60	.20
	FDC *(Oct. 19, 1995)*		1.90
	n. Pane of 20 plus label (convertible booklet)	12.00	
	n1. Pane of 15 plus label (various layouts) *(1996)*	10.00	
	n2. Pane of 16 with one stamp removed, no label, various layouts	22.50	—
	v. Vertical pair, imperforate (no die cutting between)	—	
	FDC Pane of 20		15.50

1110n2 cannot be made from 1110n1 because the label is die cut and, if removed, leaves an impression of the die cutting.

1995. MIDNIGHT ANGEL CHRISTMAS COIL ISSUE Offset by Banknote Corporation of America, vertical serpentine die cut. Plate number every 20 stamps.

1110A		MNHVF	UseVF
32¢	**multicolored** phosphored paper	.70	.45
	Pair	1.50	
	FDC *(Oct. 19, 1995)*		1.90
	Coil strip of 20	15.00	

1995. CONTEMPORARY CHRISTMAS BOOKLET ATM ISSUE Gravure for Avery Dennison, straight-line die cut.

1111 *Children sledding*

1111		MNHVF	UseVF
32¢	**multicolored** phosphored lacquer on surface of stamps	.75	.45
	FDC *(Oct. 19, 1995)*		1.25
	n. Pane of 18	12.00	
	FDC Pane of 18		10.00
	nv. Pane of 18, untagged (error)	—	

1995. TRADITIONAL CHRISTMAS ISSUE adapted from an altar panel, *Enthroned Madonna and Child,* by 14th century Florentine artist Giotto di Bodone, was offered in conventional sheet form and booklet form. *Offset and intaglio by Bureau of Engraving and Printing.*

1112, 1113, B258 Enthroned Madonna and Child *by Giotto*

1112		MNHVF	UseVF
32¢	**multicolored** phosphored paper, perforated 11 1/4	.75	.20
	Plate block of 4	3.50	
	FDC *(Oct. 19, 1995)*		1.90

1113		MNHVF	UseVF
32¢	**multicolored** phosphored paper, perforated 9 3/4x11	.75	.20

n. Pane of 10, plate number next to LL   6.50
    stamp
FDC *(Oct. 19, 1995)*   1.90
FDC booklet pane   8.50
nv. Booklet pane of 10, miscut with a plate 25.00
    number next to UL stamp

1995. RUTH BENEDICT ISSUE in the Great Americans Series celebrated a social anthropologist (1887-1948) whose 1934 text, *Patterns of Culture,* was influential throughout the world and who fought racism and intolerance through numerous other publications. Issued to pay the 1/2-ounce letter rate to Canada and the ounce letter rate to Mexico. *Intaglio by Bureau of Engraving and Printing, perforated   11 1/4x11.*

1114 *Ruth Benedict*

1114		MNHVF	UseVF
46¢	**carmine** phosphored paper (mottled tagging)	1.00	.25
	Plate block of 4	4.75	
	FDC *(Oct. 20, 1995)*		1.60

1996. AMERICAN KESTREL COIL ISSUE in the Flora and Fauna Series. *Offset in gummed coils of 500 and 3,000 stamps by Bureau of Engraving and Printing, perforated 9 3/4 vertically. Plate number every 24 stamps.*

1115, 1247, 1263 *American Kestrel*

1115		MNHVF	UseVF
1¢	**multicolored** untagged	.25	.20
	Pair	.30	
	FDC *(Jan. 20, 1996)*		1.50

First printed on the Bureau of Engraving and Printing "D" press with the colors of the plate number in the order of KYCM (black, yellow, cyan, magenta), a second version printed on the Optiforma press was printed in KCYM, and first seen in August 1996. See Nos. 1229 for YMCK version.

For sheet version see No. 1079. For version inscribed "USA 01," see No. 959.

1996. FLAG OVER PORCH ISSUE Self-adhesive booklet with stamps showing "1996" in blue. Gravure by Avery Dennison, serpentine die cut 11 1/4.

1116 *Flag over porch*

1116		MNHVF	UseVF
32¢	**multicolored** phosphored paper	.75	.30
	n. Pane of 10	8.00	
	FDC *(Jan. 20, 1996)*		2.00
	FDC pane of 10		8.50

See also 1078, 1080-83, 1125-28, and 1150-51.

> **Listings and prices for plate number coil strips and singles appear at the end of this definitives section of the Krause-Minkus catalog.**

1996. POSTAGE AND MAILING CENTER (PMC) COIL ISSUE another Unisys stamp with variable denomination. Coil stamp showing "1996" in red at bottom-left corner of design. *Gravure by Bureau of Engraving and Printing with black variable denomination (20¢-$99.99) in digital type preceded by dollar sign, perforated 9 3/4 vertically. Plate number every 24 stamps.*

1117 *Shield and bunting*

1117		MNHVF	UseVF
(variable rate) red & blue denomination in black, phosphored paper		.50	.50
	FDC *(Jan. 26, 1996)*		20.00

See also Nos. 986, 1040 and 1053. Also located in On Demand Postage section. See Nos. OD3, OD4, OD5, and OD6.

1996. RED-HEADED WOODPECKER ISSUE in the Flora and Fauna Series. *Offset by Bureau of Engraving and Printing, perforated 11 1/4x11.*

1118 *Red-headed Woodpecker*

1118		MNHVF	UseVF
2¢	**multicolored** untagged	.25	.20
	Plate block of 4	.50	
	FDC *(Feb. 2, 1996)*		1.50

See also Nos. 1227 for coil version.

1996. SPACE SHUTTLE CHALLENGER ISSUE stamps show "1996" in bottom-left corner. *Offset and intaglio (panes of 20) by Ashton-Potter (USA) Ltd., perforated 11. No first day cancel. (Issued March 1996.) (See No. 1088.)*

1119 *Space Shuttle* Challenger

1119		MNHVF	UseVF
$3	**multicolored** phosphored paper	6.00	3.00
	Plate block of 4	25.00	

1996. JACQUELINE COCHRAN ISSUE in the Pioneers of Aviation Series memorialized the first woman to break the sound barrier, a highly skilled pilot who won the Bendix Transcontinental air race in 1938, and founded the Women's Air Force Service Pilots (WASP) program during World War II (1910-1980). Issued to pay the international postcard rate. *Offset and intaglio by Bureau of Engraving and Printing, perforated 11 1/4.*

1120 *Jacqueline Cochran*

1120		MNHVF	UseVF
50¢	**multicolored** phosphored paper	1.20	.40
	Plate block of 4	5.00	
	FDC *(March 9, 1996)*		2.00
	v. Intaglio black (inscriptions) omitted	150.00	

DECODING THE CATALOG

The $3 definitive picturing the Space Shuttle Challenger was issued on June 22, 1995, to pay the then recently increased U.S. Priority Mail rate. Little remarked upon at the time that the stamp was issued was the presence of the year date "1995" below the bottom-left corner under the offset and intaglio printed stamp design. (Below the bottom-right corner is the inscription "Challenger STS-7." The year date was something of an oddity. It wasn't quite small enough to qualify as microprinting as the U.S. Postal Service (which has incorporated most of its microprinting in the printed stamp design) has conventionally used that term. Neither was it big enough to see with the naked eye, as the year dates have been on most U.S. definitives in recent years.

This would have made no difference, except that additional printings of the stamp produced the following March clearly showed a new date — "1996" — indicating that they had been made from new plates.

The "1995" and "1996" versions of the stamp also appear to show slight differences in the offset color of the earth on some copies. However, these may represent mere minor inking varieties.

The "1995" stamp (Minkus 1088) and the "1996" $3 stamp (Minkus 1119) both have the same catalog value at present. In the absence of additional printing information, it may be years before any difference in the relative scarcity of the two versions is fully recognized by collectors.

1088

1119

1996. MOUNTAIN COIL ISSUE in the Non-denominated Service-Inscribed Series. *Purple outlines on inscription letters, and small "1996" in purple in bottom-left corner. Gravure by Bureau of Engraving and Printing, perforated 9 3/4 vertically. Plate number every 24 stamps.*

1121, 1122, 1131, 1152 *Mountains*

1121		MNHVF	UseVF
(5¢)	**purple & multicolored** untagged	.25	.20
	Pair	.50	
	FDC *(March 16, 1996)*		1.25
	z. Tagged (error)	4.00	3.50

1996. MOUNTAIN COIL ISSUE in the Non-denominated Service-Inscribed Series. No outlines on inscription letters, large "1996" in blue in bottom-left corner. *Gravure by J.W. Fergusson & Sons for Stamp Venturers, perforated 9 3/4 vertically. Plate number every 14 stamps. Back number every 10 stamps.*

1122		MNHVF	UseVF
5¢	**blue & multicolored** untagged	.25	.20
	Pair	.50	
	FDC *(March 16, 1996)*		1.25
	Pair, imperforate	500.00	

1996. EASTERN BLUEBIRD ISSUE in the Flora and Fauna Series. Redesigned denomination. *Offset by Bureau of Engraving and Printing, perforated 11 1/4x11.*

1123 *Eastern Bluebird*

1123		MNHVF	UseVF
3¢	**multicolored** untagged	.25	.20
	Plate block of 4	.65	
	FDC *(April 3, 1996)*		1.50

For version inscribed "USA03" see No. 960.

1996. CAL FARLEY ISSUE in the Great Americans Series recognized the founder (1895-1967) of the Cal Farley's Boys Ranch foster home near Amarillo, Texas. Issued to pay standard First Class letter rate. *Intaglio by Banknote Corporation of America, perforated 11 1/4x11.*

1124 *Cal Farley*

1124		MNHVF	UseVF
32¢	**green** phosphored paper (solid tagging)	.65	.20
	Plate block of 4	3.75	
	FDC *(April 26, 1996)*		1.75

1996. FLAG OVER PORCH BOOKLET STAMP ISSUE Self-adhesive booklet stamps with small red "1996." Gravure by Bureau of Engraving and Printing, serpentine die cut 9 3/4 on two or three sides.

1125, 1126, 1127, 1128, B268 *Flag over porch*

1125		MNHVF	UseVF
32¢	**multicolored** phosphored paper	.75	.30
	n. Booklet pane of 10	6.50	
	FDC single *(May 21, 1996)*		2.00
	FDC booklet pane		8.50

See also Nos. 1078, 1080-83, 1116, 1150, and 1151.

1996. FLAG OVER PORCH COIL STAMP ISSUE Self-adhesive coil stamps with small red "1996." Gravure by Bureau of Engraving and Printing, serpentine die cut 9 3/4 vertically. Plate number every 24 stamps.

1126		MNHVF	UseVF
32¢	multicolored phosphored paper	1.00	.30
	Pair	2.00	.60
	FDC (May 21, 1996)		2.00
	v. Pair imperforate	—	

1996. FLAG OVER PORCH COIL STAMP ISSUE Self-adhesive coil stamps with small red "1996." Gravure by Bureau of Engraving and Printing, serpentine die cut 11 vertically. Plate number every 24 stamps.

1127		MNHVF	UseVF
32¢	multicolored phosphored paper	1.50	.50
	Pair	3.00	1.00
	FDC (May 21, 1996)		1.50

1996. FLAG OVER PORCH COIL STAMP ISSUE Self-adhesive coil. Serpentine die cut 11 1/2 vertically with large blue "1996." Plate number every 21 stamps.

1128		MNHVF	UseVF
32¢	multicolored phosphored paper	.70	.20
	Pair	1.25	
	FDC (June 15, 1996)		2.00

On this issue, stamps are spaced apart on the 10,000 stamp coil roll.

1996. EAGLE AND SHIELD NON-DENOMINATED SELF-ADHESIVE COIL ISSUE Gravure by J.W. Fergusson & Sons for Stamp Venturers, serpentine die cut 11 1/2 vertically. Plate number every 21 stamps. Back number every 10 stamps.

1129 *Eagle and shield*

1129		MNHVF	UseVF
(10¢)	multicolored untagged	.25	.20
	Pair	.50	
	FDC (May 21, 1996)		1.50

1996. BUTTE COIL ISSUE in the Non-denominated Service-Inscribed Series. *Self-adhesive coils with "1996." Gravure by J.W. Fergusson & Sons for Stamp Venturers, serpentine die cut 11 1/2 vertically. Plate number every 21 stamps. Back number every 10 stamps.*

1130, 1070 *Butte*

1130		MNHVF	UseVF
(5¢)	yellow, blue & red untagged	.25	.20
	Pair	.50	.25
	FDC (June 15, 1996)		1.50

1996. MOUNTAINS COIL ISSUE in the Non-denominated Service-Inscribed Series. *Self-adhesive coils with "1996." Gravure by J.W. Fergusson & Sons for Stamp Venturers, serpentine die cut 11 1/4 vertically. Plate number every 15 stamps. Back number every stamp.*

1131, 1121, 1122, 1152 *Mountains*

1131		MNHVF	UseVF
(5¢)	purple & multicolored untagged	.25	.20
	Pair	.50	.25
	FDC (June 15, 1996)		1.50

Listings and prices for plate number coil strips and singles appear at the end of this definitives section of the Krause-Minkus catalog.

1996. AUTOMOBILE COIL ISSUE in the American Culture Series. *Self-adhesive coils with "1996." Gravure by J.W. Fergusson & Sons for Stamp Venturers, serpentine die cut 11 1/2 vertically. Plate number every 21 stamps. Back number every 10 stamps.*

1132, 1071 *Auto*

1132		MNHVF	UseVF
(10¢)	black, brown & red brown untagged	.25	.20
	Pair	.50	.25
	FDC		1.50

1996. AUTO TAIL FIN COIL ISSUE in the American Culture Series. Self-adhesive coils with "1996." *Gravure by J.W. Fergusson & Sons for Stamp Venturers, serpentine die cut 11 1/2 vertically. Plate number every 21 stamps. Back number every 10 stamps.*

1133, 1072, 1073 *Auto tail fin*

1133		MNHVF	UseVF
(15¢)	buff & multicolored untagged	.35	.30
	Pair	.70	.60
	FDC (June 15, 1996)		1.90

1996. JUKE BOX COIL ISSUE in the American Culture Series. *Self-adhesive coils with "1996." Gravure by J.W. Fergusson & Sons for Stamp Venturers, serpentine die cut vertically. Plate number every 21 stamps. Back number every 10 stamps.*

1134, 1074, 1075, 1153, 1161 *Juke box*

1134		MNHVF	UseVF
(25¢)	orange red, bright yellow green & multicolored untagged	.60	.30
	Pair	1.20	.60
	FDC (June 15, 1996)		1.90

1996. BLUE JAY BOOKLET ISSUE in the Flora and Fauna Series. *Self-adhesive Blue jay booklets and coils with "1996." Gravure by J.W. Fergusson & Sons for Stamp Venturers, serpentine die cut perforations.*

1135, 1136, B276 *Blue Jay*

1135		MNHVF	UseVF
20¢	multicolored phosphored paper, serpentine die cut 10 1/2x10 3/4 on three sides	.45	.25
	n. Pane of 10 (convertible booklet)	4.50	
	FDC (Aug. 2, 1996)		1.50
	FDC Pane of 10		8.50

1996. BLUE JAY COIL ISSUE in the Flora and Fauna Series.
Serpentine die cut 11 1/2 vertically. Plate number every 14 stamps.

1136		MNHVF	UseVF
20¢	**multicolored** phosphored paper	.40	.20
	Pair	.80	.30
	FDC *(Aug. 2, 1996)*		1.50
	v. Coil pair, imperforate	1,000.00	

1996. CONTEMPORARY CHRISTMAS ISSUE included se-tenant sheets and self-adhesive booklets of four Christmas Family scenes and a generic Holiday Skater design for sale in ATMs offered in self-adhesive booklets only. *Offset by Ashton-Potter (USA) Ltd., perforated 11 1/4.*

1137, 1141 *Family at yule hearth*

1138, 1142 *Family trimming tree*

1139, 1143 *Dreaming of Santa*

1140, 1144 *Holiday shopping*

1137		MNHVF	UseVF
32¢	Family at yule hearth, phosphored paper	.60	.20
1138		MNHVF	UseVF
32¢	Family trimming tree, phosphored paper	.60	.20
1139		MNHVF	UseVF
32¢	Dreaming of Santa, phosphored paper	.60	.20
1140		MNHVF	UseVF
32¢	Holiday shopping, phosphored paper	.60	.20
	y. Se-tenant block or strip of 4 (Nos. 1137-40)	3.00	.50
	FDC *(Oct. 8, 1996)* any single		2.00
	Plate block of 4	3.50	
	FDC block of 4		4.25

1996. CONTEMPORARY SELF-ADHESIVE BOOKLET ISSUE *Offset by Banknote Corporation of America, serpentine die cut 11 3/4x11 1/2.*

1141		MNHVF	UseVF
32¢	Family at yule hearth, phosphored paper	.60	.20
1142		MNHVF	UseVF
32¢	Family trimming tree, phosphored paper	.60	.20
1143		MNHVF	UseVF
32¢	Dreaming of Santa, phosphored paper	.60	.20
1144		MNHVF	UseVF
32¢	Holiday shopping, phosphored paper	.60	.20
	n. Pane of 20 (five each of Nos. 1141-44) plus label (convertible booklet)	15.00	
	FDC *(Oct. 8, 1996)* any single		1.50
	FDC Nos. 1141-1144 on one cover		8.00

1996. HOLIDAY SKATERS BOOKLET ATM ISSUE *Gravure by Avery Dennison, imperforate (die cut).*

1145 *Holiday skaters*

1145		MNHVF	UseVF
32¢	**multicolored,** phosphored lacquer on surface of stamps	.75	.30
	n. Booklet pane of 18	14.00	
	FDC *(Oct. 8, 1996)*		2.00
	FDC Pane of 18		14.75

1996. TRADITIONAL CHRISTMAS ISSUE The traditional stamp taken from a detail of *Adoration of the Shepherds* by the 18th century Italian artist Paolo de Matteis, was offered in conventional sheets and self-adhesive booklets, supplemented by new stocks of the Midnight Angel stamps that had proven popular the previous year. *Offset and intaglio by Bureau of Engraving and Printing.*

1146, 1147, B280 Madonna and Child *from Virginia Museum of Fine Arts*

1146		MNHVF	UseVF
32¢	**multicolored** phosphored paper, perforated 11 1/4	.70	.20
	Plate block of 4	3.50	
	FDC *(Nov. 1, 1996)*		1.80
1147		MNHVF	UseVF
32¢	**multicolored** tagged, serpentine die cut 10	.95	.30
	n. Pane of 20 plus label (convertible booklet)	15.00	
	FDC *(Nov. 1, 1996)*		2.00
	v. No die cutting (pair)	80.00	

No. 1148 is not assigned.

1996. YELLOW ROSE ISSUE in the Flora and Fauna Series got a renewed lease on life in a new color, issued in self-adhesive form convertible booklets of 20 and vending booklets of 15 and 30. *Gravure by J.W. Fergusson & Sons for Stamp Venturers, serpentine die cut 11 1/4x11 3/4.*

1149, 1163, B282, B283 *Yellow rose*

1149		MNHVF	UseVF
32¢	**yellow & multicolored** phosphored paper	.65	.20
	n. Pane of 20 plus label (convertible booklet)	14.00	
	pn1. Plate number single (bottom left corner of pane of 5)	1.00	
	pn2. Plate number single (bottom left corner of pane of 6)	1.00	
	n1. Booklet pane of 4 *(Dec. 1996)*	2.75	
	n2. Booklet pane of 5 plus label *(Dec. 1996)*	3.25	
	n3. Booklet pane of 6, with or without plate number *(Dec. 1996)*	3.00	
	FDC *(Oct. 24, 1996)* single		2.00

1997. FLAG OVER PORCH BOOKLET ISSUE Self-adhesive booklet stamps with red "1997." Gravure by Bureau of Engraving and Printing, serpentine die cut 9 3/4 on two or three sides.

1150, 1151, 1162, B284, B285 *Flag over porch*

1150		MNHVF	UseVF
32¢	**multicolored** phosphored paper	.75	.30
	FDC *(Jan. 24, 1997)*		1.90
	n. Booklet pane of 5 plus label	3.50	
	n1. Booklet pane of 10 *(May 21, 1997)*	6.50	

See also Nos. 1078, 1080-83, 1116, and 1125-28.

1997. FLAG OVER PORCH COIL ISSUE Self-adhesive coil stamps with red "1997." Gravure by Bureau of Engraving and Printing, serpentine die cut 9 3/4 vertically. Plate number every 21 stamps.

1151		MNHVF	UseVF
32¢	multicolored phosphored paper	.75	.30
	Pair	1.50	.30
	FDC (Jan. 24, 1997)		1.90

1997. MOUNTAIN COIL ISSUE in the Non-denominated Service-Inscribed Series. *Self-adhesive, 3,000 stamp coil with "1997." Gravure by Bureau of Engraving and Printing, serpentine die cut 9 3/4 vertically. Plate number every 21 stamps. Back number every 20 stamps.*

1152, 1121, 1122, 1131 *Mountains*

1152		MNHVF	UseVF
(5¢)	purple & multicolored untagged	.25	.20
	Pair	.50	.25
	FDC (Jan. 24, 1997)		1.25

1997. JUKE BOX COIL ISSUE in the American Culture Series. *Self-adhesive, 3,000 stamp coils with "1997." Gravure by Bureau of Engraving and Printing, serpentine die cut 9 3/4 vertically. Plate number every 21 stamps. Back number every 10 stamps.*

1153, 1074, 1075, 1134, 1161 *Juke box*

1153		MNHVF	UseVF
(25¢)	multicolored untagged	.60	.20
	Pair	1.20	.30
	FDC (Jan. 24, 1997)		1.25

> *Listings and prices for plate number coil strips and singles appear at the end of this definitives section of the Krause-Minkus catalog.*

1997. STATUE OF LIBERTY BOOKLET ISSUE revised denomination version of the 1994 design for use at the 32¢ First Class domestic letter rate. *Self-adhesive vending booklets of 15 and 30 and convertible booklets of 20. Gravure by Avery Dennison, serpentine die cut 11 on two, three or four sides.*

1154, B286, B287, B288 *Statue of Liberty*

1154		MNHVF	UseVF
32¢	multicolored phosphored paper	.75	.20
	pn. Plate number single (bottom left corner of pane of 5 or 6)	—	
	n. Booklet pane of 4	2.50	
	n1. Booklet pane of 5 plus label	3.25	
	n2. Booklet pane of 6 with or without plate number	4.00	
	n3. Pane of 20 plus label	13.00	
	FDC (Feb. 1, 1997)		1.25
	v. Serpentine die cut 11 1/2x11 3/4	1.40	
	n2v. Booklet pane of 6, with or without plate number	4.00	
	n3v. Pane of 20 plus label (convertible booklet)	40.00	

1997. CITRON AND INSECT ISSUE Self-adhesive convertible-booklet stamps in two distinct sizes and die-cutting gauges, based upon two botanical prints made by Anna Maria Sibylla Merian during her 1699-1701 travels in Surinam. *Gravure by Stamp Venturers.*

Design 20x27mm, serpentine die cut 10 3/4x10 1/4 on two, three or four sides.

1155, 1157, 1159, B289 *Citron and insects*

1155		MNHVF	UseVF
32¢	multicolored phosphored paper	.75	.20
	FDC (March 3, 1997)		2.00
	n. Pane of 20 (10 each Nos. 1155-56 plus label) (convertible booklet)	12.00	

1997. FLOWERING PINEAPPLE ISSUE

1156, 1158, 1160 *Flowering pineapple*

1156		MNHVF	UseVF
32¢	multicolored phosphored paper	.75	.20
	y. Se-tenant pair 1155 and 1156	1.50	
	FDC (March 3, 1997)		2.00

1997. CITRON AND INSECT BOOKLET ISSUE *Vending booklet, design 18 1/2x24mm, serpentine die cut 11 1/4x10 3/4 on two or three sides (Nos. 1157-58).*

1157		MNHVF	UseVF
32¢	multicolored phosphored paper	.75	.20
	FDC (March 3, 1997)		2.00

1997. FLOWERING PINEAPPLE BOOKLET ISSUE *Design 18 1/2x24mm.*

1158		MNHVF	UseVF
32¢	multicolored phosphored paper	.75	.20
	y. Se-tenant pair 1157 and 1158	1.50	
	FDC (March 3, 1997)		2.00

1997. CITRON AND INSECT BOOKLET ISSUE *Design 18 1/2x24mm, serpentine die cut 11 1/4x11 1/4x11 1/4x10 3/4 (Nos. 1159-60) on two or three sides.*

1159		MNHVF	UseVF
32¢	multicolored phosphored paper	1.25	.50
	FDC (March 3, 1997)		2.00
	n. Booklet pane of 5 (one No. 1159 sideways, two each of No. 1157-58)	3.25	

1997. FLOWERING PINEAPPLE BOOKLET ISSUE *Design 18 1/2x24mm.*

1160		MNHVF	UseVF
32¢	multicolored phosphored paper	1.25	.50
	FDC (March 3, 1997)		2.00
	n. Booklet pane of 5 (one No. 1160 sideways, two each of No. 1157-58)	3.50	

Nos. 1159-60, which are die cut on all four sides, have a single irregular large serration near the middle of the right side created by die cutting.

1997. JUKE BOX COIL ISSUE in the American Culture Series. *Self-adhesive 10,000- and 30,000-stamp experimental linerless (no backing paper) coils, manufactured by 3M Corp. and finished by Stamp Venturers, gravure, imperforate with simulated perforations (black circles) and black bars at top and bottom. Plate number every 7 stamps.*

3

2

22222

1161, 1074, 1075, 1134, 1153 *Juke box with simulated perforations*

1161
		MNHVF	UseVF
(25¢)	multicolored untagged	.60	.20
	Pair	1.20	.40
	FDC (March 14, 1997)		1.50

1997. FLAG OVER PORCH COIL ISSUE Self-adhesive 100-stamp experimental linerless (no backing paper) coils, manufactured by 3M Corp. and finished by Stamp Venturers, gravure, serpentine die cut 10 vertically. Plate number every 7 stamps.

1162 *Flag over porch*

1162
		MNHVF	UseVF
32¢	multicolored phosphored paper	.60	.20
	Pair	1.25	
	FDC (March 14, 1997)		2.00

See also Nos. 1078, 1080-83, 1116, 1125-28, 1150-51.

Listings and prices for plate number coil strips and singles appear at the end of this definitives section of the Krause-Minkus catalog.

1997. YELLOW ROSE COIL ISSUE in the Flora and Fauna Series. *Self-adhesive coil. Gravure by Bureau of Engraving and Printing, serpentine die cut 9 3/4 vertically. Plate number every 24 stamps.*

1163, 1149 *Yellow rose*

1163
		MNHVF	UseVF
32¢	yellow & multicolored phosphored paper	.65	.20
	Pair	1.25	.35
	FDC (Aug. 1, 1997)		2.00
	v. Coil pair, imperforate	150.00	

1997. CHRISTMAS ISSUE For the first time in several years the Traditional and Contemporary Christmas stamps were issued in moderation — only one design of each, and in a total of four formats. The Traditional design depicts Sano di Pietro's *Madonna and Child with Saints* from the collection of the National Gallery of Art. *Offset by the Bureau of Engraving and Printing, in self-adhesive panes of 20. The Contemporary design depicts American holly. Offset by Banknote Corporation of America in self-adhesive panes of 20, and self-adhesive booklets of 15 and 30. All with serpentine die-cut perforations on two, three or four sides.*

1164 *Sano di Pietro's* Madonna and Child with Saints

1164
		MNHVF	UseVF
32¢	multicolored phosphored paper, serpentine die cut 10	.50	.20

FDC (Oct. 27, 1997) single		2.00
n. Pane of 20 plus label (convertible booklet)	10.00	

1165, B294, B295 *American holly*

1165
		MNHVF	UseVF
32¢	multicolored phosphored paper, serpentine die cut 11 1/4x11 3/4	.50	.20
	n. Booklet pane of 4	2.50	
	n1. Booklet pane of 5 plus label	3.00	
	n2. Booklet pane of 6	3.75	
	n3. Pane of 20 plus label	12.00	
	FDC (Oct. 30, 1997)		2.00

1997. MARS PATHFINDER ISSUE This Priority Mail stamp commemorated the Pathfinder's Mission to Mars and the successful landing of July 4, 1997, and the subsequent deployment of the *Sojourner* rover. The view on the sheetlet is based on one of the first views sent back showing the rover and the Ares Vallis region of Mars. The stamp design incorporates hidden images, repeated "USPS" and "Mars Pathfinder July 4, 1997," visible with a decoder lens. *Gravure, Stamp Venturers, perforated 11.*

1166 *Sojourner rover on Mars surface*

1166
		MNHVF	UseVF
$3	multicolored block tagged (15,000,000 printed)	4.50	2.50
	FDC (Dec. 10, 1997)		4.50

1998. MARS PATHFINDER PRESS SHEET ISSUE Uncut, but perforated press sheets of 18 subjects of the $3.00 Mars Pathfinder were made available in January 1998. There are vertical perforations between the three columns; thus the single subject measures 152mm wide, rather than the 146mm wide on the single imperforate examples of December 1997.

Varieties exist with perforations on left, right or on both sides. Once the stamp is removed from the pane, it is undistinguishable from No. 1166.

1167
		MNHVF	UseVF
$3	multicolored phosphored paper (single)	15.00	—
	Uncut press sheet of 18	110.00	
	Pair with horizontal gutter	13.50	
	Pair with vertical gutter	13.50	
	Cross-gutter block of 4	27.50	

1998. HENRY R. LUCE ISSUE in the Great Americans Series honored the magazine editor and publisher, founder of *Time, Fortune, Life,* and *Sports Illustrated.* Luce (1898-1967) also had interests in radio. Design is based on an Alfred Eisenstadt photo. *Intaglio, printed by Banknote Corporation of America, perforated 11.*

1168 *Henry R. Luce*

1168

		MNHVF	UseVF
32¢	**lake** phosphored paper (grainy tagging)	.50	.20
	Plate block of 4	2.00	
	FDC *(April 3, 1998)*		1.00

1998. SWAMP COIL ISSUE in the Non-denominated Service-Inscribed Series. Nonprofit organization rate. *Printed by Sennett Security Products in 10,000 stamp coils, perforated 10 vertically. Plate number every 14 stamps. Back number every 10 stamps.*

1169, 1169A *Swamp*

1169

		MNHVF	UseVF
(5¢)	**multicolored** untagged	.25	.20
	Pair	.30	
	FDC *(June 5, 1998)*		1.00

1998. SWAMP SELF-ADHESIVE COIL ISSUE in the Non-denominated Service-Inscribed Series. *Self-adhesive coil, untagged, serpentine die cut 9 3/4 vertically. Plate number every 21 stamps. Back number every 20 stamps.*

1169A

		MNHVF	UseVF
(5¢)	**multicolored** untagged	.20	.20
	Pair	.25	
	FDC *(Dec. 14, 1998)*		1.25

1998. DINER NON-DENOMINATED COIL ISSUE in the American Culture Series. Presorted First-Class rate. *Printed by Sennett Security Products in 10,000 stamp coils, perforated 10 vertically. Plate number every 14 stamps. Back number every 10 stamps.*

1170, 1177 *Diner*

1170

		MNHVF	UseVF
(25¢)	**multicolored** untagged	.40	.20
	Pair	.80	
	FDC *(June 5, 1998)*		1.00

> *Listings and prices for plate number coil strips and singles appear at the end of this definitives section of the Krause-Minkus catalog.*

1998. LILA AND DE WITT WALLACE ISSUE in the Great Americans Series honored the founders of *Reader's Digest* magazine. Later in life, Lila (1889-1984) and DeWitt (1889-1981) Wallace contributed millions of dollars to charitable causes and set up several charitable foundations. *Printed by Ashton-Potter (USA) Ltd., perforated 11.*

1171 *Lila & DeWitt Wallace*

1171

		MNHVF	UseVF
32¢	**blue** phosphored paper (solid tagging)	.50	.20
	Plate block of 4	2.00	
	FDC *(July 16, 1998)*		1.00

1998. RING-NECKED PHEASANT COIL ISSUE in the Flora and Fauna Series. *Self-adhesive coil, rolls of 100 stamps. Printed by Bureau of Engraving and Printing, serpentine die cut 9 3/4 vertically. Plate number every 24 stamps.*

1172, 1173, 1248 *Ring-necked Pheasant*

1172

		MNHVF	UseVF
20¢	**multicolored** phosphored paper	.40	.20
	Pair	.80	
	FDC *(July 30, 1998)*		1.00
	v. Pair, imperforate	—	

1998. RING-NECKED PHEASANT BOOKLET ISSUE in the Flora and Fauna Series. *Self-adhesive convertible booklet, printed by Avery Dennison, serpentine die cut 11 1/4 on two or three sides.*

1173

		MNHVF	UseVF
20¢	**multicolored** phosphored paper	.40	.20
	n. Pane of 10	3.50	
	FDC *(July 30, 1998)* single		1.00

1998. RED FOX ISSUE in the Flora and Fauna Series. A hidden image silhouette of a walking fox is visible with a decoder lens above the rear foot. *Printed by Banknote Corp. of America, serpentine die cut 11 1/2x11 1/4.*

1174 *Red Fox*

1174

		MNHVF	UseVF
$1	**multicolored** phosphored paper	1.50	.75
	Plate block of 4	10.00	
	y. Pane of 20	30.00	
	FDC *(Aug. 14, 1998)*		2.00
	v. Die cut 11 3/4x11 *(Mid July 2002)*	1.50	.75
	Plate block of 4	10.00	
	vy. Pane of 20	30.00	

1998. BICYCLE COIL ISSUE non-denominated presorted standard rate with large date. *Printed by Sennett Security Products in coils of 500 and 10,000 stamps with water-activated gum, perforated 10 vertically. (In April 2000 this stamp was issued in coils of 3,000 with no noticeable differences.) Plate number every 14 stamps. Back number every 10 stamps.*

1175 *Bicycle*

1175

		MNHVF	UseVF
(10¢)	**multicolored** untagged	.30	.20
	Pair	.60	
	FDC *(Aug. 14, 1998)*		1.00

1998. BICYCLE COIL ISSUE presorted standard rate with small date. *Printed by Sennett Security Products in coils of 500 and 10,000, and Bureau of Engraving and Printing in coils of 3,000 with no distinguishing markings, serpentine die cut 9 3/4. Plate number every 21 stamps. Back number every 20 stamps.*

1176

		MNHVF	UseVF
(10¢)	**multicolored** untagged	.30	.20
	Pair, large date, small date	.60	
	FDC *(Aug. 14, 1998)*		1.00

1998. DINER COIL ISSUE in the American Culture Series. *Self-adhesive 3,000 stamp coil. Printed by Bureau of Engraving and Printing, serpentine die cut 9 3/4. Plate number every 21 stamps. Back number every 20 stamps.*

1177

		MNHVF	UseVF
(25¢)	**multicolored** untagged	.30	.20
	Pair	.60	
	FDC *(Sept. 30, 1998)*		1.00

See also No. 1170.

1998. TRADITIONAL CHRISTMAS ISSUE A Florentine terracotta from about 1425 by unknown artisan. It is in the collection of the National Gallery of Art. *Self-adhesive booklet of 20, serpentine die cut 10 on two, three or four sides.*

1178 *Florentine terracotta*

1178		MNHVF	UseVF
32¢	**multicolored** phosphored paper	.50	.20
	n. Pane of 20 plus label (convertible booklet)	7.50	
	FDC *(Oct. 15, 1998),* any single		1.00

1998. CONTEMPORARY CHRISTMAS ISSUE Festive holiday wreaths in a traditional, colonial, chili and tropical design. *Stamp measures 23x30mm. Serpentine die cut 11 1/2, on two, three or four sides. Panes of 20, offset by Banknote Corporation of America.*

1179, 1183, 1187 *Traditional wreath*

1180, 1184, 1188 *Colonial wreath*

1181, 1185, 1189 *Chili wreath*

1182, 1186, 1190 *Tropical wreath*

B299

1179		MNHVF	UseVF
32¢	Traditional wreath, phosphored paper	.50	.20
1180		MNHVF	UseVF
32¢	Colonial wreath, phosphored paper	.50	.20
1181		MNHVF	UseVF
32¢	Chili wreath, phosphored paper	.50	.20
1182		MNHVF	UseVF
32¢	Tropical wreath, phosphored paper	.50	.20
	FDC *(Oct. 15, 1998),* any single		2.00
	FDC Nos. 1179-82 on one cover		4.00
	v. Block, red omitted	—	
	y. Se-tenant block of 4 Nos. 1179-82	2.00	

1998. CONTEMPORARY CHRISTMAS BOOKLET ISSUE had wreathes in traditional, chili, colonial and tropical order and two distinct sizes. *Serpentine die cut 11 1/2 on two, three or four sides. Offset by Bureau of Engraving and Printing (1186n); convertible booklet, 23x30mm, Banknote Corporation of America (1190n).*

1183		MNHVF	UseVF
32¢	Traditional wreath, phosphored paper	.50	.20
1184		MNHVF	UseVF
32¢	Colonial wreath, phosphored paper	.50	.20
1185		MNHVF	UseVF
32¢	Chili wreath, phosphored paper	.50	.20
1186		MNHVF	UseVF
32¢	Tropical wreath, phosphored paper	.50	.20
	FDC *(Oct. 15, 1998),* any single		1.00
	FDC Nos. 1183-86 on one cover		4.00
	n. Pane of 20 (5 each of Nos. 1183-86 plus label)	7.50	
	y. Se-tenant block of 4 Nos. 1183-86	2.00	

Vending booklet, 21x24mm, serpentine die cut 11 1/4x11 1/2.

1187		MNHVF	UseVF
32¢	Traditional wreath	.50	.20
1188		MNHVF	UseVF
32¢	Colonial wreath	.50	.20
1189		MNHVF	UseVF
32¢	Chili wreath	.50	.20

1190		MNHVF	UseVF
32¢	Tropical wreath	.50	.20
	FDC *(Oct. 15, 1998),* any single		1.00
	n. Booklet pane of 4 (Nos. 1187-90)	2.00	
	n1. Booklet pane of 5 (1 each of Nos. 1187, 1189-90, 2 of No. 1188) plus label	2.50	
	n2. Booklet pane of 6 (2 each of Nos. 1187, 1189, 2 each of Nos. 1188, 1190)	3.00	
	y. Se-tenant block of 4 Nos. 1187-90	2.00	

1998. "H" MAKE-UP RATE, USA WHITE ISSUE showed a weather vane rooster, a 1¢ stamp to be added to the 32¢ to make the new 33¢ First Class rate of Jan. 10, 1999. The inscription "USA" was in white. *Pane of 50. Printed by Ashton Potter, perforated 11 1/4.*

1191 *Rooster, white "USA"*

1191		MNHVF	UseVF
(1¢)	**multicolored** untagged	.25	.20
	Plate block of 4	.30	
	FDC *(Nov. 9, 1998)*		1.00
	v. black omitted	—	

1998. "H" MAKE-UP RATE, USA LIGHT BLUE ISSUE Weather vane rooster with inscription "USA" in light blue. *Panes of 50, printed by Banknote Corporation of America, perforated 11 1/4.*

1192 *Rooster, blue "USA"*

1192		MNHVF	UseVF
(1¢)	**multicolored** untagged	.25	.20
	Plate block of 4	.30	
	FDC *(Nov. 9, 1998)*		1.00

1998. HAT "H" FIRST CLASS ISSUE used Uncle Sam's hat to continue the "alphabet primer" stamps. *Gummed pane of 50. Printed by Stamp Venturers, perforated 11 1/4.*

1193-1197, 1203, B300 *Hat "H"*

1193		MNHVF	UseVF
(33¢)	**multicolored** phosphored paper	.50	.20
	Plate block of 4	2.00	
	FDC *(Nov. 9, 1998)*		1.90

1998. HAT "H" FIRST CLASS COIL ISSUE *Gummed coil of 100 and 3,000. Printed by Bureau of Engraving and Printing, perforated 10 vertically. Plate number every 24 stamps.*

1194		MNHVF	UseVF
(33¢)	**multicolored** phosphored paper	.50	.20
	Pair	1.00	
	FDC *(Nov. 9, 1998)*		1.90

1998. HAT "H" FIRST CLASS BOOKLET ISSUE *Self-adhesive. Printed by Avery Dennison, serpentine die cut 11.*

1195		MNHVF	UseVF
(33¢)	**multicolored** phosphored paper	.50	.20
	n. Booklet pane of 10 (convertible booklet)	4.00	1.00
	n1. Booklet pane of 20 plus label (convertible booklet)	7.00	
	FDC *(Nov. 9, 1998)*		1.90

1998. HAT "H" FIRST CLASS BOOKLET ISSUE *Self-adhesive.*
Printed by Bureau of Engraving and Printing, with tiny date, folded booklet, serpentine die cut 10 on two or three sides.

1196		MNHVF	UseVF
(33¢)	**multicolored** phosphored paper	.50	.20
	n. Booklet pane of 10	7.00	
	FDC *(Nov. 9, 1998)*		1.90

1998. HAT "H" FIRST CLASS COIL ISSUE *Self-adhesive coils of 100 or 3,000. The coils of 100 have no space between the stamps, the backing paper is the same height as the stamps, and the corners of the stamps are square. The coils of 3,000 have spaces between stamps, the backing paper is larger than the stamps, and the corners of the stamps are rounded. Printed by Bureau of Engraving and Printing, serpentine die cut 10 vertically. Plate number every 24 stamps.*

1197		MNHVF	UseVF
(33¢)	**multicolored** phosphored paper	.50	.20
	Pair	1.00	
	FDC *(Nov. 9, 1998)*		1.90
	a. Backing paper larger than stamps	.50	
	(back numbers exist)		
	FDC *(Nov. 9, 1998)*		1.90
	v. Coil pair, imperforate (no die cut)	150.00	
	v1. red omitted (coil pair)	1,500.00	
	v2. black omitted	—	

1998. UNCLE SAM ISSUE Nine months after the first depiction of the venerable symbol of America on a stamp (CM1968i), Uncle Sam got his own definitive. *Panes of 20, serpentine die cut 10 3/4. Printed by Sennett Security Products.*

1198, 1199, 1233 *Saluting Uncle Sam*

1198		MNHVF	UseVF
22¢	**multicolored** phosphored paper	.50	.20
	Plate block of 4	2.00	
	FDC *(Nov. 9, 1998)*		1.90

1998. UNCLE SAM COIL ISSUE *Self-adhesive, coil rolls of 100. Printed by Bureau of Engraving and Printing, serpentine die cut 10 vertically. Plate number every 24 stamps.*

1199		MNHVF	UseVF
22¢	**multicolored** tagged	.50	.20
	Pair	1.00	
	FDC *(Nov. 9, 1998)*		1.90

See No. 1233.

1998. MARY BRECKINRIDGE ISSUE was the first in the Great Americans Series to be issued in a self-adhesive format. Breckinridge (1881-1965) founded the Frontier Nursing Service, which brought healthcare to remote Appalachian homesteads and communities. *Printed by Banknote Corp. of America, serpentine die cut 11 3/4x11 1/2.*

1200 *Mary Breckinridge*

1200		MNHVF	UseVF
77¢	**blue** phosphored paper (solid tagging)	1.50	.20
	Plate block of 4	6.00	
	FDC *(Nov. 9, 1998)*		2.00

1998. SHUTTLE LANDING ISSUE met the Jan.10, 1999, Priority Mail rate. The names of the six space shuttles cover the face of the stamp when viewed through a decoder lens (*Endeavour* is Bmisspelled "Endeavor"). *Self-adhesive, printed by Banknote Corporation of America, serpentine die cut 11 1/2.*

1201 *Shuttle landing*

1201		MNHVF	UseVF
$3.20	**multicolored** phosphored paper	6.00	2.75
	Plate block of 4	25.00	
	FDC *(Nov. 9, 1998)*		6.00

1998. SHUTTLE PIGGYBACK TRANSPORT ISSUE Jan. 10, 1999, Express Mail rate. The Piggyback Shuttle on a converted jumbo jet is how the powerless shuttles are transported from the landing field at Edwards Air Force Base in California to the Kennedy Space Center in Florida to prepare for re-use. The names of the six space shuttles cover the face of the stamp when viewed through a decoder lens (*Endeavour* is misspelled "Endeavor"). *Printed by Banknote Corporation of America, serpentine die cut 11 1/2.*

1202 *Shuttle piggyback transport*

1202		MNHVF	UseVF
$11.75	**multicolored** phosphored paper	22.00	10.00
	Plate block of 4	90.00	
	FDC *(Nov. 17, 1998)*		22.00

1998. HAT "H" FIRST CLASS ATM VENDING ISSUE *Self-adhesive pane of 18 on thin paper, serpentine die cut 8. Gravure by Avery Dennison.*

1203		MNHVF	UseVF
(33¢)	**multicolored** phosphored lacquer on	.50	.20
	surface of stamps		
	FDC *(Nov. 9, 1998)*		1.90
	n. Pane of 18	9.00	

1998. EAGLE AND SHIELD COIL ISSUE in the Non-denominated Service-Inscribed Series featured another redesign of Bulk Rate stamps issued in 1991, 1993 and 1996, but with new nomenclature, "USA Presorted Std." *Gravure, perforated 9 3/4 vertically. Plate number every 24 stamps.*

1204 *Eagle and shield*

1204		MNHVF	UseVF
(10¢)	**multicolored** untagged	.20	.20
	Pair	.25	
	FDC *(Dec. 14, 1998)*		1.25
	v. Large date	.20	.20
	Pair	.25	

See U.S. Nos. 980 ("Bulk Rate USA"), 1011 and 1012 ("USA Bulk Rate") and 1129 ("USA Bulk Rate").

1998. EAGLE AND SHIELD COIL ISSUE in the Non-denominated Service-Inscribed Series. *Self-adhesive coil, serpentine die cut 10 vertically. Plate number every 21 stamps. Back number every 20 stamps.*

1205 *Eagle and shield*

1205		MNHVF	UseVF
(10¢)	**multicolored** untagged	.20	.20
	Pair	.25	
	FDC *(Dec. 14, 1998)*		1.25
	v. Large date	.20	.20
	Pair	.25	
	v1. Phosphored paper (error)	1.25	1.00
	Pair	2.50	

1999. FLAG AND SKYSCRAPERS ISSUE Artist Hiro Kimura recalled that, growing up in Japan, he imagined the United States as a land where the American flag flew before skyscrapers that reached to a cloudless sky. Designed by Richard Sheaff. *Glossy gummed panes of 100, gravure by Bureau of Engraving and Printing (200 million printed), perforated 11 1/4.*

1206, 1207, 1208, 1209, 1210, 1211, 1212, B301, B302 *Flag and skyscrapers*

1206		MNHVF	UseVF
33¢	**multicolored,** phosphored paper	.50	.20
	Plate block of four	2.00	
	FDC *(Feb. 25, 1999)*		1.50

1999. FLAG AND SKYSCRAPERS COIL ISSUE designed by Richard Sheaff. *Gummed coil rolls of 100, 3,000 and 10,000, gravure by the Bureau of Engraving and Printing (1.2 billion printed), perforated 10 vertically. Plate number every 24 stamps. Back number on rolls of 3,000 and 10,000 every 20 stamps.*

1207		MNHVF	UseVF
33¢	**multicolored,** phosphored paper, small date	.50	.20
	Pair	1.00	
	FDC *(Feb. 25, 1999)*		1.90
	v. Large date	.50	.20
	Pair	1.00	.25

1999. FLAG AND SKYSCRAPERS COIL ISSUE designed by Richard Sheaff, from art by Hiro Kimura, Brooklyn, N.Y. *Self-adhesive coil rolls of 100, gravure by the Bureau of Engraving and Printing (7 billion printed), serpentine die cut 9 3/4 vertically, tiny red year date. Corners of stamps are square, backing is same height as stamps. Plate number every 24 stamps.*

1208		MNHVF	UseVF
33¢	**multicolored,** phosphored paper, small date	.50	.20
	Pair	1.00	
	FDC *(Feb. 25, 1999)*		1.90
	v. Large date	.50	.20
	Pair	1.00	
	v1. Pair, imperforate	—	

1999. FLAG AND SKYSCRAPERS COIL ISSUE designed by Richard Sheaff, from art by Hiro Kimura, Brooklyn, N.Y. *Self-adhesive coils of 3,000 and 10,000, gravure by the Bureau of Engraving and Printing (2 million printed), serpentine die cut 9 3/4 vertically, tiny red year date. Corners of stamps are rounded, backing is higher than stamps. Plate number every 21 stamps. Back number every 20 stamps.*

1209		MNHVF	UseVF
33¢	**multicolored,** phosphored paper	.50	.20
	Pair	1.00	
	FDC *(Feb. 25, 1999)*		1.90

Listings and prices for plate number coil strips and singles appear at the end of this definitives section of the Krause-Minkus catalog.

1999. FLAG AND SKYSCRAPERS BOOKLET ISSUE designed by Richard Sheaff, from art by Hiro Kimura, Brooklyn, N.Y. *Self-adhesive booklets of 20, gravure by the Bureau of Engraving and Printing, serpentine die cut 9 3/4, tiny red year date.*

1210		MNHVF	UseVF
33¢	**multicolored,** phosphored paper	.50	.20
	FDC *(Feb. 25, 1999)*		1.90
	n. Booklet pane of 10 (convertible booklet)	8.00	

1999. FLAG AND SKYSCRAPERS BOOKLET ISSUE designed by Richard Sheaff, from art by Hiro Kimura, Brooklyn, N.Y. *Printed in self-adhesive convertible booklets of 10 and 20 and vending booklets of 15. Gravure by Avery Dennison, serpentine die cut 11 on two, three or four sides, black year date.*

1211		MNHVF	UseVF
33¢	**multicolored,** phosphored paper	.60	.20
	FDC *(Feb. 25, 1999)*		1.90
	pn. Plate number single (bottom left corner of pane of 5)	.80	.90
	n. Booklet pane of 4	2.50	
	n1. Booklet pane of 5 plus label	3.00	
	n2. Booklet pane of 6	3.75	
	n3. Pane of 10	6.50	
	n4. Pane of 20 plus label (convertible booklet)	15.00	
	v. Serpentine die cut 11 1/2x11 3/4	.60	.20
	nv. Pane of 20 plus label (convertible booklet)	15.00	

1999. FLAG AND SKYSCRAPERS ISSUE designed by Richard Sheaff, from art by Hiro Kimura, Brooklyn, N.Y. *Gravure in self-adhesive panes of 20, with narrow perforated tips at upper left of all stamps by Avery Dennison (500 million printed), serpentine die cut 11, with black year date.*

1212		MNHVF	UseVF
33¢	**multicolored,** phosphored paper	.60	.20
	Plate block of 4	2.50	
	FDC *(Feb. 25, 1999)*		1.90

1999. FLAG IN CLASSROOM ATM ISSUE designed by Richard Sheaff. *Printed in self-adhesive automatic teller machine booklets, serpentine die cut 8.*

1213 *Flag in classroom*

1213		MNHVF	UseVF
33¢	**multicolored,** phosphored lacquer on surface	.50	.20
	FDC *(March 13, 1999)*		1.90
	n. Pane of 18	12.00	

1999. FRUIT BERRIES ISSUE in the Flora and Fauna Series. Designed by Howard Paine, Delaplane, Va., illustrated by Ned Seidler, Hampton Bay, N.Y. Pictured four luscious se-tenant illustrations of edible berries — blueberries, raspberries, strawberries, and blackberries. The sequences of the designs are different in each of three formats. *Self-adhesive convertible booklet of 20, gravure by Banknote Corporation of America, (1.2 billion printed), serpentine die cut 11 1/4x11 3/4 on two, three or four sides.*

1214, 1218, 1224, 1251, 1257
Blueberries

1215, 1220, 1225, 1252, 1256
Raspberries

1216, 1219, 1223, 1253, 1258
Strawberries

1217, 1221, 1222, 1254, 1259
Blackberries

B303

1214		MNHVF	UseVF
33¢	Blueberries, phosphored paper	.50	.20
1215		MNHVF	UseVF
33¢	Raspberries, phosphored paper	.50	.20
1216		MNHVF	UseVF
33¢	Strawberries, phosphored paper	.50	.20
1217		MNHVF	UseVF
33¢	Blackberries, phosphored paper	.50	.20
	y. Se-tenant block of 4 (Nos. 1214-17)	2.00	
	FDC block of 4		5.50
	FDC *(April 10, 1999),* any single		2.00
	n. Pane of 20 plus label (convertible booklet)	13.00	

See also Nos. 1218-25, 1251-54, 1256-59.

1999. Fruit Berries Issue in the Flora and Fauna Series. Designed by Howard Paine, Delaplane, Va., illustrated by Ned Seidler, Hampton Bay, N.Y. *Self-adhesive vending booklets of 15, gravure by Banknote Corporation of America, (153,750,000 printed), serpentine die cut 9 1/2x10.*

1218		MNHVF	UseVF
33¢	Blueberries, phosphored paper	.50	.20
1219		MNHVF	UseVF
33¢	Strawberries, phosphored paper	.50	.20
1220		MNHVF	UseVF
33¢	Raspberries, phosphored paper	.50	.20
1221		MNHVF	UseVF
33¢	Blackberries, phosphored paper	.50	.20
	FDC *(April 10, 1999),* any single		2.00
	y. Se-tenant block of 4 (Nos. 1218-21)	2.00	—
	FDC block of 4		5.50
	n. Booklet pane of 4 (Nos. 1218-21)	2.50	—
	n1. Booklet pane of 5 (1 each Nos. 1218-19, 1221, 2 No. 1220) plus label	3.25	—
	n2. Booklet pane of 6 (2 each Nos. 1218-19, 1 each Nos. 1220-21)	4.00	—

1999. Fruit Berries Coil Issue in the Flora and Fauna Series. Designed by Howard Paine, Delaplane, Va., illustrated by Ned Seidler, Hampton Bay, N.Y. *Self-adhesive horizontal coils of 100, gravure by Banknote Corporation of America, (2 billion printed), serpentine die cut 8 1/2 vertically. Plate number every 12 stamps.*

1222 *Blackberries;* 1223 *Strawberries;* 1224 *Blueberries;* 1225 *Raspberries*

1222		MNHVF	UseVF
33¢	Blackberries, phosphored paper	.50	.20
1223		MNHVF	UseVF
33¢	Strawberries, phosphored paper	.50	.20
1224		MNHVF	UseVF
33¢	Blueberries, phosphored paper	.50	.20
1225		MNHVF	UseVF
33¢	Raspberries, phosphored paper	.50	.20

	y. Coil strip of 4 (Nos. 1222-25)	2.00	
	FDC *(Feb. 25, 1999),* any single		2.00
	FDC, strip of 4		8.00

See also Nos. 1256-59.

Scenic America Series

1999. Niagara Falls Issue first in the Scenic America Series, designed by Ethel Kesler, Bethesda, Md., from photo by Kurt Ross, North Tonawanda, N.Y. Paid a new rate for letters under one-half ounce to Canada and featured a view of the mighty falls on the border of the United States and Canada, over which 20% of the world's freshwater supply flows. *Self-adhesive panes of 20, gravure by Avery Dennison, (100,750,000 printed), serpentine die cut 11.*

1226 *Niagara Falls*

1226		MNHVF	UseVF
48¢	**multicolored,** phosphored paper	1.00	.20
	Plate block of 4	4.00	
	FDC *(May 12, 1999)*		2.00

With this stamp, the USPS began to add the silhouette of a jetliner next to the denomination on some stamps, indicating they paid an international rate for which air service was used. For many years, virtually all letters and cards have been moved by air. The last U.S. stamp to bear an "Airmail" designation was the William T. Piper Issue of 1993 (A132), and Minkus ceased to classify stamps as airmail after that issue. (See Minkus Nos. 1097, 1120 and 1250.)

1999. Red-headed Woodpecker Coil Issue in the Flora and Fauna Series with "1999" date (see No. 1118). Designed by Michael R. Matherly. *Offset by the Bureau of Engraving and Printing, (100 million printed), in gummed coils of 10,000, perforated 9 3/4 vertically. Plate number every 24 stamps.*

1227 *Red-headed Woodpecker*

1227		MNHVF	UseVF
2¢	**multicolored,** untagged	.25	.20
	Pair	.40	
	FDC *(June 22, 1999)*		1.50

See No. 1118 for sheet stamp.

1999. Justin S. Morrill Issue in the Great Americans Series honored a Vermont statesman who served 12 years in the House of Representatives and 32 years in the U.S. Senate. Morrill (1810-1898), who had to leave school at the age of 15, was the chief proponent of the federal college Land Grant Acts of 1862 and 1890, which spawned 105 colleges and universities. Designed by Howard Paine, Delaplane, Va., illustrated by Burt Silverman, New York, N.Y. *Self-adhesive panes of 20, intaglio by the Banknote Corporation of America, (100 million printed), serpentine die cut 11 3/4x11 1/2.*

1228 *Justin S. Morrill*

1228		MNHVF	UseVF
55¢	**black,** phosphored paper, (solid tagging)	1.00	.20
	Plate block of four	8.00	
	FDC *(July 17, 1999)*		2.00

1999. AMERICAN KESTREL COIL ISSUE in the Flora and Fauna Series bore the same date (1996) as an earlier version (see No. 1115) but in larger type (1.5mm versus 1mm). *Gummed coils, offset by Bureau of Engraving and Printing, perforated 9 3/4 vertically. Plate number every 24 stamps.*

1229, 1247, 1263 *American Kestrel*

1229		MNHVF	UseVF
1¢	**multicolored,** untagged	.25	.20
	Pair	.50	
	v. Tagged	—	—
	EKU *(July 19, 1999)*		—

See also Nos. 1079 and 1115.

1999. RIO GRANDE ISSUE in the Scenic America Series, designed by Ethel Kessler, Bethesda, Md., from photo by Bruce Dale, Arlington, Va., a view of the river in the southwestern United States from Big Bend Ranch State Park, Texas. The denomination was the rate to mail postcards to Mexico. *Self-adhesive panes of 20, gravure by Avery Dennison, (100,750,000 printed), serpentine die cut 11.*

1230 *Rio Grande*

1230		MNHVF	UseVF
40¢	**multicolored,** phosphored paper	.75	.20
	Plate block of four	3.00	
	FDC *(July 30, 1999)*		2.00

1999. BILLY MITCHELL ISSUE designed by Phil Jordan, Falls Church, Va., illustrated by Paul Salmon, Burke, Va. Honored a former Army brigadier general who, before World War I and beyond, foresaw the potential of military air power and so irritated his superiors with his vitriolic and single-minded pursuit of the revolutionary concept that he was court-marshaled for insubordination and retired from the service in 1926. Mitchell (1879-1936) predicted, years before the occurrence, Japanese aggressiveness in the Pacific and warned of an attack on Pearl Harbor at 7:30 a.m. on a Sunday. *Self-adhesive panes of 20, gravure by Guilford Gravure, (100,750,000 printed), serpentine die cut 9 3/4x10.*

1231 *Billy Mitchell*

1231		MNHVF	UseVF
55¢	**multicolored,** phosphored paper	1.00	.40
	Plate block of four	4.00	
	FDC *(July 30, 1999)*		2.25

1999. CORAL PINK ROSE BOOKLET ISSUE designed by Derry Noyes, Washington, D.C., illustrated by Ned Seidler, Hampton Beach, N.Y. Provided a popular flower image in convenient *self-adhesive convertible booklets of 20 and vending booklets of 15. Gravure by Armotek Industries for Sennett Security Products, (1 billion printed), serpentine die cut 11 1/2 on two, three or four sides.*

1232, B305 *Coral pink rose*

1232		MNHVF	UseVF
33¢	**multicolored** phosphored paper	.50	.20
	FDC *(Aug. 13, 1999)*		1.50
	n. Booklet pane of 4	2.50	—
	n1. Booklet pane of 5 plus label	3.00	—
	n2. Booklet pane of 6 (plate number on reverse)	3.75	—
	n3. Pane of 20 plus label (convertible booklet)	13.00	—

1999. UNCLE SAM COIL ISSUE designed by Richard Sheaff, Scottsdale, Ariz., illustrated by David LaFleur, Derby, Kan. A saluting Uncle Sam filled the need for a first-class second-ounce stamp with conventional, water-activated gum (see Nos. 1198-99). *Gummed coil of 3,000. Gravure by Bureau of Engraving and Printing, (150 million printed), perforated 9 3/4 vertically. Plate number every 24 stamps. Back number every 20 stamps.*

1233, 1199 *Saluting Uncle Sam*

1233		MNHVF	UseVF
22¢	**multicolored,** phosphored paper	.50	.20
	Pair	1.00	
	FDC *(Oct. 8, 1999)*		1.50

1999. MADONNA AND CHILD BOOKLET ISSUE designed by Richard Sheaff, Scottsdale, Ariz., from 15th century art by Venetian artist Bartolomeo Vivarini in the National Gallery of Art in Washington, D.C. Painted in tempera on a wood panel. It is the second *self-adhesive, two-sided convertible booklet* from the USPS (the first: Tropical Flowers, CM2056-59, issued May 1, 1999). *Booklet of 20, offset by the Banknote Corporation of America, (1,555,560,000 printed) (77,778,000 booklets), serpentine die cut 11 1/4 on two or three sides.*

1234 *Madonna and Child*

1234		MNHVF	UseVF
33¢	**multicolored,** phosphored paper	.50	.20
	FDC *(Oct. 20, 1999)*		1.50
	n. Pane of 20 (convertible booklet)	12.00	

1999. GREETINGS REINDEER ISSUE designed by Tom Nikosey, Bell Canyon, Calif. Featured a leaping stag in antique gold against four different colored backgrounds. *Self-adhesive panes of 20 in four designs, offset by the Banknote Corporation of America, (116,500,000 printed) (5,825,000 panes, 1,456,250 each stamp), serpentine die cut 11 1/4. No stamps have natural straight edges, background color block measures 26x19mm, and lower left corner begins between the "1" and first "9" of the "1999" date; on some corners, gold border appears notched.*

1235-1238, B307 *Leaping reindeer*

1235		MNHVF	UseVF
33¢	**red** background, phosphored paper	.50	.20
1236		MNHVF	UseVF
33¢	**blue** background, phosphored paper	.50	.20
1237		MNHVF	UseVF
33¢	**violet** background, phosphored paper	.50	.20
1238		MNHVF	UseVF
33¢	**green** background, phosphored paper	.50	.20
	Plate block of four	2.00	
	y. Block or strip of 4 (Nos. 1235-38)	2.00	
	FDC *(Oct. 20, 1999)*, any single		2.00
	FDC, block of 4		8.00

1999. GREETINGS REINDEER BOOKLET ISSUE designed by Tom Nikosey, Bell Canyon, Calif. *Self-adhesive convertible booklets of 20 in four designs, offset by the Banknote Corporation of America, (1,785,060,000 printed) (89,253,000 booklets), (22,313,250 of each stamp), serpentine die cut 11 1/4 on two or three sides. All but six stamps have at least one natural straight edge, the color block measures 25 1/2x18 1/2mm and lower left corner starts between the first and second "9" of the "1999" date, gold border appears thicker than on sheet version.*

1239-1242 *Leaping reindeer*

1239		MNHVF	UseVF
33¢	**red** background, phosphored paper	.50	.20
1240		MNHVF	UseVF
33¢	**blue** background, phosphored paper	.50	.20
1241		MNHVF	UseVF
33¢	**violet** background, phosphored paper	.50	.20
1242		MNHVF	UseVF
33¢	**green** background, phosphored paper	.50	.20
	y. Se-tenant block of 4 (Nos. 1239-42)	2.00	—
	FDC *(Oct. 20, 1999)*, any single		2.00
	n. Pane of 20 (convertible booklet)	12.00	
	FDC, block of 4		8.00

1999. GREETINGS REINDEER VENDING BOOKLET ISSUE designed by Tom Nikosey, Bell Canyon, Calif. *Self-adhesive vending booklets of 15. Offset by Banknote Corporation of America, (118,125,000 printed) (7,875,000 booklets) (1,968,750 of each stamp), serpentine die cut 11 1/2 on two or three sides. All stamps have at least one straight edge, color block measures 20 1/2x7 1/2mm, lower left corner of color block begins between the "1" and first "9" of the "1999" date.*

1243-1246 *Leaping reindeer*

1243		MNHVF	UseVF
33¢	**red** background, phosphored paper	.50	.20
1244		MNHVF	UseVF
33¢	**blue** background, phosphored paper	.50	.20
1245		MNHVF	UseVF
33¢	**violet** background, phosphored paper	.50	.20
1246		MNHVF	UseVF
33¢	**green** background, phosphored paper	.50	.20
	FDC *(Oct. 20, 1999)*		1.50
	n. Booklet pane of 4	2.50	—
	n1. Booklet pane of 5 plus label	3.00	—
	n2. Booklet pane of 6	3.75	—

1999. AMERICAN KESTREL ISSUE in the Flora and Fauna Series. *Self-adhesive panes of 50 with "1999" date (see Nos. 1115 and 1229). Offset and intaglio by Bureau of Engraving and Printing (1 billion printed), serpentine die cut 10 1/2.*

1247, 1263 *American Kestrel*

1247		MNHVF	UseVF
1¢	**multicolored,** untagged	.25	.20
	Plate block of four	.50	
	FDC *(Nov. 19, 1999)*		1.50

See also Nos. 1079, 1115, 1229.

1999. RING-NECKED PHEASANT BOOKLET ISSUE in the Flora and Fauna Series. *Self-adhesive vending booklets of 10, serpentine die cut 10 1/2x11 (8 upright stamps) or 10 1/2 (2 sideways stamps). (See No. 1173.)*

1248, B308 *Ring-necked pheasant*

1248		MNHVF	UseVF
20¢	**multicolored,** phosphored paper, die cut 10 1/2x11	.40	.20
	v. sideways stamps, serpentine die cut 10 1/2	.40	.20
	n. Booklet pane of 5 (4 No. 1248, 1 No. 1248v at top)	2.00	
	n1. Booklet pane of 5 (4 No. 1248, 1 No. 1248v at bottom)	2.00	
	EKU *(July 1999)*		—

See No. 1172 for coil version.

2000. GRAND CANYON ISSUE in the Scenic America Series, designed for release in 1999, the stamp included a notation that placed Arizona's scenic natural wonder in Colorado. It was reprinted and released in 2000 and then found to have a reversed image. The rate covered the aerogram rate, the rate for printed matter up to 1-ounce to Mexico and the international 1/2-ounce letter rate to countries other than Canada and Mexico. Designed by Ethel Kessler, Bethesda, Md. *Self-adhesive, offset with microprinting USPS by Banknote Corporation of America, (100 million printed), serpentine die cut 11 1/4x11 1/2.*

1249 *Grand Canyon*

1249		MNHVF	UseVF
60¢	**multicolored,** block tagged	1.20	.30
	Plate block of 4	5.00	
	FDC *(Jan. 20, 2000)*		1.50

DECODING THE CATALOG

The 12 33¢ Reindeer stamps issued for Christmas use in three formats in 1999 have size and design differences that give them all major-variety status. One of the factors that determine a major variety is whether it is easily distinguished on a mint or used single stamp, and these stamps easily pass that test. All production of the Reindeer issue was done by Banknote Corporation of America (BCA) in self-adhesive sheet, convertible booklet and conventional booklet formats. All versions were produced by offset lithography on phosphored paper, using red, blue, green, violet and two shades of gold.

The most notable visual difference between versions is that the stamps produced in the conventional-style booklet are physically smaller than the other two. Die-cut perforations of the larger two types measure 11, while the small stamps measure 11 1/2.

Sheet version

The sheet version of the Reindeer Stamp has been assigned Minkus Nos. 1235 (red), 1236 (blue), 1237 (violet) and 1238 (green). There is no printing on the backside of the liner, and there is selvage surrounding the flat panes of 20. As a result, there are no natural straight edges that occur on these stamps. The simulated die-cut perforations measure 11.

Under long wave ultraviolet light (fluorescent), the gold deer glow slightly. The sheet version is the only one that glows. Another diagnostic is the positioning of the color block near the back hoof, in relation to the date. On sheet-version stamps, the left side of the color block is positioned between the "1" and first "9" in "1999." Both the top antler and rear hoof nearly (and sometimes do) break the color frame. The color block measures about 26 millimeters by 19mm. This makes the overall gold border appear thinner than on the convertible booklet.

Convertible booklet

At first glance, the stamps from the convertible booklet look nearly identical to those from the sheet. But several important distinctions warrant major variety status. The stamps are numbered 1239 (red), 1240 (blue), 1241 (violet) and 1242 (green).

The booklet itself, which contains 20 stamps, has printing on the back of the liner and removable strip down the center, so the pane can be folded. Because the pane is straight cut, there are one or two naturally occurring straight edges on all but six of the stamps. This is the easiest distinguishable feature for most single stamps. The simulated die-cut perforations measure 11.

Under long wave UV light, the reindeer turn almost black, in contrast to the glow found on the sheet version.

The color block positioning near the rear hoof also is significant. The vertical line of the block is positioned between the first and second "9" of "1999." In addition, there is a strong line of color between both the top antler and rear hoof and the frame line.

The color block is smaller than on the sheet version. It measures only 25 1/2mm by 18 1/2mm. This difference is easily noted when a cut stamp is

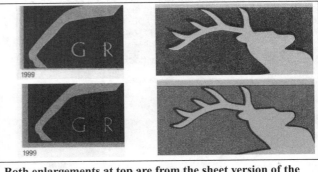

Both enlargements at top are from the sheet version of the Reindeer stamps. The vertical line of color falls between the "1" and "9," and there is a very thin line of color between the antler, rear hoof and outer frame. The convertible booklet (bottom) features a thicker line of color, and the vertical color line falls between two "9" figures in "1999."

used as a template overlay. This size difference also makes the gold border surrounding the design appear much thicker on the convertible booklet than on the sheet version. This is probably the most obvious visible difference between the two.

Conventional booklet

Although there should be no confusion between this version and the other two types, here's a quick run-down of features. The stamps have been numbered 1243 (red), 1244 (blue), 1245 (violet) and 1246 (green). Because the pane of 15 consists of a long strip of two rows, all copies of the stamps have at least one naturally occurring straight edge, and the upper-right stamp has two. The booklet is trifolded and has appropriate printing on the liner's reverse. The simulated die-cut perforations measure 11 1/2, and the stamps are physically smaller than the other versions.

The remaining features of this issue are not diagnostic, due to the diminutive size of the stamps, but are worth noting as they are a bit of a hybrid.

Under long wave UV light, the reindeer turn almost black, much like the convertible booklet. However, the color block and date positioning match the sheet version (between the "1" and "9" of "1999").

There is a strong line of color between both top antler and rear hoof and the gold border. The size of the color block is 20 1/2mm by 17 1/2mm.

Gold features

As a side note, it would seem that gold-omitted errors on this issue would be likely to be easily overlooked. The gold frame, lettering, denomination and deer design were laid down before the color was overprinted. This is why the frame line looks thicker with the smaller color block of the convertible booklet. Why two golds were used remains a mystery. They don't seem to have been printed separately. In fact, the two appear to be printed on top of each other. Because two colors of gold (that are almost indistinguishable) were used for the same design area, even a slight misregistration makes the frame line appear to be doubled.

When a cut stamp is used as a template, it is easy to see that the color block is larger on stamps from the sheet version. This also makes the gold frame line appear thicker.

Two colors of gold used in the production of the Reindeer stamp give some stamps the appearance of a doubled frame line.

2000. EDDIE RICKENBACKER ISSUE in the Pioneers of Aviation Series honored the World War I flying ace. Large "1995" date. (See No. 1097 of 1995.) *Gummed pane of 50, gravure by Bureau of Engraving and Printing, perforated 11 1/4.*

1250 *Eddie Rickenbacker*

1250			MNHVF	UseVF
60¢	**multicolored,** phosphored paper		1.00	.30
	Plate block of 4		6.50	
	EKU *(Jan. 2000) (printed 10/99)*			1.50

2000. FRUIT BERRIES BOOKLET ISSUE in the Flora and Fauna Series. Illustrated by Ned Seidler, Hampton Bay, N.Y., and designed by Howard Paine, Delaplane, Va. (See Nos. 1214-17 and 1218-21 of 1999.) *In a two-sided convertible booklet format with "2000" date, blueberries, raspberries, strawberries, and blackberries. Gravure by Banknote Corporation of America (2.85 billion printed). Serpentine die cut 11 1/2x11 3/4 on two or three sides.*

1251 *Blueberries*

1252 *Raspberries*

1253 *Strawberries*

1254 *Blackberries*

B303

1251		MNHVF	UseVF
33¢	Blueberries, phosphored paper	.60	.20
1252		MNHVF	UseVF
33¢	Raspberries, phosphored paper	.60	.20
1253		MNHVF	UseVF
33¢	Strawberries, phosphored paper	.60	.20
1254		MNHVF	UseVF
33¢	Blackberries, phosphored paper	.60	.20
	y. Se-tenant block of 4 (Nos. 1251-54)	2.40	—
	FDC *(March 15, 2000),* any single		2.00
	n. Pane of 20	12.00	
	FDC, block of 4		8.00

2000. CORAL PINK ROSE BOOKLET ISSUE designed by Derry Noyes, Washington, D.C., (see No. 1232 of 1999) in a *two-sided self-adhesive convertible booklet of 20, gravure by Sennett Security Products at American Packaging Corp., (350 million printed). Serpentine die cut 10 3/4x10 1/2 on two or three sides.*

1255 *Coral pink rose*

1255		MNHVF	UseVF
33¢	**multicolored,** phosphored paper	.60	.20
	FDC *(April 7, 2000)*		1.50
	n. Booklet pane of 20 (convertible booklet)	12.00	

DECODING THE CATALOG

A 60¢ stamp picturing World War I flying ace and commercial aviation mogul Eddie Rickenbacker (Minkus No. 1097) was issued on Sept. 25, 1995. The Bureau of Engraving and Printing produced the stamps with the copyright date "1995" printed in the bottom-left corner of the design.

After four years of service, the stamp was scheduled for replacement in summer 1999 by a 60¢ self-adhesive Grand Canyon definitive (No. 1249), release of which was postponed by an erroneous inscription that would have placed the canyon in Colorado, not Arizona. In the meantime, the Postal Service ordered an additional printing of the 60¢ Rickenbacker (No. 1250). These stamps, also printed by the BEP, were sent to post offices without public notice, and their presence was not detected until 2000.

1097   1250

The difference in the size of the copyright date on each stamp — 1.2 millimeters on the original, 1.8mm on the new version — means the stamps were printed from new plates, making them identifiably different and justifying separate major catalog listings.

The original stamps were printed on LP-748V paper, which does not fluoresce under ultraviolet light, whereas the later Rickenbakers were printed on LP-840 Universal paper, which has a "high bright" appearance, shining brilliantly under UV light.

A reported modest "color variation" may be the result of this difference in papers, rather than any difference in the ink or printing. Examples of the new stamp may have a flatter, less crisp and colorful appearance than the originals.

2000. FRUIT BERRIES VERTICAL COIL ISSUE was a *linerless coil version* of the design introduced in 1999 as part of the Flora and Fauna Series. Designed by Howard Paine, Delaplane, Va. *Serpentine die cut 8 1/2 horizontally. (See Nos. 1222-25). Self-adhesive coils of 100, gravure by Guilford Gravure (330 million printed). Plate number every 12 stamps.*

1256 *Raspberries*

1257 *Blueberries*

1258 *Strawberries*

1259 *Blackberries*

1256		MNHVF	UseVF
33¢	Raspberries, phosphored paper	.60	.20

1257		MNHVF	UseVF
33¢	Blueberries, phosphored paper	.60	.20

1258		MNHVF	UseVF
33¢	Strawberries, phosphored paper	.60	.20

1259		MNHVF	UseVF
33¢	Blackberries, phosphored paper	.60	.20
	y. Strip of 4 (Nos. 1256-1259)	2.40	
	FDC *(June 16, 2000),* any single		2.00
	FDC strip of 4		8.00

Distinguished Americans Series

2000. JOSEPH W. STILWELL ISSUE The first in the Distinguished Americans Series, honored Gen. "Vinegar Joe" Stilwell (1883-1946), who spent most of World War II in Asia. He was chief of staff for Chiang Kaishek and commander of U.S. forces in China-Burma-India 1942-44. Designed by Mark Summers, Waterdown, Ontario, Canada. *Offset and intaglio by Banknote Corporation of America (100 million printed), perforated 11.*

1260 *Joseph W. Stilwell*

1260		MNHVF	UseVF
10¢	black & red phosphored paper	.20	.20
	Plate block of 4	.80	
	FDC *(Aug. 24, 2000)*		1.25

2000. CLAUDE PEPPER ISSUE in the Distinguished Americans Series. Pepper (1900-1989) served in both the House of Representatives and the Senate and became known for advocating programs for the elderly. When he died at age 88, he was the oldest member of Congress. Designed by Richard Sheaff, Scottsdale, Ariz., illustration by Mark Summers, Waterdown, Ontario, Canada. *Offset and intaglio in gummed panes of 20, by Banknote Corporation of America (56 million printed), perforated 11.*

1261 *Claude Pepper*

1261		MNHVF	UseVF
33¢	black & red phosphored paper	.50	.20
	Plate block of 4	2.00	
	FDC *(Sept. 7, 2000)*		1.50

2000. THE NEW YORK PUBLIC LIBRARY LION COIL ISSUE featured a stylized image of one of the trademark stone lions, sculpted by Edward Clark Potter, that flank the 5th Ave. entrance to the New York Public Library, the largest in the United States. After the original design was revealed, the library insisted that its name be included on the stamp. Designed by Carl Herrman, Carlsbad, Calif., from the illustration by Nancy Stahl, New York, N.Y. *Issued in nonphosphored, self-adhesive coils of 10,000, printed by American Packaging Corp., Columbus, Wis., for Sennett Security Products (100 million printed), die cut 11 1/2. Plate number every 21 stamps. Back number every 10 stamps.*

1262, 1394 *New York Public Library lion*

1262		MNHVF	UseVF
(10¢)	multicolored untagged	.20	.20
	Pair	.25	
	FDC *(Nov. 9, 2000)*		1.50

2000. BLUE KESTREL ISSUE in the Flora and Fauna Series had the identification "American Kestrel" in blue. It was issued without notice. *Self-adhesive panes of 50, offset by Banknote Corporation of America, serpentine die cut 11 1/4.*

1263 *Blue Kestrel*

1263		MNHVF	UseVF
1¢	multicolored untagged	.20	.20
	Plate block of 4	.80	
	EKU *(Oct. 2000)*		—

See also Nos. 1079, 1115, 1229, 1247.

2000. FARM FLAG ISSUE featured an American flag against a farm field, with a tiny "USPS" over the doors on the shed in the background. Designed by Richard Sheaff, based on an illustration by Hiro Kimura, Brooklyn, N.Y. *No. 1264 offset by Ashton Potter (USA) Ltd., with microprinting "USPS" on shed, gummed panes of 20, perforated 11 1/2 (25 million printed). No. 1265 self-adhesive panes of 20, offset by Ashton Potter (USA) Ltd. with microprinting "USPS" on shed, serpentine die cut 11.*

1264, 1265 *Farm flag*

1264		MNHVF	UseVF
(34¢)	multicolored block tagged	.50	.20
	Plate block of 4	2.00	
	FDC *(Dec. 15, 2000)*		1.50

1265		MNHVF	UseVF
(34¢)	multicolored phosphored paper	.50	.20
	Plate block of 4	2.00	
	FDC *(Dec. 15, 2000)*		1.90

2000. FARM FLAG ATM PANE ISSUE had no tiny inscription over the doors on the shed in the background. *ATM pane of 18, gravure by Avery Dennison, serpentine die cut 8.*

1266 *Farm flag*

1266
(34¢)   multicolored phosphored Lacquer on surface

	MNHVF	UseVF
	.50	.20
FDC (Dec. 15, 2000)	1.90	
n. Pane of 18	12.00	

2000. STATUE OF LIBERTY COIL ISSUE featured a view of the icon of freedom in a vertical-format, water-activated-gum coil. Designed by Derry Noyes, from photo by Paul Hardy, New York, N.Y. No. 1267, *gummed, vertical coil of 3,000, gravure by Bureau of Engraving and Printing, perforated 9 3/4 vertically (200 million printed). No. 1268, self-adhesive, vertical coils of 100, gravure by Bureau of Engraving and Printing, serpentine die cut 9 3/4 vertically (1 billion printed).*

1267, 1268, 1282, 1294, 1295 *Statue of Liberty*

Plate number every 24 stamps. Back number every 20 stamps.

1267
(34¢)   multicolored phosphored paper

	MNHVF	UseVF
	.50	.20
Pair	1.00	
FDC (Dec. 15, 2000)	1.90	

Plate number every 24 stamps.

1268
(34¢)   multicolored phosphored paper

	MNHVF	UseVF
	.50	.20
Pair	1.00	
FDC (Dec. 15, 2000)	1.90	

2000. STATUE OF LIBERTY BOOKLET ISSUE featured a view of the icon of freedom in horizontal-format, self-adhesive booklets. Die cuts on four sides of some convertible booklet stamps and a plate number on one of the vending booklet stamps help to distinguish them. *Booklets of 20, gravure by Avery Dennison (1.5 billion convertible booklets and 200 million vending booklets), serpentine die cut 11 on 2, 3 or 4 sides.*

1269, B310 *Statue of Liberty*

1269
(34¢)   multicolored phosphored paper

	MNHVF	UseVF
	.50	.20
n. Booklet pane of 4 (without plate number)	2.00	
n1. Booklet pane of 6	3.00	
n2. Booklet pane of 4 (with plate number)	2.00	
pn. Plate number single (bottom right corner of pane)	.60	
n3. Pane of 20 (convertible booklet)	12.50	
FDC (Dec. 15, 2000)	1.90	

2000. FLOWERS COIL ISSUE featured close-up photos of four flowers — freesia (green backgound), Asian hybrid lily (red), cymbidium orchid (tan), and longiflorum lily (purple). Designed by Derry Noyes from photos by Robert Peak, Winter Park, Fla. *Self-adhesive coil of 100, gravure by Banknote Corporation of America, serpentine die cut 8 1/2 vertically (500 million printed). Plate number every 12 stamps.*

1270-1273, 1286-89, 1290-93 *Flowers*

1270
(34¢)   Freesia, green background, phosphored paper

	MNHVF	UseVF
	.50	.20

1271
(34¢)   Asian hybrid lily, red background, phosphored paper

	MNHVF	UseVF
	.50	.20

1272
(34¢)   Cymbidium orchid, tan background, phosphored paper

	MNHVF	UseVF
	.50	.20

1273
(34¢)   Longiflorum lily, purple background, phosphored paper

	MNHVF	UseVF
	.50	.20
FDC (Dec. 15, 2000), any single	1.90	
y. Coil strip of 4 (1 each Nos. 1270-73)	2.00	
FDC coil strip of 4	2.50	

> *Listings and prices for plate number coil strips and singles appear at the end of this definitives section of the Krause-Minkus catalog.*

2000. FLOWERS BOOKLET ISSUE featured four flowers — longiflorum lily (purple background), cymbidium orchid (tan), freesia (green), and Asian hybrid lily (red). *Self-adhesive vending booklet of 20 and convertible (two-sided) booklet of 20, gravure by Sennett Security Products (200 million vending, 1.5 billion convertible), serpentine die cut 10 1/4x10 3/4; some convertible booklets serpentine die cut 11 1/2x11 3/4 on 12-stamp side or 8-stamp side.*

1274-1277, 1278-1281, B311 *Flowers*

1274
(34¢)   Longiflorum lily, purple background, phosphored paper

	MNHVF	UseVF
	.50	.20

1275
(34¢)   Cymbidium orchid, tan background, phosphored paper

	MNHVF	UseVF
	.50	.20

1276
(34¢)   Freesia, green background, phosphored paper

	MNHVF	UseVF
	.50	.20

1277
(34¢)   Asian hybrid lily, red background, phosphored paper

	MNHVF	UseVF
	.50	.20
y. Block of 4 (Nos. 1274-77)	2.00	
n. Booklet pane of 4 (Nos. 1274-77)	2.00	
n1. Booklet pane of 6 (2 each Nos. 1274-75, 1 each Nos. 1276-77)	3.00	
n2. Booklet pane of 6 (1 each Nos. 1274-75, 2 each Nos. 1276-77)	3.00	
n3. Double-sided pane of 20 (convertible booklet)	13.50	
FDC (Dec. 15, 2000), any single	1.90	
FDC Nos. 1274-77 on one cover	2.50	

Serpentine die cut 10 1/4x10 3/4 on two or three sides.

1278
(34¢)   Longiflorum lily, purple background, phosphored paper

	MNHVF	UseVF
	.50	.20

1279
(34¢)   Cymbidium orchid, tan background, phosphored paper

	MNHVF	UseVF
	.50	.20

1280
(34¢)   Freesia, green background, phosphored paper

	MNHVF	UseVF
	.50	.20

1281
(34¢)

		MNHVF	UseVF
Asian hybrid lily, **red** background, phosphored paper		.50	.20
y. Block of 4 (Nos. 1278-81)		2.00	
n. Double-sided pane of 20 (2 No. 1281y on 8-stamp side 3 No. 1277y on 12-stamp side)		13.50	
n1. Double-sided pane of 20 (2 No. 1277y on 8-stamp side, 3 No. 1281y on 12-stamp side) (convertible booklet)		13.50	
FDC *(Dec. 15, 2000)*, any single			1.90
FDC Nos. 1278-81 on one cover			1.90

Serpentine die cut 11 1/2x11 3/4 on two or three sides.

2001. STATUE OF LIBERTY COIL ISSUE A denominated version of the self-adhesive coil stamp released in December 2000 for a mail rate increase. Designed by Derry Noyes, Washington, D.C., based on photo by Paul Hardy, New York, N.Y. *Self-adhesive, vertically formatted, rolls of 3,000 and 10,000 with rounded corners and backing paper higher than the stamp, gravure by Bureau of Engraving and Printing on phosphored paper, serpentine die cut 9 3/4 vertically, tagged. Plate number every 21 stamps. Back number every 20 stamps.*

1282, 1267, 1294, 1295 *Statue of Liberty*

1282
34¢

		MNHVF	UseVF
multicolored phosphored paper		.65	.20
Pair		1.30	
FDC *(Jan. 7, 2001)*			1.50

National Monuments Series

2001. CAPITOL DOME ISSUE featured a night-time photo of the Capitol Dome taken by Robert Llewellyn, Earlysville, Va. The stamp paid the newly-established Priority Mail rate. *Self-adhesive, panes of 20, offset with hidden image of a line, "Priority Mail," gravure by Banknote Corporation of America (800 million printed) on phosphored paper, serpentine die cut 11 1/4x11 1/2.*

1283 *Capitol Dome*

1283
$3.50

		MNHVF	UseVF
multicolored		7.00	3.00
Plate block of 4		28.00	
FDC *(Jan. 29, 2001)*			7.00

2001. WASHINGTON MONUMENT ISSUE featured a photo of the Washington Monument by Patricia Fisher, Washington, D.C., with other distinctive Washington, D.C., landmarks in the background. Designed by Derry Noyes, Washington, D.C. The stamp paid the newly-established Express Mail rate up to one pound. *Self-adhesive, panes of 20, offset with hidden image of a line, "Express Mail," gravure by Banknote Corporation of America (35 million) printed on phosphored paper, serpentine die cut 11 1/4x11 1/2.*

1284 *Washington Monument*

1284
$12.25

		MNHVF	UseVF
multicolored		24.50	10.00
Plate block of 4		100.00	
FDC *(Jan. 29, 2001)*			24.00

2001. FARM FLAG ISSUE A denominated version of the rate-change stamp issued late in 2000. *Gummed pane of 100, offset by Ashton Potter (USA) Ltd., perforated 11 1/4.*

1285 *Farm flag*

1285
34¢

		MNHVF	UseVF
multicolored block tagged		.65	.20
Plate block of 4		2.60	
FDC *(Feb. 7, 2001)*			1.50

2001. FLOWERS COIL ISSUE in the Flora and Fauna Series, denominated versions of the rate-change stamps issued late in 2000— freesia (green background), Asian hybrid lily (red), cymbidium orchid (tan), and longiflorum lily (purple). *Self-adhesive coil, offset in coils of 100 by Guilford Gravure for Banknote Corporation of America, serpentine die cut 8 1/2 vertically. Plate number every 12 stamps.*

1286-1289 *Flowers*

1286
34¢

		MNHVF	UseVF
Freesia, **green** background, phosphored paper		.65	.20

1287
34¢

		MNHVF	UseVF
Asian hybrid lily, **red** background, phosphored paper		.65	.20

1288
34¢

		MNHVF	UseVF
Cymbidium orchid, **tan** background, phosphored paper		.65	.20

1289
34¢

		MNHVF	UseVF
Longiflorum lily, **purple** background, phosphored paper		.65	.20
y. Strip of 4 (Nos. 1286-89)		2.60	
FDC *(Feb. 7, 2001)*, any single			1.50
FDC *(Feb. 7, 2001)*, coil strip of 4			2.00

2001. FLOWERS BOOKLET ISSUE in the Flora and Fauna Series. Denominated versions of the rate-change stamps issued late in 2000— longiflorum lily (purple background), cymbidium orchid (tan), freesia (green), and Asian hybrid lily (red). *Gravure by Guilford Gravure for Banknote Corporation of America, serpentine die cut 10 1/4x10 3/4 on 2 or 3 sides.*

1290-1293, B312 *Flowers*

1290
34¢

	MNHVF	UseVF
Longiflorum lily, **purple** background, phosphored paper	.65	.20

1291
34¢

	MNHVF	UseVF
Cymbidium orchid, **tan** background, phosphored paper	.65	.20

1292
34¢

	MNHVF	UseVF
Freesia, **green** background, phosphored paper	.65	.20

1293
34¢

	MNHVF	UseVF
Asian hybrid lily, **red** background, phosphored paper	.65	.20
y. Block of 4 (Nos. 1290-93)	2.60	
n. Booklet pane of 4 (Nos. 1290-93)	2.60	
n1. Booklet pane of 6 (2 each Nos. 1290-91, 1 each Nos. 1292-93)	3.90	
n2. Booklet pane of 6 (1 each Nos. 1290-91, 2 each Nos. 1292-93)	3.90	
n3. Double-sided pane of 20 (convertible booklet)	13.50	
FDC (Feb. 7, 2001), any single		1.50
FDC Nos. 1290-93 on one cover		2.50

2001. STATUE OF LIBERTY COIL ISSUE A *water-activated-gum* version of the coil stamp released in late 2000. *Gummed, vertically formatted in coils of 3,000 and 10,000, gravure by Bureau of Engraving and Printing on phosphored paper, perforated 9 3/4 vertically, tagged. Plate number every 24 stamps. Back number every 20 stamps.*

1294, 1267, 1282, 1295 *Statue of Liberty*

1294
34¢

	MNHVF	UseVF
multicolored	.65	.20
Pair	1.30	
FDC (Feb. 7, 2001)		1.50

2001. STATUE OF LIBERTY COIL ISSUE A second *self-adhesive* version of the coil stamp released in late 2000. *Vertically formatted, gravure by Bureau of Engraving and Printing on phosphored paper, with square corners and backing paper the same height as the stamp, serpentine die cut 9 3/4 vertically, tagged. Plate number every 24 stamps.*

1295, 1267, 1282, 1294 *Statue of Liberty*

1295
34¢

	MNHVF	UseVF
multicolored	.65	.20
Pair	1.30	
FDC (Feb. 7, 2001)		1.50
v. Pair imperforate	—	

Listings and prices for plate number coil strips and singles appear at the end of this definitives section of the Krause-Minkus catalog.

2001. STATUE OF LIBERTY BOOKLET ISSUE A *self-adhesive* booklet version of the coil stamp released in late 2000. *Gravure on phosphored paper, serpentine die cut 11 on 2, 3 or 4 sides.*

1296, B313 *Statue of Liberty*

1296
34¢

	MNHVF	UseVF
multicolored	.65	.20
FDC (Feb. 7, 2001)		1.50
n. Booklet pane of 4 (without plate number)	2.60	
n1. Booklet pane of 6	3.90	
n2. Booklet pane of 4 (with plate number)	2.60	
pn. Plate number single (bottom right corner of pane)	.70	.30
n3. Pane of 10 (convertible booklet)	6.50	
n4. Pane of 20 (convertible booklet)	13.50	

2001. HATTIE CARAWAY ISSUE Third in the Distinguished Americans Series, honored the first woman elected to the U.S. Senate. In November 1931, Caraway (1878-1950) was appointed to the Senate after the death of her husband, Sen. Thaddeus Caraway (D-Ark.), and on Jan. 12, 1932, she won a special election to the post and was re-elected in 1938. She left the Senate in 1945. *Self-adhesive pane of 20 on phosphored paper, designed by Richard Sheaff, offset and intaglio by Banknote Corporation of America, serpentine die cut 11.*

1297 *Hattie Caraway*

1297
76¢

	MNHVF	UseVF
black & red	1.50	.20
Plate block of 4	6.00	
FDC (Feb. 21, 2001)		1.75
v. Diecut variety 11 1/2x11	3.00	
Pane of 20	60.00	

2001. GEORGE WASHINGTON BOOKLET ISSUE featured a bust of the nation's first president by French sculptor Jean Antoine Houdon. The bust, housed at Mount Vernon, was also used as the basis for CM99 and (facing left) for the Washington-Franklin series. The stamp was issued on the 269th anniversary of Washington's birth. *Self-adhesive pane of 10 and vending booklet of 10, designed by Richard Sheaff, offset by Ashton Potter (USA) Ltd., on phosphored paper, serpentine die cut 11 1/4 on 3 sides.*

1298 *George Washington*

1298
20¢

	MNHVF	UseVF
dark carmine	.40	.20
n. Booklet pane of 4	1.60	
n1. Booklet pane of 6	2.40	
n2. Pane of 10 (convertible booklet)	4.00	
FDC (Feb. 22, 2001)		1.50

2001. GEORGE WASHINGTON BOOKLET ISSUE Designed by Richard Sheaff. *Self-adhesive pane of 10 on phosphored paper, serpentine die cut 10 1/2x11 1/4 on 3 sides.*

1299, B315, B316, B317 *George Washington*

1299		MNHVF	UseVF
20¢	**dark carmine**	.40	.20
	n. Booklet pane of 4, 2 of 1298 at left, 2 of 1299 at right	1.60	
	n1. Booklet pane of 4, 2 of 1299 at left, 2 of 1298 at right	1.60	
	n2. Booklet pane of 6, 3 of 1298 at left, 3 of 1299 at right	2.40	
	n3. Booklet pane of 6, 3 of 1298 at left, 3 of 1298 at right	2.40	
	n4. Pane of 10, 5 of 1298 at left, 5 of 1299 at right (convertible booklet)	4.00	
	n5. Pane of 10, 5 of 1299 at left, 5 of 1298 at right (convertible booklet)	4.00	
	FDC (Feb. 22, 2001)		1.50

2001. BISON ISSUE glorified the majestic symbol of the American Wild West. *Self-adhesive pane of 20 on phosphored paper, designed by Carl Herrman from an illustration by Tom Nikosey, Bell Canyon, Calif., gravure by Avery Dennison (200 million stamps), serpentine die cut 11.*

1300, 1301, 1313 *Bison*

1300		MNHVF	UseVF
21¢	**multicolored**	.40	.20
	Plate block of 4	1.60	
	FDC (Feb. 22, 2001)		1.50

2001. BISON COIL ISSUE Self-adhesive coil of 100 on phosphored paper, designed by Carl Herrman, gravure by Avery Dennison (600 million stamps), serpentine die cut 8 1/2 vertically. Plate number every 5 stamps.

1301		MNHVF	UseVF
21¢	**multicolored**	.40	.20
	Pair	.80	
	FDC (Feb. 22, 2001)		1.50

2001. ART DECO EAGLE ISSUE Bronze-look illustration based on a 1930s lobby mailbox design. *Self-adhesive pane of 20 on phosphored paper, designed by Carl Herrman from an illustration by Nancy Stahl, New York, N.Y. Gravure by American Packaging Corp. for Sennett Security Products (100 million stamps), serpentine die cut 10 3/4.*

1302 *Eagle*

1302		MNHVF	UseVF
55¢	**multicolored**	1.00	.20
	Plate block of 4	4.00	
	FDC (Feb. 22, 2001)		1.50

2001. APPLE AND ORANGE ISSUE in the Flora and Fauna Series showed the two fruits as a se-tenant pair. The stamps were designed at the same time as the 1995 Peaches and Pear Issue (Nos. 1089-90). *Self-adhesive convertible booklet of 20 on phosphored paper, designed by Ned Seidler, offset by Banknote Corporation of America, serpentine die cut 11 1/4 on 2, 3 or 4 sides.*

1303, 1304 *Apple & Orange*

1303		MNHVF	UseVF
34¢	**multicolored** (Apple)	.65	.20

1304		MNHVF	UseVF
34¢	**multicolored** (Orange)	.65	.20
	FDC (March 6, 2001), either single		1.50
	y. Se-tenant pair, Nos. 1303-04	1.30	
	n. Pane of 20 (5 No. 1304y) (convertible booklet)	14.00	
	FDC (March 6, 2001), pair		2.50

2001. NINE-MILE PRAIRIE ISSUE Seventh in the Scenic America Series featured a native prairie near Lincoln, Neb. While its design included the silhouette of an airliner adjacent to the denomination, representing the postcard rate to foreign destinations outside Canada and Mexico, it was not classified by the USPS as an airmail stamp. *Self-adhesive pane of 20 on phosphored paper, designed by Ethel Kessler, offset by Ashton Potter (USA) Ltd., die cut 11 1/4x11 1/2, tagged.*

1305 *Nine-Mile Prairie*

1305		MNHVF	UseVF
70¢	**multicolored**	1.40	.30
	Plate block of 4	5.70	
	FDC (March 6, 2001)		1.60

2001. FARM FLAG ISSUE a denominated version of the "first class" stamps issued to meet the requirements of a rate change in early 2001. *Self-adhesive pane of 20 on phosphored paper, designed by Richard Sheaff, offset by Ashton Potter (USA) Ltd., serpentine die cut 11 1/4.*

1306 *Farm flag*

1306		MNHVF	UseVF
34¢	**multicolored**	.65	.20
	Plate block of 4	2.60	
	FDC (March 6, 2001)		1.50

2001. MOUNT MCKINLEY ISSUE Eighth in the Scenic America Series featured the highest mountain in North America (20,320 feet), which is part of Alaska's Denali National Park and Preserve. *Self-adhesive pane of 20 on phosphored paper, designed by Ethel Kessler from a photo by John Eastcott and Yva Momatiuk, gravure by Avery Dennison (85 million printed), serpentine die cut 11.*

1307 *Mount McKinley*

1307		MNHVF	UseVF
80¢	**multicolored**	1.50	.35
	Plate block of 4	6.00	
	FDC (April 17, 2001)		2.00

2001. APPLE AND ORANGE ISSUE in the Flora and Fauna Series showed the two fruits as a se-tenant pair in a *self-adhesive vending booklet of 20 (see 1303-04) on phosphored paper. The USPS did not announce the issue date, probably April 2001. Designed by Ned Seidler, offset by Banknote Corporation of America, serpentine die cut 11 1/2x10 3/4.*

1308, 1309, B318 *Apple & Orange*

1308		MNHVF	UseVF
34¢	multicolored (Apple)	.65	.20

1309		MNHVF	UseVF
34¢	multicolored (Orange)	.65	.20
	y. Se-tenant pair, Nos. 1308-09	1.30	
	n. Booklet pane of 4 (2 No. 1309y), No. 1308 upper left	2.60	
	n1. Booklet pane of 6 (3 No. 1309y), No. 1308 upper left	3.90	
	n2. Booklet pane of 6 (3 No. 1309y), No. 1309 upper left	3.90	
	n3. Booklet pane of 4 (2 No. 1309y), No. 1308 upper left, plate number on 1309	2.60	
	pn. Plate number single (bottom left corner of pane)	.70	.50

2001. ACADIA NATIONAL PARK ISSUE Ninth in the Scenic America Series, highlighted the park in Maine, the first national park established east of the Mississippi River. *Self-adhesive pane of 20 on phosphored paper, designed by Ethel Kessler from a photo by Carr Clifton, Taylorsville, Calif., offset with microprinting "USPS" by Banknote Corporation of America (100 million printed) serpentine die cut 11 1/4x11 1/2.*

1310, 1398, 1412 *Acadia National Park*

1310		MNHVF	UseVF
60¢	multicolored	1.20	.30
	Plate block of 4	4.80	
	FDC (May 30, 2001)		2.00

2001. ATLAS STATUE COIL ISSUE Nondenominated "Presorted Std" coil of 10,000 in the American Culture Series featured a closely cropped image from a photo by Horst Hamann of the statue at Rockefeller Center in New York City by Lee Lawrie. *Self-adhesive rolls of 10,000, serpentine die cut 8 1/2 vertically. Printed by Guilford Gravure for Banknote Corporation of America. Plate number every 21 stamps. Back number every 10 stamps.*

1311 *Atlas statue*

1311		MNHVF	UseVF
(10¢)	multicolored untagged	.20	.20
	Pair	.40	
	FDC (June 29, 2001)		1.50

2001. WOODY WAGON PRESORTED FIRST CLASS COIL ISSUE in the American Culture Series featured the wood-paneled station wagon popularized in surfer lore. *Self-adhesive coil of 10,000, serpentine die cut 8 1/2 vertically. Printed by Guilford Gravure for*

Sennett Security Products. Plate number every 21 stamps. Back number every 10 stamps.

1312 *Woody wagon*

1312		MNHVF	UseVF
(15¢)	multicolored untagged	.30	.20
	Pair	.60	
	Plate number strip of 5	1.50	
	FDC (Aug. 3, 2001)		1.50

2001. BISON ISSUE A design introduced earlier (see Nos. 1300, 1301) got a new lease on life after a midyear rate increase for postal cards. *Gummed panes of 100, perforated 11 1/4. Printed by Sterling Sommer for Ashton-Potter USA.*

1313-1315, B319, B320, B321 *Bison*

1313		MNHVF	UseVF
21¢	multicolored phosphored paper	.40	.20
	Plate block of 4	1.60	
	FDC (Sept. 20, 2001)		1.50

See Nos. 1300 and 1301 for coil version.

2001. BISON CONVERTIBLE BOOKLET ISSUE Booklet of 10, *die cut 11 1/4 on 3 sides, printed by Ashton-Potter USA.*

1314		MNHVF	UseVF
21¢	multicolored phosphored paper	.40	.20
	n. Booklet pane of 4	1.60	
	n1. Booklet pane of 6	2.40	
	n2. Booklet pane of 10 (convertible booklet)	4.00	
	FDC (Sept. 20, 2001)		1.50

2001. BISON VENDING BOOKLET ISSUE Booklet of 10, *die cut 10 1/2x11 1/4 on 3 sides, printed by Ashton-Potter USA.*

1315		MNHVF	UseVF
21¢	multicolored phosphored paper	.40	.20
	n. Booklet pane of 4, 2 of 1314 at left, 2 of 1315 at right	1.60	
	n1. Booklet pane of 4, 2 of 1315 at left, 2 of 1314 at right	1.60	
	n2. Booklet pane of 6, 3 of 1314 at left, 3 of 1315 at right	2.40	
	n3. Booklet pane of 6, 3 of 1315 at left, 3 of 1314 at right	2.40	
	n4. Pane of 10, 5 of 1314 at left, 3 of 1315 at right (convertible booklet)	4.00	
	n5. Pane of 10, 5 of 1315 at left, 5 of 1314 at right (convertible booklet)	4.00	
	FDC (Sept. 20, 2001)		1.50

2001. ART DECO EAGLE ISSUE Same design as No. 1302 with new color and denomination reflecting a new two-ounce First-Class rate. *Self-adhesive pane of 20. Serpentine die cut 10 3/4.*

1316 *Eagle*

1316		MNHVF	UseVF
57¢	multicolored phosphored paper	1.00	.50
	Plate block of 4	4.00	
	FDC (Sept. 20, 2001)		1.90

2001. GEORGE WASHINGTON ISSUE in a new denomination reflecting a higher second-ounce rate in a pane of 20. *Printed by BCA. Serpentine die cut 11 1/4x11 3/4.*

1317		MNHVF	UseVF
23¢	**green** phosphored paper	.45	.20
	Plate block of 4	1.80	
	FDC *(Sept. 20, 2001)*		1.50

2001. GEORGE WASHINGTON COIL ISSUE The new denomination design in a *self-adhesive coil of 100. Printed by Guilford Gravure for BCA, serpentine die cut 9 3/4 vertically.* Plate number every 12 stamps.

1318, 1342 *George Washington*

1318		MNHVF	UseVF
23¢	**green** phosphored paper	.45	.20
	Pair	.90	
	FDC *(Sept. 20, 2001)*		1.50

See Nos. 1343 and 1344 for vending booklets.

> *Listings and prices for plate number coil strips and singles appear at the end of this definitives section of the Krause-Minkus catalog.*

2001. OLD WORLD SANTAS ISSUE in three formats featured four chromolithograph images of Santa Claus dating as far back as the 1880s. The Santas carrying holly (1319 with a rocking horse and 1322 with a poodle dog) are thought to have been designed in England and printed in Germany in the 1880s; the Santas carrying imitation trees (1320 dressed in blue and 1321 dressed in red) were printed in Germany, probably between 1915 and 1920. They were the first Christmas stamps since 1999. *Self-adhesive pane of 20 gravure by American Packaging Corp. for Sennett Security Products, denomination and "USA" in black. Serpentine die cut 10 3/4x11.*

1319 *Rocking horse*

1320 *Santa dressed in blue*

1321 *Santa dressed in red*

1322 *Santa with a poodle dog*

1319		MNHVF	UseVF
34¢	**multicolored** phosphored paper	.65	.20
1320		MNHVF	UseVF
34¢	**multicolored** phosphored paper	.65	.20
1321		MNHVF	UseVF
34¢	**multicolored** phosphored paper	.65	.20
1322		MNHVF	UseVF
34¢	**multicolored** phosphored paper	.65	.20
	Plate block of 4	2.60	
	FDC *(Oct. 10, 2001)* any single		2.50
	FDC Nos. 1319-22 on one cover		3.00
	y. Se-tenant block of 4 (Nos. 1319-22)	2.60	

2001. OLD WORLD SANTAS BOOKLET ISSUE featured the four designs in a two-sided *self-adhesive booklet of 20. Gravure by American Packaging Corp. for Sennett Security Products. Serpentine die cut 10 3/4x11 on 2 or 3 sides.*

1323-1326, B322 *Old World Santas*

1323		MNHVF	UseVF
34¢	**multicolored** phosphored paper	.65	.20
1324		MNHVF	UseVF
34¢	**multicolored** phosphored paper	.65	.20
1325		MNHVF	UseVF
34¢	**multicolored** phosphored paper	.65	.20
1326		MNHVF	UseVF
34¢	**multicolored** phosphored paper	.65	.20
	FDC *(Oct. 10, 2001)* any single		2.50
	FDC *(Oct. 10, 2001)* Nos. 1323-26 on one cover		3.00
	y. Se-tenant block of 4 (Nos. 1323-26)	2.60	
	n. Pane of 20 (convertible booklet)	13.00	

2001. OLD WORLD SANTAS VENDING BOOKLET ISSUE contained four smaller versions of the designs in a *self-adhesive vending booklet of 20. Gravure by Avery Dennison, "34" denomination in green, "USA" in red. Serpentine die cut 11 on 2 or 3 sides.*

1327-1330 *Old World Santas*

1327		MNHVF	UseVF
34¢	**multicolored** phosphored paper	.65	.20
1328		MNHVF	UseVF
34¢	**multicolored** phosphored paper	.65	.20
1329		MNHVF	UseVF
34¢	**multicolored** phosphored paper	.65	.20
1330		MNHVF	UseVF
34¢	**multicolored** phosphored paper	.65	.20
	y. Se-tenant block of 4 (Nos. 1327-30)	2.60	
	n. Booklet pane of 4 (Nos. 1327-30)	2.60	
	n1. Booklet pane of 6 (2 each Nos. 1327-28, 1 each 1329-30)	3.90	
	n2. Booklet pane of 6 (1 each Nos. 1327-28, 2 each Nos. 1329-30)	3.90	

FDC *(Oct. 10, 2001)* any single   2.50
FDC *(Oct. 10, 2001)* Nos. 1327-30 on one   3.00
  cover

2001. MADONNA AND CHILD (COSTA) ISSUE The image is from a painting *Virgin and Child* (c.1490) by Italian Lorenzo Costa (1460-1535) in the Philadelphia Museum of Art. *Self-adhesive convertible booklet of 20, gravure by Guilford Gravure for Banknote Corporation of America. Serpentine die cut 11 1/2 on 2 or 3 sides.*

1331 *Madonna and Child*

1331

		MNHVF	UseVF
34¢	**multicolored** phosphored paper	.65	.20
	Plate block of 4	2.60	
	n. Pane of 20 (convertible booklet)	13.00	
	FDC *(Oct. 10, 2001)*		1.50

2001. UNITED WE STAND ISSUE used a previously prepared design to help build patriotic fervor after the murderous attacks on the World Trade Center in New York City with hijacked jetliners. *Self-adhesive convertible booklet of 20, offset with microprinting "USPS" by Banknote Corporation of America. Serpentine die cut 11 1/4 on 2 or 3 sides.*

1332, 1333, 1334, 1336 *United We Stand*

1332

		MNHVF	UseVF
34¢	**multicolored** phosphored paper	.65	.20
	n. Pane of 20 (convertible booklet)	13.00	
	n1. Pane of 10	6.50	
	FDC *(Oct. 24, 2001)*		1.50

2001. UNITED WE STAND COIL ISSUE Designed by Terry McCaffrey, USPS. *Self-adhesive in coils of 100. 4.7 billion stamps gravure printed by the Bureau of Engraving and Printing.* The first day was October 24, but the nationwide sale was delayed until November 5. *The stamps are connected within the coil, the backing is the same height as the stamp, and the corners are square. Die cut 9 3/4 vertically. Plate number every 24 stamps.*

1333, 1334 *United We Stand*

1333

		MNHVF	UseVF
34¢	**multicolored** pre-phosphored paper	.65	.20
	Pair	1.30	.20
	FDC *(Oct. 24, 2001 - Washington, D.C.)*		1.50

2001. UNITED WE STAND COIL ISSUE Designed by Terry McCaffrey, USPS. *Self-adhesive in coils of 10,000. 75 million stamps gravure printed by the Bureau of Engraving and Printing.* The first day was October 24, but the nationwide sale was delayed until November 5. *The stamps are separated within the coil, the backing is higher than the stamp, and the corners are rounded. Die cut 9 3/4 vertically. Blue 4 digit back numbers every 20 stamps. Plate number every 21 stamps.*

1334

		MNHVF	UseVF
34¢	**multicolored** pre-phosphored paper	.65	.20
	Pair	1.30	.20
	FDC *(Oct. 24, 2001 - Washington, D.C.)*		1.50

2001. FARM FLAG ATM ISSUE Self-adhesive ATM booklet of 18. Gravure by Avery Dennison. Serpentine die cut 8 on 2, 3 or 4 sides.

1335 *Farm flag*

1335

		MNHVF	UseVF
34¢	**multicolored** pre-phosphored lacquer on stamps	.65	.20
	n. Pane of 20	13.00	
	FDC *(Dec. 17, 2001)*		1.50

2002. UNITED WE STAND BOOKLET ISSUE offered new formats for the flag stamp issued in panes of 20 and two coil sizes on Oct. 24, 2001. Issued without notice, the 2002 stamps bear a small "2002" in the lower left. *Two-sided convertible booklets of 20 (1.2 billion) and vending booklets of 20 (440.99 million) printed by American Packaging Corp. for Sennett Security Products. Serpentine die cut 10 1/2x10 3/4 on 2 or 3 sides.*

1336

		MNHVF	UseVF
34¢	**multicolored** pre-phosphored paper	.65	.20
	n. Pane of 4	2.60	
	n1. Pane of 6	3.40	
	n2. Pane of 20 (B323)	13.00	
	n3. Pane of 20 (convertible booklet)	13.00	
	FDC *(Oct. 24, 2001)*		1.50

2002. AMERICAN TOLEWARE COIL ISSUE Designed by Derry Noyes, Washington, D.C. *Water-activated gum in coils of 10,000. 300 million stamps gravure printed by American Packaging Corp. for Sennett Security Products.* This stamp features a painted detail of a black toleware coffeepot. Toleware is japanned (varnished) or painted tinware fashioned into a variety of objects, including teapots, coffeepots, cups, and candlesticks, and often decorated with designs such as fruits, flowers, and leaves. Typically, these designs in colors such as deep red, green, and pumpkin yellow are either hand painted or stenciled into a black background of asphaltum mixed with varnish, giving the items a velvety finish. The coffeepot featured on the stamp is now in the collection of the Winterthur Museum in Delaware. It is believed that this piece was manufactured in Philadelphia, Pennsylvania, between 1850 and 1875. The *American Toleware* stamp is the first stamp in the new *American Design* series. The stamps in this series will vary in denomination from 1 through 10 cents. *Perforated 9 3/4 vertically with pink 5-digit back numbers every 10 stamps. Plate number every 14 stamps.*

1337 *American toleware*

1337

		MNHVF	UseVF
5¢	**multicolored** untagged	.20	.20
	Pair	.20	.20
	FDC *(May 31, 2002 - McLean, Va.)*		1.50

2002. STAR ISSUE used primarily as a make-up rate stamp. Designed by Phil Jordan, Falls Church, Va. *Self-adhesive offset sheets of 400 in eight panes of 50. Printed by Banknote Corporation of America. Serpentine die cut 11.*

1338, 1339, 1340 *Star*

1338

		MNHVF	UseVF
3¢	**red, white & blue** lithographed, untagged	.20	.20
	year at lower left		

Plate block of 4		.75	
FDC (June 7, 2002)			.75

2002. STAR ISSUE
Self-adhesive gravure pane of 50 printed by Guilford Gravure for Banknote Corporation of America. Serpentine die cut 10.

1339		MNHVF	UseVF
3¢	**red, white & blue** photogravure, untagged year at lower right	.20	.20
	Plate block of 4	.75	
	FDC (June 7, 2002)		.75

2002. STAR COIL ISSUE
Designed by Phil Jordan, Falls Church, Va. *Water-activated gum in coils of 3,000. 400 million stamps gravure printed by American Packaging Corp. for Sennett Security Products. This Star definitive stamp features a red, white, and blue graphic star and was not available until the end of July. Perforated 10 vertically. Pink 5-digit back numbers every 10 stamps. Plate number every 14 stamps.*

1340		MNHVF	UseVF
3¢	**multicolored** untagged	.20	.20
	Pair	.20	.20
	FDC (June 7, 2002 - Washington, D.C.)		1.50
	EKU (July 29, 2002)		

> *Listings and prices for plate number coil strips and singles appear at the end of this definitives section of the Krause-Minkus catalog.*

2002. GEORGE WASHINGTON ISSUE
Designed by Richard Sheaff, Scottsdale, Ariz. *Water activated panes of 100 printed by Ashton-Potter. Perforated 11 1/4.*

1341, 1342, 1343, 1344, B324, B325, B326 *George Washington*

1341		MNHVF	UseVF
23¢	**green** pre-phosphored paper	.45	.20
	Plate block of 4	1.80	
	FDC (June 7, 2002)		1.50

2002. GEORGE WASHINGTON COIL ISSUE
Designed by Richard Sheaff, Scottsdale, Ariz. *Self-adhesive in coils of 100. 750 million stamps gravure printed by Avery Dennison. This stamp, first issued September 20, 2001, and printed by BCA, was not available on the first day of issue. Die cut 8 1/2 vertically. All plate numbers are known either Peak/Valley (P/V) or Valley/Peak (V/P). Plate number every 11 stamps. See also 1318.*

1342		MNHVF	UseVF
23¢	**green** pre-phosphored paper	.45	.20
	Pair	.90	.20
	FDC (June 7, 2002 - Washington, D.C.)		1.50

2002. GEORGE WASHINGTON BOOKLET ISSUE
Self-adhesive convertible booklet of 10 printed by Ashton-Potter. Serpentine die cut 11 1/4, 10 1/2x11 1/4, on three sides.

1343		MNHVF	UseVF
23¢	**green** pre-phosphored paper	.45	.20
	FDC (June 7, 2002)		1.50
	n. Booklet pane of 4, die cut 11 1/4	2.00	
	n1. Booklet pane of 6, die cut 11 1/4	3.00	
	n2. Booklet pane of 10, die cut 11 1/4	5.00	
	n3. Booklet pane of 4, die cut 10 1/2x11 1/4 in left column and 11 1/4 on right side of stamp	3.20	
	n4. Booklet pane of 6, die cut 10 1/2x11 1/4 in left column and 11 1/4 on right side of stamp	4.80	
	n5. Booklet pane of 10, die cut 10 1/2x11 1/4 in left column and 11 1/4 on right side of stamp	8.00	
	n6. Booklet pane of 4, die cut 10 1/2x11 1/4 in right column and 11 1/4 on left side of stamp	3.20	
	n7. Booklet pane of 6, die cut 10 1/2x11 1/4 in right column and 11 1/4 on left side of stamp	4.80	
	n8. Booklet pane of 10, die cut 10 1/2x11 1/4 in right column and 11 1/4 on left side of stamp	8.00	

2002. GEORGE WASHINGTON VENDING BOOKLET ISSUE
Self-adhesive pane of 10 printed by Ashton-Potter. Serpentine die cut 11 1/4, 10 1/2x11 1/4 on three sides.

1344		MNHVF	UseVF
23¢	**green** pre-phosphored paper	.45	.25
	FDC (June 7, 2002)		1.50
	n. Booklet pane of 4, die cut 11 1/4	3.00	
	n1. Booklet pane of 6, die cut 11 1/4	4.50	
	n2. Booklet pane of 10, die cut 11 1/4 (B324)	7.50	
	n3. Booklet pane of 4, die cut 10 1/2x11 1/4 in left column and 11 1/4 on right side of stamp	6.00	
	n4. Booklet pane of 6, die cut 10 1/2x11 1/4 in left column and 11 1/4 on right side of stamp	9.00	
	n5. Booklet pane of 10, die cut 10 1/2x11 1/4 in left column and 11 1/4 on right side of stamp (B325)	15.00	
	n6. Booklet pane of 4, die cut 10 1/2x11 1/4 in right column and 11 1/4 on left side of stamp	6.00	
	n7. Booklet pane of 6, die cut 10 1/2x11 1/4 in right column and 11 1/4 on left side of stamp	9.00	
	n8. Booklet pane of 10, die cut 10 1/2x11 1/4 in right column and 11 1/4 on left side of stamp (B326)	15.00	

Nos. 1343 and 1344 appear to be identical as single stamps. They can only be identified correctly if part of larger pane.

2002. U.S.A. FIRST-CLASS FLAG ISSUE
Designed by Terry McCaffrey, USPS. *Non-denominated, water activated gummed panes of 100. Printed by Ashton-Potter. The stars and stripes of "Old Glory" are featured on this non-denominated rate change definitive stamp. Perforated 11 1/4x11.*

1345, 1346, 1347, 1348, 1349, 1350, B327 *Non-denominated U.S. Flag*

1345		MNHVF	UseVF
(37¢)	**multicolored** pre-phosphored paper	.70	.25
	Plate block of 4	2.80	
	FDC (June 7, 2002 - Washington, D.C.)		1.50

2002. U.S.A. FIRST-CLASS FLAG ISSUE
Designed by Terry McCaffrey, USPS. *Issued in non-denominated, self-adhesive panes of 20. Printed by Ashton-Potter. Serpentine die cut 11 1/4x11.*

1346		MNHVF	UseVF
(37¢)	**multicolored** pre-phosphored paper	.70	.25
	Palte block of 4	2.80	
	FDC (June 7, 2002 - Washington, D.C.)		1.50

2002. U.S.A. FIRST-CLASS FLAG COIL ISSUE
Self-adhesive, non-denominated in coils of 100. 2.5 billion stamps gravure printed by the Bureau of Engraving and Printing. Die cut 9 3/4 vertically. Plate number every 24 stamps.

1347		MNHVF	UseVF
(37¢)	**multicolored** pre-phosphored paper	.70	.25
	Pair	1.40	.25
	FDC (June 7, 2002 - Washington, D.C.)		1.50

2002. U.S.A. FIRST-CLASS FLAG BOOKLET ISSUE
Self-adhesive, non-denominated flat convertible booklet of 20. Printed by Banknote Corporation of America. Serpentine die cut 11 1/4x11 1/2.

1348		MNHVF	UseVF
(37¢)	**multicolored** pre-phosphored paper	.70	.25
	n. Booklet pane of 10	7.50	

		MNHVF	UseVF
n1. Booklet pane of 20		15.00	
FDC (June 7, 2002 - Washington, D.C.)			1.50

2002. U.S.A. FIRST-CLASS FLAG BOOKLET ISSUE Self-adhesive, non-denominated folded vending booklet of 20 and flat double-sided convertible booklet of 20. Printed by Sennett Security Products. Serpentine die cut 10 1/2x10 3/4. FDC not offered.

1349		MNHVF	UseVF
(37¢)	**multicolored** pre-phosphored paper	.70	.25
	n. Booklet pane of 4 (B327)	2.80	
	n1. Booklet pane of 6	4.20	
	n2. Folded vending booklet of 20 (B327)	15.00	
	n3. Flat double-sided convertible booklet of 20	15.00	

2002. U.S.A. FIRST-CLASS FLAG ATM ISSUE Self-adhesive, non-denominated pane of 18, printed by Avery Dennison. Serpentine die cut 8.

1350		MNHVF	UseVF
(37¢)	**multicolored** pre-phosphored	.70	.25
	n. Pane of 18	13.50	
	FDC (June 7, 2002 - Washington, D.C.)		1.50

2002. ANTIQUE TOYS BOOKLET ISSUE Designed by Derry Noyes, Washington, D.C. *Non-denominated, self-adhesive convertible booklet of 20 and vending booklet of 20. Printed by Avery Dennison.* The Antique Toys definitive stamps feature four antique American toy vehicles from the Strong Museum in Rochester, New York: a bright red U.S. Mail truck with a spring wound mechanism, a yellow taxicab, a mechanical locomotive of cast iron and stamped tin, and a fiery red steam pumper complete with two firemen. Made primarily of cast iron, the toys were manufactured between 1880 and 1925. *Serpentine die cut 11 on 2, 3 or 4 sides.*

1351 *U.S. Mail truck*

1352 *Fiery red steam pumper*

1353 *Yellow taxicab*

1354 *Mechanical locomotive*

B328

1351		MNHVF	UseVF
(37¢)	**multicolored** pre-phosphored paper	.70	.25
1352		MNHVF	UseVF
(37¢)	**multicolored** pre-phosphored paper	.70	.25
1353		MNHVF	UseVF
(37¢)	**multicolored** pre-phosphored paper	.70	.25
1354		MNHVF	UseVF
(37¢)	**multicolored** pre-phosphored paper	.70	.25
	n. Booklet pane of 10	7.50	
	n1. Booklet pane of 20 (convertible or folded booklet) (B328)	15.00	
	FDC (June 7, 2002) block of 4		3.00

2002. U.S. FLAG ISSUE Designed by Terry McCaffrey, USPS. *Self-adhesive in pane of 20. Printed by Ashton-Potter. Serpentine die cut 11 1/4x11.*

1355, 1356, 1357, 1358, 1359, 1360, 1360A, 1361, 1393, 1399, 1413 *U.S. Flag*

1355		MNHVF	UseVF
37¢	**multicolored** pre-phosphored paper	.70	.25
	Plate block of 4	3.00	
	y. Pane of 20 (B329)	15.00	
	FDC (June 7, 2002 - Washington, D.C.)		1.50

2002. U.S. FLAG COIL ISSUE Designed by Terry McCaffrey, USPS. *Water activated gum in coils of 100, 3,000, and 10,000. 3.75 million stamps gravure printed by American Packaging Corp. for Sennett Security Products. Only the coil of 3,000 was available on the first day. The other two appeared about a month later. Perforated 9 3/4 vertically. Coils of 3,000 and 10,000 have pink 4- or 5-digit back numbers every 10 stamps. Plate number every 14 stamps.*

1356		MNHVF	UseVF
37¢	**multicolored** pre-phosphored paper	.70	.25
	Pair	1.40	.25
	FDC (June 7, 2002 - Washington, D.C.)		1.50

2002. U.S. FLAG BOOKLET ISSUE Designed by Terry McCaffrey, USPS. *Self-adhesive flat convertible booklet of 20. Printed by Banknote Corporation of America. Serpentine die cut 11 1/4x11 1/4 on 2, 3 or 4 sides.*

1357		MNHVF	UseVF
37¢	**multicolored** pre-phosphored paper	.70	.25
	n. Booklet pane of 10	7.50	
	n1. Booklet pane of 20 (convertible booklet)	15.00	
	FDC (June 7, 2002 - Washington, D.C.)		1.50

2002. U.S. FLAG COIL ISSUE Designed by Terry McCaffrey, USPS. *Self-adhesive in coils of 3,000 and 10,000. 250 million stamps gravure printed by Banknote Corporation of America. This stamp was not available until the middle of June. Die cut 8 1/2 vertically. Black back numbers every 10 stamps. Plate number every 20 stamps.*

1358		MNHVF	UseVF
37¢	**multicolored** pre-phosphored paper	.70	.25
	Pair	1.40	.25
	FDC (June 7, 2002 - Washington, D.C.)		1.50

2002. U.S. FLAG COIL ISSUE Designed by Terry McCaffrey, USPS. *Self-adhesive in coils of 100. 2.9 billion stamps gravure printed by the Bureau of Engraving and Printing. This stamp was not available until almost the end of July. Die cut 9 3/4 vertically. Plate number every 24 stamps.*

1359		MNHVF	UseVF
37¢	**multicolored** pre-phosphored paper	.70	.25
	Pair	1.40	.25
	FDC (June 7, 2002 - Washington, D.C.)		1.50

2002. U.S. FLAG BOOKLET ISSUE Designed by Terry McCaffrey, USPS. *Self-adhesive flat double-sided convertible booklet of 20. Printed by Sennett Security Products. Serpentine die cut 10 1/2x10 3/4 on 2 or 3 sides.*

1360		MNHVF	UseVF
37¢	**multicolored** pre-phosphored paper	.70	.25
	n. Booklet pane of 4	3.00	
	n1. Booklet pane of 20 (double-sided convertible booklet)	15.00	
	FDC (June 7, 2002 - Washington, D.C.)		1.50

2002. U.S. FLAG BOOKLET ISSUE Designed by Terry McCaffrey, USPS. *Self-adhesive folded vending booklet of 20. Printed by Sennett Security Products. Serpentine die cut 11 1/4x11 1/4 on 2, 3 or 4 sides.*

1360A		MNHVF	UseVF
37¢	**multicolored** pre-phosphored paper	.70	.25
	n1. Booklet pane of 4	3.00	
	n2. Booklet pane of 6	4.50	
	n. Booklet of 20 (B329)	15.00	
	FDC (June 7, 2002 - Washington, D.C.)		1.50

2002. U.S. FLAG BOOKLET ISSUE Designed by Terry McCaffrey, USPS. *Self-adhesive flat convertible booklet of 10. Printed by Avery Dennison. Serpentine die cut 11.*

1361		MNHVF	UseVF
37¢	**multicolored** pre-phosphored paper	.70	.25
	n. Booklet pane of 4	3.00	
	n1. Booklet pane of 6	4.50	
	n2. Booklet pane of 10 (convertible booklet)	7.50	
	FDC (June 7, 2002 - Washington, D.C.)		1.50

2002. COVERLET EAGLE ISSUE features an artistic rendering, in watercolor and graphite on paper by Arthur G. Merkley, of a detail from a coverlet made circa 1853 by Harry Tyler (1801-1858). The detail from the coverlet is an eagle pattern that resembles the Great Seal of the United States. This stamp was issued to meet a new two-ounce letter rate. Designed by Richard Shaeff, Scottsdale, Ariz. *Printed offset lithography on pre-phosphored paper by Ashton-Potter in self-adhesive panes of 20. Serpentine die cut 11x11 1/4.*

1362 *Coverlet eagle*

1362		MNHVF	UseVF
60¢	**multicolored** pre-phosphored paper	1.00	.25
	Plate block of 4	4.00	
	y. Pane of 20	20.00	
	FDC *(July 12, 2002 - Oak Brook, Ill.)*		2.00

2002. ANTIQUE TOYS BOOKLET ISSUE Designed by Derry Noyes, Washington, D.C. Reissued as a denominated *self-adhesive convertible booklet of 20 and vending booklet of 20. Printed by Avery Dennison. Serpentine die cut 11 1/4 on 2, 3 or 4 sides.*

1363, 1415 *U.S. Mail Truck*

1364, 1416 *Fiery red steam pumper*

1365, 1417 *Yellow taxicab*

1366, 1418 *Mechanical locomotive*

B330

1363		MNHVF	UseVF
37¢	**multicolored** pre-phosphored paper	.70	.20
1364		MNHVF	UseVF
37¢	**multicolored** pre-phosphored paper	.70	.20
1365		MNHVF	UseVF
37¢	**multicolored** pre-phosphored paper	.70	.20
1366		MNHVF	UseVF
37¢	**multicolored** pre-phosphored paper	.70	.20
	n. Booklet pane of 10	7.50	
	n1. Booklet pane of 20 (convertible or folded booklet)	15.00	
	(B330)		
	FDC *(July 26, 2002) block of 4*		3.00

2002. ANTIQUE TOYS COIL ISSUE Designed by Derry Noyes, Washington, D.C. *Self-adhesive in coils of 100. 1.5 billion stamps gravure printed by Banknote Corporation of America.* The 37-cent Antique Toys definitive stamps feature four antique American toy vehicles from the Strong Museum in Rochester, New York: a bright red U.S. Mail truck with a spring wound mechanism, a yellow taxicab, a mechanical locomotive of cast iron and stamped tin, and a fiery red steam pumper complete with two firemen. Made primarily of cast iron, the toys were manufactured between 1880 and 1925. The plate number appears on one of the Fire Pumper stamps. *Die cut 8 1/2 horizontally. Plate number every 12 stamps.*

Input from stamp collectors regarding the content of this catalog and ideas to make it more useful is eagerly sought. Send your comments to:

Minkus Catalog Editor

Krause Publications

700 E. State St.

Iola, WI 54990

 1367-1370 *Antique toys*

1367		MNHVF	UseVF
37¢	**multicolored** pre-phosphored paper	.70	.25
1368		MNHVF	UseVF
37¢	**multicolored** pre-phosphored paper	.70	.25
1369		MNHVF	UseVF
37¢	**multicolored** pre-phosphored paper	.70	.25
1370		MNHVF	UseVF
37¢	**multicolored** pre-phosphored paper	.70	.25
	Pair	1.40	.25
	FDC *(July 26, 2002 - Rochester, N.Y.)*		1.50

> *Listings and prices for plate number coil strips and singles appear at the end of this definitives section of the Krause-Minkus catalog.*

2002. EDNA FERBER ISSUE from the Distinguished Americans Series was issued to meet the three ounce letter rate. Edna Ferber (1885-1968) was called the greatest American woman novelist of her day. She began her career in writing while in high school as an editor for the school paper. Later, writing for the *Milwaukee Journal,* she collapsed in exhaustion. While recuperating, she wrote her first short stories and novel. By 1924, she won the Pulitzer Prize for *So Big.* Other best known books are *Showboat* (1926), *Cimarron* (1929), *Giant* (1952), and *Ice Palace* (1958). *Printed by Banknote Corporation of America in self-adhesive panes of 20. Year date 2002. Serpentine die cut 11x11 1/2.*

 1371, 1414 *Edna Ferber*

1371		MNHVF	UseVF
83¢	**black & red** pre-phosphored paper	1.50	.25
	Plate block of 4	6.00	
	y. Pane of 20	30.00	
	FDC *(July 29, 2002 - Appleton, Wis.)*		1.50

National Monuments Series

2002. JEFFERSON MEMORIAL ISSUE of the National Monuments Series featured a photograph of the Jefferson Memorial lit at night. The stamp was issued to pay the new one-pound priority rate. *Printed* offset by Banknote Corporation of America in self-adhesive panes of 20. Serpentine die cut 11 1/4.

1372 Jefferson Memorial

1372
$3.85   **multicolored** pre-phosphored paper
	MNHVF	UseVF
	7.50	3.25
Plate block of 4 — 30.00
FDC *(July 30, 2002 - Washington, D.C.)* — 7.50

2002. U.S. CAPITOL DOME ISSUE of the National Monuments Series featured a photograph of the Capitol Dome lit at night. The stamp was issued to pay the new half-pound express mail rate. *Printed offset by Banknote Corporation of America in self-adhesive panes of 20. Serpentine die cut 11 1/4.*

1373 Capitol dome

1373
$13.65   **multicolored** pre-phosphored paper
	MNHVF	UseVF
	25.00	10.00
Plate block of 4 — 100.00
FDC *(July 30, 2002 - Washington, D.C.)* — 25.00

2002. MADONNA AND CHILD BOOKLET ISSUE continues to honor the Christmas tradition with the reproduction of the painting of Jan Gossaert's *Madonna and Child*. Gossaert was a painter from the early 16th century from the Netherlands. *Printed offset by Banknote Corporation of America as a self-adhesive convertible booklet of 20. Serpentine die cut 11 1/4.*

1374 Madonna and Child

1374
37¢   **multicolored** pre-phosphored paper
	MNHVF	UseVF
	.75	.25
n. Booklet pane of 10 — 7.50
n1. Booklet pane of 20 (convertible booklet) — 15.00
FDC *(Oct. 10, 2002 - Chicago, Ill.* — 1.50

American Scenes Series

2002. SEA COAST COIL ISSUE Designed by Tom Engemen, Brunswick, Md. *Self-adhesive in coils of 10,000. 1 billion stamps gravure printed by Banknote Corporation of America. Die cut 8 1/2 vertically. Back number every 10 stamps. Plate number every 20 stamps.*

1375, 1397, 1401 Sea Coast

1375
(5¢)   **multicolored** pre-phosphored paper
	MNHVF	UseVF
	.20	.20
Pair — .20 / .20
FDC *(Oct. 21, 2002 - Washington, D.C.)* — 1.50
See also *1397, 1401.*

2002. HOLIDAY CRAFTS SNOWMEN ISSUE Designed by Derry Noyes, Washington, D.C. The Snowmen stamps feature photographs of four whimsical snowmen figurines. Popular in folklore, literature, and song, snowmen have come to symbolize the joy and magic of the holiday season and often evoke fond childhood memories of playing in the snow. *Printed by gravure by Avery Dennison in self-adhesive panes of 20. Serpentine die cut 11.*

1376-1379, 1380-1383, 1384-1387, 1388-1391 Snowmen

1376
37¢   **multicolored** pre-phosphored paper — MNHVF .75 / UseVF .25
1377
37¢   **multicolored** pre-phosphored paper — MNHVF .75 / UseVF .25
1378
37¢   **multicolored** pre-phosphored paper — MNHVF .75 / UseVF .25
1379
37¢   **multicolored** pre-phosphored paper — MNHVF .75 / UseVF .25
y. Plate block of 4 — 3.00
y1. Pane of 20 — 15.00
FDC *(Oct. 28, 2002)* any single — 1.50

2002. HOLIDAY CRAFTS SNOWMEN BOOKLET ISSUE Designed by Derry Noyes, Washington, D.C., on a *self-adhesive double-sided convertible booklet of 20. Printed gravure by Sennett Security Products. Serpentine die cut 11.*

1380-1383 Snowmen

1380
37¢   **multicolored** pre-phosphored paper — MNHVF .75 / UseVF .25
1381
37¢   **multicolored** pre-phosphored paper — MNHVF .75 / UseVF .25
1382
37¢   **multicolored** pre-phosphored paper — MNHVF .75 / UseVF .25
1383
37¢   **multicolored** pre-phosphored paper — MNHVF .75 / UseVF .25

n. Booklet pane of 4	3.00	
n1. Booklet pane of 20 (convertible booklet)	15.00	
FDC *(Oct. 28, 2002)* any single		1.50

2002. HOLIDAY CRAFTS SNOWMEN BOOKLET ISSUE Designed by Derry Noyes, Washington, D.C., on a *self-adhesive folded vending booklet of 20. Printed gravure by Sennett Security Products. Serpentine die cut 11.*

1384-1387 *Snowmen*

		MNHVF	UseVF
1384			
37¢	**multicolored** pre-phosphored paper	.75	.25
1385		MNHVF	UseVF
37¢	**multicolored** pre-phosphored paper	.75	.25
1386		MNHVF	UseVF
37¢	**multicolored** pre-phosphored paper	.75	.25
1387		MNHVF	UseVF
37¢	**multicolored** pre-phosphored paper	.75	.25
	n. Booklet pane of 4	3.00	
	n1. Booklet pane of 6 (1 each 1383-84, 2 each 1385-86)	4.50	
	n2. Booklet pane of 6 (1 each 1385-86, 2 each 1383-84)	4.50	
	n3. Booklet pane of 20 (B331)	4.50	
	FDC *(Oct. 28, 2002)* any single		1.50

2002. HOLIDAY CRAFTS SNOWMEN COIL ISSUE Designed by Derry Noyes, Washington, D.C. *Self-adhesive in linerless coils of 100. 300 million stamps gravure printed by Guilford Gravure. The plate number appears on one of the Snowmen wearing a top hat stamp. Die cut 8 1/2 vertically. Plate number every 12 stamps.*

1388-1391 *Snowmen*

		MNHVF	UseVF
1388			
37¢	**multicolored** pre-phosphored paper	.70	.20
1389		MNHVF	UseVF
37¢	**multicolored** pre-phosphored paper	.70	.20
1390		MNHVF	UseVF
37¢	**multicolored** pre-phosphored paper	.70	.20
1391		MNHVF	UseVF
37¢	**multicolored** pre-phosphored paper	.70	.20
	Pair	1.40	.20
	FDC *(Oct. 28, 2002 - Houghton, Mich.)*		1.50

American Design Series

2003. AMERICAN CLOCK ISSUE is the second stamp of the American Design Series. The American clock stamp features the work of Simon Willard, a clockmaker in the early 19th century. Designed by Derry Noyes, Washington, D.C. *Printed offset by Ashton-Potter in self-adhesive panes of 20. Die cut 11 1/4x11.*

1392 *American clock*

		MNHVF	UseVF
1392			
10¢	**multicolored** untagged	.30	.20
	Plate block of 4	1.20	
	y. Pane of 20	6.00	
	FDC *(Jan. 24, 2003 - Tucson, Ariz.)*		1.50

2003. U.S. FLAG BOOKLET ATM ISSUE Designed by Terry McCaffrey, USPS. *Self-adhesive ATM booklet of 18. Printed gravure by Avery Dennison. Serpentine die cut 8.*

		MNHVF	UseVF
1393			
37¢	**multicolored** overall tagging	.70	.25
	n. Pane of 9	7.00	
	n1. Pane of 18	14.00	
	FDC *(Feb. 4, 2003 - Washington, D.C.)*		1.50

2003. NEW YORK LIBRARY LION STATUE COIL ISSUE Designed by Carl Herrman, Carlsbad, Calif. *Water-activated gum in coils of 500 and 3,000. 250 million stamps gravure printed by American Packaging Corp. for Sennett Security Products.* This stamp, in the American Culture Series, features one of the two lions guarding the entrance to the New York Public Library. Sculpted by Edward Clark Potter, these trademarked beasts - nicknamed Patience and Fortitude - have been adopted by the library as official mascots. The Lion Statue nonprofit stamp was previously issued on November 9, 2000, in a self-adhesive (PSA) coil of 10,000. *Perforated 10 vertically with pink 3- or 4-digit back numbers every 10 stamps. Plate number every 14 stamps.*

1394 *New York Library lion*

		MNHVF	UseVF
1394			
(10¢)	**multicolored** untagged	.30	.20
	Pair	2.25	.60
	FDC *(Feb. 4, 2003 - Washington, D.C.)*		1.50

See also 1262.

> *Listings and prices for plate number coil strips and singles appear at the end of this definitives section of the Krause-Minkus catalog.*

2003. WISDOM ISSUE in the American Culture Series features Nancy Stahl's illustration of the Wisdom statue at the Rockefeller Center in New York City. *Printed by offset by Ashton-Potter in self-adhesive panes of 20. Die cut 11 1/4.*

1395 *Wisdom*

		MNHVF	UseVF
1395			
$1	**multicolored** pre-phosphored paper	1.50	.50
	Plate block of 4	6.00	
	y. Pane of 20	30.00	
	FDC *(Feb. 28, 2003 - Biloxi, Miss.)*		2.50

2003. TIFFANY LAMP COIL ISSUE Designed by Derry Noyes, Washington, D.C. *Water-activated gum in coils of 3,000. 250 million stamps gravure printed by American Packaging Corp. for Sennett Security Products.* The Tiffany Lamp stamp features the work of Louis

Comfort Tiffany (1848-1933), a designer of glass, ceramics, jewelry, enamelware, and metalwork, who transformed everyday objects into works of art. Considered one of the greatest designers of glass in his era, Tiffany is also remembered as a leader in the art nouveau movement, a style in the visual arts that transformed design in the United States and Europe from the 1890s to World War I. *Perforated 9 3/4 vertically with pink back numbers every 10 stamps. Plate number every 14 stamps.*

1396 *Tiffany lamp*

1396			MNHVF	UseVF
1¢	**multicolored** untagged		.20	.20
	Pair		.20	
	FDC *(March 1, 2003 - Biloxi, Miss.)*			1.50

Scenic America Series

2003. Sea Coast Coil Issue Designed by Tom Engemen, Brunswick, Md. *Water-activated gum in coils of 500 and 10,000. 200 million stamps gravure printed by Banknote Corporation of America.* The Sea Coast nonprofit stamp was previously issued on October 21, 2002, in a self-adhesive (PSA) coil of 10,000. *Perforated 9 3/4 vertically with pink 3- or 5-digit back numbers every 10 stamps. Plate number every 10 stamps.*

1397 *Sea coast*

1397			MNHVF	UseVF
(5¢)	**multicolored** untagged		.20	.20
	Pair		.20	.20
	FDC *(March 19, 2003 - Washington, D.C.)*			1.50

2003. Acadia National Park Issue in the Scenic America Series featured the first national park established east of the Mississippi. *Reissued and printed by Ashton-Potter. Serpentine die cut 11 1/2x11 3/4.*

1398 *Acadia National Park*

1398		MNHVF	UseVF
60¢	**multicolored**		
	Plate block of 4	2.80	
	y. Pane of 20	24.00	

See also No. 1310.

2003. U.S. Flag Coil Issue Designed by Terrence W. McCaffrey, USPS. *Self-adhesive in coils of 100. Nine hundred ninety-two million stamps gravure printed by Banknote Corporation of America.* This U.S. Flag stamp was first reported available from Kansas City on April 18, 2003, although it apparently was available before that, perhaps as early as April 6. *The date is 2003 and the corners are cut at a 90-degree angle. Die cut 8 1/2 vertically. Plate number every 12 stamps.*

1399 *U.S. flag*

1399			MNHVF	UseVF
37¢	**multicolored** pre-phosphored paper		.70	.20
	Pair		1.40	
	FDC (Earliest known use - *April 24, 2003*)			1.50

2003. Purple Heart Issue honors the sacrifices of the men and women who defend our nation. Originally known as the Badge of Military Merit during the Revolutionary War, the Purple Heart was reinstated in 1932 after almost 150 years of nonuse. It is now the world's oldest military decoration. Designed by Carl T. Herrman. *Printed Offset/Microprint "USPS" by Banknote Corporation of America in self-adhesive panes of 20. Die cut 11 1/4x11.*

1400, 1412 *Purple Heart medal*

1400			MNHVF	UseVF
37¢	**multicolored** phosphored block tagged		.75	.25
	Plate block of 4		3.00	
	y. Pane of 20		15.00	
	EKU *(May 30, 2003 - Mount Vernon, Va.)*			1.50
	FDC			

2003. Sea Coast Coil Issue Designed by Tom Engemen, Brunswick, Md. *Self-adhesive in coils of 10,000. Gravure printed by Ashton-Potter USA Ltd. Die cut 10x9 1/2 on all four sides. Back number every 20 stamps. Plate number every 22 stamps.*

1401 *Sea coast*

1401			MNHVF	UseVF
(5¢)	**multicolored** untagged		.20	.20
	Pair		.20	.20
	FDC *(June 3, 2003 - Washington, D.C.)*			1.50

2003. American Eagle Coil Issue Designed by Tom Engemen, Brunswick, Md. *Self-adhesive in coils of 10,000. Three hundred ten million stamps gravure printed by American Packaging Corp. for Sennett Security Products.* These Presorted First-Class Mail coil stamps feature an artistic rendering of a detail of the Great Seal of the United States. In his 1782 design, Charles Thomson, secretary of the Continental Congress, gave prominence to the American bald eagle. This majestic raptor, a native of North America, became a symbol of freedom as well as the emblem of our country. The designs for the stamps feature the head and outstretched right wing of the American bald eagle and a portion of the shield is on its breast, with the tip of the olive branch held in its right talon. The coil has 10 versions of the eagle - in gold, green, blue, red, and gray - that appear against a background of a contrasting color. *Die cut 11 1/2 vertically. Black or pink back numbers every 10 stamps. Plate number every 20 stamps on the stamp with gold eagle and green background.*

1402-1411 *American eagle*

1402		MNHVF	UseVF
(25¢)	**gray & gold** untagged	.45	.20
1403		MNHVF	UseVF
(25¢)	**gold & red** untagged	.45	.20
1404		MNHVF	UseVF
(25¢)	**dull blue & gold** untagged	.45	.20
1405		MNHVF	UseVF
(25¢)	**gold & Prussian blue** untagged	.45	.20
1406		MNHVF	UseVF
(25¢)	**green & gold** untagged	.45	.20
1407		MNHVF	UseVF
(25¢)	**gold & gray** untagged	.45	.20
1408		MNHVF	UseVF
(25¢)	**Prussian blue & gold** untagged	.45	.20
1409		MNHVF	UseVF
(25¢)	**gold & dull blue** untagged	.45	.20
1410		MNHVF	UseVF
(25¢)	**red & gold** untagged	.45	.20
1411		MNHVF	UseVF
(25¢)	**gold & green** (plate#) untagged	.45	.20
	Pair	.80	.20
	y. Plate number strip of 11	8.75	
	FDC *(June 26, 2003 - Santa Clara, Calif.)*		1.50

2003. PURPLE HEART ISSUE reprinted by Ashton-Potter in a self-adhesive pane of 20. Serpentine die cut 10 3/4x10 1/4. See also No. 1398.

1412		MNHVF	UseVF
37¢	**multicolored**	.75	.25
	Plate block of 4	3.00	
	y. Pane of 20	15.00	
	FDC *(Aug. 1, 2003)*		1.50

2003. U.S.A. FLAG COIL ISSUE *reprinted by Sennett Security Products in self-adhesive rolls of 100 with a "2003" date. Serpentine die cut 10 1/4. See No. 1359. Plate interval of 14.* No FDC offered. Issued to post offices in sticks of 5 with tabs holding rolls together. Issued with leaderstrips that show a barcode, description of the stamps and a reduced size image of the stamp. The last U.S. coil stamp to have a leaderstrip was issued during the Liberty Series era.

1413 *Flag*

1413		MNHVF	UseVF
37¢	**multicolored** pre-phosphored paper	.75	.25
	Pair	1.50	

For stamps with similar design, see Nos. 1355, 1356, 1357, 1358, 1359, 1360, 1361, 1393, B329.

> Listings and prices for plate number coil strips and singles appear at the end of this definitives section of the Krause-Minkus catalog.

2003. EDNA FERBER ISSUE from the Distinguished Americans Series was reissued to meet the three-ounce letter rate. (See No. 1371.) Edna Ferber (1885-1968) was called the greatest American woman novelist of her day. She began her career in writing while in high school as an editor for the school paper. Later, writing for the *Milwaukee Journal,* she collapsed in exhaustion. While recuperating, she wrote her first short stories and novel. By 1924, she won the Pulitzer Prize for *So Big.* Other best known books are *Showboat* (1926), *Cimarron* (1929), *Giant* (1952), and *Ice Palace* (1958). *Printed by Ashton-Potter in self-adhesive panes of 20. Year date 2003. Serpentine die cut 11 1/4.*

1414 *Edna Ferber*

1414		MNHVF	UseVF
83¢	**black & red** pre-phosphored paper	1.50	.25
	Plate block of 4	6.00	
	y. Pane of 20	30.00	
	EKU - Aug. 8, 2003		—

2003. ANTIQUE TOYS BOOKLET ISSUE Designed by Derry Noyed, Washington, D.C. Reissued in a *double-sided self-adhesive booklet of 20. Printed by Avery Dennison. Serpentine die cut.* See also Nos. 1363-1366, B330.

1415 *U.S. Mail truck*

1416 *Fiery red steam pumper*

1417 *Yellow taxicab*

1418 *Mechanical locomotive*

1415		MNHVF	UseVF
37¢	**multicolored** pre-phosphored paper	.70	.25
1416		MNHVF	UseVF
37¢	**multicolored** pre-phosphored paper	.70	.25
1417		MNHVF	UseVF
37¢	**multicolored** pre-phosphored paper	.70	.25
1418		MNHVF	UseVF
37¢	**multicolored** pre-phosphored paper	.70	.25
	n. Booklet pane of 10		
	n1. Booklet pane of 20 (double-sided booklet)	15.00	
	FDC *(Sept. 3, 2003 - Washington, D.C.)*		1.50

K/M #	WAG SA	Denomination, Name, Date	Details	Plate #	Imperf Pair $	Strip 5	Imperf Strip 5	Strip 3	Used Sgl	Back# on Plate#	Interval Plate #	Interval Back #	Back# Positions	Roll 100	Roll 500	Roll 3000
806		1¢ Omnibus (1983)	Overall Tag, Joint Line	1, 2, 3, 4, 5, 6		0.50		0.40	0.30		24				X	X
806v	WAG		Imperf, Overall Tag, Joint Line	5, 6	675.00						24					
867	WAG	1¢ Omnibus (1986)	Large Block Tag	1, 2		0.60		0.55	0.45		52				X	X
867pz			Mottled Tag, Shiny Gum (Error)	3		13.00		13.00	13.00		48					
867zxm			Untagged, Dull Gum	2, 3		0.65		0.55	0.45		52,48				X	X
867zxs	WAG	1¢ Omnibus (1991)	Untagged, Shiny Gum	3		0.80		0.60	0.65		48				X	X
867zxm			Untagged, Lo Gloss(?)	3		0.80		0.70	0.65		48					
867v			Imperf Tagged	2	2,400.00						52					X
1115	WAG	1¢ Kestrel (1996) Type I	Black, Yellow, Cyan, Magenta	1111		0.65		0.55	0.40		24				X	X
		1¢ Kestrel (1997) Type II	Black, Cyan, Yellow, Magenta	1111		0.65		0.55	0.40		24				X	X
1229v	WAG	1¢ Kestrel (1999) Type III	Yellow, Magenta, Cyan, Black, Tagged (Error)	1111							24					X
1229	WAG		Yellow, Magenta, Cyan, Black, Untagged	1111, 2222, 3333, 4444		0.85		0.55	0.55		24					X
1396	WAG	1¢ Tiffany Lamp	Untagged	S11111		0.75		0.60	0.20	15.00	14	10	Pink 4M		X	X
										1.00	14	10	Pink 4T,4B			X
790	WAG	2¢ Locomotive (1982)	Overall Tag, Joint Line	2, 3, 4, 6, 8, 10		0.50		0.45	0.40		24				X	X
790zo			Untagged (Error)	8							24					
790v	WAG		Imperf, Overall Tag, Joint Line	3, 4, 8, 10	50.00		250.00				24					
873	WAG	2¢ Locomotive (1987)	Block Tag	1		0.70		0.60	0.45		52				X	X
873zxs	WAG	2¢ Locomotive (1993)	Untagged, Shiny Gum	2		1.50		1.10	1.30		48				X	X
873zxm			Untagged, Dull Gum	2		0.70		0.60	0.50		48					X
1227	WAG	2¢ Woodpecker (1999)	Untagged	11111		0.80		0.65	0.65	5.00	24	20	Green 4T, 4B		X	X
										12.00	24	20	Green 4M			X
				22222						7.00	24	20	Green 4T, 4B			
800	WAG	3¢ Handcar (1983)	Overall Tag, Joint Line	1, 2, 3, 4		0.70		0.65	0.50		24				X	X
883	WAG	3¢ Conestoga Wagon (1988)	Block Tag	1		0.90		0.70	0.60		52				X	X
883zxm			Untagged, Dull Gum	2, 3		1.25		1.00	0.90		48			B		X
				3		1.25		1.00	0.85		48					X
883zxs	WAG	3¢ Conestoga Wagon (1992)	Untagged, Shiny Gum	6		2.15		1.60	2.00		48				X	X
				5 (Large #)		2.10		2.00	2.00		48					X
			Untagged, Lo-Gloss Gum	5 (Small #)		3.75		3.00	3.50		48					X
1340	WAG	3¢ Star (2002)	Untagged	S111		1.25		1.00	0.20	2.50	14	10				X
843	WAG	3.4¢ School Bus (1985)	Overall Tag	1, 2		0.90		0.80	0.75		24				X	
843zx			Precancel	1, 2		4.25		4.00	3.75		24				X	X
791			Overall Tag, Joint Line	1, 2, 3, 4		1.00		0.95	0.75		24				X	X
				5, 6		2.20		2.10	2.00		24					X
791v	WAG	4¢ Stagecoach (1982)	Imperf, Overall Tag	1, 2	275.00		1,500.00				24					
791zo			Untagged, Not Precanceled	3, 4							24					
791zx			Precancel	3, 4, 5, 6		5.00		5.00	4.25	5.00	24	10	Pink 5T, 5B		X	X
791zxv			Imperf Precancel	5, 6	750.00						24	10	Pink 5M			
868	WAG	4¢ Stagecoach (1986)	Block Tag	1		1.30		1.20	0.95		52				X	X
868z	WAG	4¢ Stagecoach (1990)	Overall Tag	1		11.00		10.50	9.00		52					X

Roll Size columns (read from vertical headers): 100, 500, 1000, 3000

K/M #	WAG/SA	Denomination, Name, Date	Details	Plate #	Imperf Pair $	Strip5	Imperf Strip 5	Strip 3	Used Sgl	Back# on Plate#	Interval Plate #	Interval Back #	Back# Positions (T=Top, M=Middle, B=Bottom, U=Upside Down, D=Double)	Roll Size
943	WAG	4¢ Steam Carriage (1991)	Overall Tag	1							52			X X
943v			Imperf, Overall Tag	1	600.00						52			
943zx			Untagged	1		1.00		1.00	0.95		52			X X
846	WAG	4.9¢ Buckboard (1985)	Overall Tag	3, 4		0.85		0.80	0.80		24			X
846zx			Precancel	1, 2, 3, 4, 5 6		1.40		1.30	1.25		24			X X
808	WAG	5¢ Motorcycle (1983)	Overall Tag	1, 2, 3, 4		0.90		0.80	0.75		24			X X
808zo			Tagging Omitted (Error)		2,750.00						24			? ?
808v			Imperf, Overall Tag	1, 2							24		B	X
879	WAG	5¢ Milk Wagon (1987)	Block Tag	1		0.90		0.85	0.75		52			X X
931	WAG	5¢ Circus Wagon (1990)	Overall Tag	1		1.20		1.00	0.90		52			X X
			Untagged, Matte Gum	1		1.20		1.10	0.90		52			X X
931z			Untagged, Low Gloss	2		1.40		1.30	1.00		52			X
931v			Imperf	1	750.00						52			
1007	WAG	5¢ Circus Wagon (1992)	Untagged	A1, A2		1.45		1.45	1.10		24			X
1007z			Untagged with Luminescent Ink	A3		2.00		2.00	2.00		24			X
1077			Untagged	S1		1.45		1.35	1.25	3.25	14	10	Black 5T, Purple 5TB	X
				S2							14	10	Pink 5TB	X
1077v	WAG	5¢ Circus Wagon (1995)	Imperf	S2	175.00	1.45		1.35	1.25		14	10	Pink 5T, 5B	X
											14	10	Pink 5M	X
1077z			Tagged (Luminescent Ink)	S2		1.45		1.35	1.25	3.25	14	10	Pink 5T, 5B	X
				S3		1.45		1.35	1.25	4.25	14	10	Pink 5T, 5B	X
955	WAG	5¢ Canoe (1991)	Untagged, Brown Ink	1, 2, 3		1.45		1.35	1.00		48			X X
955v			Imperf, Brown Ink	1	250.00						48			
979	WAG	5¢ Canoe (1991)	Red Ink, Shiny Gum	S11		1.35		1.35	1.20		33			X
979g			Red Ink, Low Gloss Gum	S11		10.00		9.50			33			X
1069	WAG	(5¢) G (1995)	Untagged	A11111, A21111		1.90		1.75	1.45		24			X X
				S111		1.45		1.40	1.00	3.25	14	10	Black 4TB & 5TB	X X
											14	10	Purple 4TB & 5TB	X
											14	10	Pink 4T, 4B	X
1070	WAG	(5¢) Butte (1995)	Untagged	S222		1.45		1.40	1.00	3.25	14	10	Black 4T	X
											14	10	Purple, Pink 4TB	X
				S333		1.45		1.40	1.00	3.25	14	10	Black, Purple 4TB	X X
											14	10	Pink 4TB & 5TB	X
1070v			Imperf	S111	650.00						14	10		
1130	SA	(5¢) Butte (1996)	Untagged	S111		1.45		1.40	1.10	8.00	21	10	Black 5TB, Pink TBM	X
1121	WAG	(5¢) Mountain (1996)	Untagged	11111		1.40		1.40	1.00		24			X X
1121z			Tagged (Error)	11111		84.00		82.00	72.00		24			
1122	WAG	(5¢) Mountain (1996)	Untagged	S111		1.45		1.35	1.00	3.25	14	10	Pink 5T, 5B	X X
1122v	WAG		Untagged, Imperf	S111	450.00	1.45		1.35	1.00		14	10	Pink 5T, 5B	X X
1131	SA	(5¢) Mountain (1996)		V333323, V333342		1.75		1.60	1.25		15	1	Blue 5M	X
				V222222		1.75		1.60	1.25		15	1	Blue 5M-U	X
			Untagged	V333333		1.75		1.60	1.25		15	1	Blue 5M, 5M-U	X
				V333343		2.45		2.15	2.15		15	1	Blue 5M	X
1152	SA	(5¢) Mountain (1997)	Untagged	1111		1.50		1.50	1.25	5.40	21	20	Green 4T, 4B	X

Back# Positions: T=Top, B=Bottom, M=Middle, D=Double, U=Upside Down

K/M #	WAG/SA	Denomination, Name, Date	Details	Plate #	Imperf Pair $	Strip 5	Imperf Strip 5	Strip 3	Used Sgl	Back# on Plate#	Interval Plate	Interval Back	Back# Positions	10000	3000	5000	1000
1169	WAG	(5¢ Wetlands (1998))	Untagged, Small Perf Holes	S1111		1.50		1.40	1.00	2.75	14	10	Pink 41TB & 51MB	X			X
			Untagged, Large Perf Holes	S1111		1.50		1.40	1.00	2.90	14	10	Pink 5T, 5B		X		
1169A	SA	(5¢ Wetlands - 3000 (1998))	Untagged	1111 (3K), 1111 (10K)						7.00	21	20	Green 4TB	X			
				2222						5.00	21	20	Green 4TB				X
				3333 (3K), 3333 (10K)		1.50		1.40	1.00	7.00	21	20	Green 4B	X			
				3333						9.00	21	20	Green 4T				X
		(5¢ Wetlands — 10,000 (1998))		1111, 2222, 3333, 4444, 5555, 6666						5.00	21	20	Green 4T, 4B	X			X
1337	WAG	5¢ American Toleware (2002)	Untagged	S1111111		1.50		1.40	1.00	2.90	14	10	Pink 5T, 5B	X			X
										NA	14	10	Pink 5M				X
1375	SA	(5¢ Sea Coast (2002))	Tagged, PSA	B111		3.00		2.50	1.50	NA	20	10	Black 5TB			X	
1397	WAG	(5¢ Sea Coast (2003))	Untagged, Shiny Gum	B111		3.00		2.50	1.50	NA	10	10	Pink 3TB, 5TB			X	
1399	SA	(5¢ Sea Coast (2003))	Die Cut All 4 Sides	P1111		3.00		2.75	2.00	4.00	22	20	Green 5TU				X
799	WAG	5.2¢ Sleigh (1983)	Overall Tag, Joint Line	1		8.25		6.00	5.50		24		Green 3TU	X			
				2							24						X
				3		260.00		170.00	160.00		24				X		
				5		190.00		140.00	135.00		24				X		
799zx	WAG		Precancel, Joint Line	4, 6		12.50		12.00	9.00		24				X		X
				1, 2, 3, 5		10.00		9.50	3.00		24				X		X
906	WAG	5.3¢ Elevator (1988)	Untagged	1		1.05		1.00	0.70		24				X		X
865	WAG	5.5¢ Star Route Truck (1986)	Untagged	1		1.50		1.40	1.25		52				X		X
865zx			Precancel	2		1.75		1.65	1.00		52				X		X
787	WAG	5.9¢ Bicycle (1982)	Untagged, Joint Line	3, 4		2.15		2.10	1.75		52				X		X
787zx			Precancel, Joint Line	3, 4		13.25		6.75	5.75		24				X		X
				5, 6		30.00		24.00	5.50		24				X		X
787zxv			Imperf, Precancel, Joint Line	3, 4	150.00	105.00	1,500.00	80.00	75.00		24						
841	WAG	6¢ Tricycle (1985)	Block Tag	1		1.45		1.40	1.00		52						X
841zx			Precancel	1		1.70		1.60	1.00		52				X		X
				2		7.00		6.75	2.75		52				X		X
841zxv			Imperf, Precancel	2	225.00						52						
870	WAG	7.1¢ Tractor (1987)	Block Tag	1		2.10		2.00	1.50		52						X
870zx			Precancel, Untagged, Nonprofit Org.	1		3.00		2.90	1.75		52				X		X
870zx1		7.1¢ Tractor (1989)	Precancel, Untagged, Zip + 4	1		1.50		1.50	1.25		52				X		X
814	WAG	7.4¢ Baby Buggy (1984)	Block Tag	2		8.25		8.00	6.00		52				X		X
814zx			Precancel, Untagged	2		5.50		5.00	4.00		52				X		X
903	WAG	7.6¢ Carreta (1998)	Precancel, Untagged	1, 2		2.00		2.00	1.50		52				X		X
				3		5.65		5.50	4.00		52				X		X
845	WAG	8.3¢ Ambulance (1985)	Overall Tag, Joint Line	1, 2		1.50		1.40	1.00		24				X		X
845zx			Precancel, Untagged, Joint Line	1, 2		1.50		1.45	1.25		24				X		X
				3, 4		4.50		4.25	3.65		24				X		X
845A	WAG	8.3¢ Ambulance (1986)	Precancel, Untagged, No Joint Line	1		5.25		4.25	3.00		52				X		X
				2		5.75		5.25	4.75		52				X		X
901	WAG	8.4¢ Wheel Chair (1988)	Precancel, Untagged	1, 2		1.90		1.75	1.00		52, 48				X		X
901v			Imperf	1, 2	650.00	13.25		12.00	5.50		52				X		X

K/M #	WAG/SA	Denomination, Name, Date	Details	Plate #	Imperf Pair $	Strip5	Imperf Strip 5	Strip 3	Used Sgl	Back# on Plate#	Interval (Plate #)	Back# Positions	Roll 100	Roll 500	Roll 3000
869			Block Tag	1		2.90		2.65	2.25		52		X		
869zx	WAG	8.5¢ Tow Truck (1987)	Precancel, Untagged	1		2.65		2.25	2.00		52			X	X
				2		11.85		11.50	8.00		52			X	X
778			Overall Tag, Joint Line	1, 2		12.00		7.50	7.00		24		X		
				3, 4		32.50		20.00	17.50		24		X		
				5, 6		285.00		245.00	185.00		24		X		
778zx	WAG	9.3¢ Mail Wagon (1981)	Precancel, Untagged, Joint Line	1		12.15		11.50	10.00		24			X	X
				2		11.00		10.50	10.00		24			X	X
				3		25.75		21.00	12.50		24			X	X
				4		18.00		16.00	10.00		24			X	X
				5, 6		2.75		2.75	1.75		24			X	X
				8		255.00		240.00	240.00		24			X	X
778zxv			Imperf, Precancel, Untagged, Joint Line	1, 2, 3, 4	115.00		1,500.00				24				
874			Block Tag, Dull Gum	1		2.55		2.00	1.00		52		B	X	X
874zm	WAG	10¢ Canal Boat (1987)	Overall Tag, Dull Gum	1		4.00		3.60	3.25		52			X	X
874zs			Overall Tag, Shiny Gum	4		4.00		3.70	2.75		48				X
874v			Imperf.	1							52				
874pz	WAG	10¢ Canal Boat (199?)	Mottled Tag, Shiny Gum	1		3.00		3.20	2.50		48			X	X
				2		3.75		3.65	2.75		48			X	X
				3, 4							48				X
		10¢ Canal Boat (?)	Solid Tag, Low Gloss Gum	5		5.75		4.00	4.00		48		X	X	X
980	WAG	(10¢) Eagle & Shield (1991) Untagged		A11111, A11112, A22113							24			X	X
				A21112							24			X	X
				A22112		2.40		2.30	2.00		24			X	X
				A43324, A43325, A43326, A43335							24			X	X
				A43334							24				X
				A53335							24				X
				A2113, A43426							24			X	X
				A12213, A33335, A54444		18.50		17.00	16.85		24			X	
				A1411101010							24			X	X
			A33333, A1010101010, A1011101011, A1011101012, A1110111010, A1111101010, A1111111010, A1411101011	A1412111110		2.80		2.70	2.70		24				X
			A54445, A89999, A99998, A99999, A1011101011	A34424, A34426		4.00		3.50	3.00		24			X	X
				A32333		280.00		275.00	275.00		24				X
				A33334, A88888, A88889		85.00		84.00	80.00		24				X
				A77777							24			X	
				A1412111111		3.25		3.00	2.50		24			X	X
				A1011101010		5.00		4.75	3.50		24			X	X

Back# Positions: T=Top, M=Middle, B=Bottom, D=Double, U=Upside Down

K/M #	WAG SA	Denomination, Name, Date	Details	Plate #	Imperf Pair $	Strip5	Imperf Strip 5	Strip 3	Used Sgl	Back# on Plate#	Int. Plate	Int. Back	Back# Positions (T=Top M=Middle B=Bottom D=Double U=Upside Down)	Roll 3000	Roll 5000	Roll 10000
980	WAG	(10¢) Eagle & Shield (1991)	Untagged	A1211101010		4.80		4.75	4.50		24			X		
980v				A1110101011		11.70		11.25	9.00		24			X		
			Imperf, Untagged\	A43335							24					
1011g			Untagged, Low Gloss Gum	22222, 33333, 44444		2.95		2.90	1.75		24			X		
				11111		65.00		60.00	60.00		24				X	
1011	WAG	(10¢) Eagle & Shield (1993)	Untagged, Shiny Gum	11111, 22221, 22222		3.00		2.90	1.75		24			X	X	
1011v			Imperf, Untagged, Shiny Gum	11111, 22221, 22222	15.00		150.00				24			X	X	
1011z			Tagged (Error) (Shiny Gum)	11111, 22221		12.50		12.00	12.00		24			X	X	
				22222							24			X		
1011zv			Imperf, Tagged (Error)	22221		310.00			300.00		24			X		
1012	WAG	(10¢) Eagle & Shield (1993)	Untagged, Lo-Gloss Gum	S11111		3.00		2.50	2.00		24					X
				S22222		3.00		2.50	2.00	7.00	24	10	Black 5T, 5B			X
1012s			Untagged, Shiny Gum	S22222		3.20		2.90	1.75	5.00	24	10	Purple 5T, 5TU,5B			X
										8.00	24	10	Pink 5T, 5B			X
1129	SA	(10¢) Eagle & Shield (1996)	Untagged	S11111		2.85		2.50	1.75	10.00	21	10	Pink 5B			X
										8.00	21	10	Pink 5TM			X
											21	10	Black 5B, Purple 5T			X
1204	WAG	(10¢) Eagle & Shield - 10,000 (1998)	Untagged, Presort Std., Small 1998 Date	11111		2.50		2.40	1.75		24			X		
			Untagged, Presort Std., Large 1998 Date	22222		2.50		2.40	1.75		24			X		
1205	SA	(10¢) Eagle & Shield (1998)	Untagged, Presort Std., Small 1998 Date	11111							21				X	
				22222		2.80		2.50	1.75	8.00	21	20	Green 4T, 4B		X	
1205v			Untagged, Presort Std., Large 1998 Date	33333						12.00	21	20	Green 4T		X	
1205v1			Tagged (Error), Presort Std., Small 1998 Date	11111		7.50		7.00	5.00	50.00	21	20	Green 4B		X	
										30.00	21	20	Green 4T		X	
1205a			Anaconda (Color Error), Presort Std., Small 1998 Date	11111						22.50	21	20	Green 4T		X	
										15.00	21	20	Green 4B		X	
954	WAG	10¢ Tractor Trailer (1991)	Untagged, Intaglio	1		2.10		2.00	1.50		48					X
954v	WAG		Imperf, Untagged, Intaglio	1	150.00		400.00				48			X		
1042	WAG	10¢ Tractor Trailer (1994)	Untagged, Gravure	11, 22		2.10		2.00	1.80		24			X		
1071	WAG	(10¢) Auto (1995)	Untagged	S111		2.50		2.00	1.75	5.00	14	10	Black 3TBM, 4T, 5TB	X	X	X
				S222		2.50		2.00	1.75	5.00	14	10	Purple 3TBD, 4TBM, 5TB	X	X	X
										8.00	14	10	Purple 4M		X	
				S333		2.50		2.00	1.75	NA	14	10	Black 5TB, Purple 3TB, 5TB		X	
										5.00	14	10	Black 5TB			X
										5.00	14	10	Pink 3TB, 3B-U, 4TB	X	X	
1132	SA	(10¢) Auto (1996)	Untagged, Presort Std.	S111y		2.50		2.00	1.75	6.00	21	10	Black 5M			X
										10.00	21	10	Black 5T			X
1176	SA	(10¢) Green Bicycle (1998)	Untagged, Small 1998 date	111, 221, 222, 333, 344, 444, 555		2.75		2.55	1.75	10.50	21	20	Green 4T, 4B	X	X	
1176a	SA		Untagged, Large 1998 date	666, 777, 888, 999		2.75		2.55	1.75	8.00	21	20	Green 4T, 4B	X	X	

Back# Positions legend: T=Top, M=Middle, B=Bottom, D=Double, U=Upside Down. Interval columns: Plate / Back. Roll Size columns: 10000, 3000, 5000, 100.

K/M #	WAG/SA	Denomination, Name, Date	Details	Plate #	Imperf Pair $	Strip 5	Imperf Strip 5	Strip 3	Used Sgl	Back# on Plate#	Int. Plate	Int. Back	Back# Positions	Roll 10000	Roll 3000	Roll 5000	Roll 100
1175	WAG	(10¢) Green Bicycle (1998)	Untagged, Presort Std.	S111		2.50		2.40	1.75	4.00	14	10	Pink 3TB, 4TB, 5TB	X	X	X	
										8.00	14	10	Pink 3M		X		
1262	SA	(10¢) Library Lion (2000)		S11111		4.00		2.50	0.50	15.00	14	10	Pink 5M		X	X	
				S11111, S22222						5.00	21	10	Pink 5M			X	X
			Untagged	S33333		4.00		2.50	0.50		21	10	Black 5M	X			
1394	WAG	(10¢) Library Lion (2003)	Untagged	S11111		2.25		2.00	1.50	5.00	21	10	Pink 5TB, Black 5TB	X	X		
										8.00	14	10	Pink 3M, 4M	X	X		
										4.00	14	10	Pink 3TB, 4TB	X	X		
1311	SA	(10¢) Atlas (2001)	Untagged	B1111, B1111 (Reverse Die Cut)		3.00		2.50	1.50	NA	21	10	Black 5TB	X	X		
837	WAG	10.1¢ Oil Wagon (1985)	Block Tag	1		2.50		2.40	2.00		52					X	
837zx			Precanceled - Black Overprint	1, 2		2.50		2.40	1.75		52				X	X	
837zxv	WAG		Imperf, Precanceled - Black Overprint	1	85.00		400.00				52				X	X
837zx1		10.1¢ Oil Wagon (1988)	Precanceled - Red Overprint	2, 3		2.25		2.15	2.00		52						
837zx1v			Imperf, Precanceled - Red Overprint	3	15.00		200.00				52						
788	WAG	10.9¢ Hansom Cab (1982)	Overall Tag, Joint Line	1, 2		29.00		15.00	12.00		24					X	
788zx			Precancel Bars	1, 2		29.00		20.00	8.75		24				X	X	
			Precancel Bars	3, 4		345.00		300.00	70.00		24				X	X	
788zxv			Imperf, Precancel Bars	1, 2	160.00						24				X	X
812	WAG	11¢ Caboose (1984)	Block Tag	1		3.85		3.65	3.00		52					X	
812zx			Untagged, Precancel Bars	1		3.20		3.10	2.75		52				X	X	
812zx1		11¢ Caboose (1991)	Untagged, No Precancel Bars	2		2.75		2.30	2.00		48				X		X
844	WAG	11¢ Stutz Bearcat (1985)	Overall Tag	1, 2, 3, 4		1.40		1.30	1.00		24				X	X	
831	WAG	12¢ Stanley Steamer (1985)	Overall Tag	1, 2		2.20		2.00	1.50		24				X	X	
831zx			Untagged, Precancel, Type I	1, 2		2.40		2.15	1.75		24				X	X	
831v			Untagged (Error), Type I	1,2							24						
831A	WAG	12¢ Stanley Steamer (1987)	Untagged, Precancel, Type II	1, 2		18.75		18.00	17.00		52				X	X	
838	WAG	12.5¢ Pushcart (1985)	Block Tag	1		3.00		2.50	2.25		52					X	
				2		4.60		4.60	3.00		52				X	X	
838zx	WAG		Untagged, Precancel, Lt. Olive	1		3.00		2.70	1.75		52				X	X	
				2		3.60		3.30	3.00		52				X	X	
838zx1			Untagged, Precancel, Dk Olive	1		3.00		2.70	1.75		52						
838zxv			Imperf, Untagged, Precancel	1	50.00		250.00				52				X	X	
914	WAG	13¢ Patrol Wagon (1988)	Untagged, Precancel	1		3.25		3.00	2.00		52				X	X	
900	WAG	13.2¢ Coal Car (1988)	Untagged, Precancel	1, 2		2.70		2.60	1.50		52				X	X	X
900v			Imperf	1, 2	100.00		275.00				52				X	X	
827	WAG	14¢ Iceboat (1985)	Overall Tag, Joint Line	1, 2, 3, 4		2.20		2.00	1.50		24				X	X	
827v			Imperf	1, 2	100.00		450.00				24				X	X	
827A	WAG	14¢ Iceboat (1986)	Block Tag	2		3.30		3.10	2.50		52				X	X	
899	WAG	15¢ Tugboat (1988)	Block Tag	1		2.00		1.80	1.25		52				X	X	
			Block Tag	2		2.50		2.25	1.50		52				X	X	
899z	WAG		Overall Tag	2		3.30		2.90	2.75		52				X	X	
899zo			Untagged (Error)	2		170.00					52				X	X	
899v			Imperf	1	750.00						52				X	X	
1072	WAG	(15¢) Tail Fin (1995)	Untagged	11111		2.90		2.75	2.00		24							X

K/M #	WAG/SA	Denomination, Name, Date	Details	Plate #	Imperf Pair $	Strip 5	Imperf Strip 5	Strip 3	Used Sgl	Back# on Plate#	Interval Plate#	Interval Back#	Back# Positions (T=Top M=Middle B=Bottom D=Double U=Upside Down)
1073	WAG	(15¢) Tail Fin (1995)	Untagged	S11111		2.80		2.65	1.75	6.50	14	10	Purple 5T, 5B
1133	SA	(15¢) Tail Fin (1996)	Untagged	S11111		2.85		2.65	1.75	10.00	21	10	Pink 5M
										8.00	21	10	Pink 5TB
											21	10	Black 5TBM
1312	SA	(15¢) Woody Wagon (2001)	Untagged	S11111		3.00		2.75	1.75	15.00	21	10	Pink 5M
										6.80	21	10	Pink 5T, 5B
898	WAG	16.7¢ Popcorn Wagon (1988)	Untagged	1		2.80		2.60	1.75		52		
				2		3.70		3.65	2.75		52		
898v			Imperf, Untagged	1	175.00						52		
771			Overall Tag, Joint Line	1, 2, 3, 4, 5		2.20		2.00	1.50		24		
				6		13.50		13.00	12.00		24		
				7		5.30		5.20	4.80		24		
771zx1	WAG	17¢ Electric Auto (1981)	Untagged, Precancel (Type A)	3, 4, 5		3.85		3.60	3.00		24		
				6, 7		11.50		11.00	9.00		24		
771zx2			Untagged, Precancel (Type B)	3		25.50		23.00	20.00		24		
				4		23.50		22.00	20.00		24		
				5,6		28.30		27.00	27.00		24		
771zx3			Untagged, Precancel (Type C)	1, 2, 3, 4		9.35		9.00	7.35		24		
				5		33.75		32.00	31.00		24		
				7		28.15		25.00	24.00		24		
771	WAG	17¢ Electric Auto (1981)	Untagged, Precancel (Type B-A combination)	5		69.00					24		
				6		75.00					24		
771v			Imperf, Overall Tag, Joint Line	1, 2, 3, 4	165.00		1,000.00				24		
771zv			Imperf, Untagged, Precancel	5, 7	575.00						24		
859	WAG	17¢ Dog Sled (1986)	Block Tag	2		3.10		2.90	1.50		52		
859v			Imperf, Block Tag	2	425.00						52		
880	WAG	17.5¢ Racing Car (1987)	Block Tag	1		3.00		2.90	2.50		52		
880zx			Untagged, Precancel	1		3.50		2.90	2.75		52		
880v			Imperf, Block Tag	1	2,250.00						52		
768	WAG	18¢ Surrey (1981)		2, 5, 6, 8, 13, 14		94.00		65.00	9.50		24		
				3, 4		3.00		2.75	1.00		24		
				7		82.50		62.00	9.25		24		
			Overall Tag, Joint Line	9, 10, 11, 12		32.00		32.00	9.50		24		
				15, 16		13.00		11.75	4.00		24		
				17, 18		23.00		19.00	18.00		24		
768v			Imperf, Overall Tag, Joint Line	2, 8, 9, 10, 13	125.00	3.00		3.60	3.60		24		
754	WAG	18¢ Flag (1981)	Block Tag	1		355.00		85.00	2.50		52		
				2		50.00		16.50	1.00		52		
				3		865.00		225.00	10.00		52		
				4		7.00		6.00	1.00		52		
754	WAG	18¢ Flag (1981)	Block Tag	5		4.75		4.00	1.00		52		
				6		29.75		1,450.00	575.00		52		
				7		175.00		27.50	25.00		52		
754v			Imperf, Block Tag	2, 3, 4	18.00	500.00					52		

Roll Size columns (10000 / 3000 / 5000 / 100): marked with X (and B in the 100-position column for rows 768, 880, 880v, 771 which show "X, B" / "B").

K/M #	WAG SA	Denomination, Name, Date	Details	Plate #	Imperf Pair $	Strip 5	Imperf Strip 5	Strip 3	Used Sgl	Back# on Plate#	Interval Plate #	Interval Back #	Back# Positions	Roll 100	Roll 500	Roll 3000	Roll 10000
852			Block Tag	1112		2.75		2.75	2.00		24					X	
				3333		4.25		3.90	3.25		24					X	X
852zx			Untagged, Precancel, Shiny Gum	11121		6.00		5.50	5.00		24					X	X
				33333		2.80		2.80	2.00		24					X	X
852zm	WAG	18¢ Washington (1985)	Untagged, Precancel, Dull Gum	33333		4.00		3.85	1.75		24					X	X
				43444		6.50		6.25	5.50		24					X	X
852v			Imperf, Block Tag	1112	975.00						24					X	
852zxo			Imperf, Untagged, Shiny Gum	33333	800.00						24						
852zo			Untagged (Error)	3333							24						
852zmo			Tagged (Error), Precancel, Dull Gum	33333		150.00			125.00		24					X	X
965	WAG	19¢ Fishing Boat (1991)	Tagged, Type I	A1111		3.10		3.00	2.25		36					X	
				A1112		6.15		6.00	5.00		36					X	X
				A2424		3.10		3.00	2.25		36					X	X
				A1212							36					X	
965a	WAG	19¢ Fishing Boat (1993)	Tagged, Type II	A5555, A5556, A7667, A7779		3.80		3.50	2.50		36					X	
				A6667, A7766							36					X	X
				A7679							36						X
965zo			Untagged (Error), Type I	A5555		7.40		7.25	5.00		36						X
965v	WAG	19¢ Fishing Boat (1991)	Imperf, Tagged, Type I	A1112, (from printers waste)	40.00						36						
965av	WAG	19¢ Fishing Boat (1993)	Imperf, Tagged, Type II	A7667	75.00		275.00				36					X	
1044	WAG	19¢ Fishing Boat (1994)	One loop of rope	S111		5.15		3.90	2.35		33					X	X
780	WAG	20¢ Flag Over Supreme Court (1981)	Wide Block Tag (B Press)	1		72.50		5.00	0.75		52			X			
				2		8.00		7.75	0.50		52		X, B	X			
				3		5.00		3.50	0.50		52		X, B	X			
				5		4.25		3.50	0.50		52		X, B	X			
				11		80.00		29.00	1.00		52			X			
				13					1.00		52		X, B	X			
				14		4.35		3.30	1.00		52			X	X		
780			Narrow Block Tag (C Press)	4		575.00		35.00	1.00		48		X	X			
				6		155.00		85.00	2.50		48		X	X			
				8		12.50		3.50	0.75		48		X	X			
				9		4.25		3.50	0.50		48		X	X			
				10		5.00		3.50	0.50		48		X	X			
				12		8.35		6.50	1.00		48		X	X			
780zo	WAG		Untagged (Error)	5							52			X			
				8, 9, 10							48			X			
780v2	WAG	20¢ Flag Over Supreme Court (1981)	Imperf	4, 11, 14		165.00					48, 52			X			
				8, 9, 10		325.00								X			
				2, 5		850.00								X			
				12	10.00	950.00								X			
				13		750.00					48, 52						
				11		1,250.00											
				6, 14		425.00											
				3, 4													
780zx	WAG	20¢ Flag Over Supreme Court (1984)	Untagged, Precancel	14		60.00		60.00	50.00		52					X	X

Back# Positions legend: T=Top, M=Middle, B=Bottom, D=Double, U=Upside Down

K/M #	WAG/SA	Denomination, Name, Date	Details	Plate #	Imperf Pair $	Strip5	Imperf Strip 5	Strip 3	Used Sgl	Back# on Plate#	Interval	Back# Positions	Roll Size 100	300	500	1000
777	WAG	20¢ Fire Pumper (1981)	Overall Tag, Joint Line	1		140.00		30.00	1.00		24			X	X	
				2		755.00		165.00	8.00		24			X	X	
				3, 4		4.30		3.85	0.65		24			X	X	
				5		2.75		2.00	0.75		24		X	X	X	
				6		34.50		33.00	1.20		24		X	X	X	
				7, 8		182.00		86.00	1.00		24		X	X	X	
				9, 10		2.75		2.00	0.75		24			X	X	
				11		80.00		29.00	1.00		24			X	X	
				12, 14		8.50		7.00	6.25							
				13, 15, 16		4.30		3.85	0.65		24			X	X	
777v			Imperf	1, 2, 3, 4, 5, 9, 10, 15, 16	1,000.00						24			X	X	
789	WAG	20¢ Consumer Education	Overall Tag, Joint Line	1, 2		157.00		25.00	1.50		24	X, B		X	X	
				3, 4		100.00		25.00	1.50		24	X, B		X	X	
789v			Imperf	1, 2, 3, 4	95.00						24					
789zo			Untagged, Joint Line	3, 4							24					
913	WAG	20¢ Cable Car (1988)	Block Tag	1, 2		3.40		3.20	1.50		48	B				X
913v			Imperf	2	75.00						48					
913z			Overall Tag	2		8.10		5.25	5.00		48					X
1086	WAG	20¢ Cog Railway (1995)	Tagged	1		4.10		3.85	2.25		48	B		X	X	
				2							48	B		X	X	
1086v				1							48					X
1136	SA	20¢ Blue Jay	Imperf, Tagged	S1111		3.15		3.00	2.00		14	B				X
1172	SA	20¢ Pheasant (1998)		1111, 2222		3.40		3.15	2.25		24	B		X	X	
1172v			Imperf	?							24					X
OF130	WAG	20¢ Official (1983)	Block Tag (B Press)	1		57.00		16.00	16.00		52	X, B				
OF130v			Imperf	1	2,000.00						52					
907	WAG	20.5¢ Fire Engine (1988)	Untagged	1		4.75		3.75	3.25		52			X	X	
902	WAG	21¢ Railroad Mail Car (1988)	Untagged	1, 2		3.50		3.40	2.50		52, 48			X	X	
902v			Untagged	1	65.00						52			X	X	
1301	SA	21¢ Bison (2001)	Imperf, Untagged	V1111, V2222		2.50		1.50	0.50		5	B				X
849	WAG	21.1¢ Letters (1985)	Block Tag	111111		3.20		2.80	2.50		24					X
849zx			Untagged, Precancel	111121		4.75		4.25	3.65		24					X
				111111		3.25		2.80	2.50		24			X	X	
				111121		4.70		4.25	3.75		24			X	X	
821	WAG	(22¢) D Eagle (1985)	Block Tag	1, 2		6.50		5.00	0.50		38	X, B		X	X	
821v			Imperf	1, 2							38					
821vzo			Imperf, Untagged	1, 2							38					
829	WAG	22¢ Flag Over Capitol (1985)	Block Tag (B Press)	4		5.90		5.00	0.55		52			X	X	
				6		6.50		6.50	6.50		52			X	X	
				13		12.50		10.50	9.00		52			X	X	
				14		28.00		24.00	27.00		52			X	X	
				15		3.25		3.00	0.60		52			X	X	

K/M #	WAG SA	Denomination, Name, Date	Details	Plate #	Imperf Pair $	Strip5	Imperf Strip 5	Strip 3	Used Sgl	Back# on Plate#	Interval Plate	Interval Back #	Back# Positions (T=Top, M=Middle, B=Bottom, D=Double, U=Upside Down)	Roll 100	Roll 3000	Roll 5000	Roll 100
829			Block Tag (B Press)	16, 21		6.00		5.00	2.25		52				X	X	
				2, 10		3.25		3.00	0.60		52		X	X			
			Block Tag (C Press)	1		12.25		10.00	0.55		48		X	X			
				3		49.00		10.50	0.50		48		X	X			
				5, 11		5.90		5.00	0.55		48		X	X			
			Block Tag (C or D Press)	7		12.25		10.00	0.55		48		X	X			
				8, 12, 19, 22		3.25		3.00	0.60		48		X	X			
				17, 18		6.00		5.00	2.25		48		X	X			
	WAG	22¢ Flag Over Capitol (1985)		1, 7, 10, 19, 22	15.00		450.00				48, 52						
				2, 8			175.00				48, 52						
				5, 18			665.00				48, 52						
				15, 20			925.00				48, 52						
829v			Imperf	3			1,000.00				48, 52						
				12			350.00				48, 52						
				17							48, 52						
				4, 6, 13	15.00		750.00				48, 52						
829zo			Untagged	1, 2, 3, 4 ((?))							48, 52		X				
876	WAG	22¢ Flag Over Capitol (Test) (1987)	Surface Phosphor Coated	T1		3.50		3.00	3.00		48		B		X		
1199	SA	22¢ Uncle Sam (1998)		1111		3.50		3.25	2.50		24		B				
1199v	WAG	22¢ Uncle Sam (1999)	Imperf	1111							24		B				
1233	WAG		Block Tag (B Press)	1111		3.25		3.25	2.50	8.00	24	20	Blue 4T, 4B	B		X	
OF132	WAG	(22¢) D - Official (1985)		1	150.00	6.50		5.00	0.50		52		B		X	X	
949			Prephos. Solid Tag	2, 3		3.75		3.00	2.00		48		B		X	X	
949v			Prephos. Solid Tag, Imperf	2, 3	150.00						48						
949pm	WAG	23¢ Lunch Wagon (1991)	Mottled Tag, Dull Gum	3		4.40		3.45	2.75		48		B				
949ps			Mottled Tag, Shiny Gum	4		5.00		4.75	2.75		48		B				
949pmv	WAG	23¢ Lunch Wagon (1991)	Imperf, Mottled Tag, Dull Gum	5		11.00		10.00	5.00		48				X		
969	WAG	23¢ Presort Flag (1991)	Untagged, Fat Red 2	A111, A112, A122, A212, A222, A333		3.40		3.00	2.00		24				X	X	
			Untagged, Thin Red 2	A222		3.90		3.30	2.25		24				X	X	
985	WAG	23¢ USA Presort (1992)	Untagged	A1111, A2222, A2232, A2233, A3333, A4364, A4443, A4444, A4453		3.95		3.40	2.50		24					X	
994		23¢ USA Presort (1992)	Untagged, Shiny Gum	1111		3.95		3.40	2.50		24				X	X	
994m			Untagged, Low Gloss Gum	1111		4.00		3.50	2.25		24				X		
994v	WAG		Imperf, Shiny Gum	1111	125.00		250.00				24				X	X	
994z			Tagged (Error)	1111		135.00			65.00		24				X		
1010	WAG	23¢ USA Presort (1993)	Untagged	S111		4.35		3.70	2.50		33		B		X	X	
1010v			Imperf	S111							33				X	X	
1318	SA	23¢ George Washington (2001) (BCA)	Green	B11		4.25		3.00	2.50		12		B				
1342	SA	23¢ George Washington (2002) (AVD)	Tagged	V11, V13, V21, V22, V24, V35, V36, V46		4.25		3.00	2.50		11		B				
912	WAG	24.1¢ Tandem Bicycle (1988)	Untagged	1		3.90		3.00	2.50		52				X	X	

Plate Numbered Prices

K/M #	WAG/SA	Denomination, Name, Date	Details	Plate #	Imperf Pair $	Strip5	Imperf Strip 5	Strip 3	Used Sgl	Back# on Plate#	Interval Plate	Interval Back#	Positions (T=Top M=Middle B=Bottom D=Double U=Upside Down)	Roll Size
866	WAG	25¢ Bread Wagon (1986)	Block Tag	1, 5		3.60		3.30	2.50		52		B	X X
				2, 3, 4		3.55		3.25	0.65		48		B	X X
866v			Imperf, Block Tag	1, 5	10.00						52			
				2, 3, 4			225.00				48			
885	WAG	(25¢) E Earth (1988)	Block Tag	1111, 1211		2.85		2.50	0.65		24		B	X X
				1222		4.15		3.80	1.25		24		B	X X X
				2222		4.50		4.50	3.50		24		B	X X X
885v	WAG		Imperf, Block Tag	1111	100.00						24		B	X
				1211, 1222, 2222			475.00				24			
891	WAG	25¢ Flag Over Yosemite (1988)	Block Tag	7		6.35		5.65	2.50		52		B	X X
				1							52			
				9		9.35		8.50	2.00		52		B	X X
				5							52			
				2		3.40		3.00	0.75		52		B	X X X
				3, 4, 8							52		B	X X X
891v	WAG	25¢ Flag Over Yosemite (1989)	Phosphored Tag	1		38.00		36.00	30.00		48			X X X
				2, 3		3.40		3.00	0.75		48		B	X X X
				7, 9, 10, 11, 13, 14		6.40		5.50	2.00		48		X	X X X
				8		11.25		10.50	5.65		48		B	X X
891v1		25¢ Flag Over Yosemite (1988)	Imperf, Block Tag	5, 8, 9			725.00				52			
				3			425.00				52			
				4	25.00		500.00				52			
				7			600.00				52			
				2			365.00				52			
891pzv	WAG		Imperf, Phosphored Tag	9, 10, 14			725.00				48			
				3, 5, 7, 8			175.00				48			
				2	10.00		900.00				48		B	
				13, 15			600.00				48		B	X X
				11							48		B	X X
891pzv			Untagged (Error)	2, 3, 5, 7, 8, 9, 10, 11, 13, 14, 15							48, 52		X	X
891pzv	WAG	25¢ Flag Over Yosemite (1988)	Untagged (Error)	2, 3, 8							48			X X
891a			Black Trees	4(?) 5, 6(?), 9, 15(?)							48, 52			X X
905	WAG	25¢ Honeybee (1988)	Block Tag, (Truncated Pl # 1)	1, 2		3.80		3.00	0.65		48		B	X
			Block Tag, (original "tall" # 1)	1							48		B	X
905v3			Imperf, Block Tag	1, 2	55.00		250.00				48			
1064	WAG	(25¢) G (1994)	Black G	S11111		4.55		3.95	2.50		33			X X
1074	WAG	(25¢) Juke Box (1995)	Untagged, WAG	111111, 212222, 332000		4.25		4.00	2.50		24		X	X X
				222222		4.75		4.20	3.00		24		X	X
1075	WAG	(25¢) Juke Box (1995)		S11111		3.75		3.50	2.25	NA	14	10	Black 5M	X
										7.75	14	10	Purple 5B	X
											14	10	Black 5TB, Purple 5T	X
				S22222						10.00	14	10	Pink 5TB	X

K/M #	WAG/SA	Denomination, Name, Date	Details	Plate #	Imperf Pair $	Strip5	Imperf Strip 5	Strip 3	Used Sgl	Back# on Plate#	Int. Plate	Int. Back	Back# Positions	Roll 1000	Roll 3000	Roll 5000	Roll 10000
1134	SA	(25¢) Juke Box (1996)	96 Black	S11111, S22222		3.85		3.55	2.00	10.50	21	10	Pink 5T				X
										9.50	21	10	Pink 5B		X		
1153	SA	(25¢) Juke Box (1997)	97 Blue	111111		4.25		3.55	2.00	18.00	21	10	Green 4TB				X
				222222							21	10	Green 4TB				X
1161	SA	(25¢) Juke Box (1997)	Linerless	M11111		4.85		3.00	2.50		7						X
1170	WAG	(25¢) Diner (1998)	Sm. Perfs	S11111		3.85		3.60	2.00	6.75	14	10	Pink 5TB				X
										NA	14	10	Pink 5M				X
			Large Perfs							6.75	14	10	Pink 5TB				X
1177	SA	(25¢) Diner (1998)		11111, 22211, 22222		4.00		3.65	2.00	19.00	21	20	Green 4TB				X
				33333, 44444, 55555						16.80	21	20	Green 4TB				X
1400-09	SA	(25¢) American Eagle	PNC strip of 11	S1111111, S2222222		8.75			3.50	9.00	20	10	Black, Pink 5M				X
										6.00	20	10	Black, Pink 5TB				X
1038	SA	29¢ Pine Cone (1993)	Roll Size 5000	B1		6.85		5.90	5.00		22			B		X	
940	WAG	29¢ F - Flower (1991)	Tagged	1111, 1222, 2222		3.60		3.25	0.75		24			B		X	X
				1211		18.50		17.75	14.00		24			B		X	X
				2211		4.85		4.25	3.00		24			B		X	X
940v	WAG	29¢ F - Flower (1991)	Imperf	1111, 1222, 2211, 2222	35.00		225.00				24			B			
945		29¢ Flag Over Mt. Rushmore (1991)		1, 3, 4, 7		4.20		3.85	0.50		48			B		X	X
				5, 6							48					X	X
			Phosphored Tag	2		6.00		5.35	2.00		48			B		X	X
				8		9.50		9.00	2.00		48			B			
				9							48			B			
945v	WAG		Imperf	1			450.00				48			B			
				2, 9	25.00		250.00							X			
				7			365.00							X			
				3, 4, 6													
945A		Toledo Brown	1		3,750.00		2,000.00	150.00		48					X	
				7		176.00		166.00	160.00		48					X	
945p		Solid Tag (Lenz paper)	2		550.00		300.00	150.00		48					X	
				6		195.00		187.00	145.00		48					X	
963	WAG	29¢ Flag Over Mt. Rushmore (1991)	Gravure	A11111, A22211		4.00		3.85	2.50		24						X
966	WAG	29¢ Flower (1991)	Rouletted	S1111, S2222		4.50		4.00	0.75		33			B			
982	WAG	29¢ Flower (1992)	Perfed	S2222		4.50		4.00	2.50		33				X		
1039	SA	29¢ Eagle (1994)	Roll Sixe 5004	111		6.85		5.90	3.75		18						
1043	SA	29¢ Statue of Liberty (1994)	Roll Size 5004	D1111		6.80		5.90	4.00		36						
984	WAG	29¢ Flag Over White House (1992)	Phosphored Tagging	1, 6, 7, 8							48			B		X	X
				3		4.50		4.30	0.75		48			B		X	
				4							48			B		X	X
				2							48			B		X	X
				5		4.50		4.30	2.25		48			B		X	
984			Phosphored Tagging	10, 11, 12, 13, 16, 18							48			B		X	X
				9		5.50		5.20	1.00		48			B		X	
				14, 15							48			B		X	X
984v	WAG	29¢ Flag Over White House (1992)	Imperf	1, 6, 7, 8, 10, 11, 12, 13	20.00						48			B		X	X
				2, 3, 4, 5, 9							48			B		X	X
1029-32	SA	29¢ Christmas Contemporary (1993)	Roll Size 3336	V1111111		5.90		3.75			24						

K/M #	WAG/SA	Denomination, Name, Date	Details	Plate #	Imperf Pair $	Strip 5	Imperf Strip 5	Strip 3	Used Sgl	Back# on Plate#	Interval Plate	Interval Back	Back# Positions	Positions	Roll Size
CM1616	SA	29¢ Sunrise Love (1994)	Roll Size 5004	B1		6.80		5.90	3.75		18					
1050	SA	29¢ Christmas Santa (1994)	Roll Size 3336	V1111		6.80		5.90	3.75		36					
1084	SA	32¢ Pink Rose (1995)	Roll Size 5000	S111		6.00		5.00	3.00		22					
1091A-92A	SA	32¢ Two Fruits (Peach/Pear) (1995)	Roll Size 5000	V11111		6.25		5.00	3.50		40					
1062	SA	(32¢) G (1994)	Roll Size 5004	V11111		5.50		5.00	3.25		36					
1059	WAG	(32¢) G (1994)	Black G	1111, 2222		11.35		9.00	6.00		24				B	
1059v		(32¢) G (1994)	Imperf, Black G	1111	300.00						24				B	
1060	WAG	(32¢) Blue G 1994	Tagged	A4435		222.00		220.00	210.00		24				B	
				A1222, A3426		6.50		6.00	4.50		24				B	
				A3423, A5437		8.30		5.00	4.50		24				B	
				A2223, A2313, A3315		10.40		6.00	5.95		24				B	
				A1417, A1433, A3114		9.50		8.00	6.75		24				B	
				A1113, A1314, A1222		5.75		4.30	4.00		24				B	
1060	WAG	(32¢) Blue G 1994	Tagged	A1311, A1313, A1324, A2213, A2214, A3113, A3314, A3315, A3323, A3324, A3423, A3433, A3435, A3436, A4426, A4427, A5327, A5427		4.50		4.30	3.25		24				B	
				A1211, A1212, A2211							24				B	
				A2212							24				B	X
				A5417							24				B	X X
				A1112							24				B	X X
				A1111							24				B	X X
1061	WAG	(32¢) G (1994)	Red G	S1111		5.00		4.65	1.00	22.00	33	10	Black, Purple 4TB	B	X X
1061A	WAG	(32¢) G (1994)	Red G, Rouletted	S1111, S2222		6.00		5.25	1.00	27.50	33	10	Purple 5TB	B	X
1085		32¢ Ferryboat (1995)	Tagged, Shiny Gum	5		10.75		10.00	2.75		33			B	X
				2, 3, 4		5.60		5.00	2.30		48			B	X
1085v			Imperf, Shiny Gum	2	275.00						48			B	X
1085gv	WAG		Imperf, Low Gloss Gum	3, 5	275.00						48			B	X
1085a			Tag, Shiny Gum (Bronx Blue)	5		120.00		118.00	115.00		48			B	X
1085gv			Phosphored Tag, Low Gloss Gum	4		15.00		13.00	2.50		48			B	X
			Gum	3, 5		6.25		5.00	2.50		48			B	X
1082	WAG	32¢ Flag Over Porch (1995)	Shiny Gum, Red 1995	11111, 22222		5.50		5.00	1.00		24			B	X X
				22221		5.25		5.00	3.50		24				X
				45444, 77767		5.25		5.00	1.00		24			B	
						5.00		5.00	1.75		24			B	
1082m	WAG	32¢ Flag Over Porch (1995)	Dull Gum, Red 1995	66646, 66666, 78767, 91161, 99969		5.00		4.75	2.50		24			B	
				22322		12.00		9.00	6.50		24			B	X X
				44444							24			B	X X
				33333		5.00		4.75	2.50		24			B	X X
				34333		5.00		5.00	1.75		24				X X

K/M #	WAG SA	Denomination, Name, Date	Details	Plate #	Imperf Pair $	Strip 5	Imperf Strip 5	Strip 3	Used Sgl	Back# on Plate#	Interval Plate	Interval Back	Back# Positions (T=Top M=Middle B=Bottom D=Double U=Upside Down)	Roll Size
1082v	WAG	32¢ Flag Over Porch (1995)	Imperf	11111, 22222, 45444,66646, 66666, 77767, 78767, 91161, 99969	35.00						24			B
1083	WAG	32¢ Flag Over Porch (1995)	Blue 1995	44444, 77767			350.00				24			
				S11111		4.55		4.00	2.50	NA	14	10	Pink 5TB, Black5D	X
1078	SA	32¢ Flag Over Porch (1995)	Blue 1995 Roll Size 5000	V11111		6.00		5.00	3.00	11.50	14	10	Black, Purple 5TB	X
1126	SA	32¢ Flag Over Porch (1996)	Self Adhesive, Red 1996. 10 x 10 die cuts with PV/VP die cuts. The following also have die 11 x 10; 66666, 78777, 87898, 88888, 89878, 89888, 97898, 99899, 99999 * = more than one die cut type. A* = has both PV/VP & VP/PV die cuts	11111, 22222, 23222, 33333, 44444, 45444, 55555, 66666, 88888*, 99999, 11111A, 12321A, 13311A, 22222A, 33333A, 44444A, 55555A, 66666A, 77777A, 78777A, 88888A		5.00		5.00	1.00		24			B
				78777		27.50		20.00	525.00		24			
				87888, 89888		15.00		15.00	4.75		24			
				87898				5.00	5.00		24			
				88898		300.00		295.00	225.00		24			
				89878		1,550.00		67.50	67.50		24			
				89898		8.00		7.00	3.00		24			
				89899		450.00		445.00	225.00		24			
				97898		7.00		6.50	3.50		24			
				99899		33.00		35.00	33.00		24			
				13211A		97.50		12.00	75.00		24			
1126v	SA	32¢ Flag Over Porch (1996)	Imperf S/A, Back #s, Red 1996	11111, 44444, 45444, 55555, 66666,78777	35.00						24			B
			Red 1996	99999, 11111A, 13231A, 22222A										
				88888	35.00		175.00							
1126v	SA	32¢ Flag Over Porch (1996)	Imperf S/A, Back #s, Red 1996	89898, 44444A, 55555A							24			
				23222A, 66666A, 88888A							24			
1128	SA	32¢ Flag Over Porch (1996)	Blue 1996	S11111		5.00		4.50	2.75	13.00	21	10	Black, Purple 5TB, Pink 5TBDM	X
1127	SA	32¢ Flag Over Porch (1996)	Red 1996 55555 & 66666 have 12x12 die cuts, 66666 also has 11x12 & 12x11	55555, 66666, 88888		14.00		12.00	3.75		24 24 24 24			B
1151	SA	32¢ Flag Over Porch (1997)	Red 1997	11111		5.50		5.00	3.25	20.00	21	20	Green 4TB	X
1162	SA	32¢ Flag Over Porch (1997)	Linerless	M11111		6.00		5.50	3.25		7			B
1102-05	SA	32¢ Child Holding Tree (1995)	Strip of 8 ($9.00) Roll Size 5000	V1111		5.00		3.00	3.00		20			
1110A	SA	32¢ Midnight Angel (1995)	Roll Size 5000	B1111		6.25		3.00	3.00		20			

K/M #	WAG SA	Denomination, Name, Date	Details	Plate #	Imperf Pair $	Strip 5	Imperf Strip 5	Strip 3	Used Sgl	Back# on Plate#	Interval Plate	Interval Back	Back# Positions (T=Top M=Middle B=Bottom D=Double U=Upside Down)	B	Roll 100	Roll 3000	Roll 5000	Roll 10000
1163				2233, 3444, 6677, 6777		6.85		6.00	3.75		24			B				
1163	SA	32¢ Yellow Rose		1111, 1112, 1122, 2222, 2223, 2333, 3344, 4455, 5455, 5555, 5556, 5566, 5666, 6666, 7777, 8888		5.35		5.00	2.50		24			B				
1163v			Imperf	1112, 1122, 2223, 4455	90.00													
1163v	SA		Imperf	5555, 5556, 5566, 5666, 6666, 7777	90.00		750.00				24			B				
1194	WAG	(33¢) H - Uncle Sam's Hat (1998)		1111, 3333, 3343, 3444		5.00		4.50	2.50		24			B				
				3344		10.75		10.50	7.00		24			B				
				1111		5.00		4.50	2.50		24			B				X
1197	SA	(33¢) H - Uncle Sam's Hat (1998)		1111, 1131, 2222, 3333		5.20		5.00	2.00		24			B				
			Controversial # but certified	1141							24			B				
1197v	SA	(33¢) H - Uncle Sam's Hat (1998)	Imperf	1111, 1131, 2222, 3333	95.00						24			B				
1197a	SA	(33¢) H - Uncle Sam's Hat (1998)	Small "1999" year, No back #	1111		5.00		4.50	3.50	19.00	21	20	Green 4TB					X
				2222							24			B				
1207	WAG	33¢ City Flag (1999)	Small "1999" year	1111		5.00		4.50	2.60	105.00	24	20	Pink 4TB, 5TB & Blue 4TB			X		X
											24	20	Pink 4M					X
				2222							24	20	Blue 4M			X		X
1207v		33¢ City Flag (1999)	Large "1999" year	3333						10.50	24	20	Blue 4TB			X		X
										NA	24	20	Blue 4TBM			X		X
1208v	SA	33¢ City Flag (1999)	Large Date	6666, 7777, 8888, 9999, 1111A, 2222A, 3333A, 4444A, 5555A, 6666A, 7777A, 8888A, 1111B, 2222B		5.00		4.50	2.00		24			B				
1208	SA	33¢ City Flag (1999)	Small Date	1111, 2222, 3333, 3433, 4443, 4444, 5555, 9999A		5.00		4.50			24			B				
1209	SA	33¢ City Flag (1999)	Gap between stamps	1111, 2222		5.00		4.50	1.50	19.00	21	20	Green 4TB					X
1222-25	SA	33¢ Blackberry (1999)	Strip of 9 ($6.60)	B1111, B1112, B2211, B2221, B2222		5.00			1.50		12			B				
1256-59	SA	33¢ Blackberry (2000)	Linerless	G1111		5.00			1.50		12			B				
1267	WAG	(34¢) Statue of Liberty (2000)		1111		5.00		4.50	2.50		20	20	Blue 4TB					X
1268	SA	(34¢) Statue of Liberty (2000)	Small Date	1111		5.00		4.00	3.00		24			B				
1268	SA	(34¢) Statue of Liberty (2000)	Large Date			6.25		5.25	3.25		24							
1270-73	SA	(34¢) Cymbidium Orchid (2000)	Strip of 9 ($6.50)	B1111		4.50		4.00	2.50		12			B				
1282	SA	34¢ Statue of Liberty (2001)		1111		5.00		4.00	2.50	17.00	21	20	Green 4TB			X		X
	SA			2222							21	20				X		X

K/M #	WAG SA	Denomination, Name, Date	Details	Plate #	Imperf Pair $	Strip 5	Imperf Strip 5	Strip 3	Used Sgl	Back# on Plate#	Interval Plate#	Interval Back#	Back# Positions (T=Top, B=Bottom, M=Middle, D=Double, U=Upside Down)	Roll Size
1294	WAG	(34¢) Statue of Liberty (2001)		1111		5.00		4.00	2.50	10.50	24	20	Blue 4TB	X X
1295	SA	34¢ Statue of Liberty (2001)		1111, 2222, 3333, 4444, 5555, 6666, 7777		4.50		4.00	2.50		24			B
1286-89	SA	34¢ Cymbidium Orchid (2001)		B1111, B2111, B2122, B2211, B2222		4.50		4.00	2.00		12			B (X)
1333	SA	34¢ United We Stand (2001)		1111, 2222, 3333		4.50		4.00	2.00		24			B
1334	SA	34¢ United We Stand (2001)		1111		4.50		4.00	2.00	17.00	21	20	Green 4TB	B
1347	SA	34¢ United We Stand (2001)		1111, 2222		5.50		4.50	2.50		24			B
1347v	SA	(37¢) US Flag (2002)	Imperf	1111	50.00		1,000.00				12			B
1356	WAG	37¢ US Flag (2002)	Back #s on 3K&10K only	S1111		5.50		4.50	2.50	12.00	20	10	Pink 4M	X
										10.50	20	10	Pink 4TBD, 5TB	X X
1359	SA	37¢ US Flag (2002)	PSA	1111, 2222, 3333, 4444, 5555, 6666, 7777, 8888		5.50		4.50	2.50		24			B (X X)
1354	SA	37¢ US Flag (2002)	PSA, Back #s on 10k only	B1111		5.50		4.50	2.50	NA	20	10	Black 4TB, 5TB	B
1367-69	SA	37¢ Antique Toys (2002)	PSA Strip of 9 ($8.28)	B11111, B12222				3.50			12			B
1388-91	SA	37¢ Snowmen (2002)	PSA, Linerless	G1111		8.25		4.50	2.00		12			B
				G1112							12			B
1397A	SA	37¢ US Flag (2003)		B1111		5.50		4.50	2.50		12			B
1411	SA	37¢ US Flag (2003)		S1111		5.50		4.50	2.50		14			B
				S111		8.00		6.00	3.00		14			B
OF154	WAG	37¢ Official (2002)	Overall Tag, Dull Gum	1		9.00		7.50	3.00		52			X
928	WAG	$1 Seaplane (1990)	Imperf, Overall Tag, Dull Gum	1	2,750.00						52			X
928v	WAG	$1 Seaplane (1993)	Mottled Tag, Shiny Gum	3		9.00		7.50	3.00		48			X
928pz	WAG	$1 Seaplane (1993)	Solid Tag, Shiny Gum	3		9.00		7.50	3.00		48			X
986	WAG	(Variable Denomination) (1992)	Solid Tag, Dull Gum	1		8.60		8.00	5.75		48			X
986pz	WAG	(Variable Denomination)	Mottled Tag, Shiny Gum, Type I	1		8.60		8.00	5.75		48			X
1053pz	WAG	(Variable Denomination) (1994)	Solid Tag, Low Gloss Gum, Type II	1		15.00		13.00	7.50		48			X
1053	WAG	(Variable Denomination) (1994)	Mottled Tag, Shiny Gum, Type II	1		14.00		12.00	7.00		48			X
1040	WAG	(Variable Denomination) (1994)	Solid Tag, Low Gloss Gum	A11		8.50		7.40	6.00		24			X
1117	WAG	(Variable Denomination) (1996)	Mottled Tag, 1996 Date	11		8.50		7.40	6.00		24			X
TT101	SA	White FTPO (1996)	Black Print, Die Cut 9 3/4	V1		15.00		15.00		30.00	15	20	Black 4T	X
TT103	SA	Blue FTPO (1996)	Black Print, Straight Die Cut	1111		15.00		15.00		20.00	21	20	Black 4B	X
T107	SA	Eagle (Linerless)	Imperf (Simulated Perfs)	1111		750.00		750.00			27			X
T116	SA	Blue FTPO (2001)	Black Print, Die Cut 9 3/4	1111		10.00		10.00		35.00	21	20	Black 4B	X

U.S. Government Commemorative Issues

1893. COLUMBIAN ISSUES released in connection with the World's Columbian Exposition held in Chicago, Ill., commemorated the 400th anniversary of the first voyage to America by Christopher Columbus. They are considered to be the first true commemoratives. All the stamps except the 8¢ were issued Jan. 2. The 8¢ value, not originally planned with the others, appeared on March 3, 1893, to meet a new, lower registry rate. It was the first 8¢ stamp in U.S. history.

Christoforo Colombo was born in Genoa, Italy, ca. 1451. He went to sea at an early age and settled in Portugal. His wife was Felipa Perestrello, daughter of a distinguished navigator who left many charts that Columbus studied with care. He conceived the idea of reaching Asia by sailing due west and vainly sought support in Portugal, Spain, Italy and England for such an expedition.

In 1491, Columbus (CM15, CM16) was on his way to France when he paused to stay with old friends at the monastery of La Rabida (CM10) in Spain. Juan Perez, former confessor to Queen Isabella, obtained for him an audience with the queen, who listened to his theories (CM5) and brought him before King Ferdinand.

Columbus was turned down by the sovereigns, whose treasury had been depleted by war with the Moors. Setting out overland for France, he had gone only six miles when a royal courier overtook him (CM11) to summon him back to court. Isabella (CM15) had decided to raise the needed money, tradition says, by pledging her jewels (CM12). An agreement was signed giving Columbus three caravels: the *Santa Maria* (CM3), a 100-ton ship with a crew of 52; the 50-ton *Pinta*; and the 40-ton *Niña*. The latter two each had a crew of 18. The little fleet sailed from Palos on Aug. 2, 1492 (CM4).

After rebellious outbursts among the crews, on the night of Oct. 11, 1492, Columbus thought he saw a light. The next morning Rodrigo de Triana sighted land (CM1): Guanahani, now believed to be Watling's Island in the Bahamas. Naming the place San Salvador (Holy Savior), Columbus kissed the soil and gave thanks to God (CM2).

Excited by the native tales of gold, the fleet sailed south, finding Cuba on Oct. 28 and Hispaniola on Dec. 6. Leaving a colony of 40 men to build a fort at Hispaniola, where the *Santa Maria* had run aground, Columbus returned to Spain. At court, in Barcelona, he was given a great welcome (CM6), reported his discoveries (CM9) and displayed the natives he brought back with him (CM8).

Columbus sailed again Sept. 25, 1493, with 3 galleons, 14 caravels, and 1,500 men. He reached Dominica, Guadaloupe, and Puerto Rico, found his Haitian colony destroyed by natives, and returned to Spain in March with 225 men and 30 natives.

Charged by enemies in court with mistreating the natives, he successfully defended himself, but his third voyage was delayed until May 1498. Given six vessels, he sent three to Hispaniola and took the others south to explore.

Returning to Hispaniola, he was put in chains (CM13) by Francisco de Bobadilla, sent from Spain to investigate new rumors of mistreatment of natives. Stripped of his honors and returned to Spain, he was released by the queen (CM7). Telling of the discoveries of his third expedition (CM14), he obtained four vessels and set out again in May 1502, discovering Honduras and Panama. The queen's death after his return in 1504 marked the end of his fortunes. He died at Valladolid in 1504, convinced that he had discovered the coast of Asia.

Intaglio by the American Bank Note Company, the last U.S. stamps of the 19th century produced by a private printer, unwatermarked paper, perforated 12.

CM1 *Columbus in Sight of Land, from a painting by William H. Powell*

CM1

1¢		UnFVF	UseFVF
deep blue *(449,195,550)*		20.00	.35
pale blue		20.00	.35
Plate strip of 3, w/imprint		85.00	
Plate strip of 4, w/imprint & letter		100.00	
Plate block of 6, w/imprint		325.00	
Plate block of 8, w/imprint & letter		500.00	
Double transfer		25.00	1.00
Cracked plate		90.00	5.00
On cover			.75
FDC *(Jan. 2, 1893)*			8,000.00

CM2 *Columbus Landing on Guanahani, from a painting by Vanderlyn in the Rotunda of the Capitol in Washington, D.C.*

CM2v *The Broken Hat variety is found in the hat of the knight to the left of Columbus.*

CM2

2¢		UnFVF	UseFVF
dull purple *(1,464,588,750)*		20.00	.20
brown violet		20.00	.20
gray violet		20.00	.20
Plate strip of 3, w/imprint		75.00	
Plate strip of 4, w/imprint & letter		110.00	
Plate block of 6, w/imprint		235.00	
Plate block of 8, w/imprint & letter		475.00	
Double transfer		25.00	.30

	UnFVF	UseFVF
Triple transfer	65.00	
Quadruple transfer	90.00	
v. Broken Hat variety	65.00	.50
v1. Broken frame line	25.00	.30
Recut frame lines	25.00	.30
Cracked plate	90.00	
On cover		.50
FDC *(Jan. 2, 1893)*; EKU *(Jan. 1, 1893)*		5,000.00

Imperforate 2¢ Columbians are from printer's waste.

CM3 *Columbus' flagship,* Santa Maria, *from a Spanish engraving*

CM3

3¢		UnFVF	UseFVF
deep bluish green *(11,501,250)*		60.00	15.00
dull green		60.00	15.00
Plate strip of 3, w/imprint		240.00	
Plate strip of 4, w/imprint & letter		300.00	
Plate block of 6, w/imprint		725.00	
Plate block of 8, w/imprint & letter		1,200.00	
Double transfer		75.00	
On cover			35.00
FDC *(Jan. 2, 1893)*			15,000.00

CM4 Santa Maria, Pinta *and* Niña, *from a Spanish engraving*

CM4

4¢		UnFVF	UseFVF
gray blue *(19,181,550)*		85.00	7.50
dull ultramarine		85.00	
Plate strip of 3, w/imprint		330.00	
Plate strip of 4, w/imprint & letter		440.00	
Plate block of 6, w/imprint		1,100.00	
Plate block of 8, w/imprint & letter		2,200.00	
Double transfer		125.00	25.00

DECODING THE CATALOG

Although the 2¢ Columbian issue of 1893 is not particularly complicated, there are three main types that every collector should know, as they are widely collected minor varieties listed in most catalogs. These are the normal, Broken Hat and broken frame line varieties. There are many types of the latter two varieties, but most of them are visually similar.

"Broken Hat" Variety

Broken frame line (lower right) variety

Recutting

The 2¢ Columbian (Minkus CM2) is part of what is generally considered to be the first United States commemorative set. The set was produced by the American Bank Note Co. and marked the last stamps of the 19th century produced by a private printer.

A group of 15 stamps, with denominations ranging from 1¢ to $5, was placed on sale Jan. 2, 1893. The 8¢ value, not originally planned as part of the set, was released March 3, 1893, to meet the new registry rate. Of all stamps produced until that time, the 2¢ Columbian had the largest printing. A total of about 1.5 billion stamps were produced, leading to a wealth of varieties for the specialized collector.

The first variety of the 2¢ Columbian is the so-called normal type, which is the most common form of this stamp. This simply means there are no noticeable major varieties.

The second is the famous "Broken Hat" variety, shown in the illustration at left. Note the notched hat on the third figure to the left of Columbus. This variety, one of the best known in all U.S. collecting, has frequently been erroneously referred to as a plate variety. It is not. The Broken Hat variety was caused by a flaw on one or more of the transfer rolls used to create the printing plate.

The third variety, also caused by a relief break on a transfer roll, is known as the broken frame line variety. An example of that stamp is shown at left center. When the image on the transfer roll (a relief) is rocked into the printing plate (a depressed image), bits of the metal can break off the roll, leaving no impression on the steel of the printing plate. The resulting unprinted area is called a relief break. It will appear on every stamp produced from any image on the printing plate created from that transfer roll.

This is different from plate varieties in that several stamps from a pane may exhibit the same transfer roll variety, whereas only a single stamp will show a plate variety. For example, a plate crack must always appear on the same stamp from the same position of the same plate. A relief break may affect several positions on several different printing plates until the use of a particular transfer roll is discontinued.

In the case of the Broken Hat and broken frame line varieties, there are different stages and different breaks, all of which are classified the same but have slightly different appearances.

Although of less consequence to the average collector, the illustration on the canceled stamp at lower left illustrates yet another type of variety that frequently occurs on stamps with long printing histories: recut designs. Recutting is usually done to solidify fading details and to gain extra life from a worn-out printing plate.

If you take a look at the figures in the enlargements, you'll note that the men each look different from one stamp to another. This is because portions of the design and shading have been recut (more than likely directly on the printing plate), resulting in altered appearances. These, too, are collectible.

	UnFVF	UseFVF
On cover		22.50
FDC *(Jan. 2, 1893)*		15,000.00
v. blue (error)	19,000.00	15,000.00
Plate strip of 4, w/imprint & letter	140,000.00	

CM5 *Columbus Soliciting Aid of Isabella, from a painting by Brozik in the Metropolitan Museum of Art, New York*

CM5
5¢

	UnFVF	UseFVF
brown *(35,248,250)*	95.00	8.00
pale brown	95.00	8.00
yellow brown	95.00	8.00
Plate strip of 3, w/imprint	375.00	
Plate strip of 4, w/imprint & letter	525.00	
Plate block of 6, w/imprint	1,400.00	
Plate block of 8, w/imprint & letter	2,750.00	
Double transfer	145.00	25.00
On cover		25.00
FDC *(Jan. 2, 1893)*		20,000.00

CM6 *Columbus Welcomed at Barcelona, from a panel by Randolph Rogers in the bronze doors of the Capitol, Washington, D.C.*

CM6
6¢

	UnFVF	UseFVF
dark lilac *(4,707,550)*	85.00	22.50
dull purple	85.00	22.50
Plate strip of 3, w/imprint	325.00	
Plate strip of 4, w/imprint & letter	425.00	
Plate block of 6, w/imprint	1,175.00	
Plate block of 8, w/imprint & letter	2,150.00	
Double transfer	125.00	30.00
On cover		50.00
FDC *(Jan. 2, 1893)*		22,500.00
a. red violet	85.00	22.50

CM7 *Columbus Restored to Favor, from a painting by Francesco Jover*

CM7
8¢

	UnFVF	UseFVF
brown purple *(10,656,550)*	75.00	11.00
pale brown purple	75.00	11.00
Plate strip of 3, w/imprint	290.00	
Plate strip of 4, w/imprint & letter	400.00	
Plate block of 6, w/imprint	825.00	
Plate block of 8, w/imprint & letter	1,450.00	
Double transfer	85.00	
On cover		25.00
Earliest known use *(March 3, 1893)*		

CM8 *Columbus Presenting Natives, from a painting by Luigi Gregori at the University of Notre Dame, South Bend, Ind.*

CM8
10¢

	UnFVF	UseFVF
black brown *(16,516,950)*	140.00	8.00
a. dark brown	140.00	8.00
gray black	140.00	8.00
Plate strip of 3, w/imprint	575.00	
Plate strip of 4, w/imprint & letter	700.00	
Plate block of 6, w/imprint	3,350.00	
Plate block of 8, w/imprint & letter	4,900.00	
Double transfer	180.00	12.00

	UnFVF	UseFVF
Triple transfer	—	
On cover		35.00
FDC *(Jan. 2, 1893)*		25,000.00

CM9 *Columbus Announcing His Discovery, from a painting by R. Baloca in Madrid, Spain*

CM9
15¢

	UnFVF	UseFVF
deep bluish green *(1,576,950)*	240.00	65.00
a. dull green	240.00	65.00
Plate strip of 3, w/imprint	950.00	
Plate strip of 4, w/imprint & letter	1,200.00	
Plate block of 6, w/imprint	4,000.00	
Plate block of 8, w/imprint & letter	6,500.00	
Double transfer	—	
On cover		250.00
Earliest known use *(Jan. 26, 1893)*		

CM10 *Columbus at La Rabida, from a painting by R. Maso*

CM10
30¢

	UnFVF	UseFVF
orange brown *(617,250)*	300.00	85.00
bright orange brown	300.00	85.00
Plate strip of 3, w/imprint	1,250.00	
Plate strip of 4, w/imprint & letter	1,600.00	
Plate block of 6, w/imprint	8,500.00	
Plate block of 8, w/imprint & letter	11,500.00	
On cover		400.00
Earliest known use *(Feb. 8, 1893)*		

CM11 *Recall of Columbus, from a painting by Augustus G. Heaton in the Capitol, Washington, D.C.*

CM11
50¢

	UnFVF	UseFVF
slate black *(243,750)*	600.00	160.00
dull slate black	600.00	160.00
Plate strip of 3, w/imprint	2,500.00	
Plate strip of 4, w/imprint & letter	3,750.00	
Plate block of 6, w/imprint	14,000.00	
Plate block of 8, w/imprint & letter	22,500.00	
Double transfer	—	
Triple transfer	—	
On cover		650.00
Earliest known use *(Feb. 8, 1893)*		

CM12 *Isabella pledging her jewels, from a painting by Muñoz Degrain in the Hall of Legislature in Madrid, Spain*

CM12
$1

	UnFVF	UseFVF
Venetian red *(55,050)*	1,400.00	650.00
pale Venetian red	1,400.00	650.00
Plate strip of 3, w/imprint	5,600.00	
Plate strip of 4, w/imprint & letter	7,250.00	
Plate block of 6, w/imprint	47,500.00	
Plate block of 8, w/imprint & letter	80,000.00	
Double transfer	—	
On cover		2,000.00
Earliest known use *(Jan. 21, 1893)*		

CM13 *Columbus In Chains, from a painting by K. Leutze, Germantown, Pa. It was the first dollar-value U.S. stamp.*

CM13 $2		UnFVF	UseFVF
	brown red *(45,550)*	1,450.00	600.00
	dark brown red	1,450.00	600.00
	Plate strip of 3, w/imprint	6,000.00	
	Plate strip of 4, w/imprint & letter	9,500.00	
	Plate block of 6, w/imprint	67,500.00	
	Plate block of 8, w/imprint & letter	85,000.00	
	On cover		2,100.00
	FDC *(Jan. 2, 1893)*		65,000.00

CM14 *Columbus Describing His Third Voyage, from a painting by Francesco Jover*

CM14 $3		UnFVF	UseFVF
	bronze green *(27,650)*	2,250.00	1,000.00
	pale bronze green	2,250.00	1,000.00
	Plate strip of 3, w/imprint	9,250.00	
	Plate strip of 4, w/imprint & letter	12,500.00	
	Plate block of 6, w/imprint	85,000.00	
	Plate block of 8, w/imprint & letter	110,000.00	
	On cover		2,600.00
	a. olive green	2,250.00	1,000.00
	Earliest known use *(April 4, 1893)*		

CM15 *Queen Isabella and Columbus, Isabella from a painting in Madrid, Columbus by Lotto*

CM15 $4		UnFVF	UseFVF
	deep rose *(26,350)*	3,000.00	1,350.00
	pale analine rose	3,000.00	1,350.00
	Plate strip of 3, w/imprint	11,500.00	
	Plate strip of 4, w/imprint & letter	17,000.00	
	Plate block of 6, w/imprint	250,000.00	
	Plate block of 8, w/imprint & letter	310,000.00	
	On cover		4,000.00
	a. rose carmine	3,000.00	1,350.00
	Earliest known use *(Jan. 6, 1893)*		

CM16 *Profile of Columbus, from the sculpture of the commemorative half dollar*

CM16 $5		UnFVF	UseFVF
	black *(27,350)*	3,500.00	1,600.00
	gray black	3,500.00	1,600.00
	Plate strip of 3, w/imprint	15,000.00	
	Plate strip of 4, w/imprint & letter	25,000.00	
	Plate block of 6, w/imprint	190,000.00	
	Plate block of 8, w/imprint & letter	250,000.00	
	On cover		4,750.00
	Earliest known use *(Jan. 6, 1893)*		

For stamps of these designs, but with "1992" instead of "1893" in the top-right corner, see Nos. CM1456-61.

1898. TRANS-MISSISSIPPI ISSUE was released for the Trans-Mississippi Exposition held at Omaha, Neb., commemorating the settling of the Middle West.

All denominations issued June 17. *Printed in intaglio, Bureau of Engraving and Printing, Washington, D.C., on paper with double-line "USPS" watermark.*

CM17 *Marquette Exploring the Mississippi, from a painting by Lamprecht. (The scene is actually on the Wisconsin River.) French Jesuit Jacques Marquette founded a mission, and in 1673 explored the Mississippi with Louis Jolliet.*

CM17 1¢		UnFVF	UseFVF
	green *(70,993,400)*	30.00	6.25
	dark yellow green	30.00	6.25
	yellow green	30.00	6.25
	Plate pair, w/imprint	70.00	
	Plate strip of 3, w/imprint	110.00	
	Plate block of 4, w/imprint	225.00	
	Plate block of 6, w/imprint	300.00	
	Margin block of 4, w/arrow	125.00	
	Double transfer	40.00	7.50
	On cover		10.00
	FDC *(June 17, 1898)*		14,500.00

CM18 *Farming in the West, from a photograph, was the first U.S. stamp to portray people still alive: Evan Nybakken (foreground, partially obscured by his arm) and Arthur John De Lance (facing front with wide-brimmed hat and holding dog).*

CM18 2¢		UnFVF	UseFVF
	brown red *(159,720,800)*	27.50	1.60
	pale brown red	27.50	1.60
	Plate pair, w/imprint	67.00	
	Plate strip of 3, w/imprint	110.00	
	Plate block of 4, w/imprint	190.00	
	Plate block of 6, w/imprint	275.00	
	Margin block of 4, w/arrow	125.00	
	Double transfer	42.00	2.50
	Worn plate	30.00	2.00
	On cover		2.50
	FDC *(June 17, 1898)*		12,000.00
	Earliest known use *(June 16, 1898)*		

CM19 *Indian Hunting Buffalo, from an engraving in Schoolcraft's* History of the Indian Tribes

CM19 4¢		UnFVF	UseFVF
	orange red *(94,924,500)*	150.00	24.00
	orange	150.00	24.00
	Plate pair, w/imprint	350.00	
	Plate strip of 3, w/imprint	600.00	20.00
	Plate block of 4, w/imprint	900.00	
	Plate block of 6, w/imprint	1,500.00	
	Margin block of 4, w/arrow	675.00	
	On cover		58.00
	FDC *(June 17, 1898)*		20,000.00

CM20 *Fremont on Rocky Mountains, from old wood engraving. John Charles Fremont mapped the Oregon Trail in 1842 and later surveyed railway routes in the Southwest.*

CM20 5¢		UnFVF	UseFVF
	deep blue *(7,694,180)*	140.00	21.00
	bright blue	140.00	21.00
	dull blue	140.00	21.00
	Plate pair, w/imprint	325.00	

Plate strip of 3, w/imprint	475.00
Plate block of 4, w/imprint	825.00
Plate block of 6, w/imprint	1,300.00
Margin block of 4, w/arrow	675.00
On cover	50.00
FDC (June 17, 1898)	20,000.00

CM21 *Troops Guarding Train, from a drawing by Frederic Remington*

CM21
8¢

	UnFVF	UseFVF
chocolate (2,927,200)	180.00	42.50
violet brown	180.00	42.50
Plate pair, w/imprint	390.00	
Plate strip of 3, w/imprint	725.00	
Plate block of 4, w/imprint	1,800.00	
Plate block of 6, w/imprint	2,750.00	
Margin block of 4, w/arrow	800.00	
On cover		115.00
FDC (June 17, 1898)		25,000.00
v. Vertical pair, imperforate horizontally between	22,000.00	
v1. Plate block of 4, w/imprint	75,000.00	

CM22 *Hardships of Emigration, from a painting by A.G. Heaton*

CM22
10¢

	UnFVF	UseFVF
violet black (4,629,760)	180.00	27.50
gray violet	180.00	27.50
Plate pair, w/imprint	425.00	
Plate strip of 3, w/imprint	650.00	
Plate block of 4, w/imprint	1,900.00	
Plate block of 6, w/imprint	3,000.00	
Margin block of 4, w/arrow	800.00	
On cover		90.00
FDC (June 17, 1898)		30,000.00

CM23 *Western Mining Prospector, from a drawing by Frederic Remington*

CM23
50¢

	UnFVF	UseFVF
bronze green (530,400)	650.00	190.00
dark bronze green	650.00	190.00
Plate pair, w/imprint	1,800.00	
Plate strip of 3, w/imprint	2,600.00	
Plate block of 4, w/imprint	13,000.00	
Plate block of 6, w/imprint	25,000.00	
Margin block of 4, w/arrow	3,250.00	
On cover		1,750.00
FDC (June 17, 1898)		35,000.00

CM24 *Western Cattle in a Storm, based on a painting,* The Vanguard, *by John A. MacWhirter of cattle in the Scottish highlands during a snowstorm*

CM24
$1

	UnFVF	UseFVF
black (56,900)	1,250.00	550.00
Plate pair, w/imprint	3,000.00	
Plate strip of 3, w/imprint	5,500.00	
Plate block of 4, w/imprint	35,000.00	
Plate block of 6, w/imprint	50,000.00	
Margin block of 4, w/arrow	6,000.00	

On cover	1,750.00
FDC (June 17, 1898)	60,000.00

CM25 *Mississippi River Bridge at St. Louis, Mo., from a photograph*

CM25
$2

	UnFVF	UseFVF
red brown (56,200)	2,100.00	1,000.00
dark red brown	2,100.00	1,000.00
Plate pair, w/imprint	5,000.00	
Plate strip of 3, w/imprint	8,500.00	
Plate block of 4, w/imprint	80,000.00	
Plate block of 6, w/imprint	150,000.00	
Margin block of 4, w/arrow	9,500.00	
On cover		12,500.00
FDC (June 17, 1898); EKU (June 24, 1898)		—

For bicolor versions of the Trans-Mississippi Issue, see Nos. CM1985 and CM1986.

1901. PAN-AMERICAN ISSUE commemorated the Pan-American Exposition at Buffalo, N.Y., promoting friendly relations among the countries of the New World. The stamps illustrating engineering achievements of the age were printed in two colors, and the first three denominations are known with inverted centers (actually, inverted frames, because the black vignettes were printed first). The stamps were on sale only during the exposition, from May 1 to Oct. 31. *Intaglio, perforated 12.*

CM26 *Navigation on the Great Lakes* (S.S. City of Alpena)

CM26v

CM26
1¢

	UnFVF	UseFVF
emerald & black (91,401,500)	18.00	3.00
dark blue green & black	18.00	3.00
Plate strip of 3, w/imprint	78.00	
Plate block of 4, w/imprint & arrow	—	
Plate strip of 5 (2 numbers), w/imprint	120.00	
Plate block of 6, w/imprint	225.00	
Plate block of 10 (2 numbers), w/imprint	425.00	
Margin block of 4, w/imprint and arrow	80.00	
Double transfer	25.00	5.25
On cover		5.00
FDC (May 1, 1901)		6,000.00
v. Center inverted (1,000 reported)	10,500.00	8,000.00
v1. Center inverted plate strip of 4, w/imprint	75,000.00	
v2. Center inverted single on cover		18,500.00

CM27 *Fast rail transportation (Empire State Express)*

CM27v

CM27
2¢

	UnFVF	UseFVF
rose red & black (209,759,700)	17.50	1.00
carmine & gray black	17.50	1.00
Plate strip of 3, w/imprint	70.00	
Plate block of 4, w/imprint & arrow	77.50	
Plate strip of 5 (2 numbers), w/imprint	130.00	
Plate block of 6, w/imprint	225.00	
Plate block of 10 (2 numbers), w/imprint	450.00	
Margin block of 4, w/imprint & arrow	75.00	
Double transfer	25.00	2.25
On cover		1.50
FDC (May 1, 1901)		3,500.00
v. Center inverted (158 known)	42,500.00	17,500.00
v1. Center inverted block of 4	375,000.00	

CM28 *Columbia Electric Vehicle Co. automobile, world's first*

CM28v *depiction of an auto on a stamp*

CM28 4¢		UnFVF	UseFVF
	orange brown & black *(5,737,100)*	82.50	15.00
	red brown & black	82.50	15.00
	Plate strip of 3, w/imprint	350.00	
	Plate block of 4, w/imprint & arrow	375.00	
	Plate strip of 5 (2 numbers), w/imprint	600.00	
	Plate block of 6, w/imprint	2,100.00	
	Plate block of 10 (2 numbers), w/imprint	4,500.00	
	Margin block of 4, w/imprint & arrow	350.00	
	On cover		37.50
	FDC *(May 1, 1901)*		15,000.00
	v. Center inverted *(206 known)*	22,500.00	
	v1. Center inverted plate strip of 4, w/imprint	140,000.00	
	v2. Center inverted, overprinted "Specimen"	—	

CM29 *Bridge at Niagara Falls*

CM29 5¢		UnFVF	UseFVF
	gray blue & black *(7,201,300)*	95.00	14.00
	dark gray blue & black	95.00	14.00
	Plate strip of 3, w/imprint	375.00	
	Plate block of 4, w/imprint & arrow	450.00	
	Plate strip of 5 (2 numbers), w/imprint	700.00	
	Plate block of 6, w/imprint	2,250.00	
	Plate block of 10 (2 numbers), w/imprint & arrow	4,250.00	
	Margin block of 4, w/imprint & arrow	425.00	
	On cover		40.00
	FDC *(May 1, 1901)*		19,500.00

CM30 *Canal Locks, Sault Ste. Marie*

CM30 8¢		UnFVF	UseFVF
	chocolate & black *(4,921,700)*	120.00	50.00
	purple brown & black	120.00	50.00
	Plate strip of 3, w/imprint	475.00	
	Plate block of 4, w/imprint & arrow	550.00	
	Plate strip of 5 (2 numbers), w/imprint	875.00	
	Plate block of 6, w/imprint	4,000.00	
	Plate block of 10 (2 numbers), w/imprint	7,000.00	
	Margin block of 4, w/imprint & arrow	525.00	
	On cover		100.00
	FDC *(May 1, 1901)*		19,500.00

CM31 *Fast Ocean Navigation* (S.S. St. Paul)

CM31 10¢		UnFVF	UseFVF
	yellow brown & black *(5,043,700)*	170.00	25.00
	dark yellow brown & black	170.00	25.00
	Plate strip of 3, w/imprint	675.00	
	Plate block of 4, w/imprint & arrow	775.00	
	Plate strip of 5 (2 numbers), w/imprint	1,250.00	
	Plate block of 6, w/imprint	7,000.00	
	Plate block of 10 (2 numbers), w/imprint	10,000.00	
	Margin block of 4, w/imprint & arrow	750.00	
	On cover		110.00
	FDC *(May 1, 1901)*		—

1904. LOUISIANA PURCHASE EXPOSITION ISSUE prepared for the World's Fair at St. Louis, Mo., commemorating the 1803 acquisition of the Louisiana Territory from France. All values were placed on sale April 30, the opening day of the fair.

Robert Livingston (CM32) was appointed minister to France in 1801. In 1803 President Jefferson (CM33) instructed him to negotiate with Napoleon for the purchase of New Orleans and the mouth of the Mississippi. James Monroe (CM34), former minister to France, was sent to aid in the negotiations. Francois de Barbe-Marbois, Napoleon's finance minister, astounded them by offering to sell the entire Louisiana Territory, an offer which they accepted without delay or authority. The price was $11,250,000; claims and interest accruals raised it to $27,000,000, about 4¢ an acre. The territory (CM36) eventually became 10 entire states and parts of three others. President McKinley (CM35) signed the Act of Congress approving the 1904 World's Fair but never lived to see it. In September 1901 he was assassinated while attending the Pan-American Exposition. *Intaglio, perforated 12.*

CM32 *Robert Livingston, from a painting by Gilbert Stuart*

CM32 1¢		UnFVF	UseFVF
	green *(79,779,200)*	20.00	3.50
	dark green	20.00	3.50
	Plate pair, w/imprint	65.00	
	Plate strip of 3, w/imprint	100.00	
	Plate block of 4, w/imprint	160.00	
	Plate block of 6, w/imprint	175.00	
	Margin block of 4, w/arrow	75.00	
	Diagonal line through left "1"	50.00	10.00
	Double transfer	—	
	On cover		75.00
	FDC *(April 30, 1904)*		6,500.00

CM33 *Thomas Jefferson, from a painting attributed to Gilbert Stuart*

CM33 2¢		UnFVF	UseFVF
	carmine *(192,732,400)*	19.00	1.25
	bright carmine	19.00	1.25
	Plate pair, w/imprint	75.00	
	Plate strip of 3, w/imprint	125.00	
	Plate block of 4, w/imprint	160.00	
	Plate block of 6, w/imprint	175.00	
	Margin block of 4, w/arrow	100.00	
	On cover		6.00
	FDC *(April 30, 1904)*		5,000.00
	v. Vertical pair, imperforate horizontally	9,000.00	

CM34 *James Monroe, from a painting by Vanderlyn in New York City Hall*

CM34 3¢		UnFVF	UseFVF
	dark red violet *(4,542,600)*	60.00	25.00
	Plate pair, w/imprint	150.00	
	Plate strip of 3, w/imprint	275.00	
	Plate block of 4, w/imprint	550.00	
	Plate block of 6, w/imprint	800.00	
	Margin block of 4, w/arrow	325.00	
	Double transfer	—	
	On cover		75.00
	FDC *(April 30, 1904)*		18,000.00

CM35 *William McKinley*

CM35

5¢		UnFVF	UseFVF
	indigo *(6,926,700)*	75.00	17.50
	Plate pair, w/imprint	200.00	
	Plate strip of 3, w/imprint	325.00	
	Plate block of 4, w/imprint	625.00	
	Plate block of 6, w/imprint	900.00	
	Margin block of 4, w/arrow	350.00	
	On cover		75.00
	FDC *(April 30, 1904)*		26,000.00

CM36 *Map of Louisiana Purchase*

CM36

10¢		UnFVF	UseFVF
	red brown *(4,011,200)*	125.00	25.00
	dark red brown	125.00	25.00
	Plate pair, w/imprint	325.00	
	Plate strip of 3, w/imprint	500.00	
	Plate block of 4, w/imprint	1,250.00	
	Plate block of 6, w/imprint	1,750.00	
	Margin block of 4, w/arrow	575.00	
	On cover		125.00
	FDC *(April 30, 1904)*		27,500.00

1907. JAMESTOWN ISSUE was created for the Jamestown Exposition at Hampton Roads, Va., commemorating the 300th anniversary of the oldest permanent English settlement in America. In 1607, on their way to reattempt a settlement at Roanoke Island, three London Company ships with 105 men were blown off course and discovered the entrance to Chesapeake Bay. Sailing 50 miles up a river they named the James (for King James I), they began a settlement called Jamestown (CM38). Constant Indian trouble brought out the leadership qualities of Capt. John Smith (CM37). Captured while foraging and condemned to death by the Indian Chief Powhatan, Smith is said by legend to have been saved by the chief's beautiful daughter Pocahontas (CM39). Married to a settler named John Rolfe, she was received with royal honors in England, where she died in 1617. The 1¢ and 2¢ stamps were placed on sale April 25, 1907. The 5¢ value was first sold May 3, 1907. *Intaglio, perforated 12.*

CM37 *Captain John Smith, from a painting in the State Library, Virginia*

CM37

1¢		UnFVF	UseFVF
	deep bluish green *(77,728,794)*	17.50	3.00
	dark green	17.50	3.00
	Plate strip of 3, w/imprint	65.00	
	Plate block of 6, w/imprint	275.00	
	Margin block of 4, w/arrow	75.00	
	Double transfer	25.00	8.00
	On cover		12.50
	FDC *(April 6, 1907)*		12,000.00

CM38 *Founding of Jamestown, from a lost painting*

CM38

2¢		UnFVF	UseFVF
	rose red *(149,497,994)*	22.50	2.75
	bright rose red	22.50	2.75

Plate strip of 3, w/imprint	75.00	
Plate block of 6, w/imprint	375.00	
Margin block of 4, w/arrow	90.00	
Double transfer		6.00
On cover		7.50
FDC *(April 6, 1907)*		12,000.00

CM39 *Pocahontas, from a painting in Norfolk, England*

CM39

5¢		UnFVF	UseFVF
	indigo *(7,980,594)*	85.00	22.50
	blue	85.00	22.50
	Plate strip of 3, w/imprint	300.00	
	Plate block of 6, w/imprint	2,100.00	
	Margin block of 4, w/arrow	350.00	
	Double transfer	125.00	45.00
	On cover		75.00
	EKU *(May 8, 1907)*		

1909. LINCOLN MEMORIAL CENTENNIAL ISSUE commemorated the 100th anniversary of the birth of Abraham Lincoln. It was designed, using the existing Washington-Franklin series frame, and produced within 31 days. As an experiment to counteract the shrinking caused by printing on wet paper, some rows of stamps were separated by 3mm spacing instead of the usual 2mm. Some of the perforated stamps were printed on a 35-percent-rag stock known as "bluish paper," which is actually grayish in appearance. *Intaglio, perforated 12 and imperforate.*

CM40-42 *Abraham Lincoln, from The Head of State statue by Augustus Saint-Gaudens, Grant Park, Chicago*

Perforated 12.

CM40

2¢		UnFVF	UseFVF
	carmine *(148,387,191)*	5.00	1.75
	bright carmine	5.00	1.75
	Block of 4 (2mm spacing)	25.00	17.50
	Block of 4 (3mm spacing)	25.00	17.50
	Plate block of 6, w/imprint	125.00	
	Double transfer	12.50	5.00
	On cover		9.00
	FDC *(Feb. 12, 1909)*		500.00

Imperforate.

CM41

2¢		UnFVF	UseFVF
	carmine *(1,273,900)*	22.50	20.00
	Block of 4 (2mm spacing)	100.00	
	Block of 4 (3mm spacing)	100.00	
	Plate block of 6, w/imprint	225.00	
	Center line block	200.00	
	Margin block of 4, w/arrow	100.00	
	Double transfer	60.00	30.00
	On cover		50.00
	FDC *(Feb. 12, 1909)*		17,000.00

Bluish gray paper, perforated 12 (Feb. 1909).

CM42

2¢		UnFVF	UseFVF
	carmine *(637,000)*	175.00	195.00
	Block of 4 (2mm spacing)	900.00	750.00
	Block of 4 (3mm spacing)	900.00	750.00
	Plate block of 6, w/imprint	3,000.00	
	On cover		450.00
	EKU *(March 27, 1909)*		

1909. ALASKA-YUKON ISSUE released in connection with a Seattle, Wash., exposition commemorating the development of the Alaska-Yukon-Pacific Territory. William H. Seward, Secretary of State under Lincoln and Johnson, negotiated the purchase of Alaska from Russia, begun in 1859 but postponed by the Civil War. The treaty of March 30, 1867, set the purchase price at $7,200,000. The formal transfer was made Oct. 18 at Sitka. *Intaglio, perforated 12 and imperforate.*

CM43, 44 *William Seward, from a drawing by Marcus W. Baldwin*

Perforated 12.

CM43			UnFVF	UseFVF
2¢	**carmine** (152,887,311)		7.00	1.50
	bright carmine		7.00	1.50
	Plate block of 6, w/imprint		250.00	
	Double transfer		1,750.00	6.00
	On cover			7.50
	FDC (June 1, 1909)			4,500.00

Imperforate.

CM44			UnFVF	UseFVF
2¢	**carmine** (525,400)		30.00	22.50
	Plate block of 6, w/imprint		275.00	
	Center line block		175.00	150.00
	Margin block of 4, w/arrow		150.00	120.00
	Double transfer		55.00	35.00
	On cover			45.00
	EKU (June 9, 1909)			

1909. HUDSON-FULTON ISSUE commemorated historic voyages, 200 years apart, up the Hudson River to Albany, N.Y. Henry Hudson, an English navigator commanding the Dutch East India Company ship, *Half Moon,* explored the river when he sailed into New York Bay Sept. 3, 1609. Robert Fulton, aided by Robert Livingston (CM32), constructed the first practical steamship, named *Clermont* after Livingston's home, and steamed to Albany and back Aug. 17-22, 1807. *Intaglio, perforated 12 and imperforate.*

CM45 Half Moon *and* S.S. Clermont

Perforated 12.

CM45			UnFVF	UseFVF
2¢	**carmine** (72,634,631)		10.00	3.50
	Plate block of 6, w/imprint		350.00	
	Double transfer		25.00	7.50
	On cover			800.00
	FDC (Sept. 25, 1909); EKU (Sept. 23, 1909)			—

Imperforate.

CM46			UnFVF	UseFVF
2¢	**carmine** (216,480)		35.00	22.50
	Plate block of 6, w/imprint		350.00	
	Center line block		275.00	140.00
	Margin block of 4, w/arrow		175.00	120.00
	Double transfer		55.00	35.00
	On cover			45.00
	FDC (Sept. 25, 1909)			7,500.00

1913-15. PANAMA-PACIFIC ISSUE commemorated Balboa's sighting of the Pacific Ocean in 1513; the opening of the Panama Canal in 1914; and the Panama-Pacific Exposition at San Francisco, Calif., in 1915.

Vasco Nuñez de Balboa (CM47), Spanish governor of Darien (Panama), marched across the isthmus and from the peak of Mount Darien sighted the waters of "the South Sea" on Sept. 25, 1513. Ferdinand Magellan named it the Pacific Ocean in 1520. A canal connecting the Atlantic and Pacific oceans (CM48) was built by the United States during 1904-14 at a cost of $336,650,000. San Francisco Bay (CM99) is said to have been sighted by Francis Drake in 1579, but the city's site was discovered (CM50) in 1770 by Don Gaspar de Portola, Spanish governor of the Californias, who, with the Franciscan missionary Junipero Serra (A116), led a 1,000-mile march establishing settlements from Lower California to Monterey. *Stamps issued on paper with single-line "USPS" watermark. Intaglio, perforated 12 (1913) and perforated 10 (1914-15). (Quantities shown include both perforation types.)*

CM47, 52 *Vasco Nuñez de Balboa*

CM47		UnFVF	UseFVF
1¢	**green** (334,796,926)	15.50	1.25
	yellow green	15.50	1.25
	Plate block of 6	160.00	
	Double transfer	25.00	5.00
	On cover		7.50
	FDC (Jan. 1, 1913)		5,000.00

CM48, CM53 *Panama Canal, from a model of the Pedro Miguel Locks*

CM48		UnFVF	UseFVF
2¢	**rose red** (503,713,086)	20.00	.50
	deep carmine	20.00	.50
	brown lake	—	
	Plate block of 6	250.00	
	Double transfer	45.00	5.00
	On cover		4.00
	FDC (Jan. 18, 1913)		2,000.00
	a. carmine lake	575.00	
	EKU (Jan. 17, 1913)		

CM49, CM54 *The Golden Gate, from a photograph*

CM49		UnFVF	UseFVF
5¢	**blue** (29,088,726)	75.00	9.00
	dark blue	75.00	9.00
	Plate block of 6	2,000.00	
	On cover		45.00
	FDC (Jan. 1, 1913)		22,000.00

CM50-51, CM55 *Discovery of San Francisco Bay, from a painting by Charles F. Matthews, San Francisco Art Museum*

CM50		UnFVF	UseFVF
10¢	**orange yellow** (16,968,365)	125.00	20.00
	Plate block of 6	2,500.00	
	On cover		100.00
	FDC (Jan. 1, 1913)		17,500.00

CM51		UnFVF	UseFVF
10¢	**orange** (16,968,365) (Aug. 1913)	200.00	15.00
	Plate block of 6	10,250.00	
	On cover		125.00

1914-15. PANAMA-PACIFIC ISSUE Perforated 10.

CM52		UnFVF	UseFVF
1¢	**green**	22.00	5.25
	dark green	22.00	5.25
	Plate block of 6	330.00	
	On cover		30.00
	EKU (Dec. 21, 1914)		

CM53		UnFVF	UseFVF
2¢	**rose red**	70.00	1.50
	dark carmine	70.00	1.50
	red	70.00	1.50
	Plate block of 6	1,700.00	
	On cover		12.50
	EKU (Jan. 13, 1915)		

CM54		UnFVF	UseFVF
5¢	**blue**	160.00	14.50

DECODING THE CATALOG

The Panama-Pacific stamps of 1913-15 are notable among early United States commemorative issues by virtue of their extraordinary longevity, which gave rise to collectible perforation and color varieties. At first, most U.S. commemoratives were issued at and used for the duration of various expositions. When the show ended, the stamps were taken off sale, and unsold remainders were soon destroyed. The idea of releasing stamps prior to an event for advance publicity and promotion came to fruition with the Panama-Pacific commemoratives.

The issue ostensibly celebrated three events — the 400th anniversary of Balboa's sighting of the Pacific Ocean in 1513, the opening of the Panama Canal in 1914 and the Panama-Pacific Exposition in 1915. However, the impetus behind the stamps and the exposition was the surprisingly rapid recovery of San Francisco from the devastating earthquake and fire of April 18, 1906. Unlike the first U.S. commemoratives, which had been widely opposed by collectors, the Panama-Pacific issue actually had some respected philatelic publications calling for the stamps, in addition to local civic boosters.

The first of the stamps, perforated 12, were issued Jan. 1, 1913 — more than two years before the exhibition, which ran from Feb. 20 to Dec. 4, 1915. The final stamps were shipped in mid-January 1916 — an unprecedented run.

In the middle of that run, the Bureau of Engraving and Printing changed perforations to 10 gauge in late 1914 to increase the strength of the sheets, and as the perf 12 stock became low additional quantities were given gauge 10 perforations. "This later group was current for only about a year, and as the majority of collectors paid little or no attention to the change of perforation it is very much scarcer than the early perf 12," Max Johl noted in *U.S. Postage Stamps of the 20th Century.*

The reprinting of the 10¢ stamp in a darker orange perf 12 version in August 1913 was no accident. It was done at the behest of the Post Office Department in response to complaints that the original orange yellow was too light a shade. The perf 10 orange, Johl wrote, "was current for less than six months and was almost entirely overlooked by both collectors and dealers," accounting for its higher value today.

Johl rated the perf 12 2¢ carmine lake as extremely scarce. "Only 40 copies from one pane of 70 of this shade were said to have been found... although it hardly seems possible that only one sheet could have been printed in this darker color," he wrote.

---

	dark blue	160.00	14.50
	Plate block of 6	4,250.00	
	On cover		75.00
	EKU *(Feb. 6, 1915)*		

CM55			
10¢		**UnVFF**	**UseFVF**
	orange	900.00	60.00
	Plate block of 6	13,000.00	
	On cover		225.00
	EKU *(Aug. 27, 1915)*		

1919. VICTORY ISSUE commemorated the winning of World War I by the Allies. The design shows a female allegory of "Victory" and the U.S. flag flanked by the flags of Great Britain, Belgium, Italy and France. *Intaglio, perforated 11.*

CM56 *"Victory" and flags*

CM56			
3¢		**UnVFF**	**UseFVF**
	dark lilac *(99,585,200)*	8.50	3.00
	Plate block of 6	100.00	
	FDC *(March 3, 1919)*		800.00
	a. dark red lilac	1,400.00	3,000.00
	Plate block of 6	10,000.00	
	b. pale red lilac	9.50	3.50
	Plate block of 6	100.00	
	c. bright red lilac	50.00	15.00
	Plate block of 6	425.00	

1920. PILGRIM TERCENTENARY ISSUE marked the 300th anniversary of the landing of the Pilgrims at Plymouth, Mass. (CM58), in December 1620. Of the *Mayflower's* (CM57) 102 passengers, 41 Pilgrim "fathers" en route signed a compact (CM59) in which they pledged to adhere to the principles of self-government in the colony. *Intaglio, perforated 11.*

CM57 *The* Mayflower, *from a watercolor by Harrison Eastman, Smithsonian Institution, Washington, D.C.*

CM57			
1¢		**UnVFF**	**UseFVF**
	green *(137,978,207)*	3.50	2.50
	dark green	3.50	2.00
	Plate block of 6	35.00	
	Double transfer	—	
	On cover		8.00
	FDC *(Dec. 21, 1920)*		1,600.00

CM58 *Landing of the Pilgrims, from an 1846 engraving by Burt based on a sketch by White*

CM58			
2¢		**UnVFF**	**UseFVF**
	rose red *(196,037,327)*	5.25	1.75
	carmine	5.25	1.75
	rose	5.25	1.75
	Plate block of 6	50.00	
	On cover		5.00
	FDC *(Dec. 20, 1920)*		1,500.00

CM59 *Signing of the Compact, from a painting by Edwin White*

CM59			
5¢		**UnVFF**	**UseFVF**
	deep blue *(11,321,607)*	35.00	12.50
	dark blue	35.00	12.50

Plate block of 6	375.00
On cover	30.00
FDC (Dec. 21, 1920)	3,000.00

1923. HARDING MEMORIAL ISSUE honored President Warren G. Harding, who died Aug. 2, 1923, in San Francisco, Calif. An Ohio newspaper editor elected to the U.S. Senate in 1914, he won the presidency in 1920 on a platform pledging a "return to normalcy." First President to visit Alaska, he died on the way home. An immediate scramble to release a memorial stamp ensued. Unlike today, there was no one-year waiting period for a president. By Sept. 1, 1923, 30 days after Harding's death, a stamp had been designed, engraved, printed, distributed and issued. This rush led to several varieties of the stamp, due primarily to changing printing technology. Four varieties of the stamp exist: two printed by flat plate *(perforated 11 and imperforate)* and two produced by rotary press *(perforated 10 and the rare perforated 11). No. CM63 is known only in used condition, and only 43 examples are recorded. Intaglio.*

The printed design of the flat plate printing measures 19x21 7/8mm. Small specks of black color usually are seen on the backs of these stamps, a characteristic of almost all flat-press-printed stamps. The color is a true black.

The printed design of the rotary press printings measures 19x22 1/2mm. Color specks are almost always absent from the backs of these stamps. The color is a grayish black.

Some consider these commemorative mourning stamps to be part of the 1922-34 Regular Issue Series. In fact, a similar design with 1 1/2¢ value (No. 420) is part of that series.

CM60-63 *Warren G. Harding*

Flat plate printing, perforated 11.

CM60

		UnFVF	UseFVF
2¢	black *(1,459,487,085)*	.60	.20
	grayish black	.60	.20
	Plate block of 6	27.50	
	Double transfer	3.00	.75
	On cover		1.00
	FDC (Sept. 1, 1923)		40.00
	v. Horizontal pair, imperforate vertically	1,500.00	

Flat plate printing, imperforate.

CM61

		UnFVF	UseFVF
2¢	black *(770,000)*	6.50	4.50
	Plate block of 6	90.00	
	Block of 4, w/arrow	50.00	
	Center line block of 4	75.00	
	On cover		12.50
	FDC (Nov. 15, 1923)		125.00

Rotary press printing, perforated 10.

CM62

		UnFVF	UseFVF
2¢	gray black *(99,950,300)*	15.00	1.75
	black	15.00	1.75
	Plate block of 4	275.00	
	Pair, gutter between	400.00	
	On cover		6.00
	FDC (Sept. 12, 1923)		175.00

Rotary press printing, perforated 11.

CM63

		UnFVF	UseFVF
2¢	gray black		30,000.00
	Pair		60,000.00

1924. HUGUENOT-WALLOON ISSUE commemorated the 300th anniversary of the Walloon settlement of New York, and the restoration of a monument to earlier Huguenot settlements in the South.

During the religious wars of the 16th century, thousands of French and Belgian Protestants, known as Huguenots, settled in Holland, where they were called Walloons (foreigners). Although Dutch traders had visited Manhattan since 1613, the first Dutch immigrants were 30 Walloon families sent by the Dutch West India Company in 1624. Under Peter Minuit, they bought Manhattan from the Indians and tried founding settlements all the way from the Delaware River to Fort

Orange, now Albany (CM65). In 1562, French Huguenots unsuccessfully had tried a settlement at Port Royal, S.C. In 1564 a colony was established at Fort Caroline (now Mayport) on the St. Johns River in Florida, and had a stone column erected bearing the French coat of arms. The colony was massacred in 1565 by the Spanish under Pedro Menendez de Aviles. This column was replaced and dedicated May 2, 1924. *Intaglio, perforated 11.*

CM64 *The* New Netherland

CM64

		UnFVF	UseFVF
1¢	green *(51,378,023)*	2.75	2.75
	dark green	2.75	2.75
	Plate block of 6	30.00	
	Double transfer	10.00	6.50
	On cover		7.00
	FDC (May 1, 1924)		40.00

CM65 *Landing of Walloons at Fort Orange, from* History of New York *by Martha Lamb*

CM65

		UnFVF	UseFVF
2¢	carmine red *(77,753,423)*	5.00	2.00
	Plate block of 6	55.00	
	Double transfer	15.00	4.25
	On cover		5.00
	FDC (May 1, 1924)		60.00

CM66 *Monument of Huguenots at Mayport, Fla.*

CM66

		UnFVF	UseFVF
5¢	Prussian blue *(5,659,023)*	27.50	14.00
	dark blue	27.50	14.00
	Plate block of 6	250.00	
	On cover (UPU rate)		30.00
	FDC (May 1, 1924)		85.00
	v. Broken circle below right numeral "5"	65.00	22.50

1925. LEXINGTON-CONCORD ISSUE commemorated the 150th anniversary of the first armed conflicts of the American Revolution, which took place on April 19, 1775.

When Gen. Thomas Gage, colonial governor of Massachusetts, sent 800 troops to Lexington and Concord to destroy military supplies stored there by the colonists, Paul Revere made his famous ride on horseback to warn the colonists. Calling themselves the Minute Men (ready to fight on a minute's notice) (CM69), the colonists gathered on the Green at Lexington with the watchword, "If they mean to have a war, let it begin here" (CM68). Eight of the 70 Minute Men were killed; the rest fell back, and the British went to Concord. In fighting on the North Bridge there, and continuing all the way back to the protection of naval guns at Charlestown Harbor, the British suffered 273 casualties; the colonists 93. Chosen to head a Continental Army, George Washington took command at Cambridge in July (CM67). *Intaglio, perforated 11.*

CM67 *Washington at Cambridge, from an engraving in the Cambridge Public Library*

CM67

		UnFVF	UseFVF
1¢	**green** (15,615,000)	2.75	2.50
	dark green	2.75	2.50
	Plate block of 6	40.00	
	On cover		5.00
	FDC (April 4, 1925)		30.00

CM68 Battle of Lexington, *painting by Henry Sandham, Town Hall, Lexington, Mass.*

CM68

		UnFVF	UseFVF
2¢	**carmine red** (26,596,600)	5.00	3.50
	Plate block of 6	65.00	
	On cover		7.50
	FDC (April 4, 1925)		35.00

CM69 *The Minute Man, from a statue by Daniel Chester French in Concord; poetry by Ralph Waldo Emerson*

CM69

		UnFVF	UseFVF
5¢	**Prussian blue** (5,348,800)	25.00	14.00
	Plate block of 6	225.00	
	On cover (UPU rate)		22.50
	FDC (April 4, 1925)		85.00
	v. Line over head	65.00	25.00

1925. NORSE-AMERICAN ISSUE commemorated the 100th anniversary of the first Norwegian immigrants' arrival on the *Restaurationen* on Oct. 9, 1825. Sagas tell of Norse exploration of the North American coast ca. 1000 A.D. *Intaglio, perforated 11.*

CM70 *Sloop* Restaurationen, *adapted from a drawing of a sister ship*

CM70

		UnFVF	UseFVF
2¢	**carmine & black** (9,104,983)	4.00	3.00
	dark carmine and black	4.00	3.00
	Plate block of 8 w/2 numbers & arrow	200.00	
	Plate block of 8, w/carmine number (only) & arrow	3,250.00	
	Center line block of 4	27.50	
	Margin block of 4, w/arrow	35.00	
	On cover		8.00
	FDC (May 18, 1925)		20.00

CM71 *Viking ship built in Norway, by popular subscription, as a gift to the people of the United States*

CM71

		UnFVF	UseFVF
5¢	**indigo & black** (1,900,983)	15.00	12.50
	Plate block of 8, w/2 numbers & arrow	575.00	
	Center line block of 4	90.00	
	Margin block of 4, w/arrow	85.00	
	On cover (UPU rate)		22.50
	FDC (May 18, 1925)		30.00
	FDC CM70 & 71 on one cover		50.00

1926. SESQUICENTENNIAL ISSUE in connection with the exposition at Philadelphia, Pa., commemorated the 150th anniversary of the Declaration of Independence. *Intaglio, perforated 11.*

CM72 *The Liberty Bell, designed from the entrance to the exposition*

CM72

		UnFVF	UseFVF
2¢	**carmine red** (307,731,900)	2.50	.50
	Plate block of 6	35.00	
	Double transfer	—	
	FDC (May 10, 1926)		10.00

1926. ERICSSON MEMORIAL ISSUE honored John Ericsson, the Swedish-born engineer who built the ironclad *USS Monitor,* which engaged the Confederate ironclad *Virginia* (formerly *USS Merrimac*) off Hampton Roads, Va., in 1862. Ericsson's inventions included a screw propeller that revolutionized shipbuilding. The stamp shows a statue of him unveiled in Washington by the Crown Prince of Sweden. *Intaglio, perforated 11.*

CM73 *Statue of John Ericsson, sculpted by James Earl Fraser, Washington, D.C.*

CM73

		UnFVF	UseFVF
5¢	**slate violet** (20,280,500)	6.00	2.50
	Plate block of 6	75.00	
	FDC (May 29, 1929)		25.00

1926. WHITE PLAINS ISSUE commemorated the 150th anniversary of the Battle of White Plains, N.Y., Oct. 28, 1776. The British, attempting to outflank Washington's forces in upper Manhattan, caused him to withdraw his main force northward. In a sharp battle at White Plains, the British captured a key hill, but Washington escaped while they were awaiting reinforcements. *Intaglio, perforated 11.*

CM74 *Alexander Hamilton's battery, from a painting by E.C. Ward (1892-) specifically for the stamp.*

CM74

		UnFVF	UseFVF
2¢	**carmine red** (40,639,485)	2.00	1.50
	Plate block of 6	40.00	
	FDC (Oct. 18, 1926)		8.00
	v. Vertical pair, imperforate between	2,500.00	

1926. WHITE PLAINS PHILATELIC EXHIBITION ISSUE Sheets of 25 stamps with marginal inscription noting the International Philatelic Exhibition, Oct. 16-23, 1926, in New York, N.Y. *Sheet size 161x149mm.*

CM75 *White Plains souvenir sheet of 25*

CM75			UnFVF	UseFVF
2¢	carmine red *(107,398)*		400.00	425.00
	v. Dot over first "S" of "States" on stamp in		425.00	450.00
	position 9 of lower left pane of plate			
	18774 or position 11 of the lower left			
	pane of plate 18773.			
	FDC Full sheet *(Oct. 18, 1926)*			1,700.00

1927. VERMONT SESQUICENTENNIAL ISSUE commemorated the 150th anniversary of the Battle of Bennington and the independence of the State of Vermont. In 1777, badly needing supplies at Saratoga, N.Y., British Gen. John Burgoyne sent a force to capture American military stores at Bennington, Vt. In a battle Aug. 16 with 2,600 militiamen (the "Green Mountain Boys") under Gen. John Stark, almost the entire British force was killed or captured. *Intaglio, perforated 11.*

CM76 *Green Mountain Boy*

CM76		UnFVF	UseFVF
2¢	carmine red *(39,974,900)*	1.25	1.00
	Plate block of 6	40.00	
	FDC *(Aug. 3, 1927)*		6.00

1927. BURGOYNE CAMPAIGN ISSUE commemorated the Battle of Bennington, Oriskany, Fort Stanwix and Saratoga. On Oct. 17, 1777, surrounded by a force three times his own, British Gen. John Burgoyne surrendered to the Americans at Saratoga. His 5,700 men went back to England, pledged not to fight again in the war. *Intaglio, perforated 11.*

CM77 *Surrender of Gen. John Burgoyne, from a painting by John Trumbull in the Capitol Rotunda, Washington, D.C.*

CM77		UnFVF	UseFVF
2¢	carmine red *(25,628,450)*	3.50	2.25
	Plate block of 6	40.00	
	FDC *(Aug. 3, 1927)*		11.00

1928. VALLEY FORGE ISSUE recalled the 150th anniversary of Washington's winter encampment at Valley Forge, about 20 miles northwest of Philadelphia, Pa. Beaten at Brandywine and

Germantown, desperately short of food, clothing and supplies, the American troops at Valley Forge showed courage in the darkest period of American history. *Intaglio, perforated 11.*

CM78 *General Washington at Prayer, from an engraving by John C. McRae*

CM78		UnFVF	UseFVF
2¢	carmine red *(101,330,328)*	1.00	.50
	Plate block of 6	25.00	
	FDC *(May 26, 1928)*		5.00

1928. HAWAIIAN SESQUICENTENNIAL ISSUE marked the 150th anniversary of the arrival in the Hawaiian Islands of English navigator Capt. James Cook. These makeshift commemoratives, made by overprinting ordinary definitive stamps (Nos. 476 and 479), disappointed collectors who expected something more elaborate. The overprints available only in the Territory of Hawaii and at the Philatelic Sales Agency in Washington, D.C., caused confusion when some postal clerks would not honor them because they thought they were precancels. *Intaglio, perforated 11x10 1/2.*

CM79 2¢ overprint

CM80 5¢ overprint

CM79		UnFVF	UseFVF
2¢	carmine *(5,519,897)*	4.50	4.50
	Plate block of 4	100.00	
	Vertical pair with wide spacing (28mm	100.00	
	rather than 18mm)		
	FDC *(Aug. 13, 1928)*		15.00
CM80		**UnFVF**	**UseFVF**
5¢	blue *(1,459,897)*	12.50	12.50
	Plate block of 4	200.00	
	FDC *(Aug. 13, 1928)*		20.00
	FDC CM79 & 80 on one cover		40.00

1928. MOLLY PITCHER ISSUE another two-line overprint of No. 476, commemorated the 150th anniversary of the Battle of Monmouth, N.J., June 28, 1778, and honored Mary Ludwig Hays McCauly, whose husband was a cannoneer in the battle. Called "Molly Pitcher" because she carried water to the tired and wounded soldiers, she also took her husband's place when he was wounded, and manned his cannon throughout the rest of the battle. (See also the 1978 10¢ postal card, No. PC73.) *Intaglio, perforated 11.*

CM81 *2¢ Molly Pitcher overprint*

CM81		UnFVF	UseFVF
2¢	carmine *(9,779,896)*	1.00	1.25
	Plate block of 4	25.00	
	Vertical pair with wide spacing (28mm	27.50	
	rather than 18mm)		
	FDC *(Oct. 20, 1928)*		12.50

1928. AERONAUTICS CONFERENCE ISSUE in connection with the International Civil Aeronautics Conference held Dec. 12-14 in Washington, D.C., commemorated the 25th anniversary of the first airplane flight (Dec. 17, 1903) by the Wright brothers at Kitty Hawk, N.C. The plane (CM80), in England for 20 years, was returned to the United States in 1948 and is now on view at the Smithsonian Institution in Washington, D.C. *Intaglio, perforated 11.*

CM82 *Wright airplane*

CM82
2¢ **carmine red** *(51,342,273)*

	UnFVF	UseFVF
carmine red *(51,342,273)*	1.25	1.00
Plate block of 6	12.50	
FDC *(Dec. 12, 1928)*		6.00

CM83 *Globe and airplane*

CM83
5¢

	UnFVF	UseFVF
Prussian blue *(10,319,700)*	5.00	3.00
Plate block of 6	55.00	
"Prairie dog" plate flaw (position 50 of bottom-lower left pane of plate 19658)	30.00	
FDC *(Dec. 12, 1928)*		10.00

1929. GEORGE ROGERS CLARK ISSUE commemorated the 150th anniversary of Clark's recapture of Fort Sackville (now Vincennes, Ind.), from a force of British, Loyalists and Indians commanded by Col. Henry Hamilton. From winter quarters at Kaskaskia, Clark sent 40 men by boat, led another 130 across the flooded plains, tricked Hamilton's Indians into deserting, took the fort on Feb. 25, and secured the Northwest for the colonists. *Intaglio, perforated 11.*

CM84 *Surrender of Fort Sackville, from a painting by Frederick C. Yohn*

CM84
2¢

	UnFVF	UseFVF
carmine & black *(16,684,674)*	.60	.50
Plate block of 6, w/two numbers & "TOP"	12.50	
Plate block of 10, w/red number only	—	
Margin block of 4, w/arrow	3.50	
Double transfer	5.50	3.00
FDC *(Feb. 25, 1929)*		5.00

1929. EDISON COMMEMORATIVE ISSUE celebrated the 50th anniversary of the invention of the incandescent electric lamp by Thomas Alva Edison (CM287). *Issued in both flat and rotary press intaglio printings and as a rotary press coil stamp. The rotary press sheet version is taller than the other two, and the coil version is wider, due to the stretching of the plates as they were curved to fit the continuous rotary press. Huge quantities of the rotary press stamps were used (and subsequently destroyed) on business mailings, leaving relatively few for the philatelic trade.*

CM85-87 *Edison's first electric lamp*

Flat press, perforated 11.
CM85
2¢

	UnFVF	UseFVF
carmine red *(31,679,200)*	.75	.75
Plate block of 6	30.00	
FDC *(June 5, 1929)*		40.00

Rotary press, perforated 11x10 1/2.
CM86
2¢

	UnFVF	UseFVF
carmine red *(210,119,474)*	.75	.25

Plate block of 4	35.00	
FDC *(June 11, 1929)*		375.00

Rotary press coil, perforated 10 vertically.
CM87
2¢

	UnFVF	UseFVF
carmine red *(133,530,000)*	12.50	1.50
Pair	22.50	7.00
Joint line pair	60.00	40.00
FDC *(June 11, 1929)*		375.00

1929. SULLIVAN EXPEDITION ISSUE noted the 150th anniversary of the campaign by Gens. John Sullivan and James Clinton against the Loyalists and Iroquois Indians ravaging Pennsylvania and New York frontier settlements. They defeated the Iroquois at Newtown (now Elmira), N.Y., Aug. 29, 1779. *Intaglio, perforated 11.*

CM88 *Maj. Gen. John Sullivan*

CM88
2¢

	UnFVF	UseFVF
carmine red *(51,451,880)*	.75	.75
Plate block of 6	25.00	
FDC *(June 17, 1929)* w/o cachet		4.00
FDC w/cachet		27.50

1929. BATTLE OF FALLEN TIMBERS ISSUE commemorated Gen. Anthony Wayne's defeat of Chief Little Turtle, Aug. 1794, near what is now Toledo, Ohio. His victory led to the settlement of Ohio. *Intaglio, perforated 11.*

CM89 *Gen. Wayne Memorial, monument by Bruce W. Laville at Fallen Timbers Park, Ohio*

CM89
2¢

	UnFVF	UseFVF
carmine red *(29,338,274)*	.75	.75
Plate block of 6	25.00	
FDC *(Sept. 14, 1929)* w/o cachet		3.50
FDC w/cachet		35.00

1929. OHIO RIVER CANALIZATION ISSUE saluted the Army Engineers' completion of America's most extensive canal system. Its 46 locks and dams provided a dependable 9-foot channel between Pittsburgh, Pa., and Cairo, Ill., a distance of 981 miles. *Intaglio, perforated 11.*

CM90 *Monongahela River lock*

CM90
2¢

	UnFVF	UseFVF
carmine red *(32,680,900)*	.50	.75
Plate block of 6	17.50	35.00
FDC *(Oct. 19, 1929)* w/o cachet		3.50
FDC w/cachet		30.00

1930. MASSACHUSETTS BAY COLONY ISSUE commemorated the 300th anniversary of the arrival of the Puritans under Gov. John Winthrop. When the charter given to the Massachusetts Bay Company neglected to specify where its annual meetings were to be held, the company took advantage of the oversight by moving itself to New England as a self-governing commonwealth, the first in the New World. *Intaglio, perforated 11.*

CM91 *Seal of the Massachusetts Bay Colony*

CM91		**UnFVF**	**UseFVF**
2¢	carmine red (74,000,774)	.75	.45
	Plate block of 6	25.00	
	FDC (April 8, 1930) w/o cachet		3.50
	FDC w/cachet		35.00

1930. CAROLINA-CHARLESTON ISSUE commemorated the 260th anniversary of the Province of Carolina and 250th anniversary of the City of Charleston. In 1670, Gov. William Sayle and 150 colonists landed at Albemarle Point on the Ashley River, founding a settlement called Charles Town. In 1680 they moved into a walled city they had built at Oyster Point, present site of Charleston. This was the first permanent settlement in the Carolinas. *Intaglio, perforated 11.*

CM92 *Colonial governor and Indian*

CM92		**UnFVF**	**UseFVF**
2¢	carmine red (25,215,574)	1.25	1.00
	Plate block of 6	40.00	
	FDC (April 10, 1930) w/cachet		35.00
	FDC w/o cachet		3.50

1930. BRADDOCK'S FIELD ISSUE commemorated the 175th anniversary of the Battle of the Wilderness in the French and Indian War. Advancing on Fort Duquesne (now Pittsburgh), Gen. Braddock's forces were defeated, and Braddock was killed. Lt. Col. George Washington, 23, commanding Braddock's colonials, led the remnant troops in a safe retreat. *Intaglio, perforated 11.*

CM93 *Col. George Washington, monument by Frank Vittor, at Braddock's Field, Pa.*

CM93		**UnFVF**	**UseFVF**
2¢	carmine red (25,609,470)	1.00	1.00
	Plate block of 6	30.00	
	FDC (July 9, 1930) w/cachet		30.00
	FDC w/o cachet		4.00

1930. VON STEUBEN ISSUE commemorated the 200th birthday of Baron Friedrich Wilhelm von Steuben, a Prussian officer who joined Washington at Valley Forge to serve as inspector general. Von Steuben reorganized and trained the army, lifted its morale, and fought at Monmouth and Yorktown. Naturalized in 1783, he was given 16,000 acres of land by New York State and an annual pension by Congress. *Intaglio, perforated 11.*

CM94 *Gen. von Steuben, from a memorial tablet by Karl Dautert, Magdeburg, Germany*

CM94		**UnFVF**	**UseFVF**
2¢	carmine red (66,487,000)	.50	.50
	Plate block of 6	20.00	
	FDC (Sept. 17, 1930) w/cachet		30.00
	FDC w/o cachet		4.00
	v. Pair, imperforate	3,000.00	
	Plate block of 6, imperforate	12,000.00	

1931. PULASKI ISSUE tardily commemorated the 150th anniversary of the Oct. 11, 1779, death of Count Casimir Pulaski, Polish patriot and hero of the American Revolution. Known as the Father of the U.S. Cavalry, he was mortally wounded leading a cavalry charge against the British at Savannah, Ga. *Intaglio, perforated 11.*

CM95 *Gen. Casimir Pulaski, from an etching by H.B. Hall*

CM95		**UnFVF**	**UseFVF**
2¢	carmine red (96,559,400)	.25	.20
	dark carmine red	.25	.20
	Plate block of 6	12.50	
	FDC (Jan. 16, 1931) w/cachet		30.00
	FDC w/o cachet		4.00

1931. RED CROSS ISSUE commemorated the 50th anniversary of the founding of the American Red Cross Society at Dansville, N.Y. Clara Barton (see CM309, CM1723) was its first president. The design of the stamp is adapted from the popular poster, *The Greatest Mother*, by Lawrence Wilbur. *Intaglio, perforated 11.*

CM96 *Red Cross nurse and globe*

CM96		**UnFVF**	**UseFVF**
2¢	black & scarlet (99,074,600)	.25	.20
	Plate block of 4	2.00	
	Margin block of 4, w/arrow	1.00	
	Double transfer	1.25	
	FDC (May 21, 1931) w/cachet		30.00
	FDC w/o cachet		3.00
	v. Red (cross) omitted	40,000.00	

1931. YORKTOWN ISSUE commemorated the 150th anniversary of Lord Cornwallis' surrender at Yorktown, the last important battle of the Revolutionary War. When Lafayette's small force in Virginia was joined in June 1781 by Wayne and von Steuben, Cornwallis moved to Yorktown to maintain sea communication with Clinton's forces in New York. The sudden arrival of De Grasse's French fleet with 3,000 troops hemmed Cornwallis in completely. Washington, who had been preparing an attack on New York, suddenly marched his troops and the French forces of Rochambeau to Virginia, where, with almost 17,000 men, he began the siege of Yorktown. Cornwallis' attempt to escape across the York River by night was thwarted by a storm. On Oct. 19 he surrendered almost 8,000 British and Hessian troops.

Flat press, two plate layouts used. Most panes have a straight edge along one side, but about 10% of printing was from plates that permitted perforation all around, and thus these sheets have no straight edges. Perforated 11.

CM97 *Rochambeau, Washington, De Grasse, from paintings by J.D. Court and J. Trumbull (see CM105) and an engraving*

CM97		**UnFVF**	**UseFVF**
2¢	carmine red & black (25,006,400)	.35	.20
	Plate block of 4, 2 numbers	3.00	
	Plate block of 4, 2 numbers & arrow	3.50	
	Plate block of 6, 2 numbers, "TOP" & arrow	3.75	
	Plate block of 8, 2 numbers & "TOP"	4.00	
	Center line block of 4	2.75	
	Margin block of 4, w/arrow	2.75	
	Double transfer	4.50	
	a. dark lake & black	400.00	
	Plate block of 4, 2 numbers	2,200.00	
	b. lake & black	4.50	
	v. Horizontal pair, imperforate vertically	4,500.00	
	FDC (Oct. 19, 1931)		45.00

1932. WASHINGTON BICENTENNIAL ISSUE commemorated the 200th birthday of George Washington, Feb. 22, 1932, in Westmoreland County, Va. *Intaglio, perforated 11x10 1/2.*

CM98 *Washington at 45, after miniature by Charles W. Peale, Metropolitan Museum of Art, New York, N.Y.*

CM98

		UnFVF	UseFVF
1/2¢	**olive brown** *(87,969,700)*	.25	.20
	Plate Block of 4	3.75	
	Broken circle (position 8 of top-right pane of plate No. 20560)	.60	
	FDC *(Jan. 1, 1932)*		17.50

CM99 *Washington at 53, from bust by Jean A. Houdon, Mount Vernon, Va.*

CM99

		UnFVF	UseFVF
1¢	**yellow green** *(1,265,555,100)*	.25	.20
	Plate block of 4	3.75	
	Gripper cracks (top left & top-right panes of plate No. 20742)	2.50	
	FDC *(Jan. 1, 1932)*		17.50

CM100 *Washington at 40, after painting by Peale, Washington & Lee University, Lexington, Va.*

CM100

		UnFVF	UseFVF
1 1/2¢	**yellow brown** *(304,926,800)*	.50	.20
	Plate block of 4	19.00	
	FDC *(Jan. 1, 1932)*		17.50

CM101 *Washington at 64, after painting by Gilbert Stuart, Boston   Museum, Boston, Mass.*

CM101

		UnFVF	UseFVF
2¢	**carmine red** *(4,222,198,300)*	.25	.20
	Plate block of 4	2.00	
	Pair, gutter between	—	
	Gripper cracks	1.75	
	FDC *(Jan. 1, 1932)*		17.50

CM102 *Washington at 46, painted by Peale at Valley Forge, West Chester (Pa.) State University*

CM102

		UnFVF	UseFVF
3¢	**slate purple** *(456,198,500)*	.50	.20
	Plate block of 4	15.00	
	Broken top frame line (position 8 of bottom-left pane of plate No. 20847)	3.75	
	Double transfer	1.60	
	FDC *(Jan. 1, 1932)*		17.50

CM103 *Washington at 49, after painting by Polk, Rhinebeck, N.Y.*

CM103

		UnFVF	UseFVF
4¢	**yellow brown** *(151,201,300)*	.40	.20
	Plate block of 4	7.50	
	Broken bottom frame line (position 100 of bottom-right pane of plate No. 20568)	1.50	
	Retouch in eyes (position 89 of bottom-right pane of plate No. 20568)	2.00	
	Double transfer	1.50	
	FDC *(Jan. 1, 1932)*		17.50

CM104 *Washington at 63, after painting by Peale, New York Historical Society, New York, N.Y.*

CM104

		UnFVF	UseFVF
5¢	**Prussian blue** *(170,656,100)*	1.75	.20
	Plate block of 4	19.00	
	Cracked plate (position 80 of top-right pane of plate No. 20637)	5.00	
	FDC *(Jan. 1, 1932)*		17.50

CM105 *Washington at 60, after a painting by John Trumbull, Yale University, New Haven, Conn.*

CM105

		UnFVF	UseFVF
6¢	**orange** *(111,739,400)*	3.50	.20
	Plate block of 4	65.00	
	FDC *(Jan. 1, 1932)*		17.50

CM106 *Washington at 48, after painting by Trumbull, Metropolitan Museum of Art, New York, N.Y.*

CM106

		UnFVF	UseFVF
7¢	**black** *(83,257,400)*	.40	.20
	Plate block of 4	7.00	
	Double transfer	—	
	FDC *(Jan. 1, 1932)*		20.00

CM107 *Washington at 66, after drawing by Charles Saint Memin, Brooklyn, N.Y.*

CM107

		UnFVF	UseFVF
8¢	**bister** *(96,506,100)*	3.00	.75
	Plate block of 4	65.00	
	FDC *(Jan. 1, 1932)*		20.00

CM108 *Washington at 62, after drawing by W. Williams, Alexandria, Va.*

CM108		UnFVF	UseFVF
9¢	**salmon** *(75,706,200)*	2.50	.20
	orange red	2.50	.20
	Plate block of 4	40.00	
	FDC *(Jan. 1, 1932)*		20.00

CM109 *Washington at 63, after portrait by Gilbert Stuart, Metropolitan Museum of Art, New York, N.Y.*

CM109		UnFVF	UseFVF
10¢	**orange yellow** *(147,216,000)*	12.50	.20
	Plate block of 4	125.00	
	FDC *(Jan. 1, 1932)*		20.00

1932. OLYMPIC WINTER GAMES ISSUE anticipated the Third Winter games, Feb. 4-13 at Lake Placid, N.Y. *Intaglio, perforated 11.*

CM110 *Ski jumper*

CM110		UnFVF	UseFVF
2¢	**carmine red** *(51,102,800)*	.40	.25
	dark carmine red	.40	.25
	Plate block of 6	12.50	
	Cracked plate	5.00	
	Recut (position 61 of top-right pane of plate No. 20823)	3.00	
	"Snowball" (position 64 of top-right pane of plate No. 20815)	25.00	
	FDC *(Jan. 25, 1932)*		25.00

1932. ARBOR DAY ISSUE hailed the 60th anniversary of Arbor Day, observed in many individual states for the planting of trees. First celebrated in Nebraska, it was originated by Julius Sterling Morton, agriculturist, newspaper editor, secretary of the Nebraska Territory, and national secretary of agriculture from 1893 to 1897. *Intaglio, perforated 11x10 1/2.*

CM111 *Children planting tree*

CM111		UnFVF	UseFVF
2¢	**carmine red** *(100,869,300)*	.25	.20
	Plate block of 4	7.00	
	FDC *(April 22, 1932)*		15.00

1932. OLYMPIC SUMMER GAMES ISSUE anticipated the 10th modern Olympic Games, held July 30-Aug. 14 in Los Angeles, Calif. The ancient games began in 776 B.C. and were banned in 394 A.D. Through the efforts of Pierre de Coubertin, French educator and sportsman, they were revived in 1896 in Greece. *Intaglio, perforated 11x10 1/2.*

CM112 *Modern athlete preparing to run*

CM112		UnFVF	UseFVF
3¢	**reddish violet** *(168,885,300)*	1.50	.20
	dark reddish violet	1.50	.20
	Plate block of 4	15.00	
	Gripper cracks	4.00	
	FDC *(June 15, 1932)*		25.00

CM113 Discus Thrower, *by Myron, 5 B.C.*

CM113		UnFVF	UseFVF
5¢	**blue** *(52,376,100)*	2.25	.30
	dark blue	2.25	.30
	Plate block of 4	27.50	
	Gripper cracks	4.00	
	FDC *(June 15, 1932)*		25.00

1932. WILLIAM PENN ISSUE commemorated the 250th anniversary of the arrival of William Penn (1644-1718) to found a colony. A Quaker at 18, Penn was imprisoned three times for religious nonconformity before he was 26. Inheriting a £16,000 claim against King Charles II, he asked for a grant of land in America and was given Pennsylvania in 1681. Landing Oct. 24, 1682, at New Castle, Del., he organized the colony on a liberal basis guaranteeing freedom of conscience, made fair treaties with the Indians, laid out the city of Philadelphia and established the first successful postal system in America. *Intaglio, perforated 11.*

CM114 *Young William Penn, from a painting, Pennsylvania Historical Society, Philadelphia, Pa.*

CM114		UnFVF	UseFVF
3¢	**reddish violet** *(49,949,000)*	.35	.25
	Plate block of 6	12.50	
	Vertical pair, imperforate horizontally	—	
	FDC *(Oct. 24, 1932)*		17.50

1933. DANIEL WEBSTER ISSUE commemorated the 150th anniversary of the birth of Daniel Webster and the 80th anniversary of his death. Famed orator, constitutional lawyer and statesman, Webster was elected five times to the U.S. House and four times to the Senate and twice appointed secretary of state. In 1840 he submitted a Senate resolution advocating reduced postal rates and the use of postage stamps in America. *Intaglio, perforated 11.*

CM115 *Daniel Webster, from a bust by Daniel Chester French, Franklin, N.H.*

CM115		UnFVF	UseFVF
3¢	**reddish violet** *(49,538,500)*	.35	.40
	light violet	.35	.40
	Plate block of 6	20.00	
	FDC *(Oct. 24, 1932)*		17.50

1933. OGLETHORPE ISSUE commemorated the 200th anniversary of the founding of Georgia and the city of Savannah, and honored Gen. James Edward Oglethorpe. A philanthropist concerned with religious tolerance and the relief of debtors, Oglethorpe obtained a royal charter and led 120 immigrants in settling the colony. He successfully repulsed Spanish attacks and attempted a siege of St. Augustine, Fla. *Intaglio, perforated 11.*

CM116 *Gen. James Edward Oglethorpe, from a painting at Oglethorpe University, Atlanta, Ga.*

CM116		UnFVF	UseFVF
3¢	**reddish violet** *(61,719,200)*	.35	.25

Plate block of 6	14.00	
FDC *(Feb. 12, 1933)*	17.50	

1933. NEWBURGH ISSUE commemorated the 150th anniversary of the Proclamation of Peace issued by Gen. George Washington from his headquarters at Newburgh, ending the Revolutionary War. *Perforated 10 1/2x11.*

CM117, CM142 *Washington's headquarters at Newburgh, N.Y., from an engraving by James Smille*

CM117		UnFVF	UseFVF
3¢	**reddish violet** *(73,382,400)*	.25	.20
	Plate block of 4	6.00	
	Block of 4, horizontal gutter between	—	
	Block of 4, vertical gutter between	—	
	Center block, w/crossed gutters	—	
	FDC *(April 19, 1933)*	17.50	

For ungummed stamps (Farley Issue), see CM142.

Although not regularly issued that way, CM117 was also available in full sheets of 400 subjects.

1933. CENTURY OF PROGRESS ISSUE commemorated the World's Fair held in Chicago, Ill., to honor the 100th anniversary of its incorporation as a city. *Intaglio, perforated 10 1/2x11.*

CM118, CM156 *Fort Dearborn blockhouse, from a painting by Dwight Benton*

CM118		UnFVF	UseFVF
1¢	**yellow green** *(348,266,800)*	.25	.20
	Plate block of 4	3.00	
	Block of 4, horizontal gutter between	—	
	Block of 4, vertical gutter between	—	
	Center block, w/crossed gutters	—	
	Gripper cracks	—	
	FDC *(May 25, 1933)*	17.50	

CM119, CM157 *Federal building at fair*

CM119		UnFVF	UseFVF
3¢	**reddish violet** *(480,239,300)*	.25	.20
	Plate block of 4	3.00	
	Block of 4, horizontal gutter between	—	
	Block of 4, vertical gutter between	—	
	Center block, w/crossed gutters	—	
	FDC *(May 25, 1933)*	17.50	

Although not regularly issued that way, CM118 and CM119 were also available in full sheets of 400 subjects.

1933. CENTURY OF PROGRESS SOUVENIR SHEETS were issued in honor of the American Philatelic Society convention held in Chicago in August. *Each sheet measures 134x120mm, contains 25 ungummed, imperforate stamps and is inscribed in the margin: "* PRINTED BY THE TREASURY DEPARTMENT, BUREAU OF ENGRAVING AND PRINTING / UNDER AUTHORITY OF JAMES A. FARLEY, POSTMASTER GENERAL AT A CENTURY OF PROGRESS / IN COMPLIMENT TO THE AMERICAN PHILATELIC SOCIETY FOR ITS CONVENTION AND EXHIBITION / CHICAGO, ILLINOIS, AUGUST 1933." *Intaglio, imperforate.*

CM120, CM156 *Sheet of 25*

CM120		UnFVF	UseFVF
1¢	**yellow green** *(456,704)*	35.00	32.50
	FDC *(Aug. 25, 1933)*		200.00
	a. Single stamp	.75	.20
	FDC (single stamp)		15.00

CM121, CM157 *Sheet of 25*

CM121		UnFVF	UseFVF
3¢	**reddish violet** *(441,172)*	30.00	27.50
	FDC *(Aug. 25, 1933)*		200.00
	a. Single stamp	.75	.50
	FDC (single stamp)		15.00

For similar Farley issues, see CM156 & CM157.

1933. NRA ISSUE publicized the National Recovery Administration, one of the first acts of the New Deal aimed at recovery from the Depression of the 1930s. The NRA was declared unconstitutional in 1935. In the original drawing for this stamp, the second figure was said by some to resemble President Franklin D. Roosevelt. A mustache was added since postal custom is against depicting a living person on a stamp. *Intaglio, perforated 10 1/2x11.*

CM122 *Workers Marching Forward, from a poster drawn by Rudolph L. Bortel*

CM122		UnFVF	UseFVF
3¢	**reddish violet** *(1,978,707,300)*	.25	.20
	Plate block of 4	2.00	
	Gripper cracks	—	
	Recut at right (position 47 of top-right pane of plate No. 21151)	—	
	FDC *(Aug. 15, 1933)*		17.50

1933. BYRD ANTARCTIC ISSUE publicized the second expedition of Rear Adm. Richard E. Byrd to the South Pole. Flight routes used by Byrd, as well as proposed new routes, are indicated on the stamp. Letters mailed with this 3¢ stamp from the camp at Little America, Antarctica, were subject to an additional service charge of 50¢ each. *Intaglio, perforated 11.*

CM123, CM143, CM158 *Globe with Antarctic routes*

CM123		UnFVF	UseFVF
3¢	blue *(5,735,944)*	.75	.60
	Plate block of 6	17.50	
	Double transfer	—	
	FDC *(Oct. 9, 1933)*		25.00

For ungummed stamps (Farley issue), see CM143.

1933. KOSCIUSZKO ISSUE commemorated Polish patriot Tadeusz Kosciuszko and the 150th anniversary of his naturalization as an American citizen. Gen. Kosciuszko fought throughout the Revolutionary War, served as aide to Washington, and laid out the fortifications of West Point. Afterward he led a rebellion that briefly liberated his native Poland from Russia. *Intaglio, perforated 11.*

CM124 *Gen. Tadeusz Kosciuszko, from a statue by Anton Popiel, Lafayette Park, Washington, D.C.*

CM124		UnFVF	UseFVF
5¢	blue *(45,137,700)*	.75	.35
	Plate block of 6	35.00	
	Cracked plate	—	
	FDC *(Oct. 13, 1933)*		17.50
	v. Horizontal pair, imperforate vertically	2,250.00	

1934. BYRD SOUVENIR SHEET honored the National Stamp Exhibition held in New York. *It measured 87x93mm and contained six imperforate stamps without gum. The margins of the sheets inscribed:* "PRINTED BY THE TREASURY DEPARTMENT, BUREAU OF ENGRAVING AND PRINTING / UNDER AUTHORITY OF JAMES A. FARLEY, POSTMASTER GENERAL / IN COMPLIMENT TO THE NATIONAL STAMP EXHIBITION OF 1934 / NEW YORK, N.Y. FEBRUARY 10-18, 1934." *Intaglio, imperforate.*

CM125, CM158 *Globe with Antarctic routes, souvenir sheet of 6*

CM125		UnFVF	UseFVF
3¢	blue *(811,404)*	17.50	16.50
	FDC *(Feb. 10, 1934)*		75.00
	a. Single stamp	3.00	2.75
	FDC (single stamp)		15.00

For similar Farley issue, see CM158.

1934. MARYLAND TERCENTENARY ISSUE marked the 300th anniversary of the settlement of Maryland by about 200 colonists under a charter held by Cecilius Calvert, second Lord Baltimore, a Catholic. He made the colony a haven of religious tolerance. The *Ark* and the *Dove* were sailing vessels used in the voyage to America. *Intaglio, perforated 11.*

CM126 *The* Ark *and the* Dove, *from a drawing by Edwin Tunis*

CM126		UnFVF	UseFVF
3¢	carmine red *(46,258,300)*	.25	.20
	Plate block of 6	10.00	
	Double transfer (position 1 of top-left pane of plate No. 21190)	—	
	FDC *(March 23, 1934)*		15.00
	v. Horizontal pair, imperforate horizontally	6,500.00	

1934. MOTHER'S DAY ISSUE commemorated the 20th anniversary of Woodrow Wilson's proclamation of the second Sunday in May as Mother's Day. The design shows an adaptation of the painting popularly known as "Whistler's Mother," a world symbol of motherhood, although the painter, James Abbott McNeill Whistler (1834-1903), called the picture simply *Arrangement in Grey and Black: The Painter's Mother (1871)*. Stamp issued in both rotary and flat-press printings. *Intaglio.*

CM127-128, CM144 *Whistler's Mother, from a painting by James McNeill Whistler, the first painting by an American in the Louvre Museum, Paris, France*

Rotary press, perforated 11x10 1/2.

CM127		UnFVF	UseFVF
3¢	reddish violet *(193,239,100)*	.25	.20
	Plate block of 4	1.25	
	FDC *(May 2, 1934)*		15.00

Flat press, perforated 11.

CM128		UnFVF	UseFVF
3¢	reddish violet *(15,432,200)*	.25	.20
	Plate block of 6	5.00	
	FDC *(May 2, 1934)*		1.00

For ungummed stamps (Farley issue), see CM144.

1934. WISCONSIN TERCENTENARY ISSUE memorialized the 300th anniversary of the arrival of the French explorer Jean Nicolet onto the shores of Green Bay on Lake Michigan. The first white man to reach that region, he appears in oriental garb as he thought he was landing in China. *Intaglio.*

CM129, CM145 *Nicolet's Landing on Green Bay, from a painting by Edward W. Deming, Wisconsin Historical Society*

CM129		UnFVF	UseFVF
3¢	reddish violet *(64,525,400)*	.25	.20
	violet	.25	.20
	Plate block of 6	4.00	
	FDC *(July 7, 1934)*		15.00
	v. Horizontal pair, imperforate vertically	325.00	
	v1. Vertical pair, imperforate horizontally	275.00	

For ungummed stamps (Farley issue), see CM145.

1934. NATIONAL PARKS ISSUE commemorated National Parks Year and publicized the great American park system. *Intaglio.*

CM130, CM146, CM159 *El Capitan, Yosemite (California)*

CM130		UnFVF	UseFVF
1¢	**green** *(84,896,350)*	.25	.20
	light green	.25	.20
	Plate block of 6	1.50	
	Recut	—	
	FDC *(July 16, 1934)*		10.00
	v. Vertical pair, imperforate horizontally	550.00	
	(with gum)		

CM131, CM147 *Grand Canyon (Arizona)*

CM131		UnFVF	UseFVF
2¢	**red** *(74,400,200)*	.25	.20
	Plate block of 6	1.75	
	Double transfer	—	
	FDC *(July 24, 1934)*		10.00
	v. Horizontal pair, imperforate vertically	300.00	
	(with gum)		
	v1. Vertical pair, imperforate horizontally	400.00	
	(with gum)		

CM132, CM148, CM160 *Mt. Rainier and Mirror Lake (Washington)*

CM132		UnFVF	UseFVF
3¢	**reddish violet** *(95,089,000)*	.25	.20
	Plate block of 6	2.00	
	Recut	—	
	FDC *(Aug. 3, 1934)*		10.00
	v. Vertical pair, imperforate horizontally	450.00	
	(with gum)		

CM133, CM149 *The Cliff Palace, Mesa Verde (Colorado)*

CM133		UnFVF	UseFVF
4¢	**yellow brown** *(19,178,650)*	.50	.35
	light brown	8.00	
	Plate block of 6	—	
	FDC *(Sept. 25, 1934)*		10.00
	v. Vertical pair, imperforate horizontally	650.00	
	(with gum)		

CM134, CM150 *Old Faithful, Yellowstone (Wyoming)*

CM134		UnFVF	UseFVF
5¢	**light blue** *(30,980,100)*	1.00	.75
	blue	1.00	.75
	Plate block of 6	10.00	
	FDC *(July 30, 1934)*		10.00
	v. Horizontal pair, imperforate vertically	475.00	
	(with gum)		

CM135, CM151 *Crater Lake (Oregon)*

CM135		UnFVF	UseFVF
6¢	**blue** *(16,923,350)*	1.25	1.00
	Plate block of 6	20.00	
	FDC *(Sept. 5, 1934)*		22.50

CM136, CM152 *Great Head, Bar Harbor, Acadia (Maine)*

CM136		UnFVF	UseFVF
7¢	**black** *(15,988,250)*	1.00	.75
	Plate block of 6	12.50	
	Double transfer	—	
	FDC *(Oct. 2, 1934)*		10.00
	v. Horizontal pair, imperforate vertically	550.00	
	(with gum)		

CM137, CM153 *Great White Throne, Zion (Utah)*

CM137		UnFVF	UseFVF
8¢	**gray green** *(15,288,700)*	2.00	1.75
	Plate block of 6	20.00	
	FDC *(Sept. 18, 1934)*		10.00

CM138, CM154 *Mt. Rockwell and Two Medicine Lake, Glacier (Montana)*

CM138		UnFVF	UseFVF
9¢	**orange red** *(17,472,600)*	2.00	.75
	orange	2.00	.75
	Plate block of 6	20.00	
	FDC *(Aug. 17, 1934)*		10.00

CM139, CM155 *Great Smoky Mountains (North Carolina)*

CM139		UnFVF	UseFVF
10¢	gray black *(18,874,300)*	3.25	1.25
	gray	3.25	1.25
	Plate block of 6	30.00	
	FDC *(Oct. 8, 1934)*		10.00

For ungummed stamps (Farley issue), see CM146-CM155.

1934. TRANS-MISSISSIPPI PHILATELIC EXPOSITION ISSUE was released in honor of the Philatelic Exposition and Convention held at Omaha, Nebr. *The sheet measured 94x99mm, contained six imperforate, gummed 1¢ National Parks stamps, and was inscribed in the margin:* "PRINTED BY THE TREASURY DEPARTMENT, BUREAU OF ENGRAVING AND PRINTING / UNDER AUTHORITY OF JAMES A. FARLEY, POSTMASTER GENERAL / IN COMPLIMENT TO THE TRANS-MISSISSIPPI PHILATELIC EXPOSITION AND CONVENTION / OMAHA, NEBRASKA, OCTOBER 1934."

CM140, CM159 *El Capitan, Yosemite (California)*

CM140		UnFVF	UseFVF
1¢	**green,** sheet of 6 *(793,551)*	14.00	12.50
	FDC *(Oct. 10, 1934)*		75.00
	a. Single stamp	2.00	1.75
	FDC, single stamp		20.00

For ungummed stamps (Farley issue), see CM159.

1934. AMERICAN PHILATELIC SOCIETY ISSUE honored the American Philatelic Society convention and exhibition held at Atlantic City, N.J. *The sheet measured 97x99mm, contained six imperforate, gummed 3¢ National Parks stamps, and was inscribed in the margin:* "PRINTED BY THE TREASURY DEPARTMENT, BUREAU OF ENGRAVING AND PRINTING / UNDER AUTHORITY OF JAMES A. FARLEY, POSTMASTER GENERAL / IN COMPLIMENT TO THE AMERICAN PHILATELIC SOCIETY FOR ITS CONVENTION AND EXHIBITION / ATLANTIC CITY, NEW JERSEY, AUGUST 1934."

CM141, CM160 *Mt. Rainier and Mirror Lake (Washington)*

CM141		UnFVF	UseFVF
3¢	**reddish violet,** sheet of 6 *(511,391)*	40.00	30.00
	FDC *(Aug. 28, 1934)*		75.00
	a. Single stamp	4.50	4.00
	FDC, single stamp		20.00

For ungummed stamps (Farley issue), see CM160.

The Farley Series (CM142-CM161) is a collective term commonly applied to 20 stamps issued to the public as a direct result of protests by collectors against the practice of presenting to a few favored collectors full sheets of stamps in forms not available to the general public. Original "Farley Sheets" — signed by government officials,

including Franklin D. Roosevelt, president; Harold L. Ickes, secretary of the interior; and James A. Farley, postmaster general — were given as philatelic favors to political friends.

The full sheets of the Farley Series contained four or more post office panes separated by spaces (called gutters) or by guidelines and arrows (to guide the cutting machine). Blocks showing two crossed gutters or crossed lines are called "cross gutter" and "center line" blocks, respectively.

All of the Farley stamps were issued ungummed. In 1940, the Post Office Department gummed full sheets of CM144-61 sent in by collectors for that purpose. With the exception of CM142-43, all Farley stamps were imperforate.

The Farley Series sheets were first placed on sale March 15, 1935, at the Philatelic Agency in Washington, D.C., and were sold through June 15, 1935.

1935. NEWBURGH FARLEY ISSUE was printed in sheets of 400 stamps: 4 panes of 100 stamps, separated by gutters. Newburgh Farley stamps differ slightly in color from the original Newburgh issue (CM117); there seems to be a tinge of blue in the violet. They usually are not well-centered and the perforations are ragged. *Intaglio, ungummed and perforated 10 1/2x11.*

CM142		UnFVF	UseFVF
3¢	**reddish violet** *(3,274,556)*	.25	.20
	Plate block of 4	16.50	
	Plate block of 4, w/arrow at top or bottom	15.00	
	Plate block of 4, w/arrow at side	8.50	
	Pair w/vertical gutter	7.50	
	Pair w/horizontal gutter	4.00	
	Center line block	50.00	
	FDC *(March 15, 1935)*		35.00

1935. BYRD FARLEY ISSUE was printed in sheets of 200, so that arrows and guidelines, along which the sheets normally were cut into panes of 50 before being sent to the post office, are complete. The stamps were issued *without gum and perforated 11.* Since it is virtually impossible to distinguish between a used copy of this and the original Byrd stamp (CM123), they must be considered interchangeable in used condition.

CM143		UnFVF	UseFVF
3¢	**blue** *(2,040,760)*	.50	.45
	Plate block of 6	17.50	
	Pair, w/vertical line	2.00	
	Pair, w/horizontal line	40.00	
	Block of 4, w/arrow at top or bottom	85.00	
	Block of 4, w/arrow at side	4.00	
	Center line block	90.00	
	FDC *(March 15, 1935)*		35.00

1935. MOTHER'S DAY FARLEY ISSUE was printed on a flat-plate press in sheets of 200 with arrows and guidelines, identical in design to CM127, but issued *without gum* and *imperforate.*

CM144		UnFVF	UseFVF
3¢	**reddish violet** *(2,389,288)*	.60	.60
	Plate block of 6	18.50	
	Block of 4, w/arrow at top or bottom	—	
	Block of 4, w/arrow at side	4.50	
	Pair, w/vertical line	1.75	
	Pair, w/horizontal line	2.25	
	Center line block	10.00	
	FDC *(March 15, 1935)*		35.00

1935. WISCONSIN FARLEY ISSUE was printed in sheets of 200 with arrows and guidelines, identical in design to CM129, but issued *without gum* and *imperforate.*

CM145		UnFVF	UseFVF
3¢	**reddish violet** *(2,294,948)*	.60	.60
	Plate block of 6	18.50	
	Block of 4, w/arrow at top or bottom	3.50	
	Block of 4, w/arrow at side	4.50	
	Pair, w/vertical line	1.75	
	Pair, w/horizontal line	2.25	
	Center line block	10.00	
	FDC *(March 15, 1935)*		35.00

1935. NATIONAL PARKS FARLEY ISSUE were printed in sheets of 200 with arrows and guidelines. The designs are identical to CM130-39, but the Farley versions were issued *without gum* and *imperforate.*

CM146		UnFVF	UseFVF
1¢	**green** *(3,217,636)*	.25	.20
	Plate block of 6	6.50	

Block of 4, w/arrow at top or bottom	1.25		
Block of 4, w/arrow at sides	1.00		
Pair, w/vertical line	.60		
Pair, w/horizontal line	.45		
Center line block	4.50		
FDC *(March 15, 1935)*		30.00	

CM147

		UnFVF	UseFVF
2¢	**red** *(2,746,640)*	.25	.20
	Plate block of 6	7.50	
	Block of 4, w/arrow at top or bottom	1.50	
	Block of 4, w/arrow at sides	1.50	
	Pair, w/vertical line	.60	
	Pair, w/horizontal line	.65	
	Center line block	5.00	
	Double transfer	—	
	FDC *(March 15, 1935)*		30.00

CM148

		UnFVF	UseFVF
3¢	**reddish violet** *(2,168,088)*	.50	.45
	Plate block of 6	17.50	
	Block of 4, w/arrow at top or bottom	3.00	
	Block of 4, w/arrow at sides	3.75	
	Pair, w/vertical line	1.25	
	Pair, w/horizontal line	1.75	
	Center line block	12.50	
	FDC *(March 15, 1935)*		30.00

CM149

		UnFVF	UseFVF
4¢	**yellow brown** *(1,822,684)*	1.25	1.25
	Plate block of 6	22.50	
	Block of 4, w/arrow at top or bottom	5.50	
	Block of 4, w/arrow at sides	6.50	
	Pair, w/vertical line	2.50	
	Pair, w/horizontal line	3.00	
	Center line block	12.50	
	FDC *(March 15, 1935)*		30.00

CM150

		UnFVF	UseFVF
5¢	**light blue** *(1,724,576)*	1.75	1.75
	Plate block of 6	27.50	
	Block of 4, w/arrow at top or bottom	12.00	
	Block of 4, w/arrow at sides	10.00	
	Pair, w/vertical line	5.25	
	Pair, w/horizontal line	4.25	
	Center line block	20.00	
	Double transfer	—	
	FDC *(March 15, 1935)*		30.00

CM151

		UnFVF	UseFVF
6¢	**blue** *(1,647,696)*	2.25	2.25
	Plate block of 6	40.00	
	Block of 4, w/arrow at top or bottom	12.50	
	Block of 4, w/arrow at sides	15.00	
	Pair, w/vertical line	6.00	
	Pair, w/horizontal line	6.75	
	Center line block	22.50	
	FDC *(March 15, 1935)*		30.00

CM152

		UnFVF	UseFVF
7¢	**black** *(1,682,948)*	2.00	1.75
	Plate block of 6	37.50	
	Block of 4, w/arrow at top or bottom	10.00	
	Block of 4, w/arrow at sides	12.00	
	Pair, w/vertical line	4.50	
	Pair, w/horizontal line	5.00	
	Center line block	2.00	
	Double transfer	—	
	FDC *(March 15, 1935)*		30.00

CM153

		UnFVF	UseFVF
8¢	**gray green** *(1,638,644)*	2.00	2.00
	Plate block of 6	45.00	
	Block of 4, w/arrow at top or bottom	14.00	
	Block of 4, w/arrow at sides	12.50	
	Pair, w/vertical line	6.50	
	Pair, w/horizontal line	5.00	
	Center line block	22.50	
	FDC *(March 15, 1935)*		30.00

CM154

		UnFVF	UseFVF
9¢	**orange red** *(1,625,224)*	2.00	2.00
	Plate block of 6	47.50	
	Block of 4, w/arrow at top or bottom	12.50	
	Block of 4, w/arrow at sides	14.00	
	Pair, w/vertical line	12.50	
	Pair, w/horizontal line	10.00	
	Center line block	35.00	
	FDC *(March 15, 1935)*		30.00

CM155

		UnFVF	UseFVF
10¢	**gray black** *(1,644,900)*	4.00	3.50
	Plate block of 6	55.00	
	Block of 4, w/arrow at top or bottom	25.00	
	Block of 4, w/arrow at sides	22.50	
	Pair, w/vertical line	12.50	
	Pair, w/horizontal line	10.00	
	Center line block	35.00	
	FDC *(March 15, 1935)*		30.00

1935. CENTURY OF PROGRESS SOUVENIR SHEET, FARLEY ISSUE contained nine souvenir sheets of 25 stamps each, separated by gutters, issued *without gum* and *imperforate*. Identification of single stamps is possible only with stamps that come from the outside rows of the miniature sheets, in which the margins are wider than those from the regular sheets, CM120-21.

CM156

		UnFVF	UseFVF
1¢	**yellow green** *(2,467,800)*	22.50	22.50
	Horizontal gutter block	—	
	Vertical gutter block	—	
	Cross-gutter block	12.50	
	a. Single stamp	.75	.30
	FDC *(March 15, 1935)*		40.00

CM157

		UnFVF	UseFVF
3¢	**reddish violet** *(2,147,856)*	20.00	20.00
	Horizontal gutter block	—	
	Vertical gutter block	—	
	Cross-gutter block	12.50	
	a. Single stamp	.75	.30
	FDC *(March 15, 1935)*		40.00

1935. BYRD SOUVENIR SHEET, FARLEY ISSUE contained 25 souvenir sheets of six stamps each, separated by gutters, issued *without gum* and *imperforate*. Identification of single stamps is possible only if their margins are wider than those from the regular sheet, CM125.

CM158

		UnFVF	UseFVF
3¢	**blue** *(1,603,200)*	17.50	12.50
	Horizcntal gutter block	—	
	Vertical gutter block	—	
	Cross-gutter block	17.50	
	a. Single stamp	2.75	2.25
	FDC *(March 15, 1935)*		40.00

1935. NATIONAL PARKS SOUVENIR SHEETS, FARLEY ISSUE contained 20 souvenir sheets of six stamps each, separated by gutters, issued *without gum* and *imperforate*. Identification of single stamps is possible only if their margins are wider than those from the regular sheets, CM140-41.

CM159

		UnFVF	UseFVF
1¢	**green** *(1,679,760)*	10.00	9.00
	Horizontal gutter block	—	
	Vertical gutter block	—	
	Cross-gutter block	12.50	
	a. Single stamp	1.75	1.75
	FDC *(March 15, 1935)*		40.00

CM160

		UnFVF	UseFVF
3¢	**reddish violet** *(1,295,520)*	25.00	20.00
	Horizontal gutter block	—	
	Vertical gutter block	—	
	Cross-gutter block	25.00	
	a. Single stamp	3.00	2.75
	FDC *(March 15, 1935)*		40.00

1935. AIRMAIL SPECIAL DELIVERY FARLEY ISSUE was printed in sheets of 200 stamps with arrows and guidelines. It is listed in this section of the catalog because it always has been considered an integral part of the Farley Series. *Intaglio, without gum, imperforate.*

CM161

		UnFVF	UseFVF
16¢	**blue** *(1,370,560)*	2.75	2.50
	Plate block of 6	70.00	
	Block of 4, w/arrow at top or bottom	13.50	
	Block of 4, w/arrow at sides	17.00	
	Horizontal gutter block	—	
	Vertical gutter block	—	
	Center line block	77.50	
	FDC *(March 15, 1935)*		40.00

1935. CONNECTICUT TERCENTENARY ISSUE commemorated the 300th anniversary of the settlement of Connecticut by dissatisfied members of the Massachusetts Bay Colony. The tree depicted is the oak in which the Colonial charter was hidden when it was demanded by the British in 1687. *Intaglio, perforated 11x10 1/2.*

CM162 *The Charter Oak, from a painting by Charles D. Brownell (1822-1909), State Library, Hartford, Conn.*

CM162		UnFVF	UseFVF
3¢	purple *(70,726,800)*	.25	.20
	rose violet	.25	.20
	Plate block of 4	2.00	
	Defect in ¢ sign (position 4 of top-right pane of plate No. 21395)	—	
	FDC *(April 26, 1935)*		10.00

For imperforates, see No. CM168.

1935. CALIFORNIA-PACIFIC ISSUE commemorated the California-Pacific Exposition at San Diego, Calif. *Intaglio, perforated 11x10 1/2.*

CM163 *View of the San Diego Exposition, from a sketch by Larrinague*

CM163		UnFVF	UseFVF
3¢	dark lilac *(100,839,600)*	.25	.20
	Plate block of 4	1.50	
	Pair, gutter between	—	
	FDC *(May 29, 1935)*		12.50

For imperforates, see No. CM168.

1935. BOULDER DAM ISSUE commemorated the dedication of the largest dam on the Colorado River. Built to supply power, water and flood control, its name was changed in 1933 to Boulder Dam, which appears on the stamp. Its original name, Hoover Dam, was restored in 1947. *Intaglio, perforated 11.*

CM164 *Boulder (Hoover) Dam*

CM164		UnFVF	UseFVF
3¢	dark lilac *(73,610,650)*	.25	.20
	purple	.25	.20
	Plate block of 6	2.25	
	FDC *(Sept. 30, 1935)*		15.00

1935. MICHIGAN CENTENNIAL ISSUE commemorated the 100th anniversary of the admission of Michigan as the 26th state. *Intaglio, perforated 11x10 1/2.*

CM165 *Michigan state seal*

CM165		UnFVF	UseFVF
3¢	dark lilac *(75,823,900)*	.25	.20
	Plate block of 4	1.50	
	FDC *(Nov. 1, 1935)*		12.50

For imperforates, see No. CM168.

1936. TEXAS CENTENNIAL ISSUE commemorated the 100th anniversary of Texas independence, established after the Texans under Gen. Sam Houston defeated the Mexicans at the Battle of San Jacinto. The first Texas colony was founded by Stephen P. Austin under a Mexican charter in 1821. *Intaglio, perforated 11x10 1/2.*

CM166 *Sam Houston, Stephen F. Austin and The Alamo, from artwork by S. Salamo, T.A. Butler and F. Pauling*

CM166		UnFVF	UseFVF
3¢	dark lilac *(124,324,500)*	.25	.20
	Plate block of 4	1.50	
	FDC *(March 2, 1936)*		15.00

For imperforates, see No. CM168.

1936. RHODE ISLAND TERCENTENARY ISSUE honored the 300th anniversary of the founding of Rhode Island as a haven of tolerance by Roger Williams. This was the only New England colony to tolerate a permanent Jewish community in the 17th century. *Intaglio, perforated 10 1/2x11.*

CM167 *Roger Williams, a statue by Franklin Simmons in Williams Park, Providence, R.I.*

CM167		UnFVF	UseFVF
3¢	dull purple *(67,127,650)*	.25	.20
	rose violet	.25	.20
	Plate block of 4	1.50	
	Pair, gutter between	—	
	FDC *(May 4, 1936)*		10.00

1936. TIPEX SOUVENIR SHEET was issued in complement to the Third International Philatelic Exhibition held in New York City. *The sheet measures 98x66mm and contains one each of the Connecticut, California-Pacific, Michigan and Texas stamps. Intaglio, imperforate. The sheet is inscribed in the margins:* "PRINTED BY THE TREASURY DEPARTMENT, BUREAU OF ENGRAVING AND PRINTING / UNDER AUTHORITY OF JAMES A. FARLEY, POSTMASTER GENERAL / IN COMPLIMENT TO THE THIRD INTERNATIONAL PHILATELIC EXHIBITION OF 1936 / NEW YORK, N.Y., MAY 9-17, 1936."

CM168 *TIPEX souvenir sheet of 4*

CM168		UnFVF	UseFVF
4x3¢	reddish purple *(2,809,039)*	2.75	2.50
	FDC *(May 9, 1936)*		17.50
	a. Connecticut single from souvenir sheet	.75	.60
	b. California single from souvenir sheet	.75	.60
	c. Michigan single from souvenir sheet	.75	.60
	d. Texas single from souvenir sheet	.75	.60

1936. ARKANSAS CENTENNIAL ISSUE commemorated the 100th anniversary of the admission of Arkansas into the Union as the 25th state. *Intaglio, perforated 11x10 1/2.*

CM169 *Old State House in Little Rock, Ark.*

CM169

3¢	**dark lilac** *(72,992,650)*	UnFVF	UseFVF
		.25	.20
	Plate block of 4	1.50	
	FDC *(June 15, 1936)*		10.00

1936. OREGON TERRITORY CENTENNIAL ISSUE commemorated the 100th anniversary of the opening of the Oregon Territory, comprising the present states of Oregon, Washington, Idaho and parts of Montana and Wyoming. *Intaglio, perforated 11x10 1/2.*

CM170 *Map of Oregon Territory*

CM170

3¢	**dark lilac** *(74,407,450)*	UnFVF	UseFVF
		.25	.20
	Plate block of 4	1.25	
	Double transfer	—	
	FDC *(July 14, 1936)*		1.50

1936. SUSAN B. ANTHONY ISSUE in an election year, honored the 16th anniversary of the ratification of the 19th Amendment, which granted suffrage to women. Anthony (1820-1906) was a pioneer in temperance and social reform, and in part through her leadership and effort, women in the United States won the right to vote. Beginning with this issue, plate numbers were placed 4mm from the frame line of the nearest stamp. Previously, they were separated by less than 2mm. *Intaglio, perforated 11x10 1/2.*

CM171 *Susan B. Anthony*

CM171

3¢	**reddish purple** *(269,522,200)*	UnFVF	UseFVF
		.25	.20
	Plate block of 4	1.25	
	FDC *(Aug. 20, 1936)*		10.00

1936-37. ARMY ISSUE honored the U.S. Army and paid tribute to its early leaders and heroes. *Intaglio, perforated 11x10 1/2.*

CM172 *George Washington commanded the Continental Army throughout the Revolutionary War. (See CM98-CM109) Mount Vernon was his home in Virginia. Nathanael Greene led the patriot forces in the Southern theater. Both portraits are from Trumbull paintings.*

CM172

1¢	**green** *(105,196,150)*	UnFVF	UseFVF
		.25	.20
	Plate block of 4	1.00	
	FDC *(Dec. 15, 1936)*		7.50

CM173 *Andrew Jackson (from a statue by Belle Scholtz in the U.S. Hall of Fame) defeated the Creek Indians at Horseshoe Bend in 1814, and the British at New Orleans in 1815. The Hermitage was his Tennessee home. Winfield Scott (from a statue by Launt*

Thomas in the U.S. Soldiers' Home at Washington) fought gallantly at Chippewa and Lundy's Lane in the War of 1812 and led the U.S. Army in the Mexican War.

CM173

2¢	**rose red** *(93,848,500)*	UnFVF	UseFVF
		.25	.20
	Plate block of 4	1.00	
	FDC *(Jan. 15, 1937)*		10.00

CM174 *William Tecumseh Sherman has been called "the first modern general." His march from Atlanta to the sea in the Civil War aimed at weakening his adversaries by the destruction of supplies rather than lives. Ulysses S. Grant split the Confederacy in two by capturing Vicksburg in 1863. After his successful Tennessee campaigns, he was given command under Lincoln of all Union forces and fought a war of attrition that brought the war to an end in 1865. Philip H. Sheridan, a cavalry commander, distinguished himself at Chickamauga and Chattanooga, and commanded the army that laid waste to the Shenandoah Valley.*

CM174

3¢	**dull purple** *(87,741,150)*	UnFVF	UseFVF
		.25	.20
	Plate block of 4	1.50	
	FDC *(Feb. 18, 1937)*		7.50

CM175 *Robert E. Lee, to whom Lincoln offered command of the Union field forces in 1861, resigned his commission instead to command the forces of Virginia. After his defeat at Gettysburg, July 1863, he fought bravely and brilliantly against hopeless odds, surrendering to Grant in 1865. Stratford Hall was his birthplace. Thomas J. Jackson, greatest of Lee's generals, won his nickname "Stonewall" by holding off strong Union assaults at the first Battle of Bull Run. After forcing back the Union troops at Chancellorsville, he was mistakenly shot by one of his own pickets.*

CM175

4¢	**slate** *(35,794,150)*	UnFVF	UseFVF
		.50	.20
	Plate block of 4	10.00	
	FDC *(March 23, 1937)*		7.50

CM176 *The U.S. Military Academy at West Point, N.Y., was established in 1802. Upon completion of a four-year course, cadets are eligible for commission as second lieutenants in the Army. Its graduates include all five generals pictured on CM174 and CM175. Among its civilian alumni were James Abbott McNeill Whistler (CM227) and Edgar Allan Poe (CM328).*

CM176

5¢	**gray blue** *(36,839,250)*	UnFVF	UseFVF
		.75	.20
	Plate block of 4	12.50	
	FDC *(May 26, 1937)*		7.50

1936-37. NAVY ISSUE honored the U.S. Navy and paid tribute to early naval leaders and heroes. *Intaglio, perforated 11x10 1/2.*

CM177 *John Paul Jones (from a painting by Peale) destroyed British ships, preyed upon the British coast and captured the man-of-war Serapis in a battle in which his own flagship Bonhomme Richard (shown) was sunk. John Barry (from a painting by Stuart) commanded the Lexington when he captured the first ship ever taken by a commanding officer of the U.S. Navy.*

CM177		UnFVF	UseFVF
1¢	green (104,773,450)	.25	.20
	Plate block of 4	1.00	
	FDC (Dec. 15, 1936)		7.50

CM178 *Stephen Decatur (from a painting by Alonzo Chappel), fighting the Tripolitan pirates, effected the daring recapture of the frigate Philadelphia. He commanded the ship United States in the War of 1812. The stamp shows a contemporary warship under full sail. Thomas Macdonough (from a painting by Carl Becker), commanded the American fleet on Lake Champlain, where his brilliant victory over the British in 1814 saved New York and Vermont from invasion. The Saratoga was his flagship.*

CM178		UnFVF	UseFVF
2¢	rose red (92,054,550)	.25	.20
	Plate block of 4	1.00	
	FDC (Jan. 15, 1937)		7.50

CM179 *David Farragut (from a photograph by Brady), in 1862 destroyed the Confederate fleet at New Orleans. His foster brother David Dixon Porter aided him there and at Vicksburg; later, as superintendent of the U.S. Naval Academy, Porter greatly improved its organization and curriculum. The stamp mentions ships commanded and depicts a warship of the period.*

CM179		UnFVF	UseFVF
3¢	dull purple (93,291,650)	.25	.20
	Plate block of 4	1.50	
	FDC (Feb. 18, 1937)		7.50

CM180 *William T. Sampson commanded the North Atlantic Squadron that destroyed the Spanish fleet at Santiago, Cuba, in 1898, sharing the victory with Winfield S. Schley, his second in command. Schley earlier had led the expedition that rescued the Arctic explorer Adolphus Greely in 1884. George Dewey, commanding the Asiatic Squadron, destroyed the Spanish fleet in the Philippines in 1898.*

CM180		UnFVF	UseFVF
4¢	slate (34,521,950)	.50	.20
	Plate block of 4	10.00	
	FDC (March 23, 1937)		7.50

CM181 *The U.S. Naval Academy at Annapolis, Md., was established in 1805. Upon completion of a four-year course, midshipmen are eligible for commissions as ensigns in the Navy. Its graduates include all three admirals pictured on CM180. The stamp pictures the academy's seal and cadets of early days and the 1930s.*

CM181		UnFVF	UseFVF
5¢	gray blue (36,819,050)	.75	.20
	Plate block of 4	12.50	
	Pair, gutter between	—	
	FDC (May 26, 1937)		7.50

1937. NORTHWEST ORDINANCE ISSUE OF 1787 marked the 150th anniversary of the adoption of the Northwest Ordinance by the Congress of the Confederation. The confederation's greatest achievement, the ordinance provided for the governing of the Northwest Territory, dividing it into five parts that are now Ohio, Indiana, Illinois, Wisconsin and Michigan. The Rev. Manasseh Cutler, a distinguished botanist, aided in drafting the ordinance and organizing the colonization. Rufus Putnam led the first settlers (see CM192), who founded Marietta, Ohio. *Intaglio, perforated 11x10 1/2.*

CM182 *Manasseh Cutler (from an engraving by J.C. Buttre), Rufus Putnam (from a Trumbull miniature), map of the Northwest Territory*

CM182		UnFVF	UseFVF
3¢	dull purple (84,825,250)	.25	.20
	Plate block of 4	8.50	
	FDC (July 13, 1937)		10.00

1937. VIRGINIA DARE ISSUE commemorated the 350th birthday of Virginia Dare, first child of English parentage born in America, at Roanoke Island off the North Carolina coast. Her grandfather, John White, leader of the expedition for Sir Walter Raleigh, returned to England for supplies a week after her birth in 1579. The Spanish War delayed his return until 1591, by which time the entire colony had mysteriously vanished. The stamps were printed 48 to the pane. *Flat plate printing, intaglio, perforated 11.*

CM183 *Virginia Dare and parents, from a drawing by William A. Roache*

CM183		UnFVF	UseFVF
5¢	light slate blue (25,040,400)	.25	.20
	Plate block of 6	8.50	
	FDC (Aug. 18, 1937)		10.00

1937. SOCIETY OF PHILATELIC AMERICANS SOUVENIR SHEET was issued for the 43rd annual convention of the S.P.A. at Asheville, N.C. It consisted of a single stamp, the 10¢ Great Smokey Mountains National Park design (CM139), *printed in blue green on a sheet measuring 67x78mm. Intaglio, imperforate. The margin is inscribed:* "PRINTED BY THE TREASURY DEPARTMENT, BUREAU OF ENGRAVING AND PRINTING / UNDER THE AUTHORITY OF JAMES A. FARLEY, POSTMASTER GENERAL / IN COMPLIMENT TO THE 43RD ANNUAL CONVENTION OF THE SOCIETY OF PHILATELIC AMERICANS / ASHEVILLE, N.C., AUGUST 26-28, 1937."

CM184 *Society of Philatelic Americans souvenir sheet*

CM184		UnFVF	UseFVF
10¢	blue green (5,277,445)	.75	.65
	FDC (Aug. 26, 1937)		10.00

1937. CONSTITUTION SESQUICENTENNIAL ISSUE marked the 150th anniversary of the signing of the U.S. Constitution. The Articles of Confederation having proved ineffectual, a convention was called in Philadelphia to revise and strengthen them. The convention, presided over by Washington, sat for four months in closed sessions, scrapping the Articles altogether and vigorously debating a new constitution point by point. On Sept. 17, 1787, a final draft was signed by 39 of the 42 delegates present and sent to Congress for submission to the states. *Intaglio, perforated 11x10 1/2.*

CM185 *Adoption of the Constitution, from a painting by J.B. Sterns*

CM185		UnFVF	UseFVF
3¢	bright purple *(99,882,300)*	.25	.20
	Plate block of 4	1.75	
	FDC *(Sept. 17, 1937)*		7.50

1937. HAWAII TERRITORY ISSUE honored Hawaii, which voluntarily joined the United States in 1898. King Kamehameha the Great (1737-1819) united the Hawaiian Islands under one rule and allowed the first foreign traders to settle there. *Intaglio, perforated 10 1/2x11.*

CM186 *Kamehameha I, from a statue by T.R. Gould, Iolani Castle, Honolulu*

CM186		UnFVF	UseFVF
3¢	violet *(78,454,450)*	.25	.20
	Plate block of 4	1.50	
	FDC *(Oct. 18, 1937)*		20.00

1937. ALASKA TERRITORY ISSUE honored Alaska, purchased from Russia in 1867 (see CM43). Mount McKinley, pictured on the stamp, is the highest North American peak. *Intaglio, perforated 10 1/2x11.*

CM187 *Mount McKinley*

CM187		UnFVF	UseFVF
3¢	violet *(77,004,200)*	.25	.20
	Plate block of 4	1.50	
	Pair, gutter between	—	
	FDC *(Nov. 12, 1937)*		15.00

1937. PUERTO RICO TERRITORY ISSUE honored Puerto Rico, ceded to the United States by Spain after the Spanish-American War of 1898. The stamp shows the old Governor's Palace in San Juan, known as La Fortaleza. *Intaglio, perforated 10 1/2x11.*

CM188 *La Fortaleza Palace*

CM188		UnFVF	UseFVF
3¢	light reddish violet *(81,292,450)*	.25	.20
	Plate block of 4	1.50	
	FDC *(Nov. 25, 1937)*		15.00

1937. VIRGIN ISLANDS ISSUE honored the Virgin Islands Territory, purchased from Denmark in 1917 to serve as a naval base for the defense of the Panama Canal. *Intaglio, perforated 10 1/2x11.*

CM189 *Harbor at Charlotte Amalie, St. Thomas, Virgin Islands*

CM189		UnFVF	UseFVF
3¢	lilac *(76,474,550)*	.25	.20
	Plate block of 4	.50	
	Pair, gutter between	—	
	FDC *(Dec. 15, 1937)*		15.00

1938. CONSTITUTION RATIFICATION ISSUE commemorated the 150th anniversary of the ratification of the Constitution of the United States. The endorsement of nine states was needed to make the Constitution effective. Maryland was the first state to ratify it. New Hampshire became the ninth (June 21, 1788). *Intaglio, perforated 11x10 1/2.*

CM190 *Colonial Court House, Williamsburg, Va.*

CM190		UnFVF	UseFVF
3¢	violet *(73,043,650)*	.50	.20
	Plate block of 4	4.50	
	FDC *(June 21, 1938)*		10.00

1938. SWEDES AND FINNS ISSUE commemorated the 300th anniversary of the settlement by Swedish and Finnish colonists of Fort Christina (now Wilmington, Del.). They were led by Peter Minuit, who was a leader in the earlier settlement of New York (see CM64). The stamps were printed 48 to the sheet. *Intaglio, perforated 11.*

CM191 *Landing of the Swedes and Finns, from a painting by Stanley M. Arthurs, Wilmington, Del.*

CM191		UnFVF	UseFVF
3¢	carmine purple *(58,564,368)*	.25	.20
	Plate block of 6	3.25	
	FDC *(June 27, 1938)*		10.00

1938. NORTHWEST TERRITORY ISSUE commemorated the 150th anniversary of the settlement of the Northwest Territory after the Northwest Ordinance of 1787 (see CM182). *Intaglio, perforated 11x10 1/2.*

CM192 *Colonization of the West, from a statue by Gutzon Borglum, Marietta, Ohio*

CM192		UnFVF	UseFVF
3¢	light reddish violet *(65,939,500)*	.25	.20
	violet	.25	.20
	Plate block of 4	10.00	
	FDC *(July 15, 1938)*		10.00

1938. IOWA TERRITORY ISSUE commemorated the 100th anniversary of the establishment of the Iowa Territory, July 3, 1838. The stamp was placed on sale in Des Moines at the opening of the Iowa State Fair. The building pictured was the old Iowa capitol in Iowa City. *Intaglio, perforated 11x10 1/2.*

CM193 *Old Capitol Building, Iowa City, Iowa*

CM193		UnFVF	UseFVF
3¢	violet *(47,064,300)*	.25	.20
	Plate block of 4	7.50	
	Pair, gutter between	—	
	FDC *(Aug. 24, 1938)*		10.00

1939. GOLDEN GATE EXPOSITION ISSUE commemorated the international fair held in San Francisco, Calif. The exposition's Tower of the Sun is shown. *Intaglio, perforated 10 1/2x11.*

CM194 *Tower of the Sun*

CM194		UnFVF	UseFVF
3¢	light reddish violet *(114,439,600)*	.25	.20
	Plate block of 4	1.75	
	FDC *(Feb. 18, 1939)*		10.00

1939. NEW YORK WORLD'S FAIR ISSUE commemorated the enormous fair and exhibition, "The World of Tomorrow," held in New York City during 1939-40. The futuristic Trylon and Perisphere served as a focal point for the fair. *Intaglio, perforated 10 1/2x11.*

CM195 *Trylon and Perisphere*

CM195		UnFVF	UseFVF
3¢	bluish violet *(101,699,550)*	.25	.20
	Plate block of 4	2.25	
	FDC *(April 1, 1939)*		12.00

1939. WASHINGTON INAUGURATION ISSUE commemorated the 150th anniversary of George Washington's inauguration as first President of the United States. The oath of office was administered on the balcony of Federal Hall, at the corner of Wall and Broad Streets in New York City, by Robert Livingston, chancellor of New York State. *Intaglio, perforated 11.*

CM196 *Washington taking the oath of office, from an engraving by Alonzo Chappel*

CM196		UnFVF	UseFVF
3¢	bright purple *(73,764,550)*	.25	.20
	Plate block of 6	5.50	
	FDC *(April 30, 1939)*		9.00

1939. BASEBALL CENTENNIAL ISSUE commemorated the 100th anniversary of this popular American sport. According to a story now generally held to be spurious, while attending school at Cooperstown, N.Y., in 1839, Abner Doubleday laid out the base and player pattern still used today. The National Baseball Hall of Fame and Museum at Cooperstown was selected as the first-day site. *Intaglio, perforated 11x10 1/2.*

CM197 *Sandlot baseball game*

CM197		UnFVF	UseFVF
3¢	violet *(81,269,600)*	2.25	.20
	Plate block of 4	11.00	
	FDC *(June 12, 1939)*		40.00

1939. PANAMA CANAL ISSUE commemorated the 25th anniversary of the opening of the Panama Canal (see CM48). Authorized by President Theodore Roosevelt, who arranged the requisite treaty with Panama in 1904, it was built under the direction of Col. George W. Goethals. *Intaglio, perforated 11.*

CM198 *Theodore Roosevelt, George W. Goethals and a ship in the Gaillard Cut of the Panama Canal*

CM198		UnFVF	UseFVF
3¢	deep reddish purple *(67,813,350)*	.50	.20
	Plate block of 6	4.00	
	FDC *(Aug. 15, 1939)*		10.00

1939. PRINTING TERCENTENARY ISSUE recalled the 300th anniversary of printing in Colonial America. The press shown was brought to the colonies by the Rev. Joseph Glover, who died en route. Stephen Daye set up the press at Cambridge, Mass. Its first publication, in March 1639, was a single sheet, "Oath of a Free-man." In 1640 it printed *The Bay Psalm Book,* the first American book in English. The press is now in the Harvard University Museum. *Intaglio, perforated 10 1/2x11.*

CM199 *Stephen Daye press*

CM199		UnFVF	UseFVF
3¢	violet *(71,394,750)*	.25	.20
	Plate block of 4	1.50	
	FDC *(Sept. 25, 1939)*		8.00

1939. FOUR STATES ISSUE commemorated the 50th anniversary of the states of North Dakota, South Dakota, Montana, and Washington. The stamp had three different first-day dates (Nov. 2 for the Dakotas, Nov. 8 for Montana, and Nov. 11 for Washington) before being placed on general sale Nov. 13. *Intaglio, perforated 11x10 1/2.*

CM200 *Map of North Dakota, South Dakota, Montana, and Washington*

CM200

		UnFVF	UseFVF
3¢	**reddish purple** *(66,835,000)*	.25	.20
	Plate block of 4	1.50	
	FDC *(Nov. 2, 1939)*		7.50

1940. FAMOUS AMERICANS SERIES issued over a nine-month period, paid tribute to America's men and women who had distinguished themselves and their country in their creative dedication to the betterment of all mankind. They were grouped by the following topics: authors, poets, educators, scientists, musicians, artists, and inventors. Honorees were chosen mainly through a poll conducted by the National Federation of Stamp Clubs. *Intaglio, perforated 10 1/2x11.*

 CM201 *Washington Irving (1783-1859), America's first internationally accepted man of letters, is best remembered for his stories such as* The Legend of Sleepy Hollow *(see CM754) and* Rip Van Winkle.

CM201

		MNHVF	UseVF
1¢	**emerald** *(56,348,320)*	.25	.20
	Plate block of 4	1.25	
	FDC *(Jan. 29, 1940)*		4.00

 CM202 *James Fenimore Cooper (1789-1851) lives on through his adventure stories, notably* The Leather-Stocking Tales, *five novels about a pioneer scout named Natty Bumppo.*

CM202

		MNHVF	UseVF
2¢	**carmine** *(53,177,110)*	.25	.20
	Plate block of 4	1.25	
	FDC *(Jan. 29, 1940)*		4.00

 CM203 *Ralph Waldo Emerson (1803-82), New England philosopher, is known for the practical idealism of his essays and for poems such as "The Concord Hymn."*

CM203

		MNHVF	UseVF
3¢	**bright purple** *(53,260,270)*	.25	.20
	Plate block of 4	1.25	
	FDC *(Feb. 5, 1940)*		4.00

 CM204 *Louisa May Alcott (1832-88), teacher, social reformer and Civil War nurse, wrote the spectacularly popular novel* Little Women *and many others.*

CM204

		MNHVF	UseVF
5¢	**gray blue** *(22,104,950)*	.40	.25
	Plate block of 4	12.00	
	FDC *(Feb. 5, 1940)*		5.00

 CM205 *Samuel Langhorne Clemens (1835-1910) is known to the world as Mark Twain. His best-known character is Tom Sawyer, his greatest work is* Adventures of Huckleberry Finn, *published in 1884.*

CM205

		MNHVF	UseVF
10¢	**sepia** *(13,201,270)*	2.25	1.75
	Plate block of 4	45.00	
	FDC *(Feb. 13, 1940)*		10.00

 CM206 *Henry Wadsworth Longfellow (1807-1882), Harvard professor and America's best-loved poet, wrote "The Song of Hiawatha," "Evangeline," and "The Village Blacksmith."*

CM206

		MNHVF	UseVF
1¢	**emerald** *(51,603,580)*	.25	.20
	Plate block of 4	2.00	
	FDC *(Feb. 16, 1940)*		4.00

 CM207 *John Greenleaf Whittier (1807-92), poet and abolitionist, is best remembered for his "Snow-Bound," "The Barefoot Boy," "Maude Muller," and "Barbara Frietchie."*

CM207

		MNHVF	UseVF
2¢	**carmine** *(52,100,510)*	.25	.20
	Plate block of 4	2.00	
	FDC *(Feb. 16, 1940)*		4.00

 CM208 *James Russell Lowell (1819-91), also was a diplomat, teacher and satirist. His best-known works are "The Biglow Papers" and "The Vision of Sir Launfal."*

CM208

		MNHVF	UseVF
3¢	**bright purple** *(51,666,580)*	.25	.20
	Plate block of 4	2.75	
	FDC *(Feb. 20, 1940)*		4.00

 CM209 *Walt Whitman (1819-92), poet of democracy and the individual, pioneered the free-verse form with a collection of poems called* Leaves of Grass, *first published in 1855.*

CM209

		MNHVF	UseVF
5¢	**gray blue** *(22,207,780)*	.45	.25
	Plate block of 4	12.00	
	FDC *(Feb. 20, 1940)*		5.00

 CM210 *James Whitcomb Riley (1849-1916) wrote kindly, cheerful poems in Indiana dialect. His best-known works are "Little Orphan Annie" and "The Raggedy Man."*

CM210

		MNHVF	UseVF
10¢	**sepia** *(11,835,530)*	2.25	1.75
	Plate block of 4	50.00	
	FDC *(Feb. 24, 1940)*		10.00

 CM211 *Horace Mann (1796-1859) founded the nation's first normal school and revolutionized the organization and teaching of the American public school system.*

CM211

		MNHVF	UseVF
1¢	**emerald** *(52,471,160)*	.25	.20
	Plate block of 4	2.75	
	FDC *(March 14, 1940)*		4.00

CM212 *Mark Hopkins (1802-87), for 36 years president of Williams College in Massachusetts, did much to raise American educational standards.*

CM212

2¢		MNHVF	UseVF
	carmine *(52,366,440)*	.25	.20
	Plate block of 4	1.25	
	FDC *(March 14, 1940)*		4.00

CM213 *Charles W. Eliot (1834-1926), president of Harvard, 1869-1909, made the school America's leading university and edited the* Harvard Classics, *commonly known as "Dr. Eliot's Five-Foot Shelf of Books."*

CM213

3¢		MNHVF	UseVF
	bright purple *(51,636,270)*	.25	.20
	Plate block of 4	2.75	
	FDC *(March 28, 1940)*		4.00

CM214 *Frances E. Willard (1839-98), dean of women at Northwestern University, was a pioneer worker for the improvement of education for women.*

CM214

5¢		MNHVF	UseVF
	gray blue *(20,729,030)*	.40	.30
	Plate block of 4	12.00	
	FDC *(March 28, 1940)*		5.00

CM215 *Booker T. Washington (1856-1910), born a slave, was America's leading Black educator. In 1881, he founded Tuskegee Normal and Industrial Institute.*

CM215

10¢		MNHVF	UseVF
	sepia *(14,125,580)*	2.50	1.75
	Plate block of 4	42.50	
	FDC *(April 7, 1940)*		10.00

CM216 *John James Audubon (1785-1851), ornithologist, painted birds from life. His* Birds of America, *published 1827-38, has been called "the most magnificent monument yet raised by art to science."*

CM216

1¢		MNHVF	UseVF
	emerald *(59,409,000)*	.25	.20
	Plate block of 4	1.25	
	FDC *(April 8, 1940)*		4.00

CM217 *Dr. Crawford W. Long (1815-78), a Georgia physician, is believed to have been the first surgeon to use ether as an anaesthetic in 1842.*

CM217

2¢		MNHVF	UseVF
	carmine *(57,888,600)*	.25	.20
	Plate block of 4	1.25	
	FDC *(April 8, 1940)*		4.00

CM218 *Luther Burbank (1849-1926), horticulturist, developed the Burbank potato and many new and better varieties of fruits, flowers and vegetables.*

CM218

3¢		MNHVF	UseVF
	bright purple *(58,273,180)*	.25	.20
	Plate block of 4	1.25	
	FDC *(April 17, 1940)*		4.00

CM219 *Dr. Walter Reed (1851-1902), led the experiments in Cuba establishing that yellow fever is transmitted by a variety of mosquito, a discovery that made possible the virtual elimination of that disease.*

CM219

5¢		MNHVF	UseVF
	gray blue *(23,779,000)*	.50	.20
	Plate block of 4	7.75	
	FDC *(April 17, 1940)*		5.00

CM220 *Jane Addams (1860-1935), noted humanitarian, in 1889 founded Hull House, a social settlement to improve community life in the slums of Chicago. It was the first institution of its kind in the United States.*

CM220

10¢		MNHVF	UseVF
	sepia *(15,112,580)*	1.50	1.50
	Plate block of 4	32.50	
	FDC *(April 26, 1940)*		6.00

CM221 *Stephen Collins Foster (1826-64), most popular of all American composers, wrote such songs as "O Susanna," "Swanee River," "Camptown Races," and "Jeannie with the Light Brown Hair."*

CM221

1¢		MNHVF	UseVF
	emerald *(57,322,790)*	.25	.20
	Plate block of 4	1.25	
	FDC *(May 3, 1940)*		4.00

CM222 *John Philip Sousa (1854-1932), a bandmaster and composer, was known as the March King. His most popular march is "The Stars and Stripes Forever." (See CM1941.)*

CM222

2¢		MNHVF	UseVF
	carmine *(58,281,580)*	.25	.20
	Plate block of 4	1.25	
	FDC *(May 3, 1940)*		4.00

CM223 *Victor Herbert (1859-1924), Irish-born cellist and conductor, wrote many operettas, including* Babes in Toyland, The Red Mill, *and* Naughty Marietta. *His best-known song is "Ah, Sweet Mystery of Life."*

CM223
		MNHVF	UseVF
3¢	**bright purple** *(56,398,790)*	.25	.20
	Plate block of 4	1.25	
	FDC *(May 13, 1940)*		4.00

CM224 *Edward A. MacDowell (1861-1908), composed piano and orchestral works and songs. He is best known for his "Woodland Sketches" and "To a Wild Rose."*

CM224
		MNHVF	UseVF
5¢	**gray blue** *(21,147,000)*	.75	.30
	Plate block of 4	12.50	
	FDC *(May 13, 1940)*		5.00

CM225 *Ethelbert Nevin (1862-1901) composed 70 songs, including "Narcissus," "The Rosary," and "Mighty Like a Rose."*

CM225
		MNHVF	UseVF
10¢	**sepia** *(13,328,000)*	5.00	2.00
	Plate block of 4	50.00	
	FDC *(June 10, 1940)*		6.00

226 *Gilbert Charles Stuart (1755-1828), was one of the first eminent American painters. His portraits of contemporaries, especially George Washington, have been used on many U.S. stamps.*

CM226
		MNHVF	UseVF
1¢	**emerald** *(54,389,510)*	.25	.20
	Plate block of 4	1.00	
	FDC *(Sept. 5, 1940)*		4.00

CM227 *James Abbott McNeill Whistler (1834-1903), a brilliant American painter and etcher, made his success in Europe. His portrait of his mother (see CM127) is his best-known work.*

CM227
		MNHVF	UseVF
2¢	**carmine** *(53,636,580)*	.25	.20
	Plate block of 4	1.00	
	FDC *(Sept. 5, 1940)*		4.00

CM228 *Augustus Saint-Gaudens (1848-1907), great Irish-born sculptor, is best known for his equestrian statue of Sherman in New York City and his statue of Lincoln.*

CM228
		MNHVF	UseVF
3¢	**bright purple** *(55,313,230)*	.25	.20

Plate block of 4	1.25
FDC *(Sept. 16, 1940)*	4.00

CM229 *Daniel Chester French (1850-1931), New Hampshire sculptor, created* The Minute Man *(CM69) on Lexington Green and the seated Abraham Lincoln in the Lincoln Memorial at Washington, D.C.*

CM229
		MNHVF	UseVF
5¢	**gray blue** *(21,720,580)*	.75	.30
	Plate block of 4	11.00	
	FDC *(Sept. 16, 1940)*		5.00

CM230 *Frederic Remington (1861-1909) was a painter, illustrator, and sculptor, known for his depiction of lively action in Western scenes. His artwork is seen on CM21, CM23, CM496 and CM993.*

CM230
		MNHVF	UseVF
10¢	**sepia** *(13,600,580)*	2.00	1.75
	Plate block of 4	35.00	
	FDC *(Sept. 30, 1940)*		6.00

CM231 *Eli Whitney (1765-1825), revolutionized the cotton industry in 1793 by inventing the cotton gin, a machine that separated cotton seed from the fiber 50 times faster than it could be done by hand.*

CM231
		MNHVF	UseVF
1¢	**emerald** *(47,599,580)*	.25	.20
	Plate block of 4	2.00	
	FDC *(Oct. 7, 1940)*		4.00

CM232 *Samuel F.B. Morse (1791-1872), a portrait painter, invented the electric telegraph (CM266) and the telegraphic alphabet known as Morse Code.*

CM232
		MNHVF	UseVF
2¢	**carmine** *(53,766,510)*	.25	.20
	Plate block of 4	1.25	
	FDC *(Oct. 7, 1940)*		4.00

CM233 *Cyrus Hall McCormick (1809-84), in 1831, invented a reaping machine with all key features of the harvesting machines of today. It increased American farm output and settlement of the West.*

CM233
		MNHVF	UseVF
3¢	**bright purple** *(54,193,580)*	.25	.20
	Plate block of 4	2.00	
	FDC *(Oct. 14, 1940)*		4.00

CM234 *Elias Howe (1819-67) invented the sewing machine in 1846, which revolutionized clothesmaking, lowered costs, increased quality, and eventually brought many women into American industry.*

CM234		MNHVF	UseVF
5¢	**gray blue** *(20,264,580)*	1.25	.50
	Plate block of 4	17.50	
	FDC *(Oct. 14, 1940)*		7.50

CM235 *Alexander Graham Bell (1847-1922), whose interest in acoustics stemmed from his work in teaching the deaf, invented the telephone in 1876.*

CM235		MNHVF	UseVF
10¢	**sepia** *(13,726,580)*	15.00	3.25
	Plate block of 4	70.00	
	FDC *(Oct. 28, 1940)*		7.50

1940. PONY EXPRESS ISSUE marked the 80th anniversary of the Central Overland California and Pike's Peak Express Company, the "Pony Express" that carried letters at $5 an ounce from St. Joseph, Mo., to Sacramento, Calif. Using 80 young riders, 420 horses, and 190 relay stations, it made the 1,900-mile trip in 10 days (winter) or eight days (summer). *Intaglio, perforated 11x10 1/2.*

CM236 *Pony Express rider*

CM236		MNHVF	UseVF
3¢	**chestnut** *(46,497,400)*	.35	.20
	Plate block of 4	3.50	
	FDC *(April 3, 1940)*		7.50

1940. PAN-AMERICAN UNION ISSUE commemorated the 50th anniversary of the founding of the International Bureau of American Republics, now known as the Pan-American Union. It was created by the various republics of North, Central and South America for the development of trade relations and peace. *Intaglio, perforated 10 1/2x11.*

CM237 *Three Graces, from Botticelli's painting,* Spring

CM237		MNHVF	UseVF
3¢	**lilac** *(47,700,000)*	.30	.20
	Plate block of 4	4.25	
	FDC *(April 14, 1940)*		5.00

1940. IDAHO STATEHOOD ISSUE commemorated the 50th anniversary of Idaho's admission as the 43rd state. The region, crossed by Lewis and Clark in 1806, was a part of the Oregon Territory (CM170) in 1848-63, before becoming Idaho Territory. *Intaglio, perforated 11x10 1/2.*

CM238 *State Capitol at Boise*

CM238		MNHVF	UseVF
3¢	**light reddish violet** *(50,618,150)*	.25	.20
	Plate block of 4	2.50	
	FDC *(July 3, 1940)*		5.00

1940. WYOMING STATEHOOD ISSUE commemorated the 50th anniversary of Wyoming's admission as the 44th state. The state seal's central figure, a female on a pedestal under the banner "Equal Rights," is a reminder that in Wyoming Territory women were given the right to vote in 1869. *Intaglio, perforated 10 1/2x11.*

CM239 *Wyoming state seal*

CM239		MNHVF	UseVF
3¢	**purple brown** *(50,034,400)*	.25	.20
	Plate block of 4	2.25	
	FDC *(July 10, 1940)*		5.00

1940. CORONADO EXPEDITION ISSUE observed the 400th anniversary of the expedition by Francisco Vasquez de Coronado, seeking the fabled Seven Cities of Cibola. Coronado's men discovered the Grand Canyon, explored what is now southern California and the Rio Grande, captured Zuni Indian settlements in New Mexico, and crossed the Arkansas River into Kansas. *Intaglio, perforated 11x10 1/2.*

CM240 Coronado and His Captains, *painting by Gerald Cassidy*

CM240		MNHVF	UseVF
3¢	**reddish lilac** *(60,943,700)*	.25	.20
	Plate block of 4	1.75	
	FDC *(Sept. 7, 1940)*		5.00

1940. NATIONAL DEFENSE ISSUE focused attention upon the necessity for building an adequate national defense. Original sketches by President Roosevelt were the basis for the final designs. *Intaglio, perforated 11x10 1/2.*

CM241 *The Statue of Liberty, rising 305 feet above the waters of New York harbor, is the work of Alsatian sculptor Frederic Auguste Bartholdi (CM1163), who conceived the idea on a visit to the United States. A centennial gift from the people of France, it was up to America to supply the funds to build the pedestal, which was completed 10 years later in 1886, after the* efforts of Pulitzer and his New York World *newspaper. Its full name is "Liberty Enlightening the World", and it has become a universal symbol of the freedom and security of democracy in America.*

CM241		MNHVF	UseVF
1¢	**emerald** *(6,081,409,300)*	.25	.20
	Plate block of 4	.50	
	Cracked plate	—	
	Gripper cracks	—	
	Pair, gutter between	—	
	FDC *(Oct. 16, 1940)*		5.00
	x. Bureau precancel (316 diff.)	.25	
	Plate block of 4	1.25	
	v. Horizontal pair, imperforate between	35.00	
	v1. Vertical pair, imperforate between	500.00	
	vx. Bureau precancel Glendale	150.00	

CM242 *90mm anti-aircraft gun*

CM242

		MNHVF	UseVF
2¢	**rose** *(5,211,708,200)*	.25	.20
	Plate block of 4	.50	
	Pair, gutter between	—	
	FDC *(Oct. 16, 1940)*		5.00
	v. Horizontal pair, imperforate between	40.00	
	x. Bureau precancel (25 diff.)	.50	
	Plate block of 4	3.00	

CM243 *Torch symbolizing enlightenment*

CM243

		MNHVF	UseVF
3¢	**light reddish violet** *(8,384,867,600)*	.25	.20
	Plate block of 4	.75	
	Pair, gutter between	—	
	FDC *(Oct. 16, 1940)*		5.00
	v. Horizontal pair, imperforate between	25.00	
	x. Bureau precancel (22 diff.)	1.00	
	Plate block of 4	5.00	

1940. THIRTEENTH AMENDMENT ISSUE commemorated the abolition of slavery in the United States. President Lincoln's Emancipation Proclamation of 1863 freed only the slaves in states that had seceded from the Union, leaving the status of nearly a million others in northern and border states unchanged. The Thirteenth Amendment, proclaimed in force Dec. 18, 1865, abolished all involuntary servitude except as a punishment for crime. *Intaglio, perforated 10 1/2x11.*

CM244 *Emancipation Monument of President Lincoln and Archer Alexander, an escaped slave who won freedom in Missouri, by Thomas Ball (1819-1911), in Lincoln Park, Washington, D.C.*

CM244

		MNHVF	UseVF
3¢	**violet** *(44,389,550)*	.35	.20
	Plate block of 4	3.75	
	FDC *(Oct. 20, 1940)*		7.50

1941. VERMONT STATEHOOD ISSUE commemorated the 150th anniversary of Vermont's admission into the Union as the 14th state. *Intaglio, perforated 11x10 1/2.*

CM245 *State Capitol at Montpelier, Vt.*

CM245

		MNHVF	UseVF
3¢	**violet** *(54,574,550)*	.25	.20
	Plate block of 4	2.00	
	FDC *(March 4, 1941)*		7.50

1942. KENTUCKY STATEHOOD ISSUE commemorated the 150th anniversary of its admission as the 15th state. Kentucky was explored in 1767 by Daniel Boone, who, in 1775, led a party of settlers through the Cumberland Gap and over the Wilderness Road to erect a fort at what later became Boonesborough. *Intaglio, perforated 11x10 1/2.*

CM246 *Daniel Boone and frontiersmen, mural by Gilbert White, State Capitol, Frankfort, Ky.*

CM246

		MNHVF	UseVF
3¢	**reddish violet** *(63,558,400)*	.25	.20
	Plate block of 4	1.25	
	FDC *(June 1, 1942)*		5.00

1942. WIN THE WAR ISSUE following Pearl Harbor, replaced the 3¢ National Defense stamp (CM243) and symbolized the nation's war effort and its goal of victory. *Intaglio, perforated 11x10 1/2.*

CM247 *Victory eagle*

CM247

		MNHVF	UseVF
3¢	**violet** *(20,642,793,300)*	.25	.20
	light violet	.25	.20
	Plate block of 4	.75	
	Pair, gutter between	—	
	FDC *(July 4, 1942)*		5.00
	x. Bureau precancel (26 diff.)	.50	
	Plate block of 4	7.50	
	a. purple		
	ax. Bureau precancel (2 diff.)	75.00	
	Plate block of 4	—	

1942. CHINESE COMMEMORATIVE ISSUE honored five years of Chinese resistance to Japanese aggression. Chinese characters below the portrait of Sun Yat-sen, founder of the Republic, are Abraham Lincoln's words: "of the people, by the people, for the people." *Intaglio, perforated 11x10 1/2.*

CM248 *Abraham Lincoln, map of China, Sun Yat-sen*

CM248

		MNHVF	UseVF
5¢	**Prussian blue** *(21,272,800)*	.60	.30
	Plate block of 4	12.00	
	FDC *(July 7, 1942)*		10.00

1943. ALLIED NATIONS ISSUE commemorated the strength and unity with which nations of the free world were fighting to establish peace and freedom. *Intaglio, perforated 11x10 1/2.*

CM249 *Nations United for Victory*

CM249

		MNHVF	UseVF
2¢	**carmine** *(1,671,564,200)*	.25	.20
	Plate block of 4	.50	
	Pair, gutter between	—	
	FDC *(Jan. 14, 1943)*		5.00
	x. Bureau precancel (2 diff.)	2.00	
	Plate block of 4	—	

1943. FOUR FREEDOMS ISSUE symbolized principles enunciated by President Roosevelt in the 1941 State of the Union message to Congress: freedom of speech and expression, freedom of worship, freedom from want, and freedom from fear. *Intaglio, perforated 11x10 1/2.*

CM250 *Liberty bearing the torch of freedom and enlightenment*

CM250		MNHVF	UseVF
1¢	**emerald** *(1,227,334,200)*	.25	.20
	Plate block of 4	.60	
	FDC *(Feb. 12, 1943)*		5.00
	x. Bureau precancel (20 diff.)	1.50	
	Plate block of 4	—	

1943-44. OVERRUN COUNTRIES ISSUE recognized the countries occupied by the Axis powers, which implied the free world's determination to liberate them.

For the first time since 1893, the Bureau of Engraving and Printing contracted with a private firm, the American Bank Note Co., so that the stamps could be printed in color. *The frames of all values were engraved slate violet. The vignettes were printed by offset in two or three colors of the flags. Letterpress and offset, perforated 12.*

CM251 *Flag of Poland*

CM251		MNHVF	UseVF
5¢	**slate violet, scarlet & black** *(19,999,646)*	.25	.20
	"Poland" block of 4	7.25	
	"Poland" block of 6, w/guide markings	—	
	FDC *(June 22, 1943)*		5.00

CM252 *Flag of Czechoslovakia*

CM252		MNHVF	UseVF
5¢	**slate violet, blue, scarlet & black** *(19,999,646)*	.25	.20
	"Czechoslovakia" block of 4	4.00	
	"Czechoslovakia" block of 6 w/guide markings	—	
	v. Doubled inscription "Czechoslovakia"	1,400.00	
	FDC *(July 12, 1943)*		5.00

CM253 *Flag of Norway*

CM253		MNHVF	UseVF
5¢	**slate violet, rose red, ultramarine & black** *(19,999,616)*	.25	.20
	"Norway" block of 4	1.75	
	"Norway" block of 6, w/guide markings	—	
	FDC *(July 27, 1943)*		5.00
	v. Doubled inscription "Norway"	1,400.00	

CM254 *Flag of Luxembourg*

CM254		MNHVF	UseVF
5¢	**slate violet, rose red, light blue & black** *(19,999,646)*	.25	.20
	"Luxembourg" block of 4	1.75	
	"Luxembourg" block of 6, w/guide markings	—	
	FDC *(Aug. 10, 1943)*		5.00

CM255 *Flag of Netherlands*

CM255		MNHVF	UseVF
5¢	**slate violet, scarlet, blue & black** *(19,999,646)*	.25	.20
	"Netherlands" block of 4	1.75	
	"Netherlands" block of 6, w/guide markings	—	
	FDC *(Aug. 24, 1943)*		5.00

CM256 *Flag of Belgium*

CM256		MNHVF	UseVF
5¢	**slate violet, scarlet, greenish yellow & black** *(19,999,646)*	.25	.20
	"Belgium" block of 4	1.75	
	"Belgium" block of 6, w/guide markings	—	
	FDC *(Sept. 14, 1943)*		5.00
	v. Doubled inscription "Belgium"	1,400.00	

CM257 *Flag of France*

CM257		MNHVF	UseVF
5¢	**slate violet, blue, red & black** *(19,999,648)*	.25	.20
	"France" block of 4	1.75	
	"France" block of 6, w/guide markings	—	
	FDC *(Sept. 28, 1943)*		5.00

CM258 *Flag of Greece*

CM258		MNHVF	UseVF
5¢	**slate violet, pale light blue & black** *(14,999,646)*	.50	.20
	"Greece" block of 4	15.00	
	"Greece" block of 6, w/guide markings	—	
	FDC *(Oct. 12, 1943)*		5.00

CM259 *Flag of Yugoslavia*

CM259		MNHVF	UseVF
5¢	**slate violet, blue, rose red & black** *(14,999,646)*	.30	.20

"Yugoslavia" block of 4   8.00
"Yugoslavia" block of 6, w/guide markings   —
FDC *(Oct. 26, 1943)*   5.00

CM260 *Flag of Albania*

CM260
5¢		MNHVF	UseVF
slate violet, red & black *(14,999,646)*		.30	.20
"Albania" block of 4		8.00	
"Albania" block of 6, w/guide markings		—	
FDC *(Nov. 9, 1943)*			5.00

CM261 *Flag of Austria*

CM261
5¢		MNHVF	UseVF
slate violet, red & black *(14,999,646)*		.30	.20
"Austria" block of 4		5.25	
"Austria" block of 6, w/guide markings		—	
v. Doubled inscription "Austria"		1,400.00	
FDC *(Nov. 23, 1943)*			5.00

CM262 *Flag of Denmark*

CM262
5¢		MNHVF	UseVF
slate violet, scarlet & black *(14,999,646)*		.30	.20
"Denmark" block of 4		6.25	
"Denmark" block of 6, w/guide markings		—	
FDC *(Dec. 7, 1943)*			5.00

CM263 *Flag of Korea*

"KORPA" flaw

CM263
5¢		MNHVF	UseVF
slate violet, scarlet, bright blue & gray *(14,999,646)*		.30	.20
"Korea" block of 4		5.25	
"Korea" block of 6, w/guide markings		—	
v. "KORPA" plate flaw		27.50	
FDC *(Nov. 2, 1944)*			5.00

1944. TRANSCONTINENTAL RAILROAD ISSUE marked the 75th anniversary of the completion of the first transcontinental railroad. A golden spike driven at Promontory Point, near Ogden, Utah, on May 10, 1869, marked the meeting of the Union Pacific tracks from the west with the Central Pacific from the east. *Intaglio, perforated 11x10 1/2.*

CM264 *Golden Spike Ceremony, mural by John McQuarrie, Union Pacific Station, Salt Lake City, Utah*

CM264
3¢		MNHVF	UseVF
violet *(61,303,000)*		.30	.20
Plate block of 4		1.75	
FDC *(May 10, 1944)*			7.50

1944. STEAMSHIP ISSUE commemorated the 125th anniversary of the first steamship crossing of the Atlantic. The first-day date was National Maritime Day. The ship *Savannah,* sailing with an auxiliary steam engine, crossed from Savannah, Ga., to Liverpool, England, in 19 days. *Intaglio, perforated 11x10 1/2.*

CM265 *S.S. Savannah, from ship model, Marine Museum, Newport News, Va.*

CM265
3¢		MNHVF	UseVF
violet *(61,001,450)*		.25	.20
Plate block of 4		1.50	
FDC *(May 22, 1944)*			7.50

1944. TELEGRAPH CENTENNIAL ISSUE commemorated the 100th anniversary of the first message sent by telegraph. The inventor, Samuel F.B. Morse (CM232), sent the historic words, "What hath God wrought!" from Washington, D.C., to Baltimore, Md., where they were received by his associate, Alfred Vail. *Intaglio, perforated 11x10 1/2.*

CM266 *Telegraph wires and posts*

CM266
3¢		MNHVF	UseVF
bright purple *(60,605,000)*		.25	.20
Plate block of 4		1.00	
FDC *(May 24, 1944)*			7.50

1944. CORREGIDOR ISSUE paid tribute to the gallant resistance of Gen. Jonathan M. Wainwright's American and Philippine troops besieged there by the Japanese in 1942. After the fall of Bataan, the surviving forces withdrew to Corregidor in Manila Bay and withstood the invaders for almost a month before surrendering May 6, 1942. *Intaglio, perforated 11x10 1/2.*

CM267 *Corregidor Island*

CM267
3¢		MNHVF	UseVF
violet *(50,129,350)*		.25	.20
Plate block of 4		1.25	
FDC *(Sept. 27, 1944)*			7.50

1944. MOTION PICTURE ISSUE commemorated the 50th anniversary of motion pictures and paid tribute to the cinema industry's contributions to the war effort. *Intaglio, perforated 11x10 1/2.*

CM268 *Motion pictures for the troops*

CM268		**MNHVF**	**UseVF**
3¢	**violet** *(53,479,400)*	.25	.20
	Plate block of 4	1.00	
	FDC *(Oct. 31, 1944)*		7.50

1945. FLORIDA CENTENNIAL ISSUE marked the 100th anniversary of Florida's admission as the 27th state. Explored by Juan Ponce de Leon in 1513, Florida was not settled by Europeans until 1565 when Pedro Menendez de Aviles set up a colony at St. Augustine, now the oldest city in the United States. West Florida was seized by the United States in 1813; East Florida was ceded by Spain in 1819. *Intaglio, perforated 11x10 1/2.*

CM269 *Gates of St. Augustine, state seal and State Capitol*

CM269		**MNHVF**	**UseVF**
3¢	**bright purple** *(61,617,350)*	.25	.20
	Plate block of 4	.75	
	FDC *(March 3, 1945)*		7.50

1945. UNITED NATIONS CONFERENCE ISSUE honored the conference in San Francisco at which the delegates of 50 nations drafted the charter of the United Nations. President Roosevelt, who had invited them there, approved the design April 2 and died 10 days later, 13 days before the conference. His words, "Toward United Nations, April 25, 1945," were inscribed on the stamp and his name added after the original plate had been prepared. *Intaglio, perforated 11x10 1/2.*

CM270 *"Toward United Nations, April 25, 1945"*

CM270		**MNHVF**	**UseVF**
5¢	**ultramarine** *(75,500,000)*	.25	.20
	Plate block of 4	.75	
	FDC *(April 25, 1945)*		8.00

1945-46. ROOSEVELT SERIES paid tribute to President Franklin Delano Roosevelt (1882-1945), who died April 12, 1945. The only American president for whom the "no third term" tradition was set aside, he was elected to the presidency four times. First taking office in a time of grave economic depression, he began the vast economic and social program known as the New Deal. He gave substantial support to Great Britain after the fall of France in 1940, wrote (with British Prime Minister Winston S. Churchill) the Atlantic Charter in 1941, defined the Four Freedoms (CM250), helped lead the fight to victory in World War II, and called the conference to organize the United Nations. Thirteen days before it opened, he died of a cerebral hemorrhage at the "Summer White House" in Warm Springs, Ga. (CM272), where he had set up a foundation for children who had, like himself, been stricken by infantile paralysis. He was buried in the garden of his home at Hyde Park, N.Y. (CM271).

An ardent stamp collector for 56 years, Roosevelt added greatly to the popularity of the hobby and suggested the designs of a number of postage stamps issued during his presidency. "I owe my life to my hobbies," he said, "especially stamp collecting." Many countries have honored him on their postage stamps. *Intaglio, perforated 11x10 1/2.*

CM271 *Roosevelt and Hyde Park*

CM271		**MNHVF**	**UseVF**
1¢	**blue green** *(128,140,000)*	.25	.20

			.50	
	Plate block of 4			
	FDC *(July 26, 1945)*			4.00
	p. printed on thin, translucent paper		—	

CM272 *Roosevelt and "Little White House" at Warm Springs, Ga.*

CM272		**MNHVF**	**UseVF**
2¢	**carmine red** *(67,255,000)*	.25	.20
	Plate block of 4	.50	
	FDC *(Aug. 24, 1945)*		4.00

CM273 *Roosevelt and the White House*

CM273		**MNHVF**	**UseVF**
3¢	**lilac** *(138,870,000)*	.25	.20
	Plate block of 4	.50	
	FDC *(June 27, 1945)*		4.00

CM274 *Roosevelt, globe and Four Freedoms*

CM274		**MNHVF**	**UseVF**
5¢	**light blue** *(76,455,400)*	.25	.20
	Plate block of 4	.75	
	FDC *(Jan. 30, 1946)*		3.00

1945-46. Armed Forces Series of five stamps paid tribute to the nation's fighting forces and Merchant Marine for their valiant efforts toward victory in World War II.

1945. MARINE COMMEMORATIVE honored the U.S. Marine Corps. The design is taken from the famous photograph by Joseph Rosenthal of the Associated Press, showing the Marines raising the American Flag on Mount Suribachi on the Japanese island of Iwo Jima. The color was intended to match that of the Marine uniform. *Intaglio, perforated 10 1/2x11.*

CM275 *U.S. Marines raising the flag on Mount Suribachi, Iwo Jima*

CM275		**MNHVF**	**UseVF**
3¢	**dark yellow green** *(137,321,000)*	.25	.20
	Plate block of 4	.75	
	FDC *(July 11, 1945)*		7.50

1945. ARMY COMMEMORATIVE honored the U.S. Army, particularly the infantry, in World War II. The design was devised from a group of photographs of the 28th Division marching through Paris. The color was selected to match the olive-drab uniform of the Army. *Intaglio, perforated 11x10 1/2.*

CM276 *U.S. infantry, bombers, and L'Arc de Triomphe, Paris, France*

CM276

		MNHVF	UseVF
3¢	**brown olive** *(128,357,750)*	.25	.20
	Plate block of 4	.65	
	FDC *(Sept. 28, 1945)*		7.50

1945. NAVY COMMEMORATIVE honored the U.S. Navy in World War II. The design reproduces an official Navy photograph made at the Corpus Christi Naval Air Station. It may be the first U.S. stamp to show people smiling. *Intaglio, perforated 11x10 1/2.*

CM277 *U.S. Navy sailors*

CM277

		MNHVF	UseVF
3¢	**blue** *(138,863,000)*	.25	.20
	Plate block of 4	.65	
	FDC *(Oct. 27, 1945)*		7.50

1945. COAST GUARD COMMEMORATIVE honored the U.S. Coast Guard service in World War II. The nation's oldest uniformed service, the Coast Guard participated in every major invasion of the war. *Intaglio, perforated 11x10 1/2.*

CM278 *Coast Guard landing craft and supply ship*

CM278

		MNHVF	UseVF
3¢	**blue green** *(111,616,700)*	.25	.20
	Plate block of 4	.65	
	FDC *(Nov. 10, 1945)*		7.50

1946. MERCHANT MARINE COMMEMORATIVE honored the achievements of the U.S. Merchant Marine in World War II. Photographs of two Liberty Ships, the *James Madison* and the *John W. Troy*, were used in the composite design. *Intaglio, perforated 11x10 1/2.*

CM279 *Liberty ship and goods*

CM279

		MNHVF	UseVF
3¢	**blue green** *(135,927,000)*	.25	.20
	Plate block of 4	.65	
	FDC *(Feb. 26, 1946)*		7.50

1945. ALFRED E. SMITH ISSUE honored the colorful and popular American who rose from humble beginnings to serve four terms as governor of New York. Known as "The Happy Warrior," he was the Democratic candidate for president in 1928, but was defeated by Herbert Hoover. He died in 1944. *Intaglio, perforated 11x10 1/2.*

CM280 *Alfred E. Smith*

CM280

		MNHVF	UseVF
3¢	**dark lilac** *(308,587,700)*	.25	.20
	Plate block of 4.	.55	
	Pair, gutter between	—	
	FDC *(Nov. 26, 1945)*		5.00

1945. TEXAS STATEHOOD ISSUE commemorated the 100th anniversary of Texas as the 28th state. A former Mexican state whose American settlers revolted in 1836 and set up a republic (CM166), Texas was granted Congressional authority to divide its vast territory into as many as five states of "convenient size" and "sufficient population" without further permission of Congress. *Intaglio, perforated 11x10 1/2.*

CM281 *U.S. and Texas flags and the "Lone Star"*

CM281

		MNHVF	UseVF
3¢	**Prussian blue** *(170,640,000)*	.25	.20
	Plate block of 4	.55	
	FDC *(Dec. 29, 1945)*		5.00

1946. HONORABLE DISCHARGE STAMP honored the members of the armed forces who were returning to civilian life after having served their country in World War II. *Intaglio, perforated 10x11 1/2.*

CM282 *Honorable discharge emblem*

CM282

		MNHVF	UseVF
3¢	**violet** *(269,339,100)*	.25	.20
	Plate block of 4	.55	
	FDC *(May 9, 1946)*		5.00

1946. TENNESSEE STATEHOOD ISSUE commemorated the 150th anniversary of Tennessee as the 16th state. First settled in 1757 as part of North Carolina, it was ceded in 1784 to the federal government, which gave it neither administration nor protection. Settlers under John Sevier set up the independent State of Franklin in 1785-88, and he later served as first governor of Tennessee. *Intaglio, perforated 11x10 1/2.*

CM283 *Capitol at Nashville, Andrew Jackson, and John Sevier*

CM283

		MNHVF	UseVF
3¢	**violet** *(132,274,500)*	.25	.20
	Plate block of 4	.55	
	FDC *(June 1, 1946)*		3.00

1946. IOWA STATEHOOD ISSUE commemorated the 100th anniversary of Iowa's admission as the 29th state. *Intaglio, perforated 11x10 1/2.*

CM284 *Iowa map and flag*

CM284

		MNHVF	UseVF
3¢	**Prussian blue** *(132,430,000)*	.25	.20
	Plate block of 4	.55	
	FDC *(Aug. 3, 1946)*		3.00

1946. SMITHSONIAN INSTITUTION ISSUE commemorated the 100th anniversary of its establishment at Washington, D.C. James Smithson, an English chemist, willed more than £100,000 as a gift to the United States for "an establishment for the increase and diffusion of knowledge among men." Today it includes a great library and several museums, including the National Postal Museum (CM1589-92). *Intaglio, perforated 11x10 1/2.*

CM285 *Smithsonian Institution*

CM285		MNHVF	UseVF
3¢	brown purple *(139,209,500)*	.25	.20
	Plate block of 4	.55	
	FDC *(Aug. 10, 1946)*		3.00

1946. KEARNY EXPEDITION ISSUE commemorated the 100th anniversary of the march of Gen. Stephen W. Kearny's Army of the West from Fort Leavenworth, Kans., to New Mexico. Kearny's unopposed entry into Santa Fe on Aug. 18, 1846, ended the Mexican War and established New Mexico as a part of the United States. *Intaglio, perforated 11x10 1/2.*

CM286 Capture of Santa Fe, *from a painting by Kenneth M. Chapman*

CM286		MNHVF	UseVF
3¢	brown purple *(114,684,450)*	.25	.20
	Plate block of 4	.55	
	FDC *(Oct. 16, 1946)*		3.00
	Plate block of 4 FDC *(Feb. 1947)*	3.00	

1947. THOMAS A. EDISON ISSUE commemorated the 100th anniversary of the birth of America's greatest practical scientist. Thomas Alva Edison's more than 1,200 inventions include the incandescent electric bulb (CM85), the automatic telegraph repeater, teleprinter, mimeograph, phonograph, microphone, Ediphone, storage battery, electric dynamo, electric automobile, electric locomotive, carbon telephone transmitter, many motion picture developments, and telegraphic communication with moving trains. *Intaglio, perforated 10 1/2x11.*

CM287 *Thomas A. Edison*

CM287		MNHVF	UseVF
3¢	bright purple *(156,540,510)*	.25	.20
	Plate block of 4	.55	
	FDC *(Feb. 11, 1947)*		3.00

1947. JOSEPH PULITZER ISSUE commemorated the 100th anniversary of the birth of Joseph Pulitzer, the Hungarian-born journalist who published the *St. Louis Post-Dispatch* and the *New York World*. It was a drive by Pulitzer's *World* that raised the funds to build the base for the Statue of Liberty. He founded and endowed the Columbia School of Journalism, which awards annual Pulitzer Prizes in journalism and letters. *Intaglio, perforated 11x10 1/2.*

CM288 *Joseph Pulitzer and the Statue of Liberty*

CM288		MNHVF	UseVF
3¢	dark lilac *(120,452,600)*	.25	.20
	Plate block of 4	.55	
	FDC *(April 10, 1947)*		3.00

1947. POSTAGE STAMP CENTENARY ISSUE marked the 100th anniversary of the first regular issue U.S. postage stamps. *Intaglio, perforated 11x10 1/2.*

CM289 *Washington, Franklin, and new methods of carrying the mail*

CM289		MNHVF	UseVF
3¢	blue *(127,104,300)*	.25	.20
	Plate block of 4	.55	
	FDC *(May 17, 1947)*		3.00
		.55	

1947. CIPEX SOUVENIR SHEET featured reproductions of the two stamps of the 1847 issue produced for the Centenary International Philatelic Exhibition. Stamps cut out of the sheet are valid for postage and sometimes are mistaken for the 1847 originals by those who have not checked the colors. The reproduced 5¢ Franklin is light blue instead of the original red brown and the 10¢ Washington reproduction is Venetian red instead of black. The sheet is inscribed in the margin: "PRINTED BY THE TREASURY DEPARTMENT, BUREAU OF ENGRAVING AND PRINTING / UNDER AUTHORITY OF ROBERT E. HANNEGAN, POSTMASTER GENERAL / IN COMPLIMENT TO THE CENTENARY INTERNATIONAL PHILATELIC EXHIBITION / NEW YORK, N.Y., MAY 17-25, 1947." *Intaglio (flat plate), imperforate.*

CM290 *CIPEX souvenir sheet*

CM290		MNHVF	UseVF
15¢	Complete sheet of 2 stamps	.75	.65
	(10,299,600)		
	a. 5¢ light blue, from sheet	.30	.25
	b. 10¢ Venetian red, from sheet	.45	.25
	FDC *(May 19, 1947)*		4.00

1947. THE DOCTORS ISSUE paid tribute to the physicians of America. *Intaglio, perforated 11x10 1/2.*

CM291 The Doctor, *from a painting by Sir Luke Fildes*

CM291

3¢	brown purple *(132,902,000)*	MNHVF	UseVF
		.25	.20
	Plate block of 4	.75	
	FDC *(June 9, 1947)*		7.00

1947. UTAH ISSUE commemorated the 100th anniversary of the settlement of Utah by the Mormons under Brigham Young. Driven out of the Midwest by religious persecution, members of the Church of Jesus Christ of Latter-Day Saints made a mass migration to the valley of the Great Salt Lake and founded a territory called Deseret, which in 1850 became the Utah Territory. *Intaglio, perforated 11x10 1/2.*

CM292 *Pioneers entering the Valley of Great Salt Lake, Utah*

CM292

3¢	violet *(131,968,000)*	MNHVF	UseVF
		.25	.20
	Plate block of 4	.75	
	FDC *(July 24, 1947)*		3.00

1947. U.S. FRIGATE CONSTITUTION ISSUE commemorated the 150th anniversary of the launching of the great fighting ship *Constitution.* Ordered dismantled in 1830, she was saved by public sentiment aroused by Oliver Wendell Holmes' poem, "Old Ironsides." *Intaglio, perforated 11x10 1/2.*

CM293 *Drawing of the U.S. frigate* Constitution

CM293

3¢	blue green *(131,488,000)*	MNHVF	UseVF
		.25	.20
	Plate block of 4	.55	
	FDC *(Oct. 21, 1947)*		3.50

1947. EVERGLADES NATIONAL PARK ISSUE commemorated the dedication of the park on Dec 6. The park contains more than a million acres of subtropical land in southern Florida, with extensive watercourses and profuse bird life. *Intaglio, perforated 11x10 1/2.*

CM294 *Great white heron and map of Florida*

CM294

3¢	emerald *(122,362,000)*	MNHVF	UseVF
		.25	.20
	Plate block of 4	.75	
	FDC *(Dec. 5, 1947)*		3.00

1948. GEORGE WASHINGTON CARVER ISSUE memorialized the fifth anniversary of the death of the agricultural chemist. Born into slavery, and illiterate until he was almost 20, Dr. Carver (1864-1943) spent 47 years as director of agricultural research at Tuskegee Institute, discovered hundreds of industrial uses for the peanut, sweet potato and soybean, aided Southern agriculture, and developed a

new cotton strain known as Carver's Hybrid. *Intaglio, perforated 10 1/2x11.*

CM295 *George Washington Carver*

CM295

3¢	bright purple *(121,548,000)*	MNHVF	UseVF
		.25	.20
	Plate block of 4	.55	
	FDC *(Jan. 5, 1948)*		4.00

1948. CALIFORNIA GOLD CENTENNIAL ISSUE celebrated the 100th anniversary of the discovery of gold by James W. Marshall at Sutter's Mill in California. News of the discovery brought 100,000 gold-seeking "Forty-Niners" to the state from all parts of the world. *Intaglio, perforated 11x10 1/2.*

CM296 *Sutter's Mill, California*

CM296

3¢	violet *(131,109,500)*	MNHVF	UseVF
		.25	.20
	Plate block of 4	.55	
	FDC *(Jan. 24, 1948)*		2.00

1948. MISSISSIPPI TERRITORY ISSUE commemorated the 150th anniversary of the establishment of the Mississippi Territory, comprising the present states of Mississippi and Alabama. Winthrop Sargent was its first governor. *Intaglio, perforated 11x10 1/2*

CM297 *Map and original seal of the territory, and Sargent*

CM297

3¢	brown purple *(122,650,500)*	MNHVF	UseVF
		.25	.20
	Plate block of 4	.55	
	FDC *(April 7, 1948)*		2.00

1948. FOUR CHAPLAINS ISSUE honored the heroic chaplains — George L. Fox, Clark V. Poling, John P. Washington and Alexander D. Goode — who sacrificed themselves for their comrades when the S.S. *Dorchester* sank on Feb. 3, 1943. Two ministers, a priest, and a rabbi, they gave up their life preservers so that others might live. *Intaglio, perforated 11x10 1/2.*

CM298 *Four chaplains and the sinking* S.S. Dorchester

CM298

3¢	black *(121,953,500)*	MNHVF	UseVF
		.25	.20
	Plate block of 4	.55	
	FDC *(May 28, 1948)*		2.00

1948. WISCONSIN CENTENNIAL ISSUE commemorated the 100th anniversary of Wisconsin's admission as the 30th state. First explored by Jean Nicolet in 1634, it was surrendered by France to the British in 1760 and ceded by the British to the United States in 1783. It was part of the Northwest, Indiana, Illinois, and Michigan Territories before becoming the Wisconsin Territory in 1836. *Intaglio, perforated 11x10 1/2.*

CM299 *Scroll with map of Wisconsin and State Capitol at Madison*

CM299

		MNHVF	UseVF
3¢	violet *(115,250,000)*	.25	.20
	Plate block of 4	.75	
	FDC *(May 29, 1948)*		2.00

1948. SWEDISH PIONEERS ISSUE hailed the 100th anniversary of the arrival of Swedish pioneers in the Midwest. The 12 stars on the stamp represent the 12 states in which the immigrants settled. *Intaglio, perforated 11x10 1/2.*

CM300 *Swedish pioneer and covered wagon*

CM300

		MNHVF	UseVF
5¢	blue *(64,198,500)*	.25	.20
	Plate block of 4	.75	
	FDC *(June 4, 1948)*		2.00

1948. THE PROGRESS OF WOMEN ISSUE observed the 100th anniversary of the first women's rights convention, held at Seneca Falls, N.Y., July 19-20, 1848. The convention, called by pioneer feminists Elizabeth Stanton and Lucretia Mott, began the women's suffrage movement to which both devoted the rest of their lives. Carrie Chapman Catt led the suffrage campaign to its final victory in 1920, when the 19th Amendment gave women the vote. *Intaglio, perforated 11x10 1/2.*

CM301 *Elizabeth Stanton, Carrie Chapman Catt, and Lucretia Mott*

CM301

		MNHVF	UseVF
3¢	violet *(117,642,500)*	.25	.20
	Plate block of 4	.55	
	FDC *(July 19, 1948)*		2.00

1948. WILLIAM ALLEN WHITE ISSUE honored the distinguished editor of the *Emporia Gazette,* from 1896, when his editorial "What's the Matter with Kansas?" attracted nationwide attention, until his death in 1944. White was known for his intellectual greatness and honesty, and he made the *Gazette* one of the most notable newspapers in American history. *Intaglio, perforated 10 1/2x11.*

CM302 *William Allen White*

CM302

		MNHVF	UseVF
3¢	bright purple *(77,649,000)*	.25	.20
	Plate block of 4	.55	
	FDC *(July 31, 1948)*		2.00

1948. UNITED STATES - CANADA FRIENDSHIP ISSUE commemorated a century of friendship between the United States and Canada. The 3,000-mile frontier between the two countries is the longest undefended border in the world. *Intaglio, perforated 11x10 1/2.*

CM303 *The Niagara Gorge railway suspension bridge joining the United States and Canada*

CM303

		MNHVF	UseVF
3¢	blue *(113,474,500)*	.25	.20
	Plate block 4	.55	
	FDC *(Aug. 2, 1948)*		2.00

1948. FRANCIS SCOTT KEY ISSUE honored the author of our national anthem, "The Star Spangled Banner." Negotiating the exchange of an American held by the British fleet off Baltimore, Key was detained aboard a warship while the British bombarded Fort McHenry on Sept. 13, 1814. After the fort endured a 25-hour bombardment of more than 1,500 shells, Key was thrilled to see the American flag still flying over the parapet. The verses were written there on the back of an envelope, published as "The Defense of Fort McHenry," and set to an old English tune, "To Anacreon in Heaven." The song was made the U.S. national anthem March 3, 1931. *Intaglio, perforated 11x10 1/2.*

CM304 *Francis Scott Key and American flags*

CM304

		MNHVF	UseVF
3¢	carmine *(120,868,500)*	.25	.20
	Plate block of 4	.55	
	FDC *(Aug. 9, 1948)*		2.00

1948. AMERICAN YOUTH ISSUE paid tribute to the young people of America and was a part of the celebration of Youth Month. *Intaglio, perforated 11x10 1/2.*

CM305 *Girl and boy*

CM305

		MNHVF	UseVF
3¢	blue *(77,800,500)*	.25	.20
	Plate block of 4	.55	
	FDC *(Aug. 11, 1948)*		2.00

1948. OREGON TERRITORY ISSUE commemorated the 100th anniversary of the signing of the Oregon Bill by President James Polk. The bill, passed after seven months' wrangling between slavery and anti-slavery elements in Congress, established a non-slaveholding Oregon Territory. Jason Lee, a Methodist minister, had petitioned Congress for territorial status as early as 1836. Dr. John McLoughlin, who founded Fort Vancouver in 1824 and for 22 years served as administrator for the Hudson's Bay Company, is known as the "Father of Oregon." *Intaglio, perforated 11x10 1/2.*

CM306 *John McLoughlin, Jason Lee, and wagon on Oregon Trail*

CM306

		MNHVF	UseVF
3¢	Venetian red *(52,214,000)*	.25	.20
	Plate block of 4	.55	
	FDC *(Aug. 14, 1948)*		2.00

1948. HARLAN FISKE STONE ISSUE honored the great American jurist, appointed to the U.S. Supreme Court by President Calvin

Coolidge in 1925. Stone was named 12th chief justice of the United States by President Franklin D. Roosevelt in 1941, and served until his death in 1946. *Intaglio, perforated 10 1/2x11.*

CM307 *Harlan Fiske Stone*

CM307

3¢		MNHVF	UseVF
	bright purple *(53,958,100)*	.25	.20
	Plate block of 4	.75	
	FDC *(Aug. 25, 1948)*		2.00

1948. PALOMAR MOUNTAIN OBSERVATORY ISSUE
commemorated the dedication of the world's largest telescope on Palomar Mountain, 66 miles north of San Diego, Calif. The 200-inch reflecting telescope, named in honor of the astronomer George Ellery Hale, penetrates a billion light years into the sky. *Intaglio, perforated 10 1/2x11.*

CM308 *Palomar Mountain Observatory*

CM308

3¢		MNHVF	UseVF
	blue *(61,120,010)*	.25	.20
	Plate block of 4	1.00	
	FDC *(Aug. 30, 1948)*		2.00
	v. Vertical pair, imperforate between	450.00	

1948. CLARA BARTON ISSUE honored the founder of the American Red Cross (CM96, CM358). A humanitarian, Barton organized supply and nursing services for Union casualties in the Civil War (CM1723), successfully campaigned for an American society of the International Red Cross, and served as its first president, 1882-1904. *Intaglio, perforated 11x10 1/2.*

CM309 *Clara Barton and red cross*

CM309

3¢		MNHVF	UseVF
	carmine *(57,823,000)*	.25	.20
	Plate block of 4	.60	
	FDC *(Sept. 7, 1948)*		2.00

1948. POULTRY INDUSTRY CENTENNIAL ISSUE marked the 100th anniversary of the establishment of the American poultry industry. *Intaglio, perforated 11x10 1/2.*

CM310 *Light Brahma rooster*

CM310

3¢		MNHVF	UseVF
	sepia *(52,975,000)*	.25	.20
	Plate block of 4	.60	
	FDC *(Sept. 9, 1948)*		2.00

1948. GOLD STAR MOTHERS ISSUE honored mothers of those members of the armed forces who lost their lives in both World Wars. *Intaglio, perforated 10 1/2x11.*

CM311 *Gold star and palm branch*

CM311

3¢		MNHVF	UseVF
	yellow *(77,149,000)*	.25	.20
	Plate block of 4	.60	
	FDC *(Sept. 21, 1948)*		2.00

1948. FORT KEARNY ISSUE commemorated the 100th anniversary of the establishment of Fort Kearny, Neb., an important frontier post in protecting settlers. *Intaglio, perforated 11x10 1/2.*

CM312 *Fort Kearny and pioneers*

CM312

3¢		MNHVF	UseVF
	violet *(58,332,000)*	.25	.20
	Plate block of 4	.60	
	FDC *(Sept. 22, 1948)*		2.00

1948. VOLUNTEER FIREMAN ISSUE commemorated the 300th anniversary of the organization of America's first volunteer fire department in New Amsterdam (now New York City) by Peter Stuyvesant, director-general of the Dutch colony of New Netherland. *Intaglio, perforated 11x10 1/2.*

CM313 *Peter Stuyvesant and fire engines*

CM313

3¢		MNHVF	UseVF
	rose carmine *(56,228,000)*	.25	.20
	Plate block of 4	.60	
	FDC *(Oct. 4, 1948)*		2.00

1948. INDIAN CENTENNIAL ISSUE commemorated the arrival of the five civilized Indian tribes in the Indian Territory, which later became the State of Oklahoma. The Cherokee, Choctaw, Chickasaw, Muskogee (Creek), and Seminole tribes were called "civilized" because of their willingness to adopt the ways of white culture. *Intaglio, perforated 11x10 1/2.*

CM314 *Map of Oklahoma and the seals of the five civilized tribes*

CM314

3¢		MNHVF	UseVF
	brown *(57,832,000)*	.25	.20
	Plate block of 4	.60	
	FDC *(Oct. 15, 1948)*		2.00

1948. ROUGH RIDERS ISSUE marked the 50th anniversary of the First U.S. Volunteer Calvalry Regiment, composed of cowboys and adventurous young Easterners, and known as the Rough Riders. Commanded by Col. Leonard Wood and Lt. Col. Theodore Roosevelt, they fought a spectacular dismounted action in the Battle of San Juan Hill, Cuba (July 1, 1898), seizing the heights and exposing Santiago and the Spanish fleet to artillery bombardment. Capt. William "Bucky"

O'Neill, killed in the battle, was one of 1,572 American casualties. *Intaglio, perforated 11x10 1/2.*

CM315 *Capt. William O'Neill on horse, from statue by Solon H. Borglum, Prescott, Ariz.*

CM315		MNHVF	UseVF
3¢	brown purple (53,875,000)	.25	.20
	Plate block of 4	.60	
	FDC (Oct. 27, 1948)		2.00

1948. JULIETTE LOW ISSUE honored the Girl Scouts of America and the memory of founder Juliette Gordon Low, who organized its first troop in Savannah, Ga., in 1912. *Intaglio, perforated 11x10 1/2.*

CM316 *Juliette Gordon Low and Girl Scout emblem*

CM316		MNHVF	UseVF
3¢	blue green (63,834,000)	.25	.20
	Plate block of 4	.60	
	FDC (Oct. 9, 1948)		1.00

1948. WILL ROGERS ISSUE memorialized America's beloved cowboy philosopher and humorist. A part-Indian native of Oklahoma, Rogers began as a vaudeville entertainer, delivering humorous monologues while doing lasso tricks. As a lecturer, movie actor, and newspaper columnist, he was known for his shrewd but kindly commentary on current events. He died in an airplane crash at Point Barrow, Ak., in 1935 with his friend Wiley Post (A96-97), holder of the 'round-the-world flight record. (See also CM929.) *Intaglio, perforated 10 1/2x11.*

CM317 *Will Rogers*

CM317		MNHVF	UseVF
3¢	bright purple (67,162,200)	.25	.20
	Plate block of 4	.60	
	FDC (Nov. 4, 1948)		1.00

1948. FORT BLISS CENTENNIAL ISSUE commemorated the 100th anniversary of Fort Bliss, Texas, largest cavalry post in America and later a center for guided-missile training. *Intaglio, perforated 10 1/2x11.*

CM318 *Fort Bliss and rocket launch*

CM318		MNHVF	UseVF
3¢	chestnut (64,561,000)	.35	.20
	Plate block of 4	1.50	
	FDC (Nov. 5, 1948)		1.00

1948. MOINA MICHAEL ISSUE honored the originator of the Memorial Poppy. John McCrae's poem, "In Flanders Fields," spoke of wild poppies growing in the cemeteries of the dead of World War I. By an annual Memorial Day sale of poppies made by disabled veterans,

Moina Michael used this symbol of the dead to assist the living. *Intaglio, perforated 11x10 1/2.*

CM319 *Moina Michael and poppies*

CM319		MNHVF	UseVF
3¢	rose carmine (64,079,500)	.25	.20
	Plate block of 4	.55	
	FDC (Nov. 9, 1948)		1.00

1948. GETTYSBURG ADDRESS ISSUE commemorated the 85th anniversary of the brief speech with which Abraham Lincoln dedicated the military cemetery at Gettysburg, Pa., (CM174), Nov. 19, 1863. The 11 sentences, which Lincoln said "the world will little note nor long remember," have since been recognized as one of the noblest and most eloquent orations in the English language. *Intaglio, perforated 11x10 1/2.*

CM320 *Abraham Lincoln, from the statue by Daniel Chester French, State Capitol, Lincoln, Neb.*

CM320		MNHVF	UseVF
3¢	light blue (63,388,000)	.25	.20
	Plate block of 4	.55	
	FDC (Nov. 19, 1948)		1.00

1948. AMERICAN TURNERS ISSUE recalled the centennial of the formation in Cincinnati of an association of gymnasts and athletes, known as the American Turners Society, which comes from the German *"turnverein,"* meaning an exercise club. The organizer was Friedrich Hecker, a German refugee. *Intaglio, perforated 10 1/2x11.*

CM321 *American Turners emblem*

CM321		MNHVF	UseVF
3¢	carmine (62,285,000)	.25	.20
	Plate block of 4	.80	
	FDC (Nov. 20, 1948)		1.00

1948. JOEL CHANDLER HARRIS ISSUE commemorated the 100th anniversary of the birth of the Georgia journalist and author of *Uncle Remus* and *Br'er Rabbit*. His stories, written for children, also are treasured by adults for their insights into human nature. The richness of their background and humor rank them among the greatest works in the school of folk literature. *Intaglio, perforated 10 1/2x11.*

CM322 *Joel Chandler Harris*

CM322		MNHVF	UseVF
3¢	bright purple (57,492,610)	.25	.20
	Plate block of 4	.60	
	FDC (Dec. 9, 1948)		1.00

1949. MINNESOTA TERRITORY ISSUE commemorated the 100th anniversary of the Minnesota Territory, with Alexander Ramsey as its first governor. It encompassed part of the Northwest Territory and part of the Louisiana Purchase. *Intaglio, perforated 11x10 1/2.*

CM323 *Pioneer and ox cart*

CM323

3¢		MNHVF	UseVF
	blue green *(99,190,000)*	.25	.20
	Plate block of 4	.55	
	FDC *(March 3, 1949)*		1.00

1949. WASHINGTON AND LEE UNIVERSITY ISSUE commemorated the 200th anniversary of the founding of Augusta Academy at Lexington, Va. In 1776, as a patriotic gesture, it was renamed Liberty Hall Academy. In 1798, endowed with $50,000 by George Washington, it became Washington Academy. It was renamed Washington and Lee University in 1871 after the death of its president, Gen. Robert E. Lee (CM175). *Intaglio, perforated 11x10 1/2.*

CM324 *George Washington, University, and Robert E. Lee*

CM324

3¢		MNHVF	UseVF
	bright blue *(104,790,000)*	.25	.20
	Plate block of 4	.55	
	FDC *(April 12, 1949)*		1.00

1949. PUERTO RICO ELECTION ISSUE celebrated Puerto Rico's first gubernatorial election, Nov. 2, 1948. Acquired from Spain in 1898, the island was an unorganized territory until 1917, when its residents were made U.S. citizens. A bill signed by President Harry Truman in 1947 gave it the right to choose its own chief executive by popular vote. Luis Muñoz Marin (stamp No. 927), its first elected governor, was sworn into office Jan. 2, 1949. *Intaglio, perforated 11x10 1/2.*

CM325 *Puerto Rican farmer with cog wheel and ballot box*

CM325

3¢		MNHVF	UseVF
	dull green *(108,805,000)*	.25	.20
	Plate block of 4	.55	
	FDC *(April 27, 1949)*		1.00

1949. ANNAPOLIS TERCENTENARY ISSUE marked the 300th anniversary of the founding of Annapolis by the colonists of Lord Baltimore's Maryland Plantation (CM126). Named for Queen Anne of England, it is the site of the U.S. Naval Academy (CM181). *Intaglio, perforated 11x10 1/2.*

CM326 *Map of 1718 and seal of Lord Baltimore*

CM326

3¢		MNHVF	UseVF
	turquoise green *(107,340,000)*	.25	.20
	Plate block of 4	.55	
	FDC *(May 23, 1949)*		1.00

1949. GAR ISSUE commemorated the 83rd and final encampment, Aug. 28 at Indianapolis, Ind., of the Civil War Union-veterans'

organization known as the Grand Army of the Republic. Founded in 1866 by Benjamin Franklin Stevenson, its members had included five presidents of the United States. *Intaglio, perforated 11x10 1/2.*

CM327 *Union soldier and GAR veteran*

CM327

3¢		MNHVF	UseVF
	carmine *(117,020,000)*	.25	.20
	Plate block of 4	.55	
	FDC *(Aug. 19, 1949)*		1.00

1949. EDGAR ALLAN POE ISSUE commemorated the 100th anniversary of the death of a world-renowned American writer. Born 1809 in Richmond, he was expelled from the University of Virginia for bad debts and from the U.S. Military Academy for disobedience and neglect of duty, and went on to a brilliant but erratic career. Now recognized as one of the world's great lyric poets, he also was one of the originators of the modern detective story. *Intaglio, perforated 10 1/2x11.*

CM328 *Edgar Allan Poe*

CM328

3¢		MNHVF	UseVF
	bright purple *(122,633,000)*	.25	.20
	Plate block of 4	.65	
	Top inner frame line missing (position 42 of bottom-left pane of plate 24143)	—	
	FDC *(Oct. 7, 1949)*		1.00

1950. AMERICAN BANKERS ASSOCIATION ISSUE commemorated the 75th anniversary of its founding at Saratoga Springs, N.Y. The group made valuable contributions to the growth and development of American industry and life. *Intaglio, perforated 11x10 1/2.*

CM329 *Areas of banking service*

CM329

3¢		MNHVF	UseVF
	green *(130,960,000)*	.25	.20
	Plate block of 4	.55	
	FDC *(Jan. 3, 1950)*		1.00

1950. SAMUEL GOMPERS ISSUE commemorated the 100th anniversary of the birth of the British-born labor leader who helped to found the American Federation of Labor and served as its president from 1886 until his death in 1924. Acknowledged leader of the American labor movement, Gompers concentrated on the betterment of wages, hours and working conditions. *Intaglio, perforated 10 1/2x11.*

CM330 *Samuel Gompers*

CM330

3¢		MNHVF	UseVF
	bright purple *(128,478,000)*	.25	.20
	Plate block of 4	.55	
	FDC *(Jan. 27, 1950)*		1.00

1950. NATIONAL CAPITAL SESQUICENTENNIAL ISSUE celebrated 150 years of the U.S. Capitol in Washington, D.C. *Intaglio, perforated 10 1/2x11 (CM331) and 11x10 1/2 (CM332-34).*

CM331 *The statue of Armed Freedom by Thomas Crawford tops the Capitol dome (see No. 442)*

CM331		MNHVF	UseVF
3¢	light blue *(132,090,000)*	.25	.20
	Plate block of 4	.60	
	FDC *(April 20, 1950)*		1.00

CM332 *The Executive Mansion, which Congress in 1902 officially designated The White House, was designed in 1792 by James Hoban (CM994-95), who is believed to have patterned it after the Duke of Leinster's palace in Dublin. Its sandstone walls were painted white after the British burned it in 1814. It was enlarged by William Howard Taft and by both Roosevelts. In 1951-52, in bad disrepair, it was completely reconstructed within its original walls during the presidency of Harry Truman.*

CM332		MNHVF	UseVF
3¢	dull green *(130,050,000)*	.25	.20
	Plate block of 4	.65	
	FDC *(June 12, 1950)*		1.00

CM333 *The Supreme Court building is the home of the chief judicial offices in the United States*

CM333		MNHVF	UseVF
3¢	bluish violet *(131,350,000)*	.25	.20
	Plate block of 4	.60	
	FDC *(Aug. 2, 1950)*		1.00

CM334 *The U.S. Capitol is the seat of the Congress. Designed by William Thornton, it was built during 1793-1800, restored in 1814-17 after being burned by British troops in the War of 1812, and greatly enlarged in 1861-65, when the central dome was added.*

CM334		MNHVF	UseVF
3¢	bright purple *(129,980,000)*	.25	.20
	Plate block of 4	.80	1.00
	Gouge marks at "GT" and "ITA"	1.00	.50
	FDC *(Nov. 22, 1950)*		1.00

1950. RAILROAD ENGINEERS ISSUE paid tribute to American railway and pictured the fabled hero, "Casey" Jones. Born John Luther Jones in 1864, he acquired the nickname "Casey" for having lived at one time in Cayce, Ky. A railroader from boyhood, he spent the last 10 years of his life as an engineer with the Illinois Central Railroad. The "big eight-wheeler" in which he won his fame was a part of the Cannonball Express between Chicago and New Orleans, and Jones' run was between Canton, Miss., and Memphis, Tenn. He was killed April 30, 1900, when his train crashed into the rear of a freight train near Vaughn, Miss. The ballad about the wreck is known throughout America. *Intaglio, perforated 11x10 1/2.*

CM335 *"Casey" Jones, steam and diesel locomotives*

CM335		MNHVF	UseVF
3¢	brown purple *(122,315,000)*	.25	.20
	Plate block of 4	.60	
	FDC *(April 29, 1950)*		1.00

1950. KANSAS CITY CENTENNIAL ISSUE commemorated the 100th anniversary of the incorporation of Kansas City, Mo. The "Gateway to the West" was first settled by a French fur trapper named Louis Barthelot. *Intaglio, perforated 11x10 1/2.*

CM336 *Kansas City in 1950 and Westport Landing in 1850*

CM336		MNHVF	UseVF
3¢	violet *(122,170,000)*	.25	.20
	Plate block of 4	.55	
	FDC *(June 3, 1950)*		1.00

1950. BOY SCOUT ISSUE honored the 40th anniversary of the Boy Scouts of America, and the second National Jamboree at Valley Forge, Pa. The organization (CM454, CM1173) was incorporated Feb. 8, 1910, formed by uniting Ernest Thompson Seton's *Woodcraft Indians* with Daniel Beard's *Sons of Daniel Boone*, with ideas from the English program of Robert Baden-Powell. *Intaglio, perforated 11x10 1/2.*

CM337 *Scouts, Statue of Liberty, and Scout badge*

CM337		MNHVF	UseVF
3¢	sepia *(131,635,000)*	.25	.20
	Plate block of 4	.60	
	FDC *(June 30, 1950)*		1.00

1950. INDIANA TERRITORY SESQUICENTENNIAL ISSUE marked the 150th anniversary of the Indiana Territory. William Henry Harrison, later a military hero and ninth president, was the territory's first governor. *Intaglio, perforated 11x10 1/2.*

CM338 *Gov. William Henry Harrison and first capitol at Vincennes*

CM338		MNHVF	UseVF
3¢	light blue *(121,860,000)*	.25	.20
	Plate block of 4	.55	
	FDC *(July 4, 1950)*		1.00

1950. CALIFORNIA STATEHOOD CENTENNIAL ISSUE commemorated the 100th anniversary of California's admission as the 31st state. First settled by the Spaniards under Gaspar de Portola, the territory was ceded to the United States by Mexico in 1848. Its development was greatly accelerated by the discovery of gold that year at Sutter's Mill (CM296). *Intaglio, perforated 11x10 1/2.*

CM339 *Gold miner, pioneers, and S.S. Oregon*

CM339

		MNHVF	UseVF
3¢	yellow *(121,120,000)*	.25	.20
	Plate block of 4	.55	
	FDC *(Sept. 9, 1950)*		1.00

1951. CONFEDERATE VETERANS ISSUE commemorated the final reunion, May 30 at Norfolk, Va., of the United Confederate Veterans, organized in New Orleans in 1889. *Intaglio, perforated 11x10 1/2.*

CM340 *Confederate soldier and veteran*

CM340

		MNHVF	UseVF
3¢	gray *(119,120,000)*	.25	.20
	Plate block of 4	.60	
	FDC *(May 30, 1951)*		1.00

1951. NEVADA CENTENNIAL ISSUE commemorated the first settlement of Nevada in 1851. The discovery of the Comstock Lode in 1856 led to rapid development of the territory; by 1863 it had 40,000 inhabitants and was producing as much as $30,000,000 worth of silver a year. Nevada was admitted to statehood in 1864. *Intaglio, perforated 11x10 1/2.*

CM341 *Carson Valley homestead*

CM341

		MNHVF	UseVF
3¢	light olive green *(112,125,000)*	.25	.20
	Plate block of 4	.55	
	FDC *(July 14, 1951)*		1.00

1952. DETROIT ISSUE noted the 250th anniversary of the landing of Antoine de la Mothe Cadillac, at what is now Detroit, with a charter from King Louis XIV of France. Established by Cadillac as a military post to protect his fur trade, Detroit became the automotive capital of the world. *Intaglio, perforated 11x10 1/2.*

CM342 *Landing of Cadillac at Detroit, modern skyline*

CM342

		MNHVF	UseVF
3¢	light blue *(114,140,000)*	.25	.20
	Plate block of 4	.55	
	FDC *(July 24, 1951)*		1.00

1951. COLORADO STATEHOOD ISSUE commemorated the 75th anniversary of Colorado's admission as the 38th state. Formed of lands that were once part of the Louisiana Purchase and of the Texas and Mexican cessions, it became a territory in 1861. *Intaglio, perforated 11x10 1/2.*

CM343 *Capitol at Denver, Mount of the Holy Cross, bronco buster*

CM343

		MNHVF	UseVF
3¢	violet blue *(114,490,000)*	.25	.20
	Plate block of 4	.55	
	FDC *(Aug. 1, 1951)*		1.00

1951. AMERICAN CHEMICAL SOCIETY ISSUE marked the 75th anniversary of the American Chemical Society. *Intaglio, perforated 11x10 1/2.*

CM344 *ACS Emblem, industrial chemical equipment*

CM344

		MNHVF	UseVF
3¢	brown purple *(117,200,000)*	.25	.20
	Plate block of 4	.55	
	FDC *(Sept. 4, 1951)*		1.00

1951. BATTLE OF BROOKLYN ISSUE commemorated the 175th anniversary of the Battle of Long Island, Aug. 27, 1776. British and Hessian troops, under Clinton, Howe, Percy, Cornwallis, and DeHesiter, attacked the American fortifications at what is now Prospect Park in Brooklyn, overpowered the desperate Americans and captured their commander, Gen. John Sullivan (CM88). General Washington arrived late in the day with additional troops, saw the futility of making a stand, and withdrew the remaining American forces in a skillful night retreat. *Intaglio, perforated 11x10 1/2.*

CM345 *Gen. George Washington evacuating the army*

CM345

		MNHVF	UseVF
3¢	violet *(16,130,000)*	.25	.20
	Plate block of 4	.60	
	FDC *(Dec. 10, 1951)*		1.00

1952. BETSY ROSS ISSUE celebrated the 200th birthday of Betsy Ross, the Philadelphia upholsterer whom the Continental Congress engaged in 1777 to make the first American flag. The legend that she designed the original Stars and Stripes generally is disputed, and the credit given to Francis Hopkinson, one of the signers of the Declaration of Independence. *Intaglio, perforated 11x10 1/2.*

CM346 Birth of Our Nation's Flag, *from a painting by C.H. Weisgerber*

CM346

		MNHVF	UseVF
3¢	carmine red *(116,175,000)*	.25	.20
	Plate block of 4	.55	
	FDC *(Jan. 2, 1952)*		1.00

1952. 4-H CLUB ISSUE honored the farm youth organization whose emblem — the letter H on each leaf of a four-leaf clover — signifies the 4-H pledge: "I pledge My Head to clear thinking; My Heart to great loyalty; My Hands to larger service; My Health to better living, for my club, my community, and my country." *Intaglio, perforated 11x10 1/2.*

CM347 *American farm, 4-H emblem and members*

CM347

		MNHVF	UseVF
3¢	blue green *(115,945,000)*	.25	.20

Plate block of 4   .55
FDC *(Jan. 15, 1952)*   1.00

1952. AMERICAN RAILROADS ISSUE commemorated the 125th anniversary of the chartering of the B & O Railroad by the Maryland Legislature. The first passenger railroad in the United States, it was begun on July 4, 1828, with Charles Carroll of Carrollton, the last living signer of the Declaration of Independence, in attendance. The first 14-mile section opened to horse-drawn traffic May 24, 1830. *Intaglio, perforated 11x10 1/2.*

CM348 *Charter, horse-drawn car, Tom Thumb, and modern diesel*

		MNHVF	UseVF
CM348			
3¢	**light blue** *(112,540,000)*	.25	.20
	Plate block of 4	.55	
	FDC *(Feb. 28, 1952)*		1.00

1952. AAA ISSUE commemorated the 50th anniversary of the American Automobile Association (the Triple-A), and honored its contribution to motoring safety and convenience. *Intaglio, perforated 11x10 1/2.*

CM349 *Children and crossing guard, automobiles of 1902 and 1952*

		MNHVF	UseVF
CM349			
3¢	**blue** *(117,415,000)*	.25	.20
	Plate block of 4	.55	
	FDC *(March 4, 1952)*		1.00

1952. NATO ISSUE commemorated the third anniversary of the signing of the North Atlantic Treaty Organization, in which the United States, Canada and 10 Western European nations pledged that an armed attack against any of them would be considered an attack against all. *Intaglio, perforated 11x10 1/2.*

CM350 *The torch of liberty, globe*

		MNHVF	UseVF
CM350			
3¢	**violet** *(2,899,580,000)*	.25	.20
	Plate block of 4	.55	
	FDC *(April 4, 1952)*		1.00
	v. thin, translucent paper	—	

1952. GRAND COULEE DAM ISSUE commemorated 50 years of federal cooperation in developing western rivers, and paid tribute to the world's largest concrete dam, the Grand Coulee, built and operated by the Bureau of Reclamation on Washington's Columbia River. *Intaglio, perforated 11x10 1/2.*

CM351 *Grand Coulee Dam spillway*

		MNHVF	UseVF
CM351			
3¢	**blue green** *(114,540,000)*	.25	.20
	Plate block of 4	.55	
	FDC *(May 15, 1952)*		1.00

1952. LAFAYETTE ISSUE commemorated the 175th anniversary of the arrival in America of Marquis de Lafayette (CM409, CM866) to fight for American freedom. Commissioned a major general at 20 by the Continental Congress, he fought valiantly at Brandywine and Monmouth, and in the Virginia campaign ending in the British surrender at Yorktown (CM97). After the war, he was a significant figure in the French Revolution. He returned briefly to the United States in 1784, and again for a triumphant tour in 1824. *Intaglio, perforated 11x10 1/2.*

CM352 *Lafayette, flags of the United States and France*

		MNHVF	UseVF
CM352			
3¢	**bright blue** *(113,135,000)*	.25	.20
	Plate block of 4	.55	
	FDC *(June 13, 1952)*		1.00

1952. MOUNT RUSHMORE MEMORIAL ISSUE marked the 25th anniversary of the dedication of the monument in the Black Hills of South Dakota. The first such memorial authorized by the government, it was financed by South Dakota. The sculptor Gutzon Borglum designed and carved the enormous heads of Washington, Jefferson, Lincoln, and Roosevelt from the solid rock of the mountain. *Intaglio, perforated 11x10 1/2.*

CM353 *Mount Rushmore*

		MNHVF	UseVF
CM353			
3¢	**blue green** *(116,255,000)*	.25	.20
	Plate block of 4	.55	
	FDC *(Aug. 11, 1952)*		1.00

1952. ENGINEERING CENTENNIAL ISSUE commemorated the 100th anniversary of the American Society of Civil Engineers. The George Washington Bridge in New York City, shown on the stamp, was chosen as a symbol of the great engineering projects for which society members are responsible. *Intaglio, perforated 11x10 1/2.*

CM354 *The George Washington Bridge and an old covered bridge*

		MNHVF	UseVF
CM354			
3¢	**ultramarine** *(113,860,000)*	.25	.20
	Plate block of 4	.55	
	FDC *(Sept. 6, 1952)*		1.00

1952. SERVICE WOMEN ISSUE honored women in the U.S. armed services. More than 40,000 women served in World War II and contributed immeasurably to Allied victory. *Intaglio, perforated 11x10 1/2.*

CM355 *Marine Corps., Army, Navy, and Air Force service women*

CM355

3¢		MNHVF	UseVF
	blue *(124,260,000)*	.25	.20
	Plate block of 4	.55	
	FDC *(Sept. 11, 1952)*		1.00

1952. GUTENBERG BIBLE ISSUE commemorated the 500th anniversary of the first European book published from movable type, attributed to Johann Gutenberg of Mainz, Germany. Movable type replaced the tedious and costly process of hand copying. It made books available to many people, thus spreading knowledge on an unprecedented scale. *Intaglio, perforated 11x10 1/2.*

CM356 *Gutenberg showing a proof to the elector of Mainz, from a mural by Edward Laning in the New York Public Library*

CM356

3¢		MNHVF	UseVF
	violet *(115,735,000)*	.25	.20
	Plate block of 4	.55	
	FDC *(Sept. 30, 1952)*		1.00

1952. NEWSPAPERBOYS OF AMERICA ISSUE recognized America's newsboys and the value of their early business training. It also complemented the meeting of the International Circulation Managers Association, at Philadelphia, Pa., in October. *Intaglio, perforated 11x10 1/2.*

CM357 *Paperboy, torch of "free enterprise," and neighborhood*

CM357

3¢		MNHVF	UseVF
	violet *(115,430,000)*	.25	.20
	Plate block of 4	.55	
	FDC *(Oct. 4, 1952)*		1.00

1952. INTERNATIONAL RED CROSS ISSUE honored the humanitarian society founded by Jean Henri Dunant and others in 1864. Its headquarters in Geneva, Switzerland, provides an exchange for all the Red Cross societies of the world. Maintaining strict neutrality, the organization extends relief to civilian victims of war, furnishes aid to war prisoners, and monitors their treatment by their captors. (See also CM96, CM525, and CM969.) *Intaglio and letterpress, perforated 11x10 1/2.*

CM358 *Red Cross enlightening the world*

CM358

3¢		MNHVF	UseVF
	ultramarine & scarlet *(136,220,000)*	.25	.20
	Plate block of 4	.55	
	FDC *(Nov. 21, 1952)*		1.00

1953. NATIONAL GUARD ISSUE honored the oldest military organization in the United States, a service older than the nation itself. The Guard, under state control except in war, has served with distinction in every national conflict. In peacetime, it aids in disasters such as floods, forest fires, and hurricanes. *Intaglio, perforated 11x10 1/2.*

CM359 *National Guard in war and peace*

CM359

3¢		MNHVF	UseVF
	light blue *(114,894,600)*	.25	.20
	Plate block of 4	.55	
	FDC *(Feb. 23, 1953)*		1.00

1953. OHIO SESQUICENTENNIAL ISSUE commemorated the 150th anniversary of Ohio as the 17th state. A part of the Northwest Territory, Ohio became a state March 1, 1803, with Chillicothe as its capital. Columbus has been the capital since 1817. Ohio has given the nation eight presidents, and its history is reflected in many U.S. stamps. *Intaglio, perforated 11x10 1/2.*

CM360 *Ohio map and seal*

CM360

3¢		MNHVF	UseVF
	sepia *(117,706,000)*	.25	.20
	Plate block of 4	.55	
	FDC *(March 2, 1953)*		1.00

1953. WASHINGTON TERRITORY ISSUE commemorated the 100th anniversary of the Washington Territory. Visited by the Lewis and Clark Expedition in 1803, it was settled in 1811. *Intaglio, perforated 11x10 1/2.*

CM361 *Centennial crest, pioneer, and vista*

CM361

3¢		MNHVF	UseVF
	blue green *(114,190,000)*	.25	.20
	Plate block of 4	.55	
	FDC *(March 2, 1953)*		1.00

1953. LOUISIANA PURCHASE ISSUE commemorated the 150th anniversary of the Louisiana Purchase from France. (See CM32-CM36.) *Intaglio, perforated 11x10 1/2.*

CM362 *Monroe, Livingston, and de Barbe-Marbois signing transfer, from the sculpture by Karl Bitter in the Jefferson Memorial, St. Louis, Mo.*

CM362

3¢		MNHVF	UseVF
	brown purple *(113,990,000)*	.25	.20
	Plate block of 4	.55	
	FDC *(April 30, 1953)*		1.00

1953. OPENING OF JAPAN ISSUE commemorated the centennial of negotiations between Commodore Matthew C. Perry and representatives of the emperor of Japan, leading to the Treaty of Kanagawa in 1854. Japan, isolated since the early 17th century, agreed to open two ports to U.S. trade and make provision for shipwrecked American seamen. In 1858 Japan opened additional ports, granted residence rights to Americans, and exchanged diplomatic representatives. *Intaglio, perforated 11x10 1/2.*

CM363 *Commodore Perry and vessels in Tokyo Bay*

CM363

5¢		MNHVF	UseVF
	blue green *(89,289,600)*	.25	.20
	Plate block of 4	.75	
	FDC *(July 14, 1953)*		1.00

1953. AMERICAN BAR ASSOCIATION ISSUE honored the organization's 75th anniversary and its efforts in securing uniform state laws, promoting sound legislation and advancing the administration of justice. *Intaglio, perforated 11x10 1/2.*

CM364 *Wisdom, Justice, Divine Inspiration, and Truth, frieze on a wall of the Supreme Court*

CM364		MNHVF	UseVF
3¢	light reddish violet *(114,865,000)*	.25	.20
	Plate block of 4	.75	
	FDC *(Aug. 24, 1953)*		1.00

1953. SAGAMORE HILL ISSUE commemorated its dedication as a national shrine, June 14. Sagamore Hill was the Oyster Bay, N.Y., home of Theodore Roosevelt, and it was there that Roosevelt died on Jan. 6, 1919. *Intaglio, perforated 11x10 1/2.*

CM365 *Sagamore Hill, home of Theodore Roosevelt*

CM365		MNHVF	UseVF
3¢	green *(115,780,000)*	.25	.20
	Plate block of 4	.55	
	FDC *(Sept. 14, 1953)*		1.00

1953. FUTURE FARMERS OF AMERICA ISSUE honored the 25th anniversary of the founding of the Future Farmers of America under the auspices of the U.S. Office of Education. *Intaglio, perforated 11x10 1/2.*

CM366 *Future farmer and farmland*

CM366		MNHVF	UseVF
3¢	bright blue *(115,224,600)*	.25	.20
	Plate block of 4	.55	
	FDC *(Oct. 13, 1953)*		1.00

1953. TRUCKING INDUSTRY ISSUE marked the 50th anniversary of the American Trucking Association and its convention in Los Angeles. *Intaglio, perforated 11x10 1/2.*

CM367 *Truck, farm, and city*

CM367		MNHVF	UseVF
3¢	violet *(123,709,600)*	.25	.20
	Plate block of 4	.55	
	FDC *(Oct. 27, 1953)*		1.00

1953. GENERAL PATTON ISSUE honored Gen. George S. Patton Jr. (1885-1945), and the armored forces of the U.S. Army. Patton was a hero of the Battle of the Bulge in World War II. *Intaglio, perforated 11x10 1/2.*

CM368 *Gen. Patton and Patton tanks in action*

CM368		MNHVF	UseVF
3¢	bluish violet *(114,789,600)*	.25	.20
	Plate block of 4	.65	
	FDC *(Nov. 11, 1953)*		1.00

1953. NEW YORK CITY TERCENTENARY ISSUE commemorated the 300th anniversary of the incorporation of New Amsterdam as a city, Feb. 2, 1653. *Intaglio, perforated 11x10 1/2.*

CM369 *Dutch ship and New Amsterdam, modern New York City skyline*

CM369		MNHVF	UseVF
3¢	bright purple *(115,759,600)*	.25	.20
	Plate block of 4	.55	
	FDC *(Nov. 20, 1953)*		1.00

1953. GADSDEN PURCHASE ISSUE commemorated the 100th anniversary of the purchase of territory from Mexico to add territory to the states of Arizona and New Mexico and settle a dispute dating from the Guadelupe-Hildalgo Treaty of 1848. *Intaglio, perforated 11x10 1/2.*

CM370 *Gadsden Purchase map and pioneers*

CM370		MNHVF	UseVF
3¢	Venetian red *(115,759,600)*	.25	.20
	Plate block of 4	.55	
	FDC *(Dec. 30, 1953)*		1.00

1953. COLUMBIA UNIVERSITY ISSUE commemorated the 200th anniversary of King's College, which closed during the Revolution to reopen as Columbia College. It now includes many colleges such as Teacher's College, Barnard College, and schools of medicine, pharmacy, engineering, law, architecture, and journalism among others. Located in New York City, it is one of the oldest and largest U.S. universities. *Intaglio, perforated 11x10 1/2.*

CM371 *Low Memorial Library*

CM371		MNHVF	UseVF
3¢	cobalt blue *(118,540,000)*	.25	.20
	Plate block of 4	.55	
	FDC *(Jan. 4, 1954)*		1.00

1954. NEBRASKA TERRITORIAL CENTENNIAL ISSUE honored the centennial of the Nebraska Territory, under the Kansas-Nebraska Bill. *Intaglio, perforated 11x10 1/2.*

CM372 *Mitchell Pass, Scotts Bluff, and The Sower, from a statue by Lee Lawrie from a painting by Millet*

CM372

		MNHVF	UseVF
3¢	violet (115,810,000)	.25	.20
	Plate block of 4	.55	
	FDC (May 7, 1954)		1.00

1954. KANSAS TERRITORIAL CENTENNIAL ISSUE commemorated the centennial of the Kansas Territory from unorganized Indian reservations. The Kansas-Nebraska bill repealed the 1820 Missouri Compromise that had drawn a line, north of which slavery could not exist. The politicians intended Kansas to be a slave state and Nebraska free, by "popular sovereignty." The rivalry for settling the status of these two new territories was one of the direct causes of the War   Between the States. *Intaglio, perforated 11x10 1/2.*

CM373 *Wagon train and wheat field*

CM373

		MNHVF	UseVF
3¢	salmon (113,603,700)	.25	.20
	Plate block of 4	.55	
	FDC (May 31, 1954)		1.00

1954. GEORGE EASTMAN ISSUE commemorated the 100th birthday of George Eastman at Waterville, N.Y. At an early age, he went to Rochester where he gained fame as an inventor and philanthropist. His inventions made photography possible for virtually everyone, and his invention of transparent film created motion pictures. He gave $100 million to educational and musical institutions and dental clinics around the world. He was a proponent of the Community Chest, and profit sharing with employees. *Intaglio, perforated 10 1/2x11.*

CM374 *George Eastman*

CM374

		MNHVF	UseVF
3¢	brown purple (121,100,000)	.25	.20
	Plate block of 4	.55	
	FDC (July 12, 1954)		1.00

1954. LEWIS AND CLARK EXPEDITION ISSUE commemorated the exploration by Meriwether Lewis and William Clark (brother of George Rogers Clark) at the request of President Jefferson to secure more information about the country west of the Mississippi. The party of 30 made its way overland to Oregon and the Pacific Ocean, leaving St. Louis in May 1804, and returning in 1806 after having been given up as lost. They owed much of the success of the venture to Sacagawea (Birdwoman), a Shoshone Indian woman who acted as their guide (CM1690). *Intaglio, perforated 11x10 1/2.*

CM375 *Lewis and Clark, from a statue by Charles Keck at Charlottesville, Va., and Sacagawea from a statue by Leonard Crunekle at Bismark, N.D.*

CM375

		MNHVF	UseVF
3¢	brown (116,078,150)	.25	.20
	Plate block of 4	.55	
	FDC (July 28, 1954)		1.00

1955. PENNSYLVANIA ACADEMY OF FINE ARTS ISSUE honored the 150th anniversary of that institution. The design of the stamp is a reproduction of the painting *Peale in his Museum*, a self-portrait of Charles Willson Peale (1741-1827), now in the collection of the Pennsylvania Academy, of which Peale was one of the founders. *Intaglio, perforated 10 1/2x11.*

CM376 *Charles Willson Peale in his museum*

CM376

		MNHVF	UseVF
3¢	brown purple (116,139,800)	.25	.20
	Plate block of 4	.55	
	FDC (Jan. 15, 1955)		1.00

1955. FIRST LAND-GRANT COLLEGE ISSUE commemorated the centennial of the establishment of Michigan State University and Pennsylvania State University. Land grants, originally intended for settlers and homesteaders, were extended in 1854 to various groups for services for the national welfare. *Intaglio, perforated 11x10 1/2.*

CM377 *Open book and symbols of agriculture, mining, chemistry, engineering*

CM377

		MNHVF	UseVF
3¢	emerald green (120,484,800)	.25	.20
	Plate block of 4	.55	
	FDC (Feb. 12, 1955)		1.00

1955. ROTARY INTERNATIONAL ISSUE marked the 50th anniversary of the organization founded Feb. 23, 1905, by Chicago lawyer Paul P. Harris. Rotary became national in 1910, international in 1912. It is an organization of business and professional men founded to further the ideal of service to others in all relationships. *Intaglio, perforated 11x10 1/2.*

CM378 *Rotary insignia, globe and torch*

CM378

		MNHVF	UseVF
8¢	deep blue (53,854,750)	.25	.20
	Plate block of 4	1.95	
	FDC (Feb. 23, 1955)		1.00

1955. THE ARMED FORCES RESERVE ISSUE honored the Reserves of all the U.S. armed forces. *Intaglio, perforated 11x10 1/2.*

CM379 *Marines, Coast Guard, Army, Navy, and Air Force Reservists*

CM379

		MNHVF	UseVF
3¢	bright purple (176,075,000)	.25	.20
	Plate block of 4	.55	
	FDC (May 21, 1955)		1.00

1955. OLD MAN OF THE MOUNTAINS ISSUE commemorated the sesquicentennial of the discovery of New Hampshire's famous landmark of that name (see also CM1312). Also called "The Great Stone Face," it was immortalized in prose by Hawthorne. *Intaglio, perforated 10 1/2x11.*

CM380 *Old Man of the Mountains as seen from Franconia, N.H.*

CM380		MNHVF	UseVF
3¢	blue green *(125,944,400)*	.25	.20
	Plate block of 4	.55	
	FDC *(June 21, 1955)*		1.00

1955. SOO LOCKS CENTENNIAL ISSUE was released in conjuction with the opening of the Soo Locks Exposition at Sault Ste. Marie, Mich., celebrating a century of Great Lakes transportation. *Intaglio, perforated 11x10 1/2.*

CM381 *Map of the Great Lakes and freighter*

CM381		MNHVF	UseVF
3¢	blue *(122,284,600)*	.25	.20
	Plate block of 4	.55	
	FDC *(June 28, 1955)*		1.00

1955. ATOMS FOR PEACE ISSUE symbolized the intention of the United States to put atomic energy to peaceful uses. The stamp features the words "To find the way by which the inventiveness of man shall be consecrated to his life" from President Eisenhower's speech before the U.N. General Assembly on Dec. 8, 1953. *Intaglio, perforated 11x10 1/2.*

CM382 *Atomic emblem and hemispheres*

CM382		MNHVF	UseVF
3¢	deep blue *(133,638,850)*	.25	.20
	Plate block of 4	.55	
	FDC *(July 28, 1955)*		1.00

1955. FORT TICONDEROGA BICENTENNIAL ISSUE marked the building of the fort in 1755 by the French, who named it Fort Carillon. During the French & Indian War it was unsuccessfully attacked by Abercrombie in 1758, but a year later was captured by Lord Amherst. Ethan Allen and his Green Mountain Boys (see CM76) took the fort at the outbreak of the Revolution (1775). *Intaglio, perforated 11x10 1/2.*

CM383 *Plan of Fort Ticonderoga, officer, and cannon*

CM383		MNHVF	UseVF
3¢	dark red brown *(118,664,600)*	.25	.20
	Plate block of 4	.55	
	FDC *(Sept. 18, 1955)*		1.00

1955. ANDREW MELLON ISSUE commemorated the 100th anniversary of the birth of Mellon (1855-1937), Secretary of the Treasury under Harding, Coolidge, and Hoover. He negotiated the payment of war debts owed to the United States, and reduced internal debt and income taxes. He later served as ambassador to England. He donated a gallery and his very valuable art collection to the United States. *Intaglio, perforated 10 1/2x11.*

CM384 *Andrew W. Mellon, portrait by O. Birely*

CM384		MNHVF	UseVF
3¢	carmine red *(112,434,000)*	.25	.20
	Plate block of 4	.55	
	FDC *(Dec. 20, 1955)*		1.00

1956. FRANKLIN 250TH ANNIVERSARY ISSUE commemorated the birth of the great inventor, writer and public official Benjamin Franklin (see 524). *Intaglio, perforated 10 1/2x11.*

CM385 Franklin Taking Electricity from the Sky, *Benjamin West painting*

CM385		MNHVF	UseVF
3¢	carmine *(129,384,550)*	.25	.20
	Plate block of 4	.55	
	FDC *(Jan. 17, 1956)*		1.00

1956. BOOKER T. WASHINGTON ISSUE commemorated the 100th anniversary of the great educator's birth (CM215). *Intaglio, perforated 11x10 1/2.*

CM386 *Log cabin*

CM386		MNHVF	UseVF
3¢	deep blue *(121,184,600)*	.25	.20
	Plate block of 4	.55	
	FDC *(April 5, 1956)*		1.00

1956. FIPEX ISSUE celebrated the fifth International Philatelic Exhibition (April 28 to May 6, 1956). Stamp, photography, and auto exhibitions, held simultaneously, opened the New York Coliseum at Columbus Circle, New York City. *Intaglio, perforated 11x10 1/2.*

CM387 *New York Coliseum and Columbus Monument*

CM387		MNHVF	UseVF
3¢	violet *(119,784,200)*	.25	.20
	Plate block of 4	.55	
	FDC *(April 28, 1956)*		1.00

1956. FIFTH INTERNATIONAL PHILATELIC EXHIBITION (FIPEX) SOUVENIR SHEET pictured two oversize versions of stamps from the Liberty Definitive Series (see 573, 578). *Measures 108x73mm, flat plate printing, intaglio, imperforate.*

CM388 *FIPEX souvenir sheet*

CM388		**MNHVF**	**UseVF**
11¢	**Complete sheet of 2 stamps** *(9,802,025)*	2.50	2.00
	a. 3¢ dark violet, from sheet		.80
	b. 8¢ deep blue and rose, from sheet		1.00
	FDC *(April 28, 1956)*		2.50

Wildlife Conservation Series highlighted the importance of protecting wildlife.

1956. WILD TURKEY ISSUE in the Wildlife Conservation Series called attention to this aspect of America's heritage. The turkey had once been proposed as the national bird. *Intaglio, perforated 11x10 1/2.*

CM389 *Wild turkey*

CM389		**MNHVF**	**UseVF**
3¢	**brown purple** *(123,159,400)*	.25	.20
	Plate block of 4	.55	
	FDC *(May 5, 1956)*		1.00

1956. PRONGHORN ANTELOPE ISSUE in the Wildlife Conservation Series showed a buck and two does. This species had dwindled to only 17,000, but multiplied rapidly under protection and now is widely hunted. *Intaglio, perforated 11x10 1/2.*

CM390 *Pronghorn antelope*

CM390		**MNHVF**	**UseVF**
3¢	**sepia** *(123,138,800)*	.25	.20
	Plate block of 4	.55	
	FDC *(June 22, 1956)*		1.00

1956. KING SALMON ISSUE in the Wildlife Conservation Series showed salmon migrating to spawning ground. Construction of fish ladders and elevators, and elimination of log jams and high waterfalls aid salmon migration and reproduction. *Intaglio, perforated 11x10 1/2.*

CM391 *King salmon*

CM391		**MNHVF**	**UseVF**
3¢	**blue green** *(109,275,000)*	.25	.20
	Plate block of 4	.55	
	FDC *(Nov. 9, 1956)*		1.00

1956. PURE FOOD AND DRUG LAWS ISSUE commemorated the 50th anniversary of their passage. Harvey W. Wiley (1844-1930) was a chemist and teacher who single-handedly devoted himself to the cause of pure food. While chief of the Bureau of Chemistry in the U.S. Department of Agriculture, he secured passage of the 1906 laws, which required government inspection and accurate labeling of foods and drugs. Wiley was the author of hundreds of scientific papers and pamphlets. *Intaglio, perforated 10 1/2x11.*

CM392 *Harvey W. Wiley*

CM392		**MNHVF**	**UseVF**
3¢	**blue green** *(112,932,200)*	.25	.20
	Plate block of 4	.55	
	FDC *(June 27, 1956)*		1.00

1956. WHEATLAND ISSUE honored President James Buchanan and his Pennsylvania home, Wheatland. *Intaglio, perforated 11x10 1/2.*

CM393 *Wheatland, Lancaster, Pa.*

CM393		**MNHVF**	**UseVF**
3¢	**black brown** *(125,475,000)*	.25	.20
	Plate block of 4	.55	
	FDC *(Aug. 5, 1956)*		1.00

1956. LABOR DAY ISSUE celebrated the national holiday honoring workers. The movement for a Labor Holiday was begun by the Knights of Labor, who paraded on the first Monday of September in 1882-84. The holiday first was recognized by Oregon (1887), then by New York, New Jersey, and Colorado, and by the U.S. Congress in 1894. *Intaglio, perforated 10 1/2x11.*

CM394 Labor is Life *mural by L. Winter in AFL-CIO headquarters building, Washington, D.C.*

CM394		**MNHVF**	**UseVF**
3¢	**deep blue** *(117,855,000)*	.25	.20
	Plate block of 4	.55	
	FDC *(Sept. 3, 1956)*		1.00

1956. NASSAU HALL ISSUE commemorated the 200th anniversary of the oldest building at Princeton University. Named for William of Nassau (later King William III of England), it was at its completion the largest academic building in the American colonies. In 1783, in Nassau Hall, Congress formally thanked George Washington for his leadership in the Revolutionary War. *Intaglio, perforated 11x10 1/2.*

CM395 *Nassau Hall, from the Henry Dawkins engraving of 1764. The first U.S. postage stamp on colored paper featured Princeton's school colors — orange and black.*

CM395

3¢	black on orange (122,100,00)	MNHVF .25	UseVF .20
	Plate block of 4	.55	
	FDC (Sept. 22, 1956)		1.00

1956. DEVILS TOWER ISSUE commemorated the 50th anniversary of the establishment of the 1,200-acre area as the first U.S. national monument. The natural 600-foot rock formation is the eroded core of a long-extinct volcano. *Intaglio, perforated 10 1/2x11.*

CM396 *Devils Tower National Monument, Wyoming*

CM396

3¢	lilac (118,180,000)	MNHVF .25	UseVF .20
	Plate block of 4	.55	
	Pair, gutter between		
	FDC (Sept. 24, 1956)		1.00

1956. CHILDREN'S ISSUE featured the theme "Friendship — The Key to World Peace," and promoted friendship among children throughout the world. The stamp design, by Ronald Dias, a 1956 high school graduate, was selected in a nationwide competition. *Intaglio, perforated 11x10 1/2.*

CM397 *Children of the world and key of friendship*

CM397

3¢	blue (100,975,000)	MNHVF .25	UseVF .20
	Plate block of 4	.55	
	FDC (Dec. 15, 1956)		1.00

1957. ALEXANDER HAMILTON BICENTENNIAL ISSUE commemorated the 200th anniversary of the birth of this great patriot, the first secretary of the treasury and one of the signers of the Constitution. *Intaglio, perforated 11x10 1/2.*

CM398 *Alexander Hamilton and Federal Hall, New York, N.Y.*

CM398

3¢	rose red (115,299,450)	MNHVF .25	UseVF .20
	Plate block of 4	.55	
	FDC (Jan. 11, 1957)		1.00

1957. ANTI-POLIO ISSUE was a tribute to those who helped fight this dread disease, from children who contributed pennies to scientists who devoted their lives to the battle against a terrifying affliction. It marked the 20th anniversary of the National Foundation for Infantile Paralysis and the March of Dimes. *Intaglio, perforated 10 1/2x11.*

CM399 *Boy, girl and allegorical figure with shield Caduceus*

CM399

3¢	bright purple (186,949,250)	MNHVF .25	UseVF .20
	Plate block of 4	.55	
	FDC (Jan. 15, 1957)		1.00

1957. COAST AND GEODETIC SURVEY ISSUE commemorated the 150th anniversary of this government service, devoted to charting and surveying America's coasts and harbors and land masses. *Intaglio, perforated 11x10 1/2.*

CM400 *Coast and Geodetic Survey flag and ships*

CM400

3¢	deep blue (115,235,000)	MNHVF .25	UseVF .20
	Plate block of 4	.55	
	FDC (Feb. 11, 1957)		1.00

1957. ARCHITECTS OF AMERICA ISSUE honored the centennial of the founding of the American Institute of Architects, and its members who create buildings, structures and communities of lasting beauty and usefulness. *Intaglio, perforated 11x10 1/2.*

CM401 *Corinthian capitol and modern pillar*

CM401

3¢	rose lilac (106,647,500)	MNHVF .25	UseVF .20
	Plate block of 4	.55	
	FDC (Feb. 23, 1957)		1.00

1957. STEEL INDUSTRY IN AMERICA ISSUE marked the centennial of this great industry, which has contributed to social progress, economic welfare, and comforts in daily life. *Intaglio, perforated 10 1/2x11.*

CM402 *Eagle and pouring ladle*

CM402

3¢	bright blue (112,010,000)	MNHVF .25	UseVF .20
	Plate block of 4	.55	
	FDC (May 22, 1957)		1.00

1957. INTERNATIONAL NAVAL REVIEW ISSUE commemorated the Jamestown Festival and the naval review. Its theme was "Freedom of the Seas," and it was the largest representation of nations in an event of this type. *Intaglio, perforated 11x10 1/2.*

CM403 *Aircraft carrier and Jamestown festival emblem*

CM403			MNHVF	UseVF
3¢	blue green *(118,399,600)*		.25	.20
	Plate block of 4		.55	
	FDC *(June 10, 1957)*			1.00

1957. OKLAHOMA STATEHOOD ISSUE celebrated the 50th anniversary of statehood, growth, and progress of a land that was once the Indian Territory. *Intaglio, perforated 11x10 1/2.*

CM404 *Arrow, atom and Oklahoma map*

CM404			MNHVF	UseVF
3¢	bright blue *(102,209,500)*		.25	.20
	Plate block of 4		.55	
	FDC *(June 14, 1957)*			1.00

1957. TEACHERS OF AMERICA ISSUE honored the National Education Association and the teaching profession that has contributed to the development of America through its school systems. *Intaglio, perforated 11x10 1/2.*

CM405 *Teacher, students, and globe*

CM405			MNHVF	UseVF
3¢	brown purple *(103,045,000)*		.25	.20
	Plate block of 4		.55	1.00
	FDC *(July 1, 1957)*			1.00

1957. AMERICAN FLAG ISSUE saluted "Old Glory," symbol of freedom throughout the world. *Intaglio (Giori Press), perforated 11.*

CM406 *48-star American flag*

CM406			MNHVF	UseVF
4¢	deep blue & carmine *(84,054,400)*		.25	.20
	Plate block of 4		.55	
	FDC *(July 4, 1957)*			1.00

1957. VIRGINIA OF SAGADAHOCK ISSUE commemorated the 350th anniversary of shipbuilding in the United States, and featured the first American-built ship to participate in world commerce. *Intaglio, perforated 10 1/2x11.*

CM407 Virginia of Sagadahock *and state seal of Maine*

CM407			MNHVF	UseVF
3¢	violet *(126,266,000)*		.25	.20
	Plate block of 4		.55	
	FDC *(Aug. 15, 1957)*			1.00

Champions of Liberty Series was a five-year-long series honoring Champions of Liberty and freedom fighters of other nations.

1957. RAMON MAGSAYSAY ISSUE honored a man of humble birth, who became president of the Philippines. (See also CM419-20, CM423-24, CM434-35, CM445-46, CM456-57, CM474-75, CM477-78 and CM483-84.) *Intaglio (Giori Press), perforated 11.*

CM408 *Ramon Magsaysay*

CM408			MNHVF	UseVF
8¢	scarlet, deep ultramarine & ocher *(39,489,600)*		.25	.20
	Plate block of 4, 2 numbers		.75	
	v. Plate block of 4, deep ultramarine number omitted		—	
	FDC *(Aug. 31, 1957)*			1.00

1957. LAFAYETTE ISSUE commemorated the 200th birthday of the French officer who came to America in 1777 and helped the fight for independence. *Intaglio, perforated 10 1/2x11.*

CM409 *Lafayette, flintlock rifle, and sword*

CM409			MNHVF	UseVF
3¢	brown purple *(122,990,000)*		.25	.20
	Plate block of 4		.55	
	FDC *(Sept. 6, 1957)*			1.00

1957. WHOOPING CRANE ISSUE in the Wildlife Conservation Series brought to the attention of the American public the need to protect and preserve wildlife resources (see CM389-CM391). The whooping crane at the time was almost extinct. *Intaglio (Giori Press), perforated 11.*

CM410 *Whooping cranes*

CM410			MNHVF	UseVF
3¢	gray blue, yellow & blue green *(174,372,800)*		.25	.20
	Plate block of 4		.55	
	FDC *(Nov. 22, 1957)*			1.00

1957. FLUSHING REMONSTRANCE ISSUE recalled a 1657 demonstration for religious freedom and liberty by the citizens of Flushing, N.Y. *Intaglio, perforated 10 1/2x11.*

CM411 *Bible, hat, pen, and inkwell*

CM411

		MNHVF	UseVF
3¢	brown black (114,365,000)	.25	.20
	Plate block of 4	.55	
	FDC (Dec. 27, 1957)		1.00

1958. GARDEN AND HORTICULTURAL ISSUE marked the 100th birthday of Liberty Hyde Bailey, famous botanist, author, and teacher whose horticultural achievements contributed to American prosperity. *Intaglio, perforated 10 1/2x11.*

CM412 *Allegory of the Good Earth with Horn of Plenty*

CM412

		MNHVF	UseVF
3¢	dull green (122,765,200)	.25	.20
	Plate block of 4	.55	
	FDC (March 15, 1958)		1.00

1958. BRUSSELS UNIVERSAL AND INTERNATIONAL EXHIBITION ISSUE paid tribute to the World's Fair and U.S. participation in it. *Intaglio, perforated 11x10 1/2.*

CM413 *U.S. fair pavilion*

CM413

		MNHVF	UseVF
3¢	brown purple (113,660,200)	.25	.20
	Plate block of 4	.55	
	FDC (April 17, 1958)		1.00

1958. JAMES MONROE ISSUE commemorated the 200th birthday of the fifth president of the United States. *Intaglio, perforated 11x10 1/2.*

CM414 *James Monroe, from a portrait by Gilbert Stuart*

CM414

		MNHVF	UseVF
3¢	violet (120,196,580)	.25	.20
	Plate block of 4	.55	
	FDC (April 28, 1958)		1.00

1958. MINNESOTA STATEHOOD CENTENNIAL ISSUE commemorated the 100th anniversary of Minnesota's admission as the 32nd state. *Intaglio, perforated 11x10 1/2.*

CM415 *Minnesota lake scene*

CM415

		MNHVF	UseVF
3¢	emerald green (120,805,200)	.25	.20
	Plate block of 4	.55	
	FDC (May 11, 1958)		1.00

1958. INTERNATIONAL GEOPHYSICAL YEAR ISSUE paid tribute to geophysicists in more than 60 countries who pool their knowledge for mankind's welfare in exploring outer space, the oceans, and Earth. *Intaglio (Giori Press), perforated 11.*

CM416 *Detail from Michelangelo's* The Creation of Adam *and solar surface*

CM416

		MNHVF	UseVF
3¢	black & red (125,815,200)	.25	.20
	Plate block of 4	.55	
	FDC (May 31, 1958)		1.00

1958. GUNSTON HALL BICENTENNIAL ISSUE honored the completion of the home of George Mason, Revolutionary patriot and friend of George Washington. The house, about 15 miles south of Alexandria, Va., was opened to the public in 1952. *Intaglio, perforated 11x10 1/2.*

CM417 *Gunston Hall*

CM417

		MNHVF	UseVF
3¢	dull green (108,415,200)	.25	.20
	Plate block of 4	.55	
	FDC (June 12, 1958)		1.00

1958. MACKINAC STRAITS BRIDGE ISSUE marked the formal opening and dedication of the suspension span that connects St. Ignace and Mackinaw City, in Michigan's Upper and Lower Peninsulas. *Intaglio, perforated 10 1/2x11.*

CM418 *Ore boat under Mackinac Bridge*

CM418

		MNHVF	UseVF
3¢	turquoise blue (107,195,200)	.25	.20
	Plate block of 4	.55	
	FDC (June 25, 1958)		1.00

1958. SIMON BOLÍVAR ISSUE The first two-stamp installment in the Champions of Liberty Series honored the South American freedom fighter known as "The Liberator" who dedicated his life to bringing happiness, social security, and political stability to his countrymen. *Intaglio, perforated 10 1/2x11.*

CM419-20 *Simon Bolívar, from portrait by Acevedo Bernal*

CM419

		MNHVF	UseVF
4¢	**olive buff** *(115,745,280)*	.25	.20
	Plate block of 4	.60	
	FDC *(July 24, 1958)*		1.00

1958. SIMON BOLÍVAR ISSUE *Intaglio (Giori Press), perforated 11*

CM420

		MNHVF	UseVF
8¢	**scarlet, deep ultramarine & deep ocher**	.25	.20
	(39,743,640)		
	Plate block of 4, 2 numbers	1.30	
	v. Plate block of 4, ocher number only	—	
	FDC *(July 25, 1958)*		1.00

1958. ATLANTIC CABLE CENTENNIAL ISSUE commemorated the linking by cable of the eastern and western hemispheres in 1858. The first formal messages were exchanged by President Buchanan and Queen Victoria. *Intaglio, perforated 11x10 1/2.*

CM421 *Globe, Neptune, and mermaid*

CM421

		MNHVF	UseVF
4¢	**red violet** *(114,570,200)*	.25	.20
	Plate block of 4	.60	
	FDC *(Aug. 15, 1958)*		1.00

1958. LINCOLN DOUGLAS DEBATE ISSUE The first of four stamps issued to note the 150th anniversary of Lincoln's birth, marked the 100th anniversary of the Lincoln-Douglas debates held as part of the 1859 campaign for U.S. Senator. Although Douglas was re-elected, Lincoln gained national prominence and two years later was elected to the presidency. *Intaglio, perforated 11x10 1/2.*

CM422 *Lincoln and Douglas debating*

CM422

		MNHVF	UseVF
4¢	**brown** *(114,860,200)*	.25	.20
	Plate block of 4	.85	
	FDC *(Aug. 27, 1958)*		1.00

1958. LAJOS KOSSUTH ISSUE The third honoree in the Champions of Liberty Series honored the famous Hungarian patriot who fought to liberate Hungary from Austrian control. He lived in exile until his death in 1894, never giving up hope that some day his beloved country would be free. *Intaglio, perforated 10 1/2x11.*

CM423-24 *Lajos Kossuth, from a photo taken in the United States in 1852*

CM423

		MNHVF	UseVF
4¢	**dull green** *(120,561,280)*	.25	.20
	Plate block of 4	.60	
	FDC *(Sept. 19, 1958)*		1.00

1958. LAJOS KOSSUTH ISSUE *Intaglio (Giori Press), perforated 11.*

CM424

		MNHVF	UseVF
8¢	**scarlet, deep ultramarine & deep ocher**	.25	.20
	(44,064,576)		
	Plate block of 4	1.30	
	FDC *(Sept. 19, 1958)*		1.00

1958. JOURNALISM AND FREEDOM OF THE PRESS ISSUE marked the 50th anniversary of the establishment of the world's first school of journalism at the University of Missouri. *Intaglio, perforated 10 1/2x11.*

CM425 *Symbols of a free press*

CM425

		MNHVF	UseVF
4¢	**gray black** *(118,390,200)*	.25	.20
	Plate block of 4	.60	
	FDC *(Sept. 22, 1958)*		1.00

1958. OVERLAND MAIL CENTENNIAL ISSUE honored the pioneer mail service established in 1858. "The Great Overland Mail Route" started its run from Memphis and St. Louis and went to San Francisco. It was important in the settlement of the Southwest. *Intaglio, perforated 11x10 1/2.*

CM426 *Overland mail coach and map of route*

CM426

		MNHVF	UseVF
4¢	**orange red** *(125,770,200)*	.25	.20
	Plate block of 4	.60	
	FDC *(Oct. 10, 1958)*		1.00

1958. NOAH WEBSTER BICENTENNIAL ISSUE commemorated the 200th birthday of the noted lexicographer. He fought for American independence in the Revolutionary War, and his *Elementary Spelling Book* sold a million copies. *Intaglio, perforated 10 1/2x11.*

CM427 *Noah Webster, from a painting by James Herring*

CM427

		MNHVF	UseVF
4¢	**magenta** *(114,114,280)*	.25	.20
	Plate block of 4	.60	
	FDC *(Oct. 16, 1958)*		1.00

1958. FOREST CONSERVATION ISSUE honored the 100th birthday of Theodore Roosevelt, one of the first leaders in the movement to preserve the nation's natural resources. *Intaglio (Giori Press), perforated 11.*

CM428 *Forest and deer*

CM428

		MNHVF	UseVF
4¢	**deep green, yellow & brown** *(156,600,200)*	.25	.20
	Plate block of 4	.60	
	FDC *(Oct. 27, 1958)*		1.00

1958. FORT DUQUESNE BICENTENNIAL ISSUE commemorated the 200th anniversary of the historic site that was so important in the conflict between England and France for control of North America. *Intaglio, perforated 11x10 1/2.*

CM429 *Composite drawing showing Gen. Forbes, Col. Washington, and Col. Henry Bouquet*

CM429

		MNHVF	UseVF
4¢	**light blue** *(124,200,200)*	.25	.20
	Plate block of 4	.60	
	FDC *(Nov. 25, 1958)*		1.00

1959. LINCOLN SESQUICENTENNIAL ISSUE Intaglio, perforated 10 1/2x11.

CM430 Beardless Lincoln, *painting by George P.A. Healy*

CM430

		MNHVF	UseVF
1¢	**deep green** *(120,400,200)*	.25	.20
	Plate block of 4	.45	
	FDC *(Feb. 12, 1959)*		1.00

1959. HEAD OF LINCOLN ISSUE Intaglio, perforated 11x10 1/2.

CM431 Head of Lincoln, *sculpture by Gutzon Borglum*

CM431

		MNHVF	UseVF
3¢	**deep plum** *(91,160,200)*	.25	.20
	Plate block of 4	.60	
	FDC *(Feb. 27, 1959)*		1.00

1959. LINCOLN STATUE ISSUE Intaglio, perforated 11x10 1/2.

CM432 Lincoln statue, *by Daniel Chester French, taken from a line and pastel drawing by Fritz Busse*

CM432

		MNHVF	UseVF
4¢	**blue** *(126,500,000)*	.25	.20
	Plate block of 4	1.25	
	FDC *(May 30, 1959)*		1.00

1959. OREGON STATEHOOD ISSUE commemorated the 100th anniversary of Oregon's admission as a state. *Intaglio, perforated 11x10 1/2.*

CM433 *Mount Hood and covered wagon*

CM433

		MNHVF	UseVF
4¢	**blue green** *(120,740,200)*	.25	.20
	Plate block of 4	.60	
	FDC *(Feb. 14, 1959)*		1.00

1959. JOSÉ DE SAN MARTIN ISSUE The fourth of the Champions of Liberty Series paid tribute to the "hero of the Andes," a great general who fought for freedom in his native Argentina and other South American nations. *Intaglio, perforated 10 1/2x11.*

CM434-35 *Portrait of José de San Martin, from a print provided by the Library of Congress*

CM434

		MNHVF	UseVF
4¢	**blue** *(113,623,280)*	.25	.20
	Plate block of 4	.60	
	FDC *(Feb. 25, 1959)*		1.00
	v. Horizontal pair, imperforate between	1,250.00	

CM435

		MNHVF	UseVF
8¢	**carmine, blue & ocher** *(45,569,088)*	.25	.20
	Plate block of 4	1.25	
	FDC *(Feb. 25, 1959)*		1.00

1959. NATO ISSUE honored the 10th anniversary of the North Atlantic Treaty Organization, binding 15 nations "to safeguard the freedom, common heritage and civilization of their people, founded on the principles of democracy, individual liberty and the rule of law." *Intaglio, perforated 10 1/2x11.*

CM436 *NATO emblem*

CM436

		MNHVF	UseVF
4¢	**blue** *(122,493,280)*	.25	.20
	Plate block of 4	.60	
	FDC *(April 1, 1959)*		1.00

1959. ARCTIC EXPLORATIONS ISSUE marked the conquest of the north polar regions and commemorated the 50th anniversary of Adm. Peary's expedition. The nuclear-powered submarine, USS *Nautilus*, joined the anniversary celebration, making the first underwater crossing of the North Pole. *Intaglio, perforated 11x10 1/2.*

CM437 *Dog team and USS* Nautilus

CM437

		MNHVF	UseVF
4¢	turquoise blue *(131,260,200)*	.25	.20
	Plate block of 4	.60	
	FDC *(April 6, 1959)*		1.00

1959. PEACE THROUGH TRADE ISSUE was released in association with the 17th Congress of the International Chamber of Commerce, held in Washington, D.C., April 19-25. *Intaglio, perforated 11x10 1/2.*

CM438 *Globe and laurel spray*

CM438

		MNHVF	UseVF
8¢	brown purple *(47,125,200)*	.25	.20
	Plate block of 4	.60	
	FDC *(April 20, 1959)*		1.00

1959. SILVER CENTENNIAL ISSUE commemorated the 100th anniversary of the discovery of the Comstock Lode, which produced about $300,000,000 worth of silver in its first 20 years. *Intaglio, perforated 11x10 1/2.*

CM439 *Henry Comstock and miners*

CM439

		MNHVF	UseVF
4¢	black *(123,105,000)*	.25	.20
	Plate block of 4	.60	
	FDC *(June 8, 1959)*		1.00

1959. ST. LAWRENCE SEAWAY ISSUE commemorated the opening of a link joining the United States and Canada in friendship and commerce, and providing a source of electric energy for both countries. Canada issued a commemorative stamp on the same day (Canada 480). Artists of both nations contributed to the design of both stamps, which are identical in design except for captions and denominations. *Intaglio (Giori Press), perforated 11.*

CM440 *Linked eagle and maple leaf over Great Lakes*

CM440

		MNHVF	UseVF
4¢	blue & red *(126,105,050)*	.25	.20
	Plate block of 4	.60	
	Pair, gutter between	—	
	FDC *(June 26, 1959)*		1.00

1959. 49-STAR FLAG ISSUE commemorated the admission of Alaska as the 49th state. *Intaglio (Giori Press), perforated 11.*

CM441 *49-star American flag*

CM441

		MNHVF	UseVF
4¢	deep blue & carmine *(209,170,000)*	.25	.20
	Plate block of 4	.60	
	FDC *(July 4, 1959)*		1.00

1959. SOIL CONSERVATION ISSUE was a tribute to the effort to prevent erosion and conserve soil, vital to successful farming and ranching. *Intaglio (Giori Press), perforated 11.*

CM442 *Soil conservation methods*

CM442

		MNHVF	UseVF
4¢	blue green & yellow orange *(120,835,000)*	.25	.20
	Plate block of 4	.60	
	FDC *(Aug. 26, 1959)*		1.00
	v. orange brown omitted	5,280.00	

1959. PETROLEUM INDUSTRY CENTENNIAL ISSUE marked the 100th anniversary of the completion of the first oil well at Titusville, Pa., by Edwin L. Drake. *Intaglio, perforated 10 1/2x11.*

CM443 *Oil derrick*

CM443

		MNHVF	UseVF
4¢	brown *(115,715,000)*	.25	.20
	Plate block of 4	.60	
	FDC *(Aug. 27, 1959)*		1.00

1959. DENTAL HEALTH ISSUE honored the centennial of the American Dental Association. *Intaglio, perforated 11x10 1/2.*

CM444 *Children playing and smiling girl with feather-cut hair style*

CM444

		MNHVF	UseVF
4¢	dark green *(118,445,000)*	.25	.20
	Plate block of 4	.90	
	FDC *(Sept. 14, 1959)*		1.00

1959. ERNST REUTER ISSUE The fifth in the Champions of Liberty Series honored Ernst Reuter (1889-1953). He was persecuted and imprisoned by the Nazis, went into exile, and after World War II returned to help rebuild his country. He was elected mayor of Berlin in 1947, holding that office until his death. *Intaglio, perforated 10 1/2x11.*

CM445-46 *Ernst Reuter*

CM445

		MNHVF	UseVF
4¢	black *(111,685,000)*	.25	.20
	Plate block of 4	.60	
	FDC *(Sept. 29, 1959)*		1.00

1959. ERNST REUTER ISSUE Intaglio (Giori Press), perforated 11.

CM446		MNHVF	UseVF
8¢	carmine, blue & ocher *(43,099,200)*	.25	.20
	Plate block of 4	1.25	
	FDC *(Sept. 29, 1959)*		1.00

1959. EPHRAIM MCDOWELL ISSUE paid tribute to an American who performed the first successful abdominal operation of its kind in the world at Danville, Ky., in 1809. *Intaglio, perforated 10 1/2x11.*

CM447 *Ephraim McDowell*

CM447		MNHVF	UseVF
4¢	brown purple *(115,444,000)*	.25	.20
	Plate block of 4	.65	
	FDC *(Dec. 3, 1959)*		1.00
	v. Vertical pair, imperforate between	500.00	
	v1. Vertical pair, imperforate horizontally	300.00	

1960. GEORGE WASHINGTON ISSUE Intaglio (Giori Press), perforated 11.

CM448 *"Observe good faith and justice toward all nations," George Washington*

CM448		MNHVF	UseVF
4¢	deep blue & carmine *(126,470,000)*	.25	.20
	Plate block of 4	.65	
	FDC *(Jan. 20, 1960)*		1.00

1960. BENJAMIN FRANKLIN ISSUE Intaglio (Giori Press), perforated 11.

CM449 *"Fear to do ill, and you need fear nought else," Benjamin Franklin*

CM449		MNHVF	UseVF
4¢	brown bister & emerald *(124,460,000)*	.25	.20
	Plate block of 4	.65	
	FDC *(March 31, 1960)*		1.00

1960. THOMAS JEFFERSON ISSUE Intaglio (Giori Press), perforated 11.

CM450 *"I have sworn hostility against every form of tyranny over the mind of man," Thomas Jefferson*

CM450		MNHVF	UseVF
4¢	gray & scarlet *(115,445,000)*	.25	.20
	Plate block of 4	.65	
	FDC *(May 18, 1960)*		1.00

1960. FRANCIS SCOTT KEY Intaglio (Giori Press), perforated 11.

CM451 *"And this be our motto, in God is our Trust," Francis Scott Key*

CM451		MNHVF	UseVF
4¢	carmine red & deep blue *(122,060,000)*	.25	.20
	Plate block of 4	.65	
	FDC *(Sept. 14, 1960)*		1.00

1960. ABRAHAM LINCOLN ISSUE Intaglio (Giori Press), perforated 11.

CM452 *"Those who deny freedom to others deserve it not for themselves,"* Abraham Lincoln

CM452		MNHVF	UseVF
4¢	bright purple & green *(120,540,000)*	.25	.20
	Plate block of 4	.90	
	FDC *(Nov. 19, 1960)*		1.00

1960. PATRICK HENRY ISSUE Intaglio (Giori Press), perforated 11.

CM453 *"Give me liberty or give me death," Patrick Henry*

CM453		MNHVF	UseVF
4¢	green & brown *(113,075,000)*	.25	.20
	Plate block of 4	.90	
	Pair, gutter between	—	
	FDC *(Jan. 11, 1961)*		1.00

1960. BOY SCOUT ISSUE commemorated the 50th anniversary of the Boy Scout movement in America. Norman Rockwell designed the stamp. *Intaglio (Giori Press), perforated 11.*

CM454 *Boy Scout giving the Scout sign*

CM454		MNHVF	UseVF
4¢	red, deep blue & deep ocher *(139,325,000)*	.25	.20
	Plate block of 4	.90	
	FDC *(Feb. 8, 1960)*		1.00

1960. WINTER OLYMPIC GAMES ISSUE marked the eighth Winter Games at Squaw Valley, Calif. It was the second time this important athletic contest was held in the United States (see CM110). *Intaglio, perforated 10 1/2x11.*

CM455 *Olympic emblem and snowflake*

CM455		MNHVF	UseVF
4¢	turquoise blue *(124,445,000)*	.25	.20
	Plate block of 4	.60	
	FDC *(Feb. 18, 1960)*		1.00

1960. TOMAS G. MASARYK ISSUE The sixth in the Champions of Liberty Series honored the first president of Czechoslovakia, who rose from humble origin to lead the movement for an independent nation. The two stamps were issued on the 41st anniversary of the republic. *Intaglio, perforated 10 1/2x11.*

CM456-57 *Tomas G. Masaryk*

CM456

		MNHVF	UseVF
4¢	blue *(113,792,000)*	.25	.20
	Plate block of 4	.60	
	v. Vertical pair, imperforate between	3,250.00	
	FDC *(March 7, 1960)*		1.00

CM457

		MNHVF	UseVF
8¢	carmine, deep blue & ocher *(44,215,200)*	.25	.20
	Plate block of 4	1.10	
	v. Horizontal pair, imperforate	—	
	FDC *(March 7, 1960)*		1.00

1960. WORLD REFUGEE YEAR ISSUE focused attention on the world's homeless and destitute and the importance of universal participation in aiding them. *Intaglio, perforated 11x10 1/2.*

CM458 *Family facing doorway to a new life*

CM458

		MNHVF	UseVF
4¢	gray black *(113,195,000)*	.25	.20
	Plate block of 4	.60	
	FDC *(April 7, 1960)*		1.00

1960. WATER CONSERVATION ISSUE in conjunction with the Seventh National Watershed Congress, emphasized the importance of conserving this precious natural resource. *Intaglio (Giori Press), perforated 11.*

CM459 *Watershed and dependent farm and factories*

CM459

		MNHVF	UseVF
4¢	blue, green & orange brown *(120,570,000)*	.25	.20
	Plate block of 4	.60	
	FDC *(April 18, 1960)*		1.00

1960. SEATO ISSUE commemorated the South East Asia Treaty Organization Conference (May 31-June 3) and the organization's efforts on behalf of peace and freedom. This defensive alliance of nations includes Australia, France, New Zealand, Pakistan, Philippines, Thailand, United Kingdom, and the United States. *Intaglio, perforated 10 1/2x11.*

CM460 *SEATO emblem*

CM460

		MNHVF	UseVF
4¢	blue *(115,353,000)*	.25	.20
	Plate block of 4	.60	
	FDC *(May 31, 1960)*		1.00
	v. Vertical pair, imperforate between	150.00	

1960. AMERICAN WOMEN ISSUE emphasized the important contributions American women have made to social, spiritual, economic, and political progress. *Intaglio, perforated 11x10 1/2.*

CM461 *Mother, daughter, and open book*

CM461

		MNHVF	UseVF
4¢	violet *(111,080,000)*	.25	.20
	Plate block of 4	.60	
	FDC *(June 2, 1960)*		1.00

1960. 50-STAR FLAG ISSUE commemorated the admission of Hawaii as the 50th state. *Intaglio (Giori Press), perforated 11.*

CM462 *50-star American flag*

CM462

		MNHVF	UseVF
4¢	deep blue & scarlet *(153,025,000)*	.25	.20
	Plate block of 4	.60	
	FDC *(July 4, 1960)*		1.00

1960. PONY EXPRESS CENTENARY ISSUE commemorated the contribution to progress by this pioneer transportation service, which provided a faster mail service vitally needed at the time. A stamped envelope (EN844) also was issued in conjunction with this event (see also CM236). *Intaglio, perforated 11x10 1/2.*

CM463 *Pony Express rider and map of route*

CM463

		MNHVF	UseVF
4¢	sepia *(119,665,000)*	.25	.20
	Plate block of 4	.70	
	FDC *(July 19, 1960)*		1.00

1960. EMPLOY THE HANDICAPPED ISSUE focused on the need to promote employment of physically handicapped people who could be trained for gainful activity in American industry. *Intaglio, perforated 10 1/2x11.*

CM464 *Drill press operator in wheelchair*

CM464

		MNHVF	UseVF
4¢	blue *(117,855,000)*	.25	.20
	Plate block of 4	.60	
	FDC *(Aug. 28, 1960)*		1.00

1960. FIFTH WORLD FORESTRY CONGRESS ISSUE paid tribute to the 2,000 foresters from more than 60 nations who gathered to explore the many uses of forest land. The congress was sponsored by the Food and Agriculture Organization of the United Nations. *Intaglio, perforated 10 1/2x11.*

CM465 *Seal of World Forestry Congress*

CM465		MNHVF	UseVF
4¢	blue green *(118,185,000)*	.25	.20
	Plate block of 4	.60	
	FDC *(Aug. 29, 1960)*		1.00

1960. MEXICAN INDEPENDENCE ISSUE marked the 150th anniversary of the Republic of Mexico. Mexico issued a stamp on the same day (Mexico 1373), different only in captions and denomination. *Intaglio (Giori Press), perforated 11.*

CM466 *Freedom Bell of the National Palace, Mexico City*

CM466		MNHVF	UseVF
4¢	deep green & carmine red *(112,260,000)*	.25	.20
	Plate block of 4	.60	
	FDC *(Sept. 16, 1960)*		1.00

1960. UNITED STATES OF AMERICA-JAPAN CENTENNIAL ISSUE commemorated the 100th anniversary of the first treaty between the two countries to promote good will and understanding. *Intaglio (Giori Press), perforated 11.*

CM467 *Washington Monument and cherry blossoms*

CM467		MNHVF	UseVF
4¢	light blue & carmine *(125,010,000)*	.25	.20
	Plate block of 4	.65	
	FDC *(Sept. 28, 1960)*		1.00

1960. IGNACE JAN PADEREWSKI ISSUE The seventh in the Champions of Liberty Series honored the world-famous statesman, pianist, and Polish patriot. *Intaglio, perforated 10 1/2x11.*

CM468-69 *Ignace Jan Paderewski*

CM468		MNHVF	UseVF
4¢	blue *(119,798,000)*	.25	.20
	Plate block of 4	.60	
	FDC *(Oct. 8, 1960)*		1.00

CM469		MNHVF	UseVF
8¢	red, blue & ocher *(42,696,000)*	.25	.20
	Plate block of 4	1.10	
	FDC *(Oct. 8, 1960)*		1.00

1960. ROBERT A. TAFT ISSUE honored the memory of an American (1889-1953) who served his country as a senator from 1939 until his death on July 31, 1953. A native of Ohio, he distinguished himself as Senate majority leader. *Intaglio, perforated 10 1/2x11.*

CM470 *Robert A. Taft*

CM470		MNHVF	UseVF
4¢	violet *(115,171,000)*	.25	.20
	Plate block of 4	.60	
	FDC *(Oct. 10, 1960)*		1.00

1960. WHEELS OF FREEDOM ISSUE was issued as a tribute to the automotive industry. It was released in conjunction with the National Automobile Show in Detroit. *Intaglio, perforated 11x10 1/2.*

CM471 *Hemispheres and steering wheel, symbol of automobile industry*

CM471		MNHVF	UseVF
4¢	blue *(109,695,000)*	.25	.20
	Plate block of 4	.60	
	FDC *(Oct. 15, 1960)*		1.00

1960. BOYS' CLUB OF AMERICA ISSUE commemorated the 100th anniversary of the movement that provided excellent recreational facilities for the underprivileged. *Intaglio (Giori Press), perforated 11.*

CM472 *American youth*

CM472		MNHVF	UseVF
4¢	deep blue, black & red *(123,690,000)*	.25	.20
	Plate block of 4	.60	
	FDC *(Oct. 18, 1960)*		1.00

1960. FIRST AUTOMATED POST OFFICE ISSUE commemorated the establishment of the first fully automated post office at Providence, R.I. Considered a milestone in postal progress, the specially created machinery was expected to speed mail delivery. *Intaglio (Giori Press), perforated 11.*

CM473 *Automated post office*

CM473		MNHVF	UseVF
4¢	deep blue & scarlet *(127,970,000)*	.25	.20
	Plate block of 4	.60	
	FDC *(Oct. 20, 1960)*		1.00

1960. BARON KARL GUSTAF EMIL MANNERHEIM ISSUE The eighth of the Champions of Liberty Series honored the great Finnish soldier, statesman, and leader for his heroic devotion to his country, in peace and war. Born in Askainen, June 4, 1867, he rose to the rank of marshal and led Finnish forces three times in his country's struggle for independence. He served twice as Finland's chief of state. *Intaglio, perforated 10 1/2x11.*

CM474-75 *Karl Gustaf Emil Mannerheim*

CM474		MNHVF	UseVF
4¢	blue *(124,796,000)*	.25	.20
	Plate block of 4	.60	
	FDC *(Oct. 26, 1960)*		1.00

CM475		MNHVF	UseVF
8¢	red, blue & ocher *(42,076,800)*	.25	.20
	Plate block of 4	1.10	
	FDC *(Oct. 26, 1960)*		1.00

1960. CAMP FIRE GIRLS ISSUE commemorated the Golden Jubilee Convention celebration of the organization that was created in 1910 for girls 7 to 18 years of age. *Intaglio (Giori Press), perforated 11.*

CM476 *Camp Fire Girls insignia*

CM476		MNHVF	UseVF
4¢	blue & red *(116,215,000)*	.25	.20
	Plate block of 4	.60	
	FDC *(Nov. 1, 1960)*		1.00

1960. GIUSEPPE GARIBALDI ISSUE The ninth of the Champions of Liberty Series commemorated Italy's great patriot and fighter for freedom. A born leader, Garibaldi helped unify Italy and fought for the cause of liberty in South America and Europe. *Intaglio, perforated 10 1/2x11.*

CM477-78 *Giuseppe Garibaldi*

CM477		MNHVF	UseVF
4¢	green *(126,252,000)*	.25	.20
	Plate block of 4	.60	
	FDC *(Nov. 2, 1960)*		1.00

CM478		MNHVF	UseVF
8¢	red, blue & ocher *(42,746,400)*	.25	.20
	Plate block of 4	1.10	
	FDC *(Nov. 2, 1960)*		1.00

1960. WALTER F. GEORGE ISSUE honored the distinguished public servant (1878-1957) who served as a senator from Georgia and as special assistant for President Eisenhower to NATO in 1957. *Intaglio, perforated 10 1/2x11.*

CM479 *Walter F. George*

CM479		MNHVF	UseVF
4¢	violet *(124,117,000)*	.25	.20
	Plate block of 4	.60	
	FDC *(Nov. 5, 1960)*		1.00

1960. JOHN FOSTER DULLES ISSUE paid tribute to an American (1888-1959) who died while serving as secretary of state. His long, distinguished career included service as secretary to the Hague Peace Conference in 1907 and as U.S. senator from New York. *Intaglio, perforated 10 1/2x11.*

CM480 *John Foster Dulles*

CM480		MNHVF	UseVF
4¢	violet *(177,187,000)*	.20	.20
	Plate block of 4	.60	
	FDC *(Dec. 6, 1960)*		1.00

1960. ANDREW CARNEGIE ISSUE honored the industrialist on his 125th birthday and the 50th anniversary of the establishment of the Carnegie Endowment for International Peace. Born in Scotland, Carnegie (1835-1919) came to the United States as a young boy and became one of the great leaders of world industry. He devoted a good portion of his life and wealth to the cause of social and educational advancements and the promotion of international peace. In 1910, in an effort to abolish the horrors of war, he founded the Carnegie Endowment for International Peace with a gift of $10 million. *Intaglio, perforated 10 1/2x11.*

CM481 *Andrew Carnegie*

CM481		MNHVF	UseVF
4¢	claret *(119,840,000)*	.20	.20
	Plate block of 4	.60	
	FDC *(Nov. 25, 1960)*		1.00

1960. ECHO I SATELLITE ISSUE commemorated the world's first communications satellite launched by NASA into orbit on Aug. 12, 1960. *Intaglio, perforated 11x10 1/2.*

CM482 *Echo I satellite in orbit*

CM482		MNHVF	UseVF
4¢	violet *(125,290,000)*	.25	.20
	Plate block of 4	1.00	
	FDC *(Dec. 15, 1960)*		1.00

1961. MAHATMA GANDHI ISSUE The 10th and final issue in the Champions of Liberty Series honored the Indian who led his country to freedom. A physically frail man, he endured many hardships that inspired his countrymen to work non-violently for independence, equality, and social justice. *Intaglio, perforated 10 1/2x11.*

CM483-84 *Mahatma Gandhi*

CM483		MNHVF	UseVF
4¢	**red orange** *(112,966,000)*	.20	.20
	Plate block of 4	.60	
	FDC *(Jan. 26, 1961)*		1.00

CM484		MNHVF	UseVF
8¢	**red, blue & ocher** *(41,644,200)*	.25	.20
	Plate block of 4	1.20	
	FDC *(Jan. 26, 1961)*		1.00

1961. RANGE CONSERVATION ISSUE was released in conjunction with the annual meeting of the American Society of Range Management, devoted to conservation, forestry, livestock, and land management. *Intaglio (Giori Press), perforated 11.*

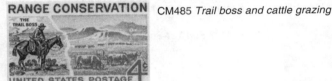

CM485 *Trail boss and cattle grazing*

CM485		MNHVF	UseVF
4¢	**blue, orange & indigo** *(110,850,000)*	.20	.20
	Plate block of 4	.60	
	FDC *(Feb. 2, 1961)*		1.00

1961. HORACE GREELEY ISSUE honored the publisher and editor (1811-1872) who advised the youth of America, "Go West, young man, go West." He established the *New York Tribune* in 1841. *Intaglio, perforated 10 1/2x11.*

CM486 *Horace Greeley*

CM486		MNHVF	UseVF
4¢	**violet** *(98,616,000)*	.20	.20
	Plate block of 4	.60	
	FDC *(Feb. 3, 1961)*		1.00

1961-65. Civil War Centennial Series saluted the 100th anniversary of the bloodiest conflict in the nation's history with one centennial stamp for each of the war's five years.

1961. FORT SUMTER ISSUE in the Civil War Centennial Series marked the anniversary of the assault and capture of the Charleston fort. This attack committed the Confederate states to war. *Intaglio, perforated 10 1/2x11.*

CM487 *Coastal gun at Fort Sumter*

CM487		MNHVF	UseVF
4¢	**green** *(101,125,000)*	.25	.20
	Plate block of 4	1.65	
	FDC *(April 12, 1961)*		1.00

1962. BATTLE OF SHILOH ISSUE in the Civil War Centennial Series commemorated the valiant stand of Confederate troops under Gen. Albert S. Johnston and Union soldiers under Gen. Ulysses S. Grant in the fields of Tennessee. (See also CM1725.) *Intaglio, perforated 11x10 1/2.*

CM488 *Infantryman in action*

CM488		MNHVF	UseVF
4¢	**black on pink** *(124,865,000)*	.25	.20
	Plate block of 4	1.10	
	FDC *(April 7, 1962)*		1.00

1963. BATTLE OF GETTYSBURG ISSUE in the Civil War Centennial Series honored the heroes of one of the most important battles of the Civil War, which was fought July 1-3, 1863, in eastern Pennsylvania. (See CM1740.) *Intaglio (Giori Press), perforated 11.*

CM489 *Union and Confederate soldiers fighting*

CM489		MNHVF	UseVF
5¢	**gray & blue** *(79,905,000)*	.25	.20
	Plate block of 4	1.75	
	FDC *(July 1, 1963)*		1.00

1964. BATTLE OF THE WILDERNESS ISSUE in the Civil War Centennial Series saluted the fierce battle between the armies of Grant and Lee that took place in densely wooded terrain near Fredericksburg, Va. *Intaglio (Giori Press), perforated 11.*

CM490 *Artillery in action*

CM490		MNHVF	UseVF
5¢	**brown, purple & black** *(125,410,000)*	.25	.20
	Plate block of 4	1.50	
	FDC *(May 5, 1964)*		1.00

1965. APPOMATTOX ISSUE in the Civil War Centennial Series celebrated the end of the War Between the States. At Appomattox Court House, Va., on Sunday, April 9, 1865, the Confederate Army under the command of Gen. Robert E. Lee surrendered to Gen. Ulysses S. Grant and the Union forces. *Intaglio (Giori Press), perforated 11.*

CM491 *Civil War soldier and rifles*

CM491		MNHVF	UseVF
5¢	**blue & black** *(112,845,000)*	.25	.20
	Plate block of 4	3.75	
	FDC *(April 9, 1965)*		1.00
	v. Horizontal pair, imperforate vertically	—	

1961. KANSAS STATEHOOD CENTENNIAL ISSUE marked 100 years of statehood for Kansas, admitted in 1861 as the 34th state. *Intaglio (Giori Press), perforated 11.*

CM492 *Sunflower, pioneers, and fort*

CM492
4¢		MNHVF	UseVF
	brown, lake & green on yellow paper	.20	.20
	(106,210,000)		
	Plate block of 4	.60	
	FDC *(May 10, 1961)*		1.00

1961. GEORGE WILLIAM NORRIS ISSUE honored the Nebraska senator on his 100th birthday. Among his many achievements was a key role in the creation of the Tennessee Valley Authority. *Intaglio, perforated 11x10 1/2.*

CM493 *George W. Norris and Norris Dam*

CM493
4¢		MNHVF	UseVF
	blue green *(110,810,000)*	.20	.20
	Plate block of 4	.60	
	FDC *(July 11, 1961)*		1.00

1961. NAVAL AVIATION ISSUE saluted the golden jubilee of the Navy's participation and development in aviation. *Intaglio, perforated 11x10 1/2.*

CM494 *Naval air wings and first naval airplane (1911 Curtis A-1)*

CM494
4¢		MNHVF	UseVF
	blue *(116,995,000)*	.20	.20
	Plate block of 4	.65	
	Pair, gutter between	—	
	FDC *(Aug. 20, 1961)*		1.00

1961. WORKMAN'S COMPENSATION ISSUE marked the 50th anniversary of the first U.S. legislation to compensate workers injured on the job. The Wisconsin law of 1911 set a pattern that was followed by nine other states that year. *Intaglio, perforated 10 1/2x11.*

CM495 *Factory and family in scales of justice*

CM495
4¢		MNHVF	UseVF
	ultramarine on bluish paper	.20	.20
	(121,015,000)		
	Plate block of 4	.60	
	v. Plate block of 4, plate number inverted	.60	
	FDC *(Sept. 4, 1961)*		1.00

Fine Arts Series

1961. FREDERIC REMINGTON ISSUE First stamp in a Fine Arts Series, honored the 100th birthday of this American artist of the West (CM230) who won fame for his paintings and sculptures of North

American Indians, U.S. soldiers, and cowboys on the western plains. (See also CM993.) *Intaglio (Giori Press), perforated 11.*

CM496 *Detail from* The Smoke Signal *by Remington (left side of painting)*

CM496
4¢		MNHVF	UseVF
	blue, red & yellow *(111,600,000)*	.20	.20
	Plate block of 4	.65	
	FDC *(Oct. 4, 1961)*		1.00

1961. 50TH ANNIVERSARY OF THE REPUBLIC OF CHINA ISSUE honored Sun Yat-Sen (1866-1925), the founder of the republic who fought against dynastic rule for the freedom of China. (See also CM248.) *Intaglio, perforated 10 1/2x11.*

CM497 *Sun Yat-Sen*

CM497
4¢		MNHVF	UseVF
	blue *(110,620,000)*	.20	.20
	Plate block of 4	.85	
	FDC *(Oct. 10, 1961)*		1.00

1961. NAISMITH-BASKETBALL ISSUE commemorated the 100th birthday of Dr. James A. Naismith (1861-1939), Canadian-born inventor of basketball. An athletic instructor at the YMCA, Naismith saw the need for a fast-moving, exciting indoor sport that could be played in the winter. In 1891 he founded the game, which today draws millions of participants and spectators. *Intaglio, perforated 10 1/2x11.*

CM498 *Basketball, hand, and net*

CM498
4¢		MNHVF	UseVF
	brown *(109,110,000)*	.25	.20
	Plate block of 4	1.00	
	FDC *(Nov. 6, 1961)*		1.00

1961. NURSING ISSUE noted the 100th anniversary of the nursing profession in the United States. An urgent need for skilled nurses was created by the Civil War. The training programs then established laid the foundations for the profession, which thousands of Americans enter each year. *Intaglio (Giori Press), perforated 11.*

CM499 *Nurse lighting candle*

CM499		MNHVF	UseVF
4¢	**blue, black, orange & flesh**	.20	.20
	(145,350,000)		
	Plate block of 4	.60	
	FDC *(Dec. 28, 1961)*		1.00

1962. NEW MEXICO STATEHOOD ISSUE commemorated the 50th anniversary of its admission as the 47th state (see CM286). *Intaglio (Giori Press), perforated 11.*

CM500 *Shiprock Mesa*

CM500		MNHVF	UseVF
4¢	**light blue, bister & brown purple**	.20	.20
	(112,870,000)		
	Plate block of 4	.60	
	FDC *(Jan. 6, 1962)*		1.00

1962. ARIZONA STATEHOOD ISSUE marked the 50th anniversary of the admission of the 48th state. *Intaglio (Giori Press), perforated 11.*

CM501 *Giant Saguaro cactus in bloom at night*

CM501		MNHVF	UseVF
4¢	**scarlet, deep blue & green**	.20	.20
	(121,820,000)		
	Plate block of 4	.60	
	FDC *(Feb. 14, 1962)*		1.00

1962. PROJECT MERCURY ISSUE paid tribute to the successful three-orbit flight of Lt. Col. John H. Glenn Jr. The stamp was released at the moment the flight was completed — the first time the United States honored a historic event with an unannounced, simultaneous commemorative. Glenn, the first American astronaut to orbit the earth, traveled at 17,500 miles per hour in his Mercury capsule, *Friendship 7. Intaglio (Giori Press), perforated 11.*

CM502 *Mercury capsule circling Earth*

CM502		MNHVF	UseVF
4¢	**deep blue & yellow** *(289,240,000)*	.20	.20
	Plate block of 4	.80	
	FDC *(Feb. 20, 1962)*		1.00

1962. MALARIA ERADICATION ISSUE pledged U.S. support to the World Health Organization in its campaign to eliminate malaria, a disease that claims countless lives each year. *Intaglio (Giori Press), perforated 11.*

CM503 *United States seal and WHO emblem*

CM503		MNHVF	UseVF
4¢	**blue & bister** *(120,155,000)*	.20	.20
	Plate block of 4	.60	
	FDC *(March 30, 1962)*		1.00

1962. CHARLES EVANS HUGHES ISSUE honored the 100th birthday of a statesman-jurist (1862-1948) who served as governor of New York, secretary of state under President Harding, and chief justice of the U.S. Supreme Court (1930-41). *Intaglio, perforated 10 1/2x11.*

CM504 *Charles Evans Hughes*

CM504		MNHVF	UseVF
4¢	**black** on yellow paper *(124,595,000)*	.20	.20
	Plate block of 4	.60	
	FDC *(April 11, 1962)*		1.00

1962. SEATTLE WORLD'S FAIR ISSUE marked the International Exposition held in Seattle, Wash., April 21-Oct. 21, 1962. This was America's first space-age world's fair, with the 550-foot-high Space Needle as its most distinctive structure and symbol. *Intaglio (Giori Press), perforated 11.*

CM505 *Space Needle and monorail*

CM505		MNHVF	UseVF
4¢	**red & deep blue** *(147,310,000)*	.20	.20
	Plate block of 4	.60	
	FDC *(April 25, 1962)*		1.00

1962. LOUISIANA STATEHOOD COMMEMORATIVE ISSUE marked the 150th anniversary of the admission of Louisiana as the 18th state. *Intaglio (Giori Press), perforated 11.*

CM506 *Mississippi riverboat*

CM506		MNHVF	UseVF
4¢	**gray green, blue & vermilion**	.20	.20
	(118,690,000)		

Plate block of 4 .60
FDC *(April 30, 1962)* 1.00

1962. HOMESTEAD ACT ISSUE commemorated the 100th anniversary of the act signed by Abraham Lincoln that opened the Great Plains to settlers. A homesteader could acquire 160 acres by living and working on the land for five years. *Intaglio, perforated 11 1/4x10 1/2.*

CM507 *Sod hut and homesteaders*

CM507 | | **MNHVF** | **UseVF**
4¢ | slate blue *(122,730,000)* | .20 | .20
 | Plate block of 4 | .60 |
 | FDC *(May 20, 1962)* | | 1.00

1962. GIRL SCOUTS OF AMERICA ISSUE commemorated the 50th anniversary of the movement, which has grown into an organization of millions. (See CM316.) *Intaglio, perforated 11 1/4x10 1/2.*

CM508 *Girl Scout, American flag*

CM508 | | **MNHVF** | **UseVF**
4¢ | red *(126,515,000)* | .20 | .20
 | Plate block of 4 | .60 |
 | Pair, gutter between | — |
 | FDC *(July 24, 1962)* | | 1.00

1962. BRIEN MCMAHON ISSUE honored the Connecticut senator who saw the vast potential of the atom for medical, industrial, and scientific purposes. McMahon (1903-1952) formed the Atomic Energy Commission. (See CM382.) *Intaglio, perforated 11 1/4x10 1/2.*

CM509 *James O'Brien McMahon and atomic symbol*

CM509 | | **MNHVF** | **UseVF**
4¢ | violet *(130,960,000)* | .20 | .20
 | Plate block of 4 | .60 |
 | FDC *(July 28, 1962)* | | 1.00

1962. NATIONAL APPRENTICESHIP ISSUE marked the 25th anniversary of the program under which the U.S. Department of Labor, unions, and management join in sponsoring apprenticeship training. *Intaglio, perforated 11 1/4x10 1/2.*

CM510 *Young hand receiving micrometer*

CM510 | | **MNHVF** | **UseVF**
4¢ | black on buff *(120,055,000)* | .20 | .20
 | Plate block of 4 | .60 |
 | FDC *(Aug. 31, 1962)* | | 1.00

1962. SAM RAYBURN ISSUE honored the Texan who served as a Congressman from 1913 until 1961. Rayburn (1882-1961) was Speaker of the House of Representatives for 17 years, longer than any other. *Intaglio (Giori Press), perforated 11.*

CM511 *Sam Rayburn and Capitol dome*

CM511 | | **MNHVF** | **UseVF**
4¢ | brown & blue *(120,715,000)* | .20 | .20
 | Plate block of 4 | .60 |
 | FDC *(Sept. 16, 1962)* | | 1.00

1962. DAG HAMMARSKJÖLD ISSUE honored the secretary-general of the United Nations who lost his life while on a peace mission in Africa. *Intaglio (Giori Press), perforated 11.*

CM512-13 *Dag Hammarskjöld and U.N. building*

CM512 | | **MNHVF** | **UseVF**
4¢ | black, brown & yellow *(121,440,000)* | .20 | .20
 | Plate block of 4 | .60 |
 | FDC *(Oct. 23, 1962)* | | 1.00

1962. DAG HAMMARSKJÖLD SPECIAL ISSUE Shortly after the commemorative was released, a yellow inverted error was discovered by collectors in New Jersey and Ohio. The Post Office Department deliberately reprinted this error — the first U.S. invert error since the 24¢ Jenny airmail of 1918. Only the yellow is inverted and there are three distinct varieties as noted below. *Intaglio (Giori Press), perforated 11.*

CM513 *Inverted yellow*

CM513 | | **MNHVF** | **UseVF**
4¢ | black, brown & yellow *(40,270,000)* | .55 | .25
 | Type I, the non-yellow strip at left is 3.5mm wide | .55 | .25
 | Type II, the non-yellow strip at left is 11.5mm wide | .55 | .25
 | Type III, the non-yellow strip at left is 9.75mm wide | .55 | .25

1962. HIGHER EDUCATION ISSUE commemorated the centennial of the law creating land-grant colleges and universities and pointed out the role higher education has played in the development of the United States (see also CM377). *Intaglio (Giori Press), perforated 11.*

CM514 *Lamp of learning and U.S. map*

CM514 | | **MNHVF** | **UseVF**
4¢ | blue, green & black *(120,035,000)* | .20 | .20
 | Plate block of 4 | .65 |
 | FDC *(Nov. 14, 1962)* | | 1.00

1962. WINSLOW HOMER ISSUE honored the American artist who painted *Breezing Up,* on display in the National Gallery of Art in Washington, D.C. This is the second issue in the Fine Arts Series. *Intaglio (Giori Press), perforated 11.*

CM515 Breezing Up *by Winslow Homer*

CM515		MNHVF	UseVF
4¢	**multicolored** *(117,870,000)*	.20	.20
	Plate block of 4	.65	
	v. Horizontal pair, imperforate between	6,750.00	
	FDC *(Dec. 15, 1962)*		1.00

1963. CAROLINA CHARTER ISSUE commemorated the 300th anniversary of the granting of the charter by Charles II to eight supporters who helped him regain the English throne. The land grant covered 1.5 million square miles. *Intaglio (Giori Press), perforated 11.*

CM516 *Charter and quill pen*

CM516		MNHVF	UseVF
5¢	**dark carmine & brown** *(129,445,000)*	.20	.20
	Plate block of 4	.65	
	FDC *(April 6, 1963)*		1.00

1963. FOOD FOR PEACE ISSUE paid tribute to the World Food Congress and joined nearly 150 other nations and territories in publicizing the international Freedom from Hunger campaign on stamps. *Intaglio (Giori Press), perforated 11.*

CM517 *Stalk of wheat*

CM517		MNHVF	UseVF
5¢	**green, yellow & red** *(135,620,000)*	.20	.20
	Plate block of 4	.65	
	FDC *(June 4, 1963)*		1.00

1963. WEST VIRGINIA STATEHOOD ISSUE commemorated the 100th anniversary of the admission of the Mountain State to the union as the 35th state. *Intaglio (Giori Press), perforated 11.*

CM518 *Map and State Capitol of West Virginia*

CM518		MNHVF	UseVF
5¢	**green, red & black** *(137,540,000)*	.20	.20
	Plate block of 4	.65	
	FDC *(June 20, 1963)*		1.00

1963. EMANCIPATION PROCLAMATION ISSUE commemorated the centennial of President Lincoln's action to abolish slavery in the United States. *Intaglio (Giori Press), perforated 11.*

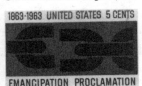

CM519 *Broken chain*

CM519		MNHVF	UseVF
5¢	**bright blue, scarlet & indigo**	.20	.20
	(132,435,000)		
	Plate block of 4	.85	
	FDC *(Aug. 16, 1963)*		1.00

1963. ALLIANCE FOR PROGRESS ISSUE marked the second anniversary of an inter-American program for peaceful coexistence and economic improvement. Other members of the Organization of American States to issue stamps honoring the event include Argentina, Bolivia, Costa Rica, Uruguay, and Canal Zone. *Intaglio (Giori Press), perforated 11.*

CM520 *Torch of progress*

CM520		MNHVF	UseVF
5¢	**bright blue & green** *(135,520,000)*	.20	.20
	Plate block of 4	.65	
	FDC *(Aug. 17, 1963)*		1.00

1963. CORDELL HULL ISSUE paid tribute to the secretary of state during the administration of Franklin Roosevelt, from 1933 until 1944. Hull (1871-1955) was awarded the Nobel Peace Prize in 1945. *Intaglio, perforated 10 1/2x11.*

CM521 *Cordell Hull*

CM521		MNHVF	UseVF
5¢	**blue green** *(131,420,000)*	.20	.20
	Plate block of 4	.65	
	FDC *(Oct. 5, 1963)*		1.00

1963. ELEANOR ROOSEVELT ISSUE honored Franklin D. Roosevelt's widow (1884-1962), a champion of liberty and a formidable fighter for human rights. The likeness on the stamp was taken from a photograph she liked best. *Intaglio, perforated 11x10 1/2.*

CM522 *Eleanor Roosevelt*

CM522		MNHVF	UseVF
5¢	**purple** *(133,170,000)*	.20	.20
	Plate block of 4	.65	
	FDC *(Oct. 11, 1963)*		1.00

1963. NATIONAL ACADEMY OF SCIENCE ISSUE saluted this organization on its 100th anniversary. Abraham Lincoln signed into law the legislation that created the academy, which was originally composed of 50 American scientists. *Intaglio (Giori Press), perforated 11.*

CM523 *Astral belt over globe*

CM523		MNHVF	UseVF
5¢	**turquoise, blue & black** *(139,195,000)*	.20	.20

Plate block of 4   .65
FDC *(Oct. 14, 1963)*   1.00

1963. CITY MAIL DELIVERY ISSUE marked the centennial of the service begun at the suggestion of Postmaster General Montgomery Blair, who convinced Congress to pass a law providing for the free delivery of city mail. Designed by Norman Rockwell, this commemorative is considered the first expression of humor on a U.S. stamp. It was the first U.S. issue tagged with an invisible compound of zinc-orthosilicate that glows green under ultraviolet light. This allowed automated handling equipment to differentiate between surface-rate stamps and airmail-rate stamps, which glowed red under ultraviolet light. *Intaglio (Giori Press), perforated 11.*

CM524 *Postman flanked by boy and dog*

CM524

		MNHVF	UseVF
5¢	**red, gray & blue,** tagged type OP *(128,450,000)*	.20	.20
	Plate block of 4	.65	
	FDC *(Oct. 26, 1963)*		1.00
	zo. Tagging omitted	15.00	

Untagged "gripper space" on lower pane margins of this issue is normal.

1963. INTERNATIONAL RED CROSS ISSUE marked the centennial of the organization and saluted the Red Cross for its participation in the Cuban prisoner exchange program. *Intaglio (Giori Press), perforated 11.*

CM525 *Cuban refugees on S.S. Morning Light*

CM525

		MNHVF	UseVF
5¢	**deep gray & red** *(116,665,000)*	.20	.20
	Plate block of 4	.65	
	FDC *(Oct. 29, 1963)*		1.00

1963. JOHN JAMES AUDUBON ISSUE honored the great American artist and ornithologist who died in 1851. This was the third in the Fine Arts Series and the third time Audubon was honored with a stamp (see CM216 and A71 and 839). *Intaglio (Giori Press), perforated 11.*

CM526 *Audubon's Columbia jays*

CM526

		MNHVF	UseVF
5¢	**multicolored** *(175,175,000)*	.20	.20
	Plate block of 4	.80	
	FDC *(Dec. 7, 1963)*		1.00

1964. SAM HOUSTON ISSUE saluted the first president of the Republic of Texas, commander of the army that defeated Santa Ana in 1836 and thus gained independence for the Lone Star state. This was the first use of the Mr. ZIP marginal inscription. (See also CM166 and CM168.) *Intaglio, perforated 10 1/2x11.*

CM527 *Sam Houston*

CM527

		MNHVF	UseVF
5¢	**black** *(125,995,000)*	.20	.20
	Plate block of 4	.85	
	FDC *(Jan. 10, 1964)*		1.00

1964. CHARLES M. RUSSELL ISSUE noted the 100th anniversary of the artist's birth with the fourth stamp in the Fine Arts Series. Famous for his Western themes, Russell's art has themes of gunmen, longhorn steers, broncos, and dancehall girls. *Intaglio (Giori Press), perforated 11.*

CM528 *Russell's* Jerked Down

CM528

		MNHVF	UseVF
5¢	**multicolored** *(128,025,000)*	.20	.20
	Plate block of 4	.85	
	FDC *(March 19, 1964)*		1.00

1964. NEW YORK WORLD'S FAIR ISSUE commemorated the opening of the international exposition dedicated to "Peace Through Understanding." Approximately 175 separate pavilions and other structures presented the achievements of more than 509 nations, states and major industries. *Intaglio, perforated 11x10 1/2.*

CM529 *Unisphere and World's Fair mall*

CM529

		MNHVF	UseVF
5¢	**green** *(145,700,000)*	.20	.20
	Plate block of 4	.85	
	FDC *(April 22, 1964)*		1.00

1964. JOHN MUIR ISSUE honored the naturalist and conservationist (1838-1914) whose efforts helped save California's priceless forests. *Intaglio (Giori Press), perforated 11.*

CM530 *John Muir and redwoods*

CM530

		MNHVF	UseVF
5¢	**brown, green, brownish gray & olive green** *(120,310,000)*	.20	.20
	Plate block of 4	.85	
	FDC *(April 29, 1964)*		1.00

1964. JOHN F. KENNEDY MEMORIAL ISSUE paid tribute to the 35th president of the United States, assassinated in Dallas, Texas, Nov. 22, 1963. Many nations mourned his passing and issued stamps in his memory. Although Boston was the official first-day city, the stamp was released nationwide that same day. *Intaglio, perforated 11x10 1/2.*

CM531 *John F. Kennedy and eternal flame*

CM531		MNHVF	UseVF
5¢	gray blue *(500,000,000)*	.20	.20
	Plate block of 4	1.85	
	FDC *(May 29, 1964)*		1.00

1964. NEW JERSEY TERCENTENARY ISSUE marked the 300th anniversary of the colonization of the Garden State by the British. The stamp was first issued in Elizabeth, the state's first capital and oldest city. *Intaglio, perforated 10 1/2x11.*

CM532 *Philip Carteret at Elizabethtown*

CM532		MNHVF	UseVF
5¢	ultramarine *(123,845,000)*	.20	.20
	Plate block of 4	.65	
	FDC *(June 15, 1964)*		1.00

1964. NEVADA STATEHOOD ISSUE commemorated the centenary of the entry of Nevada as the 36th state. *Intaglio (Giori Press), perforated 11.*

CM533 *Virginia City and map of Nevada*

CM533		MNHVF	UseVF
5¢	multicolored *(122,825,000)*	.20	.20
	Plate block of 4	.65	
	FDC *(July 22, 1964)*		1.00

1964. REGISTER AND VOTE ISSUE encouraged Americans to take part in the forthcoming election and was endorsed by both the Democratic and Republican parties. *Intaglio (Giori Press), perforated 11.*

CM534 *U.S. flag*

CM534		MNHVF	UseVF
5¢	blue & red *(325,000,000)*	.20	.20
	Plate block of 4	.65	
	FDC *(Aug. 1, 1964)*		1.00

1964. WILLIAM SHAKESPEARE ISSUE commemorated the 400th birthday of the Bard of Avon. His contributions to the world included such masterpieces as *Romeo & Juliet, Hamlet, Othello, Macbeth,* and *King Lear. Intaglio, perforated 10 1/2x11.*

CM535 *William Shakespeare*

CM535		MNHVF	UseVF
5¢	brown on tan paper *(123,245,000)*	.20	.20
	Plate block of 4	.65	
	FDC *(Aug. 14, 1964)*		1.00

1964. DOCTORS MAYO ISSUE honored the birth of William J. Mayo and his brother Charles H. Mayo and the 50th anniversary of the founding of the world-famous Mayo Clinic in Rochester, Minn. *Intaglio, perforated 10 1/2x11.*

CM536 *Statue of the Mayo brothers*

CM536		MNHVF	UseVF
5¢	green *(123,355,000)*	.20	.20
	Plate block of 4	1.50	
	FDC *(Sept. 11, 1964)*		1.00

1964. AMERICAN MUSIC ISSUE commemorated the 50th anniversary of the American Society of Composers, Authors, and Publishers. *Intaglio (Giori Press), perforated 11.*

CM537 *Lute and horn, music score, oak, and laurel*

CM537		MNHVF	UseVF
5¢	red, gray & blue on granite paper *(126,370,000)*	.20	.20
	Plate block of 4	.85	
	v. blue omitted	1,000.00	
	FDC *(Oct. 15, 1964)*		1.00

1964. HOMEMAKERS ISSUE commemorated the 50th anniversary of the Smith-Lever Act that improved home life in America. It was issued in conjunction with the annual meeting of the National Extension Homemakers Council. This was the first time the Bureau of Engraving and Printing combined offset and intaglio printing on a stamp, a method used by the American Bank Note Co. to print the Overrun Countries stamps (CM251-63). *Intaglio (Giori Press) and offset, perforated 11.*

CM538 *Needlepoint sampler of American farm scene*

CM538

		MNHVF	UseVF
5¢	multicolored on buff *(121,250,000)*	.20	.20
	Plate block of 4	.85	
	FDC *(Oct. 26, 1964)*		1.00

1964. VERRAZANO-NARROWS BRIDGE ISSUE marked the dedication of what was the longest single suspension bridge in the world. Named for the Florentine explorer who discovered New York Bay in 1524, the span links Staten Island and Brooklyn, N.Y. *Intaglio, perforated 10 1/2x11.*

CM539 *Verrazano-Narrows Bridge and map*

CM539

		MNHVF	UseVF
5¢	green *(125,005,000)*	.20	.20
	Plate block of 4	.65	
	FDC *(Nov. 21, 1964)*		1.00

1964. ABSTRACT ART ISSUE is the fifth in the Fine Arts Series commemoratives. It is based on a lithograph by the late Stuart Davis. *Intaglio (Giori Press), perforated 11.*

CM540 Melange of Squiggles *by Stuart Davis*

CM540

		MNHVF	UseVF
5¢	blue, black & red *(125,800,000)*	.20	.20
	Plate block of 4	.65	
	FDC *(Dec. 2, 1964)*		1.00

1964. AMATEUR RADIO OPERATORS ISSUE paid tribute to the nation's 250,000 "hams" and their long record of service to the country in emergencies and marked the 50th anniversary of the American Radio Relay League. *Intaglio, perforated 10 1/2x11.*

CM541 *Radio dial and wave*

CM541

		MNHVF	UseVF
5¢	purple *(122,230,000)*	.20	.20
	Plate block of 4	.90	
	FDC *(Dec. 15, 1964)*		1.00

1965. BATTLE OF NEW ORLEANS ISSUE saluted 150 years of peace between England and the United States and the sesquicentennial of the famous battle between American forces under Gen. Andrew Jackson and the British troops led by Sir Edward Packenham. *Intaglio (Giori Press), perforated 11.*

CM542 *Gen. Andrew Jackson leading troops in battle and sesquicentennial medal*

CM542

		MNHVF	UseVF
5¢	carmine, blue & slate *(115,695,000)*	.20	.20
	Plate block of 4	.65	
	FDC *(Jan. 8, 1964)*		1.00

1965. SOKOL CENTENNIAL — PHYSICAL FITNESS ISSUE paid tribute to the program initiated by President Kennedy and the 100th anniversary of the Sokol educational and physical fitness organization. *Intaglio (Giori Press), perforated 11.*

CM543 *Discus thrower*

CM543

		MNHVF	UseVF
5¢	lake & deep slate *(115,095,000)*	.20	.20
	Plate block of 4	.65	
	FDC *(Feb. 15, 1965)*		1.00

1965. CRUSADE AGAINST CANCER ISSUE publicized the importance of medical checkups and prompt treatment and saluted the efforts of those dedicated to eradicating cancer. *Intaglio (Giori Press), perforated 11.*

CM544 *Stethoscope and microscope*

CM544

		MNHVF	UseVF
5¢	reddish violet, black & red *(116,560,000)*	.20	.20
	Plate block of 4	.65	
	FDC *(April 1, 1965)*		1.00

1965. WINSTON CHURCHILL MEMORIAL ISSUE honored the World War II British leader (1874-1965) who was an honorary American citizen. *Intaglio, perforated 10 1/2x11.*

CM545 *Winston Churchill*

CM545

		MNHVF	UseVF
5¢	black *(125,180,000)*	.20	.20
	Plate block of 4	.65	
	FDC *(May 13, 1965)*		1.00

1965. MAGNA CARTA ISSUE commemorated the 750th anniversary of the document signed by King John that became the first detailed statement of English feudal law esteemed by many as a cornerstone of later British and American law. *Intaglio (Giori Press), perforated 11.*

CM546 Triumph of the People Over the King, *symbolic design by Brook Temple*

CM546

5¢		MNHVF	UseVF
	black, yellow & reddish-violet *(120,135,000)*	.20	.20
	Plate block of 4 (2 numbers)	.65	
	v. Plate block of 4, black plate number omitted	—	
	FDC *(June 15, 1965)*		1.00

1965. UN INTERNATIONAL COOPERATION YEAR ISSUE commemorated the 20th anniversary of the United Nations. The United States and other U.N. member nations issued stamps dedicated to the theme, and the United Nations issued a set of two stamps and a souvenir sheet on the same day as this U.S. stamp. *Intaglio (Giori Press), perforated 11.*

CM547 *International Cooperation Year emblem*

CM547

5¢		MNHVF	UseVF
	turquoise blue & slate *(115,405,000)*	.20	.20
	Plate block of 4	.65	
	FDC *(June 26, 1965)*		1.00

1965. SALVATION ARMY ISSUE marked the 100th anniversary of this non-sectarian international organization. Founded in London by William Booth in 1865, the Salvation Army was established in the United States in 1880. *Intaglio (Giori Press), perforated 11.*

CM548 *Salvation Army*

CM548

5¢		MNHVF	UseVF
	red, black & deep blue *(115,855,000)*	.20	.20
	Plate block of 4	.65	
	FDC *(July 2, 1965)*		1.00

1965. DANTE ALIGHIERI ISSUE marked the 700th birthday of Italy's poet who wrote *The Divine Comedy. Intaglio, perforated 10 1/2x11.*

CM549 *Dante Alighieri, adapted from a 16th-century painting*

CM549

5¢		MNHVF	UseVF
	carmine red on light Venetian red paper *(115,340,000)*	.20	.20
	Plate block of 4	.65	
	FDC *(July 17, 1965)*		1.00

1965. HERBERT HOOVER ISSUE paid tribute to the 31st president of the United States (1874-1964) who died Oct. 20, 1964. He was a talented mining engineer and served the country in many capacities, including secretary of commerce under Harding. *Intaglio, perforated 10 1/2x11.*

CM550 *Herbert Hoover*

CM550

5¢		MNHVF	UseVF
	red *(114,840,000)*	.20	.20
	Plate block of 4	.65	
	FDC *(Aug. 10, 1965)*		1.00

1965. ROBERT FULTON ISSUE commemorated the 200th birthday of the inventor (1765-1815) who built the first successful steamship, *The Clermont*, in 1807. *Intaglio (Giori Press), perforated 11.*

CM551 *Robert Fulton and* The Clermont

CM551

5¢		MNHVF	UseVF
	blue & black *(116,140,000)*	.20	.20
	Plate block of 4	.65	
	FDC *(Aug. 19, 1965)*		1.00

1965. EUROPEAN SETTLEMENT ISSUE commemorated the 400th anniversary of the establishment by Spanish colonists of a permanent settlement in Florida in September 1565. Spain released a joint issue marking this event (Spain 1715). *Intaglio (Giori Press), perforated 11.*

CM552 *Spanish explorer and ships*

CM552

5¢		MNHVF	UseVF
	yellow, red & black *(116,900,000)*	.20	.20
	Plate block of 4	.65	
	v. yellow omitted	400.00	
	FDC *(Aug. 28, 1965)*		1.00

1965. TRAFFIC SAFETY ISSUE called attention to the urgent need to reduce automotive accidents. *Intaglio (Giori Press), perforated 11.*

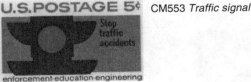

CM553 *Traffic signal*

CM553

5¢		MNHVF	UseVF
	green, black & red *(114,085,000)*	.20	.20
	Plate block of 4	.65	
	FDC *(Sept. 3, 1965)*		1.00

1965. JOHN SINGLETON COPLEY ISSUE The sixth stamp in the Fine Arts Series featured a portrait of the artist's daughter, part of a family group painted in 1776 by Copley. The original hangs in the National Gallery of Art, Washington, D.C. *Intaglio (Giori Press), perforated 11.*

CM554 *Elizabeth Clarke Copley*

CM554		MNHVF	UseVF
5¢	black & tones of brown & olive *(114,880,000)*	.20	.20
	Plate block of 4	.65	
	FDC *(Sept. 17, 1965)*		1.00

1965. INTERNATIONAL TELECOMMUNICATION UNION ISSUE commemorated the 100th anniversary of this international organization created in 1865 to develop electronic communication among nations. *Intaglio (Giori Press), perforated 11.*

CM555 *World map and radio wave*

CM555		MNHVF	UseVF
11¢	yellow, red & black *(26,995,000)*	.20	.20
	Plate block of 4	5.50	
	FDC *(Oct. 6, 1965)*		1.00

1965. ADLAI STEVENSON ISSUE paid tribute to the late U.S. ambassador to the United Nations, governor of Illinois, and presidential candidate (1900-1965). *Intaglio (Giori Press) and offset, perforated 11.*

CM556 *Adlai Stevenson, U.N. wreath and U.S. colors*

CM556		MNHVF	UseVF
5¢	light blue gray, black, red & blue *(128,495,000)*	.20	.20
	Plate block of 4	.65	
	FDC *(Oct. 23, 1965)*		1.00

1966. MIGRATORY BIRD TREATY ISSUE marked the 50th anniversary of cooperation between the United States and Canada in protecting birds. *Intaglio (Giori Press), perforated 11.*

CM557 *Birds over the Great Lakes*

CM557		MNHVF	UseVF
5¢	red, blue & light blue *(116,835,000)*	.25	.20
	Plate block of 4	.65	
	FDC *(March 16, 1966)*		

1966. HUMANE TREATMENT OF ANIMALS ISSUE paid tribute to The American Society for the Prevention of Cruelty to Animals, founded in 1866 by Henry Bergh. *Intaglio (Giori Press) and offset, perforated 11.*

CM558 *"Babe" the dog*

CM558		MNHVF	UseVF
5¢	reddish brown & black *(117,470,000)*	.25	.20
	Plate block of 4	.65	
	FDC *(April 9, 1966)*		1.00

1966. INDIANA STATEHOOD ISSUE marked the 150th anniversary of Indiana's admission to the union as the 19th state. The event was officially celebrated at Corydon, the first capital of Indiana. *Intaglio (Giori Press), perforated 11.*

CM559 *Map of Indiana and old capitol*

CM559		MNHVF	UseVF
5¢	blue, yellow & brown *(123,770,000)*	.25	.20
	Plate block of 4	.65	
	FDC *(April 16, 1966)*		1.00

1966. AMERICAN CIRCUS ISSUE saluted the Big Top and those who bring fun and thrills to audiences throughout the nation. *Intaglio (Giori Press), perforated 11.*

CM560 *Circus clown*

CM560		MNHVF	UseVF
5¢	red, blue, pink & black *(131,270,000)*	.25	.20
	Plate block of 4	.90	
	FDC *(May 2, 1966)*		1.00

1966. SIXTH INTERNATIONAL PHILATELIC EXHIBITION ISSUE commemorated the show, held in Washington, D.C., May 21-30. This commemorative stamp and souvenir sheet (and a related airmail postal card, PCA5) were issued to mark the event. *Intaglio (Giori Press) and offset, perforated 11.*

CM561 *Envelope with stamps*

CM561		MNHVF	UseVF
5¢	multicolored *(122,285,000)*	.25	.20
	Plate block of 4	.65	
	FDC *(May 21, 1966)*		1.00

1966. SIPEX SOUVENIR SHEET dedicated to stamp collectors also features the words "Discover America," the theme of President Johnson's program to stimulate travel and tourism in the United States. *Intaglio (Giori Press) and offset, imperforate.*

CM562 *Envelope and Capitol scene*

CM562		MNHVF	UseVF
5¢	multicolored *(14,680,000)*	.30	.25
	FDC *(May 23, 1966)*		1.00

1966. BILL OF RIGHTS ISSUE commemorated the 175th anniversary of the first 10 amendments to the U.S. Constitution. The stamp was designed by Herbert L. Block, renowned editorial cartoonist. *Intaglio (Giori Press), perforated 11.*

CM563 *"Freedom Conquers Tyranny"*

CM563		MNHVF	UseVF
5¢	red & blue *(114,160,000)*	.25	.20
	Plate block of 4	.65	
	FDC *(July 1, 1966)*		1.00

1966. POLISH MILLENNIUM ISSUE commemorated the 1,000th anniversary of Poland and paid tribute to the longstanding friendship between Americans and the Polish people. *Intaglio, perforated 10 1/2x11.*

CM564 *Polish eagle*

CM564		MNHVF	UseVF
5¢	red *(126,475,000)*	.25	.20
	Plate block of 4	.65	
	FDC *(July 30, 1966)*		1.00

1966. NATIONAL PARK SERVICE ISSUE paid tribute to the 50th anniversary of the National Park Service. Although the national park system dates back to 1872, it was first established as a bureau under the Department of Interior Aug. 25, 1916. *Intaglio (Giori Press) and offset, perforated 11.*

CM565 *National Park Service emblem*

CM565		MNHVF	UseVF
5¢	multicolored *(119,535,000)*	.25	.20
	Plate block of 4	.80	
	FDC *(Aug. 25, 1966)*		1.00
	z. Tagged	.30	.25
	Plate block of 4, tagged	2.00	
	FDC, tagged *(Aug. 26, 1966)*	—	30.00
	z1. Tagged after perforating	.30	
	Plate block of 4, with untagged left margin	2.00	
	FDC (Washington, D.C.) *(Aug. 26, 1966)*		—
	z2. Tagging inverted		
	Plate block of 4	—	
	z3. Error (untagged), side-margin strip of 20 with plate and ZIP, with tagged and untagged errors on same piece	1.40	

Stamps tagged after perforation can be distinguished by a grid of tagging which connects the perforation holes on the gummed side of unused stamps and perforation-sized disc-like blemishes in the tagging on the face of the stamps. Untagged gripper margins, about 3/8-inch in width, were intended to appear in left sheet margins, but some sheets were put through the offset tagging press with the underlying design inverted, resulting in errors with tagging absent in the opposite margins.

Values shown for the untagged errors are for strips of at least five stamps with both tagged and untagged specimens on a single piece.

For more information on tagging, see the introduction.

1966. MARINE CORPS RESERVE ISSUE celebrated the 50th anniversary of the military organization. *Intaglio (Giori Press) and offset, perforated 11.*

CM566 *U.S. Marines 1775-1966*

CM566		MNHVF	UseVF
5¢	black, olive, red & blue *(125,110,000)*	.25	.20
	Plate block of 4	.65	
	FDC *(Aug. 29, 1966)*		1.00
	z. Tagged, type OP	.30	.25
	Plate block of 4, tagged	2.00	
	FDC, tagged *(Aug. 29, 1966)*		30.00
	z1. Error (untagged), strip of 5 showing both tagged and untagged on same piece	—	
	v. black and olive omitted	15,400.00	

1966. GENERAL FEDERATION OF WOMEN'S CLUBS ISSUE commemorated 75 years of service ranging from aiding school dropouts to aiding international understanding, and the millions of women who are members of the clubs and associate organizations. *Intaglio (Giori Press), perforated 11.*

CM567 *Women of 1890s and 1960s*

CM567		MNHVF	UseVF
5¢	pink, blue & black *(114,853,000)*	.25	.20
	Plate block of 4	.65	
	FDC *(Sept. 12, 1966)*		30.00
	z. Tagged, type OP	.30	.25
	Plate block of 4	2.00	
	FDC *(Sept. 13, 1966)*		30.00

American Folklore Series

1966. JOHNNY APPLESEED ISSUE The inaugural stamp in the American Folklore Series honored John Chapman, eccentric nurseryman who devoted his life to planting apple trees in Pennsylvania, Ohio, and Indiana. It is reputed that he covered over 100,000 square miles before his death in 1845. *Intaglio (Giori Press), perforated 11.*

CM568 *Johnny Appleseed and apple*

CM568		MNHVF	UseVF
5¢	black, red & green *(124,290,000)*	.25	.20
	Plate block of 4	.65	
	FDC *(Sept. 24, 1966)*		1.00
	z. Tagged, type OP	.30	.25
	Plate block of 4	2.00	
	FDC *(Sept. 26, 1966)*		1.00

1966. BEAUTIFICATION OF AMERICA ISSUE publicized the campaign to restore and enhance the beauty of the country. *Intaglio (Giori Press), perforated 11.*

CM569 *Jefferson Memorial and cherry blossoms*

CM569		MNHVF	UseVF
5¢	black, green & pink *(128,460,000)*	.25	.20
	Plate block of 4	.65	
	FDC *(Oct. 5, 1966)*		1.00
	z. Tagged, type OP	.30	.25
	Plate block of 4	2.00	
	FDC *(Oct. 5, 1966)*		30.00
	z1. Tagged after perforating	.30	
	Plate block of 4, untagged right margin	2.00	
	z2. Tagged after perforating (error), untagged *left* margin	1.75	
	Plate block of 4	2.00	

1966. GREAT RIVER ROAD ISSUE publicized the longest parkway in the world, stretching from Kenora, Canada, southward to New Orleans, a distance of 5,600 miles. *Intaglio (Giori Press) and offset, perforated 11.*

CM570 *Map of Mississippi River and road*

CM570		MNHVF	UseVF
5¢	salmon, blue, olive yellow & yellow green *(127,585,000)*	.25	.20
	Plate block of 4	.65	
	FDC *(Oct. 21, 1966)*		1.00
	z. Tagged, type OP	.30	.25
	Plate block of 4	2.00	
	FDC *(Oct. 22, 1966)* tagged		30.00

1966. U.S. SAVINGS BOND ISSUE saluted 25 years of bond sales and carried the message, "We Appreciate Our Servicemen." *Intaglio (Giori Press) and offset, perforated 11.*

CM571 *Statue of Liberty and U.S. flag*

CM571		MNHVF	UseVF
5¢	red, blue & black *(115,875,000)*	.25	.20
	Plate block of 4	.75	
	FDC *(Oct. 26, 1966)*		1.00
	v. red, black & dark blue omitted	5,000.00	
	v1. dark blue omitted	8,000.00	
	z. Tagged, type OP	.30	.25
	Plate block of 4	2.00	
	FDC *(Oct. 27, 1966)* tagged		30.00

1966. MARY CASSATT ISSUE The seventh in the Fine Arts Series paid tribute to the American painter whom many critics regard as the greatest female artist. Cassatt (1844-1926) was the only American, besides Whistler, to have her work hang in the Louvre. (See No. 915.) *Intaglio (Giori Press), perforated 11.*

CM572 The Boating Party

CM572		MNHVF	UseVF
5¢	multicolored *(114,015,000)*	.25	.20
	Plate block of 4	.75	
	FDC *(Nov. 17, 1966)*		1.00
	z. Tagged, type OP	.30	.25
	Plate block of 4	—	
	FDC *(Nov. 17, 1966)* tagged		30.00

"Tagging is normal on all commemoratives after this issue."

1967. NATIONAL GRANGE ISSUE commemorated the 100th anniversary of the farmers' organization founded by Oliver H. Kelley to help farmers develop economically and culturally. Its sphere of activities has broadened to include scholarships and aid to underdeveloped nations. *Intaglio (Giori Press), perforated 11.*

CM573 *Grange poster of 1870*

CM573		MNHVF	UseVF
5¢	brownish orange, green, orange & black tagged *(121,105,000)*	.25	.20
	Plate block of 4	.65	
	FDC *(April 17, 1967)*		1.00
	zo. Tagging omitted	3.50	

1967. CANADA CENTENNIAL ISSUE commemorated the anniversary of Canada's Confederation. The stamp was first sold at the U.S. pavilion at Expo '67 in Montreal. *Intaglio (Giori Press), perforated 11.*

CM574 *Abstract Canadian landscape*

CM574		MNHVF	UseVF
5¢	blue, green, dark blue & olive green	.25	.20
	tagged (132,045,000)		
	Plate block of 4	.65	
	FDC (May 26, 1967)		1.00
	zo. Tagging omitted	4.50	

1967. ERIE CANAL SESQUICENTENNIAL ISSUE celebrated the engineering feat that linked Lake Erie with New York City. This 363-mile man-made waterway contributed to the economic development of the young nation. *Intaglio (Giori Press) and offset, perforated 11.*

CM575 *Canal boat*

CM575		MNHVF	UseVF
5¢	dark blue, light blue, black & red tagged	.25	.20
	(118,780,000)		
	Plate block of 4	.65	
	FDC (July 4, 1967)		1.00
	zo. Tagging omitted	10.00	

1967. LIONS INTERNATIONAL ISSUE saluted the world's largest volunteer service organization on its 50th anniversary. The theme of the stamp, "Search for Peace," was that of an essay contest sponsored by the Lions. *Intaglio (Giori Press), perforated 11.*

CM576 *Dove of peace and olive branch*

CM576		MNHVF	UseVF
5¢	red, blue & black on granite paper, tagged	.25	.20
	(121,985,000)		
	Plate block of 4	.80	
	FDC (July 5, 1967)		1.00
	zo. Tagging omitted	4.00	

1967. HENRY DAVID THOREAU ISSUE honored the 19th-century essayist (1817-62) on the 150th anniversary of his birth. His writings reflect his love of nature and his belief in the dignity of all mankind. *Intaglio (Giori Press) and offset, perforated 11.*

CM577 *Henry David Thoreau*

CM577		MNHVF	UseVF
5¢	red, black & green tagged (111,850,000)	.25	.20
	Plate block of 4	.65	
	FDC (July 12, 1967)		1.00
	zo. Tagging omitted	—	

1967. NEBRASKA STATEHOOD ISSUE marked the centennial of the state's entry into the union as the 37th state. *Intaglio (Giori Press), perforated 11.*

CM578 *Cattle and corn*

CM578		MNHVF	UseVF
5¢	yellow, green & brown tagged	.25	.20
	(117,225,000)		
	Plate block of 4	.65	
	FDC (July 29, 1967)		1.00
	zo. Tagging omitted	5.00	

1967. VOICE OF AMERICA ISSUE paid tribute to the radio branch of the U.S. Information Agency on its 25th anniversary. *Intaglio (Giori Press), perforated 11.*

CM579 *Radio tower transmitting*

CM579		MNHVF	UseVF
5¢	red, blue & black tagged (111,515,000)	.25	.20
	Plate block of 4	.65	
	FDC (Aug. 1, 1967)		1.00
	zo. Tagging omitted	5.00	

1967. DAVY CROCKETT ISSUE The second stamp in the American Folklore Series honored the Tennessee backwoodsman who gained fame as a trapper, hunter, soldier, and public official and died at the Alamo. *Intaglio (Giori Press), perforated 11.*

CM580 *Davy Crockett*

CM580		MNHVF	UseVF
5¢	green, black & yellow tagged	.25	.20
	(114,270,000)		
	Plate block of 4	.85	
	FDC (Aug. 17, 1967)		1.00
	v. green omitted	—	
	v1. green & black omitted	—	
	v2. green & yellow omitted	—	
	v3. Vertical pair, imperforate between	6,000.00	
	zo. Tagging omitted	4.50	

1967. SPACE TWINS ISSUE saluted America's achievements in space. For the first time, the United States printed two se-tenant stamps that blend into one complete design. *Intaglio (Giori Press) and offset, perforated 11.*

CM581-82 *Spacewalking astronaut and Gemini capsule*

CM581
5¢   **dark blue, black & red** tagged *(120,865,000)*

	MNHVF	UseVF
	1.00	.35

CM582
5¢   **dark blue, red, blue & green** tagged

	MNHVF	UseVF
	1.00	.35
y. Se-tenant pair, CM581-82	2.00	1.50
Plate block of 4	4.50	
FDC, single *(Sept. 29, 1967)*		5.00
FDC, pair		10.00
zo. Tagging omitted, any single	5.00	
zoy. Tagging omitted, pair	10.00	

1967. URBAN PLANNING ISSUE publicized the need to improve and develop American cities. *Intaglio (Giori Press), perforated 11.*

CM583 *Overhead view of model city*

CM583
5¢   **dark blue, light blue & black** tagged *(110,675,000)*

	MNHVF	UseVF
	.25	.20
Plate block of 4	.65	
FDC *(Oct. 2, 1967)*		1.00
zo. Tagging omitted	—	

1967. FINLAND INDEPENDENCE ISSUE honored the 50th anniversary of Finnish sovereignty. *Intaglio (Giori Press), perforated 11.*

CM584 *Finnish coat of arms*

CM584
5¢   **blue** tagged *(110,670,000)*

	MNHVF	UseVF
	.25	.20
Plate block of 4	.65	
FDC *(Oct. 6, 1967)*		1.00
zo. Tagging omitted	—	

1967. THOMAS EAKINS ISSUE The eighth stamp in the Fine Arts Series honored an American artist who gained fame for his paintings of athletic events, portraits, and early American life. A professor of anatomy at the Pennsylvania Academy of Fine Arts, Eakins' thorough knowledge of this subject is reflected in his works. The first U.S. postage stamp using the *gravure* method. *The issue was printed by the Photogravure and Color Co., Moonachie, N.J. Perforated 12.*

CM585 *The Biglin Brothers Racing*

CM585
5¢   **gold & multicolored** tagged *(113,825,000)*

	MNHVF	UseVF
	.25	.20
Plate block of 4	.65	
FDC *(Nov. 2, 1967)*		1.00
zo. Tagging omitted	6.00	

1967. MISSISSIPPI STATEHOOD ISSUE honored the 150th anniversary of the Magnolia State's entry into the union as the 20th state. *Intaglio (Giori Press), perforated 11.*

CM586 *Magnolia blossom*

CM586
5¢   **green blue, blue green & brown** tagged *(113,330,000)*

	MNHVF	UseVF
	.25	.20
Plate block of 4	.75	
FDC *(Dec. 11, 1967)*		1.00
zo. Tagging omitted	5.00	

1968. ILLINOIS STATEHOOD ISSUE marked the 150th anniversary of the state's entry into the union as the 21st state. *Intaglio (Giori Press), perforated 11.*

CM587 *Illinois farm scene*

CM587
6¢   **multicolored** tagged *(141,350,000)*

	MNHVF	UseVF
	.25	.20
Plate block of 4	.85	
FDC *(Feb. 12, 1968)*		1.00
zo. Tagging omitted	—	

1968. HEMISFAIR '68 ISSUE celebrated the international exposition that opened in San Antonio, Texas, April 6. The theme was "The Confluence of Civilizations in the Americas," and the stamp also commemorated the 250th anniversary of San Antonio. *Intaglio (Giori Press) and offset, perforated 11.*

CM588 *North and South America with lines converging on San Antonio*

CM588
6¢   **blue, pink & white** tagged *(117,470,600)*

	MNHVF	UseVF
	.25	.20
Plate block of 4	.85	
FDC *(March 30, 1968)*		1.00
v. white omitted	1,400.00	

1968. SUPPORT OUR YOUTH ISSUE honored the Benevolent and Protective Order of Elks' centennial year and the expansion of its youth service program. *Intaglio (Giori Press), perforated 11.*

CM589 *Young Americans*

CM589
6¢   **red & blue** tagged *(147,120,000)*

	MNHVF	UseVF
	.25	.20

		.85	
Plate block of 4		.85	
FDC *(May 1, 1968)*			1.00
zo. Tagging omitted		5.00	

1968. LAW AND ORDER ISSUE publicized the work of the law enforcement officer as a protector and friend of the people. *Intaglio (Giori Press), perforated 11.*

CM590 *Policeman and young friend*

CM590			MNHVF	UseVF
6¢	**red, blue & black** tagged *(130,125,000)*		.25	.20
	Plate block of 4		.85	
	FDC *(May 17, 1968)*			1.00
	zo. Tagging omitted		—	

1968. REGISTER AND VOTE ISSUE supported the efforts of the American Heritage Foundation and others in making the public aware of its civic obligation to vote. *Intaglio (Giori Press) and offset, perforated 11.*

CM591 *Eagle weathervane*

CM591			MNHVF	UseVF
6¢	**gold & black** tagged *(158,070,000)*		.25	.20
	Plate block of 4		.85	
	FDC *(June 27, 1968)*			1.00
	zo. Tagging omitted		—	

1968. HISTORIC FLAGS ISSUE saluted 10 banners from America's struggle for independence. Nine of the flags were selected because of their important roles in the Revolutionary War period. One flag, the one flown at Fort McHenry, inspired Francis Scott Key to write the "Star Spangled Banner" during the War of 1812. *Intaglio (Giori Press) and offset, perforated 11.*

CM592 *Fort Moultrie flag (1776)*

CM592		MNHVF	UseVF
6¢	**blue** tagged *(228,040,000)*	.40	.30

CM593 *Fort McHenry flag (1795-1818)*

CM593		MNHVF	UseVF
6¢	**red & blue** tagged	.40	.30

CM594 *Washington's Cruisers flag (1775)*

CM594		MNHVF	UseVF
6¢	**green & blue** tagged	.40	.30

CM595 *Bennington flag (1777)*

CM595		MNHVF	UseVF
6¢	**red & blue** tagged	.40	.30

CM596 *Rhode Island flag (1775)*

CM596		MNHVF	UseVF
6¢	**gold & blue** tagged	.40	.30

CM597 *First Stars and Stripes (1777)*

CM597		MNHVF	UseVF
6¢	**red & blue** tagged	.40	.30

CM598 *Bunker Hill flag (1775)*

CM598		MNHVF	UseVF
6¢	**red, green & blue** tagged	.40	.30

CM599 *Grand Union flag (1776)*

CM599		MNHVF	UseVF
6¢	**red & blue** tagged	.40	.30

CM600 *Philadelphia Light Horse flag (1775)*

CM600		MNHVF	UseVF
6¢	**multicolored** tagged	.40	.30

CM601 *First Navy Jack (1775)*

CM601

6¢		MNHVF	UseVF
	red, gold & blue tagged	.40	.30
	Plate block of 20	7.50	
	y. Se-tenant strip of 10 (CM592-601)	3.50	4.00
	FDC, *(July 4, 1968)*, any single		2.00
	FDC, strip of 10		8.50
	zo. Tagging omitted, any single	—	
	zoy. Tagging omitted se-tenant strip of 10	—	

Because the plate number is attached to a vertical column of 10 different stamps, plate block of 20 is listed.

1968. WALT DISNEY ISSUE hailed the creative genius who brought a new dimension to entertainment with his animated cartoons, full-length films, and theme parks. The creator of Mickey Mouse, Donald Duck, and other lovable characters built a multi-million dollar entertainment empire. *Gravure by Achrovure Division of Union-Camp Corp., Englewood, N.J., perforated 12.*

CM602 *Walt Disney and cartoon children*

CM602

6¢		MNHVF	UseVF
	multicolored tagged *(153,015,000)*	.25	.20
	Plate block of 4	2.10	
	FDC *(Sept. 11, 1968)*		1.00
	v. Horizontal pair, imperforate between	5,000.00	
	v1. Pair, imperforate	675.00	
	v2. Vertical pair, imperforate horizontally	650.00	
	v3. black omitted	2,000.00	
	v4. blue omitted	2,150.00	
	v5. yellow omitted	600.00	
	zo. Tagging omitted	7.50	

1968. FATHER JACQUES MARQUETTE ISSUE honored the French explorer-missionary (CM17) who, in 1668, established what is considered the oldest permanent settlement in Michigan. *Intaglio (Giori Press) and offset, perforated 11.*

CM603 *Jacques Marquette and Louis Joliet in canoe*

CM603

6¢		MNHVF	UseVF
	black, green & brown tagged *(132,560,000)*	.25	.20
	Plate block of 4	.85	
	FDC *(Sept. 20, 1968)*		1.00
	zo. Tagging omitted	6.00	

1968. DANIEL BOONE ISSUE The third commemorative in the American Folklore Series recalled the frontiersman whose exploits inspired historians and fiction writers to record the remarkable achievements of this heroic hunter, trapper, soldier, and public servant (1734-1820). *Intaglio (Giori Press) and offset, perforated 11.*

CM604 *Pipe tomahawk, powder horn, rifle, and knife*

CM604

6¢		MNHVF	UseVF
	red brown, brown, yellow & black tagged *(130,385,000)*	.25	.20
	Plate block of 4	.85	
	FDC *(Sept. 26, 1968)*		1.00
	zo. Tagging omitted	—	

1968. ARKANSAS RIVER NAVIGATION ISSUE paid tribute to this important waterway and the economic potential of the $1.2 billion project. *Intaglio (Giori Press) and offset, perforated 11.*

CM605 *Ship's wheel and transmission tower*

CM605

6¢		MNHVF	UseVF
	blue, black & dark blue tagged *(132,265,000)*	.25	.20
	Plate block of 4	.85	
	FDC *(Oct. 1, 1968)*		1.00
	zo. Tagging omitted	—	

1968. LEIF ERIKSON ISSUE honored the 11th century Norseman whose navigational skills and daring brought him to the Americas 500 years before Christopher Columbus. *Intaglio (Giori Press) and offset, perforated 11.*

CM606 *Statue of Leif Erikson by A. Stirling Calder*

CM606

6¢		MNHVF	UseVF
	brown *(128,710,000)*	.25	.20
	Plate block of 4	.85	
	FDC *(Oct. 9, 1968)*		1.00

1968. CHEROKEE STRIP ISSUE marked the 75th anniversary of the historic land run by more than 100,000 would-be homesteaders into northern Oklahoma, competing for the 40,000 available homesites. *Rotary press printing, perforated 11.*

CM607 *Racing for homesteads*

CM607

6¢		MNHVF	UseVF
	brown tagged *(124,775,000)*	.25	.20
	Plate block of 4	.85	
	FDC *(Oct. 15, 1968)*		1.00
	zo. Tagging omitted	5.00	

1968. JOHN TRUMBULL ISSUE The ninth stamp in the Fine Arts Series honored an artist noted for his paintings of Revolutionary War scenes. The design came from an original painting at Yale University, New Haven, Conn. *Intaglio (Giori Press) and offset, perforated 11.*

CM608 *Lt. Thomas Grosvenor and Peter Salem, detail from* The Battle of Bunker's Hill

CM608			MNHVF	UseVF
6¢	**multicolored** tagged *(128,295,000)*		.25	.20
	Plate block of 4		.90	
	FDC *(Oct. 18, 1968)*			1.00
	zo. Tagging omitted		20.00	
	Pane, black (engraved) omitted		21,000.00	

1968. WATERFOWL CONSERVATION ISSUE pointed out the need for protecting waterfowl and their habitats. *Intaglio (Giori Press) and offset, perforated 11.*

CM609 *Wood ducks in flight*

CM609			MNHVF	UseVF
6¢	**multicolored** tagged *(142,245,000)*		.25	.20
	Plate block of 4		1.10	
	FDC *(Oct. 24, 1968)*			1.00
	v. dark blue and red omitted		800.00	
	v1. Vertical pair, imperforate between		525.00	

1968. CHIEF JOSEPH ISSUE was released in conjunction with the dedication of the National Portrait Gallery in Washington, D.C. A portrait of the stamp subject, Chief Joseph, hangs in the gallery, which is part of the Smithsonian Institution. *Intaglio and offset, perforated 11.*

CM610 Chief Joseph, *painting by Cyrenius Hall*

CM610			MNHVF	UseVF
6¢	**multicolored** tagged *(125,100,000)*		.25	.20
	Plate block of 4		1.10	
	FDC *(Nov. 4, 1968)*			1.00
	zo. Tagging omitted		—	

1969. BEAUTIFICATION OF AMERICA ISSUE encouraged the participation of all Americans in a nationwide natural beauty campaign. Four se-tenant stamp designs appear in the same pane of 50 stamps. *Intaglio (Giori Press), perforated 11.*

CM611 *Azaleas, tulips, and Capitol building*

CM612 *Daffodils, Washington Monument, and Potomac River*

CM613 *Highway, poppies, and lupines*

CM614 *Flowering crab-apples on tree-lined street*

CM611			MNHVF	UseVF
6¢	**multicolored** tagged *(102,570,000)*		.30	.25

CM612			MNHVF	UseVF
6¢	**multicolored** tagged		.30	.25

CM613			MNHVF	UseVF
6¢	**multicolored** tagged		.30	.25

CM614			MNHVF	UseVF
6¢	**multicolored** tagged		.30	.25
	Plate block of 4		2.50	
	y. Se-tenant block of 4 (CM611-14)		2.00	
	FDC *(Jan. 16, 1969)*, any single			2.00
	FDC, block of 4			5.00
	zo. Tagging omitted, any single		—	
	zoy. Tagging omitted, se-tenant block of 4		—	

1969. AMERICAN LEGION ISSUE saluted the 50th anniversary of the veterans' organization incorporated by an act of Congress and signed by Woodrow Wilson on Sept. 16, 1919. *Intaglio (Giori Press) and offset, perforated 11.*

CM615 *Eagle with olive branch, from the Great Seal of the United States*

CM615			MNHVF	UseVF
6¢	**red, black & blue** tagged *(148,770,000)*		.25	.20
	Plate block of 4		.85	
	FDC *(March 15, 1969)*			1.00
	zo. Tagging Omitted		5.00	

1969. GRANDMA MOSES ISSUE honored the grand old lady of American painting, who took up art at the age of 76 and continued until her death at 101. *Intaglio (Giori Press) and offset, perforated 11.*

CM616 July 4th, *detail from a Grandma Moses painting*

CM616			MNHVF	UseVF
6¢	**multicolored** tagged *(139,475,000)*		.25	.20
	Plate block of 4		.85	
	FDC *(May 1, 1969)*			1.00
	v. black & Prussian blue omitted		750.00	
	v1. Horizontal pair, imperforate between		225.00	
	zo. Tagging omitted			

1969. APOLLO 8 ISSUE commemorated a vital space mission, in which the lunar surface was televised to Earth prior to the moon landing. *Intaglio (Giori Press), perforated 11.*

CM617 *Earth rising over lunar surface*

CM617

6¢	**gray, deep blue & blue** tagged	MNHVF	UseVF
	(187,165,000)	.25	.20
	Plate block of 4	1.30	
	FDC *(May 5, 1969)*		1.00
	zo. Tagging omitted	—	

Note: Imperforate varieties, from printer's waste, exist.

1969. W.C. HANDY ISSUE honored the memory of the great African-American composer and jazz musician who composed such immortal hits as "The St. Louis Blues," "The Memphis Blues," and "The Beale Street Blues." *Intaglio (Giori Press) and offset, perforated 11.*

CM618 *W.C. Handy and horn*

CM618

6¢	**multicolored** tagged *(125,555,000)*	MNHVF	UseVF
		.25	.20
	Plate block of 4	1.30	
	FDC *(May 17, 1969)*		1.00
	zo. Tagging omitted	6.00	

1969. SETTLEMENT OF CALIFORNIA ISSUE commemorated the 200th anniversary of European settlement in the state. On July 16, 1769, a Spanish expedition led by Capt. Gasper de Portola entered San Diego, which became the first European settlement in California. *Intaglio (Giori Press) and offset, perforated 11.*

CM619 *Mission bells at Carmel, Calif.*

CM619

6¢	**multicolored** tagged *(144,425,000)*	MNHVF	UseVF
		.25	.20
	Plate block of 4	.85	
	FDC *(July 16, 1969)*		1.00
	zo. Tagging omitted	5.50	

1969. JOHN WESLEY POWELL ISSUE honored the eminent geologist who, in 1869, explored the Colorado River. *Intaglio (Giori Press) and offset, perforated 11.*

CM620 *Maj. Powell leading Colorado River expedition*

CM620

6¢	**multicolored** tagged *(133,100,000)*	MNHVF	UseVF
		.25	.20
	Plate block of 4	.85	
	FDC *(Aug. 1, 1969)*		1.00
	zo. Tagging omitted	4.50	

1969. ALABAMA STATEHOOD ISSUE marked the 150th anniversary of the entry of Alabama into the union as the 22nd state. *Intaglio (Giori Press) and offset, perforated 11.*

CM621 *Camelia and yellow-shafted flicker*

CM621

6¢	**multicolored** tagged *(136,900,000)*	MNHVF	UseVF
		.25	.20
	Plate block of 4	.85	
	FDC *(Aug. 2, 1969)*		1.00
	zo. Tagging omitted	—	

1969. 11TH INTERNATIONAL BOTANICAL CONGRESS ISSUE saluted the first international meeting of botanists held in the United States. Four se-tenant stamp designs appear in the same pane of 50 stamps; each design represents a region of the country. *Intaglio (Giori Press) and offset, perforated 11.*

CM622 *Douglas fir*

CM623 *Lady's-slipper*

CM624 *Ocotillo*

CM625 *Franklinia*

CM622

6¢	**multicolored** tagged *(158,695,000)*	MNHVF	UseVF
		.30	.25

CM623

6¢	**multicolored** tagged	MNHVF	UseVF
		.30	.25

CM624

6¢	**multicolored** tagged	MNHVF	UseVF
		.30	.25

CM625

6¢	**multicolored** tagged	MNHVF	UseVF
		.30	.25
	Plate block of 4	2.75	
	y. Se-tenant block of 4 (CM622-25)	2.25	2.50
	FDC *(Aug. 23, 1969),* any single		2.00
	FDC, block of 4		6.00

1969. DARTMOUTH COLLEGE CASE ISSUE commemorated the 150th anniversary of the legal decision that protected college charters and reasserted the sanctity of contracts. Daniel Webster won the case before the U.S. Supreme Court. *Intaglio, perforated 10 1/2x11.*

CM626 *Daniel Webster and Dartmouth Hall*

CM626

6¢	**green** tagged *(124,075,000)*	MNHVF	UseVF
		.25	.20
	Plate block of 4	.95	
	FDC *(Sept. 22, 1969)*		1.00

1969. PROFESSIONAL BASEBALL ISSUE marked the 100th anniversary of the use of salaried players on a baseball team. The Red Stockings of Cincinnati, Ohio, in 1869 became the first club to pay its team members. *Intaglio (Giori Press) and offset, perforated 11.*

CM627 *Player at bat*

CM627

6¢	**yellow, red, black & green** tagged	MNHVF	UseVF
	(129,925,000)	1.25	.20
	Plate block of 4	4.95	
	FDC *(Sept. 24, 1969)*		1.00
	v. black omitted	950.00	

1969. INTERCOLLEGIATE FOOTBALL ISSUE celebrated the 100th anniversary of the popular college sport that started Nov. 6, 1869, when Rutgers defeated Princeton. *Intaglio and offset, perforated 11.*

CM628 *Coach and football player*

CM628		MNHVF	UseVF
6¢	red & green tagged *(129,860,000)*	.45	.20
	Plate block of 4	2.00	
	FDC *(Sept. 26, 1969)*		1.00
	zo. Tagging omitted	—	

The intaglio portion of CM628 was printed on a rotary press normally used for currency.

1969. DWIGHT D. EISENHOWER ISSUE paid tribute to the 34th president of the United States. Eisenhower (1890-1969) was a West Point graduate who went on to become a five-star general and the Supreme Allied Commander in Europe during World War II. *Intaglio (Giori Press), perforated 11.*

CM629 *Dwight D. Eisenhower and flag*

CM629		MNHVF	UseVF
6¢	blue, black & reddish purple tagged	.25	.20
	(138,976,000)		
	Plate block of 4	.85	
	FDC *(Oct. 14, 1969)*		1.00
	zo. Tagging omitted	—	

1969. HOPE FOR THE CRIPPLED ISSUE encouraged aid in research and therapy for the handicapped. *Intaglio (Giori Press) and offset, perforated 11.*

CM630 *Child rising from wheelchair*

CM630		MNHVF	UseVF
6¢	multicolored tagged *(124,565,000)*	.25	.20
	Plate block of 4	.85	
	FDC *(Nov. 20, 1969)*		1.00
	zo. Tagging omitted	—	

1969. WILLIAM M. HARNETT ISSUE honored an artist (1848-92) noted for his realistic work. *Intaglio (Giori Press) and offset, perforated 11.*

> Please read the introduction to this catalog carefully. It contains much valuable information for all stamp collectors, and also makes the catalog easier for you to use.

CM631 *Still life* Old Models

CM631		MNHVF	UseVF
6¢	multicolored tagged *(124,729,000)*	.25	.20
	Plate block of 4	.85	
	FDC *(Dec. 3, 1969)*		1.00

1970. NATURAL HISTORY ISSUE commemorated the centenary of the American Museum of Natural History in New York City. Four se-tenant stamp designs appear in the same 32-image pane. *Intaglio (Giori Press) and offset, perforated 11.*

CM632 *American Bald Eagle, detail from a display in The American Museum of Natural History;* CM633 *Herd of African Elephants, a display in Carl Akeley Memorial Hall;* CM634 *Northwest Coast Canoe (Haida Indians), the figures in the canoe represent a Tlingit chief and his party on their way to a marriage ceremony;* CM635 *Jurassic Dinosaurs, from a mural at Yale University's Peabody Museum of Natural History*

CM632		MNHVF	UseVF
6¢	multicolored tagged *(201,794,600)*	.25	.20
CM633		**MNHVF**	**UseVF**
6¢	multicolored tagged	.25	.20
CM634		**MNHVF**	**UseVF**
6¢	multicolored tagged	.25	.20
CM635		**MNHVF**	**UseVF**
6¢	multicolored tagged	.25	.20
	Plate block of 4	1.00	
	y. Se-tenant block of 4 (CM632-35)	1.00	
	FDC *(May 6, 1970)*, any single		2.00
	FDC, block of 4		4.00
	zo. Tagging omitted, any single	—	
	zoy. Tagging omitted, block of 4	—	

1970. MAINE STATEHOOD ISSUE honored the 150th anniversary of its entry into the union as the 23rd state. *Intaglio (Giori Press) and offset, perforated 11.*

CM636 The Lighthouse at Two Lights, *Edward Hopper oil painting in New York's Metropolitan Museum of Art*

CM636		MNHVF	UseVF
6¢	multicolored tagged *(171,850,000)*	.25	.20
	Plate block of 4	1.00	

FDC *(July 9, 1970)*   1.75
zo. Tagging omitted   —

1970. WILDLIFE CONSERVATION ISSUE reminded Americans of the continuing need to protect wildlife. Issued in Custer, S.D., near Custer State Park, home to the largest bison herd in the country. *Intaglio, perforated 11x10 1/2.*

CM637 *American bison*

CM637

		MNHVF	UseVF
6¢	**black** on tan tagged *(142,205,000)*	.25	.20
	Plate block of 4	1.00	
	FDC *(July 20, 1970)*		1.75

American Poets Series

1970. EDGAR LEE MASTERS ISSUE First in an American Poets Series paid tribute to the author of *Spoon River Anthology*. Its ruthless exposure of small-town mores won instant acclaim as well as outraged criticism. *Intaglio (Giori Press) and offset, perforated 11.*

CM638 *Edgar Lee Masters*

CM638

		MNHVF	UseVF
6¢	**black** tagged *(137,660,000)*	.25	.20
	Plate block of 4	.85	
	FDC *(Aug. 22, 1970)*		1.75
	zo. Tagging omitted	—	

1970. THE 50TH ANNIVERSARY OF WOMAN SUFFRAGE ISSUE celebrated the ratification of the 19th Amendment, which gave women the right to vote. *Intaglio (Giori Press), perforated 11.*

CM639 *Suffragettes of 1920 and modern voter*

CM639

		MNHVF	UseVF
6¢	**blue** tagged *(135,125,000)*	.25	.20
	Plate block of 4	.85	
	FDC *(Aug. 25, 1970)*		1.75

1970. SOUTH CAROLINA ISSUE marked the 300th anniversary of the state's first permanent European settlement, established by the English at Charles Town (now Charleston). *Intaglio (Giori Press) and offset, perforated 11.*

CM640 *Aspects of South Carolina*

CM640

		MNHVF	UseVF
6¢	**brown, black & red** tagged *(135,895,000)*	.25	.20
	Plate block of 4	.85	
	FDC *(Sept. 12, 1970)*		1.75

1970. STONE MOUNTAIN ISSUE commemorated the carving in a huge granite outcropping in Georgia of the mounted figures of Robert E. Lee, Jefferson Davis, and Stonewall Jackson. *Intaglio (Giori Press), perforated 11.*

CM641 *Stone Mountain Memorial*

CM641

		MNHVF	UseVF
6¢	**gray black** tagged *(132,675,000)*	.25	.20
	Plate block of 4	1.10	
	FDC *(Sept. 19, 1970)*		1.75

1970. FORT SNELLING SESQUICENTENNIAL ISSUE highlighted the importance of this outpost in settling the Northwestern United States. The fort was named after Col. Joshiah Snelling. *Intaglio (Giori Press) and offset, perforated 11.*

CM642 *Fort Snelling and surrounding area*

CM642

		MNHVF	UseVF
6¢	**multicolored** tagged *(134,795,000)*	.25	.20
	Plate block of 4	.85	
	FDC *(Oct. 17, 1970)*		1.00
	zo. Tagging omitted	—	

1970. ANTI-POLLUTION ISSUE emphasized the importance of world ecology. Four se-tenant designs appear in the pane. *Printed in gravure by the Bureau of Engraving and Printing at Guilford Gravure, Inc., perforated 11x10 1/2.*

CM643 *Save Our Soil*

CM644 *Save Our Cities*

CM645 *Save Our Water*

CM646 *Save Our Air*

CM643

		MNHVF	UseVF
6¢	**multicolored** tagged *(161,600,000)*	.25	.20

CM644

		MNHVF	UseVF
6¢	**multicolored** tagged	.25	.20

CM645

		MNHVF	UseVF
6¢	**multicolored** tagged	.25	.20

CM646

		MNHVF	UseVF
6¢	**multicolored** tagged	.25	.20
	Plate block of 4	1.50	
	y. Se-tenant block of 4 (CM643-46)	1.00	
	FDC *(Oct. 28, 1970)*, any single		2.00
	FDC, block of 4		5.00

1970. UNITED NATIONS ISSUE marked the 25th anniversary of the international organization, chartered in San Francisco on June 26, 1945. *Intaglio (Giori Press) and offset, perforated 11.*

CM647 *United Nations initials, logo*

CM647		MNHVF	UseVF
6¢	black, red & blue tagged *(127,610,000)*	.25	.20
	Plate block of 4	.85	
	Pair, gutter between	—	
	FDC *(Nov. 20, 1970)*		1.75
	zo. Tagging omitted	—	

1970. LANDING OF THE PILGRIMS ISSUE commemorated the 350th anniversary of the arrival of the *Mayflower* and the landing of the Pilgrims at Plymouth, Mass. *Intaglio (Giori Press) and offset, perforated 11.*

CM648 Mayflower *and Pilgrims*

CM648		MNHVF	UseVF
6¢	multicolored tagged *(129,785,000)*	.25	.20
	Plate block of 4	.85	
	FDC *(Nov. 21, 1970)*		1.75
	v. orange & yellow omitted	950.00	

1970. U.S. SERVICEMEN ISSUE paid tribute to the Disabled American Veterans, prisoners of war, and those missing and killed in action. Two se-tenant stamp designs alternate in the pane. *Intaglio (Giori Press) and offset, perforated 11.*

CM649 *Crest of Disabled American Veterans*

CM650 *Prisoners of war, missing and killed in action*

CM649		MNHVF	UseVF
6¢	multicolored tagged *(134,380,000)*	.25	.20

CM650		MNHVF	UseVF
6¢	dark blue, black & red tagged	.25	.20
	Plate block of 4	1.30	
	y. Se-tenant pair (CM649-50)	.50	
	FDC *(Nov. 24, 1970)*, either single		1.75
	FDC, pair		2.00
	zo. Tagging omitted, single	—	
	zoy. Tagging omitted, se-tenant pair	—	

1971. AMERICAN WOOL ISSUE commemorated the 450th anniversary of the introduction of sheep in America. *Intaglio (Giori Press) and offset, perforated 11.*

CM651 *Ewe and lamb*

CM651		MNHVF	UseVF
6¢	multicolored tagged *(135,305,000)*	.25	.20
	Plate block of 4	.85	
	FDC *(Jan. 19, 1971)*		1.75
	zo. Tagging omitted	5.00	

1971. DOUGLAS MACARTHUR ISSUE honored the five-star Army general (1880-1964) who commanded the Pacific theater Allied forces in World War II, headed occupation forces in Japan and was U.N. commander in the Korean War. *Intaglio (Giori Press), perforated 11.*

CM652 *Douglas MacArthur*

CM652		MNHVF	UseVF
6¢	red, blue & black tagged *(134,840,000)*	.25	.20
	Plate block of 4	.85	
	FDC *(Jan. 26, 1971)*		2.00
	zo. Tagging omitted	—	

1971. BLOOD DONORS ISSUE pointed out the need for more Americans to increase their participation. *Intaglio (Giori Press) and offset, perforated 11.*

CM653 *Giving Blood Saves Lives*

CM653		MNHVF	UseVF
6¢	red & blue tagged *(130,975,000)*	.25	.20
	Plate block of 4	.85	
	FDC *(March 12, 1971)*		1.75
	zo. Tagging omitted	5.00	

1971. MISSOURI STATEHOOD ISSUE honored the 150th anniversary of entry into the union of the "Show Me" state, the 24th state. *Gravure (Andreotti Press), perforated 11x10 1/2.*

CM654 Independence and the Opening of the West, *detail of a mural by Thomas Hart Benton*

CM654		MNHVF	UseVF
8¢	multicolored tagged *(161,235,000)*	.25	.20
	Plate block of 12	3.25	
	FDC *(May 8, 1971)*		1.75
	zo. Tagging omitted	—	

1971. WILDLIFE CONSERVATION ISSUE stressed the importance of preserving nature's creatures from extinction. Four different representatives of wildlife are featured in the pane of 32 stamps. *Intaglio (Giori Press) and offset, perforated 11.*

CM655 *Polar bear*
CM656 *Condor*
CM657 *Alligator*
CM658 *Trout*

CM655		MNHVF	UseVF
8¢	multicolored tagged *(175,680,000)*	.25	.20

CM656		MNHVF	UseVF
8¢	**multicolored** tagged	.25	.20

CM657		MNHVF	UseVF
8¢	**multicolored** tagged	.25	.20

CM658		MNHVF	UseVF
8¢	**multicolored** tagged	.25	.20
	Plate block of 4	1.20	
	y. Se-tenant block of 4 (CM655-58)	.75	
	FDC *(June 12, 1971),* any single		2.00
	FDC, block of 4		4.00
	v. red omitted, block of 4	9,500.00	
	v1. light green & dark green omitted, block of 4	4,500.00	
	zo. Tagging omitted, any single	—	
	zoy. Tagging omitted, se-tenant block of 4	—	

1971. ANTARCTIC TREATY ISSUE marked the 10th anniversary of the treaty that pledged 12 nations to scientific cooperation and peaceful use of Antarctica: Argentina, Australia, Belgium, Chile, France, Japan, New Zealand, Norway, South Africa, Soviet Union, United Kingdom, and United States. *Intaglio (Giori Press), perforated 11.*

CM659 *Antarctic Treaty emblem*

CM659		MNHVF	UseVF
8¢	**red & dark blue** tagged *(138,700,000)*	.25	.20
	Plate block of 4	1.00	
	FDC *(June 23, 1971)*		1.75
	zo. Tagging omitted	5.00	

American Revolution Bicentennial Series

1971. AMERICAN REVOLUTION BICENTENNIAL ISSUE commemorated the struggle that led to the birth of the United States, and was the first in a series of stamps to pay tribute to the men, women, places, and events of the Revolutionary War. *Intaglio (Giori Press) and offset, perforated 11.*

CM660 *American Revolution Bicentennial symbol*

CM660		MNHVF	UseVF
8¢	**gray, red, blue & black** tagged *(138,165,000)*	.25	.20
	Plate block of 4	1.10	
	FDC *(July 4, 1971)*		1.75
	v. gray (top legend) omitted	1,250.00	
	v1. black and gray omitted	700.00	

1971. SPACE ACHIEVEMENTS DECADE ISSUE marked 10 years of extraordinary accomplishments in space with a se-tenant pair. *Intaglio (Giori Press) and offset, perforated 11.*

CM661 *Landing craft on Moon's surface;* CM662 *Astronauts in Lunar Rover*

CM661		MNHVF	UseVF
8¢	**multicolored** tagged *(176,295,000)*	.25	.20
	v. blue & red omitted	600.00	

CM662		MNHVF	UseVF
8¢	**multicolored** tagged	.25	.20
	y. Se-tenant pair (CM661-62)	.50	
	Plate block of 4	1.15	
	FDC *(Aug. 2, 1971),* either single		1.75
	v. blue & red omitted	600.00	
	yv. Se-tenant pair, blue & red omitted	1,500.00	
	zo. Tagging omitted, any single	6.00	
	zoy. Se-tenant pair, tagging omitted	22.50	
	FDC, pair		2.50

1971. JOHN SLOAN ISSUE honored the artist on the centennial of his birth at Lock Haven, Pa. Part of the Fine Arts Series. *Intaglio (Giori Press) and offset, perforated 11.*

CM663 The Wake of the Ferry, *Phillips Gallery, Washington, D.C.*

CM663		MNHVF	UseVF
8¢	**multicolored** tagged *(152,125,000)*	.25	.20
	Plate block of 4	1.00	
	FDC *(Aug. 2, 1971)*		1.75
	zo. Tagging omitted	—	

1971. EMILY DICKINSON ISSUE in the American Poets Series honored the reclusive poet (1830-86), who was born in Amherst, Mass. Only after she died were her works widely published and acclaimed. *Intaglio (Giori Press) and offset, perforated 11.*

CM664 *Emily Dickinson*

CM664		MNHVF	UseVF
8¢	**multicolored** tagged *(142,845,000)*	.25	.20
	Plate block of 4	1.00	
	FDC *(Aug. 28, 1971)*		1.75
	v. black and olive omitted	850.00	
	v1. pale rose omitted	7,500.00	
	zo. Tagging omitted	—	

1971. SAN JUAN ISSUE marked the 450th anniversary of the founding of the Puerto Rican city. *Intaglio (Giori Press) and offset, perforated 11.*

CM665 *Battlement at El Morro Castle*

CM665		MNHVF	UseVF
8¢	**multicolored** tagged *(148,755,000)*	.25	.20
	Plate block of 4	1.00	
	FDC *(Sept. 12, 1971)*		1.75
	zo. Tagging omitted	6.00	

1971. PREVENT DRUG ABUSE ISSUE publicized drug addiction as a national menace— of concern to every American. *Gravure (Andreotti Press), perforated 10 1/2 x 11.*

CM666 *Drug addict*

CM666		MNHVF	UseVF
8¢	**blue, deep blue & black** tagged	.25	.20
	(139,080,000)		
	Plate block of 6	1.50	
	FDC (Oct. 4, 1971)		1.75
	zo. Tagging omitted	—	

1971. CARE ISSUE honored the 25th anniversary of the American-Canadian Cooperative for American Relief Everywhere. *Intaglio (Giori Press), perforated 11.*

CM667 *Hands and CARE emblem*

CM667		MNHVF	UseVF
8¢	**black, blue, violet & red lilac** tagged	.25	.20
	(130,755,000)		
	Plate block of 8	1.95	
	FDC (Oct. 27, 1971)		1.75
	v. black omitted	4,750.00	
	zo. Tagging omitted	4.00	

1971. HISTORIC PRESERVATION ISSUE paid tribute to important artifacts of America's past. *Intaglio (Giori Press) and offset, perforated.*

CM668 *Decatur House, Washington, D.C.;* CM669 *Whaling ship* Charles W. Morgan, *Mystic, Conn.;* CM670 *Cable car, San Francisco, Calif.;* CM671 *San Xavier del Bac Mission, Tucson, Ariz.*

CM668		MNHVF	UseVF
8¢	**brown & dark beige** on buff, tagged	.25	.20
	(170,208,000)		

CM669		MNHVF	UseVF
8¢	**brown & dark beige** on buff, tagged	.25	.20

CM670		MNHVF	UseVF
8¢	**brown & dark beige** on buff, tagged	.25	.20

CM671		MNHVF	UseVF
8¢	**brown & dark beige** on buff, tagged	.25	.20
	Plate block of 4	1.20	
	y. Se-tenant block of 4 (CM668-71)	.75	

FDC (Oct. 29, 1971), any single			2.00
FDC, block of 4			4.00
v. brown omitted, any single			—
v1. dark beige omitted, any single			—
vy. brown omitted, se-tenant block of 4		2,600.00	
v1y. dark beige omitted, se-tenant block of 4		—	
zo. Tagging omitted, any single			—
zoy. Tagging omitted, se-tenant block of 4		50.00	

1972. SIDNEY LANIER ISSUE in the American Poets Series honored a poet and flutist who argued that laws of music and poetry were identical and based on the physics of sound. Born in Macon, Ga., Lanier (1842-81) served with the South in the Civil War and contracted tuberculosis in prison. *Intaglio (Giori Press), perforated 11.*

CM672 *Sidney Lanier*

CM672		MNHVF	UseVF
8¢	**black, reddish brown & blue** tagged	.25	.20
	(137,355,000)		
	Plate block of 4	1.00	
	FDC (Feb. 3, 1972)		1.75
	zo. Tagging omitted	12.50	

1972. PEACE CORPS ISSUE paid tribute to a government organization created to aid developing countries. *Gravure (Andreotti Press), perforated 10 1/2x11.*

CM673 *Flag and doves, from poster by David Battle*

CM673		MNHVF	UseVF
8¢	**dark blue, light blue & red** tagged	.25	.20
	(150,400,000)		
	Plate block of 6	1.60	
	FDC (Feb. 11, 1972)		1.75
	zo. Tagging omitted	4.00	

National Parks Centennial Series released over a five-month period consisted of eight stamps (one is an airmail stamp, A82).

1972. YELLOWSTONE PARK ISSUE marked the centennial of the establishment of the first national park in the world, located in Western Wyoming. *Intaglio (Giori Press) and offset, perforated 11.*

CM674 *Old Faithful, Yellowstone Park*

CM674		MNHVF	UseVF
8¢	**multicolored** tagged *(164,096,000)*	.25	.20
	Plate block of 4	1.00	
	FDC *(March 1, 1972)*		1.75
	zo. Tagging omitted	14.00	

1972. CAPE HATTERAS ISSUE in the National Parks Centennial Series called attention to the National Seashore, established in 1937, which includes perhaps the most photographed lighthouse in the world. *Intaglio (Giori Press) and offset, perforated 11.*

CM675-78 *Cape Hatteras National Seashore scenes: squall, lighthouse, laughing gulls, and beach grass*

CM675		MNHVF	UseVF
2¢	**multicolored** tagged *(172,730,000)*	.25	.20

CM676		MNHVF	UseVF
2¢	**multicolored** tagged	.25	.20

CM677		MNHVF	UseVF
2¢	**multicolored** tagged	.25	.20

CM678		MNHVF	UseVF
2¢	**multicolored** tagged	.25	.20
	Plate block of 4	.60	
	y. Se-tenant block of 4 (CM675-78)	.30	.20
	FDC *(April 5, 1972)*, block of 4		1.75
	v. black omitted, any single	—	
	vy. black omitted, se-tenant block of 4	2,750.00	
	zo. Tagging omitted, any single	—	
	zoy. Tagging omitted, se-tenant block of 4	—	

1972. WOLF TRAP FARM ISSUE in the National Parks Centennial Series called attention to the national park for performing arts, established in 1966. *Intaglio (Giori Press) and offset, perforated 11.*

CM679 *Theater at Wolf Trap Farm, Va., at night*

CM679		MNHVF	UseVF
6¢	**multicolored** tagged *(104,090,000)*	.25	.20
	Plate block of 4	.85	
	FDC *(June 26, 1972)*		1.75
	zo. Tagging omitted	6.00	

1972. MOUNT MCKINLEY ISSUE in the National Parks Centennial Series celebrated the park including the highest peak (20,270 feet) in North America. *Intaglio (Giori Press) and offset, perforated 11.*

CM680 *Mount McKinley, Alaska*

CM680		MNHVF	UseVF
15¢	**multicolored** tagged *(53,920,000)*	.25	.20
	Plate block of 4	1.90	
	FDC *(July 28, 1972)*		1.75
	zo. Tagging omitted	19.00	

1972. FAMILY PLANNING ISSUE reminded people of the need for planning to have a better America and a better world. *Intaglio (Giori Press), perforated 11.*

CM681 *Planned family*

CM681		MNHVF	UseVF
8¢	**multicolored** tagged *(153,025,000)*	.25	.20
	Plate block of 4	1.10	
	FDC *(March 18, 1972)*		1.75
	v. dark brown omitted	9,350.00	
	v1. dark brown & olive omitted	—	
	v2. yellow omitted	1,650.00	
	zo. Tagging omitted	—	

1972. COLONIAL AMERICAN CRAFTSMEN ISSUE commemorated the contributions of Colonial artisans to the early development of America. *Intaglio, perforated 11x10 1/2.*

CM682 *Glassmaker;* CM683 *Silversmith;* CM684 *Wigmaker;* CM685 *Hatter*

CM682		MNHVF	UseVF
8¢	**deep brown** on buff paper, tagged *(201,890,000)*	.25	.20

CM683		MNHVF	UseVF
8¢	**deep brown** on buff paper, tagged	.25	.20

CM684		MNHVF	UseVF
8¢	**deep brown** on buff paper, tagged	.25	.20

CM685		MNHVF	UseVF
8¢	**deep brown** on buff paper, tagged	.25	.20
	Plate block of 4	1.25	
	y. Se-tenant block of 4 (CM682-85)	.75	
	FDC *(July 4, 1972)*, any single		2.00
	FDC, block of 4		4.00
	zo. Tagging omitted, any single	—	
	zoy. Tagging omitted, se-tenant block of 4	—	

Olympic Games Series

1972. OLYMPIC GAMES ISSUE saluted international athletic meets in Sapporo, Japan (Winter Games) and Munich, Germany (Summer Games). (See also A837.) *Gravure (Andreotti Press), perforated 11x10 1/2. (See A83.)*

CM686 *Cycling*

CM686		MNHVF	UseVF
6¢	**multicolored** tagged *(67,335,000)*	.25	.20
	Plate block of 10	2.10	
	v. Plate flaw, broken red ring (position 43 of top-left pane of plate No. 33313)	10.00	
	FDC *(Aug. 17, 1972)*		1.75

CM687 *Bobsled racing*

CM687		MNHVF	UseVF
8¢	**multicolored** tagged *(96,240,000)*	.25	.20
	Plate block of 10	2.75	
	FDC *(Aug. 17, 1972)*		1.75
	zo. Tagging omitted	5.00	

CM688 *Foot racing*

CM688		MNHVF	UseVF
15¢	**multicolored** tagged *(46,340,000)*	.25	.20
	Plate block of 10	5.25	
	FDC *(Aug. 17, 1972)*		1.75

1972. PARENT TEACHER ASSOCIATION ISSUE saluted the 75th anniversary of an organization dedicated to improving educational methods furthering development of young minds. *Gravure (Andreotti Press), perforated 11x10 1/2.*

CM689 *Blackboard, symbol of education*

CM689		MNHVF	UseVF
8¢	**yellow & black** tagged *(180,155,000)*	.25	.20
	Plate block of 4	.75	
	Plate block, yellow inverted	1.00	
	FDC *(Sept. 15, 1972)*		1.75
	zo. Tagging omitted	—	

1972. WILDLIFE CONSERVATION ISSUE showcased the importance and beauty of nature's creatures. *Intaglio (Giori Press) and offset, perforated 11.*

CM690 *Fur seal;* CM691 *Cardinal;* CM692 *Brown pelican;* CM693 *Bighorn sheep*

CM690		MNHVF	UseVF
8¢	**multicolored** tagged *(198,364,800)*	.25	.20

CM691		MNHVF	UseVF
8¢	**multicolored** tagged	.25	.20

CM692		MNHVF	UseVF
8¢	**multicolored** tagged	.25	.20

CM693		MNHVF	UseVF
8¢	**multicolored** tagged	.25	.20
	Plate block of 4	1.00	
	y. Se-tenant block of 4 (CM690-93)	.75	

FDC *(Sept. 20, 1972)*, any single			2.00
FDC, block of 4			4.00
v. brown omitted		—	
vy. Se-tenant block of 4, brown omitted		4,000.00	
v1. green & blue omitted		—	
v1y. Se-tenant block of 4, green & blue omitted		4,750.00	
v2. red & brown omitted		—	
v2y. Se-tenant block of 4, red & brown omitted		4,000.00	

1972. MAIL ORDER CENTENNIAL ISSUE marked the 100th anniversary of the introduction of merchandising by mail. *Gravure (Andreotti Press), perforated 11x10 1/2.*

CM694 *Rural Post Office store*

CM694		MNHVF	UseVF
8¢	**multicolored** tagged *(185,490,000)*	.25	.20
	Plate block of 12	3.00	
	FDC *(Sept. 27, 1972)*		1.75

Tagging on this issue typically consists of a vertical bar, 10mm wide.

1972. OSTEOPATHIC MEDICINE ISSUE marked the 75th anniversary of the American Osteopathic Association established by Dr. Andrew Still. *Gravure (Andreotti Press), perforated 10 1/2x11.*

CM695 *Osteopathic medicine*

CM695		MNHVF	UseVF
8¢	**multicolored** tagged *(162,335,000)*	.25	.20
	Plate block of 6	1.60	
	FDC *(Oct, 9, 1972)*		2.50

1972. TOM SAWYER ISSUE The fourth stamp in the American Folklore Series recalled the exciting, carefree adventures of the fictional mischievous boy created by Mark Twain (see CM205). *Intaglio (Giori Press) and offset, perforated 11.*

CM696 *Tom Sawyer, painted by Norman Rockwell*

CM696		MNHVF	UseVF
8¢	**multicolored** tagged *(162,789,950)*	.25	.20
	Plate block of 4	1.10	
	FDC *(Oct. 13, 1972)*		2.50
	v. black & red omitted	2,250.00	
	v1. yellow & tan omitted	2,100.00	
	v2. Horizontal pair, imperforate between	5,500.00	
	zo. Tagging omitted	15.00	

1972. PHARMACY ISSUE saluted the nation's druggists and their contribution to keeping Americans healthy. *Intaglio (Giori Press) and offset, perforated 11.*

CM697 *Bowl of Hygeia, mortar, and pestle*

CM697		MNHVF	UseVF
8¢	**multicolored** tagged *(165,895,000)*	.25	.20
	Plate block of 4	1.75	
	FDC *(Nov. 10, 1972)*		10.00
	v. blue omitted	2,000.00	
	v1. blue & orange omitted	875.00	
	v2. orange omitted	2,000.00	
	zo. Tagging omitted	—	

1972. STAMP COLLECTING ISSUE paid tribute to the nation's stamp collectors and the hobby of philately. *Intaglio (Giori Press) and offset, perforated 11.*

CM698 *First U.S. stamp under magnifying glass*

CM698		MNHVF	UseVF
8¢	**multicolored** tagged *(166,508,000)*	.25	.20
	Plate block of 4	1.00	
	FDC *(Nov. 17, 1972)*		2.00
	v. black omitted	900.00	
	zo. Tagging omitted	—	

Love Series

1973. LOVE ISSUE The first in a series issued for use on birthdays, anniversaries, and other occasions, featured a classic design by Robert Indiana. *Photogravure (Andreotti Press), perforated 11x10 1/2.*

CM699 *Love sculpture by Robert Indiana*

CM699		MNHVF	UseVF
8¢	**red, green, violet & blue** tagged	.25	.20
	(330,055,000)		
	Plate block of 6	1.50	
	FDC *(Jan. 26, 1973)*		2.25

1973. RISE OF THE SPIRIT OF INDEPENDENCE ISSUE highlighted the role of communications in spurring the American revolution. *Intaglio (Giori Press) and offset, perforated 11.*

CM700 *Pamphlets printed by press*

CM700		MNHVF	UseVF
8¢	**blue, greenish black & red** tagged	.25	.20
	(166,005,000)		
	Plate block of 4	1.00	
	FDC *(Feb. 16, 1973)*		1.75
	zo. Tagging omitted	12.50	

CM701 *Posting a broadside*

CM701		MNHVF	UseVF
8¢	**black, orange & ultramarine** tagged	.25	.20
	(163,050,000)		
	Plate block of 4	1.00	
	FDC *(April 13, 1973)*		1.75
	Pair, gutter between	—	
	zo. Tagging omitted	—	

CM702 *Colonial post rider*

CM702		MNHVF	UseVF
8¢	**blue, black, red & green** tagged	.25	.20
	(159,005,000)		
	Plate block of 4	1.00	
	FDC *(June 22, 1973)*		1.75
	zo. Tagging omitted	—	

CM703 *Drummer summoning minutemen*

CM703		MNHVF	UseVF
8¢	**blue, black, yellow & red** tagged	.25	.20
	(147,295,000)		
	Plate block of 4	1.00	
	FDC *(Sept. 28, 1973)*		1.75
	zo. Tagging omitted	—	

1973. GEORGE GERSHWIN ISSUE honored the American composer who created music for more than 400 songs, including "Rhapsody in Blue" and *Porgy and Bess* (CM1586), a folk opera. *Gravure (Andreotti Press), perforated 11.*

CM704 *George Gershwin and* Porgy and Bess *montage*

CM704		MNHVF	UseVF
8¢	**multicolored** *(139,152,000)*	.25	.20
	Plate block of 12	3.25	
	FDC *(Feb. 28, 1973)*		1.75
	v. Vertical pair, imperforate horizontally	225.00	

1973. NICOLAUS COPERNICUS ISSUE paid tribute to the father of modern astronomy on the 500th anniversary of his birth. *Intaglio (Giori Press) and offset, perforated 11.*

Users of this Catalog are invited to write to us if they have information which they feel will supplement or correct any material contained herein. All such communications will be answered.

CM705 *Nicolaus Copernicus*

CM705		MNHVF	UseVF
8¢	**black & yellow** tagged *(159,475,000)*	.25	.20
	Plate block of 4	1.10	
	FDC *(April 23, 1973)*		2.00
	v. Engraved black omitted	1,300.00	
	v1. yellow omitted	1,000.00	
	zo. Tagging omitted	15.00	

The yellow may be removed chemically. Competent expertization is recommended of CM705v1.

1973. POSTAL SERVICE EMPLOYEE ISSUE saluted the 700,000 employees of the U.S. Postal Service. Ten different stamps in a pane of 50 depict some of the services performed by postal employees, with text describing those activities printed on the reverse side of the stamp, under the gum, a U.S. stamp first. *Gravure (Andreotti Press), perforated 10 1/2x11.*

CM706-CM715 *Postal people performing services*

CM706		MNHVF	UseVF
8¢	**multicolored** tagged *(486,020,000)*	.25	.20
CM707		MNHVF	UseVF
8¢	**multicolored** tagged	.25	.20
CM708		MNHVF	UseVF
8¢	**multicolored** tagged	.25	.20
CM709		MNHVF	UseVF
8¢	**multicolored** tagged	.25	.20
CM710		MNHVF	UseVF
8¢	**multicolored** tagged	.25	.20
CM711		MNHVF	UseVF
8¢	**multicolored** tagged	.25	.20
CM712		MNHVF	UseVF
8¢	**multicolored** tagged	.25	.20
CM713		MNHVF	UseVF
8¢	**multicolored** tagged	.25	.20
CM714		MNHVF	UseVF
8¢	**multicolored** tagged	.25	.20
CM715		MNHVF	UseVF
8¢	**multicolored** tagged	.25	.20
	Plate block of 20	5.50	
	y. Se-tenant strip of 10 (CM706-15)	4.00	
	FDC *(April 30, 1973)*, any single		2.00
	FDC, strip of 10		20.00
	zo. Tagging omitted, any single	—	
	zoy. Tagging omitted, se-tenant strip of 10	—	

Tagging consists of a 1/2 inch high horizontal band.

1973. HARRY S. TRUMAN ISSUE honored the 33rd president of the United States, who died Dec. 26, 1972. *Intaglio (Giori Press), perforated 11.*

CM716 *Harry S. Truman, from a photograph by Leo Stern*

CM716		MNHVF	UseVF
8¢	**red, black & blue** tagged *(157,052,800)*	.25	.25
	Plate block of 4	1.10	
	FDC *(May 8, 1973)*		2.00
	zo. Tagging omitted	5.00	

1973. BOSTON TEA PARTY ISSUE used four different se-tenant designs to form a single scene depicting this historical event that preceded the War of Independence. *Intaglio (Giori Press) and offset, perforated 11.*

CM717-20 *Boston Tea Party*

CM717		MNHVF	UseVF
8¢	**multicolored** tagged *(196,275,000)*	.25	.20
CM718		MNHVF	UseVF
8¢	**multicolored** tagged	.25	.20
CM719		MNHVF	UseVF
8¢	**multicolored** tagged	.25	.20
CM720		MNHVF	UseVF
8¢	**multicolored** tagged	.25	.20
	Plate block of 4	1.15	
	y. Se-tenant block of 4 (CM717-20)	.75	
	FDC *(July 4, 1973)*, any single		2.00
	FDC, block of 4		8.00
	vy. Se-tenant block of 4, intaglio black omitted	1,500.00	
	v1y. Se-tenant block of 4, offset black omitted	1,400.00	
	zo. Tagging omitted, any single	—	
	zoy. Se-tenant block of 4, tagging omitted	—	

1973. PROGRESS IN ELECTRONICS ISSUE commemorated advances and developments in electronic communications. (See also A84.) *Intaglio (Giori Press) and offset, perforated 11.*

CM721 *Marconi spark coil and gap*

CM721		MNHVF	UseVF
6¢	**multicolored** tagged *(53,005,000)*	.25	.20
	Plate block of 4	.85	
	FDC *(July 10, 1973)*		1.75
	zo. Tagging omitted	—	

CM722 *Transistors and electronic circuit*

CM722

		MNHVF	UseVF
8¢	**multicolored** tagged *(159,775,000)*	.25	.20
	Plate block of 4	1.00	
	FDC *(July 10, 1973)*		1.75
	v. black (inscription) omitted	550.00	
	v1. lilac & tan (background) omitted	1,300.00	
	zo. Tagging omitted	—	

CM723 *Radio and television components*

CM723

		MNHVF	UseVF
15¢	**multicolored** tagged *(39,005,000)*	.25	.20
	Plate block of 4	1.85	
	FDC *(July 10, 1973)*		1.75
	v. black omitted	1,500.00	

1973. ROBINSON JEFFERS ISSUE paid tribute to the poet whose works were mainly allegories influenced by his love of the classical Greek and Roman tragedies. *Gravure (Andreotti Press), perforated 11.*

CM724 *Robinson Jeffers and children with burro*

CM724

		MNHVF	UseVF
8¢	**multicolored** tagged *(128,048,000)*	.25	.20
	Plate block of 12	3.00	
	FDC *(Aug. 13, 1973)*		1.75
	v. Vertical pair, imperforate horizontally	250.00	

1973. LYNDON B. JOHNSON ISSUE honored the 36th president of the United States, who died Jan. 22, 1973. *Gravure (Andreotti Press), perforated 11.*

CM725 *Lyndon B. Johnson*

CM725

		MNHVF	UseVF
8¢	**multicolored** *(152,624,000)*	.25	.20
	Plate block of 12	3.50	
	FDC *(Aug. 27, 1973)*		1.75
	v. Horizontal pair, imperforate vertically	350.00	

1973. HENRY O. TANNER ISSUE saluted the artist who studied art under Thomas Eakins. Many of his works were based on Biblical themes. *Gravure (Andreotti Press), perforated 11.*

CM726 *Henry O. Tanner, palette and rainbow*

CM726

		MNHVF	UseVF
8¢	**multicolored** tagged *(146,008,000)*	.25	.20
	Plate block of 12	3.00	
	FDC *(Sept. 10, 1973)*		2.50

1973. WILLA CATHER ISSUE saluted a novelist who won a 1922 Pulitzer Prize. *Gravure (Andreotti Press), perforated 11.*

CM727 *Willa Cather, pioneers, and covered wagon*

CM727

		MNHVF	UseVF
8¢	**multicolored** tagged *(139,608,000)*	.25	.20
	Plate block of 12	3.00	
	FDC *(Sept. 20, 1973)*		1.75
	v. Vertical pair, imperforate horizontally	275.00	

Rural America Series

1973. ANGUS CATTLE ISSUE First of a series of three stamps honoring rural America, saluted the 100th anniversary of the introduction of Aberdeen Angus cattle into the United States. (See also CM751-752.) *Intaglio (Giori Press) and offset, perforated 11.*

CM728 *Angus cattle and longhorn cattle on prairie*

CM728

		MNHVF	UseVF
8¢	**multicolored** tagged *(145,430,000)*	.25	.20
	Plate block of 4	1.00	
	FDC *(Oct. 5, 1973)*		1.75
	v. green & red brown omitted	975.00	
	v1. Vertical pair, imperforate between	4,500.00	
	zo. Tagging omitted	14.00	

1974. VETERANS OF FOREIGN WARS ISSUE saluted the men and women in America's military service since the Spanish-American War. *Intaglio (Giori Press), perforated 11.*

CM729 *VFW emblem*

CM729

		MNHVF	UseVF
10¢	**red & blue** tagged *(145,430,000)*	.25	.20
	Plate block of 4	1.30	
	FDC *(March 11, 1974)*		1.75
	zo. Tagging omitted	5.00	

1974. ROBERT FROST ISSUE in the American Poets Series honored the New England poet (1873-1963) and four-time winner of the Pulitzer Prize. *Intaglio, perforated 10 1/2x11.*

CM730 *Robert Frost*

CM730		MNHVF	UseVF
10¢	**black** tagged *(145,235,000)*	.25	.20
	Plate block of 4	1.30	
	FDC *(March 26, 1974)*		1.75

1974. EXPO 74 WORLD'S FAIR ISSUE featured the theme "Preserve the Environment," magically rendered by Peter Max in his images *Cosmic Jumper* and *Smiling Sage*. *Gravure (Andreotti Press), perforated 11.*

CM731 *Expo 74*

CM731		MNHVF	UseVF
10¢	**multicolored** tagged *(135,052,000)*	.25	.20
	Plate block of 12	4.25	
	FDC *(April 18, 1974)*		1.75

1974. HORSE RACING ISSUE commemorated the 100th running of the Kentucky Derby. *Gravure (Andreotti Press), perforated 11x10 1/2.*

CM732 *Horses at the turn*

CM732		MNHVF	UseVF
10¢	**multicolored** tagged *(156,750,000)*	.25	.20
	Plate block of 12	3.75	
	FDC *(May 4, 1974)*		3.00
	v. blue "Horse Racing" omitted	900.00	
	v1. red "U.S. Postage 10 cents" omitted	—	
	zo. Tagging omitted	15.00	

Beware of stamps with minute traces of red being offered as CM732b. They are printing freaks, and do not have comparable value to a full color-omitted error.

1974. SKYLAB PROJECT ISSUE paid tribute to the Skylab I program, devoted to experimentation in space.

CM733 *Skylab*

CM733		MNHVF	UseVF
10¢	**multicolored** tagged *(164,670,000)*	.25	.20
	Plate block of 4	1.30	
	FDC *(May 14, 1974)*		2.00
	v. Vertical pair, imperforate between	—	
	zo. Tagging omitted	7.50	

1974. UNIVERSAL POSTAL UNION ISSUE marked the centenary of the international organization that helped standardize mail rates and expedite mail delivery worldwide. *Gravure (Andreotti Press), perforated 11.*

CM734 Lady Writing a Letter *by Terboch;* CM735 Still Life *by Chardin;* CM736 Mrs. John Douglas *by Gainsborough;* CM737 Don Antonio Noriega *by Goya;* CM738 Portrait of Michelangelo *by Raphael;* CM739 5 Feminine Virtues *by Hokusai;* CM740 Old Scraps (Old Letter Rack) *by Peto;* CM741 The Lovely Reader *by Liotard*

CM734		MNHVF	UseVF
10¢	**multicolored** tagged *(190,154,680)*	.25	.20
CM735		**MNHVF**	**UseVF**
10¢	**multicolored** tagged	.25	.20
CM736		**MNHVF**	**UseVF**
10¢	**multicolored** tagged	.25	.20
CM737		**MNHVF**	**UseVF**
10¢	**multicolored** tagged	.25	.20
CM738		**MNHVF**	**UseVF**
10¢	**multicolored** tagged	.25	.20
CM739		**MNHVF**	**UseVF**
10¢	**multicolored** tagged	.25	.20
CM740		**MNHVF**	**UseVF**
10¢	**multicolored** tagged	.25	.20
CM741		**MNHVF**	**UseVF**
10¢	**multicolored** tagged	.25	.20
	Plate block of 10	3.50	
	y. Se-tenant block or strip of 8 (CM734-41)	2.00	
	FDC *(June 6, 1974)*		2.50
	FDC, block or strip of 8		5.00
	vy. Se-tenant block or strip of 8 imperforate vertically	7,500.00	

1974. MINERAL HERITAGE ISSUE focused attention on the significant contributions minerals have made to making the United States a leader among nations. *Intaglio (Giori Press) and offset, perforated 11.*

CM742 *Amethyst*

CM743 *Petrified wood*

CM744 *Rhodochrosite*

CM745 *Tourmaline*

CM742		MNHVF	UseVF
10¢	**multicolored** tagged *(167,212,800)*	.25	.20
	v. light blue & yellow omitted	—	

CM743		MNHVF	UseVF
10¢	**multicolored** tagged	.25	.20
	v. light blue & yellow omitted	—	

CM744		MNHVF	UseVF
10¢	**multicolored** tagged	.25	.20
	v. light blue omitted	—	
	v1. black & red omitted	—	

CM745		MNHVF	UseVF
10¢	**multicolored** tagged	.25	.20
	v. light blue omitted	—	
	v1. black & purple omitted	—	
	Plate block of 4	1.00	
	y. Se-tenant block or strip of 4 (CM742-45)	.80	
	FDC *(June 13, 1974)*, any single		2.00
	FDC, block of 4		4.00
	vy. Se-tenant block or strip of 4, light blue & yellow omitted	1,900.00	
	zo. Tagging omitted, any single	—	
	zoy. Se-tenant block or strip of 4, tagging omitted	58.00	

1974. SETTLEMENT OF KENTUCKY ISSUE saluted the 200th anniversary of the founding of Fort Harrod, the first British settlement west of the Allegheny Mountains. *Intaglio (Giori Press) and offset, perforated 11.*

CM746 *Settlers at Fort Harrod*

CM746		MNHVF	UseVF
10¢	**multicolored** tagged *(156,265,000)*	.25	.20
	Plate block of 4	1.30	
	FDC *(June 15, 1974)*		1.75
	v. Offset dull black omitted	800.00	
	v1. green & black (intaglio & offset) & blue omitted	4,250.00	
	v2. green intaglio & offset black omitted	—	
	v3. intaglio green omitted	—	
	zo. Tagging omitted	10.00	

1974. FIRST CONTINENTAL CONGRESS ISSUE commemorated the 200th anniversary of the assemblage that paved the way for the creation of the United States. *Intaglio (Giori Press), perforated 11.*

CM747 *Carpenters' Hall;* CM748 *Independence Hall;* CM749 *Quote from 1st Continental Congress;* CM750 *Quote from Declaration of Independence*

CM747		MNHVF	UseVF
10¢	**dark blue & red** tagged *(195,585,000)*	.25	.20

CM748		MNHVF	UseVF
10¢	**red & dark blue** tagged	.25	.20

CM749		MNHVF	UseVF
10¢	**gray, dark blue & red** tagged	.25	.20

CM750		MNHVF	UseVF
10¢	**gray, dark blue & red** tagged	.25	.20
	Plate block of 4	1.40	
	y. Se-tenant block of 4 (CM747-50)	.75	
	FDC *(July 4, 1974)*, any single		2.00
	FDC, block of 4		4.00
	zo. Tagging omitted, any single	—	
	zoy. Se-tenant block of 4, tagging omitted	50.00	

1974. CHAUTAUQUA TENT ISSUE The second stamp in the Rural America Series commemorated the 100th anniversary of the founding of the Chautauqua (N.Y.) Institution, which developed into a teachers' training center for Sunday school and, later, public school. *Intaglio (Giori Press) and offset, perforated 11.*

CM751 *Chautauqua tent*

CM751		MNHVF	UseVF
10¢	**multicolored** tagged *(151,335,000)*	.25	.20
	Plate block of 4	1.30	
	FDC *(Aug. 6, 1974)*		1.75
	v. black omitted	—	—

1974. WINTER WHEAT AND TRAIN ISSUE The third and final stamp in the Rural America Series marked the 100th anniversary of hard winter wheat. *Intaglio (Giori Press) and offset, perforated 11.*

CM752 *Winter wheat and train*

CM752		MNHVF	UseVF
10¢	**multicolored** tagged *(141,085,000)*	.25	.20
	Plate block of 4	1.30	
	FDC *(Aug. 16, 1974)*		1.75
	v. black & intaglio blue omitted	875.00	
	zo. Tagging omitted	15.00	

1974. ENERGY CONSERVATION ISSUE focused attention upon the national fuel shortage and the need to save energy. *Intaglio (Giori Press) and offset, perforated 11.*

CM753 *Energy conservation*

CM753		MNHVF	UseVF
10¢	**multicolored** tagged *(148,850,000)*	.25	.20
	Plate block of 4	1.30	
	FDC *(Sept. 23, 1974)*		1.75
	v. blue & orange omitted	950.00	
	v1. green omitted	875.00	
	v2. orange & green omitted	800.00	
	zo. Tagging omitted	5.00	

1974. LEGEND OF SLEEPY HOLLOW ISSUE The fifth in the American Folklore Series commemorated Washington Irving's *Legend of Sleepy Hollow. Intaglio (Giori Press) and offset, perforated 11.*

CM754 *Headless Horseman pursuing Ichabod Crane*

CM754		MNHVF	UseVF
10¢	**dark blue, black, orange, & yellow**	.25	.20
	tagged *(157,270,000)*		
	Plate block of 4	1.30	
	FDC *(Oct. 10, 1974)*		2.00

1974. HELP FOR RETARDED CHILDREN ISSUE encouraged efforts to help mentally retarded persons. *Intaglio (Giori Press), perforated 11.*

CM755 *Retarded girl and helping hand*

CM755		MNHVF	UseVF
10¢	**light & dark brown** tagged *(150,245,000)*	.25	.20
	Plate block of 4	1.30	
	FDC *(Oct. 12, 1974)*		1.75
	zo. Tagging omitted	6.00	

American Arts Series

1975. BENJAMIN WEST ISSUE Part of a brief American Arts Series, this issue commemorated Benjamin West, the first American-born painter to gain an international reputation working abroad. *Gravure (Andreotti Press), perforated 10 1/2x11.*

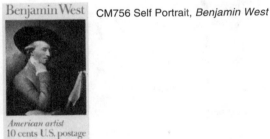

CM756 Self Portrait, *Benjamin West*

CM756		MNHVF	UseVF
10¢	**multicolored** tagged *(156,995,000)*	.25	.20
	Plate block of 10	3.25	
	FDC *(Feb. 10, 1975)*		1.75

1975. PIONEER SPACE ISSUE saluted the unmanned *Pioneer 10* space mission, which probed the planet Jupiter in 1973-74. *Intaglio (Giori Press) and offset, perforated 11.*

CM757 Pioneer 10 *and Jupiter*

CM757		MNHVF	UseVF
10¢	**dark blue, yellow & red** tagged	.25	.20
	(173,685,000)		
	Plate block of 4	1.30	
	FDC *(Feb. 28, 1975)*		1.75
	v. intaglio blue omitted	950.00	
	v1. red & yellow omitted	1,350.00	
	zo. Tagging omitted	7.50	

Imperforate varieties came from printer's waste.

1975. COLLECTIVE BARGAINING ISSUE commemorated the 40th anniversary of collective bargaining law in the Wagner Act, which stabilized labor-management relations in the United States. *Gravure (Andreotti Press), perforated 11.*

CM758 *Collective bargaining*

CM758		MNHVF	UseVF
10¢	**multicolored** tagged *(153,355,000)*	.25	.20
	Plate block of 8	2.50	
	FDC *(March 13, 1975)*		1.75
	v. Pair, imperforate	350.00	

Imperforate varieties came from printer's waste.

1975. CONTRIBUTORS TO THE CAUSE ISSUE honored four heroes of the American Revolution. Emerald green inscriptions on the back of the stamp telling the story of each individual are printed under the gum. *Gravure (Andreotti Press), perforated 11x10 1/2.*

CM759 *Sybil Ludington, Youthful Heroine*

CM759		MNHVF	UseVF
10¢	**multicolored** tagged *(63,205,000)*	.25	.20
	Plate block of 10	2.50	
	FDC *(March 25, 1975)*		1.75
	v. Inscription on back omitted	250.00	

CM760 *Salem Poor, Gallant Soldier*

CM760		MNHVF	UseVF
10¢	**multicolored** tagged *(157,865,000)*	.25	.20
	Plate block of 10	3.25	
	FDC *(March 25, 1975)*		2.50
	v. Inscription on back omitted	250.00	

CM761 *Haym Salomon, Financial Hero*

CM761		MNHVF	UseVF
10¢	**multicolored** tagged *(166,810,000)*	.25	.20
	Plate block of 10	3.25	
	FDC *(March 25, 1975)*		1.75
	v. Inscription on back omitted	250.00	
	v1. red omitted	275.00	

CM762 *Peter Francisco, Fighter Extraordinary*

CM762		MNHVF	UseVF
18¢	**multicolored** tagged *(44,825,000)*	.25	.20
	Plate block of 10	6.25	
	FDC *(March 25, 1975)*		1.75

1975. MARINER SPACE ISSUE honored the *Mariner 10* unmanned space mission to Venus and Mercury. *Intaglio (Giori Press) and offset, perforated 11.*

CM763 Mariner 10, *Venus, and Mercury*

CM763		MNHVF	UseVF
10¢	**black, red, ultramarine & bister** tagged	.25	.20
	(158,600,000)		
	Plate block of 4	1.30	
	FDC *(April 4, 1975)*		1.75
	v. red omitted	575.00	
	v1. ultramarine & bister omitted	1,750.00	
	zo. Tagging omitted	7.50	

1975. LEXINGTON AND CONCORD ISSUE commemorated these 1775 battles, the first of the Revolutionary War. *Gravure (Andreotti Press), perforated 11.*

CM764 *Lexington and Concord, based on painting* Birth of Liberty *by Henry Sandham*

CM764		MNHVF	UseVF
10¢	**multicolored** tagged *(114,028,000)*	.25	.20
	Plate block of 12	3.75	
	FDC *(April 19, 1975)*		1.75
	v. Vertical pair, imperforate horizontally	425.00	

1975. PAUL LAURENCE DUNBAR ISSUE in the American Arts Series honored the African-American poet. *Gravure (Andreotti Press), perforated 11.*

CM765 *Paul Laurence Dunbar*

CM765		MNHVF	UseVF
10¢	**multicolored** tagged *(146,365,000)*	.25	.20
	Plate block of 10	3.25	
	FDC *(May 1, 1975)*		2.50
	v. Pair, imperforate	1,300.00	

1975. D.W. GRIFFITH ISSUE of the American Arts Series commemorated motion picture pioneer D.W. Griffith. *Intaglio (Giori Press) and offset, perforated 11.*

CM766 *D.W. Griffith, motion picture camera*

CM766		MNHVF	UseVF
10¢	**multicolored** tagged *(148,805,000)*	.25	.20
	Plate block of 4	1.30	
	FDC *(May 27, 1975)*		1.75
	v. intaglio dark brown omitted	650.00	

1975. BUNKER HILL ISSUE commemorated the 200th anniversary of the Battle of Bunker Hill. *Gravure (Andreotti Press), perforated 11.*

CM767 *Detail from the painting* The Battle of Bunker Hill *by John Trumbull*

CM767		MNHVF	UseVF
10¢	**multicolored** tagged *(139,928,000)*	.25	.20
	Plate block of 12	3.75	
	FDC *(June 17, 1975)*		1.75

1975. MILITARY SERVICES BICENTENNIAL ISSUE honored the 200th anniversary year of the U.S. military services. Designs depict uniforms worn by the Continental Army, Navy, Marines, and Militia during the Revolutionary War. *Gravure (Andreotti Press), perforated 11.*

CM768 *Soldier*

CM769 *Sailor*

CM770 *Marine*

CM771 *Militiaman*

CM768		MNHVF	UseVF
10¢	**multicolored** tagged *(179,855,000)*	.25	.20
CM769		**MNHVF**	**UseVF**
10¢	**multicolored** tagged	.25	.20
CM770		**MNHVF**	**UseVF**
10¢	**multicolored** tagged	.25	.20
CM771		**MNHVF**	**UseVF**
10¢	**multicolored** tagged	.25	.20
	Plate block of 12	4.25	
	y. Se-tenant block of 4 (CM768-71)	.75	
	FDC *(July 4, 1975)*, any single		2.00
	FDC, block of 4		4.00

1975. APOLLO SOYUZ ISSUE honored the first combined space mission between the United States and Soviet Union. The se-tenant designs used by both nations are identical except for language and denomination (Russia Nos. 4472-4473). *Gravure (Andreotti Press), perforated 11.*

CM772 *Spacecraft in docked position*

CM772		MNHVF	UseVF
10¢	**multicolored** tagged *(161,863,200)*	.25	.20

CM773
Spacecraft prior to docking

CM773		MNHVF	UseVF
10¢	**multicolored** tagged	.25	.20
	Plate block of 12	4.00	
	y. Se-tenant pair (CM772-73)	.45	
	Pair, gutter between	—	
	FDC *(July 15, 1975),* either single		2.00
	FDC, pair		3.00
	v. Vertical pair, imperforate horizontally	2,500.00	
	zo. Tagging omitted, either single	—	
	zoy. Se-tenant pair, tagging omitted	25.00	
	v1. Pair, yellow omitted		

1975. WORLD PEACE THROUGH LAW ISSUE was a prelude to the Seventh World Law Conference of the World Peace Through Law Center and commemorated man's effort toward the universal goal of a peaceful world order with justice. *Intaglio (Giori Press), perforated 11.*

CM774 *Olive branch, globe, gavel, and law book*

CM774		MNHVF	UseVF
10¢	**green, gray blue & brown** tagged	.25	.20
	(146,615,000)		
	Plate block of 4	1.35	
	FDC *(Sept. 29, 1975)*		2.00
	v. Horizontal pair, imperforate vertically	14,000.00	
	(only 1 plate block)		
	zo. Tagging omitted	6.00	

1975. INTERNATIONAL WOMEN'S YEAR ISSUE celebrated the significance of women. *Gravure (Andreotti Press), perforated 11x10 1/2.*

CM775 *Stylized dove, globe, and gender sign*

CM775		MNHVF	UseVF
10¢	**blue, orange & dark blue** tagged	.25	.20
	(145,640,000)		
	Plate block of 6	1.90	
	FDC *(Aug. 26, 1975)*		1.75

1975. U.S. POSTAL SERVICE BICENTENNIAL ISSUE commemorated the 200th anniversary of Postal Service in the United States. *Gravure (Andreotti Press), perforated 11x10 1/2.*

CM776 *Stagecoach and modern trailer truck;* CM777 *Early and modern locomotives;* CM778 *Early mail plane and jumbo jet;* CM779 *Satellite for Mailgram transmissions*

CM776		MNHVF	UseVF
10¢	**multicolored** tagged *(168,655,000)*	.25	.20
CM777		MNHVF	UseVF
10¢	**multicolored** tagged	.25	.20
CM778		MNHVF	UseVF
10¢	**multicolored** tagged	.25	.20
CM779		MNHVF	UseVF
10¢	**multicolored** tagged	.25	.20
	Plate block of 12	4.25	
	y. Se-tenant block of 4 (CM776-79)	1.25	
	FDC *(Sept. 3, 1975),* any single		2.00
	FDC, block of 4		8.00
	vy. Se-tenant block of 4, red "10¢" omitted	7,500.00	

1975. BANKING AND COMMERCE ISSUE focused on the importance of these commercial activities in the nation's development. *Intaglio (Giori Press) and offset, perforated 11.*

CM780 *Coins and currency motif;* CM781 *Coins and currency motif*

CM780		MNHVF	UseVF
10¢	**multicolored** tagged *(146,196,000)*	.25	.20
CM781		MNHVF	UseVF
10¢	**multicolored** tagged	.25	.20
	Plate block of 4	1.50	
	y. Se-tenant pair (CM780-81)	.75	.50
	FDC *(Oct. 6, 1975),* either single		1.00
	FDC, pair		2.00
	vy. Se-tenant pair, brown & blue (offset) omitted	2,500.00	
	v1y. Se-tenant pair, brown, blue & yellow (offset) omitted	2,750.00	

1976. SPIRIT OF 76 ISSUE reproduced a classic image of the American Revolution. *Gravure (Andreotti Press), perforated 11.*

CM782-84 Revolutionary War Fife and Drum Trio, *painting by Archibald M. Willard*

CM782		MNHVF	UseVF
13¢	**multicolored** tagged *(219,455,000)*	.25	.20
CM783		MNHVF	UseVF
13¢	**multicolored** tagged	.25	.20
CM784		MNHVF	UseVF
13¢	**multicolored** tagged	.25	.20
	Plate block of 12	5.00	
	y. Se-tenant strip of 3 (CM782-84)	.75	1.00
	FDC *(Jan. 1, 1976),* any single		1.75
	FDC, strip of 3		5.75
	v. Vertical pair (CM784), imperforate	900.00	
	vy. Se-tenant strip of 3, imperforate	1,200.00	

1976. INTERPHIL ISSUE commemorated the Seventh International Philatelic Exhibition, May 29-June 6, 1976, in Philadelphia, Pa. *Intaglio (Giori Press) and offset, perforated 11.*

Interphil
INTERNATIONAL
PHILATELIC
EXHIBITION
PHILADELPHIA,
PENNSYLVANIA
MAY 29–JUNE 6
USA13¢

CM785 *Interphil 76*

Plate block of 4   1.60
FDC *(Jan. 17, 1976)*   1.75

1976. 50-STATE FLAG ISSUE included in one sheet the flag of every state, arranged in order of its admission to the union. (The Tennessee flag is shown on CM801 upside-down, altering subtly but discernably the orientation of the three stars.) *Gravure (Andreotti Press), perforated 11, all stamps multicolored.*

		MNHVF	UseVF
CM785			
13¢	**blue, red & ultramarine** tagged *(157,825,000)*	.25	.20

		MNHVF	UseVF
CM786			
13¢	**Delaware,** tagged *(436,005,000)*	.30	.25

CM786-CM835 *State Flags*

		MNHVF	UseVF
CM787 13¢	Pennsylvania, tagged	.30	.25
CM788 13¢	New Jersey, tagged	.30	.25
CM789 13¢	Georgia, tagged	.30	.25
CM790 13¢	Connecticut, tagged	.30	.25
CM791 13¢	Massachusetts, tagged	.30	.25
CM792 13¢	Maryland, tagged	.30	.25
CM793 13¢	South Carolina, tagged	.30	.25
CM794 13¢	New Hampshire, tagged	.30	.25
CM795 13¢	Virginia, tagged	.30	.25
CM796 13¢	New York, tagged	.30	.25
CM797 13¢	North Carolina, tagged	.30	.25
CM798 13¢	Rhode Island, tagged	.30	.25
CM799 13¢	Vermont, tagged	.30	.25
CM800 13¢	Kentucky, tagged	.30	.25
CM801 13¢	Tennessee, tagged	.30	.25
CM802 13¢	Ohio, tagged	.30	.25
CM803 13¢	Louisiana, tagged	.30	.25
CM804 13¢	Indiana, tagged	.30	.25
CM805 13¢	Mississippi, tagged	.30	.25
CM806 13¢	Illinois, tagged	.30	.25
CM807 13¢	Alabama, tagged	.30	.25
CM808 13¢	Maine, tagged	.30	.25
CM809 13¢	Missouri, tagged	.30	.25
CM810 13¢	Arkansas, tagged	.30	.25
CM811 13¢	Michigan, tagged	.30	.25
CM812 13¢	Florida, tagged	.30	.25
CM813 13¢	Texas, tagged	.30	.25
CM814 13¢	Iowa, tagged	.30	.25
CM815 13¢	Wisconsin, tagged	.30	.25
CM816 13¢	California, tagged	.30	.25
CM817 13¢	Minnesota, tagged	.30	.25
CM818 13¢	Oregon, tagged	.30	.25
CM819 13¢	Kansas, tagged	.30	.25
CM820 13¢	West Virginia, tagged	.30	.25
CM821 13¢	Nevada, tagged	.30	.25
CM822 13¢	Nebraska, tagged	.30	.25
CM823 13¢	Colorado, tagged	.30	.25
CM824 13¢	North Dakota, tagged	.30	.25

		MNHVF	UseVF
CM825 13¢	South Dakota, tagged	.30	.25
CM826 13¢	Montana, tagged	.55	.25
CM827 13¢	Washington, tagged	.55	.25
CM828 13¢	Idaho, tagged	.55	.25
CM829 13¢	Wyoming, tagged	.55	.25
CM830 13¢	Utah, tagged	.55	.25
CM831 13¢	Oklahoma, tagged	.55	.25
CM832 13¢	New Mexico, tagged	.55	.25
CM833 13¢	Arizona, tagged	.55	.25
CM834 13¢	Alaska, tagged	.55	.25
CM835 13¢	Hawaii, tagged	.55	.25
	FDC, *(Feb. 23 1976)*, any single		1.50
	y. Pane of 50	15.00	
	FDC, pane of 50		40.00

1976. TELEPHONE CENTENNIAL ISSUE honored the 100th anniversary of the first telephone call by Alexander Graham Bell (CM235). *Intaglio (Giori Press), perforated 11.*

 CM836 *Patent application of Bell's 1876 telephone*

		MNHVF	UseVF
CM836 13¢	black, purple & red on tan paper, tagged *(159,915,000)*	.25	.20
	Plate block of 4	1.60	
	FDC *(March 10, 1976)*		1.75

1976. COMMERCIAL AVIATION ISSUE saluted the 50th anniversary of the first contract airmail flights. The stamp depicts a Ford-Pullman monoplane and a Laird Swallow biplane. *Gravure (Andreotti Press), perforated 11.*

 CM837 *Early contract airmail planes*

		MNHVF	UseVF
CM837 13¢	multicolored tagged *(156,960,000)*	.25	.20
	Plate block of 10	4.70	
	FDC *(March 19, 1976)*		2.00

1976. CHEMISTRY ISSUE paid tribute to that science and saluted the 100th anniversary of the American Chemical Society. *Gravure (Andreotti Press), perforated 11.*

 CM838 *Laboratory flasks, computer tape*

		MNHVF	UseVF
CM838 13¢	multicolored tagged *(158,470,000)*	.25	.20
	Plate block of 12	4.70	
	Pair, gutter between		
	FDC *(April 6, 1976)*		1.75

1976. BICENTENNIAL SOUVENIR SHEETS issued to coincide with the Seventh International Philatelic Exhibition, held in Philadelphia, Pa., May 29-June 6. Each contained five stamps of the same denomination. *Lithographed, perforated 11.*

CM839 Surrender of Cornwallis at Yorktown, *by John Trumbull (five 13¢ stamps)*

CM839		MNHVF	UseVF
65¢	**multicolored** tagged *(1,990,500)*	4.75	4.50
	a. 13c 2 British officers	.95	.90
	b. 13c Gen. Benjamin Lincoln	.95	.90
	c. 13c Gen. George Washington	.95	.90
	d. 13c John Trumbull, Col. Cobb, von Steuben, Lafayette & Thomas Nelson	.95	.90
	e. Alexander Hamilton, John Laurens & Walter Stewart	.95	.90
	FDC *(May 29, 1976),* sheetlet		10.00
	v. "USA/13c" omitted on CM839b, CM839c & CM839d, imperforate	500.00	
	v1. "USA/13c" omitted on CM839b, CM839c & CM839d	900.00	
	v2. "USA/13c" omitted on CM839a & CM839e	500.00	
	v3. "USA/13c" omitted on CM839c & CM839d	500.00	
	v4. "USA/13c" omitted on CM839e	600.00	
	v5. "USA/13c" double on CM839b	—	
	v6. Tagging & "USA/13c" omitted, imperforate	—	
	zo. Tagging omitted	—	
	zov.Tagging omitted, imperforate	2,250.00	

CM840 Declaration of Independence, *by John Trumbull*

CM840		MNHVF	UseVF
90¢	**multicolored** tagged *(1,983,000)*	6.00	5.75
	a. 18c John Adams, Roger Sherman & Robert Livingston	1.35	1.30
	b. 18c Jefferson & Franklin	1.35	1.30
	c. 18c Thomas Nelson Jr., Francis Lewis, John Witherspoon & Samuel Huntington	1.35	1.30

		MNHVF	UseVF
	d. 18c John Hancock & Charles Thompson	1.35	1.30
	e. 18c George Read, John Dickenson & Edward Rutledge	1.35	1.30
	FDC *(May 29, 1976),* sheetlet		10.00
	v. black omitted in design	1,250.00	
	v1. Design & marginal inscriptions omitted	—	
	v2. "USA/18c" & tagging omitted, imperforate	—	
	v3. "USA/18c" omitted on CM840a & CM840c	600.00	
	v4. "USA/18c" omitted on CM840b, CM840d & CM840e	500.00	
	v5. "USA/18c" omitted on CM840d	550.00	
	v6. "USA/18c" omitted on CM840b & CM840e	550.00	
	zo. Tagging omitted	—	

CM841 Washington Crossing the Delaware, *by Emmanuel Leutze/Eastman Johnson (five 24¢ stamps)*

CM841		MNHVF	UseVF
$1.20	**multicolored** tagged *(1,953,000)*	8.25	8.00
	a. 24c Boatsman	1.80	1.70
	b. 24c Gen. George Washington	1.80	1.70
	c. 24c Flag bearer	1.80	1.70
	d. 24c Men in boat	1.80	1.70
	e. 24c Men on shore	1.80	1.70
	FDC *(May 29, 1976),* sheetlet		10.00
	v. Design & marginal inscription omitted	3,250.00	
	v1. "USA/24c" omitted, imperforate	—	
	v2. "USA/24c" omitted on CM841a, CM841b & CM841c	600.00	
	v3. "USA/24c" omitted on CM841d & CM841e	550.00	
	v4. "USA/24c" of CM841d & CM841e inverted	500.00	
	zo. Tagging omitted	—	
	zov. Tagging omitted, imperforate	2,500.00	

CM842 Washington Reviewing His Ragged Army at Valley Forge, *by William T. Trego*

CM842		MNHVF	UseVF
$1.55	**multicolored** tagged *(1,903,000)*	10.75	10.50
	a. 31c 2 officers	2.25	2.15
	b. 31c Gen. George Washington	2.25	2.15
	c. 31c Officer on black horse	2.25	2.15
	d. 31c Officer & white horse	2.25	2.15
	e. 31c 3 foot soldiers	2.25	2.15
	FDC *(May 29, 1976)*, sheetlet		10.00
	v. black omitted in design	—	
	v1."USA/31c" omitted, imperforate	2,500.00	
	v2."USA/31c" omitted on CM842a, CM842b & CM842e	—	
	v3."USA/31c" & tagging omitted on CM842a, CM842b & CM842c, imperforate	—	
	v4."USA/31c" omitted on CM842a & CM842c	550.00	
	v5."USA/31c" & tagging omitted on CM842a & CM842c, imperforate	—	
	v6."USA/31c" omitted on CM842b, CM842d & CM842e	—	
	v7."USA/31c" & tagging omitted on CM842b, CM842d & CM842e, imperforate	2,500.00	
	v8."USA/31c" omitted on CM842b & CM842d	—	
	v9."USA/31c" omitted on CM842d & CM842e	1,250.00	
	v10."USA/31c" omitted on CM842e	550.00	
	zo. Tagging omitted, imperforate	2,250.00	

1976. BENJAMIN FRANKLIN ISSUE honored America's first postmaster general, appointed by the Continental Congress. *Intaglio (Giori Press) and offset, perforated 11.*

CM843 *Benjamin Franklin and map of North America*

CM843		MNHVF	UseVF
13¢	**multicolored** tagged *(164,890,000)*	.25	.20
	Plate block of 4	1.60	
	FDC *(June 1, 1976)*		1.75
	v. light blue omitted	275.00	
	zo. Tagging omitted	4.00	

1976. DECLARATION OF INDEPENDENCE ISSUE celebrated the anniversary of the approval of the document on July 4, 1776, by the members of the Continental Congress. *Gravure (Andreotti Press), perforated 11.*

CM844-47 The Declaration of Independence, *painting by John Trumbull*

CM844		MNHVF	UseVF
13¢	**multicolored** tagged *(208,035,000)*	.25	.20
CM845		MNHVF	UseVF
13¢	**multicolored** tagged	.25	.20
CM846		MNHVF	UseVF
13¢	**multicolored** tagged	.25	.20
CM847		MNHVF	UseVF
13¢	**multicolored** tagged	.25	.20
	Plate block of 16	11.00	
	y. Se-tenant strip of 4 (CM844-47)	1.00	1.00
	FDC *(July 4, 1976)*, any single		2.00
	FDC, strip of 4		8.00

1976. OLYMPIC GAMES ISSUE saluted the 1976 Winter Games in Innsbruck, Austria, and the Summer Games in Montreal, Canada. *Gravure (Andreotti Press), perforated 11.*

CM848 *Diving*

CM849 *Skiing*

CM850 *Running*

CM851 *Skating*

CM848		MNHVF	UseVF
13¢	**multicolored** tagged *(185,715,000)*	.25	.20
CM849		MNHVF	UseVF
13¢	**multicolored** tagged	.25	.20
CM850		MNHVF	UseVF
13¢	**multicolored** tagged	.25	.20
CM851		MNHVF	UseVF
13¢	**multicolored** tagged	.25	.20
	Plate block of 12	6.50	
	y. Se-tenant block of 4 (CM848-51)	1.25	1.50
	FDC *(July 16, 1976)*, any single		2.00
	FDC, block of 4		4.00
	v. Se-tenant block of 4, imperforate	700.00	
	v1. Pair (CM848-49 or CM850-51), imperforate	275.00	

1976. CLARA MAASS ISSUE honored the 100th birthday of the nurse who gave her life during yellow fever research. *Gravure (Andreotti Press), perforated 11.*

CM852 *Nurse Clara Maass and hospital pin*

CM852		MNHVF	UseVF
13¢	**multicolored** tagged *(130,592,000)*	.25	.20
	Plate block of 12	5.75	
	FDC *(Aug. 18, 1976)*		2.00
	v. Horizontal pair, imperforate vertically	500.00	

1976. ADOLPH S. OCHS ISSUE commemorated the 125th anniversary of *The New York Times.* Ochs was the publisher of the *Times* from 1896 until his death in 1935. *Intaglio (Giori Press), perforated 11.*

CM853 Adolph S. Ochs, *from portrait by S.J. Woolf*

CM853

		MNHVF	UseVF
13¢	**gray & black** tagged *(158,332,800)*	.25	.20
	Plate block of 4	1.60	
	FDC *(Sept. 18, 1976)*		1.75

1977. WASHINGTON AT PRINCETON ISSUE commemorated the American victory at Princeton, N.J., over the British led by Lord Cornwallis. *Gravure (Andreotti Press), perforated 11.*

CM854 George Washington *painting by Charles Willson Peale*

CM854

		MNHVF	UseVF
13¢	**multicolored** tagged *(150,328,000)*	.25	.20
	Plate block of 10	3.95	
	FDC *(Jan. 3, 1977)*		1.75
	v. Horizontal pair, imperforate vertically	550.00	

1977. SOUND RECORDING ISSUE paid tribute to a century of progress in the field of sound recording. *Intaglio (Giori Press) and offset, perforated 11.*

CM855 *Early sound recorder*

CM855

		MNHVF	UseVF
13¢	**multicolored** tagged *(176,830,000)*	.25	.20
	Plate block of 4	1.60	
	FDC *(March 23, 1977)*		2.00

American Folk Art Series

1977. PUEBLO INDIAN ART ISSUE first installment in the all se-tenant American Folk Art Series showcased the artistic achievements of the Pueblo Indians in the craft of pottery. *Gravure (Andreotti Press), perforated 11.*

Input from stamp collectors regarding the content of this catalog and ideas to make it more useful is eagerly sought.

Send your comments to:
Minkus Catalog Editor
Krause Publications
700 E. State St.
Iola, WI 54990

CM856 *Zia Pueblo*

CM857 *San Ildefonso Pueblo*

CM858 *Hopi Pueblo*

CM859 *Acoma Pueblo*

CM856

		MNHVF	UseVF
13¢	**multicolored** tagged *(195,976,000)*	.25	.20

CM857

		MNHVF	UseVF
13¢	**multicolored** tagged	.25	.20

CM858

		MNHVF	UseVF
13¢	**multicolored** tagged	.25	.20

CM859

		MNHVF	UseVF
13¢	**multicolored** tagged	.25	.20
	Plate block of 10	4.50	
	y. Se-tenant block or strip of 4 (CM856-59)	.75	
	FDC *(April 13, 1977)*, any single		2.00
	FDC, block of 4		4.00
	v. Se-tenant block or strip of 4, imperforate vertically	2,500.00	

1977. 50TH ANNIVERSARY OF TRANSATLANTIC FLIGHT ISSUE commemorated the epic solo flight of Charles A. Lindbergh across the Atlantic Ocean (see A10). *Gravure (Andreotti Press), perforated 11.*

CM860 The Spirit of St. Louis *over the Atlantic Ocean*

CM860

		MNHVF	UseVF
13¢	**multicolored** tagged *(208,820,000)*	.25	.20
	Plate block of 12	4.75	
	FDC *(May 20, 1977)*		2.50
	v. Pair, imperforate	1,250.00	

Privately applied overprints on this stamp have no official status.

1977. COLORADO STATEHOOD ISSUE celebrated the centennial of Colorado's entry into the union as the 38th state. *Gravure (Andreotti Press), perforated 11.*

CM861 *Columbine and mountain peak*

CM861

		MNHVF	UseVF
13¢	**multicolored** tagged *(190,005,000)*	.25	.20
	Plate block of 12	4.75	
	FDC *(May 21, 1977)*		1.75

v. Horizontal pair, imperforate between	900.00	
v1. Horizontal pair, imperforate vertically	900.00	
v2. Perforated 11 1/4		.35

1977. BUTTERFLY ISSUE commemoratives displayed representatives of different regions of the United States. *Gravure (Andreotti Press), perforated 11.*

CM862 *Swallowtail*

CM863 *Checkerspot*

CM864 *Dogface*

CM865 *Orange-Tip*

CM862		MNHVF	UseVF
13¢	**multicolored** tagged *(219,830,000)*	.25	.20

CM863		MNHVF	UseVF
13¢	**multicolored** tagged	.25	.20

CM864		MNHVF	UseVF
13¢	**multicolored** tagged	.25	.20

CM865		MNHVF	UseVF
13¢	**multicolored** tagged	.25	.20
	Plate block of 12	5.50	
	y. Se-tenant block of 4 (CM1712-1715)	1.00	.80
	FDC *(June 6, 1977)*, any single		2.00
	FDC, block of 4		4.00
	v. Se-tenant block of 4, imperforate horizontally	13,000.00	

1977. LAFAYETTE ISSUE marked the 200th anniversary of Marquis de Lafayette's landing on the coast of South Carolina, north of Charleston. *Intaglio (Giori Press), perforated 11.*

CM866 *Marquis de Lafayette*

CM866		MNHVF	UseVF
13¢	**blue, black & red** *(159,852,000)*	.25	.20
	Plate block of 4	1.60	
	FDC *(June 13, 1977)*		1.75

1977. SKILLED HANDS OF INDEPENDENCE ISSUE saluted representatives of four American industries — blacksmiths, wheelwrights, leatherworkers, and seamstresses — who contributed to winning the Revolutionary War. *Gravure (Andreotti Press), perforated 11.*

CM867 *Seamstress*

CM868 *Blacksmith*

CM869 *Wheelwright*

CM870 *Leatherworker*

CM867		MNHVF	UseVF
13¢	**multicolored** tagged *(188,310,000)*	.25	.20

CM868		MNHVF	UseVF
13¢	**multicolored** tagged	.25	.20

CM869		MNHVF	UseVF
13¢	**multicolored** tagged	.25	.20

CM870		MNHVF	UseVF
13¢	**multicolored**	.25	.20
	Plate block of 12	5.50	
	y. Se-tenant block of 4 (CM1717-1720)	1.00	.80
	FDC *(July 4, 1977)*, any single		2.00
	FDC, block of 4		4.00

1977. PEACE BRIDGE ISSUE marked the 50th anniversary of the Peace Bridge between Buffalo (Fort Porter), N.Y., and Fort Erie, Ontario, Canada. *Intaglio, perforated 11x10 1/2.*

CM871 *Dove over Peace Bridge*

CM871		MNHVF	UseVF
13¢	**blue** tagged *(163,625,000)*	.25	.20
	Plate block of 4	1.60	
	FDC *(Aug. 4, 1977)*		1.75

1977. HERKIMER AT ORISKANY ISSUE honored Gen. Nicholas Herkimer's contribution to the American War for Independence and the 200th anniversary of the Battle of Oriskany. *Gravure (Andreotti Press), perforated 11.*

CM872 *Wounded Gen. Herkimer at Battle of Oriskany*

CM872		MNHVF	UseVF
13¢	**multicolored** tagged *(156,296,000)*	.25	.20
	Plate block of 10	3.95	
	FDC *(Aug. 6, 1977)*		1.75

1977. ALTA CALIFORNIA ISSUE commemorated the bicentennial of the first Spanish civil settlement in Alta (northern) California. *Intaglio (Giori Press) and offset, perforated 11.*

CM873 *Spanish colonial farms*

CM873		MNHVF	UseVF
13¢	**multicolored** tagged *(154,495,000)*	.25	.20
	Plate block of 4	1.60	
	FDC *(Sept. 9, 1977)*		1.75

1977. ARTICLES OF CONFEDERATION ISSUE marked the 200th anniversary of the drafting of the Articles of Confederation in 1777. *Intaglio (Giori Press), perforated 11.*

CM874 *Drafting the Articles of Confederation*

CM874		MNHVF	UseVF
13¢	**red & dark brown** on cream paper, tagged *(168,050,000)*	.25	.20
	Plate block of 4	1.60	

FDC *(Sept. 30, 1977)*		1.75
zo. Tagging omitted		10.00

1977. TALKING PICTURES ISSUE marked 50 years since the introduction of sound in films. *The Jazz Singer,* starring Al Jolson, is accepted as the first feature-length talking picture. *Intaglio (Giori Press) and offset, perforated 11.*

CM875 *Early projector and phonograph*

CM875

	MNHVF	UseVF
13¢ **multicolored** tagged *(156,810,000)*	.25	.20
Plate block of 4	1.60	
FDC *(Oct. 6, 1977)*		2.25

1977. SURRENDER AT SARATOGA marked the surrender of British Gen. John Burgoyne to Gen. Horatio Gates in 1777 (see CM77). *Gravure (Andreotti Press), perforated 11.*

CM876 Surrender of Burgoyne, *painted by John Trumbull*

CM876

	MNHVF	UseVF
13¢ **multicolored** *(153,736,000)*	.25	.20
Plate block of 10	4.00	
FDC *(Oct. 7, 1977)*		1.75

1977. ENERGY ISSUE stressed the importance of conserving energy and developing new sources. *Gravure (Andreotti Press), perforated 11.*

CM876A *"Conservation"*

CM876B *"Development"*

CM876A

	MNHVF	UseVF
13¢ **multicolored** tagged	.25	.20
Plate block of 12	5.00	
FDC *(Oct. 20, 1977)*, either single		1.50
y. Se-tenant pair CM876A & CM876B	.50	.40
FDC, se-tenant pair		3.00

CM876B

	MNHVF	UseVF
13¢ **multicolored** tagged	.25	.20
FDC *(Oct. 20, 1977)*		1.50

1978. CARL SANDBURG ISSUE honored "The Poet of the People" on the 100th anniversary of his birth. He won the Pulitzer Prize three times for his works. *Intaglio (Giori Press), perforated 11.*

CM877 *Carl Sandburg*

CM877

	MNHVF	UseVF
13¢ **brown & black** tagged *(156,560,000)*	.25	.20
Plate block of 4	1.60	
FDC *(Jan. 6, 1978)*		1.75
v. brown omitted	—	

1978. CAPTAIN COOK ISSUE featuring two stamps oriented differently in the same sheet, marked the 200th anniversary of the explorer's arrival in Hawaii and Alaska. *Intaglio (Giori Press), perforated 11.*

CM878 *Capt. James Cook*

CM879 *Cook's ships* Resolution and Discovery

CM878

	MNHVF	UseVF
13¢ **blue** tagged *(202,155,000)*	.25	.20
FDC *(Jan. 20, 1978)*		1.75

CM879

	MNHVF	UseVF
13¢ **green** tagged	.25	.20
Plate block of 4, CM878 & CM879	1.60	
Plate block of 20, 10 each CM878-79	5.25	
y. Se-tenant pair (CM878-79)	.50	
FDC *(Jan. 20, 1978)*, either single		1.75
FDC, se-tenant pair		2.00
v. Se-tenant pair, imperforate between	4,250.00	
v1. Vertical pair (CM879), imperforate horizontally	—	

Black Heritage Series

1978. HARRIET TUBMAN ISSUE First stamp in the long-running Black Heritage Series honored the woman known as the "Moses of her people" (c1820-1913). Born into slavery, she is credited with helping more than 300 slaves to escape via the "Underground Railway." (See also CM1731.) *Gravure (Andreotti Press), perforated 10 1/2x11.*

CM880 *Harriet Tubman*

CM880

	MNHVF	UseVF
13¢ **multicolored** tagged *(156,525,000)*	.25	.20
Plate block of 12	6.50	
FDC *(Feb. 1, 1978)*		2.50

1978. AMERICAN QUILTS ISSUE The second se-tenant set in the American Folk Art Series showed four different basket— design quilt patterns. *Gravure (Andreotti Press), perforated 11.*

CM881-884 *Basket design by Christopher Pullman after 1875 quilt made in New York City*

CM881		MNHVF	UseVF
13¢	multicolored tagged (165,182,000)	.25	.20

CM882		MNHVF	UseVF
13¢	multicolored tagged	.25	.20

CM883		MNHVF	UseVF
13¢	multicolored tagged	.25	.20

CM884		MNHVF	UseVF
13¢	multicolored tagged	.25	.20
	Plate block of 12	5.50	
	y. Se-tenant block of 4 (CM881-84)	1.00	.95
	FDC (May 8, 1978), any single		2.00
	FDC, block of 4		4.00

1978. AMERICAN DANCE ISSUE celebrated various styles of popular dancing. *Gravure (Andreotti Press), perforated 11.*

CM885 *Ballet*

CM886 *Theater*

CM887 *Folk*

CM888 *Modern*

CM885		MNHVF	UseVF
13¢	multicolored tagged (157,598,400)	.25	.20

CM886		MNHVF	UseVF
13¢	multicolored tagged	.25	.20

CM887		MNHVF	UseVF
13¢	multicolored tagged	.25	.20

CM888		MNHVF	UseVF
13¢	multicolored tagged	.25	.20
	Plate block of 12	5.50	
	y. Se-tenant block of 4 (CM885-88)	1.50	.95
	FDC (April 26, 1978), any single		2.00
	FDC, block of 4		4.00

1978. FRENCH ALLIANCE ISSUE marked the 200th anniversary of the signing of the French Alliance in 1778. *Intaglio (Giori Press) and offset, perforated 11.*

CM889 *King Louis XVI and Benjamin Franklin. Porcelain statuette by Charles Gabriel Sauvage*

CM889		MNHVF	UseVF
13¢	blue, black & red tagged (102,856,000)	.25	.20
	Plate block of 4	1.60	
	FDC (May 4, 1978)		1.75

1978. GEORGE PAPANICOLAOU ISSUE commemorated the noted cancer researcher for his development of an early cancer detection procedure, the use of which has saved the lives of thousands of women. *Intaglio, perforated 10 1/2x11.*

CM890 *Dr. Papanicolaou and microsope*

CM890		MNHVF	UseVF
13¢	brown tagged (152,270,000)	.25	.20
	Plate block of 4	2.10	
	FDC (May 13, 1978)		1.75

Performing Arts Series

1978. JIMMIE RODGERS ISSUE The first stamp in the Performing Arts Series commemorated the country and western singer known as the "Singing Brakeman" and the "Father of Country Music." Rodgers was the first person inducted into the Country Music Hall of Fame in 1967. *Gravure (Andreotti Press), perforated 11.*

CM891 *Jimmie Rodgers*

CM891		MNHVF	UseVF
13¢	multicolored tagged (94,600,000)	.25	.20
	Plate block of 12	5.00	
	FDC (May 24, 1978)		1.75

1978. CANADIAN INTERNATIONAL PHILATELIC EXHIBITION Souvenir Sheet commemorated the 1978 CAPEX stamp show in Toronto, Canada. The souvenir sheet contains eight perforated stamps depicting animals and birds indigenous to the United States and Canada. *Intaglio (Giori Press) and offset, perforated 11.*

CM892 *CAPEX souvenir sheet*

CM892

$1.04		MNHVF	UseVF
	multicolored *(10,400,000)*	2.75	2.00
	Souvenir sheet w/plate number attached	3.25	2.25
	a. 13¢ Cardinal, tagged	.25	.20
	b. 13¢ Mallard, tagged	.25	.20
	c. 13¢ Canada Goose, tagged	.25	.20
	d. 13¢ Blue Jay, tagged	.25	.20
	e. 13¢ Moose, tagged	.25	.20
	f. 13¢ Chipmunk, tagged	.25	.20
	g. 13¢ Red Fox, tagged	.25	.20
	h. 13¢ Raccoon, tagged	.25	.20
	y. Se-tenant block of 8 (CM892 a-h)	3.00	
	FDC *(June 6, 1978),* souvenir sheet		3.50
	FDC, any single		2.00
	v. Yellow, green, red, brown, blue & offset black omitted	7,000.00	
	v1. Strip of 4 (a-d), imperforate vertically	7,500.00	
	v2. Strip of 4 (e-h), imperforate vertically	6,500.00	

1978. PHOTOGRAPHY ISSUE celebrated the colorful, popular art form. *Gravure (Andreotti Press), perforated 11.*

CM893 *Camera, filters and photo equipment*

CM893

15¢		MNHVF	UseVF
	multicolored tagged *(161,228,000)*	.30	.20
	Plate block of 12	5.75	
	FDC *(June 26, 1978)*		1.75

1978. GEORGE M. COHAN ISSUE The second stamp in the Performing Arts Series marked the 100th birthday of George M. Cohan, a patriotic and world-renowned actor, popular songwriter, playwright and producer. *Gravure (Andreotti Press), perforated 11.*

CM894 *George M. Cohan*

CM894

15¢		MNHVF	UseVF
	multicolored tagged *(151,570,000)*	.30	.20

Plate block of 12	5.75	
FDC *(July 3, 1978)*		1.75

1978. VIKING MISSIONS ISSUE commemorated the historic Viking space voyages; issued on the second anniversary of the landing of *Viking 1* on Mars. *Intaglio (Giori Press) and offset, perforated 11.*

CM895 Viking I *lander and Mars*

CM895

15¢		MNHVF	UseVF
	multicolored tagged *(158,880,000)*	.30	.20
	Plate block of 4	2.25	
	FDC *(July 20, 1978)*		1.75

1978. WILDLIFE CONSERVATION ISSUE featured four species of owls native to the United States. *Intaglio (Giori Press) and offset, perforated 11.*

CM896 *Great Gray Owl*

CM897 *Saw-whet Owl*

CM898 *Barred Owl*

CM899 *Great Horned Owl*

CM896

15¢		MNHVF	UseVF
	Great Gray Owl, tagged *(186,550,000)*	.30	.20

CM897

15¢		MNHVF	UseVF
	Saw-whet Owl, tagged	.30	.20

CM898

15¢		MNHVF	UseVF
	Barred Owl, tagged	.30	.20

CM899

15¢		MNHVF	UseVF
	Great Horned Owl, tagged	.30	.20
	Plate block of 4	2.00	
	y. Se-tenant block of 4 (CM896-99)	1.50	1.00
	FDC *(Aug. 26, 1978),* any single		2.00
	FDC, block of 4		4.00

1978. AMERICAN TREES ISSUE highlighted four different trees native to the United States and reflected a variety in both appearance and geographic location. *Gravure, perforated 11.*

CM900 *Giant Sequoia*

CM901 *Eastern White Pine*

CM902 *White Oak*

CM903 *Gray Birch*

CM900

15¢		MNHVF	UseVF
	Giant Sequoia, tagged *(168,136,000)*	.30	.20

CM901		MNHVF	UseVF
15¢	**Eastern White Pine,** tagged	.30	.20
CM902		MNHVF	UseVF
15¢	**White Oak,** tagged	.30	.20
CM903		MNHVF	UseVF
15¢	**Gray Birch,** tagged	.30	.20
	Plate block of 12	6.00	
	y. Se-tenant block of 4 (CM900-03)	1.25	1.00
	FDC *(Oct. 9, 1978),* any single		2.00
	FDC, block of 4		4.00
	vy. Se-tenant block of 4, imperforate horizontally	12,250.00	

1979. ROBERT F. KENNEDY ISSUE honored the assassinated U.S. senator and presidential hopeful. *Intaglio, perforated 11.*

CM904 *Robert F. Kennedy*

CM904		MNHVF	UseVF
15¢	**blue** tagged *(159,297,000)*	.30	.20
	Plate block of 4	1.80	
	FDC *(Jan. 12, 1979)*		2.00
	zo. Tagging omitted	—	

1979. MARTIN LUTHER KING JR. ISSUE in the Black Heritage Series, honored the civil rights leader and his role in the struggle for racial equality. *Gravure (Andreotti Press), perforated 11.*

CM905 *Martin Luther King Jr.*

CM905		MNHVF	UseVF
15¢	**multicolored** tagged *(166,435,000)*	.30	.20
	Plate block of 12	6.25	
	FDC *(Jan. 13, 1979)*		2.50
	v. Imperforate pair	1,750.00	

1979. INTERNATIONAL YEAR OF THE CHILD ISSUE acknowledged the declaration by the U.N. General Assembly of 1979 as a year of concern for the condition and well-being of the children of the world. *Intaglio, perforated 11.*

CM906 *Portraits of four children*

CM906		MNHVF	UseVF
15¢	**light & dark brown** tagged *(162,535,000)*	.30	.20
	Plate block of 4	1.80	
	FDC *(Feb. 15, 1979)*		1.75

Literary Arts Series

1979. JOHN STEINBECK ISSUE The first release in the Literary Arts Series honored the prolific novelist (1902-68) of *The Grapes of Wrath* and *Travels With Charley* who won the Pulitzer Prize in 1940 and the Nobel Prize for Literature in 1962. *Intaglio, perforated 10 1/2x11.*

CM907 *John Steinbeck, from photograph by Philippe Halsman*

CM907		MNHVF	UseVF
15¢	**dark blue** tagged *(155,000,000)*	.30	.20
	Plate block of 4	1.80	
	FDC *(Feb. 27, 1979)*		1.75

1979. ALBERT EINSTEIN ISSUE honored the physicist, philosopher and humanitarian best known as the creator of the special and general theories of relativity. *Intaglio, perforated 10 1/2x11.*

CM908 *Albert Einstein, from photograph by Hermann Landshoff*

CM908		MNHVF	UseVF
15¢	**brown** tagged *(157,310,000)*	.30	.20
	Plate block of 4	1.80	
	Gutter pair, vertical	—	
	FDC *(March 4, 1979)*		1.75

1979. PENNSYLVANIA TOLEWARE ISSUE The third se-tenant installment in the American Folk Art Series depicted four examples of Pennsylvania Toleware, work known for its colorful design motifs. *Gravure (Andreotti Press), perforated 11, multicolored.*

CM909 *Coffee pot with straight spout*

CM910 *Tea caddy*

CM911 *Sugar bowl with lid*

CM912 *Coffee pot with gooseneck spout*

CM909		MNHVF	UseVF
15¢	**Coffee pot with straight spout** *(174,096,000)*	.30	.20
CM910		MNHVF	UseVF
15¢	**Tea caddy**	.30	.20
CM911		MNHVF	UseVF
15¢	**Sugar bowl with lid**	.30	.20
CM912		MNHVF	UseVF
15¢	**Coffee pot with gooseneck spout**	.30	.20
	Plate block of 12	5.00	
	y. Se-tenant block of 4 (CM909-12)	1.50	1.00
	FDC *(April 19, 1979),* any single		2.00
	FDC, block of 4		4.00
	vy. Se-tenant block of 4, imperforate horizontally	4,250.00	

1979. AMERICAN ARCHITECTURE ISSUE The first of four se-tenant quartets on this subject, designed by Walter D. Richards, commemorated successful early American architecture of enduring beauty, strength, and usefulness. *Intaglio (Giori Press), perforated 11, multicolored.*

CM913 *Virginia Rotunda, designed by Thomas Jefferson*

CM914 *Baltimore Cathedral, designed by Benjamin Latrobe*

CM915 *Boston State House, designed by Charles Bulfinch*

CM916 *Philadelphia Exchange, designed by William Strickland*

CM913		MNHVF	UseVF
15¢	**University of Virginia Rotunda,** tagged	.30	.20
	(164,793,000)		

CM914		MNHVF	UseVF
15¢	**Baltimore Cathedral,** tagged	.30	.20

CM915		MNHVF	UseVF
15¢	**Boston State House,** tagged	.30	.20

CM916		MNHVF	UseVF
15¢	**Philadelphia Exchange,** tagged	.30	.20
	Plate block of 4	2.50	
	y. Se-tenant block of 4 (CM913-16)	1.50	1.00
	FDC *(June 4, 1979),* any single		2.00
	FDC, block of 4		4.00

1979. ENDANGERED FLORA ISSUE portrayed four of the more than 1,700 plant species in the United States seriously threatened with extinction. *Gravure (Andreotti Press), perforated 11, multicolored.*

CM917 *Persistent Trillium*

CM918 *Hawaiian Wild Broadbean*

CM919 *Contra Costa Wallflower*

CM920 *Antioch Dunes Evening Primrose*

CM917		MNHVF	UseVF
15¢	**Persistent Trillium,** tagged	.30	.20
	(163,055,000)		

CM918		MNHVF	UseVF
15¢	**Hawaiian Wild Broadbean,** tagged	.30	.20

CM919		MNHVF	UseVF
15¢	**Contra Costa Wallflower,** tagged	.30	.20

CM920		MNHVF	UseVF
15¢	**Antioch Dunes Evening Primrose,** tagged	.30	.20
	Plate block of 12	6.50	
	FDC *(June 7, 1979),* any single		2.00
	FDC, block of 4		4.00
	Horizontal gutter block of 4	—	
	y. Se-tenant block of 4 (CM917-20)	2.00	1.00
	vy. Imperforate se-tenant block of 4	600.00	

1979. SEEING EYE DOG ISSUE commemorated the 50th anniversary of the first guide dog program in the United States, founded by Dorothy Harrison. *Gravure (Combination Press), perforated 11.*

CM921 *German shepherd leading man*

CM921		MNHVF	UseVF
15¢	**multicolored** tagged *(161,860,000)*	.30	.20
	Plate block of 20	9.00	
	FDC *(June 15, 1979)*		1.75
	v. Imperforate pair	425.00	
	zo. Tagging omitted	6.00	

1979. SPECIAL OLYMPICS ISSUE honored the international program of sports training, physical fitness, and athletic competition for mentally and physically impaired children and adults. *Gravure (Andreotti Press), perforated 11.*

CM922 *Child with Special Olympics medal*

CM922		MNHVF	UseVF
15¢	**multicolored** tagged *(165,775,000)*	.30	.20
	Plate block of 10	4.50	
	FDC *(Aug. 9, 1979)*		1.75

1979. SUMMER GAMES ISSUE *Gravure, perforated 11, multicolored.*

CM923 *Decathlete throwing javelin*

CM923		MNHVF	UseVF
10¢	**multicolored** tagged *(67,195,000)*	.25	.25
	Plate block of 12	4.50	
	FDC *(Sept. 5, 1979)*		1.75

1979. JOHN PAUL JONES ISSUE honored the naval hero (1747-92) of the American Revolution on the 200th anniversary of his victory over the British in the 1779 battle between *Bonhomme Richard* and *HMS Serapis.* This stamp was the first to be printed privately under terms of a contract awarded by the U.S. Postal Service in 1978. *Gravure by J.W. Fergusson and Sons, Richmond, Va., with perforating, cutting, and final processing by American Bank Note Co., New York, N.Y. Perforated 11x12.*

CM924, 924A, 924B *John Paul Jones, based on portrait by Charles Willson Peale in Independence National Historical Park, Philadelphia, Pa.*

CM924		MNHVF	UseVF
15¢	**multicolored** tagged *(160,000,000, all perforation types)*	.30	.20
	Plate block of 10	3.50	
	FDC *(Sept. 23, 1979)*		2.00
	v. Vertical pair, imperforate horizontally	175.00	

Imperforate errors are from printer's waste.

CM924A		MNHVF	UseVF
15¢	**multicolored** tagged, perforated 11	.65	.25
	Plate block of 10	7.50	
	FDC *(Sept. 23, 1979)*		2.00
	v. Vertical pair, imperforate horizontally	140.00	

CM924B		MNHVF	UseVF
15¢	**multicolored** tagged, perforated 12	2,800.00	1,000.00
	Plate block of 10	28,000.00	

1979. SUMMER GAMES ISSUE *Gravure, perforated 11, multicolored.*

CM925 *Women runners*

CM926 *Women swimmers*

CM927 *Pair of rowers*

CM928 *Horse and rider*

CM925		MNHVF	UseVF
15¢	**Women runners,** tagged *(186,905,000)*	.25	.20
CM926		MNHVF	UseVF
15¢	**Women swimmers,** tagged	.25	.20
CM927		MNHVF	UseVF
15¢	**Pair of rowers,** tagged	.25	.20
CM928		MNHVF	UseVF
15¢	**Horse & Rider,** tagged	.25	.20
	Plate block of 12	6.50	
	y. Se-tenant block of 4 (CM925-28)	1.50	1.10
	FDC *(Sept. 28, 1979),* any single		2.00
	FDC, block of 4		4.00
	vy. Se-tenant block of 4, imperforate	1,500.00	
	v1. Vertical pair, imperforate (either)	650.00	

1979. WILL ROGERS ISSUE in the Performing Arts Series, honored the American humorist on the 100th anniversary of his birth. (See also CM317.) *Gravure (Andreotti Press), perforated 11.*

CM929 *Will Rogers*

CM929		MNHVF	UseVF
15¢	**multicolored** tagged *(161,290,000)*	.30	.20
	Plate block of 12	6.00	

DECODING THE CATALOG

The 15¢ United States John Paul Jones issue of 1979 exists in three major types.

Printing for the American Bank Note Co. on a four-color gravure press owned by J.W. Fergusson and Sons of Richmond, Va., produced no significant printing differences on the Jones stamp. Processing by ABNC in New York City was quite another matter.

When the stamps were first processed on a line perforator, perforations on all four sides gauged 12. These stamps are cataloged as Minkus CM924B.

Shortly after production began, the perforation wheels that perforated the stamps horizontally were replaced with perf 11 wheels. The resulting stamps measured perf 11 by 12. The stamps created by this switch are Minkus CM924.

Some time later, the vertical perforations were changed as well, making the remainder of the stamps measure perf 11 all around. These stamps are Minkus CM924A.

Ironically, the rarest of the three stamp types is not a variety, but the originally intended version. Both inexpensive types are varieties. The catalog lists an inexpensive variety as the primary issue, partly so collectors won't feel compelled to acquire the rare type simply because it is the major listing. Both the perf 11 and perf 11 by 12 stamps are fairly common. However, only a few mint panes and a handful of used singles of the perf 12 type were located.

	FDC *(Nov. 4, 1979)*		1.75
	v. Imperforate pair	200.00	

1979. VIETNAM VETERANS ISSUE paid tribute to the veterans of the war in Southeast Asia. *Gravure (Andreotti Press), perforated 11.*

CM930 *Vietnam Service ribbon*

CM930		MNHVF	UseVF
15¢	**multicolored** tagged *(172,740,000)*	.30	.20
	Plate block of 10	5.95	
	FDC *(Nov. 11, 1979)*		2.50

1980. W.C. FIELDS ISSUE in the Performing Arts Series honored the juggler, actor, and comedian on the 100th anniversary of his birth. *Gravure, perforated 11.*

CM931 *W.C. Fields*

CM931		MNHVF	UseVF
15¢	**multicolored** tagged *(168,995,000)*	.30	.20
	Plate block of 12	6.00	

FDC *(Jan. 29, 1980)*
v. Pair, imperforate   —   2.50

1980. WINTER GAMES ISSUE included four commemoratives for events from the Winter Games, and honored the 13th Winter Games at Lake Placid, N.Y. *Gravure, perforated 11x10 1/2, multicolored.*

CM932, CM935A
Speed skater

CM933, CM935B
Ski jumper

CM934, CM935C
Downhill skier

CM935, CM935D
Hockey goaltender

CM932		MNHVF	UseVF
15¢	**Speed skater,** tagged *(208,295,000)*	.30	.20
	(both perforation types)		

CM933		MNHVF	UseVF
15¢	**Ski jumper,** tagged	.30	.20

CM934		MNHVF	UseVF
15¢	**Downhill skier,** tagged	.30	.20

CM935		MNHVF	UseVF
15¢	**Hockey goaltender,** tagged	.30	.20
	Plate block of 12	6.50	
	y. Se-tenant block of 4 (CM932-35)	1.50	1.10
	FDC *(Feb. 1, 1980),* any single		2.00
	FDC, block of 4		4.00

1980. WINTER GAMES ISSUE *perforated 11.*

CM935A		MNHVF	UseVF
15¢	**Speed Skater,** tagged	.80	.75

CM935B		MNHVF	UseVF
15¢	**Ski jumper,** tagged	.80	.75

CM935C		MNHVF	UseVF
15¢	**Downhill skier,** tagged	.80	.75

CM935D		MNHVF	UseVF
15¢	**Hockey goaltender,** tagged	.80	.75
	Plate block of 12	14.00	
	y. Se-tenant block of 4 (CM935A-935D)	4.00	4.00

1980. BENJAMIN BANNEKER ISSUE in the Black Heritage Series honored a pioneer American scientist and mathematician. Born free in 1731, he became both a noted astronomer and surveyor. *Gravure by J.W. Fergusson and Sons for American Bank Note Co., perforated 11.*

CM936 *Benjamin Banneker*

CM936		MNHVF	UseVF
15¢	**multicolored** tagged *(160,000,000)*	.30	.20
	Plate block of 12	5.50	
	FDC *(Feb. 15, 1980)*		2.50
	v. Horizontal pair, imperforate vertically	750.00	
	v1. Imperforate pair	50.00	

Imperforates with misregistered colors are from printer's waste, have been fraudulently perforated to simulate CM936v. Genuine examples of this error have colors correctly registered. Expert certification recommended.

1980. NATIONAL LETTER WRITING ISSUE focused attention on the importance of letter writing. Three sets of vertical pairs. *Gravure, perforated 11, multicolored.*

CM937-38 *"Letters Preserve Memories"* and *"P.S. Write Soon"*

CM939-40 *"Letters Lift Spirits"* and *"P.S. Write Soon"*

CM41-42 *"Letters Shape Opinions"* and *"P.S. Write Soon"*

CM937		MNHVF	UseVF
15¢	**"Letters Preserve Memories"**	.30	.20
	(232,134,000)		

CM938		MNHVF	UseVF
15¢	**"Write Soon," (purple),** tagged	.30	.20

CM939		MNHVF	UseVF
15¢	**"Letters Lift Spirits,"** tagged	.30	.20

CM940		MNHVF	UseVF
15¢	**"Write Soon," (green),** tagged	.30	.20

CM941		MNHVF	UseVF
15¢	**"Letters Shape Opinions,"** tagged	.30	.20

CM942		MNHVF	UseVF
15¢	**"Write Soon," (red),** tagged	.30	.20
	Plate block of 36	19.50	
	y. Se-tenant vertical strip of 6 (CM937-42)	2.00	
	FDC *(Feb. 25, 1980),* any single		1.75
	FDC, strip of 6		4.00

1980. FRANCES PERKINS ISSUE honored the first woman to serve as a member of a U.S. presidential cabinet. Perkins (1882-1965), a social reformer, was Franklin Roosevelt's Secretary of Labor. *Intaglio, perforated 10 1/2x11.*

CM943 *Frances Perkins*

CM943		MNHVF	UseVF
15¢	**blue** tagged *(163,510,000)*	.30	.20
	Plate block of 4	1.95	
	FDC *(April 10, 1980)*		1.75

1980. EMILY BISSELL ISSUE celebrated the crusader against tuberculosis who introduced Christmas seals to the United States. *Intaglio, perforated 11.*

CM944 *Emily Bissell*

CM944		MNHVF	UseVF
15¢	**black & red** tagged *(95,695,000)*	.30	.20
	Plate block of 4	1.80	
	FDC *(May 31, 1980)*		1.75
	v. Vertical pair, imperforate horizontally	375.00	

1980. HELEN KELLER AND ANNE SULLIVAN ISSUE
commemorated blind, deaf author and lecturer Helen Keller (1880-1968) and her teacher, Anne Sullivan, her constant companion for almost 50 years. *Offset and intaglio, perforated 11.*

CM945 *Helen Keller and Anne Sullivan*

CM945

		MNHVF	UseVF
15¢	**multicolored** tagged *(153,975,000)*	.30	.20
	Plate block of 4	1.80	
	FDC *(June 27, 1980)*		2.00

1980. VETERANS ADMINISTRATION ISSUE marked the 50th anniversary of the Veterans Administration. *Gravure by J.W. Fergusson and Sons for American Bank Note Co., perforated 11.*

CM946 *Veterans Administration emblem*

CM946

		MNHVF	UseVF
15¢	**red & dark blue** tagged *(160,000,000)*	.30	.20
	Plate block of 4	1.80	
	FDC *(July 21, 1980)*		2.00
	v. Horizontal pair, imperforate vertically	475.00	

1980. BERNARDO DE GALVEZ ISSUE honored the governor of Spanish Louisiana during the American Revolution, a major contributor to the winning of the war. *Intaglio and offset, perforated 11.*

CM947 *Bernardo de Galvez from statue in Spanish Plaza, Mobile, Ala.*

CM947

		MNHVF	UseVF
15¢	**multicolored** tagged *(103,850,000)*	.30	.20
	Plate block of 4	1.80	
	FDC *(July 23, 1980)*		1.75
	v. blue, brown, red & yellow omitted	1,350.00	
	v1. red, brown & blue omitted	750.00	

1980. CORAL REEFS ISSUE showcased corals found in the waters of the United States, its territories and possessions. *Gravure, perforated 11, multicolored.*

CM948 *Brain Coral: U.S. Virgin Islands*

CM949 *Elkhorn Coral: Florida*

CM950 *Chalice Coral: American Samoa*

CM951 *Finger Coral: Hawaii*

CM948

		MNHVF	UseVF
15¢	**Brain Coral,** tagged *(204,715,000)*	.30	.20

CM949

		MNHVF	UseVF
15¢	**Elkhorn Coral,** tagged	.30	.20

CM950

		MNHVF	UseVF
15¢	**Chalice Coral,** tagged	.30	.20

CM951

		MNHVF	UseVF
15¢	**Finger Coral,** tagged	.30	.20
	Plate block of 12	6.00	
	y. Se-tenant block of 4 (CM948-51)	1.50	
	FDC *(Aug. 26, 1980)*, any single		2.00
	FDC, block of 4		4.00
	vy. Se-tenant block of 4, imperforate	1,200.00	
	v1y. Se-tenant block of 4, imperforate between vertically	3,750.00	
	v2y. Se-tenant block of 4, imperforate vertically	3,000.00	

1980. ORGANIZED LABOR ISSUE honored the American labor movement, an integral part of the history of democracy and freedom in the United States. *Gravure, perforated 11.*

CM952 *Bald eagle*

CM952

		MNHVF	UseVF
15¢	**multicolored** tagged *(166,545,000)*	.30	.20
	Plate block of 12	5.50	
	FDC *(Sept. 1, 1980)*		1.75
	v. Imperforate pair	375.00	

1980. EDITH WHARTON ISSUE 2nd in the Literary Arts Series honored the Pulitzer Prize-winning author (1862-1937) of *The Age of Innocence* and other novels, as well as short stories and poetry. *Intaglio, perforated 10 1/2x11.*

CM953 *Edith Wharton*

CM953

		MNHVF	UseVF
15¢	**purple** tagged *(163,310,000)*	.30	.20
	Plate block of 4	2.00	
	FDC *(Sept. 5, 1980)*		1.75

1980. EDUCATION IN AMERICA ISSUE commemorated American education and called attention to the newly established U.S. Education Department. *Gravure by J.W. Fergusson and Sons for the American Bank Note Co., perforated 11.*

CM954 Homage to the Square: Glow, *acrylic printing by Josef Albers*

CM954

		MNHVF	UseVF
15¢	**multicolored** tagged *(160,000,000)*	.30	.20
	Plate block of 6	3.50	
	FDC *(Sept. 12, 1980)*		2.00
	v. Vertical pair, imperforate vertically	225.00	

1980. PACIFIC NORTHWEST MASKS ISSUE the fourth set in the American Folk Art Series, featured four carved masks representing the craftsmanship of tribes in the Pacific Northwest coastal region. *Gravure, perforated 11.*

CM955 *Heiltsuk Bella Bella mask*

CM956 *Chilkat Tlingit mask*

CM957 *Tlingit mask*

CM958 *Bella Coola mask*

CM955

		MNHVF	UseVF
15¢	**Heiltsuk Bella Bella mask,** tagged *(152,404,000)*	.30	.20

CM956

		MNHVF	UseVF
15¢	**Chilkat Tlingit mask,** tagged	.30	.20

CM957

		MNHVF	UseVF
15¢	**Tlingit mask,** tagged	.30	.20

CM958

		MNHVF	UseVF
15¢	**Bella Coola mask,** tagged	.30	.20
	Plate block of 10	7.00	

y. Se-tenant block of 4 (CM955-58)	2.25	1.50	
FDC *(Sept. 24, 1980),* any single		2.00	
FDC, block of 4		4.00	

1980. AMERICAN ARCHITECTURE ISSUE Second of four se-tenant quartets, represented 19th-century architecture of enduring beauty, strength, and usefulness. *Intaglio (Giori Press), perforated 11.*

CM959 *Smithsonian Institution in Washington, D.C., designed by James Renwick;* CM960 *Trinity Church in Boston, designed by Henry Hobson Richardson;* CM961 *Pennsylvania Academy of the Fine Arts in Philadelphia, designed by Frank Furness;* CM962 *Lyndhurst at Tarrytown, New York, designed by Alexander Jackson Davis*

CM959

		MNHVF	UseVF
15¢	**Smithsonian Institution,** tagged *(152,720,000)*	.30	.20

CM960

		MNHVF	UseVF
15¢	**Trinity Church,** tagged	.30	.20

CM961

		MNHVF	UseVF
15¢	**Pennsylvania Academy of the Fine Arts,** tagged	.30	.20

CM962

		MNHVF	UseVF
15¢	**Lyndhurst,** tagged	.30	.20
	Plate block of 4	2.50	
	y. Se-tenant block of 4 (CM959-62)	2.25	1.50
	FDC *(Oct. 9, 1980),* any single		2.00
	FDC, block of 4		4.00

1981. EVERETT DIRKSEN ISSUE commemorated a public servant (1896-1969) first elected from Illinois to the U.S. House of Representatives in 1932, then in 1950 to the U.S. Senate, where he served until his death. Dirksen was noted for his oratory and attention to legislative detail. *Intaglio, perforated 11.*

CM963 *Everett Dirksen*

CM963

		MNHVF	UseVF
15¢	**gray** tagged *(160,155,000)*	.30	.20
	Plate block of 4	2.50	
	FDC *(Jan. 4, 1981)*		1.75

1981. WHITNEY MOORE YOUNG ISSUE Part of the Black Heritage Series. Honored the civil rights leader who was executive director of the National Urban League at his death. Young was an author, former dean of the Atlanta School of Social Work, and a recipient of the Medal of Freedom. *Gravure, perforated 11.*

CM964 *Whitney M. Young*

CM964		MNHVF	UseVF
15¢	**multicolored** tagged *(159,505,000)*	.30	.20
	Plate block of 4	1.80	
	FDC *(Jan. 30, 1981)*		2.50

1981. FLOWER ISSUE featured the designs of four flowers cultivated in the United States, reproduced from original paintings by Lowell Nesbitt in se-tenant form. *Gravure, perforated 11, multicolored.*

CM965 *Rose*

CM966 *Camellia*

CM967 *Dahlia*

CM968 *Lily*

CM965		MNHVF	UseVF
18¢	**Rose,** tagged *(210,633,000)*	.30	.20
CM966		MNHVF	UseVF
18¢	**Camellia,** tagged	.30	.20
CM967		MNHVF	UseVF
18¢	**Dahlia,** tagged	.30	.20
CM968		MNHVF	UseVF
18¢	**Lily,** tagged	.30	.20
	Plate block of 4	2.60	
	y. Se-tenant block of 4 (CM965-68)	2.00	1.50
	FDC *(April 23, 1981),* any single		2.00
	FDC, block of 4		4.00

1981. AMERICAN RED CROSS ISSUE marked the centennial of the organization and honored the thousands of Red Cross volunteers who have given freely of their time to help people throughout the country. *Gravure, perforated 10 1/2x11.*

CM969 *Nurse and baby*

CM969		MNHVF	UseVF
18¢	**multicolored** tagged *(165,175,000)*	.30	.20
	Plate block of 4	2.80	
	FDC *(May 1, 1981)*		2.00

1981. SAVINGS AND LOANS ISSUE marked the sesquicentennial of the first savings and loans organization in the United States and emphasized the importance of thrift and home ownership. *Gravure, perforated 11.*

CM970 *Savings and loans building coin bank*

CM970		MNHVF	UseVF
18¢	**multicolored** tagged *(107,240,000)*	.30	.20
	Plate block of 4	2.50	
	FDC *(May 8, 1981)*		1.75

1981. SPACE ACHIEVEMENT ISSUE saluted the U.S. accomplishments and technology in space research. *Gravure, perforated 11, multicolored.*

CM971 *Astronaut on moon*; CM972 *Pioneer II and Saturn*; CM973 *Skylab and sun*; CM974 *Hubble Space Telescope*; CM975 *Space shuttle in orbit*; CM976 *Space shuttle with arm deployed*; CM977 *Space shuttle at launch*; CM978 *Space shuttle prior to landing*

CM971		MNHVF	UseVF
18¢	**Astronaut on moon,** tagged *(337,819,000)*	.30	.20
CM972		MNHVF	UseVF
18¢	**Pioneer II & Saturn,** tagged	.30	.20
CM973		MNHVF	UseVF
18¢	**Skylab & sun,** tagged	.30	.20
CM974		MNHVF	UseVF
18¢	**Hubble Space Telescope,** tagged	.30	.20
CM975		MNHVF	UseVF
18¢	**Space shuttle in orbit,** tagged	.30	.20
CM976		MNHVF	UseVF
18¢	**Space shuttle with arm deployed,** tagged	.30	.20
CM977		MNHVF	UseVF
18¢	**Space shuttle at launch,** tagged	.30	.20
CM978		MNHVF	UseVF
18¢	**Space shuttle at landing,** tagged	.30	.20
	Plate block of 8	6.00	
	y. Se-tenant block of 8 (CM971-78)	5.00	4.00
	FDC *(May 5, 1981),* any single		2.00
	FDC, block of 8		6.00
	vy. Se-tenant block of 8, imperforate	9,500.00	

1981. PROFESSIONAL MANAGEMENT ISSUE marked the 100th anniversary of professional management education in the United States, and honored Joseph Wharton, founder of the Wharton School of Business. *Gravure, perforated 11.*

CM979 *Joseph Wharton*

CM979

		MNHVF	UseVF
18¢	blue & black tagged *(99,420,000)*	.30	.20
	Plate block of 4	2.40	
	FDC *(June 18, 1981)*		1.75

1981. SAVE WILDLIFE HABITATS ISSUE focused on the necessity for the preservation of the natural environment of our native birds and mammals. *Gravure, perforated 11, multicolored.*

CM980 *Blue heron*

CM981 *Badger*

CM982 *Grizzly bear*

CM983 *Ruffed grouse*

CM980

		MNHVF	UseVF
18¢	Blue heron, tagged *(178,930,000)*	.30	.20

CM981

		MNHVF	UseVF
18¢	Badger, tagged	.30	.20

CM982

		MNHVF	UseVF
18¢	Grizzly bear, tagged	.30	.20

CM983

		MNHVF	UseVF
18¢	Ruffed grouse, tagged	.30	.20
	Plate block of 4	2.50	
	y. Se-tenant block of 4 (CM980-83)	2.25	1.50
	FDC *(June 26, 1981),* any single		2.00
	FDC, block of 4		4.00

1981. DISABLED PERSONS ISSUE hailed the U.N.'s International Year of Disabled Persons, and the worldwide effort to promote education, prevention of impairments, and rehabilitation. *Gravure, perforated 11.*

CM984 *Disabled man using microscope*

CM984

		MNHVF	UseVF
18¢	multicolored tagged *(100,265,000)*	.30	.20
	Plate block of 4	2.40	
	FDC *(June 29, 1981)*		1.75
	v. Vertical pair, imperforate horizontally	2,750.00	

1981. EDNA ST. VINCENT MILLAY ISSUE Third in the Literary Arts Series honored the poet and author who received, among other awards, the Pulitzer Prize for Poetry in 1923. *Offset and intaglio, perforated 11.*

CM985 *Edna St. Vincent Millay, from miniature painting by Glenora Case Richards*

CM985

		MNHVF	UseVF
18¢	multicolored tagged *(99,615,000)*	.30	.25
	Plate block of 4	2.40	
	FDC *(July 10, 1981)*		1.75
	v. Intaglio black (inscriptions) omitted	525.00	

1981. BEAT ALCOHOLISM ISSUE conveyed the message that alcoholism is a treatable disease. *Intaglio, perforated 11.*

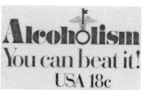

CM986 *Alcoholism - You Can Beat It!*

CM986

		MNHVF	UseVF
18¢	blue & black tagged *(97,535,000)*	.65	.20
	Plate block of 20	40.00	
	FDC *(Aug. 19, 1981)*		3.00
	v. Pair, imperforate	425.00	
	v1. Vertical pair, imperforate horizontally	1,850.00	

1981. AMERICAN ARCHITECTURE ISSUE The third of four issues on this subject featured examples of successful work by late 19th and early 20th century American architects. *Intaglio, perforated 11, multicolored.*

CM987 *New York University Library, designed by Stanford White;* CM988 *Biltmore House, Asheville, N.C., designed by Richard Morris Hunt;* CM989 *Palace of Arts, San Francisco, Calif., designed by Bernard Maybeck;* CM990 *National Farmers Bank Building, Owatonna, Minn., designed by Louis Sullivan*

CM987

		MNHVF	UseVF
18¢	N.Y. University Library, tagged *(167,308,000)*	.30	.20

CM988

		MNHVF	UseVF
18¢	Biltmore House, tagged	.30	.20

CM989

		MNHVF	UseVF
18¢	Palace of Arts, tagged	.30	.20

CM990

		MNHVF	UseVF
18¢	National Farmers Bank Building, tagged	.30	.20
	Plate block of 4	3.00	
	y. Se-tenant block of 4 (CM987-90)	2.75	
	FDC *(Aug. 28, 1981),* any single		2.00
	FDC, block of 4		4.00

American Sports Series

1981. BOBBY JONES ISSUE inaugurated the American Sports Series honoring famous American athletes. In 1930 Bobby Jones became the only golfer in history to win the Grand Slam of Golf. *Intaglio, perforated 10 1/2x11.*

CM991 *Bobby Jones*

CM991		MNHVF	UseVF
18¢	**green** tagged *(99,170,000)*	.30	.20
	Plate block of 4	7.75	
	FDC *(Sept. 22, 1981)*		12.00

1981. (MILDRED) BABE ZAHARIAS ISSUE also part of the American Sports Series, honored one of the greatest athletes of the first half of the 20th century, who broke four track records in the 1932 Olympics and then won virtually every women's golf title, both as an amateur and as a professional. *Intaglio, perforated 10 1/2x11.*

CM992 *Mildred "Babe" Didrickson Zaharias*

CM992		MNHVF	UseVF
18¢	**light violet** tagged *(101,625,000)*	.30	.20
	Plate block of 4	4.00	
	FDC *(Sept. 22, 1981)*		8.00

1981. FREDERIC REMINGTON ISSUE honored the American painter, illustrator and sculptor. *Offset and intaglio, perforated 11.*

CM993 *Frederic Remington's* Coming Through the Rye *sculpture*

CM993		MNHVF	UseVF
18¢	**multicolored** tagged *(101,155,000)*	.30	.20
	Plate block of 4	2.40	
	FDC *(Oct. 9, 1981)*		1.75
	v. brown omitted	550.00	
	v1. Vertical pair, imperforate between	250.00	

1981. JAMES HOBAN ISSUE honored the Irish-American architect of the White House. The Irish Postal Administration and the U.S. Postal Service jointly issued stamps identical in design except for country designation and denomination (Ireland 528). The issue was released by the USPS in two denominations: the lower to accommodate the then current first-class letter rate; and the higher to accommodate the rate that went into effect a little more than two weeks following the release of the stamps. *Gravure, perforated 11.*

CM994 *James Hoban and White House*

CM994		MNHVF	UseVF
18¢	**multicolored** tagged *(101,200,000)*	.30	.20
	Plate block of 4	2.40	

FDC *(Oct. 13, 1981)*   1.75

CM995 *James Hoban and White House*

CM995		MNHVF	UseVF
20¢	**multicolored** tagged *(167,360,000)*	.30	.20
	Plate block of 4	2.50	
	FDC *(Oct. 13, 1981)*		1.75

1981. BATTLE OF YORKTOWN AND THE VIRGINIA CAPES ISSUE commemorated the bicentennial of the two battles with *se-tenant* stamps. The Battle of the Virginia Capes of Sept. 6, 1781, prevented the British fleet from aiding British troops, a critical turning point in the Revolutionary War. The Battle of Yorktown, Oct. 16-19, ending with the surrender of the British, marked the end of the war. *Intaglio and offset, perforated 11.*

CM996 *Map of Yorktown Capes;* CM997 *Map of Virginia Capes*

CM996		MNHVF	UseVF
18¢	**multicolored** tagged *(162,420,000)*	.30	.20
	v. intaglio back (inscriptions) omitted	175.00	
	zo. Tagging omitted	—	

CM997		MNHVF	UseVF
18¢	**multicolored** tagged	.30	.20
	Plate block of 4	3.00	
	y. Se-tenant pair (CM996-97)	.60	.60
	FDC *(Oct. 16, 1981)*, either single		1.50
	FDC, pair		2.00
	v. Intaglio black (inscriptions) omitted	175.00	
	vy. Se-tenant pair, intaglio black, (inscriptions) omitted	425.00	
	zo. Tagging omitted	—	
	zoy. Se-tenant pair, tagging omitted	—	

1981. JOHN HANSON ISSUE commemorated the American Revolutionary leader elected first president of the Continental Congress Nov. 5, 1781. Elected "President of the United States in Congress Assembled," and therefore considered by some the first president of the United States, Hanson (1715-83) was a congressional presiding officer and had none of the powers of the president under the Constitution. *Gravure, perforated 11.*

CM998 *John Hanson*

CM998		MNHVF	UseVF
20¢	**multicolored** tagged *(167,130,000)*	.30	.20
	Plate block of 4	2.50	
	FDC *(Nov. 5, 1981)*		1.75

1981. DESERT PLANTS ISSUE depicted four plants that grow in the arid American West. Three are in the cactus family, and the agave is a succulent plant of the amaryllis family. *Intaglio, perforated 11, multicolored.*

CM999 *Barrel cactus;* CM1000 *Agave;* CM1001 *Beavertail cactus;* CM1002 *Saguaro*

CM999		MNHVF	UseVF
20¢	**Barrel cactus,** tagged *(191,560,000)*	.35	.20

CM1000		MNHVF	UseVF
20¢	**Agave,** tagged	.35	.20

CM1001		MNHVF	UseVF
20¢	**Beavertail cactus,** tagged	.35	.20

CM1002		MNHVF	UseVF
20¢	**Saguaro,** tagged	.35	.20
	Plate block of 4	3.25	
	FDC *(Dec. 11, 1981),* any single		2.00
	FDC, block of 4		4.00
	v. Vertical pair (CM1002), imperforate	6,500.00	
	y. Se-tenant block of 4 (CM999-1002)	2.00	
	vy. Se-tenant block of 4, intaglio brown omitted	8,000.00	

1982. FRANKLIN D. ROOSEVELT ISSUE commemorated the 100th birthday of the 32nd president of the United States. The only president to be elected four times, Roosevelt was inaugurated in 1933 and served as president through the New Deal era and World War II until his death in April 1945. *Intaglio, perforated 11.*

CM1003 *Franklin D. Roosevelt*

CM1003		MNHVF	UseVF
20¢	**blue** tagged *(163,939,200)*	.35	.20
	Plate block of 4	2.50	
	FDC *(Jan. 3, 1982)*		1.75

1982. LOVE ISSUE celebrated special occasions, such as birthdays, anniversaries, weddings, and other special sentiments. Flowers form the letters: "L": miniature poppy; "O": painted daisies and miniature pansies; "V": cornflower; "E": coralbells. *Gravure, perforated 11.*

CM1004-04A

CM1004		MNHVF	UseVF
20¢	**multicolored** tagged	.35	.20
	Plate block of 4	3.25	

CM1004A		MNHVF	UseVF
20¢	**multicolored** tagged, perforated 11x10 1/2	1.00	.25
	Plate block of 4	5.50	
	FDC *(Feb. 1, 1982)*		1.75
	v. Blue omitted	225.00	
	v1. Pair, imperforate	275.00	

1982. GEORGE WASHINGTON ISSUE commemorated the 250th anniversary of his birth. *Gravure, perforated 11.*

CM1005 *George Washington*

CM1005		MNHVF	UseVF
20¢	**multicolored** tagged *(180,700,000)*	.35	.20
	Plate block of 4	2.75	
	FDC *(Feb. 22, 1982)*		2.00

1982. STATE BIRDS AND FLOWERS commemorated the official birds and flowers of all 50 states. Arranged in alphabetical order in the pane, from top-left to bottom right, these stamps were designed by the father-and-son team of Arthur and Alan Singer. Arthur, the father, created the bird designs, and Alan contributed the flower designs. *Gravure, perforated 10 1/2x11 and 11 ("v" numbers).*

CM1006		MNHVF	UseVF
20¢	**Alabama, multicolored,** tagged *(666,950,000)*	1.00	.50
	v. Perforated 11	1.00	.50

CM1007		MNHVF	UseVF
20¢	**Alaska, multicolored,** tagged	1.00	.50
	v. Perforated 11	1.00	.50

CM1008		MNHVF	UseVF
20¢	**Arizona, multicolored,** tagged	1.00	.50
	v. Perforated 11	1.00	.50

CM1009		MNHVF	UseVF
20¢	**Arkansas, multicolored,** tagged	1.00	.50
	v. Perforated 11	1.00	.50

CM1010		MNHVF	UseVF
20¢	**California, multicolored,** tagged	1.00	.50
	v. Perforated 11	1.00	.50

CM1011		MNHVF	UseVF
20¢	**Colorado, multicolored,** tagged	1.00	.50
	v. Perforated 11	1.00	.50

CM1012		MNHVF	UseVF
20¢	**Connecticut, multicolored,** tagged	1.00	.50
	v. Perforated 11	1.00	.50

CM1013		MNHVF	UseVF
20¢	**Delaware, multicolored,** tagged	1.00	.50
	v. Perforated 11	1.00	.50

CM1014		MNHVF	UseVF
20¢	**Florida, multicolored,** tagged	1.00	.50
	v. Perforated 11	1.00	.50

CM1015		MNHVF	UseVF
20¢	**Georgia, multicolored,** tagged	1.00	.50
	v. Perforated 11	1.00	.50

CM1016		MNHVF	UseVF
20¢	**Hawaii, multicolored,** tagged	1.00	.50
	v. Perforated 11	1.00	.50

CM1017		MNHVF	UseVF
20¢	**Idaho, multicolored,** tagged	1.00	.50
	v. Perforated 11	1.00	.50

CM1018		MNHVF	UseVF
20¢	**Illinois, multicolored,** tagged	1.00	.50
	v. Perforated 11	1.00	.50

CM1019		MNHVF	UseVF
20¢	**Indiana, multicolored,** tagged	1.00	.50
	v. Perforated 11	1.00	.50

CM1020		MNHVF	UseVF
20¢	**Iowa, multicolored,** tagged	1.00	.50
	v. Perforated 11	1.00	.50

CM1021		MNHVF	UseVF
20¢	**Kansas, multicolored,** tagged	1.00	.50
	v. Perforated 11	1.00	.50

CM1022		MNHVF	UseVF
20¢	**Kentucky, multicolored,** tagged	1.00	.50
	v. Perforated 11	1.00	.50

CM1023		MNHVF	UseVF
20¢	**Louisiana, multicolored,** tagged	1.00	.50
	v. Perforated 11	1.00	.50

		MNHVF	UseVF
CM1024			
20¢	**Maine, multicolored,** tagged	1.00	.50
	v. Perforated 11	1.00	.50
CM1025		MNHVF	UseVF
20¢	**Maryland, multicolored,** tagged	1.00	.50
	v. Perforated 11	1.00	.50
CM1026		MNHVF	UseVF
20¢	**Massachusetts, multicolored,** tagged	1.00	.50
	v. Perforated 11	1.00	.50
CM1027		MNHVF	UseVF
20¢	**Michigan, multicolored,** tagged	1.00	.50
	v. Perforated 11	1.00	.50
CM1028		MNHVF	UseVF
20¢	**Minnesota, multicolored,** tagged	1.00	.50
	v. Perforated 11	1.00	.50
CM1029		MNHVF	UseVF
20¢	**Mississippi, multicolored,** tagged	1.00	.50
	v. Perforated 11	1.00	.50
CM1030		MNHVF	UseVF
20¢	**Missouri, multicolored,** tagged	1.00	.50
	v. Perforated 11	1.00	.50
CM1031		MNHVF	UseVF
20¢	**Montana, multicolored,** tagged	1.00	.50
	v. Perforated 11	1.00	.50
CM1032		MNHVF	UseVF
20¢	**Nebraska, multicolored,** tagged	1.00	.50
	v. Perforated 11	1.00	.50
CM1033		MNHVF	UseVF
20¢	**Nevada, multicolored,** tagged	1.00	.50
	v. Perforated 11	1.00	.50
CM1034		MNHVF	UseVF
20¢	**New Hampshire, multicolored,** tagged	1.00	.50
	v. Perforated 11	1.00	.50

		MNHVF	UseVF
CM1035			
20¢	**New Jersey, multicolored,** tagged	1.00	.50
	v. Perforated 11	1.00	.50
CM1036		MNHVF	UseVF
20¢	**New Mexico, multicolored,** tagged	1.00	.50
	v. Perforated 11	1.00	.50
CM1037		MNHVF	UseVF
20¢	**New York, multicolored,** tagged	1.00	.50
	v. Perforated 11	1.00	.50
CM1038		MNHVF	UseVF
20¢	**North Carolina, multicolored,** tagged	1.00	.50
	v. Perforated 11	1.00	.50
CM1039		MNHVF	UseVF
20¢	**North Dakota, multicolored,** tagged	1.00	.50
	v. Perforated 11	1.00	.50
CM1040		MNHVF	UseVF
20¢	**Ohio, multicolored,** tagged	1.00	.50
	v. Perforated 11	1.00	.50
CM1041		MNHVF	UseVF
20¢	**Oklahoma, multicolored,** tagged	1.00	.50
	v. Perforated 11	1.00	.50
CM1042		MNHVF	UseVF
20¢	**Oregon, multicolored,** tagged	1.00	.50
	v. Perforated 11	1.00	.50
CM1043		MNHVF	UseVF
20¢	**Pennsylvania, multicolored,** tagged	1.00	.50
	v. Perforated 11	1.00	.50
CM1044		MNHVF	UseVF
20¢	**Rhode Island, multicolored,** tagged	1.00	.50
	v. Perforated 11	1.00	.50
CM1045		MNHVF	UseVF
20¢	**South Carolina, multicolored,** tagged	1.00	.50
	v. Perforated 11	1.00	.50

CM1006-55 *State Birds and Flowers*

CM1046		MNHVF	UseVF
20¢	South Dakota, multicolored, tagged	1.00	.50
	v. Perforated 11	1.00	.50
CM1047		MNHVF	UseVF
20¢	Tennessee, multicolored, tagged	1.00	.50
	v. Perforated 11	1.00	.50
CM1048		MNHVF	UseVF
20¢	Texas, multicolored, tagged	1.00	.50
	v. Perforated 11	1.00	.50
CM1049		MNHVF	UseVF
20¢	Utah, multicolored, tagged	1.00	.50
	v. Perforated 11	1.00	.50
CM1050		MNHVF	UseVF
20¢	Vermont, multicolored, tagged	1.00	.50
	v. Perforated 11	1.00	.50
CM1051		MNHVF	UseVF
20¢	Virginia, multicolored, tagged	1.00	.50
	v. Perforated 11	1.00	.50
CM1052		MNHVF	UseVF
20¢	Washington, multicolored, tagged	1.00	.50
	v. Perforated 11	1.00	.50
CM1053		MNHVF	UseVF
20¢	West Virginia, multicolored, tagged	1.00	.50
	v. Perforated 11	1.00	.50
CM1054		MNHVF	UseVF
20¢	Wisconsin, multicolored, tagged	1.00	.50
	v. Perforated 11	1.00	.50
CM1055		MNHVF	UseVF
20¢	Wyoming, multicolored, tagged	1.00	.50
	v. Perforated 11	1.00	.50
	y. Se-tenant pane of 50	45.00	
	vy. Se-tenant pane of 50, perforated 11	47.50	
	FDC (April 14, 1982), any single		1.50
	FDC, pane of 50		45.00
	vy1. Pane of 50, imperforate	23,000.00	

Because most plate block collectors consider that a plate block contains at least one copy of each stamp in the issue, a plate block of the State Birds and Flowers Issue is considered to be a full pane of 50 stamps.

1982. NETHERLANDS ISSUE marked the 200th anniversary of Netherlands' diplomatic recognition of the United States. The Netherlands released two stamps at the same time as this one (Netherlands 1365-66). *Gravure, perforated 11.*

CM1056 *200th anniversary of Netherlands, diplomatic recognition of the United States*

CM1056		MNHVF	UseVF
20¢	orange, red, blue & dark gray tagged (109,245,000)	.35	.20
	Plate block of 6	13.95	
	FDC (April 20, 1982)		1.75
	v. Pair, imperforate	300.00	

1982. LIBRARY OF CONGRESS ISSUE saluted the library for the services and information it provides to Congress and many other organizations and researchers who use it every year. *Intaglio, perforated 11.*

CM1057 *Library of Congress*

CM1057		MNHVF	UseVF
20¢	black & red tagged (112,535,000)	.35	.20
	Plate block of 4	2.50	
	FDC (April 21, 1982)		1.75

1982. KNOXVILLE WORLD'S FAIR ISSUE commemorated the Knoxville, Tenn., World's Fair, the theme of which was energy. Four stamps depict solar, synthetic, nuclear, and fossil fuel energy sources. *Gravure, perforated 11, multicolored.*

CM1058 *Solar energy;* CM1059 *Synthetic fuels;* CM1060 *Breeder reactor;* CM1061 *Fossil fuels*

CM1058		MNHVF	UseVF
20¢	Solar energy, tagged (124,640,000)	.35	.20
CM1059		MNHVF	UseVF
20¢	Synthetic fuels, tagged	.35	.20
CM1060		MNHVF	UseVF
20¢	Breeder reactor, tagged	.35	.20
CM1061		MNHVF	UseVF
20¢	Fossil fuels, tagged	.35	.20
	Plate block of 4	3.25	
	y. Se-tenant block of 4 (CM1058-61)	2.00	1.50
	FDC (April 29, 1982), any single		1.75
	FDC, block of 4		4.00

1982. HORATIO ALGER ISSUE honored the 150th birthday of Alger, a best-selling author of books for boys, with more than 100 of his works published during his lifetime. Alger's *Phil the Fiddler, or The Story of a Young Street Musician* is credited with bringing public and legislative attention to forced child labor. The stamp is generally not considered to be part of the Literary Arts Series, although no stamp in that series was issued in 1982. *Intaglio, perforated 11.*

CM1062 *Horatio Alger, frontispiece from Ragged Dick series by Alger*

CM1062		MNHVF	UseVF
20¢	red & black on tan paper tagged (107,605,000)	.35	.20
	Plate block of 4	2.50	
	FDC (April 30, 1982)		1.75
	v. Red and black omitted	—	

1982. AGING TOGETHER ISSUE heightened awareness that older persons enrich society with their wealth of experience and creative energy. *Intaglio, perforated 11.*

CM1063 *Aging together*

CM1063		MNHVF	UseVF
20¢	brown tagged (173,160,000)	.35	.20
	Plate block of 4	2.50	
	FDC (May 21, 1982)		1.75

1982. BARRYMORE FAMILY ISSUE in the Performing Arts Series honored the distinguished American theatrical family, featuring likenesses of Lionel, Ethel, and John Barrymore. *Gravure, perforated 11.*

CM1064 *Lionel, Ethel, and John Barrymore*

CM1064		MNHVF	UseVF
20¢	multicolored tagged *(107,285,000)*	.35	.20
	Plate block of 4	2.50	
	FDC *(June 8, 1982)*		1.75

1982. MARY WALKER ISSUE commemorated the Civil War surgeon who gave care and treatment to the sick and the wounded. *Gravure, perforated 11.*

CM1065 *Dr. Mary Walker*

CM1065		MNHVF	UseVF
20¢	multicolored tagged *(109,040,000)*	.35	.20
	Plate block of 4	3.00	
	FDC *(June 10, 1982)*		1.75

1982. INTERNATIONAL PEACE GARDEN ISSUE recognized the 50th anniversary of the garden shared by Dunseith, N. Dak., and Boissevain, Manitoba. It remains a symbol of more than 150 years of peace and friendship between the United States and Canada. *Offset and intaglio, perforated 11.*

CM1066 *Maple leaf and rose*

CM1066		MNHVF	UseVF
20¢	multicolored tagged *(183,270,000)*	.35	.20
	Plate block of 4	2.50	
	FDC *(June 30, 1982)*		1.75
	v. black & intaglio green omitted	275.00	

1982. AMERICA'S LIBRARIES ISSUE honored the contribution of libraries to the growth and development of the United States. *Intaglio, perforated 11.*

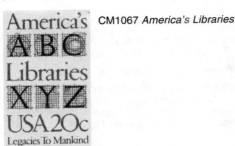

CM1067 *America's Libraries*

CM1067		MNHVF	UseVF
20¢	red & black tagged *(169,495,000)*	.35	.20
	Plate block of 4	2.50	
	FDC *(July 13, 1982)*		1.75
	v. Vertical pair, imperforate horizontally	325.00	
	zo. Tagging omitted	6.00	

1982. JACKIE ROBINSON ISSUE in the Black Heritage Series honored the athlete who broke major league baseball's racial barrier. A football star at UCLA, he was signed to play for the Brooklyn Dodgers' top farm team and then for the Dodgers in 1947. Robinson (1919-72) withstood racial hostility to become one of the most exciting baseball players of his era. *Gravure, perforated 10 1/2x11.*

CM1068 *Jackie Robinson*

CM1068		MNHVF	UseVF
20¢	multicolored tagged *(164,235,000)*	1.50	.20
	Plate block of 4	7.00	
	FDC *(Aug. 2, 1982)*		7.00

1982. TOURO SYNAGOGUE ISSUE honored the oldest existing synagogue in the United States. Designated a National Historical Site in 1946, the synagogue was built in 1763 principally by Sephardic Jews from Spain and Portugal who fled the Inquisition and found religious freedom in the Rhode Island colony. *Gravure and intaglio, perforated 11.*

CM1069 *Touro Synagogue*

CM1069		MNHVF	UseVF
20¢	multicolored tagged *(110,130,000)*	.35	.20
	Plate block of 20	13.75	
	FDC *(Aug. 22, 1982)*		3.00
	v. Pair, imperforate	2,750.00	

1982. WOLF TRAP FARM ISSUE saluted the Wolf Trap Farm Park for the Performing Arts, a theater in wooded surroundings in Virginia. (See also CM679.) *Gravure, perforated 11.*

CM1070 *Wolf Trap Farm Park*

CM1070		MNHVF	UseVF
20¢	multicolored tagged *(110,995,000)*	.35	.20
	Plate block of 4	2.50	
	FDC *(Sept. 1, 1982)*		1.75

1982. AMERICAN ARCHITECTURE ISSUE The fourth and final installment in the series, which honored key structures and architects of the 20th century. *Intaglio, perforated 11.*

> Please read the introduction to this catalog carefully. It contains much valuable information for all stamp collectors, and also makes the catalog easier for you to use.

CM1071 *Fallingwater, Mill Run, Pa., designed by Frank Lloyd Wright;* CM1072 *Illinois Institute of Technology, Chicago, Ill., designed by Ludwig Mies van der Rohe ; CM1073 Gropius House, Lincoln, Mass., designed by Walter Gropius in collaboration with Marcel Breuer;* CM1074 *Dulles International Airport, Washington, D.C., designed by Eero Saarinen*

CM1071		MNHVF	UseVF
20¢	**Falling Water,** tagged *(165,340,000)*	.35	.20

CM1072		MNHVF	UseVF
20¢	**Illinois Institute of Technology,** tagged	.35	.20

CM1073		MNHVF	UseVF
20¢	**Gropius House,** tagged	.35	.20

CM1074		MNHVF	UseVF
20¢	**Dulles International Airport,** tagged	.35	.20
	Plate block of 4	4.25	
	y. Se-tenant block of 4 (CM1071-74)	2.00	
	FDC *(Sept. 30, 1982),* any single		2.00
	FDC, block of 4		4.00

1982. FRANCIS OF ASSISI ISSUE honored the 800th birthday of the man (1182-1226) whose compassion earned him reverence transcending religious bounds. He formed the Franciscan Order, the members of which still minister to the sick and needy. *Gravure by J.W. Fergusson and Sons for American Bank Note Co., perforated 11.*

CM1075 *Francis of Assisi*

CM1075		MNHVF	UseVF
20¢	**multicolored** tagged *(174,180,000)*	.35	.20
	Plate block of 4	2.75	
	FDC *(Oct. 7, 1982)*		1.75

1982. PONCE DE LEÓN ISSUE honored the Spaniard (1527-1591) who explored Puerto Rico in 1508-09 and Florida in 1513. *Gravure (Combination Press), perforated 11.*

CM1076 *Ponce de León*

CM1076		MNHVF	UseVF
20¢	**multicolored** tagged *(110,261,000)*	.35	.20
	Plate block of 6	16.00	
	FDC *(Oct. 12, 1982)*		1.75
	v. Pair, imperforate	500.00	
	v1. Vertical pair, imperforate between	—	

1983. SCIENCE AND INDUSTRY ISSUE saluted their contributions to the growth and development of the United States. *Offset and intaglio, perforated 11.*

CM1077 *Science and Industry*

CM1077		MNHVF	UseVF
20¢	**multicolored** tagged *(118,555,000)*	.35	.20
	Plate block of 4	2.50	
	FDC *(Jan. 19, 1983)*		1.75
	a. Intaglio black omitted	1,400.00	

1983. SWEDEN ISSUE marked the 200th anniversary of the signing of the Treaty of Amity and Commerce between Sweden and the United States. A stamp of similar design was issued simultaneously by Sweden (Sweden 1247). *Intaglio, perforated 11.*

CM1078 *Benjamin Franklin and treaty seal*

CM1078		MNHVF	UseVF
20¢	**multicolored** tagged *(118,225,000)*	.30	.20
	Plate block of 4	2.50	
	FDC *(March 24, 1983)*		1.75

1983. BALLOONING ISSUE honored the sport of hot air ballooning. Balloons were successfully flown in June 1783 by two brothers, Joseph and Jacques Montgolfier, in France. Used for surveillance and scientific research over the years, they are today enjoyed by thousands of recreational enthusiasts. *Gravure, perforated 11.*

CM1079 Intrepid, *1861;* CM1080 and CM1081 *Hot air ballooning;* CM1082 Explorer II, *1935*

CM1079		MNHVF	UseVF
20¢	***Intrepid,*** tagged *(226,128,000)*	.35	.20

CM1080		MNHVF	UseVF
20¢	**Hot air ballooning,** tagged	.35	.20

CM1081		MNHVF	UseVF
20¢	**Hot air ballooning,** tagged	.35	.20

CM1082		MNHVF	UseVF
20¢	***Explorer II,*** tagged	.35	.20
	Plate block of 4	3.00	
	y. Se-tenant block of 4 (CM1079-82)	2.00	
	FDC *(March 31, 1983),* any single		2.00
	FDC, block of 4		4.00
	vy. Se-tenant block of 4, imperforate	5,500.00	

1983. CIVILIAN CONSERVATION CORPS ISSUE honored the 50th anniversary of the Great Depression programs, which recruited thousands of unemployed young men to develop and conserve the nation's natural resources. *Gravure, perforated 11.*

CM1083 *Civilian Conservation Corps*

CM1083		MNHVF	UseVF
20¢	**multicolored** tagged *(114,290,000)*	.35	.20
	Plate block of 4	2.50	
	FDC *(April 5, 1983)*		1.75
	v. Pair, imperforate	2,750.00	

1983. JOSEPH PRIESTLY ISSUE commemorated the clergyman and chemist (1733-1804) who discovered oxygen. *Gravure, perforated 11.*

CM1084 *Joseph Priestly*

CM1084		MNHVF	UseVF
20¢	**multicolored** tagged *(165,000,000)*	.35	.20
	Plate block of 4	3.00	
	FDC *(April 13, 1983)*		1.75

1983. VOLUNTEER ISSUE recognized the contribution volunteers have made to the development of the United States. *Intaglio, perforated 11.*

CM1085 *Helping hands*

CM1085		MNHVF	UseVF
20¢	**red & black** tagged *(120,430,000)*	.35	.20
	Plate block of 20	13.95	
	FDC *(April 20, 1983)*		1.75
	v. Pair, imperforate	800.00	

1983. GERMAN CONCORD ISSUE honored the 300th anniversary of the arrival of the first 13 families of German immigrants to the United States in the ship *Concord*. A stamp of similar design was issued May 5, six days after the U.S. issue, by West Germany (W. Germany 2363). *Intaglio, perforated 11.*

CM1086 Concord, *1683, German immigration tricentennial*

CM1086		MNHVF	UseVF
20¢	**brown** tagged *(117,025,000)*	.35	.20
	Plate block of 4	2.50	
	FDC *(April 29, 1983)*		1.75

1983. PHYSICAL FITNESS ISSUE saluted physical fitness activities for maintaining good physical health. *Gravure (Combination Press), perforated 11.*

CM1087 *Physical fitness*

CM1087		MNHVF	UseVF
20¢	**multicolored** tagged *(111,775,000)*	.35	.20
	Plate block of 20	13.95	
	FDC *(May 14, 1983)*		2.00

1983. BROOKLYN BRIDGE ISSUE honored the 100th anniversary of the completion of the bridge, created by 19th-century civil engineer John A. Roebling and his son Washington. It opened on May 24, 1883. *Intaglio, perforated 11.*

CM1088 *Brooklyn Bridge*

CM1088		MNHVF	UseVF
20¢	**blue** tagged *(181,700,000)*	.35	.20
	"Short bridge"	.50	.30
	Plate block of 4	2.50	
	FDC *(May 17, 1983)*		2.00
	zo. Tagging omitted		

1983. TENNESSEE VALLEY AUTHORITY ISSUE marked the 50th anniversary of its establishment, providing flood control through a system of dams and locks, developing the natural resources of the area and creating industry. *Gravure and intaglio (Combination Press), perforated 11.*

CM1089 *Norris Hydroelectric Dam*

CM1089		MNHVF	UseVF
20¢	**multicolored** tagged *(114,250,000)*	.35	.20
	Plate block of 20	13.95	
	FDC *(May 18, 1983)*		1.75

1983. MEDAL OF HONOR ISSUE saluted the United States' highest military award and all those who have been awarded the medal. It is awarded for "courage above and beyond the call of duty." *Offset and intaglio, perforated 11.*

CM1090 *Medal of Honor*

CM1090		MNHVF	UseVF
20¢	**multicolored** tagged *(108,820,000)*	.35	.20
	Plate block of 4	3.00	
	FDC *(June 7, 1983)*		6.00
	v. Red omitted	325.00	

1983. SCOTT JOPLIN ISSUE in the Black Heritage Series honored the ragtime composer (1868-1917) who successfully combined the charm of late Victorian music and the lively qualities of pioneer American folk song and dance. *Gravure, perforated 11.*

CM1091 *Scott Joplin*

CM1091

			MNHVF	UseVF
20¢	**multicolored** tagged *(115,200,000)*		.35	.20
	Plate block of 4		3.00	
	FDC *(June 9, 1983)*			2.50
	v. Pair, imperforate		550.00	

1983. BABE RUTH ISSUE The third issue in the American Sports Series commemorated the great baseball player and Hall of Fame member George Herman Ruth (1895-1948). *Intaglio, perforated 10 1/2x11.*

CM1092 *George Herman "Babe" Ruth*

CM1092

			MNHVF	UseVF
20¢	**blue** tagged *(184,950,000)*		.35	.20
	Plate block of 4		9.75	
	FDC *(July 6, 1983)*			6.00

1983. NATHANIEL HAWTHORNE ISSUE Fourth in the Literary Arts Series honored the American author of the novel, *The House of Seven Gables*. A master at writing tales, Hawthorne (1804-1864) was one of the first American writers who built his stories around the New England of his forefathers. *Gravure, perforated 11.*

CM1093 *Nathaniel Hawthorne*

CM1093

			MNHVF	UseVF
20¢	**multicolored** tagged *(110,925,000)*		.35	.20
	Plate block of 4		2.50	
	FDC *(July 8, 1983)*			1.75

1983. 1984 OLYMPIC ISSUE was the first of an array of postal paper designed by Robert Peak, commemorating the Summer Games in Los Angeles and the Winter Games in Sarajevo, Yugoslavia. (See also CM1111-14, CM1126-29, A101-12, ALS19, PC96 and PC98.) *Gravure, perforated 11, multicolored.*

CM1094 *Discus;* CM1095 *High jump;* CM1096 *Archery;* CM1097 *Boxing*

CM1094

			MNHVF	UseVF
13¢	**Discus,** tagged *(395,424,000)*		.25	.20

CM1095

			MNHVF	UseVF
13¢	**High jump,** tagged		.25	.20

CM1096

			MNHVF	UseVF
13¢	**Archery,** tagged		.25	.20

CM1097

			MNHVF	UseVF
13¢	**Boxing,** tagged		.25	.20
	Plate block of 4		3.75	
	y. Se-tenant block of 4 (CM1094-97)		2.00	
	FDC *(July 28, 1983),* any single			2.00
	FDC, block of 4			4.00

1983. TREATY OF PARIS ISSUE marked the 200th anniversary of the Treaty of Paris, which officially ended the American Revolution and was signed by John Adams, Benjamin Franklin, and John Jay. The treaty established the boundaries of the new nation at the Great Lakes, the Mississippi River and the northern border of Florida. *Gravure, perforated 11.*

CM1098 *Treaty of Paris*

CM1098

			MNHVF	UseVF
20¢	**multicolored** tagged *(104,340,000)*		.35	.20
	Plate block of 4		2.75	
	FDC *(Sept. 2, 1983)*			1.75

1983. CIVIL SERVICE ISSUE marked 100 years of federal civil service. *Gravure and intaglio, perforated 11.*

CM1099 *Civil Service*

CM1099

			MNHVF	UseVF
20¢	**beige, blue & red** tagged *(114,725,000)*		.35	.20
	Plate block of 20		13.95	
	FDC *(Sept. 9, 1983)*			1.75

1983. METROPOLITAN OPERA ISSUE celebrated the centennial of the Metropolitan Opera in New York, combining features from the original Metropolitan Opera (the proscenium arch above the stage) and the new building at Lincoln Center (the five-arched entrance). *Offset and intaglio, perforated 11.*

CM1100 *Metropolitan Opera*

CM1100

			MNHVF	UseVF
20¢	**dark carmine & yellow orange** tagged *(112,525,000)*		.35	.20
	Plate block of 4		2.75	
	FDC *(Sept. 14, 1983)*			1.75
	zo. Tagging omitted		7.00	

1983. AMERICAN INVENTORS ISSUE honored Charles Steinmetz, Edwin Armstrong, Nikola Tesla, and Philo T. Farnsworth. Steinmetz pioneered research on alternating current and high-voltage power. Armstrong's crowning achievement is wide-band frequency modulation, now used in FM radio. Tesla, creator of more than 700 inventions, is best known for the induction motor. Farnsworth, with more than 300 inventions in television and related fields, is most famous for the first all-electronic television transmission in 1927. *Offset and intaglio, perforated 11, multicolored.*

CM1101 *Charles Steinmetz;* CM1102 *Edwin Armstrong;* CM1103 *Nikola Tesla;* CM1104 *Philo T. Farnsworth*

CM1101		MNHVF	UseVF
20¢	**Charles Steinmetz,** tagged	.35	.20
	(193,055,000)		

CM1102		MNHVF	UseVF
20¢	**Edwin Armstrong,** tagged	.35	.20

CM1103		MNHVF	UseVF
20¢	**Nikola Tesla,** tagged	.35	.20

CM1104		MNHVF	UseVF
20¢	**Philo T. Farnsworth,** tagged	.35	.20
	Plate block of 4	4.25	
	y. Se-tenant block of 4 (CM1101-04)	2.00	
	FDC (Sept. 21, 1983), any single		2.00
	FDC, block of 4		4.00
	v. black (engraved) omitted, any single	100.00	
	vy. Block of 4, black (engraved) omitted	375.00	

1983. STREETCAR ISSUE paid tribute to the evolution of importance of the streetcar in the United States. *Offset and intaglio, perforated 11.*

CM1105 *1st American streetcar New York City, 1832;* CM1106 *Early electric streetcar, Montgomery, Ala., 1886;* CM1107 *"Bobtail" horsecar, Sulphur Rock, Ark., 1926;* CM1108 *St. Charles streetcar, New Orleans, La., 1923*

CM1105		MNHVF	UseVF
20¢	**NYC's first horsecar,** tagged	.35	.20

CM1106		MNHVF	UseVF
20¢	**Montgomery electric,** tagged	.35	.20

CM1107		MNHVF	UseVF
20¢	**"Bobtail" horsecar,** tagged	.35	.20

CM1108		MNHVF	UseVF
20¢	**St. Charles streetcar,** tagged	.35	.20
	Plate block of 4	4.25	
	y. Se-tenant block of 4 (CM1105-08)	2.00	
	FDC (Oct. 8, 1983), any single		2.00
	FDC, block of 4		4.00
	v. black (engraved) omitted, any single	75.00	
	vy. Block of 4, black (engraved) omitted	400.00	

1983. MARTIN LUTHER ISSUE commemorated the 500th birthday of religious reformer Martin Luther (1483-1546). *Gravure (American Bank Note Co.), perforated 11.*

CM1109 *Martin Luther*

CM1109		MNHVF	UseVF
20¢	**multicolored** tagged (165,000,000)	.35	.20
	Plate block of 4	2.50	
	FDC (Nov. 10, 1983)		1.75

1984. ALASKA STATEHOOD ISSUE honored the 25th anniversary of the 49th state. *Gravure by J.W. Fergusson & Sons for the American Bank Note Co., perforated 11.*

CM1110 *Alaska statehood*

CM1110		MNHVF	UseVF
20¢	**multicolored** tagged (120,000,000)	.35	.20
	Plate block of 4	2.50	
	FDC (Jan. 3, 1984)		1.75

1984. WINTER OLYMPICS ISSUE featured events of the games in Sarajevo, Yugoslavia. Designed by Robert Peak. *Gravure, perforated 10 1/2x11.*

CM1111 *Ice dancing*

CM1112 *Alpine skiing*

CM1113 *Cross-country skiing*

CM1114 *Ice hockey*

CM1111		MNHVF	UseVF
20¢	**Ice dancing,** tagged (319,675,000)	.35	.20

CM1112		MNHVF	UseVF
20¢	**Alpine skiing,** tagged	.35	.20

CM1113		MNHVF	UseVF
20¢	**Cross-country skiing,** tagged	.35	.20

CM1114

		MNHVF	UseVF
20¢	**Ice hockey,** tagged	.35	.20
	Plate block of 4	4.25	
	y. Se-tenant block of 4 (CM1111-14)	2.00	
	FDC (Jan. 6, 1984), any single		2.00
	FDC, block of 4		4.00

1984. FEDERAL DEPOSIT INSURANCE CORPORATION ISSUE honored the 50th anniversary of the institution, which gives bank depositors limited protection in the event of bank insolvency. *Gravure, perforated 11.*

CM1115 *Federal Deposit Insurance Corporation*

CM1115

		MNHVF	UseVF
20¢	**multicolored** tagged *(103,975,000)*	.35	.20
	Plate block of 4	2.50	
	FDC (Jan. 12, 1984)		1.75

1984. LOVE ISSUE for use on Valentine's Day as well as other special occasions. From a design by Bradbury Thompson. *Gravure and intaglio (Combination Press), perforated 11.*

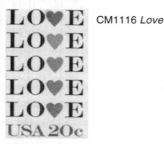

CM1116 *Love*

CM1116

		MNHVF	UseVF
20¢	**multicolored** tagged *(554,675,000)*	.35	.20
	Plate block of 20	14.50	
	FDC (Jan. 31, 1984)		1.75
	v. Horizontal pair, imperforate vertically	175.00	
	zo. Tagging omitted	5.00	

1984. CARTER G. WOODSON ISSUE part of the Black Heritage Series, honored the African-American historian, teacher and administrator, as well as editor of the *Journal of Negro History*. *Gravure by American Bank Note Co., perforated 11.*

CM1117 *Carter G. Woodson*

CM1117

		MNHVF	UseVF
20¢	**multicolored** tagged *(120,000,000)*	.35	.20
	Plate block of 4	2.75	
	FDC (Feb. 1, 1984)		2.50
	v. Horizontal pair, imperforate vertically	1,750.00	

1984. SOIL AND WATER CONSERVATION ISSUE recognized the 50th anniversary of government efforts to abate soil erosion and conserve water resources. *Gravure, perforated 11.*

CM1118 *Soil and water conservation*

CM1118

		MNHVF	UseVF
20¢	**multicolored** tagged *(106,975,000)*	.35	.20
	Plate block of 4	2.50	
	FDC (Feb. 6, 1984)		1.75

1984. CREDIT UNION ACT OF 1934 ISSUE honored the 50th anniversary of the act that enabled credit unions to be organized everywhere in the United States under charters from the federal government. *Gravure, perforated 11.*

CM1119 *Credit Union Act of 1934*

CM1119

		MNHVF	UseVF
20¢	**multicolored** tagged *(107,325,000)*	.35	.20
	Plate block of 4	2.50	
	FDC (Feb. 10, 1984)		1.75

1984. ORCHIDS ISSUE featured four different native American orchids: the Wild Pink orchid of Florida; Yellow Lady's Slipper of the Midwest; Spreading Pogonia of the Northeast; and the Pacific Calypso found along the Pacific Coast. *Gravure, perforated 11.*

CM1120 *Wild Pink Orchid*

CM1121 *Yellow Lady's-Slipper*

CM1122 *Spreading Pogonia*

CM1123 Pacific Calypso Orchid

CM1120

		MNHVF	UseVF
20¢	**Wild Pink Orchid,** tagged *(306,912,000)*	.35	.20

CM1121

		MNHVF	UseVF
20¢	**Yellow Lady's-Slipper,** tagged	.35	.20

CM1122

		MNHVF	UseVF
20¢	**Spreading Pogonia,** tagged	.35	.20

CM1123

		MNHVF	UseVF
20¢	**Pacific Calypso Orchid,** tagged	.35	.20
	Plate block of 4	3.50	
	y. Se-tenant block of 4 (CM1120-23)	2.00	
	FDC (March 6, 1984), any single		2.00
	FDC, block of 4		4.00

1984. HAWAII STATEHOOD ISSUE honored the 25th anniversary of Hawaii statehood. Hawaii was admitted as the 50th state Aug. 21, 1959. *Gravure by American Bank Note Co., perforated 11.*

CM1124 *Hawaii statehood*

CM1124		MNHVF	UseVF
20¢	**multicolored** tagged *(120,000,000)*	.35	.20
	Plate block of 4	2.75	
	FDC *(March 12, 1984)*		2.00

1984. NATIONAL ARCHIVES ISSUE marked the 50th anniversary of the National Archives in Washington, D.C., which preserves the Declaration of Independence, the Constitution of the United States, the Bill of Rights and other treasures of America's past such as photographs, maps, and sound recordings of film. *Gravure, perforated 11.*

CM1125 *National Archives*

CM1125		MNHVF	UseVF
20¢	**multicolored** tagged *(108,000,000)*	.35	.20
	Plate block of 4	2.75	
	FDC *(April 16, 1984)*		1.75

1984. SUMMER OLYMPICS ISSUE featured events at the Los Angeles Summer Games. *Gravure, perforated 11.*

CM1126 *Men's diving*

CM1127 *Women's long jump*

CM1128 *Wrestling*

CM1129 *Women's kayaking*

CM1126		MNHVF	UseVF
20¢	**Men's diving,** tagged *(313,350,000)*	.35	.20

CM1127		MNHVF	UseVF
20¢	**Women's long jump,** tagged	.35	.20

CM1128		MNHVF	UseVF
20¢	**Wrestling,** tagged	.35	.20

CM1129		MNHVF	UseVF
20¢	**Women's kayaking,** tagged	.35	.20
	Plate block of 4	5.50	
	v. Block of 4, imperforate vertically	—	
	y. Se-tenant block of 4 (CM1126-29)	2.00	
	FDC *(May 4, 1984),* any single		2.00
	FDC, block of 4		4.00
	v1. Pair (Wrestling and Kayaking), imperforate vertically	—	

1984. LOUISIANA WORLD EXPOSITION ISSUE honored the exposition that celebrated fresh water, spotlighting rivers and ports of the world through displays and exhibitions. *Gravure, perforated 11.*

CM1130 *Louisiana World Exposition*

CM1130		MNHVF	UseVF
20¢	**multicolored** tagged *(130,320,000)*	.35	.20
	Plate block of 4	2.75	
	FDC *(May 11, 1984)*		1.75

1984. HEALTH RESEARCH ISSUE hailed the professionals who have worked to prevent disease and prolong life. *Gravure by American Bank Note Co., perforated 11.*

CM1131 *Health Research*

CM1131		MNHVF	UseVF
20¢	**multicolored** tagged *(120,000,000)*	.35	.20
	Plate block of 4	3.00	
	FDC *(May 17, 1984)*		1.75

1984. DOUGLAS FAIRBANKS ISSUE recalled the actor as part of the Performing Arts Series. Together with Charlie Chaplin, D.W. Griffith and Mary Pickford, in 1919 Fairbanks (1883-1939) formed United Artists Corp. *Gravure and intaglio (Combination Press), perforated 11.*

CM1132 *Douglas Fairbanks*

CM1132		MNHVF	UseVF
20¢	**multicolored** tagged *(117,050,000)*	.35	.20
	Plate block of 20	17.50	
	FDC *(May 23, 1984)*		1.75
	v. Horizontal pair, imperforate vertically (one copy known)	—	
	zo. Tagging omitted	7.50	

1984. JIM THORPE ISSUE saluted the American athlete whose feats in track, baseball, and football are legendary. In 1912, at the Summer Olympics in Stockholm, Thorpe (1888-1953) became the first athlete to win both the pentathlon and the decathlon. Later, he was stripped of his medals when it was learned that he had briefly played semi-professional baseball in 1910. In 1938, the International Olympic Committee returned replicas of Thorpe's 1912 medals to his family, restoring his place in Olympic history. Part of the American Sports Series. *Intaglio, perforated 11.*

CM1133 *Jim Thorpe*

CM1133

		MNHVF	UseVF
20¢	**dark brown** tagged *(115,725,000)*	.75	.20
	Plate block of 4	3.00	
	FDC *(May 24, 1984)*		5.00

1984. JOHN MCCORMACK ISSUE in the Performing Arts Series honored the 100th birthday of the Irish-American singer and world-famous tenor (1884-1945) who sang with the outstanding opera companies in North America and performed Irish folk songs and ballads in major cities of the world. This stamp was released jointly with an Irish stamp (Ireland 622). *Gravure, perforated 11.*

CM1134 *John McCormack*

CM1134

		MNHVF	UseVF
20¢	**multicolored** tagged *(116,600,000)*	.35	.20
	Plate block of 4	2.50	
	FDC *(June 6, 1984)*		1.75

1984. ST. LAWRENCE SEAWAY ISSUE commemorated the 25th anniversary of the opening of the seaway, which stretches from the Atlantic Ocean to Duluth, Minn. This was a joint issue with Canada (Canada 1085). *Gravure by American Bank Note Co., perforated 11.*

CM1135 *St. Lawrence Seaway*

CM1135

		MNHVF	UseVF
20¢	**multicolored** tagged *(120,000,000)*	.35	.20
	Plate block of 4	2.50	
	FDC *(June 26, 1984)*		1.75

1984. WETLANDS PRESERVATION ISSUE marked the 50th anniversary of the Migratory Bird Hunting and Conservation Stamp Act, enacted in 1934 as a result of a proposal by conservationist Jay Norwood ("Ding") Darling for a federal revenue stamp required to be purchased by waterfowl hunters. Funds from the sale of these stamps go to buy and lease waterfowl habitats. The stamp design is the same Darling art as that on the first Duck stamp, RH1. *Intaglio, perforated 11.*

CM1136 Mallards Dropping In, *by Jay Norwood Darling*

CM1136

		MNHVF	UseVF
20¢	**blue** tagged *(123,575,000)*	.35	.20
	Plate block of 4	4.50	
	FDC *(July 2, 1984)*		1.75
	v. Horizontal pair, imperforate vertically	375.00	

1984. ROANOKE VOYAGES ISSUE commemorated the 400th anniversary of the establishment of an English colony in the New World. An expedition landed in 1584 on what is now the coast of North Carolina and took possession of the new land in the name of Queen Elizabeth. Two groups landed in 1585 and 1587. In 1590, the crew of a ship carrying supplies to the colony landed and could find no evidence of the colonists, whose fate remains a mystery. *Gravure by American Bank Note Co., perforated 11.*

CM1137 *Roanoke Voyages*

CM1137

		MNHVF	UseVF
20¢	**multicolored** tagged *(120,000,000)*	.35	.20
	Plate block of 4	2.80	
	Gutter pair	—	
	FDC *(July 13, 1984)*		1.75

1984. HERMAN MELVILLE ISSUE Fifth in the Literary Arts Series honored the 19th century American author (1819-91) of *Moby Dick*. *Intaglio, perforated 11.*

CM1138 *Herman Melville*

CM1138

		MNHVF	UseVF
20¢	**blue green** tagged *(117,125,000)*	.35	.20
	Plate block of 4	2.50	
	FDC *(Aug. 1, 1984)*		1.75

1984. HORACE MOSES ISSUE saluted the man who created Junior Achievement because of his interest in career-oriented educational opportunities for city youth. *Intaglio (Combination Press), perforated 11.*

CM1139 *Horace Moses*

CM1139

		MNHVF	UseVF
20¢	**orange & dark brown** tagged *(117,225,000)*	.35	.20
	Plate block of 20	17.00	
	FDC *(Aug. 6, 1984)*		1.75

1984. SMOKEY BEAR ISSUE celebrated the symbol for forest fire prevention used by the Forest Service of the U.S. Department of Agriculture. *Combination of offset and intaglio, perforated 11.*

CM1140 *Smokey and bear cub*

CM1140		MNHVF	UseVF
20¢	**multicolored** tagged *(95,525,000)*	.35	.20
	Plate block of 4	3.00	
	FDC *(Aug. 13, 1984)*		2.00
	v. Horizontal pair, imperforate between	275.00	
	v1. Horizontal pair, imperforate vertically	1,750.00	
	v2. Vertical pair, imperforate between	225.00	
	v3. Block of 4, imperforate between horizontally & vertically	6,000.00	

1984. ROBERTO CLEMENTE ISSUE in the American Sports Series commemorated the 18-year Pittsburgh Pirates veteran inducted into the Baseball Hall of Fame in 1973, the year following his untimely death while on a volunteer humanitarian mission. The Puerto Rican flag in the background symbolizes the place of his birth. *Gravure, perforated 11.*

CM1141 *Roberto Clemente*

CM1141		MNHVF	UseVF
20¢	**multicolored** tagged *(119,125,000)*	2.75	.20
	Plate block of 4	12.75	
	FDC *(Aug. 17, 1984)*		10.00
	v. Horizontal pair, imperforate vertically	2,000.00	

1984. AMERICAN DOGS ISSUE depicted eight pedigreed dogs that represent the types most often bred in the United States. The stamps were issued in conjunction with the American Kennel Club's centennial. *Gravure, perforated 11.*

CM1142 *Beagle, Boston Terrier;* CM1143 *Chesapeake Bay Retriever, Cocker Spaniel;* CM1144 *Alaskan Malamute, Collie;* CM1145 *Black and Tan Coonhound, American Foxhound*

CM1142		MNHVF	UseVF
20¢	**Beagle & Terrier,** tagged *(216,260,000)*	.35	.20

CM1143		MNHVF	UseVF
20¢	**Retriever & Cocker Spaniel,** tagged	.35	.20

CM1144		MNHVF	UseVF
20¢	**Malamute & Collie,** tagged	.35	.20

CM1145		MNHVF	UseVF
20¢	**Coonhound & Foxhound,** tagged	.35	.20
	Plate block of 4	4.25	
	y. Se-tenant block of 4 (CM1142-45)	2.00	
	FDC *(Sept. 7, 1984)*, any single		2.00
	FDC, block of 4		4.00

1984. CRIME PREVENTION ISSUE depicted McGruff, the Crime Dog, popularized to boost public confidence and encourage participation in citizen crime-prevention activities. *Gravure by American Bank Note Co., perforated 11.*

CM1146 *McGruff, the Crime Dog*

CM1146		MNHVF	UseVF
20¢	**multicolored** tagged *(120,000,000)*	.35	.20
	Plate block of 4	2.50	
	FDC *(Sept. 26, 1984)*		2.00

1984. FAMILY UNITY ISSUE was designed by high school student Molly LaRue. *Gravure and intaglio (Combination Press), perforated 11.*

CM1147 *Stick-figure family*

CM1147		MNHVF	UseVF
20¢	**multicolored** tagged *(117,625,000)*	.35	.20
	Plate block of 20	17.75	
	FDC *(Oct. 1, 1984)*		1.75
	v. Horizontal pair, imperforate vertically	525.00	
	v1. Vertical pair, imperforate between	—	
	zo. Tagging omitted	4.00	

1984. ELEANOR ROOSEVELT ISSUE honored the woman who distinguished herself both as the first lady and as a humanitarian who fought for human rights as a delegate to the United Nations. *Intaglio, perforated 11.*

CM1148 *Eleanor Roosevelt*

CM1148		MNHVF	UseVF
20¢	**blue** tagged *(112,896,000)*	.35	.20
	Plate block of 4	2.50	
	FDC *(Oct. 11, 1984)*		1.75

1984. NATION OF READERS ISSUE recognized the importance of reading in American society, including the traditions of public education and the public library. *Intaglio, perforated 11.*

CM1149 *Abraham Lincoln and son Tad, from a daguerreotype by Matthew Brady*

CM1149

		MNHVF	UseVF
20¢	**brown & dark red** tagged, *(116,500,000)*	.35	.20
	Plate block of 4	2.95	
	FDC *(Oct. 16, 1984)*		1.75

1984. HISPANIC AMERICANS ISSUE honored Hispanic Americans and their contribution to national defense. Many have received the nation's highest honors and awards for gallantry in the armed services. *Gravure, perforated 11.*

CM1150 *Hispanic Americans*

CM1150

		MNHVF	UseVF
20¢	**multicolored** tagged *(108,140,000)*	.35	.20
	Plate block of 4	2.50	
	FDC *(Oct. 31, 1984)*		1.75
	v. Vertical pair, imperforate horizontally	1,850.00	

1984. VIETNAM VETERANS MEMORIAL ISSUE commemorated the second anniversary of the dedication of the Vietnam Veterans Memorial. The Washington, D.C., memorial contains the names of 58,196 Americans killed or missing in action during the war. *Intaglio, perforated 11.*

CM1151 *Vietnam Veterans Memorial*

CM1151

		MNHVF	UseVF
20¢	**multicolored** tagged *(105,300,000)*	.35	.20
	Plate block of 4	4.25	
	FDC *(Nov. 10, 1984)*		1.75
	zo. Tagging omitted		

1985. JEROME KERN ISSUE in the Performing Arts Series celebrated the 100th birthday of the composer who wrote more than 108 complete theatrical scores and 1,000 songs and earned two Academy Awards. He perhaps is best known for *Show Boat*. The stamp was the first with the 22¢ First Class denomination. *Gravure by American Bank Note Co., perforated 11.*

CM1152 *Jerome Kern*

CM1152

		MNHVF	UseVF
22¢	**multicolored** tagged *(124,500,000)*	.35	.20
	Plate block of 4	3.00	
	FDC *(Jan. 23, 1985)*		1.75
	zo. Tagging omitted	7.00	

1985. MARY MCLEOD BETHUNE ISSUE in the Black Heritage Series commemorated the noted educator and social activist (1875-1955). She founded the school that became Bethune-Cookman College in Daytona, Fla., and advised president Franklin Roosevelt on minority affairs. *Gravure by American Bank Note Co., perforated 11.*

CM1153 *Mary McLeod Bethune*

CM1153

		MNHVF	UseVF
22¢	**multicolored** tagged *(120,000,000)*	.35	.20
	Plate block of 4	3.25	
	FDC *(March 5, 1985)*		2.50

1985. DUCK DECOYS ISSUE in the American Folk Art Series had designs based on actual decoys: a broadbill decoy carved by Ben Holmes of Stratford, Conn., 1890; a mallard decoy by Percy Grant of Osbornville, N.J., 1900; a canvasback by Bob McGraw of Havre de Grace, Md., 1929; and a redhead by Keyes Chadwick of Martha's Vineyard, Mass., 1925. *Gravure by American Bank Note Co., perforated 11.*

CM1154 *Broadbill decoy;* CM1155 *Mallard decoy;* CM1156 *Canvasback decoy;* CM1157 *Redhead decoy*

CM1154

		MNHVF	UseVF
22¢	**Broadbill decoy,** tagged *(300,000,000)*	.40	.20

CM1155

		MNHVF	UseVF
22¢	**Mallard decoy,** tagged	.40	.20

CM1156

		MNHVF	UseVF
22¢	**Canvasback decoy,** tagged	.40	.20

CM1157

		MNHVF	UseVF
22¢	**Redhead decoy,** tagged	.40	.20
	Plate block of 4	12.00	
	y. Se-tenant block of 4 (CM1154-57)	2.00	1.50
	FDC *(March 22, 1985),* any single		2.00
	FDC, block of 4		4.00

1985. SPECIAL OLYMPICS ISSUE saluted the largest program of sports training and athletic competition for mentally and physically impaired people in the world. With assistance of 550,000 volunteers worldwide, more than 1 million children and adults participate. *Gravure, perforated 11.*

CM1158 *Winter Special Olympics*

CM1158

		MNHVF	UseVF
22¢	**multicolored** tagged *(120,580,000)*	.35	.20
	Plate block of 4	2.95	
	FDC *(March 25, 1985)*		1.75
	v. Vertical pair, imperforate horizontally	575.00	

1985. LOVE ISSUE was the fourth issue for use on special occasions throughout the year. Color lines by Corita Kent. *Gravure, perforated 11.*

CM1159 *Love*

CM1159		MNHVF	UseVF
22¢	**multicolored** tagged *(729,700,000)*	.35	.20
	Plate block of 4	3.25	
	FDC *(April 17, 1985)*		1.75
	v. Pair, imperforate	1,500.00	

1985. RURAL ELECTRIFICATION ADMINISTRATION ISSUE marked the 50th anniversary of the organization, which has served as a lending agency as well as developing programs for rural electrification. *Gravure and intaglio (Combination Press), perforated 11.*

CM1160 *Rural Electrification Administration*

CM1160		MNHVF	UseVF
22¢	**multicolored** tagged *(124,750,000)*	.35	.20
	Plate block of 20	32.50	
	FDC *(May 11, 1985)*		1.75
	v. Vertical pair, imperforate between	—	

1985. AMERIPEX 86 ISSUE honored the 1986 international stamp show hosted by the United States in suburban Chicago, Ill. The stamp depicted is the 1¢ National Bank Note of 1870 (No. 97). *Offset and intaglio, perforated 11.*

CM1161 *Ameripex 86*

CM1161		MNHVF	UseVF
22¢	**multicolored** tagged *(203,496,000)*	.35	.20
	Plate block of 4	2.75	
	FDC *(May 25, 1985)*		1.75
	v. red omitted	2,250.00	
	v1. red & black omitted	1,250.00	
	v2. black, blue, & red omitted	200.00	

1985. ABIGAIL ADAMS ISSUE honored the wife of John Adams, second president of the United States. She acted as adviser to her husband, maintained the family estate, raised four children (son John Quincy Adams became the sixth president of the United States), and distinguished herself as one of the leading women writers of her era (1744-1818). *Gravure, perforated 11.*

CM1162 *Abigail Adams*

CM1162		MNHVF	UseVF
22¢	**multicolored** tagged *(126,325,000)*	.35	.20
	Plate block of 4	2.75	
	FDC *(June 14, 1985)*		1.75
	v. Pair, imperforate	250.00	

Examples exist with minute traces of the intaglio black remaining, which are worth far less than a complete color-omitted error. Competent expertizing is required.

1985. FREDERIC AUGUSTE BARTHOLDI ISSUE saluted the sculptor of the Statue of Liberty. *Offset and intaglio, perforated 11.*

CM1163 *F.A. Bartholdi and Statue of Liberty*

CM1163		MNHVF	UseVF
22¢	**multicolored** tagged *(130,000,000)*	.35	.20
	Plate block of 4	2.75	
	FDC *(July 18, 1985)*		1.75
	v. Intaglio black omitted	—	

1985. KOREAN WAR VETERANS ISSUE honored Americans who served during the Korean War (1950-53), the first conflict in which U.S. troops fought under the flag of the United Nations. *Intaglio, perforated 11.*

CM1164 *Troops marching, from a photograph by David Duncan*

CM1164		MNHVF	UseVF
22¢	**gray green & rose red** tagged	.35	.20
	(119,975,000)		
	Plate block of 4	3.50	
	FDC *(July 26, 1985)*		2.00

1985. SOCIAL SECURITY ACT ISSUE marked the 50th anniversary of the Social Security Act, which, along with later amendments, brought workers essential protection. These include old age, survivor, disability, and health insurance; compensation for unemployment; public assistance; and health and welfare services. *Gravure by American Bank Note Co., perforated 11.*

CM1165 *Social Security Act*

CM1165		MNHVF	UseVF
22¢	**dark blue & light blue** tagged	.35	.20
	(120,000,000)		
	Plate block of 4	3.50	
	FDC *(Aug. 14, 1985)*		1.75

1985. WORLD WAR I VETERANS ISSUE honored American sacrifice in "the War to End all Wars" based on a drawing, *The Battle of the Marne* by Capt. Harvey Dunn, one of eight official artists for the American Expeditionary Force. *Intaglio, perforated 11.*

CM1166 The Battle of the Marne by *Capt. Harvey Dunn*

CM1166		MNHVF	UseVF
22¢	**green & red** tagged *(119,975,000)*	.35	.20
	Plate block of 4	3.50	
	FDC *(Aug. 26, 1985)*		2.00

1985. AMERICAN HORSES ISSUE featured four breeds of horses representing the many types of horses, mules, and donkeys in North America. *Gravure, perforated 11.*

CM1167 *Quarter horse;* CM1168 *Morgan;*
CM1169 *Saddlebred;* CM1170 *Appaloosa*

CM1167			MNHVF	UseVF
22¢	**Quarter horse,** tagged (147,940,000)		2.75	.20
CM1168			MNHVF	UseVF
22¢	**Morgan,** tagged		2.75	.20
CM1169			MNHVF	UseVF
22¢	**Saddlebred,** tagged		2.75	.20
CM1170			MNHVF	UseVF
22¢	**Appaloosa,** tagged		2.75	.20
	Plate block of 4		15.00	
	y. Se-tenant block of 4 (CM1167-70)		13.00	6.50
	FDC *(Sept. 25, 1985),* any single			2.00
	FDC, block of 4			4.00

1985. PUBLIC EDUCATION ISSUE recognized the importance of public education in the development of America. *Gravure by American Bank Note Co., perforated 11.*

CM1171 *Pen and inkwell, glasses, penmanship drill*

CM1171			MNHVF	UseVF
22¢	**multicolored** tagged (120,000,000)		.35	.20
	Plate block of 4		6.50	
	FDC *(Oct. 1, 1985)*			2.00

1985. INTERNATIONAL YOUTH YEAR ISSUE honored youth groups with outdoor scenes and representative individuals from each group. *Gravure by American Bank Note Co., perforated 11.*

CM1172 *YMCA Youth Camping;* CM1173 *Boy Scouts;*
CM1174 *Big Brothers/Big Sisters;* CM1175 *Camp Fire*

CM1172			MNHVF	UseVF
22¢	**YMCA Youth Camping,** tagged		1.00	.20
	(130,000,000)			
CM1173			MNHVF	UseVF
22¢	**Boy Scouts,** tagged		1.00	.20
CM1174			MNHVF	UseVF
22¢	**Big Brothers/Sisters,** tagged		1.00	.20
CM1175			MNHVF	UseVF
22¢	**Camp Fire,** tagged		1.00	.20
	Plate block of 4		8.00	
	y. Se-tenant block of 4 (CM1172-75)		3.50	3.00
	FDC *(Oct. 7, 1985),* any single			2.00
	FDC, block of 4			4.00

1985. HELP END HUNGER ISSUE focused on the plight of millions suffering from hunger worldwide. *Gravure by American Bank Note Co., perforated 11.*

CM1176 *Help End Hunger*

CM1176			MNHVF	UseVF
22¢	**multicolored** tagged (129,000,000)		.35	.20
	Plate block of 4		3.00	
	FDC *(Oct. 15, 1985)*			1.75

1986. ARKANSAS STATEHOOD ISSUE marked the 150th anniversary of Arkansas' entry into the Union as the 25th state. *Gravure by American Bank Note Co., perforated 11.*

CM1177 *Old State House, Little Rock, Ark.*

CM1177			MNHVF	UseVF
22¢	**multicolored** tagged		.35	.20
	Plate block of 4		3.00	
	FDC *(Jan. 3, 1986)*			1.75
	v. Vertical pair, imperforate horizontally		—	

1986. STAMP COLLECTING BOOKLET ISSUE celebrated philately. This first booklet of commemorative stamps was issued by the U.S. Postal Service on the same day as a booklet about stamp collecting was issued by the postal administration of Sweden (Sweden 1368). The U.S. also paid tribute to the centennial of the Smithsonian Institution's first acceptance of philatelic items and to the centennial year of the American Philatelic Society. The cover of the U.S. stamp collecting booklet was an acceptable admission ticket to the international stamp show, Ameripex '86. *Offset and intaglio, perforated 10 vertically on 1 or 2 sides.*

CM1178 *Handstamp, magnifying glass, 1883 stamps;* CM1179 *Boy with his stamp collection;* CM1180 *2 Swedish stamps and U.S. CM191;* CM1181 *First-day cover of 1986 Presidents souvenir sheet* B167

CM1178			MNHVF	UseVF
22¢	**Covers & handstamp,** tagged		.40	.20
	(67,996,800)			
CM1179			MNHVF	UseVF
22¢	**Youth w/albums,** tagged		.40	.20
CM1180			MNHVF	UseVF
22¢	**Magnifier & stamp,** tagged		.40	.20

CM1181		MNHVF	UseVF
22¢	**Ameripex '86 souvenir sheet,** tagged	.40	.20
	FDC (Jan. 23, 1986), any single		2.00
	n. Booklet pane of 4 (CM1178-1181)	2.00	
	FDC, pane of 4		5.00
	nv. Booklet pane w/black omitted (CM1178 & CM1181)	45.00	150.00
	nv1. Booklet pane w/blue omitted (CM1178-CM1180)	2,500.00	
	nv2. Booklet pane w/light brown omitted	—	

1986. LOVE STAMP ISSUE was the fifth U.S. Love stamp. *Gravure, perforated 11.*

CM1182 *Puppy*

CM1182		MNHVF	UseVF
22¢	**multicolored** tagged (947,450,000)	.35	.20
	Plate block of 4	3.50	
	FDC (Jan. 30, 1986)		1.75
	zo. Tagging omitted		

1986. SOJOURNER TRUTH ISSUE in the Black Heritage Series honored the woman who, after acquiring her freedom, took a new name and dedicated her life to the enfranchisement and education of freed slaves and to the cause of human rights (1797-1853). *Gravure by American Bank Note Co., perforated 11.*

CM1183 *Sojourner Truth*

CM1183		MNHVF	UseVF
22¢	**multicolored** tagged (130,000,000)	.35	.20
	Plate block of 4	3.50	
	FDC (Feb. 4, 1986)		2.50

1986. REPUBLIC OF TEXAS ISSUE commemorated the 150th anniversary of Texan independence from Mexico. *Gravure by American Bank Note Co., perforated 11.*

CM1184 *Spur on Texas state flag*

CM1184		MNHVF	UseVF
22¢	**dark blue, dark red & dark gray** tagged (136,500,000)	.35	.20
	Plate block of 4	3.50	
	FDC (March 2, 1986)		2.00
	v. dark red omitted	2,550.00	
	v1. Horizontal pair, imperforate vertically	1,100.00	

1986. FISH BOOKLET ISSUE featured five fish common to the U.S. waters. *Gravure, perforated 10 horizontally on 1 or 2 sides.*

CM1185 *Muskellunge*

CM1186 *Atlantic cod*

CM1187 *Largemouth bass*

CM1188 *Bluefin tuna*

CM1189 *Catfish*

B168

CM1185		MNHVF	UseVF
22¢	**Muskellunge,** tagged (219,990,000)	1.75	.20

CM1186		MNHVF	UseVF
22¢	**Atlantic cod,** tagged	1.75	.20

CM1187		MNHVF	UseVF
22¢	**Largemouth bass,** tagged	1.75	.20

CM1188		MNHVF	UseVF
22¢	**Bluefin tuna,** tagged	1.75	.20

CM1189		MNHVF	UseVF
22¢	**Catfish,** tagged	1.75	.20
	FDC (March 21, 1986), any single		2.00
	n. Booklet pane of 5 (CM1185-89)	8.50	
	FDC, pane of 5		6.00

1986. PUBLIC HOSPITALS ISSUE honored U.S. public hospitals that trace their history back to Philadelphia General Hospital, which opened about 1731 (closed in 1977). *Gravure by American Bank Note Co., perforated 11.*

CM1190 *Public hospitals*

CM1190		MNHVF	UseVF
22¢	**multicolored** tagged (130,000,000)	.35	.20
	Plate block of 4	3.25	
	FDC (April 11, 1986)		1.75
	v. Horizontal pair, imperforate vertically	1,250.00	
	v1. Vertical pair, imperforate horizontally	375.00	

Where adequate pricing information for a specific item has proven to be currently unobtainable (as in the case of a recently discovered error or, more prosaically, a common plate block in used condition) in the place of a value a line appears (—).

1986. DUKE ELLINGTON ISSUE in the Performing Arts Series paid homage to the renowned jazz composer on the 75th anniversary of his birth. Edward Kennedy Ellington (1899-1974) was a creative master of jazz composition, songwriting, film scoring, ballet, and sacred music alike. *Gravure by American Bank Note Co., perforated 11.*

CM1191 *Duke Ellington*

CM1191

22¢		MNHVF	UseVF
	multicolored tagged *(130,000,000)*	.35	.20
	Plate block of 4	3.00	
	FDC *(April 29, 1986)*		2.75
	v. Vertical pair, imperforate horizontally	900.00	375.00

1986. PRESIDENTS SOUVENIR SHEETS honored U.S. presidents on four souvenir sheets of nine stamps (one for each president and one featuring the White House). The sheets were issued in conjunction with Ameripex '86, in Chicago. *Intaglio, perforated 11.*

CM1192 *Presidents I*

CM1192

$1.98		MNHVF	UseVF
	Souvenir sheet of 9 *(5,825,050)*	5.25	4.50
	a. 22¢ George Washington, tagged	.50	.40
	b. 22¢ John Adams, tagged	.50	.40
	c. 22¢ Thomas Jefferson, tagged	.50	.40
	d. 22¢ James Madison, tagged	.50	.40
	e. 22¢ James Monroe, tagged	.50	.40
	f. 22¢ John Quincy Adams, tagged	.50	.40
	g. 22¢ Andrew Jackson, tagged	.50	.40
	h. 22¢ Martin Van Buren, tagged	.50	.40
	i. 22¢ William Henry Harrison, tagged	.50	.40
	FDC *(May 22, 1986)*, any single		1.75
	FDC, souvenir sheet		8.00
	v. black (inscription) omitted	2,000.00	—
	v1. Intaglio blue omitted	3,500.00	
	v2. Pane of 9, imperforate	10,500.00	

CM1193 *Presidents II*

AMERIPEX 86
International
Stamp Show
Chicago, Illinois
May 22-June 1, 1986

CM1193

$1.98		MNHVF	UseVF
	Souvenir sheet of 9 *(5,825,050)*	5.25	4.50
	a. 22¢ John Tyler, tagged	.50	.40
	b. 22¢ James K. Polk, tagged	.50	.40
	c. 22¢ Zachary Taylor, tagged	.50	.40
	d. 22¢ Millard Fillmore, tagged	.50	.40
	e. 22¢ Franklin Pierce, tagged	.50	.40
	f. 22¢ James Buchanan, tagged	.50	.40
	g. 22¢ Abraham Lincoln, tagged	.50	.40
	h. 22¢ Andrew Johnson, tagged	.50	.40
	i. 22¢ Ulysses S. Grant, tagged	.50	.40
	FDC *(May 22, 1986)*, any single		1.75
	FDC, souvenir sheet		8.00
	v. black (inscription) omitted	3,000.00	

CM1194 *Presidents III*

AMERIPEX 86
International
Stamp Show
Chicago, Illinois
May 22-June 1, 1986

CM1194

$1.98		MNHVF	UseVF
	Souvenir sheet of 9 *(5,825,050)*	5.25	4.50
	a. 22¢ Rutherford B. Hayes, tagged	.50	.40
	b. 22¢ James A. Garfield, tagged	.50	.40
	c. 22¢ Chester A. Arthur, tagged	.50	.40
	d. 22¢ Grover Cleveland, tagged	.50	.40

e.	22¢ Benjamin Harrison, tagged	.50	.40
f.	22¢ William McKinley, tagged	.50	.40
g.	22¢ Theodore Roosevelt, tagged	.50	.40
h.	22¢ William H. Taft, tagged	.50	.40
i.	22¢ Woodrow Wilson, tagged	.50	.40
	FDC (May 22, 1986), any single		1.75
	FDC, souvenir sheet		8.00
v.	black (inscription) omitted	—	
v1.	Intaglio brown omitted	2,750.00	

CM1195 *Presidents IV*

Presidents of the United States: IV

AMERIPEX 86 International Stamp Show Chicago, Illinois May 22-June 1, 1986

CM1195		MNHVF	UseVF
$1.98	**Souvenir sheet of 9** (5,825,050)	5.25	4.50
a.	22¢ Warren G. Harding, tagged	.50	.40
b.	22¢ Calvin Coolidge, tagged	.50	.40
c.	22¢ Herbert C. Hoover, tagged	.50	.40
d.	22¢ Franklin D. Roosevelt, tagged	.50	.40
e.	22¢ White House, tagged	.50	.40
f.	22¢ Harry S. Truman, tagged	.50	.40
g.	22¢ Dwight D. Eisenhower, tagged	.50	.40
h.	22¢ John F. Kennedy, tagged	.50	.40
i.	22¢ Lyndon B. Johnson, tagged	.50	.40
	FDC (May 22, 1986), any single		2.75
	FDC, souvenir sheet		8.00
v.	Intaglio blue black inscription omitted on 6 stamps at left (a-b, d-e, g-h)	2,250.00	
zo.	Tagging omitted on 3 stamps at right (c, f, i)	—	

1986. ARCTIC EXPLORERS ISSUE honored five pioneers of popular exploration who accomplished a variety of geographical, anthropological, mapping, and other scientific work. *Gravure, perforated 11.*

CM1196 *Elisha Kent Kane;* CM1197 *Adolphus W. Greely;* CM1198 *Vilhjalmur Stefansson;* CM1199 *Robert E. Peary and Matthew Henson*

CM1196			MNHVF	UseVF
22¢	**E.K. Kane,**	(130,000,000)	1.10	.20
CM1197			**MNHVF**	**UseVF**
22¢	**A.W. Greely**		1.10	.20
CM1198			**MNHVF**	**UseVF**
22¢	**V. Stefansson**		1.10	.20
CM1199			**MNHVF**	**UseVF**
22¢	**R.E. Peary & M. Henson**		1.10	.20
	Plate block of 4		8.00	
y.	Se-tenant block of 4 (CM1196-99)		5.50	3.75
	FDC (May 28, 1986), any single			2.00
	FDC block of 4			5.00
vy.	Se-tenant block of 4, engraved black omitted		11,550.00	
vy1.	Se-tenant block of 4, engraved black omitted from CM1196-97 only		—	

1986. STATUE OF LIBERTY ISSUE commemorated the 100th anniversary of this sculpture, a gift to the United States from the people of France as a demonstration of their empathy with the nation's founding principles. France simultaneously released a 2.20-franc stamp (France 2764) with matching design. *Intaglio, perforated 11.*

CM1200 *Statue of Liberty*

Liberty 1886-1986

USA 22

CM1200		MNHVF	UseVF
22¢	**red & blue** (220,725,000)	.35	.20
	Plate block of 4	4.00	
	FDC (July 4, 1986)		2.00

1986. NAVAJO ART ISSUE depicted four Navajo blankets. This sixth issue in the Folk Art Series celebrated Native American handicrafts. *Offset and intaglio, perforated 11.*

CM1201, CM1202, CM1203, CM1204 *Navajo blankets*

CM1201		MNHVF	UseVF
22¢	**multicolored** (240,525,000)	.40	.20
CM1202		**MNHVF**	**UseVF**
22¢	**multicolored**	.40	.20
CM1203		**MNHVF**	**UseVF**
22¢	**multicolored**	.40	.20
CM1204		**MNHVF**	**UseVF**
22¢	**multicolored**	.40	.20
	Plate block of 4	6.00	
y.	Se-tenant block of 4 (CM1201-04)	3.00	1.50
	FDC (Sept. 4, 1986), any single		2.00
	FDC, block of 4		4.00
vy.	Se-tenant block of 4 (engraved) black omitted	375.00	

1986. T.S. ELIOT ISSUE Sixth in the Literary Arts Series commemorated Thomas Stearns Eliot (1888-1965), prominent poet ("The Love Song of J. Albert Prufrock"), critic, editor, and dramatist, awarded the Nobel Prize for Literature. *Gravure, perforated 11.*

CM1205 *T.S. Eliot*

CM1205

22¢	copper red *(131,700,000)*	MNHVF	UseVF
		.35	.20
	Plate block of 4	2.75	
	FDC *(Sept. 26, 1986)*		1.75

1986. WOODCARVED FIGURINES ISSUE was the seventh in the American Folk Art Series. Since Colonial times, woodcarved figurines frequently served as advertisements by merchants, displayed outside their shop doors. *Gravure by American Bank Note Co., perforated 11.*

CM1206 *Highlander figure*

CM1207 *Ship figurehead*

CM1208 *Nautical figure*

CM1209 *Cigar store figure*

CM1206

22¢	Highlander figure, tagged *(240,000,000)*	MNHVF	UseVF
		.40	.20

CM1207

22¢	Ship figurehead, tagged	MNHVF	UseVF
		.40	.20

CM1208

22¢	Nautical figure, tagged	MNHVF	UseVF
		.40	.20

CM1209

22¢	Cigar store figure, tagged	MNHVF	UseVF
		.40	.20
	Plate block of 4	4.50	
	y. Se-tenant block of 4 (CM1206-09)	3.25	1.50
	FDC *(Oct. 1, 1986)*, any single		2.00
	FDC, block of 4		4.00
	vy. Block of 4, imperforate vertically	1,450.00	
	vy1. Pair, any, imperforate vertically	300.00	

1987. MICHIGAN STATEHOOD ISSUE honored the 150th anniversary of Michigan's admission as the 26th state of the union. *Gravure, perforated 11.*

CM1210 *White pine*

CM1210

22¢	multicolored tagged *(167,430,000)*	MNHVF	UseVF
		.35	.20
	Plate block of 4	2.75	
	Pair, gutter between	—	
	FDC *(Jan. 26, 1987)*		1.75

1987. PAN-AMERICAN GAMES ISSUE commemorated the international sports competition held every four years since 1957. *Gravure, perforated 11.*

CM1211 *Runners*

CM1211

22¢	multicolored tagged *(166,555,000)*	MNHVF	UseVF
		.35	.20
	Plate block of 4	2.75	
	FDC *(Jan. 29, 1987)*		1.75
	v. metallic silver omitted	1,600.00	

1987. LOVE STAMP ISSUE The sixth in the Love Series. *Gravure, perforated 11 1/2x11.*

CM1212 *Love*

CM1212

22¢	multicolored tagged *(811,560,000)*	MNHVF	UseVF
		.35	.20
	Plate block of 4	2.75	
	FDC *(Jan. 30, 1987)*		1.75

1987. JEAN-BAPTISTE DU SABLE ISSUE in the Black Heritage Series honored the founder of Chicago in the year of that city's sesquicentennial. Du Sable played an active role in the frontier settlement on the Chicago River as a general merchant, fur trader, farmer, and Indian overseer. *Gravure, perforated 11.*

CM1213 *Jean-Baptiste du Sable*

CM1213

22¢	multicolored tagged *(142,905,000)*	MNHVF	UseVF
		.35	.20
	Plate block of 4	3.25	
	FDC *(Feb. 20, 1987)*		2.50

1987. ENRICO CARUSO ISSUE in the Performing Arts Series honored one of the most popular opera tenors (1873-1921) of all time and the world's highest paid performer in his day. *Gravure by American Bank Note Co., perforated 11.*

CM1214 *Enrico Caruso*

CM1214

22¢	multicolored tagged *(130,000,000)*	MNHVF	UseVF
		.35	.20

			MNHVF	UseVF
	Plate block of 4		2.75	
	FDC *(Feb. 27, 1987)*			1.75
	v. Intaglio black omitted		5,000.00	

1987. GIRL SCOUTS ISSUE marked the 75th anniversary of the Girl Scouts. Juliette Low (CM316) formed the first Girl Scout troop in the United States, patterned after the English Girl Guides. *Intaglio (Giori Press), perforated 11.*

CM1215 *Girl Scout badges*

CM1215		MNHVF	UseVF
22¢	**multicolored** tagged *(149,980,000)*	.35	.20
	Plate block of 4	3.25	
	FDC *(March 12, 1987)*		3.00
	v. black, yellow, magenta, cyan & green omitted	2,750.00	
	v1. Intaglio black & red omitted	—	

1987. SPECIAL OCCASIONS ISSUE consisted of eight designs (CM1216 and CM1221 each are repeated once and CM1216 has two different perforation configurations) in a booklet pane of 10. The stamps were intended for use on greeting cards and other special personal mail. *Gravure, perforated 10 on 1, 2, or 3 sides.*

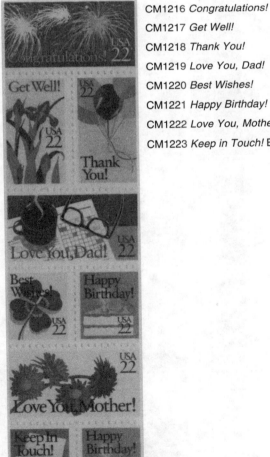

CM1216 *Congratulations!*

CM1217 *Get Well!*

CM1218 *Thank You!*

CM1219 *Love You, Dad!*

CM1220 *Best Wishes!*

CM1221 *Happy Birthday!*

CM1222 *Love You, Mother!*

CM1223 *Keep in Touch!* B169

CM1216		MNHVF	UseVF
22¢	**Congratulations,** tagged *(610,425,000)*	1.75	.40
CM1217		MNHVF	UseVF
22¢	**Get Well,** tagged	1.75	.40
CM1218		MNHVF	UseVF
22¢	**Thank You,** tagged	1.75	.40
CM1219		MNHVF	UseVF
22¢	**Love You, Dad,** tagged	1.75	.40
CM1220		MNHVF	UseVF
22¢	**Best Wishes,** tagged	1.75	.40
CM1221		MNHVF	UseVF
22¢	**Happy Birthday,** tagged	1.75	.40
CM1222		MNHVF	UseVF
22¢	**Love You, Mother,** tagged	1.75	.40
CM1223		MNHVF	UseVF
22¢	**Keep in Touch,** tagged	1.75	.40
	FDC *(April 20, 1987)*, any single		1.00
	n. Booklet pane of 10 (2 each CM1216, CM1221 and 1 each CM1217-20, CM1222-23)	16.00	12.00
	FDC, pane of 10		7.00

Nos. CM1224 and CM1225 are not assigned.

1987. UNITED WAY ISSUE celebrated the community-based charity's 100th anniversary. *Offset and intaglio, perforated 11.*

CM1226 *Faces in profile*

CM1226		MNHVF	UseVF
22¢	**multicolored** tagged *(156,995,000)*	.35	.20
	Plate block of 4	2.75	
	FDC *(April 28, 1987)*		1.75

1987. AMERICAN WILDLIFE ISSUE 50 different stamps se-tenant in one pane released during Capex 87 in Toronto, Canada. Stamps feature animals indigenous to North America and Hawaii. *Gravure, perforated 11.*

CM1227		MNHVF	UseVF
22¢	**Barn Swallow,** tagged	1.50	.55
CM1228		MNHVF	UseVF
22¢	**Monarch Butterfly,** tagged	1.50	.55
CM1229		MNHVF	UseVF
22¢	**Bighorn Sheep,** tagged	1.50	.55
CM1230		MNHVF	UseVF
22¢	**Broad-tailed Hummingbird,** tagged	1.50	.55
CM1231		MNHVF	UseVF
22¢	**Cottontail,** tagged	1.50	.55
CM1232		MNHVF	UseVF
22¢	**Osprey,** tagged	1.50	.55
CM1233		MNHVF	UseVF
22¢	**Mountain Lion,** tagged	1.50	.55
CM1234		MNHVF	UseVF
22¢	**Luna Moth,** tagged	1.50	.55
CM1235		MNHVF	UseVF
22¢	**Mule Deer,** tagged	1.50	.55
CM1236		MNHVF	UseVF
22¢	**Gray Squirrel,** tagged	1.50	.55
CM1237		MNHVF	UseVF
22¢	**Armadillo,** tagged	1.50	.55
CM1238		MNHVF	UseVF
22¢	**Eastern Chipmunk,** tagged	1.50	.55
CM1239		MNHVF	UseVF
22¢	**Moose,** tagged	1.50	.55
CM1240		MNHVF	UseVF
22¢	**Black Bear,** tagged	1.50	.55
CM1241		MNHVF	UseVF
22¢	**Tiger Swallowtail,** tagged	1.50	.55
CM1242		MNHVF	UseVF
22¢	**Bobwhite,** tagged	1.50	.55
CM1243		MNHVF	UseVF
22¢	**Ringtail,** tagged	1.50	.55
CM1244		MNHVF	UseVF
22¢	**Red-winged Blackbird,** tagged	1.50	.55

			MNHVF	UseVF				MNHVF	UseVF
CM1245 22¢	American Lobster,	tagged	1.50	.55	**CM1259** 22¢	Blue Jay,	tagged	1.50	.55
CM1246 22¢	Black-tailed Jack Rabbit, Rabbit,	tagged	1.50	.55	**CM1260** 22¢	Pika,	tagged	1.50	.55
CM1247 22¢	Scarlet Tanager,	tagged	1.50	.55	**CM1261** 22¢	Bison,	tagged	1.50	.55
CM1248 22¢	Woodchuck,	tagged	1.50	.55	**CM1262** 22¢	Snowy Egret,	tagged	1.50	.55
CM1249 22¢	Roseate Spoonbill,	tagged	1.50	.55	**CM1263** 22¢	Gray Wolf,	tagged	1.50	.55
CM1250 22¢	Bald Eagle,	tagged	1.50	.55	**CM1264** 22¢	Mountain Goat,	tagged	1.50	.55
CM1251 22¢	Alaskan Brown Bear,	tagged	1.50	.55	**CM1265** 22¢	Deer Mouse,	tagged	1.50	.55
CM1252 22¢	Iiwi,	tagged	1.50	.55	**CM1266** 22¢	Black-tailed Prairie Dog,	tagged	1.50	.55
CM1253 22¢	Badger,	tagged	1.50	.55	**CM1267** 22¢	Box Turtle,	tagged	1.50	.55
CM1254 22¢	Pronghorn,	tagged	1.50	.55	**CM1268** 22¢	Wolverine,	tagged	1.50	.55
CM1255 22¢	River Otter,	tagged	1.50	.55	**CM1269** 22¢	American Elk,	tagged	1.50	.55
CM1256 22¢	Ladybug,	tagged	1.50	.55	**CM1270** 22¢	California Sea Lion,	tagged	1.50	.55
CM1257 22¢	Beaver,	tagged	1.50	.55	**CM1271** 22¢	Mockingbird,	tagged	1.50	.55
CM1258 22¢	White-tailed Deer,	tagged	1.50	.55	**CM1272** 22¢	Raccoon,	tagged	1.50	.55

CM1227-1276 *Examples of American wildlife*

CM1273		MNHVF	UseVF
22¢	**Bobcat,** tagged	1.50	.55

CM1274		MNHVF	UseVF
22¢	**Black-footed Ferret,** tagged	1.50	.55

CM1275		MNHVF	UseVF
22¢	**Canada Goose,** tagged	1.50	.55

CM1276		MNHVF	UseVF
22¢	**Red Fox,** tagged	1.50	.55
	y. Pane of 50	65.00	20.00
	FDC (June 13, 1987), any single		1.50
	FDC, pane of 50		30.00
	v. red omitted, any single	—	

Constitution Ratification Bicentennial Series

1987. DELAWARE STATEHOOD ISSUE was the first stamp in a series commemorating the bicentennial of the Constitution. Delaware was the first state to vote for ratification. *Offset and intaglio by Bureau of Engraving and Printing, perforated 11.*

CM1277 *Delaware state seal*

CM1277		MNHVF	UseVF
22¢	**multicolored** tagged (166,725,000)	.35	.20
	Plate block of 4	3.00	
	FDC (July 4, 1987)		2.00

1987. FRIENDSHIP WITH MOROCCO ISSUE marked the bicentennial of diplomatic relations between the United States and Morocco. Morocco issued a stamp at the same time (Morocco 1281). *Intaglio (Giori Press), perforated 11.*

CM1278 *Arabesque from door of Dar Batha Palace, Fez, Morocco*

CM1278		MNHVF	UseVF
22¢	**red & black** tagged (157,475,000)	.35	.20
	Plate block of 4	2.75	
	FDC (July 17, 1987)		1.75
	v. Intaglio black omitted	350.00	

1987. WILLIAM FAULKNER ISSUE Seventh in the Literary Arts Series honored the novelist and poet (1897-1962) who won the Nobel Prize in 1955. He was noted for his writings about life in the South. *Intaglio, perforated 11.*

CM1279 *William Faulkner*

CM1279		MNHVF	UseVF
22¢	**green** tagged (156,225,000)	.35	.20
	Plate block of 4	2.75	
	FDC (Aug. 3, 1987)		1.75
	v. Single, imperforate	—	

Note: Imperforate singles are untagged and from printer's waste.

1987. LACEMAKING ISSUE in the American Folk Art Series featured four different designs of delicate needlework. *Offset and intaglio, perforated 11. Intaglio white ink was printed on top of offset blue to achieve the lace effect.*

CM1280 *Squash blossoms*

CM1281 *Floral design*

CM1282 *Floral lace*

CM1283 *Dogwood blossoms*

CM1280		MNHVF	UseVF
22¢	**Squash blossoms,** tagged (163,980,000)	.40	.20

CM1281		MNHVF	UseVF
22¢	**Floral design,** tagged	.40	.20

CM1282		MNHVF	UseVF
22¢	**Floral lace design,** tagged	.40	.20

CM1283		MNHVF	UseVF
22¢	**Dogwood blossoms,** tagged	.40	.20
	Plate block of 4	5.00	
	y. Se-tenant block of 4 (CM1280-83)	2.50	1.50
	FDC (Aug. 14, 1987), any single		2.00
	FDC, block of 4		4.00
	v1. White omitted, any single	165.00	
	vy. Se-tenant block of 4, white omitted	900.00	

1987. PENNSYLVANIA STATEHOOD ISSUE second in the Constitution Ratification Bicentennial Series. The Keystone State ratified the U.S. Constitution on Dec. 12, 1787. *Gravure by American Bank Note Co., perforated 11.*

CM1284 *Independence Hall, Philadelphia*

CM1284		MNHVF	UseVF
22¢	**multicolored** tagged (186,575,000)	.35	.20
	Plate block of 4	3.95	
	FDC (Aug. 26, 1987)		2.00

1987. CONSTITUTION BICENTENNIAL ISSUE released in booklet format, commemorated the 200th anniversary of the drafting of the U.S. Constitution with excerpts from the preamble. *Gravure, perforated 10 horizontally on 1 or 2 sides.*

The minimum stamp value in this catalog (20¢) represents the cost to a retail stamp dealer to maintain in inventory and supply to a collector on demand a single copy of even the most common stamp in fault-free condition and a grade of fine-to-very-fine.

CM1285 *The Bicentennial...*

CM1286 *We the people...*

CM1287 *Establish justice...*

CM1288 *And secure... liberty...*

CM1289 *Do ordain...*

CM1285

		MNHVF	UseVF
22¢	**The Bicentennial...,** tagged	.75	.25
	(584,340,000)		

CM1286

		MNHVF	UseVF
22¢	**We the people...,** tagged	.75	.25

CM1287

		MNHVF	UseVF
22¢	**Establish justice...,** tagged	.75	.25

CM1288

		MNHVF	UseVF
22¢	**And secure... liberty...,** tagged	.75	.25

CM1289

		MNHVF	UseVF
22¢	**Do ordain...,** tagged	.75	.25
	FDC (Aug. 28, 1987), any single		2.00
	n. Booklet pane of 5 (CM1285-89)	4.25	3.50
	FDC, pane of 5		5.00
	v. greenish gray (background) omitted	—	

1987. NEW JERSEY STATEHOOD ISSUE third in the Constitution Ratification Bicentennial Series. New Jersey ratified the document Dec. 18, 1787. *Gravure by American Bank Note Co., perforated 11.*

CM1290 *Farmer carrying produce*

CM1290

		MNHVF	UseVF
22¢	**multicolored** tagged (184,325,000)	.35	.20
	Plate block of 4	3.50	
	FDC (Sept. 11, 1987)		2.00
	v. Intaglio black omitted	6,500.00	

1987. CONSTITUTION BICENTENNIAL ISSUE honored the 200th anniversary of the signing of the document. *Offset and intaglio, perforated 11.*

CM1291 *Constitution and feather pen*

CM1291

		MNHVF	UseVF
22¢	**multicolored** tagged (168,995,000)	.35	.20
	Plate block of 4	3.25	
	FDC (Sept. 17, 1987)		2.00

1987. CERTIFIED PUBLIC ACCOUNTANTS ISSUE honored the centennial of the accounting profession in the United States. *Intaglio, perforated 11.*

CM1292 *Spreadsheet and pen*

CM1292

		MNHVF	UseVF
22¢	**multicolored** tagged (163,120,000)	1.90	.20
	Plate block of 4	8.00	
	FDC (Sept. 21, 1987)		12.00
	v. Intaglio black omitted	700.00	

1987. STEAM LOCOMOTIVE ISSUE a five-stamp booklet, paid tribute to the steam locomotives that drove the railroad revolution in America. *Offset and intaglio, perforated 10, horizontally.*

CM1293 Stourbridge Lion

CM1294 Best Friend of Charleston

CM1295 John Bull

CM1296 Brother Jonathan

CM1297 Gowan & Marx B171

CM1293

		MNHVF	UseVF
22¢	**Stourbridge Lion,** tagged	.75	.25

CM1294		MNHVF	UseVF
22¢	**Best Friend of Charleston,** tagged	.75	.25

CM1295		MNHVF	UseVF
22¢	**John Bull,** tagged	.75	.25

CM1296		MNHVF	UseVF
22¢	**Brother Jonathan,** tagged	.75	.25
	v. red omitted	1,100.00	

CM1297		MNHVF	UseVF
22¢	**Gowan & Marx,** tagged	.75	.25
	v. blue omitted	—	
	FDC *(Oct. 1, 1993),* any single		2.00
	n. Booklet pane of 5 (CM1293-97)	3.75	2.50
	FDC, pane of 5		4.00
	nv. Booklet pane of 5, black omitted	—	
	nzo. Booklet pane of 5, untagged	—	

1988. GEORGIA STATEHOOD ISSUE fourth in the Constitution Ratification Bicentennial Series. Georgia ratified the Constitution Jan. 2, 1788. *Gravure, perforated 11.*

CM1298 *Live oak and Atlanta skyline*

CM1298		MNHVF	UseVF
22¢	**multicolored** tagged *(165,845,000)*	.35	.20
	Plate block of 4	3.50	
	FDC *(Jan. 6, 1988)*		2.00

1988. CONNECTICUT STATEHOOD ISSUE fifth in the Constitution Ratification Bicentennial Series. Connecticut ratified the Constitution Jan. 9, 1788. *Offset and intaglio, perforated 11.*

CM1299 *Harbor scene*

CM1299		MNHVF	UseVF
22¢	**multicolored** tagged *(155,170,000)*	.35	.20
	Plate block of 4	3.50	
	FDC *(Jan. 9, 1988)*		2.00

1988. WINTER OLYMPICS ISSUE honored the 1988 Winter Games at Calgary, Alberta, Canada. *Gravure by American Bank Note Co., perforated 11.*

CM1300 *Alpine skier*

CM1300		MNHVF	UseVF
22¢	**multicolored** tagged *(158,870,000)*	.35	.20
	Plate block of 4	3.25	
	FDC *(Jan. 10, 1988)*		1.75

1988. AUSTRALIA BICENTENNIAL ISSUE marked the 200th anniversary of the first European settlement in Australia. The stamp was issued at the same time as one by Australia (Australia 1175). *Gravure, perforated 11.*

CM1301 *Cartoon of Australian koala and American bald eagle*

CM1301		MNHVF	UseVF
22¢	**multicolored** tagged *(145,560,000)*	.35	.20
	Plate block of 4	2.75	
	FDC *(Jan. 26, 1988)*		1.75

1988. JAMES WELDON JOHNSON ISSUE in the Black Heritage Series honored the educator, diplomat, lawyer, author and lyricist (1871-1938). *Gravure by American Bank Note Co., perforated 11.*

CM1302 *James Weldon Johnson*

CM1302		MNHVF	UseVF
22¢	**multicolored** tagged *(97,300,000)*	.35	.20
	Plate block of 4	3.00	
	FDC *(Feb. 2, 1988)*		2.50

1988. CATS ISSUE depicted eight popular feline breeds. *Gravure by American Bank Note Co., perforated 11.*

CM1303 *Siamese, Exotic Shorthair;* CM1304 *Abyssinian, Himalayan;* CM1305 *Maine Coon Cat, Burmese;* CM1306 *American Shorthair, Persian*

CM1303		MNHVF	UseVF
22¢	**Siamese, Exotic Shorthair,** tagged *(158,556,000)*	1.00	.20

CM1304		MNHVF	UseVF
22¢	**Abyssinian, Himalayan,** tagged	1.00	.20

CM1305		MNHVF	UseVF
22¢	**Maine Coon Cat, Burmese,** tagged	1.00	.20

CM1306		MNHVF	UseVF
22¢	**American Shorthair, Persian,** tagged	1.00	.20
	Plate block of 4	5.75	
	y. Se-tenant block of 4 (CM1303-06)	4.50	2.50
	FDC *(Feb. 5, 1988),* any single		3.00
	FDC, block of 4		8.00

1988. MASSACHUSETTS STATEHOOD ISSUE sixth in the Constitution Ratification Bicentennial Series. Massachusetts' own constitution was a model for the federal document, which it ratified Feb. 6, 1788. *Intaglio, perforated 11.*

CM1307 *Old Statehouse*

CM1307

		MNHVF	UseVF
22¢	**dark blue & dark red** tagged (102,100,000)	.35	.20
	Plate block of 4	3.50	
	FDC (Feb. 6, 1988)		2.00

1988. MARYLAND STATEHOOD ISSUE seventh in the Constitution Ratification Bicentennial Series. Maryland ratified the document April 28, 1788. *Offset and intaglio, perforated 11.*

CM1308 *Skipjack sailboat and Annapolis*

CM1308

		MNHVF	UseVF
22¢	**multicolored** tagged (103,325,000)	.35	.20
	Plate block of 4	3.50	
	FDC (Feb. 15, 1988)		2.00

1988. KNUTE ROCKNE ISSUE in the American Sports Series honored the famed player and Notre Dame University football coach (1888-1931) credited with helping to develop the forward pass with quarterback Gus Dorais. *Offset and intaglio, perforated 11.*

CM1309 *Knute Rockne*

CM1309

		MNHVF	UseVF
22¢	**multicolored** tagged (97,300,000)	.35	.20
	Plate block of 4	3.95	
	FDC (March 9, 1988)		4.00

1988. SOUTH CAROLINA STATEHOOD ISSUE eighth in the Constitution Ratification Bicentennial Series. South Carolina ratified the Constitution May 23, 1788. This was the first commemorative stamp paying the 25¢ First Class rate. *Gravure by American Bank Note Co., perforated 11.*

CM1310 *Palmetto trees*

CM1310

		MNHVF	UseVF
25¢	**multicolored** tagged (162,045,000)	.40	.20
	Plate block of 4	3.95	
	FDC (May 23, 1988)		2.00
	v. Horizontal strip of 3, vertically imperforate between	10,450.00	

1988. FRANCIS OUIMET ISSUE in the American Sports Series honored the 75th anniversary of his victory at the U.S. Open Golf Championship, which made him the first amateur to win the event. *Gravure by American Bank Note Co., perforated 11.*

CM1311 *Francis Ouimet*

CM1311

		MNHVF	UseVF
25¢	**multicolored** tagged (153,045,000)	.40	.20
	Plate block of 4	5.75	
	FDC (June 13, 1988)		7.50

1988. NEW HAMPSHIRE STATEHOOD ISSUE ninth in the Constitution Ratification Bicentennial Series (see also CM380). New Hampshire ratified the Constitution June 21, 1788. *Gravure by American Bank Note Co., perforated 11.*

CM1312 *Old Man of the Mountains*

CM1312

		MNHVF	UseVF
25¢	**multicolored** tagged (153,295,000)	.40	.20
	Plate block of 4	3.95	
	FDC (June 21, 1988)		2.00

1988. VIRGINIA STATEHOOD ISSUE 10th in the Constitution Ratification Bicentennial Series. Virginia ratified the document June 25, 1788. *Offset and intaglio, perforated 11.*

CM1313 *Old Capitol Building, Williamsburg*

Every reasonable effort has been made to make the values in this catalog as accurate, realistic, and up-to-date as possible.

CM1313		MNHVF	UseVF
25¢	multicolored tagged *(153,295,000)*	.40	.20
	Plate block of 4	3.95	
	FDC *(June 25, 1988)*		2.00

1988. LOVE ISSUE seventh in the series begun in 1982, featured a rose and was released in Pasadena, Calif., home of the Rose Bowl. *Gravure, perforated 11.*

CM1314 *Rose*

CM1314		MNHVF	UseVF
25¢	multicolored tagged *(841,240,000)*	.40	.20
	Plate block of 4	3.25	
	FDC *(July 4, 1988)*		1.75
	v. Pair, imperforate	2,750.00	

1988. NEW YORK STATEHOOD ISSUE 11th in the Constitution Ratification Bicentennial Series. New York ratified the Constitution July 26, 1788. *Offset and intaglio, perforated 11.*

CM1315 *Federal Hall, Wall Street, and Trinity Church steeple*

CM1315		MNHVF	UseVF
25¢	multicolored tagged *(183,290,000)*	.40	.20
	Plate block of 4	3.25	
	FDC *(July 26, 1988)*		2.00

1988. LOVE ISSUE the second of the year, this one in a 45¢ denomination, was released to cover the postal rate for 2 ounces of First Class mail (such as a standard wedding invitation and R.S.V.P. envelope). *Gravure, perforated 11.*

CM1316 *Roses*

CM1316		MNHVF	UseVF
45¢	multicolored tagged *(169,765,000)*	1.35	.20
	Plate block of 4	5.75	
	FDC *(Aug. 8, 1988)*		2.00

1988. SUMMER OLYMPIC GAMES ISSUE honored the 14th Summer Games in Seoul, Korea. *Gravure, perforated 11.*

CM1317 *Gymnast on rings*

CM1317		MNHVF	UseVF
25¢	multicolored tagged *(157,215,000)*	.40	.20
	Plate block of 4	3.50	
	FDC *(Aug. 19, 1988)*		1.75

1988. CLASSIC CARS ISSUE featured five antique automobiles in se-tenant booklet pane. *Offset and intaglio, perforated 10 horizontally on 1 or 2 sides.*

CM1318 *Locomobile, 1928*

CM1319 *Pierce-Arrow, 1929*

CM1320 *Cord, 1931*

CM1321 *Packard, 1932*

CM1322 *Duesenberg, 1935* B181

CM1318		MNHVF	UseVF
25¢	Locomobile, tagged *(635,238,000)*	2.00	.50

CM1319		MNHVF	UseVF
25¢	Pierce-Arrow, tagged	2.00	.50

CM1320		MNHVF	UseVF
25¢	Cord, tagged	2.00	.50

CM1321		MNHVF	UseVF
25¢	Packard, tagged	2.00	.50

CM1322		MNHVF	UseVF
25¢	Duesenberg, tagged	2.00	.50
	FDC *(Aug. 25, 1988)*, any single		2.00
	n. Booklet pane of 5 (CM1318-22)	10.00	
	FDC, booklet pane		4.00

1988. ANTARCTIC EXPLORERS ISSUE saluted four men who first explored the vast ice-capped continent of Antarctica. *Gravure by American Bank Note Co., perforated 11.*

CM1323 *Nathaniel Palmer*; CM1324 *Lt. Charles Wilkes*; CM1325 *Richard E. Byrd*; CM1326 *Lincoln Ellsworth*

CM1323		MNHVF	UseVF
25¢	Nathaniel Palmer, tagged *(162,142,500)*	1.00	.20

CM1324

25¢	**Lt. Charles Wilkes,** tagged	MNHVF	UseVF
		1.00	.20

CM1325

25¢	**Richard E. Byrd,** tagged	MNHVF	UseVF
		1.00	.20

CM1326

25¢	**Lincoln Ellsworth,** tagged	MNHVF	UseVF
		1.00	.20
	Plate block of 4	8.00	
	y. Se-tenant block of 4 (CM1323-26)	4.75	3.00
	FDC (Sept. 14, 1988), any single		2.00
	FDC, block of 4		4.00
	v. Block of 4, intaglio black omitted	1,500.00	
	v1. Block of 4, imperforate horizontally	3,000.00	

1988. CAROUSEL ANIMAL ISSUE in the American Folk Art Series presented examples of a popular art form. *Offset and intaglio, perforated 11.*

CM1327 *Deer*

CM1328 *Horse*

CM1329 *Camel*

CM1330 *Goat*

CM1327

25¢	**Deer,** tagged (305,015,000)	MNHVF	UseVF
		1.00	.20

CM1328

25¢	**Horse,** tagged	MNHVF	UseVF
		1.00	.20

CM1329

25¢	**Camel,** tagged	MNHVF	UseVF
		1.00	.20

CM1330

25¢	**Goat,** tagged	MNHVF	UseVF
		1.00	.20
	Plate block of 4	6.00	
	y. Se-tenant block of 4 (CM1327-30)	4.75	2.00
	FDC (Oct. 1, 1988), any single		2.00
	FDC, block of 4		6.00

1988. SPECIAL OCCASIONS ISSUE had four different designs. Each booklet pane contains six stamps, three each of two designs. The two different panes bring the total to 12 stamps (three of each design). *Gravure by American Bank Note Co., perforated 11 on 2 or 3 sides.*

CM1331, B182 *Happy Birthday*

CM1331

25¢	**multicolored** tagged (480,000,000)	MNHVF	UseVF
		1.00	.20

CM1332 *Best Wishes*

CM1332

25¢	**multicolored** tagged	MNHVF	UseVF
		1.00	.20
	n. Booklet pane of 6 (3 each CM1331-32) with gutter between	5.00	4.00
	FDC, (Oct. 22, 1988), either single		1.25
	FDC, booklet pane		5.00

CM1333 *Thinking of You*

CM1333

25¢	**multicolored** tagged	MNHVF	UseVF
		1.00	.20

CM1334 *Love You*

CM1334

25¢	**multicolored** tagged	MNHVF	UseVF
		1.00	.20
	n. Booklet pane of 6 (3 each CM1333-34) with gutter between	5.00	4.00
	nv. Booklet pane, imperforate	—	
	FDC (Oct. 22, 1988), any single		1.25
	FDC, booklet pane		5.00

1989. MONTANA STATEHOOD ISSUE commemorated the state's centennial with a design by Western artist Charles Russell (see also CM528). Montana became the 41st state Nov. 8, 1889. *Offset and intaglio, perforated 11.*

CM1335 *C.M. Russell and friends*

CM1335

25¢	**multicolored** tagged	MNHVF	UseVF
		.40	.20
	Plate block of 4	4.00	
	v. Pair, imperforate	—	
	FDC (Jan. 15, 1989)		2.00

1989. A. PHILIP RANDOLPH ISSUE in the Black Heritage Series honored a prominent, respected and indefatigable voice (1889-1979) for the rights of minority labor. *Gravure, perforated 11.*

CM1336 *Asa Philip Randolph*

CM1336

25¢	**multicolored** tagged (151,675,000)	MNHVF	UseVF
		.40	.20
	Plate block of 4	3.75	
	FDC (Feb. 3, 1989)		2.50

1989. NORTH DAKOTA STATEHOOD ISSUE marked the centennial of the 39th state to enter the Union — Nov. 2, 1889. *Gravure by American Bank Note Co., perforated 11.*

CM1337 *Grain elevator*

CM1337		MNHVF	UseVF
25¢	multicolored tagged *(163,000,000)*	.40	.20
	Plate block of 4	3.50	
	FDC *(Feb. 21, 1989)*		1.75

1989. WASHINGTON STATEHOOD ISSUE marked the centennial of the 42nd state to enter the Union — Nov. 11, 1889. *Gravure by American Bank Note Co., perforated 11.*

CM1338 *Mount Rainier*

CM1338		MNHVF	UseVF
25¢	multicolored tagged *(264,625,000)*	.40	.20
	Plate block of 4	2.00	
	FDC *(Feb. 22, 1989)*		1.75

1989. STEAMBOATS ISSUE a se-tenant five-stamp booklet issue depicted five of America's earliest and most innovative crafts. *Offset and intaglio, perforated 11 on 1 or 2 sides.*

CM1339 Experiment

CM1340 Phoenix

CM1341 New Orleans

CM1342 Washington

CM1343 Walk in the Water

B183

CM1339		MNHVF	UseVF
25¢	*Experiment,* tagged *(204,984,000)*	.75	.20
CM1340		**MNHVF**	**UseVF**
25¢	*Phoenix,* tagged	.75	.20

CM1341		MNHVF	UseVF
25¢	*New Orleans,* tagged	.75	.20
CM1342		**MNHVF**	**UseVF**
25¢	*Washington,* tagged	.75	.20
CM1343		**MNHVF**	**UseVF**
25¢	***Walk in the Water,*** tagged	.75	.20
	FDC *(March 3, 1989),* any single		2.00
	n. Booklet pane of 5 (CM1339-43)	3.60	1.00
	FDC, booklet pane		4.00

1989. WORLD STAMP EXPO 89 ISSUE honored the first-ever international stamp show to be sponsored by the U.S. Postal Service. The stamp depicted is the 90¢ Lincoln from the 1869 Pictorial Series (No. 96). *Offset and intaglio, perforated 11.*

CM1344 *World Stamp Expo 89*

CM1344		MNHVF	UseVF
25¢	red, gray & black *(103,835,000)*	.40	.20
	Plate block of 4	3.00	
	FDC *(March 16, 1989)*		1.75

1989. ARTURO TOSCANINI ISSUE in the Performing Arts Series saluted an Italian (1867-1957) who many consider the greatest orchestra conductor of all time. *Gravure by American Bank Note Co., perforated 11.*

CM1345 *Arturo Toscanini*

CM1345		MNHVF	UseVF
25¢	multicolored tagged *(152,250,000)*	.40	.20
	Plate block of 4	3.50	
	FDC *(March 25, 1989)*		1.75

Branches of Government Series

1989. HOUSE OF REPRESENTATIVES ISSUE was the first of four stamps honoring the three branches of government set by the U.S. Constitution. *Offset and intaglio, perforated 11.*

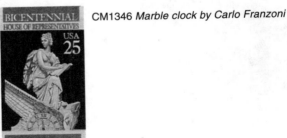

CM1346 *Marble clock by Carlo Franzoni*

CM1346		MNHVF	UseVF
25¢	multicolored tagged *(138,760,000)*	.40	.20
	Plate block of 4	3.75	
	FDC *(April 4, 1989)*		2.00

1989. SENATE ISSUE honored the bicentennial of the U.S. Senate; the second in a series to honor branches of government established by the U.S. Constitution. *Offset and intaglio, perforated 11.*

CM1347 *Old Senate Chamber eagle and shield*

CM1347

		MNHVF	UseVF
25¢	multicolored tagged *(137,985,000)*	.40	.20
	Plate block of 4	3.75	
	FDC *(April 6, 1989)*		2.00

1989. EXECUTIVE BRANCH ISSUE honored George Washington as the first person to head this government branch established by the Constitution. *Offset and intaglio, perforated 11.*

CM1348 *George Washington*

CM1348

		MNHVF	UseVF
25¢	multicolored tagged *(138,580,000)*	.40	.20
	Plate block of 4	4.25	
	FDC *(April 16, 1989)*		2.00

1989. SOUTH DAKOTA STATEHOOD ISSUE honored the centennial of the 40th state, which entered the Union — Nov. 2, 1889. *Gravure by American Bank Note Co., perforated 11.*

CM1349 *Pasque flower, pioneer woman, and sod house*

CM1349

		MNHVF	UseVF
25¢	multicolored tagged *(164,680,000)*	.40	.20
	Plate block of 4	3.00	
	FDC *(May 3, 1989)*		1.75

1989. LOU GEHRIG ISSUE in the American Sports Series recognized one of baseball's immortals (1903-1941), the "Iron Horse" of the New York Yankees. *Gravure by American Bank Note Co., perforated 11.*

CM1350 *Lou Gehrig*

CM1350

		MNHVF	UseVF
25¢	multicolored tagged *(138,760,000)*	1.10	.20
	Plate block of 4	5.25	
	FDC *(June 10, 1989)*		5.50

1989. ERNEST HEMINGWAY ISSUE Eighth in the Literary Arts Series honored the Nobel Prize-winning author (1899-1961) of *The Sun Also Rises* and *For Whom the Bell Tolls. Gravure by American Bank Note Co., perforated 11.*

CM1351 *Ernest Hemingway*

CM1351

		MNHVF	UseVF
25¢	multicolored tagged *(191,755,000)*	.40	.20
	Plate block of 4	3.00	
	Pair, imperforate horizontally	—	
	FDC *(July 17, 1989)*		1.75
	v. Vertical pair, imperforate horizontally	—	

1989. MOON LANDING ANNIVERSARY ISSUE commemorated the 20th anniversary of man's first steps on the Moon. The stamp was the first to meet the basic Priority Mail rate. *Offset and intaglio, perforated 11.*

CM1352 *Astronauts and flag on Moon*

CM1352

		MNHVF	UseVF
$2.40	multicolored tagged	6.00	2.25
	Plate block of 4	28.50	
	FDC *(July 20, 1989)*		7.00
	v. Intaglio black omitted	2,750.00	
	v1. Offset black omitted	4,500.00	
	v2. Pair, imperforate	850.00	

1989. NORTH CAROLINA STATEHOOD ISSUE the 12th in the Constitution Ratification Bicentennial Series. North Carolina ratified the Constitution Nov. 21, 1789. *Gravure by American Bank Note Co., perforated 11.*

CM1353 *Dogwood*

CM1353

		MNHVF	UseVF
25¢	multicolored tagged *(179,800,000)*	.40	.20
	Plate block of 4	3.95	
	FDC *(Aug. 22, 1989)*		2.00

1989. LETTER CARRIERS ISSUE paid tribute to those who carry America's mail to 100 million delivery points. *Gravure by American Bank Note Co., perforated 11.*

Condition refers to the overall appearance and quality of the stamp.

CM1354 *Letter carrier caricatures*

CM1354

		MNHVF	UseVF
25¢	**multicolored** tagged *(188,400,000)*	.40	.20
	Plate block of 4	3.95	
	FDC *(Aug. 30, 1989)*		2.00

1989. BILL OF RIGHTS ISSUE commemorated the freedoms guaranteed in the first 10 Amendments to the Constitution. *Offset and intaglio, perforated 11.*

CM1355 *Eagle, stars, and stripes*

CM1355

		MNHVF	UseVF
25¢	**multicolored** tagged *(191,860,000)*	.40	.20
	Plate block of 4	5.50	
	FDC *(Sept. 25, 1989)*		1.75
	v. Intaglio black omitted	350.00	

1989. DINOSAURS ISSUE celebrated the great prehistoric beasts, kicked off Stamp Collecting Month and served as a promotional tie-in with the videocassette release of the movie *The Land Before Time. Intaglio (Giori Press), perforated 11.*

CM1356
Tyrannosaurus

CM1357
Pteranodon

CM1358
Stegosaurus

CM1359
Apatosaurus
("Brontosaurus")

CM1356

		MNHVF	UseVF
25¢	**Tyrannosaurus,** tagged	1.25	.20

CM1357

		MNHVF	UseVF
25¢	**Pteranodon,** tagged	1.25	.20

CM1358

		MNHVF	UseVF
25¢	**Stegosaurus,** tagged	1.25	.20

CM1359

		MNHVF	UseVF
25¢	**Apatosaurus,** tagged	1.25	.20
	Plate block of 4	5.75	
	y. Se-tenant block of 4 (CM1356-59)	4.50	2.50
	FDC *(Oct. 1, 1989),* any single		2.00
	FDC, block of 4		5.00
	v. Any single, intaglio black omitted	175.00	
	vy. Block of 4, intaglio black omitted	1,000.00	

1989. AMERICA ISSUE honored the customs, images, and traditions of native Americans prior to Columbus. Part of a 1989-91 Columbian Series by members of the Postal Union of the Americas and Spain (PUAS). *Gravure by American Bank Note Co., perforated 11.*

CM1360 *Southwest carved figure*

CM1360

		MNHVF	UseVF
25¢	**multicolored** tagged *(137,410,000)*	.40	.20
	Plate block of 4	3.00	
	FDC *(Oct. 12, 1989)*		1.75

1989. WORLD STAMP EXPO 89 SOUVENIR SHEET featured a reproduction of the 90¢ stamp from the 1869 Pictorials (No. 96) and three trial color proofs on a single imperforate sheet. *Offset and intaglio, perforated 11.*

CM1361 *World Stamp Expo 89 souvenir sheet*

CM1361

		MNHVF	UseVF
$3.60	**Souvenir sheet of 4** *(2,017,225)*	20.00	13.50
	a. 90¢ like No. 96, carmine frame, black vignette	2.50	2.00
	b. 90¢ blue frame, brown vignette	2.50	2.00
	c. 90¢ green frame, blue vignette	2.50	2.00
	d. 90¢ scarlet frame, blue vignette	2.50	2.00
	FDC *(Nov. 17, 1989)*		14.50

1989. CLASSIC MAIL TRANSPORTATION ISSUE depicted vehicles that delivered mail in the 19th and the early 20th century. Issued in conjunction with the 20th UPU Congress. *Offset and intaglio, perforated 11.*

CM1362, 1366a
Stagecoach

CM1363, 1366b
Steamboat

CM1364, 1366c *Biplane*

CM1365, 1366d *Early automobile*

CM1362

		MNHVF	UseVF
25¢	**Stagecoach,** tagged *(163,824,000)*	.75	.20

CM1363

		MNHVF	UseVF
25¢	**Steamboat,** tagged	.75	.20

CM1364

		MNHVF	UseVF
25¢	**Biplane,** tagged	.75	.20

CM1365

		MNHVF	UseVF
25¢	**Early automobile,** tagged	.75	.20
	Plate block of 4	6.00	
	y. Se-tenant block of 4 (CM1362-65)	3.00	2.00
	FDC *(Nov. 19, 1989)*, any single		2.00
	FDC, block of 4		4.00
	v. Any single, intaglio blue omitted	200.00	
	vy. Block of 4, intaglio dark blue omitted	900.00	

1989. CLASSIC MAIL TRANSPORTATION SOUVENIR SHEET ISSUE

CM1366 *Classic Mail Transportation souvenir sheet*

CM1366

		MNHVF	UseVF
$1	**multicolored souvenir sheet,** tagged	5.00	4.00
	a. 25¢ like CM1362	1.25	.75
	b. 25¢ like CM1363	1.25	.75
	c. 25¢ like CM1364	1.25	.75
	d. 25¢ like CM1365	1.25	.75
	FDC *(Nov. 28, 1989)*		4.50
	v. Souvenir sheet, dark blue & gray omitted	5,500.00	

1990. IDAHO STATEHOOD ISSUE honored its centennial as the 43rd state to join the Union — July 3, 1890. *Gravure, American Bank Note Co., perforated 11.*

CM1367 *Mountain bluebird and Sawtooth Mountains*

CM1367

		MNHVF	UseVF
25¢	**multicolored** tagged	.40	.20
	Plate block of 4	3.00	
	FDC *(Jan. 6, 1990)*		2.00

1990. LOVE ISSUE was the first in the series to include a booklet version of the winning Pennsylvania Dutch-inspired design, which came from a design project for Yale University graduate students. *Gravure, U.S. Bank Note Co. (sheet) and Bureau of Engraving and Printing (booklet).*

CM1368-69, B186 *Lovebirds*

CM1368

		MNHVF	UseVF
25¢	**multicolored** tagged perforated 12 1/2 x 13	.40	.20
	Plate block of 4	3.00	
	FDC *(Jan. 18, 1990)*		2.00
	v. Pair, imperforate	800.00	

CM1369

		MNHVF	UseVF
25¢	**multicolored** tagged perforated 11 1/2 on 2 or 3 sides	.40	.20
	FDC *(Jan. 18, 1990)*		1.75
	v. Single, pink omitted	200.00	
	n. Booklet pane of 10	5.00	3.50
	FDC, pane of 10		8.00
	nv. Pane of 10, pink omitted	1,900.00	

1990. IDA B. WELLS ISSUE in the Black Heritage Series honored the civil rights activist (1862-1930) who was born a slave and spent her life educating others about the horrors of discrimination and lynching. *Gravure, American Bank Note Co., perforated 11.*

CM1370 *Ida B. Wells*

CM1370

		MNHVF	UseVF
25¢	**multicolored** tagged	.40	.20
	Plate block of 4	3.75	
	FDC *(Feb. 1, 1990)*		2.50

1990. SUPREME COURT ISSUE the fourth and final stamp in the series honoring the three branches of the federal government established by the U.S. Constitution, honored the 200th anniversary of the judicial branch. *Offset and intaglio, perforated 11.*

CM1371 *Bust of John Marshall, fourth chief justice of the Supreme Court*

CM1371

		MNHVF	UseVF
25¢	**multicolored** tagged	.40	.20
	Plate block of 4	4.00	
	FDC *(Feb. 2, 1990)*		2.00

1990. WYOMING STATEHOOD ISSUE commemorated the centennial of the state's entry July 10, 1890, as the 44th state in the Union. *Offset and intaglio, perforated 11.*

CM1372 High Mountain Meadows *by Conrad Schwiering*

CM1372

		MNHVF	UseVF
25¢	**multicolored** tagged	.40	.20
	Plate block of 4	3.85	
	FDC (Feb. 23, 1990)		1.75
	v. Intaglio black omitted	2,500.00	

1990. CLASSIC FILMS ISSUE showcased four works of Hollywood's Golden Era on the 50th anniversary of their nomination for the Academy Award. *Gravure, American Bank Note Co., perforated 11.*

CM1373 *Judy Garland and Toto*, The Wizard of Oz; CM1374 *Clark Gable and Vivien Leigh*, Gone with the Wind; CM1375 *Gary Cooper*, Beau Geste; CM1376 *John Wayne*, Stagecoach

CM1373

		MNHVF	UseVF
25¢	*Wizard of Oz,* tagged	2.00	.20

CM1374

		MNHVF	UseVF
25¢	*Gone with the Wind,* tagged	2.00	.20

CM1375

		MNHVF	UseVF
25¢	*Beau Geste,* tagged	2.00	.20

CM1376

		MNHVF	UseVF
25¢	*Stagecoach,* tagged	2.00	.20
	Plate block of 4	10.00	
	y. Se-tenant block of 4 (CM1373-76)	9.00	
	FDC (March 23, 1990), any single		3.00
	FDC, block of 4		7.50

1990. MARIANNE MOORE ISSUE Ninth in the Literary Arts Series paid tribute to the Pulitzer Prize-winning poet (1887-1972). *Gravure, American Bank Note Co., perforated 11.*

CM1377 *Marianne Moore*

CM1377

		MNHVF	UseVF
25¢	**multicolored** tagged	.40	.20
	Plate block of 4	3.00	
	FDC (April 18, 1990)		2.00

1990. AMERICAN LIGHTHOUSES ISSUE a se-tenant booklet issue of five designs, portrayed oceanside lighthouses. *Offset and intaglio, perforated 10 vertically on 1 or 2 sides.*

CM1378 *Admiralty Head, Wash.;* CM1379 *Cape Hatteras, N.C.;* CM1380 *West Quoddy Head, Maine;* CM1381 *American Shoals, Fla.;* CM1382 *Sandy Hook, N.J.* B188

CM1378

		MNHVF	UseVF
25¢	**Admiralty Head,** tagged	.40	.20
	v. white "25 / USA" omitted	15.00	

CM1379

		MNHVF	UseVF
25¢	**Cape Hatteras,** tagged	.40	.20
	v. white "25 / USA" omitted	15.00	

CM1380

		MNHVF	UseVF
25¢	**West Quoddy Head,** tagged	.40	.20
	v. white "25 / USA" omitted	15.00	

CM1381

		MNHVF	UseVF
25¢	**American Shoals,** tagged	.40	.20
	v. white "25 / USA" omitted	15.00	

CM1382

		MNHVF	UseVF
25¢	**Sandy Hook,** tagged	.40	.20
	FDC (April 26, 1990), any single		2.00
	v. white "25 / USA" omitted	15.00	
	n. Booklet pane of 5 (CM1378-82)	4.00	
	FDC, booklet pane		4.00
	nv. Booklet pane of 5, white omitted	75.00	

1990. RHODE ISLAND STATEHOOD ISSUE The 13th and final stamp in the Constitution Ratification Bicentennial Series. Rhode Island ratified the Constitution May 29, 1790. *Offset and intaglio, perforated 11.*

CM1383 *Slater Mill, R.I.*

CM1383

		MNHVF	UseVF
25¢	**multicolored** tagged	.40	.20
	Plate block of 4	3.95	
	FDC (May 29, 1990)		2.00

1990. OLYMPIC ATHLETES ISSUE honored five of the greatest U.S. Olympic athletes of the first half of the 20th century. *Gravure, American Bank Note Co., perforated 11.*

CM1384 *Jesse Owens;* CM1385 *Ray Ewry;* CM1386 *Hazel Wightman;* CM1387 *Eddie Eagan;* CM1388 *Helene Madison*

CM1384

		MNHVF	UseVF
25¢	**Jesse Owens,** tagged	.40	.20

CM1385

		MNHVF	UseVF
25¢	**Ray Ewry,** tagged	.40	.20

CM1386

		MNHVF	UseVF
25¢	**Hazel Wightman,** tagged	.40	.20

CM1387

		MNHVF	UseVF
25¢	**Eddie Eagan,** tagged	.40	.20

CM1388

		MNHVF	UseVF
25¢	**Helene Madison,** tagged	.40	.20
	Plate block of 10	8.00	

y. Se-tenant strip of 5 (CM1384-88)   3.00
FDC *(July 6, 1990)*, any single   2.50
FDC, strip of 5   5.00

1990. AMERICAN INDIAN HEADDRESSES ISSUE featured five different native headdresses or war bonnets. Folk Art series. *Offset and intaglio, perforated 11 on 2 or 3 sides.*

CM1389 *Assiniboine;* CM1390 *Cheyenne;* CM1391 *Commanche;* CM1392 *Flathead;* CM1393 *Shoshone* B189

CM1389		MNHVF	UseVF
25¢	**Assiniboine,** tagged	.40	.20
CM1390		MNHVF	UseVF
25¢	**Cheyenne,** tagged	.40	.20
CM1391		MNHVF	UseVF
25¢	**Commanche,** tagged	.40	.20
CM1392		MNHVF	UseVF
25¢	**Flathead,** tagged	.40	.20
CM1393		MNHVF	UseVF
25¢	**Shoshone,** tagged	.40	.20
	FDC *(Aug. 17, 1990)* any single		2.00
	v. Any single, intaglio black omitted	300.00	
	y. Se-tenant strip of 5 (CM1389-93)	8.50	7.50
	vy. Strip of 5, intaglio black omitted	1,500.00	
	n. Booklet of 10 (2 each CM1389-93)	5.00	
	nv. Booklet of 10, intaglio black omitted	3,500.00	
	FDC, booklet pane		8.00

1990. MICRONESIA AND MARSHALL ISLANDS ISSUE commemorated the relationship between the United States and the Federated States of Micronesia and the Republic of the Marshall Islands. This was a joint issue among the three postal administrations (Micronesia 188-190, Marshall Islands 300). *Offset and intaglio, perforated 11.*

CM1394 *Micronesia flag;* CM1395 *Marshall Islands flag*

CM1394		MNHVF	UseVF
25¢	**Micronesia,** tagged	.40	.20
	v. Intaglio black omitted	1,000.00	
CM1395		MNHVF	UseVF
25¢	**Marshall Islands,** tagged	.40	.20
	Plate block of 4	3.85	
	Intaglio, black omitted	1,000.00	
	FDC *(Sept. 28, 1990)*, either single		2.00
	FDC, pair		3.00
	y. Se-tenant pair (CM1394-95)	1.00	1.00
	vy. Se-tenant pair, intaglio black omitted	4,250.00	

1990. SEA MAMMALS ISSUE a joint release by the United States and the Soviet Union (Russia 6228-6231), focused on the beauty and significance of marine mammals. *Offset and intaglio, perforated 11.*

CM1396 *Killer whales*

CM1397 *Northern sea lions*

CM1398 *Sea otter*

CM1399 *Dolphin*

CM1396		MNHVF	UseVF
25¢	**Killer Whale,** tagged *(278,264,000)*	.75	.20
CM1397		MNHVF	UseVF
25¢	**Northern Sea Lion,** tagged	.75	.20
CM1398		MNHVF	UseVF
25¢	**Sea Otter,** tagged	.75	.20
CM1399		MNHVF	UseVF
25¢	**Dolphin,** tagged	.75	.20
	Plate block of 4	3.95	
	FDC *(Oct. 3, 1990)*, any single		2.00
	FDC, block of 4		5.00
	y. Se-tenant block of 4 (CM1396-99)	3.00	2.00
	v. Any single, intaglio black omitted	175.00	
	vy. Block of 4, intaglio black omitted	750.00	
	zo. Tagging omitted, any single	—	
	zoy. Block of 4, tagging omitted	—	

1990. AMERICA ISSUE honored natural wonders of the Americas as part of the joint release by the 24 participating postal administrations of the Postal Union of the Americas and Spain (PUAS). (See also A127.) *Gravure, American Bank Note Co., perforated 11.*

CM1400 *Grand Canyon*

CM1400		MNHVF	UseVF
25¢	**multicolored** tagged *(143,995,000)*	.40	.20
	Plate block of 4	3.00	
	FDC *(Oct. 12, 1990)*		2.00

1990. DWIGHT D. EISENHOWER ISSUE paid tribute on the centennial of his birth, to the 34th president. Eisenhower (1890-1969) also was the supreme commander of Allied Forces in Europe during World War II. *Gravure by American Bank Note Co., perforated 11.*

CM1401 *Dwight D. Eisenhower*

CM1401		MNHVF	UseVF
25¢	**multicolored** tagged *(142,692,000)*	.45	.20
	Plate block of 4	5.00	
	FDC *(Oct. 13, 1990)*		2.00
	v. Pair, imperforate	2,300.00	

1991. SWITZERLAND 700TH ANNIVERSARY ISSUE honored the small country founded in 1291. Switzerland issued a matching stamp at the same time (Switzerland 1579). *Gravure by American Bank Note Co., perforated 11.*

CM1402 *U.S. Capitol, Swiss Federal Palace*

CM1402		MNHVF	UseVF
50¢	**multicolored** tagged *(103,648,000)*	.75	.35
	Plate block of 4	6.50	
	FDC *(Feb. 22, 1991)*		2.00

1991. VERMONT STATEHOOD ISSUE marked the bicentennial of the Green Mountain State, which remained an independent republic until admitted to the Union as the 14th state, March 4, 1791. *Gravure by American Bank Note Co., perforated 11.*

CM1403 *Vermont farmland*

CM1403		MNHVF	UseVF
29¢	**multicolored** tagged *(179,990,000)*	.45	.20
	Plate block of 4	3.50	
	FDC *(March 1, 1991)*		2.25

1991. U.S. SAVINGS BOND ISSUE honored the 50th anniversary of the E-Series Savings Bond. *Gravure, perforated 11.*

CM1404 *Bald eagle*

CM1404		MNHVF	UseVF
29¢	**multicolored** tagged *(150,560,000)*	.45	.20
	Plate block of 4	3.95	
	FDC *(April 30, 1991)*		1.75

1991. LOVE ISSUE part of the Love Series. *Gravure (29¢ sheet by U.S. Bank Note Co., 29¢ booklet by Bureau of Engraving and Printing, 52¢ sheet by American Bank Note Co.)*

CM1405-06, B202 *Heart-shaped Earth*

CM1405		MNHVF	UseVF
29¢	**multicolored** tagged, perforated 12 1/2 x 13	.45	.20
	Plate block of 4	3.75	
	FDC *(May 9, 1991)*		1.75
	v. Pair, imperforate	2,500.00	
CM1405A		MNHVF	UseVF
29¢	**multicolored** tagged, perforated 11	.45	.20
	Plate block of 4	5.00	
CM1406		MNHVF	UseVF
29¢	**multicolored** tagged, perforated 11 on 2 or 3 sides	.45	.20
	FDC *(May 9, 1991)*, any single		1.75
	n. Booklet pane of 10	7.50	
	FDC, booklet pane		7.50

CM1407 *Fischer's Lovebirds*

CM1407		MNHVF	UseVF
52¢	**multicolored** tagged, perforated 11	.75	.35

Plate block of 4 5.75
FDC *(May 9, 1991)* 2.00

1991. WILLIAM SAROYAN ISSUE 10th in the Literary Arts Series honored the Armenian-American novelist, playwright and short story writer (1908-81). He won a Pulitzer Prize in 1940 for his play, *The Time of Your Life.* This was a joint issue with Russia (Russia 6300). *Gravure, J.W. Fergusson & Sons for American Bank Note Co., perforated 11.*

CM1408 *William Saroyan*

CM1408		MNHVF	UseVF
29¢	**multicolored** tagged *(161,498,000)*	.45	.20
	Plate block of 4	3.50	
	FDC *(May 22, 1991)*		2.25

1991. FISHING FLIES ISSUE showed classic and carefully crafted lures in a five stamp se-tenant booklet format. *Gravure by American Bank Note Co., perforated 11 horizontally on 1 or 2 sides.*

CM1409 *Royal Wulff*
CM1410 *Jock Scott*
CM1411 *Apte Tarpon Fly*
CM1412 *Lefty's Deceiver*
CM1413 *Muddler Minnow* B204

CM1409		MNHVF	UseVF
29¢	**Royal Wulff,** tagged *(744,918,000)*	.45	.20
	v. black omitted	—	
CM1410		MNHVF	UseVF
29¢	**Jack Scott,** tagged	.45	.20
	v. black omitted	—	
CM1411		MNHVF	UseVF
29¢	**Apte Tarpon,** tagged	.45	.20
	v. black omitted	—	
CM1412		MNHVF	UseVF
29¢	**Lefty's Deceiver,** tagged	.45	.20

CM1413		MNHVF	UseVF
29¢	**Muddler Minnow,** tagged	.45	.20
	FDC *(May 31, 1991),* any single		2.00
	n. Booklet pane of 5 (CM1409-13)	5.50	3.25
	FDC, booklet pane		5.00
	nv. Booklet pane, black omitted from CM1409-11		—

1991. COLE PORTER ISSUE in the Performing Arts Series, honored the 20th-century composer (1891-1964) of light, cheery songs and plays, including *Anything Goes. Gravure by American Bank Note Co., perforated 11.*

CM1414 *Cole Porter*

CM1414		MNHVF	UseVF
29¢	**multicolored** tagged *(149,848,000)*	.45	.20
	Plate block of 4	3.75	
	FDC *(June 8, 1991)*		1.75
	v. Vertical pair, imperforate between	600.00	

1991. DESERT SHIELD-DESERT STORM ISSUE paid tribute to those who served in the Gulf War. *Gravure (sheet version by J.W. Fergusson & Sons for Stamp Venturers, perforated 11.*

CM1415-16, B205 *Southwest Asia Service Medal*

CM1415		MNHVF	UseVF
29¢	**multicolored** tagged *(200,003,000)*	.45	.20
	Plate block of 4	3.50	
	FDC *(July 2, 1991)*		2.00
	v. Vertical pair, imperforate horizontally	2,000.00	

1991. DESERT SHIELD-DESERT STORM BOOKLET ISSUE by the *Multi-Color Corp. for American Bank Note Co., perforated 11 vertically on 1 or 2 sides.*

CM1416		MNHVF	UseVF
29¢	**multicolored** tagged *(200,000,000)*	.45	.20
	FDC *(July 2, 1991)*		2.00
	n. Booklet pane of 5	2.00	
	FDC, booklet pane		4.50

1991. OLYMPIC TRACK AND FIELD ISSUE promoted the USPS sponsorship of the 1992 Winter and Summer Olympics. *Gravure by American Bank Note Co., perforated 11.*

CM1417 *Pole vault;* CM1418 *Discus;* CM1419 *Women's sprint;* CM1420 *Javelin;* CM1421 *Women's hurdles*

CM1417		MNHVF	UseVF
29¢	**Pole vault,** tagged *(170,025,000)*	.45	.20
CM1418		MNHVF	UseVF
29¢	**Discus,** tagged	.45	.20
CM1419		MNHVF	UseVF
29¢	**Women's sprint,** tagged	.45	.20

CM1420		MNHVF	UseVF
29¢	**Javelin,** tagged	.45	.20
CM1421		MNHVF	UseVF
29¢	**Women's hurdles,** tagged	.45	.20
	Plate block of 10	9.75	
	y. Se-tenant strip of 5 (CM1417-21)	2.25	
	FDC *(July 12, 1991),* any single		1.00
	FDC, strip of 5		4.50

1991. NUMISMATICS ISSUE saluted the hobby of coin and currency collecting. *Offset and intaglio, perforated 11.*

CM1422 *Coins and bank notes*

CM1422		MNHVF	UseVF
29¢	**multicolored** tagged *(150,310,000)*	.45	.20
	Plate block of 4	4.50	
	FDC *(Aug. 13, 1991)*		1.00

1991. BASKETBALL CENTENNIAL ISSUE commemorated the 100th anniversary of one of the world's most popular sports. Many basketball fans pointed out the design looks like an illegal "goaltending" block. (See CM498.) *Gravure, perforated 11.*

CM1423 *Hands above basketball hoop*

CM1423		MNHVF	UseVF
29¢	**multicolored** tagged *(149,810,000)*	.45	.20
	Plate block of 4	4.50	
	FDC *(Aug. 28, 1991)*		3.00

1991. AMERICAN COMEDIANS ISSUE showcased comedians and comedy teams of the first half of the 20th century. The stamps were the first designed by the famed caricaturist Al Hirschfeld. *Offset and intaglio, perforated 11 on 2 or 3 sides.*

CM1424 *Stan Laurel, Oliver Hardy;* CM1425 *Edgar Bergen, Charlie McCarthy;* CM1426 *Jack Benny;* CM1427 *Fanny Brice;* CM1428 *Bud Abbott, Lou Costello* B206

CM1424		MNHVF	UseVF
29¢	**Laurel & Hardy,** tagged *(699,978,000)*	.45	.20
CM1425		MNHVF	UseVF
29¢	**Bergen & McCarthy,** tagged	.45	.20
CM1426		MNHVF	UseVF
29¢	**Jack Benny,** tagged	.45	.20
CM1427		MNHVF	UseVF
29¢	**Fanny Brice,** tagged	.45	.20
CM1428		MNHVF	UseVF
29¢	**Abbott & Costello,** tagged	.45	.20
	y. Se-tenant strip of 5 (CM1424-28)	3.00	
	FDC *(Aug. 28, 1991),* any single		2.00
	a. Intaglio purple & red omitted, any single	—	
	n. Booklet pane of 10 (2 each CM1424-28)	6.00	

nv. Booklet pane, intaglio purple & red omitted	850.00
FDC, strip of 5	4.50
nv1. Booklet pane, intaglio red omitted	—
nv2. Booklet pane, intaglio purple omitted	—

World War II Commemorative Series

1991. 1941: A WORLD AT WAR ISSUE was the first in an annual World War II Commemorative Series issued through 1995 to trace the history of World War II. *Offset and intaglio, perforated 11.*

CM1429		MNHVF	UseVF
$2.90	**Commemorative pane of 10**	9.00	5.00
	a. 29¢ Military Vehicles, tagged	.80	.45
	b. 29¢ Draft Recruits, tagged	.80	.45
	c. 29¢ Dockside View, tagged	.80	.45
	d. 29¢ Roosevelt and Churchill, tagged	.80	.45
	e. 29¢ Tank, tagged	.80	.45
	f. 29¢ Sinking of *Reuben James,* tagged	.80	.45
	g. 29¢ Gas Mask and Helmet, tagged	.80	.45
	h. 29¢ Liberty Ship, tagged	.80	.45
	i. 29¢ Pearl Harbor, tagged	.80	.45
	j. 29¢ Congress Declares War, tagged	.80	.45
	FDC (Sept. 3, 1991), any single		3.00
	FDC Complete pane of 10		12.00
	v. black omitted, complete sheet of 20	12,650.00	

1991. DISTRICT OF COLUMBIA BICENTENNIAL ISSUE marked the 200th anniversary of the federal district selected by George Washington as a site for the permanent capital. *Offset and intaglio, perforated 11.*

CM1430 *Early view up Pennsylvania Avenue*

CM1430		MNHVF	UseVF
29¢	**multicolored** tagged *(699,978,000)*	.45	.20
	Plate block of 4	3.50	

FDC *(Sept. 7, 1991)*		1.75
v. Intaglio black omitted	100.00
Plate block of 4, intaglio black omitted	650.00

1991. JAN E. MATZELIGER ISSUE in the Black Heritage Series honored the man (1852-89) who patented a machine for shaping shoes, which revolutionized shoe manufacturing in the United States and cut the price in half. *Gravure, J.W. Fergusson & Sons for American Bank Note Co., perforated 11.*

CM1431 *Jan E. Matzeliger*

CM1431		MNHVF	UseVF
29¢	**multicolored** tagged *(148,973,000)*	.45	.20
	Plate block of 4	4.25	
	FDC *(Sept. 15, 1991)*		2.50
	v. Horizontal pair, imperforate vertically	1,500.00	
	v1. Vertical pair, imperforate horizontally	1,500.00	
	v2. Pair, imperforate	1,250.00	

1991. SPACE EXPLORATION ISSUE a se-tenant 10-stamp booklet pane featured unmanned spacecraft launched to the Earth's Moon and each of the nine planets that orbit the sun, with the exception of Pluto, which is depicted as well. *Gravure, perforated 11 on two or three sides.*

CM1432		MNHVF	UseVF
29¢	**Mercury,** tagged *(333,948,000)*	.45	.20

CM1433		MNHVF	UseVF
29¢	**Venus,** tagged	.45	.20

CM1434		MNHVF	UseVF
29¢	**Earth,** tagged	.45	.20

CM1429 *1941: A World at War*

CM1432 *Mercury, Mariner 10;* CM1433 *Venus, Mariner 2;* CM1434 *Earth, Landsat;* CM1435 *Moon, Lunar Orbiter;* CM1436 *Mars, Viking Orbiter;* CM1437 *Jupiter, Pioneer II;* CM1438 *Saturn, Voyager 2;* CM1439 *Uranus, Voyager 2;* CM1440 *Neptune, Voyager 2;* CM1441 *Pluto*

		MNHVF	UseVF
CM1435			
29¢	**Moon,** tagged	.45	.20
CM1436		MNHVF	UseVF
29¢	**Mars,** tagged	.45	.20
CM1437		MNHVF	UseVF
29¢	**Jupiter,** tagged	.45	.20
CM1438		MNHVF	UseVF
29¢	**Saturn,** tagged	.45	.20
CM1439		MNHVF	UseVF
29¢	**Uranus,** tagged	.45	.20
CM1440		MNHVF	UseVF
29¢	**Neptune,** tagged	.45	.20
CM1441		MNHVF	UseVF
29¢	**Pluto,** tagged	.45	.20
	FDC *(Oct. 1, 1991),* any single		2.00
	n. Booklet pane of 10 (CM1432-41)	8.75	
	FDC, booklet pane		8.00

1992. WINTER OLYMPICS ISSUE honored five of the sporting events of the games held in Albertville, France. *Gravure, J.W. Fergusson & Sons for Stamp Venturers, perforated 11.*

CM1442 *Ice hockey*

		MNHVF	UseVF
CM1442			
29¢	**multicolored** tagged	.45	.20

CM1443 *Figure skating*

		MNHVF	UseVF
CM1443			
29¢	**multicolored** tagged	.45	.20

CM1444 *Speed skating*

		MNHVF	UseVF
CM1444			
29¢	**multicolored** tagged	.45	.20

CM1445 *Skiing*

		MNHVF	UseVF
CM1445			
29¢	**multicolored** tagged	.45	.20

CM1446 *Bobsledding*

		MNHVF	UseVF
CM1446			
29¢	**multicolored** tagged	.45	.20
	Plate block of 10	9.75	
	y. Se-tenant strip of 5 (CM1442-46)	3.00	
	FDC *(Jan. 11, 1992),* any single		2.00
	FDC, strip of 5		5.00

1992. WORLD COLUMBIAN STAMP EXPO '92 ISSUE promoted the international stamp show in Chicago. The stamp shows a detail from the 1869 15¢ Pictorial (No. 92). *Offset and intaglio, perforated 11.*

CM1447 *World Columbian Stamp Expo*

		MNHVF	UseVF
CM1447			
29¢	**multicolored** tagged	.45	.20
	Plate block of 4	3.50	
	FDC *(Jan. 24, 1992)*		1.75
	zo. Tagging omitted	—	

1992. W.E.B. DU BOIS ISSUE in the Black Heritage Series honored the noted writer, historian, critic, scholar and educator (1868-1963). The Niagara Movement he founded in 1905 evolved into the NAACP. *Offset and intaglio, perforated 11.*

CM1448 *W.E.B. Du Bois*

CM1448		MNHVF	UseVF
29¢	**multicolored** tagged	.45	.20
	Plate block of 4	3.75	
	FDC *(Jan. 31, 1992)*		2.50

1992. LOVE ISSUE part of the Love Series. *Gravure, American Bank Note Co., perforated 11.*

CM1449 *Heart in an envelope*

CM1449		MNHVF	UseVF
29¢	**multicolored** tagged	.45	.20
	Plate block of 4	3.50	
	FDC *(Feb. 6, 1992)*		1.75
	v. Horizontal pair, imperforate between	800.00	

1992. OLYMPIC BASEBALL ISSUE commemorated the acceptance of baseball as an official Olympic sport. *Gravure, perforated 11.*

CM1450 *Player sliding into home*

CM1450		MNHVF	UseVF
29¢	**multicolored** tagged	1.00	.20
	Plate block of 4	4.75	
	FDC *(April 3, 1992)*		3.50

1992. VOYAGE OF COLUMBUS ISSUE a joint issue with Italy (Italy 2416-2419), honored the explorer's historic first voyage to the New World with four related se-tenant designs. *Offset and intaglio, perforated 11.*

CM1451 *Seeking Queen Isabella's Support;* CM1452 *Crossing the Atlantic;* CM1453 *Approaching Land;* CM1454 *Coming Ashore*

CM1451		MNHVF	UseVF
29¢	**Seeking Support,** tagged	1.00	.20

CM1452		MNHVF	UseVF
29¢	**Atlantic Crossing,** tagged	1.00	.20

CM1453		MNHVF	UseVF
29¢	**Approaching Land,** tagged	1.00	.20

CM1454		MNHVF	UseVF
29¢	**Coming Ashore,** tagged	1.00	.20
	Plate block of 4	4.75	
	y. Se-tenant block of 4 (CM1451-54)	4.00	3.00
	FDC *(April. 24, 1992),* any single		2.00
	FDC, se-tenant block of 4		4.00

1992. NEW YORK STOCK EXCHANGE ISSUE commemorated the bicentennial of the exchange, originally formed by 24 brokers and dealers who met regularly under a tree. *Offset and intaglio by Jeffries Bank Note Co. for American Bank Note Co., perforated 11.*

CM1455 *Stock certificate*

CM1455		MNHVF	UseVF
29¢	**multicolored** tagged	.45	.20
	Plate block of 4	3.50	
	FDC *(May 17, 1992)*		3.00
	v. Intaglio black omitted	—	
	v1. Intaglio black inverted	—	

1992. COLUMBIAN SOUVENIR SHEETS were a joint issue with Italy, Portugal, and Spain at the World Columbian Expo '92 (Italy 2423-28, Portugal 2102-07, Spain 3177-82). Stamps depicted on the sheets are close in appearance to the original Columbian commemoratives of 1893 (CM1-16), but are inscribed "1992" at upper right. *Offset and intaglio by American Bank Note Co., perforated 10 1/2, block tagging on stamps over 10¢ value.*

CM1456 *Seeking Royal Support*

CM1456		MNHVF	UseVF
85¢	**Sheet of three**	3.00	
	a. 5¢ brown like CM5		.75
	b. 30¢ orange brown like CM10		1.00
	c. 50¢ slate black like CM11		1.00
	FDC *(May 22, 1992),* souvenir sheet		4.00
	v. Souvenir sheet, imperforate	—	

Note: Imperforate Columbian souvenir sheets are very probably the result of printer's waste.

CM1457 *First Sighting of Land*

CM1457

$1.05	Sheet of three	MNHVF	UseVF
		2.50	
	a. 1¢ deep blue like CM1		.50
	b. 4¢ gray blue like CM4		.75
	c. $1 Venetian red like CM12		2.50
	FDC *(May 22, 1992)*		4.00
	v. Souvenir sheet, imperforate	—	

CM1459 *Royal Favor Restored*

CM1459

$3.14	Sheet of three	MNHVF	UseVF
		8.50	
	a. 6¢ dark lilac like CM6		1.00
	b. 8¢ brown purple like CM7		1.00
	c. $3 bronze green like CM14		5.50
	FDC *(May 22, 1992)*		10.00
	v. Souvenir sheet, imperforate	—	

CM1458 *Reporting Discoveries*

CM1458

$2.25	Sheet of three	MNHVF	UseVF
		5.00	
	a. 10¢ black brown like CM8		.75
	b. 15¢ deep bluish green like CM9		.75
	c. $2 brown red like CM13		4.50
	FDC *(May 22, 1992)*		9.00
	v. Souvenir sheet, imperforate	—	

CM1460 *Claiming a New World*

CM1460

$4.05	Sheet of three	MNHVF	UseVF
		9.00	
	a. 2¢ dull purple like CM2		.75
	b. 3¢ dark bluish green like CM3		.75
	c. $4 deep rose like CM15		7.00
	FDC *(May 22, 1992)*		15.00
	v. Souvenir sheet, imperforate	—	

With few exceptions, and unlike other catalogs, Minkus catalog numbers are assigned in strict chronological sequence, and definitive issues (stamps that may go back to press for additional prints at any time to furnish new stocks) are listed separately from commemorative issues (typically printed in a single, much smaller run than their definitive counterparts).

CM1461 *Christopher Columbus*

CM1461		MNHVF	UseVF
$5	**Sheet of one, black** like CM15	12.00	8.50
	FDC *(May 22, 1992)*		20.00
	Full set of 6 s/s	40.00	37.50
	v. Souvenir sheet, imperforate	—	

1992. SPACE ACHIEVEMENTS ISSUE A joint issue with Russia (Russia 6376-79), honored a broad spectrum of space exploration by the two countries. *Gravure, perforated 11.*

CM1462 *Space Shuttle*

CM1463 *Astronaut, Space Shuttle, space station*

CM1464 *Lunar Lander, Apollo and Vostok spacecraft, Sputnik*

CM1465 *Soyuz, Mercury and Gemini spacecraft*

CM1462		MNHVF	UseVF
29¢	**Space Shuttle,** tagged	1.00	.20
CM1463		MNHVF	UseVF
29¢	**Space station,** tagged	1.00	.20
CM1464		MNHVF	UseVF
29¢	**Apollo & Vostok craft,** tagged	1.00	.20
CM1465		MNHVF	UseVF
29¢	**Soyuz, Mercury & Gemini craft,** tagged	1.00	.20
	Plate block of 4	4.50	
	y. Se-tenant block of 4 (CM1462-65)	4.00	2.50
	FDC *(May 29, 1992),* any single		2.00
	FDC, block of 4		4.00

1992. ALASKA HIGHWAY ISSUE marked the 50th anniversary of the completion of the 1,500-mile route connecting Army installations in Alaska and the contiguous United States during World War II. *Offset and intaglio, perforated 11.*

CM1466 *Alaska Highway*

CM1466		MNHVF	UseVF
29¢	**multicolored** tagged	.45	.20
	Plate block of 4	3.50	
	FDC *(May 30, 1992)*		1.75
	v. Intaglio black omitted	900.00	

1992. KENTUCKY STATEHOOD ISSUE celebrated the bicentennial of the entry of the Bluegrass State as the 15th state in the union. *Gravure, J.W. Fergusson & Sons for Stamp Venturers, perforated 11.*

CM1467 *My Old Kentucky Home State Park*

CM1467		MNHVF	UseVF
29¢	**multicolored** tagged	.45	.20
	Plate block of 4	3.50	
	FDC *(June 1, 1992)*		1.75

1992. SUMMER OLYMPIC GAMES ISSUE presented five events contested in the quadrennial games held in Barcelona, Spain. *Gravure, J.W. Fergusson & Sons for Stamp Venturers.*

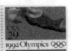

CM1468 *Soccer;* CM1469 *Gymnastics;* CM1470 *Volleyball;* CM1471 *Boxing;* CM1472 *Swimming*

CM1468		MNHVF	UseVF
29¢	**Soccer,** tagged	.45	.20
CM1469		MNHVF	UseVF
29¢	**Gymnastics,** tagged	.45	.20
CM1470		MNHVF	UseVF
29¢	**Volleyball,** tagged	.45	.20
CM1471		MNHVF	UseVF
29¢	**Boxing,** tagged	.45	.20
CM1472		MNHVF	UseVF
29¢	**Swimming,** tagged	.45	.20
	Plate block of 10	10.00	
	y. Se-tenant strip of 5 (CM1468-72)	8.00	
	FDC *(June 11, 1992),* any single		2.00
	FDC, strip of 5		5.00

1992. HUMMINGBIRDS ISSUE A popular booklet release, featured five varieties of these colorful birds. *Gravure, Multi-Color Corp. for American Bank Note Co., perforated 11 on 1 or 2 sides.*

CM1473 *Ruby-throated hummingbird;* CM1474 *Broad-billed hummingbird;* CM1475 *Costa's hummingbird;* CM1476 *Rufous hummingbird;* CM1477 *Calliope hummingbird*

		MNHVF	UseVF
CM1473		MNHVF	UseVF
29¢	**Ruby-throated,** tagged	.45	.20
CM1474		MNHVF	UseVF
29¢	**Broad-billed,** tagged	.45	.20
CM1475		MNHVF	UseVF
29¢	**Costa's,** tagged	.45	.20
CM1476		MNHVF	UseVF
29¢	**Rufous,** tagged	.45	.20
CM1477		MNHVF	UseVF
29¢	**Calliope,** tagged	.45	.20
	FDC *(June 15,1992),* any single		2.00
	n. Booklet pane of 5 (CM1473-77)	4.50	
	FDC, booklet pane		5.00
	nv. Booklet pane, imperforate	—	

1992. WILDFLOWERS ISSUE showcased 50 colorful, blooming native plants. While no specific states are attached to each flower, one or more of the flowers are found in each of the states. *Offset, Ashton Potter America, Inc., perforated 11.*

   Two simultaneous printings were produced, one with four panes (plate number positions) per sheet and the other with six panes (plate number positons) per sheet. Stamps from the four-pane press were assigned odd plate numbers and stamps from the six-pane press were assigned even plate numbers. Further, an illustration is found in the selvage of each pane depicting an uncut sheet and the location of the specific pane in hand. Screening of the "29" inscription apparently was a test leading toward microprinting, which began in 1992 (see Nos. 995-998).

		MNHVF	UseVF
CM1478		MNHVF	UseVF
29¢	**Indian Paintbrush,** tagged	.95	.60

		MNHVF	UseVF
CM1479		MNHVF	UseVF
29¢	**Fragrant Water Lily,** tagged	.95	.60
CM1480		MNHVF	UseVF
29¢	**Meadow Beauty,** tagged	.95	.60
CM1481		MNHVF	UseVF
29¢	**Jack-in-the-Pulpit,** tagged	.95	.60
CM1482		MNHVF	UseVF
29¢	**California Poppy,** tagged	.95	.60
CM1483		MNHVF	UseVF
29¢	**Large-Flowered Trillium,** tagged	.95	.60
CM1484		MNHVF	UseVF
29¢	**Tickseed,** tagged	.95	.60
CM1485		MNHVF	UseVF
29¢	**Shooting Star,** tagged	.95	.60
CM1486		MNHVF	UseVF
29¢	**Stream Violet,** tagged	.95	.60
CM1487		MNHVF	UseVF
29¢	**Bluets,** tagged	.95	.60
CM1488		MNHVF	UseVF
29¢	**Herb Robert,** tagged	.95	.60
CM1489		MNHVF	UseVF
29¢	**Marsh Marigold,** tagged	.95	.60
CM1490		MNHVF	UseVF
29¢	**Sweet White Violet,** tagged	.95	.60
CM1491		MNHVF	UseVF
29¢	**Claret Cup Cactus,** tagged	.95	.60
CM1492		MNHVF	UseVF
29¢	**White Mountain Avens,** tagged	.95	.60
CM1493		MNHVF	UseVF
29¢	**Sessile Bellwort,** tagged	.95	.60

CM1478-1527 *Wildflowers from around the nation*

		MNHVF	UseVF
CM1494 29¢	Blue Flag, tagged	.95	.60
CM1495 29¢	Harlequin Lupine, tagged	.95	.60
CM1496 29¢	Twinflower, tagged	.95	.60
CM1497 29¢	Common Sunflower, tagged	.95	.60
CM1498 29¢	Sego Lily, tagged	.95	.60
CM1499 29¢	Virginia Bluebells, tagged	.95	.60
CM1500 29¢	Ohi'a Lehua, tagged	.95	.60
CM1501 29¢	Rosebud Orchid, tagged	.95	.60
CM1502 29¢	Showy Evening Primrose, tagged	.95	.60
CM1503 29¢	Fringed Gentian, tagged	.95	.60
CM1504 29¢	Yellow Lady's Slipper, tagged	.95	.60
CM1505 29¢	Passionflower, tagged	.95	.60
CM1506 29¢	Bunchberry, tagged	.95	.60
CM1507 29¢	Pasqueflower, tagged	.95	.60
CM1508 29¢	Round-Lobed Hepatica, tagged	.95	.60
CM1509 29¢	Wild Columbine, tagged	.95	.60
CM1510 29¢	Fireweed, tagged	.95	.60
CM1511 29¢	Indian Pond Lily, tagged	.95	.60
CM1512 29¢	Turk's Cap Lily, tagged	.95	.60
CM1513 29¢	Dutchman's Breeches, tagged	.95	.60

		MNHVF	UseVF
CM1514 29¢	Trumpet Honeysuckle, tagged	.95	.60
CM1515 29¢	Jacob's Ladder, tagged	.95	.60
CM1516 29¢	Plains Prickly Pear, tagged	.95	.60
CM1517 29¢	Moss Campion, tagged	.95	.60
CM1518 29¢	Bearberry, tagged	.95	.60
CM1519 29¢	Mexican Hat, tagged	.95	.60
CM1520 29¢	Harebell, tagged	.95	.60
CM1521 29¢	Desert Five Spot, tagged	.95	.60
CM1522 29¢	Smooth Solomon's Seal, tagged	.95	.60
CM1523 29¢	Red Maids, tagged	.95	.60
CM1524 29¢	Yellow Skunk Cabbage, tagged	.95	.60
CM1525 29¢	Rue Anemone, tagged	.95	.60
CM1526 29¢	Standing Cypress, tagged	.95	.60
CM1527 29¢	Wild Flax, tagged	.95	.60
	y. Pane of 50 (CM1478-1527)	42.50	
	FDC (July 24, 1992) any single		1.75
	FDC, pane of 50		50.00

1992. 1942: INTO THE BATTLE ISSUE of the World War II Commemorative Series included a map and stamps showing events of the war in 1942. *Offset and intaglio, perforated 11.*

		MNHVF	UseVF
CM1528 $2.90	Commemorative pane of 10	9.00	5.00
	a. 29¢ B-25 Raid on Tokyo, tagged	.75	.45
	b. 29¢ Ration stamps, tagged	.75	.45
	c. 29¢ Carrier crewman & fighter, tagged	.75	.45
	d. 29¢ Prisoners of war, tagged	.75	.45

B-25s take off to raid Tokyo April 18, 1942

Food and other commodities rationed, 1942

U.S. wins Battle of the Coral Sea May 1942

Corregidor falls to Japanese May 6, 1942

Japan invades Aleutian Islands June 1942

1942: Into the Battle

Allies decipher secret enemy codes, 1942

Yorktown lost, U.S. wins at Midway, 1942

Millions of women join war effort, 1942

Marines land on Guadalcanal Aug. 7, 1942

Allies land in North Africa November 1942

e. 29¢ Attack on Aleutian Islands, tagged	.75	.45

CM1528 *1942: Into the Battle*

		MNHVF	UseVF
f.	29¢ Coded message, tagged	.75	.45
g.	29¢ *USS Yorktown,* tagged	.75	.45
h.	29¢ Woman defense worker, tagged	.75	.45
i.	29¢ Marines at Guadalcanal, tagged	.75	.45
j.	29¢ Tank in desert, tagged	.75	.45
	FDC *(Aug. 17, 1992),* any single		2.00
	FDC, complete pane of 10		10.00
	v. red omitted	6,000.00	

1992. DOROTHY PARKER ISSUE 11th in the Literary Arts Series honored the writer, poet and critic (1893-1967) noted for her wit. *Gravure by J.W. Fergusson & Sons for Stamp Venturers, perforated 11.*

CM1529 *Dorothy Parker*

CM1529

		MNHVF	UseVF
29¢	**multicolored** tagged	.45	.20
	Plate block of 4	3.50	
	FDC *(Aug. 22, 1992)*		1.75

1992. THEODORE VON KÁRMÁN ISSUE paid tribute to the aerospace scientist credited with establishing the center for rocket research that now is the Jet Propulsion Laboratory at the California Institute of Technology. *Gravure, J.W. Fergusson & Sons for Stamp Venturers, perforated 11.*

CM1530 *Theodore von Kármán*

CM1530

		MNHVF	UseVF
29¢	**multicolored** tagged	.45	.20
	Plate block of 4	3.50	
	FDC *(Aug. 31, 1992)*		1.75

1992. MINERALS ISSUE featured specimens from the Smithsonian Institution's National Museum of Natural History collection. *Offset and intaglio, perforated 11.*

CM1531 *Azurite*

CM1532 *Copper*

CM1533 *Variscite*

CM1534 *Wulfenite*

CM1531

		MNHVF	UseVF
29¢	**Azurite,** tagged	.45	.20

CM1532

		MNHVF	UseVF
29¢	**Copper,** tagged	.45	.20

CM1533

		MNHVF	UseVF
29¢	**Variscite,** tagged	.45	.20

CM1534

		MNHVF	UseVF
29¢	**Wulfenite,** tagged	.45	.20
	Plate block of 4	4.50	
	y. Se-tenant block or strip of 4 (CM1531-34)	3.00	
	FDC *(Sept. 17, 1992),* any single		2.00
	FDC, block or strip of 4		4.00
	v. silver omitted	—	

1992. JUAN RODRÍGUEZ CABRILLO ISSUE recalled the Spanish explorer who named San Miguel Harbor, later the site of San Diego, Calif. *Printed by The Press and J.W. Fergusson & Sons for Stamp Venturers, perforated 11.*

CM1535 *Juan Rodríguez Cabrillo*

CM1535

		MNHVF	UseVF
29¢	**multicolored** tagged	.45	.20
	Plate block of 4	3.50	
	FDC *(Sept. 28, 1992)*		1.75

1992. WILD ANIMALS ISSUE depicted five popular animals in U.S. zoos. *Gravure, J.W. Fergusson & Sons for Stamp Venturers, perforated 11 horizontally on 1 or 2 sides.*

CM1536 *Giraffe*

CM1537 *Giant Panda*

CM1538 *Flamingo*

CM1539 *King Penguins*

CM1540 *White Bengal Tiger*

B216

CM1536		MNHVF	UseVF
29¢	**Giraffe,** tagged	.45	.20

CM1537		MNHVF	UseVF
29¢	**Giant Panda,** tagged	.45	.20

CM1538		MNHVF	UseVF
29¢	**Flamingo,** tagged	.45	.20

CM1539		MNHVF	UseVF
29¢	**King Penquins,** tagged	.45	.20

CM1540		MNHVF	UseVF
29¢	**White Bengal Tiger,** tagged	.45	.20
	FDC *(Oct. 1, 1992),* any single		2.00
	n. Booklet pane of 5 (CM1536-40)	2.25	
	FDC, booklet pane of 5		5.00
	nv. Pane of 5, imperforate (6 reported)	3,500.00	

Lunar New Year Series

1992. YEAR OF THE ROOSTER ISSUE was the first U.S. stamp in the Lunar New Year Series to honor the Asian lunar holiday. *Offset and intaglio, American Bank Note Co., perforated 11.*

CM1541 *Rooster and Chinese characters*

CM1541		MNHVF	UseVF
29¢	**multicolored** overall tagged on phosphor-coated paper	.45	.20
	Plate block of 4	3.95	
	FDC *(Dec. 30, 1992)*		3.00
	z. Block tagging overall	3.00	
	z1. Phosphor-coated paper	40.00	

American Music Series

1993. ELVIS PRESLEY ISSUE of 500 million stamps represented a massive press run for a single commemorative, reflecting the interest in the rock 'n' roll entertainer. The public in a write-in poll voted for the design of this stamp over a second design showing an older-looking portrait of the pop icon. This stamp is also the first in a lengthy and eclectic American Music Series. *Gravure, perforated 11.*

CM1542 *Elvis Presley*

CM1542		MNHVF	UseVF
29¢	**multicolored** tagged	.45	.20
	Plate block of 4	3.50	
	FDC *(Jan. 8, 1993)*		2.00

1993. SPACE FANTASY ISSUE was reminiscent of the 1930s vision of space travel made popular in movie and comic-book adventure. *Gravure, perforated 11 vertically on 1 or 2 sides.*

CM1543; CM1544; CM1545; CM1546; CM1547; B219

CM1543		MNHVF	UseVF
29¢	**Saturn rings,** tagged	.45	.20

CM1544		MNHVF	UseVF
29¢	**Two oval crafts,** tagged	.45	.20

CM1545		MNHVF	UseVF
29¢	**Spacemen & jet pack,** tagged	.45	.20

CM1546		MNHVF	UseVF
29¢	**Craft & lights,** tagged	.45	.20

CM1547		MNHVF	UseVF
29¢	**Three craft,** tagged	.45	.20
	FDC *(Jan. 25, 1993),* any single		2.00
	n. Booklet pane of 5 (CM1541-45)	3.50	
	FDC, booklet pane		5.00

1993. PERCY LAVON JULIAN ISSUE in the Black Heritage Series honored the research chemist (1898-1975) who synthesized cortisone for treatment of arthritis. *Offset and intaglio, perforated 11.*

CM1548 *Percy Lavon Julian*

CM1548		MNHVF	UseVF
29¢	**multicolored** tagged	.45	.20
	Plate block of 4	3.50	
	FDC *(Jan. 29, 1993)*		2.50

1993. OREGON TRAIL ISSUE recalled the 2,000-mile stretch from Independence, Mo., to Oregon City, Ore., that was a popular route used by settlers traveling west. *Offset and intaglio, perforated 11.*

CM1549 *The Oregon Trail*

CM1549		MNHVF	UseVF
29¢	**multicolored** tagged	.45	.20
	Plate block of 4	3.50	
	FDC *(Feb. 12, 1993)*		1.75
	zo. Tagging omitted	—	

The official first day city was Salem, Ore., but the stamp was available Feb. 12 at 36 cities along the Trail.

1993. WORLD UNIVERSITY GAMES ISSUE celebrated the first time this biennial competition was held in the United States. *Gravure, perforated 11.*

CM1550 *World University Games*

CM1550		MNHVF	UseVF
29¢	**multicolored** tagged	.45	.20
	Plate block of 4	4.00	
	FDC *(Feb. 25, 1993)*		2.00

1993. GRACE KELLY ISSUE memorialized the American actress who became Princess of Monaco (1928-1982). Monaco and the United States jointly issued similar stamps (Monaco 2127). *Intaglio, Stamp Venturers, perforated 11.*

CM1551 *Grace Kelly*

CM1551		MNHVF	UseVF
29¢	**blue** tagged	.45	.20
	Plate block of 4	3.50	
	FDC *(March 24, 1993)*		2.50

1993. OKLAHOMA! ISSUE paid tribute to the landmark American musical. The stamp was available for sale in every post office in the state on its first day, rather than at a single outlet. American Music Series. *Gravure, perforated 10.*

CM1552 *Oklahoma!*

CM1552		MNHVF	UseVF
29¢	**multicolored** tagged	.45	.20
	Plate block of 4	3.50	
	FDC *(March 30, 1993)*		1.75

1993. CIRCUS ISSUE honored the 200th anniversary of the first circus performance in America. *Offset, Ashton Potter America, perforated 11.*

CM1553 *Trapeze Artist*

CM1554 *Elephant*

CM1555 *Clown*

CM1556 *Ringmaster*

CM1553		MNHVF	UseVF
29¢	**Trapeze Artist**, tagged	.45	.20

CM1554		MNHVF	UseVF
29¢	**Elephant**, tagged	.45	.20

CM1555		MNHVF	UseVF
29¢	**Clown**, tagged	.45	.20

CM1556		MNHVF	UseVF
29¢	**Ringmaster**, tagged	.45	.20
	Plate block of 6	6.75	
	Plate block of 4	4.00	
	y. Se-tenant block of 4 (CM1553-56)	3.00	
	FDC *(April 6, 1993)*, any single		2.50
	FDC, block of 4		4.00

1993. CHEROKEE STRIP LAND RUN CENTENNIAL ISSUE commemorated the events of Sept. 16, 1893, when more than 100,000 pioneers raced to stake out land claims in the 8 million acre parcel of land known as the "Cherokee Strip." *Offset and intaglio, by American Bank Note Co., perforated 11.*

CM1557 *Pioneers racing on wagon and horseback*

CM1557		MNHVF	UseVF
29¢	**multicolored** tagged	.45	.20
	Plate block of 4	3.50	
	FDC *(April 17, 1993)*		1.75
	y. Pane of 20	10.00	

1993. DEAN ACHESON ISSUE honored the former U.S. Secretary of State (1893-1971). *Intaglio, Stamp Venturers, perforated 11.*

CM1558 *Dean Acheson*

CM1558		MNHVF	UseVF
29¢	**green** tagged	.45	.20
	Plate block of 4	3.50	
	FDC *(April 21, 1993)*		1.75

1993. SPORTING HORSES ISSUE commemorated four equestrian events. *Offset and intaglio, Stamp Venturers, perforated 11x11 1/2.*

CM1559 *Steeplechase*; CM1560 *Thoroughbred racing*; CM1561 *Harness racing*; CM1562 *Polo*

CM1559		MNHVF	UseVF
29¢	**Steeplechase**, tagged	.45	.20

CM1560		MNHVF	UseVF
29¢	**Thoroughbred racing**, tagged	.45	.20

CM1561		MNHVF	UseVF
29¢	**Harness racing**, tagged	.45	.20

CM1562		MNHVF	UseVF
29¢	**Polo**, tagged	.45	.20
	Plate block of 4	4.25	
	FDC *(May 1, 1993)*, any single		2.00
	FDC, block of 4		4.00
	y. Se-tenant block of 4 (CM1559-62)	1.80	
	v. Any single, intaglio, black omitted	375.00	
	vy. Block of 4, intaglio black omitted	1,650.00	

Spring Garden Flowers Series

1993. GARDEN FLOWERS ISSUE The first in a Garden Flowers Series of four that showed popular spring blooms in a booklet format. *Offset and intaglio, perforated 11 vertically on 1 or 2 sides.*

CM1563 *Hyacinth;* CM1564 *Daffodil;* CM1565 *Tulip;* CM1566 *Iris;*
CM1567 *Lilac* B220

CM1563		MNHVF	UseVF
29¢	**Hyacinth,** tagged	.45	.20
CM1564		MNHVF	UseVF
29¢	**Daffodil,** tagged	.45	.20
CM1565		MNHVF	UseVF
29¢	**Tulip,** tagged	.45	.20
CM1566		MNHVF	UseVF
29¢	**Iris,** tagged	.45	.20
CM1567		MNHVF	UseVF
29¢	**Lilac,** tagged	.45	.20
	FDC *(May 15, 1993),* any single		2.00
	n. Booklet pane of 5 (CM1563-67)	5.50	
	FDC, booklet pane		5.00
	nv. Booklet pane, imperforate	2,000.00	
	nv1. Booklet pane, intaglio black omitted	275.00	

1993. 1943: TURNING THE TIDE ISSUE in the World War II
Commemorative Series included a map and stamps showing events
of the war in 1943. *Offset and intaglio, perforated 11.*

CM1568		MNHVF	UseVF
$2.90	**Commemorative pane of 10**	8.75	7.00
	a. Allied escort ships, tagged	.75	.45
	b. Military medics, tagged	.75	.45
	c. Sicily attacked, tagged	.75	.45
	d. B-24's hit Ploesti, tagged	.75	.45
	e. V-mail delivers letters, tagged	.75	.45
	f. Italy invaded (PT boat), tagged	.75	.45
	g. War bonds & stamps, tagged	.75	.45
	h. "Willie and Joe," tagged	.75	.45
	i. Gold Stars, tagged	.75	.45
	j. Marines assault Tarawa, tagged	.75	.45
	FDC *(May 31, 1993),* any single		2.00
	FDC, complete pane of 10		10.00

1993. HANK WILLIAMS ISSUE in the American Music Series honored
the country singer and composer credited with integrating country
music and rock 'n' roll. *Gravure, Stamp Venturers, perforated 11.*

CM1569 *Hank Williams*

CM1569		MNHVF	UseVF
29¢	**multicolored** tagged	.45	.20
	Plate block of 4	3.50	
	FDC *(June 9, 1993)*		1.75
	v. Perforated 11 1/4 x 11 1/2	20.00	15.00
	Plate block of 4	125.00	

1993. ROCK 'N' ROLL - RHYTHM & BLUES ISSUE honored seven
stars in a continuation of the American Music Series, including a
second Elvis Presley stamp that spells out his last name. Additional
personalities featured in this issue are Buddy Holly, Ritchie Valens,
Bill Haley, Dinah Washington, Otis Redding, and Clyde McPhatter.
The stamps were released in a pane of 35 stamps and a booklet of 20
stamps. The booklet consists of two panes of eight (with six of seven
honorees appearing once and Elvis Presley appearing twice), and one
pane of four (the bottom four stamps of the pane of eight).

Although the stamp designs are similar, the stamps in the booklet
panes are printed in magenta, cyan, yellow, and black, while the
commemorative sheet is printed in those four colors plus additional
blue and red inks. The sheet stamps are 31.5mm high, and booklet
stamps are 31.1mm high. *Gravure, Stamp Venturers, perforated 10
on 4 sides.*

CM1568 *1943: Turning the Tide*

CM1570, CM1577 *Elvis Presley*

CM1571, CM1582 *Buddy Holly*

CM1572, CM1580 *Ritchie Valens*

CM1573, CM1578 *Bill Haley*

CM1574, CM1583 *Dinah Washington*

CM1575, CM1581 *Otis Redding*

CM1576, CM1579 *Clyde McPhatter*

B221

CM1570		MNHVF	UseVF
29¢	**Elvis Presley,** tagged	.45	.20
CM1571		MNHVF	UseVF
29¢	**Buddy Holly,** tagged	.45	.20
CM1572		MNHVF	UseVF
29¢	**Ritchie Valens,** tagged	.45	.20
CM1573		MNHVF	UseVF
29¢	**Bill Haley,** tagged	.45	.20
CM1574		MNHVF	UseVF
29¢	**Dinah Washington,** tagged	.45	.20
CM1575		MNHVF	UseVF
29¢	**Otis Redding,** tagged	.45	.20
CM1576		MNHVF	UseVF
29¢	**Clyde McPhatter,** tagged	.45	.20
	Commemorative sheet of 35 (includes 4 plate nos.)	18.00	
	y. Se-tenant vertical strip of 7 (CM1570-76)	3.00	—
	y1. Pane of 35	15.00	
	FDC *(June 16, 1993),* any single		2.50
	FDC, strip of 7		8.00

Gravure, Multi-Color Corp. Perforated 11 on one or two sides.

CM1577		MNHVF	UseVF
29¢	**multicolored** tagged	.45	.20
CM1578		MNHVF	UseVF
29¢	**multicolored** tagged	.45	.20
CM1579		MNHVF	UseVF
29¢	**multicolored** tagged	.45	.20

CM1580		MNHVF	UseVF
29¢	**multicolored** tagged	.45	.20
CM1581		MNHVF	UseVF
29¢	**multicolored** tagged	.45	.20
CM1582		MNHVF	UseVF
29¢	**multicolored** tagged	.45	.20
CM1583		MNHVF	UseVF
29¢	**multicolored** tagged	.45	.20
	FDC *(June 16, 1993),* any single		2.50
	n. Booklet pane of 8 (2 of CM1577, 1 each CM-1578-83)	4.50	2.25
	FDC, booklet pane of 8		8.00
	n1. Booklet pane of 4 (CM1577 & CM1581-83)	2.50	
	FDC, booklet pane of 4		4.50

The vertically oriented pane of eight consists of the following stamps, from top to bottom: CM1577, CM1578, CM1579, CM1580, CM1581, CM1582, CM1583, CM1577. The vertically oriented pane of four consists of the following stamps, from top to bottom: CM1581, CM1582, CM1583, CM1584. A complete booklet consists of two panes of eight and one pane of four. CM1583n1 without tab is indistinguishable from a strip of the bottom four stamps of CM1583n.

1993. JOE LOUIS ISSUE honored the heavyweight boxing champion known as the "Brown Bomber" (1914-1981) and was issued on the 55th anniversary of his knockout win over Max Schmeling. *Offset and intaglio, perforated 11.*

CM1584 *Joe Louis*

CM1584		MNHVF	UseVF
29¢	**multicolored** tagged	.45	.20
	Plate block of 4	4.75	
	FDC *(June 22, 1993)*		3.00

1993. BROADWAY MUSICALS ISSUE in the American Music Series honored four of the most celebrated musicals in American theater. *Gravure, Multi-Color Corp. for American Bank Note Co., perforated 11 horizontally on 1 or 2 sides.*

CM1585 Show Boat

CM1586 Porgy & Bess

CM1587 Oklahoma!

CM1588 My Fair Lady

B222

CM1585		MNHVF	UseVF
29¢	*Show Boat,* tagged	.45	.20
CM1586		MNHVF	UseVF
29¢	*Porgy & Bess,* tagged	.45	.20
CM1587		MNHVF	UseVF
29¢	*Oklahoma!,* tagged	.45	.20
CM1588		MNHVF	UseVF
29¢	*My Fair Lady,* tagged	.45	.20
	FDC *(July 14, 1993),* any single		2.50
	n. Booklet pane of 4 (CM1585-88)	4.95	
	FDC, booklet pane of 4		5.00

1993. NATIONAL POSTAL MUSEUM ISSUE marked the opening of the Washington, D.C., facility, part of the Smithsonian Institution. *Offset and intaglio, American Bank Note Co., perforated 11.*

CM1589 *Benjamin Franklin, Liberty Hall, printing press;* CM1590 *Civil War soldier writing letter, stagecoach;* CM1591 *Mail plane, Charles Lindbergh, railway mail car, and mail truck;* CM1592 *Miner's letter, stamps, barcode, and date stamp*

CM1589		MNHVF	UseVF
29¢	**Benjamin Franklin,** tagged	.45	.20
CM1590		MNHVF	UseVF
29¢	**Civil War soldier writing letter**	.45	.20
CM1591		MNHVF	UseVF
29¢	**Charles Lindbergh,** tagged	.45	.20
CM1592		MNHVF	UseVF
29¢	**Letters & date stamp,** tagged	.45	.20
	Plate block of 4	2.00	
	y. Se-tenant block or strip of 4 (CM1589-92)	1.80	.80
	FDC *(July 30, 1993),* any single		2.50
	FDC, block of 4		4.00
	v. Block of 4, imperforate	3,500.00	

1993. RECOGNIZING DEAFNESS/AMERICAN SIGN LANGUAGE ISSUE showed nonverbal communication used with the hearing impaired. Both stamps show the sign for "I love you." *Gravure, Stamp Venturers, perforated 11 1/2.*

CM1593-CM1594 *"I Love You"*

CM1593		MNHVF	UseVF
29¢	**Mother and child,** tagged	.45	.20
CM1594		MNHVF	UseVF
29¢	**Sign "I love you"**	.45	.20
	y. Se-tenant pair (CM1593-94)	.90	.40
	Plate block of 4	3.95	
	FDC *(Sept. 20, 1993),* either single		2.00
	FDC, pair		2.25

1993. COUNTRY MUSIC ISSUE in the American Music Series included an earlier design that featured Hank Williams (CM1569). Added were The Carter Family, Patsy Cline and Bob Wills. The stamps were available as a 20-stamp pane with a large title across the top, or a booklet with each stamp appearing once on each of the five panes. Although the designs and sizes are identical, the sheet stamps used burgundy and blue in addition to yellow, magenta, cyan, and black, while the booklet stamps were produced using pink and line black in addition to the four process colors. *Gravure, Stamp Venturers, perforated 10 on 4 sides (sheet stamps) or on 1 or 2 sides (booklet stamps).*

CM1595, CM1599 *Hank Williams;* CM1596, CM1600 *The Carter Family;* CM1597, CM1601 *Patsy Cline;* CM1598, CM1602 *Bob Wills*
B223

CM1595		MNHVF	UseVF
29¢	**Hank Williams,** tagged	.45	.20
CM1596		MNHVF	UseVF
29¢	**The Carter Family,** tagged	.45	.20
CM1597		MNHVF	UseVF
29¢	**Patsy Cline,** tagged	.45	.20
CM1598		MNHVF	UseVF
29¢	**Bob Wills,** tagged	.45	.20
	Plate block of 4	3.95	
	y. Se-tenant block or strip of 4 (CM1595-98)	2.50	
	FDC *(Sept. 25, 1993),* any single		2.00
	FDC, block or strip of 4		5.00

Gravure by American Bank Note Co., perforated 11 on 1 or 2 sides, from booklet panes.

CM1599		MNHVF	UseVF
29¢	**Hank Williams,** tagged	.45	.20
CM1600		MNHVF	UseVF
29¢	**The Carter Family,** tagged	.45	.20
CM1601		MNHVF	UseVF
29¢	**Patsy Cline,** tagged	.45	.20
CM1602		MNHVF	UseVF
29¢	**Bob Wills,** tagged	.45	.20
	FDC *(Sept. 25, 1993),* any single		1.75
	n. Booklet pane of 4 (CM1599-1602)	3.50	
	FDC, booklet pane		5.00
	nv. Booklet pane, imperforate	—	

1993. YOUTH CLASSICS ISSUE was a se-tenant block showing four of the best-loved and popular stories for young readers. Louisa May Alcott's *Little Women* was published in two volumes in 1868-69. Kate Douglas Smith Wiggin's *Rebecca of Sunnybrook Farm,* the story of a fatherless little girl who goes to live with her maiden aunts, was a best-seller in 1903. Laura Ingalls Wilder drew upon her own childhood and travels on the frontier as inspiration for her books, including *Little House on the Prairie,* published in 1935. *The Adventures of Huckleberry Finn* also is a peek into the childhood of its author, Samuel Clemens (Mark Twain). *Offset and Intaglio on phosphored paper by American Bank Note Co., perforated. In addition, two stamps block tagged in one configuration, all four stamps in another configuration.*

CM1603 Rebecca of Sunnybrook Farm

CM1604 Little House on the Prairie

CM1605 The Adventures of Huckleberry Finn

CM1606 Little Women

CM1603			MNHVF	UseVF
29¢	**Rebecca,** block tagged		.45	.20

CM1604			MNHVF	UseVF
29¢	**Little House**		.60	.20
	z. Block tagged		.60	

CM1605			MNHVF	UseVF
29¢	**Huck Finn**		.60	.20
	z. Block tagged		.60	

CM1606			MNHVF	UseVF
29¢	**Little Women,** block tagged		.45	.20
	Plate block of 4		4.50	
	y. Se-tenant block or strip of 4 (CM1603-06)		3.50	
	FDC (Oct. 23, 1993), any single			2.00
	FDC, block of 4			4.00
	v. Block of 4, imperforate		3,000.00	

1993. COMMONWEALTH OF THE NORTHERN MARIANA ISLANDS ISSUE saluted a group of 16 islands in the western Pacific Ocean administered by the United States following World War II as part of the U.N. Trust Territories of the Pacific Islands. In 1978, following a referendum, the archipelago became a self-governing entity in union with the United States. Mail to and from the Mariana Islands is sent at domestic U.S. postage rates from a U.S. post office. *Offset and intaglio, perforated 11.*

CM1607 *Flag and limestone pillars*

CM1607			MNHVF	UseVF
29¢	**multicolored** tagged		.45	.20
	Plate block of 4		3.50	
	FDC (Nov. 4, 1993)			1.75

1993. COLUMBUS LANDING IN PUERTO RICO ISSUE marked the 500th anniversary of the arrival of Columbus. *Gravure, perforated 11.*

CM1608 *Caravels in Boqueron Bay*

CM1608			MNHVF	UseVF
29¢	**multicolored** tagged		.45	.20
	Plate block of 4		3.50	
	FDC (Nov. 19, 1993)			1.75

1993. AIDS AWARENESS ISSUE symbolized compassion and awareness for those afflicted by this disease. The stamps were sold nationwide on their first day of issue and were available in sheet form or in 10-stamp booklets. *Gravure, perforated 11.*

CM1609, B228 *Symbolic ribbon*

CM1609			MNHVF	UseVF
29¢	**red & black** tagged		.45	.20
	Plate block of 4		2.50	
	FDC (Dec. 1, 1993)			1.75

CM1609A			MNHVF	UseVF
29¢	**red & black** tagged, perforated 11 vertically on 1 or 2 sides		.75	.25
	FDC (Dec. 1, 1993)			1.75
	FDC, booklet pane			5.00
	n. Booklet pane of 5		2.50	

1994. WINTER OLYMPICS ISSUE honored the 1994 Winter Games. *Offset, Ashton Potter, perforated 11.*

CM1610 *Downhill skiing;* CM1611 *Luge;* CM1612 *Figure skating;* CM1613 *Cross-country skiing;* CM1614 *Hockey*

CM1610			MNHVF	UseVF
29¢	**Downhill skiing,** tagged		.45	.20

CM1611			MNHVF	UseVF
29¢	**Luge,** tagged		.45	.20

CM1612			MNHVF	UseVF
29¢	**Figure skating,** tagged		.45	.20

CM1613			MNHVF	UseVF
29¢	**Cross-country skiing,** tagged		.45	.20

CM1614			MNHVF	UseVF
29¢	**Hockey,** tagged		.45	.20
	Plate block of 10		7.50	
	y. Se-tenant strip of 5 (CM-1610-14)		3.00	
	FDC (Jan. 6, 1994), any single			2.00
	FDC, strip of 5			5.00

1994. EDWARD R. MURROW ISSUE honored the broadcast journalist (1908-65) who joined CBS in 1935 and directed its European bureau through World War II. In 1945, he was made CBS vice president in charge of news, education, and discussion programs. *Intaglio, perforated 11.*

CM1615 *Edward R. Murrow*

CM1615			MNHVF	UseVF
29¢	**brown** tagged		.45	.20
	Plate block of 4		3.50	
	FDC (Jan. 21, 1994)			1.75

1994. Love Issue in the popular Love Series was a self-adhesive stamp, one of four 1994 stamps with this theme. (See CM1619-20, CM1642.) *Offset and intaglio, straight line die cut.*

 CM1616 *Love — Heart*

CM1616		MNHVF	UseVF
29¢	**multicolored** tagged	.45	.20
	FDC *(Jan. 27, 1994)*		1.75
	n. Pane of 18	15.00	
	Coil strip of 18	15.00	

1994. Dr. Allison Davis Issue in the Black Heritage Series honored the influential social anthropologist and educator (1902-83) who challenged the cultural bias of standardized intelligence tests and helped end racial segregation. *Intaglio by Stamp Venturers, perforated 11.*

 CM1617 *Dr. William Allison Davis*

CM1617		MNHVF	UseVF
29¢	**red brown & brown** tagged	.45	.20
	Plate block of 4	4.00	
	FDC *(Feb. 1, 1994)*		2.75

1994. Year of the Dog Issue Second in the Lunar New Year Series featured the royal dog of China, a Pekinese, and marked the Year of the Dog. *Gravure, perforated 11.*

 CM1618 *Lunar New Year*

CM1618		MNHVF	UseVF
29¢	**multicolored** tagged	.45	.20
	Plate block of 4	3.75	
	FDC *(Feb. 5, 1994)*		2.50

1994. Love Issues in the Love Series were two lick-and-stick stamps released on Valentine's Day, complementing the earlier self-adhesive issue, CM1616. (See also CM1642.) *Gravure and intaglio.*

 CM1619, B229 *Love — Dove and roses*

CM1619		MNHVF	UseVF
29¢	**multicolored** tagged, perforated	.45	.20
	10 3/4x11 on 2 or 3 sides		
	FDC *(Feb. 14, 1994)*		1.75
	n. Booklet pane of 10	6.00	
	FDC, booklet pane		7.00
	v. Pair, imperforate	—	

v1. Horizontal pair, imperforate between —
nv. Booklet pane of 10, imperforate —

 CM1620 *Love — Doves and roses*

CM1620		MNHVF	UseVF
52¢	**multicolored** tagged, perforated 11 1/4	1.50	.35
	Plate block of 4	7.00	
	FDC *(Feb. 14, 1994)*		2.00

1994. Buffalo Soldiers Issue honored the U.S. Army's regiments, predominantly black cavalry and infantry, that played a major role in the settlement of the American West. Black troops of the Buffalo Soldier regiments were the first authorized to serve in the Army during peacetime. *Offset and intaglio, perforated 11 1/2x11.*

 CM1621 *Buffalo Soldiers*

CM1621		MNHVF	UseVF
29¢	**multicolored** tagged	.45	.20
	Plate block of 4	1.25	
	FDC *(April 22, 1994)*		2.50

1994. Silent Screen Stars Issue featured 10 early film stars, drawn by Al Hirschfeld. Rudolph Valentino is one of the world's best-known film stars remembered for *The Four Horsemen of the Apocalypse, The Sheik,* and *Blood and Sand.* Film star Clara Bow first arrived in Hollywood as the result of a high school beauty contest. Charlie Chaplin's "*Little Tramp*" character became famous worldwide. Lon Chaney used his incredible make-up and characterization in *The Hunchback of Notre Dame, Phantom of the Opera* and *The Unholy Three.* John Gilbert began with a stage career that led to romantic roles in such films as *The Merry Widow, The Big Parade* and *Flesh and the Devil.* Zasu Pitts began as an extra, moving to both comedy and dramatic roles. Comedian Harold Lloyd made more than 500 movies, beginning in 1914. Mack Sennett's Keystone Cops kept audiences laughing through many short films of 1914-20. Theda Bara's work in *The Vampire* led to the term "vamp." Buster Keaton is known for slapstick comedy and his deadpan stare. *Offset and intaglio, perforated 11.*

CM1622 *Rudolph Valentino;* CM1623 *Clara Bow;* CM1624 *Charlie Chaplin;* CM1625 *Lon Chaney;* CM1626 *John Gilbert;* CM1627 *Zasu Pitts;* CM1628 *Harold Lloyd;* CM1629 *Keystone Cops;* CM1630 *Theda Bara;* CM1631 *Buster Keaton*

		MNHVF	UseVF
CM1622		MNHVF	UseVF
29¢	**Rudolph Valentino,** tagged	.45	.20
CM1623		MNHVF	UseVF
29¢	**Clara Bow,** tagged	.45	.20
CM1624		MNHVF	UseVF
29¢	**Charlie Chaplin,** tagged	.45	.20
CM1625		MNHVF	UseVF
29¢	**Lon Chaney,** tagged	.45	.20
CM1626		MNHVF	UseVF
29¢	**John Gilbert,** tagged	.45	.20
CM1627		MNHVF	UseVF
29¢	**Zasu Pitts,** tagged	.45	.20
CM1628		MNHVF	UseVF
29¢	**Harold Lloyd,** tagged	.45	.20
CM1629		MNHVF	UseVF
29¢	**Keystone Cops,** tagged	.45	.20
CM1630		MNHVF	UseVF
29¢	**Theda Bara,** tagged	.45	.20
CM1631		MNHVF	UseVF
29¢	**Buster Keaton,** tagged	.45	.20
	Plate block of 10	9.00	
	y. Se-tenant block of 10 (CM1622-31)	8.00	
	vy. Block of 10, offset black omitted	—	
	vy1. Block of 10, offset black & intaglio red & purple omitted	—	
	FDC *(April 27, 1994)*, any single		2.00
	FDC, block of 10		8.00

1994. SUMMER GARDEN FLOWERS ISSUE The second in a Garden Flowers Series of five-stamp booklets showing bright and popular flowers that bloom in summer. *Offset and intaglio, perforated 11 vertically on 1 or 2 sides.*

CM1632 *Lily;* CM1633 *Zinnia;* CM1634 *Gladiola;* CM1635 *Marigold;* CM1636 *Rose* B230

		MNHVF	UseVF
CM1632		MNHVF	UseVF
29¢	**multicolored** tagged	.45	.20
CM1633		MNHVF	UseVF
29¢	**multicolored** tagged	.45	.20
CM1634		MNHVF	UseVF
29¢	**multicolored** tagged	.45	.20
CM1635		MNHVF	UseVF
29¢	**multicolored** tagged	.45	.20
CM1636		MNHVF	UseVF
29¢	**multicolored** tagged	.45	.20
	FDC *(April 28, 1994)*, any single		2.00
	n. Booklet pane of 5 (CM1632-36)	4.50	
	FDC, booklet pane of 5		5.00
	nv. Pane of 5, intaglio black omitted	375.00	
	nv1. Pane of 5, imperforate	2,250.00	

1994. WORLD CUP SOCCER CHAMPIONSHIP ISSUE of three stamps and a souvenir sheet noted the first time the United States hosted the final rounds of soccer's quadrennial World Cup. Stamps issued in panes of 20 were printed on phosphor-coated paper; those within the souvenir sheet are block tagged. The 50¢ stamp in the souvenir sheet (CM1640c) has part of the yellow map from the sheet in the lower-right corner of its design. *Gravure, perforated 11.*

CM1640 *World Cup souvenir sheet*

		MNHVF	UseVF
CM1637		MNHVF	UseVF
29¢	**multicolored** phosphored paper	.75	.20
	Plate block of 4	4.00	
	FDC *(May 26, 1994)*		1.75
CM1638		MNHVF	UseVF
40¢	**multicolored** phosphored paper	1.00	.35
	Plate block of 4	5.50	
	FDC *(May 26, 1994)*		2.00
CM1639		MNHVF	UseVF
50¢	**multicolored** phosphored paper	1.50	.50
	Plate block of 4	6.50	
	FDC *(May 26, 1994)*		2.00
CM1640		MNHVF	UseVF
$1.19	**Souvenir Sheet**	3.75	3.00
	a. 29¢ like CM1637, block tagged		.75
	b. 40¢ like CM1638, block tagged		1.00
	c. 50¢ like CM1639, block tagged		1.25

1994. 1944: ROAD TO VICTORY ISSUE in the World War II Commemorative Series included a map and stamps showing events of the war in 1944. *Offset and intaglio, perforated 11.*

		MNHVF	UseVF
CM1641		MNHVF	UseVF
$2.90	**Commemorative pane of 10,** tagged	8.75	7.00
	a. 29¢ Forces retake New Guinea	.75	.70
	b. 29¢ P-51s escort B-17s	.75	.70
	c. 29¢ Allies free Normandy	.75	.70
	d. 29¢ Airborne units	.75	.70
	e. 29¢ Submarines	.75	.70
	f. 29¢ Allies free Rome, Paris	.75	.70
	g. 29¢ U.S. troops clear Saipan	.75	.70
	h. 29¢ Red Ball Express	.75	.70
	i. 29¢ Battle of Leyte Gulf	.75	.70
	j. 29¢ Bastogne and The Bulge	.75	.70
	FDC *(June 6, 1994)*, any single		2.00
	FDC complete pane of 10		10.00

1994. LOVE ISSUE in the Love Series was a slightly longer sheet version of the 29¢ booklet stamp (CM1619) released on Valentine's Day. *Offset and intaglio, perforated 11.*

CM1642 *Love*

		MNHVF	UseVF
CM1642		MNHVF	UseVF
29¢	**multicolored** tagged	.50	.20
	Plate block of 4	3.50	
	FDC *(June 11, 1994)*		1.75

1994. NORMAN ROCKWELL ISSUE honored the artist best known as a chronicler of 20th century America for more than 4,000 works, including 321 original *Saturday Evening Post* covers between 1916 and 1963. The commemoration consisted of a single stamp and a commemorative sheet of four stamps depicting Franklin D. Roosevelt's Four Freedoms. *Offset and intaglio, perforated 11.*

CM1643 *Norman Rockwell*

CM1643		MNHVF	UseVF
29¢	**multicolored** tagged	.50	.20
	Plate block of 4	3.50	
	FDC *(July 1, 1994)*		1.75

CM1644a *Freedom from Want;* CM1644b *Freedom from Fear;*
CM1644c *Freedom of Speech;* CM1644d *Freedom of Worship*

CM1644		MNHVF	UseVF
$2	**multicolored** tagged	6.00	5.00
	a. 50¢ Freedom from Want	1.00	1.00
	b. 50¢ Freedom from Fear	1.00	1.00
	c. 50¢ Freedom of Speech	1.00	1.00
	d. 50¢ Freedom of Worship	1.00	1.00
	FDC *(July 1, 1994),* any single		2.00
	FDC, souvenir sheet		5.75

1994. MOON LANDING ANNIVERSARY ISSUE released in special
12-stamp sheetlets, celebrated the 25th anniversary of man's first
landing on the Moon. (See also No. 1045.) *Gravure, by Stamp
Venturers, perforated 11.*

CM1645 *Moon Landing, 25th anniversary*

CM1645		MNHVF	UseVF
29¢	**multicolored** tagged	.50	.25
	FDC *(July 20, 1994)*		1.75
	y. Commemorative pane of 12	9.00	7.50
	FDC, sheetlet		10.75

1994. LOCOMOTIVES ISSUE A five-stamp booklet, depicted
historically significant locomotives. (See also CM1293-97.) *Gravure,
by J.W. Fergusson & Sons for Stamp Venturers, perforated 11
horizontally on 1 or 2 sides.*

CM1641 *1944: Road to Victory*

CM1646 *Hudson's General*

CM1647 *McQueen's Jupiter*

CM1648 *Eddy's No. 242*

CM1649 *Ely's No. 10*

CM1650 *Buchannan's No. 999* B231

CM1646		MNHVF	UseVF
29¢	Hudson's General, tagged	.75	.50
CM1647		MNHVF	UseVF
29¢	McQueen's Jupiter, tagged	.75	.50
CM1648		MNHVF	UseVF
29¢	Eddy's No. 242, tagged	.75	.50
CM1649		MNHVF	UseVF
29¢	Ely's No. 10, tagged	.75	.50
CM1650		MNHVF	UseVF
29¢	Buchannan's No. 999, tagged	.75	.50
	FDC *(July 29, 1994)*, any single		2.00
	n. Booklet pane of 5 (CM1646-50)	4.50	
	FDC, booklet pane of 5		5.00
	nv. Pane of 5, imperforate	—	

1994. GEORGE MEANY ISSUE honored one of the most influential labor leaders in American history (1894-1980), president of the American Federation of Labor (AFL) from 1952-55 and first president of the AFL and Congress of Industrial Organizations (CIO) from 1955 until his retirement in 1979. *Intaglio, perforated 11.*

CM1651 *George Meany*

CM1651		MNHVF	UseVF
29¢	blue tagged	.50	.20
	Plate block of 4	3.50	
	FDC *(Aug. 16, 1994)*		1.75

1994. POPULAR SINGERS ISSUE in the American Music Series honored five showstoppers of this century. *Gravure by J.W. Fergusson & Sons for Stamp Venturers, perforated 10.*

CM1652 *Al Jolson*

CM1653 *Bing Crosby*

CM1654 *Ethel Waters*

CM1655 *Nat "King" Cole*

CM1656 *Ethel Merman*

CM1652		MNHVF	UseVF
29¢	Al Jolson, tagged	.75	.50
CM1653		MNHVF	UseVF
29¢	Bing Crosby, tagged	.75	.50
CM1654		MNHVF	UseVF
29¢	Ethel Waters, tagged	.75	.50
CM1655		MNHVF	UseVF
29¢	Nat "King" Cole, tagged	.75	.50
CM1656		MNHVF	UseVF
29¢	Ethel Merman, tagged	.75	.50
	Plate block of 6 (vertical)	6.00	
	Plate block of 12 (horizontal)	11.00	
	FDC *(Sept. 1, 1994)*, any single		2.00
	FDC, strip of 5		6.00
	y. Se-tenant vertical strip of 5 (CM1652-56)	3.75	

1994. JAMES THURBER ISSUE 12th in the Literary Arts Series hailed the author, humorist, playwright and cartoonist (1894-1961) whose 31 books gave humorous views of life in America. *Offset and intaglio, perforated 11.*

CM1657 *James Thurber*

CM1657		MNHVF	UseVF
29¢	**multicolored** tagged	.50	.20
	Plate block of 4	3.50	
	FDC *(Sept. 10. 1994)*		1.75

1994. BLUES AND JAZZ SINGERS ISSUE in the American Music Series honored seminal artists in these distinctive American musical genres. *Offset by Manhardt-Alexander for Ashton Potter (USA) Ltd., perforated 11.*

  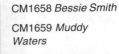

CM1658 *Bessie Smith*

CM1659 *Muddy Waters*

 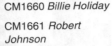

CM1660 *Billie Holiday*

CM1661 *Robert Johnson*

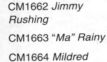

CM1662 *Jimmy Rushing*

CM1663 *"Ma" Rainy*

 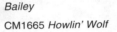

CM1664 *Mildred Bailey*

CM1665 *Howlin' Wolf*

CM1658		MNHVF	UseVF
29¢	**Bessie Smith,** tagged	.50	.25
CM1659		MNHVF	UseVF
29¢	**Muddy Waters,** tagged	.50	.25
CM1660		MNHVF	UseVF
29¢	**Billie Holiday,** tagged	.50	.25
CM1661		MNHVF	UseVF
29¢	**Robert Johnson,** tagged	.50	.25
CM1662		MNHVF	UseVF
29¢	**Jimmy Rushing,** tagged	.50	.25
CM1663		MNHVF	UseVF
29¢	**"Ma" Rainy,** tagged	.50	.25
CM1664		MNHVF	UseVF
29¢	**Mildred Bailey,** tagged	.50	.25
CM1665		MNHVF	UseVF
29¢	**Howlin' Wolf,** tagged	.50	.25
	Plate block of 10	8.00	
	y. Se-tenant block of 9 (CM1658-65) plus 1 extra stamp	5.50	
	FDC *(Sept. 17, 1994),* any single		2.00
	FDC, block of 9		10.00

1994. WONDERS OF THE SEAS ISSUE used four se-tenant stamps to form a single underwater fantasy scene. *Offset by Barton Press for the Banknote Corporation of America, perforated 11.*

CM1666 *Porcupine fish*

CM1667 *Dolphin*

CM1668 *Nautilus and ship's wheel*

CM1669 *Fish and coral*

CM1666		MNHVF	UseVF
29¢	**Porcupine fish,** tagged	.75	.25
CM1667		MNHVF	UseVF
29¢	**Dolphin,** tagged	.75	.25
CM1668		MNHVF	UseVF
29¢	**Nautilus & ship's wheel,** tagged	.75	.25
CM1669		MNHVF	UseVF
29¢	**Fish & coral,** tagged	.75	.25
	Plate block of 4	4.00	
	y. Se-tenant block of 4 (CM1666-69)	3.00	
	FDC *(Oct. 3, 1994),* any single		2.00
	vy. Block of 4, imperforate	2,500.00	
	FDC, block of 4		4.00

1994. CRANES ISSUE depicted two of the world's rarest birds, the North American Whooping Crane and the Chinese Black-necked Crane. A joint issue of the United States and the People's Republic of China (CNP3784-3785), the issues of the two countries show the same designs, with the Chinese issue as two separate stamps and the U.S. issue as a se-tenant pair. *Offset and intaglio by Barton Press for the Banknote Corporation of America, perforated 11.*

CM1670 *Black-Necked Crane*

CM1671 *Whooping Crane*

CM1670		MNHVF	UseVF
29¢	**Black-necked crane,** tagged	.45	.20
CM1671		MNHVF	UseVF
29¢	**Whooping crane,** tagged	.45	.20
	Plate block of 4	1.25	
	y. Se-tenant pair (CM1670-71)		
	FDC *(Oct. 9, 1994),* either single		2.25
	vy. Se-tenant pair, black & red omitted	2,000.00	
	FDC, pair		2.75

Classic Collections Series

1993-1994. LEGENDS OF THE WEST ISSUE Late in 1993, the Postal Service printed more than 5 million Legends of the West panes and forwarded them to postal distribution centers and post offices throughout the country, even though the stamps were not scheduled to be issued until 1994. These stamps were to be the first in a new series formatted by USPS as "*Classic Collections*"— special panes of 20 different first-class letter rate stamps with explanatory text on the back of each and a banner across the top of the pane describing its collective subject — in this case, legendary personalities and themes from the early days of the Western frontier.

At least 183 of these panes were sold at four post offices long before the planned first day of issue, beginning with a full pane that was purchased and used to frank a parcel mailed in Bend, Ore., Dec. 14, 1993. The other three post offices at which the stamps were sold early were McLean, Va., High Point, N.C., and Princeton, N.J.

About the same time, the USPS learned that one stamp in the original pane, purported to have depicted black cowboy and rodeo showman Bill Pickett, was actually a portrait of his brother, Ben. Bill Pickett's descendants demanded that the Postal Service withdraw and destroy panes with the incorrect portrait and print new ones with an accurate portrait of Bill Pickett, and the USPS agreed to do so.

However, the early release and use of the panes from the original printing made that impossible.

After a great deal of public and private debate as to the best solution (including two lawsuits), the Postal Service decided to print a second Legends of the West pane as promised with a revised, accurate portrait of Bill Pickett, but also to offer 150,000 original Legends of the West panes with the Ben Pickett portrait to the public in a special lottery. The remainder of the original Legends of the West — nearly 5 million panes — would then be destroyed.

The USPS stuck to this plan despite considerable criticism from stamp collectors, even when it was revealed that, in the revised pane, 16 of the 20 stamps in the pane were different from those in the original pane. (The red framelines around the stamps portraying people in the original pane are about half the thickness of those in the revised pane.) Because the overwhelming majority of the 150,000 original Legends of the West commemorative panes that were sold to collectors by lottery were retained as panes by collectors, it has been listed as a single number (CM1671A), with the individual stamps as minor varieties of that number. *Gravure by J.W. Fergusson & Sons for Stamp Venturers, perforated 10.*

CM1671A *Legends of the West commemorative pane (original version): a. Home on the Range; b. Buffalo Bill Cody (1846-1917); c. Jim Bridger (1804-81); d. Annie Oakley (1860-1926); e. Native American Culture; f. Chief Joseph (c. 1840-1904); g. Bill (Ben) Pickett (incorrect portrait in original pane); h. Bat Masterson (1853-1921); i. John C. Fremont (1813-90); j. Wyatt Earp (1848-1929); k. Nellie Cashman (c. 1849-1925); l. Charles Goodnight (1826-1929); m. Geronimo (1823-1909); n. Kit Carson (1809-68); o. Wild Bill Hickok (1837-76); p. Western Wildlife; q. Jim Beckwourth (c. 1798-1866); r. Bill Tilghman (1854-1924); s. Sacagawea (c. 1787-1812); t. Overland Mail*

CM1671A		MNHVF	UseVF
$5.80	**Legends of the West commemorative pane,** tagged, *(earliest known use Dec. 14, 1993)*	195.00	

1994. REVISED LEGENDS OF THE WEST ISSUE with a stamp showing an accurate portrait of Bill Pickett and thicker red framelines around the portraits on the stamps in the pane that depict individuals.

Because the revised panes were sold at face value, and stamps from them were used relatively more extensively on mail, stamps from the revised pane are listed and numbered individually. *Gravure by J.W. Fergusson & Sons for Stamp Venturers, perforated 11.*

CM1691y *Legends of the West commemorative pane (revised version)*
CM1678 *Bill Pickett (correct portrait in revised pane)*

		MNHVF	UseVF
CM1672 29¢	**Home on the Range,** tagged	.45	.20
CM1673 29¢	**Buffalo Bill,** tagged	.45	.20
CM1674 29¢	**Jim Bridger,** tagged	.45	.20
CM1675 29¢	**Annie Oakley,** tagged	.45	.20
CM1676 29¢	**Native American Culture,** tagged	.45	.20
CM1677 29¢	**Chief Joseph,** tagged	.45	.20
CM1678 29¢	**Bill Pickett,** tagged	.45	.20
CM1679 29¢	**Bat Masterson,** tagged	.45	.20
CM1680 29¢	**John Fremont,** tagged	.45	.20
CM1681 29¢	**Wyatt Earp,** tagged	.45	.20
CM1682 29¢	**Nellie Cashman,** tagged	.45	.20
CM1683 29¢	**Charles Goodnight,** tagged	.45	.20
CM1684 29¢	**Geronimo,** tagged	.45	.20
CM1685 29¢	**Kit Carson,** tagged	.45	.20
CM1686 29¢	**Wild Bill Hickok,** tagged	.45	.20
CM1687 29¢	**Western Wildlife,** tagged	.45	.20
CM1688 29¢	**Jim Beckwourth,** tagged	.45	.20

CM1689		MNHVF	UseVF
29¢	**Bill Tilghman,** tagged	.45	.20
CM1690		MNHVF	UseVF
29¢	**Sacagawea,** tagged	.45	.20
CM1691		MNHVF	UseVF
29¢	**Overland Mail,** tagged	.45	.20
	FDC *(Oct. 18, 1994),* any single		2.00
	y. Se-tenant pane of 20	16.00	14.00
	Six pane press sheet	125.00	
	FDC, pane of 20		25.00
	v. Pane of 20, imperforate	2,000.00	
	v1. Pane of 20, CM1672-76, imperforate, CM1677-81 partially imperforate	—	
	Set of 5 pairs with horizontal gutters	10.00	
	Block of 10 with horizontal gutter	11.00	
	Set of 4 pairs with vertical gutters	8.00	
	Block of 8 with vertical gutter	9.00	
	Cross-gutter block of 20	20.00	

1994. BUREAU OF ENGRAVING AND PRINTING CENTENNIAL SOUVENIR ISSUE marked the 100th anniversary of the national security printer with a souvenir sheet containing four $2 James Madison definitives of a design first used almost a century before (No. 185, 1894), when the Bureau of Engraving and Printing began printing U.S. stamps. *Offset and intaglio, perforated 11.*

CM1692 *Bureau of Engraving and Printing centennial souvenir sheet*

Close-up of Major Double Transfer with prominent areas indicated

CM1692		MNHVF	UseVF
$8	**multicolored** tagged	20.00	14.50
	a. single stamp	5.00	3.50
	Major double transfer on right $2 stamp in sheet of 4	—	
	Major double transfer, single $2 stamp	—	
	Minor double transfer on $2 stamp in sheet of 4	—	
	Minor double transfer, single $2 stamp	—	
	FDC *(Nov. 3, 1994),* any single		7.00
	FDC, souvenir sheet of 4		24.00

Listings for minor double transfers refer to any of approximately 10 different ones that are known.

1994. YEAR OF THE BOAR ISSUE in Lunar New Year Series for the Year of the Boar was the third installment. This stamp was released only two days before the first-class letter rate increased from 29¢ to 32¢. *Gravure by Stamp Venturers, perforated 11.*

CM1693 *Lunar New Year, Boar*

CM1693		MNHVF	UseVF
29¢	**multicolored** tagged	.50	.20
	Plate block of 4	3.50	
	FDC *(Dec. 30, 1994)*		2.50

1995. LOVE CHERUB ISSUE in the Love Series featured non-denominated conventional and self-adhesive stamps depicting a cherub from the 16th-century *Sistine Madonna* by Raphael. *Offset and intaglio (Bureau of Engraving and Printing), perforated 11 1/4.*

CM1694 *Love Cherub, tall design*

CM1694		MNHVF	UseVF
(32¢)	**multicolored** phosphored paper	.50	.20
	Plate block of 4	2.00	
	FDC *(Feb. 1, 1995)*		1.90

1995. LOVE CHERUB BOOKLET ISSUE *Self-adhesive booklet, offset and intaglio by Banknote Corporation of America, imperforate (die cut).*

CM1695 *Love Cherub, short design*

CM1695		MNHVF	UseVF
(32¢)	**multicolored** phosphored paper	.50	.20
	FDC *(Feb. 1, 1995)*		1.90
	n. Pane of 20, plus label (convertible booklet)	16.00	
	vn. Pane of 20, intaglio red (inscriptions) omitted	1,000.00	

1995. FLORIDA SESQUICENTENNIAL ISSUE marked the 150th anniversary of Florida statehood. It was the 27th state in the Union. *Offset by Sterling Sommer for Ashton-Potter (USA) Ltd., perforated 11.*

CM1696 *Florida statehood sesquicentennial*

CM1696		MNHVF	UseVF
32¢	**multicolored** phosphored paper	.50	.20
	Plate block of 4	3.50	
	FDC *(March 3, 1995)*		1.90

1995. EARTH DAY ISSUE showcased the four winning designs created by children in a nationwide contest to produce stamps for the 25th anniversary of Earth Day. The winning quartet was issued in a pane of 16 (four se-tenant blocks of four) with a "Kids Care!" banner across selvage at the top of the pane and the details of the contest in the selvage at the foot of the pane. *Offset by Sterling Sommer for Ashton-Potter (USA) Ltd., perforated 11.*

CM1697 *Clean Earth*

CM1698 *Solar Power*

CM1699 *Tree Planting*

CM1700 *Clean Beaches*

CM1697

		MNHVF	UseVF
32¢	**Clean Earth,** phosphored paper	.50	.20

CM1698

		MNHVF	UseVF
32¢	**Solar Power,** phosphored paper	.50	.20

CM1699

		MNHVF	UseVF
32¢	**Tree Planting,** phosphored paper	.50	.20

CM1700

		MNHVF	UseVF
32¢	**Clean Beaches,** phosphored paper	.50	.20
	Plate block of 4	3.50	
	y. Se-tenant block of 4 (CM1697-1700)	2.00	
	FDC (April 20, 1995), any single		2.00
	y1. Pane of 16	14.00	
	FDC, block of 4		4.35

1995. RICHARD M. NIXON ISSUE marked the death on April 22, 1994, of the 37th president of the United States, Richard Milhous Nixon (1913-1994). He ended the divisive Vietnam war and improved relations with the USSR and China, but he resigned from office over a burglary of Democratic offices in Washington, D.C. *Offset and intaglio by Barton Press and Banknote Corporation of America, perforated 11.*

CM1701 *Richard M. Nixon*

CM1701

		MNHVF	UseVF
32¢	**multicolored** phosphored paper	.50	.20
	Plate block of 4	3.50	
	FDC (April 26, 1995)		1.90
	v. Intaglio red ("Richard Nixon") omitted	1,500.00	

1995. BESSIE COLEMAN ISSUE in the Black Heritage Series commemorated the first African-American woman aviator, who traveled to France to learn the language in order to earn her pilot's license there in 1921 after American flying schools had refused to admit her. She died in a fall from a plane (1896-1926). *Intaglio by Bureau of Engraving and Printing, perforated 11.*

CM1702 *Bessie Coleman*

CM1702

		MNHVF	UseVF
32¢	**red & black** phosphored paper	.50	.20

Plate block of 4	3.50	
FDC (April 27, 1995)		3.00

1995. LOVE CHERUB ISSUE in the Love Series added stamps with a 32¢ face value in matching designs to follow the non-denominated versions issued in February (CM1695-96), along with 55¢ stamps showing the cherub on the right in the same Raphael painting, paying the rate for letters under 2 ounces (such as most wedding invitations with response cards and envelopes enclosed). *Offset and intaglio, by Bureau of Engraving and Printing. Perforated 11 1/4.*

CM1703, CM1704, CM1798 *Love Cherub*

CM1703

		MNHVF	UseVF
32¢	**multicolored** phosphored paper	.50	.20
	Plate block of 4	2.50	
	FDC (May 12, 1995)		1.90

1995. LOVE CHERUB BOOKLET ISSUE in the Love Series *perforated 9 3/4x11 on 2 or 3 sides (32¢) or 11 1/4 (55¢).*

CM1704

		MNHVF	UseVF
32¢	**multicolored** phosphored paper	.50	.20
	FDC (May 12, 1995)		1.90
	n. Booklet pane of 10	5.50	
	FDC, booklet pane		8.50

CM1705 *Love Cherub*

CM1705

		MNHVF	UseVF
55¢	**multicolored** phosphored paper	1.00	.35
	Plate block of 4	5.00	
	FDC (May 12, 1995)		2.25

1995. LOVE CHERUB SELF-ADHESIVE BOOKLET ISSUE in the Love Series *printed in offset and intaglio by Banknote Corporation of America, imperforate (die cut).*

CM1706 *Love Cherub*

CM1706

		MNHVF	UseVF
55¢	**multicolored** phosphored paper	1.00	.35
	FDC (May 12, 1995)		2.25
	n. Pane of 20, plus label (convertible booklet)	22.50	

1995. RECREATIONAL SPORTS ISSUE depicted popular American pastimes in five se-tenant designs. *Offset by Barton Press for Banknote Corporation of America, perforated 11x11 1/4.*

CM1707

		MNHVF	UseVF
32¢	**Bowling,** phosphored paper	.50	.20

CM1708

		MNHVF	UseVF
32¢	**Tennis,** phosphored paper	.50	.20

CM1709

		MNHVF	UseVF
32¢	**Golf,** phosphored paper	.50	.20

CM1710

		MNHVF	UseVF
32¢	**Volleyball,** phosphored paper	.50	.20

CM1711

		MNHVF	UseVF
32¢	**Baseball,** phosphored paper	.50	.20
	Plate block of 10	8.50	
	y. Se-tenant vertical strip of 5 (CM1708-11)	3.00	
	FDC (May 20, 1995), any single		2.00
	y1. Pane of 20	17.00	

		MNHVF	UseVF
vy. Strip of 5, imperforate		2,750.00	
v1y. Vertical strip of 5, yellow omitted		2,500.00	

CM1707 *Bowling*

CM1708 *Tennis*

CM1709 *Golf*

CM1710 *Volleyball*

CM1711 *Baseball*

		MNHVF	UseVF
v2y. Vertical strip of 5, yellow, cyan & magenta omitted		2,500.00	
FDC, strip of 5			5.50

1995. POW & MIA ISSUE saluted personnel in the U.S. armed forces who were prisoners of war or who were unaccounted for after the end of hostilities. *Offset by Sterling Sommer for Ashton-Potter (USA) Ltd., perforated 11.*

CM1712 *POW & MIA*

CM1712		MNHVF	UseVF
32¢	**multicolored** phosphored paper	.50	.20
	Plate block of 4	3.50	
	FDC (May 29, 1995)		1.90

Legends of Hollywood Series

1995. MARILYN MONROE ISSUE first installment in the USPS Legends of Hollywood Series, with a pane of 20 (each stamp having its corner perforations in the shape of a star), bearing the likeness and facsimile autograph of Marilyn Monroe (1926-1962), with the large all-around selvage in the commemorative pane of 20 showing an enlargement of a portrait of the movie star near the height of her appeal. *Gravure by J.W. Fergusson & Sons for Stamp Venturers, perforated 11.*

CM1713 *Marilyn Monroe*

CM1713		MNHVF	UseVF
32¢	**multicolored** block tagged	.75	.20
	Plate block of 4	3.50	
	FDC (June 1, 1995)		4.00
	y. Pane of 20	17.00	
	v. Pair, imperforate	625.00	
	Six-pane press sheet	125.00	
	Pair with horizontal gutter	3.25	
	Pair with vertical gutter	6.00	
	Block of 8 with vertical gutter	36.00	
	Cross-gutter block of 8	45.00	

1995. TEXAS SESQUICENTENNIAL ISSUE marked the 150th anniversary of Texas statehood. Texas was the 28th state in the union. *Offset by Ashton-Potter (USA) Ltd., perforated 11.*

CM1714 *Texas statehood sesquicentennial*

CM1714		MNHVF	UseVF
32¢	**multicolored** phosphored paper	.50	.20
	Plate block of 4	3.50	
	FDC (June 16, 1995)		1.90

1995. LIGHTHOUSES ISSUE used the same format and design as the 1990 Lighthouses issue (CM1378-82) to create a booklet showcasing lighthouses of the Great Lakes. *Gravure by J.W. Fergusson & Sons for Stamp Venturers, perforated 11 vertically on one or two sides.*

CM1715 *Split Rock;* CM1716 *St. Joseph;* CM1717 *Spectacle Reef;* CM1718 *Marblehead;* CM1719 *Thirty Mile Point* B254

CM1715		MNHVF	UseVF
32¢	**Split Rock,** phosphored paper	.50	.20
CM1716		MNHVF	UseVF
32¢	**St. Joseph,** phosphored paper	.50	.20
CM1717		MNHVF	UseVF
32¢	**Spectacle Reef,** phosphored paper	.50	.20
CM1718		MNHVF	UseVF
32¢	**Marblehead,** phosphored paper	.50	.20
CM1719		MNHVF	UseVF
32¢	**Thirty Mile Point,** phosphored paper	.50	.20
	FDC (June 17, 1995), any single		2.00
	n. Booklet pane of 5 (CM1715-19)	3.50	3.50
	FDC, booklet pane		5.50

1995. UNITED NATIONS ISSUE marked the 50th anniversary of that organization. *Intaglio by Banknote Corporation of America, perforated 11 1/4x11.*

CM1720 *United Nations*

CM1720		MNHVF	UseVF
32¢	**blue** phosphored paper	.50	.20
	Plate block of 4	3.00	
	FDC (June 26, 1995)		1.90

1995. CIVIL WAR ISSUE was the second release in the USPS Classic Collections Series to showcase 20 stamps on a single theme in a pane with a colorful banner across the top selvage identifying the subject — in this case, the Civil War. As on the 1994 Legends of the West pane that introduced the concept, the four corner stamps detail events (battles, in this instance) while the other 16 stamps are painstakingly researched portraits of individuals who played a significant role in the era, and text printed on the back of the stamps provides information on the subject of each. *Gravure by J.W. Fergusson & Sons for Stamp Venturers, perforated 10 1/4x10. Multicolored, block tagged.*

CM1721 Monitor *and* Virginia; CM1722 *Robert E. Lee;* CM1723 *Clara Barton;* CM1724 *Ulysses S. Grant;* CM1725 *Battle of Shiloh;* CM1726 Jefferson Davis; CM1727 *David Farragut;* CM1728 *Frederick Douglass;* CM1729 *Raphael Semmes;* CM1730 *Abraham Lincoln;* CM1731 *Harriet Tubman;* CM1732 *Stand Watie;* CM1733 *Joseph E. Johnston;* CM1734 *Winfield Hancock;* CM1735 *Mary Chesnut;* CM1736 *Battle of Chancellorsville;* CM1737 *William T. Sherman;* CM1738 *Phoebe Pember;* CM1739 *Stonewall Jackson;* CM1740 *Battle of Gettysburg*

		MNHVF	UseVF
CM1721 32¢	*Monitor* and *Virginia*	.75	.50
CM1722 32¢	Robert E. Lee	.75	.50
CM1723 32¢	Clara Barton	.75	.50
CM1724 32¢	Ulysses S. Grant	.75	.50
CM1725 32¢	Battle of Shiloh	.75	.50
CM1726 32¢	Jefferson Davis	.75	.50
CM1727 32¢	David Farragut	.75	.50
CM1728 32¢	Frederick Douglass	.75	.50
CM1729 32¢	Raphael Semmes	.75	.50
CM1730 32¢	Abraham Lincoln	.75	.50
CM1731 32¢	Harriet Tubman	.75	.50

		MNHVF	UseVF
CM1732 32¢	Stand Watie	.75	.50
CM1733 32¢	Joseph E. Johnston	.75	.50
CM1734 32¢	Winfield Hancock	.75	.50
CM1735 32¢	Mary Chesnut	.75	.50
CM1736 32¢	Battle of Chancellorsville	.75	.50
CM1737 32¢	William T. Sherman	.75	.50
CM1738 32¢	Phoebe Pember	.75	.50
CM1739 32¢	"Stonewall" Jackson	.75	.50
CM1740 32¢	Battle of Gettysburg	.75	.50
	y. Pane of 20 (CM1721-40)	16.00	14.00
	FDC *(June 29, 1995),* any single		2.00
	FDC, pane of 20		20.00
	vy. Pane of 20, imperforate	2,000.00	
	v1y. Pane with CM1721-25 imperforated, (CM1726-30) part perforated	—	
	v2y. Pane with CM1731-35 imperforated, (CM1736-40) part perforated	—	
	v3y. Block of 9 (CM1726-28, CM1731-33, CM1736-38), imperforate vertically	—	
	Six pane press sheet	150.00	
	Set of 5 pairs with horizontal gutters	16.25	
	Block of 10 with horizontal gutter	18.00	
	Set of 4 pairs with vertical gutters	13.00	
	Block of 8 with vertical gutter	14.25	
	Cross-gutter block of 20	30.00	

1995. CAROUSEL HORSES ISSUE in the American Folk Art Series used the same design and much the same format as the popular 1988 Carousel Animals issue (CM1327-30) in portraying four stalwart steeds from the classic American carnival ride. *Offset by Sterling Sommer for Ashton-Potter (USA) Ltd., perforated 11.*

CM1741 *Golden horse*

CM1742 *Black horse*

CM1743 *Armored horse*

CM1744 *Brown horse*

		MNHVF	UseVF
CM1741 32¢	**Golden horse,** phosphored paper	.50	.20
CM1742 32¢	**Black horse,** phosphored paper	.50	.20
CM1743 32¢	**Armored horse,** phosphored paper	.50	.20
CM1744 32¢	**Brown horse,** phosphored paper	.50	.20
	Plate block of 4	3.75	
	y. Se-tenant block of 4 (CM1741-44)	2.00	
	FDC *(July 21, 1995),* any single		2.00
	FDC, block of 4		4.35

1995. WOMAN SUFFRAGE ISSUE memorialized the 75th anniversary of the Aug. 18, 1920, ratification of the 19th Amendment to the Constitution: "The right of citizens of the United States to vote will not be denied or abridged by the United States or by any state on account of sex." *Offset and intaglio by Ashton-Potter (USA) Ltd., perforated 11.*

CM1745 *U.S. Constitution's 19th Amendment*

CM1745		MNHVF	UseVF
32¢	**multicolored,** phosphored paper	.50	.20
	Plate block of 4	3.50	
	FDC *(Aug. 26, 1995)*		1.90
	v. Pair, imperforate	1,500.00	
	v1. Intaglio black omitted	450.00	

1995. LOUIS ARMSTRONG ISSUE in the American Music Series honored the New Orleans-born trumpet player, composer, improviser and unofficial U.S. goodwill ambassador (1900-1971) who made giant contributions to jazz. *Offset by Sterling Sommer for Ashton-Potter (USA) Ltd., perforated 11.*

CM1746 *Louis Armstrong*

CM1746		MNHVF	UseVF
32¢	**multicolored,** phosphored paper	.50	.20
	Plate block of 4	3.50	
	FDC *(Sept. 1, 1995)*		2.75

For a similar design with "32" in black, see CM1749.

1995. 1945: VICTORY AT LAST ISSUE The final installment in the five-year, 50-stamp World War II Commemorative Series, featured a map and stamps covering events of the war in 1945. *Offset and intaglio by Bureau of Engraving and Printing, perforated 11.*

CM1747		MNHVF	UseVF
$3.20	**Commemorative pane of 10,** overall tagged	9.00	8.00
	a. 32¢ Flag raised on Iwo Jima	.80	.75
	b. 32¢ Manila freed	.80	.75
	c. 32¢ Okinawa	.80	.75
	d. 32¢ U.S. & Soviets at Elbe	.80	.75
	e. 32¢ Liberated Camps	.80	.75
	f. 32¢ Germany surrenders	.80	.75
	g. 32¢ Displaced persons	.80	.75
	h. 32¢ Japan surrenders	.80	.75
	i. 32¢ News of victory	.80	.75
	j. 32¢ Hometowns honor veterans	.80	.75
	FDC, any single		2.50
	FDC, pane of 10		10.00

1995. JAZZ MUSICIANS ISSUE in the American Music Series a se-tenant pane of 20 stamps depicting 10 jazz greats included a second version of the Louis Armstrong commemorative (CM1746) released Sept. 1. *Offset by Sterling Sommer for Ashton-Potter (USA) Ltd., perforated 11.*

CM1748		MNHVF	UseVF
32¢	**Coleman Hawkins,** phosphored paper	.50	.20

CM1749		MNHVF	UseVF
32¢	**Louis Armstrong,** phosphored paper	.50	.20

CM1750		MNHVF	UseVF
32¢	**James P. Johnson,** phosphored paper	.50	.20

CM1751		MNHVF	UseVF
32¢	**"Jelly Roll" Morton,** phosphored paper	.50	.20

CM1752		MNHVF	UseVF
32¢	**Charles Parker,** phosphored paper	.50	.20

CM1753		MNHVF	UseVF
32¢	**Eubie Blake,** phosphored paper	.50	.20

CM1754		MNHVF	UseVF
32¢	**Charlie Mingus,** phosphored paper	.50	.20

CM1755		MNHVF	UseVF
32¢	**Thelonious Monk,** phosphored paper	.50	.20

CM1756		MNHVF	UseVF
32¢	**John Coltrane,** phosphored paper	.50	.20

CM1757		MNHVF	UseVF
32¢	**Erroll Garner,** phosphored paper	.50	.20
	Plate block of 10	8.50	

CM1747 *1945: Victory at Last*

CM1748 *Coleman Hawkins*

CM1749 *Louis Armstrong*

CM1750 *James P. Johnson*

CM1751 *"Jelly Roll" Morton*

CM1752 *Charlie Parker*

CM1753 *Eubie Blake*

CM1754 *Charles Mingus*

CM1755 *Thelonious Monk*

CM1756 *John Coltrane*

CM1757 *Erroll Garner*

		MNHVF	UseVF
FDC *(Sept. 16, 1995),* any single			2.00
y. Se-tenant vertical block of 10 (CM1748-57)		9.50	
y1. Pane of 20		25.00	
vy. Pane of 20, dark blue omitted		—	
FDC, block of 10			10.00

1995. GARDEN FLOWERS ISSUE the third in a Garden Flowers Series of colorful and popular se-tenant five-stamp booklets, depicted late summer and early autumn blooms. *Offset and intaglio by Bureau of Engraving and Printing, perforated 11 vertically on one or two sides.*

CM1758 *Aster;* CM1759 *Chrysanthemum;* CM1760 *Dahlia;* CM1761 *Hydrangea;* CM1762 *Rudbeckia* B256

CM1758		MNHVF	UseVF
32¢	**Aster,** overall tagged	.50	.20
CM1759		MNHVF	UseVF
32¢	**Chrysanthemum,** overall tagged	.50	.20
CM1760		MNHVF	UseVF
32¢	**Dahlia,** overall tagged	.50	.20
CM1761		MNHVF	UseVF
32¢	**Hydrangea,** overall tagged	.50	.20
CM1762		MNHVF	UseVF
32¢	**Rudbeckia,** overall tagged	.50	.20
	FDC *(Sept. 19, 1995),* any single		2.00
	n. Booklet pane of 5 (CM1758-62)	4.00	
	FDC, booklet pane		5.50
	nv. Pane of 5, imperforate	—	

1995. REPUBLIC OF PALAU ISSUE celebrated the first anniversary of independence for this former U.S. trust territory of the western Pacific Ocean, which released a joint issue almost identical in design (Palau No. 815) on Oct. 1. This stamp also is complementary in design to those of earlier U.S. issues honoring each of the other three territories previously administered by the United States: Marshall

Islands (CM1394); Micronesia (CM1395); and the Northern Mariana Islands (CM1607). *Offset by Sterling Sommer for Ashton-Potter (USA) Ltd., perforated 11.*

CM1763 *Republic of Palau*

CM1763		MNHVF	UseVF
32¢	**multicolored** phosphored paper	.50	.20
	Plate block of 4	3.50	
	FDC *(Sept. 29, 1995)*		1.90

1995. COMIC STRIP CLASSICS ISSUE was the third USPS Classic Collection Series of 20 stamps on a single theme in a se-tenant pane with a header across the top and explanatory text on the back of each stamp. This issue, on the subject of influential U.S. comic strips, was issued to mark the 100th anniversary of *The Yellow Kid,* which appeared in the *New York World* in May 1895 and is recognized as one of the first modern comic strip characters. *Gravure by J.W. Fergusson & Sons for Stamp Venturers, perforated 10. Multicolored, block tagged. (Oct. 1, 1995)*

CM1764 *The Yellow Kid;* CM1765 *Katzenjammer Kids;* CM1766 *Little Nemo in Slumberland;* CM1767 *Bringing Up Father;* CM1768 *Krazy Kat;* CM1769 *Rube Goldberg's Inventions;* CM1770 *Toonerville Folks;* CM1771 *Gasoline Alley;* CM1772 *Barney Google;* CM1773 *Little Orphan Annie;* CM1774 *Popeye;* CM1775 *Blondie;* CM1776 *Dick Tracy;* CM1777 *Alley Oop;* CM1778 *Nancy;* CM1779 *Flash Gordon;* CM1780 *Li'l Abner;* CM1781 *Terry and the Pirates;* CM1782 *Prince Valiant;* CM1783 *Brenda Starr, Reporter*

CM1764		MNHVF	UseVF
32¢	**The Yellow Kid**	.75	.50
CM1765		MNHVF	UseVF
32¢	**Katzenjammer Kids**	.75	.50
CM1766		MNHVF	UseVF
32¢	**Little Nemo in Slumberland**	.75	.50
CM1767		MNHVF	UseVF
32¢	**Bringing Up Father**	.75	.50

CM1768		MNHVF	UseVF
32¢	Krazy Kat	.75	.50
CM1769		MNHVF	UseVF
32¢	Rube Goldberg's Inventions	.75	.50
CM1770		MNHVF	UseVF
32¢	Toonerville Folks	.75	.50
CM1771		MNHVF	UseVF
32¢	Gasoline Alley	.75	.50
CM1772		MNHVF	UseVF
32¢	Barney Google	.75	.50
CM1773		MNHVF	UseVF
32¢	Little Orphan Annie	.75	.50
CM1774		MNHVF	UseVF
32¢	Popeye	.75	.50
CM1775		MNHVF	UseVF
32¢	Blondie	.75	.50
CM1776		MNHVF	UseVF
32¢	Dick Tracy	.75	.50
CM1777		MNHVF	UseVF
32¢	Alley Oop	.75	.50
CM1778		MNHVF	UseVF
32¢	Nancy	.75	.50
CM1779		MNHVF	UseVF
32¢	Flash Gordon	.75	.50
CM1780		MNHVF	UseVF
32¢	Li'l Abner	.75	.50
CM1781		MNHVF	UseVF
32¢	Terry & the Pirates	.75	.50
CM1782		MNHVF	UseVF
32¢	Prince Valiant	.75	.50
CM1783		MNHVF	UseVF
32¢	Brenda Starr	.75	.50
	FDC (Oct. 1, 1995), any single	—	2.50
	y. Pane of 20 (CM1764-83)	15.00	14.00
	FDC, pane of 20		25.00
	vy. Pane of 20, imperforate	3,000.00	
	v1y. Pane with CM1764-71 imperforate, CM1772-75 part perforated	—	
	Six pane press sheet	125.00	
	Set of 4 pairs with horizontal gutters	13.00	
	Block of 8 with horizontal gutter	14.25	
	Set of 5 pairs with vertical gutters	16.25	
	Block of 10 with vertical gutter	18.00	
	Cross-gutter block of 20	30.00	

1995. U.S. NAVAL ACADEMY ISSUE marked the 150th anniversary of the Annapolis, Md., institution with a stamp showing the racing sloop *Swift* crewed by academy midshipmen. *Offset by Sterling Sommer for Ashton-Potter (USA) Ltd., perforated 11.*

 CM1784 *U.S. Naval Academy sesquicentennial*

CM1784		MNHVF	UseVF
32¢	multicolored phosphored paper	.50	.20
	Plate block of 4	3.50	
	FDC (Oct. 10, 1995)		1.90

1995. TENNESSEE WILLIAMS ISSUE 13th in the Literary Arts Series memorialized the Mississippi-born playwright and author. Williams (1911-1983), among the most influential U.S. dramatists of the 20th century, wrote such powerful works as *The Glass Menagerie*, *Suddenly Last Summer* and *A Streetcar Named Desire*. *Offset by Sterling Sommer for Ashton-Potter (USA) Ltd., perforated 11.*

 CM1785 *Tennessee Williams*

CM1785		MNHVF	UseVF
32¢	multicolored phosphored paper	.50	.20
	Plate block of 4	3.50	
	FDC (Oct. 13, 1995)		1.90

1995. JAMES K. POLK ISSUE with its frame design adapted from the 1932 1/2¢ Washington Bicentennial stamp (CM98), commemorated the 200th birthday of the 11th president of the United States. *Intaglio by Banknote Corporation of America, perforated 11 1/4x11.*

 CM1786 *James K. Polk*

CM1786		MNHVF	UseVF
32¢	reddish brown phosphored paper	.50	.20
	Plate block of 4	3.50	
	FDC (Nov. 2, 1995)		1.90

1995. ANTIQUE AUTOMOBILES ISSUE depicted in a se-tenant pane of 25 stamps five of the earliest types of automobiles made in the United States at the turn of the century. *Gravure by J.W. Fergusson & Sons for Stamp Venturers, perforated 10x11.*

CM1787 *Duryea*
CM1788 *Haynes*
CM1789 *Columbia*
CM1790 *Winton*
CM1791 *White*

CM1787		MNHVF	UseVF
32¢	Duryea, phosphored paper	.75	.50
CM1788		MNHVF	UseVF
32¢	Haynes, phosphored paper	.75	.50
CM1789		MNHVF	UseVF
32¢	Columbia, phosphored paper	.75	.50
CM1790		MNHVF	UseVF
32¢	Winton, phosphored paper	.75	.50
CM1791		MNHVF	UseVF
32¢	White, phosphored paper	.75	.50
	Plate block of 10	9.00	
	y. Se-tenant strip of 5 (CM1787-91)	4.00	
	FDC (Nov. 3, 1995), any single		1.70
	FDC, strip of 5		3.75

1996. UTAH CENTENNIAL ISSUE marked the 100th anniversary of Utah statehood with a colorful rendering of a natural rock formation from the state's Arches National Park. Utah was the 45th state in the union. *Offset by Sterling Sommer for Ashton-Potter (USA) Ltd., perforated 11.*

CM1792, B263 *Utah state centennial*

CM1792		MNHVF	UseVF
32¢	multicolored tagged *(120,000,000)*	.50	.20
	Plate block of 4	3.50	
	FDC *(Jan. 4, 1996)*		1.90

1996. GARDEN FLOWERS ISSUE was the fourth in a Garden Flower Series of colorful five-stamp pane booklets, this one depicting blooms that appear at various locations in the United States during the winter months. *Offset and intaglio by Bureau of Engraving and Printing, perforated 11 vertically on one or two sides.*

CM1793 *Crocus;* CM1794 *Winter Aconite;* CM1795 *Pansy;* CM1796 *Snowdrop;* CM1797 *Anemone*

CM1793		MNHVF	UseVF
32¢	Crocus, phosphored paper	.50	.20
	(160,000,000)		

CM1794		MNHVF	UseVF
32¢	Winter Aconite, phosphored paper	.50	.20

CM1795		MNHVF	UseVF
32¢	Pansy, phosphored paper	.50	.20

CM1796		MNHVF	UseVF
32¢	Snowdrop, phosphored paper	.50	.20

CM1797		MNHVF	UseVF
32¢	Anemone, phosphored paper	.50	.20
	FDC *(Jan. 19, 1996)*, any single		2.00
	n. Booklet pane of 5 (CM1793-97)	3.50	
	FDC, booklet pane		5.50
	nv. Pane of 5, imperforate	—	

1996. LOVE CHERUB ISSUE in the Love Series is slightly reformatted self-adhesive version of the 32¢ Cherub design (CM1703-04) in booklet form with "32" and "USA" side-by-side. *Offset and intaglio by Banknote Corporation of America, serpentine die cut 11 1/4x11 3/4.*

CM1798, B265, B266 *Love*

CM1798		MNHVF	UseVF
32¢	multicolored tagged *(2,550,000,000)*	.50	.20
	FDC *(Jan. 20, 1996)*		1.90
	n. Pane of 20 plus label (convertible booklet)	16.50	
	FDC, pane of 20		15.50

n1. Pane of 15 plus label, various layouts   10.00
v. red omitted   —

1996. ERNEST E. JUST ISSUE in the Black Heritage Series honored marine biologist, scientist, and professor Ernest Everett Just (1883-1941) whose research on abnormal cell development contributed to understanding leukemia, sickle-cell anemia, and cancer. *Offset by Banknote Corporation of America, perforated 11.*

CM1799 *Ernest E. Just*

CM1799		MNHVF	UseVF
32¢	black & gray tagged *(92,100,000)*	.50	.20
	Plate block of 4	3.50	
	FDC *(Feb. 1, 1996)*		2.75

1996. SMITHSONIAN INSTITUTION SESQUICENTENNIAL ISSUE marked the 150th anniversary of the national museum, begun in 1829 with a $508,318 bequest from a British chemist named Smithson, "to found at Washington...an establishment for the increase & diffusion of knowledge among men." (See also CM285 and CM959.) *Offset by Sterling Sommer for Ashton-Potter (USA) Ltd., perforated 11.*

CM1800 *Smithsonian Institution sesquicentennial*

CM1800		MNHVF	UseVF
32¢	multicolored tagged *(115,600,000)*	.50	.20
	Plate block of 4	3.50	
	FDC *(Feb. 7, 1996)*		2.00

1996. YEAR OF THE RAT ISSUE in the Lunar New Year Series for the Year of the Rat was the fourth in the on-going series celebrating the lunar holiday. *Gravure by J.W. Fergusson & Sons for Stamp Venturers, perforated 11.*

CM1801 *Year of the Rat*

CM1801		MNHVF	UseVF
32¢	multicolored tagged *(93,150,000)*	.50	.20
	Plate block of 4	3.50	
	FDC *(Feb. 8, 1996)*		2.00
	v. Single, imperforate	—	
	v1. Pair, imperforate	—	
	v2. Plate block, imperforate	—	

1996. PIONEERS OF COMMUNICATIONS ISSUE saluted a quartet of 19th-century innovators in photographic and print technology. Eadweard Muybridge (1830-1904) pioneered the conversion of photographs to moving images. Ottmar Mergenthaler (1854-99) invented the Linotype, which vastly reduced the cost of printing newspapers and boosted circulation. Chief among the many inventions of Frederic E. Ives (1856-1937) was the half-tone printing process, which enabled newspapers to reproduce photographs. William Kennedy Laurie Dickson (1860-1935), an Edison employee, devised the Kinetoscope, in which precise synchronization gives motion pictures the illusion of movement. *Offset by Ashton-Potter (USA) Ltd., perforated 11.*

CM1802 *Eadweard Muybridge;* CM1803 *Ottmar Mergenthaler;*
CM1804 *Frederic E. Ives;* CM1805 *William Dickson*

CM1802		MNHVF	UseVF
32¢	**Eadweard Muybridge,** phosphored paper	.50	.20
	(23,292,500)		

CM1803		MNHVF	UseVF
32¢	**Ottmar Mergenthaler,** phosphored paper	.50	.20

CM1804		MNHVF	UseVF
32¢	**Frederic E. Ives,** phosphored paper	.50	.20

CM1805		MNHVF	UseVF
32¢	**William Dickson,** phosphored paper	.50	.20
	Plate block of 4	3.50	
	y. Se-tenant block or strip of 4	3.00	2.50
	(CM1802-05)		
	FDC *(Feb. 22, 1996)*		1.75
	FDC, block of 4		3.50

1996. FULBRIGHT SCHOLARSHIPS ISSUE marked the 50th anniversary of the annual awards, named for Arkansas Senator and long-time Foreign Relations Committee Chairman J. William Fulbright (1905-1995), sponsor of the 1946 act that created the program. To date, about a quarter million Fulbright scholars either have traveled from the United States to study abroad or have come from abroad to study in the United States. *Offset and intaglio by Bureau of Engraving and Printing, perforated 11.*

CM1806, B267 *Fulbright scholarships*

CM1806		MNHVF	UseVF
32¢	**multicolored** tagged *(111,000,000)*	.50	.20
	Plate block of 4	3.50	
	FDC *(Feb. 28, 1996)*		2.00

1996. MARATHON ISSUE saluted the 100th running of the annual 26.2-mile Boston Marathon. *Offset by Banknote Corporation of America, perforated 11.*

CM1807 *Marathon*

CM1807		MNHVF	UseVF
32¢	**multicolored** tagged *(209,450,000)*	.50	.20
	Plate block of 4	3.50	
	FDC *(April 11, 1996)*		3.00

1996. ATLANTA 1996 CENTENNIAL OLYMPIC GAMES ISSUE was the fourth USPS Classic Collections Series of 20 stamps on a single theme in a se-tenant pane with a header across the top and descriptive text on the back of each stamp. This issue celebrated the 100th anniversary of the first modern Olympiad. *Gravure by J.W. Fergusson & Sons for Stamp Venturers, perforated 10 1/4x10. Multicolored, block tagged. (May 2, 1996)*

CM1808 *Javelin;* CM1809 *Whitewater canoeing;* CM1810 *Women's running;* CM1811 *Women's platform diving;* CM1812 *Men's cycling;* CM1813 *Freestyle wrestling;* CM1814 *Women's gymnastics;* CM1815 *Women's sailboarding;* CM1816 *Men's shot put;* CM1817 *Women's soccer;* CM1818 *Beach volleyball;* CM1819 *Men's rowing;* CM1820 *Men's sprinting event;* CM1821 *Women's swimming;* CM1822 *Women's softball;* CM1823 *Men's hurdles;* CM1824 *Men's swimming (backstroke);* CM1825 *Men's gymnastics (pommel horse);* CM1826 *Equestrian events;* CM1827 *Men's basketball*

CM1808		MNHVF	UseVF
32¢	**Javelin**	.75	.50

CM1809		MNHVF	UseVF
32¢	**Whitewater canoeing**	.75	.50

CM1810		MNHVF	UseVF
32¢	**Women's running**	.75	.50

CM1811		MNHVF	UseVF
32¢	**Women's platform diving**	.75	.50

CM1812		MNHVF	UseVF
32¢	**Men's cycling**	.75	.50

CM1813		MNHVF	UseVF
32¢	**Freestyle wrestling**	.75	.50

CM1814		MNHVF	UseVF
32¢	**Women's gymnastics**	.75	.50

CM1815		MNHVF	UseVF
32¢	**Women's sailboarding**	.75	.50

CM1816		MNHVF	UseVF
32¢	**Men's shot put**	.75	.50

CM1817		MNHVF	UseVF
32¢	**Women's soccer**	.75	.50

CM1818
32¢   Beach volleyball   MNHVF .75   UseVF .50

CM1819
32¢   Men's rowing   MNHVF .75   UseVF .50

CM1820
32¢   Men's sprinting events   MNHVF .75   UseVF .50

CM1821
32¢   Women's swimming   MNHVF .75   UseVF .50

CM1822
32¢   Women's softball   MNHVF .75   UseVF .50

CM1823
32¢   Men's hurdles   MNHVF .75   UseVF .50

CM1824
32¢   Men's swimming (backstroke)   MNHVF .75   UseVF .50

CM1825
32¢   Men's gymnastics (pommel horse)   MNHVF .75   UseVF .50

CM1826
32¢   Equestrian events   MNHVF .75   UseVF .50

CM1827
32¢   Men's basketball   MNHVF .75   UseVF .50

FDC *(May 2, 1996),* any single	2.00
y. Pane of 20 (CM1808-27)	14.00
FDC, pane of 20	20.00
vy. Pane of 20, imperforate	—
v1y. Partially perforated pane of 20	—
Six pane press sheet	150.00
Set of 5 pairs with horizontal gutters	17.50
Block of 10 with horizontal gutter	19.50
Set of 4 pairs with vertical gutters	14.00
Block of 8 with vertical gutter	15.50
Cross-gutter block of 20	32.50

1996. GEORGIA O'KEEFFE ISSUE commemorated the artist whose distinctive, vibrant presentation of images from nature in abstract, creative settings marked her as a true American original. One of 200 early flower paintings created by O'Keeffe (1887-1986) was reproduced in a 15-stamp commemorative pane with selvage picturing the painter and a quotation by her. *Gravure by J.W. Fergusson & Sons for Stamp Venturers, perforated 11 1/2.*

CM1828, B269 *Georgia O'Keeffe's Red Poppy, 1927*

CM1828
32¢   **multicolored** tagged *(156,300,000)*   MNHVF .50   UseVF .20

Plate block of 4	3.50
y. Pane of 15	16.00
FDC *(May 23, 1996)*	2.00
v. Pair, imperforate	200.00

1996. TENNESSEE BICENTENNIAL ISSUE marked the 200th anniversary of Tennessee's entering the union as the 16th state. It was the first conventional commemorative issued simultaneously both in lick-and-stick panes and self-adhesive booklets sold only in Tennessee. *Gravure by J.W. Fergusson & Sons for Stamp Venturers, perforated 11.*

CM1829-30, B270 *Tennessee statehood*

CM1829
32¢   **multicolored** tagged *(100,000,000)*   MNHVF .50   UseVF .20

Plate block of 4	3.25
FDC *(May 31, 1996)*	2.00

1996. TENNESSEE BICENTENNIAL BOOKLET ISSUE *Serpentine die cut 10 x 10 3/4.*

CM1830
32¢   **multicolored** tagged *(60,120,000)*   MNHVF .75   UseVF .20

FDC *(May 31, 1996)*	2.00
n. Pane of 20 (convertible booklet)	16.00
v. Horizontal pair, imperforate (no die cutting) between	—

1996. AMERICAN INDIAN DANCES ISSUE pictured an important component of Native American culture and ritual in a 20-stamp commemorative pane. *Gravure by Ashton-Potter (USA) Ltd., perforated 11.*

CM1831 *Fancy Dance;* CM1832 *Butterfly Dance;* CM1833 *Traditional Dance;* CM1834 *Raven Dance;* CM1835 *Hoop Dance* B271

CM1831
32¢   **Fancy Dance,** tagged *(27,850,000)*   MNHVF .75   UseVF .50

CM1832
32¢   **Butterfly Dance,** tagged   MNHVF .75   UseVF .50

CM1833
32¢   **Traditional Dance,** tagged   MNHVF .75   UseVF .50

CM1834
32¢   **Raven Dance,** tagged   MNHVF .75   UseVF .50

CM1835
32¢   **Hoop Dance,** tagged   MNHVF .75   UseVF .50

Plate block of 10	8.00
y. Se-tenant strip of 5 (CM1831-53)	3.50
FDC *(June 7, 1996),* any single	2.00
y1. Pane of 20	16.00
FDC, strip of 5	4.00

1996. PREHISTORIC ANIMALS ISSUE featured dramatic portraits of four important North American animals of the Cenozoic Era (or Age of Mammals), comprising the last 65 million years. *Offset by Ashton-Potter (USA) Ltd., perforated 11.*

CM1836 *Eohippus*

CM1837 *Woolly Mammoth*

CM1838 *Mastodon*

CM1839 *Saber-tooth Cat*

CM1836
32¢   **Eohippus,** tagged *(22,218,000)*   MNHVF .75   UseVF .50

CM1837
32¢   **Woolly Mammoth,** tagged   MNHVF .75   UseVF .50

CM1838
32¢   **Mastodon,** tagged   MNHVF .75   UseVF .50

CM1839
32¢   **Saber-tooth Cat,** tagged   MNHVF .75   UseVF .50

Plate block of 4	3.50
y. Se-tenant block or strip of 4 (CM1836-39)	3.00
FDC *(June 8, 1996),* any single	2.00
FDC, block or strip of 4	4.00

1996. BREAST CANCER AWARENESS ISSUE took note of a serious health risk to American women to raise awareness and encourage early detection. Special postmarks, clinics, and screenings in conjunction with this stamp across the nation increased public attention, and helped spark Congress to request a breast cancer semipostal stamp (CMSP1) in 1998. *Offset by Ashton-Potter (USA) Ltd., perforated 11.*

CM1840 *Breast Cancer Awareness*

CM1840		MNHVF	UseVF
32¢	**multicolored** tagged *(95,600,000)*	.50	.20
	Plate block of 4	3.25	
	FDC *(June 15, 1996)*		2.00

1996. JAMES DEAN ISSUE the second in the Legends of Hollywood Series again consisted of a 20-stamp commemorative pane with star-shaped corner perforations and a large area of selvage displaying an enlargement of the actor. Dean (1931-55) had enormous impact in three films — *East of Eden, Rebel Without a Cause* and *Giant* — before his death in a car crash at the age of 24. *Gravure by J.W. Fergusson & Sons for Stamp Venturers, perforated 11.*

CM1841, B272 *James Dean*

CM1841		MNHVF	UseVF
32¢	**multicolored** tagged *(300,000,000)*	.50	.20
	Plate block of 4	3.25	
	FDC *(June 24, 1996)*		3.00
y.	Pane of 20	15.00	
	Six pane press sheet		
	Pair with horizontal gutter	2.00	
	Pair with vertical gutter	3.25	
	Block of 8 with vertical gutter	14.00	
	Cross-gutter block of 8	20.00	
v.	Pair, imperforate	495.00	
vy.	Pane, imperforate	4,700.00	
v1y.	Partially perforate pane	—	

1996. FOLK HEROES ISSUE featured bold portraits of larger-than-life characters made famous in popular American fiction: Mighty Casey, whose turn at the bat in Ernest L. Thayer's 1888 poem tragically came to naught; legendary lumberjack Paul Bunyan, who transformed America together with Babe, his giant blue ox; John Henry, the "steel drivin' man" who beat a steam drill in carving out a West Virginia railway tunnel, but perished in the attempt; and the cyclone-taming Texas cowboy Pecos Bill, who wears a rattlesnake for a scarf on the stamp. *Offset by Ashton-Potter (USA) Ltd., perforated 11.*

CM1842		MNHVF	UseVF
32¢	**Mighty Casey,** tagged *(23,681,250)*	.50	.20
CM1843		MNHVF	UseVF
32¢	**Paul Bunyan,** tagged	.50	.20
CM1844		MNHVF	UseVF
32¢	**John Henry,** tagged	.50	.20
CM1845		MNHVF	UseVF
32¢	**Pecos Bill,** tagged	.50	.20
	Plate block of 4	3.50	

CM1842 *Mighty Casey*

CM1843 *Paul Bunyan*

CM1844 *John Henry*

CM1845 *Pecos Bill* B273

y.	Se-tenant block or strip of 4 (CM1842-45)	3.00	
	FDC *(July 11, 1996)*, any single		2.00
	FDC, block or strip of 4		4.00

1996. OLYMPIC GAMES CENTENNIAL ISSUE was another single-design 20-stamp commemorative pane to mark the 100th anniversary of the first modern Olympiad in 1896 in Athens, Greece. Left margin selvage showed an enlargement of *Discobolus*, after the original bronze created by the Greek sculptor Myron in the 5th century B.C. *Offset and intaglio by Ashton-Potter (USA) Ltd., perforated 11.*

CM1846, B274 *Discus Thrower, centennial Olympics*

CM1846		MNHVF	UseVF
32¢	**brown** tagged *(133,613,000)*	.50	.20
	Plate block of 4	3.00	
	FDC *(July 19, 1996)*		1.00
y.	Pane of 20	14.00	

1996. IOWA SESQUICENTENNIAL ISSUE marked the 150th anniversary of Iowa's entering the union as the 29th state. The conventional commemorative was available throughout the country, whereas the self-adhesive booklet version of the stamp was sold only in Iowa and at philatelic centers out of state. *Offset by Ashton-Potter (USA) Ltd., perforated 11.*

CM1847, CM1848, B275 *Iowa sesquicentennial*

CM1847		MNHVF	UseVF
32¢	**multicolored** tagged *(103,400,000)*	.50	.20
	Plate block of 4	3.00	
	FDC *(Aug. 1, 1996)*		2.00

1996. IOWA SESQUICENTENNIAL SELF ADHESIVE ISSUE

Serpentine die cut 11 1/2.

CM1848

		MNHVF	UseVF
32¢	**multicolored** tagged *(60,000,000)*	.75	.30
	FDC *(Aug. 1, 1996)*		2.00
	n. Pane of 20 (convertible booklet)	16.00	

1996. RURAL FREE DELIVERY CENTENNIAL ISSUE

saluted a century of the service that brought mail for the first time directly to the homes of America's farmers and other rural residents. *Offset and intaglio by Bureau of Engraving and Printing, perforated 11.*

CM1849, B277 *Rural Free Delivery*

CM1849

		MNHVF	UseVF
32¢	**multicolored** tagged *(134,000,000)*	.50	.20
	Plate block of 4	3.00	
	FDC *(Aug. 7, 1996)*		2.00

1996. RIVERBOATS ISSUE

is a se-tenant presentation of five self-adhesive stamps saluting historic 19th-century steamboats that carried passengers and important cargo on the inland waterways of America. *Gravure by Avery Dennison Security Printing Division, serpentine die cut 11. (CM1854y has the serpentine die cut through the backing paper and, in addition, is also die cut, in the shape of a sine wave, behind each column of stamps. CM1854vy has three 2mm gaps in the serpentine die cutting between each vertical pair of stamps. In addition, the backing paper is not die cut behind the stamps. This was done to facilitate the use of a strip of 5 on USPS created products.)*

CM1850 Robt. E. Lee

CM1851 Sylvan Dell

CM1852 Far West

CM1853 Rebecca Everingham

CM1854 Bailey Gatzert B278

CM1850

		MNHVF	UseVF
32¢	**Robt. E. Lee,** tagged *(32,000,000)*	.75	.50

CM1851

		MNHVF	UseVF
32¢	**Sylvan Dell,** tagged	.75	.50

CM1852

		MNHVF	UseVF
32¢	**Far West,** tagged	.75	.50

CM1853

		MNHVF	UseVF
32¢	**Rebecca Everingham,** tagged	.75	.50

CM1854

		MNHVF	UseVF
32¢	**Bailey Gatzert,** tagged	.75	.50
	Plate block of 10	8.00	
	y. Se-tenant vertical strip of 5 (CM1850-54)	3.50	
	vy. Strip of 5 with special die cutting	75.00	
	Pane of 20 with special die cuts	275.00	
	FDC *(Aug. 22, 1996),* any single		2.00
	FDC, strip of 5		5.50

1996. BIG BAND LEADERS ISSUE

in the American Music Series honored outstanding orchestra leaders of the Big Band era who popularized the swing music that had its heyday in the 1930s and '40s. Count Basie (1904-84), a brilliant composer whose bands for almost 50 years featured many of the nation's finest jazz soloists, is best remembered for tunes including "One O'Clock Jump," "Swingin' the Blues," and "Jumpin' at the Woodside." The Dorsey Brothers, clarinetist Jimmy (1904-57) and trombonist Tommy (1905-56), headed dance bands separately and together, notable for melodies such as "Tangerine" and "I'm Sentimental Over You." Glenn Miller (1904-44), a gifted trombonist and arranger, presided over one of the most successful Swing era orchestras, the distinctive sound of which is recognizable in classics such as "In the Mood," "Kalamazoo," and "Sunrise Serenade." Benny Goodman (1909-86), known as the "King of Swing," was a clarinet prodigy and a perfectionist as band leader, with "King Porter Stomp," "Don't Be That Way," and "Sing, Sing, Sing" among his hits. *Offset by Ashton-Potter (USA) Ltd., perforated 11.*

CM1855 *Count Basie;* CM1856 *Tommy & Jimmy Dorsey;* CM1857 *Glenn Miller;* CM1858 *Benny Goodman*

CM1855

		MNHVF	UseVF
32¢	**Count Basie,** tagged *(23,025,000)*	.50	.20

CM1856

		MNHVF	UseVF
32¢	**Tommy & Jimmy Dorsey,** tagged	.50	.20

CM1857

		MNHVF	UseVF
32¢	**Glenn Miller,** tagged	.50	.20

CM1858

		MNHVF	UseVF
32¢	**Benny Goodman,** tagged	.50	.20
	Plate block of 4	3.50	
	y. Se-tenant block or strip of 4 (CM1855-58)	3.00	
	FDC *(Sept. 11, 1996),* any single		3.00
	y1. Pane of 20	14.00	
	FDC, block or strip of 4		6.00

1996. SONGWRITERS ISSUE

in the American Music Series honored four of the finest songwriters of the 20th century. Harold Arlen (1905-86) is best known for his scores for two Judy Garland films, *The Wizard of Oz* (co-written with Yip Harburg) and *A Star is Born* (co-written with Ira Gershwin), and tunes written for Harlem's renowned Cotton Club including "Stormy Weather." Songwriter, singer, and Capitol Records founder Johnny Mercer (1909-76) penned the lyrics to more than 1,000 songs, from "I'm an Old Cowhand" to "Moon River." The nation's finest female songwriter, Dorothy Fields' (1905-74) credits include "Sunny Side of the Street," "The Way You Look Tonight," and "A Fine Romance." Hoagy Carmichael (1899-1981) may be most closely associated with "Stardust" but authored many other great songs as well, including "Heart and Soul" and "Georgia on My Mind." *Offset by Ashton-Potter (USA) Ltd., perforated 11.*

CM1859 *Harold Arlen;* CM1860 *Johnny Mercer;* CM1861 *Dorothy Fields;* CM1862 *Hoagy Carmichael*

	MNHVF	UseVF
CM1859	MNHVF	UseVF
32¢ **Harold Arlen,** tagged *(23,025,000)*	.50	.20
CM1860	MNHVF	UseVF
32¢ **Johnny Mercer,** tagged	.50	.20
CM1861	MNHVF	UseVF
32¢ **Dorothy Fields,** tagged	.50	.20
CM1862	MNHVF	UseVF
32¢ **Hoagy Carmichael,** tagged	.50	.20
Plate block of 4	3.50	
y. Se-tenant block or strip of 4 (CM1859-62)	3.00	
FDC *(Sept. 11, 1996),* any single		2.00
y1. Pane of 20	14.00	
FDC, block or strip of 4		5.00

1996. F. SCOTT FITZGERALD ISSUE 14th in the Literary Arts Series celebrated the 100th birthday of the novelist (1896-1940) who immortalized the Jazz Age of the 1920s in such works as *The Beautiful and the Damned, The Great Gatsby,* and *Tender is the Night.* The stamp prepays the 23¢ fee for each additional ounce over the basic 32¢ first-class letter rate. *Gravure by Bureau of Engraving and Printing, perforated 11.*

CM1863 *F. Scott Fitzgerald*

	MNHVF	UseVF
CM1863	MNHVF	UseVF
23¢ **multicolored** tagged *(300,000,000)*	.50	.20
Plate block of 4	2.75	
FDC *(Sept. 27, 1996)*		1.00

1996. ENDANGERED SPECIES ISSUE was a 15-stamp se-tenant commemorative pane with a banner and marginal text, each stamp featuring an indigenous American animal currently threatened with extinction. Although not a joint issue technically speaking, a pane of 24 stamps depicting native endangered species was issued simultaneously by Mexico. *Offset (14,910,000 panes) by Sterling Sommer for Ashton-Potter (USA) Ltd., perforated 11. Multicolored, block tagged.*

	MNHVF	UseVF
CM1864	MNHVF	UseVF
32¢ **Black-footed ferret**	.50	.20

Endangered Species

CM1864 *Black-footed ferret;* CM1865 *Thick-billed parrot;* CM1866 *Hawaiian Monk seal;* CM1867 *American crocodile;* CM1868 *Ocelo;* CM1869 *Schaus swallowtail butterfly;* CM1870 *Wyoming toad;* CM1871 *Brown pelican;* CM1872 *California condor;* CM1873 *Gila trout;* CM1874 *San Francisco garter snake;* CM1875 *Woodland caribou;* CM1876 *Florida panther,* CM1877 *Piping plover;* CM1878 *Florida manatee*

	MNHVF	UseVF
CM1865	MNHVF	UseVF
32¢ **Thick-billed parrot**	.50	.20
CM1866	MNHVF	UseVF
32¢ **Hawaiian Monk seal**	.50	.20
CM1867	MNHVF	UseVF
32¢ **American crocodile**	.50	.20
CM1868	MNHVF	UseVF
32¢ **Ocelot**	.50	.20
CM1869	MNHVF	UseVF
32¢ **Schaus swallowtail butterfly**	.50	.20
CM1870	MNHVF	UseVF
32¢ **Wyoming toad**	.50	.20
CM1871	MNHVF	UseVF
32¢ **Brown pelican**	.50	.20
CM1872	MNHVF	UseVF
32¢ **California condor**	.50	.20
CM1873	MNHVF	UseVF
32¢ **Gila trout**	.50	.20
CM1874	MNHVF	UseVF
32¢ **San Francisco garter snake**	.50	.20
CM1875	MNHVF	UseVF
32¢ **Woodland caribou**	.50	.20
CM1876	MNHVF	UseVF
32¢ **Florida panther**	.50	.20
CM1877	MNHVF	UseVF
32¢ **Piping plover**	.50	.20
CM1878	MNHVF	UseVF
32¢ **Florida manatee**	.50	.20
FDC *(Oct. 2, 1996),* any single		2.00
y. Se-tenant pane of 15 (CM1864-78)	11.00	
FDC, pane of 15		14.50

1996. COMPUTER TECHNOLOGY ISSUE marked the 50th anniversary of the Electronic Numerical Integrator and Calculator (ENIAC), regarded widely as the first general-purpose electronic digital computer, forerunner to the millions in use today. *Offset and intaglio, by Ashton-Potter (USA) Ltd., perforated 11.*

CM1879 *Computer Technology*

CM1879

		MNHVF	UseVF
32¢	**multicolored** tagged *(93,612,000)*	.50	.20
	Plate block of 4	3.00	
	FDC *(Oct. 8, 1996)*		1.00

Holiday Celebration Series

1996. HANUKKAH ISSUE first in a Holiday Celebration Series, honored the Jewish Festival of Lights and shared its design with a joint issue from Israel (Israel No. 1360). The self-adhesive stamp shows a stylized menorah and the colorful candles with which Jews mark the eight-day observance. Due to its popularity, it was reprinted in 1997 with no major differences. *Gravure by Avery Dennison Security Printing Division, serpentine die cut 11.*

CM1880, B281 *Hanukkah*

CM1880

		MNHVF	UseVF
32¢	**multicolored** tagged *(103,520,000)*	.75	.20
	Plate block of 4	3.00	
	FDC *(Oct. 22, 1996)*		1.00

1996. CYCLING SOUVENIR SHEET was issued to sell at international cycling meets in which the USPS Pro Cycling Team competed, to defray the team's cost. *Gravure by J.W. Fergusson & Sons for Stamp Venturers, perforated 11.*

CM1881 *Cycling souvenir sheet*

CM1881

		MNHVF	UseVF
50¢	**multicolored** tagged *(20,000,000)*	2.50	1.00
	a. 50¢ multicolored & orange	1.50	1.00
	b. 50¢ multicolored & blue green	1.50	1.00
	FDC *(Nov. 1, 1996)*		1.00

1997. YEAR OF THE OX ISSUE for the Year of the Ox in the Lunar New Year Series was the fifth in celebrating the Chinese holiday. *Gravure by J.W. Fergusson & Sons for Stamp Venturers, perforated 11 1/4.*

CM1882 *Year of the Ox*

CM1882

		MNHVF	UseVF
32¢	**multicolored** tagged *(160,000,000)*	.50	.20
	Plate block of 4	3.00	
	FDC *(Jan. 5, 1997)*		1.00

1997. BENJAMIN O. DAVIS ISSUE in the Black Heritage Series saluted with a self-adhesive stamp the nation's first black brigadier general, a soldier who began as a private and rose through the ranks in a 50-year career to become both a force for and a symbol of integration in America's military. *Offset by Banknote Corporation of America, serpentine die cut 11 1/2.*

CM1883 *Benjamin O. Davis Sr.*

CM1883

		MNHVF	UseVF
32¢	**gray, green & black** phosphored paper *(112,000,000)*	.50	.20
	Plate block of 4	3.00	
	FDC *(Jan. 28, 1997)*		1.00

1997. LOVE ISSUE in the Love Series used bilaterally symmetrical profiles of two elegant swans outlining a heart in two self-adhesive booklets paying the 32¢ standard First Class 1-ounce letter rate and the 55¢ rate for 2-ounce letters (useful for wedding invitations containing reply cards and envelopes), respectively. *Offset by Banknote Corporation of America, serpentine die cut 11 3/4x11 1/2 on two, three or four sides.*

CM1884 *32¢ Love swans*

CM1884

		MNHVF	UseVF
32¢	**multicolored** tagged	.50	.20
	FDC *(Feb. 7, 1997)*		1.00
	n. Pane of 20 plus label (convertible booklet)	13.00	
	v. Pair, imperforate (no die cutting)	275.00	
	vn. Pane of 20, imperforate (no die cutting)	—	

1997. LOVE ISSUE Serpentine die cut 11 1/2x11 3/4 on two, three or four sides.

CM1885 *55¢ Love swans*

CM1885

		MNHVF	UseVF
55¢	**multicolored** tagged	1.00	.30
	FDC *(Feb. 7, 1997)*		1.00
	n. Pane of 20 plus label	22.50	

1997. HELPING CHILDREN LEARN ISSUE a self-adhesive stamp called attention to the developmental importance and simple pleasure of reading as an activity for adults to share with children. The issue coincided with the centennial of the PTA, the nation's oldest and largest volunteer association working for children. *Gravure by Avery Dennison Security Printing Division, serpentine die cut 11 1/2x11 3/4.*

CM1886 *Helping Children Learn*

CM1886		MNHVF	UseVF
32¢	**multicolored** tagged	.50	.20
	Plate block of 4	3.00	
	FDC *(Feb. 18, 1997)*		1.00

1997. PACIFIC 97 ISSUE The first triangular stamps in U.S. philatelic history, used two early means of moving the mail — the stagecoach and the clipper ship — to promote the Pacific 97 International Philatelic Exhibition May 29 to June 8 in San Francisco, Calif. *Intaglio by Banknote Corporation of America, perforated 11 1/4.*

CM1887 *Stagecoach*

CM1887		MNHVF	UseVF
32¢	**red** phosphored paper *(65,000,000)*	.50	.20

CM1888 *Clipper ship*

CM1888		MNHVF	UseVF
32¢	**blue** phosphored paper	.50	.20
	Plate block of 4	3.00	
	y. Se-tenant pair (CM1887-88)	1.25	
	FDC *(March 13, 1997),* either single		2.00
	FDC, pair		2.50
	y1. Pane of 16	13.00	
	Six pane press sheet	80.00	
	Pair with horizontal gutter	8.00	
	Pair with vertical gutter	4.00	
	Cross-gutter block of 16	25.00	

1997. THORNTON WILDER ISSUE 15th in the Literary Arts Series celebrated the 100th birthday of the three-time Pulitzer Prize-winning author (1897-1975) of the novel *The Bridge of San Luis Rey* and the plays *Our Town* (symbolically depicted on the stamp) and *The Skin of Our Teeth.* *Offset by Ashton-Potter (USA) Ltd., perforated 11.*

CM1889 *Thornton Wilder*

CM1889		MNHVF	UseVF
32¢	**multicolored** tagged *(97,500,000)*	.50	.20
	Plate block of 4	3.00	
	FDC *(April 17, 1997)*		1.00

1997. RAOUL WALLENBERG ISSUE commemorated the Swedish diplomat who in 1944 risked his own life to save over 20,000 Hungarian Jews from Nazi genocide by issuing them falsified Swedish passes. In 1945, Wallenberg was taken prisoner by the Soviets, who only in 1957 announced that he had died a decade earlier, of a purported heart attack, while in Moscow's Lubyanka Prison. *Offset by Sterling Sommer for Ashton-Potter (USA) Ltd., perforated 11.*

CM1890 *Wallenberg and refugees*

CM1890		MNHVF	UseVF
32¢	**multicolored** tagged *(96,000,000)*	.50	.20
	Plate block of 4	3.00	
	FDC *(April 24, 1997)*		1.00

1997. THE WORLD OF DINOSAURS ISSUE A 15-stamp pane showcased two panoramic dioramas by James Gurney of life in the age of the giant reptiles: a scene in Colorado 150 million years ago in the top panel; and a 75-million-year-old scene from Montana in the bottom panel of the pane. The pane portrays many species never before shown on stamps. *Offset by Sterling Sommer for Ashton-Potter (USA) Ltd., perforated 11.*

CM1891		MNHVF	UseVF
$4.80	**Pane of 15,** tagged *(14,600,000)*	15.00	9.50
	a. 32¢ Ceratosaurus	.75	.50
	b. 32¢ Camptosaurus	.75	.50
	c. 32¢ Camarasaurus	.75	.50
	d. 32¢ Brachiosaurus	.75	.50
	e. 32¢ Goniopholis	.75	.50
	f. 32¢ Stegosaurus	.75	.50
	g. 32¢ Allosaurus	.75	.50
	h. 32¢ Opisthias	.75	.50
	i. 32¢ Edmontonia	.75	.50
	j. 32¢ Einiosaurus	.75	.50
	k. 32¢ Daspletosaurus	.75	.50
	l. 32¢ Palaeosaniwa	.75	.50
	m. 32¢ Corythosaurus	.75	.50
	n. 32¢ Ornithomimus	.75	.50
	o. 32¢ Parasaurolophus	.75	.50
	FDC *(May 1, 1997),* any single		2.00
	FDC, pane of 15		12.50
	v. All colors omitted, untagged	—	
	v1. Perforations inverted	—	
	v2. Perforate CM1891 a-g, imperforate CM1891 h-o	—	
	v3. Imperforate CM1891 a-g, perforated CM1891 h-o	6,875.00	

Warner Bros. Cartoon Characters Series

1997. BUGS BUNNY ISSUE First in the Warner Bros. Cartoon Characters Series, showcased in two types of self-adhesive 10-stamp panes (rouletted vertically through the middle) the wisecracking "Oscar-winning rabbit" with the Brooklyn accent who has been a fixture on American movie and television screens for more than half a century. *Gravure by Avery Dennison Security Printing Division, serpentine die cut 11 does not extend through backing.*

The minimum stamp value in this catalog (20¢) represents the cost to a retail stamp dealer to maintain in inventory and supply to a collector on demand a single copy of even the most common stamp in fault-free condition and a grade of fine-to-very-fine.

THE WORLD OF DINOSAURS

A scene in Colorado, 150 million years ago

A scene in Montana, 75 million years ago

CM1891 *The World of Dinosaurs*

CM1892 *Bugs Bunny*

CM1892
$3.20   Pane of 10, tagged

	MNHVF	UseVF
	7.50	

		MNHVF	UseVF
n. Right half of pane (single die cut CM1892a superimposed on enlarged image in right selvage)	1.00		
n1. Left half of pane (block of 9 CM1892a)	5.00		
a. 32¢ single	.75		.25
FDC (May 22, 1997), single			2.50
FDC, entire right side			5.00
Six pane top press sheet	350.00		
Six pane bottom press sheet with plate number	625.00		
Pair with horizontal gutter	20.00		
Pair with vertical gutter	40.00		
Cross-gutter block of 12	250.00		

Serpentine die cut 11 through stamps and backing.

CM1893

	MNHVF	UseVF
$3.20 Pane of 10, tagged	200.00	
n. Right half of pane (single imperforate CM1893a on enlarged image in right selvage)	150.00	
n1. Left half of pane (block of 9 CM1893a)	5.00	
a. 32¢ single	.75	.25
FDC, entire pane		275.00
FDC, CM1893n		250.00

This issue also was made available in top and bottom half printing sheets of six 10-stamp panes each. A single plate number, trimmed away on individual panes, appears adjacent to the bottom-left pane in the bottom half of the printing sheet only.

Note: A gummed, non-denominated, untagged item similar to CM1893n on the same backing paper as the normal stamps lacks Bugs' "autograph" and single stamp, the latter of which is replaced by "32 USA" as on the issued stamp. Though printed for the USPS, this item was an advertising piece and was not postally valid.

1997. PACIFIC 97 U.S. STAMP SESQUICENTENNIAL ISSUE
marked the 150th anniversary of the first regular-issue U.S. postage stamps (Minkus 1-2, depicted in the selvage of the souvenir sheets) and hailed the opening of the Pacific 1997 International Philatelic Exhibition in San Francisco, Calif. The souvenir sheets were sold only during the 11 days of the show. *Offset and intaglio by Bureau of Engraving and Printing, perforated 10 1/2.*

CM1894 *Benjamin Franklin souvenir sheet*

CM1894		MNHVF	UseVF
$6	Pane of 12, tagged	11.50	9.00
	a. 50¢ single	1.00	.50
	FDC (May 29, 1997), single		4.00
	FDC, pane of 12		24.00

CM1895 *George Washington souvenir sheet*

CM1895		MNHVF	UseVF
$7.20	Pane of 12, tagged	12.50	10.00
	a. 60¢ single	1.25	.75
	FDC (May 30, 1997), single		4.00
	FDC, pane of 12		24.00

1997. MARSHALL PLAN 50TH ANNIVERSARY ISSUE
saluted the post-World War II European Recovery Program unveiled in 1947 by Gen. George C. Marshall (1880-1959). The U.S.-backed, multi-billion-dollar plan to help a devastated Western Europe regain its economic health and halt the expansion of Soviet influence earned Marshall the Nobel Peace Prize. *Offset and intaglio by Stevens Security Press for Ashton-Potter (USA) Ltd., perforated 11.*

CM1896 *The Marshall Plan*

CM1896		MNHVF	UseVF
32¢	multicolored tagged (45,250,000)	.50	.20
	Plate block of 4	3.50	
	FDC (June 4, 1997)		2.00

1997. CLASSIC AMERICAN AIRCRAFT ISSUE
was the fifth USPS issue of 20 se-tenant single-theme stamps in a pane with a header across the top and descriptive text on the back of each stamp. This issue showcased 20 U.S. aircraft of the first half-century of powered flight. *Gravure (8,050,000 panes) by J.W. Fergusson & Sons for Stamp Venturers, perforated 10. Multicolored, block tagged.*

CM1897 *North American P-51 Mustang fighter;* CM1898 *Wright Model B Flyer;* CM1899 *Piper J-3 Cub;* CM1900 *Lockheed Vega;* CM1901 Northrop Alpha; CM1902 *Martin B-10 bomber;* CM1903 Chance Vought Corsair F4U fighter; CM1904 *Boeing B-47 Stratojet bomber;* CM1905 *Gee Bee Super-Sportster;* CM1906 *Beech Model C17L Staggerwing;* CM1907 *Boeing B-17 Flying Fortress bomber;* CM1908 *Stearman PT-13 training aircraft;* CM1909 *Lockheed Constellation;* CM1910 *Lockheed P-38 Lightning fighter;* CM1911 *Boeing P-26 Peashooter fighter;* CM1912 *Ford Tri-Motor;* CM1913 *Douglas DC-3 passenger plane;* CM1914 *Boeing 314 Clipper flying boat;* CM1915 *Curtiss JN-4 Jenny training aircraft;* CM1916 *Grumman F4F Wildcat fighter*

		MNHVF	UseVF
CM1897		MNHVF	UseVF
32¢	North American P-51 Mustang fighter	.75	.50
CM1898		MNHVF	UseVF
32¢	Wright Model B Flyer	.75	.50
CM1899		MNHVF	UseVF
32¢	Piper J-3 Cub	.75	.50
CM1900		MNHVF	UseVF
32¢	Lockheed Vega	.75	.50
CM1901		MNHVF	UseVF

			MNHVF	UseVF
32¢		*Northrop Alpha*	.75	.50
CM1902			MNHVF	UseVF
32¢		**Martin B-10 bomber**	.75	.50
CM1903			MNHVF	UseVF
32¢		**Chance Vought Corsair F4U fighter**	.75	.50
CM1904			MNHVF	UseVF
32¢		**Boeing B-47 Stratojet bomber**	.75	.50
CM1905			MNHVF	UseVF
32¢		**Gee Bee Super-Sportster**	.75	.50
CM1906			MNHVF	UseVF
32¢		**Beech Model C17L Staggerwing**	.75	.50
CM1907			MNHVF	UseVF
32¢		**Boeing B-17 Flying Fortress bomber**	.75	.50
CM1908			MNHVF	UseVF
32¢		**Stearman PT-13 training aircraft**	.75	.50
CM1909			MNHVF	UseVF
32¢		**Lockheed Constellation**	.75	.50
CM1910			MNHVF	UseVF
32¢		**Lockheed P-38 Lightning fighter**	.75	.50
CM1911			MNHVF	UseVF
32¢		**Boeing P-26 Peashooter fighter**	.75	.50
CM1912			MNHVF	UseVF
32¢		**Ford Tri-Motor**	.75	.50
CM1913			MNHVF	UseVF
32¢		**Douglas DC-3 passenger plane**	.75	.50
CM1914			MNHVF	UseVF
32¢		**Boeing 314 Clipper flying boat**	.75	.50
CM1915			MNHVF	UseVF
32¢		**Curtiss JN-4 Jenny training aircraft**	.75	.50
CM1916			MNHVF	UseVF
32¢		**Grumman F4F Wildcat fighter**	.75	.50

FDC *(July 19, 1997),* any single   2.00
y.   Se-tenant pane of 20 (CM1897-1916)   15.00
FDC, pane of 20   15.50
Six pane press sheet   150.00
Set of 4 pairs with horizontal gutters   8.00
Block of 8 with horizontal gutter   9.00
Set of 5 pairs with vertical gutters   10.00
Block of 10 with vertical gutter   11.00
Cross-gutter block of 20   20.00

1997. LEGENDARY FOOTBALL COACHES ISSUE recalled four of the greatest who ever coached the game in a se-tenant issue released at Canton, Ohio, home of the professional Football Hall of Fame. Slightly revised designs of all four stamps were issued in August in the states where the coaches became famous (CM1937-40). *Offset by Sterling Sommer for Ashton-Potter (USA) Ltd., perforated 11.*

CM1917 *Paul "Bear" Bryant;* CM1918 *Glenn "Pop" Warner;* CM1919 *Vince Lombardi;* CM1920 *George Halas*

CM1917			MNHVF	UseVF
32¢		**Paul "Bear" Bryant,** tagged *(22,500,000)*	.50	.20
CM1918			MNHVF	UseVF
32¢		**Glen "Pop" Warner,** tagged	.50	.20
CM1919			MNHVF	UseVF
32¢		**Vince Lombardi,** tagged	.50	.20
CM1920			MNHVF	UseVF
32¢		**George Halas,** tagged	.50	.20
		Plate block of 4	2.50	
	y.	Se-tenant block or strip of 4 (CM1917-20)	2.00	

FDC *(July 25, 1997),* any single   2.00
FDC, block or strip of 4   4.00
y1. Pane of 20   12.00

1997. CLASSIC AMERICAN DOLLS ISSUE depicted these beloved toys of childhood (and, increasingly, collectibles for adults) dating from as far back as the 1850s up to the 1960s in a commemorative 15-stamp pane with a banner and descriptions in the margins. *Offset (7 million panes) by Sterling Sommer for Ashton-Potter (USA) Ltd., perforated 11. Multicolored, tagged.*

CM1921 *"Alabama Baby" and Martha Chase Doll;* CM1922 *Rutta Sisters "The Columbian Doll";* CM1923 *Johnny Gruelle's "Raggedy Ann";* CM1924 *Martha Chase Cloth Doll;* CM1925 *Effanbee Doll Co. "American Child";* CM1926 *Ideal Novelty & Toy Co. "Baby Coos";* CM1927 *Plains Indian Doll 1920s;* CM1928 *Izannah Walker Oil-Painted Cloth Doll;* CM1929 *All-Cloth "Babyland Rag" Doll;* CM1930 *Rose O'Neill "Scootles" Doll;* CM1931 *Ludwig Greiner First U.S. Patent Doll;* CM1932 *"Betsy McCall" American Character Doll;* CM1933 *Percy Crosby's "Skippy";* CM1934 *Alexander Doll Co. "Maggie Mix-up";* CM1935 *Schoenut "All Word Perfection Art Dolls"* B290

CM1921			MNHVF	UseVF
32¢		**"Alabama Baby" and Martha Chase Doll**	.75	.50
CM1922			MNHVF	UseVF
32¢		**Rutta Sisters "The Columbian Doll"**	.75	.50
CM1923			MNHVF	UseVF
32¢		**Johnny Gruelle's "Raggedy Ann"**	.75	.50
CM1924			MNHVF	UseVF
32¢		**Martha Chase Cloth Doll**	.75	.50
CM1925			MNHVF	UseVF
32¢		**Effanbee Doll Co. "American Child"**	.75	.50
CM1926			MNHVF	UseVF
32¢		**Ideal Novelty & Toy Co. "Baby Coos"**	.75	.50
CM1927			MNHVF	UseVF
32¢		**Plains Indian Doll 1920s**	.75	.50
CM1928			MNHVF	UseVF
32¢		**Izannah Walker Oil-Painted Cloth Doll**	.75	.50
CM1929			MNHVF	UseVF
32¢		**All-Cloth "Babyland Rag" Doll**	.75	.50
CM1930			MNHVF	UseVF
32¢		**Rose O'Neill "Scootles" Doll**	.75	.50
CM1931			MNHVF	UseVF
32¢		**Ludwig Greiner First U.S. Patent Doll**	.75	.50

CM1932		MNHVF	UseVF
32¢	"Betsy McCall" American Character Doll	.75	.50
CM1933		MNHVF	UseVF
32¢	Percy Crosby's "Skippy"	.75	.50
CM1934		MNHVF	UseVF
32¢	Alexander Doll Co. "Maggie Mix-up"	.75	.50
CM1935		MNHVF	UseVF
32¢	Schoenut "All Word Perfection Art Dolls"	.75	.50
	FDC (July 28, 1997), any single		2.00
	y. Se-tenant pane of 15 (CM1921-35)	12.50	
	FDC, pane of 15		12.00

1997. HUMPHREY BOGART ISSUE Third in the Legends of Hollywood Series, was a 20-stamp commemorative pane with a large area of selvage displaying a portrait of the actor on the stamp. Bogart was one of the giants of American film in the 1930s and '40s in such movies as *Casablanca, The Maltese Falcon* and *To Have and Have Not.* Bogart was nominated for an Academy Award for *Treasure of the Sierra Madre* and *The Caine Mutiny,* and finally won an Oscar for *The African Queen. Gravure by J.W. Fergusson & Sons for Stamp Venturers, perforated 11.*

CM1936, B291 *Humphrey Bogart*

CM1936		MNHVF	UseVF
32¢	multicolored tagged (195,000,000)	.50	.20
	FDC (July 31, 1997)		2.50
	Plate block of 4	2.50	
	y. Pane of 20	8.00	
	Six pane press sheet	125.00	
	Pair with horizontal gutter	1.75	
	Pair with vertical gutter	2.50	
	Block of 8 with vertical gutter	11.00	
	Cross-gutter block of 8	15.00	

1997. VINCE LOMBARDI ISSUE recalled the legendary coach of the Green Bay Packers, a member of the Pro Football Hall of Fame, with a stamp issued in Green Bay, Wis., similar to CM1917 but with a red bar over Lombardi's name. *Printed by Sterling Sommer for Ashton-Potter (USA) Ltd., perforated 11.*

CM1937 *Vince Lombardi*

CM1937		MNHVF	UseVF
32¢	multicolored tagged (20,000,000)	.50	.20
	FDC (Aug. 5, 1997)		1.00
	Plate block of 4	2.50	

1997. PAUL "BEAR" BRYANT ISSUE honored the fabled coach of the University of Alabama — "the Crimson Tide" — with a stamp issued in Tuscaloosa, Ala., similar to CM1918 but with a red bar over Bryant's name. *Printed by Sterling Sommer for Ashton-Potter (USA) Ltd., perforated 11.*

CM1938 *Paul "Bear" Bryant*

CM1938		MNHVF	UseVF
32¢	multicolored tagged (20,000,000)	.50	.20

	FDC (Aug. 7, 1997)		1.00
	Plate block of 4	2.50	

1997. GLEN "POP" WARNER ISSUE commemorated the outstanding LaSalle University coach who gave his name to the nationwide Pop Warner Youth Football League with a stamp issued in Philadelphia, Pa., similar to CM1919 but with a red bar over Warner's name. *Printed by Sterling Sommer for Ashton-Potter (USA) Ltd., perforated 11.*

CM1939 *Glen "Pop" Warner*

CM1939		MNHVF	UseVF
32¢	multicolored tagged (10,000,000)	.50	.20
	FDC (Aug. 8, 1997)		1.00
	Plate block of 4	2.50	

1997. GEORGE HALAS ISSUE recalled the longtime coach of the Chicago Bears, a member of the Pro Football Hall of Fame, with a stamp issued in Chicago, Ill., similar to CM1920 but with a red bar over Halas' name. *Printed by Sterling Sommer for Ashton-Potter (USA) Ltd., perforated 11.*

CM1940 *George Halas*

CM1940		MNHVF	UseVF
32¢	multicolored tagged (10,000,000)	.50	.20
	FDC (Aug. 16, 1997)		1.00
	Plate block of 4	2.50	

1997. "THE STARS AND STRIPES FOREVER" ISSUE saluted the centennial of the premiere of "The Stars and Stripes Forever!" arguably the best-loved and most frequently played composition of John Philip Sousa (CM222), the celebrated "March King." *Gravure by Bureau of Engraving and Printing, perforated 11 1/4.*

CM1941, B292 *"The Stars and Stripes Forever!"*

CM1941		MNHVF	UseVF
32¢	multicolored tagged (323,000,000)	.50	.20
	Plate block of 4	2.50	
	FDC (Aug. 21, 1997)		1.00

1997. OPERA SINGERS ISSUE in the American Music Series was a se-tenant quartet of renowned vocalists in costumes from their greatest roles, celebrating the 400th anniversary of their art, which originated in 16th-century Florence, Italy. Lily Pons (1898-1976), a diminutive coloratura, made her debut at New York's Metropolitan Opera in 1931 as the heroine of *Lucia di Lammermoor.* Tenor Richard Tucker (1913-75), depicted in foreground of his stamp as the Duke in Verdi's *Rigoletto,* enjoyed a 30-year career at the Met and was regarded as the nation's foremost opera performer of the postwar era. Baritone Lawrence Tibbett (1896-1960), celebrated as the first American male to achieve operatic stardom in his own right, is portrayed as the Toreador in *Carmen,* one of many roles in which he excelled. A 21-year-old soprano, Rosa Ponselle (1897-1981), held her own opposite Caruso at the Met's premiere of Verdi's *La Forza del Destino,* much to the delight of critics and audiences as well, and is pictured in her costume from *Norma. Offset by Ashton-Potter (USA) Ltd., perforated 11.*

CM1942 *Lily Pons;* CM1943 *Richard Tucker;* CM1944 *Lawrence Tibbett;* CM1945 *Rosa Ponselle* B293

CM1942			
		MNHVF	**UseVF**
32¢	**Lily Pons,** tagged *(21,500,000)*	.50	.20

CM1943			
		MNHVF	**UseVF**
32¢	**Richard Tucker,** tagged	.50	.20

CM1944			
		MNHVF	**UseVF**
32¢	**Lawrence Tibbett,** tagged	.50	.20

CM1945			
		MNHVF	**UseVF**
32¢	**Rosa Ponselle,** tagged	.50	.20
	Plate block of 4	2.50	
	FDC *(Sept. 10, 1997),* any single		2.00
	y. Se-tenant block or strip of 4 (CM1942-45)	2.00	
	FDC, block or strip of 4		4.25
	y1. Pane of 20	12.00	

1997. CLASSICAL COMPOSERS AND CONDUCTORS ISSUE in the American Music Series celebrated four composers and four conductors in a se-tenant 20-stamp pane. Leopold Stokowski began conducting the Cincinnati Symphony at the age of 27, and in 1912 moved to Philadelphia where he was to wield the baton for more than 25 years, making that city's symphony orchestra one of the finest in the world. Arthur Fiedler, who began as a viola player in the Boston Symphony, gained world fame and brought classical music to vast new audiences as conductor of the Boston Pops Orchestra. George Szell fashioned the Cleveland Orchestra into one of the finest in the nation. Eugene Ormandy was musical director of the Philadelphia Symphony for over 35 years, and in 1948 conducted the first symphony concert on American television. Composer Samuel Barber won the Pulitzer Prize for his operas *Vanessa* and his *Piano Concerto.* Composer, pianist, and arranger Ferde Grofe brilliantly scored Gershwin's *Rhapsody In Blue* for the symphony in 1924, and merged jazz and simple ballads with equal creativity in his own compositions. Charles Ives was an innovative composer who used daring techniques to mold hymns and folk tunes into unusual symphonies. Louis Moreau Gottschalk gained international celebrity as a dazzling pianist whose compositions were built on the Creole rhythms of his native New Orleans. *Offset by Sterling Sommer for Ashton-Potter (USA) Ltd., perforated 11.*

CM1946 *Leopold Stokowski;* CM1947 *Arthur Fiedler;* CM1948 *George Szell;* CM1949 *Eugene Ormandy;* CM1950 *Samuel Barber;* CM1951 *Ferde Grofe;* CM1952 *Charles Ives;* CM1953 *Louis Moreau Gottschalk*

CM1946			
		MNHVF	**UseVF**
32¢	**Leopold Stokowski,** tagged *(4,300,000)*	.50	.20

CM1947			
		MNHVF	**UseVF**
32¢	**Arthur Fiedler,** tagged	.50	.20

CM1948			
		MNHVF	**UseVF**
32¢	**George Szell,** tagged	.50	.20

CM1949			
		MNHVF	**UseVF**
32¢	**Eugene Ormandy,** tagged	.50	.20

CM1950			
		MNHVF	**UseVF**
32¢	**Samuel Barber,** tagged	.50	.20

CM1951			
		MNHVF	**UseVF**
32¢	**Ferde Grofe,** tagged	.50	.20

CM1952			
		MNHVF	**UseVF**
32¢	**Charles Ives,** tagged	.50	.20

CM1953			
		MNHVF	**UseVF**
32¢	**Louis Moreau Gottschalk,** tagged	.50	.20
	Plate block of 8	5.00	
	FDC *(Sept. 12, 1997),* any single		2.00
	y. Se-tenant block of 8 (CM1946-53)	4.50	
	FDC, block of 8		11.00
	y1. Pane of 20	15.00	

1997. PADRE FELIX VARELA ISSUE memorialized the priest, educator, and social reformer whose humanitarian works for more than 30 years earned him high esteem. Varela (1788-1853) was educated in Cuba but is best known for his work in New York City, beginning in the 1820s, when he concentrated on helping the poor, organized the New York Catholic Temperance Association, founded nurseries and orphanages, and risked infection during an 1832 cholera epidemic. He also founded the first Hispanic newspaper in the United States, which chronicled social injustice, urged religious and ethnic tolerance, and promoted the importance of education. The stamp is notable for its use of the microprinted letters "USPS" to form Varela's portrait. *Offset by Sterling Sommer for Ashton-Potter (USA) Ltd., perforated 11 1/4.*

CM1954 *Padre Felix Varela*

CM1954			
		MNHVF	**UseVF**
32¢	**purple** tagged *(25,250,000)*	.50	.20
	FDC *(Sept. 15, 1997)*		2.00
	Plate block of 4	3.50	

1997. U.S. DEPARTMENT OF THE AIR FORCE ISSUE marked the 50th anniversary of the youngest branch of the U.S. armed forces as a separate military department. The stamp shows the Thunderbirds USAF demonstration team flying its custom-painted F-18 jet fighters in close "Diamond-Four" formation. This also was the first U.S. issue to include hidden images in the background of the stamp, designs visible only with a special USPS "Stamp Decoder." *Offset by Sterling Sommer for Ashton-Potter (USA) Ltd., perforated 11.*

CM1955 *U.S. Department of the Air Force*

CM1955			
		MNHVF	**UseVF**
32¢	**multicolored** tagged *(45,250,000)*	.50	.20
	FDC *(Sept. 18, 1997)*		3.00
	Plate block of 4	3.50	

1997. CLASSIC MOVIE MONSTERS ISSUE a 20-stamp pane with a banner across the top released for National Stamp Collecting Month saluted monsters from Universal Studios films of the 1920s, '30s, and '40s and the actors who brought them to life. The stamps included hidden images to be viewed with the USPS decoder. *Gravure by J.W. Fergusson & Sons for Stamp Venturers, perforated 10.*

CM1956 *Lon Chaney, as The Phantom of the Opera;* CM1957 *Bela Lugosi, as Dracula;* CM1958 *Boris Karloff, in* Frankenstein; CM1959 *Boris Karloff, as The Mummy;* CM1960 *Lon Chaney Jr., as The Wolf Man*

CM1956

		MNHVF	UseVF
32¢	**Lon Chaney, as Phantom of the Opera,** (29,000,000), tagged	.50	.20

CM1957

		MNHVF	UseVF
32¢	**Bela Lugosi, as Dracula,** tagged	.50	.20

CM1958

		MNHVF	UseVF
32¢	**Boris Karloff, in** *Frankenstein,* tagged	.50	.20

CM1959

		MNHVF	UseVF
32¢	**Boris Karloff, as The Mummy,** tagged	.50	.20

CM1960

		MNHVF	UseVF
32¢	**Lon Chaney Jr., as The Wolf Man,** tagged	.50	.20
	Plate block of 10	5.00	
	FDC (Sept. 30, 1997), any single		1.00
	y. Se-tenant strip of 5 (CM1956-60)	4.00	
	FDC, strip of 5		4.00
	y1. Pane of 20	8.00	
	Nine pane press sheet	100.00	
	Set of 5 pairs with horizontal gutters	8.75	
	Block of 10 with horizontal gutter	9.50	
	Set of 4 pairs with vertical gutters	7.00	
	Block of 8 with vertical gutter	8.00	
	Cross-gutter block of 8	12.50	

1997. FIRST SUPERSONIC FLIGHT ISSUE A self-adhesive stamp hailed the 50th anniversary of the historic 1947 flight at Edwards Air Force Base in which a Bell X-1 rocket aircraft piloted by Chuck Yeager became the first to break the sound barrier and travel faster than Mach 1. *Offset by Banknote Corporation of America, serpentine die cut 11 1/2.*

CM1961 *First supersonic flight*

CM1961

		MNHVF	UseVF
32¢	**multicolored** tagged (173,000,000)	.50	.20
	FDC (Oct. 14, 1997)		2.50
	Plate block of 4	3.50	

1997. WOMEN IN MILITARY SERVICE ISSUE saluted the nearly 2 million women who have served in the U.S. armed forces in conjunction with the Oct. 18 dedication of the Women in Military Service for America Memorial in Arlington National Cemetery near Washington, D.C. (See also CM355.) *Offset by Banknote Corporation of America, perforated 11.*

CM1962 *Women in military service*

CM1962

		MNHVF	UseVF
32¢	**multicolored** tagged (37,000,000)	.50	.20
	FDC (Oct. 18, 1997)		2.50
	Plate block of 4	3.50	

1997. KWANZAA ISSUE a colorful self-adhesive design and the second annual installment in the Postal Service's Holiday Celebration Series, honored the non-sectarian African-American festival of family, community, and culture that takes its name from the Swahili phrase

meaning "first fruits." Available in panes of 50. *Gravure by Avery Dennison Security Printing Division, serpentine die cut 11.*

CM1963 *Kwanzaa*

CM1963

		MNHVF	UseVF
32¢	**multicolored** tagged (133,000,000)	.50	.20
	FDC (Oct. 22, 1997)		3.00
	Plate block of 4	3.50	
	Five pane press sheet	150.00	
	Pair with vertical gutter	8.50	

1998. YEAR OF THE TIGER ISSUE The sixth in the Lunar New Year Series. *Gravure by Stamp Venturers, perforated 11.*

CM1964 *Year of the Tiger*

CM1964

		MNHVF	UseVF
32¢	**multicolored** tagged	.50	.20
	FDC (Jan. 5, 1998)		2.50
	Plate block of 4	2.00	

1998. WINTER SPORTS ISSUE celebrated alpine skiing. The USPS circumvented the licensing fee to the International Olympic Committee for use of the five-ring trademark, and still was able to honor the games held in Nagano, Japan; thus this is a substitute Winter Olympics stamp. *Offset by Banknote Corporation of America, perforated 11.*

CM1965 *Winter sports — alpine skier*

CM1965

		MNHVF	UseVF
32¢	**multicolored** tagged	.50	.20
	FDC (Jan. 22, 1998)		2.00
	Plate block of 4	2.00	1.50

1998. MADAM C.J. WALKER ISSUE in the Black Heritage Series saluted, with a self-adhesive stamp, the successful cosmetic and hair-care products businesswoman of the early 20th century. She earned praise as a philanthropist championing such causes as the NAACP and Tuskegee Institute. The portrait photo is from the Scurlock Studio. *Offset by Banknote Corporation of America, serpentine die cut 11 1/2x11 1/4.*

CM1966 *Madam C.J. Walker*

CM1966

		MNHVF	UseVF
32¢	**multicolored** tagged	.50	.20
	Plate block of 4	2.00	
	FDC (Jan. 28, 1998)		3.00

Celebrate the Century Series

1998. CELEBRATE THE CENTURY 1900S ISSUE was the first of a series of distinctive commemorative panes of 15 stamps that highlighted notable events, personalities, and things of each decade of the 20th century. Historical text is printed on the back of each stamp. *Offset, with one intaglio stamp in the pane, printed by Ashton-Potter USA, perforated 11 3/4.*

CM1967 *Celebrate the Century 1900s*

CM1967

		MNHVF	UseVF
$4.80	**Pane of 15,** tagged	12.50	9.50
	a. Model T Ford	.50	.50
	b. President Theodore Roosevelt	.50	.50
	c. The Great Train Robbery	.50	.50
	d. Crayola Crayons	.50	.50
	e. 1904 St. Louis World's Fair	.50	.50
	f. 1906 Pure Food and Drugs Act	.50	.50
	g. Kitty Hawk (1903)	.50	.50
	h. Ash Can Painters	.50	.50
	i. Immigrants Arrive	.50	.50
	j. John Muir Preservationist	.50	.50
	k. "Teddy" Bear Created	.50	.50
	l. W.E.B. DuBois, Social Activist	.50	.50
	m. Gibson Girl (intaglio)	.50	.50
	n. First World Series	.50	.50
	o. Robie House, Chicago	.50	.50
	FDC (Feb. 3, 1998), any single		2.00
	v. Pane of 15, red engraved omitted (one known)	—	
	FDC, pane of 15		35.00
	Four pane press sheet		36.00
	Set of 2 blocks with vertical gutters		10.00

1998. CELEBRATE THE CENTURY 1910S ISSUE was the second pane of 15 stamps in the series. *Offset, with one intaglio stamp in the pane, by Ashton-Potter USA, perforated 11 3/4.*

CM1968 *Celebrate the Century 1910s*

CM1968

		MNHVF	UseVF
$4.80	**Pane of 15,** tagged	12.50	9.50
	a. Charlie Chaplin	.50	.50
	b. Federal Reserve (intaglio)	.50	.50
	c. George Washington Carver	.50	.50
	d. Armory Show	.50	.50
	e. Transcontinental phone line	.50	.50
	f. Panama Canal	.50	.50
	g. Jim Thorpe	.50	.50
	h. Grand Canyon	.50	.50
	i. World War I	.50	.50
	j. Scouting	.50	.50
	k. Woodrow Wilson	.50	.50
	l. Crossword puzzle	.50	.50
	m. Jack Dempsey	.50	.50
	n. Construction toys	.50	.50
	o. Child labor reform	.50	.50
	v. Pane of 15, 5 stamps imperforate (one known)	—	
	FDC (Feb. 3, 1998), any single		2.00
	FDC, pane of 15		35.00
	Four pane press sheet		36.00
	Set of 2 blocks with vertical gutters	10.00	

1998. SPANISH AMERICAN WAR ISSUE marked the centennial of this very short hostility, which began after the sinking of the battleship *Maine* in Havana harbor. *Offset and intaglio by Bureau of Engraving and Printing, perforated 11 1/4.*

CM1969 *Battleship* Maine

CM1969

		MNHVF	UseVF
32¢	**red & black** tagged	.50	.20
	Plate block of 4	2.00	
	FDC (Feb. 15, 1998)		3.00

1998. FLOWERING TREES ISSUE highlighted in self-adhesive form these native North American trees. *Offset, serpentine die cut 11 1/4, printed by Banknote Corporation of America.*

CM1970-1974 *Flowering trees*

CM1970		MNHVF	UseVF
32¢	**Southern Magnolia,** tagged	.50	.20
CM1971		MNHVF	UseVF
32¢	**Blue Paloverde,** tagged	.50	.20
CM1972		MNHVF	UseVF
32¢	**Yellow Poplar,** tagged	.50	.20
CM1973		MNHVF	UseVF
32¢	**Prairie Crab Apple,** tagged	.50	.20
CM1974		MNHVF	UseVF
32¢	**Pacific Dogwood,** tagged	.50	.20
	FDC, *(March 19, 1998),* any single		2.00
	y. Strip of 5 (CM1970-74)	3.00	
	Plate block of 10	5.50	
	FDC, strip of 5		5.50

1998. ALEXANDER CALDER ISSUE honored the abstract sculptor on the centennial of his birth. His dramatic mobiles and stabiles helped popularize the art form. *Gravure, Stamp Venturers, perforated 10 1/4.*

CM1975-1979 *Calder sculptures*

CM1975		MNHVF	UseVF
32¢	**Black Cascade, 13 verticals,** tagged	.50	.20
CM1976		MNHVF	UseVF
32¢	**Untitled,** tagged	.50	.20
CM1977		MNHVF	UseVF
32¢	**Rearing Stallion,** tagged	.50	.20
CM1978		MNHVF	UseVF
32¢	**Portrait of a young man,** tagged	.50	.20
CM1979		MNHVF	UseVF
32¢	**Un Effet du Japonais,** tagged	.50	.20
	FDC *(March 25, 1998),* any single		2.00
	Plate block of 10	6.00	
	y. Strip of 5 (CM1975-79)	2.00	
	y1. Pane of 20	7.50	
	FDC, strip of 5		5.50
	Six pane press sheet	100.00	
	Set of 5 pairs with horizontal gutters	16.25	
	Block of 10 with horizontal gutter	18.00	
	Pair with vertical gutter	4.50	
	Block of 8 with vertical gutter	20.00	
	Cross-gutter block of 20	32.50	

1998. CINCO DE MAYO ISSUE honored the festival of Mexican Heritage commemorating the Mexican victory over French invaders at the Battle of Puebla in 1862. The stamp, a joint issue with Mexico (Mexico 2946), featured a couple dancing in traditional costumes. A 33¢ version (CM2055) with the same design was released in 1999. *Self-adhesive, gravure, Stamp Venturers, serpentine die cut 11 3/4x11.*

 CM1980 *Cinco de Mayo festival*

CM1980		MNHVF	UseVF
32¢	**multicolored** tagged	.50	.20
	FDC *(April 16, 1998)*		1.50
	Plate block of 4	2.00	
	Nine pane press sheet	100.00	
	Pair with horizontal gutter	1.75	
	Pair with vertical gutter	1.75	
	Cross-gutter block of 4	10.00	

1998. SYLVESTER AND TWEETY ISSUE Second in the Warner Bros. Cartoon Characters Series, pictured the two cartoon antagonists. *Self-adhesive, gravure, printed by Avery Dennison, serpentine die cut 11.*

CM1981 *Sylvester and Tweety*

CM1981		MNHVF	UseVF
$3.20	**Pane of 10,** tagged	5.00	
	n. Right half of pane (single die cut CM1981a superimposed on enlarged image in right selvage)	1.00	
	n1.Left half of pane (block of 9 CM1981a)	5.00	
	a. 32¢ single	.50	.25
	Six pane top press sheet	70.00	
	Six pane bottom press sheet with plate number	100.00	
	Pair with horizontal gutter	4.75	
	Pair with vertical gutter	10.00	
	Cross-gutter block of 12	36.00	
	FDC *(April 27, 1998),* single		2.00

1998. SYLVESTER AND TWEETY ISSUE *self-adhesive — gravure, printed by Avery Dennison, 9 stamps serpentine die cut, and one imperforate on right panel.*

CM1982		MNHVF	UseVF
$3.20	**Pane of 10,** tagged	5.00	
	n. Right half of pane (single imperforate CM1982a) enlarged image in right selvage	1.00	
	n1.Left half of pane (block of 9 CM1982a)	5.00	
	a. 32¢ single	.50	

This issue also was made available in top and bottom half printing sheets of six 10-stamp panes each. Vertical rouletting between the two panes is missing on these half sheets. A plate number, trimmed away or individual panes, appears adjacent to the bottom-left pane in the bottom half of the printing sheet only.

1998. CELEBRATE THE CENTURY, 1920S ISSUE was the third in the series honoring each decade of the 20th Century. *Offset, with one intaglio stamp in the pane, printed by Ashton-Potter USA, perforated 11 3/4.*

Condition refers to the overall appearance and quality of the stamp.

CM1983 *Celebrate the Century 1920s*

CM1983

		MNHVF	UseVF
$4.80	**Pane of 15,** tagged	10.00	9.50
	a. Babe Ruth	.75	.50
	b. The Gatsby Style	.75	.50
	c. Prohibition Enforced	.75	.50
	d. Electric toy trains	.75	.50
	e. 19th Amendment	.75	.50
	f. Emily Post's Etiquette	.75	.50
	g. Margaret Mead, Anthropologist	.75	.50
	h. Flappers do the Charleston	.75	.50
	i. Radio Entertains America	.75	.50
	j. Art Deco style	.75	.50
	k. Jazz flourishes	.75	.50
	l. Four Horsemen of Notre Dame	.75	.50
	m. Lindbergh Flies Atlantic (intaglio)	.75	.50
	n. American Realism	.75	.50
	o. Stock Market Crash of 1929	.75	.50
	FDC *(May 28, 1998),* any single		2.00
	FDC, pane of 15		15.00
	Four pane press sheet	36.00	
	Set of 2 blocks with vertical gutters	10.00	

1998. WISCONSIN STATEHOOD SESQUICENTENNIAL ISSUE
honored the 1848 entry of Wisconsin as the 40th state in the union.
Sale of the stamp was restricted. It contains a hidden image of a
badger, the state animal, in the sky, visible only with a USPS decoder.
*Self-adhesive, gravure by American Packaging Corp. for Sennett
Security Products, serpentine die cut 11.*

CM1984 *Door County farm scene*

CM1984

		MNHVF	UseVF
32¢	**multicolored** tagged	.50	.20
	Plate block of 4	2.00	
	FDC *(May 29, 1998)*		1.50

1998. TRANS-MISSISSIPPI COLOR ISSUE highlighted nine views of
westward expansion. Orginally issued in single colors for the 1898
Trans-Mississippi Exposition held in Omaha, Neb. The 2¢ and $2
vignettes are reversed from the issued versions but as originally
planned in 1898. CM1986 consists of nine copies of the $1 value.
*Offset and intaglio by Banknote Corporation of America, perforated
12 1/4x12 1/2.*

CM1985 *1898 Trans-Mississippi*

CM1985

		MNHVF	UseVF
$3.80	**Pane of 9,** tagged	7.50	3.50
	a. 1¢ dark green & black	.25	.20
	b. 2¢ copper red & black	.25	.20
	c. 4¢ orange & black	.25	.20
	d. 5¢ dark blue & black	.25	.20
	e. 8¢ dark lilac & black	.25	.20
	f. 10¢ purple & black	.50	.50
	g. 50¢ olive & black	1.50	.50
	h. $1.00 red & black	2.00	.50
	i. $2.00 brown & black	3.00	1.00
	FDC *(June 18, 1998),* pane of 9		10.75

CM1986 *1898 Trans-Mississippi*

CM1986

		MNHVF	UseVF
$9	**Pane,** 9 examples of CM1985h, tagged	15.00	
	FDC *(June 18, 1998),* single		2.00

FDC, pane of 9	16.50	
Six pane press sheet (3 each CM1985-86)	125.00	
Set of 4 pairs with horizontal gutters	32.00	
Block of 9 with horizontal gutter	34.00	
Set of 3 pairs with vertical gutters	24.00	
Block of 12 with vertical gutter	26.00	
Cross-gutter block of 12	47.50	

1998. BERLIN AIRLIFT ISSUE commemorated the 50th anniversary of the U.S. Air Force operation to assist the citizens of war-ravaged Berlin from a land and water blockade set up by the Soviets. The flights of C-47s and C-54s lasted from June 26, 1948, through Sept. 30, 1949. *Offset by Banknote Corporation of America, perforated 11.*

CM1987 *Berliners watching arriving C-54*

CM1987		MNHVF	UseVF
32¢	**multicolored** tagged	.50	.20
	Plate block of 4	2.00	
	FDC *(June 26, 1998)*		2.00

1998. FOLK MUSICIANS ISSUE in the American Music Series honored four performers whose songs reflected the soul of America. Woodrow "Woody" Guthrie (1912-1967), maybe the most famous folk singer of all time, wrote 1,000 songs, including "This Land Is Your Land" and "So Long, It's Been Good To Know You." Sonny Terry (1911-1986), a blind harmonica player, also produced an array of sounds on the harp. "Leadbelly" Ledbetter (1888-1949), master of the 12-string guitar, drew upon the breadth of southern black music and wrote the popular sentimental hit, "Goodnight Irene." Josh White (1908-1969) played guitar for President Franklin Roosevelt at the White House. A favorite song was "Careless Love." *Gravure, American Packaging Corp. for Sennett Security Products, perforated 10 1/4.*

CM1988 *Woody Guthrie;* CM1989 *Sonny Terry;* CM1990 *Huddie "Leadbelly" Ledbetter;* CM1991 *Josh White*

CM1988		MNHVF	UseVF
32¢	**Woody Guthrie,** tagged	.50	.20
CM1989		MNHVF	UseVF
32¢	**Sonny Terry,** tagged	.50	.20
CM1990		MNHVF	UseVF
32¢	**Huddie "Leadbelly" Ledbetter,** tagged	.50	.20
CM1991		MNHVF	UseVF
32¢	**Josh White,** tagged	.50	.20
	FDC *(June 26, 1998),* any single		2.00
	Plate block of 4	3.00	
	y. Block or strip of 4 (CM1988-91)	2.00	
	y1. Pane of 20	9.50	
	FDC, block or strip of 4		6.00

1998. SPANISH SETTLEMENT OF THE SOUTHWEST ISSUE noted the 400th anniversary of the oldest European road in the southwestern U.S., "El Camino Real de Tierra Adentro" (the royal road to the interior land), and the founding of the settlement of San Gabriel in what is now New Mexico. The mission replica in Española, N. Mex., is depicted. *Offset by Banknote Corporation of America, perforated 11 1/4.*

CM1992 *Mission de San Miguel de San Gabriel*

CM1992		MNHVF	UseVF
32¢	**multicolored** tagged	.50	.20
	FDC *(July 11, 1998)*		2.00
	Plate block of 4	2.00	

1998. GOSPEL SINGERS ISSUE in the American Music Series. Mahalia Jackson's magnificent voice and fervent faith made her gospel music's first superstar. Clara Ward was the leader of the most successful female gospel group of the 1950s. Roberta Martin founded the Roberta Martin Singers. Sister Rosetta Tharpe was the first gospel singer to record with a major record company. *Gravure. American Packaging Corp. for Sennett Security Products, perforated 10 1/4.*

CM1993 *Mahalia Jackson;* CM1994 *Roberta Martin;* CM1995 *Clara Ward;* CM1996 *Sister Rosetta Tharpe*

CM1993		MNHVF	UseVF
32¢	**Mahalia Jackson,** tagged	.50	2.00
CM1994		MNHVF	UseVF
32¢	**Roberta Martin,** tagged	.50	.20
CM1995		MNHVF	UseVF
32¢	**Clara Ward,** tagged	.50	.20
CM1996		MNHVF	UseVF
32¢	**Sister Rosetta Tharpe,** tagged	.50	.20
	FDC *(July 15, 1998),* any single		2.00
	Plate block of 4	2.40	
	y. Block or strip of 4 (CM1993-96)	2.00	
	y1. Pane of 20	12.00	
	FDC, strip or block of 4		5.00

1998. STEPHEN VINCENT BENÉT ISSUE 16th in the Literary Arts Series honored the poet (1898-1943) on his birth centennial. Pulitzer Prize winning author of *John Brown's Body* and *The Devil and Daniel Webster.* Benét's portrait is set against part of Augustus St. Gauden's Shaw Memorial on Boston Common. *Offset by Sterling Sommer for Ashton Potter, with microprinting "John Brown's Body" on rifle barrel under "B." Perforated 11.*

CM1997 *Stephen Vincent Benét*

CM1997		MNHVF	UseVF
32¢	**multicolored** tagged	.50	.20
	FDC *(July 22, 1998)*		2.00
	Plate block of 4	2.00	

1998. BREAST CANCER RESEARCH SEMIPOSTAL ISSUE The first official money-raising U.S. stamp, raised $7.8 million in one year of sales. The undenominated First Class stamp sold for 40¢, with the amount over standard postage (8¢ before the rate increase in 1999, then 7¢ and 6¢ after the rate increase to 34¢ in 2001) earmarked for cancer research. By August 2001, sales had generated $25 million for research. *Self-adhesive, gravure by Avery Dennison, serpentine die cut 11.*

CMSP1 *Breast cancer self-examination*

CMSP1		MNHVF	UseVF
(32¢ + 8¢)	**multicolored** tagged	.75	.20
	Plate block of 4	3.00	
	FDC *(July 29, 1998)*		1.25

1998. TROPICAL BIRDS ISSUE featured two birds of Puerto Rico, and one each from the the rain forest of Maui and the island of Samoa. *Offset, Banknote Corporation of America, perforated 11.*

CM1998-2001 *Tropical Birds,* B296

CM1998		MNHVF	UseVF
32¢	**Antillean Euphonia,** tagged	.50	.20
CM1999		MNHVF	UseVF
32¢	**Green-throated Carib,** tagged	.50	.20
CM2000		MNHVF	UseVF
32¢	**Crested Honeycreeper,** tagged	.50	.20
CM2001		MNHVF	UseVF
32¢	**Cardinal Honeyeater,** tagged	.50	.20
	FDC *(July 29, 1998),* any single		2.00
	Plate block of 4	2.40	
	FDC, strip or block of 4		5.50
	y. Block or strip of 4 (CM1998-2001)	2.00	

1998. ALFRED HITCHCOCK ISSUE in the Legends of Hollywood Series honored the British born director (1899-1980) who became an American citizen. He was a master of dramatic suspense. The caricature sketch at upper left on the stamp is die cut, not printed. *Gravure by American Packaging Corp. for Sennett Security Products, perforated 11 1/4.*

CM2002 *Alfred Hitchcock*

CM2002		MNHVF	UseVF
32¢	**black & gray** tagged	.60	.20
	FDC, *(Aug. 3, 1998)*		2.00
	Plate block of 4	2.40	
	y. Pane of 20	12.00	
	FDC, pane of 20		17.50
	Six pane press sheet	72.00	
	Pair with horizontal gutter	1.75	
	Pair with vertical gutter	2.50	
	Block of 8 with vertical gutter	11.00	
	Cross-gutter block of 8	15.00	

1998. ORGAN & TISSUE DONATION ISSUE called attention to a lifesaving medical practice. *Self-adhesive, gravure by Avery Dennison. Serpentine die cut 11 3/4.*

CM2003 *Organ & Tissue Donation*

CM2003		MNHVF	UseVF
32¢	**multicolored** tagged	.50	.20
	Plate block of 4	2.40	
	FDC *(Aug. 5, 1998)*		1.00

1998. BRIGHT EYES PET ISSUE aimed at children, showed bug-eyed examples of popular pets. *Self-adhesive, gravure by Guilford Gravure for Banknote Corporation of America, serpentine die cut 10.*

CM2004 *Dog*

CM2005 *Goldfish*

CM2006 *Cat*

CM2007 *Parakeet*

CM2008 *Hamster*

CM2004		MNHVF	UseVF
32¢	**Dog,** tagged	.50	.20
CM2005		MNHVF	UseVF
32¢	**Goldfish,** tagged	.50	.20
CM2006		MNHVF	UseVF
32¢	**Cat,** tagged	.50	.20
CM2007		MNHVF	UseVF
32¢	**Parakeet,** tagged	.50	.20
CM2008		MNHVF	UseVF
32¢	**Hamster,** tagged	.50	.20
	FDC *(Aug. 20, 1998),* any single		1.90
	y. Strip of 5 (CM2004-08)	2.50	—
	y1. Pane of 20	7.50	
	FDC, strip of 5		5.50

1998. KLONDIKE GOLD RUSH ISSUE dramatically portrayed the gold-seekers who crossed Alaska to the Klondike gold fields a century earlier. *Offset by Sterling Sommer for Ashton-Potter, perforated 11.*

CM2009 *Klondike Gold Rush*

CM2009		MNHVF	UseVF
32¢	**multicolored** tagged	.50	.20
	Plate block of 4	7.50	
	FDC *(Aug. 21, 1998)*		1.90

1998. AMERICAN ART ISSUE the sixth in the Classic Collections Series featured works of four centuries of American artists. *Gravure by American Packaging Corp. for Sennett Security Products, perforated 10 1/4x10.*

CM2010-2029

CM2010		MNHVF	UseVF
32¢	John Foster, tagged	.50	.20
CM2011		MNHVF	UseVF
32¢	The Freake Limner, tagged	.50	.20
CM2012		MNHVF	UseVF
32¢	Ammi Phillips, tagged	.50	.20
CM2013		MNHVF	UseVF
32¢	Rembrandt Peale, tagged	.50	.20
CM2014		MNHVF	UseVF
32¢	John J. Audubon, tagged	.50	.20
CM2015		MNHVF	UseVF
32¢	George Caleb Bingham, tagged	.50	.20
CM2016		MNHVF	UseVF
32¢	Asher B. Durand, tagged	.50	.20
CM2017		MNHVF	UseVF
32¢	Joshua Johnson, tagged	.50	.20
CM2018		MNHVF	UseVF
32¢	William M. Harnett, tagged	.50	.20
CM2019		MNHVF	UseVF
32¢	Winslow Homer, tagged	.50	.20
CM2020		MNHVF	UseVF
32¢	George Catlin, tagged	.50	.20
CM2021		MNHVF	UseVF
32¢	Thomas Moran, tagged	.50	.20
CM2022		MNHVF	UseVF
32¢	Albert Bierstadt, tagged	.50	.20
CM2023		MNHVF	UseVF
32¢	Frederic Edwin Church, tagged	.50	.20
CM2024		MNHVF	UseVF
32¢	Mary Cassatt, tagged	.50	.20
CM2025		MNHVF	UseVF
32¢	Edward Hopper, tagged	.50	.20
CM2026		MNHVF	UseVF
32¢	Grant Wood, tagged	.50	.20
CM2027		MNHVF	UseVF
32¢	Charles Sheeler, tagged	.50	.20
CM2028		MNHVF	UseVF
32¢	Franny Kline, tagged	.50	.20

CM2029		MNHVF	UseVF
32¢	Mark Rothko, tagged	.50	.20
	FDC (Aug. 27, 1998), any single		1.00
	y. Pane of 20	8.50	
	FDC, pane of 20		—
	Six pane press sheet	72.00	
	Set of 5 pairs with horizontal gutters	10.00	
	Block of 10 with horizontal gutter	11.00	
	Set of 4 pairs with vertical gutters	8.00	
	Block of 8 with vertical gutter	9.00	
	Cross-gutter block of 20	20.00	

1998. CELEBRATE THE CENTURY, 1930s ISSUE was the fourth in the series honoring each decade of the 20th century. *Printed by Ashton-Potter. Offset, with one intaglio stamp per pane, perforated 11 3/4.*

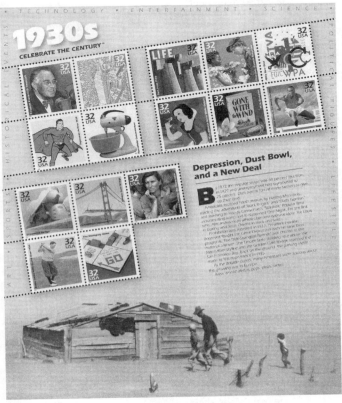

CM2030 *Celebrate the Century 1930s*

CM2030		MNHVF	UseVF
$4.80	Pane of 15, tagged	10.00	7.50
	a. Franklin D. Roosevelt	.75	.50
	b. Empire State Building (intaglio)	.75	.50
	c. *Life* magazine	.75	.50
	d. Eleanor Roosevelt	.75	.50
	e. FDR's New Deal Programs	.75	.50
	f. Superman Arrives	.75	.50
	g. Household Conveniences	.75	.50
	h. Disney's Snow White	.75	.50
	i. Gone with the Wind	.75	.50
	j. Jesse Owens	.75	.50
	k. Streamline Design	.75	.50
	l. Golden Gate Bridge	.75	.50
	m. America Survives the Depression	.75	.50
	n. Bobby Jones	.75	.50
	o. Monopoly Game	.75	.50
	FDC (Sept. 10, 1998), any single		1.50
	FDC, pane of 15		7.50
	Four pane press sheet	36.00	
	Block with vertical gutter	7.50	

1998. BALLET ISSUE Ballerina performing the step "en pointe" in an "attitude derriere" pose honored the art form. *Offset by Sterling Sommer for Ashton Potter, perforated 11.*

CM2031, B297 *Ballet*

CM2031

		MNHVF	UseVF
32¢	**multicolored** tagged	.50	.20
	FDC *(Sept. 16, 1998)*		2.00
	y. Pane of 20	12.80	
	Plate block of 4	2.00	
	Six pane press sheet	72.50	
	Pair with horizontal gutter	1.75	
	Pair with vertical gutter	1.75	
	Cross-gutter block of 4	10.00	

1998. SPACE DISCOVERY ISSUE a panoramic scene by artist Attila Hejja depicted exotic spacecraft, a city on an alien planet and colonists. There are views of space ships as hidden indicia visible only with the USPS optical decoder. *Gravure by American Packaging Corp., for Sennett Security Products, block tagged, perforated 11.*

CM2032-2036, B298

CM2032

		MNHVF	UseVF
32¢	**Land craft**	.50	.20

CM2033

		MNHVF	UseVF
32¢	**Space ship**	.50	.20

CM2034

		MNHVF	UseVF
32¢	**Figure**	.50	.20

CM2035

		MNHVF	UseVF
32¢	**Jagged hills**	.50	.20

CM2036

		MNHVF	UseVF
32¢	**Moon**	.50	.20
	Plate block of 10	5.00	
	y. Se-tenant strip of 5 (CM2032-36)	2.50	
	FDC *(Oct. 1, 1998)*, any single		1.50
	FDC, strip of 5	7.50	
	y1. Pane of 20		2.00
	Nine pane press sheet	100.00	
	Set of 5 pairs with horizontal gutters	8.75	
	Block of 10 with horizontal gutter	9.50	
	Pair with vertical gutter	1.75	
	Cross-gutter block of 10	15.00	

1998. GIVING & SHARING ISSUE paid tribute to philanthropy. The bee and flower is a metaphor for the symbolic relationship between the "giver" and the "receiver." *Gravure by Avery Dennison, serpentine die cut 11, phosphored paper, self-adhesive.*

CM2037 *Giving & Sharing*

CM2037

		MNHVF	UseVF
32¢	**multicolored**	.50	.20
	Plate block of 4	2.00	
	FDC *(Oct. 7, 1998)*		2.00

1999. YEAR OF THE HARE ISSUE was the seventh in the Lunar New Year Series designed by Clarence Lee, Honolulu, Hawaii, and executed in paper-cut style. *Gravure by American Packaging Corp. for Sennett Security Products (51 million printed), gummed, perforated 11.*

CM2038 *Year of the Hare*

CM2038

		MNHVF	UseVF
33¢	**multicolored** tagged	.50	.20
	Plate block of 4	2.50	
	FDC *(Jan. 5, 1999)*		2.25

1999. MALCOLM X ISSUE 22nd stamp in the Black Heritage Series, saluted the founder (born Malcolm Little) of the Organization of Afro-American Unity (1963). Once a fiery spokesman for the black separatism teachings of the Nation of Islam, Malcolm X (1925-1965) broke away from the organization and promoted a more neutral solution to racial inequality. He was shot to death during a speech Feb. 21, 1965. The black-and-white stamp image is from an Associated Press news photo. Designed by Richard Sheaff, Scottsdale, Ariz. *Self-adhesive, serpentine die cut 11 1/2. Offset by Banknote Corporation of America (100 million printed).*

CM2039 *Malcolm X*

CM2039

		MNHVF	UseVF
33¢	**multicolored** tagged	.50	.20
	Plate block of 4	2.00	
	FDC *(Jan. 20, 1999)*		2.50

1999. VICTORIAN HEARTS ISSUE in the Love Series initiated in 1973 constituted the first die-cut-to-shape United States postage stamps. Designed by Richard Sheaff, Scottsdale, Ariz., computer design by John Grossman and Holly Sudduth of Point Richmond, Calif. The word "love" was not included in the design for only the second time in the series (see CM1884 and CM1885). The paper-lace-and-flowers motif was reminiscent of the late 1880s. *Self-adhesive, die-cut convertible booklet (33¢) and pane (55¢) of 20. Gravure by Avery Dennison (1.5 billion printed).*

CM2040 *Victorian hearts*

CM2040

		MNHVF	UseVF
33¢	**multicolored** tagged	.50	.20
	FDC *(Jan. 28, 1999)*		1.90
	n. Pane of 20 (convertible booklet)	12.00	

1999. VICTORIAN HEARTS ISSUE in the Love Series. Designed by Richard Sheaff, Scottsdale, Ariz., computer design by John Grossman and Holly Sudduth of Point Richmond, Calif. *Self-adhesive die cut to shape. Offset by Banknote Corporation of America (300 million printed).*

CM2041 *Victorian hearts*

CM2041

		MNHVF	UseVF
55¢	**multicolored** tagged	.85	.25
	Plate block of 4	3.20	
	FDC *(Jan. 28, 1999)*		2.25

1999. HOSPICE CARE ISSUE was intended to raise awareness of the concept of a team oriented medical care program to treat and comfort terminally ill patients in a home-like setting. Designed by Phil Jordan, Falls Church, Va. *Self-adhesive serpentine die cut 11 1/2. Offset by Banknote Corporation of America (100 million printed).*

 CM2042 *Hospice care*

CM2042

		MNHVF	UseVF
33¢	**multicolored** phosphored paper	.50	.20
	Plate block of 4	2.00	
	FDC *(Feb. 9, 1999)*		2.25

1999. CELEBRATE THE CENTURY 1940S ISSUE in the Celebrate the Century Series was the fifth in the series highlighting each decade of the 20th century. Designed by Carl Herrman, Laguna Nigel, Calif., illustrated by Howard Koslow, Toms River, N.J., engraver Ron Becker (Internatinal Style of Architecture design). *Gummed pane of 15. Offset, with one intaglio stamp in the pane; by Ashton-Potter USA (188 million or 12,533,333 panes printed). Perforated 11 3/4, tagged.*

CM2043 *Celebrate the Century 1940s*

CM2043

		MNHVF	UseVF
$4.95	**Pane of 15, multicolored** tagged	10.00	7.50
a.	World War II	.75	.50
b.	Antibiotics Save Lives	.75	.50
c.	Jackie Robinson	.75	.50
d.	President Harry S. Truman	.75	.50
e.	Women Support War Effort	.75	.50
f.	TV Entertains America	.75	.50
g.	Jitterbug Sweeps Nation	.75	.50
h.	Abstract Expressionism	.75	.50
i.	GI Bill 1944	.75	.50
j.	The Big Band Sound	.75	.50
k.	International Style of Architecture (intaglio)	.75	.50
l.	Postwar Baby Boom	.75	.50
m.	Slinky Craze Begins 1945	.75	.50
n.	Broadway Hit 1947	.75	.50
o.	Orson Welles' *Citizen Kane*	.75	.50
	FDC *(Feb. 18, 1999), any single*		7.50
	FDC, pane of 15		1.90
	Four pane press sheet	40.00	
	Block with vertical gutter	7.50	

1999. IRISH IMMIGRATION ISSUE acknowledged the second-largest ancestral group in the United States on the 150th anniversary of the potato famine, which drove many Irish to America for survival. It was a joint issue with an Irish Emigration stamp from Ireland. Designed by Howard Paine, Delaplane, Va., from illustration by Dennis Lyall of Bridgeport, Conn. *Gummed pane of 20. Offset by Ashton-Potter USA (40.4 million printed). Perforated 11, tagged.*

 CM2044 *Irish immigration*

CM2044

		MNHVF	UseVF
33¢	**multicolored**	.50	.20
	Plate block of 4	2.00	
	FDC *(Feb. 26, 1999)*		1.90

1999. ALFRED LUNT AND LYNN FONTANNE ISSUE in the Performing Arts Series honored one of the greatest husband-and-wife acting teams ever to take the stage. Lunt (1892-1977) and Fontanne (1887-1983) met and first acted together in 1919, married in 1922, and never appeared separately on stage after 1928. They last appeared in the Broadway play, *The Visit,* in 1958. The illustration was based on a 1931 publicity photo for a film that was never made, *Lullaby.* The first-day ceremony took place at the Lunt-Fontanne Theatre in New York City. Designed by Carl Herrman, Laguna Nigel, Calif., from illustration by Drew Struzan, Pasadena, Calif. *Offset by Sterling Sommer for Ashton-Potter USA (42.5 million printed). Perforated 11, tagged.*

 CM2045 *Alfred Lunt & Lynn Fontanne*

CM2045

		MNHVF	UseVF
33¢	**multicolored**	.50	.20
	Plate block of 4	2.00	
	FDC *(March 2, 1999)*		1.90

1999. ARCTIC ANIMALS ISSUE pictured five animals adapted to thrive in the extreme cold of the Arctic. The stamps are based on close-up photographs. Designed by Derry Noyes, Washington, D.C., photos by Art Wolfe (Arctic Hare), Joe McDonald (Timber Wolf), Zig Leszczynski (Snowy Owl), Gary Schultz (Arctic Fox), Jeff Foott (Polar Bear), and Johnny Johnson (Polar Bear family in header). *Offset by Banknote Corporation of America, (73,155,000 or 4,877,000 panes printed), block tagged, perforated 11.*

CM2046 *Arctic Hare;* CM2047 *Arctic Fox;* CM2048 *Snowy Owl;* CM2049 *Polar Bear;* CM2050 *Gray Wolf*

CM2046

		MNHVF	UseVF
33¢	**Arctic Hare, multicolored**	.60	.20

CM2047		MNHVF	UseVF
33¢	**Arctic Fox, multicolored**	.60	.20
CM2048		MNHVF	UseVF
33¢	**Snowy Owl, multicolored**	.60	.20
CM2049		MNHVF	UseVF
33¢	**Polar Bear, multicolored**	.60	.20
CM2050		MNHVF	UseVF
33¢	**Gray Wolf, multicolored**	.60	.20
	y. Se-tenant strip of 5 (CM2046-50)	3.00	
	FDC (March 12, 1999), any single		2.00
	FDC, strip of 5		5.50
	y1. Pane of 15	9.00	
	FDC, pane of 15		18.00

Nature of America Series

1999. SONORAN DESERT ISSUE The first of the planned educational Nature of America Series, pictured a Southwestern desert scene teeming with wildlife. On the back of the pane, the USPS identified 25 species, including those not on the stamps die-cut into the scene, ranging from an elf owl in a cactus cavity, three collared peccary, and a tarantula, but not including a trail of ants near the bottom of the pane. Designed by Ethel Kessler, Bethesda, Md., illustrated by John Dawson, Hilo, Hawaii. *Self-adhesive commemorative pane of 10, offset by Banknote Corporation of America (10 million panes printed). Serpentine die cut 11 1/4.*

CM2051a *Saguaro cactus;* CM2051b *White-winged dove, prickly pear;* CM2051c *Desert mule deer;* CM2051d *Gila woodpecker;* CM2051e *Cactus wren, brittlebush, teddy bear cholla;* CM2051f *Desert tortoise;* CM2051g *Gambel quail;* CM2051h *Desert cottontail, hedgehog cactus;* CM2051i *Gila monster;* CM2051j *Western diamondback rattlesnake, cactus mouse*

CM2051		MNHVF	UseVF
$3.30	**Pane of 10, multicolored** blocked tagged	7.50	3.00
	a. Saguaro cactus	.75	.50
	b. White-winged dove, prickly pear	.75	.50
	c. Desert mule deer	.75	.50
	d. Gila woodpecker	.75	.50
	e. Cactus wren, brittlebush, teddy bear cholla	.75	.50
	f. Desert tortoise	.75	.50
	g. Gambel quail	.75	.50
	h. Desert cottontail, hedgehog cactus	.75	.50
	i. Gila monster	.75	.50
	j. Western diamondback rattlesnake, cactus mouse	.75	.50
	FDC (April 6, 1999), any single		1.00
	FDC, pane of 10		10.00
	Six pane press sheet	40.00	
	Pair with horizontal gutter	6.00	
	Pair with vertical gutter	6.00	
	Cross-gutter block of 4	13.50	

1999. DAFFY DUCK ISSUE the third in the Warner Bros. Cartoon Characters Series, featured the underachieving Looney Tunes duck famous for his lisping, "That's despicable." Designed by Ed Wleczyk,

Los Angeles, Calif. *Self-adhesive, gravure by Avery Dennison, (427 million stamps printed), (42.7 million panes). Serpentine die cut 11 on all stamps, "Double prong" tooth at upper right corner of each stamp, tagged.*

CM2052 *Daffy Duck*

CM2052		MNHVF	UseVF
$3.30	**Pane of 10,** tagged	7.50	
	n. Right half of pane (single die cut CM2052a superimposed on enlarged image)	1.00	
	n1. Left half of pane (block of 9 CM2052a)	5.00	
	a. 33¢ single	.75	.25
	FDC (April 16, 1999)		2.50
	Six pane top press sheet	40.00	
	Six pane bottom press sheet	45.00	
	Pair with horizontal gutter	1.75	
	Pair with vertical gutter	3.50	
	Cross-gutter block of 12	17.50	

A single plate number, trimmed away on individual panes, appears adjacent to the bottom-left pane in the bottom half of the printing sheet only.

1999. DAFFY DUCK ISSUE in the Warner Bros. Cartoon Characters Series. Designed by Ed Wleczyk, Los Angeles, Calif. *Self-adhesive, gravure by Avery Dennison (50 thousand panes), nine stamps serpentine die cut 11 through stamps and backing on left pane, one stamp imperforate on right pane. The two sides are separated by a vertical line of tiny perforations.*

CM2053 *Daffy Duck*

CM2053		MNHVF	UseVF
$3.30	**Pane of 10,** tagged	7.50	
	n. Right half of pane (single imperforate CM2053a superimposed on enlarged image)	1.00	1.00
	n1. Left half of pane (block of 9 CM2053a)	6.00	
	a. 33¢ single	.75	.25

1999. AYN RAND ISSUE 17th in the Literary Arts Series honored the writer (and stamp collector) whose philosophy of individual freedom and effort shaped her novels such as *Atlas Shrugged* and *The Fountainhead.* Born Alissa Rosenbaum in Russia, she came to the United States at the age of 21, became a U.S. citizen, changed her name (Ayn rhymes with fine; Rand she found on her Remington-Rand typewriter), and moved to

Hollywood, where she continued writing and worked in movies. Designed by Phil Jordan, Falls Church, Va., illustrated by Nicholas Gaetano, Fletcher, N.C. *Offset by Sterling Sommer for Ashton-Potter USA (42.5 million printed). Perforated 11, tagged.*

CM2054 *Ayn Rand*

CM2054		MNHVF	UseVF
33¢	multicolored	.50	.20
	Plate block of 4	2.00	
	FDC (April 22, 1999)		1.90

1999. CINCO DE MAYO ISSUE part of the Holiday Celebration Series. Was printed with "33" denomination and 1999 date (see CM1980). *Offset by Banknote Corporation of America (105 million printed), self-adhesive serpentine die cut 11 1/2, tagged. The 1998 version (CM1980) was printed by gravure.*

CM2055 *Cinco de Mayo*

CM2055		MNHVF	UseVF
33¢	multicolored	.50	.20
	Plate block of 4	2.00	
	FDC (April 27, 1999)		1.90

1999. TROPICAL FLOWERS ISSUE continued the USPS fascination with floral issues and included several innovations. It was the first self-adhesive convertible booklet with stamps on both sides of the pane, the first U.S. stamps printed with a 550-line screen rather than the more common 300-line screen to give the illustrations more sharpness, the first with a completely recyclable adhesive, and the first on paper stock with 20% post-consumer waste. The flowers, arranged as in a bouquet, are the bird of paradise, whose showy flowers resemble the heads of birds; the royal poinciana, a 50-foot tree with fiery blooms in the rainy season; the gloriosa lily, a climbing plant whose flowers are four inches across; and the Chinese hibiscus whose vibrant flowers last only a day each but are replaced quickly for a long-lasting bloom. Designed by Carl Herrman, Laguna Niguel, Calif., illustrations by Steve Buchanan, Winstead, Conn. *Gravure at American Packaging Corp. for Sennett Security Products on phosphored paper (1.5 billion stamps), (75 million booklets), self-adhesive serpentine die cut 11.*

CM2056 *Bird of paradise*

CM2057 *Royal poinciana*

CM2058 *Gloriosa lily*

CM2059 *Chinese hibiscus*

CM2056		MNHVF	UseVF
33¢	Bird of paradise, multicolored	.50	.20
CM2057		MNHVF	UseVF
33¢	Royal poinciana, multicolored	.50	.20
CM2058		MNHVF	UseVF

33¢	Gloriosa lily, multicolored	.50	.20
CM2059		MNHVF	UseVF
33¢	Chinese hibiscus, multicolored	.50	.20
	y. Se-tenant block of 4 (CM2056-59)		1.50
	FDC (May 1, 1999), any single		2.50
	n. Pane of 20	13.00	
	FDC, one of each stamp		5.50

1999. JOHN & WILLIAM BARTRAM ISSUE brought to attention John Bartram (1699-1777), who established in Philadelphia the oldest existing botanical garden in America. He and his son, William Bartram (1739-1823) introduced 200 native American plants there. The stamp shows a detail of a handcolored engraving by William Bartram. *Offset with microprinting "Botanists" by Banknote Corporation of America, (145,375,000 printed), self-adhesive, phosphored paper, serpentine die cut, perforated 11 1/2.*

CM2060 *Botanical engraving*

CM2060		MNHVF	UseVF
33¢	multicolored	.60	.20
	Plate block of 4	2.00	
	y. Block of 4	—	
	FDC (May 18, 1999)		1.90

1999. CELEBRATE THE CENTURY 1950S ISSUE in the Celebrate the Century Series was the sixth in the series highlighting each decade of the 20th century. Designed by Howard Paine, Delaplane, Va., with illustrations by Dean Ellis, Amagansett, N.Y. *Gummed pane of 15, offset, with one intaglio stamp in the pane, by Ashton-Potter USA (188 million printed), (12,533,333 panes). Perforated 11 1/2.*

CM2061 *Celebrate the Century 1950s*

CM2061		MNHVF	UseVF
$4.95	**Pane of 15, multicolored** tagged	10.00	7.50
	a. Polio Vaccine Developed (intaglio)	.65	.30
	b. Teen Fashions	.65	.30
	c. The "Shot Heard 'Round the World"	.65	.30
	d. U.S. Launches Satellites	.65	.30
	e. The Korean War	.65	.30
	f. Desegregating Public Schools	.65	.30
	g. Tail Fins and Chrome	.65	.30
	h. Dr. Seuss' *The Cat in the Hat*	.65	.30
	i. Drive-in Movies	.65	.30
	j. World Series Rivals	.65	.30
	k. Rockey Marciano, Undefeated	.65	.30
	l. *I Love Lucy*	.65	.30
	m. Rock 'n' Roll	.65	.30
	n. Stock Car Racing	.65	.30
	o. Movies Go 3-D	.65	.30
	FDC *(May 26, 1999)*, any single		2.25
	FDC, pane of 15		15.00
	Four pane press sheet	40.00	
	Set of 2 blocks with vertical gutters	10.00	

1999. PROSTATE CANCER AWARENESS ISSUE focused attention on the second leading cause of cancer death (after lung cancer) in men and the second most common cancer (after skin cancer) in men. Designed by Michael Cronan, San Francisco, Calif. *Gravure by Avery Dennison (78.1 million printed), phosphored paper, self-adhesive, serpentine die cut 11.*

CM2062 *Prostate Cancer Awareness*

CM2062		MNHVF	UseVF
33¢	**multicolored**	.50	.20
	Plate block of 4	2.60	
	FDC *(May 28, 1999)*		1.90

1999. CALIFORNIA GOLD RUSH ISSUE honored the thousands of hopeful "Forty-Niners" who rushed to California after gold was discovered at Sutter's Mill in January 1848. Designed by Howard Paine, Delaplane, Va., illustrated by John Berkey, Excelsior, Minn. *Offset by Sterling Sommer for Ashton-Potter USA Ltd. (89,270,000 printed) in gummed panes of 20, perforated 11.*

CM2063 *Gold miners*

CM2063		MNHVF	UseVF
33¢	**multicolored**	.50	.20
	Plate block of 4	2.00	
	FDC *(June 18, 1999)*		1.90

1999. AQUARIUM FISH ISSUE displayed on a strip of four multicolored stamps in an illustrated sheetlet a fish tank scene with corals, sea anemones, fish, and other species found at reefs in different parts of the world. Designed by Richard Sheaff, Scottsdale, Ariz., illustrations by Teresa Fasolino, New York, N.Y. *Offset by Banknote Corporation of America (152,375,000 printed), serpentine die cut 11 1/2. Block tagging (7,618,500 panes) results in an untagged strip at top and bottom of each stamp. Overall tagging variety has tagging over entire pane.*

CM2064-2067 *Aquarium fish*

CM2064		MNHVF	UseVF
33¢	**Black-and-white fish,** block tagged	.50	.20
	z. Overall tagged	3.00	

CM2065		MNHVF	UseVF
33¢	**Thermometer,** block tagged	.50	.20
	z. Overall tagged	3.00	

CM2066		MNHVF	UseVF
33¢	**Blue-and-yellow fish,** block tagged	.50	.20
	z. Overall tagged	3.00	

CM2067		MNHVF	UseVF
33¢	**red-and-white fish,** block tagged	.50	.20
	z. Overall tagged	3.00	
	y. Se-tenant strip of 4 (CM2064-67)	2.00	
	Plate block of 8	4.00	
	FDC *(June 24, 1999)*, any single		2.00
	FDC, strip of 4		4.50
	y1. Pane of 20	10.00	
	Six pane press sheet	80.00	
	Set of 4 pairs with horizontal gutters	7.00	
	Block of 8 with horizontal gutter	8.00	
	Pair with vertical gutter	1.75	
	Cross-gutter block of 8	15.00	
	zy. Se-tenant strip of 4 (CM2064z-67z)	12.00	
	Plate block of 8	24.00	
	zy1. Overall tagged pane of 20	65.00	

1999. XTREME SPORTS ISSUE designed by Carl Herrman, Laguna Nigel, Calif., from photos by J. Grant Brittain (Skateboarding), Keith Mulligan (BMX Biking), Scott Spiker (Snowboarding), and Mike Powell (Inline Skating). Captured, in four multicolored stamps on an illustrated sheetlet, the speed and action of participants in four high-excitement and daring pastimes — skateboarding, BMX biking, snowboarding and in line skating. Slang words detectable only with a special USPS decoder appear on the stamps — "Gnarly," "Rad," "Stoked," and "Phat," respectively. *Gravure by Avery Dennison on phosphored paper (7,598,750 panes), self-adhesive serpentine die cut 11.*

CM2068 *Skateboarding*

CM2069 *BMX Biking*

CM2070 *Snowboarding*

CM2071 *In line Skating*

CM2068		MNHVF	UseVF
33¢	**Skateboarding**	.50	.20

CM2069		MNHVF	UseVF
33¢	**BMX Biking**	.50	.20

CM2070		MNHVF	UseVF
33¢	**Snowboarding**	.50	.20

CM2071		MNHVF	UseVF
33¢	**In line Skating**	.50	.20
	Plate block of 4	2.00	
	FDC *(June 25, 1999),* any single		1.50
	y. Block or strip of 4 (CM2068-71)	2.00	
	FDC, block or strip of 4		4.50
	y1. Pane of 20	10.00	
	Four pane top press sheet	52.00	
	Four pane bottom press sheet	52.00	
	Set of 2 pairs with horizontal gutters	3.50	
	Block of 4 with horizontal gutter	4.50	
	Set of 4 pairs with vertical gutters	7.00	
	Block of 8 with vertical gutter	8.00	
	Cross-gutter block of 8	15.00	

1999. AMERICAN GLASS ISSUE designed by Richard Sheaff, Scottsdale, Ariz. from photos by Robert Schlowsky, Weston, Mass. (Mold-Blown and Pressed Glass) and Nicholas Williams, Corning, N.Y. (Art Glass and Freeblown Glass). Showcased on an illustrated sheetlet American glassmaking designs and techniques from 18th to 20th century. Presented are examples of freeblown, mold-blown, pressed, and art glass. They were the first U.S. stamps to feature digital photography. Tagging was in selective-cut blocks only on the glass items in the stamps. *Offset by Sterling Sommer for Ashton-Potter USA (116,083,500 printed), (7,738,900 panes), perforated 11.*

CM2072 *Freeblown glass*

CM2073 *Mold-blown glass*

CM2074 *Pressed glass*

CM2075 *Art glass* B304

CM2072		MNHVF	UseVF
33¢	**Freeblown glass**	.50	.20

CM2073		MNHVF	UseVF
33¢	**Mold-blown glass**	.50	.20

CM2074		MNHVF	UseVF
33¢	**Pressed glass**	.50	.20

CM2075		MNHVF	UseVF
33¢	**Art glass**	.50	.20
	FDC *(June 29, 1999),* any single		2.00
	y. Block or strip of 4 (CM2072-75)	2.00	
	FDC, block of 4		5.50
	y1. Pane of 15	8.00	

1999. JAMES CAGNEY ISSUE in the Legends of Hollywood Series. Designed by Howard Paine, Delaplane, Va., illustrated by Thomas Blackshear, Colorado Springs, Colo. Honored the star of stage and screen (1899-1986) who was equally proficient playing a song-and-dance man or a tough guy. He appeared in 65 films, won his only Oscar playing George M. Cohan in *Yankee Doodle Dandy* (portrayed in the selvage illustration), and turned out numerous seminal performances of bad men, including *The Public Enemy* and *White Heat. Gummed pane of 20, gravure by American Packaging Corp. for Sennett Security Products (75.5 million printed), (3,775,000 panes), block tagged, perforated 11.*

2076 *James Cagney*

CM2076		MNHVF	UseVF
33¢	**multicolored**	.50	.20
	Plate block of 4	2.00	
	FDC *(July 22, 1999)*		1.90
	y. Pane of 20	10.00	
	Six pane press sheet	80.00	
	Pair with horizontal gutter	1.75	
	Pair with vertical gutter	2.50	
	Block of 8 with vertical gutter	11.00	
	Cross-gutter block of 8	15.00	

1999. HONORING THOSE WHO SERVED ISSUE paid tribute to the millions of military veterans, firefighters, and law enforcement officers who have risked or given their lives to protect the welfare of their fellow Americans. Designed by Richard Sheaff, Scottsdale, Ariz., and Uldis Purins, Newton, Mass. *Gravure by Avery Dennison on phosphored paper, (101.8 million printed), self-adhesive pane of 20, serpentine die cut 11.*

CM2077

CM2077		MNHVF	UseVF
33¢	**multicolored**	.50	.20
	Plate block of 4	2.00	
	FDC *(Aug. 16, 1999)*		1.90

1999. UNIVERSAL POSTAL UNION ISSUE commemorated 125 years of the world governing body for postal matters. Designed by Gerald Gallo, Bethesda, Md. The stamp was issued in Beijing, China. *Tagging was in selective-cut blocks only on the stars in the stamps. Gummed pane of 20, offset by Sterling Sommer for Ashton-Potter, USA, (43,150,000 printed), perforated 11.*

CM2078

CM2078		MNHVF	UseVF
45¢	**multicolored**	.90	.40
	Plate block of 4	3.60	
	FDC *(Aug. 25, 1999)*		2.50

1999. ALL ABOARD! ISSUE pictured watercolor illustrations of five legendary passenger trains of the 1930s and 1940s. Designed by Howard Paine, Delaplane, Va., illustrated by Ted Rose, Santa Fe, N.M. The Daylight, called "the Most Beautiful Train in the World," connected Los Angeles and San Francisco along Pacific Ocean beaches. The Congressional, which ran between New York City and Washington, D.C., boasted, "Every Mile Electrified," thanks to Public Works Administration help. The 20th Century Limited offered 16 hour travel between Chicago and New York. The Hiawatha traveled over 100 mph on its twice-daily run connecting Chicago, Milwaukee, and Minneapolis-St. Paul. The Super Chief, which ran between Chicago and Los Angeles, became known as "the Train of the Stars" because it was the preferred mode of transportation for Hollywood's elite. *Gummed pane of 20, offset by Ashton-Potter USA (120 million printed), block tagged, perforated 11.*

CM2079 *Daylight*

CM2080 *Congressional*

CM2081 *20th Century Limited*

CM2082 *Hiawatha*

CM2083 *Super Chief* B306

CM2079

		MNHVF	UseVF
33¢	multicolored	.50	.20

CM2080

		MNHVF	UseVF
33¢	multicolored	.50	.20

CM2081

		MNHVF	UseVF
33¢	multicolored	.50	.20

CM2082

		MNHVF	UseVF
33¢	multicolored	.50	.20

CM2083

		MNHVF	UseVF
33¢	multicolored	.50	.20
	Plate block of 10	6.50	
	FDC *(Aug. 26, 1999)*, any single		1.90
	y. Strip of 5 stamps (CM2079-83)	2.50	
	FDC, strip of 5		10.00
	y1. Pane of 20	10.00	
	Six pane press sheet	82.00	
	Set of 4 pairs with horizontal gutters	7.00	
	Block of 8 with horizontal gutter	8.00	
	Set of 5 pairs with vertical gutters	8.75	
	Block of 10 with vertical gutter	9.50	
	Cross-gutter block of 8	15.00	

1999. FREDERIC LAW OLMSTED ISSUE called attention to the ideals and artistry of one of America's most prolific park designers, who was a founder of American landscape architecture. Among many other projects, Olmsted designed New York's Central Park and the Capitol grounds in Washington, D.C. Designed by Ethel Kessler, Bethesda, Md. *Offset by Ashton-Potter USA Ltd. (42.5 million printed), gummed pane of 10 on phosphored paper, perforated 11.*

CM2084 *Frederic Law Olmsted*

CM2084

		MNHVF	UseVF
33¢	multicolored	.50	.20
	Plate block of 4	2.00	
	FDC *(Sept. 12, 1999)*		1.90

1999. HOLLYWOOD COMPOSERS ISSUE in the Legends of American Music Series. Featured six distinguished composers of music for films. Max Steiner, a pioneer of Hollywood composing provided music for more than 200 films, including *Gone With the Wind,* and won three Academy Awards. Dimitri Tiomkin, a concert pianist, won Oscars for his music for *High Noon, The High and the Mighty,* and *The Old Man and the Sea.* Alfred Newman pioneered a method of synchronizing film music that is still in use and won Oscars for films that included *Alexander's Ragtime Band, The Song of Bernadette, Love Is a Many Splendored Thing, The King and I,* and *Camelot.* Bernard Herrmann worked with Alfred Hitchcock on films such as *Vertigo* and *Psycho.* Franz Waxman was a cabaret pianist in Berlin before moving to Hollywood, where he composed music for more than 200 films and won Academy Awards for *Sunset Boulevard* and *A Place in the Sun.* Erich Wolfgang Korngold, a child prodigy in Vienna, won Oscars for *Anthony Adverse* and *The Adventures of Robin Hood.* Designed by Howard Paine, Delaplane, Va., illustrated by Drew Struzan, Pasadena, Calif. *Offset by Sterling Sommer for Ashton-Potter USA Ltd. (42.5 million printed), (2,125,000 gummed panes). Gummed pane of 20, block tagged, perforated 11.*

CM2085 *Max Steiner*

CM2086 *Dimitri Tiomkin*

CM2087 *Bernard Herrmann*

CM2088 *Franz Waxman*

CM2089 *Alfred Newman*

CM2090 *Erich Wolfgang Korngold*

CM2085

		MNHVF	UseVF
33¢	multicolored	.50	.20

CM2086

		MNHVF	UseVF
33¢	multicolored	.50	.20

CM2087

		MNHVF	UseVF
33¢	multicolored	.50	.20

CM2088

		MNHVF	UseVF
33¢	multicolored	.50	.20

CM2089

		MNHVF	UseVF
33¢	multicolored	.50	.20

CM2090

		MNHVF	UseVF
33¢	multicolored	4.00	
	Plate block of 6	4.00	
	y. Se-tenant block of 6 (CM2085-90)	4.00	
	FDC *(Sept. 16, 1999)*, any single		2.00
	FDC, block of 6		5.50
	y1. Pane of 20	10.00	

1999. CELEBRATE THE CENTURY 1960S ISSUE in the Celebrate the Century Series. Was the seventh in the series highlighting each decade of the 20th century. Designed by Carl Herrman, Laguna Nigel, Calif., illustrated by Keith Birdsong, Muskogee, Okla. *Offset with one stamp intaglio by Ashton-Potter USA Ltd. (120 million printed), (8 million panes), perforated 11 1/2.*

CM2091a-2091o *Celebrate the Century 1960s*

CM2091		MNHVF	UseVF
$4.95	**Pane of 15, multicolored** tagged	10.00	7.50
	a. Martin Luther King Jr.	.50	.25
	b. Woodstock	.50	.25
	c. Man Walks on Moon (intaglio)	.50	.25
	d. Green Bay Packers	.50	.25
	e. Star Trek	.50	.25
	f. Peace Corps	.50	.25
	g. Vietnam War	.50	.25
	h. Ford Mustang	.50	.25
	i. Barbie Doll	.50	.25
	j. Integrated circuit	.50	.25
	k. Lasers	.50	.25
	l. Super Bowl I	.50	.25
	m. Peace symbol	.50	.25
	n. Roger Maris, "61 in '61"	.50	.25
	o. The Beatles' "Yellow Submarine"	.50	.25
	FDC *(Sept. 17, 1999),* any single		2.40
	FDC, pane of 15		15.00
	Four pane press sheet	40.00	
	Set of 2 blocks with vertical gutters	10.00	

1999. BROADWAY SONGWRITERS ISSUE Final installment in the Legends of American Music Series. Honored, on six stamps, nine world-renowned songwriters whose works on Broadway delighted music lovers for decades. Brothers Ira (lyrics) and George (music) Gershwin worked together from the early 1920s to 1937 for shows including *Of Thee I Sing* (1931), the first musical to win a Pulitzer Prize. Alan Jay Lerner and Frederick Loewe collaborated from 1942 until the 1970s on musicals including *Brigadoon, Paint Your Wagon, My Fair Lady,* and *Camelot.* Lorenz Hart is best known for memorable turns of phrase in such musicals as *Pal Joey* and *Babes in Arms.* Richard Rogers and Oscar Hammerstein II were noted for innovative integration of music and plot in musicals such as *Oklahoma!, Carousel, South Pacific, The King and I,* and *The Sound of Music.* Besides his signature *Music Man,* Meredith Willson wrote *The*

Unsinkable Molly Brown and *Here's Love.* Frank Loesser wrote *Guys and Dolls, The Most Happy Fella,* and *How To Succeed in Business Without Really Trying.* Designed by Howard Paine, Delaplane, Va., illustrated by Drew Struzan, Pasadena, Calif. *Offset by Sterling Sommer for Ashton-Potter USA Ltd. (42.5 million printed), (2,125,000 panes). Gummed pane of 20, block tagged, perforated 11.*

CM2092 *Ira & George Gershwin;* CM2093 *Alan Jay Lerner & Frederick Loewe;* CM2094 *Lorenz Hart;* CM2095 *Richard Rogers & Oscar Hammerstein II;* CM2096 *Meredith Willson;* CM2097 *Frank Loesser*

CM2092		MNHVF	UseVF
33¢	multicolored	.50	.20
CM2093		MNHVF	UseVF
33¢	multicolored	.50	.20
CM2094		MNHVF	UseVF
33¢	multicolored	.50	.20
CM2095		MNHVF	UseVF
33¢	multicolored	.50	.20
CM2096		MNHVF	UseVF
33¢	multicolored	.50	.20
CM2097		MNHVF	UseVF
33¢	multicolored	.50	.20
	Plate block of 6	3.00	
	y. Se-tenant block of 6 (CM2092-97)	3.00	
	FDC *(Sept. 21, 1999),* any single		2.00
	FDC, block of 6		5.50
	y1. Pane of 20	10.00	

1999. INSECTS AND SPIDERS ISSUE in the Classic Collection Series. Presented 20 lifelike crawly creatures aimed at appealing to children's curiosity. Designed by Carl Herrman, Laguna Nigel, Calif., illustrated by Steven Buchanan, Winsted, Conn., from specimens at the Connecticut Agriculture Experiment Station, New Haven, Conn. *Phosphor tagging on stamps took the shape of the bugs. Printing on the back of each stamp included its Latin name and a description. Offset by Ashton-Potter USA (84.7 million printed), (4,235,000 panes), perforated 11.*

CM2098		MNHVF	UseVF
33¢	**Pane of 20, multicolored**	10.00	.50
	a. Black widow spider	.50	.20
	b. Elderberry longhorn beetle	.50	.20
	c. Lady beetle	.50	.20
	d. Yellow garden spider	.50	.20
	e. Dogbane beetle	.50	.20
	f. Flower fly	.50	.20
	g. Assassin bug	.50	.20
	h. Ebony jewelring damselfly	.50	.20

INSECTS & SPIDERS

CM2098 *Insects and Spiders*

i.	Velvet ant	.50	.20
j.	Monarch caterpillar	.50	.20
k.	Monarch butterfly	.50	.20
l.	Eastern Hercules beetle	.50	.20
m.	Bombardier beetle	.50	.20
n.	Dung beetle	.50	.20
o.	Spotted water beetle	.50	.20
p.	True katydid	.50	.20
q.	Spinybacked spider	.50	.20
r.	Periodical cicada	.50	.20
s.	Scorpionfly	.50	.20
t.	Jumping spider	.50	.20
FDC *(Oct. 1, 1999),* any single			2.25
FDC, pane of 20			16.00
Four pane press sheet		52.00	
Set of 4 pairs with horizontal gutters		7.00	
Block of 8 with horizontal gutter		8.00	
Set of 5 pairs with vertical gutters		8.75	
Block of 10 with vertical gutter		9.50	
Cross-gutter block of 20		20.00	

1999. HANUKKAH ISSUE in the Holiday Celebrations Series. A redenominated version of a stamp that kicked off the series in 1996, it features a Jewish menorah for the Festival of Lights. Designed by Hannah Smotrich. *Gravure by Avery Dennison (65 million printed), serpentine die cut 11.*

CM2099 *Festival of Lights*

CM2099

		MNHVF	UseVF
33¢	multicolored	.50	.20
	Plate block of 4	2.00	
	FDC *(Oct. 8, 1999)*		1.50

1999. NORTH ATLANTIC TREATY ORGANIZATION ISSUE Featured the Dove of Peace to celebrate 50 years of the European defense organization. Its release date was delayed while NATO bombed Serbia during the Kosovo crisis. Designed by Michael Cronan, San

Francisco, Calif. *Gummed pane of 20, gravure by Sterling Sommer for Ashton-Potter USA (44.6 million printed) on phosphored paper, perforated 11.*

CM2100 *Dove of Peace*

CM2100

		MNHVF	UseVF
33¢	multicolored	.50	.20
	Plate block of 4	2.00	
	FDC *(Oct. 13, 1999)*		1.50

1999. KWANZAA ISSUE in the Holiday Celebrations Series. A redenominated version of a stamp issued in 1997, it pictures a couple in colorful African garb and the seven symbols of the relatively new year-end celebration. Designed by Synthia St. James. *Self-adhesive pane of 20, gravure by Avery Dennison (95 million printed) on phosphored paper, serpentine die cut 11.*

CM2101 *African couple*

CM2101

		MNHVF	UseVF
33¢	multicolored	.50	.20
	Plate block of 4	2.00	
	FDC *(Oct. 29, 1999)*		1.50

1999. CELEBRATE THE CENTURY 1970S ISSUE in the Celebrate the Century Series was the eighth in a series highlighting each decade of the 20th century. Designed by Howard Paine, Delaplane, Va., illustrations by Kazuhiko Sano, Mill Valley, Calif. *Offset (with one stamp intaglio) by Ashton-Potter USA (90 million printed), (6 million panes), perforated 11 1/2.*

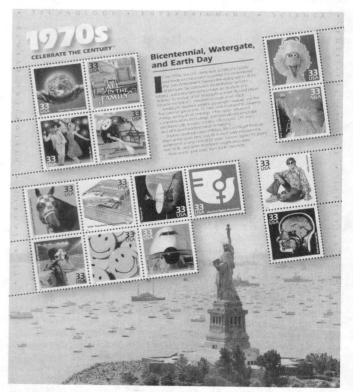

CM2102a-2102o *Celebrate the Century 1970s*

CM2102		MNHVF	UseVF
$4.95	**Pane of 15,** tagged	10.00	7.00
	a. Earth Day Celebrated	.50	.25
	b. TV Series ("All in the Family")	.50	.25
	c. "Sesame Street"	.50	.25
	d. Disco Music	.50	.25
	e. (Pittsburgh) Steelers Win Four Super Bowls	.50	.25
	f. U.S. Celebrates 200th Birthday	.50	.25
	g. Secretariat Wins Triple Crown	.50	.25
	h. VCRs Transform Entertainment (intaglio)	.50	.25
	i. "Pioneer 10"	.50	.25
	j. Women's Rights Movement	.50	.25
	k. 1970s Fashion	.50	.25
	l. "Monday Night Football"	.50	.25
	m. America Smiles	.50	.25
	n. Jumbo Jets	.50	.25
	o. Medical Imaging	.50	.25
	FDC *(Nov. 18, 1999),* any single		2.00
	FDC, pane of 15		15.00
	Four pane press sheet	40.00	
	Set of 2 blocks with vertical gutters	10.00	

1999. YEAR 2000 ISSUE used a traditional, festive "New Year's Baby" illustration by J.C. Leyendecker (1874-1951) that originally appeared on the cover of the Jan. 2, 1937, issue of the *Saturday Evening Post.* The "1999" date is included at lower right in the vignette, and a microprint "USPS" is at the bottom of the cowbell. Designed by Carl Herrman, Carlsbad, Calif. *Self-adhesive pane of 20, offset by Banknote Corporation of America (120 million printed), block tagged, self-adhesive, serpentine die cut 11.*

 CM2103 *"New Year's Baby"*

CM2103		MNHVF	UseVF
33¢	**multicolored**	.50	.20
	Plate block of 4	2.00	
	FDC *(Dec. 27, 1999)*		1.50

2000. YEAR OF THE DRAGON ISSUE in the Lunar New Year Series. Was the eighth in a series featuring the creatures of the Chinese zodiac designed in paper cut fashion and calligraphy by artist Clarence Lee, Honolulu, Hawaii. *Gummed pane of 20, offset by Ashton-Potter (56 million printed), on phosphored paper, perforated 11 1/4, (56 million printed).*

 CM2104 *Dragon*

CM2104		MNHVF	UseVF
33¢	**multicolored**	.50	.20
	Plate block of 4	2.00	
	FDC *(Jan. 6, 2000)*		1.25

2000. CELEBRATE THE CENTURY 1980S ISSUE was the ninth in the Celebrate the Century Series highlighting each decade of the 20th century. Designed by Carl Herrman, Carlsbad, Calif. *Gummed pane of 15, offset by Ashton-Potter USA (90 million printed), perforated 11 1/2.*

CM2105		MNHVF	UseVF
33¢	**Pane of 15, multicolored,** tagged	10.00	7.00
	a. Space Shuttle Program	.50	.25
	b. *Cats* Broadway Show	.50	.25
	c. San Francisco 49ers	.50	.25
	d. American Hostages Freed	.50	.25
	e. Figure Skating	.50	.25
	f. Cable TV	.50	.25

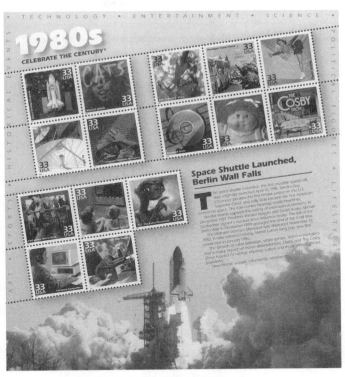

CM2105a-2105o *Celebrate the Century 1980s*

		MNHVF	UseVF
	g. Vietnam Veterans Memorial	.50	.25
	h. Compact Discs	.50	.25
	i. Cabbage Patch Kids	.50	.25
	j. *The Cosby Show*	.50	.25
	k. Fall of the Berlin Wall	.50	.25
	l. Video Games	.50	.25
	m. *ET The Extra-Terrestrial* Movie	.50	.25
	n. Personal Computers	.50	.25
	o. Hip-Hop Culture	.50	.25
	FDC *(Jan. 12, 2000),* any single		2.00
	FDC, pane of 15		15.00
	Four pane press sheet	40.00	
	Block with vertical gutter	7.50	

2000. PATRICIA ROBERTS HARRIS ISSUE in the Black Heritage Series. The daughter of a Pullman dining car waiter, Patricia Roberts Harris (1924-1985) graduated first in her law school class and became known as "a woman of firsts." She was the first African-American woman ambassador (to Luxembourg, under President Lyndon Johnson), the first black to hold a U.S. cabinet position (secretary of Housing and Urban Development under President Carter), the first to hold two cabinet posts (adding secretary of Health, Education and Welfare — then HHS), the first black woman on a major company's corporate board of directors, and the first black woman to serve as dean of the Howard University School of Law. This is the 23rd stamp in the series. Designed by Howard Paine. *Self-adhesive pane of 20, offset by Ashton Potter USA Ltd. (150 million printed) on phosphored paper, perforated 11 1/2x11 1/4.*

 CM2106 *Patricia Roberts Harris*

CM2106		MNHVF	UseVF
33¢	**multicolored**	.50	.20

Plate block of 4	2.00	
FDC *(Jan. 27, 2000)*		1.25

2000. U.S. NAVY SUBMARINES ISSUE was issued at Groton, Conn., which in World War I was named the first U.S. submarine base and in 1954 became the launch site of the USS *Nautilus,* the first nuclear-powered sub and the only other one to be pictured on a U.S. stamp (CM437). Images depict the USS *Holland* (60¢), *S*-class submarine (22¢), *Gato*-class submarine ($3.20), *Los Angeles*-class attack submarine (33¢), *Ohio*-class intercontinental ballistic missile submarine (55¢). Designed by Carl Herrman, Carlsbad, Calif. *Prestige booklet pane of 5, offset by Banknote Corporation of America (1.5 million booklets printed), (15 million stamps printed). Gummed, block tagged, perforated 11.*

CM2107 *USS* Holland; CM2108 S-*class submarine;* CM2109 Gato-*class submarine;* CM2110 Los Angeles-*class attack submarine;* CM2111 Ohio-*class ICBM submarine* B309

CM2107		**MNHVF**	**UseVF**
60¢	**USS** *Holland*	1.20	1.00
CM2108		**MNHVF**	**UseVF**
22¢	***S*-class submarine**	.40	.30
CM2109		**MNHVF**	**UseVF**
$3.20	***Gato*-class submarine**	6.00	2.50
CM2110		**MNHVF**	**UseVF**
33¢	***Los Angeles*-class attack submarine**	.60	.30
CM2111		**MNHVF**	**UseVF**
55¢	***Ohio*-class ICBM submarine**	1.00	1.00
	n. Booklet pane of 5 plus descriptive text	10.00	7.00
	FDC *(March 27, 2000),* booklet pane		12.00

CM2111n was issued with two different descriptive texts.

2000. LOS ANGELES-CLASS SUBMARINE ISSUE Designed by Carl Herrman, Carlsbad, Calif. *Gummed pane of 20, offset by Banknote Corporation of America (65,150,000 printed) with microprinting USPS at base of sail. Prephosphored paper, perforated 11.*

CM2112 Los Angeles-*class submarine*

CM2112		**MNHVF**	**UseVF**
33¢	**multicolored**	.50	.20
	Plate block of 4	2.00	
	FDC *(March 27, 2000)*		1.50

2000. PACIFIC COAST RAIN FOREST ISSUE second in the Nature of America Series, featured 10 plants and animals in an overall scene. Designed by John D. Dawson of Hilo, Hawaii (art director Ethel

Kessler of Bethesda, Md.) *Self-adhesive pane of 10, offset by Banknote Corporation of America (100 million printed), with microprinting USPS. Block tagged, serpentine die cut 11 1/4x11 1/2 (vertical stamps) or 11 1/2 (horizontal stamps).*

CM2113a *Roosevelt elk;* CM2113b *Harlequin duck;* CM2113c *Snail-eating ground beetle;* CM2113d *American dipper;* CM2113e *Winter wren;* CM2113f *Douglas squirrel;* CM2113g *Pacific giant salamander;* CM2113h *Western tiger swallowtail;* CM2113i *Banana slug;* CM2113j *Cutthroat trout*

CM2113		**MNHVF**	**UseVF**
33¢	**multicolored,** Pane of 10	7.50	—
	a. Roosevelt elk	.50	.20
	b. Harlequin duck	.50	.20
	c. Snail-eating ground beetle	.50	.20
	d. American dipper	.50	.20
	e. Winter wren	.50	.20
	f. Douglas squirrel	.50	.20
	g. Pacific giant salamander	.50	.20
	h. Western tiger swallowtail	.50	.20
	i. Banana slug	.50	.20
	j. Cutthroat trout	.50	.20
	FDC *(March 29, 2000),* any single		1.50
	FDC, pane of 10		10.00
	Six pane press sheet	40.00	
	Pair with horizontal gutter	6.00	
	Pair with vertical gutter	6.00	
	Cross-gutter block of 4	13.50	

2000. LOUISE NEVELSON ISSUE honored a pioneering sculptor who arranged carved, recycled, and painted wooden objects in boxes and stacked to create sculptural walls. Nevelson (1899-1988) was born in Kiev and came to the United States with her family in 1905. She lived and worked in New York City for most of her life. The pane selvage includes a portrait of the artist. Designed by Ethel Kessler, Bethesda, Md. *Gummed pane of 20, offset by Ashton-Potter USA Ltd. (55 million printed). Block tagged, perforated 11.*

CM2114 Silent Music I; CM2115 Royal Tide I; CM2116 Black Chord; CM2117 Night-Sphere-Light; CM2118 Wedding Chapel I

CM2114		**MNHVF**	**UseVF**
33¢	**multicolored**	.50	.20
CM2115		**MNHVF**	**UseVF**
33¢	**multicolored**	.50	.20
CM2116		**MNHVF**	**UseVF**
33¢	**multicolored**	.50	.20
CM2117		**MNHVF**	**UseVF**
33¢	**multicolored**	.50	.20

CM2118		MNHVF	UseVF
33¢	multicolored	.50	.20
	Plate block of 10	5.00	
	FDC *(April 6, 2000)*, any single		2.00
	y. Se-tenant strip of 5 (CM2114-18)	2.50	
	FDC, strip of 5		5.50
	y1. Pane of 20	10.00	

2000. EDWIN POWELL HUBBLE ISSUE honored an American astronomer who vastly expanded mankind's concept of the universe. The five designs feature remarkable images of distant celestial features captured by the orbiting Hubble Space Telescope named after him. The selvage depicts Hubble (1889-1953) at the 48-inch Schmidt Telescope at Palomar Observatory. Designed by Phil Jordan, Falls Church, Va. *Gummed pane of 20, gravure by Sennett Security Products (105,350,000 printed). Block tagged, perforated 11.*

CM2119-23

CM2119		MNHVF	UseVF
33¢	**Eagle Nebula**	.50	.20
CM2120		MNHVF	UseVF
33¢	**Ring Nebula**	.50	.20
CM2121		MNHVF	UseVF
33¢	**Lagoon Nebula**	.50	.20
CM2122		MNHVF	UseVF
33¢	**Egg Nebula**	.50	.20
CM2123		MNHVF	UseVF
33¢	**Galaxy NGC 1316**	.50	.20
	Plate block of 10	5.00	
	FDC *(April 10, 2000)*, any single		2.00
	y. Se-tenant strip of 5 (CM2119-23)	2.50	
	FDC, strip of 5		5.50
	y1. Pane of 20	10.00	

2000. AMERICAN SAMOA ISSUE marked the 100th anniversary of the union between the U.S. and the South Pacific Ocean territory. The stamp features an 'alia, the traditional double canoe of the Samoans, sailing near Sunuitao Peak on the island of Ofu. The territory consists of five volcanic islands and two coral atolls. Designed by Howard Paine, Delaplane, Va. *Gummed pane of 20, offset by Ashton-Potter USA Ltd. (16 million printed) with microprinting Samoa. Prephosphored paper, perforated 11.*

 CM2124 *American Samoa canoe*

CM2124		MNHVF	UseVF
33¢	multicolored	.50	.20
	Plate block of 4	2.00	
	FDC *(April 17, 2000)*		1.50

2000. LIBRARY OF CONGRESS ISSUE Designed by Ethel Kessler, from a photo by Michael Freeman, London, England. *Gummed pane of 20, offset with microprinting USPS by Ashton-Potter USA Ltd. (55 million printed), block tagged, perforated 11.*

 CM2125 *Library of Congress*

CM2125		MNHVF	UseVF
33¢	multicolored	.50	.20
	Plate block of 4	2.00	
	FDC *(April 24, 2000)*		1.50
	y. Pane of 20	10.00	

2000. CELEBRATE THE CENTURY 1990-1999 ISSUE The 10th and last in the Celebrate the Century Series highlighting each decade of the 20th century. Designed by Howard Paine, Delaplane, Va. *Gummed pane of 15, offset by Ashton-Potter USA Ltd. (82.5 million printed), (5.5 million panes). Block tagged, perforated 11 1/2.*

CM2126a-2126o *Celebrate the Century 1990s*

CM2126		MNHVF	UseVF
33¢	**Pane of 15, multicolored** tagged	10.00	7.00
	a. New Baseball Records	.50	.20
	b. Gulf War	.50	.20
	c. Sitcom Sensation *(Seinfeld)*	.50	.20
	d. Extreme Sports	.50	.20
	e. Improving Education	.50	.20
	f. Computer Art and Graphics	.50	.20
	g. Recovering Species	.50	.20
	h. Return to Space	.50	.20
	i. Special Olympics	.50	.20
	j. Virtual Reality	.50	.20
	k. *Jurassic Park*	.50	.20
	l. Blockbuster Film *(Titanic)*	.50	.20
	m. Sport Utlility Vehicles	.50	.20
	n. World Wide Web	.50	.20
	o. Cellular Phones	.50	.20

	MNHVF	UseVF
FDC *(May 2, 2000),* any single	2.00	
FDC, pane of 15	15.00	
Four pane press sheet	40.00	
Block with vertical gutter	7.50	

2000. WILE E. COYOTE & ROAD RUNNER ISSUE

The fourth in the Warner Bros. Cartoon Characters Series, featured the nonchalant Road Runner and his conniving but perennially thwarted nemisis, Wile E. Coyote. Designed and illustrated by Ed Wleczyk, Los Angeles, Calif. *Offset with microprinting by Banknote Corporation of America (300 million printed), (30 million panes), serpentine die cut 11.*

CM2127-CM2128 *Wile E. Coyote & Road Runner*

CM2127

33¢		MNHVF	UseVF
	multicolored	7.50	
	Pane of 10, tagged (30,000,000 panes)	7.50	
n.	Right half of pane (single die cut CM2127a superimposed on enlarged image)	1.00	1.00
n1.	Left half of pane (block of 9 CM2127a)	6.00	
a.	33¢ single	.75	.20
	FDC *(April 26, 2000),* Pane of 10		10.00
	FDC, single		2.00
	Six pane top press sheet	45.00	
	Six pane bottom press sheet	45.00	
	Pair with horizontal gutter	1.75	
	Pair with vertical gutter	3.50	
	Cross-gutter block of 9	15.00	

CM2128

33¢		MNHVF	UseVF
	multicolored	7.50	
	Pane of 10, tagged	7.50	
n.	Right half of pane (single imperforate CM2128a superimposed on enlarged image)	1.00	
n1.	Left half of pane (block of 9 CM2128a)	6.00	
a.	33¢ single	.75	.20
	FDC *(April 26, 2000),* Pane of 10, 1 imperforate		15.00
	FDC, Pane of 1 imperforate		12.00

2000. DISTINGUISHED SOLDIERS ISSUE

saluted four American war heroes. John L. Hines (1868-1968) took part in the Battle of San Juan Hill in the Spanish-American War, was adjutant to Gen. John J. Pershing in the Mexican Expedition, and was promoted from major to major general during World War I and succeeded Pershing as Army Chief of Staff in 1924. Omar Bradley (1893-1981) commanded the American ground forces in the invasion of Normandy during World War II, the largest American field command in history. He headed the Veterans Administration after the war and became the first chairman of the Joint Chiefs of Staff in 1949. Alvin C. York (1887-1964) won the Medal of Honor for his exploits in a battle at the Argonne Forest during World War I. He was credited with killing 25 Germans, capturing 132 and silencing 35 machine guns. It was "the greatest thing accomplished by any private soldier of all the armies of Europe," according to Allied Commander Marshall Ferdinand Foch. Audie L. Murphy (1924-1971) won the Medal of Honor for his actions during a German attack in World War II. Ordering the men to retreat, he

remained to man a machine gun and break up the attack, killing 240 of the enemy. He wrote a book about his war experiences and played himself in a motion picture based upon it. Designed by Phil Jordan, Falls Church, Va. *Offset by Sterling Sommer (55 million printed), (2,750,000 panes). Gummed pane of 20, block tagged, perforated 11.*

CM2129 *John L. Hines;* CM2130 *Omar Bradley;* CM2131 *Alvin C. York;* CM2132 *Audie L. Murphy*

CM2129

33¢		MNHVF	UseVF
	multicolored	.50	.20

CM2130

33¢		MNHVF	UseVF
	multicolored	.50	.20

CM2131

33¢		MNHVF	UseVF
	multicolored	.50	.20

CM2132

33¢		MNHVF	UseVF
	multicolored	.50	.20
	Plate block of 4	2.00	
y.	Se-tenant block or strip of 4 (CM2129-32)	2.00	
	FDC *(May 3, 2000),* any single		2.00
	FDC, block of 4		4.25
y1.	Pane of 20	10.00	

2000. SUMMER SPORTS ISSUE

portrayed through a blurred photograph the speed of a track event. Designed by Richard Sheaff, Scottsdale, Ariz., from a photograph by David Madison, Portola Valley, Calif. *Offset, with microprinting "USPS" under the runner's numeral 4, by Ashton-Potter, USA (90.6 million printed). Gummed pane of 20, block tagged, perforated 11.*

CM2133 *Runners*

CM2133

33¢		MNHVF	UseVF
	multicolored	.50	.20
	Plate block of 4	2.00	
	FDC *(May 5, 2000)*		1.50

2000. ADOPTION ISSUE

intended to raise awareness that more than 100,000 children are available for adoption in the United States each year. Designed by Greg Berger, Bethesda, Md. *Offset with microprinting "USPS" at corner of house, by Banknote Corporation of America. Self-adhesive pane of 20, block tagged, serpentine die cut 11 1/2.*

CM2134 *Adoption awareness*

CM2134		MNHVF	UseVF
33¢	multicolored	.50	.20
	Plate block of 4	2.00	
	FDC *(May 10, 2000)*		1.50
	y. Pane of 20	10.00	

2000. YOUTH TEAM SPORTS ISSUE captured typical moments of kids playing four popular team sports. Photos were by William Sallaz, basketball; Mike Powell, football; Zoran Milich, soccer; and Bob Wickley, baseball. Designed by Derry Noyes, Washington, D.C. *Offset by Sterling Sommer (88 million printed). Gummed pane of 20, block tagged, perforated 11.*

CM2135 *Basketball*; CM2136 *Football*; CM2137 *Soccer*; CM2138 *Baseball*

CM2135		MNHVF	UseVF
33¢	multicolored	.50	.20
CM2136		MNHVF	UseVF
33¢	multicolored	.50	.20
CM2137		MNHVF	UseVF
33¢	multicolored	.50	.20
CM2138		MNHVF	UseVF
33¢	multicolored	.50	.20
	Plate block of 4	2.00	
	FDC *(May 27, 2000)*, any single		2.00
	y. Se-tenant block or strip of 4 (CM2135-38)	2.00	
	FDC, block or strip of 4		4.25
	y1. Pane of 20	10.00	

2000. STARS AND STRIPES ISSUE in the Classic Collection Series tracked the 225-year evolution of the American flag, with text on the backs of the stamps written by Dr. Whitney Smith of the Flag Research Center. Designed by Richard Sheaff, Scottsdale, Ariz. *Offset by Sennett Security Products (80 million printed). Gummed pane of 20, block tagged, perforated 10 1/2x11.*

CM2139		MNHVF	UseVF
33¢	multicolored	.50	.20
CM2140		MNHVF	UseVF
33¢	multicolored	.50	.20
CM2141		MNHVF	UseVF
33¢	multicolored	.50	.20
CM2142		MNHVF	UseVF
33¢	multicolored	.50	.20
CM2143		MNHVF	UseVF
33¢	multicolored	.50	.20
CM2144		MNHVF	UseVF
33¢	multicolored	.50	.20
CM2145		MNHVF	UseVF
33¢	multicolored	.50	.20
CM2146		MNHVF	UseVF
33¢	multicolored	.50	.20
CM2147		MNHVF	UseVF
33¢	multicolored	.50	.20

THE STARS AND STRIPES

CM2139 *Sons of Liberty Flag, 1775*, represented the unity of the 13 colonies, probably inspired the stripes in Old Glory; CM2140 *New England Flag, 1775*, featured a pine tree and red, white and blue stripes; CM2141 *Forster Flag, 1775*, captured from the British, the altered red and white canton represented the colonies; CM2142 *Continental Colors, 1776*, carried the British Union Jack as a canton and 13 stripes; CM2143 *Francis Hopkinson Flag, 1777*, constituted the first "Stars and Stripes"; CM2144 *Brandywine Flag, 1777*, may have been a militia color carried at the Battle of Brandywine; CM2145 *John Paul Jones Flag, 1779*, was hoisted in victory when Bonhomme Richard *captured* HMS Serapis; CM2146 *Pierre L'Enfant Flag, 1783*, was sketched by the man who drew up the original plans for the layout of Washington, D.C.; CM2147 *Indian Peace Flag, 1803*, displayed the U.S. coat of arms and was presented to friendly Indian nations by the government; CM2148 *Easton Flag, 1814*, presented to volunteers from Easton, Pa., in the War of 1812, reversed the official placement of the stars and stripes; CM2149 *Star-Spangled Banner, 1814*, featured the "broad stripes and bright stars" that inspired Francis Scott Key to write the poem that became our national anthem; CM2150 *Bennington Flag, c.1820*, has an uncertain origin; CM2151 *Great Star Flag, 1837*, contained its stars in a star pattern; CM2152 *29-Star Flag, 1847*, featured a diamond pattern of stars in the canton, with stars for four more states added in the corners; CM2153 *Fort Sumter Flag, 1861*, was flying over the fort at Charleston, S.C., when the first shots of the Civil War were fired; CM2154 *Centennial Flag, 1876*, was unofficial but reflected the patriotism of the people who made it; CM2155 *38-Star Flag, 1877*, features another imaginative star design; rows did not become standard until 1912; CM2156 *Peace Flag, 1891*, carried the Stars and Stripes within a field of white; CM2157 *48-Star Flag, 1912*, was official for 47 years, the longest period for any fixed star pattern; CM2158 *50-Star Flag, 1960*, represents the current configuration

CM2148		MNHVF	UseVF
33¢	multicolored	.50	.20
CM2149		MNHVF	UseVF
33¢	multicolored	.50	.20
CM2150		MNHVF	UseVF
33¢	multicolored	.50	.20
CM2151		MNHVF	UseVF
33¢	multicolored	.50	.20

CM2152		MNHVF	UseVF
33¢	multicolored	.50	.20
CM2153		MNHVF	UseVF
33¢	multicolored	.50	.20
CM2154		MNHVF	UseVF
33¢	multicolored	.50	.20
CM2155		MNHVF	UseVF
33¢	multicolored	.50	.20
CM2156		MNHVF	UseVF
33¢	multicolored	.50	.20
CM2157		MNHVF	UseVF
33¢	multicolored	.50	.20
CM2158		MNHVF	UseVF
33¢	multicolored	.50	.20
	FDC (June 14, 2000), any single		2.00
	FDC, pane of 20		16.00
	y. Pane of 20	10.00	
	Six pane press sheet	80.00	
	Set of 4 pairs with horizontal gutters	7.00	
	Block of 8 with horizontal gutter	8.00	
	Set of 5 pairs with vertical gutters	8.75	
	Block of 10 with vertical gutter	9.50	
	Cross-gutter block of 20	20.00	

2000. LEGENDS OF BASEBALL ISSUE in the Classic Collections Series honored 20 players chosen as Major League Baseball's All-Century Team. Designed by Phil Jordan, Falls Church, Va., with illustrations by Joseph Saffold, Savannah, Ga. *Offset by Ashton-Potter, USA (225 million printed). Self-adhesive pane of 20, block tagged, serpentine die cut 11 1/4.*

CM2159 *Jackie Robinson;* CM2160 *Eddie Collins;* CM2161 *Christy Mathewson;* CM2162 *Ty Cobb;* CM2163 *George Sisler;* CM2164 *Rogers Hornsby;* CM2165 *Mickey Cochrane;* CM2166 *Babe Ruth;* CM2167 *Walter Johnson;* CM2168 *Roberto Clemente;* CM2169 *Lefty Grove;* CM2170 *Tris Speaker;* CM2171 *Cy Young;* CM2172 *Jimmie Foxx;* CM2173 *Pie Traynor;* CM2174 *Satchel Paige;* CM2175 *Honus Wagner;* CM2176 *Josh Gibson;* CM2177 *Dizzy Dean;* CM2178 *Lou Gehrig*

CM2159		MNHVF	UseVF
33¢	multicolored	.50	.20
CM2160		MNHVF	UseVF
33¢	multicolored	.50	.20

CM2161		MNHVF	UseVF
33¢	multicolored	.50	.20
CM2162		MNHVF	UseVF
33¢	multicolored	.50	.20
CM2163		MNHVF	UseVF
33¢	multicolored	.50	.20
CM2164		MNHVF	UseVF
33¢	multicolored	.50	.20
CM2165		MNHVF	UseVF
33¢	multicolored	.50	.20
CM2166		MNHVF	UseVF
33¢	multicolored	.50	.20
CM2167		MNHVF	UseVF
33¢	multicolored	.50	.20
CM2168		MNHVF	UseVF
33¢	multicolored	.50	.20
CM2169		MNHVF	UseVF
33¢	multicolored	.50	.20
CM2170		MNHVF	UseVF
33¢	multicolored	.50	.20
CM2171		MNHVF	UseVF
33¢	multicolored	.50	.20
CM2172		MNHVF	UseVF
33¢	multicolored	.50	.20
CM2173		MNHVF	UseVF
33¢	multicolored	.50	.20
CM2174		MNHVF	UseVF
33¢	multicolored	.50	.20
CM2175		MNHVF	UseVF
33¢	multicolored	.50	.20
CM2176		MNHVF	UseVF
33¢	multicolored	.50	.20
CM2177		MNHVF	UseVF
33¢	multicolored	.50	.20
CM2178		MNHVF	UseVF
33¢	multicolored	.50	.20
	FDC (July 6, 2000), any single		2.00
	FDC, pane of 20		16.00
	y. Pane of 20	10.00	
	Six pane press sheet	80.00	
	Set of 5 pairs with horizontal gutters	8.75	
	Block of 10 with horizontal gutter	9.50	
	Set of 4 pairs with vertical gutters	7.00	
	Block of 8 with vertical gutter	8.00	
	Cross-gutter block of 20	20.00	

2000. SPACE ACHIEVEMENT AND EXPLORATION ISSUE was the first holographic stamp and first circular stamp issued by the United States. The Express Mail rate hologram, on a souvenir sheet for World Stamp Expo 2000 (which had a space theme), showed the western hemisphere of the Earth from space. (For previous hologram envelopes, see Minkus Nos. EN917, EN918, EN925, and EN945.) Designed by Richard Sheaff, Scottsdale, Ariz. *Gravure and hologram by Sennett Security Products. Perforated 10 1/2. (1,695,000 printed). Untagged.*

CM2179
Earth from space

CM2179		MNHVF	UseVF
$11.75	**multicolored**	22.00	10.00
	FDC *(July 7, 2000)*		25.00
	y. Sheetlet	22.00	11.00

The foil hologram is affixed with water-soluble adhesive and may release from the stamp while soaking.

2000. LANDING ON THE MOON ISSUE was a second Express Mail rate hologram stamp issued on an illustrated sheetlet of one during World Stamp Expo 2000. It depicted the Lunar Lander blasting off from the Moon, formed with computer images and a model of the lander. The selvage illustration was a photo of astronaut Charles M. Duke Jr., taken by astronaut John W. Young during the Apollo 16 mission in April 1972. Designed by Richard Sheaff, Scottsdale, Ariz. *Gravure and hologram by Sennett Security Products. Perforated 10 1/2. (1,695,000 printed.) Untagged.*

CM2180 *Lunar Lander blasting off from the Moon*

CM2180		MNHVF	UseVF
$11.75	**multicolored**	22.00	10.00
	FDC *(July 8, 2000)*		25.00
	y. Sheetlet	22.00	11.00

The foil hologram is affixed with water-soluble adhesive and may release from the stamp while soaking.

2000. ESCAPING THE GRAVITY OF EARTH ISSUE featured two more hologram stamps on an illustrated sheetlet issued at World Stamp Expo 2000. The Priority Mail rate stamps showed a computer-generated image of a space shuttle docking with the International Space Station (CM2181) and a model of astronauts fabricating the International Space Station (CM2182). The selvage showed astronauts David Leestma (with the red stripes on his legs) and Kathryn Sullivan in the cargo bay of the Challenger space shuttle during an October 1984 mission. Designed by Richard Sheaff, Scottsdale, Ariz. *Gravure and hologram by Sennett Security Products. Perforated 10 1/2. (1,695,000 printed.) Untagged.*

ESCAPING THE GRAVITY OF EARTH

CM2181 *Space shuttle;* CM2182 *Astronauts at work*

CM2181		MNHVF	UseVF
$3.20	**multicolored**	6.50	3.00
	FDC *(July 9, 2000)*		1.50

The foil holograms are affixed with water-soluble adhesive and may release from the stamp while soaking.

CM2182		MNHVF	UseVF
$3.20	**multicolored**	6.50	3.00
	y. Pair, (CM2181-82)	15.00	6.50
	FDC, pair		15.00
	y1. Souvenir sheet of 2	15.00	7.50
	FDC *(July 9, 2000),* souvenir sheet		18.00

2000. PROBING THE VASTNESS OF SPACE ISSUE featured six International rate stamps that showed various telescopes on an illustrated six-stamp sheetlet at World Stamp Expo 2000. The selvage was a view of the Eagle Nebula, part of which was on one of the Edwin Powell Hubble stamps of 2000 (CM2119). Designed by Richard Sheaff, Scottsdale, Ariz. *Gravure by Sennett Security Products (1,695,000 printed). Block tagged, perforated 10 1/2x11.*

CM2183		MNHVF	UseVF
60¢	**multicolored**	1.10	.60

CM2184		MNHVF	UseVF
60¢	**multicolored**	1.10	.60

CM2185		MNHVF	UseVF
60¢	**multicolored**	1.10	.60

CM2186		MNHVF	UseVF
60¢	**multicolored**	1.10	.60

CM2187		MNHVF	UseVF
60¢	**multicolored**	1.10	.60

CM2188		MNHVF	UseVF
60¢	**multicolored**	1.10	.60
	FDC *(July 10, 2000),* any single		2.50
	Souvenir sheet of 6 (CM2183-88)	7.00	
	FDC, souvenir sheet		9.00

CM2183 *2.4 Meter Mirror Optical Telescopes, Hubble Space Telescope;* CM2184 *Radio Interferometer Very Large Array, National Radio Astronomy Observatory;* CM2185 *Twin 10-Meter Optical and Infrared Telescopes, Keck Observatory, Mauna Kea, Hawaii;* CM2186 *Optical Telescopes, Cerro Tololo Inter-American Observatory east of La Serena, Chile;* CM2187 *100-inch Optical Telescope, Mount Wilson Observatory near Pasadena, Calif.;* CM2188 *1,000-Foot Dish Radio Telescope, Arecibo Observatory in Puerto Rico*

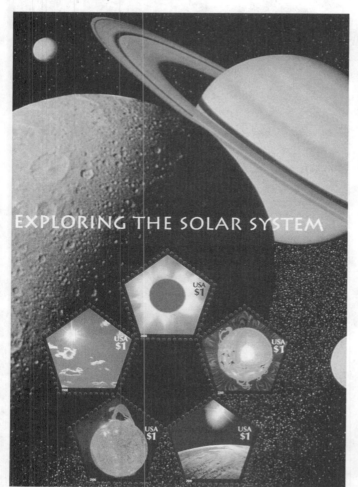

CM2189 *Solar eclipse from a satellite;* CM2190 *An illustrated cutaway view;* CM2191 *A digitally restored NASA image of sunrise from space;* CM2192 *Solar eruption taken by Skylab on Dec. 19, 1973;* CM2193 *Photo from Earth of the Sun in a partly cloudy sky*

2000. EXPLORING THE SOLAR SYSTEM ISSUE featured the first pentagonal stamps issued by the United States on an illustrated five-stamp sheetlet at World Stamp Expo. The $1 stamps offered views of the Sun. The selvage depicted a montage of Saturn and several moons, imaged by *Voyager 1* in November 1980. Designed by Richard Sheaff, Scottsdale, Ariz. *Gravure by Sennett Security Products. Perforated 10 1/2. (1,695,000 printed.) Block tagged.*

CM2189		MNHVF	UseVF
$1	multicolored	2.00	1.00
CM2190		MNHVF	UseVF
$1	multicolored	2.00	1.00
CM2191		MNHVF	UseVF
$1	multicolored	2.00	1.00
CM2192		MNHVF	UseVF
$1	multicolored	2.00	1.00
CM2193		MNHVF	UseVF
$1	multicolored	2.00	1.00
	FDC *(July 11, 2000)*, any single		2.00
	y. Souvenir sheet of 5 (CM2189-93)	10.00	
	FDC, souvenir sheet		13.50
	Five pane press sheet (CM2179y, CM2180y, CM2182y1, CM2188y, CM2193y)	75.00	
	Set of 2 blocks with gutters	35.00	

2000. STAMPIN' THE FUTURE ISSUE featured winning designs from 120,000 contest entries by U.S. children aged 8-12. Designed by Richard Sheaff, Scottsdale, Ariz., illustrators: Zachary Canter, astronauts; Sara Lipsey, children; Morgan Hill, rocket; and Ashley Young, dog. *Self-adhesive pane of 20, offset by Ashton-Potter, USA (100 million printed), block tagged, serpentine die cut 11 1/4.*

CM2194 *Astronauts;* CM2195 *Children;* CM2196 *Rocket;* CM2197 *Dog*

CM2194		MNHVF	UseVF
33¢	multicolored	.50	.20
CM2195		MNHVF	UseVF
33¢	multicolored	.50	.20
CM2196		MNHVF	UseVF
33¢	multicolored	.50	.20
CM2197		MNHVF	UseVF
33¢	multicolored	.50	.20
	Plate block of 4	2.00	
	FDC *(July 13, 2000)*, any single		2.00
	y. Se-tenant strip of 4 (CM2194-97)	2.00	
	FDC, strip of 4		4.25
	y1. Pane of 20	10.00	

2000. CALIFORNIA STATEHOOD ISSUE in the Statehood Series featured a color photograph of cliffs at the Big Sur coastline, with the invasive plant pest iceplant blooming in the foreground. Designed by Carl Herrman, Carlsbad, Calif., from photo by Art Wolfe, Seattle Wash. *Self-adhesive pane of 20, gravure by Avery Dennison, (53 million printed), phosphored paper, serpentine die cut 11.*

2198 *Cliffs at the Big Sur coastline*

CM2198		MNHVF	UseVF
33¢	multicolored	.50	.20
	Plate block of 4	2.00	
	FDC *(Sept. 8, 2000)*		1.50

2000. DEEP-SEA CREATURES ISSUE for National Stamp Collecting Month showed sea life whose normal habitat is 330 feet to more than 3,300 feet below the ocean surface. Designed by Ethel Kessler, Bethesda, Md. *Gummed panes of 15, gravure by Sennett Security Products, (85 million printed), block tagged, perforated 10x10 1/4.*

CM2199 *Fanfin anglerfish*

CM2200 *Sea cucumber*

CM2201 *Fangtooth*

CM2202 *Amphipod*

CM2203 *Medusa*

CM2199		MNHVF	UseVF
33¢	**Fanfin anglerfish**	.50	.20

CM2200		MNHVF	UseVF
33¢	**Sea cucumber**	.50	.20

CM2201		MNHVF	UseVF
33¢	**Fangtooth**	.50	.20

CM2202		MNHVF	UseVF
33¢	**Amphipod**	.50	.20

CM2203		MNHVF	UseVF
33¢	**Medusa**	.50	.20
	FDC *(Oct. 2, 2000)*, any single		1.50
	y. Se-tenant vertical strip of 5 (CM2199-2203)	2.50	
	FDC, strip of 5		5.50
	y1. Pane of 15	9.00	
	Nine pane press sheet	90.00	
	Pair with horizontal gutter	1.75	
	Set of 5 pairs with vertical gutters	8.75	
	Block of 10 with vertical gutter	9.50	
	Cross-gutter block of 10	15.00	

2000. THOMAS WOLFE ISSUE 18th in the Literary Arts Series marked the 100th birthday of Wolfe (1900-1938), author of novels including *Look Homeward, Angel, Of Time and the River,* and *You Can't Go Home Again,* based on his life in North Carolina. Wolfe died of tuberculosis. Designed by Michael J. Deas, illustrator. *Gummed pane of 20, offset by Ashton-Potter (USA) with microprinting "Author," (53 million printed), phosphored paper, perforated 11.*

CM2204 *Thomas Wolfe*

CM2204		MNHVF	UseVF
33¢	**multicolored**	.50	.20
	Plate block of 4	2.00	
	FDC *(Oct. 3, 2000)*		1.50

2000. THE WHITE HOUSE ISSUE marked the bicentennial of the construction of the house designed as the living quarters of the president of the United States. Designed by architect James Hoban (CM994 and CM995) for a site chosen by President George Washington and planner Pierre L'Enfant, construction started in 1792, and it was first occupied by President John Adams and his wife, Abigail. Designed by Derry Noyes, Washington, D.C., from a photo by Patricia Fisher, Washington, D.C. *Self-adhesive pane of 20, offset by Ashton-Potter (USA) (125 million printed), phosphored paper, serpentine die cut 11 1/4.*

CM2205 *White House on a winter evening*

CM2205		MNHVF	UseVF
33¢	**multicolored**	.50	.20
	Plate block of 4	2.00	
	FDC *(Feb. 25, 2000)*		1.50

2000. EDWARD G. ROBINSON ISSUE featured, on the sixth in the Legends of Hollywood Series, the actor known for his roles as gangsters, notably in *Little Caesar* (1931). Born in Romania, Robinson (1893-1973) immigrated to the United States with his family as a youngster and started his professional acting career in 1913. The stamp image is based on a photo by Elmer Fryer. The selvage photo is a publicity still from the film *Five Star Final* (1931), in which Robinson played a tough newspaper editor. Designed by Howard Paine, Delaplane, Va., illustrated by Drew Struzan, Pasadena, Calif. *Gummed pane of 20, gravure by Sennett Security Products (52 million printed), block tagged, perforated 11.*

CM2206 *Edward G. Robinson*

CM2206		MNHVF	UseVF
33¢	**multicolored**	.50	.20
	Plate block of 4	2.00	
	FDC *(Oct. 24, 2000)*		1.50
	y. Pane of 20	10.00	
	Six pane press sheet	80.00	
	Pair with horizontal gutter	1.75	
	Pair with vertical gutter	2.50	
	Block of 8 with vertical gutter	11.00	
	Cross-gutter block of 8	15.00	

2001. ROSE AND LOVE LETTER ISSUE in the Love Series. Featured a love letter written by John Adams, who would become the second U.S. President, to Abigail Smith, who would become his wife, on April 20, 1763. The excerpt is from a passage that reads: "I am at Braintree but I wish I was at Weymouth! What strange Revolutions take Place in our Breasts, and what curious Vicissitudes in every Part of human Life. This summer I shall like Weymouth better than Braintree but something prompts me to believe I shall like Braintree next Winter better than Weymouth. Writers who procure Reputation by flattering human Nature, tell us that Mankind grows wiser and wiser: whether they lie, or speak the Truth, I know I like it, better and better. I would feign make an original, an Exemplar, of this Letter but fear I have not an original Genius." *Designed by Lisa Catalone, Washington, D.C., from photo by Renee Cornet, Washington, D.C., offset by Banknote Corporation of America (510 million printed), phosphored paper, serpentine die cut 11 3/4 on 2, 3, or 4 sides.*

CM2207 *Rose and Love Letter*

CM2207		MNHVF	UseVF
(34¢)	multicolored	.70	.20
	n. Pane of 20 (convertible booklet)	14.00	
	FDC (Jan. 19, 2001)		1.50

2001. YEAR OF THE SNAKE ISSUE Lunar New Year Series. Was the ninth in a series featuring the creatures of the Chinese zodiac designed in paper cut fashion and calligraphy by artist Clarence Lee. *Gummed pane of 20, offset by Sterling Sommer for Ashton-Potter (USA) Ltd. (55 million printed) on phosphored paper, perforated 11 1/4.*

CM2208 *Snake*

CM2208		MNHVF	UseVF
34¢	multicolored	.75	.25
	Plate block of 4	3.00	
	FDC (Jan. 20, 2001)		1.50

2001. ROY WILKINS ISSUE Black Heritage Series. Civil rights leader Roy Wilkins (1901-81) joined the National Association for the Advancement of Colored People (NAACP) in 1931 and was executive secretary and executive director 1955-77. The traditional black-and-white stamp image was taken from a portrait photo by Morgan and Marvin Smith in the 1940s, and designed by Richard Sheaff. *Self-adhesive pane of 20, offset by Ashton-Potter (USA) Ltd. on phosphored paper, serpentine die cut 11 1/2x11 1/4.*

CM2209 *Roy Wilkins*

CM2209		MNHVF	UseVF
34¢	multicolored	.75	.25
	Plate block of 4	3.00	
	FDC (Jan. 24, 2001)		1.50

2001. AMERICAN ILLUSTRATORS ISSUE in the Classic Collection Series featured illustrations by commercial artists in the 19th and 20th centuries. Designed by Carl Herrman. *Self-adhesive pane of 20, gravure by Avery Dennison (625,000 panes printed) on phosphored paper, serpentine die cut 11 1/4.*

CM2210 *Marine Corps poster, "First in the Fight, Always Faithful," by James Montgomery Flagg;* CM2211 *"Interlude (The Lute Players)" by Maxfield Parrish;* CM2212 *Advertisement for Arrow Collars and Shirts by J.C. Leyendecker;* CM2213 *Advertisement for Carrier Corp. Refrigeration by Robert Fawcett;* CM2214 *Advertisement for Luxite Hosiery by Coles Phillips;* CM2215 *Illustration for correspondence school lesson by Al Parker;* CM2216 *"Br'er Rabbit," by A.B. Frost;* CM2217 *"An Attack on a Galleon," by Howard Pyle;* CM2218 *Kewpie and Kewpie Doodle Dog by Rose O'Neill;* CM2219 *Illustration for cover of* True *magazine by Dean Cornwell;* CM2220 *"Galahad's Departure," by Edwin Austin Abbey;* CM2221 *"The First Lesson," by Jessie Willcox Smith;* CM2222 *Illustration for cover of* McCall's *magazine by Neysa McMein;* CM2223 *"Back Home for Keeps," by Jon Whitcomb;* CM2224 *"Something for Supper," by Harvey Dunn;* CM2225 *"A Dash for the Timber," by Frederic Remington;* CM2226 *Illustration for "Moby Dick" by Rockwell Kent;* CM2227 *"Captain Bill Bones," by N.C. Wyeth;* CM2228 *Illustration for cover of* The Saturday Evening Post *by Norman Rockwell;* CM2229 *"The Girl He Left Behind," by John Held Jr.*

CM2210		MNHVF	UseVF
34¢	multicolored, tagged (single)	.75	.25
CM2211		MNHVF	UseVF
34¢	multicolored, tagged (single)	.75	.25
CM2212		MNHVF	UseVF
34¢	multicolored, tagged (single)	.75	.25
CM2213		MNHVF	UseVF
34¢	multicolored, tagged (single)	.75	.25
CM2214		MNHVF	UseVF
34¢	multicolored, tagged (single)	.75	.25
CM2215		MNHVF	UseVF
34¢	multicolored, tagged (single)	.75	.25
CM2216		MNHVF	UseVF
34¢	multicolored, tagged (single)	.75	.25

CM2217		MNHVF	UseVF
34¢	**multicolored,** tagged (single)	.75	.25

CM2218		MNHVF	UseVF
34¢	**multicolored,** tagged (single)	.75	.25

CM2219		MNHVF	UseVF
34¢	**multicolored,** tagged (single)	.75	.25

CM2220		MNHVF	UseVF
34¢	**multicolored,** tagged (single)	.75	.25

CM2221		MNHVF	UseVF
34¢	**multicolored,** tagged (single)	.75	.25

CM2222		MNHVF	UseVF
34¢	**multicolored,** tagged (single)	.75	.25

CM2223		MNHVF	UseVF
34¢	**multicolored,** tagged, (single)	.75	.25

CM2224		MNHVF	UseVF
34¢	**multicolored,** tagged (single)	.75	.25

CM2225		MNHVF	UseVF
34¢	**multicolored,** tagged (single)	.75	.25

CM2226		MNHVF	UseVF
34¢	**multicolored,** tagged (single)	.75	.25

CM2227		MNHVF	UseVF
34¢	**multicolored,** tagged (single)	.75	.25

CM2228		MNHVF	UseVF
34¢	**multicolored,** tagged (single)	.75	.25

CM2229		MNHVF	UseVF
34¢	**multicolored,** tagged (single)	.75	.25
	FDC *(Feb. 1, 2001),* any single		1.50
	y. Pane of 20	15.00	
	FDC, pane of 20		15.00
	Four pane press sheet	60.00	
	Set of 4 pairs with vertical gutters	7.00	
	Block of 8 with vertical gutter	8.00	

2001. ROSE AND LOVE LETTER ISSUE in the Love Series. Featured on a 34¢ stamp a red rose against a love letter written by John Adams, who would become the second U.S. President, to Abigail Smith, who would become his wife; and, on a 55¢ stamp a pink rose against a letter from Smith to Adams. On April 20, 1763, Adams wrote, "I am at Braintree but I wish I was at Weymouth! What strange Revolutions take Place in our Breasts, and what curious Vicissitudes in every Part of human Life. This summer I shall like Weymouth better than Braintree but something prompts me to believe I shall like Braintree next Winter better than Weymouth. Writers who procure Reputation by flattering human Nature, tell us that Mankind grows wiser and wiser: whether they lie, or speak the Truth, I know I like it, better and better. I would feign make an original, an Exemplar, of this Letter but fear I have not an original Genius." On Aug. 11, 1763, Smith wrote, "If I was sure your absence today was occasioned, by what it generally is, either to wait upon Company, or promote some good work, I freely confess my Mind would be much more at ease than at present it is. Yet this uneasiness does not arise from any apprehension of Slight or neglect, but a fear least you are indisposed, for that you said should be your only hindrance. Humanity obliges us to be affected with the distresses and Miserys of our fellow creatures. Friendship is a band yet stronger; which causes us to feel with greater tenderness the afflictions of our Friends." *Images based on photographs by Renee Comet, Washington, D.C., designed by Lisa Catalone, Washington, D.C., offset with microprinting "USPS" by Banknote Corporation of America (4 million vending booklets of CM2230 and 75,000 vending booklets of CM2231 printed) on phosphored paper, self-adhesive, serpentine die cut 11 1/4 (55¢ stamp on 2, 3 or 4 sides for 34¢ convertible booklet) or 11 1/2x10 3/4 on 2 or 3 sides (vending book).*

CM2230 *Rose and Love Letter*

CM2230		MNHVF	UseVF
34¢	**multicolored**	.70	.20
	n. Pane of 20 (convertible booklet)	14.00	
	FDC *(Feb. 14, 2001)*		2.00

CM2231, B314 *Rose and Love Letter*

CM2231		MNHVF	UseVF
34¢	**multicolored**	.70	.20
	n. Booklet pane of 4, no plate number	2.80	
	n1. Booklet pane of 6	4.20	
	n2. Booklet pane of 4, plate number on lower left stamp	2.80	
	pn. Plate number single (bottom left corner of pane)	.75	
	FDC *(Feb. 14, 2001)*		2.00

CM2232 *Rose and Love Letter*

CM2232		MNHVF	UseVF
55¢	**multicolored**	1.00	.40
	Plate block of 4	4.00	
	FDC *(Feb. 14, 2001)*		2.00

2001. DIABETES ISSUE urged people to "Know More About Diabetes," which kills one American every three minutes. *Self-adhesive pane of 20 illustrated by James Steinberg, Amherst, Mass., designed by Richard Sheaff, Scottsdale, Ariz., offset with "USPS" microprinting by Ashton-Potter (USA) Ltd. (100 million printed), serpentine die cut 11 1/4x11 1/2, phosphored paper.*

CM2233 *"Know More About Diabetes"*

CM2233		MNHVF	UseVF
34¢	**multicolored**	.70	.20
	Plate block of 4	2.80	
	FDC *(March 15, 2001)*		1.50

2001. NOBEL PRIZE CENTENNIAL ISSUE honored the founding of the world's most prestigious awards for intellectual achievement. The man who endowed the prizes for physics, chemistry, physiology or medicine, literature, and peace was Alfred Bernhard Nobel (1833-96), an immensely wealthy Swedish chemist and industrialist who invented dynamite and other explosives. Joint issue with Sweden, *engraving by Czeslaw Slania. Designed by Olof Baldursdottir, Stockholm, Sweden, intaglio and offset by De La Rue Security Printing, Dulles, Va. (35 million printed), perforated 11, phosphored paper.*

CM2234 *Alfred Bernhard Nobel (1833-96)*

CM2234		MNHVF	UseVF
34¢	**multicolored**	.65	.20
	Plate block of 4	2.60	
	FDC *(March 22, 2001)*		1.50

2001. PAN-AMERICAN EXPOSITION CENTENNIAL ISSUE reproduced three inverted-center stamps from the set issued for the 1901 Pan-American Exposition. The illustrated sheetlet also included 80¢ stamps based on the design of labels issued for the exposition.

The background is taken from an exposition poster. *Designed by Richard Sheaff, offset and intaglio by Banknote Corporation of America (14 million printed), perforated 12 1/2x12 (1¢, 2¢, and 3¢), 12 (80¢).*

CM2235-CM2238 *Pan-American*

CM2235		MNHVF	UseVF
1¢	green & black	.20	.20
	FDC *(March 29, 2001)*		1.25

CM2236		MNHVF	UseVF
2¢	carmine & black	.20	.20
	FDC *(March 29, 2001)*		1.25

CM2237		MNHVF	UseVF
4¢	red brown & black	.20	.20
	FDC *(March 29, 2001)*		1.25

CM2238		MNHVF	UseVF
80¢	red & blue	1.60	.40
	FDC *(March 29, 2001)*		—
	y. Pane of 7 (1 each CM2235-37, 4 CM2238)	7.00	
	FDC, pane of 7		6.00
	Four pane press sheet	—	

2001. GREAT PLAINS PRAIRIE ISSUE third in the Nature of America Series featured the animal and plant life in one of the world's largest grasslands, stretching from the edge of the eastern woodlands and oak savannahs to the foothills of the Rocky Mountains. *Illustrated pane of 10, designed by Ethel Kessler from illustration by John D. Dawson, Hilo, Hawaii, offset by Ashton-Potter (USA) Ltd. (89.6 million printed), serpentine die cut 10.*

CM2239		MNHVF	UseVF
34¢	multicolored, single	.65	.20
	a. Pronghorns, Canada geese	.65	.20
	b. Burrowing owls, American bison	.65	.20
	c. American bison, black-tailed prairie dogs, wild alfalfa	.65	.20
	d. Black-tailed prairie dog, American bison	.65	.20
	e. Painted lady butterfly, American bison, prairie coneflowers, prairie wild roses	.65	.20
	f. Western meadowlark, camel cricket, prairie coneflowers, prairie wild roses	.65	.20
	g. Badger, harvester ants	.65	.20
	h. Eastern short-horned lizard, plains pocket gopher	.65	.20
	i. Plains spadefoot, dung beetle	.65	.20

CM2239 *Animals of the Great Plains Prairie*

		MNHVF	UseVF
	j. Two-striped grasshopper, Ord's kangaroo rat	.65	.20
	FDC *(April 19, 2001),* any single		1.25
	y. Pane of 10	7.00	
	FDC, pane of 10		7.00
	Six pane press sheet	—	

2001. PEANUTS ISSUE celebrated the cartoon dog Snoopy, in his "Red Baron" guise, created by Charles M. Schulz. At the time of the stamp issue, a year after Schulz's death, the comic strip appeared in 2,600 newspapers in 75 countries and was translated into 21 languages. *Designed by Carl Herrman from an illustration by Paige Braddock. Offset with microprinting "USPS" by Ashton-Potter (USA) Ltd. (125 million stamps printed), self-adhesive, serpentine die cut 11 1/4x11 1/2.*

CM2240 "Red Baron"

CM2240		MNHVF	UseVF
34¢	multicolored	.65	.30
	Plate block of 4	5.00	
	FDC *(May 17, 2001)*		1.90
	y. Pane of 20	13.00	

2001. VETERANS CONTINUING TO SERVE ISSUE paid tribute to the patriotism of the almost 25 million men and women who have served in the armed forces and are members of veterans service organizations. The stamp sold out in the months following terrorist attacks with hijacked jetliners. *Designed by Carl Herrman from a photograph of a waving American flag, (200 million stamps printed) offset with microprinting "USA" by Ashton-Potter (USA) Ltd., self-adhesive, serpentine die cut 11 1/4x11 1/2.*

CM2241 *Veterans*

CM2241		MNHVF	UseVF
34¢	multicolored	.65	.20
	Plate block of 4	2.60	
	FDC *(May 23, 2001)*		1.90

2001. FRIDA KAHLO ISSUE celebrated the free-spirited Mexican artist (1907-54) who survived polio and a streetcar accident and embraced revolutionaries. Kahlo exhibited her work, predominently self-portraits with sometimes surrealistic themes, in New York, Paris and Mexico City. She is the first Mexican woman to appear on a U.S. stamp. *Designed by Richard Sheaff from Self-portrait With Necklace by Frida Kahlo, (55 million stamps printed) offset, with microprinting "USPS" by Ashton-Potter (USA) Ltd., perforated 11 1/4.*

CM2242 *Frida Kahlo*

CM2242		MNHVF	UseVF
34¢	multicolored	.65	.20
	Plate block of 4	2.80	
	FDC (June 21, 2001)		1.50
	y. Pane of 20	14.00	
	FDC, pane of 20	20.00	
	Eight pane press sheet	—	

2001. BASEBALL'S LEGENDARY PLAYING FIELDS ISSUE pictured the fields where several Major League baseball teams played. Only three were still being used by the teams: Boston's Fenway Park, Chicago's Wrigley Field, and New York's Yankee Stadium. *Designed by Phil Jordan, based on vintage postcards from the collection of Ron Menchine, a former Washington Senators announcer, gravure by Avery Dennison (125 million printed), self-adhesive, serpentine die cut 11 1/4x11 1/2.*

CM2243 *Ebbets Field, Brooklyn;* CM2244 *Tiger Stadium, Detroit;* CM2245 *Crosley Field, Cincinnati;* CM2246 *Yankee Stadium, New York City;* CM2247 *Polo Grounds, New York City;* CM2248 *Forbes Field, Pittsburgh;* CM2249 *Fenway Park, Boston;* CM2250 *Comiskey Park, Chicago;* CM2251 *Shibe Park, Philadelphia;* CM2252 *Wrigley Field, Chicago*

CM2243		MNHVF	UseVF
34¢	multicolored	.65	.20
CM2244		MNHVF	UseVF
34¢	multicolored	.65	.20
CM2245		MNHVF	UseVF
34¢	multicolored	.65	.20
CM2246		MNHVF	UseVF
34¢	multicolored	.65	.20
CM2247		MNHVF	UseVF
34¢	multicolored	.65	.20
CM2248		MNHVF	UseVF
34¢	multicolored	.65	.20
CM2249		MNHVF	UseVF
34¢	multicolored	.65	.20
CM2250		MNHVF	UseVF
34¢	multicolored	.65	.20
CM2251		MNHVF	UseVF
34¢	multicolored	.65	.20
CM2252		MNHVF	UseVF
34¢	multicolored	.65	.20
	FDC (June 27, 2001), any single		1.90
	y. Se-tenant block of 10 (CM2243-52)	7.00	
	y1. Pane of 20	13.00	
	FDC, pane of 20		
	Eight pane press sheet	—	

2001. LEONARD BERNSTEIN ISSUE honored a musical genius who distinguished himself in many genres. Bernstein (1918-90) composed symphonies, chamber music, and vocal music, as well as works for ballet, opera, film, and the musical stage. He was arguably most famous for the operetta, "West Side Story." The stamp was designed by Howard Paine, of Delaplane, Va., using a photograph by Don Hunstein. *Gummed pane of 20, offset by Sterling Sommer, Tonawanda, N.Y.*

CM2253 *Leonard Bernstein*

CM2253		MNHVF	UseVF
34¢	multicolored	.65	.20
	Plate block of 4	2.60	
	y. Pane of 20	13.00	
	FDC (July 10, 2001)		1.90

2001. LUCILLE BALL ISSUE seventh in the Legends of Hollywood Series featured the comedienne known mainly for her roles in the television shows "I Love Lucy" (1951-57), "The Lucy-Desi Comedy Hour" (1957-60), "The Lucy Show" (1962-68), "Here's Lucy" (1968-74), and "Life with Lucy" (1986). Ball (1911-89) also appeared in more than 70 movies, in radio comedy and on the Broadway stage. She was the first woman president of a major Hollywood production company, DesiLu Studios. *Self-adhesive stamps offset by Banknote Corporation of America.*

CM2254 *Lucille Ball*

CM2254		MNHVF	UseVF
34¢	multicolored	.65	.20
	Plate block of 4	2.60	
	y. Pane of 20	13.00	
	FDC (Aug. 6, 2001)		1.90

American Treasures Series

2001. AMISH QUILTS ISSUE first in the American Treasures Series, featured se-tenant stamps picturing four Amish quilts made in Lancaster County, Pennsylvania, in the first half of the 20th century: Diamond in the Square, Lone Star, Sunshine and Shadow, and Double Ninepatch (variation). *Designed by Derry Noyes, Washington, D.C., self-adhesive pane of 20 offset by Ashton-Potter (USA) Ltd.*

CM2255-2258
Amish Quilts

CM2255		MNHVF	UseVF
34¢	multicolored	.65	.20
CM2256		MNHVF	UseVF
34¢	multicolored	.65	.20
CM2257		MNHVF	UseVF
34¢	multicolored	.65	.20
CM2258		MNHVF	UseVF
34¢	multicolored	.65	.20
	Plate block of 4	2.60	
	y. Pane of 20	13.00	
	FDC *(Aug. 9, 2001)*		2.50

2001. CARNIVOROUS PLANTS ISSUE showed a Venus Flytrap with a metalmark butterfly caught in one of its cagelike leaves; a Yellow Trumpet with a fly on its lip; a Cobra Lily, which has lured a wasp to its mouth; and an English Sundew with an unlucky syrphid fly caught in its sticky leaves. The paintings are by Steve Buchanan, Winsted, Conn. *Self-adhesive pane of 20, gravure by Avery Dennison.*

CM2259-2262 *Carnivorous Plants*

CM2259		MNHVF	UseVF
34¢	multicolored	.65	.20
CM2260		MNHVF	UseVF
34¢	multicolored	.65	.20
CM2261		MNHVF	UseVF
34¢	multicolored	.65	.20
CM2262		MNHVF	UseVF

	multicolored	.65		.20
34¢				
	Plate block of 4	2.60		
	y. Pane of 20	13.00		
	FDC *(Aug. 23, 2001)*			2.50

2001. EID ISSUE in the Holiday Celebrations Series highlighted the Muslim holiday. The Islamic calligraphy by Mohamed Zakariya on the stamp is "Eid mubarak" or "blessed festival." *Self-adhesive pane of 20, gravure by Avery Dennison.*

CM2263 *Islamic calligraphy by Mohamed Zakariya*

CM2263		MNHVF	UseVF
34¢	blue & gold	.65	.20
	Plate block of 4	2.60	
	y. Pane of 20	13.00	
	FDC *(Sept. 1, 2001)*		1.50

2001. ENRICO FERMI ISSUE honored a preeminent physicist of the atomic age. Fermi (1901-54), experimenting at the University of Rome in 1934, became the first physicist to split the atom. He won the Nobel Prize in Physics in 1938. He headed the U.S. effort to design and build a nuclear reactor and assisted in the development of the first atomic bomb. Fermi became a naturalized U.S. citizen in 1944. Part of the equation shown in the blackboard on the stamp is said to be erroneous. *Gummed panes of 20, offset with microprinting "USPS" by Sterling Sommer.*

CM2264 *Enrico Fermi (1901-54)*

CM2264		MNHVF	UseVF
34¢	multicolored	.65	.20
	Plate block of 4	2.60	
	y. Pane of 20	13.00	
	FDC *(Sept. 29, 2001)*		1.50

2001. PORKY PIG ("THAT'S ALL, FOLKS")

CM2265 *Porky Pig ("That's all, folks")*

CM2265		MNHVF	UseVF
34¢	multicolored	.65	.20
	y. Pane of 10	6.50	
	FDC *(Oct. 1, 2001)*		1.50

Every reasonable effort has been made to make the values in this catalog as accurate, realistic, and up-to-date as possible.

2001. PORKY PIG ("THAT'S ALL, FOLKS") SPECIAL DIE CUT ISSUE ("imperforate").

CM2266 *Porky Pig ("That's all, folks")*

CM2266		MNHVF	UseVF
34¢	**multicolored**	.65	.20
	y. Pane of 10	6.50	
	FDC *(Sept. 1, 2001)*		1.50

2001. JAMES MADISON ISSUE honored the fourth president of the United States, known as the father of the U.S. Constitution, on the 250th anniversary of his birth. The portrait of Madison (1751-1836) shows his home, Montpelier, in Virginia. *Self-adhesive pane of 20, illustrated by John Thompson, Waterloo, Iowa, intaglio and offset by Banknote Corporation of America.*

CM2267 *James Madison (1751-1836)*

CM2267		MNHVF	UseVF
34¢	**multicolored**	.65	.20
	Plate block of 4	2.60	
	y. Pane of 20	13.00	
	FDC *(Oct. 18, 2001)*		1.50

2001. WE GIVE THANKS ISSUE in the Holiday Celebrations Series showed a cornucopia filled with fruits and vegetables. Margaret Cusack designed and made the machine-appliqued, partially quilted needlework. *Self-adhesive pane of 20, offset with microprinting "USPS" by Ashton-Potter (USA) Ltd.*

CM2268 *Cornucopia filled with fruits and vegetables*

CM2268		MNHVF	UseVF
34¢	**multicolored**	.65	.20
	Plate block of 4	2.60	
	y. Pane of 20	13.00	
	FDC *(Oct. 19, 2001)*		1.50

2001. HANUKKAH ISSUE in the Holiday Celebrations Series showed the menorah design first issued in 1996 with a third denomination (see Nos. CM1880 and CM2099). *Self-adhesive pane of 20.*

CM2269 *Menorah design*

CM2269		MNHVF	UseVF
34¢	**multicolored**	.65	.20
	Plate block of 4	2.60	
	y. Pane of 20	13.00	
	FDC *(Oct. 21, 2001)*		1.50

2001. KWANZAA ISSUE in the Holiday Celebrations Series showed the celebrating family design first issued in 1997 with a third denomination (see Nos. CM1963 and CM2101). *Self-adhesive pane of 20.*

CM2270 *Family celebrating*

CM2270		MNHVF	UseVF
34¢	**multicolored**	1.20	.30
	Plate block of 4	5.00	
	y. Pane of 50	60.00	
	FDC *(Oct. 19, 2001)*		1.50

2001. LOVE LETTER ISSUE in the Love Series featured a higher denomination to meet new two-ounce rates. *Self-adhesive convertible booklet of 20.*

CM2271 *Love Letter*

CM2271		MNHVF	UseVF
57¢	**multicolored**	.65	.20
	Plate block of 4	2.60	
	y. Pane of 20	13.00	
	FDC *(Nov. 19, 2001)*		1.50

2002. WINTER SPORTS ISSUE featured photographic images of athletes in four sports, along with line drawings of the participation sites. In support of the Winter Olympics at Salt Lake City, Utah, they represented the first U.S. stamps with the Olympics logo since 1996. *Gravure by American Packaging Corporation, Columbus, Wis., for Sennett Security Products (80 million printed), self-adhesive, die cut 11.*

CM2272 *Ski Jumping;* CM2273 *Snowboarding;* CM2274 *Ice Hockey;* CM2275 *Figure Skating*

CM2272		MNHVF	UseVF
34¢	**multicolored**	.65	.20

CM2273		MNHVF	UseVF
34¢	**multicolored**	.65	.20

CM2274		MNHVF	UseVF
34¢	**multicolored**	.65	.20

CM2275		MNHVF	UseVF
34¢	**multicolored**	.65	.20
	Plate block of 4	2.60	
	Pane of 20	13.00	
	Die cut inverted pane of 20	25.00	
	FDC *(Jan. 8, 2002)*		1.50

2002. MENTORING A CHILD ISSUE paid tribute to volunteers who guide and support youths through mentoring. *Designed by Lance Hidy, Merrimac, Mass., gravure by American Packaging Corporation,*

Columbus, Wis., for Sennett Security Products (125 million printed), self-adhesive, die cut 11 1/4.

CM2276 *Adult guiding a child*

CM2276

		MNHVF	UseVF
34¢	multicolored	.65	.20
	Plate block of 4	2.60	
	y. Pane of 20	13.00	
	FDC *(Jan. 10, 2002)*		1.90

2002. LANGSTON HUGHES ISSUE in the Black Heritage Series commemorated a Harlem Renaissance poet and author known for his insightful portrayal of black life in America. Hughes (1902-67), wrote novels, short stories, and plays as well as poetry. His first published poem, "The Negro Speaks of Rivers," became one of his most famous works. *Designed by Richard Sheaff from a 1946 photograph by Henri Cartier-Bresson, offset with microprinting "USPS" by Banknote Corporation of America (120 million printed), self-adhesive, die cut 10.*

CM2277 *Langston Hughes*

CM2277

		MNHVF	UseVF
34¢	multicolored	.65	.20
	Plate block of 4	2.60	
	Pane of 20	13.00	
	FDC *(Feb. 1, 2002)*		1.50

2002. HAPPY BIRTHDAY ISSUE encouraged the sending of birthday cards. *Designed by Harry Zelenko, New York, N.Y., gravure by Avery Dennison (75 million printed), self-adhesive, die cut 10 1/2x10 1/4.*

CM2278 *Happy Birthday*

CM2278

		MNHVF	UseVF
34¢	multicolored	.65	.20
	Plate block of 4	2.60	
	FDC *(Feb. 8, 2002)*		1.90

2002. YEAR OF THE HORSE ISSUE was the 10th in the Lunar New Year Series and the first self-adhesive stamp in the series. *Designed by Clarence Lee, Honolulu, Hawaii, offset with microprinting "USPS" by Banknote Corporation of America (70 million printed), self-adhesive, die cut 10 1/2x10.*

CM2279 *Cut paper horse*

CM2279

		MNHVF	UseVF
34¢	multicolored	.65	.20

Plate block of 4		2.60	
FDC *(Feb. 11, 2002)*			1.90

2002. U.S. MILITARY ACADEMY ISSUE commemorated the bicentennial of the school at West Point, N.Y. It featured the academy's coat of arms against a gray background. *Designed by Derry Noyes, gravure by American Packaging Corporation, for Sennett Security Products (55 million printed), self-adhesive, die cut 10 1/2.*

CM2280 *Military Academy coat of arms*

CM2280

		MNHVF	UseVF
34¢	multicolored	.65	.20
	Plate block of 4	2.60	
	FDC *(March 16, 2002)*		1.90

2002. GREETINGS FROM AMERICA ISSUE highlighted symbols of each of the 50 states with stamps that evoked the large-letters postcards from the 1930s and '40s. It was the first 50-stamp pane from the USPS since 1992. *Illustrated by Lonnie Busch, Franklin, N.C., gravure by American Packaging Corporation, for Sennett Security Products (200 million printed), self-adhesive, die cut 10 1/2.*

CM2281-CM2330 *Greetings pane*

CM2281

		MNHVF	UseVF
34¢	Alabama, multicolored	1.20	.30

CM2282

		MNHVF	UseVF
34¢	Alaska, multicolored	1.20	.30

CM2283

		MNHVF	UseVF
34¢	Arizona, multicolored	1.20	.30

	MNHVF	UseVF			MNHVF	UseVF
CM2284 34¢ Arkansas, multicolored	1.20	.30	**CM2298** 34¢ Louisiana, multicolored		1.20	.30
CM2285 34¢ California, multicolored	1.20	.30	**CM2299** 34¢ Maine, multicolored		1.20	.30
CM2286 34¢ Colorado, multicolored	1.20	.30	**CM2300** 34¢ Maryland, multicolored		1.20	.30
CM2287 34¢ Connecticut, multicolored	1.20	.30	**CM2301** 34¢ Massachusetts, multicolored		1.20	.30
CM2288 34¢ Delaware, multicolored	1.20	.30	**CM2302** 34¢ Michigan, multicolored		1.20	.30
CM2289 34¢ Florida, multicolored	1.20	.30	**CM2303** 34¢ Minnesota, multicolored		1.20	.30
CM2290 34¢ Georgia, multicolored	1.20	.30	**CM2304** 34¢ Mississippi, multicolored		1.20	.30
CM2291 34¢ Hawaii, multicolored	1.20	.30	**CM2305** 34¢ Missouri, multicolored		1.20	.30
CM2292 34¢ Idaho, multicolored	1.20	.30	**CM2306** 34¢ Montana, multicolored		1.20	.30
CM2293 34¢ Illinois, multicolored	1.20	.30	**CM2307** 34¢ Nebraska, multicolored		1.20	.30
CM2294 34¢ Indiana, multicolored	1.20	.30	**CM2308** 34¢ Nevada, multicolored		1.20	.30
CM2295 34¢ Iowa, multicolored	1.20	.30	**CM2309** 34¢ New Hampshire, multicolored		1.20	.30
CM2296 34¢ Kansas, multicolored	1.20	.30	**CM2310** 34¢ New Jersey, multicolored		1.20	.30
CM2297 34¢ Kentucky, multicolored	1.20	.30	**CM2311** 34¢ New Mexico, multicolored		1.20	.30

LONGLEAF PINE FOREST

FOURTH IN A SERIES

N A T U R E O F A M E R I C A

CM2331a *Bachman's sparrow;* CM2331b *Northern bobwhite, yellow pitcher plants;* CM2331c *Fox squirrel, red bellied woodpecker;* CM2331d *Brown-headed nuthatch;* CM2331e *Broadhead skink, yellow pitcher plants, pipeworts;* CM2331f *Eastern towhee, yellow pitcher plants, Savannah meadow beauties, toothache grass;* CM2331g *Gray fox, gopher tortoise;* CM2331h *Blind click beetle, sweetbay, pine woods treefrog;* CM2331i *Rosebud orchid, pipeworts, southern toad, yellow pitcher plants;* CM2331j *Grass-pink orchid, yellow-sided skimmer, pipeworts, yellow pitcher plants*

CM2312			MNHVF	UseVF
34¢	**New York**, multicolored		1.20	.30
CM2313			MNHVF	UseVF
34¢	**North Carolina**, multicolored		1.20	.30
CM2314			MNHVF	UseVF
34¢	**North Dakota**, multicolored		1.20	.30
CM2315			MNHVF	UseVF
34¢	**Ohio**, multicolored		1.20	.30
CM2316			MNHVF	UseVF
34¢	**Oklahoma**, multicolored		1.20	.30
CM2317			MNHVF	UseVF
34¢	**Oregon**, multicolored		1.20	.30
CM2318			MNHVF	UseVF
34¢	**Pennsylvania**, multicolored		1.20	.30
CM2319			MNHVF	UseVF
34¢	**Rhode Island**, multicolored		1.20	.30
CM2320			MNHVF	UseVF
34¢	**South Carolina**, multicolored		1.20	.30
CM2321			MNHVF	UseVF
34¢	**South Dakota**, multicolored		1.20	.30
CM2322			MNHVF	UseVF
34¢	**Tennessee**, multicolored		1.20	.30
CM2323			MNHVF	UseVF
34¢	**Texas**, multicolored		1.20	.30
CM2324			MNHVF	UseVF
34¢	**Utah**, multicolored		1.20	.30
CM2325			MNHVF	UseVF
34¢	**Vermont**, multicolored		1.20	.30
CM2326			MNHVF	UseVF
34¢	**Virginia**, multicolored		1.20	.30
CM2327			MNHVF	UseVF
34¢	**Washington**, multicolored		1.20	.30
CM2328			MNHVF	UseVF
34¢	**West Virginia**, multicolored		1.20	.30
CM2329			MNHVF	UseVF
34¢	**Wisconsin**, multicolored		1.20	.30
CM2330			MNHVF	UseVF
34¢	**Wyoming**, multicolored		1.20	.30
	y. Pane of 50		35.00	
	FDC *(April 4, 2002)*			1.50

Nature of America Series

2002. LONGLEAF PINE FOREST ISSUE is the fourth of the planned educational Nature of America Series designed to promote appreciation of North America's major plant and animal communities. Thirty-one animal and plant species are portrayed. A description of the longleaf pine forest and a numbered key to the artwork appear on the back of the pane along with a corresponding list of common and scientific names for 27 selected species. Designed by Ethel Kessler, illustrated by John D. Dawson, Hilo, Hawaii. *Self-adhesive pane of 10, 9 panes to a sheet. Photogravure by American Packaging Corp. for Sennett Security Products. Serpentine die cut 10 1/2x10 3/4, 10 3/4x11 1/2.*

CM2331		MNHVF	UseVF
$3.40	**Pane of 10, multicolored** block tagged	7.00	3.00
	9 Pane press sheet	65.00	
	FDC *(April 26, 2002)* any single		1.00
	FDC *(April 26, 2002)* pane of 10		10.00
	a. Bachman's sparrow	.75	.25
	b. Northern bobwhite	.75	.25
	c. Fox squirrel	.75	.25
	d. Brown-headed nuthatch	.75	.25
	e. Broadhead skink	.75	.25
	f. Eastern towhee	.75	.25
	g. Gray fox	.75	.25
	h. Blind click beetle	.75	.25
	i. Rosebud orchid	.75	.25
	j. Grass-pink orchid	.75	.25

2002. HEROES OF 2001 ISSUE (37¢ + 8¢) is the second semi-postal stamp issued by USPS. Artwork is from a photograph taken by Thomas E. Franklin. Sales from this special stamp were used to generate funds to provide assistance to families of emergency relief personnel killed or permanently disabled in the line of duty in connection with terrorist attacks of Sept. 11, 2001. *Self-adhesive pane of 20 printed by Ashton-Potter. Serpentine die cut 11 1/4.*

CMSP2 *Firemen hoisting the flag*

CMSP2		MNHVF	UseVF
(37¢ + 8¢) multicolored phosphored block tagged		.90	.25
	Plate block of 4	3.75	
	y. Pane of 20	18.00	
	FDC *(June 7, 2002)*		1.50

Classic Collections Series

2002. MASTERS OF AMERICAN PHOTOGRAPHY ISSUE is the ninth installment in the Classic Collections Series. Designed by Derry Noyes, Washington, D.C., the pane of 20 includes examples of portrait, documentary, landscape and fine art photography. Many of the major themes and events in U.S. history, including immigration, the Depression, and World War II, are captured in these compelling images. *Printed photogravure by Sennett Security Products on pre-phosphored paper. Self-adhesive. Serpentine die cut 10 1/2x10 3/4.*

CM2332a *Albert Sands Southworth;* CM2332b *Timothy O'Sullivan;* CM2332c *Carleton E. Watkins;* CM2332d *Gertrude Kasebier;* CM2332e *Lewis W. Hine;* CM2332f *Alvin Langdon Coburn;* CM2332g *Edward Steichen;* CM2332h *Alfred Stieglitz;* CM2332i *Man Ray;* CM2332j *Edward Weston;* CM2332k *James VanDerZee;* CM2332l *Dorothea Lange;* CM2332m *Walker Evans;* CM2332n *W. Eugene Smith;* CM2332o *Paul Strand;* CM2332p *Ansel Adams;* CM2332q *Imogen Cunningham;* CM2332r *Andre Kertesz;* CM2332s *Garry Winogrand;* CM2332t *Minor White*

CM2332		MNHVF	UseVF
37¢	**black** pre-phosphored paper	.75	.25
	y. Pane of 20	15.00	
	y1. Uncut press sheet (6 panes of 20)	90.00	
	FDC pane of 20 *(June 13, 2002)*		15.00
	a. Albert Sands Southworth	.75	.25
	b. Timothy O'Sullivan	.75	.25
	c. Carleton E. Watkins	.75	.25

d.	Gertrude Kasebier	.75	.25
e.	Lewis W. Hine	.75	.25
f.	Alvin Langdon Coburn	.75	.25
g.	Edward Steichen	.75	.25
h.	Alfred Stieglitz	.75	.25
i.	Man Ray	.75	.25
j.	Edward Weston	.75	.25
k.	James VanDerZee	.75	.25
l.	Dorothea Lange	.75	.25
m.	Walker Evans	.75	.25
n.	W. Eugene Smith	.75	.25
o.	Paul Strand	.75	.25
p.	Ansel Adams	.75	.25
q.	Imogen Cunningham	.75	.25
r.	Andre Kertesz	.75	.25
s.	Garry Winogrand	.75	.25
t.	Minor White	.75	.25

2002. JOHN JAMES AUDUBON ISSUE second in the American Treasures Series features the artwork of plate 354 from a reprint of *Birds of America*. It portrays two male Louisiana Tanagers and two Scarlet Tanagers in spring plumage. Designed by Derry Noyes, Washington, D.C. *Printed gravure by American Packaging Corp. for Sennett Security Products. Self-adhesive on pre-phosphored paper. Serpentine die cut 10 3/4.*

CM2333 *John James Audubon*

CM2333		MNHVF	UseVF
37¢	**multicolored** pre-phosphored paper	.70	.20
	Plate block of 4	2.80	
	y. Pane of 20	15.00	
	FDC *(June 27, 2002 - Santa Clara, Calif.)*		1.50

2002. HARRY HOUDINI ISSUE Born Ehrich Weiss on March 24, 1874, in Budapest, Hungary, Harry's family immigrated to the U.S. when he was four. His professional debut occurred at the age of nine when he appeared as a contortionist and trapeze performer at a five-cent circus. He went on to perform magic and escape tricks in dime museums, medicine shows, circuses, and other small performance venues. By 1915, Houdini was thrilling huge crowds with death defying escape tricks. Later in life, Houdini used his knowledge of illusion to expose fraudulent mediums. The image of Houdini reveals a hidden image of himself wrapped in chains when viewed through the official U.S. Postal Service Stamp Decoder. Designed by Richard Sheaff, Scottsdale, Ariz. *Printed by Ashton-Potter on pre-phosphored paper. Self-adhesive panes of 20. Serpentine die cut 11 1/2.*

CM2334 *Harry Houdini*

CM2334		MNHVF	UseVF
37¢	**multicolored** pre-phosphored paper	.70	.20
	Plate block of 4	2.80	
	y. Pane of 20	15.00	
	FDC *(July 3, 2002 - New York, N.Y.)*		1.50

2002. ANDY WARHOL ISSUE features Andy Warhol's *Self-Portrait*, based on a 1964 photo-booth photograph. One of the central figures in pop art, Warhol filled galleries with provocative pieces that utilized serial imagery, most notably with his Campbell's soup can of 1962. Designed by Richard Sheaff. *Printed gravure by Sennett Security Products in self-adhesive panes of 20. Serpentine die cut 10 3/4.*

CM2335 *Andy Warhol*

CM2335		MNHVF	UseVF
37¢	**multicolored** phosphored block tagging	.75	.25
	Plate block of 4	3.00	
	y. Pane of 20	15.00	
	FDC *(Aug. 9, 2002 - Pittsburgh, Penn.)*		1.50

2002. TEDDY BEAR ISSUES featured four photos of vintage bears prized by collectors and marks the 100th anniversary of the teddy bear. Featured on the top selvage of the pane are the Gund Bear circa 1948, the Bruin Bear circa 1907, an Ideal Bear circa 1905, and a Stick Bear circa 1920s. Designed by Margaret Baur. *Printed gravure by Sennett Security Products in self-adhesive panes of 20. Serpentine die cut 10 1/2.*

CM2336 *Gund Bear*

CM2337 *Bruin Bear*

CM2338 *Ideal Bear*

CM2339 *Stick Bear*

CM2336		MNHVF	UseVF
37¢	**multicolored** phosphored tagging	.75	.25

CM2337		MNHVF	UseVF
37¢	**multicolored** phosphored tagging	.75	.25

CM2338		MNHVF	UseVF
37¢	**multicolored** phosphored tagging	.75	.25

CM2339		MNHVF	UseVF
37¢	**multicolored** phosphored tagging	.75	.20
	Plate block of 4	3.00	
	y. Pane of 20	15.00	
	y1. Uncut press sheet (6 sheets)	75.00	
	FDC *(Aug. 15, 2002 - Atlantic City, N.J.)*		1.50

2002. LOVE BOOKLET ISSUE featured colorful abstract designs. Issued to pay the First-class letter rate. Designed by Michael Osborne, San Francisco, Calif. *Printed gravure by Banknote Corporation of America in self-adhesive convertible booklets of 20. Serpentine die cut 11.*

CM2340 *Love*

CM2340

		MNHVF	UseVF
37¢	**multicolored** pre-phosphored paper	.70	.25
	n. Booklet pane of 10	7.50	
	n1. Booklet pane of 20 (convertible booklet)	15.00	
	FDC (Aug. 16, 2002 - Atlantic City, N.J.)		1.50

2002. LOVE ISSUE featured colorful abstract designs. Issued to pay the two ounce rate for heavier items such as wedding invitations, announcements and RSVPs. Designed by Michael Osborne, San Francisco, Calif. *Printed gravure by Avery Dennison in self-adhesive panes of 20. Serpentine die cut 11.*

CM2341 *Love*

CM2341

		MNHVF	UseVF
60¢	**multicolored** pre-phosphored paper	1.00	.35
	Plate block of 4	4.00	
	y. Pane of 20	20.00	
	FDC (Aug. 6, 2002 - Atlantic City, N.J.)		2.00

2002. OGDEN NASH ISSUE is the eighteenth issue in the Literary Arts Series honoring Ogden Nash on the centennial of his birth. Nash's inventive use of the English language held his reader's attention. In 1950, Nash was inducted into the American Academy of Arts and Letters. Designed by Carl Herrman based on artwork by Michael Deas. *Printed gravure by Avery Dennison in self-adhesive panes of 20. Serpentine die cut 11.*

CM2342 *Ogden Nash*

CM2342

		MNHVF	UseVF
37¢	**multicolored** pre-phosphored paper	.75	.25
	Plate block of 4	3.00	
	y. Pane of 20	15.00	
	FDC (Aug. 19, 2002 - Baltimore, Md.)		1.50

2002. DUKE KAHANAMOKU ISSUE is based on an oil painting by Michael Deas from a 1918 photograph of Hawaii's unofficial ambassador of goodwill. Duke Kahanamoku's fame as a surfer was known worldwide. He also won medals in swimming for the U.S. Olympic teams in 1912, 1920, 1924, and 1932. In 1994, his name was placed on the Surfing Walk of Fame in Huntington Beach, Calif. Designed by Carl Herrman. *Printed gravure by Avery Dennison in self-adhesive panes of 20. Serpentine die cut 11 1/2x11 3/4.*

CM2343 *Duke Kahanamoku*

CM2343

		MNHVF	UseVF
37¢	**multicolored** phosphored block tagging	.75	.25
	Plate block of 4	3.00	
	y. Pane of 20	15.00	
	FDC (Aug. 24, 2002 - Honolulu, Hawaii)		1.50

2002. AMERICAN BATS ISSUE Designed by Phil Jordan and based on photographs by Merlin Tuttle, the American Bats stamps were picked to help highlight National Stamp Collecting Month October 2002. This stamp pane features four different bats that are found throughout North America. They are the Red Bat, Pallid Bat, Spotted Bat and Leaf-nosed Bat. The stamp pane's selvage shows Long-nosed bats. *Printed gravure by Sennett Security Products in self-adhesive panes of 20. Serpentine die cut 10 3/4.*

CM2344 *Red Bat;* CM2345 *Leaf-nosed Bat;* CM2346 *Pallid Bat;* CM2347 *Spotted Bat*

CM2344

		MNHVF	UseVF
37¢	**multicolored** phosphored block tagging	.75	.25

CM2345

		MNHVF	UseVF
37¢	**multicolored** phosphored block tagging	.75	.25

CM2346

		MNHVF	UseVF
37¢	**multicolored** phosphored block tagging	.75	.25

CM2347

		MNHVF	UseVF
37¢	**multicolored** phosphored block tagging	.75	.25
	Plate block of 4	3.00	
	y. Pane of 20	15.00	
	FDC (Sept. 13, 2002 - Austin, Texas)		1.50

2002. WOMEN IN JOURNALISM ISSUE depicts four different famous women in the male dominated field of journalism. Nellie Bly, known for her sensationalism during the late 19th century, Marguerite Higgins, as the first female to win a Pulitzer Prize, Ethel L. Payne, for her aggressive style, and Ida M. Tarbell, for her investigative reporting are remembered as trailblazers for future female journalists. Designed by Fred Otnes. *Printed gravure by Sennett Security Products in self-adhesive panes of 20 on pre-phosphored paper. Serpentine die cut 11x10 1/2.*

CM2348 *Nellie Bly;* CM2349 *Marguerite Higgins;* CM2350 *Ethel L. Payne;* CM2351 *Ida M. Tarbell*

CM2348

		MNHVF	UseVF
37¢	**Nellie Bly**	.75	.25

CM2349

		MNHVF	UseVF
37¢	**Marguerite Higgins**	.75	.25

CM2350

		MNHVF	UseVF
37¢	**Ethel L. Payne**	.75	.25

CM2351

		MNHVF	UseVF
37¢	**Ida M. Tarbell**	.75	.25
	Plate block of 4	3.00	
	y. Pane of 20	15.00	
	FDC (Sept. 14, 2002 - Fort Worth, Texas)		1.50

2002. IRVING BERLIN ISSUE commemorates one of the greatest songwriters of all time. Born in 1888, Irving Berlin immigrated with his family from Russia and by his early teens was making a living as a singing waiter. Published by the time he was 19, Irving Berlin went on to write more than 1,000 songs in his lifetime. Some of the most well known songs include "White Christmas" and "God Bless America." Designed by Greg Berger and based on a 1932 black and white photograph. *Printed gravure by Avery Dennison in self-adhesive panes of 20 on pre-phosphored paper. Serpentine die cut 11.*

CM2352 *Irving Berlin*

CM2352		MNHVF	UseVF
37¢	**multicolored** pre-phosphored paper	.75	.25
	Plate block of 4	3.00	
	y. Pane of 20	15.00	
	FDC (Sept. 15, 2002 - New York, N.Y.)		1.50

2002. NEUTER OR SPAY ISSUE depicts a puppy and a kitten. Designed by Derry Noyes *Printed gravure by Sennett Security Products in self-adhesive panes of 20. Serpentine die cut 10 3/4.*

CM2353 *Kitten;* CM2354 *Puppy*

CM2353		MNHVF	UseVF
37¢	**multicolored** phosphored block tagging	.75	.25

CM2354		MNHVF	UseVF
37¢	**multicolored** phosphored block tagging	.75	.25
	Plate block of 4	3.00	
	y. Pane of 20	15.00	
	FDC (Sept. 20, 2002 - Denver, Colo.)		1.50

2002. HANUKKAH ISSUE in the Holiday Celebrations Series shows the menorah design first issued in 1996 with a fourth denomination. (See Nos. CM1880, CM2099 and CM2269.) *Printed by Avery Dennison in self-adhesive panes of 20. Serpentine die cut 11.*

HANUKKAH USA 37   CM2355 *Menorah design*

CM2355		MNHVF	UseVF
37¢	**multicolored** pre-phosphored paper	.75	.25
	Plate block of 4	3.00	
	y. Pane of 20	15.00	
	FDC (Oct. 10, 2002)		1.50

2002. KWANZAA ISSUE in the Holiday Celebrations Series shows the celebrating family design first issued in 1997 with a fourth denomination. (See Nos. CM1963, CM2101 and CM2270.) *Printed by Avery Dennison in self-adhesive panes of 20. Serpentine die cut 11.*

CM2356 *Family celebrating*

CM2356		MNHVF	UseVF
37¢	**multicolored** pre-phosphored paper	.75	.25
	Plate block of 4	3.00	
	y. Pane of 20	15.00	
	FDC (Oct. 10, 2002)		1.50

2002. EID MUSLIM HOLIDAY ISSUE in the Holiday Celebrations Series highlights the Muslim holiday that was first depicted in 2001 with a second denomination. (See No. CM2263.) *Printed by Avery Dennison in self-adhesive panes of 20. Serpentine die cut 11.*

CM2357 *Islamic calligraphy by Mohamed Zakariya*

CM2357		MNHVF	UseVF
37¢	**blue & gold** phosphored block tagging	.75	.25
	Plate block of 4	3.00	
	y. Pane of 20	15.00	
	FDC (Oct. 10, 2002)		1.50

2002. CARY GRANT ISSUE eighth in the Legends of Hollywood Series features the actor as the leading debonair man that he was. Appearing in more than 70 films, Grant was always charming and sophisticated. The selvage from the pane of 20 is one of Cary Grant's most famous scenes as he is being chased by a crop duster in the film *North by Northwest. Printed gravure by Sennett Security Products in self-adhesive panes of 20. Serpentine die cut 10 3/4.*

CM2358 *Cary Grant (1904-1986)*

CM2358		MNHVF	UseVF
37¢	**multicolored** pre-phosphored small block tagging	.75	.25
	Plate block of 4	3.00	
	y. Pane of 20	15.00	
	y1. Uncut Press sheet of 6	75.00	
	FDC (Oct. 15, 2002 - Los Angeles, Calif.)		1.50

2002. HAWAIIAN MISSIONARIES ISSUE features four examples of Hawaii's first postage stamps. Included in the souvenir sheet above the reproduced stamps is the famous "Dawson Cover." It is believed to have the only known use of the 2¢ Missionary stamp. Most all uses of the original Hawaiian issues were used by Christian missionaries in their family correspondence, hence the term "Hawaiian Missionaries." *Printed offset by Banknote Corporation of America with block tagging. Perforated 11x11 1/4.*

CM2359		MNHVF	UseVF
37¢	**2¢ Hawaiian Postage, multicolored**	.75	.25

CM2360		MNHVF	UseVF
37¢	**5¢ Hawaiian Postage, multicolored**	.75	.25

CM2361		MNHVF	UseVF
37¢	**13¢ Hawaiian Postage, multicolored**	.75	.25

The "Hawaiian Missionary" Stamps of 1851-1853

The first official Hawaiian post office was established in December 1850. Postmaster Henry M. Whitney had stamps printed locally in three denominations. Philatelists call these rare stamps "Hawaiian Missionaries" because virtually all were used by Christian missionaries on outbound mail. Only 28 covers with Missionary stamps are known to exist; only the Dawson cover (right) bears the 2¢ stamp. The two 13¢ stamps were unusual as they prepaid postage in two countries–Hawaii and the U.S.

CM2359 *"2¢" Hawaiian Postage;* CM2360 *"5" Hawaiian Postage;*
CM2361 *"13¢" Hawaiian Postage;* CM2362 *"13¢" H.I. & U.S. Postage*

CM2362		MNHVF	UseVF
37¢	**13¢ H.I. & U.S. Postage, multicolored**	.75	.25
	FDC *(Oct. 24, 2002)* any single		1.50
	y. Souvenir sheet of 4 (CM2359-62)	3.00	
	y1. Uncut press sheet of 6	18.00	
	FDC, souvenir sheet		6.00

2002. HAPPY BIRTHDAY ISSUE encouraged the sending of birthday cards with a second denomination. (See No. CM2278.) Designed by Harry Zelenko, New York, N.Y. *Printed gravure by Avery Dennison in self-adhesive panes of 20. Serpentine die cut 11.*

CM2363 *Happy Birthday*

CM2363		MNHVF	UseVF
37¢	**multicolored** pre-phosphored paper	.75	.25
	Plate block of 4	3.00	
	FDC *(Oct. 25, 2002 - New York, N.Y.)*		1.50

2002. GREETINGS FROM AMERICA ISSUE highlighted symbols of each of the 50 states with stamps that evoked the large-letter postcards from the 30's and 40's with a second denomination. (See Nos. CM2281-2330.) Illustrated by Lonnie Busch, Franklin, N.C. *Printed gravure by Sennett Security Products in a self-adhesive pane of 50 on pre-phosphored paper. Serpentine die cut 10 3/4.*

CM2364		MNHVF	UseVF
37¢	**Alabama, multicolored**	.75	.25
CM2365		MNHVF	UseVF
37¢	**Alaska, multicolored**	.75	.25
CM2366		MNHVF	UseVF
37¢	**Arizona, multicolored**	.75	.25
CM2367		MNHVF	UseVF
37¢	**Arkansas, multicolored**	.75	.25
CM2368		MNHVF	UseVF
37¢	**California, multicolored**	.75	.25
CM2369		MNHVF	UseVF
37¢	**Colorado, multicolored**	.75	.25
CM2370		MNHVF	UseVF
37¢	**Connecticut, multicolored**	.75	.25

CM2371		MNHVF	UseVF
37¢	**Delaware, multicolored**	.75	.25
CM2372		MNHVF	UseVF
37¢	**Florida, multicolored**	.75	.25
CM2373		MNHVF	UseVF
37¢	**Georgia, multicolored**	.75	.25
CM2374		MNHVF	UseVF
37¢	**Hawaii, multicolored**	.75	.25
CM2375		MNHVF	UseVF
37¢	**Idaho, multicolored**	.75	.25
CM2376		MNHVF	UseVF
37¢	**Illinois, multicolored**	.75	.25
CM2377		MNHVF	UseVF
37¢	**Indiana, multicolored**	.75	.25
CM2378		MNHVF	UseVF
37¢	**Iowa, multicolored**	.75	.25
CM2379		MNHVF	UseVF
37¢	**Kansas, multicolored**	.75	.25
CM2380		MNHVF	UseVF
37¢	**Kentucky, multicolored**	.75	.25
CM2381		MNHVF	UseVF
37¢	**Louisiana, multicolored**	.75	.25
CM2382		MNHVF	UseVF
37¢	**Maine, multicolored**	.75	.25
CM2383		MNHVF	UseVF
37¢	**Maryland, multicolored**	.75	.25
CM2384		MNHVF	UseVF
37¢	**Massachusetts, multicolored**	.75	.25
CM2385		MNHVF	UseVF
37¢	**Michigan, multicolored**	.75	.25
CM2386		MNHVF	UseVF
37¢	**Minnesota, multicolored**	.75	.25
CM2387		MNHVF	UseVF
37¢	**Mississippi, multicolored**	.75	.25
CM2388		MNHVF	UseVF
37¢	**Missouri, multicolored**	.75	.25
CM2389		MNHVF	UseVF
37¢	**Montana, multicolored**	.75	.25

CM2364-CM2413 *Greetings pane*

		MNHVF	UseVF
CM2390		MNHVF	UseVF
37¢	Nebraska, multicolored	.75	.25
CM2391		MNHVF	UseVF
37¢	Nevada, multicolored	.75	.25
CM2392		MNHVF	UseVF
37¢	New Hampshire, multicolored	.75	.25
CM2393		MNHVF	UseVF
37¢	New Jersey, multicolored	.75	.25
CM2394		MNHVF	UseVF
37¢	New Mexico, multicolored	.75	.25
CM2395		MNHVF	UseVF
37¢	New York, multicolored	.75	.25
CM2396		MNHVF	UseVF
37¢	North Carolina, multicolored	.75	.25
CM2397		MNHVF	UseVF
37¢	North Dakota, multicolored	.75	.25
CM2398		MNHVF	UseVF
37¢	Ohio, multicolored	.75	.25
CM2399		MNHVF	UseVF
37¢	Oklahoma, multicolored	.75	.25
CM2400		MNHVF	UseVF
37¢	Oregon, multicolored	.75	.25
CM2401		MNHVF	UseVF
37¢	Pennsylvania, multicolored	.75	.25
CM2402		MNHVF	UseVF
37¢	Rhode Island, multicolored	.75	.25
CM2403		MNHVF	UseVF
37¢	South Carolina, multicolored	.75	.25
CM2404		MNHVF	UseVF
37¢	South Dakota, multicolored	.75	.25
CM2405		MNHVF	UseVF
37¢	Tennessee, multicolored	.75	.25
CM2406		MNHVF	UseVF
37¢	Texas, multicolored	.75	.25
CM2407		MNHVF	UseVF
37¢	Utah, multicolored	.75	.25
CM2408		MNHVF	UseVF
37¢	Vermont, multicolored	.75	.25
CM2409		MNHVF	UseVF
37¢	Virginia, multicolored	.75	.25
CM2410		MNHVF	UseVF
37¢	Washington, multicolored	.75	.25
CM2411		MNHVF	UseVF
37¢	West Virginia, multicolored	.75	.25
CM2412		MNHVF	UseVF
37¢	Wisconsin, multicolored	.75	.25
CM2413		MNHVF	UseVF
37¢	Wyoming, multicolored	.75	.25
	y. Pane of 50	40.00	
	y1. Uncut press sheet of 2	80.00	
	FDC (Oct. 25, 2002) any state		1.50

2003. THURGOOD MARSHALL ISSUE twenty sixth in the Black Heritage Series features a photograph of Thurgood Marshall from 1967 when he became the first African-American justice of the U.S. Supreme Court. Designed by Richard Sheaff, Scottsdale, Ariz. *Printed offset by Ashton-Potter in self-adhesive panes of 20. Serpentine die cut 11 1/2x11 1/4.*

CM2414 *Thurgood Marshall (1908-1993)*

		MNHVF	UseVF
CM2414			
37¢	black & gray pre-phosphored paper	.75	.25
	Plate block of 4	3.00	
	y. Pane of 20	15.00	
	FDC (Jan. 7, 2003 - Washington, D.C.)		1.50

2003. YEAR OF THE RAM ISSUE is the eleventh stamp of the Lunar New Year Series and the eighth of twelve animals associated with the Chinese New Year. The Year of the Ram started February 1, 2003, and continued until January 1, 2004. Designed by Clarence Lee, Honolulu, Hawaii. *Printed offset by Banknote Corporation of America in self-adhesive panes of 20. Die cut 11 1/2x11 3/4.*

CM2415 *Cut paper ram*

		MNHVF	UseVF
CM2415			
37¢	multicolored phosphored block tagging	.75	.25
	Plate block of 4	3.00	
	y. Pane of 20	15.00	
	FDC (Jan. 15, 2003 - Chicago, Ill.)		1.50

2003. ZORA NEALE HURSTON ISSUE is the nineteenth stamp in the Literary Arts Series and the first issue of this series to be self-adhesive. Hurston wrote many short stories, plays and essays as well as four novels including *Their Eyes Were Watching God*. *Printed gravure by Sennett Security Products in self-adhesive panes of 20. Die cut 10 3/4.*

CM2416 *Zora Neale Hurston*

		MNHVF	UseVF
CM2416			
37¢	multicolored phosphored small block tagging	.75	.25
	Plate block of 4	3.00	
	y. Pane of 20	15.00	
	FDC (Jan. 24, 2003 - Eatonville, Fla.)		1.50

2003. SPECIAL OLYMPICS ISSUE features a stylized competitor in the Olympics as he realizes his dream. Since its inception in 1968, the Special Olympics have helped more than a million athletes with mental retardation and other developmental disabilities through competition. *Printed offset by Avery Dennison in self-adhesive panes of 20. Die cut 11.*

CM2417 *Gold medallist celebrating*

		MNHVF	UseVF
CM2417			
80¢	multicolored pre-phosphored paper	1.50	.50
	Plate block of 4	6.00	
	y. Pane of 20	30.00	
	FDC (Feb. 13, 2003)		2.00

2003. AMERICAN FILMMAKING: BEHIND THE SCENES ISSUE features stamps for screenwriting, directing, costume design, music, makeup, art direction, cinematography, film editing, special effects and sound. Designed by Ethel Kessler, the stamps provide a window into the world of filmmaking. Release of the stamps coincided with the 75th anniversary of the Academy of Motion Picture Arts and Sciences. Explanatory text can be found on the backing paper of the stamps for those subjects listed below. Additional text about producing and filmmaking can be found on the stamp pane's selvage. *Printed gravure by Sennett Security Products on self-adhesive souvenir sheets of 10. Pre-phosphored paper. Die cut 10 3/4 top and bottom only.*

CM2418 *Filmmaking behind the scenes*

CM2418		MNHVF	UseVF
37¢	y. Pane of 10 multicolored	7.50	
	a. Screenwriting	.75	
	b. Directing	.75	
	c. Costume design	.75	
	d. Music	.75	
	e. Makeup	.75	
	f. Art direction	.75	
	g. Cinematography	.75	
	h. Film editing	.75	
	i. Special effects	.75	
	j. Sound	.75	
	y1. Uncut press sheet of 6	45.00	
	FDC (Feb. 25, 2003 - Beverly Hills, Calif.)		10.00

2003. OHIO STATEHOOD BICENTENNIAL ISSUE features a color photograph taken by Ian Adams near Marietta, Ohio. The photograph depicts a country lane and barn located on the edge of Wayne National Forest in Washington County. Designed by Phil Jordan, Falls Church, Va. *Printed offset/microprint "USPS" by Banknote Corporation of America in self-adhesive panes of 20. Die cut 11 3/4x11 1/2.*

CM2419 *Ohio rural scene*

CM2419		MNHVF	UseVF
37¢	multicolored phosphored block tagging	.75	.25
	Plate block of 4	3.00	
	y. Pane of 20	15.00	
	FDC (March 1, 2003 - Chillicothe, Ohio)		1.50

2003. PELICAN ISLAND NATIONAL WILDLIFE REFUGE ISSUE commemorates the 100th anniversary of the nation's first wildlife refuge located in the Indian River lagoon on the east coast of Central Florida and features a Brown Pelican. Wildlife refuges can now be found in every U.S. state or territory. Designed by Carl T. Herrman. *Printed offset/microprint "USPS" by Banknote Corporation of America in self-adhesive panes of 20. Die cut 11 3/4x11 1/2.*

CM2420 *Brown pelican*

CM2420		MNHVF	UseVF
37¢	multicolored phosphored block tagging	.75	.25
	Plate block of 4	3.00	
	y. Pane of 20	15.00	
	FDC (March 14, 2003 - Sebastian, Fla.)		1.50

2003. OLD GLORY PRESTIGE BOOKLET ISSUE is the second prestige booklet published by USPS. Designed by Richard Sheaff, a 28 page booklet with over 200 photos of flag history is included along with 20 stamps. Handpicked Americana at its best. *Printed offset by Ashton-Potter in self-adhesive 2 panes of 10 stamps. Serpentine die cut 10. No plate numbers.*

CM2421 *Uncle Sam on high wheeler bike;* CM2422 *1888 Campaign badge;* CM2423 *Old Glory and Star Spangled Banner ribbon;* CM2424 *Modern folding flag fan;* CM2425 *Lady Liberty and sword*

CM2421		MNHVF	UseVF
37¢	multicolored pre-phosphored paper	.75	.25
CM2422		**MNHVF**	**UseVF**
37¢	multicolored pre-phosphored paper	.75	.25
CM2423		**MNHVF**	**UseVF**
37¢	multicolored pre-phosphored paper	.75	.25
CM2424		**MNHVF**	**UseVF**
37¢	multicolored pre-phosphored paper	.75	.25
CM2425		**MNHVF**	**UseVF**
37¢	multicolored pre-phosphored paper	.75	.25
	n. Booklet pane of 10	7.50	
	n1. Booklet of 20 (Prestige booklet) (B332)	15.00	
	FDC (April 3, 2003 - New York, N.Y.) any single		1.50
	FDC (all five different designs)		7.50

2003. CESAR E. CHAVEZ ISSUE features the civil rights and farm labor leader who worked successfully to protect the rights and dignity of farm workers for over 30 years. The 1975 California Agricultural Labor Relations Act was a direct result of his influence and the only law in the nation that protects the rights of farm workers to unionize. Designed by Carl T. Herrman. *Printed offset/microprint "USPS" by Banknote Corporation of America in self-adhesive panes of 20. Die cut 11 3/4x11 1/2.*

CM2426 *Cesar E. Chavez (1927-1993)*

CM2426		MNHVF	UseVF
37¢	**multicolored** phosphored block tagging	.75	.25
	Plate block of 4	3.00	
	y. Pane of 20	15.00	
	FDC *(April 23, 2003 - Los Angeles, Calif.)*		1.50

2003. LOUISIANA PURCHASE BICENTENNIAL ISSUE commemorates the greatest real estate deal ever. In 1803, the United States doubled the size of the country by purchasing a block of land from cash-strapped France. Eventually, the parcel was divided into thirteen states and paved the way for western expansion. Designed by Richard Sheaff, Scottsdale, Ariz. *Printed gravure by Sennett Security Products in self-adhesive panes of 20. Die cut 10 3/4.*

CM2427 *Finalizing the deal*

CM2427		MNHVF	UseVF
37¢	**multicolored** pre-phosphored paper	.75	.25
	Plate block of 4	3.00	
	y. Pane of 20	15.00	
	FDC *(April 30, 2003 - New Orleans, La.)*		1.50

2003. FIRST POWERED FLIGHT CENTENNIAL ISSUE commemorates Orville and Wilbur Wright's 100th anniversary of a controlled, powered flight near Kitty Hawk, North Carolina. The "Wright Flyer" is shown on front and a detail of a 1909 photograph of the Wright Brothers in Pau, France, on the reverse. Designed by McRay Magleby, Provo, Utah. *Printed gravure by Avery Dennison on self-adhesive souvenir sheets of 10. Die cut 11.*

CM2428 *Wright flyer*

CM2428		MNHVF	UseVF
37¢	**multicolored** pre-phosphored paper	.75	.25
	y. Souvenir sheet of 10	7.50	
	FDC *(May 22, 2003 - Dayton, Ohio)*		1.50
	FDC *(May 22, 2003 - Kill Devil Hills, N.C.)*		1.50

2003. AUDREY HEPBURN ISSUE is ninth in the Legends of Hollywood Series. Hepburn not only graced the silver screen with her beauty and charm but also used the world as her stage. A great humanitarian as well, she spent her later years as a goodwill ambassador for UNICEF. Designed by Michael Deas. *Printed gravure by Sennett Security Products in self-adhesive panes of 20. Die cut 10 3/4.*

CM2429 *Audrey Hepburn (1929-1993)*

CM2429		MNHVF	UseVF
37¢	**multicolored** phosphored block tagging	.75	.25
	Plate block of 4	3.00	
	y. Pane of 20	15.00	
	y1. Uncut press sheet of 6	90.00	
	FDC *(June 11, 2003 - Los Angeles, Calif.)*		1.50

2003. SOUTHEASTERN LIGHTHOUSES ISSUE depicts paintings of 5 historic lighthouses found along the east coast from Virginia to Florida. Designed by Howard E. Paine. *Printed offset by Sennett Security Products in self-adhesive panes of 20. Die cut 10 3/4.*

CM2430 *Old Cape Henry, Va.*

CM2431 *Cape Lookout, N.C.*

CM2432 *Morris Island, S.C.*

CM2433 *Tybee Island, Ga*

CM2434 *Hillsboro Inlet, Fla.*

CM2430		MNHVF	UseVF
37¢	**multicolored** phosphored block tagging	.75	.25

CM2431		MNHVF	UseVF
37¢	**multicolored** phosphored block tagging	.75	.25

CM2432		MNHVF	UseVF
37¢	**multicolored** phosphored block tagging	.75	.25

CM2433		MNHVF	UseVF
37¢	**multicolored** phosphored block tagging	.75	.25

CM2434		MNHVF	UseVF
37¢	**multicolored** phosphored block tagging	.75	.25
	v. mis-registered "37¢" in position 2	.75	.25
	Strip of 5	3.75	
	y. Pane of 20	15.00	
	FDC *(June 13, 2003 - Tybee Island, Ga.)*		1.50

2003. ARCTIC TUNDRA ISSUE Fifth in the Nature of America Series features the plant and animal life in North America's coldest ecosystem. The arctic tundra stretches across northern Alaska and Canada. Illustrated from a painting by John D. Dawson, Hilo, Hawaii. *Printed offset by Banknote Corporation of America in a pane of 10. Self-adhesive and serpentine die cut 10 1/2.*

CM2435		MNHVF	UseVF
37¢	**Pane of 10** phosphored block tagging	7.50	
	y. Eight pane uncut press sheet	65.00	
	FDC *(July 2, 2003)* any single		1.50
	FDC, pane of 10		15.00

a. Gyrfalcon .75
b. Gray wolf .75
c. Common raven .75
d. Musk oxen and caribou .75
e. Grizzly bears and caribou .75
f. Caribou and willow ptarmigans .75
g. Arctic ground squirrel .75
h. Willow ptarmigan and bearberry .75
i. Arctic grayling .75
j. Singing vole, thin-legged wolf spider, lingonberry & Labrador tea

2003. KOREAN WAR VETERANS MEMORIAL ISSUE features John W. Alli's photograph of 19 stainless-steel statues that depict American soldiers from the Army, Navy, Air Force and Marines. This stamp honors the brave Americans who served in a war that has come to be known as the "forgotten war." *Printed offset by Banknote Corporation of America in self-adhesive panes of 20. Serpentine die cut 11 3/4x11 1/2.*

CM2436 *Statues of U.S. soldiers in wedge formation*

CM2436
37¢

		MNHVF	UseVF
multicolored phosphored block tagging		.75	.25
Plate block of 4		3.00	
y. Pane of 20		15.00	
FDC (July 27, 2003 - Washington, D.C.)			1.50

2003. MARY CASSATT BOOKLET ISSUE third in the American Treasures Series features four of Mary Cassatt's impressionist paintings. Her unique style made her internationally famous. Many of her paintings left you with the feeling you personally knew her subjects. *Printed gravure by Sennett Security Products in a flat double sided convertible booklet format. Self-adhesive and serpentine die cut 10 3/4 on 2 or 3 sides.*

CM2437 *Young Mother 1888*

CM2438 *Children Playing on the Beach*

CM2439 *On a Balcony*

CM2440 *Child in a Straw Hat*

CM2435 *Plant and animals of the Arctic Tundra*

CM2437		MNHVF	UseVF
37¢	**multicolored** pre-phosphored paper	.75	.25

CM2438		MNHVF	UseVF
37¢	**multicolored** pre-phosphored paper	.75	.25

CM2439		MNHVF	UseVF
37¢	**multicolored** pre-phosphored paper	.75	.25

CM2440		MNHVF	UseVF
37¢	**multicolored** pre-phosphored paper	.75	.25
	n. Booklet pane of 4	3.00	
	n1. Booklet pane of 20 (convertible booklet)	15.00	
	FDC *(Aug. 7, 2003 - Columbus, Ohio)* any single		1.50
	FDC (pane of 4)		6.00

2003. EARLY FOOTBALL HEROES ISSUE honors four legends from football's past. Bronko Nagurski, Ernie Nevers, and Red Grange had many accomplishments on the field while Walter Camp is credited with many new innovations of the game. Designed by Richard Sheaff. *Printed gravure by Avery Dennison in self-adhesive sheets of 20. Serpentine die cut 11.*

CM2441 *Bronko Nagurski (1908-1990)*

CM2442 *Ernie Nevers (1903-1976)*

CM2443 *Walter Camp (1859-1925)*

CM2444 *Red Grange (1903-1991)*

CM2441		MNHVF	UseVF
37¢	**multicolored** pre-phosphored paper	.75	.25

CM2442		MNHVF	UseVF
37¢	**multicolored** pre-phosphored paper	.75	.25

CM2443		MNHVF	UseVF
37¢	**multicolored** pre-phosphored paper	.75	.25

CM2444		MNHVF	UseVF
37¢	**multicolored** pre-phosphored paper	.75	.25
	Plate block of 4	3.00	
	y. Pane of 20	15.00	
	FDC *(Aug. 8, 2003 - South Bend, Ind.)*		1.50

2003. ROY ACUFF ISSUE celebrates his long life as an entertainer that thrilled generations with his fiddle and innovative sound. Once called "King of Country Music," Roy Acuff and his band, The Smokey Mountain Boys, performed many times at the Grand Ole Opry in Nashville where he eventually moved. He was also the first living member of the Country Music Hall of Fame. Designed by Richard Sheaff, Scottsdale, Ariz. *Printed gravure by Avery Dennison in self-adhesive non-phosphored paper in sheets of 20. Serpentine die cut.*

CM2445 *Roy Acuff (1903-1992)*

CM2445		MNHVF	UseVF
37¢	**multicolored** phosphored block tagging	.75	.25
	Plate block of 4	3.00	
	y. Pane of 20	15.00	
	FDC *(Sept. 13, 2003 - Nashville, Tenn.)*		1.50

Airmail

The first Airmail Series got under way in 1918, when the U.S. Post Office Department announced that an airmail service from New York to Philadelphia to Washington, D.C., would begin May 15.

Two days before the initial flight, the world's first stamp designed expressly for airmail was issued to pay the rate between any two of the three cities: 24¢ for the first ounce, including special delivery.

Later in the year, when the rate dropped to 16¢, another stamp was issued. Near the end of the year, a 6¢ stamp was issued to pay the airmail rate without special delivery.

All three stamps were of the same design, an Army Curtiss biplane used by the Air Corps, since the carrying of airmail had been entrusted to Army pilots flying Army planes. The Curtiss biplanes were called "Jennys" from their official designation, which began with the initials "JN."

All airmail issues were printed by the Bureau of Engraving and Printing unless otherwise noted. Prices for FDC are uncacheted for A1-A20.

Intaglio (flat plate press), perforated 11.

1918. CURTISS BIPLANE ISSUE

A1 Curtiss biplane

A1
6¢

		UnFVF	UseFVF
red orange (3,395,854)		75.00	30.00
pale orange		75.00	30.00
Plate block of 6 w/arrow		700.00	
Block of 4 w/arrow		280.00	150.00
Center line block		300.00	150.00
Double transfer		90.00	40.00
On cover			50.00
First flight cover (Dec. 16, 1918)			2,700.00
FDC (Dec. 10, 1918)			25,000.00

A2 Curtiss biplane

A2
16¢

		UnFVF	UseFVF
green (3,793,887)		90.00	40.00
dark green		90.00	40.00
Plate block of 6 w/arrow		1,200.00	
Block of 4 w/arrow		425.00	150.00
Center line block		450.00	175.00
On cover			50.00
First flight cover (July 15, 1918)			850.00
FDC (July 11, 1918)			25,000.00

A3 Curtiss biplane

A3v "Inverted Jenny"

A3
24¢

	UnFVF	UseFVF
carmine red & blue (2,134,888)	90.00	40.00
dark carmine red & blue	90.00	40.00
Plate block of 4 blue plate number & "TOP"	450.00	
Plate block of 4 red plate number & "TOP"	450.00	
Plate block of 4 red plate number only	450.00	
Plate block of 12, 2 plate numbers, arrow, & 2 "TOP" inscriptions	1,300.00	
Plate block of 12, 2 plate numbers, arrow, & blue "TOP" only	12,000.00	
Block of 4 w/arrow at top or left	425.00	125.00
Block of 4 w/arrow at bottom	420.00	120.00
Block of 4 w/arrow at right	450.00	175.00
Center line block	450.00	175.00
On cover		75.00
First flight cover (May 15, 1918)		850.00

	UnFVF	UseFVF
FDC (May 13, 1918)	26,000.00	
v. Center inverted, single	160,000.00	—
Block of 4 center inverted	750,000.00	
Plate block of 4 center inverted	1200,000.00	

Note: One sheet of 100 stamps with the blue vignette of the airplane upside down was purchased in a post office at Washington, D.C., by William T. Robey, who sold it to Eugene Klein of Philadelphia, who in turn sold it to Col. Edward H.R. Green. Green retained some of the errors, including the position pieces, and through Klein disposed of the rest. No. A3v is one of the most famous post office finds in U.S. stamp history.

1923. THE SECOND AIRMAIL SERIES ISSUE was issued for use on airmail service between New York and San Francisco. Three airmail zones were established: New York to Chicago; Chicago to Cheyenne; and Cheyenne to San Francisco. The rate of postage was 8¢ an ounce for each zone. The stamps were available through the Philatelic Agency at Washington, D.C., before they were issued to postmasters. *Intaglio, perforated 11.*

A4 Propeller and plane radiator

A4
8¢

	UnFVF	UseFVF
green (6,414,576)	25.00	15.00
dark green	25.00	15.00
Plate block of 6	250.00	
Double transfer	40.00	20.00
On cover		22.50
FDC (Aug. 15, 1923)		350.00

A5 Airmail service insignia

A5
16¢

	UnFVF	UseFVF
indigo (5,309,275)	85.00	30.00
Plate block of 6	1,800.00	
Double transfer	125.00	40.00
On cover		45.00
FDC (Aug. 17, 1923)		525.00

A6 De Havilland biplane

A6
24¢

	UnFVF	UseFVF
carmine (5,285,775)	95.00	30.00
Plate block of 6	2,250.00	
Double transfer	175.00	40.00
On cover		40.00
FDC (Aug. 21, 1923)		650.00

1926-27. MAP ISSUE consisted of three denominations: 10¢, 15¢, and 20¢, reflecting new rates: 10¢ per ounce up to 1,000 miles; 15¢ to 1,500 miles; and 20¢ for distances greater than 1,500 miles or Contract Airmail routes. *Intaglio, perforated 11.*

A7-A9 Relief map of United States and two mail planes

A7
10¢

	UnFVF	UseFVF
blue (42,092,800)	3.00	.45
light blue	3.00	.45
Plate block of 6	40.00	
Double transfer	5.50	1.00
FDC (Feb. 13, 1926)		80.00

A8		UnFVF	UseFVF
15¢	olive brown *(15,597,307)*	3.75	2.50
	light brown	3.75	2.50
	Plate block of 6	45.00	
	FDC *(Sept. 18, 1926)*		90.00

A9		UnFVF	UseFVF
20¢	yellow green *(17,616,350)*	9.00	2.00
	green	9.00	2.00
	Plate block of 6	100.00	
	FDC *(Jan. 25, 1927)*		100.00

1927. LINDBERGH AIRMAIL ISSUE honored Charles Augustus Lindbergh (1902-1974), the 25-year-old former airmail pilot who made the first non-stop solo flight from New York to Paris, May 20-21, 1927. Stamp collectors welcomed one of the few U.S. stamps ever to honor a living person. The stamp pictures Lindbergh's Ryan monoplane, *The Spirit of St. Louis,* which is now on display in the Smithsonian Institution at Washington, D.C. *Intaglio, perforated 11.*

A10 *Lindbergh's monoplane, The Spirit of St. Louis*

A10		UnFVF	UseFVF
10¢	indigo *(20,379,179)*	8.00	2.00
	Plate block of 6	145.00	
	Double transfer	11.00	3.00
	FDC *(June 18, 1927)*		175.00
	n. Booklet pane of 3	75.00	50.00
	Single, perforated 11 horizontally	12.50	
	FDC *(May 26, 1928)*		200.00

Note: First-day covers for No. A10 are from Washington, D.C., Little Falls, Minn. (where Lindbergh grew up), St. Louis, Mo., and Detroit, Mich. (his birthplace). FDCs for No. A10n are from Washington, D.C., and Cleveland, Ohio.

1928. AIR MAIL BEACON ISSUE the first airmail bicolor produced since the Curtiss Jenny stamp of 1918, reflects the 5¢-per-ounce rate that went into effect Aug. 1, 1928. Major shifts in the blue vignette are not uncommon. *Intaglio, flat plate press, perforated 11.*

A11 *Sherman Hill airmail beacon light*

A11		UnFVF	UseFVF
5¢	carmine red & blue *(106,887,675)*	4.50	.75
	Plate block of 6, 2 plate numbers & red "TOP"	45.00	
	Plate block of 6, 2 plate numbers & blue "TOP"	65.00	
	Plate block of 6, 2 plate numbers & double "TOP"	100.00	
	Plate block of 8, 2 plate numbers only	185.00	
	Block of 4 w/arrow	20.00	4.25
	Double transfer	—	
	Recut frame line at left	6.50	1.20
	FDC *(July 25, 1928)*		225.00
	v. Vertical pair, imperforate between	6,000.00	

1930. WINGED GLOBE ISSUE is sometimes confused with the 5¢ rotary-press version of 1931 (A16) but is smaller — 46 3/4mm by 18 3/4mm. *Intaglio (flat plate press), perforated 11.*

A12 *Winged globe*

A12		UnFVF	UseFVF
5¢	purple *(97,641,200)*	10.00	.50
	Plate block of 6	140.00	
	Double transfer	18.00	1.25
	FDC *(Feb. 10, 1930)*		90.00
	v. Horizontal pair, imperforate between	5,000.00	

1930. GRAF ZEPPELIN ISSUE was issued for use on mail carried by the German dirigible, built and commanded by Hugo Eckener, during various stages of a single flight from Friedrichshafen, Germany, to Seville, Spain, Pernambuco, Brazil, and Lakehurst, N.J., and back to Germany during May and June. A former newspaper reporter and an early critic of Count Ferdinand von Zeppelin's experiments with dirigibles, Eckener became a pilot and in 1921 manager of the Zeppelin firm.

The three values covered postal cards or letters on various legs of the trip; a round trip letter cost $3.90. Although more than a million copies of each value were printed, sales were disappointing. After the stamps were withdrawn from circulation June 30, more than 90 percent of them were destroyed.

A13 *Graf Zeppelin in flight*

A13		UnFVF	UseFVF
65¢	green *(93,536)*	325.00	240.00
	Plate block of 6	2,750.00	
	On flight cover		325.00
	FDC *(April 19, 1930)*		2,500.00

A14 *Zeppelin spanning the Atlantic*

A14		UnFVF	UseFVF
$1.30	yellow brown *(72,428)*	650.00	450.00
	Plate block of 6	5,750.00	
	On flight cover		550.00
	FDC *(April 19, 1930)*		2,500.00

A15 *Zeppelin circling globe*

A15		UnFVF	UseFVF
$2.60	blue *(61,296)*	975.00	700.00
	Plate block of 6	8,750.00	
	On flight cover		850.00
	FDC *(April 19, 1930)*		2,500.00

1931-34. WINGED GLOBE ISSUE had three values: 5¢, 6¢ and 8¢. The 5¢ stamp is sometimes confused with the 5¢ flat-plate issue of 1930 (A12), but is larger — 47 3/4mm by 19 1/4mm. *Intaglio (rotary press), perforated 10 1/2x11.*

A16-A18 *Winged globe*

A16		UnFVF	UseFVF
5¢	reddish violet *(57,340,000)*	5.50	.60
	Plate block of 4	95.00	
	FDC *(Aug. 19, 1931)*		175.00

A17		UnFVF	UseFVF
6¢	orange *(302,205,100)*	2.50	.35
	Plate block of 4	22.50	
	Pair, gutter between	400.00	

		UnFVF	UseFVF
	FDC *(July 1, 1934)*		40.00
	FDC *(June 30, 1934)*, Baltimore, Md.		600.00
A18		UnFVF	UseFVF
8¢	**yellow olive** *(76,648,803)*	2.50	.35
	Plate block of 4	40.00	
	Pair, gutter between	400.00	
	FDC *(Sept. 26, 1932)*		50.00

1933. CENTURY OF PROGRESS ZEPPELIN ISSUE was released in connection with the flight of the *Graf Zeppelin* to the Chicago World's Fair, as a goodwill gesture to publicize the event. The stamp, now known as the "Baby Zepp," remained on sale at the Philatelic Agency at Washington until 1935, but sales were disappointing, and more than 90 percent of the issue was destroyed. *Intaglio, perforated 11.*

A19 *Airship* Graf Zeppelin

A19		UnFVF	UseFVF
50¢	**green** *(324,070)*	90.00	75.00
	Plate block of 6	800.00	
	On flight cover		80.00
	FDC *(Oct. 2, 1933)*		250.00

1935-37. CHINA CLIPPER OVER PACIFIC ISSUE released primarily to pay postage on mail carried over the transpacific airmail route. *Intaglio, perforated 11.*

A20 *China Clipper over Pacific*

A20		UnFVF	UseFVF
20¢	**green** *(12,794,600)*	10.00	1.50
	dark green	10.00	1.50
	Plate block of 6	110.00	
	FDC *(Feb. 15, 1937)*		55.00
A21		UnFVF	UseFVF
25¢	**blue** *(10,205,400)*	1.50	1.00
	Plate block of 6	22.50	
	FDC *(Nov. 22, 1935)*		45.00
A22		UnFVF	UseFVF
50¢	**carmine** *(9,285,300)*	10.00	4.50
	Plate block of 6	110.00	
	FDC *(Feb. 15, 1937)*		60.00

1938. EAGLE AND SHIELD ISSUE originally designed by Franklin D. Roosevelt, was issued to coincide with the U.S. Post Office Department's promotion of National Air Mail Week. *Intaglio, perforated 11.*

A23 *Eagle and shield*

A23		UnFVF	UseFVF
6¢	**indigo & carmine** *(349,946,500)*	.50	.20
	ultramarine & carmine	.40	.20
	Block of 4 w/arrow	7.50	
	Center line block	2.50	.90
	Plate block of 10, 2 plate numbers, arrow, 2 "TOP" & 2 registration markers	15.00	
	FDC *(May 14, 1938)*		17.50
	v. Horizontal pair, imperforate vertically	10,000.00	
	v1. Vertical pair, imperforate horizontally	350.00	

1939. TRANSATLANTIC ISSUE A final Winged Globe design, celebrates the inauguration of transatlantic Airmail service. *Intaglio, perforated 11.*

A24 *Winged globe*

A24		UnFVF	UseFVF
30¢	**slate blue** *(19,768,150)*	9.00	1.50
	Plate block of 6	150.00	
	On flight cover		5.00
	FDC *(May 16, 1939)*		60.00

1941-44. TWIN MOTORED TRANSPORT PLANE ISSUE consisted of seven denominations intended to cover all airmail postage requirements. Except for the color and denomination, all of the stamps are of the same design. *Intaglio, perforated 11x10 1/2.*

A25, BA2, BA3 *Twin motored transport plane*

A25		MNHVF	UseVF
6¢	**rose red** *(4,746,527,700)*	.25	.20
	Plate block of 4	1.00	
	Vertical pair, gutter between	200.00	
	Horizontal pair, gutter between	—	6.00
	FDC *(June 25, 1941)*		7.50
	v. Horizontal pair, imperforate between	1,500.00	
	n. Booklet pane of 3	3.50	3.00
	FDC *(March 18, 1943)*, single		10.00
A26		MNHVF	UseVF
8¢	**light olive green** *(1,744,878,650)*	.30	.20
	Plate block of 4	2.00	
	Pair, gutter between	300.00	
	FDC *(March 21, 1944)*		6.00
A27		MNHVF	UseVF
10¢	**violet** *(67,117,400)*	1.40	.20
	Plate block of 4	11.00	
	FDC *(Aug. 15, 1941)*		9.00
A28		MNHVF	UseVF
15¢	**brown carmine** *(78,434,800)*	2.75	.40
	Plate block of 4	12.50	
	FDC *(Aug. 19, 1941)*		9.00
A29		MNHVF	UseVF
20¢	**emerald** *(42,359,850)*	2.75	.40
	Plate block of 4	12.50	
	FDC *(Aug. 27, 1941)*		12.50
A30		MNHVF	UseVF
30¢	**light blue** *(59,880,850)*	2.75	.50
	Plate block of 4	14.00	
	FDC *(Sept. 25, 1941)*		20.00
A31		MNHVF	UseVF
50¢	**orange** *(11,160,600)*	14.00	4.00
	Plate block of 4	90.00	
	FDC *(Oct. 29, 1941)*		30.00

1946. SKYMASTER ISSUE was released to prepay the new 5¢ airmail rate. *Intaglio, perforated 11x10 1/2.*

A32 *DC-4 Skymaster*

A32		MNHVF	UseVF
5¢	**carmine** *(864,753,100)*	.25	.20
	Plate block of 4	.75	
	FDC *(Sept. 25, 1946)*		1.75

1947. SMALL 5¢ SKYMASTER ISSUE replaced the large 5¢ stamp of 1946. *Intaglio, perforated 10 1/2x11.*

A33, A34 *DC-4 Skymaster*

A33		MNHVF	UseVF
5¢	**carmine** *(971,903,700)*	.25	.20
	Plate block of 4	1.00	
	FDC *(March 26, 1947)*		1.75

1947. SMALL 5¢ SKYMASTER COIL ISSUE Intaglio perforated 10 horizontally.

A34		MNHVF	UseVF
5¢	**carmine** *(33,244,500)*	1.00	.80
	Pair	2.20	1.70
	Line pair	10.00	3.00
	FDC *(Jan. 15, 1948)*		1.75

1947. PICTORIAL AIRMAIL ISSUE consisted of three denominations intended to cover international air postage rates. *Intaglio, perforated 11x10 1/2.*

A35 *Pan-American Union Building, Washington, D.C.*

A35		MNHVF	UseVF
10¢	**black** *(207,976,550)*	.30	.20
	Plate block of 4	1.30	
	FDC *(Aug. 30, 1947)*		1.75
	p. Dry print	.50	.25
	Plate block of 4	2.25	

A36 *Statue of Liberty and skyline of New York City*

A36		MNHVF	UseVF
15¢	**blue green** *(756,186,350)*	.40	.20
	Plate block of 4	1.75	
	Pair, gutter between	625.00	
	FDC *(Aug. 20, 1947)*		2.00
	p. Dry print	.50	.25
	Plate block of 4	2.50	
	v. Horizontal pair, imperforate between	2,250.00	

A37 *San Francisco-Oakland Bay Bridge*

A37		MNHVF	UseVF
25¢	**blue** *(132,956,100)*	1.00	.20
	Plate block of 4	5.00	
	FDC *(July 31, 1947)*		2.50
	p. Dry print	1.00	.20
	Plate block of 4	4.25	

1948. NEW YORK CITY ISSUE commemorated the 50th anniversary of the consolidation of the five boroughs of New York City. *Intaglio, perforated 11x10 1/2.*

A38 *Map of the five boroughs encompassed by ring and airplanes*

A38		MNHVF	UseVF
5¢	**carmine red** *(38,449,100)*	.25	.20
	Plate block of 4	4.00	
	FDC *(July 31, 1948)*		2.00

1949. SMALL 6¢ SKYMASTER ISSUE reflected the raise in rates to 6¢ for domestic airmail. *Intaglio, perforated 10 1/2x11.*

A39-A40, BA4, BA5, BA6, BA7, BA8 *DC-4 Skymaster*

A39		MNHVF	UseVF
6¢	**carmine** *(5,070,095,200)*	.25	.20
	Plate block of 4	1.00	
	FDC *(Jan. 18, 1949)*		1.75
	n. Booklet pane of 6	9.50	7.50
	FDC *(Nov. 18, 1949),* pane of 6		12.50
	p. Dry print	.75	.30
	Plate block of 4	3.50	
	pn. Booklet pane of 6	15.00	

1949. SMALL 6¢ SKYMASTER COIL ISSUE Intaglio, perforated 10 horizontally.

A40		MNHVF	UseVF
6¢	**carmine**	3.50	.20
	Pair	7.00	
	Line pair	14.00	
	FDC *(Aug. 25, 1949)*		1.75

1949. ALEXANDRIA BICENTENNIAL ISSUE commemorated the 200th anniversary of the founding of Alexandria, Va. *Intaglio, perforated 11x10 1/2.*

A41 *Carlyle House, Alexandria seal & Gadsby's Tavern*

A41		MNHVF	UseVF
6¢	**carmine** *(75,085,000)*	.20	.20
	Plate block of 4	.80	
	FDC *(May 11, 1949)*		2.00

1949. UNIVERSAL POSTAL UNION ISSUE commemorated the 75th anniversary of the formation of the Universal Postal Union.

A42 *Post Office Department Building, Washington, D.C.*

A42		MNHVF	UseVF
10¢	**violet** *(21,061,300)*	.30	.30
	Plate block of 4	1.60	
	FDC *(Nov. 18, 1949)*		1.75

A43 *Globe surrounded by letter-carrying doves*

A43		MNHVF	UseVF
15¢	**cobalt** *(36,613,100)*	.30	.25
	Plate block of 4	1.25	
	FDC *(Oct. 7, 1949)*		3.00

A44 *Plane and globe*

A44

25¢	**carmine** (16,217,100)	MNHVF	UseVF
		.50	.40
	Plate block of 4	6.00	
	FDC (Nov. 30, 1949)		4.00

1949. WRIGHT BROTHERS ISSUE commemorated the 46th anniversary of Wilbur and Orville Wright's first flight. On Dec. 17, 1903, at Kill Devil Hill, south of Kitty Hawk, N.C., Orville took the plane aloft for 12 seconds over a distance of 120 feet. Wilbur flew 59 seconds over a distance of 825 feet in the fourth flight that day. *Intaglio, perforated 11.*

A45 *Wright brothers and their plane*

A45

6¢	**carmine purple** (80,405,000)	MNHVF	UseVF
		.30	.20
	Plate block of 4	1.25	
	FDC (Dec. 17, 1949)		3.00

1952. HAWAII AIRMAIL ISSUE provided a stamp to pay postage on one pound of air parcel post to the eight domestic zones (over 1,800 miles). *Intaglio, perforated 11x10 1/2.*

A46 *Diamond Head at Honolulu, Hawaii*

A46

80¢	**bright purple** (18,876,800)	MNHVF	UseVF
		5.00	1.25
	Plate block of 4	22.50	
	FDC (March 26, 1952)		15.00

1953. POWERED FLIGHT ISSUE marked the 50th anniversary of the Wright brothers' first flight. *Intaglio, perforated 11x10 1/2.*

A47 *Old and new planes with slogan*

A47

6¢	**carmine** (78,415,000)	MNHVF	UseVF
		.25	.20
	Plate block of 4	1.00	
	FDC (May 29, 1953)		2.50

1954. EAGLE ISSUE was intended primarily for use on domestic airmail postcards. *Intaglio, perforated 11x10 1/2.*

A48, 50 *Eagle in flight*

A48

4¢	**blue** (40,483,600)	MNHVF	UseVF
		.25	.20
	Plate block of 4	1.50	
	FDC (Sept. 3, 1954)		1.75

1957. AIR FORCE ISSUE marked the 50th anniversary of the U.S. Air Force. *Intaglio, perforated 11x10 1/2.*

A49 *U.S. military aircraft*

A49

6¢	**bright Prussian blue** (63,185,000)	MNHVF	UseVF
		.25	.20
	Plate block of 4	1.00	
	FDC (Aug. 1, 1957)		2.00

1958. EAGLE ISSUE used the flying eagle design with a 5¢ denomination because of the increase in postage rates Aug. 1. *Intaglio, perforated 11x10 1/2.*

A50

5¢	**carmine red** (72,480,000)	MNHVF	UseVF
		.25	.20
	Plate block of 4	1.50	
	FDC (July 31, 1958)		1.75

1958. JET SILHOUETTE ISSUE met the change in domestic airmail rates Aug. 1. *Intaglio, perforated 10 1/2x11.*

A51-A52, A60-A61 *Jet airliner*

A51

7¢	**blue** (1,326,960,000)	MNHVF	UseVF
		.25	.20
	Plate block of 4	1.00	
	FDC (July 31, 1958)		1.75
	n. Booklet pane of 6	13.00	6.75
	FDC, booklet pane		7.00
	v. Vertical pair, imperforate between	—	

1958. JET SILHOUETTE COIL ISSUE Coil stamp, perforated 10 horizontally.

A52

7¢	**blue** (large hole perforations)	MNHVF	UseVF
		2.25	.20
	(157,035,000)		
	Pair	4.50	.40
	Line pair	19.00	1.25
	FDC (July 31, 1958)		1.75
	s. (Small hole perforations)	10.00	
	Pair	25.00	10.00
	Line pair	200.00	
	v. Pair, imperforate	200.00	

1959. ALASKA STATEHOOD ISSUE commemorated the addition to the union of the 49th state. *Intaglio, perforated 11x10 1/2.*

A53 *The Big Dipper and North Star superimposed on map of Alaska*

A53

7¢	**deep blue** (90,055,200)	MNHVF	UseVF
		.25	.20
	Plate block of 4	1.00	
	FDC (Jan. 3, 1959)		2.00

1959. BALLOON JUPITER ISSUE commemorated the 100th anniversary of the first U.S. transmission of airmail by balloon from Lafayette to Crawfordsville, Ind., a distance of 35 miles. *Intaglio (Giori Press), perforated 11.*

A54 *Crowd watching John Wise ascending on first flight, Aug. 17, 1859*

A54		MNHVF	UseVF
7¢	deep blue & scarlet *(79,290,000)*	.30	.20
	Plate block of 4	1.20	
	FDC *(Aug. 17, 1959)*		3.00

1959. PAN AMERICAN GAMES ISSUE marked the opening of the Pan American Games in Chicago, Ill. *Intaglio (Giori Press), perforated 11.*

A55 *Runner holding torch*

A55		MNHVF	UseVF
10¢	deep blue & scarlet *(38,770,000)*	.35	.30
	Plate block of 4	1.50	
	FDC *(Aug. 27, 1959)*		2.00

1959. HAWAII STATEHOOD ISSUE commemorated the admission of Hawaii to the union as the 50th state. *Intaglio, perforated 11x10 1/2.*

A56 *Hawaiian warrior and map of islands*

A56		MNHVF	UseVF
7¢	dull scarlet *(84,815,000)*	.25	.20
	Plate block of 4	1.20	
	FDC *(Aug. 21, 1959)*		2.00

International Airmail Series was created to meet the demand for specific foreign airmail rates. The 10¢ value covered airmail to Central and South America and the West Indies exclusive of Mexico. The 15¢ denomination prepaid airmail postage to Europe and North Africa. The 25¢ stamp was for use to Asia, Africa, and the Middle East. *Intaglio (Giori Press), perforated 11.*

1960. LIBERTY BELL ISSUE in the International Airmail Series.

A57 *Liberty Bell*

A57		MNHVF	UseVF
10¢	black & green *(39,960,000)*	1.25	.80
	Plate block of 4	5.50	
	FDC *(June 10, 1960)*		2.00

1959. STATUE OF LIBERTY ISSUE in the International Airmail Series.

A58 *Statue of Liberty*

A58		MNHVF	UseVF
15¢	black & orange *(98,160,000)*	.35	.20
	Plate block of 4	1.50	
	FDC *(Nov. 20, 1959)*		1.75

1966. ABRAHAM LINCOLN ISSUE in the International Airmail Series.

A59 *Abraham Lincoln*

A59		MNHVF	UseVF
25¢	black & brown purple	.50	.20
	Plate block of 4	2.00	
	FDC *(April 22, 1960)*		1.75
	z. Tagged, type OP	.70	.40
	Plate block of 4	2.80	
	FDC, tagged *(Dec. 29, 1966)*		60.00

Untagged "gripper space" on lower pane margins of this issue is normal.

1960. JET SILHOUETTE ISSUE returned in a new color to facilitate handling of domestic airmail letters. *Intaglio, perforated 10 1/2x11.*

A60		MNHVF	UseVF
7¢	bright red *(BA9, BA10)* *(1,289,460,000)*	.25	.20
	Plate block of 4	1.25	
	Pair, gutter between	250.00	
	z. Tagged, Type II	.25	.20
	Plate block of 4	1.25	
	z1. Tagged, Type IIa	.25	.20
	Plate block of 4	—	
	FDC *(Aug. 12, 1960)*		1.75
	n. Booklet pane of 6	15.00	
	FDC *(Aug. 19, 1960),*		9.00
	n1. Booklet pane of 6, tagged Type I	—	
	n2. Booklet pane of 6, tagged Type II	—	
	p. Hi-brite	—	—

1960. JET SILHOUETTE COIL ISSUE Coil stamp, perforated 10 horizontally.

A61		MNHVF	UseVF
7¢	bright red *(87,140,000)*	4.25	.30
	Pair	8.50	.60
	Line pair	37.50	
	FDC *(Oct. 22, 1960)*		1.75

1961. STATUE OF LIBERTY ISSUE in the International Airmail Series was a revision of the 1959 15¢ Statue of Liberty airmail stamp (A58), showing a revised frame line around the statue engraving. *Intaglio and offset by Bureau of Engraving and Printing (Giori Press), perforated 11.*

A62 *Statue of Liberty, redesigned frame line*

A62		MNHVF	UseVF
15¢	black & orange	.50	.20
	Plate block of 4	2.00	
	FDC *(Jan. 13, 1961)*		1.75
	z. Tagged, Type OP	.75	.50
	Plate block of 4	6.50	
	FDC *(Jan. 11, 1967)*		1.75
	vz. Horizontal pair, imperforate vertically	11,500.00	

DECODING THE CATALOG

There is no particular difficulty in distinguishing the two types of the 15¢ Statue of Liberty airmail stamp.

Type I of this issue (Krause-Minkus A58) was released Nov. 20, 1959. The Bureau of Engraving and Printing produced an initial total of 98.1 million. A double-line orange frame line surrounds the entire design, and the bottom part of Liberty's book is cropped.

On Jan. 13, 1961, and Jan. 11, 1967, respectively, two versions of the Type II 15¢ LIberty airmail were released. Type II stamps feature the same basic design as Type I, but the orange frame line has been removed from the Statue of Liberty and is replaced by a black frame. This creates the appearance of two framed images and a vertical white gutter down the center. Liberty's book is now fully seen.

The Type II version released informally on Jan. 13, 1961, in Buffalo, N.Y., is untagged. The version released six years later in Washington, D.C. (A62), has an all-over coating of phosphorescent tagging that glows orange-red under shortwave ultraviolet light.

None of the major types of the 15¢ Statue of Liberty airmail bears any particular value premium, but it is important to learn what to search for when decoding the catalog.

1961. LIBERTY BELL ISSUE in the International Airmail Series was a new denomination and color required because of new increased postal rates. *Intaglio (Giori Press), perforated 11.*

A63 *Liberty Bell*

A63 13¢		MNHVF	UseVF
	black & scarlet	.50	.20
	Plate block of 4	2.00	
	FDC *(June 28, 1961)*		1.75
	z. Tagged	.70	.40
	Plate block of 4	2.80	
	FDC *(Feb. 15, 1967)*		60.00

1962. AIRLINER OVER CAPITOL ISSUE was made available to meet the increase in postage rates. *Rotary press printing, perforated 10 1/2x11.* Although this stamp was issued Dec. 6, 1962, an experiment was started Aug. 1, 1963, in Dayton, Ohio, in which a luminescent was applied to these airmail stamps. The phosphor-tagged stamps, in conjunction with an ultraviolet sensing device, sped up airmail service.

A64, A65, BA11, BA12, BA13, B14, BA15, BA16, BA17, BA18, BA19, BA20, BA21 *Jet over Capitol dome*

A64 8¢		MNHVF	UseVF
	carmine	.30	.20
	Plate block of 4	1.25	
	FDC *(Dec. 5, 1962)*		1.75
	n. Booklet pane of 5 plus Mailman label	6.75	
	FDC *(Dec. 5, 1962)*		1.75
	n1. Booklet pane of 5 plus Zone # label (1963)	47.50	
	n2. Booklet pane of 5 plus ZIP label (1964)	12.50	
	p1. Printed on Hi-brite paper	—	—
	Plate block of 4	1.50	
	p1n. Booklet pane of 5 plus Mailman label	—	—
	z. Tagged, Type I or II	.35	.20
	Plate block of 4	1.75	
	FDC *(Aug. 1, 1963), Dayton, Ohio*		1.75
	zn. Booklet pane of 5 plus ZIP label	1.65	1.25

Type I tagging: mat tagging, using four separate mats that did not cover entire sheet of 400 stamps (untagged areas identify the variety). Stamps from the four corners of a pane have two untagged margins.

Type II tagging: roll tagging, where continuous rolls replaced the tagging mats. Only the plate number selvage margin is partially tagged.

Type IIa tagging: wide roll tagging, where all margins are fully tagged.

1962. AIRLINER OVER CAPITOL COIL ISSUE Coil stamp, perforated 10 horizontally.

A65 8¢		MNHVF	UseVF
	carmine	.40	.20
	Pair	.80	.20
	Line pair	3.50	
	FDC *(Dec. 5, 1962)*		1.75
	p1. On Hi-brite paper	—	
	Pair	—	
	Line pair	—	
	z. Tagged, Type I	.40	.20
	Pair	.80	.20
	Line pair	2.00	
	FDC, *(Jan. 14, 1965),* tagged		60.00
	z1. Tagged, Type II	.35	.20
	Pair	1.00	
	Line pair	2.75	

1963. MONTGOMERY BLAIR ISSUE recalled Abraham Lincoln's postmaster general (1861-64). Blair (1813-83) called the first international postal conference in Paris in 1863, which led to the Universal Postal Union. *Intaglio (Giori Press), perforated 11.*

A66 *Montgomery Blair and mail circling the globe*

A66 15¢		MNHVF	UseVF
	red, maroon & blue *(42,245,000)*	.60	.50
	Plate block of 4	2.50	
	FDC *(May 3, 1963)*		2.50

1963. BALD EAGLE ISSUE was prepared for use on domestic airmail postcards. *Intaglio, perforated 11x10.*

A67 *Bald eagle on crag*

A67 6¢		MNHVF	UseVF
	carmine	.25	.20
	Plate block of 4	2.00	
	FDC *(July 12, 1963)*		1.75
	z. Tagged	4.50	3.50
	Plate block of 4	55.00	
	FDC *(Feb. 15, 1967)*		60.00

1963. AMELIA EARHART ISSUE marked the 65th birthday of America's most prominent female aviatrix, the first woman to fly across the Atlantic Ocean, and the first woman to fly across the United States non-stop. Earhart (1898-1937) was lost at sea while attempting to fly around the world. *Intaglio (Giori Press), perforated 11.*

A68 *Amelia Earhart and Lockheed Electra*

A68		MNHVF	UseVF
8¢	**carmine red & brown purple**	.25	.20
	(63,890,000)		
	Plate block of 4	1.50	
	FDC (July 24, 1963)		4.00

1964. ROBERT H. GODDARD ISSUE marked the 50th anniversary of the first patents granted to Goddard for his multi-stage booster rockets using liquid and solid fuels. *Intaglio (Giori Press), perforated 11.*

A69 *Dr. Goddard, Atlas rocket and launching pad*

A69		MNHVF	UseVF
8¢	**multicolored** tagged Type OP	.45	.20
	(65,170,000)		
	Plate block of 4	2.00	
	FDC (Oct. 5, 1964)		3.00
	zo. Tagging omitted	—	

1967. ALASKA PURCHASE ISSUE celebrated the 100th anniversary of the acquisition of Alaska from Russia. The date of issue, March 30, is a state holiday honoring Secretary of State William H. Seward, who arranged the sale for $7,200,000. *Intaglio (Giori Press), perforated 11.*

A70 *Tlingit Totem pole in the Alaska State Museum, Juneau*

A70		MNHVF	UseVF
8¢	**brown & light brown** tagged (64,710,000)	.25	.20
	Plate block of 4	1.50	
	FDC (March 20, 1967)		2.00

1967. COLUMBIA JAYS ISSUE prepared to meet the increase in airmail rates to Europe and Mediterranean Africa. The design is similar to the 1963 5¢ Audubon commemorative (CM526) and was used again because of its aesthetic and technical excellence. *Intaglio (Giori Press), perforated 11.*

A71 *John James Audubon's* Columbia Jays

A71		MNHVF	UseVF
20¢	**blue, brown & yellow,** tagged	.80	.20
	(165,430,000)		
	Plate block of 4	5.00	
	FDC (April 26, 1967)		2.50
	zo. Tagging omitted	10.00	

1968. STAR RUNWAY ISSUE met the increase in airmail rates that went into effect Jan. 7, 1968. *Intaglio, perforated 11x10 1/2.*

A72, A73, BA22, BA23 *Poster type art showing 50 stars*

A72		MNHVF	UseVF
10¢	**red** tagged	.20	.20
	Plate block of 4	1.60	
	FDC (Jan. 5, 1968)		1.75
	n. Booklet pane of 5 plus Mail Early label	3.75	3.50
	n1. Booklet pane of 5 plus ZIP slogan label	3.75	3.50
	n2. Booklet pane of 8	2.00	.75
	n2z. Booklet pane of 8, tagging glows yellow rather than red orange	—	
	zo. Tagging omitted	10.00	
	nzo. Booklet pane of 5 plus Mail Early label	—	
	n1zo. Booklet pane of 5 plus ZIP slogan label	—	
	n2zo. Booklet pane of 8	—	
	v. Booklet pair, imperforate between vertically (one known)	8,000.00	

1968. STAR RUNWAY COIL ISSUE Coil stamp, perforated 10 vertically.

A73		MNHVF	UseVF
10¢	**red** tagged	.30	.20
	Pair	.80	
	Line pair	2.00	
	FDC (Jan. 5, 1968)		1.75
	v. Pair, imperforate	625.00	

1968. AIRMAIL SERVICE ISSUE commemorated the 50th anniversary of the service, established May 15, 1918, when mail was carried by biplane on the Washington-New York flight. *Intaglio (Giori Press) and offset, perforated 11.*

A74 *Curtiss Jenny, the same plane number as on the first airmail stamp*

A74		MNHVF	UseVF
10¢	**black, red & blue** tagged (74,180,000)	.25	.20
	Plate block of 4	2.00	
	FDC (May 15, 1968)		2.00
	v. red stripe on tail omitted	3,000.00	
	zo. Tagging omitted	7.50	

1968. USA AND JET ISSUE intended primarily for mail to Europe and points in North Africa. *Intaglio and offset, perforated 11.*

A75, A81 *"USA" and airplane*

A75		MNHVF	UseVF
20¢	**multicolored** tagged	.35	.20
	Plate block of 4	1.75	
	FDC (Nov. 22, 1968)		1.75
	zo. Tagging omitted	10.00	

1969. MOON LANDING ISSUE paid tribute to the landing of a man on the Moon July 20, 1969, when Neil A. Armstrong and Col. Edwin E. Aldrin Jr., became the first humans to land on the lunar surface. The engraved master die from which the stamps were printed was carried to the Moon by the astronauts. *Intaglio and offset, perforated 11.*

A76 *First man on the Moon*

A76		MNHVF	UseVF
10¢	**multicolored** tagged *(152,364,800)*	.25	.20
	Plate block of 4	1.50	
	FDC *(Sept. 9, 1969)*		5.00
	v. Offset red omitted	500.00	

Note: No. A76v must have missing red from the entire design, including the dots on top of the yellow area as well as the astronaut's shoulder patch. Stamps with any red present are worth far less than the true red-omitted error.

1971. DELTA WING SILHOUETTE ISSUE created to meet increased domestic and international rates. *Intaglio, perforated 10 1/2x11.*

A77 *Silhouette of Delta wing plane*

A77		MNHVF	UseVF
9¢	**red** tagged *(25,830,000)*	.25	.20
	Plate block of 4	1.00	
	FDC *(May 15, 1971)*		1.75

1971. JET SILHOUETTE ISSUE Intaglio, perforated 11x10 1/2.

A78-A79, BA24 *Silhouette of jet airliner*

A78		MNHVF	UseVF
11¢	**red** tagged *(317,810,000)*	.25	.20
	Plate block of 4	1.60	
	FDC *(May 7, 1971)*		1.75
	n. Booklet pane of 4 plus 2 labels	1.60	
	zo. Tagging omitted	7.50	
	zx. Untagged & Bureau precancel Washington D.C.	.50	.30
	Plate block of 4	2.75	
	zx1. Untagged & Bureau precancel Washington D.C.	1.50	
	Plate block of 4	25.00	
	FDC booklet pane		3.00
	FDC booklet single		4.00

1971. JET SILHOUETTE COIL ISSUE Coil stamp, perforated 10 vertically.

A79		MNHVF	UseVF
11¢	**red** tagged	.25	.20
	Pair	.50	
	Line pair	.90	
	FDC *(May 7, 1971)*		1.75
	v. Pair, imperforate	250.00	

1971. HEAD OF LIBERTY ISSUE Intaglio (Giori Press), perforated 11.

A80 *Head of Liberty*

A80		MNHVF	UseVF
17¢	**multicolored** tagged	.35	.20
	Plate block of 4	1.50	
	FDC *(July 13, 1971)*		1.75
	zo. Tagging omitted	10.00	

1971. JET AND "USA" ISSUE *Intaglio (Giori Press) and offset, perforated 11.*

A81		MNHVF	UseVF
21¢	**multicolored** tagged *(49,815,000)*	.40	.20
	Plate block of 4	2.00	
	FDC *(May 21, 1971)*		1.75
	zo. Tagging omitted	10.00	
	v. black omitted	12,100.00	

National Parks Centennial Series

released over a five-month period consisted of eight stamps (one is an airmail stamp, A82).

1972. NATIONAL PARK ISSUE was part of the National Parks Centennial Series (see CM674-CM680). The City of Refuge depicted is an ancient sanctuary, for taboo breakers or victims of wars, on a lava ledge on the southwestern part of the island of Hawaii. *Intaglio (Giori Press) and offset, perforated 11.*

A82 *Wooden statue and palisaded temple*

A82		MNHVF	UseVF
11¢	**multicolored** tagged *(78,210,000)*	.25	.20
	Plate block of 4	1.00	
	FDC *(May 3, 1972)*		1.75
	v. blue & green omitted	925.00	—
	zo. Tagging omitted	—	

1972. OLYMPIC ISSUE released as part of the Olympic Games Series (see CM686) for the Winter and Summer Games held in Japan and Germany. *Gravure, perforated 11x10 1/2.*

A83 *Skiing*

A83		MNHVF	UseVF
11¢	**multicolored** tagged *(92,710,000)*	.25	.20
	Plate block of 10	2.75	
	FDC *(Aug. 17, 1972)*		1.75

1973. PROGRESS IN ELECTRONICS ISSUE was the fourth stamp and only airmail in a set commemorating advances in electronic communication. (See CM721-CM723.) *Intaglio (Giori Press) and offset, perforated 11.*

A84 *Lee DeForest's audion*

A84		MNHVF	UseVF
11¢	**multicolored** tagged *(56,000,000)*	.25	.20

Plate block of 4	1.00		
FDC *(July 10, 1973)*		1.75	
v. vermilion and olive omitted	1,150.00		
zo. Tagging omitted	20.00		
v1. Olive omitted	—		

1973. WINGED ENVELOPE ISSUE was created to meet the basic domestic airmail letter rate increase. *Intaglio, perforated 11x10 1/2.*

A85, A86, B138, BA25 *Flying envelope*

A85		MNHVF	UseVF
13¢	**red** tagged	.25	.20
	Plate block of 4	1.00	
	FDC *(Nov. 16, 1973)*		1.75
	zx. Untagged & Bureau precancel Washington D.C.	.35	.30
	Plate block of 4	4.00	
	n. Booklet pane of 5 plus label *(Dec. 27, 1973)*	1.50	.75
	nz. Pane of 5 plus label yellow-green, tagging (error) (rare)	—	
	zo. Tagging omitted (without precancel)	7.50	

1973. WINGED ENVELOPE COIL ISSUE Rotary Press, perforated 10 vertically.

A86		MNHVF	UseVF
13¢	**red** tagged	.30	.20
	Pair	.60	
	Line pair	1.00	
	FDC *(Dec. 27, 1973)*		1.75
	v. Pair, imperforate	75.00	

1974. STATUE OF LIBERTY ISSUE met increases in airmail rates to foreign destinations. *Intaglio (Giori Press), perforated 11.*

A87 *Statue of Liberty*

A87		MNHVF	UseVF
18¢	**multicolored** tagged	.35	.25
	Plate block of 4	1.50	
	FDC *(Jan. 11, 1974)*		1.75
	zo. Tagging omitted	18.00	

1974. MOUNT RUSHMORE ISSUE

A88 *Mount Rushmore*

A88		MNHVF	UseVF
26¢	**multicolored** tagged	.50	.20
	Plate block of 4	2.50	
	Pair, gutter between	200.00	
	FDC *(Jan. 2, 1974)*		2.00
	z. yellow-green tagging (error) (rare)	—	
	zo. Tagging omitted	18.00	

1976. PLANE AND GLOBES ISSUE met increases in airmail rates to foreign destinations. *Intaglio (Giori Press), perforated 11.*

A89 *Stylized aircraft and globes*

A89		MNHVF	UseVF
25¢	**multicolored** tagged	.50	.20
	Plate block of 4	2.25	
	FDC *(Jan. 2, 1976)*		1.75
	zo. Tagging omitted	—	

A90 *Stylized aircraft and flag, with globes*

A90		MNHVF	UseVF
31¢	**multicolored** tagged	.60	.20
	Plate block of 4	2.50	
	FDC *(Jan. 2, 1976)*		1.75
	zo. Tagging omitted	10.00	

Pioneers of Aviation Series

1978. ORVILLE AND WILBUR WRIGHT ISSUE The first stamps in the Pioneers of Aviation Series, marked the 75th anniversary of Orville (1871-1948) and Wilbur (1867-1912) Wright's historic first powered flight in 1903. *Intaglio (Giori Press) and offset, perforated 11.*

A91, A92 *Orville and Wilbur Wright, Aviation Pioneers*

A91		MNHVF	UseVF
31¢	**multicolored large portraits & biplane** tagged	.60	.30

A92		MNHVF	UseVF
31¢	**multicolored, small portraits, biplane & hangar** tagged	.60	.30
	Plate block of 4	3.00	
	y. Se-tenant pair (A91-92)	1.40	
	FDC, pair *(Sept. 23, 1978)*		1.00
	vy. Pair with intaglio black omitted	—	
	v1y. Pair with intaglio black & ultramarine omitted	700.00	
	v2y. Pair with offset black, yellow, magenta, blue & brown omitted	2,250.00	

1978. OCTAVE CHANUTE ISSUE in the Pioneers of Aviation Series honored the biplane hang glider designed by Chanute (1832-1910), which became a standard for future glider design and aided the Wright brothers. *Intaglio (Giori Press) and offset, perforated 11.*

A93, A94 *Octave Chanute, Aviation Pioneer*

A93

		MNHVF	UseVF
21¢	**multicolored, large portrait** tagged	.70	.30

A94

		MNHVF	UseVF
21¢	**multicolored, small portrait** tagged	.70	.30
	Plate block of 4	3.25	
	y. Se-tenant pair (A93-94)	1.40	1.00
	FDC, pair *(March 29, 1978)*		2.50
	vy. Pair with intaglio black omitted	—	
	v1y. Pair with intaglio black & ultramarine omitted	4,500.00	

1979. HIGH JUMPER ISSUE in the Olympic Games Series featured a high jumper in action. (See also CM925-28, CM932-35.) *Gravure, perforated 11.*

A95 *High jumper*

A95

		MNHVF	UseVF
31¢	**multicolored** tagged	.75	.30
	Plate block of 12	10.00	
	FDC *(Nov. 1, 1979)*		2.50

1979. WILEY POST ISSUE in the Pioneers of Aviation Series honored the aviator famous for record-making flights, scientific research and aircraft designs. Post (1900-1935) died with humorist Will Rogers while on a flight to Alaska. *Intaglio (Giori Press) and offset, perforated 11.*

A96, A97 *Wiley Post, Aviation Pioneer*

A96

		MNHVF	UseVF
25¢	**multicolored, large portrait,** tagged	1.20	.40

A97

		MNHVF	UseVF
25¢	**multicolored, small portrait,** tagged	1.20	.40
	Plate block of 4	6.00	
	y. Se-tenant pair (A96-97)	2.75	1.25
	FDC, pair *(Nov. 20, 1979)*		2.50

1982. PHILIP MAZZEI ISSUE honored the Italian-American patriot. He collaborated with the leaders of Virginia on political ideas and promoted independence through writings published in America and in Europe. *Gravure, perforated 11.*

A98 *Philip Mazzei*

A98

		MNHVF	UseVF
40¢	**multicolored** tagged	1.25	.25
	Plate block of 12	15.00	
	FDC *(Oct. 13, 1980)*		2.50

	v. Horizontal pair, imperforate vertically	—	
	v1. Pair, imperforate	3,500.00	
	v2. Perforated 10 1/2x11 *(1982)*	—	
	zo. Tagging omitted	—	

1980. BLANCHE STUART SCOTT ISSUE in the Pioneers of Aviation Series commemorated the first American woman to make a solo flight in early September 1910. *Gravure, perforated 11.*

A99 *Blanche Stuart Scott*

A99

		MNHVF	UseVF
28¢	**multicolored** tagged	.90	.25
	Plate block of 12	12.50	
	FDC *(Dec. 30, 1980)*		2.50
	v. Pair, imperforate	—	

1980. GLENN CURTISS ISSUE in the Pioneers of Aviation Series honored an early aviator and noted aircraft designer and manufacturer (1878-1930) principally remembered for his invention and development of the aileron, and for his design and production of the first successful seaplanes and amphibious airplanes. *Gravure, perforated 11.*

A100 *Glenn Curtiss*

A100

		MNHVF	UseVF
35¢	**multicolored** tagged	1.00	.25
	Plate block of 12	12.50	
	FDC *(Dec. 30, 1980)*		2.50

1983. OLYMPIC ISSUES consisted of three se-tenant blocks of four commemorating the 1984 Summer Olympic Games in Los Angeles, Calif. (See CM1094-97, CM1111-14, CM1126-29, ALS19, PC96, and PC98.) *Gravure, bull's-eye perforated 11 1/4.*

A101 *Men's shot put*

A102 *Men's gymnastics*

A103 *Women's swimming*

A104 *Men's weight lifting*

A101

		MNHVF	UseVF
40¢	**Men's shot put,** tagged	1.25	.25
	v. Line perforated 11	—	

A102

		MNHVF	UseVF
40¢	**Men's gymnastics,** tagged	1.25	.25
	v. Line perforated 11	—	

A103

		MNHVF	UseVF
40¢	**Women's swimming,** tagged	1.25	.25
	v. Line perforated 11	—	

A104

		MNHVF	UseVF
40¢	**Men's weight lifting,** tagged	1.25	.25
	Plate block of 4	6.50	
	y. Se-tenant block of 4 (A101-104)	4.00	
	FDC *(April 8, 1983)*, block		4.50
	v. Line perforated 11	1.35	
	Plate block of 4 line perforated 11	6.00	
	vy. Se-tenant block of 4 line perforated 11	5.00	
	v1y. Block of 4, imperforate	1,250.00	

1983. OLYMPICS SECOND ISSUE Gravure, perforated 11.

A105 *Women's gymnastics*

A106 *Men's hurdles*

A107 *Women's basketball*

A108 *Soccer*

A105		MNHVF	UseVF
28¢	**Women's gymnastics,** tagged	1.25	.25
A106		MNHVF	UseVF
28¢	**Men's hurdles,** tagged	1.25	.25
A107		MNHVF	UseVF
28¢	**Women's basketball,** tagged	1.25	.25
A108		MNHVF	UseVF
28¢	**Soccer,** tagged	1.25	.25
	Plate block of 4	6.50	
	y. Se-tenant block of 4 (A105-108)	4.00	
	FDC *(June 17, 1983),* block		4.00
	v. Block of 4, imperforate	1,250.00	

1983. OLYMPICS THIRD ISSUE Gravure, perforated 11.

A109 *Fencing*

A110 *Cycling*

A111 *Women's volleyball*

A112 *Pole vaulting*

A109		MNHVF	UseVF
35¢	**Fencing,** tagged	1.25	.25
A110		MNHVF	UseVF
35¢	**Cycling,** tagged	1.25	.25
A111		MNHVF	UseVF
35¢	**Women's volleyball,** tagged	1.25	.25
A112		MNHVF	UseVF
35¢	**Pole vaulting,** tagged	1.25	.25
	Plate block of 4	12.50	
	y. Se-tenant block of 4 (A109-112)	6.50	
	FDC *(Nov. 4, 1983),* block		4.50

1985. ALFRED V. VERVILLE ISSUE in the Pioneers of Aviation Series honored the man (1890-1970) who designed and produced aircraft with Lawrence Sperry and Glenn Curtiss. *Gravure press, perforated 11.*

A113 *Alfred V. Verville, Aviation Pioneer*

A113		MNHVF	UseVF
33¢	**multicolored** tagged	1.00	.30
	Plate block of 4	4.50	
	FDC *(Feb. 13, 1985)*		2.50
	v. Pair, imperforate	850.00	

1985. LAWRENCE AND ELMER SPERRY ISSUE in the Pioneers of Aviation Series commemorated the father-and-son duo of Elmer Sperry (father, 1860-1930) who was awarded over 400 patents, such as the gyro-compass which revolutionized flying, and Lawrence Sperry (son, 1892-1923) who helped develop and test such aviation innovations as the automatic pilot and retractable landing gear. *Gravure press, perforated 11.*

A114 *Lawrence and Elmer Sperry, Aviation Pioneers*

A114		MNHVF	UseVF
39¢	**multicolored** tagged	1.25	.40
	Plate block of 4	5.50	
	FDC *(Feb. 13, 1985)*		2.50
	v. Pair, imperforate	1,850.00	

1986. TRANSPACIFIC AIRMAIL ISSUE marked the 50th anniversary of airmail service between the United States and the Far East. *Gravure, perforated 11.*

A115 *Martin M-130 China Clipper*

A115		MNHVF	UseVF
44¢	**multicolored** tagged	1.25	.40
	Plate block of 4	6.00	
	FDC *(Feb. 15, 1985)*		3.00
	v. Pair, imperforate	800.00	

1985. JUNIPERO SERRA ISSUE honored the Franciscan friar (1713-84) who founded the California missions. *Gravure, perforated 11.*

A116 *Junipero Serra and San Gabriel Mission*

A116		MNHVF	UseVF
44¢	**multicolored** tagged	1.75	.60
	Plate block of 4	11.50	
	FDC *(Aug. 22, 1985)*		2.50
	v. Pair, imperforate	1,500.00	

1988. SETTLEMENT OF NEW SWEDEN ISSUE honored the 350th anniversary of the colony established by Peter Minuit. Sweden and Finland released stamps the same day (Sweden 1460, Finland 1077) with a common design to that issued by the United States. *Intaglio and offset, perforated 11.*

A117 *Illustration from a 1602 book on the New Sweden Colony*

A117		MNHVF	UseVF
44¢	**multicolored** tagged *(22,975,000)*	1.40	.50
	Plate block of 4	9.00	
	FDC *(March 29, 1988)*		2.50

1988. SAMUEL P. LANGLEY ISSUE in the Pioneers of Aviation Series honored the early pioneer flight engineer (1834-1906) and the 70th anniversary of airmail service. Langley's early experiments in mechanical flight laid the groundwork for the Wright brothers, Glenn Curtiss, and others. *Intaglio and offset, perforated 11.*

A118 *Samuel P. Langley, unmanned Aerodrome No. 5*

A118		MNHVF	UseVF
45¢	**multicolored** block tagged	1.40	.30
	Plate block of 4	6.00	
	FDC *(May 14, 1988)*		2.50
	v. Overall tagged	2.00	.50
	Plate block of 4	10.00	

1988. IGOR SIKORSKY ISSUE in the Pioneers of Aviation Series paid tribute to the man (1889-1972) who designed and built many early helicopters. *Intaglio and offset, perforated 11.*

A119 *Igor Sikorsky and VS-300*

A119		MNHVF	UseVF
36¢	**multicolored** tagged	1.25	.40
	Plate block of 4	6.00	
	FDC *(June 23, 1988)*		2.50

Note: Traces of red have been detected in all copies of a so-called "red-omitted" error of this stamp. Such stamps, on which even minute traces of red are present, are worth far less than a genuine color-omitted error would be.

1989. FRENCH REVOLUTION BICENTENNIAL ISSUE part of a joint issue with France, was released both in Washington, D.C., and in Paris. *Offset and intaglio, perforated 11 1/2x11.*

A120 *Liberte, Egalite, and Fraternite*

A120		MNHVF	UseVF
45¢	**multicolored** tagged *(38,532,000)*	1.40	.40
	Plate block of 4	6.00	
	FDC *(July 14, 1989)*		2.50

1989. AMERICA ISSUE depicted a rare wooden native sculpture of the pre-Columbian era. It was one of a pair of U.S. stamps (with CM1360) that were the first stamps issued by 24 postal administrations commemorating the 500th anniversary of Christopher Columbus' arrival in America. It was part of a 1989-91 Columbian series by members of the Postal Union of the Americas and Spain (PUAS). (See A127.) *Gravure by American Bank Note Co., perforated 11.*

A121 *Key Marco Cat, Calusa culture, pre-Columbian period*

A121		MNHVF	UseVF
45¢	**multicolored** tagged *(39,325,000)*	1.50	.30
	Plate block of 4	7.50	
	FDC *(Oct. 12, 1989)*		2.50

1989. FUTURE MAIL TRANSPORTATION SOUVENIR SHEET was part of a group of 11 postal items issued during World Stamp Expo '89 and the 20th Congress of the Universal Postal Union in Washington, D.C. *Offset and intaglio, imperforate.*

A122a *Hypersonic airliner*

A122b *Hovercraft*

A122c *Service rover*

A122d *Space shuttle*

A122		MNHVF	UseVF
$1.80	**multicolored,** souvenir sheet, tagged	7.00	5.00
	(1,944,000)		
	FDC *(Nov. 24, 1989)*		8.00
	a. 45¢ multicolored, tagged		
	b. 45¢ multicolored, tagged		
	c. 45¢ multicolored, tagged		
	d. 45¢ multicolored, tagged		

1989. FUTURE MAIL TRANSPORTATION ISSUE Offset and intaglio, perforated 11.

A123 *Hypersonic airliner*

A124 *Hovercraft*

A125 *Service rover*

A126 *Space shuttle*

A123		MNHVF	UseVF
45¢	**Hypersonic airliner,** tagged	1.25	.25

A124		MNHVF	UseVF
45¢	**Hovercraft,** tagged	1.25	.25

A125		MNHVF	UseVF
45¢	**Service rover,** tagged	1.25	.25

A126		MNHVF	UseVF
45¢	**Space shuttle,** tagged	1.25	.25
	Plate block of 4	8.00	
	y. Se-tenant block of 4 (A123-26)	7.00	
	FDC *(Nov. 28, 1989),* block		8.00
	vy. Plate block of 4 w/light blue omitted	900.00	

1990. AMERICA ISSUE was the second in the PUAS Columbian Series depicting scenes of the natural beauty of America prior to Columbus. *Gravure, perforated 11.*

A127 *Caribbean coast*

A127		MNHVF	UseVF
45¢	**multicolored** tagged	1.50	.50
	Plate block of 4	7.50	
	FDC *(Oct. 12, 1990)*		2.50

1991. HARRIET QUIMBY ISSUE in the Pioneers of Aviation Series honored the journalist, drama critic, and first licensed American woman pilot (1875-1912). *Gravure by Stamp Venturers, perforated 11 on L perforator with USPS logo and Olympic rings in selvage; reissued*

1993 perforated 11 1/4 on bullseye perforator without logo and rings and plate number horizontal instead of vertical.

A128 *Harriet Quimby, Bleriot airplane*

A128		MNHVF	UseVF
50¢	**multicolored** tagged	1.00	.30
	Plate block of 4	5.50	
	FDC *(April 27, 1991)*		2.50
v.	Vertical pair, imperforate horizontally	2,000.00	
v1.	Perforated 11 1/4 bullseye (1993)	1.10	.30
	Plate block of 4	6.00	

1991. WILLIAM T. PIPER ISSUE in the Pioneers of Aviation Series honored the "Henry Ford of Aviation," the developer of the Piper Cub aircraft. (See also A132.) *Gravure by J.W. Fergusson & Sons for the American Bank Note Co., perforated 11.*

A129 *William T. Piper, Piper Cub*

A129		MNHVF	UseVF
40¢	**multicolored** tagged	1.40	.50
	Plate block of 4	6.00	
	FDC *(May 17, 1991)*		2.50

1991. ANTARCTIC TREATY ISSUE honored the 30th anniversary of the 1961 treaty dedicating the region to peaceful purposes. *Gravure by Stamp Venturers, perforated 11.*

A130 *View of McMurdo Sound*

A130		MNHVF	UseVF
50¢	**multicolored** tagged	1.50	.60
	Plate block of 4	7.00	
	FDC *(June 21, 1991)*		2.50

1991. AMERICA ISSUE had as its theme "Pre-Columbian Voyages of Discovery," and depicted a prehistoric Asian and the Bering land bridge by which the first native Americans are believed to have come to the Western Hemisphere thousands of years ago. *Gravure, perforated 11.*

A131 *Asian overlooking Bering land bridge*

A131		MNHVF	UseVF
50¢	**multicolored** tagged	1.50	.50
	Plate block of 4	7.00	
	FDC *(Oct. 12, 1991)*		2.50

1993. WILLIAM T. PIPER ISSUE differs from the 1991 version (A129) in that Piper's hair touches the top edge of the design of this stamp. There was no official first day of issue for the redesigned stamp. *Printed in gravure by Stamp Venturers, perforated 11 1/4.*

A132 *William T. Piper*

A132		MNHVF	UseVF
40¢	**multicolored,** tagged	1.50	.50
	Plate block of 4	7.00	
	FDC *(July 1993)*		—

Special Delivery Stamps

A special delivery stamp on any letter or article of mailable matter entitled the addressee to immediate delivery between the hours of 7 a.m. and midnight. This service began Oct. 1, 1885, and was limited to free delivery offices and post offices in towns of 4,000 population or more. At that time there were 555 such post offices. The Act of Aug. 4, 1886, extended the service to all post offices.

1885. MESSENGER, FIRST ISSUE inscribed "At a special delivery office." *Printed by American Bank Note Co., flat press, unwatermarked, perforated 12.*

 SD1 *Messenger on foot*

SD1

		UnFVF	UseFVF
10¢	Prussian blue	325.00	45.00
	dark blue	325.00	45.00
	Plate block of 8	14,000.00	
	Double transfer at top	450.00	
	FDC (Oct. 1, 1885); EKU (Sept. 30, 1885)		12,500.00

1888. MESSENGER, SECOND ISSUE inscribed "At any post office." *Printed by American Bank Note Co., flat press, unwatermarked, perforated 12.*

 SD2, SD3 *Messenger on foot*

SD2

		UnFVF	UseFVF
10¢	Prussian blue	300.00	17.50
	dark blue	300.00	17.50
	Plate block of 8	11,000.00	
	FDD (Sept. 6, 1888)		
	EKU (Dec. 18, 1888)		

1893. MESSENGER, THIRD ISSUE had a change of color and was released to avoid confusion with the 1- and 4-cent Columbian commemorative stamps. SD2 went on sale again in January 1894 and remained in use until it was replaced by SD4. *Printed by American Bank Note Co., flat press, unwatermarked, perforated 12.*

SD3

		UnFVF	UseFVF
10¢	orange yellow	200.00	22.50
	dark orange	200.00	22.50
	Plate block of 8	7,000.00	
	FDD (Jan. 24, 1893)		
	EKU (Feb. 11, 1893)		

1894. MESSENGER ISSUE similar to SD2, with a line drawn under the words "Ten Cents." *Printed intaglio by the Bureau of Engraving and Printing, perforated 12.*

 SD4, SD5 *Messenger on foot*

SD4

		UnFVF	UseFVF
10¢	deep blue	750.00	30.00
	bright blue	750.00	30.00
	dark blue	750.00	30.00
	Plate block of 4 w/arrow	2,000.00	
	Plate block of 6	15,000.00	
	Double transfer	—	—
	v. Plate block of 6, imperforate & without gum	8,800.00	
	v1. horizontal pair, imperforate	4,675.00	—
	FDD (Oct. 10, 1894)		
	EKU (Oct. 24, 1894)		

1895. MESSENGER ISSUE same design as SD4. *Intaglio, perforated 12, watermarked double-line USPS (wmk 187).*

SD5

		UnFVF	UseFVF
10¢	blue	160.00	3.50
	dark blue	160.00	3.50
	deep blue	160.00	3.50
	Plate block of 6	4,000.00	
	Block of 4 w/arrow	725.00	
	Colored line through "POSTAL DELIVERY"	250.00	25.00
	Dots in frame (curved) above messenger	200.00	9.00
	Double transfer	—	10.00
	v. Printed on both sides	—	
	v1. Imperforate pair	4,500.00	
	FDD (Aug. 16, 1895)		
	EKU (Oct. 3, 1895)		

1902. MESSENGER ON BICYCLE ISSUE intaglio, perforated 12, watermarked double-line USPS (wmk 187).

 SD6 *Messenger on bicycle*

SD6

		UnFVF	UseFVF
10¢	ultramarine	110.00	3.25
	blue	110.00	3.25
	dark blue	110.00	3.25
	Plate block of 6	2,400.00	
	Plate block of 6, from plates 5240, 5243, 5244 or 5245, with "09" added to number	2,100.00	
	Plate block of 4 w/arrow	475.00	
	Double transfer	—	—
	Transfer "damage" under "N" of "CENTS"	140.00	3.75
	FDD (Dec. 9, 1902)		
	EKU (Jan. 22, 1903)		

1908. HELMET OF MERCURY ISSUE the "Merry Widow" is the nickname for this stamp due to the resemblance to a contemporary lady's hat, of the same name. *Intaglio, perforated 12, watermarked double-line USPS (wmk 187).*

 SD7 *Helmet of Mercury*

SD7

		UnFVF	UseFVF
10¢	green	60.00	40.00
	dark green	60.00	40.00
	yellowish green	60.00	40.00
	Plate block of 6	925.00	
	Double transfer	140.00	75.00
	On cover		85.00
	FDD (Dec. 12, 1908)		
	EKU (Dec. 14, 1908)		

1911. MESSENGER ON BICYCLE ISSUE intaglio, watermarked single-line USPS (wmk 273), perforated 12.

 SD8-SD11 *Messenger on bicycle*

SD8

		UnFVF	UseFVF
10¢	ultramarine	100.00	5.25
	dark ultramarine	100.00	5.25
	pale ultramarine	100.00	5.25
	violet blue	100.00	5.25
	Plate block of 6	1,800.00	
	Plate block of 6 w/imprint	2,000.00	
	v. Top frame line missing	140.00	12.50
	FDD (Jan. 1911)		
	EKU (Jan. 14, 1911)		

1914. MESSENGER ON BICYCLE ISSUE intaglio, watermarked single-line USPS (wmk 273), perforated 10.

SD9

		UnFVF	UseFVF
10¢	ultramarine	180.00	6.50
	blue	180.00	6.50
	pale ultramarine	180.00	6.50

Plate block of 6	3,250.00	
Plate block of 6 w/imprint	4,000.00	
FDD *(Sept. 1914)*		
EKU *(Oct. 26, 1914)*		

1916. MESSENGER ON BICYCLE ISSUE intaglio, unwatermarked, perforated 10.

SD10

		UnFVF	UseFVF
10¢	pale ultramarine	275.00	27.50
	blue	300.00	27.50
	ultramarine	275.00	27.50
	Plate block of 6	5,000.00	
	Plate block of 6 w/imprint	5,500.00	
	FDD *(Oct. 19, 1916)*		
	EKU *(Nov. 4, 1916)*		

1917. MESSENGER ON BICYCLE ISSUE intaglio, unwatermarked, perforated 11.

SD11

		UnFVF	UseFVF
10¢	ultramarine	20.00	.50
	blue	50.00	.50
	dark ultramarine	20.00	.50
	gray violet	20.00	.50
	pale ultramarine	20.00	.50
	Plate block of 6	550.00	
	Plate block of 6 w/imprint	1,900.00	
	v. Perforated 10 at left	—	
	FDD *(May 2, 1917)*		

1922. MESSENGER AND MOTORCYCLE ISSUE intaglio, unwatermarked, perforated 11.

SD12, SD13, SD15-SD18 *Messenger and motorcycle*

SD12

		UnFVF	UseFVF
10¢	gray blue	35.00	.50
	deep ultramarine	40.00	.60
	Plate block of 6	400.00	
	Double transfer	—	1.00
	FDC *(July 12, 1922)*		375.00

SD13

		UnFVF	UseFVF
15¢	red orange	24.00	1.00
	Plate block of 6	300.00	
	Double transfer	32.50	1.50
	FDC *(April 11, 1925)*		225.00

1925. POST OFFICE DELIVERY TRUCK ISSUE intaglio, unwatermarked, perforated 11.

SD14, SD19 *Post office delivery truck*

SD14

		UnFVF	UseFVF
20¢	black	2.00	1.00
	Plate block of 6	30.00	
	FDC *(April 25, 1925)*		110.00

1927. MESSENGER AND MOTORCYCLE ISSUE rotary press printing, previous designs, perforated 11x10 1/2.

SD15

		UnFVF	UseFVF
10¢	dark lilac	.60	.20
	gray lilac	.60	.20
	red lilac	.60	.20
	violet	.60	.20
	Plate block of 4	4.00	
	Cracked plate	35.00	
	Gouged plate	100.00	
	FDC *(Nov. 29, 1927)*		95.00
	FDC, *(Sept. 8, 1941)* electric eye plate		25.00
	v. Horizontal pair, imperforate between	300.00	
	v1. Plate block of 4, imperforate vertically between	850.00	

1944. MESSENGER AND MOTORCYCLE ISSUE

SD16

		MNHVF	UseVF
13¢	blue	.60	.20
	Plate block of 4	3.00	
	FDC *(Oct. 30, 1944)*		10.00

1931. MESSENGER AND MOTORCYCLE ISSUE

SD17

		MNHVF	UseVF
15¢	yellow orange	.75	.20
	Plate block of 4	4.00	
	FDC *(Aug. 13, 1931)*, Washington, D.C.		125.00
	FDC *(Aug. 6, 1931)*, Easton, Pa.		2,300.00

1944. MESSENGER AND MOTORCYCLE ISSUE

SD18

		MNHVF	UseVF
17¢	yellow	2.75	1.75
	Plate block of 4	20.00	
	FDC *(Oct. 30, 1944)*		10.00

1951. POST OFFICE DELIVERY TRUCK ISSUE

SD19

		MNHVF	UseVF
20¢	black	1.25	.20
	Plate block of 4	5.50	
	FDC *(Nov. 30, 1951)*		4.50

1954. LETTER AND HANDS ISSUE Rotary press printing, perforated 11x10 1/2.

SD20, SD21 *Two hands and letter*

SD20

		MNHVF	UseVF
20¢	gray blue	.40	.20
	light blue	.40	.20
	Plate block of 4	2.00	
	FDC *(Oct. 13, 1954)*		2.00

1957. LETTER AND HANDS ISSUE

SD21

		MNHVF	UseVF
30¢	maroon	.50	.20
	Plate block of 4	2.50	
	FDC *(Sept. 3, 1957)*		2.00

1969. DUAL ARROWS ISSUE for new rate. *Giori Press, perforated 11.*

SD22, SD23 *Arrows pointing in opposite directions.*

SD22

		MNHVF	UseVF
45¢	carmine & violet blue	1.25	.20
	Plate block of 4	6.00	
	FDC *(Nov. 21, 1969)*		2.25

1971. DUAL ARROWS ISSUE new rates, same design as SD22.

SD23

		MNHVF	UseVF
60¢	violet blue & carmine	1.25	.25
	Plate block of 4	5.50	
	FDC *(May 10, 1971)*		2.50

Airmail/Special Delivery

1934. BLUE AIRMAIL SPECIAL DELIVERY STAMP ISSUE prepaid, with one stamp, air postage and the special delivery fee. The stamp was designed by President Franklin D. Roosevelt. The first day of issue was Aug. 30 at the convention of the American Air Mail Society at Chicago. *Intaglio, unwatermarked, perforated 11.*

ASD1 *Great Seal*

ASD1

		UnFVF	UseFVF
16¢	**Prussian blue** (9,215,750)	.60	.65
	blue	.60	.65
	Plate block of 6	17.50	
	FDC (Aug. 30, 1934)		30.00

Note: An imperforate, ungummed version of the blue airmail special delivery issue, CM161, is listed with other so-called Farley Series stamps among the commemorative listings.

1936. RED AND BLUE AIRMAIL SPECIAL DELIVERY STAMP ISSUE used the same design as the 1934 stamp, but in two colors.

ASD2 *Great Seal*

ASD2

		UnFVF	UseFVF
16¢	**carmine & blue**	.40	.25
	Center line block of 4	2.50	2.25
	Plate block of 4, Type I, thin red & blue registration line above plate nos.	6.50	—
	Plate block of 4, Type II, thick red, thin blue registration line above plate nos.	50.00	
	Plate block of 4, Type III, dotted blue, thin red registration line above plate nos.	65.00	
	Plate block of 4, Type IV, thick red and blue registration line above plate nos.	15.00	6.00
	Arrow block of 4, bottom or side arrow	2.00	1.50
	v. Horizontal pair, imperforate between	3,750.00	
	v1. Center line block of 4, imperforate vertically	8,625.00	
	FDC (Feb. 10, 1936)		25.00

Offices in China

1919. OFFICES IN CHINA ISSUE Postage stamps of the 1917 United States Series were overprinted and issued to the U.S. postal agency at Shanghai. The overprints are in black, except OC7 and OC16, which are in red. Sold in Shanghai at the local currency, which was one-half the value of U.S. currency at the time. These stamps were good for mail to addresses in the United States. After the closing of the China office in December 1922, the stamps were sold for a short time at the Philatelic Agency at Washington, D.C. *Intaglio, unwatermarked, perforated 11.*

OC1-OC16 *U.S. stamps 380-398 overprinted with "¢."*

Overprint

SHANGHAI

2¢

CHINA

OC1

		UnFVF	UseFVF
2¢ on 1¢ **green** (380)		20.00	50.00
	Plate block of 6	275.00	

OC2

		UnFVF	UseFVF
4¢ on 2¢ **rose red** (381)		20.00	50.00
	Plate block of 6	275.00	

OC3

		UnFVF	UseFVF
6¢ on 3¢ **violet** (382)		40.00	55.00
	Plate block of 6	475.00	

OC4

		UnFVF	UseFVF
8¢ on 4¢ **yellow brown** (383)		45.00	50.00
	Plate block of 6	600.00	

OC5

		UnFVF	UseFVF
10¢ on 5¢ **blue** (384)		50.00	55.00
	Plate block of 6	650.00	

OC6

		UnFVF	UseFVF
12¢ on 6¢ **red orange** (386)		65.00	80.00
	Plate block of 6	750.00	

OC7

		UnFVF	UseFVF
14¢ on 7¢ **black** (387)		65.00	80.00

Plate block of 6	850.00	

OC8

		UnFVF	UseFVF
16¢ on 8¢ **yellow olive** (388)		50.00	55.00
	a. olive green	40.00	45.00
	Plate block of 6	600.00	

OC9

		UnFVF	UseFVF
18¢ on 9¢ **salmon** (389)		50.00	60.00
	Plate block of 6	700.00	

OC10

		UnFVF	UseFVF
20¢ on 10¢ **orange yellow** (390)		45.00	50.00
	Plate block of 6	650.00	

OC11

		UnFVF	UseFVF
24¢ on 12¢ **brown purple** (392)		50.00	60.00
	a. claret brown	70.00	85.00
	Plate block of 6	850.00	

OC12

		UnFVF	UseFVF
30¢ on 15¢ **gray black** (394)		60.00	75.00
	Plate block of 6	1,000.00	

OC13

		UnFVF	UseFVF
40¢ on 20¢ **pale blue** (395)		90.00	120.00
	Plate block of 6	1,350.00	

OC14

		UnFVF	UseFVF
60¢ on 30¢ **orange red** (396)		85.00	100.00
	Plate block of 6	1,000.00	

OC15

		UnFVF	UseFVF
$1 on 50¢ **reddish violet** (397)		325.00	425.00
	Plate block of 6	9,000.00	

OC16

		UnFVF	UseFVF
$2 on $1 **black purple** (398)		300.00	350.00
	Plate block of 6	6,500.00	
	Arrow block of 4	1,400.00	

1922. OFFICES IN CHINA ISSUE overprinted on No. 380. *Intaglio.*

OC17, OC18 *Overprinted "Cts."*

Overprint

SHANGHAI

2 Cts.

CHINA

OC17

		UnFVF	UseFVF
2¢ on 1¢ **green** (380)		90.00	90.00
	Plate block of 6	725.00	

1922. OFFICES IN CHINA ISSUE overprinted on No. 404. *Offset.*

OC18

		UnFVF	UseFVF
4¢ on 2¢ **rose red** (404)		75.00	75.00
	Plate block of 6	725.00	
	"CHINA" only	—	—
	"SHANGHAI" omitted	—	—

Parcel Post Stamps

1912. PARCEL POST STAMPS were provided to cover the rates of postage on Fourth Class mail, set up by the Act of Congress of Aug. 24, 1912. Less than a year later, on July 1, 1913, the Postmaster General directed that ordinary postage stamps be valid for parcel post and that parcel post stamps be valid for postage purposes and be continued on sale until the supply was exhausted. The 75¢ value (PP11) outlasted all the others, and in September 1921 the remainders, consisting of 3,510,345 copies, were destroyed. The 20¢ value was the first stamp in the world to depict an airplane. *Intaglio, watermarked single-line USPS (wmk 273) and perforated 12; marginal imprints (the denomination in words) were added to the plates on Jan. 27, 1913.*

PP1 *Post Office clerk*

			UnFVF	UseFVF
PP1				
1¢	**carmine** *(209,691,094)*		5.25	1.50
	Double transfer		8.75	4.00
	Plate block of 6 w/imprint		110.00	
	FDC *(Nov. 27, 1912)*			3,500.00

PP2 *City carrier*

			UnFVF	UseFVF
PP2				
2¢	**carmine** *(206,417,253)*		6.75	1.25
	lake		6.75	
	Double transfer		100.00	
	Plate block of 6 w/imprint		125.00	
	FDC *(Nov. 27, 1912)*			4,500.00

PP3 *Railway postal clerk*

			UnFVF	UseFVF
PP3				
3¢	**carmine** *(29,027,433)*		13.50	4.50
	Double transfer		26.00	
	Lower right corner retouched		26.00	
	Plate block of 6 w/imprint		260.00	
	FDC *(April 5, 1913)*			4,500.00

PP4 *Rural carrier*

			UnFVF	UseFVF
PP4				
4¢	**carmine** *(76,743,813)*		37.50	2.50
	Double transfer		—	
	Plate block of 6 w/imprint		1,050.00	
	FDC *(Dec. 12, 1912)*			5,500.00

PP5 *Mail train*

			UnFVF	UseFVF
PP5				
5¢	**carmine** *(108,153,993)*		32.50	2.25
	Double transfer		45.00	
	Plate block of 6 w/imprint		1,000.00	
	FDC *(Nov. 27, 1912)*			4,000.00

PPy6 *Steamship & mail tender*

			UnFVF	UseFVF
PP6				
10¢	**carmine** *(56,896,653)*		52.50	3.00
	Double transfer		—	—
	Plate block of 6 w/imprint		1,150.00	
	FDC *(Dec. 9, 1912)*			—

PP7 *Automobile*

			UnFVF	UseFVF
PP7				
15¢	**carmine** *(21,147,033)*		67.50	12.00
	Plate block of 6 w/imprint		2,600.00	
	FDC *(Dec. 16, 1912)*			—

PP8 *Airplane carrying mail*

			UnFVF	UseFVF
PP8				
20¢	**carmine** *(17,142,393)*		140.00	25.00
	Plate block of 6 w/imprint		6,500.00	
	FDC *(Dec. 16, 1912)*			—

PP9 *Manufacturing*

			UnFVF	UseFVF
PP9				
25¢	**carmine** *(21,940,653)*		67.50	5.00
	Plate block of 6 w/imprint		2,700.00	
	FDC *(Nov. 27, 1912)*			—

PP10 *Dairying*

			UnFVF	UseFVF
PP10				
50¢	**carmine** *(2,117,793)*		280.00	40.50
	Plate block of 6 w/imprint		22,500.00	
	FDC *(March 15, 1913)*			—

PP11 *Harvesting*

			UnFVF	UseFVF
PP11				
75¢	**carmine** *(2,772,615)*		95.00	35.00
	Plate block of 6 w/imprint		3,600.00	
	FDC *(Dec. 18, 1912)*			—

PP12 *Fruit growing*

			UnFVF	UseFVF
PP12				
$1	**carmine** *(1,053,273)*		350.00	35.00
	Plate block of 6 w/imprint		20,000.00	
	FDC *(Jan. 3, 1913)*			—

Parcel Post/Postage Due Stamps

1912. PARCEL POST POSTAGE DUE STAMPS were used to indicate the amount due by the addressee when parcel post was insufficiently prepaid by the sender. *Watermarked single-line USPS (wmk 273), intaglio, perforated 12.*

PPD1-PPD5

			UnFVF	UseFVF
PPD1				
1¢	**green** *(7,322,400)*		6.00	3.50
	FDD *(Nov. 27, 1912)*			
PPD2			UnFVF	UseFVF
2¢	**green** *(3,132,000)*		55.00	15.00
	FDD *(Dec. 9, 1912)*			
PPD3			UnFVF	UseFVF
5¢	**green** *(5,840,100)*		9.00	3.50
	FDD *(Nov. 27, 1912)*			
PPD4			UnFVF	UseFVF
10¢	**green** *(2,124,540)*		125.00	40.00
	FDD *(Dec. 12, 1912)*			
PPD5			UnFVF	UseFVF
25¢	**green** *(2,117,700)*		65.00	3.75
	FDD *(Dec. 16, 1912)*			

Special Handling Stamps

1925-29. ISSUE The Postal Service Act of 1925 provided the same service for Fourth Class matter as normally accorded First Class by payment of a 25¢ fee, for which a stamp was issued. The other denominations were issued to meet rate changes. *Intaglio, unwatermarked, perforated 11.*

The 10¢, 15¢ and 20¢ denominations were dry-printed on pre-gummed paper (1955). They were issued in much smaller quantities than the usual wet-printed stamps. There is a minute size difference between the wet and dry printings; the latter are on a whiter, thicker and stiffer paper.

SH1-SH5

		UnFVF	UseFVF
SH1			
25¢	**green**	22.50	5.50
	Plate block of 6	75.00	
	FDC *(April 11, 1925)*		225.00
SH2		UnFVF	UseFVF
10¢	**yellow green**	2.25	1.00
	FDC *(June 25, 1928)*		50.00
	p. Dry print *(1955)*	1.25	.90
	Plate block of 6	5.50	
SH3		UnFVF	UseFVF
15¢	**yellow green**	2.25	1.00
	FDC *(June 25, 1928)*		50.00
	p. Dry print *(1955)*	2.00	1.50
	Plate block of 6	25.00	
SH4		UnFVF	UseFVF
20¢	**yellow green**	3.00	1.75
	FDC *(June 25, 1928)*		50.00
	p. Dry print *(1955)*	2.00	1.50
	Plate block of 6	—	
SH5		UnFVF	UseFVF
25¢	**yellow green** *(1929)*	17.50	7.50
	Plate block of 6	500.00	
	"A" and "T" of "STATES" joined at top	40.00	20.00

"A" and "T" of "STATES" & "T" and "A" of	40.00	40.00
"POSTAGE" joined at top		
FDC *(April 11, 1929)*		225.00

Registration Stamp

1911. REGISTRATION STAMP Although we have had a registry since 1855, the Registry Stamp of 1911 was the only stamp issued for the specific purpose of paying registration fees. The stamp was valid for the fees only, not postage; regular postage stamps could be used to pay the fees. The Postmaster General abolished the issuance of these stamps in 1913 but allowed remaining stock to be used up. *Intaglio, single-line USPS watermark (wmk 273), perforated 12.*

REG1

		MNHVF/UnFVF	UseFVF
REG1			
10¢	**bright blue**	75.00	7.50
	Plate block of 6 w/imprint	1,600.00	
	FDC *(Dec. 1, 1911)*		19,500.00

Certified Mail Stamp

1955. CERTIFIED MAIL STAMP This service provided the mailer with a receipt of mailing and required signatures of addressees or agent on delivery. *Intaglio, perforated 10 1/2x11.*

CER1 *U.S. mail carrier*

		MNHVF	UseVF
CER1			
15¢	**red**	.50	.35
	Plate block of 4	4.00	
	FDC *(June 6, 1955)*		2.00

On-demand Postage

These stamps are printed and dispensed by various machines, usually computerized. Although the borderline between postage meter imprints and postage stamps is blurred, the way to determine the difference is this: If the vended item can be taken from the point of sale and used at a later date, at a different location, to mail something, it is a stamp.

Five major efforts by the USPS have tested experimental on-demand postage systems. Autopost, the first, lasted only nine months. Postal Buddy, a program that produced postal cards with the stamp imprinted on the card by the machine at the time of sale, followed. The Variable Rate Coil program was next, pitting Eca-Gard against Unisys. The Automated Postal Center tests began in 1999, with the NCR machines bowing to those of IBM/Neopost in 2001. Neopost kiosks, the latest experimental stamp vending program, have had several iterations.

AUTOPOST

Strategic Financial Planning Systems, Inc.

A total of six of these self-service coin- and currency-operated mailing systems were installed in three post office lobbies: two at the Martin Luther King Jr. Station in Washington, D.C. (Aug. 23, 1989, to May 7, 1990); two at the White Flint Mall Station in Kensington, Md. (Sept. 1, 1989, to May 7, 1990); and two at a temporary postal station set up for the UPU Congress of 1989 in Washington, D.C., which was not open to the public (Nov. 13 to Dec. 14, 1989). The machines would print stamps for First Class, Third Class, Fourth Class, Priority, and Express. The stamps for Fourth Class and Priority weighing more than one pound contained a destination bar code. The other stamps contained a stylized "USA" with stars. Autopost stamps were printed on white, peel-and-stick labels with a fluorescent orange stripe at the left.

Autopost was part of an experimental computerized system called Quickpost, consisting of Infopost and Autopost. The Infopost interactive touch screen computer provided information about mailing services, rates, and requirements. Autopost, a full-service automated mailing service, weighed and rated letters and parcels, accepted payment, and dispensed metered postage strips.

Although the stamps showed a town and state, as well as a date, they were and remain usable on any domestic mail from any location in the country. This is no doubt because sets of Autopost stamps were at one time sold by the Philatelic Sales Division of the USPS.

For each transaction, along with a paper receipt, an advertising label was dispensed, printed on the same orange-striped peelable material as the stamps. Three varieties of the advertising label exist: 1 "We Deliver..."; 2 "We Deliver... / United States Postal Serivce" (replaced first type in November 1989); and 3 "Developed by / Technology Resource Department" (from the UPU machines only).

When a machine was "rebooted" after being powered down, it dispensed a receipt-like paper slip containing the words "Welcome to Autopost" and "Please Discard - Not a Receipt" along with a stamp-like label, on the same orange-striped peel-and-stick material, with the words "Please Dispose of Properly." Two types of this test label are known, with and without a bar code.

Unsevered multiples, squished and elongated prints, and other errors are known to exist. Mint sets of Autopost stamps were subsequently marketed by the Philatelic Sales Division bearing the first-day dates for Washington and Kensington, so covers and stamps should be accompanied by dated postmarks or dated receipts to verify first-day status.

Postal Buddy

Postal Buddy Corp.

Postal Buddy was introduced July 5, 1990; the last machine was removed from service Sept. 16, 1993. Overall, 31 Postal Buddy I machines and 171 Postal Buddy II machines were used in 40 locations in northern Virginia.

These machines were designed primarily to reduce the amount of forwarded mail by providing automated change-of-address services. The machines would notify specified publishers of a customer's new address as well as dispense pre-printed address change cards with postage printed on them. The machines also would dispense other blank or decorated versions of the cards, which could be taken home by the patron and used later.

The machines were all connected electronically to the Postal Buddy corporate headquarters in San Diego, Calif.

The Postal Buddy I design was an unframed USPS eagle logo with "USA" and the denomination at right. Data printed beneath the indicia contained a location code, a two-digit year, a three-digit Julian date, and a transaction number. They are known in 15¢ and 19¢ denominations, as appropriate for the date of issue.

The Postal Buddy II design was a star and stripes enclosed in a faux-perforation rectangle. "USA" and the denomination are to the right. Data similar to that of the Postal Buddy I is printed beneath and outside the design. Postal Buddy II is known only in the 19¢ denomination.

Postal Mailing Center

ECA GARD Corp.
Unisys Corp.

These self-service machines were installed in post office lobbies and in non-postal sites such as convenience stores and shopping malls. They dispensed adhesive coil stamps with a pre-printed design upon which the denomination was applied when vended.

Automated Postal Center

National Cash Register
IBM and Neopost

The Automated Postal Center testing began in 1999 in and around Orlando, Fla. The machines computed postage and dispensed thermal-printed postage labels, plus pre-printed forms for certified and express mail.

The first phase of the testing pitted 16 NCR machines against 16 by a collaboration of IBM and Neopost. The machines were placed in post offices and Gooding's grocery stores. After two years, USPS announced that it was dropping the NCR machines. The remaining IBM/Neopost machines were redistributed to area post offices only because the grocery chain had closed shop in the area.

The stamps from both types of machines during the first phase were available as regular labels with an identification number printed beneath a large two-dimensional bar code, and with "PRIORITY MAIL," "EXPRESS MAIL" and "POST CARD" beneath the bar code if such services were selected by the patron. The labels were self-adhesive, with a fluorescent orange bar along the bottom edge. In addition, the IBM/Neopost stamps included a narrow strip of microprinting just above the orange bar.

Virtually coinciding with the start of phase two, the IBM/Neopost stamps were printed on a new label with rounded corners and "U.S. POSTAGE" vertically at right. In addition, the microprinting was discontinued about the same time.

In the second phase, the stamps were printed as regular stamps with an identification number, or with "PRIORITY MAIL," or with "PRIORITY MAIL" with a string of text beneath the barcode.

Phase two testing continues. Two of the machines were relocated to the West Palm Beach, Fla., area and one was installed in New York City.

SnapStamps

Neopost

SnapStamps appeared sometime in 2001 with little or no fanfare. They are dispensed by small wall-mounted kiosks on small sheets of four stamps. The basic design of the stamp has undergone several changes in the short time it has been available.

The first design is the only one with four serpentine sides and a mail class indicated. All subsequent varieties are serpentined only at the right along the fluorescent orange bar. A stylized eagle and stars was used for a short while, but it was changed to a stylized waving flag. Other variations exist, but these relate to marginal inscriptions and text on the back of the sheets and do not affect the stamps. These stamps apparently are available only in the prevailing first class rate.

Values are for mint stamps on backing paper and used stamps on cover.

1989. AUTOPOST ISSUE Design is 25x54mm, fluorescent orange band at left, "USA" with stars in rectangle, mail classification in small box at lower left, machine number, transaction number, and item weight in box at lower right, "U.S. Postage," denomination date, and sequence number in box at upper right, and city, state, and ZIP code along bottom. Each transaction also generated an advertising label printed on the same peel-and-stick paper as the stamps; the first type, which simply read, "We Deliver..." was dispensed for less than three months, then changed to the second type. Test labels, closely resembling the actual stamps, were generated each time the machine was rebooted; these labels were supposed to be destroyed by the technicians, but some ended up in collectors' hands.

 OD1

OD1

	MNHVF	UseVF
First Class, orange & black	5.00	25.00
Priority, orange & black	10.00	75.00
Express Mail, orange & black	30.00	300.00
Third-Class, orange & black	5.00	30.00
Auxilliary labels: We Deliver	10.00	
We Deliver/United States Postal Service	5.00	
Test label	50.00	
Test label with bar code	100.00	
FDC (Aug. 23, 1989)		200.00

1989. AUTOPOST ISSUE Design same as OD1 except "USA" and stars of main design replaced by bar code for delivery ZIP code. Available only for Parcel Post and Priority over one pound.

 OD2

OD2

	MNHVF	UseVF
Parcel Post, orange & black	15.00	50.00
Priority, orange & black	75.00	250.00

1992. POSTAGE AND MAILING CENTER ISSUE The basic ECA GARD design is a printed coil stamp of striped bunting around a wavy-lined background, with a blue shield at top center, oriented horizontally with perforations at top and bottom. The denomination (1¢-$99.99) was printed on site by the machine. A small, solid asterisk takes the place of a dollar sign, and a large dot indicates the decimal point. Errors with misaligned or missing denominations are known, caused mostly by collectors tinkering with the machines. *Intaglio by Bureau of Engraving and Printing, perforated 10 horizontally, shiny or matte gum. (See Krause-Minkus No. 986.)*

 OD3

OD3

	MNHVF	UseVF
red and blue	.50	2.00
embedded taggant, shiny gum	1.50	.50
FDC (Aug. 20, 1992)		7.50

1994. POSTAGE AND MAILING CENTER ISSUE Similar to OD3 but the Unisys stamp is oriented vertically with perforations at left and right. Digital type face with dollar sign, denominations 19¢-$99.99. *Gravure by Guilford Gravure for American Bank Note Co., perforated 10, matte gum. (See Krause-Minkus No. 1040).*

 OD4

OD4

	MNHVF	UseVF
red & blue	.50	2.00
FDC (Feb. 19, 1994)		7.50

1994. POSTAGE AND MAILING CENTER ISSUE As OD3 but improved font for denomination. A hollow-center asterisk takes the place of a dollar sign, and the decimal point is in the normal position. *(See Krause-Minkus No. 1053.)*

 OD5

OD5

	MNHVF	UseVF
red & blue	.50	1.00
FDC (Nov. 9, 1994)		20.00

1996. POSTAGE AND MAILING CENTER ISSUE As OD4 but date (1996) added at bottom-left of design. *Gravure by Bureau of Engraving and Printing, perforated 9 3/4. (See Krause-Minkus No. 1117.)*

 OD6

OD6

	MNHVF	UseVF
red & blue	.50	1.00
FDC (Jan. 26, 1996)		1.25

1999. AUTOMATED POSTAL CENTER ISSUE The NCR stamp is printed on a 41mmx79mm self-adhesive label with square corners and a fluorescent band along the bottom. It has an identification number printed to the right beneath a large two-dimensional bar code, and with "PRIORITY MAIL," "EXPRESS MAIL" or "POST CARD" beneath the bar code if such services were selected by the patron. The labels had a fluorescent orange bar along the bottom edge.

 OD7

OD7

	MNHVF	UseVF
black	—	—
EKU (Aug. 30, 1999)	—	—

1999. AUTOMATED POSTAL CENTER ISSUE The first IBM/Neopost stamp is similar to OD6 but the design is taller. There is a small USPS logo at the upper right, and the line of text is aligned to the left beneath the bar code. There is a line of micro-printing just above the orange band at the bottom.

 OD8

OD8		MNHVF	UseVF
	black & orange	—	—

1999. AUTOMATED POSTAL CENTER ISSUE IBM/Neopost stamps similar to OD7 but printed on a 41mmx72mm label with rounded corners, "U.S. POSTAGE" in orange vertically at right, and no micro-printing.

OD9
Regular

OD9
Priority

OD9
Priority and text string

OD9		MNHVF	UseVF
	Regular print, black & orange	1.00	3.00
	PRIORITY MAIL print, black & orange	5.00	5.00
	PRIORITY MAIL and text string, black & orange	5.00	5.00

2001. SNAPSTAMPS ISSUE This first Neopost design has four serpentine sides, red fluorescent bar at right, a stylized yellow envelope in the center, a quartered two-dimensional bar code at right above the denomination, and a line of micro-printing at left with "FIRST CLASS."

OD10

OD10		MNHVF	UseVF
33¢	black, red & yellow		

2001. SNAPSTAMPS ISSUE This and all subsequent SnapStamp types are printed on small sheetlets of four stamps with quartered two-dimensional bar code and fluorescent bar at right. They have a serpentine edge at right, with straight edges otherwise and rounded corners. This type has a stylized eagle and stars at left above the denomination.

OD11

OD11		MNHVF	UseVF
34¢	black	—	—

2001. SNAPSTAMPS ISSUE Same as OD10 but machine number added at upper left.

OD12

OD12		MNHVF	UseVF
34¢	black	—	—

2001. SNAPSTAMPS ISSUE Similar to OD11 but eagle replaced by waving blue flag.

OD13

OD13		MNHVF	UseVF
34¢	black & blue	—	—

2001. SNAPSTAMPS ISSUE Same as OD13 but "U.S. POSTAGE" beneath denomination and machine number moved to lower left.

OD14 *Sheetlet*

OD14		MNHVF	UseVF
34¢	black, blue & red	5.00	3.00

2002. SNAPSTAMPS ISSUE Similar design to OD14 with two changes. The words "simplypostage.com" was replaced with "neopostage.com" and the twelve digit number under "US Postage" was placed above the scrambled square. Printed in sheets of ten. Entire sheet consisted of same denomination. Denominations available included $0.23, $0.37, $0.50, $0.60, $0.70, $0.80, $3.85, $13.65. $0.34 is known but on a very limited basis.

OD15		MNHVF	UseVF
37¢	black, blue & red	5.00	3.00
	n. Pane of 10	50.00	

NetStamps

Internet postage that can be printed from the user's personal computer. Postage can be printed in any denomination. Stamps.com, for a monthly subscription fee, sells supplies and self-adhesive sheets of 25 labels which are used to print postage. Initially, the order of prined information on the stamp was 1) Denomination, 2) "US POSTAGE," 3) Zip Code, 4) "FIRST-CLASS," 5) Control number and then a scrambled square (Type 1A). If the postage required was not for a first-class use, then "FIRST-CLASS" did not print (Type 1A). After a trial period, the order of printed information was changed to 1) Denomination, 2) "US POSTAGE," 3) "FIRST-CLASS," 4) Control number, 5) Zip Code and then a scrambled square (Type 2). If the postage required was not a first-class use, then "FIRST-CLASS" did not print (Type 2A).

Type 1

Type 1A

Type 2

Type 2A

2002. NetStamps Flag and Star Issue "Stamps.com" printed in orange bar on right side of label. Blue star behind a waving blue flag. *Self-adhesive and serpentine die cut 3 1/2 on left side and straight die cuts on top, bottom and right side. Type 1 and Type 1A printing.*

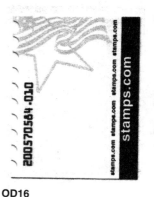

OD16, OD17 *Flag and Star*

OD16

	MNHVF	UseVF
black, blue & orange (Type 1)	.75	.25
v. Type 1A	.75	.25

2002. NetStamps Flag and Star Issue Same design as OD16 except uses Type 2 and Type 2A printing.

OD17

	MNHVF	UseVF
black, blue & orange (Type 2)	.75	.25
v. Type 2A	.75	.25

2003. NetStamps Love Issue Three light violet hearts make up the background image with the word "LOVE" printed in the side orange bar. Released for Valentine's Day. *Self-adhesive and serpentine die cut 3 1/2 on left side and straight die cuts on top, bottom and right side.*

OD18 *Love*

OD18

	MNHVF	UseVF
black, violet & orange (Type 2)	.75	.25
v. Type 2A	.75	.25

2003. NetStamps Statue of Liberty and Flag Issue First of five new designs that form the Liberty Series. Each row on a sheet of 25 labels features a scene depicting Liberty. "Liberty" is printed in orange bar on right. *Self-adhesive and serpentine die cut 3 1/2 on left side and straight die cuts on top, bottom and right side.*

OD19 *Statue of Liberty and Flag*

OD19

	MNHVF	UseVF
black, blue & orange (Type 2)	.75	.25
v. Type 2A	.75	.25

2003. NETSTAMPS LIBERTY BELL AND FLAG ISSUE Second of five new designs that form the Liberty Series. "Liberty" is printed in orange bar on right. Each row on a sheet of 25 labels features a scene depicting Liberty. *Self-adhesive and serpentine die cut 3 1/2 on left side and straight die cuts on top, bottom and right side.*

OD20 *Liberty Bell and Flag*

OD20

	MNHVF	UseVF
black, blue & orange (Type 2)	.75	.25
v. Type 2A	.75	.25

2003. NETSTAMPS EAGLE AND FLAG ISSUE Third of five new designs that form the Liberty Series. "Liberty" is printed in orange bar on right. Each row on a sheet of 25 labels features a scene depicting Liberty. *Self-adhesive and serpentine die cut 3 1/2 on left side and straight die cuts on top, bottom and right side.*

OD21 *Eagle and Flag*

OD21

	MNHVF	UseVF
black, blue & orange (Type 2)	.75	.25
v. Type 2A	.75	.25

2003. NETSTAMPS GEORGE WASHINGTON AND FLAG ISSUE Fourth of five new designs that form the Liberty Series. "Liberty" is printed in orange bar on right. Each row on a sheet of 25 labels features a scene depicting Liberty. *Self-adhesive and serpentine die cut 3 1/2 on left side and straight die cuts on top, bottom and right side.*

OD22 *George Washington and Flag*

OD22

	MNHVF	UseVF
black, blue & orange (Type 2)	.75	.25
v. Type 2A	.75	.25

2003. NETSTAMPS CAPITOL BUILDING AND FLAG ISSUE Fifth of five new designs that form the Liberty Series. "Liberty" is printed in orange bar on right. Each row on a sheet of 25 labels features a scene depicting Liberty. *Self-adhesive and serpentine die cut 3 1/2 on left side and straight die cuts on top, bottom and right side.*

OD23 *Capitol Building and Flag*

OD23

	MNHVF	UseVF
black, blue & orange (Type 2)	.75	.25
v. Type 2A	.75	.25

2003. NETSTAMPS SNOWMAN ISSUE First of five new designs that form the Happy Holidays Series. "Happy Holidays" is printed in the orange side bar on right. Each row on a sheet of 25 labels features a scene depicting a holiday scene. *Self-adhesive and serpentine die cut 3 1/2 on left side and straight die cuts on top, bottom and right side.*

OD24 *Snowman*

OD24

	MNHVF	UseVF
black, green & orange (Type 2)	.75	.25
v. Type 2A	.75	.25

2003. NETSTAMPS SNOWFLAKES ISSUE Second of five new designs that form the Happy Holidays Series. "Happy Holidays" is printed in the orange side bar on right. Each row on a sheet of 25 labels features a scene depicting a holiday scene. *Self-adhesive and serpentine die cut 3 1/2 on left side and straight die cuts on top, bottom and right side.*

OD25 *Snowflakes*

OD25

		MNHVF	UseVF
black, green & orange (Type 2)		.75	.25
v. Type 2A		.75	.25

2003. NETSTAMPS HOLLY ISSUE Third of five new designs that form the Happy Holidays Series. "Happy Holidays" is printed in the orange side bar on right. Each row on a sheet of 25 labels features a scene depicting a holiday scene. *Self-adhesive and serpentine die cut 3 1/2 on left side and straight die cuts on top, bottom and right side.*

OD26 *Holly*

OD26

		MNHVF	UseVF
black, green & orange (Type 2)		.75	.25
v. Type 2A		.75	.25

2003. NETSTAMPS DOVE ISSUE Fourth of five new designs that form the Happy Holidays Series. "Happy Holidays" is printed in the orange side bar on right. Each row on a sheet of 25 labels features a scene depicting a holiday scene. *Self-adhesive and serpentine die cut 3 1/2 on left side and straight die cuts on top, bottom and right side.*

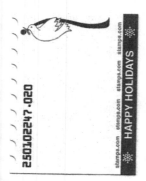

OD27 *Dove*

OD27

		MNHVF	UseVF
black, green & orange (Type 2)		.75	.25
v. Type 2A		.75	.25

2003. NETSTAMPS GINGERBREAD MAN AND CANDY ISSUE Fifth of five new designs that form the Happy Holidays Series. "Happy Holidays" is printed in the orange side bar on right. Each row on a sheet of 25 labels features a scene depicting a holiday scene. *Self-adhesive and serpentine die cut 3 1/2 on left side and straight die cuts on top, bottom and right side.*

OD28 *Gingerbread Man and Candy*

OD28

		MNHVF	UseVF
black, green & orange (Type 2)		.75	.25
v. Type 2A		.75	.25

1990. POSTAL BUDDY ISSUE Design is USPS eagle logo with "USA" and denomination at right, with data string beneath. Printed directly on 110x140mm (approx. 4 1/2 by 5 1/2 inches) white cards.

ODPC1

10001-90-186-064

ODPC1

		MNHVF	UseVF
15¢	black	5.00	10.00
	FDC (July 5, 1990)		5.00

1991. POSTAL BUDDY ISSUE

ODPC2

		MNHVF	UseVF
19¢	black	5.00	10.00
	FDC (Feb. 3, 1991)		75.00

1992. POSTAL BUDDY ISSUE Design is a star and stripes enclosed in a faux-perforation rectangle. "USA" and the denomination are to the right. Data similar to that of ODPC1 is printed beneath and outside the design.

ODPC3

22021-011-21113-052

ODPC3

		MNHVF	UseVF
19¢	black	5.00	25.00
	FDC (Nov. 13, 1992)		40.00

Newspaper/Periodical Stamps

First issued in September 1865 to prepay postage on bulk shipments of newspapers and periodicals, they were not attached to the items mailed, but rather to the statement of mailing, which was canceled and retained by the Post Office. The stamps were discontinued July 1, 1898.

1865. FIRST NEWSPAPER STAMP ISSUE *embossed and printed in letterpress, National Bank Note Co. Thin, hard, unwatermarked paper, without gum, and perforated 12. The design size is 51x95mm, colored border.*

N1, N4 *George Washington*

N1		UnFVF	UseFVF
5¢	**dark blue**	250.00	—
	a. light blue	275.00	—

N2 *Benjamin Franklin*

N5-N11 *"Freedom" after Crawford's statue on the dome of the Capitol*

N5		UnFVF	UseFVF
2¢	**black**	25.00	12.50
	gray black	25.00	12.50
	greenish black	25.00	12.50
N6		**UnFVF**	**UseFVF**
3¢	**black**	27.50	15.00
	gray black	27.50	15.00
N7		**UnFVF**	**UseFVF**
4¢	**black**	27.50	15.00
	gray black	27.50	15.00
	greenish black	27.50	15.00
N8		**UnFVF**	**UseFVF**
6¢	**black**	30.00	20.00
	gray black	30.00	20.00
	greenish black	30.00	20.00
N9		**UnFVF**	**UseFVF**
8¢	**black**	45.00	24.00
	gray black	45.00	32.50
	greenish black	45.00	
N10		**UnFVF**	**UseFVF**
9¢	**black**	65.00	52.00
	gray black	85.00	60.00
	greenish black	65.00	52.00
	Double transfer	100.00	75.00
N11		**UnFVF**	**UseFVF**
10¢	**black**	45.00	32.50
	gray black	45.00	32.50
	greenish black	45.00	32.50

N2		UnFVF	UseFVF
10¢	**green**	100.00	—
	a. blue green	100.00	—
	p. Pelure paper	125.00	—

N3 *Abraham Lincoln*

N3		UnFVF	UseFVF
25¢	**orange red**	150.00	—
	a. carmine red	175.00	—
	p. Pelure paper	150.00	—
N4		**UnFVF**	**UseFVF**
5¢	**blue**	75.00	—
	a. dark blue	75.00	—
	p. Pelure paper	75.00	—

1875. First Special Printing of the 1865 Issue *by the Continental Bank Note Co. The 5¢ with white border, the 10¢ and 25¢ with colored border. Hard, white paper, unwatermarked, issued without gum, perforated.*

SPN1		UnFVF	UseFVF
5¢	**blue**	75.00	
SPN2		**UnFVF**	**UseFVF**
10¢	**bluish green**	85.00	
SPN3		**UnFVF**	**UseFVF**
25¢	**carmine**	100.00	

1881. Second Special Printing of 1865 Issue *by the American Bank Note Co. White border, soft, porous paper, unwatermarked, perforated 12.*

SPN4		UnFVF	UseFVF
5¢	**dark blue**	175.00	—

1875. Allegory Design Issue *Intaglio, Continental Bank Note Co. Issued Jan. 1, 1875, on thin, hard paper. Design size 24x35mm.*

N12-19 *Astraea, Goddess of Justice*

N12		UnFVF	UseFVF
12¢	**rose**	100.00	50.00
	pale rose	100.00	50.00
N13		**UnFVF**	**UseFVF**
24¢	**rose**	125.00	65.00
	pale rose	125.00	65.00
N14		**UnFVF**	**UseFVF**
36¢	**rose**	150.00	75.00
	pale rose	150.00	75.00
N15		**UnFVF**	**UseFVF**
48¢	**rose**	250.00	125.00
	pale rose	250.00	125.00
N16		**UnFVF**	**UseFVF**
60¢	**rose**	140.00	65.00
	pale rose	140.00	65.00
N17		**UnFVF**	**UseFVF**
72¢	**rose**	300.00	175.00
	pale rose	300.00	175.00
N18		**UnFVF**	**UseFVF**
84¢	**rose**	450.00	200.00
	pale rose	450.00	200.00
N19		**UnFVF**	**UseFVF**
96¢	**rose**	250.00	125.00
	pale rose	250.00	125.00

N20 *Ceres*

N21 *Victory*

N22 *Clio*

N20		UnFVF	UseFVF
$1.92	brown	350.00	225.00
	dark brown	350.00	225.00
N21		UnFVF	UseFVF
$3	vermilion	475.00	175.00
N22		UnFVF	UseFVF
$6	ultramarine	750.00	150.00

N23 *Minerva*

N24 *Vesta*

N25 *Peace*

N23		UnFVF	UseFVF
$9	yellow	850.00	325.00
N24		UnFVF	UseFVF
$12	blue green	1,000.00	450.00
N25		UnFVF	UseFVF
$24	dark gray violet	1,000.00	450.00

N26 *"Commerce"*

N27 *Hebe*

N25 *Indian Maiden*

N26		UnFVF	UseFVF
$36	brown rose	1,150.00	600.00
N27		UnFVF	UseFVF
$48	red brown	1,600.00	650.00
N28		UnFVF	UseFVF
$60	violet	1,600.00	650.00

1875. SPECIAL PRINTING OF THE 1875 ISSUE *by the Continental Bank Note Co. Hard, white paper, unwatermarked, without gum, perforated 12.*

SPN5		UnFVF	UseFVF
2¢	gray black *(19,514, quantity issued probably includes SPN 29)*	125.00	
SPN6		UnFVF	UseFVF
3¢	gray black *(6,952)*	140.00	
SPN7		UnFVF	UseFVF
4¢	gray black *(4,451)*	150.00	
SPN8		UnFVF	UseFVF
6¢	gray black *(2,348)*	200.00	

SPN9		UnFVF	UseFVF
8¢	gray black *(1,930)*	250.00	
SPN10		UnFVF	UseFVF
9¢	gray black *(1,795)*	275.00	
SPN11		UnFVF	UseFVF
10¢	gray black *(1,499)*	350.00	
SPN12		UnFVF	UseFVF
12¢	rose *(1,313)*	425.00	
SPN13		UnFVF	UseFVF
24¢	rose *(411)*	600.00	
SPN14		UnFVF	UseFVF
36¢	rose *(330)*	700.00	
SPN15		UnFVF	UseFVF
48¢	rose *(268)*	800.00	
SPN16		UnFVF	UseFVF
60¢	rose *(222)*	850.00	
SPN17		UnFVF	UseFVF
72¢	rose *(174)*	1,000.00	
SPN18		UnFVF	UseFVF
84¢	rose *(164)*	1,250.00	
SPN19		UnFVF	UseFVF
96¢	rose *(141)*	1,750.00	
SPN20		UnFVF	UseFVF
$1.92	dark brown *(41)*	4,500.00	
SPN21		UnFVF	UseFVF
$3	vermilion *(20)*	8,000.00	
SPN22		UnFVF	UseFVF
$6	ultramarine *(14)*	10,000.00	
SPN23		UnFVF	UseFVF
$9	yellow *(4)*	17,500.00	
SPN24		UnFVF	UseFVF
$12	bluish green *(5)*	16,000.00	
SPN25		UnFVF	UseFVF
$24	gray violet *(2)*	—	
SPN26		UnFVF	UseFVF
$36	brown rose *(2)*	—	
SPN27		UnFVF	UseFVF
$48	red brown *(1)*	—	
SPN28		UnFVF	UseFVF
$60	violet	—	
SPN29		UnFVF	UseFVF
2¢	black	325.00	

1879. ALLEGORY DESIGN ISSUE *American Bank Note Co., soft, porous paper, unwatermarked, perforated 12.*

N29		UnFVF	UseFVF
2¢	black	10.00	5.00
	gray black	10.00	5.00
	greenish black	19.00	5.00
	Double transfer at top	12.00	9.00
	Cracked plate	—	
	v. Imperforate	—	

1879. ALLEGORY DESIGN ISSUE

N30		UnFVF	UseFVF
3¢	black	12.50	5.50
	gray black	12.50	5.50
	greenish black	12.00	5.50
	Double transfer at top	14.00	10.00
	v. Imperforate	—	
N31		UnFVF	UseFVF
4¢	black	12.50	5.50
	gray black	12.50	5.50
	greenish black	12.50	5.50
	intense black	12.50	5.50
	Double transfer at top	15.00	10.00
	v. Imperforate	—	
N32		UnFVF	UseFVF
6¢	black	22.50	12.50
	gray black	22.50	12.50
	greenish black	22.50	12.50
	intense black	22.50	12.50
	Double transfer at top	27.50	22.50
	v. Imperforate	—	
N33		UnFVF	UseFVF
8¢	black	22.50	12.50
	gray black	22.50	12.50
	greenish black	22.50	12.50
	Double transfer at top	27.50	22.50
	v. Imperforate	—	

			UnFVF	UseFVF
N34	10¢	black	25.00	12.50
		gray black	25.00	12.50
		greenish black	25.00	12.50
		Double transfer at top	27.50	—
		v. Imperforate	—	
N35	12¢	red	90.00	35.00
		v. Imperforate	—	
N36	24¢	red	90.00	35.00
		v. Imperforate	—	
N37	36¢	red	250.00	125.00
		v. Imperforate	—	
N38	48¢	red	225.00	75.00
		v. Imperforate	—	
N39	60¢	red	175.00	75.00
		v. Imperforate	—	
N40	72¢	red	350.00	150.00
		v. Imperforate	—	
N41	84¢	red	250.00	125.00
		v. Imperforate	—	
N42	96¢	red	175.00	75.00
		pink carmine	175.00	75.00
		v. Imperforate	—	
N43	$1.92	pale brown	125.00	100.00
		brown	125.00	100.00
		Cracked plate	175.00	
		v. Imperforate	—	
N44	$3	red vermilion	125.00	75.00
		v. Imperforate	—	
N45	$6	blue	225.00	125.00
		ultramarine	225.00	125.00
		v. Imperforate	—	
N46	$9	orange	150.00	75.00
		v. Imperforate	—	
N47	$12	yellow green	225.00	100.00
		v. Imperforate	—	
N48	$24	dark violet	300.00	150.00
		v. Imperforate	—	
N49	$36	Indian red	350.00	150.00
		v. Imperforate	—	
N50	$48	yellow brown	450.00	225.00
		v. Imperforate	—	
N51	$60	purple	450.00	225.00
		bright purple	450.00	225.00
		v. Imperforate	—	

1885. ALLEGORY DESIGN ISSUE *Intaglio, American Bank Note Co., soft, porous paper, perforated 12.*

			UnFVF	UseFVF
N52	1¢	black	12.50	5.50
		gray black	12.50	5.50
		intense black	12.50	5.50
		Double transfer at top	15.00	9.00
N53	12¢	carmine	40.00	15.00
		deep carmine	40.00	15.00
		rose carmine	40.00	15.00
N54	24¢	carmine	40.00	17.50
		deep carmine	40.00	17.50
		rose carmine	40.00	17.50
N55	36¢	carmine	60.00	25.00
		deep carmine	60.00	25.00
		rose carmine	60.00	25.00
N56	48¢	carmine	85.00	40.00
		deep carmine	85.00	40.00
N57	60¢	carmine	125.00	50.00
		deep carmine	125.00	50.00
N58	72¢	carmine	150.00	60.00
		deep carmine	150.00	60.00
		rose carmine	150.00	60.00
N59	84¢	carmine	300.00	140.00
		rose carmine	300.00	140.00
N60	96¢	carmine	225.00	100.00
		rose carmine	225.00	100.00

Imperforates of N52-N60 exist, but they were not regularly issued.

1894. ALLEGORY DESIGN ISSUE *Intaglio, Bureau of Engraving and Printing, soft wove paper, perforated 12.*

			UnFVF	UseFVF
N61	1¢	black	100.00	—
		Double transfer at top	125.00	
N62	2¢	black	100.00	—
		Double transfer at top	125.00	
N63	4¢	black	125.00	—
N64	6¢	black	1,500.00	
N65	10¢	black	225.00	—
N66	12¢	pink	700.00	
N67	24¢	pink	700.00	—
N68	36¢	pink	4,500.00	
N69	60¢	pink	4,500.00	—
N70	96¢	pink	5,500.00	—
N71	$3	scarlet	6,500.00	
N72	$6	pale blue	8,500.00	—

1895. NEW ALLEGORY DESIGNS ISSUE *Intaglio, Bureau of Engraving and Printing, soft wove paper, perforated 12.*

N73-N76 "Freedom"

N77-N78 "Astraea"

			UnFVF	UseFVF
N73	1¢	black	40.00	10.00
N74	2¢	black	40.00	10.00
		gray black	30.00	10.00
		Double transfer at top	45.00	
N75	5¢	black	50.00	15.00
		gray black	50.00	15.00
N76	10¢	black	100.00	45.00
N77	25¢	carmine	150.00	50.00
N78	50¢	carmine	325.00	125.00

N79 *"Victory"*

N80 *"Clio"*

N81 *"Vista"*

			UnFVF	UseFVF
N79 $2	**scarlet**		400.00	100.00
N80 $5	**ultramarine**		600.00	200.00
N81 $10	**green**		550.00	225.00

N82 *"Peace"*

N83 *"Commerce"*

N84 *Indian maiden*

		UnFVF	UseFVF
N82 $20	**slate**	825.00	400.00
N83 $50	**dull rose**	850.00	400.00
N84 $100	**purple**	1,000.00	450.00
N85 1¢	**black**	4.00	3.25
	gray black	4.00	3.25
N86 2¢	**black**	4.50	3.75
	gray black	4.50	3.75
N87 5¢	**black**	7.00	5.50
	gray black	7.00	5.50
N88 10¢	**black**	4.50	3.75
	gray black	4.50	3.75
N89 25¢	**carmine**	8.50	8.50
	lilac rose	8.50	8.50
N90 50¢	**carmine**	12.50	14.00
	rose carmine	12.50	14.00
	lilac rose	12.50	14.00
N91 $2	**scarlet**	15.00	17.50
	scarlet vermilion	15.00	17.50
N92 $5	**dark blue**	25.00	30.00
	light blue	125.00	50.00
N93 $10	**green**	25.00	30.00
N94 $20	**slate**	25.00	35.00
N95 $50	**dull rose**	30.00	40.00
N96 $100	**purple**	35.00	42.50

1899. REPRINTS OF THE 1895 ISSUE SPECIAL PRINTING In 1899 the U.S. Government sold 26,898 sets of the Newspaper Series of 1895-97 to collectors at $5 per set. Since the supply of high values was not great enough to make up the number of sets required, the values from the $5 through the $100 were reprinted. These special printings can be distinguished from the originals by the shade and whiteness of the paper and gum.

Bureau of Engraving and Printing. Designs of 1895 issue but on double-line USPS watermark paper, with white instead of yellowish gum, perforated 12.

		UnFVF	UseFVF
SPN30 $5	**blue**	—	
SPN31 $10	**green**	—	
SPN32 $20	**slate**	—	
SPN33 $50	**rose**	—	
SPN34 $100	**purple**	—	

Official Carrier Stamps

1851. OFFICIAL CARRIER STAMP In the early days of the U.S. postal system the regular postage charge paid only for the delivery of mail from post office to post office. For an additional charge, the post office would act as a carrier and deliver letters to the addressee. Two stamps were issued for this purpose. *Printed by Toppan, Carpenter, Casilear and Company, they were unwatermarked and imperforate.* They were both of the 1¢ denomination, although the Franklin stamp had no denomination indicated on its face.

OCS1 *Benjamin Franklin*

		UnFVF	UseFVF
OCS1 1¢	**blue on rose paper**	4,000.00	4,500.00
	Cracked plate	4,500.00	
	Double transfer	—	—
	On cover		7,750.00

OCS2 *Eagle*

		UnFVF	UseFVF
OCS2 1¢	**blue on yellowish paper**	20.00	35.00
	Double transfer	—	—
	On cover (alone)		125.00

1875. REPRINT OFFICIAL CARRIER STAMP Special Printing reprint of the Official Carrier Stamps of 1851. The Franklin carrier was printed in a darker blue than the originals and appears on rose-colored paper as well as on a paler, thicker paper. The Eagle reprints are on hard white paper and also on a coarse paper. *Printed by the Continental Bank Note Co., intaglio, imperforate, without gum.*

		UnFVF	UseFVF
SPOCS1 1¢	**blue on rose paper**	50.00	
	v. Perforated 12	2,500.00	
SPOCS2 1¢	**blue**	25.00	
	v. Perforated 12	175.00	

Official Stamps

The franking privilege for the various government departments was abolished July 1, 1873. On that date, official stamps were issued to be used by the departments. In addition to the name of the department, inscribed at the top, the Post Office Department stamps have large numerals as the central design, while the stamps of the other departments feature busts of the following men, as on the then-current Banknotes:

1¢ Benjamin Franklin	2¢ Andrew Jackson
3¢ George Washington	6¢ Abraham Lincoln
7¢ Edwin Stanton	10¢ Thomas Jefferson
12¢ Henry Clay	15¢ Daniel Webster
24¢ Winfield Scott	30¢ Alexander Hamilton
90¢ Oliver Perry	

William Seward is shown on the $2-$20 State Department stamps.

The first official stamps were printed in intaglio by the Continental Bank Note Co. on thin, hard paper; but in 1879 the American Bank Note Co., using the same plates, made printings on soft, porous paper. This is the principal way that they can be identified, since all the paper is unwatermarked, and all the stamps are *perforated 12*. A marginal imprint reading "Continental" does not necessarily indicate the printer. *Intaglio on thin, hard paper, unwatermarked, perforated 12.*

1873. AGRICULTURE DEPT. ISSUE *Intaglio on thin, hard paper, unwatermarked, perforated 12.*

 OF1

OF1		UnFVF	UseFVF
1¢	**yellow**	95.00	75.00
	golden yellow	110.00	80.00
	olive yellow	110.00	80.00
	p. Ribbed paper	125.00	80.00
	On cover	—	

OF2		UnFVF	UseFVF
2¢	**yellow**	85.00	32.50
	golden yellow	75.00	25.00
	olive yellow	75.00	27.50
	p. Ribbed paper	80.00	30.00
	On cover	—	

OF3		UnFVF	UseFVF
3¢	**yellow**	65.00	6.00
	golden yellow	70.00	6.50
	olive yellow	73.00	6.50
	Double transfer	—	—
	p. Ribbed paper	73.00	7.00
	On cover	—	

OF4		UnFVF	UseFVF
6¢	**yellow**	80.00	25.00
	golden yellow	80.00	27.50
	olive yellow	80.00	27.50
	On cover	—	

OF5		UnFVF	UseFVF
10¢	**yellow**	150.00	100.00
	golden yellow	165.00	110.00
	olive yellow	175.00	115.00
	On cover	—	

OF6		UnFVF	UseFVF
12¢	**yellow**	195.00	100.00
	golden yellow	210.00	110.00
	olive yellow	225.00	110.00
	On cover	—	

OF7		UnFVF	UseFVF
15¢	**yellow**	160.00	95.00
	golden yellow	170.00	100.00
	olive yellow	175.00	100.00
	On cover	—	

OF8		UnFVF	UseFVF
24¢	**yellow**	160.00	85.00
	golden yellow	175.00	85.00
	On cover	—	

OF9		UnFVF	UseFVF
30¢	**yellow**	225.00	115.00
	olive yellow	250.00	150.00
	golden yellow	235.00	140.00

1879. AGRICULTURE DEPT. ISSUE *American Bank Note Co., intaglio on soft, porous paper, unwatermarked, perforated 12.*

OF10		UnFVF	UseFVF
1¢	**yellow,** issued without gum	2,000.00	
	issued without gum	1,500.00	
	Plate pair	—	

Some consider No. OF10 a special printing, circa 1883.

OF11		UnFVF	UseFVF
3¢	**yellow**	225.00	40.00

1873. EXECUTIVE DEPT. ISSUE *Intaglio on thin, hard paper, unwatermarked, perforated 12.*

OF12		UnFVF	UseFVF
1¢	**carmine**	335.00	200.00
	dark carmine	335.00	200.00

OF13		UnFVF	UseFVF
2¢	**carmine**	210.00	100.00
	dark carmine	210.00	100.00
	Double transfer	—	

OF14		UnFVF	UseFVF
3¢	**carmine**	260.00	100.00
	lilac red	260.00	100.00

 OF15

OF15		UnFVF	UseFVF
6¢	**carmine**	400.00	275.00
	dark carmine	400.00	275.00
	dull carmine	400.00	275.00

OF16		UnFVF	UseFVF
10¢	**carmine**	350.00	300.00
	dark carmine	350.00	300.00
	dull carmine	350.00	300.00

1873. INTERIOR DEPT. ISSUE *Intaglio on thin, hard paper, unwatermarked, perforated 12.*

OF17		UnFVF	UseFVF
1¢	**orange red**	21.00	5.25
	bright orange red	21.00	5.25
	dull orange red	21.00	5.25
	p. Ribbed paper	25.00	6.00

OF18		UnFVF	UseFVF
2¢	**orange red**	16.50	3.25
	bright orange red	16.50	3.25
	dull orange red	16.50	3.25

OF19		UnFVF	UseFVF
3¢	**orange red**	28.00	3.00
	bright orange red	28.00	3.00
	dull orange red	28.00	3.00
	p. Ribbed paper	30.00	5.25

OF20		UnFVF	UseFVF
6¢	**orange red**	**21.00**	**3.25**
	bright orange red	21.00	3.25
	dull orange red	21.00	3.25

OF21		UnFVF	UseFVF
10¢	**orange red**	20.00	6.25
	bright orange red	20.00	6.25
	dull orange red	20.00	6.25

OF22		UnFVF	UseFVF
12¢	**orange red**	32.50	4.75
	bright orange red	32.50	4.75
	dull orange red	32.50	4.75

 OF23

OF23		UnFVF	UseFVF
15¢	**orange red**	50.00	10.00
	bright orange red	50.00	10.00
	dull orange red	50.00	10.00
	Double transfer	90.00	25.00
	p. Ribbed paper	—	

OF24		UnFVF	UseFVF
24¢	**orange red**	37.50	8.50
	bright orange red	37.50	8.50
	dull orange red	37.50	8.50

OF25		UnFVF	UseFVF
30¢	**orange red**	50.00	8.50
	bright orange red	50.00	8.50
	dull orange red	50.00	8.50

OF26		UnFVF	UseFVF
90¢	**orange red**	115.00	22.50
	bright orange red	115.00	22.50
	dull orange red	115.00	22.50
	Double transfer	160.00	—

1879. INTERIOR DEPT. ISSUE *Intaglio on soft, porous paper, unwatermarked, perforated 12.*

OF27		UnFVF	UseFVF
1¢	**orange red**	135.00	125.00
	dull orange red	135.00	125.00

OF28		UnFVF	UseFVF
2¢	**orange red**	2.50	1.25
	dull orange red	2.50	1.25

OF29		UnFVF	UseFVF
3¢	**orange red**	2.25	.75
	dull orange red	2.25	.75

OF30		UnFVF	UseFVF
6¢	**orange red**	3.50	3.75
	dull orange red	3.50	3.75

OF31		UnFVF	UseFVF
10¢	**orange red**	45.00	35.00
	dull orange red	45.00	35.00

OF32		UnFVF	UseFVF
12¢	**orange red**	90.00	60.00
	dull orange red	90.00	60.00

OF33		UnFVF	UseFVF
15¢	**orange red**	200.00	150.00
	dull orange red	200.00	150.00
	Double transfer, left side	275.00	—

OF34		UnFVF	UseFVF
24¢	**orange red**	2,500.00	—
	dull orange red	2,500.00	—

1873. JUSTICE DEPT. ISSUE *Intaglio on thin, hard paper, unwatermarked, perforated 12.*

OF35		UnFVF	UseFVF
1¢	**purple**	65.00	47.50
	dark purple	65.00	47.50

OF36		UnFVF	UseFVF
2¢	**purple**	100.00	50.00
	dark purple	100.00	50.00

OF37		UnFVF	UseFVF
3¢	**purple**	100.00	10.00
	dark purple	100.00	10.00
	Double transfer	—	—

OF38		UnFVF	UseFVF
6¢	**purple**	95.00	16.00
	bluish purple	95.00	16.00
	dull purple	95.00	16.00

OF39		UnFVF	UseFVF
10¢	**purple**	110.00	35.00
	bluish purple	110.00	35.00
	Double transfer	—	—

OF40

OF40		UnFVF	UseFVF
12¢	**purple**	85.00	22.50
	dark purple	85.00	22.50

OF41		UnFVF	UseFVF
15¢	**purple**	160.00	75.00
	Double transfer	—	

OF42		UnFVF	UseFVF
24¢	**purple**	425.00	165.00

OF43		UnFVF	UseFVF
30¢	**purple**	375.00	95.00
	Double transfer	400.00	95.00

OF44		UnFVF	UseFVF
90¢	**purple**	700.00	240.00
	dark purple	700.00	240.00

1879. JUSTICE DEPT. ISSUE *Intaglio on soft, porous paper, unwatermarked, perforated 12.*

OF45		UnFVF	UseFVF
3¢	**bluish purple**	65.00	40.00
	dark bluish purple	65.00	40.00

OF46		UnFVF	UseFVF
6¢	**dark bluish purple**	150.00	100.00

1873. NAVY DEPT. ISSUE *Intaglio on thin, hard paper, unwatermarked, perforated 12.*

OF47		UnFVF	UseFVF
1¢	**ultramarine**	45.00	22.50
	dark ultramarine	45.00	22.50
	dull blue	45.00	22.50

OF48		UnFVF	UseFVF
2¢	**ultramarine**	35.00	10.00
	dark ultramarine	35.00	10.00
	dull blue	45.00	12.50
	gray blue	45.00	12.50
	Double transfer	—	—

OF49

OF49		UnFVF	UseFVF
3¢	**ultramarine**	35.00	5.25
	dark ultramarine	35.00	5.25
	dull blue	35.00	5.25
	pale ultramarine	35.00	5.25
	Double transfer		

OF50		UnFVF	UseFVF
6¢	**ultramarine**	37.50	8.50
	bright ultramarine	37.50	8.50
	dull blue	45.00	8.50
	Double transfer		
	Vertical line through "N" of "NAVY"	65.00	14.00

OF51		UnFVF	UseFVF
7¢	**ultramarine**	210.00	85.00
	dark ultramarine	210.00	85.00
	dull blue	210.00	85.00
	Double transfer	—	—

OF52		UnFVF	UseFVF
10¢	**ultramarine**	47.50	17.50
	dark ultramarine	46.50	17.50
	dull blue	50.00	17.50
	pale ultramarine	47.50	17.50
	Cracked plate	—	125.00
	p. Ribbed paper	75.00	40.00

OF53		UnFVF	UseFVF
12¢	**ultramarine**	55.00	15.00
	dark ultramarine	55.00	15.00
	pale ultramarine	55.00	15.00
	Double transfer, left side	175.00	50.00

OF54		UnFVF	UseFVF
15¢	**ultramarine**	100.00	35.00
	dark ultramarine	100.00	35.00

OF55		UnFVF	UseFVF
24¢	**ultramarine**	100.00	35.00
	dark ultramarine	100.00	35.00
	dull blue	125.00	

OF56		UnFVF	UseFVF
30¢	**ultramarine**	80.00	17.50
	dark ultramarine	80.00	17.50
	Double transfer	100.00	20.00

OF57		UnFVF	UseFVF
90¢	**ultramarine**	425.00	110.00
	v. Double impression	—	7,500.00

1873. POST OFFICE DEPT. ISSUE *Intaglio on thin, hard paper, unwatermarked, perforated 12.*

OF58		UnFVF	UseFVF
1¢	**gray black**	7.50	3.50
	black	7.50	3.50

OF59		UnFVF	UseFVF
2¢	**gray black**	8.50	3.00
	black	8.50	3.00
	v. Double impression	325.00	—

OF60		UnFVF	UseFVF
3¢	**black**	3.00	1.00
	gray black	3.00	1.00
	Cracked plate	10.00	7.00
	Double transfer	—	—
	p. Ribbed paper	—	—
	v. Printed on both sides	—	3,500.00

OF61		UnFVF	UseFVF
6¢	**black**	9.00	2.25
	gray black	9.00	2.25
	p. Ribbed paper	—	9.00
	y. Diagonal half used as 3¢ on cover	—	4,500.00

OF62

OF62		UnFVF	UseFVF
10¢	**black**	40.00	20.00
	gray black	40.00	20.00

OF63		UnFVF	UseFVF
12¢	**black**	20.00	5.50
	gray black	20.00	5.50

OF64		UnFVF	UseFVF
15¢	**black**	27.50	9.00
	gray black	27.50	9.00
	Double transfer	—	—
	v. Pair, imperforate	—	550.00

OF65		UnFVF	UseFVF
24¢	**black**	35.00	10.00
	gray black	35.00	10.00

OF66		UnFVF	UseFVF
30¢	**black**	35.00	10.00
	gray black	35.00	10.00

OF67		UnFVF	UseFVF
90¢	**black**	50.00	10.00
	gray black	50.00	10.00
	Double transfer	—	—

1879. POST OFFICE DEPT. ISSUE *Intaglio on soft, porous paper, unwatermarked, perforated 12.*

OF68		UnFVF	UseFVF
3¢	**black**	9.00	3.25
	gray black	9.00	3.25
	Block of 4	200.00	—

1873. STATE DEPT. ISSUE *Intaglio on thin, hard paper, unwatermarked, perforated 12.*

OF69		UnFVF	UseFVF
1¢	**green**	65.00	25.00
	dark yellow green	65.00	25.00
	pale green	65.00	25.00

OF70		UnFVF	UseFVF
2¢	**green**	130.00	40.00
	dark yellow green	130.00	40.00
	yellow green	130.00	40.00
	Double transfer	—	—

OF71		UnFVF	UseFVF
3¢	**green**	50.00	9.50
	bright green	50.00	9.50
	yellow green	50.00	9.50

OF72		UnFVF	UseFVF
6¢	**green**	50.00	11.50
	bright green	50.00	11.50
	yellow green	50.00	11.50
	Double transfer	—	—

OF73		UnFVF	UseFVF
7¢	**green**	90.00	25.00
	dark yellow green	90.00	25.00
	p. Ribbed paper	125.00	27.50

OF74

OF74		UnFVF	UseFVF
10¢	**green**	70.00	16.00
	bright green	70.00	16.00
	yellow green	70.00	16.00
	Short transfer	150.00	30.00

OF75		UnFVF	UseFVF
12¢	**green**	115.00	50.00
	yellow green	115.00	50.00

OF76		UnFVF	UseFVF
15¢	**green**	125.00	35.00
	dark yellow green	125.00	35.00

OF77		UnFVF	UseFVF
24¢	**green**	256.00	90.00
	dark yellow green	250.00	90.00

OF78		UnFVF	UseFVF
30¢	**green**	225.00	65.00
	dark yellow green	225.00	65.00

OF79		UnFVF	UseFVF
90¢	**green**	450.00	140.00
	dark yellow green	450.00	140.00

OF80		UnFVF	UseFVF
$2	**green & black**	525.00	400.00
	yellow green & black	525.00	400.00

OF81

OF81		UnFVF	UseFVF
$5	**green & black**	4,250.00	1,800.00
	dark green & black	4,250.00	1,800.00
	yellow green & black	4,250.00	1,800.00
	Plate block of 6	42,500.00	

OF82		UnFVF	UseFVF
$10	**green & black**	2,800.00	1,400.00
	dark green & black	2,800.00	1,400.00
	yellow green & black	2,800.00	1,400.00

OF83		UnFVF	UseFVF
$20	**green & black**	1,950.00	950.00
	dark green & black	1,950.00	950.00
	yellow green & black	1,950.00	950.00

1873. TREASURY DEPT. ISSUE *Intaglio on thin, hard paper, unwatermarked, perforated 12.*

OF84		UnFVF	UseFVF
1¢	**brown**	25.00	3.00
	dark brown	25.00	3.00
	yellow brown	25.00	3.00
	Double transfer	35.00	5.00

OF85		UnFVF	UseFVF
2¢	**brown**	27.50	3.00
	dark brown	27.50	3.00
	yellow brown	27.50	3.00
	Cracked plate	40.00	—
	Double transfer	—	—

yellow green ... 50.00 ... 11.50 (OF72 continued — top of right column)
Double transfer — —

OF86
3¢

	UnFVF	UseFVF
brown	17.50	1.50
dark brown	17.50	1.50
yellow brown	17.50	1.50
t. Shaded circle to right of right frame line	—	—
t1. Double impression	—	—

OF87
6¢

	UnFVF	UseFVF
brown	23.00	2.50
dark brown	23.00	2.50
yellow brown	23.00	2.50
Double transfer	—	—
Worn plate	23.00	3.00

OF88
7¢

	UnFVF	UseFVF
brown	55.00	15.00
dark brown	55.00	15.00
yellow brown	55.00	15.00

OF89
10¢

	UnFVF	UseFVF
brown	60.00	5.50
dark brown	60.00	5.50
yellow brown	60.00	5.50
Double transfer	—	—

OF90
12¢

	UnFVF	UseFVF
brown	60.00	4.00
dark brown	60.00	4.00
yellow brown	60.00	4.00

OF91
15¢

	UnFVF	UseFVF
brown	55.00	5.50
dark brown	55.00	5.50
yellow brown	55.00	5.50

OF92
24¢

	UnFVF	UseFVF
brown	250.00	45.00
dark brown	250.00	45.00
yellow brown	250.00	45.00
Double transfer	—	—

OF93
30¢

	UnFVF	UseFVF
brown	85.00	6.00
dark brown	85.00	6.00
yellow brown	85.00	6.00
Short transfer	—	—

OF94

OF94
90¢

	UnFVF	UseFVF
brown	85.00	6.00
dark brown	85.00	6.00
yellow brown	85.00	6.00

1879. TREASURY DEPT. ISSUE *Intaglio on soft, porous paper, unwatermarked, perforated 12.*

OF95
3¢

	UnFVF	UseFVF
brown	30.00	4.50
yellow brown	30.00	4.50

OF96
6¢

	UnFVF	UseFVF
brown	40.00	4.00
yellow brown	40.00	4.00

OF97
10¢

	UnFVF	UseFVF
brown	85.00	25.00
dark brown	85.00	25.00
yellow brown	85.00	25.00

OF98
30¢

	UnFVF	UseFVF
brown	800.00	175.00
yellow brown	800.00	175.00

OF99
90¢

	UnFVF	UseFVF
brown	1,000.00	175.00
dark brown	1,000.00	175.00
yellow brown	1,000.00	175.00

1873. WAR DEPT. ISSUE *Intaglio on thin, hard paper, unwatermarked, perforated 12.*

OF100
1¢

	UnFVF	UseFVF
Venetian red	80.00	4.50
rose red	80.00	4.50

OF101
2¢

	UnFVF	UseFVF
Venetian red	70.00	6.50
rose red	70.00	6.50
p. Ribbed paper	65.00	9.00

OF102
3¢

	UnFVF	UseFVF
Venetian red	70.00	1.75
rose red	70.00	1.75

OF103
6¢

	UnFVF	UseFVF
Venetian red	225.00	4.00
dull Venetian red	225.00	4.00

OF104
7¢

	UnFVF	UseFVF
Venetian red	70.00	40.00
dull Venetian red	70.00	40.00
rose red	70.00	40.00

OF105
10¢

	UnFVF	UseFVF
Venetian red	25.00	7.50
rose red	25.00	7.50

The crack at lower left of OF105 was on the original die and is found on all copies.

OF106
12¢

	UnFVF	UseFVF
Venetian red	80.00	5.50
p. Ribbed paper	110.00	7.50

OF107
15¢

	UnFVF	UseFVF
Venetian red	19.00	6.75
dull Venetian red	19.00	6.75
rose red	22.50	7.50
p. Ribbed paper	30.00	10.00

OF108

OF108
24¢

	UnFVF	UseFVF
Venetian red	19.00	4.00
dull Venetian red	19.00	4.00
rose red	19.00	4.00

OF109
30¢

	UnFVF	UseFVF
Venetian red	20.00	4.00
rose red	20.00	4.00
p. Ribbed paper	40.00	7.50

OF110
90¢

	UnFVF	UseFVF
Venetian red	55.00	25.00
rose red	55.00	25.00

1879. WAR DEPT. ISSUE *Intaglio on soft, porous paper, unwatermarked, perforated 12.*

OF111
1¢

	UnFVF	UseFVF
dull rose	3.00	2.00
Venetian red	60.00	27.50
rose red	60.00	27.50

OF112
2¢

	UnFVF	UseFVF
dull rose	3.50	2.00
dark rose	3.50	2.00
dull vermilion	3.50	2.00

OF113
3¢

	UnFVF	UseFVF
dull rose	3.50	1.25
rose red	3.50	1.25
Double transfer	6.00	4.00
v1. Double impression	1,000.00	—
v2. Pair, imperforate	1,500.00	—

OF114
6¢

	UnFVF	UseFVF
dull rose	4.00	1.25
dull vermilion	4.00	1.25
rose red	4.00	1.25

OF115
10¢

	UnFVF	UseFVF
dull rose	25.00	20.00
rose red	25.00	20.00

OF116
12¢

	UnFVF	UseFVF
dull rose	20.00	7.50
rose red	20.00	7.50

OF117
30¢

	UnFVF	UseFVF
dull rose	65.00	42.50
rose red	65.00	42.50

1910-1911. POSTAL SAVINGS ISSUE When Postal Savings Depositories were set up in 1910 under the Post Office Department, special stamps were provided for that division. Their use was discontinued in 1914, and all remainders destroyed. *Intaglio by the Bureau of Engraving and Printing, perforated 12.*

OF118 and OF119 are watermarked double-line USPS. OF120, OF121, OF122 and OF123 are watermarked single-line USPS.

 OF118, OF122

OF118
		UnFVF	UseFVF
2¢	**black**	17.50	1.75
	FDC *(Dec. 22, 1910)*		—
	Plate block of 6 w/imprint	250.00	
	Block of 4 (2mm apart)	45.00	6.50
	Block of 4 (3mm apart)	42.00	5.50
	Double transfer	15.00	2.50

OF119
		UnFVF	UseFVF
50¢	**green**	150.00	32.50
	FDC *(Feb. 1, 1911)*		—
	Plate block of 6 w/imprint	2,400.00	
	Block of 4 (2mm apart)	550.00	170.00
	Block of 4 (3mm apart)	535.00	170.00
	Margin block of 4 w/arrow	560.00	

 OF120

OF120
		UnFVF	UseFVF
$1	**bright blue**	150.00	10.00
	FDC *(Feb. 1, 1911)*		—
	Plate block of 6 w/imprint	1,900.00	375.00
	Block of 4 (2mm apart)	400.00	45.00
	Block of 4 (3mm apart)	390.00	45.00
	Margin block of 4 w/arrow	425.00	

OF121
		UnFVF	UseFVF
1¢	**dark red violet**	8.50	1.25
	FDC *(March 27, 1911)*		—
	Plate block of 6 w/imprint	110.00	
	Block of 4 (2mm apart)	21.00	5.00
	Block of 4 (3mm apart)	20.00	4.75

OF122
		UnFVF	UseFVF
2¢	**black**	45.00	4.25
	FDC *(March 27, 1911)*		—
	Plate block of 6 w/imprint	525.00	
	Block of 4 (2mm apart)	120.00	19.00
	Block of 4 (3mm apart)	118.00	19.00
	Double transfer	32.00	4.75

OF123
		UnFVF	UseFVF
10¢	**carmine**	17.50	1.25
	FDC *(Feb. 1, 1911)*		—
	Plate block of 6 w/imprint	225.00	
	Block of 4 (2mm apart)	35.00	5.50
	Block of 4 (3mm apart)	33.00	5.00
	Double transfer	14.00	2.50

1983. OFFICIAL MAIL ISSUE *Intaglio, perforated 11.*

OF124   OF125   OF126

OF124
		MNHVF	UseVF
1¢	**blue, red & black**	.25	.25
	Plate block of 4	.60	
	FDC *(Jan. 12, 1983)*		1.75

OF125
		MNHVF	UseVF
4¢	**blue, red & black**	.25	.25
	Plate block of 4	.75	
	FDC *(Jan. 12, 1983)*		1.75

OF126
		MNHVF	UseVF
13¢	**blue, red & black**	.45	.75
	Plate block of 4	2.00	
	FDC *(Jan. 12, 1983)*		1.75

OF127   OF128   OF129

OF127
		MNHVF	UseVF
17¢	**blue, red & black**	.50	.40
	Plate block of 4	2.50	
	FDC *(Jan. 12, 1983)*		1.75

OF128
		MNHVF	UseVF
$1	**blue, red & black**	3.00	1.25
	Plate block of 4	14.00	
	FDC *(Jan. 12, 1983)*		5.00

OF129
		MNHVF	UseVF
$5	**blue, red & black**	10.00	5.00
	Plate block of 4	45.00	
	FDC *(Jan. 12, 1983)*		15.00

1985. OFFICIAL MAIL COIL ISSUE *Intaglio, perforated 9 3/4 vertically.*

 OF130

OF130
		MNHVF	UseVF
20¢	**blue, red & black**	2.00	2.25
	Pair	4.50	4.50
	FDC *(Jan. 12, 1983)*		1.75
	Pair, imperforate	2,000.00	

1985. OFFICIAL MAIL NON-DENOMINATED ISSUE Postal Card "D" rate, *intaglio. Perforated 11.*

 OF131

OF131
		MNHVF	UseVF
(14¢)	**blue, red & black**	4.50	5.50
	Plate block of 4	35.00	
	FDC *(Feb. 4, 1985)*		1.75

1985. OFFICIAL MAIL COIL ISSUE *Intaglio, perforated 9 3/4 vertically.*

 OF132

OF132
		MNHVF	UseVF
(22¢)	**blue, red & black,** non-denominated	4.75	3.00
	Pair	7.50	—
	FDC *(Feb. 4, 1985)*		1.00

1985. OFFICIAL MAIL ISSUE *Intaglio, perforated 11.*

 OF133

OF133		MNHVF	UseVF
14¢	**blue, red & black**	.40	.65
	FDC *(May 15, 1985)*		2.00

1985. OFFICIAL MAIL COIL ISSUE *Intaglio, perforated 9 3/4 vertically.*

 OF134

OF134		MNHVF	UseVF
22¢	**blue, red & black**	.75	2.25
	Pair	1.50	4.50
	FDC *(May 15, 1985)*		1.00

1988. OFFICIAL MAIL NON-DENOMINATED COIL ISSUE *Design similar to OF133 but without the 'USA' prior to denomination. Offset, perforated 9 3/4 vertically.*

 OF135

OF135		MNHVF	UseVF
(25¢)	**blue, red & black**	1.00	2.00
	Pair	2.00	
	FDC *(March 22, 1988)*		1.00

1988. OFFICIAL MAIL COIL ISSUE *Design similar to OF133 but without "USA" prior to the denomination. Offset, perforated 10 vertically.*

OF136   OF137   OF138

OF136		MNHVF	UseVF
20¢	**blue, red & black**	.45	.35
	Pair	1.00	.75
	FDC *(May 19, 1988)*		1.00

OF137		MNHVF	UseVF
15¢	**blue, red & black**	.45	.65
	Pair	.75	
	FDC *(June 11, 1988)*		1.00

OF138		MNHVF	UseVF
25¢	**blue, red & black**	.75	.50
	Pair	1.50	.75
	FDC *(June 11, 1988)*		1.75
	v. Pair, imperforate	2,000.00	

1989. OFFICIAL MAIL ISSUE Similar to OF133, but without the "USA" prior to the denomination, *offset, perforated 11.*

 OF139

OF139

OF139		MNHVF	UseVF
1¢	**blue, red & black**	.25	.25
	FDC *(July 5, 1989)*		1.75

1991. OFFICIAL MAIL COIL ISSUE "F" rate non-denominated stamp. *Coil, offset, perforated 9 3/4 vertically.*

 OF140

OF140		MNHVF	UseVF
29¢	**blue, red & black**	.75	.50
	Pair	1.00	
	FDC *(Jan. 22, 1991)*		1.25

1991. OFFICIAL MAIL ISSUE Similar to OF139, *offset, perforated 11.*

 OF141

OF141		MNHVF	UseVF
4¢	**blue, red & black**	.25	.30
	FDC *(April 6, 1991)*		1.25

1991. OFFICIAL MAIL ISSUE Similar to OF139, *offset, perforated 11.*

OF142   OF143

OF142		MNHVF	UseVF
19¢	**blue, red & black**	.40	.60
	FDC *(May 24, 1991)*		1.25

OF143		MNHVF	UseVF
23¢	**blue, red & black**	.45	.60
	FDC *(May 24, 1991)*		1.75
	Pair, imperforate	475.00	

1991. OFFICIAL MAIL COIL ISSUE Similar to OF139, *coil, printed by offset, perforated 9 3/4 vertically.*

 OF144

OF144		MNHVF	UseVF
29¢	**blue, red & black**	.75	.50
	Pair	1.25	1.00
	FDC *(May 24, 1991)*		1.25

1993. OFFICIAL MAIL ISSUE Similar to OF139, included a line of microprinting between the Great Seal and the denomination, *offset, perforated 11.*

 OF145

OF145		MNHVF	UseVF
10¢	**blue, red & black**	.35	.55
	FDC *(Oct. 19, 1993)*		1.75

OF146

OF146
$1   **blue, red & black**   MNHVF 2.10   UseVF 1.75
No official FDC issued *(Sept. 1993)*

1994. OFFICIAL MAIL COIL ISSUE "G" Rate non-denominated stamp. *Offset, perforated 9 3/4 vertically.*

 OF147

OF147
(32¢)   **blue, red & black**   MNHVF .75   UseVF .50
Pair   1.50   1.00
FDC *(Dec. 13, 1994)*   1.00

1995. OFFICIAL MAIL ISSUE Similar to OF139, with line of microprinting, *offset, perforated 11 1/4.*

OF148   OF149   OF150   OF151

OF148
1¢   **blue, red & black**   MNHVF .25   UseVF .25
FDC *(May 9, 1995)*   1.90

OF149
20¢   **blue, red & black**   MNHVF .45   UseVF .55
FDC *(May 9, 1995)*   1.25

OF150
23¢   **blue, red & black**   MNHVF .55   UseVF .65
FDC *(May 9, 1995)*   1.25

OF151
32¢   **blue, red & black**   MNHVF .75   UseVF .40
Pair   1.50
FDC *(May 9, 1995)*   1.00

1999. GREAT SEAL ISSUE showed the Great Seal of the United States in the current First Class denomination, with a line under it consisting of microprinting of the repeated phrase, "USA 1999." *Gummed coil of 100, offset by Bureau of Engraving and Printing, perforated 9 3/4 vertically.*

 OF152

OF152
33¢   **multicolored**   MNHVF .65   UseVF .20
Pair   1.30
FDC *(Oct. 8, 1999)*   1.50

2001. OFFICIAL MAIL COIL ISSUE Great Seal with a line under it consisting of microprinting of the repeated phrase, "USA 2001." *Gummed coil of 100, offset by Bureau of Engraving and Printing, perforated 9 3/4 vertically.*

 OF153

OF153
34¢   **blue, red & black**   MNHVF .65   UseVF .30
Pair   1.30
FDC *(Feb. 27, 2001)*   1.50

2002. THE GREAT SEAL OFFICIAL COIL ISSUE Designed by Bradbury Thompson (Citizens Stamp Advisory Committee). *Water-activated gum in coils of 100. Twenty-five million stamps gravure printed by American Packaging Corp. for Sennett Security Products.* This stamp features the Great Seal of the United States and was only available from Kansas City. *Perforated 9 3/4 vertically. Plate number every 14 stamps.*

 OF154 *The Great Seal*

OF154
37¢   **blue, red & black** pre-phosphored paper   MNHVF .70   UseVF .20
Pair   1.40   .20
FDC *(Aug. 2, 2002 - Washington, DC)*   1.50

Postage Due

1879. POSTAGE DUE STAMPS ISSUE were authorized in 1879. They were created to denote the amount due, by the addressee, on mail that was insufficiently prepaid. The stamps were to come into use on July 1, 1879, but the four lowest denominations are known used almost two months before that date. *Engraved and printed by American Bank Note Co., on unwatermarked paper, perforated 12.*

 PD1-28
First Printing

PD1
1¢   **yellow brown**   UnFVF 55.00   UseFVF 8.50

PD2
2¢   **yellow brown**   UnFVF 350.00   UseFVF 7.50

PD3
3¢   **yellow brown**   UnFVF 50.00   UseFVF 5.00

PD4
5¢   **yellow brown**   UnFVF 575.00   UseFVF 42.00

PD5
10¢   **yellow brown**   UnFVF 620.00   UseFVF 25.00
Pair, imperforate   2,000.00

PD6
30¢   **yellow brown**   UnFVF 300.00   UseFVF 50.00

PD7
50¢   **yellow brown**   UnFVF 450.00   UseFVF 60.00

Later Printings

PD8
1¢   **brown**   UnFVF 55.00   UseFVF 8.50

PD9
2¢   **brown**   UnFVF 350.00   UseFVF 7.00

PD10
3¢   **brown**   UnFVF 50.00   UseFVF 5.00

PD11
5¢	brown	UnFVF	UseFVF
		575.00	42.00

PD12
10¢	brown	UnFVF	UseFVF
		620.00	25.00

PD13
30¢	brown	UnFVF	UseFVF
		300.00	50.00

PD14
50¢	brown	UnFVF	UseFVF
		450.00	60.00

1887. Previous designs in changed colors.

PD15
1¢	brown red	UnFVF	UseFVF
		55.00	5.00

PD16
2¢	brown red	UnFVF	UseFVF
		65.00	5.00

PD17
3¢	brown red	UnFVF	UseFVF
		1,000.00	175.00

PD18
5¢	brown red	UnFVF	UseFVF
		500.00	25.00

PD19
10¢	brown red	UnFVF	UseFVF
		450.00	15.00

PD20
30¢	brown red	UnFVF	UseFVF
		165.00	50.00

PD21
50¢	brown red	UnFVF	UseFVF
		1,625.00	175.00

1891. Previous designs in changed colors. *Imperforate varieties of PD22-28 exist, but they were not regularly issued.*

PD22
1¢	claret	UnFVF	UseFVF
		25.00	1.00

PD23
2¢	claret	UnFVF	UseFVF
		32.00	1.00

PD24
3¢	claret	UnFVF	UseFVF
		60.00	8.00

PD25
5¢	claret	UnFVF	UseFVF
		75.00	8.00

PD26
10¢	claret	UnFVF	UseFVF
		125.00	17.50

PD27
30¢	claret	UnFVF	UseFVF
		500.00	150.00

 PD28

PD28
50¢	claret	UnFVF	UseFVF
		525.00	150.00

1879. SPECIAL PRINTINGS of the then current first issue of postage dues usually have mutilated perforations for they were cut apart by scissors. Known only unused.

Despite the quantities issued, the first three values are comparatively scarce. *American Bank Note Co. on soft, porous paper, unwatermarked, perforated 12.*

SPD1
1¢	brown (9,420)	UnFVF	UseFVF
		12,000.00	

SPD2
2¢	brown (1,361)	UnFVF	UseFVF
		8,500.00	

SPD3
3¢	brown (436)	UnFVF	UseFVF
		12,500.00	

SPD4
5¢	brown (249)	UnFVF	UseFVF
		7,500.00	

SPD5
10¢	brown (174)	UnFVF	UseFVF
		3,750.00	

SPD6
30¢	brown (179)	UnFVF	UseFVF
		3,750.00	

SPD7
50¢	brown (179)	UnFVF	UseFVF
		3,750.00	

1894. NEW DESIGNS ISSUE appear in many shades. Care should be observed in soaking these stamps as the colors may run. *Printed by the Bureau of Engraving and Printing, unwatermarked, perforated 12.*

 PD29-68

PD29
1¢	vermilion (1894)	UnFVF	UseFVF
		1,700.00	500.00

PD30
1¢	brown carmine (Aug. 14, 1894)	UnFVF	UseFVF
		47.50	6.00

PD31
2¢	vermilion (1894)	UnFVF	UseFVF
		700.00	175.00

PD32
2¢	brown carmine (July 20, 1894)	UnFVF	UseFVF
		40.00	4.00

PD33
3¢	brown carmine (April 27, 1895)	UnFVF	UseFVF
		160.00	30.00

PD34
5¢	brown carmine (April 27, 1895)	UnFVF	UseFVF
		240.00	35.00

PD35
10¢	brown carmine (Sept. 24, 1894)	UnFVF	UseFVF
		240.00	25.00

PD36
30¢	brown carmine (April 27, 1895)	UnFVF	UseFVF
		400.00	90.00

PD37
50¢	brown carmine (April 27, 1895)	UnFVF	UseFVF
		1,300.00	350.00

1895. Same as previous designs. *Double-line USPS watermark.*

PD38
1¢	brown carmine (Aug. 29, 1895)	UnFVF	UseFVF
		8.50	.75

PD39
2¢	brown carmine (Sept. 14, 1895)	UnFVF	UseFVF
		8.50	.70

PD40
3¢	brown carmine (Oct. 30, 1895)	UnFVF	UseFVF
		57.50	1.75

PD41
5¢	brown carmine (Oct. 15, 1895)	UnFVF	UseFVF
		65.00	1.75

PD42
10¢	brown carmine (Sept. 14, 1895)	UnFVF	UseFVF
		67.50	3.50

PD43
30¢	brown carmine (Aug. 21, 1897)	UnFVF	UseFVF
		550.00	50.00

PD44
50¢	brown carmine (March 17, 1896)	UnFVF	UseFVF
		350.00	37.00

1910. Same as previous designs. *Single-line USPS watermark.*

PD45
1¢	brown carmine (Aug. 30, 1910)	UnFVF	UseFVF
		32.50	3.00

PD46
2¢	brown carmine (Nov. 25, 1910)	UnFVF	UseFVF
		30.00	1.25

PD47
3¢	brown carmine (Aug. 31, 1910)	UnFVF	UseFVF
		600.00	30.00

PD48
5¢	brown carmine (Aug. 31, 1910)	UnFVF	UseFVF
		95.00	6.25

PD49
10¢	brown carmine (Aug. 31, 1910)	UnFVF	UseFVF
		115.00	12.50

PD50
50¢	brown carmine (Sept. 23, 1912)	UnFVF	UseFVF
		1,000.00	120.00

1914. Same as previous designs. *Perforated 10.*

PD51
1¢	rose red	UnFVF	UseFVF
		60.00	11.00

PD52
2¢	vermilion	UnFVF	UseFVF
		50.00	.40

PD53
2¢	rose red	UnFVF	UseFVF
		50.00	.40

PD54
3¢	rose red	UnFVF	UseFVF
		875.00	38.00

PD55
5¢	rose red	UnFVF	UseFVF
		37.00	2.50

PD56
10¢	rose red	UnFVF	UseFVF
		57.00	2.00

PD57
30¢	rose red	UnFVF	UseFVF
		240.00	17.00

PD58
50¢	rose red	UnFVF	UseFVF
		10,000.00	900.00

1916. Same as previous designs. *Unwatermarked.*

PD59
1¢	rose red	UnFVF	UseFVF
		3,000.00	325.00
x.	Experimental Bureau (precancel - New Orleans, La.)		100.00

PD60		UnFVF	UseFVF
2¢	**rose red**	160.00	25.00
	x. Experimental Bureau precancel - New Orleans, La.		7.50

1917-25. Same as previous designs. *Perforated 11.*

PD61		UnFVF	UseFVF
1/2¢	**carmine** *(April 13, 1925)*	1.00	.25
PD62		UnFVF	UseFVF
1¢	**carmine**	2.50	.25
PD63		UnFVF	UseFVF
2¢	**carmine**	2.50	.25
PD64		UnFVF	UseFVF
3¢	**carmine**	10.00	.25
PD65		UnFVF	UseFVF
5¢	**carmine**	11.00	.25
PD66		UnFVF	UseFVF
10¢	**carmine**	17.00	.30
PD67		UnFVF	UseFVF
30¢	**carmine**	85.00	.75

 PD68

PD68		UnFVF	UseFVF
50¢	**carmine**	110.00	.30

1930. NEW DESIGNS ISSUE *Flat press printing, perforated 11.*

 PD69-76, 79-86

PD69		UnFVF	UseFVF
1/2¢	**carmine**	4.00	1.35
PD70		UnFVF	UseFVF
1¢	**carmine**	3.00	.25
PD71		UnFVF	UseFVF
2¢	**carmine**	4.00	.25
PD72		UnFVF	UseFVF
3¢	**carmine**	20.00	1.75
PD73		UnFVF	UseFVF
5¢	**carmine**	19.00	2.50
PD74		UnFVF	UseFVF
10¢	**carmine**	40.00	1.00
PD75		UnFVF	UseFVF
30¢	**carmine**	110.00	2.00

 PD76

PD76		UnFVF	UseFVF
50¢	**carmine**	150.00	.75

 PD77, 87

PD77		UnFVF	UseFVF
$1	**carmine**	30.00	.25

 PD78

PD78		UnFVF	UseFVF
$5	**carmine**	40.00	.25

1931. Same as previous design. *Rotary press printing, perforated 11x10 1/2.*

PD79		UnFVF	UseFVF
1/2¢	**vermilion**	1.00	.20
PD80		UnFVF	UseFVF
1¢	**vermilion**	.20	.20
PD81		UnFVF	UseFVF
2¢	**vermilion**	.20	.20
PD82		UnFVF	UseFVF
3¢	**vermilion**	.25	.20
PD83		UnFVF	UseFVF
5¢	**vermilion**	.40	.20
PD84		UnFVF	UseFVF
10¢	**vermilion**	1.00	.20
PD85		UnFVF	UseFVF
30¢	**vermilion**	8.00	.25
PD86		UnFVF	UseFVF
50¢	**vermilion**	10.00	.25

1956. *Perforated 10 1/2x11.*

PD87		UnFVF	UseFVF
$1	**vermilion**	33.00	.25

1959-85. NEW DESIGNS ISSUE for the first time in 29 years featured an adaptation of the design of the 1930 stamps with the lathe-turned background and denominations removed. Printed in two colors with the addition of values never before used in dues stamps. Black denomination added within intaglio frame with rubber-mat letterpress on rotary press. *Unwatermarked, perforated 11x10 1/2.*

 PD88-99, 102-04

PD88		UnFVF	UseFVF
1/2¢	**red & black** *(June 19, 1959)*	1.50	1.00
PD89		UnFVF	UseFVF
1¢	**red & black** *(June 19, 1959)*	.20	.20
	black denomination omitted	300.00	
	Pair, one with denomination omitted	500.00	
	m. Matte gum	.25	
PD90		UnFVF	UseFVF
2¢	**red & black** *(June 19, 1959)*	.20	.20
	m. Matte gum	.25	
PD91		UnFVF	UseFVF
3¢	**red & black** *(June 19, 1959)*	.20	.20
	Pair, one with black denomination omitted	725.00	
	m. Matte gum	.25	
PD92		UnFVF	UseFVF
4¢	**red & black** *(June 19, 1959)*	.20	.20
PD93		UnFVF	UseFVF
5¢	**red & black** *(June 19, 1959)*	.20	.20
	Pair, one with black denomination omitted	1,250.00	
	m. Matte gum	.25	
PD94		UnFVF	UseFVF
6¢	**red & black** *(June 19, 1959)*	.20	.20
	Pair, one with black denomination omitted	850.00	
	m. Matte gum	100.00	
PD95		UnFVF	UseFVF
7¢	**red & black** *(June 19, 1959)*	.20	.20
	m. Matte gum	400.00	
PD96		UnFVF	UseFVF
8¢	**red & black** *(June 19, 1959)*	.20	.20
	Pair, one with black denomination omitted	850.00	

PD97
10¢   **red & black** *(June 19, 1959)*   UnFVF   UseFVF
        m. Matte gum   .20   .20
                                                    .35

PD98
30¢   **red & black** *(June 19, 1959)*   UnFVF   UseFVF
        m. Matte gum   .75   .20
                                                    .90

PD99
50¢   **red & black** *(June 19, 1959)*   UnFVF   UseFVF
        m. Matte gum   1.00   .20
                                                    1.50

PD100
$1   **red & black** *(June 19, 1959)*   UnFVF   UseFVF
        m. Matte gum   2.00   .20
                                                    2.50

     PD100-101

PD101
$5   **red & black**   UnFVF   UseFVF
        m. Matte gum   9.00   .20
                                                    10.00

PD102
11¢   **red & black** *(Jan. 2, 1978)*   UnFVF   UseFVF
                                                    .25   .20

PD103
13¢   **red & black** *(Jan. 2, 1978)*   UnFVF   UseFVF
                                                    .25   .20

PD104
17¢   **red & black** *(June 10, 1985)*   UnFVF   UseFVF
                                                    .40   .30

Envelopes and Wrappers

Government stamped envelopes first were authorized by the United States under an Act of Congress on Aug. 31, 1852. From the very first issue until the present they have been produced by private manufacturers under contract to the government. It is believed the first envelopes were issued some time in April 1853. The exact date is not known.

Unlike adhesive stamps, stamped envelopes are produced one at a time. Until 1965 the blanks were cut to shape by means of a cutting die (called a "knife" by collectors) much as one operates a cookie cutter. This die was placed on a pile of sheets of paper and was forced through by means of a press. Then a complex machine printed the stamp and whatever corner card might be requested, folded, gummed and sealed the flaps, applied gum to the top back flap, and counted the finished envelopes into multiples of 100 or any number desired.

Beginning in 1965 envelopes have been made from a continuous roll (web) of paper.

The embossed printing of the stamp is accomplished with a recessed printing die that strikes against a resilient undersurface, or "tympan." The tympan forces the paper into the recesses, causing the embossed effect. Later issues are printed by more contemporary processes.

Paper

While our envelopes have been made from paper of various colors, the usual color is "white." During the first issue, the customer had the choice of "white" or "buff" paper envelopes, and at various times the choice of colors available was as many as six or seven. Since 1942, envelopes have been made of white paper only.

The paper colors used throughout the issues are:

White - and various shades thereof.

Buff - in early issues from a brownish color to a yellow.

Amber - a yellowish cast that can be quite pronounced or very pale.

Cream - an intermediate shade between a yellow and a brown, was discontinued in 1886 and "buff" (sometimes known as "oriental buff") substituted.

Blue - and various shades thereof.

Orange - and various shades thereof.

Fawn - a brownish shade.

Manila - made of manila fibers.

Amber-manila - manila paper dyed yellowish.

Canary - bright yellow (used for Post Office Department envelopes only).

It will be seen that all colors vary greatly in shades. Such variation is not intentional, but merely reflects the inability to match colors exactly in various batches of paper. Even the "white" of one issue may differ by a wide margin from the "white" of another issue. Thus the colors of paper, while important to the collector, are not standardized and may be considered only within each individual issue of envelopes.

From 1853 to 1915, all envelopes were made of laid paper, and the laid lines will appear diagonal. This is the result of turning the cutting knife on the bias to the edge of the pile of paper in order to reduce waste. On the other hand, wrappers, which are rectangular in shape, presented no great waste of paper, so they were cut parallel to the edge of the paper. The laid lines on wrappers will appear horizontal or vertical, depending on how they were inserted in the press. This is the principle method of distinguishing between cut squares from wrappers and envelopes.

From 1915 to the present, envelopes have been made of wove paper, and thus show no laid lines.

Albinos and Misprints

Until the web-printing process was adopted in 1965, two envelope blanks occasionally were fed into the envelope-making machine at one time. The top sheet received an inked impression, and the bottom sheet an impression without ink. Such colorless impressions look like white "stamps" and are called "albinos." They are quite common for recent issues, including those even after web printing of envelopes began, but rather rare for early 19th century envelopes. Although they are interesting, they do not command near the premium as do envelopes with two impressions of the stamp in color (one over or partially over the other).

Collecting Envelopes and Wrappers

Envelopes and wrappers are collected as "entires" by size and watermarks and as cut squares. Cut squares are popular because, like postage stamps, they may be mounted easily into albums. Cut squares always should provide adequate margins, which in most instances would be no less than 1/4 inch of paper margin beyond the design of the stamp on all four sides.

Prices in this catalog are for cut squares with such margins. Larger squares, "full corners," or extra large corners with all back flaps attached may bring premium prices, especially for earlier issues.

Envelopes are manufactured in a variety of sizes and shapes. Thus, a single basic stamp may appear on several different-size envelopes, and some of these sizes may be more valuable than others although the stamp remains the same. Certain envelopes exist in large sizes only. In the listing that follows, an asterisk (*) designates entires available only in large size.

Catalog values are for entires of the least value. It is required by law that all envelopes be manufactured with watermarked paper. From 1853 to 1870, a single style watermark was used for all issues (wmk1), but with a new manufacturer in 1870 a new watermark was introduced, and beginning in 1874 it became the custom to change the watermark with the letting of each new contract (about every four years) through the late 1960s. It has been customary to allow remaining stocks of paper to be used up before the new watermarked paper is introduced. Most issues of envelopes, therefore, exist on at least two styles of watermarked paper and, when an issue extended over a very long period of years, there might be several watermarks involved. Indicated at the beginning of each issue are watermarks to be found on envelopes of that issue.

Watermark No. 5 "STAR"
(1878-82)

Watermark No. 6
(1882-86)

Watermark No. 1, 1A
(1853-70)

Watermark No. 9
(1886-87)

Watermark No. 7
(1886-90)

Watermark No. 8
(1890-94)

Watermark No. 2
(1870-78)

Watermark No. 10
(1886-99)

Watermark No. 3
"Centennial"
(1876)

Watermark No. 11
(1893)

Watermark No. 4
(1877-82)
Used only on
Offical stamped
envelopes

Watermark No. 12
(1894-98

'99

Watermark No. 13
(1899-1902)

Watermark No. 14
(1903-1907)

Watermark No. 15
(1907-1911)

Watermark No. 15a
(1907-1911)

Watermark
No. 16

U S S E
1911

Watermark No. 17
(1911-1915)

US–S E
1911

Watermark No. 18
(1911-1915)

1853-55. ISSUE All envelopes issued from 1853 to 1870 were manufactured in New York City by the George F. Nesbitt Manufacturing Company and are known to collectors as the "Nesbitt Issues." The Nesbitt firm was established in 1795, and, at the time it was awarded the contract to produce the first U.S. government stamped envelopes in 1852, it was said to be the largest firm of manufacturing stationers in the country. Following the death of the owner in 1869, the firm lost the contract for manufacturing government envelopes, and although it entered bids on succeeding contracts for many years thereafter, it never again was successful.

Issued some time in April 1853, this issue featured the portrait of George Washington, after Houdon's bust. The complete design would appear to be adapted from the "Wyon" essay for the first stamped envelopes of Great Britain.

Watermark No. 1, also No. 1A on EN1. Wmk. 1 has the lines horizontal in the background with the letters "POD" and "US" horizontal. Background lines on wmk. 1A are diagonal.

EN1-EN2 *"THREE" within short label with curved ends. Die A, 13mm wide, 12 varieties.*

EN1		UnFVF	UseFVF
3¢	**red** on white	190.00	16.00
	entire	—	—
	entire, wmk No. 1	1,200.00	25.00
EN2		UnFVF	UseFVF
3¢	**red** on buff	70.00	10.00
	entire	750.00	20.00

EN3-EN4 *"THREE" within short label with straight ends. Die B, 16mm wide, 3 varieties.*

EN3		UnFVF	UseFVF
3¢	**red** on white	680.00	35.00
	entire	3,000.00	70.00
EN4		UnFVF	UseFVF
3¢	**red** on buff	195.00	15.00
	entire	1,500.00	32.00

EN5-EN6 *"THREE" within short, curved octagonal label, forming the letter "K." Die C, 2 varieties.*

EN5		UnFVF	UseFVF
3¢	**red** on white	3,500.00	360.00
	entire	12,500.00	500.00
EN6		UnFVF	UseFVF
3¢	**red** on buff	190.00	40.00
	entire	1,000.00	75.00

EN7-EN8 *"THREE" within wide label with straight ends. Die D, 25mm wide.*

EN7		UnFVF	UseFVF
3¢	**red** on white	500.00	80.00
	entire	6,200.00	130.00
EN8		UnFVF	UseFVF
3¢	**red** on buff	1,100.00	90.00
	entire	4,500.00	95.00

EN9-EN10 *"THREE" within medium wide label with curved ends. Die E. 20mm wide, 20 varieties.*

EN9		UnFVF	UseFVF
3¢	**red** on white	18.00	2.50
	entire	75.00	9.00
	reprint, cut square	80.00	
EN10		UnFVF	UseFVF
3¢	**red** on buff	14.00	2.25
	entire	60.00	6.00
	reprint, cut square	80.00	

EN11-EN14 *"SIX" within short label with straight ends. Die F, 4 varieties.*

EN11		UnFVF	UseFVF
6¢	**green** on white	175.00	100.00
	entire	300.00	150.00
	reprint, cut square	—	
EN12		UnFVF	UseFVF
6¢	**green** on buff	135.00	65.00
	entire	235.00	115.00
	reprint, cut square	80.00	
EN13		UnFVF	UseFVF
6¢	**red** on white	90.00	60.00
	entire*	210.00	105.00
	reprint, cut square	80.00	
EN14		UnFVF	UseFVF
6¢	**red** on buff	175.00	100.00
	entire*	300.00	150.00
	reprint, cut square	80.00	

EN15, EN16 *"TEN" within short label with straight ends. Die G, 16mm wide.*

EN15		UnFVF	UseFVF
10¢	**green** on white	175.00	100.00
	entire	325.00	150.00
EN16		UnFVF	UseFVF
10¢	**green** on buff	65.00	50.00
	entire	200.00	80.00

EN17, EN18 *"TEN" within wide label. Die H.*

EN17		UnFVF	UseFVF
10¢	**green** on white	200.00	100.00
	entire	350.00	150.00
	reprint, cut square	80.00	
EN18		UnFVF	UseFVF
10¢	**green** on buff	100.00	65.00
	entire	170.00	80.00
	reprint, cut square	80.00	

Reprints EN9-14, 17, 18, are on white and buff wove or vertically laid paper. Known also only as cut squares.

1860. "STAR DIE" ISSUE so-called because of the small stars at either side of the design, which do not appear on any other envelope stamp. The stars of the 1¢ denomination have five points; those of all other denominations have six points. With this series, 1¢ envelopes and newspaper wrappers were introduced for the first time. The series also introduced the 3¢ + 1¢ envelope. This was to provide for the carrier service, the fee for which was 1¢, for transporting the letter from the lamp-post letter boxes to the post office. Use of the "compound envelopes" apparently was reserved for large cities and very possibly New York City only.

A very few are known used in Baltimore, Chicago, and a few other cities where carrier service was operated. Usages in any city other than New York are rare and command premium values.

The series was introduced some time during the summer of 1860 (3¢ envelopes are known used in August) and remained in use for about one year. When the Civil War broke out, steps were taken to replace the issue with a new design. However, the 1¢ and 3¢ + 1¢ envelopes continued in use and were not subjected to the general demonetization order.

Envelopes used by Southern states after their secession, as evidenced by cancellation, are scarce and command considerable premium values. Likewise, envelopes of this series overprinted (over the stamp) "CONFEDERATE STATES OF AMERICA" and other suitable indicia, used by the Confederate States postal department for official mail, are of considerable interest and value to collectors.

The buff paper for all envelopes of this series, and throughout the Nesbitt issues, exists in a multitude of shades that extend from a yellow through dark brown. None of these differences were intentional. They merely indicate various batches of paper, all of which were supposed to be "buff." Likewise, there are many shades of green of the 6¢ and 10¢ stamps, extending from "yellow green" to "dark green." The interested collector may be advised that the extreme dark shades are less numerous than the pale or yellow shades.

Wrappers. Newspaper wrappers were introduced with this series, and were continued with succeeding series up to 1934, when they were discontinued. Wrappers may be distinguished from envelopes in that they are on paper with either vertical or horizontal laid lines. Envelopes almost invariably are on paper with diagonally laid lines.

EN19-EN23 *Franklin. Period after "POSTAGE"*

EN19		UnFVF	UseFVF
1¢	**blue** on buff	28.00	13.00
	entire	55.00	25.00
EN20		UnFVF	UseFVF
1¢	**blue** on orange, wove paper	—	—
	entire	1,750.00	—
EN21		UnFVF	UseFVF
1¢	**blue** on buff, wrapper	65.00	50.00
	entire	100.00	65.00
	v1. Double impression	—	
EN22		UnFVF	UseFVF
1¢	**blue** on manila, wrapper	45.00	45.00
	entire	85.00	85.00
EN23		UnFVF	UseFVF
1¢	**blue** on orange, wrapper	1,800.00	—
	entire	2,800.00	—

EN24, EN25 *Franklin. Bust touches frame front and back*

EN24		UnFVF	UseFVF
1¢	**blue** on orange	410.00	360.00
	entire	480.00	425.00
EN25		UnFVF	UseFVF
1¢	**blue** on white	—	—

EN26, EN27 *No period after "POSTAGE," 2 varieties*

EN26		UnFVF	UseFVF
1¢	**blue** on amber	—	—
	entire	—	—
EN27		UnFVF	UseFVF
1¢	**blue** on manila, wrapper	2,600.00	2,000.00
	entire	11,000.00	3,800.00

EN28, EN29 *Washington*

EN28		UnFVF	UseFVF
3¢	**red** on white	27.00	13.00
	entire	37.00	23.00
	reprint, cut square	150.00	
EN29		UnFVF	UseFVF
3¢	**red** on buff	25.00	23.00
	entire	35.00	30.00
	reprint, cut square	150.00	

EN30, EN31 *Franklin. Bust does not touch frame.*

EN30		UnFVF	UseFVF
3¢ + 1¢	**red & blue** on white	335.00	235.00
	entire	775.00	500.00

EN31
3¢ + 1¢   **red & blue** on buff

	UnFVF	UseFVF
	250.00	210.00
entire	825.00	500.00

Nos. EN32-33 are not assigned.

EN34, EN35

EN34
6¢   **red** on white

	UnFVF	UseFVF
	2,000.00	1,300.00
entire*	3,700.00	
reprint, cut square	80.00	

EN35
6¢   **red** on buff

	UnFVF	UseFVF
	1,700.00	950.00
entire*	4,300.00	4,500.00
reprint, cut square	80.00	

EN36, EN37

EN36
10¢   **green** on white

	UnFVF	UseFVF
	1,000.00	350.00
entire	10,000.00	475.00
reprint, cut square	80.00	

EN37
10¢   **green** on buff

	UnFVF	UseFVF
	1,000.00	275.00
entire	3,800.00	475.00
reprint, cut square	80.00	

Reprints are cut squares on vertical laid paper.

1861. ISSUE was introduced in the summer of 1861. The previous "Star Die" series was declared invalid for postage, due to the outbreak of the Civil War (except the 1¢ and 3¢ + 1¢ envelopes). The series presents a novelty as the higher-value envelope stamps were printed in more than one color. These also are the first bi-colored postal emissions from the United States. Still another innovation was the introduction of Letter Sheets, which, it has been stated, were issued to provide soldiers in the field with stationery and stamps in a single package. Their use did not prove popular, and they were withdrawn in April 1864.

EN38-EN41

EN38
3¢   **pink** on white

	UnFVF	UseFVF
	18.00	5.00
entire	45.00	15.00

EN39
3¢   **pink** on buff

	UnFVF	UseFVF
	16.00	6.00
entire	18.00	12.00

EN40
3¢   **pink** on blue, letter sheet

	UnFVF	UseFVF
	70.00	55.00
entire	200.00	90.00

EN41
3¢   **pink** on orange

	UnFVF	UseFVF
	2,300.00	—
entire	3,900.00	—

EN42, EN43

EN42
6¢   **pink** on white

	UnFVF	UseFVF
	90.00	85.00
entire*	145.00	145.00
reprint, cut square	—	—

EN43
6¢   **pink** on buff

	UnFVF	UseFVF
	65.00	60.00
entire*	100.00	145.00
reprint, cut square	—	—

Reprints, known in cut squares only, are on vertically laid paper.

EN44-EN46

EN44
10¢   **green** on white

	UnFVF	UseFVF
	28.00	28.00
entire	26.00	26.00

EN45
10¢   **green** on buff

	UnFVF	UseFVF
	27.00	19.00
entire	60.00	35.00

No. EN46 is not assigned.

EN47

EN47
12¢   **brown & red** on amber

	UnFVF	UseFVF
	175.00	150.00
entire*	460.00	650.00

EN48

EN48
20¢   **blue & red** on amber

	UnFVF	UseFVF
	175.00	150.00
entire*	460.00	775.00

EN49, EN50

EN49
24¢   **green & red** on amber

	UnFVF	UseFVF
	185.00	145.00
entire*	650.00	775.00

EN50
24¢   **dark green & maroon** on **amber**

	UnFVF	UseFVF
	190.00	180.00
entire*	650.00	1,000.00

EN51

EN51		UnFVF	UseFVF
40¢	**red & black** on amber	280.00	280.00
	entire*	850.00	1,800.00

1863-65. ISSUE To provide for the higher postal rates on drop letters and circular matter, it was necessary to provide 2¢ envelopes and wrappers (called "Black Jacks" because of the portrait of Andrew Jackson). At the same time, new designs were adopted for the 3¢, 6¢ and higher denominations.

EN52, EN53 *Andrew Jackson. Die A. "U.S. POSTAGE" at top. Down stroke of "2" and bottom stroke merge.*

EN52		UnFVF	UseFVF
2¢	**black** on buff	30.00	15.00
	entire	60.00	30.00
EN53		UnFVF	UseFVF
2¢	**black** on manila, wrapper	42.00	38.00
	entire	70.00	55.00

EN54, EN55 *Andrew Jackson. Die B, down stroke of figure "2" joins but does not merge with bottom stroke.*

EN54		UnFVF	UseFVF
2¢	**black** on buff	1,700.00	—
	entire	3,600.00	—
EN55		UnFVF	UseFVF
2¢	**black** on orange	1,000.00	—
	entire	2,500.00	—

EN56-EN59 *Andrew Jackson. Die C, "U.S. POST" at top. Width of design 24 to 25mm.*

EN56		UnFVF	UseFVF
2¢	**black** on buff	10.00	9.00
	entire	27.00	15.00
EN57		UnFVF	UseFVF
2¢	**black** on orange	12.00	8.00
	entire	22.00	10.00
EN58		UnFVF	UseFVF
2¢	**black** on buff, wrapper	160.00	160.00
	entire	260.00	260.00
EN59		UnFVF	UseFVF
2¢	**black** on dark manila, wrapper	35.00	22.00
	entire	120.00	60.00

EN60-EN64 *Andrew Jackson. Die D. "U.S. POST" at top. 25 1/2mm.*

EN60		UnFVF	UseFVF
2¢	**black** on buff	12.00	10.00
	entire	22.00	14.00

No. EN61 is not assigned.

EN62		UnFVF	UseFVF
2¢	**black** on orange	12.00	8.00
	entire	17.00	11.00
EN63		UnFVF	UseFVF
2¢	**black** on buff, wrapper	80.00	50.00
	entire	125.00	85.00
EN64		UnFVF	UseFVF
2¢	**black** on light manila, wrapper	12.00	11.00
	entire	25.00	20.00

EN65-EN68

EN65		UnFVF	UseFVF
3¢	**pink** on white	6.00	2.00
	entire	10.00	3.50
EN66		UnFVF	UseFVF
3¢	**pink** on buff	5.00	1.50
	entire	10.00	2.50
EN67		UnFVF	UseFVF
3¢	**brown** on white	38.00	20.00
	entire*	75.00	75.00
EN68		UnFVF	UseFVF
3¢	**brown** on buff	40.00	22.00
	entire*	80.00	60.00

EN69-EN73

EN69		UnFVF	UseFVF
6¢	**pink** on white	50.00	30.00
	entire*	85.00	50.00
EN70		UnFVF	UseFVF
6¢	**pink** on buff	30.00	25.00
	entire*	85.00	50.00
EN71		UnFVF	UseFVF
6¢	**purple** on white	45.00	25.00
	entire	70.00	50.00

No. EN72 is not assigned.

EN73		UnFVF	UseFVF
6¢	**purple** on buff	42.00	18.00
	entire	60.00	50.00

EN74, EN75

EN74		UnFVF	UseFVF
9¢	**lemon** on buff	325.00	200.00
	entire*	500.00	500.00
EN75		UnFVF	UseFVF
9¢	**orange** on buff	95.00	75.00
	entire*	150.00	200.00

EN76, EN77

EN76		UnFVF	UseFVF
12¢	**brown** on buff	340.00	200.00
	entire*	500.00	950.00
EN77		UnFVF	UseFVF
12¢	**red brown** on buff	90.00	55.00
	entire*	130.00	185.00

EN78

EN78
18¢   **red** on buff
entire*

	UnFVF	UseFVF
	90.00	85.00
	180.00	800.00

EN79

EN79
24¢   **blue** on buff
entire*

	UnFVF	UseFVF
	95.00	80.00
	180.00	800.00

EN80

EN80
30¢   **green** on buff
entire*

	UnFVF	UseFVF
	60.00	50.00
	150.00	800.00

EN81

EN81
40¢   **pink** on buff
entire*

	UnFVF	UseFVF
	80.00	225.00
	250.00	9,300.00

1870. ISSUE By the end of 1869 there were various designs of stamps in use for envelopes and wrappers, none of which even closely resembled the designs of the adhesive stamps then in use. To remedy this situation and bring order to confusion, as well as to meet the public clamor against awarding the envelope contract by negotiated bid, the government advertised for bids to supply the envelopes needed for the next four years. One provision of the proposal was that the new envelopes be in denominations of the adhesive stamps then in use and that the designs of the envelope stamps be as near as possible, in color and design, to the adhesive stamps in use. After considerable controversy, the contract was awarded to George H. Reay of Brooklyn, N.Y., a former associate of Nesbitt. Reay proceeded to produce what has almost unanimously been considered the most beautiful designs and envelopes our post office ever has issued. The finely executed engravings, the beautiful inks, and careful printing on fine quality paper have earned for them the name "cameos" among collectors.

Although the contract provided that envelopes be manufactured in all denominations from 1¢ to 90¢, there was little use for envelopes in the denominations over 10¢. Hence, used examples of these high denominations are practically unknown.

 EN82-EN85 *Franklin. Die A, front of the bust is narrow, back rounded. It points at letter "N" of "ONE." The neck forms a straight line between chest and chin. (Compare with EN120 and EN128.) (Watermark 2.)*

Die A

EN82
1¢   **blue** on white
entire

	UnFVF	UseFVF
	28.00	23.00
	50.00	28.00

EN83
1¢   **blue** on amber
entire

	UnFVF	UseFVF
	28.00	23.00
	50.00	28.00

EN84
1¢   **blue** on orange
entire

	UnFVF	UseFVF
	18.00	10.00
	26.00	17.00

EN85
1¢   **blue** on manila, wrapper
entire

	UnFVF	UseFVF
	40.00	25.00
	70.00	60.00

 EN86-EN89 *Die B, the choker around the neck is notched top and bottom.*

Die B

EN86
1¢   **blue** on white
entire

	UnFVF	UseFVF
	—	—
	—	—

EN87
1¢   **blue** on amber
entire

	UnFVF	UseFVF
	—	—
	—	—

EN88
1¢   **blue** on orange
entire

	UnFVF	UseFVF
	—	—
	—	—

EN89
1¢   **blue** on manila, wrapper
entire

	UnFVF	UseFVF
	—	—
	—	—

 EN90-EN93 *Andrew Jackson. The figure "2" at right and left are within small circles. The top loop of "P" of "POSTAGE" is well formed. (Compare with EN142.)*

EN90
2¢   **brown** on white
entire

	UnFVF	UseFVF
	40.00	13.00
	50.00	20.00

EN91
2¢   **brown** on amber
entire

	UnFVF	UseFVF
	15.00	8.00
	30.00	15.00

EN92
2¢   **brown** on orange
entire

	UnFVF	UseFVF
	10.00	7.00
	13.00	10.00

EN93
2¢   **brown** on manila, wrapper
entire

	UnFVF	UseFVF
	20.00	15.00
	40.00	30.00

 EN94-EN96 *Small figure "3" within circles. The ponytail projects below the bust. (Compare with EN183 and EN187.)*

EN94
3¢   **green** on white
entire

	UnFVF	UseFVF
	7.00	1.00
	12.00	2.50

EN95
3¢   **green** on amber
entire

	UnFVF	UseFVF
	5.00	2.00
	12.00	3.00

EN96
3¢   **green** on cream
entire

	UnFVF	UseFVF
	8.00	3.00
	16.00	5.00

EN97-EN99 *Abraham Lincoln. The neck is long at the back. (Compare with EN211.)*

EN97
6¢   **red** on white
entire

	UnFVF	UseFVF
	17.00	13.00
	18.00	16.00

EN98
6¢   **red** on amber
entire

	UnFVF	UseFVF
	22.00	13.00
	38.00	14.00

EN99

		UnFVF	UseFVF
6¢	**red** on cream	27.00	13.00
	entire	45.00	19.00

EN97-EN99 exist in a variety of shades from dark red to vermilion.

EN100 *Edwin Stanton. The down strokes of the figure "7" do not curl up. (Compare with EN215.)*

EN100

		UnFVF	UseFVF
7¢	**vermilion** on amber	40.00	200.00
	entire	60.00	750.00

EN101-EN104 *Thomas Jefferson. The end of the ponytail does not project. (Compare with EN219.)*

EN101

		UnFVF	UseFVF
10¢	**olive-black** on white	375.00	375.00
	entire	475.00	850.00

EN102

		UnFVF	UseFVF
10¢	**olive-black** on amber	375.00	375.00
	entire	475.00	850.00

EN103

		UnFVF	UseFVF
10¢	**brown** on white	50.00	70.00
	entire	70.00	75.00

EN104

		UnFVF	UseFVF
10¢	**brown** on amber	70.00	50.00
	entire	85.00	70.00

EN105-EN107 *Henry Clay. The hair hides the ear. The nose is long and sharp. (Compare with EN227.)*

EN105

		UnFVF	UseFVF
12¢	**violet-black** on white	100.00	65.00
	entire*	200.00	375.00

EN106

		UnFVF	UseFVF
12¢	**violet-black** on amber	110.00	85.00
	entire*	180.00	500.00

EN107

		UnFVF	UseFVF
12¢	**violet-black** on cream	220.00	190.00
	entire*	335.00	—

EN108-EN110 *Daniel Webster. Hair not parted, cheeks with sideburns. (Compare with EN230.)*

EN108

		UnFVF	UseFVF
15¢	**red orange** on white	60.00	60.00
	entire*	140.00	—

EN109

		UnFVF	UseFVF
15¢	**red orange** on amber	140.00	170.00
	entire*	360.00	—

EN110

		UnFVF	UseFVF
15¢	**red orange** on cream	235.00	210.00
	entire*	325.00	—

EN111-EN113 *Winfield Scott. Ornamental lines around inner oval end in squares. (Compare with EN233.)*

EN111

		UnFVF	UseFVF
24¢	**purple** on white	100.00	90.00
	entire	150.00	—

EN112

		UnFVF	UseFVF
24¢	**purple** on amber	180.00	225.00
	entire*	335.00	—

EN113

		UnFVF	UseFVF
24¢	**purple** on cream	180.00	250.00
	entire*	325.00	—

EN108-EN113 exist in various shades.

EN114-EN116 *Alexander Hamilton. The horizontal rectangles containing numerals are in alignment. Back of bust ends in narrow point. (Compare with EN236.)*

EN114

		UnFVF	UseFVF
30¢	**black** on white	70.00	85.00
	entire*	280.00	—

EN115

		UnFVF	UseFVF
30¢	**black** on amber	180.00	210.00
	entire*	500.00	—

EN116

		UnFVF	UseFVF
30¢	**black** on cream	200.00	325.00
	entire*	385.00	—

EN117-EN119 *Oliver Perry. The shields containing the numerals of value do not project beyond the inner circle. (Compare with EN242.)*

EN117

		UnFVF	UseFVF
90¢	**carmine** on white	135.00	190.00
	entire*	190.00	—

EN118

		UnFVF	UseFVF
90¢	**carmine** on amber	300.00	335.00
	entire*	800.00	—

EN119

		UnFVF	UseFVF
90¢	**carmine** on cream	335.00	550.00
	entire*	875.00	—

1874-76. ISSUE In 1874, the Post Office advertised for bids to supply envelopes. After considerable legal difficulties with George H. Reay and other bidders, the contract was awarded to the Plimpton Manufacturing Co. Reay refused to surrender his printing dies and, to futher embarrass the new contractor, is said to have engaged the services of all known die engravers. The new contractors were thus forced to employ less skilled engravers to try to duplicate the Reay designs. The resulting delay embarrassed the Post Office officials, who were forced to purchase supplies of envelopes from Reay until the new contractors could produce acceptable dies. Several unsuitable designs were accepted to take care of the situation until better dies could be made, which accounts for some of the designs of the lower denomination stamps.

Eventually the Plimpton Manufacturing Co. overcame its difficulties and, in combination with the Morgan Envelope Co., continued to be the successful bidders for the manufacture of envelopes until 1903.

The struggle George H. Reay put up to retain his contract is one of the classic stories of philately. In the end, to prevent his competitors from ever using his dies, it is stated that he finally agreed to turn them over to the authorities, only to instruct his wife to throw them overboard from a Brooklyn-Manhattan ferry. There seems to be much evidence to substantiate this story.

EN120-EN127 *Franklin. A copy of the Reay design (EN82). Die A, back of bust angles in sharp point. "O" of "POSTAGE" without network. (Compare with EN82.) (Watermarks 2, 5, 6, 7, 9.)*

		UnFVF	UseFVF
EN120 1¢	**dark blue** on white	85.00	40.00
	entire	100.00	80.00
EN121 1¢	**dark blue** on amber	100.00	67.50
	entire	140.00	100.00
EN122 1¢	**dark blue** on cream	775.00	—
EN123 1¢	**dark blue** on orange	17.50	15.00
	entire	27.50	20.00
EN124 1¢	**dark blue** on manila, wrapper	50.00	32.50
	entire	67.50	60.00
EN125 1¢	**light blue** on white	100.00	70.00
	entire	130.00	100.00
EN126 1¢	**light blue** on orange	20.00	12.50
	entire	25.00	20.00
EN127 1¢	**light blue** on manila, wrapper	—	—
	entire	—	—

EN128-EN141 *A copy of Reay design (EN82). Die B, back of bust is a straight line. Front of bust broad and blunt. "O" in "POSTAGE" with network. (Compare with EN82.)*

		UnFVF	UseFVF
EN128 1¢	**dark blue** on white	6.00	6.00
	entire	15.00	15.00
EN129 1¢	**dark blue** on amber	12.50	8.00
	entire	15.00	10.00
EN130 1¢	**dark blue** on cream	15.00	6.00
	entire	22.50	15.00
EN131 1¢	**dark blue** on orange	2.50	3.00
	entire	7.00	5.00
EN132 1¢	**dark blue** on manila, wrapper	6.00	7.50
	entire	10.00	12.50
EN133 1¢	**blue** on white	1.50	1.00
	entire	2.25	1.50
EN134 1¢	**blue** on amber	4.00	3.00
	entire	8.00	4.00
EN135 1¢	**blue** on cream	4.50	4.50
	entire	7.00	5.00
EN136 1¢	**blue** on orange	.60	.50
	entire	.75	.50
EN137 1¢	**blue** on blue	6.00	5.00
	entire	8.00	6.00
EN138 1¢	**blue** on fawn	6.00	5.00
	entire	7.00	6.00
EN139 1¢	**blue** on manila	6.00	4.00
	entire	7.00	6.00

		UnFVF	UseFVF
EN140 1¢	**blue** on amber-manila	11.00	9.00
	entire	13.00	10.00
EN141 1¢	**blue** on manila, wrapper	1.50	1.50
	entire	3.00	2.00

The "dark blue" of EN128-EN132 is very dark, almost indigo. The "blue" of EN133-EN141 is in various shades of "blue," "pale blue," etc.

EN142-EN147 *Andrew Jackson. A copy of Reay design (EN90). Die A, thin narrow figure "2" within circles. Top loop of "P" in "POSTAGE" is very narrow. (Compare with EN90.) (Watermark 2.)*

		UnFVF	UseFVF
EN142 2¢	**brown** on white	80.00	37.00
	entire	95.00	75.00
EN143 2¢	**brown & amber**	50.00	40.00
	entire	80.00	65.00
EN144 2¢	**brown** on cream	675.00	—
EN145 2¢	**brown** on orange	7,200.00	—
	entire	15,000.00	—
EN146 2¢	**brown** on manila, wrapper	80.00	40.00
	entire	85.00	60.00
EN147 2¢	**vermilion** on manila, wrapper	1,000.00	260.00
	entire	1,500.00	—

EN148-EN151 *A copy of the Reay design (EN90). Die B, Figure "2" within tall ovals. "O" in "TWO" has plain center. (Compare with EN90, EN142 and following.)*

		UnFVF	UseFVF
EN148 2¢	**brown** on white	38.00	28.00
	entire	75.00	65.00
EN149 2¢	**brown** on amber	65.00	40.00
	entire	80.00	60.00
EN150 2¢	**brown** on cream	22,000.00	—
EN151 2¢	**brown** on manila, wrapper	15.00	14.00
	entire	20.00	18.00

EN152, EN153 *Andrew Jackson. Die B2, similar to last except tail of left figure "2" touches the oval at right.*

		UnFVF	UseFVF
EN152 2¢	**brown** on white	55.00	25.00
	entire	75.00	65.00
EN153 2¢	**brown** on amber	160.00	55.00
	entire	175.00	85.00

EN154-EN161 *Die B3, same as EN148 but "O" in "TWO" with network in center.*

EN154			UnFVF	UseFVF
2¢	**brown** on white		600.00	100.00
	entire		700.00	125.00
EN155			UnFVF	UseFVF
2¢	**brown** on amber		375.00	110.00
	entire		500.00	130.00
EN156			UnFVF	UseFVF
2¢	**brown** on orange		37.50	27.50
	entire		60.00	40.00
EN157			UnFVF	UseFVF
2¢	**brown** on manila, wrapper		50.00	32.50
	entire		65.00	35.00
EN158			UnFVF	UseFVF
2¢	**vermilion** on white		17,000.00	—
EN159			UnFVF	UseFVF
2¢	**vermilion** on amber		17,000.00	—
EN160			UnFVF	UseFVF
2¢	**vermilion** on orange		17,000.00	—
EN161			UnFVF	UseFVF
2¢	**vermilion** on manila, wrapper		6,000.00	—

EN162-EN172 *Andrew Jackson. Die C, short, thick figure "2" within small size ovals. (Compare with preceding and following; also with EN90.)*

EN162			UnFVF	UseFVF
2¢	**brown** on white		37.50	35.00
	entire		50.00	40.00
EN163			UnFVF	UseFVF
2¢	**brown** on amber		70.00	55.00
	entire		85.00	60.00
EN164			UnFVF	UseFVF
2¢	**brown** on manila, wrapper		35.00	25.00
	entire		40.00	35.00
EN165			UnFVF	UseFVF
2¢	**brown red** on orange		—	—
	entire		—	—
EN166			UnFVF	UseFVF
2¢	**vermilion** on orange		—	—
(Watermarks 2, 5 and 6.)				
EN167			UnFVF	UseFVF
2¢	**red** on white		5.50	2.50
	entire		7.00	4.50
EN168			UnFVF	UseFVF
2¢	**red** on amber		5.00	2.50
	entire		6.00	4.00
EN169			UnFVF	UseFVF
2¢	**red** on cream		11.00	5.50
	entire		13.00	8.00
EN170			UnFVF	UseFVF
2¢	**red** on blue		120.00	28.00
	entire		180.00	135.00
EN171			UnFVF	UseFVF
2¢	**red** on fawn		6.50	4.50
	entire		12.00	7.00
EN172			UnFVF	UseFVF
2¢	**red** on manila, wrapper		4.00	4.00
	entire		7.00	6.00

EN173-EN176 *Die C1, similar to last except ovals containing numerals are much heavier and there is a diagonal white line from about the letter "U" to the outer frame. (Compare with EN177.)*

EN173			UnFVF	UseFVF
2¢	**red** on white		50.00	30.00
	entire		55.00	35.00
EN174			UnFVF	UseFVF
2¢	**red** on amber		25.00	15.00
	entire		28.00	17.00
EN175			UnFVF	UseFVF
2¢	**red** on blue		10.00	8.00
	entire		9.00	10.00
EN176			UnFVF	UseFVF
2¢	**red** on fawn		10.00	4.00
	entire		13.00	10.00

EN177-EN179 *Andrew Jackson. Die C2, similar to last except there is no diagonal line and the middle stroke of "N" in "CENTS" is as thin as the vertical strokes. (Compare with EN173.)*

EN177			UnFVF	UseFVF
2¢	**red** on white		50.00	25.00
	entire		70.00	27.00
EN178			UnFVF	UseFVF
2¢	**red** on amber		250.00	75.00
	entire		335.00	100.00
EN179			UnFVF	UseFVF
2¢	**red** on manila, wrapper		16.00	9.00
	entire		40.00	12.00

EN180-EN182 *Die D, the bottom of the bust forms a complete quarter circle. (Compare with EN162.)*

EN180			UnFVF	UseFVF
2¢	**red** on white		525.00	100.00
	entire		625.00	300.00
EN181			UnFVF	UseFVF
2¢	**red** on amber		16,000.00	16,000.00
	entire		57,000.00	—
EN182			UnFVF	UseFVF
2¢	**red** on manila, wrapper		80.00	55.00
	entire		115.00	95.00

EN183-EN186 *Washington. Copy of Reay design (EN94). Die A, thin lettering. Long thin figures of value within tall ovals. (Compare with EN94 and EN187.) (Watermarks 2, 3, 4, 5, and 6.)*

EN183			UnFVF	UseFVF
3¢	**green** on white		18.00	5.50
	entire		33.00	14.00
EN184			UnFVF	UseFVF
3¢	**green** on amber		23.00	10.00
	entire		38.00	14.00
EN185			UnFVF	UseFVF
3¢	**green** on cream		33.00	10.00
	entire		40.00	15.00

EN186
3¢   **green** on blue   UnFVF   UseFVF
—   —

EN187-EN191 *Die B, thick lettering. Thick figures of value in short ovals. (Compare with EN183 and following.)*

EN187
3¢   **green** on white   UnFVF   UseFVF
entire   1.25   .35
2.25   1.00

EN188
3¢   **green** on amber   UnFVF   UseFVF
entire   1.50   .75
2.50   1.25

EN189
3¢   **green** on cream   UnFVF   UseFVF
entire   8.00   7.00
12.00   8.50

EN190
3¢   **green** on blue   UnFVF   UseFVF
entire   8.00   5.00
13.00   8.50

EN191
3¢   **green** on fawn   UnFVF   UseFVF
entire   5.00   3.00
8.00   4.00

EN192-EN195 *Washington. Similar to last. Die C, the top of the head is flat at back and there is a notch above and below the knot of the ponytail. (Compare with EN187.)*

EN192
3¢   **green** on white   UnFVF   UseFVF
entire   460.00   45.00
1,800.00   75.00

EN193
3¢   **green** on amber   UnFVF   UseFVF
entire   190.00   100.00
280.00   120.00

EN194
3¢   **green** on blue   UnFVF   UseFVF
entire   8,000.00   1,800.00
17,000.00   4,300.00

EN195
3¢   **green** on fawn   UnFVF   UseFVF
entire   25,000.00   1,700.00
—   15,000.00

EN196-EN200 *Zachary Taylor. Die A, the numerals "5" with short thick top strokes. (Compare with EN201.) (Watermarks 2 and 5.)*

EN196
5¢   **blue** on white   UnFVF   UseFVF
entire   10.00   8.00
12.00   12.00

EN197
5¢   **blue** on amber   UnFVF   UseFVF
entire   10.00   8.00
12.00   15.00

EN198
5¢   **blue** on cream   UnFVF   UseFVF
entire*   82.00   38.00
105.00   100.00

EN199
5¢   **blue** on blue   UnFVF   UseFVF
entire   15.00   13.00
18.00   20.00

EN200
5¢   **blue** on fawn   UnFVF   UseFVF
entire*   100.00   50.00
175.00   —

EN201-EN205 *Zachary Taylor. Die B, the numerals "5" with long thin top strokes. (Compare with EN196.)*

EN201
5¢   **blue** on white   UnFVF   UseFVF
entire   6.00   5.50
11.00   20.00

EN202
5¢   **blue** on amber   UnFVF   UseFVF
entire   5.50   5.50
13.00   25.00

EN203
5¢   **blue** on cream   UnFVF   UseFVF
entire*   2,500.00   —
4,200.00   —

EN204
5¢   **blue** on blue   UnFVF   UseFVF
entire   13.00   8.00
16.00   20.00

EN205
5¢   **blue** on fawn   UnFVF   UseFVF
entire*   88.00   43.00
110.00   100.00

EN206-EN210 *James Garfield. (Watermarks 5, 6.)*

EN206
5¢   **brown** on white   UnFVF   UseFVF
entire   3.00   2.00
5.50   15.00

EN207
5¢   **brown** on amber   UnFVF   UseFVF
entire   4.00   2.25
7.50   18.00

EN208
5¢   **brown** on buff   UnFVF   UseFVF
entire   90.00   60.00
120.00   —

EN209
5¢   **brown** on blue   UnFVF   UseFVF
entire   50.00   30.00
65.00   —

EN210
5¢   **brown** on fawn   UnFVF   UseFVF
entire*   200.00   —
250.00   —

EN211-EN214 *Abraham Lincoln. Copy of Reay design (EN97). The neck is short at the back. Lock of hair curves upward from forehead. (Compare with EN97.) (Watermarks 2, 3, 4, 5, 6.)*

EN211
6¢   **red** on white   UnFVF   UseFVF
entire   6.00   6.00
10.00   8.00

EN212
6¢   **red** on amber   UnFVF   UseFVF
entire   10.00   6.00
16.00   11.00

EN213
6¢   **red** on cream   UnFVF   UseFVF
entire   16.00   10.00
20.00   16.00

EN214
6¢   **red** on fawn   UnFVF   UseFVF
entire*   17.00   9.00
25.00   14.00

Users of this Catalog are invited to write to us if they have information which they feel will supplement or correct any material contained herein. All such communications will be answered.

EN215, EN216 *Edwin Stanton. Copy of Reay design (EN100). The down strokes of the figure "7" curve sharply upward. (Compare with EN100.) (Watermark 2.)*

EN215		UnFVF	UseFVF
7¢	**vermilion** on white	1,500.00	—
EN216		UnFVF	UseFVF
7¢	**vermilion** on amber	90.00	55.00
	entire	120.00	

EN217, EN218 *Thomas Jefferson. Die A, very large head, called the "booby-head." (Compare with EN101 and following.)*

EN217		UnFVF	UseFVF
10¢	**brown** on white	30.00	17.00
	entire	55.00	
EN218		UnFVF	UseFVF
10¢	**brown** on amber	55.00	25.00
	entire	80.00	—

EN219-EN226 *Copy of Reay design (EN101). Die B, the end of the ponytail projects prominently and the head tilts downward. (Compare with EN101.)*

EN219		UnFVF	UseFVF
10¢	**brown** on white	6.00	4.00
	entire	10.00	8.00
EN220		UnFVF	UseFVF
10¢	**brown** on amber	8.00	6.00
	entire	10.00	8.00
EN221		UnFVF	UseFVF
10¢	**brown** on buff	10.00	7.00
	entire	11.00	8.00
EN222		UnFVF	UseFVF
10¢	**brown** on blue	12.00	8.00
	entire	14.00	9.00

EN219-EN222 exist in various shades.

EN223		UnFVF	UseFVF
10¢	**brown** on manila	12.00	8.00
	entire	13.00	13.00
	a. red brown on manila	12.00	9.00
	entire	15.00	15.00
EN224		UnFVF	UseFVF
10¢	**brown** on amber-manila	12.00	7.00
	entire*	15.00	13.00
	a. red brown on amber-manila	16.00	7.00
	entire	22.00	17.00
EN225		UnFVF	UseFVF
10¢	**ocher yellow** on white	1,050.00	—
	entire*	1,500.00	—
EN226		UnFVF	UseFVF
10¢	**ocher yellow** on amber	1,050.00	—
	entire*	1,500.00	—

EN227-EN229 *Henry Clay. Copy of Reay design (EN105). The head is round and small. The ear is clearly defined. (Compare with EN105.) (Watermark 2.)*

EN227		UnFVF	UseFVF
12¢	**violet black** on white	150.00	75.00
	entire*	160.00	—
EN228		UnFVF	UseFVF
12¢	**violet black** on amber	160.00	135.00
	entire*	235.00	—
EN229		UnFVF	UseFVF
12¢	**violet black** on cream	175.00	145.00
	entire*	720.00	—

EN230-EN232 *Daniel Webster. Copy of Reay design (EN108). Bust without sideburns. The hair parted. (Compare with EN108.) (Watermarks 2, 5.)*

EN230		UnFVF	UseFVF
15¢	**orange** on white	40.00	30.00
	entire*	80.00	38.00
EN231		UnFVF	UseFVF
15¢	**orange** on amber	120.00	90.00
	entire*	175.00	—
EN232		UnFVF	UseFVF
15¢	**orange** on cream	335.00	335.00
	entire*	825.00	—

EN233-EN235 *Winfield Scott. Copy of Reay design (EN111). The ornaments around the inner oval end in points. (Compare with EN111.) (Watermark 2.)*

EN233		UnFVF	UseFVF
24¢	**purple** on white	150.00	110.00
	entire*	220.00	—
EN234		UnFVF	UseFVF
24¢	**purple** on amber	150.00	110.00
	entire*	220.00	—
EN235		UnFVF	UseFVF
24¢	**purple** on cream	150.00	110.00
	entire*	700.00	—

EN236-EN241 *Alexander Hamilton. Copy of Reay design (EN114). The octagonal labels containing the figures of value are not in alignment; the one at the right tilts sharply downward. (Compare with EN114.) For brown stamps in this design, issued in 1887, see EN375-EN380. (Watermarks 2, 5, 6, 7, 9, 10.)*

EN236		UnFVF	UseFVF
30¢	**black** on white	55.00	30.00
	entire*	65.00	65.00
EN237		UnFVF	UseFVF
30¢	**black** on amber	70.00	55.00
	entire*	125.00	275.00
EN237A		UnFVF	UseFVF
30¢	**black** on cream (see note)	400.00	380.00
	entire*	725.00	—

The only way to distinguish EN237A and EN243A— which both appear on cream paper— from the same designs on buff paper (EN238 and EN244) is to examine the watermark. Wmk. 2 signifies cream paper.

EN238		UnFVF	UseFVF
30¢	**black** on buff	95.00	75.00
	entire	135.00	—
EN239		UnFVF	UseFVF
30¢	**black** on blue	100.00	75.00
	entire	110.00	—
EN240		UnFVF	UseFVF
30¢	**black** on manila	90.00	75.00
	entire	135.00	—
EN241		UnFVF	UseFVF
30¢	**black** on amber-manila	110.00	75.00
	entire	140.00	—

EN242-EN247 *Oliver Perry. Copy of Reay design (EN117). The shields containing the numerals of value project considerably within the inner circle. (Compare with EN117.) For purple stamps of same design, issued in 1887, see EN381-EN386. (Watermarks 2, 6, 7, 9.)*

			UnFVF	UseFVF
EN242				
90¢	**carmine** on white		110.00	75.00
	entire*		120.00	85.00
EN243			UnFVF	UseFVF
90¢	**carmine** on amber		150.00	195.00
	entire*		235.00	—
EN243A			UnFVF	UseFVF
90¢	**carmine** on cream (see note following EN237A)		1,100.00	—
	entire*		2,000.00	—
EN244			UnFVF	UseFVF
90¢	**carmine** on buff		200.00	230.00
	entire		235.00	
EN245			UnFVF	UseFVF
90¢	**carmine** on blue		175.00	210.00
	entire		235.00	—
EN246			UnFVF	UseFVF
90¢	**carmine** on manila		115.00	210.00
	entire*		195.00	—
EN247			UnFVF	UseFVF
90¢	**carmine** on amber-manila		110.00	175.00
	entire*		195.00	—

1876. CENTENNIAL ISSUE Just before the great Centennial Exposition at Philadelphia in 1876, the Plimpton Morgan Envelope Co. had developed a machine that would gum the top back flap of envelopes. Previously the machines in use would perform all operations of folding, printing and gluing together, but the gum on the top back flaps had to be applied by hand. To publicize this mechanical achievement, the company requested permission to demonstrate its new machine at the exposition. The Post Office consented and provided that a specially designed stamp should be used to commemorate the exposition, thus authorizing the world's first commemorative postage stamp. Two envelopes were authorized: The small one would have the stamp printed in green; the slightly larger one would have the stamp in red. Also, paper bearing a special watermark (wmk. 3) was ordered for these envelopes. The demand proved so great that the envelopes were manufactured at Hartford, Conn., as well as on the demonstration machine at the exposition. In all, 8 million envelopes were issued, approximately 4 million of each size.

EN248, EN249 *Old and new methods of carrying the post.*
There is a single line forming the bottom of the label containing the word "POSTAGE." (Compare with EN250.) (Watermarks 2 and 3.)

			UnFVF	UseFVF
EN248				
3¢	**green** on white		50.00	13.00
	entire		60.00	35.00
EN249			UnFVF	UseFVF
3¢	**red** on white		55.00	25.00
	entire		70.00	45.00

EN250, EN251 *The line at the bottom of the label containing the word "POSTAGE" is made up of two thin lines which sometimes merge.*

			UnFVF	UseFVF
EN250				
3¢	**green** on white		55.00	18.00
	entire		80.00	50.00
EN251			UnFVF	UseFVF
3¢	**red** on white		19,500.00	—
	entire		28,000.00	—

1883-86. ISSUE With the change of the First Class rate from 3¢ to 2¢, new envelopes of the 2¢ and 4¢ denominations were called for, and new designs were adopted. The first design submitted was not considered entirely satisfactory, but so that envelopes would be available on time, it was approved. In the meantime, the new approved die was prepared and put into use in November, just one month after the new envelopes had been issued. Despite its short life, the first design (EN252-EN255) is not rare; apparently a very large supply was made. In May 1884, the color of the 2¢ envelope stamp was changed from carmine to brown to coincide with the color of the 2¢ adhesive stamp then in use. It is stated that the brown ink, because of its chemical construction, destroyed the printing dies and much recutting had to be done.

EN252-EN255 *Washington. Background of frame composed of scroll work ending in points around inner circle. (Watermarks 5, 6.)*

			UnFVF	UseFVF
EN252				
2¢	**red** on white		3.00	1.75
	entire		7.00	2.00
	a. brown on white (error), entire		2,250.00	—
EN253			UnFVF	UseFVF
2¢	**red** on amber		5.00	2.00
	entire		8.00	3.50
EN254			UnFVF	UseFVF
2¢	**red** on blue		7.00	5.00
	entire		9.00	6.00
EN255			UnFVF	UseFVF
2¢	**red** on fawn		7.00	3.50
	entire		13.00	4.00

EN256-EN265 *Four clear ornamental wavy lines within the circular frame of the design. (Compare with EN266 and EN302.) EN256-EN260 Nov. 1883. EN261-EN265 May 1884. EN266 June 1894.*

			UnFVF	UseFVF
EN256				
2¢	**red** on white		3.00	1.50
	entire		7.00	3.00
EN257			UnFVF	UseFVF
2¢	**red** on amber		4.00	2.50
	entire		8.50	4.00
EN258			UnFVF	UseFVF
2¢	**red** on blue		7.00	5.00
	entire		11.00	6.00
EN259			UnFVF	UseFVF
2¢	**red** on fawn		5.00	3.00
	entire		7.00	4.00
EN260			UnFVF	UseFVF
2¢	**red** on manila, wrapper		8.00	4.00
	entire		13.00	8.50
EN261			UnFVF	UseFVF
2¢	**brown** on white		3.00	1.50
	entire		7.00	3.00
EN262			UnFVF	UseFVF
2¢	**brown** on amber		4.00	3.00
	entire		8.00	4.00
EN263			UnFVF	UseFVF
2¢	**brown** on blue		7.00	4.00
	entire		11.00	6.00
EN264			UnFVF	UseFVF
2¢	**brown** on fawn		5.00	3.00
	entire		7.00	4.00
EN265			UnFVF	UseFVF
2¢	**brown** on manila, wrapper		8.00	4.00
	entire		13.00	8.00

EN266		UnFVF	UseFVF
2¢	red on white	6.00	4.00
	entire	9.00	6.00

EN267-EN274 *Washington. Retouched dies. Similar to EN256-EN266 but the pairs of wavy lines are no longer continuous, but merge at various points.*

EN267		UnFVF	UseFVF
2¢	red on amber	10.00	7.00
	entire	15.00	10.00
EN268		UnFVF	UseFVF
2¢	red on blue	13.00	8.00
	entire	20.00	10.00
EN269		UnFVF	UseFVF
2¢	red on fawn	10.00	7.00
	entire	13.00	8.00
EN270		UnFVF	UseFVF
2¢	brown on white	13.00	5.00
	entire	18.00	10.00
EN271		UnFVF	UseFVF
2¢	brown on amber	60.00	35.00
	entire	18.00	10.00
EN272		UnFVF	UseFVF
2¢	brown on blue	12.00	6.00
	entire	13.00	8.00
EN273		UnFVF	UseFVF
2¢	brown on fawn	10.00	9.00
	entire	14.00	13.00
EN274		UnFVF	UseFVF
2¢	brown on manila, wrapper	18.00	13.00
	entire	24.00	13.00

EN275-EN277 *There are 3 1/2 links above the left figure "2."*

EN275		UnFVF	UseFVF
2¢	red on white	50.00	35.00
	entire	65.00	50.00
EN276		UnFVF	UseFVF
2¢	red on amber	600.00	300.00
	entire	875.00	525.00
EN277		UnFVF	UseFVF
2¢	red on fawn	—	6,500.00

EN278-EN284 *Washington. There are two links below the right figure "2." Center link below left figure "2" touches at left.*

EN278		UnFVF	UseFVF
2¢	red on white	65.00	45.00
	entire	85.00	70.00
EN279		UnFVF	UseFVF
2¢	red on amber	120.00	65.00
	entire	135.00	85.00
EN280		UnFVF	UseFVF
2¢	red on blue	270.00	110.00
	entire	400.00	135.00
EN281		UnFVF	UseFVF
2¢	red on fawn	280.00	110.00
	entire	350.00	200.00

EN282		UnFVF	UseFVF
2¢	brown on white	80.00	35.00
	entire	180.00	90.00
EN283		UnFVF	UseFVF
2¢	brown on amber	180.00	90.00
	entire	260.00	200.00
EN284		UnFVF	UseFVF
2¢	brown on fawn	2,100.00	925.00
	entire	4,000.00	2,100.00

EN285-EN291 *A round "O" in "TWO," upright of letter "T" in "TWO" slants to right.*

EN285		UnFVF	UseFVF
2¢	red on white	1,200.00	300.00
	entire	1,600.00	650.00
EN286		UnFVF	UseFVF
2¢	red on amber	2,100.00	775.00
	entire	3,000.00	1,000.00
EN287		UnFVF	UseFVF
2¢	red on fawn	650.00	350.00
	entire	950.00	450.00
EN288		UnFVF	UseFVF
2¢	brown on white	140.00	70.00
	entire	160.00	225.00
EN289		UnFVF	UseFVF
2¢	brown on amber	160.00	70.00
	entire	180.00	90.00
EN290		UnFVF	UseFVF
2¢	brown on blue	—	5,000.00
EN291		UnFVF	UseFVF
2¢	brown on fawn	775.00	625.00
	entire	1,100.00	750.00

EN292-EN297 *Andrew Jackson. Die A, the numeral "4" at left is narrow (2 3/4mm) and has a sharp point. (Compare with EN298.) (Watermarks 6, 7.) Oct. 1883.*

EN292		UnFVF	UseFVF
4¢	green on white	3.00	3.00
	entire	5.00	5.00
EN293		UnFVF	UseFVF
4¢	green on amber	4.00	3.00
	entire	6.00	5.00
EN294		UnFVF	UseFVF
4¢	green on buff	7.00	7.00
	entire	11.00	10.00
EN295		UnFVF	UseFVF
4¢	green on blue	7.00	6.00
	entire	10.00	7.00
EN296		UnFVF	UseFVF
4¢	green on manila	8.00	6.00
	entire	11.00	11.00
EN297		UnFVF	UseFVF
4¢	green on amber-manila	16.00	9.00
	entire	23.00	12.00

EN298-EN301 *Die B, the numeral "4" at left is wide (3mm) and has a blunt point.*

EN298

4¢	**green** on white	**UnFVF** 5.00	**UseFVF** 4.00
	entire	11.00	6.00

EN299

4¢	**green** on amber	**UnFVF** 10.00	**UseFVF** 6.00
	entire	15.00	9.00

EN300

4¢	**green** on manila	**UnFVF** 10.00	**UseFVF** 6.00
	entire	14.00	10.00

EN301

4¢	**green** on amber-manila	**UnFVF** 9.00	**UseFVF** 6.00
	entire	12.00	9.00

1884. JULY ISSUE The previous printing dies having proved completely unsatisfactory, new designs were introduced in July 1884. The principal change consisted of simplifying the old design by removing one pair of the wavy lines from the inner and outer circles.

At first a few impressions were made in red ink, and these are comparatively scarce. Later the stamps were printed in brown ink.

EN302-EN312 *Washington. Only two ornamental wavy lines in frame (compare with EN256), and the back of the bust forms an angle. (Compare with EN314.) (Watermarks 6, 7, 9, 10.)*

EN302

2¢	**red** on white	**UnFVF** 500.00	**UseFVF** —
	entire	1,200.00	—

EN303

2¢	**red** on blue	**UnFVF** 225.00	**UseFVF** —
	entire	275.00	—

EN304

2¢	**red** on manila, wrapper	**UnFVF** 100.00	**UseFVF** —
	entire	150.00	—

EN305

2¢	**lake** on white	**UnFVF** 25.00	**UseFVF** 20.00
	entire	30.00	24.00

EN306

2¢	**brown** on white	**UnFVF** .50	**UseFVF** .25
	entire	.75	.30

EN307

2¢	**brown** on amber	**UnFVF** .65	**UseFVF** .45
	entire	1.25	.55

EN308

2¢	**brown** on buff	**UnFVF** 3.00	**UseFVF** 2.00
	entire	4.00	2.50

EN309

2¢	**brown** on blue	**UnFVF** 2.50	**UseFVF** .50
	entire	3.50	1.75

EN310

2¢	**brown** on fawn	**UnFVF** 3.00	**UseFVF** 2.00
	entire	3.50	2.25

EN311

2¢	**brown** on manila	**UnFVF** 9.00	**UseFVF** 3.50
	entire	13.00	5.00

EN312

2¢	**brown** on amber-manila	**UnFVF** 6.00	**UseFVF** 6.00
	entire	10.00	7.00

EN313

2¢	**brown** on manila, wrapper	**UnFVF** 5.25	**UseFVF** 5.00
	entire	7.00	6.00

EN314-EN318 *The back of the bust is rounded. (Compare with EN302.)*

EN314

2¢	**brown** on white	**UnFVF** 150.00	**UseFVF** 40.00
	entire	375.00	70.00

EN315

2¢	**brown** on amber	**UnFVF** 14.00	**UseFVF** 12.00
	entire	18.00	14.00

EN316

2¢	**brown** on blue	**UnFVF** 700.00	**UseFVF** 125.00
	entire	775.00	225.00

EN317

2¢	**brown** on fawn	**UnFVF** 20.00	**UseFVF** 17.50
	entire	27.50	20.00

EN318

2¢	**brown** on manila, wrapper	**UnFVF** 20.00	**UseFVF** 15.00
	entire	22.50	18.00

1886-87. ISSUE Letter sheet. Despite the failed attempt in 1861 to popularize letter sheets, Congress authorized the Postmaster General, by an Act of March 3, 1879, to make letter sheets available to the public. It stipulated, however, that no royalty should be paid for any patents on such devices. This caused the Postmaster General much difficulty, since existing letter sheets had been patented. Eventually an arrangement was made with the American Bank Note Co. to produce letter sheets under a patent owned by the United States Postal Card Co. The sheets again proved unpopular and were discontinued in 1894.

EN319 *Ulysses S. Grant. Unwatermarked or watermark "US."*

Letter sheet watermark.

EN319

2¢	**green** on white	**UnFVF** —	**UseFVF** —
	entire	22.00	11.00

Letter sheets exist with three varieties of perforations at top: 83, 41, or 33, and with guide perforations for folding at either right or left. Watermarked sheets are inscribed "Series 1" through "Series 7" and always have 41 perforations at top.

1887-99. ISSUE The new contract in 1886 again changed the designs and colors of the stamps on envelopes. The contractor, as before, was the Plimpton Morgan Envelope Co. In 1894 the contractor lost the contract to James Purcell, whose factory was at Holyoke, Mass. Purcell had great difficulty completing the terms of his contract and soon was forced to enter into negotiations with the Plimpton Morgan Co. to complete the work. Purcell's work principally is noted by the 1¢ envelopes, which he printed in a very rare dark blue ink, the 4¢ envelopes which he printed in a scarlet and sometimes orange ink, and the 5¢ envelopes for which he prepared a new printing die on which the neckline of Gen. Grant had been eliminated (EN373-374).

EN320 *Franklin. The bust leans forward and has a tremendously large lower portion. This is the so-called "Tiffany Die," which was rejected.*

EN320

1¢	**blue** on white	**UnFVF** —	**UseFVF** —
	entire	—	—

Watermarks 7, 8, 9, 10, 12. Wmk. 10 was intended primarily for Post Office Dept. penalty envelopes.

EN321-EN331 *The illustration at the right shows the "Spur Die," a sharp "spur" projecting downward from lower portion of the bust.*

EN321

1¢	**blue** on white	**UnFVF** .60	**UseFVF** .25
	entire	1.00	.35
	v. "Spur Die"	—	—

	UnFVF	UseFVF
entire	2.00	—
v1. Double impression	—	—

EN322
1¢ blue on amber

	UnFVF	UseFVF
	3.00	1.50
entire	6.00	4.00
v. "Spur Die"	—	—
entire	10.00	

EN323
1¢ blue on buff

	UnFVF	UseFVF
	2,000.00	—
entire	4,100.00	—
v. "Specimen"	—	

EN324
1¢ blue on blue

	UnFVF	UseFVF
	3,300.00	—
entire	4,400.00	—

EN325
1¢ blue on manila

	UnFVF	UseFVF
	.65	.35
entire	1.00	.50

EN326
1¢ blue on amber-manila

	UnFVF	UseFVF
	5.00	4.00
entire	7.00	6.00

EN327
1¢ blue on manila, wrapper

	UnFVF	UseFVF
	.45	.30
entire	1.00	.50

EN328
1¢ dark blue on white

	UnFVF	UseFVF
	7.00	3.00
entire	10.00	7.00

EN329
1¢ dark blue on amber

	UnFVF	UseFVF
	45.00	25.00
entire	60.00	30.00

EN330
1¢ dark blue on manila

	UnFVF	UseFVF
	20.00	9.00
entire	27.50	20.00

EN331
1¢ dark blue on manila, wrapper

	UnFVF	UseFVF
	12.00	10.00
entire	20.00	13.00

Nos. EN332-EN337 are not assigned.

EN338-EN343 *Washington. Die A, the bust points at the third colored tooth of the frame. "G" in "POSTAGE" has no cross bar. (Compare with EN344.)*

EN338
2¢ green on white

	UnFVF	UseFVF
	9.00	8.00
entire	18.00	11.00

EN339
2¢ green on amber

	UnFVF	UseFVF
	18.00	12.00
entire	25.00	13.00

EN340
2¢ green on buff

	UnFVF	UseFVF
	65.00	30.00
entire	85.00	35.00

EN341
2¢ green on blue

	UnFVF	UseFVF
	2,700.00	700.00
entire	—	4,200.00

EN342
2¢ green on manila

	UnFVF	UseFVF
	1,750.00	500.00
entire	1,500.00	500.00

EN343
2¢ green on amber-manila

	UnFVF	UseFVF
	1,500.00	550.00
entire	4,750.00	1,800.00

EN344-EN350 *Washington. Die B, bust points between first and second colored teeth of frame. "G" in "POSTAGE" has a cross bar. This is the common die of the series. (Compare with EN338.) The illustration at right shows the cap on "2" variety.*

EN344
2¢ green on white

	UnFVF	UseFVF
	.30	.25
entire	.60	.25
v. Cap on "2"	—	—
entire	—	—
v1. Double impression		

EN345
2¢ green on amber

	UnFVF	UseFVF
	.45	.25
entire	.60	.30
v. Cap on "2"	—	—
entire	—	—

EN346
2¢ green on buff

	UnFVF	UseFVF
	.60	.25
entire	1.00	.45
v. Cap on "2"	—	—
entire	—	—

EN347
2¢ green on blue

	UnFVF	UseFVF
	.60	.25
entire	1.00	.40
v. Cap on "2"	—	—
entire	—	—

EN348
2¢ green on manila

	UnFVF	UseFVF
	2.00	.60
entire	2.50	1.50
v. Cap on "2"	—	—
entire	—	—

EN349
2¢ green on amber-manila

	UnFVF	UseFVF
	2.50	2.00
entire	5.00	2.50
v. Cap on "2"	—	—
entire	—	—

EN350
2¢ green on manila, wrapper

	UnFVF	UseFVF
	3.00	2.50
entire	7.00	6.00

EN351-EN356 *Washington. Die C, similar to last, but head larger and well rounded. The ear is formed by two lines and there are two locks of hair in front of it. (Compare with EN355.)*

EN351
2¢ green on white

	UnFVF	UseFVF
	100.00	13.00
entire	125.00	40.00

EN352
2¢ green on amber

	UnFVF	UseFVF
	125.00	20.00
entire	135.00	40.00

EN353
2¢ green on buff

	UnFVF	UseFVF
	150.00	40.00
entire	160.00	60.00

EN354
2¢ green on blue

	UnFVF	UseFVF
	175.00	60.00
entire	185.00	65.00

EN355
2¢ green on manila

	UnFVF	UseFVF
	125.00	65.00
entire	160.00	90.00

EN356
2¢ green on amber-manila

	UnFVF	UseFVF
	325.00	80.00
entire	375.00	120.00

EN357-EN362 *Die D, similar to EN344 but the bust has no ear.*

EN357
2¢ green on white

	UnFVF	UseFVF
	—	—
entire	—	—

EN358
2¢ green on amber

	UnFVF	UseFVF
	—	—
entire	—	—

EN359
2¢ green on buff

	UnFVF	UseFVF
	—	—
entire	—	—

EN360
2¢ green on blue

	UnFVF	UseFVF
	—	—
entire	—	—

EN361
2¢ green on manila

	UnFVF	UseFVF
entire		

EN362
2¢   **green** on amber-manila

	UnFVF	UseFVF
entire	—	—
	—	—

EN363-EN368 *Andrew Jackson. The scarlet and orange shades of the 4¢ stamps were manufactured by James Purcell, who obtained the contract in 1894 but due to lack of adequate machinery shortly thereafter was forced to sublet his contract to the previous manufacturer.*

EN363
4¢   **carmine** on white

	UnFVF	UseFVF
	1.65	1.25
entire	3.25	1.50
a. scarlet	2.25	1.50
entire	5.00	4.00
b. orange	—	—
entire	—	—

EN364
4¢   **carmine** on amber

	UnFVF	UseFVF
	3.00	2.00
entire	5.00	3.50
a. scarlet	3.00	3.25
entire	6.00	4.00
b. orange	—	—
entire	—	—

EN365
4¢   **carmine** on buff

	UnFVF	UseFVF
	6.00	3.00
entire	9.00	4.00

EN366
4¢   **carmine** on blue

	UnFVF	UseFVF
	5.00	4.50
entire	7.00	6.00

EN367
4¢   **carmine** on manila

	UnFVF	UseFVF
	7.00	6.00
entire	9.00	7.50

EN368
4¢   **carmine** on amber-manila

	UnFVF	UseFVF
	5.00	3.50
entire	3.00	4.00

EN369-EN372 *Ulysses S. Grant. There is a space between the chin and the coat. (Compare with EN373.)*

EN369
5¢   **blue** on white

	UnFVF	UseFVF
	4.00	3.50
entire	6.00	15.00

EN370
5¢   **blue** on amber

	UnFVF	UseFVF
	4.50	2.50
entire	8.00	18.00

EN371
5¢   **blue** on buff

	UnFVF	UseFVF
	5.00	4.00
entire	10.00	20.00

EN372
5¢   **blue** on blue

	UnFVF	UseFVF
	6.00	5.00
entire	10.00	16.00

EN373, EN374 *Ulysses S. Grant. There is no space between the chin and the coat. (Compare with EN369.)*

EN373
5¢   **blue** on white

	UnFVF	UseFVF
	10.00	5.00
entire	14.00	20.00

EN374
5¢   **blue** on amber

	UnFVF	UseFVF
	10.00	6.00
entire	15.00	20.00

EN375-EN380 *Alexander Hamilton. Re-issue of old design with value labels not in alignment.*

EN375
30¢   **red brown** on white

	UnFVF	UseFVF
	40.00	43.00
entire	50.00	225.00

EN376
30¢   **red brown** on amber

	UnFVF	UseFVF
	45.00	55.00
entire	55.00	325.00

EN377
30¢   **red brown** on buff

	UnFVF	UseFVF
	40.00	45.00
entire	50.00	360.00

EN378
30¢   **red brown** on blue

	UnFVF	UseFVF
	40.00	45.00
entire	50.00	350.00

EN379
30¢   **red brown** on manila

	UnFVF	UseFVF
	45.00	45.00
entire	50.00	275.00

EN380
30¢   **red brown** on amber-manila

	UnFVF	UseFVF
	50.00	30.00
entire	55.00	275.00

EN381-EN386 *Oliver Perry. Re-issue of old design.*

EN381
90¢   **purple** on white

	UnFVF	UseFVF
	65.00	70.00
entire	80.00	450.00

EN382
90¢   **purple** on amber

	UnFVF	UseFVF
	75.00	75.00
entire	100.00	450.00

EN383
90¢   **purple** on buff

	UnFVF	UseFVF
	75.00	80.00
entire	100.00	450.00

EN384
90¢   **purple** on blue

	UnFVF	UseFVF
	75.00	85.00
entire	120.00	450.00

EN385
90¢   **purple** on manila

	UnFVF	UseFVF
	80.00	85.00
entire	120.00	450.00

EN386
90¢   **purple** on amber-manila

	UnFVF	UseFVF
	90.00	90.00
entire	120.00	450.00

EN375-EN380 are known in various shades of brown. EN381-EN386 exist in both dark and bright purple.

1893. COLUMBIAN EXPOSITION ISSUE To commemorate the Columbian Exposition, the Post Office Department ordered a special series of stamped envelopes in the 1¢, 2¢, 4¢, 5¢, and 10¢ denominations. For reasons not known, the 4¢ envelope never was issued.

The designs of all denominations are identical, except in the face value of the stamp. Four varieties are widely recognized by collectors:
- A period after "CENT"; a meridian behind head of Columbus
- A period; no meridian
- No period; a meridian
- No period; no meridian

The first three will be found on the 1¢ stamps. All four are found on the 2¢ stamps; only the first two on the 5¢ stamps. The 10¢ stamp exists only without the period, but with the meridian.

EN387-EN390 *Christopher Columbus, "Liberty," American eagle. Designs identical except for face value. (Watermark 11.)*

EN387		UnFVF	UseFVF
1¢	**blue** on white	2.00	1.50
	entire	3.00	1.75
EN388		UnFVF	UseFVF
2¢	**violet** on white	1.50	.75
	entire	2.50	.75
	a. slate (error)	1,900.00	—
	entire	—	—
EN389		UnFVF	UseFVF
5¢	**brown** on white	9.00	8.00
	entire*	15.00	12.00
	a. slate (error)	750.00	750.00
	entire	800.00	1,200.00
EN390		UnFVF	UseFVF
10¢	**slate** on white	40.00	30.00
	entire	60.00	45.00

1899. ISSUE With this issue all denominations of stamps above 5¢ values were discontinued; envelopes in higher denominations had been found to be of little use or in little demand. This was the last issue manufactured by the Plimpton Morgan Envelope Co.

EN391-EN396 *Franklin. (Watermarks 12, 13.)*

EN391		UnFVF	UseFVF
1¢	**green** on white	.75	.25
	entire	1.50	.75
EN392		UnFVF	UseFVF
1¢	**green** on amber	4.75	1.50
	entire	7.75	3.00
EN393		UnFVF	UseFVF
1¢	**green** on buff	10.00	4.00
	entire	13.50	4.00
EN394		UnFVF	UseFVF
1¢	**green** on blue	10.00	7.00
	entire	13.00	20.00
EN395		UnFVF	UseFVF
1¢	**green** on manila	2.00	1.00
	entire	6.50	2.50
EN396		UnFVF	UseFVF
1¢	**green** on manila, wrapper	2.00	1.00
	entire	8.75	3.00

EN397-EN400 *Washington. Die A, point of bust broad and ends over the left corner of the shield containing numeral. (Compare with EN401.)*

EN397		UnFVF	UseFVF
2¢	**carmine** on white	4.00	2.00
	entire	8.50	3.00
EN398		UnFVF	UseFVF
2¢	**carmine** on amber	17.50	10.00
	entire	27.50	12.00
EN399		UnFVF	UseFVF
2¢	**carmine** on buff	17.50	8.00
	entire	30.00	9.00
EN400		UnFVF	UseFVF
2¢	**carmine** on blue	60.00	30.00
	entire	75.00	35.00

EN401-EN405 *George Washington. Die B, point of bust elongated and points to the second tooth. Hair tied with ribbon at back. (Compare with EN397 and following.)*

EN401		UnFVF	UseFVF
2¢	**carmine** on white	.30	.25
	entire	.75	.50
EN402		UnFVF	UseFVF
2¢	**carmine** on amber	1.25	.25
	entire	3.25	.75
EN403		UnFVF	UseFVF
2¢	**carmine** on buff	1.00	.25
	entire	2.75	.75
EN404		UnFVF	UseFVF
2¢	**carmine** on blue	1.25	.50
	entire	3.50	1.75
EN405		UnFVF	UseFVF
2¢	**carmine** on manila, wrapper	6.00	3.00
	entire	12.50	6.00

EN406-EN409 *Die C, re-cut die. Similar to last but the hair is without ribbon. Many varieties of the re-cutting exist, some of which show the hair in flowing curves; some with hair pulled straight down; and others with the ribbon obliterated with short lines. (Compare with EN401.)*

EN406		UnFVF	UseFVF
2¢	**carmine** on white	5.00	2.50
	entire	9.50	7.00
EN407		UnFVF	UseFVF
2¢	**carmine** on amber	12.00	8.00
	entire	22.50	15.00
EN408		UnFVF	UseFVF
2¢	**carmine** on buff	25.00	15.00
	entire	35.00	17.50
EN409		UnFVF	UseFVF
2¢	**carmine** on blue	10.00	7.00
	entire	22.50	15.00

There are many shades for Nos. EN406-EN409.

EN410, EN411 *Abraham Lincoln. Die A, bust pointed and undraped. Inner oval with teeth. (Compare with following.)*

EN410		UnFVF	UseFVF
4¢	**brown** on white	17.00	12.00
	entire	30.00	15.00
EN411		UnFVF	UseFVF
4¢	**brown** on amber	17.00	12.00
	entire	30.00	25.00

EN412 *Die B, bust is draped and point broad. Inner oval with teeth.*

EN412		UnFVF	UseFVF
4¢	**brown** on white	5,000.00	325.00
	entire	5,700.00	—

EN413-EN415 *Abraham Lincoln. Die C, no teeth in inner oval. Bust broad and draped. (Watermarks 12, 13, 14.)*

EN413

4¢	**brown** on white	UnFVF	UseFVF
		10.00	7.00
	entire	25.00	11.00

EN414

4¢	**brown** on amber	UnFVF	UseFVF
		37.50	15.00
	entire	50.00	20.00

EN415

4¢	**brown** on manila, wrapper	UnFVF	UseFVF
		15.00	8.00
	entire	25.00	12.50

EN416, EN417 *Ulysses S. Grant. (Watermark 13.)*

EN416

5¢	**blue** on white	UnFVF	UseFVF
		10.00	9.50
	entire	14.00	13.00

EN417

5¢	**blue** on amber	UnFVF	UseFVF
		13.00	10.00
	entire	22.50	15.00

1903. ISSUE This contract is the first for the Hartford Manufacturing Co. as producers of stamped envelopes.

EN418-EN423 *Franklin. (Watermarks 13, 14.)*

EN418

1¢	**green** on white	UnFVF	UseFVF
		.50	.25
	entire	1.25	.50

EN419

1¢	**green** on amber	UnFVF	UseFVF
		12.00	3.00
	entire	18.50	4.00

EN420

1¢	**green** on buff	UnFVF	UseFVF
		13.00	3.00
	entire	17.00	4.00

EN421

1¢	**green** on blue	UnFVF	UseFVF
		13.00	3.00
	entire	20.00	4.00

EN422

1¢	**green** on manila	UnFVF	UseFVF
		3.00	1.50
	entire	4.50	2.00

EN423

1¢	**green** on manila, wrapper	UnFVF	UseFVF
		1.50	.75
	entire	2.00	1.00

EN424-EN428 *Washington. A short and two long lines of colorless shading are found in the right side of the ribbon containing the value. (Compare with EN434.)*

EN424

2¢	**carmine** on white	UnFVF	UseFVF
		.50	.25
	entire	1.00	.50

EN425

2¢	**carmine** on amber	UnFVF	UseFVF
		1.75	.50
	entire	3.75	1.50

EN426

2¢	**carmine** on buff	UnFVF	UseFVF
		2.00	.50
	entire	2.50	.75

EN427

2¢	**carmine** on blue	UnFVF	UseFVF
		1.50	.75
	entire	3.25	.75

EN428

2¢	**carmine** on manila, wrapper	UnFVF	UseFVF
		15.00	8.00
	entire	22.50	14.00

EN429-EN431 *Ulysses S. Grant*

EN429

4¢	**brown** on white	UnFVF	UseFVF
		20.00	12.00
	entire*	27.50	15.00

EN430

4¢	**brown** on amber	UnFVF	UseFVF
		20.00	12.00
	entire*	27.50	15.00

EN431

4¢	**brown** on manila, wrapper	UnFVF	UseFVF
		18.00	11.00
	entire*	40.00	30.00

EN432, EN433 *Abraham Lincoln*

EN432

5¢	**blue** on white	UnFVF	UseFVF
		17.00	10.00
	entire	25.00	17.50

EN433

5¢	**blue** on amber	UnFVF	UseFVF
		18.00	13.00
	entire	25.00	20.00

EN434-EN438 *Washington. Re-cut die. The colorless shading lines at the right of the ribbon containing the value are all short. Lettering throughout is heavier. (Compare with EN424.)*

EN434

2¢	**carmine** on white	UnFVF	UseFVF
		.50	.25
	entire	1.00	.50

EN435

2¢	**carmine** on amber	UnFVF	UseFVF
		7.00	.75
	entire	12.00	2.00

EN436

2¢	**carmine** on buff	UnFVF	UseFVF
		6.00	2.00
	entire	7.50	2.00

EN437

2¢	**carmine** on blue	UnFVF	UseFVF
		4.00	2.00
	entire	6.00	2.50

EN438

2¢	**carmine** on manila, wrapper	UnFVF	UseFVF
		12.00	7.00
	entire	22.50	12.50

1907-16. ISSUE New contractors, The Mercantile Corp., brought a change from Hartford, Conn., where envelopes had been manufactured since 1874, to Dayton, Ohio. In 1915 the Middle West Supply Co. obtained the contract and in 1929 the International Envelope Co. was the successful bidder. These new names did not change the site of manufacture itself, and appear to reflect the merger of the corporations named. From 1929 until 1965, envelopes were manufactured by the International Envelope Co., Dayton, Ohio.

Beginning in 1915, laid paper was dropped for all envelopes in favor of wove paper, and from then on all watermarks were of the same or similar design. The watermark was changed every four years to mark each new contract. The various arrangement of the dates, at top, bottom or diagonal, is identification of the paper manufacturer. From 1929 until 1958, the diagonally placed numerals identified "Extra quality" paper. Since 1958, all envelopes are of a single quality paper.

19

20

21

Typical examples of watermarks 1915-60 (reduced size).

EN439-EN444 *Franklin. Die A, wide "D" in "UNITED."
(Compare with EN445 and following.) (Watermarks
12, 14, 15, 16, 17, 18.)*

		UnFVF	UseFVF
EN439		.30	.25
1¢	**green** on white		
	entire	.50	.40
	v. "NITED" instead of "UNITED," entire	—	—
	v1. with added impression of 2¢	—	—
	Washington (EN466)		
EN440		UnFVF	UseFVF
1¢	**green** on amber	.75	.50
	entire	1.25	.75
EN441		UnFVF	UseFVF
1¢	**green** on buff	4.00	2.00
	entire	6.00	2.50
EN442		UnFVF	UseFVF
1¢	**green** on blue	5.00	2.00
	entire	6.00	3.00
EN443		UnFVF	UseFVF
1¢	**green** on manila	3.00	2.00
	entire	4.50	2.50
EN444		UnFVF	UseFVF
1¢	**green** on manila, wrapper	.50	.25
	entire	.75	.50

EN445-EN449 *Die B, narrow "D" in "UNITED."
(Compare with EN439 and following.)*

		UnFVF	UseFVF
EN445		UnFVF	UseFVF
1¢	**green** on white	1.00	.50
	entire	1.25	.60
EN446		UnFVF	UseFVF
1¢	**green** on amber	1.00	.75
	entire	1.50	1.00
EN447		UnFVF	UseFVF
1¢	**green** on buff	4.00	2.00
	entire	6.00	2.50
EN448		UnFVF	UseFVF
1¢	**green** on blue	5.00	2.00
	entire	6.00	3.00
EN449		UnFVF	UseFVF
1¢	**green** on manila, wrapper	37.50	20.00
	entire	42.50	27.50

EN450-EN455 *Franklin. Die C, both "Ss" in
"STATES" are broad. (Compare with other 1¢ dies.)*

		UnFVF	UseFVF
EN450		UnFVF	UseFVF
1¢	**green** on white	1.00	.50
	entire	1.25	.75
EN451		UnFVF	UseFVF
1¢	**green** on amber	1.00	.80
	entire	2.00	1.00
EN452		UnFVF	UseFVF
1¢	**green** on buff	6.00	2.00
	entire	7.00	3.00
EN453		UnFVF	UseFVF
1¢	**green** on blue	5.00	4.00
	entire	5.50	4.50
EN454		UnFVF	UseFVF
1¢	**green** on manila	4.00	3.00
	entire	6.00	5.00
EN455		UnFVF	UseFVF
1¢	**green** on manila, wrapper	6.00	4.00
	entire	11.00	6.00

EN450-EN455 *So-called "Dayton Dies" of which there are 13 varieties.
See note after illustration of EN492.*

EN456-EN460 *Die D, back of bust forms angle
opposite "T" in "CENT." (Compare with other 1¢ dies.)*

		UnFVF	UseFVF
EN456		.70	.35
1¢	**green** on white		
	entire	.85	.50
EN457		UnFVF	UseFVF
1¢	**green** on amber	1.00	.75
	entire	1.25	1.00
EN458		UnFVF	UseFVF
1¢	**green** on buff	4.00	2.00
	entire	5.00	3.00
EN459		UnFVF	UseFVF
1¢	**green** on blue	4.00	2.00
	entire	6.00	4.00
EN460		UnFVF	UseFVF
1¢	**green** on manila	50.00	
	entire	—	

Watermarks 15 to 23 (1907-1919).

EN461-EN470 *Washington. Die A, both the "O" in
"TWO" and the "C" in "CENTS" are ovals. (Compare
with the following.)*

		UnFVF	UseFVF
EN461		UnFVF	UseFVF
2¢	**brown red** on white	1.00	.50
	entire	1.75	.75
EN462		UnFVF	UseFVF
2¢	**brown red** on amber	6.00	3.00
	entire	8.50	7.00
EN463		UnFVF	UseFVF
2¢	**brown red** on buff	7.00	2.00
	entire	11.00	4.50
EN464		UnFVF	UseFVF
2¢	**brown red** on blue	5.00	2.50
	entire	7.00	4.00
EN465		UnFVF	UseFVF
2¢	**brown red** on manila, wrapper	40.00	30.00
	entire	60.00	40.00
EN466		UnFVF	UseFVF
2¢	**carmine** on white	.30	.25
	entire	.60	.40
	v1. with added impression of 1¢ Franklin	325.00	400.00
	(EN439) on reverse		
	v2. with added impression of 4¢ Franklin	300.00	
	(EN509)		
EN467		UnFVF	UseFVF
2¢	**carmine** on amber	.30	.25
	entire	1.00	.25
EN468		UnFVF	UseFVF
2¢	**carmine** on buff	.50	.25
	entire	.75	.25
EN469		UnFVF	UseFVF
2¢	**carmine** on blue	.50	.25
	entire	1.00	.25
EN470		UnFVF	UseFVF
2¢	**carmine** on manila, wrapper	5.00	3.00
	entire	9.50	5.00

EN471-EN479 *Die A2, similar to last except there is
a prominent wedge-shaped lock of hair in the center
of the head. (Compare with other 2¢ dies.)*

			UnFVF	UseFVF
EN471 2¢	**brown red** on white entire		30.00 40.00	8.00 25.00
EN472 2¢	**brown red** on amber entire		110.00 130.00	50.00 75.00
EN473 2¢	**brown red** on buff entire		135.00 150.00	60.00 100.00
EN474 2¢	**brown red** on blue entire		135.00 170.00	110.00 140.00
EN475 2¢	**carmine** on white entire		.40 .75	.20 .40
EN476 2¢	**carmine** on amber entire		.40 .80	.25 .60
EN477 2¢	**carmine** on buff entire		.60 .90	.55 .60
EN478 2¢	**carmine** on blue entire		.45 .80	.40 .50
EN479 2¢	**carmine** on manila, wrapper entire		5.00 7.00	3.00 5.00

EN480-EN487 *Washington. Die B, head is large, hair arranged in bumps. The "O" in "TWO" is circular. (Compare with EN488 and other 2¢ dies.)*

			UnFVF	UseFVF
EN480 2¢	**brown red** on white entire		.60 .90	.40 .50
EN481 2¢	**brown red** on amber entire		3.50 5.00	2.00 2.00
EN482 2¢	**brown red** on buff entire		7.00 10.00	3.25 6.00
EN483 2¢	**brown red** on blue entire		5.00 7.00	2.25 4.00
EN484 2¢	**carmine** on white entire		.75 1.25	.40 .60
EN485 2¢	**carmine** on amber entire		1.35 1.75	.50 .80
EN486 2¢	**carmine** on buff entire		7.00 11.00	4.00 6.00
EN487 2¢	**carmine** on blue entire		.90 1.50	.70 .75

EN488-EN491 *Die C, prominent slits in hair resembling the gills of a shark. Lettering clear and sharp. (Compare with EN480 and other 2¢ dies.)*

			UnFVF	UseFVF
EN488 2¢	**carmine** on white entire		.50 .75	.25 .50
EN489 2¢	**carmine** on amber entire		.40 .75	.30 .50
EN490 2¢	**carmine** on buff entire		.45 .70	.35 .50

			UnFVF	UseFVF
EN491 2¢	**carmine** on blue entire		.50 .60	.35 .50

EN492-EN496 *Die D, the so-called "Dayton Dies" as they were made by a private die engraver on order from the factory at Dayton, Ohio. There are 13 varieties, some of which are quite valuable.*

			UnFVF	UseFVF
EN492 2¢	**carmine** on white entire		.60 1.00	.40 .60
EN493 2¢	**carmine** on amber entire		.60 1.00	.40 .60
EN494 2¢	**carmine** on buff entire		3.00 4.00	1.50 3.75
EN495 2¢	**carmine** on blue entire		.75 1.50	.50 .75
EN496 2¢	**carmine** on manila, wrapper entire		5.00 8.00	3.00 3.00

EN497-EN500 *Washington. Die E, front of bust tapers and the end is rounded. (Compare with EN461 and others.)*

			UnFVF	UseFVF
EN497 2¢	**carmine** on white entire		.40 .85	.25 .40
EN498 2¢	**carmine** on amber entire		.65 1.00	.45 .60
EN499 2¢	**carmine** on buff entire		.75 1.25	.50 .70
EN500 2¢	**carmine** on blue entire		.75 1.25	.50 .50

EN501-EN505 *Washington. Die F, upright lines of the "2s" taper. There is a very thin line where it meets the base of the numeral. The upper corner of the front end of the bust is usually, but not always, cut away in varying degrees.*

			UnFVF	UseFVF
EN501 2¢	**carmine** on white entire a. vermilion entire		14.00 16.00 — —	12.00 14.00 — —
EN502 2¢	**carmine** on amber entire		12.00 14.00	9.00 12.00
EN503 2¢	**carmine** on buff entire		40.00 50.00	20.00 30.00
EN504 2¢	**carmine** on blue entire		15.00 20.00	9.00 16.00
EN505 2¢	**carmine** on manila, wrapper entire		45.00 55.00	40.00 45.00

> ## Condition refers to the overall appearance and quality of the stamp.

EN506-EN508 *Die G, hair arranged as in EN471 (a wedge-shape lock in center). (Compare with EN501 and others.)*

EN506		UnFVF	UseFVF
2¢	carmine on white	15.00	13.00
	entire	20.00	15.00
EN507		UnFVF	UseFVF
2¢	carmine on buff	13.00	10.00
	entire	20.00	13.00
EN508		UnFVF	UseFVF
2¢	carmine on blue	15.00	10.00
	entire	18.00	16.00

EN509, EN510 *Franklin. Die A, the "F" in "FOUR" is only 1mm from the "4." (Compare with EN511.)*

EN509		UnFVF	UseFVF
4¢	black on white	4.00	3.00
	entire*	9.00	5.00
EN510		UnFVF	UseFVF
4¢	black on amber	6.00	3.00
	entire*	10.00	5.00

EN511, EN512 *Die B, the "F" in "FOUR" is 1 3/4mm from the figure "4."*

EN511		UnFVF	UseFVF
4¢	black on white	5.00	4.00
	entire*	10.00	6.00
EN512		UnFVF	UseFVF
4¢	black on amber	6.00	3.00
	entire*	12.50	7.00

EN513-EN515 *Washington. Die A, large "F" in "FIVE" (2 3/4mm high). (Compare with EN516.)*

EN513		UnFVF	UseFVF
5¢	blue on white	7.00	3.00
	entire	11.00	7.00
EN514		UnFVF	UseFVF
5¢	blue on amber	13.00	12.00
	entire	16.00	14.00
EN515		UnFVF	UseFVF
5¢	blue on blue	1,200.00	—
	entire	1,800.00	—

EN516-EN519 *Die B, small "F" in "FIVE" (2 1/2mm tall). (Compare with EN513.)*

EN516		UnFVF	UseFVF
5¢	blue on white	7.00	3.00
	entire	12.50	6.00
EN517		UnFVF	UseFVF
5¢	blue on amber	13.00	12.00
	entire	22.50	15.00

EN518		UnFVF	UseFVF
5¢	blue on buff	1,000.00	—
	entire	—	—
EN519		UnFVF	UseFVF
5¢	blue on blue	1,000.00	—
	entire	—	—

1916-50. ISSUE The circular design used on these envelopes was introduced in 1916 and continued without change until 1950. Many dies wore out through this long tenure and many new master dies were required, which accounts for the several different dies for each denomination. The 3¢ envelopes were issued in 1917, when the rate of postage was increased from 2¢ to 3¢. The stamps were printed in a violet ink. Twenty months later the First Class rate was returned to 2¢ and the 3¢ envelopes were discontinued.

After the reduction of First Class postal rates from 3¢ (a war measure) to 2¢, the Post Office found itself with an enormous supply of 3¢ envelopes for which there was no practical use. The envelopes were revalued (1920) by running them through canceling machines with appropriate slugs to indicate the new value (2¢) inserted into them. It is estimated that some 63 million envelopes were revalued in the process.

When, in 1925, the rate for circular letters was advanced from 1¢ to 1 1/2¢, the government again found itself with an unusable supply of envelopes, this time the 1¢ denomination. Again revaluing was done by the use of canceling machines.

In July 1932, First Class rates were advanced to 3¢, which called for production of 3¢ envelopes. This new issue was printed in a bright purple ink. Wrappers were discontinued in 1934.

EN520-EN528 *Franklin. Die A, "UNITED" small and nearer inner than outer circle. (Compare with following.) Watermarks 19 to 42 (1915-1949).*

EN520		UnFVF	UseFVF
1¢	green on white	.25	.25
	entire	.40	.25
EN521		UnFVF	UseFVF
1¢	green on amber	.40	.35
	entire	.75	.50
EN522		UnFVF	UseFVF
1¢	green on buff	2.00	1.25
	entire	2.75	1.75
EN523		UnFVF	UseFVF
1¢	green on blue	.50	.40
	entire	.75	.50
EN524		UnFVF	UseFVF
1¢	green on manila	7.00	5.00
	entire	9.50	6.00
EN525		UnFVF	UseFVF
1¢	green on manila, wrapper	.25	.25
	entire	.75	.25
EN526		UnFVF	UseFVF
1¢	green on brown (glazed)	35.00	20.00
	entire	40.00	22.00
EN527		UnFVF	UseFVF
1¢	green on brown, (glazed) wrapper	65.00	—
	entire	75.00	—
EN528		UnFVF	UseFVF
1¢	green on brown (unglazed)	10.00	10.00
	entire	12.50	11.00

EN529, EN530 *Die B, the first "S" in "STATES" is larger than the last "S." "NT" in "CENT" are large. "U" in "UNITED" is close to circle. (Compare with EN531 and others.)*

EN529		UnFVF	UseFVF
1¢	green on white	85.00	65.00
	entire*	100.00	75.00
EN530		UnFVF	UseFVF
1¢	green on amber	325.00	200.00
	entire*	500.00	250.00

EN531-EN533 *Franklin. Die C, hair projects strongly at back, forming a "bun." (Compare with EN529 and others.)*

EN531
1¢   green on white
           entire

	UnFVF	UseFVF
	.35	.25
	.40	.30

EN532
1¢   green on amber
           entire

	UnFVF	UseFVF
	1.35	.75
	1.75	1.00

EN533
1¢   green on blue
           entire

	UnFVF	UseFVF
	1.00	.75
	1.50	.90

EN533A
1¢   green on manila, wrapper
           entire

	UnFVF	UseFVF
	150.00	135.00
	175.00	150.00

EN534-EN537 *Die D, "UNITED" large and closer to outer than inner circle. (Compare with EN520 and others.)*

EN534
1¢   green on white
           entire

	UnFVF	UseFVF
	.40	.30
	.50	.35

EN535
1¢   green on amber
           entire

	UnFVF	UseFVF
	1.50	1.00
	2.00	1.50

EN536
1¢   green on buff
           entire

	UnFVF	UseFVF
	4.00	1.50
	.50	.35

EN537
1¢   green on blue
           entire

	UnFVF	UseFVF
	1.00	.50
	1.50	.75

EN538-EN540 *"C" in "CENTS," "G" in "POSTAGE," and "U" in "UNITED" are very narrow. (Compare with all other dies.)*

EN538
1¢   green on white
           entire

	UnFVF	UseFVF
	.40	.30
	.55	.50

EN539
1¢   green on amber
           entire

	UnFVF	UseFVF
	1.25	.75
	1.50	1.00

EN540
1¢   green on blue
           entire

	UnFVF	UseFVF
	.75	.40
	1.10	.75

EN541-EN545 *Washington. Die A, large head, well formed thick letters.*

EN541
1 1/2¢   brown on white
           entire
           a. purple (error)
           entire

	UnFVF	UseFVF
	.25	.25
	.60	.25
	95.00	—
	120.00	—

EN542
1 1/2¢   brown on amber
           entire

	UnFVF	UseFVF
	1.00	.50
	1.50	.70

EN543
1 1/2¢   brown on blue
           entire

	UnFVF	UseFVF
	1.75	1.10
	2.00	1.50

EN544
1 1/2¢   brown on manila
           entire

	UnFVF	UseFVF
	7.00	4.00
	12.00	7.00

EN545
1 1/2¢   brown on manila, wrapper
           entire

	UnFVF	UseFVF
	.90	.25
	1.50	.60

EN546-EN548 *Die H2, slightly different head from EN541. Lettering thin and sharp; "T" with long top strokes.*

EN546
1 1/2¢   brown on white
           entire

	UnFVF	UseFVF
	.70	.35
	.90	.60

EN547
1 1/2¢   brown on amber
           entire

	UnFVF	UseFVF
	1.50	.85
	2.00	.90

EN548
1 1/2¢   brown on blue
           entire

	UnFVF	UseFVF
	2.00	1.50
	2.25	1.50

EN549-EN555 *Washington. Die A, head large. Base line of "2s" horizontal. Lettering heavy and well formed. (Compare with following.)*

EN549
2¢   carmine on white
           entire
           a. green (error), entire
           p. laid paper
           entire
           v. with added impression of 1¢ green (EN520)
           v1. with added impression of 1¢ green (EN439)
           v2. with added impression of 4¢ black (EN509)

	UnFVF	UseFVF
	.25	.25
	.50	.25
	7,500.00	—
	—	—
	—	—
	750.00	—
	750.00	—
	600.00	—

EN550
2¢   carmine on amber
           entire
           p. laid paper
           entire

	UnFVF	UseFVF
	.30	.25
	.50	.25
	—	—
	—	—

EN551
2¢   carmine on buff
           entire

	UnFVF	UseFVF
	2.00	.75
	4.50	2.00

EN552
2¢   carmine on blue
           entire

	UnFVF	UseFVF
	.25	.25
	.75	.25

EN553
2¢   carmine on manila, wrapper
           entire

	UnFVF	UseFVF
	.25	.25
	.50	.25

EN554
2¢   carmine on brown (glazed), wrapper
           entire

	UnFVF	UseFVF
	80.00	55.00
	100.00	70.00

EN555
2¢   carmine on brown (unglazed), wrapper
           entire

	UnFVF	UseFVF
	75.00	55.00
	100.00	70.00

EN556-EN559 *Washington. Die B, head very large. Base line of both "2s" slope down to right. "U" in "UNITED" far from circle. (Compare with other 2¢ dies.)*

EN556
2¢   carmine on white
           entire

	UnFVF	UseFVF
	10.00	7.00
	16.00	10.00

EN557
2¢   carmine on amber
           entire

	UnFVF	UseFVF
	10.00	8.00
	16.00	11.00

EN558		UnFVF	UseFVF
2¢	**carmine** on buff	110.00	50.00
	entire	135.00	90.00

EN559		UnFVF	UseFVF
2¢	**carmine** on blue	20.00	15.00
	entire	25.00	22.50

EN560, EN561 *Die C, as EN556 except the large inner circle and circles around the figure "2s" are very thin. (The rejected die.)*

EN560		UnFVF	UseFVF
2¢	**carmine** on white	35.00	30.00
	entire	50.00	40.00

EN561		UnFVF	UseFVF
2¢	**carmine** on blue	80.00	75.00
	entire	150.00	125.00

EN562-EN565 *Washington. Die D, "C" in "CENTS" very close to circle. Base line of right "2" slopes downward to right. Head slightly smaller. (Compare with EN549 and others.)*

EN562		UnFVF	UseFVF
2¢	**carmine** on white	10.00	8.00
	entire	13.00	11.00

EN563		UnFVF	UseFVF
2¢	**carmine** on amber	25.00	15.00
	entire	30.00	17.00

EN564		UnFVF	UseFVF
2¢	**carmine** on buff	35.00	35.00
	entire	45.00	45.00

EN565		UnFVF	UseFVF
2¢	**carmine** on blue	20.00	17.50
	entire	25.00	22.50

EN566-EN569 *Die E, smaller head than all other dies. "T" and "S" in "CENTS" close.*

EN566		UnFVF	UseFVF
2¢	**carmine** on white	.55	.35
	entire	.75	.50

EN567		UnFVF	UseFVF
2¢	**carmine** on amber	.60	.40
	entire	1.60	.70

EN568		UnFVF	UseFVF
2¢	**carmine** on buff	3.00	2.00
	entire	6.00	3.00

EN569		UnFVF	UseFVF
2¢	**carmine** on blue	.75	.25
	entire	1.75	.60

EN570-EN573 *Washington. Die F, base line of left "2" slopes downward to right. Heavy strands of hair resemble bumps. "T" and "S" in "CENTS" widely spaced. (Compare with other 2¢ dies.)*

EN570		UnFVF	UseFVF
2¢	**carmine** on white	.70	.40
	entire	1.10	.70

EN571		UnFVF	UseFVF
2¢	**carmine** on amber	1.00	.45
	entire	1.85	.85

EN572		UnFVF	UseFVF
2¢	**carmine** on buff	4.50	3.00
	entire	7.00	3.50

EN573		UnFVF	UseFVF
2¢	**carmine** on blue	.75	.30
	entire	1.25	.50

EN574-EN577 *Die H, base lines of "2s" slope downward to right. Clear sharp impressions. Thin lettering. "Ts" have short top strokes.*

EN574		UnFVF	UseFVF
2¢	**carmine** on white	.70	.30
	entire	1.00	.80

EN575		UnFVF	UseFVF
2¢	**carmine** on amber	.80	.40
	entire	1.60	1.00

EN576		UnFVF	UseFVF
2¢	**carmine** on buff	4.00	2.50
	entire	6.00	4.00

EN577		UnFVF	UseFVF
2¢	**carmine** on blue	.80	.40
	entire	1.50	.70

EN577A		UnFVF	UseFVF
2¢	**carmine** on manila	—	—
	entire	—	—

EN578-EN580 *Washington. Die H2, similar to EN574 except all "Ts" have long top strokes.*

EN578		UnFVF	UseFVF
2¢	**carmine** on white	.50	.25
	entire	.75	.55

EN579		UnFVF	UseFVF
2¢	**carmine** on amber	.70	.40
	entire	1.00	.50

EN580		UnFVF	UseFVF
2¢	**carmine** on blue	.50	.25
	entire	1.00	.50

EN581-EN585 *Die I, the letters "C," "U," and "G" are very narrow. (Compare with all other 2¢ dies.)*

EN581		UnFVF	UseFVF
2¢	**carmine** on white	.50	.30
	entire	.75	.50

EN582		UnFVF	UseFVF
2¢	**carmine** on amber	.60	.30
	entire	.70	.40

EN583		UnFVF	UseFVF
2¢	**carmine** on blue	.80	.25
	entire	2.25	.50

EN584-EN590 *Washington. Die A, similar to the 2¢ die (EN549). Dark violet stamps were issued from 1916-17, at which time the postage rate was reduced to 2¢. When rate again was raised to 3¢, in 1932, this denomination was reissued in a bright purple.*

EN584		UnFVF	UseFVF
3¢	**dark violet** on white	.60	.25
	entire	.75	.25
	a. carmine (error)	35.00	30.00
	entire	40.00	35.00
	v. with added impression of EN520, entire	650.00	—
	v1. with added impression of EN549, entire	750.00	—

EN585		UnFVF	UseFVF
3¢	**dark violet** on amber	2.50	1.50

entire	7.00	2.75
a. black (error)	175.00	—
entire	210.00	—

EN586
3¢

	UnFVF	UseFVF
dark violet on buff	25.00	2.00
entire	32.50	3.00

EN587
3¢

	UnFVF	UseFVF
dark violet on blue	7.00	1.75
entire	11.00	7.50

EN588
3¢

	UnFVF	UseFVF
purple on white	.25	.20
entire	.50	.25

EN589
3¢

	UnFVF	UseFVF
purple on amber	.50	.25
entire	.75	.40

EN590
3¢

	UnFVF	UseFVF
purple on blue	.30	.25
entire	.75	.30

EN591-EN594 *Die E, similar to 2¢ (EN566).*

EN591
3¢

	UnFVF	UseFVF
dark violet on white	1.75	1.00
entire	3.25	1.00
a. carmine (error)	35.00	30.00
entire	40.00	35.00

EN592
3¢

	UnFVF	UseFVF
dark violet on amber	5.00	3.00
entire	9.00	4.00
a. carmine (error)	375.00	265.00
entire	425.00	350.00

EN593
3¢

	UnFVF	UseFVF
dark violet on buff	30.00	1.75
entire	27.50	1.25

EN594
3¢

	UnFVF	UseFVF
dark violet on blue	7.00	4.50
entire	9.00	5.00
a. carmine (error)	300.00	300.00
entire	425.00	775.00

EN595-EN598 *Die F, similar to 2¢ (EN570).*

EN595
3¢

	UnFVF	UseFVF
dark violet on white	2.50	1.75
entire	4.00	2.00

EN596
3¢

	UnFVF	UseFVF
dark violet on amber	6.50	3.00
entire	8.00	3.50

EN597
3¢

	UnFVF	UseFVF
dark violet on buff	33.00	2.00
entire	35.00	3.00

EN598
3¢

	UnFVF	UseFVF
dark violet on blue	7.00	5.00
entire	10.00	5.00

EN599-EN602 *Die H, similar to 2¢, die H (EN574).*
EN603-EN605 *Die I, similar to 2¢. (See EN581.)*

EN599
3¢

	UnFVF	UseFVF
dark violet on white	1.50	1.00
entire	3.00	2.50

EN600
3¢

	UnFVF	UseFVF
dark violet on amber	4.00	2.00
entire	6.00	3.00

EN601
3¢

	UnFVF	UseFVF
dark violet on buff	32.00	4.00
entire	37.00	8.00

EN602
3¢

	UnFVF	UseFVF
dark violet on blue	9.00	5.00
entire	13.00	7.00

EN603
3¢

	UnFVF	UseFVF
purple on white	.50	.25
entire	.50	.35

EN604
3¢

	UnFVF	UseFVF
purple on amber	.60	.25
entire	1.10	.40

EN605
3¢

	UnFVF	UseFVF
purple on blue	.60	.25
entire	1.10	.55

Nos. EN606-EN608 are not assigned.

EN609-EN611 *Franklin*

EN609
4¢

	UnFVF	UseFVF
black on white	1.25	.75
entire*	3.25	2.55
v. with added impression of 2¢ (EN549)	—	—
entire*	275.00	—

EN610
4¢

	UnFVF	UseFVF
black on amber	2.75	1.00
entire	5.50	2.00

EN611
4¢

	UnFVF	UseFVF
black on blue	3.00	1.00
entire	5.50	2.00

EN612-EN614 *Washington*

EN612
5¢

	UnFVF	UseFVF
blue on white	3.00	2.50
entire	6.50	3.50

EN613
5¢

	UnFVF	UseFVF
blue on amber	4.00	1.75
entire	7.00	3.50

EN614
5¢

	UnFVF	UseFVF
blue on blue	4.00	3.00
entire	9.00	4.50

EN615-EN617

EN615
6¢

	UnFVF	UseFVF
orange on white	6.00	3.50
entire*	8.00	6.00

EN616
6¢

	UnFVF	UseFVF
orange on amber	11.00	8.00
entire*	15.00	10.00

EN617
6¢

	UnFVF	UseFVF
orange on blue	11.00	8.00
entire*	15.00	10.00

1920. TYPE 1 SURCHARGE REVALUED ENVELOPES When a double or triple overprint is listed it indicates that all of the overprints either are directly over the stamp or partly on the stamp. Envelopes which show overprints in various places other than on the stamp are freaks and command little or no premium value.

On 3¢ envelopes of 1916-50 issue.

2 CENTS

Type 1 *surcharge - black overprint*

EN618
2¢ on 3¢ on white, Die A (EN584)
entire

	UnFVF	UseFVF
	11.00	10.00
entire	16.00	12.00

EN619
2¢ on 3¢ on white, Die E (EN591)
entire

	UnFVF	UseFVF
	11.00	10.00
entire	14.00	12.00

1920. TYPE 2 SURCHARGE REVALUED ENVELOPES

Type 2 *surcharge - rose overprint*

EN620
2¢ on 3¢ on white, Die A, (EN584)

entire

	UnFVF	UseFVF
	7.00	6.00
entire	8.50	8.00

EN621
2¢ on 3¢ on white, Die F (EN595)
entire

	UnFVF	UseFVF
	7.00	6.00
entire	9.50	9.00

EN621A
2¢ on 3¢ on white, Die A (EN549)
entire

	UnFVF	UseFVF
	1,600.00	—
entire	—	—

EN621B
2¢ on 3¢ on amber, Die A (EN550)
entire*

	UnFVF	UseFVF
	—	—
entire*	—	—

EN622
2¢ on 3¢ on white, Die A (EN584)
entire

	UnFVF	UseFVF
	2.50	2.00
entire	3.00	2.50

EN623
2¢ on 3¢ on amber, Die A (EN585)
entire

	UnFVF	UseFVF
	6.00	6.00
entire	7.00	7.00

EN624
2¢ on 3¢ on buff, Die A (EN586)
entire

	UnFVF	UseFVF
	15.00	13.00
entire	18.00	17.00

EN625
2¢ on 3¢ on blue, Die A (EN587)
entire

	UnFVF	UseFVF
	12.00	11.00
entire	13.00	11.00

EN626
2¢ on 3¢ on white, Die E (EN591)
entire

	UnFVF	UseFVF
	—	—
entire	—	—

EN627
2¢ on 3¢ on amber, Die E (EN592)
entire

	UnFVF	UseFVF
	—	—
entire	—	—

EN628
2¢ on 3¢ on buff, Die E (EN593)
entire

	UnFVF	UseFVF
	—	—
entire	—	—

EN629
2¢ on 3¢ on blue, Die E (EN594)
entire

	UnFVF	UseFVF
	—	—
entire	—	—

EN630
2¢ on 3¢ on white, Die F (EN595)
entire

	UnFVF	UseFVF
	—	—
entire	—	—

EN631
2¢ on 3¢ on amber, Die F (EN596)
entire

	UnFVF	UseFVF
	—	—
entire	—	—

EN632
2¢ on 3¢ on buff, Die F (EN597)
entire

	UnFVF	UseFVF
	—	—
entire	—	—

EN633
2¢ on 3¢ on blue, Die F (EN598)
entire

	UnFVF	UseFVF
	—	—
entire	—	—

EN634
2¢ on 3¢ on white, Die H (EN599)
entire

	UnFVF	UseFVF
	—	—
entire	—	—

EN635
2¢ on 3¢ on amber, Die H (EN600)
entire

	UnFVF	UseFVF
	—	—
entire	—	—

EN636
2¢ on 3¢ on buff, Die H (EN601)
entire

	UnFVF	UseFVF
	—	—
entire	—	—

EN637
2¢ on 3¢ on blue, Die H (EN602)
entire

	UnFVF	UseFVF
	—	—
entire	—	—

1920. TYPE 3 SURCHARGE REVALUED ENVELOPES On 4¢ brown envelope of 1899 issue.

Type 3 *surcharge - black overprint*

EN638A
2¢ on 4¢ on white (EN413)
entire*

	UnFVF	UseFVF
	—	—
entire*	—	—

1920. TYPE 3 SURCHARGE REVALUED ENVELOPES On 4¢ brown envelope of 1903 issue.

EN639
2¢ on 4¢ on white (EN429)
entire*

	UnFVF	UseFVF
	350.00	175.00
entire*	400.00	200.00

1920. TYPE 3 SURCHARGE REVALUED ENVELOPES On 4¢ brown envelope of 1899 issue.

EN640
2¢ on 4¢ on amber (EN430)
entire*

	UnFVF	UseFVF
	350.00	125.00
entire*	400.00	175.00

1920. TYPE 3 SURCHARGE REVALUED ENVELOPES On envelopes of 1907-16 issue.

EN641
2¢ on 1¢ on white, Die A (EN439)
entire

	UnFVF	UseFVF
	21,700.00	—
entire	—	—

EN642
2¢ on 2¢ on white, Die A (EN466)
entire

	UnFVF	UseFVF
	900.00	—
entire	1,300.00	—

EN643
2¢ on 2¢ on buff, Die A (EN468)
entire

	UnFVF	UseFVF
	675.00	—
entire	775.00	—

EN644
2¢ on 2¢ on white, Die C (EN488)
entire

	UnFVF	UseFVF
	900.00	—
entire	1,300.00	—

EN645
2¢ on 2¢ on buff, Die E (EN499)
entire

	UnFVF	UseFVF
	700.00	550.00
entire	800.00	—

EN646
2¢ on 2¢ on blue, Die E (EN500)
entire

	UnFVF	UseFVF
	700.00	—
entire	800.00	—

EN647
2¢ on 4¢ on white, Die B (EN511)
entire

	UnFVF	UseFVF
	750.00	—
entire	825.00	—

1920. TYPE 3 SURCHARGE REVALUED ENVELOPES On 1¢ circular dies of 1916-50.

EN648
2¢ on 1¢ on white, Die A (EN520)
entire

	UnFVF	UseFVF
	900.00	—
entire	1,100.00	—

EN649
2¢ on 1¢ on white, Die C (EN531)
entire

	UnFVF	UseFVF
	2,500.00	—
entire	3,250.00	—

1920. TYPE 3 SURCHARGE REVALUED ENVELOPES On 2¢ circular dies of 1916-1950.

EN650
2¢ on 2¢ on white, Die A (EN549)
entire

	UnFVF	UseFVF
	200.00	—
entire	250.00	—

EN651
2¢ on 2¢ on amber, Die A (EN550)
entire

	UnFVF	UseFVF
	950.00	—
entire	1,300.00	—

EN652
2¢ on 2¢ on buff, Die B (EN558)
entire

	UnFVF	UseFVF
	150.00	—
entire	185.00	—

EN653
2¢ on 2¢ on white, Die E (EN566)
entire

	UnFVF	UseFVF
	300.00	—
entire	500.00	—

EN654
2¢ on 2¢ on buff, Die E (EN568)
entire

	UnFVF	UseFVF
	275.00	—
entire	300.00	—

EN655
2¢ on 2¢ on blue, Die E (EN569)
entire

	UnFVF	UseFVF
	275.00	—
entire	350.00	—

EN656

	UnFVF	UseFVF
2¢ on 2¢ on white, Die F (EN570)	85.00	—
entire	160.00	—

EN657

	UnFVF	UseFVF
2¢ on 2¢ on blue, Die F (EN573)	275.00	—
entire	300.00	—

EN658

	UnFVF	UseFVF
2¢ on 2¢ on white, Die H (EN574)	—	—
entire	—	—

EN659

	UnFVF	UseFVF
2¢ on 2¢ on buff, Die H (EN576)	275.00	—
entire	300.00	—

EN660

	UnFVF	UseFVF
2¢ on 2¢ on blue, Die H (EN577)	500.00	—
entire	550.00	—

1920. TYPE 3 SURCHARGE REVALUED ENVELOPES *On 3¢ circular dies of 1916-50.*

EN661

	UnFVF	UseFVF
2¢ on 3¢ on white, Die A (EN584)	.50	.40
entire	.70	.50
v. Double overprint	15.00	8.00
entire	40.00	—
v1. Triple overprint	—	—
entire	35.00	—
v2. with added impression of 3¢ dark violet	—	—

EN662

	UnFVF	UseFVF
2¢ on 3¢ on amber, Die A (EN585)	3.00	1.50
entire	4.50	2.00
v. Double overprint	19.00	—
entire	—	—

EN663

	UnFVF	UseFVF
2¢ on 3¢ on buff, Die A (EN586)	3.00	1.50
entire	3.50	1.50
v. Double overprint	13.00	—
entire	—	—
v1. Triple overprint	30.00	—
entire	—	—

EN664

	UnFVF	UseFVF
2¢ on 3¢ on blue, Die A (EN587)	4.50	1.50
entire	6.00	2.00
v. Double overprint	16.00	—
entire	—	—

EN665

	UnFVF	UseFVF
2¢ on 3¢ on white, Die E (EN591)	—	—
entire	—	—
v. Double overprint	—	—
entire	—	—
v1. Triple overprint	—	—
entire	—	—

EN666

	UnFVF	UseFVF
2¢ on 3¢ on amber, Die E (EN592)	3.00	1.50
entire	4.50	2.00

EN667

	UnFVF	UseFVF
2¢ on 3¢ on buff, Die E (EN593)	—	—
entire	—	—
v. Double overprint	—	—
entire	—	—

EN668

	UnFVF	UseFVF
2¢ on 3¢ on blue, Die E (EN594)	4.25	1.00
entire	6.25	1.50
v. Double overprint	12.50	—
entire	—	—
v1. Triple overprint	—	—
entire	—	—

EN669

	UnFVF	UseFVF
2¢ on 3¢ on white, Die F (EN595)	—	—
entire	—	—
v. Double overprint	—	—
entire	—	—

EN670

	UnFVF	UseFVF
2¢ on 3¢ on amber, Die F (EN596)	—	—
entire	—	—
v. Double overprint	—	—
entire	—	—
v1. Triple overprint	—	—
entire	—	—

EN671

	UnFVF	UseFVF
2¢ on 3¢ on buff, Die F (EN597)	—	—
entire	—	—

EN672

	UnFVF	UseFVF
2¢ on 3¢ on blue, Die F (EN598)	—	—
entire	—	—

EN673

	UnFVF	UseFVF
2¢ on 3¢ on white, Die H (EN599)	—	—
entire	—	—
v. Double overprint	—	—
entire	—	—
v1. Triple overprint	—	—
entire	—	—

EN674

	UnFVF	UseFVF
2¢ on 3¢ on amber, Die H (EN600)	—	—
entire	—	—
v. Double overprint	—	—
entire	—	—
v1. Triple overprint	—	—
entire	—	—

EN675

	UnFVF	UseFVF
2¢ on 3¢ on blue, Die H (EN602)	—	—
entire	—	—

1920. TYPE 3 SURCHARGE REVALUED ENVELOPES *On 5¢ circular dies of 1916-50.*

EN676

	UnFVF	UseFVF
2¢ on 5¢ on white (EN612)	900.00	—
entire	1,100.00	—

1920. TYPE 3 SURCHARGE REVALUED ENVELOPES Type 3 over Type 7a - black overprint. *On 3¢ violet circular dies of 1916-50.*

EN677

	UnFVF	UseFVF
2¢ on 3¢ on white, Die F (EN595)	—	—
entire	—	—

1920. TYPE 4 SURCHARGE REVALUED ENVELOPES *On 2¢ circular dies of 1874-76.*

Type 4 *surcharge - black overprint*

EN678

	UnFVF	UseFVF
2¢ on 3¢ on white (EN187)	225.00	—
entire*	275.00	—

1920. TYPE 4 SURCHARGE REVALUED ENVELOPES *On 4¢ brown envelopes of 1903 issue.*

EN679

	UnFVF	UseFVF
2¢ on 4¢ on white (EN429)	12.00	9.00
entire*	25.00	15.00
v. Double overprint	40.00	—
entire*	—	—

EN680

	UnFVF	UseFVF
2¢ on 4¢ on amber (EN430)	14.00	10.00
entire	22.00	13.00

1920. TYPE 4 SURCHARGE REVALUED ENVELOPES *On 2¢ carmine envelope of 1907-16 issue.*

EN681

	UnFVF	UseFVF
2¢ on 2¢ on white, Die E (EN497)	12,000.00	—
entire	23,700.00	—

1920. TYPE 4 SURCHARGE REVALUED ENVELOPES *On 1¢ circular dies of 1916-21.*

EN682

	UnFVF	UseFVF
2¢ on 1¢ on white, Die A (EN520)	750.00	—
entire	950.00	—

EN683

	UnFVF	UseFVF
2¢ on 1¢ on white, Die C (EN531)	1,400.00	—
entire	2,250.00	—

1920. TYPE 4 SURCHARGE REVALUED ENVELOPES *On 2¢ circular dies of 1874-76.*

EN684

	UnFVF	UseFVF
2¢ on 2¢ on white, Die A (EN549)	225.00	—
entire	275.00	—

1920. TYPE 4 SURCHARGE REVALUED ENVELOPES *On 2¢ circular dies of 1916-50.*

EN685

	UnFVF	UseFVF
2¢ on 2¢ on amber, Die A (EN550)	1,750.00	—
entire	2,000.00	—

EN686
	UnFVF	UseFVF
2¢ on 2¢ on white, Die E (EN566)	375.00	—
entire		

EN687
	UnFVF	UseFVF
2¢ on 2¢ on white, Die H (EN574)	1,000.00	—
entire	1,500.00	—

1920. TYPE 4 SURCHARGE REVALUED ENVELOPES On 3¢ circular dies of 1916-50.

EN688
	UnFVF	UseFVF
2¢ on 3¢ on white, Die A (EN584)	.70	.50
entire	.90	.80
v. Double overprint	16.00	—
entire	—	—
v1. Triple overprint	25.00	—
entire	—	—

EN689
	UnFVF	UseFVF
2¢ on 3¢ on amber, Die A (EN585)	3.25	2.00
entire	5.00	3.00
v. Double overprint	—	—
entire	—	—

EN690
	UnFVF	UseFVF
2¢ on 3¢ on buff, Die A (EN586)	5.00	3.00
entire	7.00	5.00
v. Double overprint	20.00	—
entire	—	—

EN691
	UnFVF	UseFVF
2¢ on 3¢ on blue, Die A (EN587)	3.50	1.50
entire	10.00	4.00
v. Double overprint	20.00	—
entire	—	—

1920. TYPE 4 SURCHARGE REVALUED ENVELOPES On Die E.

EN692
	UnFVF	UseFVF
2¢ on 3¢ on white (EN591)	—	—
entire	—	—
v. Double overprint	—	—
entire	—	—

EN693
	UnFVF	UseFVF
2¢ on 3¢ on amber (EN592)	—	—
entire	—	—

EN694
	UnFVF	UseFVF
2¢ on 3¢ on buff (EN593)	—	—
entire	—	—

EN695
	UnFVF	UseFVF
2¢ on 3¢ on blue (EN594)	—	—
entire	—	—
v. Double overprint	—	—
entire	—	—

1920. TYPE 4 SURCHARGE REVALUED ENVELOPES On Die F.

EN696
	UnFVF	UseFVF
2¢ on 3¢ on white (EN595)	—	—
entire	—	—
v. Double overprint	—	—
entire	—	—

EN697
	UnFVF	UseFVF
2¢ on 3¢ on amber (EN596)	—	—
entire	—	—
v. Double overprint	—	—
entire	—	—

EN698
	UnFVF	UseFVF
2¢ on 3¢ on buff (EN597)	—	—
entire	—	—

EN699
	UnFVF	UseFVF
2¢ on 3¢ on blue (EN598)	—	—
entire	—	—

1920. TYPE 4 SURCHARGE REVALUED ENVELOPE On Die H.

EN700
	UnFVF	UseFVF
2¢ on 3¢ on white (EN599)	—	—
entire	—	—
v. Double overprint	—	—
entire	—	—

EN701
	UnFVF	UseFVF
2¢ on 3¢ on amber (EN600)	—	—
entire	—	—

EN702
	UnFVF	UseFVF
2¢ on 3¢ on buff (EN601)	—	—
entire	—	—

EN703
	UnFVF	UseFVF
2¢ on 3¢ on blue (EN602)	—	—
entire	—	—

1920. TYPE 4 OVER TYPE 7A SURCHARGE REVALUED ENVELOPES Black overprints. On 3¢ circular dies of 1916-50.

EN704
	UnFVF	UseFVF
2¢ on 3¢ on white, Die A (EN584)	—	—
entire	—	—

EN705
	UnFVF	UseFVF
2¢ on 3¢ on amber, Die A (EN585)	—	—
entire	—	—

EN706
	UnFVF	UseFVF
2¢ on 3¢ on white, Die E (EN591)	325.00	—
entire	450.00	—

EN707
	UnFVF	UseFVF
2¢ on 3¢ on white, Die H (EN599)	750.00	—
entire	900.00	—

1920. TYPE 4 OVER TYPE 2 SURCHARGE REVALUED ENVELOPES Black overprints. On 3¢ circular dies of 1916-50. On Die A.

EN708
	UnFVF	UseFVF
2¢ on 3¢ on white (EN584)	75.00	—

EN709
	UnFVF	UseFVF
2¢ on 3¢ on amber (EN585)	60.00	—
entire		

EN710
	UnFVF	UseFVF
2¢ on 3¢ on buff (EN586)	60.00	—
entire		

EN711
	UnFVF	UseFVF
2¢ on 3¢ on blue (EN587)	180.00	—
entire	—	—

1920. TYPE 4 OVER TYPE 2 SURCHARGE REVALUED ENVELOPES On Die E.

EN712
	UnFVF	UseFVF
2¢ on 3¢ on amber (EN592)	—	—
entire	—	—

EN713
	UnFVF	UseFVF
2¢ on 3¢ on buff (EN593)	—	—
entire	—	—

EN714
	UnFVF	UseFVF
2¢ on 3¢ on blue (EN594)	—	—
entire	—	—

1920. TYPE 4 OVER TYPE E SURCHARGE REVALUED ENVELOPES On Die F.

EN715
	UnFVF	UseFVF
2¢ on 3¢ on buff (EN597)	—	—
entire	—	—

EN716
	UnFVF	UseFVF
2¢ on 3¢ on blue (EN598)	—	—
entire	—	—

EN717
	UnFVF	UseFVF
2¢ on 3¢ on white, Die H (EN599)	—	—
entire	—	—

1920. TYPE 4 OVER TYPE 3 SURCHARGE REVALUED ENVELOPES Black overprints. On 3¢ circular dies of 1916-50. On Die A.

EN718
	UnFVF	UseFVF
2¢ on 3¢ on white (EN584)	—	—
entire	—	—

EN719
	UnFVF	UseFVF
2¢ on 3¢ on amber (EN585)	—	—
entire	—	—

EN720
	UnFVF	UseFVF
2¢ on 3¢ on buff (EN586)	—	—
entire	—	—

EN721
	UnFVF	UseFVF
2¢ on 3¢ on blue (EN587)	—	—
entire	—	—

1920. TYPE 4 OVER TYPE 3 SURCHARGE REVALUED ENVELOPES On Die E.

EN722
	UnFVF	UseFVF
2¢ on 3¢ on amber (EN592)	—	—
entire	—	—

EN723
	UnFVF	UseFVF
2¢ on 3¢ on buff (EN593)	—	—
entire	—	—

EN724
	UnFVF	UseFVF
2¢ on 3¢ on blue (EN594)	—	—
entire	—	—

EN725

	UnFVF	UseFVF
2¢ on 3¢ on blue, Die F (EN598)	—	—
entire	—	—

EN726

	UnFVF	UseFVF
2¢ on 3¢ on white, Die H (EN599)	—	—
entire	—	—

1920. Type 5 Surcharge Revalued Envelopes On 3¢ circular dies of 1916-50.

Type 5 *surcharge - black overprint*

EN727

	UnFVF	UseFVF
2¢ on 3¢ on amber, Die A (EN585)	100.00	—
entire	130.00	—

EN728

	UnFVF	UseFVF
2¢ on 3¢ on amber, Die F (EN596)	—	—
entire	—	—

1920. Type 6 Surcharge Revalued Envelopes On 3¢ circular dies of 1916-50. On Die A.

2 Type 6 *surcharge - black overprint*

EN729

	UnFVF	UseFVF
2¢ on 3¢ on white (EN584)	100.00	—
entire	130.00	—
x. Double overprint	—	—
entire	—	—

EN730

	UnFVF	UseFVF
2¢ on 3¢ on amber (EN585)	200.00	—
entire	220.00	—

EN731

	UnFVF	UseFVF
2¢ on 3¢ on white, Die E (EN591)	—	—
entire	—	—

EN732

	UnFVF	UseFVF
2¢ on 3¢ on white, Die F (EN595)	—	—
entire	—	—

EN733

	UnFVF	UseFVF
2¢ on 3¢ on white, Die H (EN599)	—	—
entire	—	—

1920. Type 7 Surcharge Revalued Envelopes On 3¢ circular dies of 1916-50.

Type 7 *surcharge - black overprint*

EN734

	UnFVF	UseFVF
2¢ on 3¢ on white, Die A (EN584)	275.00	—
entire	325.00	—

EN735

	UnFVF	UseFVF
2¢ on 3¢ on white, Die E (EN591)	—	—
entire	—	—

EN736

	UnFVF	UseFVF
2¢ on 3¢ on white, Die H (EN599)	—	—
entire	—	—

1920. Type 7A Surcharge Revalued Envelopes

Type 7A *surcharge - violet overprint*

1 CENT

EN737

	UnFVF	UseFVF
2¢ on 3¢ on white, Die H (EN599)	200.00	—
entire	225.00	—

1920. Type 7A Surcharge Revalued Envelopes On 2¢ circular dies of 1916-50.

EN738

	UnFVF	UseFVF
1¢ on 2¢ on white, Die A (EN549)	—	—
entire	—	—

EN739

	UnFVF	UseFVF
1¢ on 2¢ on white, Die H (EN574)	—	—
entire	—	—

1920. Type 7A Surcharge Revalued Envelopes On 3¢ circular dies of 1916-50.

EN740

	UnFVF	UseFVF
1¢ on 3¢ on white, Die E (EN591)	200.00	—
entire	225.00	—
v1. with added 2¢ Type 4 surcharge (error)	—	—

1925. Type 8 Surcharge Revalued Envelopes On 2¢ green envelopes of 1887 issue.

Type 8 *surcharge - black overprint*

EN741

	UnFVF	UseFVF
1 1/2¢ on 2¢ on white (EN344)	600.00	—
entire	650.00	—

EN742

	UnFVF	UseFVF
1 1/2¢ on 2¢ on amber (EN345)	700.00	—
entire	800.00	—

1925. Type 8 Surcharge Revalued Envelopes On 1¢ green envelopes of 1899 issue.

EN743

	UnFVF	UseFVF
1 1/2¢ on 1¢ on white (EN391)	350.00	—
entire	650.00	—

EN744

	UnFVF	UseFVF
1 1/2¢ on 1¢ on amber (EN392)	75.00	65.00
entire	120.00	100.00

1925. Type 8 Surcharge Revalued Envelopes On 1¢ green envelopes of 1907-16. On Die A.

EN745

	UnFVF	UseFVF
1 1/2¢ on 1¢ on white (EN439)	5.00	4.00
entire	6.00	6.00

EN746

	UnFVF	UseFVF
1 1/2¢ on 1¢ on amber (EN440)	8.00	3.00
entire	12.00	7.00

EN747

	UnFVF	UseFVF
1 1/2¢ on 1¢ on manila (EN443)	200.00	75.00
entire	250.00	100.00

1925. Type 8 Surcharge Revalued Envelopes On Die B.

EN748

	UnFVF	UseFVF
1 1/2¢ on 1¢ on white (EN445)	13.00	10.00
entire	15.00	13.00

EN749

	UnFVF	UseFVF
1 1/2¢ on 1¢ on amber (EN446)	80.00	70.00
entire	200.00	90.00

EN750

	UnFVF	UseFVF
1 1/2¢ on 1¢ on buff (EN447)	200.00	100.00
entire	225.00	110.00

EN751

	UnFVF	UseFVF
1 1/2¢ on 1¢ on blue (EN448)	75.00	55.00
entire	100.00	65.00

1925. Type 8 Surcharge Revalued Envelopes On Die C.

EN751A

	UnFVF	UseFVF
1 1/2¢ on 1¢ on white (EN450)	7.00	3.00
entire	9.00	5.00

EN751B

	UnFVF	UseFVF
1 1/2¢ on 1¢ on amber (EN450)	4.50	2.50
entire*	8.00	5.00

EN751C

	UnFVF	UseFVF
1 1/2¢ on 1¢ on manila (EN454)	—	—
entire	—	—

1925. Type 8 Surcharge Revalued Envelopes *On Die D.*

EN752

	UnFVF	UseFVF
1 1/2¢ on 1¢ on white (EN456)	—	—
entire	—	—

EN753

	UnFVF	UseFVF
1 1/2¢ on 1¢ on amber (EN457)	4.50	2.50
entire	8.00	5.00

EN754

	UnFVF	UseFVF
1 1/2¢ on 1¢ on buff (EN458)	75.00	55.00
entire	100.00	65.00

EN755
1 1/2¢ on 1¢ on blue (EN459) | UnFVF — | UseFVF —
entire | — | —

1925. TYPE 8 SURCHARGE REVALUED ENVELOPES *On 1¢ circular dies of 1916-50. On Die A.*

EN756	UnFVF	UseFVF
1 1/2¢ on 1¢ on white (EN520)	.35	.30
entire	.60	.50
v. Double overprint	5.00	2.50
entire		

EN757	UnFVF	UseFVF
1 1/2¢ on 1¢ on amber (EN521)	14.00	13.00
entire	21.00	16.00

EN758	UnFVF	UseFVF
1 1/2¢ on 1¢ on buff (EN522)	4.00	2.50
entire	6.00	2.75

EN759	UnFVF	UseFVF
1 1/2¢ on 1¢ on blue (EN523)	1.25	1.00
entire	2.50	1.50

EN760	UnFVF	UseFVF
1 1/2¢ on 1¢ on manila (EN524)	11.00	7.00
entire	16.00	8.00

EN761	UnFVF	UseFVF
1 1/2¢ on 1¢ on brown (glazed) (EN526)	60.00	30.00
entire	70.00	40.00

EN762	UnFVF	UseFVF
1 1/2¢ on 1¢ on brown (unglazed) (EN528)	60.00	35.00
entire	70.00	40.00

1925. TYPE 8 SURCHARGE REVALUED ENVELOPES *On Die B.*

EN762A	UnFVF	UseFVF
1 1/2¢ on 1¢ on white (EN529)	2.00	.75
entire	—	—

1925. TYPE 8 SURCHARGE REVALUED ENVELOPES *On Die C.*

EN763	UnFVF	UseFVF
1 1/2¢ on 1¢ on white (EN531)	2.00	1.00
entire	—	—
x. Double overprint	—	—
entire	—	—

EN764	UnFVF	UseFVF
1 1/2¢ on 1¢ on blue (EN533)	—	—
entire	—	—

1925. TYPE 8 SURCHARGE REVALUED ENVELOPES *On Die D.*

EN765	UnFVF	UseFVF
1 1/2¢ on 1¢ on white (EN534)	—	—
entire	—	—
x. Double overprint	—	—
entire	—	—

EN766	UnFVF	UseFVF
1 1/2¢ on 1¢ on amber (EN535)	—	—
entire	—	—

EN767	UnFVF	UseFVF
1 1/2¢ on 1¢ on blue (EN537)	—	—
entire	—	—
x. Double overprint	—	—
entire	—	—

1925. TYPE 8 SURCHARGE REVALUED ENVELOPES *On 1 1/2¢ circular dies of 1916-50.*

EN768	UnFVF	UseFVF
1 1/2¢ on 1 1/2¢ on white, Die A (EN541)	400.00	—
entire	475.00	—

EN769	UnFVF	UseFVF
1 1/2¢ on 1 1/2¢ on blue, Die H2 (EN548)	350.00	—
entire	400.00	—

1925. TYPE 8 SURCHARGE REVALUED ENVELOPES *On 2¢ circular dies of 1916-50.*

EN770	UnFVF	UseFVF
1 1/2¢ on 2¢ on white, Die A (EN549)	250.00	—
entire*	300.00	—

EN771	UnFVF	UseFVF
1 1/2¢ on 2¢ on buff, Die E (EN568)	275.00	—
entire	300.00	—

EN772	UnFVF	UseFVF
1 1/2¢ on 2¢ on blue, Die F (EN573)	250.00	—
entire	300.00	—

1925. TYPE 9 SURCHARGE REVALUED ENVELOPES *On 1¢ blue envelope of 1887 issue.*

Type 9 *surcharge - black overprint*

EN773	UnFVF	UseFVF
1 1/2¢ on 1¢ on white (EN321)	1,000.00	—
entire	1,200.00	—

1925. TYPE 9 SURCHARGE REVALUED ENVELOPES *On 1¢ green envelope of 1899.*

EN774	UnFVF	UseFVF
1 1/2¢ on 1¢ on amber (EN392)	60.00	—
entire	70.00	—

1925. TYPE 9 SURCHARGE REVALUED ENVELOPES *On 1¢ green envelopes of 1903 issue.*

EN775	UnFVF	UseFVF
1 1/2¢ on 1¢ on white (EN418)	1,500.00	—
entire	2,400.00	—

EN776	UnFVF	UseFVF
1 1/2¢ on 1¢ on amber (EN419)	14.00	12.00
entire	25.00	17.00
x. Double overprint	27.00	
entire	33.00	

EN777	UnFVF	UseFVF
1 1/2¢ on 1¢ on buff (EN420)	60.00	50.00
entire	70.00	60.00

1925. TYPE 9 SURCHARGE REVALUED ENVELOPES *On 1¢ oval dies of 1907-16. On Die A.*

EN778	UnFVF	UseFVF
1 1/2¢ on 1¢ on white (EN439)	2.00	1.50
entire	3.50	2.00
x. Double overprint	8.00	—
entire	—	—

EN779	UnFVF	UseFVF
1 1/2¢ on 1¢ on amber (EN440)	175.00	80.00
entire	200.00	100.00

EN780	UnFVF	UseFVF
1 1/2¢ on 1¢ on buff (EN441)	7.00	5.00
entire	12.00	7.00
x. Double overprint	—	—
entire	—	—

EN781	UnFVF	UseFVF
1 1/2¢ on 1¢ on blue (EN442)	6.00	3.00
entire	8.00	5.00

EN782	UnFVF	UseFVF
1 1/2¢ on 1¢ on manila (EN443)	25.00	11.00
entire	35.00	25.00

EN783	UnFVF	UseFVF
1 1/2¢ on 1¢ on white, Die B (EN445)	7.00	5.00

1925. TYPE 9 SURCHARGE REVALUED ENVELOPES *On Die C.*

EN784	UnFVF	UseFVF
1 1/2¢ on 1¢ on white (EN450)	17.00	9.00
entire	25.00	13.00

EN785	UnFVF	UseFVF
1 1/2¢ on 1¢ on manila (EN454)	55.00	40.00
entire	60.00	50.00

1925. TYPE 9 SURCHARGE REVALUED ENVELOPES *On Die D.*

EN786	UnFVF	UseFVF
1 1/2¢ on 1¢ on white (EN456)	4.00	1.50
entire	7.00	3.00

EN787	UnFVF	UseFVF
1 1/2¢ on 1¢ on buff (EN458)	18.00	15.00
entire	25.00	19.00

EN788	UnFVF	UseFVF
1 1/2¢ on 1¢ on blue (EN459)	6.00	5.00
entire	8.00	6.00

1925. TYPE 9 SURCHARGE REVALUED ENVELOPES *On 1¢ circular dies of 1916-50. On Die A.*

EN789	UnFVF	UseFVF
1 1/2¢ on 1¢ on white (EN520)	.40	.30
entire	.70	.40
x. Double overprint	7.00	—
entire	—	—
x1. Triple overprint	13.00	
entire	—	—

		UnFVF	UseFVF
	x2. Inverted overprint	11.00	—
	entire	—	—
EN790		**UnFVF**	**UseFVF**
1 1/2¢ on 1¢	on amber (EN521)	50.00	35.00
	entire	60.00	45.00
EN791		**UnFVF**	**UseFVF**
1 1/2¢ on 1¢	on buff (EN522)	5.00	2.00
	entire	6.00	2.00
EN792		**UnFVF**	**UseFVF**
1 1/2¢ on 1¢	on blue (EN523)	5.00	2.00
	entire	6.00	2.00
	x. Double overprint	11.00	—
	entire	—	—
EN793		**UnFVF**	**UseFVF**
1 1/2¢ on 1¢	on manila (EN524)	20.00	12.00
	entire	28.00	15.00
EN794		**UnFVF**	**UseFVF**
1 1/2¢ on 1¢	on white, Die B (EN529)	—	—
	entire	—	—

1925. Type 9 Surcharge Revalued Envelopes *On Die C.*

		UnFVF	UseFVF
EN795		**UnFVF**	**UseFVF**
1 1/2¢ on 1¢	on white (EN531)	—	—
	entire	—	—
	x. Double overprint	—	—
	entire	—	—
EN796		**UnFVF**	**UseFVF**
1 1/2¢ on 1¢	on blue (EN533)	—	—
	entire	—	—

1925. Type 9 Surcharge Revalued Envelopes *On Die D.*

		UnFVF	UseFVF
EN797		**UnFVF**	**UseFVF**
1 1/2¢ on 1¢	on white (EN534)	—	—
	entire	—	—
	x. inverted overprint	—	—
	entire	—	—
EN798		**UnFVF**	**UseFVF**
1 1/2¢ on 1¢	on amber (EN535)	—	—
	entire	—	—
EN799		**UnFVF**	**UseFVF**
1 1/2¢ on 1¢	on buff (EN536)	—	—
	entire	—	—
EN800		**UnFVF**	**UseFVF**
1 1/2¢ on 1¢	on blue (EN537)	—	—
	entire	—	—

1925. Type 9 Surcharge Revalued Envelopes *On 2¢ carmine envelopes of 1916-50 issue.*

		UnFVF	UseFVF
EN801		**UnFVF**	**UseFVF**
1 1/2¢ on 2¢	on white, Die A (EN549)	175.00	
	entire	225.00	—
EN801A		**UnFVF**	**UseFVF**
1 1/2¢ on 2¢	on white, Die E (EN566)	—	—
	entire	—	—
EN801B		**UnFVF**	**UseFVF**
1 1/2¢ on 2¢	on amber, Die E (EN567)	—	—
	entire	—	—
EN802		**UnFVF**	**UseFVF**
1 1/2¢ on 2¢	on white, Die F (EN570)	—	—
	entire	—	—
EN803		**UnFVF**	**UseFVF**
1 1/2¢ on 2¢	on white, Die H (EN574)	—	—
	entire	—	—

1925. Type 9 Surcharge Revalued Envelopes Type 9 - *magenta overprint on 1¢ green envelope of 1916-50 issue.*

		UnFVF	UseFVF
EN804		**UnFVF**	**UseFVF**
1 1/2¢ on 1¢	on white (EN531)	5.00	4.00
	entire	5.00	6.00
	x. Double overprint	30.00	—
	entire	—	—

1925. Type 10 Surcharge Revalued Envelopes *On 1¢ circular dies of 1916-50.*

½c Paid   Type 10 *surcharge - black overprint*
Santa Rosa, Cal.

		UnFVF	UseFVF
EN805		**UnFVF**	**UseFVF**
1¢ + 1/2¢	on white (EN520)	—	—
	entire	—	—

1926. Sesquicentennial Exposition Envelope

EN806 *Liberty Bell, Center bar of "E" of "POSTAGE" shorter than top bar. Watermark 27 (1925).*

		UnFVF	UseFVF
EN806		**UnFVF**	**UseFVF**
2¢	carmine on white	2.00	1.00
	entire	2.75	1.75

EN807 *The center bar of "E" in "POSTAGE" is the same length as top bar.*

		UnFVF	UseFVF
EN807		**UnFVF**	**UseFVF**
2¢	carmine on white	10.00	7.00
	entire	12.50	10.00
	FDC *(July 27, 1926)*		30.00

1932. Washington Bicentennial Issue

EN808-EN813 *Mount Vernon. All of the same design; only the denomination changes. Watermark 29 (1929).*

		UnFVF	UseFVF
EN808		**UnFVF**	**UseFVF**
1¢	green on white *(Jan. 1, 1932)*	2.00	1.50
	entire	2.50	1.75
EN809		**UnFVF**	**UseFVF**
1 1/2¢	brown on white *(Jan. 1, 1932)*	3.50	2.00
	entire	3.75	2.75
EN810		**UnFVF**	**UseFVF**
2¢	carmine on white *(Jan. 1, 1932)*	.50	.25
	entire	.75	.30
	a. carmine on blue (error), entire	27,000.00	—
	v. "S" of "POSTAGE" high	—	—
	entire	90.00	50.00
EN811		**UnFVF**	**UseFVF**
3¢	purple on white *(June 16, 1932)*	2.50	.30
	entire	4.00	.50
EN812		**UnFVF**	**UseFVF**
4¢	black on white *(Jan. 1, 1932)*	25.00	20.00
	entire*	30.00	25.00
EN813		**UnFVF**	**UseFVF**
5¢	blue on white *(Jan. 1, 1932)*	6.00	4.00
	entire	6.50	5.50

1950. Issue New Oval Design. As far back as 1941, the Post Office had submitted new designs for its envelope stamps and had ordered the necessary new printing dies to be made. The outbreak of World War II interfered with plans for the new design, and the new printing dies were not put into use. After the war, collectors brought ever-increasing pressure to bear on the Post Office Department to change the circular design, which was well into a third decade of use.

In 1950 the Post Office determined to put some of the printing dies that had been prepared in 1941 into production and ordered 1¢, 2¢ and 3¢ envelopes printed on a demonstration machine at the annual stamp exhibition sponsored by the American Stamp Dealers Association in New York. Only a very few of the old dies were found to be usable in the more modern machines then in use. However, at least one printing die in each denomination was put into use, and the envelopes were then printed and sold at the ASDA stamp show.

New printing dies immediately were developed so that the new design could replace completely the old design. These first-printed envelopes are in very short supply. *These envelopes were issued on white paper only.*

EN814 *Franklin. Die A, thick, short, "1" within heavy circle.*

EN814

		UnFVF	UseFVF
1¢	**green,** Die A *(Nov. 16, 1950)*	6.00	2.00
	entire*	8.00	3.00

EN815 *Die B, thin, long "1" within thin circle, "E" in "ONE" has long bars and is close. (1mm) to circle.*

EN815

		UnFVF	UseFVF
1¢	**green,** Die B	7.00	4.00
	entire	9.00	4.50

EN816 *Die C, thin long "1." "E" in "ONE" with short bars and far (1 1/2mm) from circle.*

EN816

		UnFVF	UseFVF
1¢	**green,** Die C	7.00	4.00
	entire	9.00	4.50
	v. precanceled, entire	1.00	1.00

EN817 *Washington*

EN817

		UnFVF	UseFVF
1 1/2¢	**brown**	5.00	4.00
	entire	6.00	5.00
	v. precanceled, entire	1.25	1.25

EN818 *Washington. Die A, figure "2" set low in heavy circle.*

EN818

		UnFVF	UseFVF
2¢	**carmine,** Die A *(Nov. 17, 1950)*	.80	.35
	entire*	1.50	.50

EN818A *Die B, thin "2" with long hook. Center cross bar of "E" in "STATES" shorter than top or bottom bars.*

EN818A

		UnFVF	UseFVF
2¢	**carmine,** Die B	1.50	1.00
	entire	2.00	1.10

EN819 *Die C, thin "2" set high in thin circle.*

EN819

		UnFVF	UseFVF
2¢	**carmine,** Die C	.80	.30
	entire	1.50	.50

EN819A *Washington. Die D, thick cross bar in "A" of "STATES."*

EN819A

		UnFVF	UseFVF
2¢	**carmine,** Die D	1.50	.70
	entire	1.60	.70

EN820 *Die A, tall, thick "3" within thick circle. Narrow "Es" in "THREE."*

EN820

		UnFVF	UseFVF
3¢	**purple,** Die A *(Nov. 18, 1950)*	2.25	.85
	entire*	.30	1.50

EN821 *Die B, tall, thin, "3" in thin circle. Narrow "Es" in "THREE."*

EN821

		UnFVF	UseFVF
3¢	**purple,** Die B *(Nov. 19, 1950)*	.85	.60
	entire*	1.60	.65

EN822 *Die C, short "3" in thin circle. Wide "Es" in "THREE." Line from left stand of "N" in "UNITED" to stand in "E" in "POSTAGE" well below chin.*

EN822

		UnFVF	UseFVF
3¢	**purple,** Die C	.60	.35
	entire	1.00	.50

EN823 *Die D, short "3" in thin circle. Wide "Es" in "THREE." Line from left stand of "N" in "UNITED" to stand of "E" in "POSTAGE" almost touches chin. "N" in "UNITED" short; thin cross bar in "A" in "STATES."*

EN823

		UnFVF	UseFVF
3¢	**purple,** Die D	.50	.25
	entire	.65	.30

EN824 *Die E, similar to EN823 except "N" in "UNITED" tall, and thick cross bar in "A" in "STATES."*

EN824

		UnFVF	UseFVF
3¢	**purple,** Die E	.90	.50
	entire	1.35	.75

1958. ISSUE On Aug. 1, 1958, First Class postage rates were raised to 4¢. This necessitated new 4¢ stamped envelopes. In addition, to use up surplus stocks of 2¢ and 3¢ envelopes, the Post Office Department again revalued existing stocks.

EN825 *Franklin. Die A, head high in oval. Circle around "4" low (1mm from outer edge of color). Watermarks 46, 47, 48.*

EN825

		UnFVF	UseFVF
4¢	**lilac,** Die A *(Aug. 1, 1958)*	.90	.25
	entire	1.00	.30

EN826 *Die B, head low in oval. Circle around "4" high (1 1/2mm from outer edge of color). To verify: right leg of "A" in "POSTAGE" shorter than left leg. Short leg on "P."*

EN826

		UnFVF	UseFVF
4¢	**lilac,** Die B	1.10	.25
	entire	1.40	.35

EN827 *Die C, head centered in oval. Circle around "4" high as on Die B. To verify: legs of "A" in "POSTAGE" are about equal in length. Long leg on "P."*

EN827

		UnFVF	UseFVF
4¢	**lilac,** Die C	1.25	.25
	entire	1.40	.35

1958. TYPE 11 SURCHARGE REVALUED ENVELOPES

Type 11 *surcharge - overprint in green to left of stamp. On 3¢ purple of 1916-50 issue.*

EN828

		UnFVF	UseFVF
3¢ + 1¢	**purple,** Die A (EN588)	15.00	11.00
	entire	16.00	—

EN829

		UnFVF	UseFVF
3¢ + 1¢	**purple,** Die H (EN603)	12.00	10.00
	entire	15.00	—

EN830

		UnFVF	UseFVF
3¢ + 1¢	**purple,** Die I (EN606)	35.00	20.00
	entire	40.00	—

1958. TYPE 11 SURCHARGE REVALUED ENVELOPES *On 3¢ purple of 1950.*

EN831

		UnFVF	UseFVF
3¢ + 1¢	**purple,** Die B (EN821)	—	—
	entire	1,100.00	—

EN832

		UnFVF	UseFVF
3¢ + 1¢	**purple,** Die C (EN822)	.60	.25
	entire	.70	.35

EN833

		UnFVF	UseFVF
3¢ + 1¢	**purple,** Die D (EN823)	.85	.25
	entire	1.00	.25
	quintuple surcharge	—	—

EN834

		UnFVF	UseFVF
3¢ + 1¢	**purple,** Die E (EN824)	.85	.25
	entire	1.10	.25

1958. TYPE 12 SURCHARGE REVALUED ENVELOPES *On 2¢ circular dies of 1916-1950.*

Type 12 *surcharge - overprint in red to left of stamp.*

EN835

		UnFVF	UseFVF
2¢ + 2¢	**carmine,** Die A (EN549)	4.00	2.00
	entire	4.50	—
	Double surcharge	—	

EN836

		UnFVF	UseFVF
2¢ + 2¢	**carmine,** Die H (EN574)	11.00	8.00
	entire	13.00	—

EN837

		UnFVF	UseFVF
2¢ + 2¢	**carmine,** Die I (EN581)	6.00	6.00
	entire	7.50	—

1958. TYPE 12 SURCHARGE REVALUED ENVELOPES *On 2¢ oval die of 1950.*

EN838

		UnFVF	UseFVF
2¢ + 2¢	**carmine,** Die A (EN818)	.90	.40
	entire	1.10	.50

EN839

		UnFVF	UseFVF
2¢ + 2¢	**carmine,** Die B (EN818A)	1.10	—
	entire	1.50	—

EN840

		UnFVF	UseFVF
2¢ + 2¢	**carmine,** Die C (EN819)	.90	.35
	entire	1.10	—

EN841

		UnFVF	UseFVF
2¢ + 2¢	**carmine,** Die D (EN819A)	.90	—
	entire	1.25	—

1960. ISSUE Effective July 1, 1960, the Third Class postage rate for bulk mailing was raised to 2 1/2¢ for commercial users and 1 1/4¢ for non-profit organizations. These envelopes are available only precanceled and were sold only to holders of proper permits. The small size of each (No. 6 3/4), however, were made available to collectors at COMPEX in Chicago (commercial rate) and DIXIPEX in Birmingham, Ala. (non-profit rate), and were on sale at the Philatelic Agency until Dec. 31, 1960. These unprecanceled envelopes have gum on the top back flap, and the precanceled envelopes are without such gum.

EN842 *Washington*

EN842

		UnFVF	UseFVF
2 1/2¢	**blue** on white *(May 28, 1960)*	.90	.60
	entire	1.00	.70
	v. precanceled	.25	.25
	entire	.30	.30

EN843 *Die A, small "1 1/4." 2 1/4mm across bar of "4." Leaf cluster 2mm under "U."*

EN843

		UnFVF	UseFVF
1 1/4¢	**turquoise** on white, Die A *(June 25, 1960)*	.85	.60
	entire*	1.00	.65
	v. precanceled	.25	.25
	entire	.25	.25

EN843A *Die B, large "1 1/4." 2 3/4mm across bar of "4." Leaf cluster 1mm under "U."*

EN843A

		UnFVF	UseFVF
1 1/4¢	**turquoise** on white		2.00
	precanceled	3.00	3.00
	entire	3.50	3.50

EN844 *Pony Express Rider. Watermark 46.*

EN844		UnFVF	UseFVF
4¢	**brown** on white, blue inside *(July 19, 1960)*	.65	.35
	entire	.85	.50

1963. ISSUE Effective Jan. 7, 1963, First Class postage rates were raised to 5¢. A new stamped envelope was prepared showing a bust of Lincoln. However, a sufficient number of working dies were unable to be delivered to service all of the machines at the factory. Hence the factory was authorized to continue printing 4¢ stamped envelopes and revalue them to 5¢. This was accomplished by using the Type 11 surcharge printed in green to the left of the stamp. The revaluing was done on unfolded envelope blanks on the regular printing machines at the factory. These blanks were then passed to another machine, which printed the 4¢ stamps and folded the envelopes. At least two different dies were used to print the added 1¢ value.

While the effective date for the new postage rates was not until Jan. 7, 1963, the Post Office made the new envelopes available as rapidly as they could be supplied. The authorized first day of issue for the 5¢ Lincoln envelope was Nov. 19, 1962. No announcement was made regarding the 4¢ revalued envelopes, but they began making their appearance at post offices in December 1962.

All of these new envelopes are known with *watermarks 47 and 48.*

Note: EN846v and EN847v are the result of using the O'Connell machines to fold blanks on which the stamps already had been printed by the Huckins (Die B) and Harris (Die C) machines, which were incapable of folding. To accomplish the folding operation, the ink fountains were removed from some of the O'Connell machines still idle for lack of working dies of the 5¢ stamp. By error, the old 4¢ die was not removed on at least one of the O'Connell machines, and this caused an albino impression of the 4¢ stamp to be printed over the 5¢ stamp. The error was not discovered until the O'Connell machine(s) had been performing the folding operation for some time.

EN845 *Abraham Lincoln. Die A, figure "5" centered in circle. Middle bar of "E" in "FIVE" equal length as top. Center bar in "E" in "POSTAGE" off center to top. Verification: small head, sharp pointed nose. Watermarks 47, 48.*

Watermark 47.

Beginning in May 1961, a new watermark was introduced to mark the letting of the new contract. Two types were adopted: a star preceding the letters "USA" for paper manufactured by the International Paper Co. (wmk. 47); star following the letters "USA" (wmk. 48) for paper manufactured by the Howard Paper Co.

EN845		UnFVF	UseFVF
5¢	**dark blue,** Die A	1.00	.35
	entire	1.00	.35

EN846 *Die B, "5" centered in circle. "FI" in "FIVE" close together. "C" in "CENTS" higher than "E." Verification: large wide head with blunt nose.*

EN846		UnFVF	UseFVF
5¢	**dark blue,** Die B	.75	.25
	entire	1.00	.30
	v. with albino impression of 4¢, entire	75.00	—

EN847 *Die C, "5" to right in circle. Short leg on "P" in "POSTAGE."*

EN847		UnFVF	UseFVF
5¢	**dark blue,** Die C *(Nov. 19, 1962)*	1.00	.40
	entire	1.25	.50
	v. with albino impression of 4¢, entire	75.00	—

1963. TYPE 11 SURCHARGE REVALUED ENVELOPES Two types of the surcharge are known:

Type I: large word "CENT," dot after "U" and "S" far from letters, long angle serif on center bar of "E."
Type II: small word "CENT," dot after "U" and "S."

Type 11 *surcharge - printed in green to left of stamp on 4¢ envelope EN825.*

EN848		UnFVF	UseFVF
4¢ + 1¢	**lilac, green** Type I (EN825)	1.50	.50
	entire	1.75	.75
	v. Type II	1.50	.50
	entire	1.75	.75

1964. NEW YORK WORLD'S FAIR ISSUE

EN849 *Globe and orbit rings*

EN849		UnFVF	UseFVF
5¢	**red** on white *(April 22, 1964)*	.70	.50
	entire	.80	.50

1965. NEW ISSUE Beginning Jan. 1, 1965, the United States Envelope Co. was awarded the contract for making envelopes. This firm established a new facility at Williamsburg, Pa., and equipped it with new machinery that would produce envelopes from a continuous web (roll) of paper. The process is very rapid, with each individual machine being capable of producing one million envelopes every 24 hours. Envelopes produced by this method are of the old low-back design.

Watermark 49

New watermarks were introduced, as illustrated. Watermarks 47 and 48 also are known on these envelopes. Watermark 49 has the star below the letter "S" of "USA" and signifies the product of the Oxford Paper Co. Watermark 50 has the star above the "S" and distinguishes the product of Crown Zellerbach.

Also, a new watermark closely resembling Watermark 47 (star before "USA") but with a star somewhat larger distinguishes the product of the Champion Paper Co.

The small size (No. 6 3/4) and large size (No. 10) of the 5¢ envelopes (EN852), both regular and window, also exist tagged, consisting of a vertical luminescent rectangle to the left of the stamp. This method of tagging also was used for the 8¢ air mail envelopes in both sizes (AEN38).

EN850 *Liberty Bell. The wavy lines at the sides indicate the stamp is precanceled.*

EN850

1 1/4¢	brown on white *(Jan. 6, 1965)*	UnFVF	UseFVF
		.25	.25
	entire	1.00	.25

EN851 *USS Constitution "Old Ironsides" under sail*

EN851

4¢	bright blue on white *(Jan. 6, 1965)*	UnFVF	UseFVF
		.85	.25
	entire	1.00	.25

EN852 *Eagle*

EN852

5¢	purple on white *(Jan. 5, 1965)*	UnFVF	UseFVF
		.80	.25
	entire	.90	.30
	z. Tagged *(Aug. 15, 1967)*	1.10	.25
	entire	1.35	.35

1968. Type 12 Surcharge Envelopes *Printed in red to left of stamp on 4¢ envelope (EN851).*

EN853

4¢ + 2¢	bright blue, red on white *(Feb. 1968)*	UnFVF	UseFVF
		3.50	2.00
	entire	4.50	2.50

1968. Type 11 Surcharge Envelopes *Printed in green to left of stamp on 5¢ envelope (EN852).*

EN854

5¢ + 1¢	purple, green on white *(Feb. 1968)*	UnFVF	UseFVF
		3.50	2.00
	entire	4.25	2.50
	z. Tagged *(Feb. 5, 1968)*	3.50	2.00
	entire	4.25	2.50

1968. Type 12 Surcharge Error Envelopes *Printed in red to left of stamp on 5¢ envelope (EN852).*

EN854A

5¢ + 2¢	purple, red on white	UnFVF	UseFVF
		—	—
	entire	200.00	

EN855 *Statue of Liberty*

EN855

6¢	turquoise green on white, tagged *(Jan. 4, 1968)*	UnFVF	UseFVF
		.75	.25
	entire	1.00	.35

EN855 is tagged with luminescent materials mixed with the printing ink.

EN856 *Liberty Bell. The wavy lines at sides indicate the envelope is precanceled.*

EN856

1.4¢	brown on white *(March 26, 1968)*	UnFVF	UseFVF
		.25	.25
	entire	1.25	.35

EN857

1.6¢	orange on white *(June 16, 1969)*	UnFVF	UseFVF
		.25	.25
	entire	1.00	.25

EN858

1.7¢	purple on white *(May 10, 1971)*	UnFVF	UseFVF
		.25	.25
	entire	.50	.25

1970. Herman Melville Issue honored the writer and the whaling industry.

EN859 *Herman Melville's* Moby Dick

EN859

6¢	light blue on white, tagged *(March 7, 1970)*	UnFVF	UseFVF
		.50	.25
	entire	.70	.35

1971. White House Conference on Youth

EN860 *White House Conference on Youth emblem*

EN860

6¢	light blue on white, tagged *(Feb. 24, 1971)*	UnFVF	UseFVF
		.75	.25
	entire	1.00	.50

1971. Issue Issued to meet new first class postage rate.

EN861 *Eagle*

EN861

8¢	ultramarine on white, tagged *(May 6, 1971)*	UnFVF	UseFVF
		.50	.25
	entire	.75	.30

1971. Type 13 Surcharge Envelopes

Type 13 *surcharge - in green to left of stamp on EN855 or EN860.*

EN862

6¢	turquoise green (EN855), + 2¢ green on white, tagged *(May 16, 1971)*	UnFVF	UseFVF
		1.00	.50
	entire	1.25	.50

EN863

6¢	light blue (EN860) + 2¢ green on white, tagged *(May 16, 1971)*	UnFVF	UseFVF
		2.00	1.00
	entire	2.75	1.50

Sale of EN863, of which one million were produced, was limited to Washington D.C.

> Generally speaking, the more nearly equal in width all margins of a stamp are, and the farther those equal margins are from the printed design, the more desirable the stamp will be to the collector.

1971. BOWLING ISSUE honored the seventh World Tournament of the International Bowling Federation.

EN864 *Bowling ball and pin*

EN864		UnFVF	UseFVF
8¢	red on white, tagged *(Aug. 21, 1971)*	.50	.25
	entire	.75	.25

Available in both #6 small and #10 large size. EN864 is the first commemorative envelope since the Washington Bicentennial of 1932 to be available in two sizes.

1971. THE WHITE HOUSE CONFERENCE ON AGING ISSUE

EN865 *Snowflake*

EN865		UnFVF	UseFVF
8¢	blue on white, tagged *(Nov. 15, 1977)*	.50	.25
	entire	.75	.25

1972. FIRST U.S. INTERNATIONAL TRANSPORTATION EXPOSITION ISSUE

EN866 *Transpo 72 emblem*

EN866		UnFVF	UseFVF
8¢	red and blue on white, tagged *(May 2, 1972)*	.75	.25
	entire	1.00	.25

1973. ISSUE Issued to meet new First Class postage rate.

EN867 *Liberty Bell*

EN867		UnFVF	UseFVF
10¢	turquoise green on white, tagged *(Dec. 5, 1973)*	.50	.25
	entire	.50	.25

1973. TYPE 12 SURCHARGE ENVELOPES

Type 12 *surcharge - in ultramarine to left of stamp on EN861.*

EN868		UnFVF	UseFVF
8¢ + 2¢	ultramarine, ultramarine on white, tagged *(Dec. 1, 1973)*	.50	.25
	entire	.50	.20

1974. TENNIS CENTENNIAL

EN869 *Tennis centennial*

EN869		UnFVF	UseFVF
10¢	yellow, green and blue on white, tagged, *(Aug. 31, 1974)*	.85	.50
	entire	.85	.50

1974. NON-PROFIT BULK MAILING

EN870 *Volunteerism*

EN870		UnFVF	UseFVF
1.8¢	blue green on white, tagged, *(Aug. 23, 1974)*	.35	.25
	entire	—	—

Bicentennial Era Series

1975. SEAFARING TRADITION ISSUE in the Bicentennial Era Series.

EN871 *Compass rose*

EN871		UnFVF	UseFVF
10¢	brown and blue on light brown, tagged, *(Oct. 13, 1975)*	.50	.25
	entire	.50	.30
	a. Brown omitted, entire	125.00	
	FDC		1.75

1975. ISSUE in the Bicentennial Era Series met new First Class postage rate.

EN872 *Liberty tree*

EN872		UnFVF	UseFVF
13¢	brown on white, tagged, *(Nov. 8, 1975)*	.50	.25
	entire	.50	.30
	FDC		1.75

1976. THE AMERICAN HOME MAKER ISSUE in the Bicentennial Era Series.

EN873 *Quilt pattern*

EN873

		UnFVF	UseFVF
13¢	**brown and bluish green** on light brown, tagged, *(Feb. 2, 1976)*	.50	.25
	entire	.50	.30
	a. Brown omitted, entire	125.00	
	FDC		1.75

1976. AMERICAN FARMER ISSUE in the Bicentennial Era Series.

EN874 *Sheaf of wheat*

EN874

		UnFVF	UseFVF
13¢	**brown and green** on light brown, tagged, *(March 15, 1976)*	.50	.25
	entire	.50	.30
	a. Brown omitted, entire	125.00	
	FDC		1.25

1976. AMERICAN DOCTOR ISSUE in the Bicentennial Era Series.

EN875 *Mortar and pestle*

EN875

		UnFVF	UseFVF
13¢	**orange and brown** on light brown, tagged, *(June 30, 1976)*	.50	.25
	entire	.50	.30
	a. Brown omitted, entire	—	
	FDC		2.50

1976. AMERICAN CRAFTSMAN ISSUE in the Bicentennial Era Series.

EN876 *Craftsman's tools*

EN876

		UnFVF	UseFVF
13¢	**red and brown** on light brown, tagged, *(Aug. 6, 1976)*	.50	.25
	entire	.50	.30
	a. Brown omitted, entire	125.00	
	FDC		1.75

1976. NON-PROFIT MAILING ISSUE

EN877 *Star in pinwheel*

EN877

		UnFVF	UseFVF
2¢	**red** on white, *(Sept. 10, 1976)*	.35	.25
	entire	.35	.50
	FDC		1.75

1976. ISSUE in the Bicentennial Era Series.

EN878 *Centennial envelope design*

EN878

		UnFVF	UseFVF
13¢	**green** on white, tagged, *(Oct. 15, 1976)*	.50	.25
	entire	.50	.25
	FDC		1.75

1977. GOLF ISSUE *Printed by gravure, in addition to embossing.*

EN879 *Golf club in motion and ball*

EN879

		UnFVF	UseFVF
13¢	**blue, black and yellow green** on white, tagged, *(April 7, 1977)*	1.00	.50
	entire	1.00	.50
	a. black omitted, entire*	250.00	
	b. black and blue omitted, entire*	250.00	
	c. blue, black and yelllow green omitted, entire*	250.00	
	FDC		7.00

1977. NON-PROFIT MAILING ISSUE

EN880 *"2.1¢" in octagon*

EN880

		UnFVF	UseFVF
2.1¢	**yellow green** on white, *(June 3, 1977)*	.50	.25
	entire	.50	.25
	FDC		1.75

1977. ENERGY ISSUE

EN881 *Energy conservation*

EN881

		UnFVF	UseFVF
13¢	**black, red and yellow** on white, tagged, *(Oct. 20, 1977)*	.50	.25
	entire	.50	.25
	a. black omitted, entire	—	
	b. black and red omitted, entire	475.00	
	c. red and yellow omitted, entire		
	d. yellow omitted, entire FDC *(Oct. 20, 1977)*	—	
	e. black, red, yellow and tagging omitted		

EN882 *Energy development*

EN882		UnFVF	UseFVF
13¢	**black, red and yellow** on white	.60	.30
	entire	.60	.30
	FDC		1.75

1978. "A" NON-DENOMINATED ISSUE to accommodate new 15¢ First Class postage rate. The envelope was printed in 1975 and 1976 and stored for contingency use.

EN883 *Stylized eagle and "A"*

EN883		UnFVF	UseFVF
15¢	**orange** on white, tagged, *(May 22, 1978)*	.60	.25
	entire	.70	.25
	FDC		2.00

1978. UNCLE SAM ISSUE

EN884 *Stylized Uncle Sam hat and shield*

EN884		UnFVF	UseFVF
15¢	**red** on white, tagged *(June 3, 1978)*	.50	.25
	entire	.60	.25
	FDC		1.75

1978. NON-PROFIT MAILING ISSUE

EN885 *"2.7¢" over "USA"*

EN885		UnFVF	UseFVF
2.7¢	**green** on white *(July 5, 1978)*	.25	.25
	entire	.40	.25
	FDC		1.75

1978. TYPE 14 SURCHARGE REVALUED ISSUE *Downward re-valuing.*

Type 14 *surcharge - in black to left of stamp.*

EN886		UnFVF	UseFVF
15¢ on 16¢	**blue** on white, tagged *(July 28, 1978)*	.45	.25
	entire	.60	.25
	t. Surcharge omitted, entire	400.00	—
	z. Tagging omitted	—	—
	FDC		1.75

1978. AUTO RACING ISSUE

EN887 *Indianapolis 500 racer*

EN887		UnFVF	UseFVF
15¢	**black, blue and red** on white, tagged *(Sept. 2, 1975)*	.45	.25
	entire	.50	.25
	a. black omitted, entire	175.00	—
	b. black and blue omitted, entire	—	—
	c. red omitted, entire	—	—
	d. red and blue omitted, entire	—	—
	e. black, blue and red omitted, entire	—	—
	z. Tagging omitted	—	—
	FDC		1.75

1978. TYPE 14 SURCHARGE REVALUED ISSUE *(EN872) Liberty tree re-valued.*

Type 14 *surcharge - in black to left of stamp*

EN888		UnFVF	UseFVF
15¢ on 13¢	**brown** on white (EN872), tagged *(Nov. 28, 1978)*	.40	.25
	entire	.55	.25
	FDC		1.75

1979. NON-PROFIT MAILING ISSUE

EN889 *Authorized nonprofit organization*

EN889		UnFVF	UseFVF
3.1¢	**blue** on white *(May 18, 1979)*	.25	.25
	entire	.30	.25
	FDC		1.75

1979. VETERINARY MEDICINE ISSUE

EN890 *"V" on staff of Aesculapius*

EN890		UnFVF	UseFVF
15¢	**gray and brown** on white, tagged *(July 24, 1979)*	.40	.25
	entire	.55	.25
	a. gray omitted, entire	700.00	—
	b. brown omitted, entire	—	—
	c. gray, brown and tagging omitted, entire	—	—
	FDC		1.75

1979. OLYMPIC GAMES ISSUE *Soccer*

EN891 *1980 Moscow Olympics, soccer players on envelope*

EN891

15¢	**red, green and black** on white, tagged *(Dec. 10, 1979)*	UnFVF .75	UseFVF .25
	entire	1.00	.25
	a. black omitted, entire	175.00	—
	b. black and green omitted, entire	175.00	—
	c. red omitted, entire	—	—
	d. red and green omitted, entire	175.00	—
	e. red, green and black omitted, entire	—	—
	f. red, green black and tagging omitted, entire	—	—
	FDC		1.75

1980. BICYCLING ISSUE

EN892 *High-wheel bicycle*

EN892

15¢	**blue and maroon** on white, tagged *(May 16, 1980)*	UnFVF .50	UseFVF .25
	entire	.65	.25
	a. blue omitted, entire	150.00	—
	FDC		1.75

1980. NON-PROFIT MAILING ISSUE

EN893 *Weaver violins*

EN893

3.5¢	**purple** on white *(June 23, 1980)*	UnFVF .25	UseFVF .25
	entire	.35	.25
	FDC		1.75

1980. AMERICA'S CUP YACHT RACES ISSUE

EN894 *Yacht*

EN894

15¢	**red & blue** on white, tagged *(Sept. 15, 1980)*	UnFVF .50	UseFVF .25
	entire	.65	.25
	FDC		1.75

1980. HONEYBEE ISSUE *Printed by gravure, in addition to embossing.*

EN895 *Orange blossom and honeybee*

EN895

15¢	**green and yellow** on white, tagged *(Oct. 10, 1980)*	UnFVF .50	UseFVF .25
	entire	.55	.25

	a. brown omitted, entire	200.00	—
	FDC		1.75

1981. "B" NON-DENOMINATED ISSUE to accommodate new First Class postage rate.

EN896 *Stylized eagle and "B"*

EN896

18¢	**purple** on white, tagged *(March 15, 1981)*	UnFVF .50	UseFVF .25
	entire	.55	.25
	FDC		1.75

1981. STAR ISSUE Denominated to meet new First Class postage rate.

EN897 *Star*

EN897

18¢	**blue** on white, tagged *(April 2, 1981)*	UnFVF .50	UseFVF .25
	entire	.55	.25
	FDC		1.75

1981. BLINDED VETERANS ASSOCIATION ISSUE

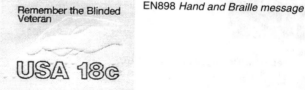

EN898 *Hand and Braille message*

EN898

18¢	**blue** on white, tagged *(Aug. 13, 1981)*	UnFVF .40	UseFVF .25
	entire	.60	.25
	a. red omitted, entire	250.00	
	blue omitted, entire	—	
	FDC		1.75

The hand and Braille message are embossed without color.

1981. "C" NON-DENOMINATED ISSUE met the new First Class postage rate.

EN899 *Stylized eagle and "C"*

EN899

20¢	**brown** on white, tagged *(Oct. 11, 1981)*	UnFVF .50	UseFVF .25
	entire	.55	.25
	FDC		1.75

1981. CAPITOL DOME ISSUE

EN900 *Dome of U.S. Capitol*

EN900		UnFVF	UseFVF
20¢	**dark red** on white, tagged *(Nov. 13, 1981)*	.50	.25
	entire	5.15	.25
	z. Bar tagged	2.00	2.00
	FDC		1.75

1982. NON-PROFIT BULK MAILING ISSUE

 EN901

EN901		UnFVF	UseFVF
5.9¢	**brown** on white *(Feb. 17, 1982)*	.25	.25
	entire	.35	.25
	FDC		1.75

1982. GREAT SEAL OF THE UNITED STATES BICENTENNIAL ISSUE

 EN902 *Great Seal*

EN902		UnFVF	UseFVF
20¢	**blue, black and red** on white, tagged *(June 15, 1982)*	.50	.25
	entire	.55	.25
	a. blue omitted, entire	165.00	
	blue and red omitted	—	—
	FDC		1.75

1982. PURPLE HEART BICENTENNIAL ISSUE

 EN903 *Purple Heart medal*

EN903		UnFVF	UseFVF
20¢	**purple and black** on white, tagged *(Aug. 6, 1982)*	.50	.25
	entire	.55	.25
	FDC		2.00

1983. NON-PROFIT MAILING ISSUE

 EN904 *Olive branches*

EN904		UnFVF	UseFVF
5.2¢	**orange** on white *(March 21, 1983)*	.25	.25
	entire	.25	.25
	FDC		1.75

1983. PARALYZED VETERANS ISSUE

 EN905 *Wheelchair*

EN905		UnFVF	UseFVF
20¢	**red, blue and black** on white, tagged *(Aug. 3, 1983)*	.50	.25

entire		.55	.25
a. blue omitted, entire		350.00	
b. blue and black omitted, entire		150.00	
c. red omitted, entire		350.00	
d. red and black omitted, entire		150.00	
e. black omitted, entire		325.00	
FDC			1.75

1984. SMALL BUSINESS ISSUE

 EN906 *Business signs*

EN906		UnFVF	UseFVF
20¢	**multicolored** on white, tagged *(May 7, 1984)*	.60	.25
	entire	.65	.25
	FDC		1.75

1985. "D" NON-DENOMINATED ISSUE met the new First Class postage rate.

 EN907 *Stylized eagle and "D"*

EN907		UnFVF	UseFVF
22¢	**green** on white, tagged *(Feb. 1, 1985)*	.50	.25
	entire	.65	.25
	FDC		1.75

1985. AMERICAN BISON ISSUE

 EN908 *Bison*

EN908		UnFVF	UseFVF
22¢	**brown** on white, tagged *(Feb. 25, 1985)*	.50	.25
	entire	.60	.25
	z. Double tagged, phosphorescent ink and separate bar tagging	—	
	z1. Untagged (precanceled)		
	FDC		1.75

1985. NON-PROFIT MAILING ISSUE

 EN909 *U.S.S. Constitution*

EN909		UnFVF	UseFVF
6¢	**aqua** on white *(May 3, 1985)*	.25	.25
	entire	.30	.25
	black omitted	—	
	FDC		1.75

1986. THE *MAYFLOWER* ISSUE

 EN910 *Mayflower, gulls*

EN910
		UnFVF	UseFVF
8.5¢	**black and gray** on white, precanceled (Dec. 4, 1986)	.25	.25
	entire	.35	.25
	FDC		1.75

1988. STARS ISSUE *Printed by letterpress in addition to embossing.*

EN911 *Circle of stars*

EN911
		UnFVF	UseFVF
25¢	**red and blue** on white, tagged (March 26, 1988)	.60	.25
	entire	.75	.35
	a. red omitted, entire	95.00	
	b. red and tagging omitted, entire	125.00	—
	z. Tagging omitted, entire	—	—
	FDC		1.75

1988. NON-PROFIT MAILING ISSUE *U.S.S. Constellation.*

EN912 *U.S.S. Constellation*

EN912
		UnFVF	UseFVF
8.4¢	**black and blue** on white, precanceled (April 12, 1988)	.30	.25
	entire	.50	.25
	a. black omitted, entire	—	—
	z. Tagging omitted	—	—
	FDC		1.75

1988. HOLIDAY GREETING SNOWFLAKE ISSUE *Printed by letterpress.*

EN913 *Snowflake*

EN913
		UnFVF	UseFVF
25¢	**red and green** on white, tagged (Sept. 8, 1988)	.60	.30
	entire	.75	.35
	FDC		1.75

1989. PHILATELIC ISSUE *Printed by letterpress.*

EN914 *Circle of stars in stamp field*

EN914
		UnFVF	UseFVF
25¢	**red and blue on white,** tagged (March 10, 1989)	.50	.25
	entire*	.65	.30
	FDC		1.75

1989. SECURITY MAIL ISSUE *Printed by letterpress.*

EN915 *Circle of stars*

EN915
		UnFVF	UseFVF
25¢	**red and blue** on white, tagged (July 10, 1989)	.50	.25
	entire	.60	.30
	FDC		1.75

Envelope is blue on inside to provide security for enclosures.

1989. LOVE ISSUE *Printed by offset and letterpress.*

EN916 *Love*

EN916
		UnFVF	UseFVF
25¢	**red and blue** on white, tagged (Sept. 22, 1989)	.50	.25
	entire	.60	.30
	a. blue omitted, entire	—	—
	b. red and blue omitted, entire	—	—
	FDC		1.75

1989. WORLD STAMP EXPO '89 ISSUE *Printed by letterpress, with foil hologram used for first time by U.S.*

EN917 *Space station and shuttle*

EN917
		UnFVF	UseFVF
25¢	**ultramarine,** tagged (Dec. 3, 1989)	.50	.30
	entire	1.00	.75
	a. ultramarine omitted, entire	575.00	
	FDC		1.75

A hologram is affixed at upper right inside, visible through a die cut window.

1990. FOOTBALL ISSUE *Printed by letterpress, with hologram.*

EN918 *Football players and Lombardi trophy*

EN918
		UnFVF	UseFVF
25¢	**vermilion,** tagged (Sept. 9, 1990)	.50	.30
	entire	1.00	.75
	FDC		4.00

A hologram is affixed at upper right inside, visible through a die cut window.

1991. STAR ISSUE met the new First Class postage rate. *Printed by letterpress, with embossing.*

EN919 *Star*

EN919		UnFVF	UseFVF
29¢	**ultramarine and rose** on white, tagged	.70	.35
	(Jan. 24, 1991)		
	entire	.85	.45
	a. ultramarine omitted	750.00	
	b. rose omitted	325.00	
	FDC		1.75

1991. NON-PROFIT MAILING ISSUE *Printed by letterpress.*

EN920 *Sparrows on wires*

EN920		UnFVF	UseFVF
11.1¢	**red and blue** on white, tagged,	.25	.25
	precanceled *(May 3, 1991)*		
	entire	.40	.30
	FDC		1.75

1991. LOVE ISSUE in the Love Series. *Printed by offset.*

EN921 *Love*

EN921		UnFVF	UseFVF
29¢	**blue, maroon and rose** on white, tagged	.65	.35
	(May 9, 1991)		
	entire	.75	.40
	a. rose omitted	—	
	FDC		1.75

1991. SECURITY ISSUE *Printed by letterpress.*

EN922 *Star*

EN922		UnFVF	UseFVF
29¢	**ultramarine and rose** on white, tagged	.65	.35
	(July 20, 1991)		
	entire*	.75	.40
	a. ultramarine omitted, entire	575.00	
	b. rose omitted, entire	—	
	FDC		1.75

The inside of the envelope has a blue design as a security precaution for enclosures.

1991. MAGAZINE INDUSTRY ISSUE *Printed by offset and letterpress, with gravure-printed vignette affixed through a die-cut window.*

EN923 *Stylized globe 250th anniversary, magazine industry*

Creating a Brighter World

EN923		UnFVF	UseFVF
29¢	**multicolored** on white, tagged	.65	.35
	(Oct. 7, 1991)		
	entire*	.75	.40
	FDC		1.75

1991. COUNTRY GEESE ISSUE *Printed by offset and letterpress.*

EN924 *Geese*

EN924		UnFVF	UseFVF
29¢	**bluish gray and yellow,** tagged	.65	.35
	(Nov. 8, 1990)		
	entire	.75	.40
	FDC		1.75

1992. SPACE STATION HOLOGRAM ISSUE *Printed by letterpress, with hologram.*

EN925 *Space station and shuttle*

EN925		UnFVF	UseFVF
29¢	**yellow green** on white, tagged	.65	.35
	(Jan. 21, 1992)		
	entire*	.75	.40
	FDC		1.75

A hologram is affixed at upper right inside, visible through a die cut window.

1992. WESTERN AMERICANA ISSUE *Printed by offset and letterpress.*

EN926 *Western saddle*

EN926		UnFVF	UseFVF
29¢	**multicolored** on white, tagged	.60	.35
	(April 10, 1992)		
	entire*	.75	.40
	FDC		1.75

A vignette, printed by offset, is affixed through a die cut window at upper right.

1992. PROTECT THE ENVIRONMENT ISSUE *Printed by offset and letterpress.*

EN927 *Hillebrandia*

EN927		UnFVF	UseFVF
29¢	**multicolored** on white, tagged	.60	.35
	(April 22, 1992)		
	entire*	.75	.40
	FDC		1.75

A vignette, printed by offset, is affixed at upper right inside, visible through a die cut window.

1992. RE-ISSUES ON RECYCLED PAPER ISSUE

All of the envelopes in this series have the "Recycle" tri-arrow logo on the reverse. Unwatermarked envelopes and/or those available only in large (No. 10) size are marked. This series is listed only as entires, to enable inclusion both of the "Recycle" logo and to verify watermarking. *Issued May 1, 1992.*

EN928		UnFVF	UseFVF
29¢	**ultramarine** on white, unwatermarked, tagged, entire (EN919)	.80	.40

EN929		UnFVF	UseFVF
11.1¢	**red and blue** on white, unwatermarked, tagged, entire (EN920)	.40	.30

EN930		UnFVF	UseFVF
29¢	**blue, maroon and rose** on white, tagged, entire (EN921)	.80	.40

EN931		UnFVF	UseFVF
29¢	**red and blue** on white, tagged, entire* (EN922)	.80	.40

EN932		UnFVF	UseFVF
29¢	**bluish gray and yellow,** unwatermarked, tagged, entire (EN924)	.80	.40

EN933		UnFVF	UseFVF
29¢	**yellow green,** with hologram, tagged, entire* (EN925)	.80	.40

1992. BULK MAILING ISSUE *Printed by offset and letterpress.*

EN934 *Star*

EN934		UnFVF	UseFVF
19.8¢	**red and blue** on white, tagged,	.55	.40
	(May 19, 1992)		
	entire*	.55	.45
	FDC		1.75

1992. DISABLED AMERICAN ISSUE *Printed by letterpress.*

EN935 *Woman in wheelchair*

EN935		UnFVF	UseFVF
29¢	**red and blue** on white, tagged,	.75	.40
	(July 22, 1992)		
	entire	.75	.40
	FDC		1.75

1993. KITTEN ISSUE *Printed by offset and letterpress.*

EN936 *Siamese kitten*

EN936		UnFVF	UseFVF
29¢	**cyan, black and purple** on white, tagged,	.75	.40
	(Oct. 2, 1993)		
	entire*	.75	.40
	FDC		1.75

A vignette, printed by offset, is affixed at upper right inside, visible through a die cut window.

1994. FOOTBALL ISSUE *Printed by offset and letterpress.*

EN937 *Football*

EN937		UnFVF	UseFVF
29¢	**brown and black** on white, tagged,	.75	.40
	(Sept. 17, 1994)		
	entire*	.75	.40
	FDC		3.00

1994. OLD GLORY ISSUE *Number 6 3/4 and 10 envelopes.*

EN938, EN939 *Flag — design continues to back of envelope*

EN938		UnFVF	UseFVF
32¢	**red and blue** on white, tagged, (No. 6 3/4)	.75	.40
	entire	.75	.40
	FDC (Dec. 13, 1994)		2.00

EN939		UnFVF	UseFVF
32¢	**red and blue** on white, tagged, (No. 10)	.75	.40
	entire	.75	.40
	a. red omitted, entire	—	
	b. blue omitted, entire	—	
	FDC (Dec. 13, 1994)		2.00

Announced Jan. 12, 1995, envelopes were initially available only through mail order and received first-day cancels of Dec. 13, 1994.

1995. LIBERTY BELL ISSUE

EN940, EN944 *Liberty Bell*

EN940		UnFVF	UseFVF
32¢	**greenish blue and blue** on white, tagged,	.75	.40
	(Jan. 3, 1995)		
	entire*	.75	.40
	a. greenish blue omitted	—	
	b. blue omitted	125.00	
	c. greenish blue and blue omitted, entire	200.00	—
	d. blue and tagging omitted		
	FDC		2.00

1995. NON-PROFIT ISSUE

EN941 *Sheep — design continues to back of envelope*

EN941		UnFVF	UseFVF
5¢	**green and red brown** on white, *(March 10, 1995)*	.75	.40
	entire	.75	.40
	FDC		2.00

1995. BULK RATE ISSUE

EN942 *Eagle*

EN942		UnFVF	UseFVF
10¢	**dark red and blue** on white, *(March 10, 1995)*	.75	.40
	entire*	.75	.40
	FDC		2.00

1995. HEART SPIRAL ISSUE

EN943 *Heart*

EN943		UnFVF	UseFVF
32¢	**red** on light blue, *(March 12, 1995)*	.75	.40
	entire	.75	.40
	FDC		2.00

1995. LIBERTY BELL ISSUE *Number 9 size security envelope.*

EN944		UnFVF	UseFVF
32¢	**greenish blue and blue** on security paper, *(May 16, 1995)*	.75	.40
	entire	.75	.40

1995. SPACE HOLOGRAM ISSUE

EN945 *Space station*

EN945		UnFVF	UseFVF
32¢	**red** on white, *(Sept. 22, 1995)*	.75	.40
	entire*	.75	.40
	FDC		2.00

1996. SAVE OUR ENVIRONMENT ISSUE

EN946 *Landscape*

EN946		UnFVF	UseFVF
32¢	**multicolored** on white, *(April 20, 1996)*	.75	.40
	entire*	.75	.40
	FDC		2.00

A vignette, printed by offset, is affixed at upper right inside, visible through a die cut window.

1996. PARALYMPIC GAMES ISSUE

EN947 *Star, flame*

EN947		UnFVF	UseFVF
32¢	**multicolored** on white, *(May 2, 1996)*	.75	.40
	entire	.75	.40
	a. blue and gold omitted	—	
	b. blue omitted	—	
	c. black and red omitted	—	
	FDC		2.00

1999. FLAG ISSUE portrayed a stylized, wavy-lined American flag with a yellow staff. *Printed by Westvaco U.S. Envelope.*

EN948 *American flag with yellow staff*

EN948		UnFVF	UseFVF
33¢	**red, blue and yellow** on white	.75	.50
	entire	.75	.50
	FDC *(Jan. 11, 1999)*		1.25

1999. FLAG ISSUE portrayed a stylized, wavy-lined American flag with a blue staff on security paper. *Printed by Westvaco U.S. Envelope.*

EN949 *American flag with blue staff*

EN949		UnFVF	UseFVF
33¢	**red and blue** on white	.75	.50
	entire	.75	.50
	FDC *(Jan. 11, 1999)*		1.25

Love Series

1999. CALLIGRAPHIC LOVE ISSUE in the Love Series featured "Love" and hearts in calligraphy. *Printed by Westvaco U.S. Envelope.*

EN950 *Love*

EN950		UnFVF	UseFVF
33¢	**purple** on white	.75	.50

		UnFVF	UseFVF
entire		.75	.50
FDC *(Jan. 28, 1999)*			1.25

1999. LINCOLN ISSUE portrayed a bust of Abraham Lincoln, printed to appear embossed. *Offset by Westvaco U.S. Envelope.*

EN951 *Abraham Lincoln*

EN951

33¢		UnFVF	UseFVF
blue and gray on white		.75	.50
entire		.75	.50
FDC *(June 5, 1999)*			1.25

2001. FEDERAL EAGLE ISSUE featured a simple bald eagle design reminiscent of some postal meters but in blue-gray with a gray "34" denomination. Designed by Michael Doret, Hollywood, Calif. Plain- and window-front envelopes were issued in each of three standard sizes: No. 10 business size, No. 9 security, and No. 6 3/4 personal size. *Typographed, tagged. 75 million (#10) printed, 29 million (#10 window), 20 million (6 3/4), 20 million (6 3/4 window), 2.5 million (#9 security), 1.8 million (#9 security window).*

EN952 *Federal Eagle*

EN952

34¢		UnFVF	UseFVF
blue-gray & gray		.75	.30
entire		.75	.30
FDC *(Jan. 7, 2001)*			1.50

2001. LOVEBIRDS ISSUE featured a heart-shaped line drawing of two birds as mirror images. Designed by Robert Brangwynne, Boston, Mass. Envelopes were issued in two standard sizes: No. 10 business size and No. 6 3/4 personal size. *Offset by Westvaco, tagged, (15 million each).*

EN953 *Lovebirds*

EN953

34¢		UnFVF	UseFVF
purple & red		.75	.30
entire		.75	
FDC *(Feb. 14, 2001)*			1.50

2001. COMMUNITY COLLEGES ISSUE showed a student reading while riding public transportation. Plain and window-front envelopes in No. 10 business size and No. 6 3/4 personal size. *Designed by Howard Paine from illustration by Steve McCracken, Washington, D.C. Flexographically printed by Westvaco.*

EN954 *Student reading while riding public transportation*

EN954

34¢		UnFVF	UseFVF
blue & red-brown		.75	.30
entire		.75	.30
No. 10		.75	.30
No. 10 window		.75	.30
No. 6 3/4		.75	.30
No. 6 3/4 window		.75	.30
FDC *(Feb. 20, 2001)*			1.50

2002. RIBBON STAR ISSUE shows the outline of a star that is surrounded by flowing ribbons. *Printed by MeadWestvaco U.S. Envelope. Rectangular block tagging to left of design. Three different printings on papers exist.*

EN955 *Ribbon around star*

EN955

37¢		UnFVF	UseFVF
red, white, blue & gray on white		.75	.30
entire		.75	.30
No. 6 3/4		.75	.30
No. 6 3/4 window		.75	.30
No. 9 security		.75	.30
No. 9 window security		.75	.30
No. 10		.75	.30
No. 10 window		.75	.30
FDC *(June 7, 2002 - Washington, DC)*			1.50

2002. USA PRESORTED STANDARD GRAPHIC EAGLE ISSUE was the second time the same graphic eagle was used for an envelope but with the phrase "Presorted Standard" instead of "Bulk Rate" as required by USPS bulk mailing rules. *Printed by MeadWestvaco U.S. Envelope. Untagged.*

EN956 *Eagle*

EN956

10¢		UnFVF	UseFVF
dark red & blue on white		.75	.30
entire		.75	.30
No. 10		.75	.30
FDC *(Aug. 8, 2002 - Washington, DC)*			1.50

2003. NURTURING LOVE ISSUE in the Love Series featured two plants in the shape of a heart being watered by a caregiver in silhouette. *Printed by MeadWestvaco U.S. Envelope. Rectangular block tagging to right of design.*

EN957 *Love*

EN957

37¢		UnFVF	UseFVF
green & orange on white		.75	.30
entire		.75	.30
No. 6 3/4		.75	.30
No. 10		.75	.30
FDC *(Jan. 24, 2003 - Tucson, AZ)*			1.50

Airmail Envelopes

The order authorizing airmail envelopes expressly provided they be printed on white paper and have red, white, and blue borders, which became known as "barber pole" borders.

Some experimenting was needed to produce these borders. On the first issues, five different types of borders are known to collectors.

Red Lozenge at Upper Right

Border 1: The lozenges (parallelograms) along the top edge and parallel to the edge measure 9 to 10mm, and with the top flap open measure along the oblique side 11 to 13mm. Small size envelopes only.

Border 2: Like Border 1 except that the lozenges measure only 7 to 8mm along the oblique side (with the top flap open). Small size envelopes only.

Border 3: Like Border 1 except the lozenges measure 11 to 12mm parallel to the edge of the envelope. Large size envelopes only.

Blue Lozenge at Upper Right — Large size envelopes only.

Border 4: Like Border 2 except with a blue lozenge at upper right corner.

Border 5: Like Border 4 except the lozenges at top point to the right (all others point to the left).

The borders are of importance to collectors, and cut squares should be preserved to include them.

After the experimentation on the first issue (AEN1-AEN2), the borders were standardized as Border 2 (red lozenge at upper right) for small size envelopes and Border 4 (blue lozenge at upper right) for large size envelopes.

1929. First Airmail Issue The U.S. domestic airmail rate from 1929 to 1932 was 5¢, as evidenced by the 5¢ stamps (AEN1-AEN2) which were the world's first postal stationery that totally prepaid airmail postage. The airmail rate to or from Puerto Rico, however, was 10¢. Persons desiring to send airmail to or from Puerto Rico simply used a 5¢ airmail envelope to which they affixed a 5¢ adhesive stamp.

In 1932 the domestic airmail rate for the United States was advanced to 8¢, and new 8¢ airmail envelopes were issued (AEN3). In 1934 the rate was reduced to 6¢ with a resulting change in the stamps on the airmail envelopes (AEN4-AEN7).

AEN1 *Vertical rudder slopes off to the left*

AEN1		UnFVF	UseFVF
5¢	**blue,** Border 1	4.00	2.50
	entire	5.50	3.00
	v. Border 2	4.00	2.50
	entire	5.50	3.00
	v1. Border 3	4.00	2.50
	entire	7.50	6.00
	v2. Border 4	4.00	2.50
	entire	9.00	6.00
	v2a. entire, 1933 watermark	750.00	—
	v2b. entire, 1937 watermark	—	—
	v3. Border 5	4.00	2.50
	entire	9.00	6.00
	v4. Border omitted	700.00	
	FDC *(Jan. 12, 1929),* size 13		40.00
	FDC *(Feb. 1, 1929),* size 5		75.00
	FDC *(Feb. 1, 1929),* size 8		75.00

AEN2 *Vertical rudder is semi-circular*

AEN2		UnFVF	UseFVF
5¢	**blue,** Border 2	12.50	6.00
	entire	17.50	7.00
	entire, 1933 watermark	700.00	—

	v. Border 4	12.00	6.00
	entire	20.00	13.00
	va. entire, 1933 watermark	350.00	—
	v1. Border 5	—	—
	entire	—	—

1932. Issue

AEN3

AEN3		UnFVF	UseFVF
8¢	**olive,** Border 4	15.00	5.00
	entire	20.00	7.00
	v. Border 2	—	—
	entire	—	—
	FDC *(Sept. 26, 1932),* size 8		30.00
	FDC, size 13		11.00

1934-44. Issue With the change of the airmail rate to 6¢, the 6¢ orange design copied the old 5¢ design. The old master die of the 5¢ was used to produce blank printing dies, into each of which the figure "6" then was cut by hand. Eleven of these dies were so made; each, of course, differs materially from the other. To simplify the collecting of these, collectors divided the 11 varieties into three general classifications, as follows:

1 (AEN4): the figure "6" measures 6 1/2mm wide
2 (AEN5): the figure "6" measures 6mm wide
3 (AEN6): the figure "6" measures 5 1/2mm wide

Finally, in 1942, a new master 6¢ airmail die was made (AEN7), from which were struck as many printing dies as were necessary. All such printing dies struck from this master die were identical and may not be individually identified.

With the outbreak of World War II, there was an enormous demand by the armed forces overseas for airmail envelopes. To expedite manufacturing, the borders were ordered dropped. All borderless airmail envelopes were shipped overseas and were not available to the civilian population in this country until after the war.

AEN4-AEN6 *Vertical rudder is semi-circular*

AEN4		UnFVF	UseFVF
6¢	**orange,** Border 2	1.75	.50
	entire	2.00	.70
	v. Border 4	—	—
	entire	—	—
	v1. w/out border, entire	3.00	1.75
	FDC *(July 1, 1934),* size 13		14.00
	FDC, size 8		25.00
AEN5		**UnFVF**	**UseFVF**
6¢	**orange,** Border 2 (1942)	3.00	2.25
	entire	60.00	25.00
	v. Border 4	—	—
	entire	—	—
	v1. w/out border, entire	5.00	2.50
AEN6		**UnFVF**	**UseFVF**
6¢	**orange,** no border (1944)	1.00	.35
	entire	1.25	.50

AEN7 *Vertical rudder slopes forward*

AEN7		UnFVF	UseFVF
6¢	**orange,** Border 2 (1942)	1.75	.75

		UnFVF	UseFVF
entire		2.50	1.00
v. Border 4			
entire		—	—
v1. w/out border, entire		3.00	1.25
v2. on blue paper (error) no border, entire		4,000.00	2,700.00
v3. red lozenges of border omitted, entire		1,200.00	

1945. ISSUE In March, to alleviate the enormous demand for airmail envelopes that the printer had not been able to supply, the Post Office approved the overprinting of 60 million ordinary 2¢ envelopes (AEN8-AEN14). The overprinting was done in New York, and great care was taken to keep any envelopes other than those authorized from being re-valued. All were shipped to the armed forces.

By the following September, the airmail rates had been reduced from 6¢ to 5¢, and re-valuing of the 6¢ airmail borderless envelopes was performed.

Following the war, remainders of these revalued envelopes were called in and destroyed, because they were confusing to the postal clerks. Adequate supplies, however, reached philatelic hands.

AEN8-AEN14

AEN8
		UnFVF	UseFVF
6¢ on 2¢ **carmine** (EN549), Die A		1.50	.75
entire		2.00	1.25

AEN9
		UnFVF	UseFVF
6¢ on 2¢ **carmine** (EN574), Die H		—	—
entire		—	—

AEN10
		UnFVF	UseFVF
6¢ on 2¢ **carmine** (EN578), Die H2		—	—
entire		—	—

AEN11
		UnFVF	UseFVF
6¢ on 2¢ **carmine** (EN581), Die I		—	—
entire		—	—

AEN12
		UnFVF	UseFVF
6¢ on 2¢ **carmine** (EN810)		80.00	45.00
entire		125.00	75.00

AEN13
		UnFVF	UseFVF
6¢ on 1¢ **green** (EN520), Die A		1,900.00	—
entire		2,700.00	—

On 1¢ green envelope of 1916-50 issue (error).

AEN14
		UnFVF	UseFVF
6¢ on 3¢ **purple** (EN588), Die I		1,900.00	—
entire		2,700.00	—

On 3¢ purple envelope of 1916-50 issue (error).

REVALUED AEN15-AEN18
5¢
P.O.DEPT.

AEN15
		UnFVF	UseFVF
5¢ on 6¢ **orange** (AEN4v1)		3.50	2.00
entire		4.00	3.00
v. Double overprint, entire		75.00	—

AEN16
		UnFVF	UseFVF
5¢ on 6¢ **orange** (AENv1)		10.00	6.00
entire		12.50	8.00
v. Double overprint, entire		65.00	—

AEN17
		UnFVF	UseFVF
5¢ on 6¢ **orange** (AEN6)		.75	.55
entire		1.50	.75
v. Double overprint, entire		65.00	—

AEN18
		UnFVF	UseFVF
5¢ on 6¢ **orange** (AEN7v1)		1.00	.75
entire		125.00	.75
v. Double overprint, entire		65.00	—

Black overprint on 6¢ orange airmail envelopes, without borders, of 1934-44 issue.

1946. DC 4 SKYMASTER ISSUE

AEN19 *DC-4 Skymaster. The small projection directly below the rudder is rounded.*

AEN19
		UnFVF	UseFVF
5¢ **carmine**, Border 2		.85	.25
entire		1.25	.50
FDC *(Sept. 25, 1946)*			2.25

AEN20 *The small projection directly below the rudder is a sharp point.*

AEN20
		UnFVF	UseFVF
5¢ **carmine**, Border 2		1.00	.35
entire		1.25	.50
v. w/Border 4		—	—
entire		—	—

1947. U.S. POSTAGE STAMP CENTENARY ISSUE complemented the Centenary International Philatelic Exhibition in New York City. The envelopes were printed on a demonstration machine at the exhibition. The envelopes also were produced at the factory in Dayton, Ohio, from both a flat and a rotary die, for distribution throughout the country. Approximately 8 million envelopes were issued, of which the rotary die printings are more common. *Flat die measures 21 3/4mm high; rotary die measures 22 1/2mm high.*

 AEN21

AEN21
		UnFVF	UseFVF
5¢ **carmine**, Border 2, rotary die		.50	.35
entire		.75	.45
v. Flat die		.60	.40
entire		.75	.50
FDC *(May 21, 1947)*			2.50

1950. ISSUE

AEN22 Type 1: figure "6s" lean to the right

Type 2: figure "6s" are upright

AEN22
		UnFVF	UseFVF
6¢ **carmine**, Border 2, Type 1		.50	.25
entire		.75	.40
v. Type 2		.90	.35
entire		1.15	.40
v1. Border 4, Type 1		—	—
entire		—	—
v2. Border 4, Type 2		—	—
entire		—	—
FDC *(Sept. 22, 1950)*			35.00

1951-52. ISSUE The return to a 6¢ airmail rate in 1950 caused the Post Office to revalue existing supplies of 5¢ airmail envelopes in some larger post offices. The re-valuing was done on a "Ticometer," a new machine developed by Pitney-Bowes Co. This process first was done in 1951 and again in 1952. Different styles of slugs were used to make the overprint on each occasion.

 AEN23, AEN24

AEN23

		UnFVF	UseFVF
6¢ on 5¢ carmine, Border 2 (AEN19)		1.00	.65
entire		1.50	1.00
FDC *(Sept. 29, 1951)*			—

AEN24

		UnFVF	UseFVF
6¢ on 5¢ carmine, Border 2 (AEN20)		.95	.65
entire		1.40	1.10
v. w/Border 4 (AEN20v)		—	—
entire		—	—

Overprint in red to left of stamp on 5¢ airmail envelopes of 1946 issue.

 AEN25, AEN26, AEN27

AEN25

		UnFVF	UseFVF
6¢ on 5¢ (AEN19)		30.00	20.00
entire		35.00	25.00

AEN26

		UnFVF	UseFVF
6¢ on 5¢ (AEN20)		4.00	3.00
entire		6.00	5.00
v. w/Border 4 (AEN20v)		—	—
entire		—	—
FDC *(Aug. 29, 1952)*			—

AEN27

		UnFVF	UseFVF
6¢ on 5¢ carmine (AEN21)		—	—
entire		1,400.00	—

Overprint in red to left of stamp on 5¢ airmail envelopes of 1946 and 1947 issues.

1956. ISSUE FIPEX Envelope. Issued in celebration of the Fifth International Philatelic Exhibition. The embossed stamp shows an eagle in flight.

 AEN28 *Eagle in flight*

 Type I: *(Left) short cloud*

 Type 2: *(Right) long cloud*

AEN28

		UnFVF	UseFVF
6¢ carmine red, Type 1		.90	.65
entire		1.25	1.00
v. Type 2		—	—
entire		—	—
FDC *(May 2, 1956)*			1.25

1958. ISSUE

 AEN29 *DC-4 Skymaster*

AEN29

		UnFVF	UseFVF
7¢ blue, Border 2		.80	.70
entire		1.25	.75
v. Border 4		—	—
entire		—	—
FDC *(July 31, 1958)*			1.25

1958. ISSUE

 AEN30, AEN36 *Jet Airliner*

AEN30

		UnFVF	UseFVF
7¢ blue, Border 2		.70	.35
entire		.80	.40
v. w/Border 4		—	—
entire		—	—
FDC *(Nov. 21, 1958)*			1.25

1958. ISSUE On Aug. 1, 1958, airmail rates were advanced to 7¢, necessitating new envelopes and the re-valuing of surplus stocks of the 6¢ airmail envelopes. The same surcharging device was used as for re-valuing the 3¢ regular postage envelopes.

 Type 11 *surcharge — printed in green to left of stamp*

AEN31

		UnFVF	UseFVF
6¢ + 1¢ orange, Die 1 (AEN4v1)		250.00	250.00
entire		300.00	400.00

AEN32

		UnFVF	UseFVF
6¢ + 1¢ orange, Die 2 (AEN5v1)		70.00	80.00
entire		100.00	150.00

AEN33

		UnFVF	UseFVF
6¢ + 1¢ orange, Die 3 (AEN6)		40.00	55.00
entire		50.00	100.00

Overprinted in green to left of stamp on 6¢ orange of 1934-44 (circular die) issue, no borders.

AEN34

		UnFVF	UseFVF
6¢ + 1¢ carmine, Border 2, Type 1 (AEN22)		1.25	.65
entire		1.35	.80
v. Type 2 (AEN22v)		1.25	.65
entire		1.35	.80
v1. Border 4, Type 1 (AEN22v2)		—	—
entire		—	—
v2. Border 4, Type 2 (AEN22v3)		—	—
entire		—	—

On 6¢ carmine of 1950 (Skymaster design) issue.

AEN35

		UnFVF	UseFVF
6¢ + 1¢ carmine, Type 1 (AEN28)		1.25	.75
entire		1.75	1.00
v. Type 2		—	—
entire		—	—

On 6¢ carmine of 1956 (FIPEX) issue.

1960. ISSUE Type AEN30 in new color.

AEN36

		UnFVF	UseFVF
7¢ red, Border 2		.75	.40
entire		1.00	.45
v. Border 4		—	—
entire		—	—
FDC *(Aug. 18, 1960)*			1.75

1962. AIRLINER ISSUE

 AEN37 *Airliner in flight*

AEN37

		UnFVF	UseFVF
8¢ red, Border 2		.75	.25
entire		1.00	.40
v. Border 4		—	—
entire		—	—
FDC *(Nov. 17, 1962)*			1.25

1965. ISSUE

 AEN38 *Jet liner with denomination*

AEN38

		UnFVF	UseFVF
8¢ red, Border 6		.50	.25

entire	.60	.40
v. Border 7 (error)	—	—
entire	25.00	—
FDC *(Jan. 7, 1965)*		1.25
z. Tagged *(Aug. 15, 1967)*	1.50	.50
entire	2.00	1.00
FDC *(Aug. 15, 1967)*		3.50

Border 6 has a blue lozenge above and to left of stamp. Border 7 has a red lozenge above and to left of stamp.

1968. ISSUE

AEN39 *Type 12 surcharge printed in red to left of stamp on 8¢ airmail envelopes AEN38*

		UnFVF	UseFVF
AEN39			
8¢ + 2¢	**red,** Border 6	.80	.25
	entire	1.25	.50
	FDC *(Feb. 5, 1968)*		

1968. ISSUE

AEN40 *Jet liner without denomination*

		UnFVF	UseFVF
AEN40			
10¢	**red,** Border 6, tagged	.60	.25
	entire	1.00	.25
	FDC *(Jan. 8, 1968)*		1.25

1971. ISSUE

AEN41 *Three circles*

		UnFVF	UseFVF
AEN41			
11¢	**red & blue**	.60	.25
	entire	.75	.25
	FDC *(May 6, 1971)*		1.25

1971. ISSUE *Revalued at left of stamp, printed on AEN40.*

Type 13: *surcharge — printed in green to left of stamp*

		UnFVF	UseFVF
AEN42			
10¢ + 1¢	**red**	1.75	.30
	entire	2.25	.65
	FDC *(June 28, 1971)*		8.00

1973. ISSUE

AEN43 *Stylized bird*

		UnFVF	UseFVF
AEN43			
13¢	**red,** luminescent ink	.40	.25
	entire	.50	.25
	FDC *(Dec. 1, 1973)*		1.25

Air Letter Sheets, Aerogrammes

Listings are for entires only.

1947. ISSUE *Printed by letterpress.* There are four types of inscriptions:

Type A: "AIR LETTER" on face; two-line inscription on back (when folded).

Type B: "AIR MAIL" on face; four-line inscription on back (when folded).

Type C: "AIR LETTER - AEROGRAMME" on face; four-line inscription on back (when folded).

Type D: "AIR LETTER - AEROGRAMME" on face; three-line inscription on back (when folded).

ALS1

		UnFVF	UseFVF
ALS1			
10¢	**carmine on bluish,** Type A	9.00	7.00
	v. blue overlay on inner side omitted	—	—
	v1. Reverse die cutting	125.00	—
	v2. Type B *(Sept. 1951)*	18.50	16.00
	v2a. chocolate (error of color)	450.00	—
	v2a. Reverse die cutting	300.00	—
	v3. Type C *(Nov. 1953)*	55.00	15.00
	v3a. Reverse die cutting	—	—
	v4. Type D *(1955)*	9.00	9.00
	v4a. Reverse die cutting	70.00	—
	FDC *(April 29, 1947)*		2.00

1958. ISSUE Paper tinted blue without overlay. *Printed by letterpress.* New inscriptions:

Type A: two-line inscription on back (when folded).

Type B: three-line inscription on back (when folded).

ALS2

		UnFVF	UseFVF
ALS2			
10¢	**blue & red,** Type A	7.50	6.00
	v. red omitted	—	—
	v1. blue omitted	—	—
	v2. Reverse die cutting	80.00	—
	v3. Type B	12.50	7.50
	FDC *(Sept. 12, 1958)*		1.25

1961. ISSUE *Printed by typography.*

ALS3

		UnFVF	UseFVF
ALS3			
11¢	**red & blue** on bluish	3.50	2.50
	v. red omitted	900.00	—
	v1. blue omitted	900.00	—
	v2. Reverse die cutting	40.00	—
	FDC *(June 16, 1961)*		1.25

1965. ISSUE "AEROGRAMME PAR AVION" on face at bottom; two-line inscription on back.

ALS4 *John F. Kennedy*

		UnFVF	UseFVF
ALS4			
11¢	**red & blue** on bluish	4.00	3.00
	v. Reverse die cutting	45.00	—
	FDC *(May 29, 1965)*		1.25

1967. ISSUE Same design as ALS4.

ALS5		UnFVF	UseFVF
13¢	**red & blue** on bluish	3.50	3.00
	v1. blue omitted	600.00	—
	v2. red omitted	600.00	—
	v3. Reverse die cutting	—	—
	FDC *(May 29, 1967)*		1.25

1968. HUMAN RIGHTS ISSUE Commemorated the 20th Anniversary of Universal Declaration of Human Rights.

ALS6

ALS6		UnFVF	UseFVF
13¢	**multicolored** on bluish, tagged GB	10.00	5.50
	v. black omitted	—	—
	v1. brown omitted	400.00	—
	v2. orange omitted	—	—
	z. Untagged (error)	—	—
	zo. Tagging omitted (error)	—	—
	FDC *(Dec. 3, 1968)*		1.25

1971. BIRDS ISSUE used the same indicium with two inscriptions — "VIA AIR MAIL • PAR AVION" for ALS7 and "AEROGRAMME • VIA AIR MAIL • PAR AVION" for ALS8.

ALS7, ALS8 *Birds in flight*

ALS7		UnFVF	UseFVF
15¢	**multicolored** on bluish	2.00	1.50
	FDC *(May 28, 1971)*		1.25

ALS8		UnFVF	UseFVF
15¢	**multicolored** on bluish	2.00	1.50
	FDC *(Dec. 13, 1971)*		1.25

1973. HOT-AIR BALLOONING ISSUE

ALS9 *Hot-air balloons (same stamp indicium as previous two issues)*

ALS9		UnFVF	UseFVF
15¢	**multicolored** on bluish	1.00	1.50
	FDC *(Feb. 10, 1973)*		1.25

1974. GLOBE AND JET ISSUE

ALS10

ALS10		UnFVF	UseFVF
18¢	**red & blue** on bluish, tagged	1.25	1.50
	v. red omitted	—	—
	v1. Reverse die cutting	—	—
	FDC *(Jan. 4, 1974)*		1.25

1974. NATO ISSUE Commemorated the 25th anniversary of the North Atlantic Treaty Organization.

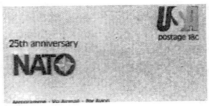

ALS11

ALS11		UnFVF	UseFVF
18¢	**red & blue** on bluish, tagged	1.25	2.00
	FDC *(April 4, 1974)*		1.25

1976. ISSUE

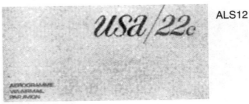

ALS12

ALS12		UnFVF	UseFVF
22¢	**red & blue** on bluish, tagged	1.25	.50
	v. Reverse die cutting	15.00	—
	FDC *(Jan. 16, 1976)*		1.25

1978. ISSUE

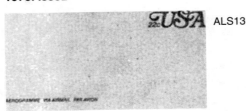

ALS13

ALS13		UnFVF	UseFVF
22¢	**blue** on bluish, tagged	1.25	.40
	v. Reverse die cutting	30.00	—
	FDC *(Nov. 3, 1978)*		1.25

1979. OLYMPICS ISSUE

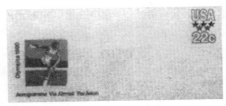

ALS14

ALS14		UnFVF	UseFVF
22¢	**red, green, & black** on bluish, tagged	1.75	1.00
	FDC *(Dec. 5, 1979)*		1.25

1980. TOURISM AND TRAVEL ISSUE

ALS15

ALS15		UnFVF	UseFVF
30¢	**blue, red, & brown** on bluish, tagged	1.00	.40
	v. red omitted	100.00	—
	v1. Reverse die cutting	20.00	—
	FDC *(Dec. 29, 1980)*		1.25

1981. TOURISM AND TRAVEL ISSUE

ALS16		UnFVF	UseFVF
30¢	**yellow, red, blue, & black** on blue, tagged	1.00	.40
	v. Reverse die cutting	25.00	—
	FDC *(Sept. 21, 1981)*		1.25

1982. WORLD TRADE ISSUE

ALS17 *Made in USA*

ALS17
30¢   **multicolored** on blue, tagged
FDC *(Sept. 16, 1982)*

	UnFVF	UseFVF
	1.25	.40
		1.25

1983. WORLD COMMUNICATIONS ISSUE

ALS18

ALS18
30¢   **multicolored** on blue, tagged
v. Reverse die cutting
FDC *(Jan. 7, 1983)*

	UnFVF	UseFVF
	1.25	.40
	35.00	—
		1.25

1983. OLYMPICS ISSUE

ALS19

ALS19
30¢   **multicolored,** tagged
v. Reverse die cutting
FDC *(Oct. 14, 1983)*

	UnFVF	UseFVF
	1.25	1.00
	—	—
		1.25

1985. LANDSAT ISSUE

ALS20

ALS20
36¢   **multicolored** on blue, tagged
v. Reverse die cutting
FDC *(Feb. 14, 1985)*

	UnFVF	UseFVF
	1.25	1.00
	35.00	—
		1.25

1985. TRAVEL ISSUE

ALS21 *City skyline*

ALS21
36¢   **multicolored** on blue, tagged
v. black omitted
v1. Reverse die cutting
FDC *(May 21, 1985)*

	UnFVF	UseFVF
	1.25	1.00
	—	—
	30.00	—
		1.25

1985. MARK TWAIN/HALLEY'S COMET ISSUE

ALS22 *Halley's Comet*

ALS22
36¢   **multicolored,** tagged
v. Reverse die cutting
FDC *(Dec. 4, 1985)*

	UnFVF	UseFVF
	3.00	2.00
	30.00	—
		1.35

1988. ISSUE Stylized envelope.

ALS23

ALS23
39¢   **multicolored,** tagged
FDC *(May 9, 1988)*

	UnFVF	UseFVF
	1.25	1.00
		1.50

1988. UPU ISSUE Abraham Lincoln and Montgomery Blair are depicted.

ALS24

ALS24
39¢   **multicolored,** tagged
FDC *(Nov. 20, 1988)*

	UnFVF	UseFVF
	1.25	1.00
		1.50

1991. ISSUE

ALS25, ALS26 *Eagle*

ALS25
45¢   **blue, gray, & red** on white, tagged
FDC *(May 17, 1991)*

	UnFVF	UseFVF
	1.50	.65
		1.50

ALS26
45¢   **blue, gray, & red** on blue, tagged

	UnFVF	UseFVF
	1.50	.65

1995. THADDEUS LOWE (BALLOONIST) ISSUE

ALS27 *Thaddeus Lowe*

ALS27		UnFVF	UseFVF
50¢	**multicolored** on blue, tagged	1.50	.65
	FDC (Sept. 23, 1995)		1.50

Scenic America Series

1999. VOYAGEURS NATIONAL PARK ISSUE in the Scenic American Landmarks Series portrayed park scenes including the indicia, a swimming loon, a common resident of the park near International Falls, Minn. The park is named for the French traders and trappers who worked in the fur trade in the 18th and 19th centuries. *Offset by the Bureau of Engraving and Printing.*

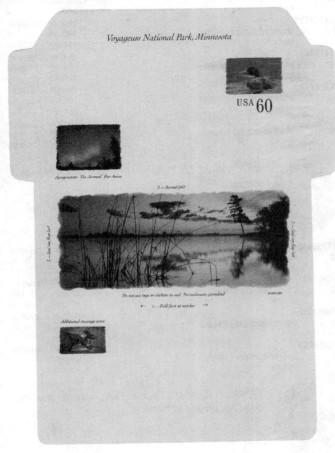

ALS28 *Voyageurs National Park*

ALS28		UnFVF	UseFVF
60¢	**multicolored**	1.50	1.50
	FDC (May 15, 1999)		1.50

Official Envelopes

When the franking privilege for government officials and departments was abolished in 1873, envelopes were issued for the Post Office and War Departments only. They were discontinued after 1879, although the War Department continued to use them for some years thereafter. Official envelope production resumed in 1983.

1873. POST OFFICE DEPARTMENT ISSUE manufactured by George H. Reay. *Envelope Watermark 2.*

 PDEN1 *Small, finely executed numeral "2"*

PDEN1		UnFVF	UseFVF
2¢	**black** on canary	11.00	7.00
	entire	15.00	11.00

 PDEN2-PDEN3 *Small, finely executed numeral "3"*

PDEN2		UnFVF	UseFVF
3¢	**black** on canary	6.00	5.00
	entire	10.00	8.00
PDEN3		UnFVF	UseFVF
3¢	**black** on white	7,000.00	—
	entire	16,000.00	—

 PDEN4 *Small, finely executed numeral "6"*

PDEN4		UnFVF	UseFVF
6¢	**black** on canary	13.00	11.00
	entire	19.00	16.00

1874. POST OFFICE DEPARTMENT ISSUE manufactured by Plimpton Manufacturing Co. *Watermark 2, 4, 5.*

 PDEN5, PDEN6 *Tall, heavy "2"*

PDEN5		UnFVF	UseFVF
2¢	**black** on canary	5.00	4.00
	entire	8.00	5.00
PDEN6		UnFVF	UseFVF
2¢	**black** on white	50.00	30.00
	entire	55.00	35.00

 PDEN7-PDEN11 *Tall "3"*

PDEN7		UnFVF	UseFVF
3¢	**black** on canary	3.00	1.00
	entire	4.00	1.50
PDEN8		UnFVF	UseFVF
3¢	**black** on white	900.00	900.00
	entire	1,000.00	—
PDEN9		UnFVF	UseFVF
3¢	**black** on amber	40.00	29.00
	entire	50.00	45.00
PDEN10		UnFVF	UseFVF
3¢	**black** on blue	16,000.00	—
	entire	19,000.00	—

PDEN11

			UnFVF	UseFVF
3¢	**blue** on blue		15,000.00	—
	entire		17,000.00	—

PDEN12, PDEN13 *Tall "6"*

PDEN12

			UnFVF	UseFVF
6¢	**black** on canary		4.50	4.25
	entire		9.00	4.50

PDEN13

			UnFVF	UseFVF
6¢	**black** on white		550.00	—
	entire		750.00	—

1877. POSTAL SERVICE DEPARTMENT ISSUE *Unwatermarked and watermark 2, 4, 5.*

PDEN14-PDEN17

PDEN14

			UnFVF	UseFVF
	black on white		4.00	3.50
	entire		6.00	5.00

PDEN15

			UnFVF	UseFVF
	black on amber		30.00	21.00
	entire		90.00	40.00

PDEN16

			UnFVF	UseFVF
	blue on amber		35.00	25.00
	entire		90.00	45.00

PDEN17

			UnFVF	UseFVF
	blue on blue		6.00	6.00
	entire		8.00	8.00

1873. WAR DEPARTMENT ISSUE *manufactured by George H. Reay. Watermarks 2, 3, 4, 5, 6.*

WDEN18-WDEN20 *Benjamin Franklin, point of bust narrow and points at "N" of "ONE"*

WDEN18

			UnFVF	UseFVF
1¢	**dark red** on white		500.00	300.00
	entire		750.00	350.00

WDEN19

			UnFVF	UseFVF
1¢	**vermilion** on white		200.00	—
	entire		275.00	—

WDEN20

			UnFVF	UseFVF
1¢	**vermilion** on manila, wrapper		11.00	8.00
	entire		20.00	15.00

WDEN21-WDEN23 *Andrew Jackson, point of bust broad and square*

WDEN21

			UnFVF	UseFVF
2¢	**dark red** on white		650.00	350.00
	entire		750.00	—

WDEN22

			UnFVF	UseFVF
2¢	**vermilion** on white		260.00	—
	entire		5,000.00	—

WDEN23

			UnFVF	UseFVF
2¢	**vermilion** on manila, wrapper		200.00	—
	entire		300.00	—

WDEN24-WDEN29 *George Washington, the ponytail projects below the bottom of the bust*

WDEN24

			UnFVF	UseFVF
3¢	**dark red** on white		50.00	40.00
	entire		150.00	—

WDEN25

			UnFVF	UseFVF
3¢	**dark red** on amber		13,000.00	—
	entire		17,000.00	—

WDEN26

			UnFVF	UseFVF
3¢	**dark red** on cream		450.00	200.00
	entire		550.00	225.00

WDEN27

			UnFVF	UseFVF
3¢	**vermilion** on white		75.00	40.00
	entire		150.00	—

WDEN28

			UnFVF	UseFVF
3¢	**vermilion** on amber		85.00	—
	entire		250.00	—

WDEN29

			UnFVF	UseFVF
3¢	**vermilion** on cream		13.00	7.00
	entire		40.00	20.00

WDEN30-WDEN33 *Abraham Lincoln, back of neck is long*

WDEN30

			UnFVF	UseFVF
6¢	**dark red** on white		170.00	70.00
	entire		200.00	—

WDEN31

			UnFVF	UseFVF
6¢	**dark red** on cream		1,400.00	350.00
	entire*		2,400.00	1,500.00

WDEN32

			UnFVF	UseFVF
6¢	**vermilion** on white		—	—
	entire		—	—

WDEN33

			UnFVF	UseFVF
6¢	**vermilion** on cream		350.00	—
	entire*		6,500.00	—

WDEN34, WDEN35 *Thomas Jefferson, the ponytail does not project at back*

WDEN34

			UnFVF	UseFVF
10¢	**dark red** on white		2,700.00	280.00
	entire*		5,000.00	550.00

WDEN35

			UnFVF	UseFVF
10¢	**vermilion** on white		200.00	—
	entire*		350.00	—

WDEN36, WDEN37 *Henry Clay, ear covered by hair*

WDEN36

			UnFVF	UseFVF
12¢	**dark red** on white		100.00	40.00
	entire*		140.00	—

WDEN37

			UnFVF	UseFVF
12¢	**vermilion** on white		150.00	—
	entire*		200.00	—

WDEN38, WDEN39 *Daniel Webster, face with sideburns*

WDEN38		UnFVF	UseFVF
15¢	**dark red** on white	100.00	45.00
	entire*	125.00	400.00

WDEN39		UnFVF	UseFVF
15¢	**vermilion** on white	250.00	—
	entire*	2,500.00	—

WDEN40, WDEN41 *Winfield Scott*

WDEN40		UnFVF	UseFVF
24¢	**dark red** on white	135.00	35.00
	entire*	100.00	—

WDEN41		UnFVF	UseFVF
24¢	**vermilion** on white	375.00	—
	entire*	400.00	—

WDEN42, WDEN43 *Alexander Hamilton, bust at back ends in a narrow point*

WDEN42		UnFVF	UseFVF
30¢	**dark red** on white	400.00	110.00
	entire*	450.00	180.00

WDEN43		UnFVF	UseFVF
30¢	**vermilion** on white	375.00	—
	entire*	475.00	—

1875. WAR DEPARTMENT ISSUE produced by Plimpton Manufacturing Co. *Watermarks 2, 3, 4, 5, 6.*

WDEN44-WDEN46 *Benjamin Franklin, point of bust is broad*

WDEN44		UnFVF	UseFVF
1¢	**red** on white	125.00	100.00
	entire	135.00	—

WDEN45		UnFVF	UseFVF
1¢	**red** on amber	750.00	—

WDEN45A		UnFVF	UseFVF
1¢	**red** on orange	18,000.00	—

WDEN46		UnFVF	UseFVF
1¢	**red** on manila, wrapper	3.00	1.75
	entire	6.00	4.00

WDEN47-WDEN50 *Andrew Jackson, forward slope of bust is rounded*

WDEN47		UnFVF	UseFVF
2¢	**red** on white	100.00	—
	entire	125.00	—

WDEN48		UnFVF	UseFVF
2¢	**red** on amber	25.00	15.00
	entire	35.00	25.00

WDEN49		UnFVF	UseFVF
2¢	**red** on orange	45.00	13.00
	entire	45.00	20.00

WDEN50		UnFVF	UseFVF
2¢	**red** on manila, wrapper	70.00	45.00
	entire	90.00	—

WDEN51-WDEN55 *George Washington, the ponytail does not project below bust but protrudes toward rear*

WDEN51		UnFVF	UseFVF
3¢	**red** on white	11.00	9.00
	entire	12.00	10.00

WDEN52		UnFVF	UseFVF
3¢	**red** on amber	12.00	9.00
	entire	15.00	13.00

WDEN53		UnFVF	UseFVF
3¢	**red** on cream	6.00	3.00
	entire	8.00	5.00

WDEN54		UnFVF	UseFVF
3¢	**red** on blue	4.00	3.00
	entire	5.00	4.00

WDEN55		UnFVF	UseFVF
3¢	**red** on fawn	5.00	2.00
	entire	7.00	3.00

WDEN56-WDEN58 *Abraham Lincoln, back of bust is short*

WDEN56		UnFVF	UseFVF
6¢	**red** on white	35.00	22.00
	entire	70.00	—

WDEN57		UnFVF	UseFVF
6¢	**red** on amber	70.00	30.00
	entire	75.00	—

WDEN58		UnFVF	UseFVF
6¢	**red** on cream	170.00	70.00
	entire	200.00	—

WDEN59, WDEN60 *Thomas Jefferson, the ponytail projects at back*

WDEN59		UnFVF	UseFVF
10¢	**red** on white	150.00	90.00
	entire	175.00	—

WDEN60		UnFVF	UseFVF
10¢	**red** on amber	1,100.00	—
	entire	1,400.00	—

WDEN61-WDEN63 *Henry Clay, clearly defined ear*

WDEN61		UnFVF	UseFVF
12¢	**red** on white	40.00	35.00
	entire*	100.00	—

WDEN62		UnFVF	UseFVF
12¢	**red** on white	650.00	—
	entire*	700.00	—

WDEN63		UnFVF	UseFVF
12¢	**red** on cream	600.00	—
	entire*	750.00	—

WDEN64-WDEN67 *Daniel Webster, face without sideburns*

WDEN64

		UnFVF	UseFVF
15¢	**red** on white	175.00	135.00
	entire*	200.00	—

WDEN65

		UnFVF	UseFVF
15¢	**red** on amber	700.00	—
	entire*	750.00	—

WDEN66

		UnFVF	UseFVF
15¢	**red** on cream	650.00	—
	entire*	700.00	—

WDEN67-WDEN69 *Alexander Hamilton, bust at back is broad*

WDEN67

		UnFVF	UseFVF
30¢	**red** on white	150.00	125.00
	entire*	180.00	—

WDEN68

		UnFVF	UseFVF
30¢	**red** on amber	1,000.00	—
	entire*	1,100.00	—

WDEN69

		UnFVF	UseFVF
30¢	**red** on cream	1,000.00	—
	entire*	1,100.00	—

1910. UNITED STATES POSTAL SAVINGS ISSUE *Watermarks 15, 16, 17, 18.*

PSEN72 *Watermarks 15, 16, 17, 18*

PSEN70

		UnFVF	UseFVF
1¢	**green** on white	60.00	15.00
	entire*	75.00	45.00

PSEN71

		UnFVF	UseFVF
1¢	**green** on buff	185.00	60.00
	entire*	220.00	75.00

PSEN72

		UnFVF	UseFVF
2¢	**carmine** on white	8.00	3.00
	entire*	13.00	9.00

PSEN73

		UnFVF	UseFVF
2¢	**carmine** on manila	1,700.00	—
	entire*	2,500.00	—

1983. OFFICIAL MAIL ISSUE

OEN74 *Great Seal*

OEN74

		UnFVF	UseFVF
20¢	**blue** on white, entire	1.00	25.00
	FDC *(Jan. 12, 1983)*		1.25

1985. OFFICIAL MAIL ISSUE

OEN75 *Great Seal*

OEN75

		UnFVF	UseFVF
22¢	**blue** on white, entire	.75	5.00
	FDC *(Feb. 26, 1985)*		1.25

1987. OFFICIAL MAIL ISSUE Used exclusively to mail U.S. Savings Bonds. *Typographed.*

OEN76 *Great Seal*

OEN76

		UnFVF	UseFVF
22¢	**blue** on white, entire	.90	20.00
	FDC *(March 2, 1987)*		1.25

1988. NON-DENOMINATED "E" ISSUE Used exclusively to mail U.S. Savings Bonds. *Typographed.*

OEN77 *Great Seal and "E"*

OEN77

		UnFVF	UseFVF
25¢	**black & blue** on white, entire	1.00	20.00
	FDC *(March 22, 1988)*		1.25

1988. DENOMINATED 25¢ ISSUE *Printed by letterpress and embossed.*

OEN78 *Great Seal*

OEN78

		UnFVF	UseFVF
25¢	**black & blue** on white, entire	.75	5.00
	FDC *(April 11, 1988)*		1.25
	v. lettering as on OEN79, entire	—	—

OEN79 *Great Seal. Used exclusively to mail U.S. Savings Bonds. Typographed.*

OEN79

		UnFVF	UseFVF
25¢	**black & blue** on white, thick lettering, entire	.85	25.00

FDC *(April 11, 1988)* 1.25
v. lettering as on OEN78, entire — —

1990. OFFICIAL MAIL ISSUE Stars and "E Pluribus Unum" barely legible, lettering heavy. "Official" measures 13mm; "USA" measures 16mm. *Printed by letterpress.*

 OEN80 *Great Seal*

OEN80		UnFVF	UseFVF
45¢	**black & blue** on white, entire	1.25	—
	FDC *(March 17, 1990)*		1.50

 OEN81 *Great Seal. Used exclusively to mail U.S. passports. Typographed.*

OEN81		UnFVF	UseFVF
65¢	**black & blue** on white, entire	1.60	—
	FDC *(March 17, 1990)*		2.25

1990. OFFICIAL MAIL ISSUE Similar to above. *Printed by offset.* "Official" measures 14.5mm; "USA" measures 17mm.

 OEN82 *Great Seal. Used exclusively to mail U.S. passports. Lithographed.*

OEN82		UnFVF	UseFVF
45¢	**black & blue** on white, entire	1.25	—
	FDC *(Aug. 10, 1990)*		1.50

 OEN83 *Great Seal*

OEN83		UnFVF	UseFVF
65¢	**black & blue** on white, entire	1.50	—
	FDC *(Aug. 10, 1990)*		2.25

1991. OFFICIAL NON-DENOMINATED ISSUE Non-denominated "F" envelope. Used exclusively to mail U.S. Savings Bonds. *Typographed.*

OEN84 *Great Seal*

OEN84
		UnFVF	UseFVF
29¢	**black & blue** on white, entire	1.10	20.00
	FDC *(Jan. 22, 1991)*		1.25

1991. DENOMINATED OFFICIAL ISSUE *Issued initially watermarked; unwatermarked evelopes are on recycled paper, and have an imprint under the flap. Lithographed and embossed.*

 OEN85 *Great Seal*

OEN85
		UnFVF	UseFVF
29¢	**black & blue** on white, entire	.70	2.00
	FDC *(April 6, 1991)*		1.25
	entire, unwatermarked *(May 1, 1992)*	.70	—

1991. OFFICIAL ISSUE Used exclusively to mail U.S. Savings Bonds. *Typographed, unwatermarked evelopes are on recycled paper and have an imprint under the flap.*

 OEN86 *Great Seal*

OEN86
		UnFVF	UseFVF
29¢	**black & blue** on white, entire	.70	20.00
	FDC *(April 17, 1991)*		1.25
	v. entire, unwatermarked *(May 1, 1992)*	.70	—

1992. CONSULAR SERVICE BICENTENNIAL ISSUE The first commemorative Official Mail postage items were used exclusively to mail U.S. passports. *Designed by Zebulon Rogerson, Washington, D.C., lithograph by Westvaco, unwatermarked, special size 4 3/8x8 7/8 inches, self-adhesive.*

 OEN87 *Globe, U.S. flag*

OEN87
		UnFVF	UseFVF
52¢	**blue & red** on white, entire	2.00	—
	FDC *(July 10, 1992)*		2.25
	v. "© USPS 1992" at right under flap	2.00	—

 OEN88 *Globe, U.S. flag*

OEN88
		UnFVF	UseFVF
75¢	**blue & red** on white, entire	3.00	—

FDC *(July 10, 1992)*
v. *"© USPS 1992" at right under flap*   3.00   3.25
—

1995. OFFICIAL MAIL ISSUE *Typographed and embossed, unwatermarked.*

OEN89 *Great Seal*

OEN89

		UnFVF	UseFVF
32¢	**blue & red** on white, entire	.75	10.00
	FDC *(May 9, 1995)*		1.25

1999. OFFICIAL MAIL ISSUE *featured the Great Seal of the United States. Westvaco U.S. Envelope (2 million), offset and embossed, tagged.*

OEN90 *Great Seal*

OEN90

		UnFVF	UseFVF
33¢	**blue & red** on white, entire	.75	—
	FDC *(Feb. 22, 1999)*		1.50

2001. GREAT SEAL ISSUE *typographed and embossed by Westvaco, unwatermarked, tagged.*

OEN91 *Great Seal*

OEN91

		UnFVF	UseFVF
34¢	**blue & red**, entire	.85	.50
	FDC *(Feb. 27, 2001)*		1.50

2002. THE GREAT SEAL OFFICIAL ISSUE *features the Great Seal of the United States. Printed by MeadWestvaco U.S. Envelope. Rectangular block tagging to right of design.*

OEN92 *Great Seal*

OEN92

		UnFVF	UseFVF
37¢	**blue & red** entire (No. 10)	.90	.50
	FDC *(Aug. 2, 2002 - Washington, DC)*		1.75

Postal Cards

Postal cards vary greatly in size. Card sizes are not indicated except in those cases where the difference is important in making proper identification. So, too, the text on the face of the cards has been changed on numerous occasions. The exact wording is not indicated except when it is the determining factor of identification.

Postal cards normally are collected intact in one of the following three conditions: mint; unused (preprinted with address or messages, but no postal marking); or used (with postal marking).

Prices for used examples of Universal Postal Union cards or other international rate cards are for overseas usages. Such cards used domestically sell for much less. Similarly, inflated values for recent used cards are based on proper use during the appropriate period.

1873. PROFILE OF LIBERTY ISSUE *watermarked with large (90mmx60mm) "USPOD."*

PC1, PC2, *Profile of Liberty*

PC1 *Watermark*

PC1

		UnFVF	UseFVF
1¢	**reddish brown** on buff	350.00	25.00
	Preprinted	60.00	
	v. Unwatermarked	—	—
	Date of Issue *(May 12, 1873)*;		
	EKU: *May 11, 1873*		

Watermark with small (55mmx38mm) "USPOD."

PC2

		UnFVF	UseFVF
1¢	**reddish brown** on buff	75.00	3.00
	Preprinted	22.50	
	v. Unwatermarked	—	—
	Date of Issue unknown; EKU: *June 5, 1873*		

1875. LIBERTY ISSUE *inscribed "WRITE THE ADDRESS ON THIS SIDE - THE MESSAGE ON THE OTHER." Watermarked small (52mmx36mm) "USPOD."*

PC3, PC4 *Liberty, 21 teeth below "One Cent"*

PC3

		UnFVF	UseFVF
1¢	**black** on buff	2,500.00	325.00
	Preprinted	650.00	
	Date of Issue unknown; EKU: *Dec. 1, 1875*		

Unwatermarked. All subsequent U.S. postal cards also are without watermarks.

PC4

		UnFVF	UseFVF
1¢	**black** on buff	65.00	1.00
	Preprinted	6.50	
	Date of Issue *(Sept. 30, 1875)*		

1879. UNIVERSAL POSTAL UNION CARD ISSUE *frame around card. Size 5 1/8 inches x 3 inches.*

PC5, PC12, PC15, *Liberty*

PC5			UnFVF	UseFVF
2¢	**blue** on buff		25.00	30.00
	Preprinted		12.50	
	a. dark blue on buff		30.00	25.00
	Preprinted		12.50	
	Date of Issue *(Dec. 1, 1879)*			

1881. LIBERTY ISSUE inscribed: "NOTHING BUT THE ADDRESS CAN BE PLACED ON THIS SIDE." There are 21 teeth or 23 teeth below "ONE CENT."

PC6 *23 teeth below "One Cent"*

PC6			UnFVF	UseFVF
1¢	**black** on buff, 21 teeth		55.00	1.00
	Preprinted		5.00	
	v. 23 teeth		950.00	50.00
	Preprinted		220.00	
	v1. Printed on both sides		1,000.00	750.00
	Date of Issue *(Oct. 17, 1881)*;			
	EKU: *Aug. 3, 1881*			

1885. THOMAS JEFFERSON ISSUE was in production only 9 months because of difficulties in formulating a suitable ink and due to public uproar over the way Jefferson's eyes were drawn.

PC7 *Thomas Jefferson*

PC7			UnFVF	UseFVF
1¢	**brown** on buff		50.00	2.50
	Preprinted		5.00	
	a. chocolate		95.00	20.00
	Preprinted		25.00	
	b. orange brown		50.00	2.50
	Preprinted		5.00	
	c. red brown		50.00	3.00
	Preprinted		5.00	
	v. Double impression		1,100.00	
	v1. Double impression, 1 inverted		1,200.00	
	v2. Printed on both sides, same color		—	
	Date of Issue *(Aug. 24, 1885)*;			
	EKU: *Aug. 29, 1885*			

1886. THOMAS JEFFERSON ISSUE

PC8 *Thomas Jefferson*

PC8			UnFVF	UseFVF
1¢	**black** on buff		20.00	1.00
	Preprinted		2.00	
	a. black on glossy dark buff		40.00	2.50
	Preprinted		5.50	
	v. Double impression		—	
	v1. Double impression, 1 inverted		—	

	v2. Missing keystone in arc above "UNITED STATES"		—	
	Date of Issue *(Dec. 1, 1886)*;			
	EKU: *May 7, 1886*			

1891. ULYSSES S. GRANT ISSUE has the same indicium on two different cards, distinguishable by their size (PC10 is known as the "Ladies Card" for short, personal notes) and by the ornate front printing (PC9 has a small, angled "of" in "United States of America"; PC10 has a small shield as part of the design).

PC9, PC10 *Ulysses S. Grant*

PC9			UnFVF	UseFVF
1¢	**black** on buff, 155mm x 95mm		35.00	1.50
	Preprinted		4.50	
	v. Double impression		1,200.00	
	Date of Issue *(Dec. 16, 1891)*; EKU: *Dec. 23, 1891*			

PC10			UnFVF	UseFVF
1¢	**blue** on grayish, 117mmx75mm		15.00	3.00
	Preprinted		7.50	
	v. Double impression, 1 inverted		1,000.00	
	v2. "Picture hanger" loop in top of portrait frame line		400.00	125.00
	Date of Issue *(Dec. 16, 1891)*;			
	EKU: *Dec. 21, 1891*			

1894. THOMAS JEFFERSON ISSUE

PC11 *Thomas Jefferson with small wreath*

PC11			UnFVF	UseFVF
1¢	**black** on buff		37.00	1.00
	Preprinted		1.50	
	v. Double impression		—	
	Date of Issue *(Jan. 2, 1894)*;			
	EKU: *Jan. 4, 1894*			

1897. UNIVERSAL POSTAL UNION same design as PC5, but larger (5 1/2 inches x 3 1/2 inches).

PC12			UnFVF	UseFVF
2¢	**blue** on light blue		165.00	90.00
	Preprinted		65.00	
	Date of Issue *(Jan. 25, 1897)*;			
	EKU: *April 17, 1897*			

1897. THOMAS JEFFERSON ISSUE

PC13 *Thomas Jefferson with large wreath*

PC13			UnFVF	UseFVF
1¢	**black** on buff		30.00	2.00
	Preprinted		3.00	
	v. Double impression, 1 inverted		—	
	v1. Printed on both sides		—	
	Date of Issue *(Dec. 1, 1897)*			

1898. JOHN ADAMS ISSUE

PC14 *John Adams*

PC14
		UnFVF	UseFVF
1¢	**black** on buff	45.00	27.50
	Preprinted	12.00	

Date of Issue *(March 31, 1898)*

1898. UNIVERSAL POSTAL UNION same design as PC5 and PC12, but without frame around card (140mmx82mm).

PC15
		UnFVF	UseFVF
2¢	**black** on buff	12.50	10.00
	Preprinted	5.50	

1902. WILLIAM MCKINLEY (FULL-FACE) ISSUE Rejected and ordered destroyed by the Post Office as being of inferior quality, one box of 500 postal cards with this design (out of 1,625,000 printed) was inadvertently sold and subsequently imprinted with "Messrs. Booth, Dailey & Ivins," which held a garbage-hauling contract for the city of New York. By the end of 1902, 149 unused and 318 used cards were in collectors' hands. Many used cards were subsequently destroyed in a fire, and today the unused cards probably outnumber the used ones. The contrarily nicknamed "Garbage Card" is the most valuable U.S. postal card.

PC16 *U.S. seal (at left); William McKinley, full face (at right)*

PC16
		UnFVF	UseFVF
1¢	**black** on buff	6,500.00	3,200.00
	Preprinted	3,250.00	

Earliest known use: *May 26, 1902*

1902. WILLIAM MCKINLEY (PROFILE) ISSUE

PC17 *U.S. seal (at left); William McKinley, profile (at right)*

PC17
		UnFVF	UseFVF
1¢	**black** on buff	12.50	2.00
	Preprinted	2.00	
	v. Double impression	—	

Earliest known use: *July 10, 1902*

1907. WILLIAM MCKINLEY

PC18, PC19 *William McKinley*

PC18
		UnFVF	UseFVF
1¢	**black** on buff	40.00	1.50
	Preprinted	2.00	

Date of Issue *(June 1907)*

1908. WILLIAM MCKINLEY same design as PC18. Message space at left side. Inscribed (vertically) at side: "THE SPACE BELOW MAY BE USED FOR CORRESPONDENCE."

PC19
		UnFVF	UseFVF
1¢	**black** on buff	50.00	7.50
	Preprinted	8.00	

Date of Issue *(Jan. 2, 1908)*

1910. WILLIAM MCKINLEY ISSUE

PC20 *William McKinley, area around head shaded*

PC20
		UnFVF	UseFVF
1¢	**blue** on bluish	100.00	7.50
	Preprinted	16.50	
	a. bronze blue on bluish	170.00	15.00
	Preprinted	27.50	
	b. Pointed arcs on 4 outer areas above & below "IS" in inscription to left of imprinted stamp	2,000.00	550.00
	Preprinted	1,000.00	
	v1. Double impression	—	
	v2. Double impression, 1 inverted	—	
	v3. Triple impression	—	

Date of Issue *(Feb. 12, 1910)*

PC21, PC23 *William McKinley, area around head without shading*

PC21
		UnFVF	UseFVF
1¢	**blue** on bluish	15.00	.50
	Preprinted	1.75	
	p. Printed on thin paper (0.008 inches thickness)	—	—
	v. Double impression, normal position	—	

Date of Issue *(April 13, 1910)*

1911. ABRAHAM LINCOLN ISSUE

PC22, PC25 *Abraham Lincoln*

PC22
		UnFVF	UseFVF
1¢	**red** on cream, 127mmx76mm	10.00	7.50
	Preprinted	3.50	
	v. Double impression	—	

Date of Issue *(Jan. 21, 1911)*

1911. WILLIAM MCKINLEY ISSUE same design as PC21.

PC23
		UnFVF	UseFVF
1¢	**carmine** on cream	12.50	7.50
	Preprinted	1.75	
	a. scarlet	—	
	v. Double impression	—	

Date of Issue *(Aug. 10, 1911)*

1911. GRANT INTERNATIONAL RATE ISSUE

PC24 *Ulysses S. Grant*

PC24		UnFVF	UseFVF
2¢	**carmine** on cream	1.75	9.00
	Preprinted	1.00	
	v. Double impression	—	
	Date of Issue *(Oct. 27, 1911)*		

1913. ABRAHAM LINCOLN ISSUE same design as PC22; same size: 5x3 inches.

PC25		UnFVF	UseFVF
1¢	**green** on cream	12.50	7.50
	Preprinted		
	Date of Issue *(July 29, 1913)*		

1914. THOMAS JEFFERSON ISSUE

PC26, PC27 *Thomas Jefferson*

PC26		UnFVF	UseFVF
1¢	**green** on buff	.40	.30
	Preprinted	.25	
	a. green on cream	3.75	.75
	Preprinted	1.25	
	b. green on off-white	3.75	.75
	Preprinted	1.25	
	v. Double impression	—	
	Date of Issue *(June 4, 1914)*		

1916. THOMAS JEFFERSON ISSUE same design as PC26. Due to wartime shortages, an inferior rough-textured bluish gray paper was used for a short period. PC27 and PC28 were printed on this substitute paper.

PC27		UnFVF	UseFVF
1¢	**dark green** on bluish gray	2,700.00	175.00

1916. THOMAS JEFFERSON ISSUE recut die consisting of heavy hair lines and distinct hair lines in queue.

PC28 *Recut die*

PC28		UnFVF	UseFVF
1¢	**dark green** on bluish gray	3,000.00	140.00
	Date of Issue *(Dec. 22, 1916)*		

1917. ABRAHAM LINCOLN ISSUE Small "library" size: 5x3 inches.

PC29 *Abraham Lincoln*

PC29		UnFVF	UseFVF
1¢	**green** on cream	.75	.50
	Preprinted	.35	
	a. green on dark buff	1.75	.75
	Preprinted	.65	
	b green on canary	—	—
	v. Double impression	—	
	Date of Issue *(March 14, 1917)*		

1917. THOMAS JEFFERSON ISSUE

PC30 *Die 1, coarse impression. Points on numerals.*

PC30		UnFVF	UseFVF
2¢	**carmine** on cream	50.00	3.00
	Preprinted	7.50	
	a. vermilion on cream	300.00	70.00
	Preprinted	75.00	
	b. lake on cream	50.00	3.00
	Preprinted	7.50	
	c. carmine on buff	40.00	3.00
	Preprinted	6.00	
	Date of Issue *(Oct. 22, 1917)*		

1918. THOMAS JEFFERSON ISSUE

PC31 *Die 2, clear impression. Balls on numerals.*

PC31		UnFVF	UseFVF
2¢	**carmine** on cream	30.00	2.75
	Preprinted	4.50	
	Date of Issue *(Jan. 23, 1918)*		

1920. JEFFERSON SURCHARGE ISSUE surcharged "1 CENT" in black on PC30 (die 1).

The overprints were applied by a canceling machine (below left) or a printing press (below right).

 PC32, PC33

PC32		UnFVF	UseFVF
1¢ on 2¢	**red** on cream, *canceling machine*	55.00	12.50
	Preprinted	16.00	
	a. Press printing	550.00	50.00
	Preprinted	110.00	
	v. Double surcharge	—	
	v1. Inverted surcharge	—	
	Date of Issue *(April 1920)*		

1920. JEFFERSON SURCHARGE (DIE 2) ISSUE

PC33		UnFVF	UseFVF
1¢ on 2¢	**red** on cream	15.00	12.50
	Preprinted	2.50	
	a. Press printing	225.00	35.00
	Preprinted	60.00	
	v. Double surcharge	90.00	
	v1. Double surcharge, 1 inverted	300.00	
	v2. Inverted surcharge	60.00	
	v3. Triple surcharge	375.00	
	Date of Issue *(April 1920)*		

1920. JEFFERSON ISSUE

PC34 *Overprinted in black on PC31 (Die 2)*

PC34

		UnFVF	UseFVF
1¢ on 2¢	**red** on cream	4,000.00	4,500.00
	Preprinted	3,000.00	
	Date of Issue *(April 1920)*		

1920. GRANT INTERNATIONAL RATE SURCHARGE ISSUE 2 line 1¢ surcharge on 2¢ Grant postal card (PC24). Only three or four examples known.

PC34A

		UnFVF	UseFVF
1¢ on 2¢	**carmine** on cream	—	75,000.00
	Earliest known usage: *Dec. 16, 1920*		—

1926. UNIVERSAL POSTAL UNION

PC35 *William McKinley*

PC35

		UnFVF	UseFVF
3¢	**red orange** on cream	5.00	10.00
	Preprinted	2.00	
	a. red on canary	5.50	12.50
	b. deep carmine on canary	—	—
	c. orange red on dark buff	—	—
	FDC *(Feb. 1, 1926)*		225.00

1951. BENJAMIN FRANKLIN ISSUE

PC36 *Benjamin Franklin*

PC36

		UnVF	UseVF
2¢	**carmine** on buff	.50	.30
	Preprinted	.30	
	a. lake on buff	—	—
	b. Damaged (missing) LR stamp corner	40.00	15.00
	v. Double impression	225.00	
	FDC *(Nov. 16, 1951)*		1.00

1952. 2¢ OVPT. ON THOMAS JEFFERSON ISSUE

PC37 *Overprinted in green on PC26*

PC37

		UnVF	UseVF
2¢ on 1¢	**green** on buff	.75	.40
	Preprinted	.35	
	v. Double surcharge	20.00	25.00
	v1. Surcharge vertical at left	7.50	9.00
	v2. Surcharge vertical below stamp	—	
	FDC *(Jan. 1, 1952)*		12.50

Tickometer surcharge.

PC37A

		UnVF	UseVF
2¢ on 1¢	**green** on buff	5.50	2.50
	Preprinted	2.00	
	v. Inverted surcharge, lower left	80.00	130.00
	Preprinted	60.00	
	v1. Double surcharge	—	
	v2. Split surcharge, top & bottom	—	
	FDC *(March 22, 1952)*		

Press-printed surcharge.

1952. 2¢ OVPT. ON LINCOLN ISSUE PC29. *Surcharged, printed by Pitney Bowes Tickometer.*

PC38

		UnVF	UseVF
2¢ on 1¢	**green** on buff	.75	.50
	Preprinted	.40	
	a. green on cream	.75	.50
	Preprinted	.40	
	b. green on canary	.75	.50
	Preprinted	.40	
	v. Double surcharge, normal position	—	
	v1. Inverted surcharge, lower left	—	
	v2. Double surcharge, 1 inverted	—	
	v3. Vertical surcharge, left of stamp, reading down	7.00	5.50
	FDC *(March 22, 1952)*		110.00

PC38A

		UnVF	UseVF
2¢ on 1¢	**green** on buff	6.00	2.50
	Preprinted	3.00	
	v. Surcharge on back	85.00	

Press-printed surcharge.

1952. SMALL "LIBRARY" SIZE ISSUE 5x3 inches.

PC39 *Abraham Lincoln*

PC39

		UnVF	UseVF
2¢	**carmine** on buff	.30	1.50
	Preprinted	.15	
	a. lake on buff	—	
	FDC *(July 31, 1952)*		1.00

1956. FIPEX ISSUE

PC40 *Liberty*

PC40

		UnVF	UseVF
2¢	**red & dark violet blue** on buff	.30	2.00
	a. rose & dark violet blue	1.75	1.25
	v. dark violet blue omitted	475.00	250.00
	v1. Double impression of dark violet blue	18.00	11.00
	FDC *(May 4, 1956)*		1.00

1956. STATUE OF LIBERTY ISSUE International postal card.

PC41, MRC15 *Liberty*

PC41

		UnVF	UseVF
4¢	**scarlet & ultramarine** on buff	1.75	75.00
	FDC *(Nov. 16, 1956)*		1.00

1958. STATUE OF LIBERTY ISSUE Domestic postal card.

PC42, MRC16 *Liberty*

PC42

		UnVF	UseVF
3¢	**violet** on buff	.60	.30
	v. Double impression	—	
	v1. "I" of "IN" omitted	13.00	26.00
	x. printed precancel bars *(Sept. 15, 1961)*	4.00	3.00
	FDC *(Aug. 1, 1958)*		1.00

1958. BENJAMIN FRANKLIN ISSUE PC36 revalued in black.

PC43 *Overprinted in black at left of PC36*

PC43

		UnVF	UseVF
2¢ & 1¢	**carmine** on buff, preprinted	175.00	500.00
	v. Surcharge inverted lower left	—	

This surcharge was authorized for use by the General Electric Co. in Owensboro, Ky., which had prepared a large number of cards for an advertising campaign prior to the 1958 rate increase. In all, some 750,000 cards were surcharged by Pitney Bowes Tickometer.

1962. ABRAHAM LINCOLN ISSUE

PC44, MRC17 *Abraham Lincoln*

PC44

		UnVF	UseVF
4¢	**lilac** on white, precanceled	.30	.25
	p. Non-fluorescent paper, non-phosphorescent ink	.30	.25
	p1. Fluorescent paper, non-phosphorescent ink	.45	.25
	p2. Non-fluorescent paper, phosphorescent ink	.75	.25
	v. Double impression	—	
	FDC (Nov. 19, 1962)		1.00

The phosphorescent ink was experimental tagging for expediting mail processing (cards placed on sale July 6, 1966).

1963. VACATIONLAND ISSUE International postal card. Designed to promote tourism to the United States.

PC45, MRC18 *Map of North America*

PC45

		UnVF	UseVF
7¢	**red & blue** on white	4.50	50.00
	v. blue omitted	—	
	v1. red omitted	—	
	FDC (Aug. 30, 1963)		1.00

1964. U.S. CUSTOMS SERVICE ISSUE honoring the 175th anniversary of the service.

PC46 *Map of United States and flags*

PC46

		UnVF	UseVF
4¢	**red & blue** on white	.55	1.50
	a. blue omitted	600.00	
	v1. red omitted	—	
	FDC (Feb. 22, 1964)		1.00

1964. SOCIAL SECURITY ISSUE in complement to the International Social Security Association conference.

PC47

PC47

		UnVF	UseVF
4¢	**red & blue** on white	.50	1.50
	p. Fluorescent paper	—	—
	v. red omitted	—	
	v1. blue omitted	750.00	
	FDC (Sept. 22, 1964)		1.00

1965. U.S. COAST GUARD ISSUE honoring its 175th anniversary.

PC48 *U.S. Coast Guard flag*

PC48

		UnVF	UseVF
4¢	**red & blue** on white	.50	1.50
	v. blue omitted	—	
	FDC (Aug. 4, 1965)		1.00

1965. U.S. CENSUS BUREAU ISSUE honoring its 175th anniversary.

PC49 *Census anniversary*

PC49

		UnVF	UseVF
4¢	**blue, light blue, & black** on white	.40	1.50
	FDC (Oct. 21, 1965)		1.00

1967. VACATIONLAND ISSUE International postal card, design of PC45.

PC50

		UnVF	UseVF
8¢	**red & blue** on white	4.25	40.00
	FDC (Dec. 4, 1967)		1.00

1968. ABRAHAM LINCOLN ISSUE

PC51, MRC20 *Abraham Lincoln*

PC51

		UnVF	UseVF
5¢	**green** on white	.35	.50
	v. Double impression	—	
	FDC (Jan. 4, 1968)		1.00

1968. WOMEN MARINES ISSUE honoring their 25th anniversary.

PC52 *Women Marines*

PC52

		UnVF	UseVF
5¢	**olive green & rose red** on white	.40	1.50
	v. damaged "M" in "WOMEN"	—	—
	FDC (July 26, 1968)		1.00

1970. WEATHER SERVICES CENTENNIAL ISSUE

PC53 *Weather recording equipment*

PC53

		UnVF	UseVF
5¢	**yellow, blue, red, & black** on white, tagged	.35	1.50
	v. black omitted	600.00	
	v1. black & yellow omitted	700.00	
	v2. blue omitted	650.00	
	FDC (Sept. 1, 1970)		1.00

Patriot Series

1971. PAUL REVERE ISSUE was the first in the Patriot Series.

PC54, MRC21 *Paul Revere*

PC54

6¢		UnVF	UseVF
	brown on white, tagged	.35	2.00
	v. Double impression	325.00	—
	FDC *(May 15, 1971)*		1.00

1971. VACATIONLAND ISSUE design of PC45, Vacationland.

PC55

10¢		UnVF	UseVF
	red & blue on white, tagged	4.75	50.00
	FDC *(June 10, 1971)*		1.00

1971. NEW YORK HOSPITAL BICENTENNIAL ISSUE

PC56 *New York Hospital*

PC56

6¢		UnVF	UseVF
	multicolored on white, tagged	.35	2.00
	v. blue & yellow omitted	700.00	
	v1. red omitted	—	
	v2. red & black omitted	—	
	v3. yellow omitted	—	
	v4. red & black impressions shifted 25mm left	—	
	za. Tagging omitted	—	
	FDC *(Sept. 16, 1971)*		1.00

1972. TOURISM YEAR OF THE AMERICAS ISSUE A luminescent panel of tagging was printed at the left of the stamp. The reverse of each card is printed overall with four scenes and the words "TOURISM YEAR OF THE AMERICAS '72." (See PCA12-13.)

PC57 *Eastern Point Lighthouse, Gloucester, Mass.*

PC57

6¢		UnVF	UseVF
	black on manila, tagged	.50	4.50
	v. Reverse blank	400.00	
	v1. Reverse inverted to front	275.00	
	zo. Tagging omitted	75.00	
	FDC *(June 29, 1972)*		1.00

PC58 *Monument Valley*

PC58

6¢		UnVF	UseVF
	black on manila, tagged	.50	.45
	v. Reverse blank	400.00	
	v1. black missing on reverse	400.00	
	zo. Tagging omitted	75.00	
	FDC *(June 29, 1972)*		1.00

PC59 *U.S. Frigate* Constellation

PC59

6¢		UnVF	UseVF
	black on manila, tagged	.50	.45
	v. Address side blank	400.00	
	v1. Reverse blank	400.00	
	v2. black missing on reverse	400.00	
	zo. Tagging omitted	75.00	
	FDC *(June 29, 1972)*		1.00

First-day cancels were available from any post office that had the cards in stock that day.

1972. JOHN HANSON ISSUE in the Patriot Series.

PC60, MRC22 *John Hanson*

PC60

6¢		UnVF	UseVF
	blue on white, tagged, smooth paper	.30	1.00
	FDC *(Sept. 1, 1972)*		1.00
	p. Coarse paper	1.00	1.00

1973. U.S. POSTAL CARD CENTENNIAL ISSUE

PC61 *Design similar to PC1*

PC61

6¢		UnVF	UseVF
	magenta on manila	.30	2.00
	FDC *(Sept. 14, 1973)*		1.00
	zo. Tagging omitted	75.00	
	zv. Tagging inverted to lower left	—	

1973. SAMUEL ADAMS ISSUE in the Patriot Series.

PC62, MRC23 *Samuel Adams*

PC62

8¢		UnVF	UseVF
	orange on white, tagged, smooth paper	.50	1.00
	FDC *(Dec. 16, 1973)*		1.00
	v. Double impression	—	
	p. Printed on coarse paper	.50	1.00
	v1. Double impression	250.00	

1974. SHIP'S FIGUREHEAD ISSUE International surface mail.

PC63 *Ship's figurehead*

PC63

12¢		UnVF	UseVF
	multicolored on white, tagged	.40	35.00

FDC *(Jan. 4, 1974)* 1.00
v. yellow omitted 1,000.00

1975. CHARLES THOMSON ISSUE in the Patriot Series.

PC64, MRC24 *Charles Thomson*

PC64		**UnVF**	**UseVF**
7¢	**emerald green** on white, tagged, smooth paper	.40	7.50
	If used after Dec. 31, 1975		.35
	FDC *(Sept. 14, 1975)*		1.00
	v1. Left tip of lower precancel bar raised	—	—
	p. printed on coarse paper	.40	8.00

1975. JOHN WITHERSPOON ISSUE in the Patriot Series.

PC65, MRC25 *John Witherspoon*

PC65		**UnVF**	**UseVF**
9¢	**yellow brown** on white, tagged	.40	1.00
	FDC *(Nov. 10, 1975)*		1.00

1976. CAESAR RODNEY ISSUE in the Patriot Series.

PC66, MRC26 *Caesar Rodney*

PC66		**UnVF**	**UseVF**
9¢	**blue** on white, tagged	.35	1.00
	v. Double impression	—	
	FDC *(July 1, 1976)*		1.00

Historic Preservation Series

1977. FEDERAL COURT HOUSE, GALVESTON, TEXAS ISSUE was the first in a long-running Historic Preservation Series.

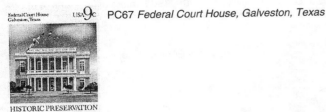

PC67 *Federal Court House, Galveston, Texas*

PC67		**UnVF**	**UseVF**
9¢	**multicolored** on white, tagged	.40	1.50
	FDC *(July 20, 1977)*		1.00
	v. black omitted	—	
	zo. Tagging omitted	100.00	

1977. NATHAN HALE ISSUE in the Patriot Series.

PC68, MRC27 *Nathan Hale*

PC68		**UnVF**	**UseVF**
9¢	**green** on white, tagged	.35	1.00

FDC *(Oct. 14, 1977)* 1.00
v. Double impression 250.00
v1. Missing "¢" 75.00

1978. THE MUSIC HALL, CINCINNATI, OHIO ISSUE 2nd in the Historic Preservation Series.

PC69 *Music Hall, Cincinnati, Ohio*

PC69		**UnVF**	**UseVF**
10¢	**multicolored** on white, tagged	.40	1.50
	FDC *(May 12, 1978)*		1.00

1978. JOHN HANCOCK (NON-DENOMINATED) ISSUE in the Patriot Series.

PC70, MRC28 *John Hancock (for domestic use only)*

PC70		**UnVF**	**UseVF**
10¢	**brown orange** on white, tagged	.40	1.50
	FDC *(May 19, 1978)*		1.00

1978. JOHN HANCOCK (DENOMINATED) ISSUE in the Patriot Series.

PC71, MRC29 *John Hancock (denomination as numeral)*

PC71		**UnVF**	**UseVF**
10¢	**orange** on white, tagged	.35	.20
	FDC *(June 20, 1978)*		1.00

1978. U.S.C.G. EAGLE ISSUE International surface mail rate.

PC72 *U.S. Coast Guard Cutter Eagle*

US Coast Guard Eagle USA 14c

PC72		**UnVF**	**UseVF**
14¢	**multicolored** on white, tagged	.45	2.00
	FDC *(Aug. 4, 1978)*		1.00

American Revolution Series

1978. MOLLY PITCHER ISSUE was the first in the American Revolution Series.

PC73 *Molly Pitcher (Mary Ludwig Hays)*

Molly Pitcher, Monmouth, 1778

PC73		**UnVF**	**UseVF**
10¢	**multicolored** on white, tagged	.35	2.00
	FDC *(Sept. 8, 1978)*		1.00

1979. GEORGE ROGERS CLARK ISSUE in the American Revolution Series.

PC74 *George Rogers Clark*

George Rogers Clark, Vincennes, 1779

PC74
10¢   **multicolored** on white, tagged   UnVF .35   UseVF 2.00
                 FDC *(Feb. 23, 1979)*   1.00
             v. yellow omitted   —

1979. SUMMER OLYMPICS ISSUE

PC75 *Sprinter*

PC75
10¢   **multicolored,** tagged   UnVF .75   UseVF 2.00
                 FDC *(Sept. 17, 1979)*   1.00
             zo. Tagging omitted   —

1979. IOLANI PALACE, HONOLULU, HAWAII ISSUE 3rd in the Historic Preservation Series.

PC76 *Iolani Palace, Hawaii*

Historic Preservation

PC76
10¢   **multicolored** on white, tagged   UnVF .35   UseVF 2.00
                 FDC *(Oct. 1, 1979)*   1.00
             zo. Tagging omitted   —

1979. CASIMIR PULASKI ISSUE in the American Revolution Series.

PC77 *Gen. Casimir Pulaski*

Casimir Pulaski, Savannah, 1779

PC77
10¢   **multicolored** on white, tagged   UnVF .35   UseVF 2.00
                 FDC *(Oct. 11, 1979)*   1.00

1980. WINTER OLYMPICS ISSUE International airmail rate.

PC78 *Figure skater*

PC78
14¢   **multicolored,** tagged   UnVF .75   UseVF 12.50
                 FDC *(Jan. 15, 1980)*   1.00

1980. SALT LAKE TEMPLE ISSUE 4th in the Historic Preservation Series.

PC79 *Mormon Temple, Salt Lake City, Utah*

PC79
10¢   **multicolored,** tagged   UnVF .35   UseVF 2.00
                 FDC *(April 5, 1980)*   1.00
             zo. Tagging omitted   —

1980. LANDING OF ROCHAMBEAU ISSUE in the American Revolution Series.

PC80 *Fleet of Count Jean-Baptiste de Rochambeau*

Landing of Rochambeau, 1780

PC80
10¢   **multicolored** on white, tagged   UnVF .35   UseVF 2.00
                 FDC *(July 11, 1980)*   1.00
             v. black & yellow printed on reverse, front   —
                 normal

1980. BATTLE OF KINGS MOUNTAIN ISSUE in the American Revolution Series.

PC81 *Battle of Kings Mountain, 1780*

Battle of Kings Mountain, 1780

PC81
10¢   **multicolored,** tagged   UnVF .35   UseVF 2.00
                 FDC *(Oct. 7, 1980)*   1.00

1980. DRAKE'S *GOLDEN HINDE* ISSUE International surface rate. Celebrated the 300th anniversary of the circumnavigation of the globe by Drake.

PC82 The Golden Hinde, *ship of Sir Francis Drake*

Drake's Golden Hinde 1580

PC82
19¢   **multicolored** on white, tagged   UnVF .75   UseVF 15.00
                 FDC *(Nov. 21, 1980)*   1.00

1981. BATTLE OF COWPENS ISSUE in the American Revolution Series.

PC83 *Battle of Cowpens, 1781*

Battle of Cowpens, 1781

PC83
10¢   **multicolored**, tagged
        FDC *(Jan. 17, 1981)*

	UnVF	UseVF
	.35	4.00
		1.00

1981. NON-DENOMINATED EAGLE ISSUE

PC84, MRC30 *Stylized eagle*

PC84
12¢   **purple** on white
        FDC *(March 15, 1981)*

	UnVF	UseVF
	.40	1.00
		1.00

1981. ISAIAH THOMAS ISSUE in the Patriot Series.

PC85, MRC31 *Isaiah Thomas*

PC85
12¢   **blue** on white
        FDC *(May 5, 1981)*

	UnVF	UseVF
	.35	1.00
		1.00

1981. NATHANAEL GREENE, EUTAW SPRINGS ISSUE in the American Revolution Series.

PC86 *Nathanael Greene and The Battle at Eutaw Springs, 1781*

Nathanael Greene, Eutaw Springs, 1781

PC86
12¢   **multicolored** on white
        FDC *(Sept. 8, 1981)*
        v. magenta & yellow omitted

	UnVF	UseVF
	.35	3.00
		1.00
	—	

1981. LEWIS AND CLARK EXPEDITION ISSUE

PC87 *Lewis and Clark expedition, 1806*

Lewis and Clark Expedition, 1806

PC87
12¢   **multicolored**
        FDC *(Sept. 23, 1981)*

	UnVF	UseVF
	.35	4.00
		1.00

1981. ROBERT MORRIS (NON-DENOMINATED) ISSUE in the Patriot Series.

PC88, MRC32 *Robert Morris (for Domestic use only)*

PC88
(13¢)   **brown** on white
          FDC *(Oct. 11, 1981)*

	UnVF	UseVF
	.35	1.00
		1.00

1981. ROBERT MORRIS (DENOMINATED) ISSUE in the Patriot Series.

PC89, MRC33 *Robert Morris (denomination as numeral)*

PC89
13¢   **brown** on white
        FDC *(Nov. 10, 1981)*
        v. Stamp missing (copyright normal)

	UnVF	UseVF
	.35	1.00
		1.00

1982. "SWAMP FOX" FRANCIS MARION ISSUE in the American Revolution Series.

PC90 *Gen. Francis Marion*

"Swamp Fox" Francis Marion, 1782

PC90
13¢   **multicolored** on white
        FDC *(April 3, 1982)*

	UnVF	UseVF
	.35	1.00
		1.00

1982. LASALLE CLAIMS LOUISIANA ISSUE

PC91 *LaSalle Expedition, 1682*

La Salle claims Louisiana, 1682

PC91
13¢   **multicolored** on white
        FDC *(April 7, 1982)*

	UnVF	UseVF
	.35	1.00
		1.00

1982. PHILADELPHIA ACADEMY OF MUSIC ISSUE 5th in the Historic Preservation Series.

PC92 *Philadelphia Academy of Music*

PC92
13¢   **brown, dark beige, red** on tan
        FDC *(June 18, 1982)*
        v. brown & dark beige omitted

	UnVF	UseVF
	.35	1.00
		1.00
	400.00	

1982. OLD POST OFFICE, ST. LOUIS ISSUE 6th in the Historic Preservation Series.

Old Post Office St. Louis, Missouri   USA 13c   PC93 *Old St. Louis Post Office*

Historic Preservation

PC93
13¢   **multicolored** on white
        FDC *(Oct. 14, 1982)*

	UnVF	UseVF
	.35	1.00
		1.00

1983. LANDING OF GEN. OGLETHORPE, GEORGIA ISSUE

PC94 *Landing of James Oglethorpe in Georgia*

Landing of Oglethorpe, Georgia, 1733

PC94		UnVF	UseVF
13¢	**multicolored** on white	.35	1.00
	FDC *(Feb. 12, 1983)*		1.00

1983. OLD POST OFFICE, WASHINGTON, D.C. ISSUE 7th in the Historic Preservation Series.

PC95 *Old Post Office, Washington, D.C.*

Old Post Office, Washington, D.C.

PC95		UnVF	UseVF
13¢	**multicolored** on white	.35	1.00
	FDC *(April 19, 1983)*		1.00

1983. SUMMER OLYMPICS ISSUE

PC96 *Yachting*

PC96		UnVF	UseVF
13¢	**multicolored** on white	.35	1.00
	FDC *(Aug. 5, 1983)*		1.00
	v. black, magenta & yellow omitted		

1984. ARK AND DOVE, MARYLAND, 1634 ISSUE

PC97 Ark *and* Dove

Ark and Dove, Maryland, 1634

PC97		UnVF	UseVF
13¢	**multicolored** on white	.35	1.00
	FDC *(March 25, 1984)*		1.00

1984. SUMMER OLYMPICS ISSUE

PC98 *Olympic torch carrier*

PC98		UnVF	UseVF
13¢	**multicolored** on white	.35	1.00
	FDC *(April 30, 1984)*		1.00
	v. yellow & black inverted	—	
	zo. Tagging omitted	125.00	

1984. FREDERIC BARAGA ISSUE

PC99 *Frederic Baraga*

Frederic Baraga, Michigan, 1835

PC99		UnVF	UseVF
13¢	**multicolored** on white	.35	1.00
	FDC *(June 29, 1984)*		1.00

1984. RANCHO SAN PEDRO ISSUE 8th in the Historic Preservation Series.

PC100 *Rancho San Pedro*

PC100		UnVF	UseVF
13¢	**multicolored**	.35	1.00
	FDC *(Sept. 16, 1984)*		1.00
	v. black & blue omitted	—	
	zo. Tagging omitted	75.00	

1985. CHARLES CARROLL (NON-DENOMINATED) ISSUE in the Patriot Series.

PC101, MRC34 *Charles Carroll (for Domestic use only)*

PC101		UnVF	UseVF
14¢	**green** on white, non-denominated	.35	.50
	FDC *(Feb. 1, 1985)*		1.00

1985. CLIPPER FLYING CLOUD ISSUE International surface rate.

PC102 *Clipper* Flying Cloud, *1852*

PC102		UnVF	UseVF
25¢	**multicolored** on white	.75	7.50
	x. Cachet for CUP.PEX '87, Perth, Australia	1.25	—
	FDC *(Feb. 27, 1985)*		1.00

1985. CHARLES CARROLL (DENOMINATED) ISSUE in the Patriot Series.

PC103, MRC35 *Charles Carroll (denomination as numeral)*

PC103		UnVF	UseVF
14¢	**green** on white	.35	.25
	FDC *(March 6, 1985)*		1.00

1985. GEORGE WYTHE ISSUE in the Patriot Series.

PC104, MRC36 *George Wythe*

PC104			UnVF	UseVF
14¢	**olive green** on white		.35	.50
	FDC *(June 20, 1985)*			1.00

1986. SETTLING OF CONNECTICUT ISSUE

PC105 *Settling of Connecticut*

PC105		UnVF	UseVF
14¢	**multicolored** on white	.30	1.00
	FDC *(April 18, 1986)*		1.00

1986. STAMP COLLECTING ISSUE

PC106

PC106		UnVF	UseVF
14¢	**multicolored** on white	.35	1.00
	x. Cachet for NAJUBRIA '86, Germany	7.50	—
	FDC *(May 23, 1986)*		1.00

1986. FRANCIS VIGO ISSUE in the American Revolution Series.

PC107 *Francis Vigo, Battle of Vincennes*

PC107		UnVF	UseVF
14¢	**multicolored** on white	.35	1.00
	FDC *(May 24, 1986)*		1.00

1986. SETTLING OF RHODE ISLAND ISSUE

PC108 *Roger Williams landing at Providence, 1636*

PC108		UnVF	UseVF
14¢	**multicolored** on white	.35	1.00
	FDC *(June 26, 1986)*		1.00

Users of this Catalog are invited to write to us if they have information which they feel will supplement or correct any material contained herein. All such communications will be answered.

1986. WISCONSIN TERRITORY SESQUICENTENNIAL ISSUE

PC109 *Wisconsin Territory 150th anniversary*

PC109		UnVF	UseVF
14¢	**multicolored** on white	.35	1.00
	FDC *(July 3, 1986)*		1.00

1986. NATIONAL GUARD ISSUE

PC110 *National Guard, 350th anniversary*

PC110		UnVF	UseVF
14¢	**multicolored** on white	.35	1.00
	FDC *(Dec. 12, 1986)*		1.00

1987. SELF-SCOURING PLOW ISSUE

PC111 *150th anniversary, steel plow by John Deere*

PC111		UnVF	UseVF
14¢	**multicolored** on white	.35	1.00
	FDC *(May 22, 1987)*		1.00

1987. CONSTITUTIONAL CONVENTION ISSUE in the American Revolution Series.

PC112 *Constitutional Convention, 1787*

PC112		UnVF	UseVF
14¢	**multicolored** on white	.35	1.00
	FDC *(May 25, 1987)*		1.00

1987. U.S. FLAG ISSUE

PC113, MRC37 *Flag*

PC113		UnVF	UseVF
14¢	**black, blue, & red** on white	.35	.50
	FDC *(June 14, 1987)*		1.00
	x. Cachet for Philatelia '87 (exhibition in Koln (Cologne), Germany	1.00	
	vz. Tagging double, 1 normal & 1 split top & bottom	—	

1987. PRIDE IN AMERICA ISSUE

PC114 *Landscape*

PC114
14¢   **multicolored** on white
   FDC *(Sept. 22, 1987)*

	UnVF	UseVF
	.35	1.00
		1.00

1987. TIMBERLINE LODGE, MOUNT HOOD, OREGON ISSUE 9th in the Historic Preservation Series.

PC115 *Timberline Lodge, Mt. Hood, Ore.*

PC115
14¢   **multicolored** on white
   FDC *(Sept. 28, 1987)*

	UnVF	UseVF
	.35	1.00
		1.00

America the Beautiful Series

1988. PRAIRIE SCENE ISSUE was the first of the America the Beautiful Series.

PC116, MRC38 *Bison on the prairie*

PC116
15¢   **multicolored** on white, non-fluorescent
     paper
   FDC *(March 28, 1988)*
   p. Non-fluorescent paper
   v. printed on both sides
   v1. black & blue on reverse, front normal
   v2. Double magenta & blue & triple black
      impressions
   v3. Added printing on both sides for Myrtle
      Beach

	UnVF	UseVF
	.35	1.00
		1.00
	—	
	650.00	
	650.00	
	—	
	2.00	1.50

1988. BLAIR HOUSE ISSUE 10th in the Historic Preservation Series.

PC117 *Blair House, Washington, D.C.*

PC117
15¢   **multicolored** on white
   FDC *(May 4, 1988)*

	UnVF	UseVF
	.35	1.00
		1.00

1988. SQUARE-RIGGED PACKET SHIP *YORKSHIRE* ISSUE International surface rate.

PC118 Yorkshire

PC118
28¢   **multicolored**
   FDC *(June 29, 1988)*

	UnVF	UseVF
	.75	4.00
		1.00

1988. IOWA TERRITORY SESQUICENTENNIAL ISSUE

PC119 *Corn harvesting*

PC119
15¢   **multicolored** on white
   FDC *(July 2, 1988)*

	UnVF	UseVF
	.35	1.00
		1.00

1988. SETTLING OF OHIO ISSUE recalled the Bicentennial of the settling of Ohio, then in the Northwest Territory.

PC120 *Flatboat ferry transporting settlers*

PC120
15¢   **multicolored** on white
   FDC *(July 15, 1988)*

	UnVF	UseVF
	.35	1.00
		1.00

1988. HEARST CASTLE ISSUE 11th in the Historic Preservation Series. Featured the estate at San Simeon, Calif., built by the newspaper magnate.

PC121 *Hearst Castle, San Simeon, Calif.*

PC121
15¢   **multicolored** on white
   FDC *(Sept. 20, 1988)*

	UnVF	UseVF
	.35	1.00
		1.00

1988. FEDERALIST PAPERS ISSUE

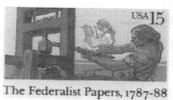

PC122 *Colonial Pressman*

PC122
15¢   **multicolored** on white
   FDC *(Oct. 27, 1988)*

	UnVF	UseVF
	.35	1.00
		1.00

1989. SONORA DESERT ISSUE in the America the Beautiful Series.

PC123 *Hawk and Sonora Desert sunset*

PC123
15¢   **multicolored** on white
   FDC *(Jan. 13, 1989)*

	UnVF	UseVF
	.35	1.00
		1.00

College Series

1989. GEORGETOWN UNIVERSITY ISSUE was the first of the College Series, which became intertwined with the Historic Preservation Series (12th of the series).

PC124 *Healy Hall, Georgetown University*

PC124		UnVF	UseVF
15¢	**multicolored** on white	.35	1.00
	FDC *(Jan. 23, 1989)*		1.00

1989. BLUE HERON AND MARSH ISSUE in the America the Beautiful Series.

PC125 *Great blue heron in marsh scene*

PC125		UnVF	UseVF
15¢	**multicolored** on white	.35	1.00
	FDC *(March 17, 1989)*		1.00

1989. SETTLING OF OKLAHOMA ISSUE

PC126 *Land rush scene*

PC126		UnVF	UseVF
15¢	**multicolored** on white	.35	.35
	FDC *(April 22, 1989)*		1.00

1989. MOUNTAIN SCENE, GEESE ISSUE in the America the Beautiful Series. Card paid surface rate to Canada.

PC127 *Geese in flight*

PC127		UnVF	UseVF
21¢	**multicolored** on white	.65	5.00
	FDC *(May 5, 1989)*		1.00

1989. SEASHORE ISSUE in the America the Beautiful Series.

PC128 *Seashore*

PC128		UnVF	UseVF
15¢	**multicolored** on white	.35	1.00
	FDC *(June 17, 1989)*		1.00

1989. FOREST STREAM ISSUE in the America the Beautiful Series.

PC129 *Deer in forest*

PC129		UnVF	UseVF
15¢	**multicolored** on white	.35	1.00
	FDC *(Aug. 26, 1989)*		1.00

1989. HULL HOUSE ISSUE 13th in the Historic Preservation Series.

PC130 *Jane Addams' Hull House Community Center, Chicago*

PC130		UnVF	UseVF
15¢	**multicolored** on white	.35	1.00
	FDC *(Sept. 16, 1989)*		1.00

1989. INDEPENDENCE HALL ISSUE in the America the Beautiful Series.

PC131, PC136A *Independence Hall, Philadelphia*

PC131		UnVF	UseVF
15¢	**multicolored** on white	.35	1.00
	FDC *(Sept. 25, 1989)*		1.00

1989. BALTIMORE HARBOR ISSUE in the America the Beautiful Series.

PC132, PC136 USS Constellation; *Inner Harbor, Baltimore, Md.*

PC132		UnVF	UseVF
15¢	**multicolored** on white	.35	1.00
	FDC *(Oct. 7, 1989)*		1.00

1989. MANHATTAN SKYLINE ISSUE in the America the Beautiful Series.

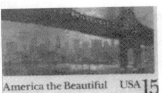

PC133, PC136C *Manhattan skyline, Queensboro Bridge*

PC133		UnVF	UseVF
15¢	**multicolored** on white	.35	1.00
	FDC *(Nov. 8, 1989)*		1.00

1989. U.S. CAPITOL BUILDING ISSUE in the America the Beautiful Series.

PC134, PC136B *U.S. Capitol building*

PC134
15¢   multicolored on white   UnVF   UseVF
          FDC *(Nov. 26, 1989)*   .35   1.00
                                                    1.00

1989. WHITE HOUSE POSTAL CARD ISSUE sold for 50¢ each with the illustration of the White House enlarged on the reverse.

PC135 *White House*

PC135
15¢   multicolored on white   UnVF   UseVF
          FDC *(Nov. 30, 1989)*   1.25   5.00
                                                    2.00

1989. AMERICA THE BEAUTIFUL SE-TENANT SHEET ISSUE in the America the Beautiful Series. Designs of PC131-PC134 were issued in a se-tenant sheet of four cards, with rouletting between them for separation, for World Stamp Expo '89. The sheet included two labels showing the emblems of either World Stamp Expo '89 or the 20th UPU Congress. These cards do not include inscription and copyright symbols at lower left. *Rouletted 9 1/2 on two or three sides.*

PC136
15¢   multicolored on white, design of PC132   UnVF   UseVF
          FDC *(Dec. 1, 1989)*   2.00   5.00
                                                               1.00

PC136A
15¢   multicolored on white, design of PC131   UnVF   UseVF
          FDC   2.00   5.00
                                                               1.00

PC136B
15¢   multicolored on white, design of PC134   UnVF   UseVF
          FDC   2.00   5.00
                                                               1.00

PC136C
15¢   multicolored on white, design of PC133   UnVF   UseVF
          FDC   2.00   5.00
                                                               1.00
          y. Se-tenant block of 4 (PC136-136C) w/2   12.50
              labels

1989. JEFFERSON MEMORIAL PICTURE POSTAL CARD ISSUE sold for 50¢ each, with a different view of the Jefferson Memorial covering the reverse.

PC137 *Jefferson Memorial*

PC137
15¢   multicolored on white   UnVF   UseVF
          FDC *(Dec. 2, 1989)*   1.25   4.00
                                                    2.00

1990. AMERICAN PAPERMAKING ISSUE

PC138 *Rittenhouse Paper Mill, Germantown, Pa.*

PC138
15¢   multicolored on white   UnVF   UseVF
          FDC *(March 13, 1990)*   .35   1.00
                                                    1.00

1990. WORLD LITERACY YEAR ISSUE

PC139 *Book and globe, World Literacy Year*

PC139
15¢   multicolored on white   UnVF   UseVF
          FDC *(March 22, 1990)*   .35   .50
                                                    1.00

1990. GEORGE CALEB BINGHAM PICTURE POSTAL CARD ISSUE sold for 50¢, with the painting *Fur Traders Descending the Missouri* covering the reverse.

PC140 *Fur traders on the Missouri*

PC140
15¢   multicolored on white   UnVF   UseVF
          FDC *(May 4, 1990)*   1.25   5.00
                                                    1.00

1990. ISAAC ROYALL HOUSE ISSUE 14th in the Historic Preservation Series.

PC141 *Isaac Royall House, Medford, Mass.*

PC141
15¢   multicolored on white   UnVF   UseVF
          FDC *(June 16, 1990)*   .45   1.00
                                                    1.00

1990. POSTAL BUDDY ISSUE computer-generated and printed USPS Eagle card, available from a vending machine under a special license agreement. The cards cost 33¢, plus state sales tax, from one of a group of test machines in Virginia. A variety of borders, messages and backs are known. The cards also were produced in sheets of four.

PC142 *Postal Buddy card*

PC142
15¢   black on white   UnVF   UseVF
          FDC *(July 5, 1990)*   8.50   15.00
                                                    2.50

1990. STANFORD UNIVERSITY ISSUE 15th in the Historic Preservation Series and 2nd in the College Series.

PC143 *Quadrangle, Stanford University*

PC143
15¢   multicolored on white   UnVF   UseVF
          FDC *(Sept. 11, 1990)*   .35   1.00
                                                    1.00

1990. CONSTITUTION HALL PICTURE POSTAL CARD ISSUE sold for 50¢ with an enlarged picture of Memorial Continental Hall, Washington, D.C., covering the reverse. Issued for the Centennial of the Daughters of the American Revolution. It is the 16th in the Historic Preservation Series.

PC144 *Constitution Hall, Washington, D.C.*

PC144		UnVF	UseVF
15¢	**multicolored** on white	1.25	5.00
	FDC *(Oct. 11, 1990)*		1.00

1990. CHICAGO ORCHESTRA HALL ISSUE 17th in the Historic Preservation Series.

PC145 *Chicago Orchestra Hall*

PC145		UnVF	UseVF
15¢	**multicolored** on white	.45	1.00
	FDC *(Oct. 19, 1990)*		1.00

1991. FLAG ISSUE

PC146, MRC39 *Flag*

PC146		UnVF	UseVF
19¢	**black, blue & red** on white	.50	.50
	FDC *(Jan. 24, 1991)*		1.00

1991. POSTAL BUDDY USPS EAGLE CARD ISSUE available in sheets of four from vending machines. (See PC142.)

PC147 *Postal Buddy card*

PC147		UnVF	UseVF
19¢	**black** on white	4.00	15.00
	FDC *(Feb. 3, 1991)*		25.00

1991. CARNEGIE HALL CENTENNIAL ISSUE 18th in the Historic Preservation Series.

PC148 *Carnegie Hall, New York City*

PC148		UnVF	UseVF
19¢	**multicolored** on white	.50	1.00
	FDC *(April 1, 1991)*		1.00

1991. UNIVERSITY OF TEXAS MEDICAL BRANCH AT GALVESTON ISSUE 19th in the Historic Preservation Series and 3rd in the College Series.

PC149 *Old Red, University of Texas Medical Branch, Galveston*

PC149		UnVF	UseVF
19¢	**multicolored** on white	.50	1.00
	FDC *(June 14, 1991)*		1.00

1991. NIAGARA FALLS ISSUE in the America the Beautiful Series. International surface rate and airmail to Canada and Mexico.

PC150 *Niagara Falls*

PC150		UnVF	UseVF
30¢	**multicolored** on white	1.00	5.00
	FDC *(Aug. 21, 1991)*		1.00

1991. BILL OF RIGHTS ISSUE

PC151 *Ratification of the Bill of Rights*

PC151		UnVF	UseVF
19¢	**black, blue & red** on white	.50	.75
	FDC *(Sept. 25, 1991)*		1.00

1991. UNIVERSITY OF NOTRE DAME ISSUE 20th in the Historic Preservation Series and 4th in the College Series.

PC152 *Main Building, University of Notre Dame, South Bend, Ind.*

PC152		UnVF	UseVF
19¢	**multicolored** on white	.50	1.00
	FDC *(Oct. 15, 1991)*		1.00

1991. UNIVERSITY OF VERMONT ISSUE 21st in the Historic Preservation Series and 5th in the College Series.

PC153 *The Old Mill, University of Vermont*

PC153		UnVF	UseVF
19¢	**multicolored** on white	.50	1.00
	FDC *(Oct. 29, 1991)*		1.00

1992. WADSWORTH ATHENEUM SESQUICENTENNIAL ISSUE 22nd in the Historic Preservation Series.

PC154 *Wadsworth Atheneum, Hartford, Conn.*

PC154
19¢   **multicolored** on white   UnVF UseVF
FDC *(Jan. 16, 1992)*   .50   1.00
                                             1.00

1992. UNIVERSITY OF CHICAGO ISSUE 23rd in the Historic Preservation Series and 6th in the College Series.

PC155 *Cobb Hall, University of Chicago*

PC155
19¢   **multicolored** on white   UnVF UseVF
FDC *(Jan. 23, 1992)*   .50   .75
                                             1.00

1992. WILLAMETTE UNIVERSITY ISSUE 24th in the Historic Preservation Series and 7th in the College Series.

PC156 *Waller Hall, Willamette University, Salem, Ore.*

PC156
19¢   **multicolored** on white   UnVF UseVF
FDC *(Feb. 1, 1992)*   .50   .75
                                             1.00

1992. AMERICA'S CUP PICTURE POSTAL CARD ISSUE sold for 50¢ with a picture of *The Ranger*, USA 1937, covering the reverse.

PC157 *America's Cup.* The Reliance, USA 1903

PC157
19¢   **multicolored** on white   UnVF UseVF
FDC *(May 6, 1992)*   1.25 2.00
                                             1.00

1992. COLUMBIA RIVER GORGE ISSUE

PC158 *Columbia River Gorge*

PC158
19¢   **multicolored** on white   UnVF UseVF
FDC *(May 9, 1992)*   .50   .75
                                             1.00

1992. ELLIS ISLAND CENTENNIAL ISSUE 25th in the Historic Preservation Series.

PC159 *Ellis Island Immigration Museum*

PC159
19¢   **multicolored** on white   UnVF UseVF
FDC *(May 11, 1992)*   .50   .75
                                             1.00

1992. POSTAL BUDDY ISSUE available only in sheets of four from vending machines. Price raised to 39¢ per card, plus any state sales tax (see PC142, PC147).

PC160 *Postal Buddy post card*

PC160
19¢   **multicolored** on white, tagged   UnVF   UseVF
FDC *(Nov. 13, 1992)*   15.00 35.00
p. Fluorescent paper   —   27.00

1993. WASHINGTON NATIONAL CATHEDRAL ISSUE 26th in the Historic Preservation Series.

PC161 *Washington National Cathedral*

PC161
19¢   **multicolored** on white   UnVF UseVF
FDC *(Jan. 6, 1993)*   .50   .75
                                             1.00

1993. COLLEGE OF WILLIAM & MARY ISSUE 27th in the Historic Preservation Series and 8th in the College Series.

PC162 *Wren Building, College of William & Mary*

PC162
19¢   **multicolored** on white   UnVF UseVF
FDC *(Feb. 8, 1993)*   .50   .75
                                             1.00

1993. HOLOCAUST MEMORIAL PICTURE POSTAL CARD ISSUE sold for 50¢ with an aerial view of the museum covering the reverse.

PC163 *Holocaust Memorial Museum*

PC163
19¢   **multicolored** on white   UnVF UseVF
FDC *(March 23, 1993)*   1.25 2.00
                                             3.00

1993. FORT RECOVERY ISSUE 28th in the Historic Preservation Series.

PC164 *Fort Recovery, Ohio*

PC164		UnVF	UseVF
19¢	multicolored on white	.50	.75
	FDC (June 13, 1993)		1.00

1993. UNIVERSITY OF NORTH CAROLINA ISSUE 29th in the Historic Preservation Series and 9th in the College Series.

PC165 *Playmaker's Theatre at Chapel Hill, N.C.*

PC165		UnVF	UseVF
19¢	multicolored on white	.50	.75
	FDC (Sept. 14, 1993)		1.00

1993. COLLEGE OF THE HOLY CROSS ISSUE 30th in the Historic Preservation Series and 10th in the College Series.

PC166 *O'Kane Hall, College of the Holy Cross, Worcester, Mass.*

PC166		UnVF	UseVF
19¢	multicolored on white	.50	.45
	FDC (Sept. 17, 1993)		1.00

1993. ILLINOIS COLLEGE ISSUE 31st in the Historic Preservation Series and 11th in the College Series.

PC167 *Beecher Hall, Illinois College, Jacksonville, Ill.*

PC167		UnVF	UseVF
19¢	multicolored	.50	.45
	FDC (Oct. 9, 1993)		1.00

1993. BOWDOIN COLLEGE ISSUE 32nd in the Historic Preservation Series and 12th in the College Series.

PC168 *Massachusetts Hall, Bowdoin College, Brunswick, Maine*

PC168		UnVF	UseVF
19¢	multicolored	.50	.75
	FDC (Oct. 14, 1993)		1.00

1994. LINCOLN HOME ISSUE 33rd in the Historic Preservation Series.

PC169 *Lincoln's Home, Springfield, Ill.*

PC169		UnVF	UseVF
19¢	multicolored	.50	.60
	FDC (Feb. 12, 1994)		1.00

1994. WITTENBERG UNIVERSITY ISSUE 34th in the Historic Preservation Series and 13th in the College Series.

PC170 *Meyers Hall, Wittenberg University, Springfield, Ohio*

PC170		UnVF	UseVF
19¢	multicolored	.50	.75
	FDC (March 11, 1994)		1.00

1994. CANYON DE CHELLY ISSUE

PC171 *Canyon de Chelly, Arizona*

PC171		UnVF	UseVF
19¢	multicolored	.50	.75
	FDC (Aug. 11, 1994)		1.00

1994. ST. LOUIS UNION STATION ISSUE 35th in the Historic Preservation Series.

PC172 *St. Louis Union Station, St. Louis, Mo.*

PC172		UnVF	UseVF
19¢	multicolored	.50	.75
	FDC (Sept. 3, 1994)		1.00

1994. LEGENDS OF THE WEST PICTURE POSTAL CARD ISSUE issued in conjunction with the 20-stamp sheetlet depicting 16 individuals and four "themes" from the Old West. Each card depicts a double-framed design from the sheetlet with the 19¢ postal card rate, while the reverse of the card is an enlarged version of the stamp design. The cards were issued Oct. 18, 1994. Sold in sets for $7.95.

PC173

PC174

PC175

PC173
19¢   Home on the Range   UnVF   UseVF
                                            .60   5.00
PC174
19¢   Buffalo Bill   UnVF   UseVF
                                            .60   5.00
PC175
19¢   Jim Bridger   UnVF   UseVF
                                            .60   5.00

PC176   PC177   PC178

PC176
19¢   Annie Oakley   UnVF   UseVF
                                            .60   5.00
PC177
19¢   Native American Culture   UnVF   UseVF
                                            .60   5.00
PC178
19¢   Chief Joseph   UnVF   UseVF
                                            .60   5.00

PC179   PC180   PC181

PC179
19¢   Bill Pickett   UnVF   UseVF
                                            .60   5.00
PC180
19¢   Bat Masterson   UnVF   UseVF
                                            .60   5.00
PC181
19¢   John Fremont   UnVF   UseVF
                                            .60   5.00

PC182   PC183   PC184

PC182
19¢   Wyatt Earp   UnVF   UseVF
                                            .60   5.00
PC183
19¢   Nellie Cashman   UnVF   UseVF
                                            .60   5.00
PC184
19¢   Charles Goodnight   UnVF   UseVF
                                            .60   5.00

PC185   PC186   PC187

PC185
19¢   Geronimo   UnVF   UseVF
                                            .60   5.00
PC186
19¢   Kit Carson   UnVF   UseVF
                                            .60   5.00
PC187
19¢   Wild Bill Hickok   UnVF   UseVF
                                            .60   5.00

PC188   PC189   PC190

PC188
19¢   Western Wildlife   UnVF   UseVF
                                            .60   5.00
PC189
19¢   Jim Beckwourth   UnVF   UseVF
                                            .60   5.00
PC190
19¢   Bill Tilghman   UnVF   UseVF
                                            .60   5.00

PC191   PC192

PC191
19¢   Sacagawea   UnVF   UseVF
                                            .60   5.00
PC192
19¢   Overland Mail   UnVF   UseVF
                                            .60   5.00
       FDC (any card) (Oct. 18, 1994)   1.25

1994. OLD GLORY "G" NON-DENOMINATED ISSUE

PC193 *Old Glory, "G"*

PC193
20¢   multicolored   UnVF   UseVF
                                            .40   .50
       FDC (Dec. 13, 1994)   1.00

1995. RED BARN ISSUE

PC194, MRC40 *Red Barn*

PC194
20¢   multicolored   UnVF   UseVF
                                            .40   .50
       FDC (Jan. 3, 1995)   1.00

1995. CIVIL WAR PICTURE POSTAL CARD ISSUE issued in

conjunction with the 20 stamp sheetlet. Each card depicted a design
from the sheetlet with the 20¢ post card rate, while the reverse of the
card was an enlarged version of the stamp design. Issued June 29,
1995. Sold in sets for $7.95.

PC195   PC196   PC197

			UnVF	UseVF
PC195				
20¢	*Monitor Virginia*		.75	3.50
PC196			UnVF	UseVF
20¢	Robert E. Lee		.75	3.50
PC197			UnVF	UseVF
20¢	Clara Barton		.75	3.50

PC198 PC199 PC200

			UnVF	UseVF
PC198				
20¢	Ulysses S. Grant		.75	3.50
PC199			UnVF	UseVF
20¢	Battle of Shiloh		.75	3.50
PC200			UnVF	UseVF
20¢	Jefferson Davis		.75	3.50

PC201 PC202 PC203

			UnVF	UseVF
PC201				
20¢	David Farragut		.75	3.50
PC202			UnVF	UseVF
20¢	Frederick Douglass		.75	3.50
PC203			UnVF	UseVF
20¢	Raphael Semmes		.75	3.50

PC204 PC205 PC206

			UnVF	UseVF
PC204				
20¢	Abraham Lincoln		.75	3.50
PC205			UnVF	UseVF
20¢	Harriet Tubman		.75	3.50
PC206			UnVF	UseVF
20¢	Stand Watie		.75	3.50

PC207 PC208 PC209

			UnVF	UseVF
PC207				
20¢	Joseph E. Johnston		.75	3.50
PC208			UnVF	UseVF
20¢	Winfield Hancock		.75	3.50
PC209			UnVF	UseVF
20¢	Mary Chesnut		.75	3.50

PC210 PC211 PC212

			UnVF	UseVF
PC210				
20¢	Battle of Chancellorsville		.75	3.50
PC211			UnVF	UseVF
20¢	William T. Sherman		.75	3.50
PC212			UnVF	UseVF
20¢	Phoebe Pember		.75	3.50

PC213 PC214 PC215

			UnVF	UseVF
PC213				
20¢	Stonewall Jackson		.75	3.50
PC214			UnVF	UseVF
20¢	Battle of Gettysburg		.75	3.50
	FDC (any card) *(June 29, 1995)*			1.10

1995. AMERICAN CLIPPER SHIPS ISSUE

PC215 *American Clipper Ships*

			UnVF	UseVF
PC215				
20¢	multicolored		.40	.50
	FDC *(Sept. 3, 1995)*			1.00

1995. COMIC STRIP CLASSICS PICTURE POSTAL CARD ISSUE

issued in conjunction with the sheetlet of 20 stamps commemorating the centennial of the comic strip. An enlarged version of the design appears on the reverse. Issued Oct. 1, 1995. Sold in sets for $7.95.

PC216 PC217 PC218

			UnVF	UseVF
PC216				
20¢	The Yellow Kid		.60	3.00
PC217			UnVF	UseVF
20¢	Katzenjammer Kids		.60	3.00
PC218			UnVF	UseVF
20¢	Little Nemo in Slumberland		.60	3.00

 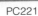

PC219 PC220 PC221

PC219
20¢   Bringing up Father

	UnVF	UseVF
	.60	3.00

PC220
20¢   Krazy Kat

	UnVF	UseVF
	.60	3.00

PC221
20¢   Rube Goldberg's Inventions

	UnVF	UseVF
	.60	3.00

PC222   PC223   PC224

PC222
20¢   Toonerville Folks

	UnVF	UseVF
	.60	3.00

PC223
20¢   Gasoline Alley

	UnVF	UseVF
	.60	3.00

PC224
20¢   Barney Google

	UnVF	UseVF
	.60	3.00

PC225   PC226   PC227

PC225
20¢   Little Orphan Annie

	UnVF	UseVF
	.60	3.00

PC226
20¢   Popeye

	UnVF	UseVF
	.60	3.00

PC227
20¢   Blondie

	UnVF	UseVF
	.60	3.00

PC228   PC229   PC230

PC228
20¢   Dick Tracy

	UnVF	UseVF
	.60	3.00

PC229
20¢   Alley Oop

	UnVF	UseVF
	.60	3.00

PC230
20¢   Nancy

	UnVF	UseVF
	.60	3.00

PC231   PC232   PC233

PC231
20¢   Flash Gordon

	UnVF	UseVF
	.60	3.00

PC232
20¢   Li'l Abner

	UnVF	UseVF
	.60	3.00

PC233
20¢   Terry and the Pirates

	UnVF	UseVF
	.60	3.00

PC234   PC235

PC234
20¢   Prince Valiant

	UnVF	UseVF
	.60	3.00

PC235
20¢   Brenda Starr, Reporter

	UnVF	UseVF
	.60	3.00
FDC (any card) *(Oct. 1, 1995)*		1.00

1996. WINTER FARM SCENE ISSUE

PC236 *Winter farm scene*

PC236
20¢   **multicolored**

	UnVF	UseVF
	.40	.50
FDC *(Feb. 23, 1996)*		1.00

1996. ATLANTA OLYMPICS PICTURE POSTAL CARD ISSUE issued
in conjunction with the 20 stamp sheetlet. The reverse features an enlargement of the stamp image. Issued May 2, 1996. Sold in booklets of 20 for $12.95.

PC237   PC238   PC239

PC237
20¢   Men's Cycling

	UnVF	UseVF
	.90	5.00

PC238
20¢   Women's Diving

	UnVF	UseVF
	.90	5.00

PC239
20¢   Women's Running

	UnVF	UseVF
	.90	5.00

PC240   PC241   PC242

PC240
20¢   Men's Canoeing

	UnVF	UseVF
	.90	5.00

PC241
20¢   Decathlon (Javelin)

	UnVF	UseVF
	.90	5.00

PC242
20¢   Women's Soccer

	UnVF	UseVF
	.90	5.00

PC243   PC244   PC245

PC243
20¢   Men's Shot Put   UnVF .90   UseVF 5.00

PC244
20¢   Women's Sailboarding   UnVF .90   UseVF 5.00

PC245
20¢   Women's Gymnastics   UnVF .90   UseVF 5.00

PC246   PC247   PC248

PC246
20¢   Freestyle Wrestling   UnVF .90   UseVF 5.00

PC247
20¢   Women's Softball   UnVF .90   UseVF 5.00

PC248
20¢   Women's Swimming   UnVF .90   UseVF 5.00

PC249   PC250   PC251

PC249
20¢   Men's Sprints   UnVF .90   UseVF 5.00

PC250
20¢   Men's Rowing   UnVF .90   UseVF 5.00

PC251
20¢   Volleyball   UnVF .90   UseVF 5.00

PC252   PC253   PC254

PC252
20¢   Men's Basketball   UnVF .90   UseVF 5.00

PC253
20¢   Equestrian   UnVF .90   UseVF 5.00

PC254
20¢   Men's Gymnastics   UnVF .90   UseVF 5.00

PC255   PC256

PC255
20¢   Men's Swimming   UnVF .90   UseVF 5.00

PC256
20¢   Men's Hurdles   UnVF .90   UseVF 5.00
    Booklet of 20   16.00
    FDC (any card) *(May 2, 1996)*   1.10

1996. ST. JOHN'S COLLEGE ISSUE 36th in the Historic Preservation Series and 14th in the College Series.

PC257 *McDowell Hall, St. John's College, Annapolis, Md.*

St. John's College, Annapolis, Maryland

PC257
20¢   multicolored   UnVF .50   UseVF .50
    FDC *(June 1, 1996)*   1.00

1996. PRINCETON UNIVERSITY ISSUE 37th in the Historic Preservation Series and 15th in the College Series.

PC258 *Alexander Hall, Princeton University*

PRINCETON UNIVERSITY • 250TH ANNIVERSARY

PC258
20¢   multicolored   UnVF .50   UseVF .50
    FDC *(Sept. 20, 1996)*   1.00

1996. ENDANGERED SPECIES PICTURE POSTAL CARD ISSUE issued in conjunction with the 15-stamp sheetlet. Each card features an enlargement of the stamp image. Issued Oct. 2, 1996. Sold in a 5-panel booklet for $11.95. *Printed by Art Litho Co.*

PC259   PC260   PC261

PC259
20¢   Florida panther   UnVF 1.10   UseVF 5.00

PC260
20¢   Black-footed ferret   UnVF 1.10   UseVF 5.00

PC261
20¢   American crocodile   UnVF 1.10   UseVF 5.00

PC262   PC263   PC264

PC262
20¢   Piping plover   UnVF 1.10   UseVF 5.00

PC263
20¢   Gila trout   UnVF 1.10   UseVF 5.00

PC264
20¢   Florida manatee   UnVF 1.10   UseVF 5.00

PC265   PC266   PC267

PC265
20¢   Schaus swallowtail butterfly   UnVF 1.10   UseVF 5.00

PC266				UnVF	UseVF
20¢	Woodland caribou			1.10	5.00
PC267				UnVF	UseVF
20¢	Thick-billed parrot			1.10	5.00

PC268

PC269

PC270

PC268		UnVF	UseVF
20¢	San Francisco garter snake	1.10	5.00
PC269		UnVF	UseVF
20¢	Ocelot	1.10	5.00
PC270		UnVF	UseVF
20¢	Wyoming toad	1.10	5.00

PC271

PC272

PC273

PC271		UnVF	UseVF
20¢	California condor	1.10	5.00
PC272		UnVF	UseVF
20¢	Hawaiian monk seal	1.10	5.00
PC273		UnVF	UseVF
20¢	Brown pelican	1.10	5.00
	Booklet of 15	15.00	
	FDC (any card) (Oct. 2, 1996)		1.50

Love Series

1997. LOVE SWANS PICTURE POSTAL CARD ISSUE Current and previous Love stamp designs enlarged on back. Issued Feb. 4, 1997. Sold in sets of 12 cards (2 panels each of designs a.-d.; 1 panel of designs e.-h.) for $6.95. *Offset by Ashton-Potter (USA) Ltd.*

PC274 *Swans*

PC274		UnVF	UseVF
	multicolored		
a.	Bird in Rose Heart (1994)	.75	2.25
b.	2 Birds in Rose Basket (1994)	.75	2.25
c.	Swans, vert. (1997)	.75	2.25
d.	Swans, horiz. (1997)	.75	2.25
e.	Puppy (1986)	.75	2.25
f.	Paper cut-out Heart (1987)	.75	2.25
g.	Pennsylvania-Dutch 2 birds & Heart (1990)	.75	2.25
h.	Heart Sunrise (1994)	.75	2.25
	FDC (any card) (Feb. 4, 1997)		1.00

1997. CITY COLLEGE OF NEW YORK ISSUE 38th in the Historic Preservation Series and 16th in the College Series.

PC275 *City College of New York*

PC275				UnVF	UseVF
20¢	multicolored			.60	1.50
	FDC (May 7, 1997)				1.00

1997. GOLDEN GATE BRIDGE AND SAN FRANCISCO HARBOR ISSUE issued in conjunction with Pacific '97 World Stamp Exhibition.

PC276 *Golden Gate Bridge, San Francisco Harbor (in daylight)*

PC276		UnVF	UseVF
20¢	multicolored	.60	1.00
	FDC (June 2, 1997)		1.00

PC277 *Golden Gate Bridge at sunset*

PC277		UnVF	UseVF
50¢	multicolored	.60	1.00
	FDC (June 2, 1997)		1.00

Warner Bros. Cartoon Characters Series

1997. BUGS BUNNY PICTURE POSTAL CARD ISSUE issued in conjunction with the self-adhesive stamp; an enlarged image appears on the back. Booklet of 10 cards sold for $5.95. *Offset by Banknote Corporation of America.*

PC278 *Bugs Bunny*

PC278		UnVF	UseVF
20¢	multicolored	.75	2.50
	Booklet of 10	7.50	
	FDC (May 22, 1997)		1.00

1997. FORT MCHENRY ISSUE 39th in the Historic Preservation Series.

PC279 *Fort McHenry, Baltimore, Md.*

PC279		UnVF	UseVF
20¢	multicolored	.50	.75
	FDC (Sept. 9, 1997)		1.00

1997. MOVIE MONSTER PICTURE POSTAL CARD ISSUE issued in conjuction with the 20-image sheetlet. Each postcard featured an enlargement of the stamp image. Booklet of 20 cards (four of each design) sold for $5.95. *All multicolored, tagged, offset by Ashton-Potter (USA) Ltd.*

PC280   PC281   PC282

		UnVF	UseVF
PC280		**UnVF**	**UseVF**
20¢	Lon Chaney, Phantom of the Opera	.75	3.50
PC281		**UnVF**	**UseVF**
20¢	Bela Lugosi, Dracula	.75	3.50
PC282		**UnVF**	**UseVF**
20¢	Boris Karloff, Frankenstein	.75	3.50

PC283   PC284

		UnVF	UseVF
PC283		**UnVF**	**UseVF**
20¢	Boris Karloff, The Mummy	.75	3.50
PC284		**UnVF**	**UseVF**
20¢	Lon Chaney Jr., The Wolf Man	.75	3.50
	Booklet of 20	9.00	
	FDC (any card) (Sept. 30, 1997)		1.00

1998. UNIVERSITY OF MISSISSIPPI ISSUE 40th in the Historic Preservation Series and 17th in the College Series.

PC285 *The Lyceum, University of Mississippi, Oxford*

		UnVF	UseVF
PC285		**UnVF**	**UseVF**
20¢	**multicolored**	.50	.75
	FDC (April 20, 1998)		1.00

1998. SYLVESTER & TWEETY PICTURE POSTAL CARD ISSUE in the Warner Bros. Cartoon Character Series. An enlargement of the stamp image appears on the back. Booklet of 10 cards sold for $5.95. *Offset by Ashton-Potter (USA) Ltd.*

PC286 *Sylvester & Tweety*

		UnVF	UseVF
PC286		**UnVF**	**UseVF**
20¢	**multicolored**	.75	3.50
	Booklet of 10	7.50	
	FDC (April 27, 1998)		1.00

1998. GIRARD COLLEGE ISSUE 41st in the Historic Preservation Series and 18th in the College Series.

PC287 *Founders Hall, Girard College, Philadelphia*

		UnVF	UseVF
PC287		**UnVF**	**UseVF**
20¢	**multicolored**	.50	.75
	FDC (May 1, 1998)		1.00

1998. TROPICAL BIRDS PICTURE POSTAL CARD ISSUE an enlargement of the stamp image appears on the back. Booklet of 20 cards (5 of each design) sold for $6.95. *Offset by Ashton-Potter (USA) Ltd., (2 million printed, 100,000 sets).*

PC288   PC289

		UnVF	UseVF
PC288		**UnVF**	**UseVF**
20¢	Antillean Euphonia of Puerto Rico	.60	3.00
PC289		**UnVF**	**UseVF**
20¢	Green-throated Carib of Puerto Rico	.60	3.00

PC290   PC291

		UnVF	UseVF
PC290		**UnVF**	**UseVF**
20¢	Crested Honeycreeper of Hawaii	.60	3.00
PC291		**UnVF**	**UseVF**
20¢	Cardinal Honeyeater of Western Samoa	.60	3.00
	Booklet of 20	10.00	
	FDC (any card) (July 29, 1998)		2.50

1998. AMERICAN BALLET PICTURE POSTAL CARD ISSUE an enlargement of the stamp image appears on the back. Booklet of 10 cards sold for $5.95. *Offset by Milken Companies for Ashton-Potter (USA) Ltd.*

PC292 *Ballet dancer*

		UnVF	UseVF
PC292		**UnVF**	**UseVF**
20¢	**multicolored,** tagged (1,000,000)	.75	3.00
	n. Booklet of 10	7.50	
	FDC (Sept. 16, 1998)		1.00

1998. NORTHEASTERN UNIVERSITY ISSUE 42nd in the Historic Preservation Series and 19th in the College Series, featured a stylized window detail of Kerr Hall, a residence hall noted on the National Register of Historic Places. The institution in Boston, Mass., was founded Oct. 3, 1898. *Offset by Government Printing Office.*

PC293 *Kerr Hall, Northeastern University*

PC293

	UnVF	UseVF
20¢ **multicolored,** tagged *(21,000,000)*	.50	.75
FDC *(Oct. 3, 1998)*		1.00

1998. BRANDEIS UNIVERSITY ISSUE 43rd in the Historic Preservation Series and 20th in the College Series, portrayed a photo of Usen Castle, which was built of colonial fieldstone between 1928 and 1940 and is an undergraduate residence hall. The nation's youngest private research university, in Waltham, Mass., was named for Louis Dembitz Brandeis, an associate justice of the U.S. Supreme Court. It was founded in 1948. *Offset by Government Printing Office.*

PC294 *Usen Castle, Brandeis University*

PC294

	UnVF	UseVF
20¢ **multicolored,** tagged *(21,000,000)*	.50	.75
FDC *(Oct. 17, 1998)*		1.00

1999. VICTORIAN LOVE PICTURE POSTAL CARD ISSUE in the Love Series designed to be used for special greetings of affection, featured a paper-lace-and-flowers motif reminiscent of the late 1800s. An enlargement of the stamp design appears on the back. Sold in packs of 20 cards (5 panels of 4 cards each) for $6.95. *Offset by Banknote Corporation of America.*

PC295 *Victorian Valentine*

PC295

	UnVF	UseVF
20¢ **multicolored,** tagged *(2,000,000)*	.50	2.50
Pane of 4 cards	2.40	
FDC *(Jan. 28, 1999)*		1.00

1999. UNIVERSITY OF WISCONSIN-MADISON ISSUE 44th in the Historic Preservation Series and 21st in the College Series, portrayed an old lithograph of Bascom Hill, a campus landmark. *Offset by Government Printing Office.*

PC296 *Bascom Hill, University of Wisconsin, Madison*

PC296

	UnVF	UseVF
20¢ **multicolored** *(6,000,000)*	.50	.75
FDC *(Feb. 5, 1999)*		1.00

1999. WASHINGTON AND LEE UNIVERSITY ISSUE 45th in the Historic Preservation Series and 22nd in the College Series, noted the 250th anniversary of the nation's sixth oldest college. It was named for George Washington, who contributed to its endowment in 1796, and Gen. Robert E. Lee, who was its president 1865-70 (see CM324). *Offset by Government Printing Office.*

PC297 *Colonnade, Washington and Lee University, Lexington, Va.*

PC297

	UnVF	UseVF
20¢ **multicolored**	.50	.75
FDC *(Feb. 11, 1999)*		1.00

1999. REDWOOD LIBRARY & ATHENAEUM ISSUE 46th in the Historic Preservation Series, commemorated the 250th anniversary of the nation's oldest lending library. Its original building is said to be the oldest building in the United States. The design, an old view of Newport, R.I., is based on an 1871 illustration. *Offset by Government Printing Office.*

PC298 *View of Newport, R.I., from 1871*

PC298

	UnVF	UseVF
20¢ **red & black** *(6,000,000)*	.50	.75
FDC *(March 11, 1999)*		1.00

1999. DAFFY DUCK PICTURE POSTAL CARD ISSUE in the Warner Bros. Cartoon Character Series. An enlargement of the stamp image appears on the back. Booklet of 10 cards sold for $6.95. *Printed by Ashton-Potter (USA) Ltd.*

PC299 *Daffy Duck*

PC299

	UnVF	UseVF
20¢ **multicolored**	.85	2.50
Booklet of 10	8.50	
FDC *(April 16, 1999)*		1.00

1999. MOUNT VERNON ISSUE 47th in the Historic Preservation Series, was based on a painting, *A View of Mount Vernon,* from about 1792. The estate overlooking the Potomac River was inherited by George Washington in 1751, and he lived there 1759-99. George and Martha Washington are buried there. (See EN808-13, CM172, 571.) *Offset by Government Printing Office.*

PC300 *Mount Vernon*

PC300

	UnVF	UseVF
20¢ **multicolored** *(6,000,000)*	.50	.75
FDC *(May 14, 1999)*		1.00

1999. MOUNT RAINIER ISSUE in the Scenic American Landmarks Series paid a new international postal card rate to all countries other than Canada and Mexico and portrayed the snow-clad mountain that dominates the Cascade Mountain Range southeast of Tacoma, Wash. The card coincided with the 100th anniversary of Mount Rainier National Park. *Printed by Government Printing Office.*

PC301 *Mount Rainier*

		UnVF	UseVF
PC301		1.00	3.50
55¢	**multicolored**		
	FDC *(May 15, 1999)*		1.50

1999. BLOCK ISLAND LIGHTHOUSE ISSUE in the Scenic America Series portrayed the highest lighthouse in New England, 200 feet above the shoals and ledges that sank dozens of ships off Rhode Island. The lighthouse was established in 1875 on the island, nine miles from the mainland of Rhode Island. *Offset by Government Printing Office.*

PC302 *Block Island Lighthouse*

		UnVF	UseVF
PC302		.50	.75
20¢	**multicolored**		
	FDC *(July 24, 1999)*		1.00
	40-card sheets *(Nov. 10, 1999)*	20.00	

1999. ALL ABOARD! ISSUE Depicted five illustrated postal cards with the same designs as the 33¢ stamps and corresponding 20¢ postcard-rate stamp indicia. Booklet of 20 cards sold for $6.95. *Printed by Ashton-Potter (USA) Ltd.*

PC303 *Daylight;* PC304 *20th Century;* PC305 *Superchief;* PC306 *Congressional;* PC307 *Hiawatha*

		UnVF	UseVF
PC303		.50	2.50
20¢	Daylight, **multicolored**		
PC304		.50	2.50
20¢	20th Century Limited, **multicolored**		
PC305		.50	2.50
20¢	Superchief, **multicolored**		
PC306		.50	2.50
20¢	Congressional, **multicolored**		
PC307		.50	2.50
20¢	Hiawatha, **multicolored**		
	Booklet of 20	10.00	—
	FDC (any card) *(Aug. 26, 1999)*		1.00

2000. UNIVERSITY OF UTAH ISSUE 48th in the Historic Preservation Series and 23rd in the College Series, was released as part of the sesquicentennial celebration at the university in Salt Lake City, Utah. *Offset by the Government Printing Office.*

PC308 *University of Utah*

		UnVF	UseVF
PC308		.50	.75
20¢	**multicolored**		
	FDC *(Feb. 28, 2000)*		1.50

2000. RYMAN AUDITORIUM ISSUE 49th in the Historic Preservation Series saluted the former home of the Grand Ole Opry in Nashville, Tenn. *Offset by the Government Printing Office.*

PC309 *Ryman Auditorium*

		UnVF	UseVF
PC309		.50	.75
20¢	**multicolored**		
	FDC *(March 18, 2000)*		1.50

2000. WILE E. COYOTE & ROAD RUNNER ISSUE Warner Bros. Cartoon Character Series. An enlargement of the stamp image appears on the back. Booklet of 10 cards sold for $6.95. Designed and illustrated by Ed Wleczyk, Los Angeles. *Offset by Banknote Corporation of America.* 1 million printed, (100,000 books).

PC310 *Wile E. Coyote & Road Runner*

		UnVF	UseVF
PC310		.85	2.50
20¢	**multicolored**		
	Booklet of 10	8.50	—
	FDC *(April 26, 2000)*		1.50

2000. ADOPTION ISSUE intended to raise awareness that more than 100,000 children are available for adoption in the United States each year. Booklet of 10 cards sold for $6.95. *Offset by Banknote Corporation of America.*

PC311 *Drawing of family*

PC311
20¢   **multicolored**

	UnVF	UseVF
	.85	2.50
Booklet of 10	9.00	—
FDC *(May 10, 2000)*		1.50

2000. MIDDLEBURY COLLEGE ISSUE 50th in the Historic Preservation Series and 24th in the College Series, featured the Vermont college's original three buildings, which date to 1815-61 and are known as Old Stone Row. Designed by Howard Paine, Delaplane, Va., illustrated by Arnold Holeywell, Warrenton, Va. *Offset by Government Printing Office.*

PC312 *Middlebury College, Old Stone Row*

PC312
20¢   **multicolored** *(4,000,000 printed)*

	UnVF	UseVF
	.50	.75
FDC *(May 19, 2000)*		1.50

2000. STARS AND STRIPES ISSUE Designed by Richard Sheaff, Scottsdale, Ariz. Sold in packs of 20 cards (5 panels of 4 cards each) for $8.95. *Offset by Ashton-Potter USA.* 2 million cards printed, 100,000 sets of 20 cards.

PC313
Sons of Liberty Flag

PC314
New England Flag

PC313
20¢   **multicolored**

	UnVF	UseVF
	.65	2.50

PC314
20¢   **multicolored**

	UnVF	UseVF
	.65	2.50

PC315
Forster Flag

PC316
Continental Colors

PC315
20¢   **multicolored**

	UnVF	UseVF
	.65	2.50

PC316
20¢   **multicolored**

	UnVF	UseVF
	.65	2.50

PC317
Francis Hopkinson Flag

PC318
Brandywine Flag

PC317
20¢   **multicolored**

PC318
20¢   **multicolored**

	UnVF	UseVF
	.65	2.50
	UnVF	UseVF
	.65	2.50

PC319
John Paul Jones Flag

PC320
Pierre L'Enfant Flag

PC319
20¢   **multicolored**

PC320
20¢   **multicolored**

	UnVF	UseVF
	.65	2.50
	UnVF	UseVF
	.65	2.50

PC321
Indian Peace Flag

PC322
Easton Flag

32321
20¢   **multicolored**

PC322
20¢   **multicolored**

	UnVF	UseVF
	.65	2.50
	UnVF	UseVF
	.65	2.50

PC323
Star-Spangled Banner

PC324
Bennington Flag

PC323
20¢   **multicolored**

PC324
20¢   **multicolored**

	UnVF	UseVF
	.65	2.50
	UnVF	UseVF
	.65	2.50

Please read the introduction to this catalog carefully. It contains much valuable information for all stamp collectors, and also makes the catalog easier for you to use.

PC325
Great Star Flag

PC326
29-Star Flag

		UnVF	UseVF
PC325		.65	2.50
20¢	multicolored		
PC326		UnVF	UseVF
20¢	multicolored	.65	2.50

PC327
Fort Sumter Flag

PC328
Centennial Flag

		UnVF	UseVF
PC327		.65	2.50
20¢	multicolored		
PC328		UnVF	UseVF
20¢	multicolored	.65	2.50

PC329
38-Star Flag

PC330
Peace Flag

		UnVF	UseVF
PC329		.65	2.50
20¢	multicolored		
PC330		UnVF	UseVF
20¢	multicolored	.65	2.50

PC331
48-Star Flag

PC332
50-Star Flag

		UnVF	UseVF
PC331		.65	2.50
20¢	multicolored		
PC332		UnVF	UseVF
20¢	multicolored	.65	2.50
	FDC *(June 14, 2000),* any single		1.50

2000. LEGENDS OF BASEBALL ISSUE Designed by Derry Noyes, Washington, D.C. Booklet of 20 cards sold for $8.95. *Gravure by Sennett Security Products.*

		UnVF	UseVF
PC333		.65	2.50
20¢	multicolored		

PC333
Jackie Robinson

PC334
Eddie Collins

PC335
Christy Mathewson

		UnVF	UseVF
PC334		.65	2.50
20¢	multicolored		
PC335		UnVF	UseVF
20¢	multicolored	.65	2.50

PC336
Ty Cobb

PC337
George Sisler

PC338
Rogers Hornsby

		UnVF	UseVF
PC336		.65	2.50
20¢	multicolored		
PC337		UnVF	UseVF
20¢	multicolored	.65	2.50
PC338		UnVF	UseVF
20¢	multicolored	.65	2.50

PC339
Mickey Cochrane

PC340
Babe Ruth

PC341
Walter Johnson

		UnVF	UseVF
PC339		.65	2.50
20¢	multicolored		
PC340		UnVF	UseVF
20¢	multicolored	.65	2.50
PC341		UnVF	UseVF
20¢	multicolored	.65	2.50

PC342
Roberto Clemente

PC343
Lefty Grove

PC344
Tris Speaker

PC342		UnVF	UseVF
20¢	multicolored	.65	2.50
PC343		UnVF	UseVF
20¢	multicolored	.65	2.50
PC344		UnVF	UseVF
20¢	multicolored	.65	2.50

PC345 *Cy Young*   PC346 *Jimmie Foxx*   PC347 *Pie Traynor*

PC345		UnVF	UseVF
20¢	multicolored	.65	2.50
PC346		UnVF	UseVF
20¢	multicolored	.65	2.50
PC347		UnVF	UseVF
20¢	multicolored	.65	2.50

PC348 *Satchel Paige*   PC349 *Honus Wagner*   PC350 *Josh Gibson*

PC348		UnVF	UseVF
20¢	multicolored	.65	2.50
PC349		UnVF	UseVF
20¢	multicolored	.65	2.50
PC350		UnVF	UseVF
20¢	multicolored	.65	2.50

PC351 *Dizzy Dean*   PC352 *Lou Gehrig*

PC351		UnVF	UseVF
20¢	multicolored	.65	2.50
PC352		UnVF	UseVF
20¢	multicolored	.65	2.50
	Booklet of 20	12.00	—
	FDC (any card) (July 6, 2000)		1.50

Holiday Contemporary Series

2000. DEER POSTAL CARD ISSUE in the Holiday Contemporary Series had the same design as Christmas-season stamps issued in three formats in 1998. Designed by Tom Nikosey, Canoga Park, Calif.

Issued in packs of 5 sheets of 4 cards ($8.95) (blue, red, purple, green), offset by Ashton-Potter (USA), (2 million printed, 100,000 sets of 5 sheets).

PC353, PC354, PC355, PC356
Leaping reindeer

PC353		UnVF	UseVF
20¢	red & gold	.65	2.50
PC354		UnVF	UseVF
20¢	blue & gold	.65	2.50
PC355		UnVF	UseVF
20¢	purple & gold	.65	2.50
PC356		UnVF	UseVF
20¢	green & gold	.65	2.50
	Sheet of 4	2.75	
	FDC (Oct. 12, 2000) any card		1.50

2001. BADLANDS NATIONAL PARK ISSUE in the Scenic American Landscapes Series, international rate, highlighted the 244,000-acre national park in southwestern South Dakota, which constitutes the largest protected mixed-grasses prairie in the United States. *Offset by the Government Printing Office.*

PC357 *Badlands scene*

PC357		UnVF	UseVF
70¢	multicolored	1.40	2.50
	FDC (Feb. 22, 2001)		2.00

2001. YALE UNIVERSITY ISSUE in the Historic Preservation Series helped to commemorate the 300th anniversary of the founding of the school in New Haven, Conn. A contemporary photo of Connecticut Hall is featured. Designed by Derry Noyes, *offset by Government Printing Office (6 million).*

PC358 *Yale's Connecticut Hall*

PC358		UnVF	UseVF
20¢	multicolored	.50	.75
	FDC (March 30, 2001)		1.50

2001. UNIVERSITY OF SOUTH CAROLINA ISSUE 52nd in the Historic Preservation Series helped to commemorate the 200th anniversary of the founding of the school in Columbia, S.C. It featured a detail from a painting ©1820 of the historic Horseshoe district on the main campus. Designed by Ethel Kessler, *offset by Government Printing Office (6 million).*

PC359 *USC's Horseshoe District*

PC359		UnVF	UseVF
20¢	multicolored	.50	.75
	FDC *(April 26, 2001)*		1.50

2001. NORTHWESTERN UNIVERSITY ISSUE in the Historic Preservation Series helped to commemorate the 150th anniversary of the founding of the school in Evanston, Ill. A drawing of the tower of University Hall, built in 1869 and the oldest building on campus, is featured. *Designed by Howard Paine from the illustration by Arnold C. Holeywell, Warrenton, Va., offset by Government Printing Office (6 million).*

PC360 *Northwestern's University Hall tower*

PC360		UnVF	UseVF
20¢	multicolored	.50	.75
	FDC *(April 28, 2001)*		1.50

2001. UNIVERSITY OF PORTLAND ISSUE 54th in the Historic Preservation Series helped to commemorate the 100th anniversary of the founding of the school in Portland, Ore. A computer-generated illustration of Waldschmidt Hall, the oldest building on the campus, is featured. *Designed by Richard Sheaff from an illustration by John Pirman, New York, N.Y., offset by Government Printing Office (6 million).*

PC361 *University of Portland's Waldschmidt Hall*

PC361		UnVF	UseVF
20¢	multicolored	.50	.75
	FDC *(May 1, 2001)*		1.50

2001. BASEBALL'S LEGENDARY PLAYING FIELDS ISSUE featured 10 historic baseball parks, only three of which were still in use. Designs were taken from contemporary picture postcards, and the cards, issued in an attached booklet, had the design of the original card in full size on the reverse. Booklet of 10 cards sold for $6.95. *Designed by Phil Jordan based on postcards from the collection of Ron Menchine, a former Washington Senators announcer, printed by Avery Dennison.*

> Every reasonable effort has been made to make the values in this catalog as accurate, realistic, and up-to-date as possible.

PC362

PC363

PC362		UnVF	UseVF
21¢	multicolored	.90	2.50
PC363		UnVF	UseVF
21¢	multicolored	.90	2.50

PC364

PC365

PC364		UnVF	UseVF
21¢	multicolored	.90	2.50
PC365		UnVF	UseVF
21¢	multicolored	.90	2.50

PC366

PC367

PC366		UnVF	UseVF
21¢	multicolored	.90	2.50
PC367		UnVF	UseVF
21¢	multicolored	.90	2.50

PC368

PC369

PC368		UnVF	UseVF
21¢	multicolored	.90	2.50
PC369		UnVF	UseVF
21¢	multicolored	.90	2.50

PC370

PC371

PC370		UnVF	UseVF
21¢	multicolored	.90	2.50
PC371		UnVF	UseVF
21¢	multicolored	.90	2.50
	FDC *(June 27, 2001)* any card		1.50
	Booklet of 10	9.00	

2001. WHITE BARN POSTAL CARD ISSUE showed a white barn behind a field.

PC372 *White barn*

PC372		UnVF	UseVF
21¢	multicolored	.50	.75
	FDC (Sept. 20, 2001)		1.50

2001. PORKY PIG ("THAT'S ALL, FOLKS") ISSUE in the Warner Bros. Cartoon Character Series featured the final Looney Tunes stamp design in a 21¢ denomination and as an enlarged illustration on the reverse of the postal card. Booklet of 10 cards sold for $7.25. *Offset by Banknote Corporation of America.*

PC373 *Porky Pig ("That's All, Folks")*

PC373		UnVF	UseVF
21¢	multicolored	.70	2.50
	FDC (Oct. 1, 2001)		1.50
	Booklet of 10	9.75	

2001. OLD WORLD SANTAS ISSUE in the Christmas Series featured the 2001 Christmas stamp images with 21¢ denominations as stamp indicia and as enlarged illustrations on the reverse. Sold in packs of 20 cards (5 panels of 4 cards) for $9.25. *Offset by Banknote Corporation of America.*

PC374

PC375

PC376

PC377

PC374		UnVF	UseVF
21¢	multicolored	.70	2.50
PC375		UnVF	UseVF
21¢	multicolored	.70	2.50
PC376		UnVF	UseVF
21¢	multicolored	.70	2.50
PC377		UnVF	UseVF
21¢	multicolored	.70	2.50
	FDC (Oct. 1, 2001) any card		1.50

2002. CARLSBAD CAVERNS ISSUE in the Scenic America Series shows the natural wonder of a cave ecosystem with its many stalagmites and stalactites. *Printed by Government Printing Office. Rectangular block tagging to right of design.*

PC378 *Carlsbad Caverns*

PC378		UnVF	UseVF
23¢	multicolored on white	.50	.25
	FDC (June 7, 2002 - Carlsbad, N.M.)		1.50

2002. TEDDY BEARS ISSUE featured four different photos of vintage bears prized by collectors and marks the 100th anniversary of the teddy bear. *Printed by Banknote Corporation of America. FDC not offered. Issued in 5 sheets of 4.*

PC379 *Gund Bear*

PC380 *Bruin Bear*

PC381 *Ideal Bear*

PC382 *Stick Bear*

PC379		UnVF	UseVF
23¢	multicolored	.80	.25
PC380		UnVF	UseVF
23¢	multicolored	.80	.25
PC381		UnVF	UseVF
23¢	multicolored	.80	.25
PC382		UnVF	UseVF
23¢	multicolored	.80	.25
	y. Sheet of 4	4.00	

2002. HOLIDAY CRAFTS SNOWMEN ISSUE featured four colorful and loveable snowmen ready for the holidays. *Printed by Banknote Corporation of America. FDC not offered. Issued in 5 sheets of 4.*

PC383

PC384

PC385

PC386

PC383		UnVF	UseVF
23¢	multicolored	.80	.30
PC384		UnVF	UseVF
23¢	multicolored	.80	.30
PC385		UnVF	UseVF
23¢	multicolored	.80	.30
PC386		UnVF	UseVF
23¢	multicolored	.80	.30
	y. Sheet of 4	4.25	

2003. OLD GLORY ISSUE featured five different aspects of Americana. Designed by Dick Sheaff. *Printed by Ashton-Potter. Issued in pads of 20 cards.*

PC387 *Uncle Sam on a bicycle*

PC388 *Old Glory hanging from golden eagle*

PC389 *Old Glory & Star Spangled Banner*

PC390 *Old Glory on fan*

PC391 *Liberty fighting for Old Glory*

PC387		UnVF	UseVF
23¢	multicolored	1.00	.30
PC388		UnVF	UseVF
23¢	multicolored	1.00	.30
PC389		UnVF	UseVF
23¢	multicolored	1.00	.30

PC390		UnVF	UseVF
23¢	multicolored	1.00	.30
PC391		UnVF	UseVF
23¢	multicolored	1.00	.30

2003. SOUTHEASTERN LIGHTHOUSES ISSUE featured five different paintings of lighthouses on the southeast coast from Virginia to Florida. *Issued in pads of 20 cards.*

PC392 *Old Cape Henry*

PC393 *Cape Lookout*

PC394 *Morris Island*

PC395 *Tybee Island*

PC396 *Hillsboro Inlet*

PC392		UnVF	UseVF
23¢	multicolored	1.00	.30
PC393		UnVF	UseVF
23¢	multicolored	1.00	.30
PC394		UnVF	UseVF
23¢	multicolored	1.00	.30
PC395		UnVF	UseVF
23¢	multicolored	1.00	.30
PC396		UnVF	UseVF
23¢	multicolored	1.00	.30

Airmail Postal Cards

1949. INSCRIBED. "AIR MAIL-POSTAL CARD" ISSUE

 PCA1 *Eagle*

PCA1			UnVF	UseVF
4¢	**red orange** on buff		.75	1.00
	a. deep red on buff		.75	1.50
	FDC *(Jan. 10, 1949)*			2.00

1958. INSCRIBED. "AIR MAIL-POSTAL CARD" ISSUE

 PCA2, PCA3 *Eagle in flight*

PCA2		UnVF	UseVF
5¢	**red** on buff	1.60	.80
	FDC *(July 31, 1958)*		2.00

1960. EAGLE IN FLIGHT ISSUE with no inscription but red and blue border.

PCA3		UnVF	UseVF
5¢	**red** on buff	6.50	2.25
	v. red omitted	—	
	v1. Thinned dividing line at top	—	
	v2. Thinned dividing line at bottom	—	
	FDC *(June 18, 1960)*		2.00

1963. BALD EAGLE ISSUE with red and blue border.

 PCA4 *Bald eagle*

PCA4		UnVF	UseVF
6¢	**red** on white	.75	1.00
	p. Fluorescent paper	10.00	—
	FDC *(Feb. 15, 1963)*		5.00

1966. VISIT THE USA ISSUE with red and blue border. International rate.

PCA5 *Map, flag and VISIT THE USA. Photos of Mt. Rainier, Washington; New York City skyline; Miami Beach, Florida; Indian on horseback.*

PCA5		UnVF	UseVF
11¢	**red & blue** on white	.75	15.00
	Fluorescent paper	—	
	FDC *(May 27, 1966)*		1.75

1967. 50TH ANNIVERSARY OF PURCHASE OF THE VIRGIN ISLANDS ISSUE with red and blue lines at bottom.

 PCA6 *Virgin Islands and flag*

PCA6		UnVF	UseVF
6¢	**multicolored** on white	.50	7.50
	v. magenta & yellow omitted	—	
	FDC *(March 31, 1967)*		1.75

1967. 12TH BOY SCOUT WORLD JAMBOREE ISSUE Idaho, USA.

 PCA7 *Boy Scout emblem and Borah Peak.*

PCA7		UnVF	UseVF
6¢	**multicolored** on white	.50	7.50
	v. cyan (blue) omitted	—	
	v1. cyan (blue) & black omitted	—	
	v2. magenta & yellow omitted	—	
	FDC *(Aug. 4, 1967)*		1.75

1967. VISIT THE USA ISSUE with design as PCA5, but without scenic pictures at left and with red and blue lines at bottom instead of border. International rate.

 PCA8 *Eagle*

PCA8		UnVF	UseVF
13¢	**red & blue** on white	1.75	10.00
	FDC *(Sept. 8, 1967)*		1.75

1968. STYLIZED EAGLE ISSUE with red and blue border.

 PCA9 *Stylized eagle*

PCA9		UnVF	UseVF
8¢	**red & blue** on white, non-fluorescent paper, tagged	.75	.50
	FDC *(March 1, 1968)*		1.75
	p. Slightly fluorescent paper, tagged	2.50	3.00
	p1. Tagging omitted	—	
	FDC *(March 1, 1969)*		15.00

Fluorescent paper noted in No. PCA9 and later issues was a function of paper manufacturers' attempt at producing whiter paper stock with the use of brighteners; such fluorescence was not a function of the tagging schemes to aid in automated canceling.

1971. STYLIZED EAGLE ISSUE with design as PCA9.

 PCA10

PCA10		UnVF	UseVF
9¢	**red & blue** on white, tagged	.70	2.00
	FDC *(May 15, 1971)*		1.75

1971. VISIT THE USA ISSUE with design as PCA8. International rate.

PCA11		UnVF	UseVF
15¢	**red & blue** on white, tagged	2.25	15.00
	v. Card w/ printed cachet for sale at LUPOSTA 1971 in Berlin, Germany	—	
	FDC *(June 10, 1971)*		1.75

1972. TOURISM YEAR OF THE AMERICAS ISSUE

PCA12 *Grand Canyon with Statue of Liberty, Hawaii, Alaska, and San Francisco on reverse.*

PCA12		UnVF	UseVF
9¢	**black** on manila, tagged	.65	10.00
	v. red & blue lozenges of border omitted	—	
	v1. red lozenges omitted	—	
	zo. Tagging omitted	—	
	FDC *(June 29, 1972)*		1.75

PCA13 *Niagara Falls with Mount Vernon, Washington, D.C., Abraham Lincoln, and Liberty Bell on reverse. For international rate.*

PCA13		UnVF	UseVF
15¢	**black** on manila, tagged	.70	15.00
	v. red & blue lozenges omitted	—	
	v1 Stamp & vertical line omitted	600.00	
	zo. Tagging omitted	—	
	FDC *(June 29, 1972)*		1.75

1974. STYLIZED EAGLE ISSUE

PCA14 *Stylized eagle*

PCA14		UnVF	UseVF
11¢	**red, white & blue** on white, non-fluorescent paper, tagged	.75	3.00
	p. Fluorescent paper	2.00	
	zo. Tagging omitted	—	
	zv. Inverted tag bar at lower left	250.00	
	zvl. Tag bar printed double in normal position	250.00	
	FDC *(Jan. 4, 1974)*		1.75

1974. EAGLE WEATHERVANE ISSUE International rate.

PCA15 *Eagle weathervane*

PCA15		UnVF	UseVF
18¢	**multicolored** on white, non-fluorescent paper, tagged	1.00	17.50
	p. Fluorescent paper	3.00	17.50

		UnVF	UseVF
	v. black & yellow omitted	—	
	zo. Tagging omitted	—	
	FDC *(Jan. 4, 1974)*		1.75

1975. ANGEL WEATHERVANE ISSUE International rate.

PCA16 *Angel Gabriel weathervane*

PCA16		UnVF	UseVF
21¢	**multicolored** on white, non-fluorescent paper, tagged	.90	9.50
	v. cyan (blue) & magenta omitted	—	
	zo. Tagging omitted	150.00	
	FDC *(Dec. 17, 1975)*		1.75

1978. AIRPLANE ISSUE International rate.

PCA17 *Curtiss "Jenny"*

PCA17		UnVF	UseVF
21¢	**multicolored** on white, non-fluorescent paper, tagged	.85	7.50
	FDC *(Sept. 16, 1978)*		1.75

1979. OLYMPIC GAMES ISSUE International rate.

PCA18 *Gymnast*

PCA18		UnVF	UseVF
21¢	**multicolored** on white, fluorescent or non-fluorescent paper, tagged	1.25	12.50
	FDC *(Dec. 1, 1979)*		1.75

1981. 50TH ANNIVERSARY OF TRANSPACIFIC FLIGHT ISSUE International rate.

PCA19 *Clyde Pangborn, Hugh Herndon, and plane Miss Veedol.*

PCA19		UnVF	UseVF
28¢	**multicolored** on white, fluorescent or non-fluorescent paper, tagged	1.00	7.50
	zo. Tagging omitted	—	
	FDC *(Jan. 2, 1981)*		1.75

1982. 50TH ANNIVERSARY OF THE FOUNDING OF THE SOARING SOCIETY OF AMERICA ISSUE International rate.

PCA20 *Sailplanes*

PCA20		UnVF	UseVF
28¢	multicolored on white, tagged	1.00	7.50
	FDC (March 5, 1982)		1.75

1984. OLYMPICS ISSUE International rate.

PCA21 *Speed skater*

PCA21		UnVF	UseVF
28¢	multicolored on white	1.00	7.50
	v. 40mm left shift of magenta & yellow	—	
	FDC (Dec. 29, 1983)		1.75

1985. CHINA CLIPPER ISSUE International rate.

IPCA22 *China Clipper*

PCA22		UnVF	UseVF
33¢	multicolored on white	1.00	7.50
	FDC (Feb. 15, 1985)		1.75

1986. AMERIPEX '86 ISSUE International rate.

PCA23 *Chicago skyline*

PCA23		UnVF	UseVF
33¢	multicolored on white	.90	7.50
	v. Card w/printed cachet to left, sold by U.S. Postal Service at SUDPOSTA '87, Sindelfingen, Germany	2.00	9.00
	FDC (Feb. 1, 1986)		1.75
	SUDPOSTA FDC (Oct. 22, 1987)		—

1988. DC-3 ISSUE International rate.

PCA24 *Douglas DC-3*

PCA24		UnVF	UseVF
36¢	multicolored on white, fluorescent paper, tagged	1.00	7.00
	p. Non-fluorescent paper	1.50	7.00
	v. Card w/printed cachet to left, sold by U.S. Postal Service at SYDPEX '88, Sydney, Australia	1.50	9.00
	FDC (May 14, 1988)		2.00
	SYDPEX FDC (July 30, 1988)		—

1991. YANKEE CLIPPER ISSUE International rate.

PCA25 *Yankee Clipper*

PCA25		UnVF	UseVF
40¢	multicolored on white	1.00	7.50
	FDC (June 28, 1991)		2.00

1995. SOARING EAGLE ISSUE International rate.

PCA26 *Soaring eagle*

PCA26		UnVF	UseVF
50¢	multicolored on white	1.25	8.00
	FDC (Aug. 24, 1995)		2.00

Defects of condition on stamps include (but are not necessarily limited to) tears, scrapes, thins (places where some of the paper is missing from the back of a stamp, often due to inept removal of a hinge), stains, foxing (a yellowish-brown staining) and so-called tropical toning (brown spots on the gum or perforation tips), absence of original gum, the presence of substantial hinge remnants, inclusions (pieces of foreign matter accidentally embedded in the stamp paper during manufacture), heavy, smeared or otherwise disfiguring cancellations or postal markings, pulled, torn or clipped perforations, creases, pinholes, missing corners, and faded, bleached or oxidated pigments and other color changelings (wherein the color of the stamp has changed after it was produced).

Official Postal Cards

1913. POSTAL SAVINGS ISSUE produced for Postal Savings System monthly reports. In use for a very short time. 5x3 inches.

 OPC1 *U.S. Postal Savings*

OPC1		UnVF	UseVF
1¢	black	325.00	150.00
	FDC *(July 1913)*		

1983. GREAT SEAL ISSUE

OPC2 *Great Seal*

OPC2		UnVF	UseVF
13¢	blue	.60	35.00
	FDC *(Jan. 12, 1983)* at Washington, D.C.		1.75

OCP3 *Great Seal*

OPC3		UnVF	UseVF
14¢	blue	.60	35.00
	FDC *(Feb. 26, 1985)* at Washington, D.C.		1.75

1988. GREAT SEAL ISSUE

OPC4 *Great Seal*

OPC4		UnVF	UseVF
15¢	multicolored	.60	35.00
	FDC *(June 10, 1988)* at New York City		1.75

1991. GREAT SEAL ISSUE

 OPC5 *Great Seal*

OPC5		UnVF	UseVF
19¢	multicolored	.55	30.00
	FDC *(May 24, 1991)* at Seattle, Wash.		1.75

1995. GREAT SEAL ISSUE

OPC6 *Great Seal*

OPC6		UnVF	UseVF
20¢	multicolored	.40	—
	FDC *(May 9, 1995)* at Washington, D.C.		1.75

Message & Reply Cards

First issued in 1892, message and reply cards consist of two postal cards attached to each other. One card is used for sending the message, and the other card, when separated, is used to send the reply. The term "used" when referring to the unsevered card signifies a used message card and an unused reply card. Listings are for unsevered and severed (individual) cards.

1892. Issue frame around edge of card.

MRC1 *Ulysses S. Grant*

MRC1		UnFVF	UseFVF
1¢ + 1¢	**black** on buff, unsevered	37.50	8.00
m.	Message card	7.00	1.50
r.	Reply card	7.00	1.50
t.	Message card printed on both sides, reply card blank	275.00	—
t1.	Message card blank, reply card printed on both sides	325.00	—
FDC (Oct. 25, 1892)			350.00

1893. Universal Postal Union Card frame around edge of card.

MRC2, MRC10 *Liberty*

MRC2		UnFVF	UseFVF
2¢ + 2¢	**blue** on grayish white, unsevered	18.50	25.00
a.	dark blue on grayish white	20.00	25.00
m.	Message card	6.00	7.00
r.	Reply card	6.00	7.00
t.	Message card printed on both sides, reply card blank	325.00	—
t1.	Message card blank, reply card printed on both sides	—	—
t2.	Message card normal, reply card blank	325.00	—
FDC (March 1, 1893)			

1898. Issue same design as MRC1, but without frame around edge of card.

MRC3		UnFVF	UseFVF
1¢ + 1¢	**black** on buff, unsevered	70.00	20.00
m.	Message card	15.00	3.00
r.	Reply card	15.00	3.00
t.	Message card printed on both sides, reply card blank	275.00	—

t1.	Message card blank, reply card printed on both sides	275.00	—
t2.	Message card blank, reply card normal	—	275.00
t3.	Message card normal, reply card printed on both sides	—	—
t4.	Message card without "detach annexed card/for answer"	275.00	160.00
t5.	Message card printed on both sides, reply card normal	—	—
t6.	Message card printed on both halves	—	—
No official date of issue			

1904. Issue

MRC4m *William T. Sherman*

MRC4r *Philip H. Sheridan*

MRC4		UnFVF	UseFVF
1¢ + 1¢	**black** on buff, unsevered	50.00	6.00
m.	Message card	10.00	2.00
r.	Reply card	10.00	2.00
t.	Message card printed on both sides, reply card blank	300.00	—
t1.	Message card blank, reply card printed on both sides	—	185.00
t2.	Message card blank, reply card normal	—	300.00
t3.	Message card normal, reply card blank	300.00	—
FDC (March 31, 1904)			

1910. Issue

MRC5m *George Washington*

MRC5r *Martha Washington*

MRC5		UnFVF	UseFVF
1¢ + 1¢	**dark blue** on bluish, unsevered	150.00	25.00
m.	Message card	11.00	4.00
r.	Reply card	11.00	4.00
t.	Message card normal, reply card blank	220.00	—
FDC (Sept. 14, 1910)			

1911. Issue same design.

MRC6m *George Washington*

MRC6r *Martha Washington*

MRC6		UnFVF	UseFVF
1¢ + 1¢	**green** on cream, unsevered	150.00	25.00
m.	Message card	25.00	6.00
r.	Reply card	40.00	45.00
t.	Message card normal, reply card blank	—	—
FDC (Oct. 27, 1911)			

1915. ISSUE same design. Single frame around inscription.

 MRC7

MRC7	UnFVF	UseFVF
1¢ + 1¢ **green** on cream, unsevered	1.50	.55
dark green on buff	1.50	.55
m. Message card	.30	.25
r. Reply card	.30	.25
t. Message card normal, reply card blank	—	—
FDC *(Sept. 18, 1915)*		

1918. ISSUE

MRC8m *George Washington*

MRC8r *Martha Washington*

MRC8	UnFVF	UseFVF
2¢ + 2¢ **red** on cream, unsevered	80.00	45.00
m. Message card	22.50	7.50
r. Reply card	22.50	7.50
FDC *(Aug. 2, 1918)*		

1920-21. ISSUE re-valued. *Surcharged in black by canceling machine.*

MRC9m *Overprinted on MRC8m*

MRC9r *Overprinted on MRC8r*

MRC9	UnFVF	UseFVF
1¢ on 2¢ + 1¢ on 2¢ **red** on cream, unsevered	20.00	10.00
m. Message card	6.00	4.00
r. Reply card	6.00	4.00
x. Message card double surcharge, reply card normal	80.00	—
x1. Message card normal, reply card no surcharge	90.00	—
x2. Message card normal, reply card double surcharge	80.00	—
x3. Message card no surcharge, reply card normal	80.00	—
x4. Message card no surcharge, reply card double surcharge	80.00	—
x5. Message card double surcharge, reply card no surcharge	—	—
x6. Message card no surcharge, reply card double surcharge, one inverted	—	—

MRC9A	UnFVF	UseFVF
1¢ on 2¢ + 1¢ on 2¢ **red** on cream, unsevered	325.00	200.00
m. Message card	95.00	45.00
p. red on buff	—	—
r. Reply card	95.00	45.00
x. Message card no surcharge, reply card normal	—	—
x1. Message card double surcharge, reply card no surcharge	—	—
x2. Message card no surcharge, reply card double surcharge	—	—

Same surcharge press printed.

1924. UNIVERSAL POSTAL UNION CARD same design and size as MRC2.

MRC10	UnFVF	UseFVF
2¢ + 2¢ **red** on buff, unsevered	3.00	50.00
m. Message card	.50	20.00
r. Reply card	.50	20.00
FDC *(March 18, 1924)*		

1926. UNIVERSAL POSTAL UNION CARD same size as PC11.

MRC11 *William McKinley*

MRC11	UnFVF	UseFVF
3¢ + 3¢ **red** on cream, unsevered	15.00	35.00
a. carmine on cream	—	—
b. pale red on cream	—	—
c. scarlet on cream	—	—
m. Message card	3.00	16.00
p. red on buff	—	—
p1. red on canary	10.00	17.50
p2. red on light buff	—	—
p3. red on yellow buff	—	—
r. Reply card	3.00	6.00
FDC *(Feb. 1, 1926)*		250.00

1951. ISSUE same size as PC13.

MRC12 *George Washington, message card; Martha Washington, reply card.*

MRC12	UnVF	UseVF
2¢ + 2¢ **carmine** on cream, unsevered		
m. Message card		
r. Reply card		
FDC *(Dec. 29, 1951)*		

1952. ISSUE re-valued, overprinted in green by Pitney-Bowes Tickometer.

 MRC13 *Overprinted on MRC7*

MRC13	UnVF	UseVF
2¢ on 1¢ + 2¢ on 1¢ **light green** on buff, unsevered	1.75	4.00
m. Message card	.50	2.00
r. Reply card	.50	2.00
x. Both cards double surcharge	55.00	40.00
x1. Inverted surcharge horizontal, to left of stamps	150.00	100.00
x2. Message card double surcharge, reply card normal	45.00	30.00
x3. Message card no surcharge, reply card normal	40.00	45.00
x4. Message card normal, reply card double surcharge	45.00	30.00
x5. Message card normal, reply card no surcharge	40.00	45.00
x6. Surcharge horizontal, to left of stamp	15.00	15.00
x7. Surcharge vertical, to left of stamp	7.00	7.00
x8. Surcharge vertical below stamp	—	—
x9. Black surcharge vertical below stamp	—	—
x10. Message card no surcharge, reply card double surcharge	—	—

	UnVF	UseVF
x11. Message card double surcharge, reply card no surcharge	—	—
FDC (Jan. 1, 1952)		50.00

1952. ISSUE same as MRC13, but dark green horizontal overprint applied by printing press.

MRC14

	UnVF	UseVF
2¢ on 1¢ + 2¢ on 1¢ **green** on cream, unsevered	135.00	55.00
m. Message card	20.00	12.50
r. Reply card	20.00	12.50
x. Message card normal plus one on back, reply card no surcharge	—	—
x1. Reply card normal plus one on back, with Tickometer surcharge vertical below stamp on message card	—	—

1956. UNIVERSAL POSTAL UNION CARD ISSUE Design of PC41, Liberty.

MRC15 *Statue of Liberty*

MRC15

	UnVF	UseVF
4¢ + 4¢ **scarlet & ultramarine** on cream, unsevered	1.50	60.00
m. Message card	.50	40.00
r. Reply card	.50	35.00
t. Message card printed on both halves	140.00	—
t1. Reply card printed on both halves	140.00	—
FDC (Nov. 16, 1956)		2.00
FDC (Message card printed both halves)		75.00
FDC (Reply card printed both halves)		50.00

1958. ISSUE Design of PC42, Liberty; the two cards are identical.

MRC16

	UnVF	UseVF
3¢ + 3¢ **purple** on buff, unsevered	4.00	5.00
t. One card blank	140.00	—
t1. Printed by electrotype	—	—
t2. Printed by steel plate	—	—
FDC (July 31, 1958)		2.00

1962. LINCOLN PRECANCEL ISSUE Design of PC44, Abraham Lincoln; the two cards are identical.

MRC17 *Abraham Lincoln*

MRC17

	UnVF	UseVF
4¢ + 4¢ **red violet** on white, unsevered	4.50	5.00
a. light violet	—	—
p. Fluorescent paper, non-fluorescent ink	—	—
t. Printed by electrotype	—	—
t1. Printed by steel plate	—	—
z. Non-fluorescent paper, fluorescent ink (March 7, 1967)	6.50	3.50
FDC (Nov. 19, 1962)		1.75

1963. UNIVERSAL POSTAL UNION CARD ISSUE Design of PC45, Vacationland.

MRC18 *Map of North America*

MRC18

	UnVF	UseVF
7¢ + 7¢ **red & blue** on white, unsevered	3.00	50.00
m. Message card	.90	25.00
r. Reply card	.90	25.00

	UnVF	UseVF
t. Message card blank, reply card normal	140.00	—
t1. Message card normal, reply card blank	140.00	—
FDC (Aug. 30, 1963)		2.50

1968. UNIVERSAL POSTAL UNION CARDS ISSUE Design of MRC18 (PC45), Vacationland, with 8¢ denomination.

MRC19 *Map of North America*

MRC19

	UnVF	UseVF
8¢ + 8¢ **red & blue** on white, unsevered	3.50	50.00
m. Message card	.90	25.00
r. Reply card	.90	25.00
FDC (Dec. 4, 1967)		

1968. ABRAHAM LINCOLN ISSUE Design of PC51, Abraham Lincoln; the two cards are identical.

MRC20 *Abraham Lincoln*

MRC20

	UnVF	UseVF
5¢ + 5¢ **emerald green** on white, unsevered	1.75	3.00
t. One half blank (printed one side only)	—	—
FDC (Jan. 4, 1968)		1.50

1971. ISSUE Design of PC54, Paul Revere; the two cards are identical.

MRC21 *Paul Revere*

MRC21

	UnVF	UseVF
6¢ + 6¢ **brown** on white, unsevered, tagged	1.25	2.50
FDC (May 15, 1971)		1.50

1972. ISSUE Design of PC60, John Hanson; the two cards are identical.

MRC22

	UnVF	UseVF
6¢ + 6¢ **cobalt blue** on white, unsevered, tagged	1.25	2.00
FDC (Sept. 1, 1972)		1.00

1973. ISSUE Design of PC62, Samuel Adams; the two cards are identical.

MRC23

	UnVF	UseVF
8¢ + 8¢ **orange** on white, unsevered, tagged	1.25	2.00
p. Smooth paper	—	—
p1. Coarse paper	1.35	4.00
t. One half blank (printed one side only)	—	—
FDC (Dec. 16, 1973)		1.00

1975. ISSUE Design of PC64, Charles Thomson; the two cards are identical.

MRC24

	UnVF	UseVF
7¢ + 7¢ **emerald green** on white, unsevered, tagged	1.25	5.00
FDC (Sept. 14, 1975)		2.00

1975. ISSUE Design of PC65, John Witherspoon; the two cards are identical.

MRC25

	UnVF	UseVF
9¢ + 9¢ **brown** on white, unsevered, tagged	1.25	5.00
FDC (Nov. 10, 1975)		1.00

1976. ISSUE Design of PC66, Caesar Rodney; the two cards are identical.

	UnVF	UseVF
MRC26		
9¢ + 9¢ blue on white, unsevered, tagged	1.25	2.00
FDC *(July 1, 1976)*		1.00

1977. ISSUE Design of PC68, Nathan Hale; the two cards are identical.

	UnVF	UseVF
MRC27		
9¢ + 9¢ green on white, unsevered, tagged	1.25	2.00
FDC *(Oct. 14, 1977)*		1.00

1978. ISSUE Design of PC70, John Hancock (non-denominated), two cards are identical.

	UnVF	UseVF
MRC28		
10¢ + 10¢ brown orange on white, unsevered, tagged	11.00	9.00
t. Printed with MRC28 one side, MRC29 on back side	—	—
FDC *(May 19, 1978)*		3.50

1978. ISSUE Design of PC71, John Hancock (with denomination); the two cards are identical.

	UnVF	UseVF
MRC29		
10¢ + 10¢ brown orange on white, unsevered, tagged	1.25	3.00
t. One half blank (printed one side only)	—	—
FDC *(June 20, 1978)*		1.00

1981. ISSUE Design of PC84, stylized eagle; the two cards are identical.

	UnVF	UseVF
MRC30		
12¢ + 12¢ purple on white, unsevered, tagged	1.25	3.00
FDC *(March 15, 1981)*		1.00

1981. ISSUE Design of PC85, Isaiah Thomas; the two cards are identical.

	UnVF	UseVF
MRC31		
12¢ + 12¢ blue on white, unsevered, tagged	1.50	4.00
t. Large stamp die on both sides	—	—
t1. Large stamp die on one side, small stamp die on back	3.00	2.25
FDC *(May 5, 1981)*		1.00

1981. ISSUE Design of PC88, Robert Morris (non-denominated); the two cards are identical.

	UnVF	UseVF
MRC32		
13¢ + 13¢ brown on white, unsevered, tagged	2.25	4.00
FDC *(Oct. 11, 1981)*		1.25

1981. ISSUE Design of PC89, Robert Morris (with denomination); the two cards are identical.

	UnVF	UseVF
MRC33		
13¢ + 13¢ brown on white, unsevered, tagged	1.25	3.00
t. One half blank (printed one side only)	—	—
t1. Additional copyright notice, inverted on back of message card	—	—
FDC *(Nov. 10, 1981)*		1.00

1985. ISSUE Design of PC101, Charles Carroll (non-denominated); the two cards are identical.

	UnVF	UseVF
MRC34		
14¢ + 14¢ green on white, unsevered, tagged	3.50	5.00
FDC *(Feb. 1, 1985)*		1.25

1985. ISSUE Design of PC103, Charles Carroll (with denomination); the two cards are identical.

	UnVF	UseVF
MRC35		
14¢ + 14¢ green on white, unsevered, tagged	1.25	3.00
t. One half blank (printed one side only)	—	—
FDC *(March 6, 1985)*		1.25

1985. ISSUE Design of PC104, George Wythe; the two cards are identical.

	UnVF	UseVF
MRC36		
14¢ + 14¢ olive green on white, unsevered, tagged	1.20	3.00
t. One half blank (printed one side only)	—	—
FDC *(June 20, 1985)*		1.25

1987. ISSUE Design of PC113, U.S. Flag; the two cards are identical.

	UnVF	UseVF
MRC37		
14¢ + 14¢ black, blue & red on white, unsevered, tagged	1.25	3.00
FDC *(Sept. 1, 1987)*		1.50

1988. ISSUE Design of PC116, America the Beautiful; the two cards are identical.

	UnVF	UseVF
MRC38		
15¢ + 15¢ multicolored on white, unsevered, tagged	1.25	3.00
p. Fluorescent paper	—	—
FDC *(July 11, 1988)*		1.25

1991. ISSUE Design of PC146, U.S. Flag; the two cards are identical.

	UnVF	UseVF
MRC39		
19¢ + 19¢ black, blue & red on white, unsevered, tagged	1.25	3.00
FDC *(March 27, 1991)*		1.00

1995. ISSUE Design of PC194, Red Barn; the two cards are identical.

	UnVF	UseVF
MRC40		
20¢ + 20¢ multicolored, unsevered	1.25	3.00
t. One half blank (printed one side only)	—	—
FDC *(Feb. 1, 1995)*		1.25

1999. BLOCK ISLAND LIGHTHOUSE ISSUE Design of PC302 in the Scenic America Series. The two cards are identical. *Offset by Government Printing Office.*

MRC41 *Block Island Lighthouse, Rhode Island*

	UnVF	UseVF
MRC41		
20¢ + 20¢ multicolored, unsevered	1.25	3.00
FDC *(Nov. 10, 1999)*		1.50

2001. WHITE BARN POSTAL CARD ISSUE

MRC42 *White barn*

	UnVF	UseVF
MRC42		
21¢ + 21¢ multicolored	1.25	.30
FDC *(Sept. 20, 2001)*		1.00

2002. CARLSBAD CAVERNS ISSUE Design of PC378 in the Scenic America Series shows the natural wonder of a cave ecosystem with its many stalagmites and stalactites. *Printed by Government Printing Office. Rectangular block tagging to right of design.*

MRC43 *Carlsbad Caverns*

	UnVF	UseVF
MRC43		
23¢ + 23¢ multicolored unsevered	1.25	.30
FDC *(June 7, 2002 - Carlsbad, N.M.)*		1.50

Savings Stamps

United States Savings Stamps fall into five classifications: Postal Savings and Defense Postal Savings, both issued by the Post Office Department; and War Savings, Treasury Savings, and Savings, issued by the Treasury Department.

For many years the Treasury Department objected to the listings of Savings Stamps as collectors' items, but in a letter dated July 13, 1942, these objections were withdrawn, and since that date the collecting of these stamps has been encouraged.

Postal Savings Stamp Series

In 1910 the U.S. Post Office Department started a Postal Savings Department where accounts could be opened in even-dollar amounts. To enable small depositors to accumulate dollar deposits, stamps were provided with a face value of 10¢ each so that when nine were secured they could be mounted on a card with one integral stamp. The Postal Savings Department, as a banking activity, was closed April 27, 1966.

1911. FIRST ISSUE Inscribed "U.S. POSTAL SAVINGS 10 CENTS." *Intaglio, watermark double-line "USPS" (wmk. 187), perforated 12.*

PS1, PS3

PS1

		UnFVF	UseFVF
10¢	orange	7.00	1.25
	Plate block of 6, w/imprint and open star	450.00	—
	Plate strip of 3, w/imprint and open star	45.00	—
	Block of 4, 2mm spacing between stamps	30.00	—
	Block of 4, 3mm spacing between stamps	35.00	—
	FDC (Jan. 3, 1911)		

1911. IMPRINTED CARD ISSUE Same design as No. PS1. Imprinted on deposit card with spaces for nine additional stamps. *Intaglio, unwatermarked, imperforate.*

PS2

After being redeemed, these cards were canceled with a large killer device, and interesting combinations of stamps are found.

Proofs in red and blue on thin paper and a deposit card in blue, with an entirely different design showing the head of George Washington in a circle and space for nine stamps are known. It is believed that they were not issued.

PS2

		UnFVF	UseFVF
10¢	orange	150.00	40.00
	Canceled with nine additional stamps	—	—
	FDC (Jan. 3, 1911)		

1911. SECOND ISSUE Aug. 14. Same design as No. PS1. *Intaglio, watermark single-line "USPS" (wmk. 237), perforated 12.*

PS3

		UnFVF	UseFVF
10¢	blue	4.25	1.00

	Plate block of 6, w/imprint and open star	150.00	—
	Plate strip of 3, w/imprint and open star	27.50	—
	Block of 4, 2mm spacing between stamps	22.50	—
	Block of 4, 3mm spacing between stamps	25.00	—

1911. SECOND CARD ISSUE Design type of No. PS2, with change in color. Imprinted on deposit card. *Intaglio, unwatermarked, imperforate.*

PS4

		UnFVF	UseFVF
10¢	blue	100.00	22.50
	Canceled with 9 additional stamps	—	—
	FDC (Aug. 14, 1911)		

In September 1920, the Post Office Department issued a new type of deposit card (Form PS333) without imprint of the first stamp. These are not listed as regular postal issues, but can be found canceled with 10 stamps of either No. PS1 or No. PS3.

1936. THIRD ISSUE Type of No. PS1. *Intaglio, unwatermarked, perforated 11.*

PS5

		UnFVF	UseFVF
10¢	blue	4.75	1.25
	violet blue	4.75	1.25
	Plate block of 6, w/imprint and closed star	125.00	—

1940. ISSUE Inscribed "UNITED STATES" at top, "POSTAL SAVINGS" at bottom, and either "CENTS" or "DOLLAR" diagonally in center, with denomination above and below. *Intaglio, unwatermarked, perforated 11.*

PS6-PS9

PS6

		MNHVF	UseVF
10¢	blue	12.50	6.00
	Plate block of 6	225.00	—
	FDC (April 3, 1940)		

PS7

		MNHVF	UseVF
25¢	red	17.50	9.00
	Plate block of 6	325.00	—
	FDC (April 1, 1940)		

PS8

		MNHVF	UseVF
50¢	green	50.00	16.00
	Plate block of 6	1,400.00	—
	FDC (April 1, 1940)		

PS9

		MNHVF	UseVF
$1	black	150.00	15.00
	Plate block of 6	1,900.00	—
	FDC (April 1, 1940)		

Both a yellow and a manila card for 25 10¢ stamps, a salmon card for 25 25¢ stamps, a green card for 25 50¢ stamps and a manila card for 18 $1 stamps and 3 25¢ stamps were produced. Any total of $18.75 was redeemable for a $25 U.S. Savings bond.

Defense Postal Savings Stamp Series

On May 1, 1941, the Post Office Department issued Defense Postal Savings Stamps, redeemable in U.S. Treasury Defense or War Bonds. Daniel Chester French, who created the Minute Man used in the design, was one of the artists honored on the Famous Americans Series of commemorative stamps (CM229).

1941. ISSUE. May 1. Inscribed "AMERICA ON GUARD/U.S. POSTAL SAVINGS/1941." *Intaglio, unwatermarked. First four values perforated 11x10 1/2; $5 perforated 11.*

PS10-PS14 Minute Man

PS10

		MNHVF	UseVF
10¢	red	.60	

Plate block of 4	7.25	
Booklet pane of 10, w/horizontal edges trimmed *(July 30, 1941)*	55.00	
n. Booklet pane of 10, w/trimmed edges, electric eye marks at left	60.00	
Booklet pane of 10, perforated at horizontal edges	120.00	
Booklet pane of 10, perforated at edges, electric eye marks at left	135.00	
FDC *(May 1, 1941)*		175.00

PS11		**MNHVF**	**UseVF**
25¢	**green**	1.85	—
Plate block of 4	16.00
Booklet pane of 10 *(July 30, 1941)*	65.00
n. Booklet pane of 10, electric eye marks at left	70.00

PS12		**MNHVF**	**UseVF**
50¢	**ultramarine**	4.50	—
Plate block of 4	40.00

PS13		**MNHVF**	**UseVF**
$1	**black**	10.00	—
Plate block of 4	77.00

PS14		**MNHVF**	**UseVF**
$5	**sepia**	37.00	—
Plate block of 6	535.00

War Savings Stamp Series

In 1917, the Treasury Department brought out the first of a series of War Savings Stamps, which were redeemable in Treasury War Certificates, War Bonds, or Defense Bonds. A 25¢ Thrift Stamp was issued to enable small purchasers to accumulate them on a Deposit Card exchangeable for a $5 stamp when full.

1917. ISSUE Dec. 1. *Intaglio, unwatermarked, perforated 11.*

 WS1

WS1		**UnFVF**	**UseFVF**
25¢	**green**	7.00	2.25
Plate block of 6	750.00
Plate strip of 3	50.00

1918. ISSUE In 1918, 1919, 1920, and 1921, $5 stamps were issued. They sold at $4.12 when first issued and increased in value each month until they became worth par in five years and could be cashed or applied on bonds at the face value of $5.

Nov. 17. *Intaglio, unwatermarked, perforated 11.*

 WS2 *George Washington*

WS2		**UnFVF**	**UseFVF**
$5	**green**	70.00	22.00
Single with plate number	80.00
v. Vertical pair, imperforate horizontally	—

WS2A		**UnFVF**	**UseFVF**
$5	**green**	1,100.00	—
Single w/plate number	1,350.00

Rouletted 7

1919. ISSUE July 3. *Intaglio, unwatermarked, perforated 11.*

 WS3 *Benjamin Franklin*

WS3		**UnFVF**	**UseFVF**
$5	**blue**	275.00	—
Single w/plate number	300.00
Single w/inverted plate number	325.00

1920. ISSUE Dec. 11. *Intaglio, unwatermarked, perforated 11.*

 WS4 *George Washington*

WS4		**UnFVF**	**UseFVF**
$5	**carmine**	675.00	160.00
Single w/plate number	700.00

1921. ISSUE Dec. 21. *Intaglio, unwatermarked, perforated 11.*

 WS5 *Abraham Lincoln*

WS5		**UnFVF**	**UseFVF**
$5	**orange** on green paper	2,600.00	—
Single w/plate number	2,750.00

1942. ISSUE Early in 1942 the Treasury Department issued a new series of War Savings Stamps to replace the Defense Postal Savings Stamps of 1941 issued by the Post Office Department. *Intaglio, unwatermarked.*

 WS6-WS10 *Minute Man*

WS6		**MNHVF**	**UseVF**
10¢	**red**	.55	—
Plate block of 4	5.25
n. Booklet pane of 10 *(Oct. 27, 1942)*	40.00
n1. Booklet pane of 10 w/electric eye mark at left	45.00
a. carmine rose	.55
FDC *(Oct. 29, 1942)*	

WS7

		MNHVF	UseVF
25¢	**green**	1.25	—
	Plate block of 4	8.50	
	Booklet pane of 10 *(Oct. 15, 1942)*	50.00	
	Booklet pane of 10 w/electric eye mark at left	55.00	
	FDC *(Oct. 15, 1942)*		

WS8

		MNHVF	UseVF
50¢	**ultramarine**	2.75	—
	Plate block of 4	27.50	
	FDC *(Nov. 12, 1942)*		

WS9

		MNHVF	UseVF
$1	**black**	9.00	—
	Plate block of 4	60.00	
	FDC *(Nov. 17, 1942)*		

Perforated 11x10 1/2.

WS10

		MNHVF	UseVF
$5	**violet brown**	45.00	—
	Plate block of 6	475.00	
	FDC *(1945)*		

Perforated 11.

1943. COIL ISSUE *Coil stamps.* Although plates for coil stamps were prepared for the 1941 issue, they were not used. Thus, this is the first Savings Stamp issued in coil form: 500 stamps to a roll.

Aug. 5. Type of No. WS6. *Intaglio, unwatermarked, perforated 10 vertically.*

WS11

		MNHVF	UseVF
10¢	**red**	2.75	—
	Pair	6.00	—
	Line pair	11.00	—

WS12

		MNHVF	UseVF
25¢	**green**	4.50	—
	Pair	9.50	—
	Line pair	21.00	—

Treasury Savings Stamp Series
While the $5 orange-on-green paper (No. WS5) was still current, the Treasury Department brought out a $1 stamp redeemable in War Savings Stamps or Treasury Savings Certificates. It is the scarcest of the Savings Stamps.

1921. ISSUE Dec. 21. *Intaglio, unwatermarked, perforated 11.*

TS1 *Alexander Hamilton*

TS1

		UnFVF	UseFVF
$1	**red** on green paper	3,250.00	—
	Single with plate number	3,000.00	

Savings Stamp Series
Issued by the Treasury Department.

1954. ISSUE Figure of Minute Man, same as 1942 War Savings Stamps. Inscribed "UNITED STATES SAVINGS STAMP." *Intaglio, unwatermarked.*

S1 *Minute Man*

S1

		MNHVF	UseVF
10¢	**red**	.60	—
	Plate block of 4	3.75	
	Booklet pane of 10 *(April 22, 1955)*	145.00	
	v. Booklet w/electric eye mark at left	155.00	
	FDC *(Nov. 30, 1954)*		

1954. ISSUE

S2

		MNHVF	UseVF
25¢	**green**	5.75	—
	Plate block of 4	30.00	
	Booklet pane of 10 *(Aug. 15, 1955)*	145.00	
	v. Booklet pane w/electric eye mark at left	800.00	
	FDC *(Dec. 30, 1954)*		

1956. ISSUE

S3

		MNHVF	UseVF
50¢	**ultramarine**	8.00	—
	Plate block of 4	45.00	
	FDC *(Dec. 31, 1956)*		

1957. ISSUE

S4

		MNHVF	UseVF
$1	**black**	22.50	—
	Plate block of 4	110.00	
	FDC *(March 13, 1957)*		

1956. ISSUE *Perforated 11.*

S5

		MNHVF	UseVF
$5	**violet brown**	70.00	—
	Plate block of 6	725.00	
	FDC *(Nov. 30, 1956)*		

1959. ISSUE Nov. 18. Figure of Minute Man and 48-star U.S. flag. *Intaglio (Giori Press), unwatermarked, perforated 11.*

S6 *Minute Man, flag*

S6

		MNHVF	UseVF
25¢	**dark blue & carmine**	1.75	—
	Plate block of 4	8.50	
	Booklet pane of 10	65.00	
	FDC *(Nov. 18, 1959)*		

1961. ISSUE Figure of Minute Man and 50-star U.S. flag. *Intaglio (Giori Press), unwatermarked, perforated 11.*

S7 *Minute Man, flag*

S7

		MNHVF	UseVF
25¢	**dark blue & carmine**	1.25	—
	Plate block of 4	8.00	
	Booklet pane of 10	275.00	

Revenue Stamps
Documentary Stamps

For both sides, the costs of the War Between the States were appallingly high. In human terms, the casualty rates rose to possibly 40 percent, and almost half a million American men died for the causes of the Union and the Confederacy. In financial terms, a week before the war ended the government of the United States already had spent $3.25 billion— a figure larger than the total previously spent since the founding of the republic. (The final cost to both sides was more than $10 billion) During the war the Union borrowed $2.6 billion, issued paper money to an extent that brought the value of the dollar down to 39 cents, and introduced a variety of new taxes.

In collecting some of the taxes, the government issued receipts in the form of tax stamps, which we call Revenue Stamps.

1862-64. THE FIRST DOCUMENTARY ISSUE In August 1862, the Commissioner of Internal Revenue advertised for bids for the printing of revenue stamps. The contract was awarded to Butler & Carpenter, and most of the first issue of revenues appeared near the end of 1862 and early in 1863. At first the stamps paid specific taxes on official documents, according to the designation on the stamp, but after Dec. 25, 1862, they were used indiscriminately. Different kinds of paper were used from time to time, and wide differences in shades and colors exist due to chemical reactions or fading. They are noticeable in the violets or lilacs, which often look gray, and in the reds, which are often on the brown side. Usually these stamps were canceled with pen and ink, and they are priced accordingly in this catalog. Printed cancellations are worth more; cancellations that cut into the paper are worth less.

All of the stamps came unwatermarked and perforated 12, but most of them also exist imperforate. Some stamps are perforated only horizontally and imperforate vertically, or vice versa. These are called "part perfs."

The collector should be careful of these, and make sure that they have good margins on the imperforate sides; people have been known to trim a perforated stamp in an attempt to make it look like a part perf or an imperforate stamp.

1862-64. U.S. INTERNAL REVENUE ISSUE included the first U.S. bicolor stamp, R3.

		Perf	Part Perf	Imperf
R1		.20	—	
2¢	orange			
R2		Perf	Part Perf	Imperf
$50	green	75.00		75.00

R3

		Perf	Part Perf	Imperf
R3		500.00		1,200.00
$200	red & green			

1862-64. AGREEMENT ISSUE

		Perf	Part Perf	Imperf
R4		.20		
5¢	red			

1862-64. BANK CHECK ISSUE

R5

		Perf	Part Perf	Imperf
R5		.20	1.50	1.50
2¢	blue			

		Perf	Part Perf	Imperf
R6		.20	.85	
2¢	orange			

1862-64. BILL OF LADING ISSUE

		Perf	Part Perf	Imperf
R7		.75	150.00	50.00
10¢	blue			

1862-64. BOND ISSUE

R8   R15   R18

		Perf	Part Perf	Imperf
R8		2.00	6.00	125.00
25¢	red			

1862-64. CERTIFICATE ISSUE

		Perf	Part Perf	Imperf
R9		25.00		10.00
2¢	blue			
R10		Perf	Part Perf	Imperf
2¢	orange	25.00		
R11		Perf	Part Perf	Imperf
5¢	red	.20	10.00	2.50
R12		Perf	Part Perf	Imperf
10¢	blue	.25	165.00	190.00
R13		Perf	Part Perf	Imperf
25¢	red	.20	5.00	7.50

1862-64. CHARTER PARTY ISSUE

		Perf	Part Perf	Imperf
R14		4.50		900.00
$3	green			
R15		Perf	Part Perf	Imperf
$5	red	6.00		225.00
R16		Perf	Part Perf	Imperf
$10	green	20.00		450.00

1862-64. CONTRACT ISSUE

		Perf	Part Perf	Imperf
R17		.35	140.00	
10¢	blue			
	a. ultramarine	.40	160.00	

1862-64. CONVEYANCE ISSUE

		Perf	Part Perf	Imperf
R18		.20	1.25	12.50
50¢	blue			
	a. ultramarine	25.00		

 R19   R20

Cat.	Denom	Color	Perf	Part Perf	Imperf
R19	$1	red	3.50	375.00	10.00
R20	$2	red	2.50	1,250.00	90.00
R21	$5	red	6.00		35.00
R22	$10	green	55.00		80.00
R23	$20	orange	45.00		100.00

1862-64. ENTRY OF GOODS ISSUE

Cat.	Denom	Color	Perf	Part Perf	Imperf
R24	25¢	red	.60	50.00	15.00
R25	50¢	blue	.25	11.50	
R26	$1	red	1.50		27.50

1862-64. EXPRESS ISSUE

 R27

Cat.	Denom	Color	Perf	Part Perf	Imperf
R27	1¢	red	1.00	40.00	50.00
R28	2¢	blue	.25	16.00	10.00
R29	2¢	orange	6.00		
R30	5¢	red	.30	450.00	4.00

1862-64. FOREIGN EXCHANGE ISSUE

Cat.	Denom	Color	Perf	Part Perf	Imperf
R31	3¢	green	3.00	225.00	
R32	5¢	red	.35		
R33	10¢	blue	6.50		
	a.	ultramarine	8.00		
R34	15¢	brown	12.50		
R35	20¢	red	27.50		40.00
R36	30¢	lilac	35.00	825.00	65.00
R37	50¢	blue	5.00	32.50	35.00
R38	70¢	green	6.50	75.00	275.00
R39	$1	red	.75		60.00

R31

 R40

Cat.	Denom	Color	Perf	Part Perf	Imperf
R40	$1.30	orange	50.00		

Cat.	Denom	Color	Perf	Part Perf	Imperf
R41	$1.60	green	85.00		800.00
R42	$1.90	brown violet	65.00		2,000.00

1862-64. INLAND EXCHANGE ISSUE

Cat.	Denom	Color	Perf	Part Perf	Imperf
R43	4¢	brown	1.75		
R44	5¢	red	.20	3.50	4.25
R45	6¢	orange	15.00		
R46	10¢	blue	.25	3.50	165.00
R47	15¢	brown	1.20	10.00	25.00
R48	20¢	red	.50	15.00	14.50
R49	30¢	lilac	3.00	55.00	45.00
R50	40¢	brown	3.00	6.00	475.00
R51	60¢	orange	6.00	45.00	75.00
R52	$1	red	.50	275.00	12.50
R53	$1.50	blue	3.00		20.00
R54	$2.50	red violet	3.50		1,850.00
R55	$3.50	blue	45.00		1,500.00

1862-64. INSURANCE ISSUE

Cat.	Denom	Color	Perf	Part Perf	Imperf
R56	25¢	red	.25	10.00	9.00

1862-64. LEASE ISSUE

Cat.	Denom	Color	Perf	Part Perf	Imperf
R57	50¢	blue	6.50	55.00	22.50
R58	$1	red	1.75		30.00

1862-64. LIFE INSURANCE ISSUE

Cat.	Denom	Color	Perf	Part Perf	Imperf
R59	25¢	red	6.00	175.00	30.00
R60	50¢	blue	.75	50.00	30.00
R61	$1	red	5.00		125.00

1862-64. MANIFEST ISSUE

Cat.	Denom	Color	Perf	Part Perf	Imperf
R62	$1	red	22.50		45.00
R63	$3	green	20.00		100.00
R64	$5	red	75.00		100.00

1862-64. MORTGAGE ISSUE

Cat.	Denom	Color	Perf	Part Perf	Imperf
R65	50¢	blue	.35	2.25	10.00
R66	$1	red	140.00		17.50
R67	$2	red	2.25		85.00
R68	$5	red	17.50		90.00
R69	$10	green	20.00		325.00

Please read the introduction to this catalog carefully. It contains much valuable information for all stamp collectors, and also makes the catalog easier for you to use.

R70

R70		Perf	Part Perf	Imperf
$15	blue	100.00		850.00
	a. ultramarine	125.00		
R71		Perf	Part Perf	Imperf
$25	red	90.00		800.00

1862-64. ORIGINAL PROCESS ISSUE

R72		Perf	Part Perf	Imperf
50¢	blue	.40	475.00	3.00

1862-64. PASSAGE TICKET ISSUE

R73		Perf	Part Perf	Imperf
50¢	blue	.70	125.00	65.00
R74		Perf	Part Perf	Imperf
$1	red	150.00		225.00

1862-64. POWER OF ATTORNEY ISSUE

R75		Perf	Part Perf	Imperf
10¢	blue	.45	20.00	425.00
R76		Perf	Part Perf	Imperf
25¢	red	.25	25.00	5.00
R77		Perf	Part Perf	Imperf
$1	red	1.75		60.00

1862-64. PROBATE OF WILL ISSUE

R78		Perf	Part Perf	Imperf
50¢	blue	17.50	50.00	30.00
R79		Perf	Part Perf	Imperf
$1	red	32.50		60.00
R80		Perf	Part Perf	Imperf
$2	red	47.50		1,750.00
R81		Perf	Part Perf	Imperf
$5	red	17.50		400.00
R82		Perf	Part Perf	Imperf
$10	green	20.00		1,000.00
R83		Perf	Part Perf	Imperf
$20	orange	900.00		1,000.00

1862-64. PROTEST ISSUE

R84		Perf	Part Perf	Imperf
25¢	red	7.00	225.00	22.50

1862-64. SURETY BOND ISSUE

R85		Perf	Part Perf	Imperf
50¢	blue	.25	2.50	140.00
	a. ultramarine	1.50		

1862-64. TELEGRAPH ISSUE

R86		Perf	Part Perf	Imperf
$1	red	10.00		400.00
R87		Perf	Part Perf	Imperf
$3	green	2.50	17.50	50.00

1862-64. WAREHOUSE RECEIPT ISSUE

R88		Perf	Part Perf	Imperf
25¢	red	20.00	200.00	40.00

For stamps inscribed: **Playing Cards** *see numbers RPC1-6 in the Playing Cards Revenues Section.*

For stamps inscribed: **Proprietary** *see numbers RP1-8 in the Proprietary Revenues Section.*

1871. THE SECOND DOCUMENTARY ISSUE

Unscrupulous people soon found that the First Issue could be cleaned and used over again, thus avoiding the payment of taxes and cheating the government. Experiments were made and a special patented paper, violet in shade, and with tiny silk threads woven into it, was placed in use. The ink too, was special, so that any attempt to clean the stamps was disastrous. All the stamps, except for the last two values, were bi-colored, with the frames printed in blue and Washington's head in black. Each value had its individual frame. The first nine values were all small in size, and the head of Washington was enclosed in an octagon. From the 25¢ value on, they were quite tall and narrow and the Washington head was enclosed in a circle. In bi-colored printings there is a chance that a sheet after having been printed in one color, may be reversed before being put through the machine for the second color. That happened with some of these stamps, for eight of the values are known with "inverted centers," and are quite valuable. Excellent imitations of inverted centers exist; the collector interested in buying one should inspect it carefully and do business only with a firm he can trust. **Prices given are for the normal "herringbone" cancellation, a row of arrowheads, one within the other, impressed or cut into the paper.** *These stamps were printed by Joseph R. Carpenter of Philadelphia, on unwatermarked paper and perforated 12.*

R89, 120   R90, 121, 137   R90a

R89			Uncut	CutCnl
1¢	blue & black		30.00	17.00
	a. Inverted center		900.00	
R90			Uncut	CutCnl
2¢	blue & black		1.00	.20
	a. Inverted center		3,250.00	

R91   R92, 122   R93, 123

R91			Uncut	CutCnl
3¢	blue & black		12.50	8.00
R92			Uncut	CutCnl
4¢	blue & black		55.00	25.00
R93			Uncut	CutCnl
5¢	blue & black		1.40	.40
	a. Inverted center		1,400.00	

R94, 124   R95   R96, 125

R94			Uncut	CutCnl
6¢	blue & black		85.00	45.00
R95			Uncut	CutCnl
10¢	blue & black		.85	.20
	a. Inverted center		1,400.00	

R96
15¢   **blue & black**

	Uncut	CutCnl
	22.50	12.00

 R97

R97
20¢   **blue & black**
   a. Inverted center

	Uncut	CutCnl
	5.00	2.00
	7,000.00	

R98   R99, 126   R100, 127

R98
25¢   **blue & black**
   a. Inverted center

	Uncut	CutCnl
	.60	.20
	7,500.00	

R99
30¢   **blue & black**

	Uncut	CutCnl
	60.00	30.00

R100
40¢   **blue & black**

	Uncut	CutCnl
	40.00	20.00

R101   R102, 128   R103, 129

R101
50¢   **blue & black**
   a. Inverted center
   b. Inverted center, punch cancellation
   c. Sewing machine perf.

	Uncut	CutCnl
	.60	.20
	750.00	
		200.00
	70.00	

R102
60¢   **blue & black**

	Uncut	CutCnl
	85.00	40.00

R103
70¢   **blue & black**
   a. Inverted center

	Uncut	CutCnl
	30.00	15.00
	2,500.00	

R104, 130   R105   R106

R104
$1   **blue & black**
   a. Inverted center
   b. Inverted center, punch cancellation

	Uncut	CutCnl
	3.00	1.50
	4,000.00	
		700.00

R105
$1.30   **blue & black**

	Uncut	CutCnl
	250.00	150.00

R106
$1.50   **blue & black**
   a. Sewing machine perf.

	Uncut	CutCnl
	12.50	7.00
		450.00

 R107

R108

R107
$1.60   **blue & black**

	Uncut	CutCnl
	325.00	200.00

R108
$1.90   **blue & black**

	Uncut	CutCnl
	160.00	90.00

 R109

R110,132

R109
$2   **blue & black**

	Uncut	CutCnl
	12.50	7.00

R110
$2.50   **blue & black**

	Uncut	CutCnl
	25.00	15.00

R111

R112

R117

R118

R111		Uncut	CutCnl
$3	**blue & black**	30.00	17.00

R112		Uncut	CutCnl
$3.50	**blue & black**	150.00	75.00

R117		Uncut	CutCnl
$50	**blue & black**	325.00	220.00

R118		Uncut	CutCnl
$200	**blue, red & black**	4,500.00	2,500.00

R113,134

R114,135

R113		Uncut	CutCnl
$5	**blue & black**	17.50	9.00
	a. Inverted center	2,000.00	
	b. Inverted center, punch cancellation		600.00

R114		Uncut	CutCnl
$10	**blue & black**	90.00	50.00

R115,136

R16

R115		Uncut	CutCnl
$20	**blue & black**	300.00	200.00

R116		Uncut	CutCnl
$25	**blue & black**	300.00	200.00

R119 *("Persian rug")*

R119		Uncut	CutCnl
$500	**green & red, black**	10,000.00	

1871-72. THE THIRD DOCUMENTARY ISSUE The second issue was a great success in preventing the cleaning and re-use of stamps. There were, however, complaints that the stamps were difficult to distinguish because the colors were uniform in nearly all values. A third issue was therefore prepared, again by Joseph R. Carpenter of Philadelphia, using the same plates but this time with varying colors, so that identification might be much easier. *They are on violet paper with silk threads, unwatermarked and perforated 12.*

R120		Uncut	CutCnl
1¢	**claret & black**	25.00	15.00

R121		Uncut	CutCnl
2¢	**orange & black**	.20	.20
	a. Inverted center	275.00	
	b. claret and gray black (error of color)	500.00	

R122		Uncut	CutCnl
4¢	**brown & black**	30.00	16.00

R123		Uncut	CutCnl
5¢	**orange & black**	.20	.20
	a. Inverted center	3,000.00	

R124		Uncut	CutCnl
6¢	**orange & black**	30.00	15.00

R125		Uncut	CutCnl
15¢	**brown & black**	7.50	3.50
	a. Inverted center	7,500.00	

R126		Uncut	CutCnl
30¢	**orange & black**	12.50	6.00
	a. Inverted center	2,000.00	

R127		Uncut	CutCnl
40¢	**brown & black**	30.00	15.00

R128		Uncut	CutCnl
60¢	**orange & black**	55.00	28.00

R129		Uncut	CutCnl
70¢	**green & black**	35.00	28.00

R130		Uncut	CutCnl
$1	**green & black**	1.25	.50
	a. Inverted center	5,000.00	

R131		Uncut	CutCnl
$2	**vermilion & black**	17.50	11.00

R132		Uncut	CutCnl
$2.50	**claret & black**	30.00	18.00
	a. Inverted Center	12,500.00	

R133		Uncut	CutCnl
$3	**green & black**	30.00	20.00

R134		Uncut	CutCnl
$5	**vermilion & black**	17.50	10.00

R135		Uncut	CutCnl
$10	**green & black**	70.00	35.00

R136		Uncut	CutCnl
$20	**orange & black**	450.00	225.00
	a. vermilion and black	550.00	

1874. U.S. INTERNAL REVENUE ISSUE The design of the 2¢ stamp No. R121 was issued on green paper, perforated 12.

R137		Uncut	CutCnl
2¢	**orange & black** on green paper	.20	.20
	a. Inverted center	325.00	

1875-78. U.S. INTERNAL REVENUE ISSUE *The Profile of Liberty was used as the central design of the new 2¢ stamps printed on blue silk or watermarked paper. The stamps were perforated 12, imperforate or rouletted 6.*

R138-R141 *Silk paper, unwatermarked, perforated 12*

R138		UnCnl	UseFVF
2¢	**blue,** on blue paper	.75	.20
	Pair	2.50	.50
	Block of 4	8.00	1.25

1875-78. U.S. INTERNAL REVENUE ISSUE *Double-line USIR watermark, perforated 12.*

      R139 *Watermark*

R139		UnCnl	UseFVF
2¢	**blue,** on blue paper	1.50	.20
	Pair	3.50	
	Block of 4	8.00	
	v. Pair, imperforate		225.00
	v1. Vertical pair, imperforate horizontally	400.00	

Note: No. R140, an imperforate version of the issue of 1875-78, has been eliminated and the stamp included as a variety of R139.

1875-78. U.S. INTERNAL REVENUE *Double-line USIR watermark, rouletted 6.*

R141		UnCnl	UseFVF
2¢	**blue,** on blue paper	30.00	30.00
	Pair	125.00	

1898. U.S. INTERNAL REVENUE ISSUE Regular Issue Nos. 189, 191, overprinted.

    R142 *Overprint A*

R142		UnCnl	UseFVF
1¢	**deep green,** red overprint A	3.00	3.00

    R143, R144 *Overprint B*

R143		UnCnl	UseFVF
1¢	**deep green,** red overprint B	.25	.20
	a. Inverted overprint	20.00	17.50

R144		UnCnl	UseFVF
2¢	**carmine,** blue overprint B	.30	.20
	a. Inverted overprint	2.50	1.50

The 8¢ purple brown, 10¢ dark green, and 15¢ indigo of the 1895 regular postage issue exist with overprint B in magenta, but they were not officially issued. They are valued at approximately $4,000 each.

The 1¢ value of the Trans-Mississippi Exposition Issue (CM17) was overprinted provisionally with "I.R." and "L.H.C." or "P.I.D. & Son," both in red. Used copies of these sold in a range of $6,600-$22,500. The 250 overprints of each stamp were done by Purvis Printing Co. for use by the Chapman Line and P.I. Daprix & Son, which operated freight steamboats on the Erie Canal.

1898. NEWSPAPER STAMP ISSUE Newspaper Stamp No. N92, overprinted.

    R145-158

R145		UnCnl	UseFVF
$5	**dark blue,** red overprint A, reading down	225.00	150.00

R146		UnCnl	UseFVF
$5	**dark blue,** red overprint B, reading up	100.00	75.00

1898. DOCUMENTARY ISSUE "The Battleship Issue" featured a new design, officially designated as a "Battleship, second class." The blowing-up of the battleship *Maine* in the harbor of Havana on Feb. 15, 1898, had touched off the Spanish-American War and the slogan "Remember the Maine." Many people thought the new design represented the unfortunate *Maine,* but this was officially denied. *The stamps were printed on paper with double-line watermark USIR, and rouletted 5 1/2 or hyphen-hole perforated 7.* Stamps identical with these, except that the word "Proprietary" is printed on the base instead of "Documentary" are found listed with the Proprietary stamps later on.

R147

R147		UnCnl	UseFVF	
1/2¢	**orange,** rouletted	2.25	6.00	

R148		UnCnl	UseFVF	
1/2¢	**dark gray,** rouletted	.30	.20	

R148a		UnCnl	UseFVF	
1/2¢	**dark gray,** hyphen-hole	.30	.20	

R149		UnCnl	UseFVF	
1¢	**pale blue,** rouletted	.35	.20	

R149a		UnCnl	UseFVF	
1¢	**pale blue,** hyphen-hole	.35	.20	

R150		UnCnl	UseFVF	
2¢	**rose,** rouletted	.25	.20	

R150a		UnCnl	UseFVF	
2¢	**rose,** hyphen-hole	.25	.20	

R151		UnCnl	UseFVF	
3¢	**indigo,** rouletted	1.25	.20	

R151a		UnCnl	UseFVF	
3¢	**indigo,** hyphen-hole	1.25	.20	

R152		UnCnl	UseFVF	
4¢	**pale rose,** rouletted	.75	.20	

R152a		UnCnl	UseFVF	
4¢	**pale rose,** hyphen-hole	.75	.20	

R153		UnCnl	UseFVF	
5¢	**lilac,** rouletted	.25	.20	

R153a		UnCnl	UseFVF	
5¢	**lilac,** hyphen-hole	.25	.20	

R154		UnCnl	UseFVF	
10¢	**gray brown,** rouletted	1.25	.20	

R154a		UnCnl	UseFVF	
10¢	**gray brown,** hyphen-hole	1.25	.20	

R155		UnCnl	UseFVF	
25¢	**lilac brown,** rouletted	1.25	.20	

R155a		UnCnl	UseFVF	
25¢	**lilac brown,** hyphen-hole	1.25	.20	

R156		UnCnl	UseFVF	
40¢	**blue lilac,** rouletted	110.00	2.00	

R156a		UnCnl	UseFVF	
40¢	**blue lilac,** hyphen-hole	150.00	2.00	

R157		UnCnl	UseFVF	
50¢	**violet gray,** rouletted	10.00	.20	

R157a		UnCnl	UseFVF	
50¢	**violet gray,** hyphen-hole	20.00	.20	

R158		UnCnl	UseFVF	
80¢	**bistre,** rouletted	55.00	.40	

R158a		UnCnl	UseFVF	
80¢	**bistre,** hyphen-hole	150.00	.40	

1898-1900. DOCUMENTARY ISSUE Allegorical Figure of Commerce design on the $1 through $50 values. *These stamps are rouletted 5 1/2 or hyphen-hole perforated 7, all on the double-line USIR watermark paper. The canceled stamps usually are without gum.*

 R159

R159		UnCnl	UseFVF	CutCnl
$1	**green** *(1898),* rouletted	7.00	.20	

R159a		UnCnl	UseFVF	CutCnl
$1	**green,** hyphen-hole	7.00	.20	

R160		UnCnl	UseFVF	CutCnl
$1	**carmine** *(1900),* hyphen-hole	14.00	.50	

R161		UnCnl	UseFVF	CutCnl
$3	**brown** *(1898),* rouletted	14.00	.75	.20

R161a		UnCnl	UseFVF	CutCnl
$3	**brown,** hyphen-hole	14.00	.75	.20

R162		UnCnl	UseFVF	CutCnl
$3	**lake** *(1900),* hyphen-hole	45.00	100.00	8.00

R163		UnCnl	UseFVF	CutCnl
$5	**red orange** *(1898),* rouletted	17.50	1.50	.25

R164		UnCnl	UseFVF	CutCnl
$10	**black,** rouletted	55.00	2.50	.75

R165		UnCnl	UseFVF	CutCnl
$30	**red,** rouletted	175.00	85.00	40.00

R166		UnCnl	UseFVF	CutCnl
$50	**gray brown,** rouletted	80.00	6.00	2.00

1899. DOCUMENTARY ISSUE Portraits in various ornate frames, each stamp inscribed: "Series of 1898." *Double-line watermark, imperforate.*

R167 *Marshall*   R168 *Hamilton*   R169 *Madison*

R167		UnCnl	UseFVF	CutCnl
$100	**pale brown & black** (Marshall)	90.00	30.00	17.50

R168		UnCnl	UseFVF	CutCnl
$500	**carmine lake & black** (Hamilton)	600.00	425.00	225.00

R169		UnCnl	UseFVF	CutCnl
$1,000	**dark green & black** (Madison)	600.00	350.00	100.00

1900. DOCUMENTARY ISSUE Allegorical Figure of Commerce, same designs as 1898-1900, but different colors and overprinted with large outline numerals of value. *Hyphen-hole perforation 7, double-line USIR watermark.*

 R170 *Outline numeral overprint*

R170		UnCnl	UseFVF	CutCnl
$1	**olive gray**	8.00	.25	.20

R171		UnCnl	UseFVF	CutCnl
$2	**olive gray**	8.00	.25	.20

R172		UnCnl	UseFVF	CutCnl
$3	**olive gray**	45.00	10.50	2.25

R173		UnCnl	UseFVF	CutCnl
$5	**olive gray**	35.00	8.50	1.25

R174		UnCnl	UseFVF	CutCnl
$10	**olive gray**	60.00	17.50	3.50

R175		UnCnl	UseFVF	CutCnl
$50	**olive gray**	600.00	350.00	75.00

1902. DOCUMENTARY ISSUE Allegorical figure of Commerce, overprinted in black with large filigree numerals of value. A small square of water-soluble varnish was printed on the face of each stamp before it was overprinted; the part of the overprint that is on this small square of varnish will disappear when the stamp is soaked in water. *Double-line USIR watermark, hyphen-hole roulette perforated 7.*

 R176 *Filigree numeral overprint*

R176		UnCnl	UseFVF	CutCnl
$1	green	17.50	3.50	.25
	a. inverted surcharge		175.00	
R177		UnCnl	UseFVF	CutCnl
$2	green	15.00	1.50	.25
R178		UnCnl	UseFVF	CutCnl
$5	green	125.00	30.00	4.50
	a. Overprint omitted	55.00		

R179 *Filigree numeral overprint*

R179		UnCnl	UseFVF	CutCnl
$10	green	300.00	140.00	50.00
R180		UnCnl	UseFVF	CutCnl
$50	green	900.00	750.00	225.00

1914. DOCUMENTARY ISSUE A white numeral in a circle was the new design of the small-size stamps, printed in one color. They are inscribed "Series of 1914," *offset printed on single-line USPS watermark paper, and are perforated 10.* The unused stamps valued are with gum.

R181-R191 *Single-line USPS watermark*

R181		UnFVF	UseFVF
1/2¢	rose	6.50	3.50
R182		UnFVF	UseFVF
1¢	rose	1.50	.20
R183		UnFVF	UseFVF
2¢	rose	1.75	.20
R184		UnFVF	UseFVF
3¢	rose	45.00	27.50
R185		UnFVF	UseFVF
4¢	rose	11.00	2.00
R186		UnFVF	UseFVF
5¢	rose	4.00	.20
R187		UnFVF	UseFVF
10¢	rose	3.25	.20
R188		UnFVF	UseFVF
25¢	rose	27.50	.75
R189		UnFVF	UseFVF
40¢	rose	17.50	1.00
R190		UnFVF	UseFVF
50¢	rose	5.50	.20
R191		UnFVF	UseFVF
80¢	rose	80.00	10.00

1914. DOCUMENTARY ISSUE Same design as the preceding stamps, Nos. R181-R191, but on *double-line USIR watermark paper, perforated 10.*

R192		UnFVF	UseFVF
1/2¢	red	1.50	.60
R193		UnFVF	UseFVF
1¢	red	.20	.20
R194		UnFVF	UseFVF
2¢	red	.20	.20
R195		UnFVF	UseFVF
3¢	red	.60	.20
R196		UnFVF	UseFVF
4¢	red	3.50	.40
R197		UnFVF	UseFVF
5¢	red	.75	.30

R198		UnFVF	UseFVF
10¢	red	.50	.20
R199		UnFVF	UseFVF
25¢	red	5.00	1.25
R200		UnFVF	UseFVF
40¢	red	60.00	12.50
R201		UnFVF	UseFVF
50¢	red	12.50	.35
R202		UnFVF	UseFVF
80¢	red	90.00	17.50

1914. DOCUMENTARY ISSUE Head of Liberty design, inscribed "Series 1914," *flat press printing. Double-line USIR watermark, perforated 10.*

 R203

R203		UnFVF	UseFVF	CutCnl
$1	yellow green	30.00	.30	.20
R204		UnFVF	UseFVF	CutCnl
$2	carmine	45.00	.50	.20
R205		UnFVF	UseFVF	CutCnl
$3	purple	55.00	2.50	.20
R206		UnFVF	UseFVF	CutCnl
$5	dark blue	45.00	3.00	.50
R207		UnFVF	UseFVF	CutCnl
$10	yellow	100.00	5.00	1.00
R208		UnFVF	UseFVF	CutCnl
$30	vermilion orange	225.00	12.50	2.50
R209		UnFVF	UseFVF	CutCnl
$50	violet	1,200.00	750.00	300.00

1914-15. DOCUMENTARY ISSUE Portraits are featured on high values *printed on double-line USIR watermark paper, perforated 12.* These stamps always come with one or two straight edges, since they were printed in strips of four that were imperforate at the top, bottom, and right side.

 R210   R211

R210		UnFVF	UseFVF	CutCnl
$60	brown (Lincoln)		115.00	45.00
R211		UnFVF	UseFVF	CutCnl
$100	green (Washington)		40.00	17.50
R212		UnFVF	UseFVF	CutCnl
$500	blue (Hamilton)		475.00	200.00
R213		UnFVF	UseFVF	CutCnl
$1,000	yellow (Madison)		475.00	200.00

1917. DOCUMENTARY ISSUE White numerals in ovals were used on horizontal stamps 21mm wide and 18mm high. *Double-line USIR watermark, perforated 11.* See Nos. R237-249 for stamps of the same designs but with different perforations. *Offset printed.*

R214		UnCnl	UseFVF
1¢	rose	.30	.20
R215		UnCnl	UseFVF
2¢	rose	.30	.20

R216		UnCnl	UseFVF
3¢	rose	1.50	.40
R217		UnCnl	UseFVF
4¢	rose	.50	.20
R218		UnCnl	UseFVF
5¢	rose	.30	.20
R219		UnCnl	UseFVF
8¢	rose	1.75	.30

 R220

 R223

R220		UnCnl	UseFVF
10¢	rose	.50	.20
R221		UnCnl	UseFVF
20¢	rose	1.25	.20
R222		UnCnl	UseFVF
25¢	rose	1.25	.20
R223		UnCnl	UseFVF
40¢	rose	1.50	.40
R224		UnCnl	UseFVF
50¢	rose	2.00	.20
R225		UnCnl	UseFVF
80¢	rose	4.50	.20

1917-33. DOCUMENTARY ISSUE UNDATED Head of Liberty design (No. R203) but without dates. *Double-line USIR watermark, perforated 11.*

 R226-R231 *Head of Liberty*

R226		UnCnl	UseFVF	CutCnl
$1	green	6.00	.20	
R227		UnCnl	UseFVF	CutCnl
$2	rose	10.00	.20	
R228		UnCnl	UseFVF	CutCnl
$3	violet	30.00	.75	.20

R229 *Head of Liberty*

R229		UnCnl	UseFVF	CutCnl
$4	ochre	22.50	1.75	.20
R230		UnCnl	UseFVF	CutCnl
$5	blue	15.00	.30	.20
R231		UnCnl	UseFVF	CutCnl
$10	yellow	27.50	1.00	.20

1917. DOCUMENTARY ISSUE Portraits in various frames without dates. *Double-line USIR watermark, perforated 12.*

 R232 *Grant*

R233 *Lincoln*

R232		UnCnl	UseFVF	CutCnl
$30	**orange,** green numerals (Grant)	45.00	10.00	1.50
	a. blue numerals	70.00	20.00	1.50
R233		UnCnl	UseFVF	CutCnl
$60	**brown** (Lincoln)	50.00	7.50	1.00

 R234 *George Washington*

R234		UnCnl	UseFVF	CutCnl
$100	**pale green** (Washington)	27.50	1.50	.50
R235		UnCnl	UseFVF	CutCnl
$500	**blue** (Hamilton), red numerals	200.00	35.00	10.00
	a. orange numerals	—50.00	20.00	
R236		UnCnl	UseFVF	CutCnl
$1,000	**orange yellow** (Madison)	125.00	15.00	5.00

1928-29. DOCUMENTARY ISSUE Similar to the 1917 issue but *perforated 10.*

R237		UnCnl	UseFVF	CutCnl
1¢	**pale red**	2.00	1.50	
R238		UnCnl	UseFVF	CutCnl
2¢	**pale red**	.60	.25	
R239		UnCnl	UseFVF	CutCnl
4¢	**pale red**	6.00	4.00	
R240		UnCnl	UseFVF	CutCnl
5¢	**pale red**	1.25	.60	
R241		UnCnl	UseFVF	CutCnl
10¢	**pale red**	1.75	1.25	
R242		UnCnl	UseFVF	CutCnl
20¢	**pale red**	6.00	5.25	
R243		UnCnl	UseFVF	CutCnl
$1	**green**	80.00	27.50	5.00
R244		UnCnl	UseFVF	CutCnl
$2	**rose**	30.00	2.50	
R245		UnCnl	UseFVF	CutCnl
$10	**yellow**	100.00	40.00	22.50

1929-30. DOCUMENTARY ISSUE Similar to the 1917 issue but *perforated 11x10.*

R246		UnCnl	UseFVF	CutCnl
2¢	**carmine rose**	1.00	.80	
R247		UnCnl	UseFVF	CutCnl
5¢	**carmine rose**	.45	.40	
R248		UnCnl	UseFVF	CutCnl
10¢	**carmine rose**	3.50	3.50	
R249		UnCnl	UseFVF	CutCnl
20¢	**carmine rose**	5.50	5.25	

1940. DOCUMENTARY ISSUE Stamps of 1917 *overprinted in black "Series 1940" and perforated 11.*

R250		UnCnl	UseVF	PunchCnl
1¢	**pink**	2.50	2.00	.30

R251		UnCnl	UseVF	PunchCnl
2¢	pink	2.50	1.75	.40
R252		UnCnl	UseVF	PunchCnl
3¢	pink	8.00	4.00	.60
R253		UnCnl	UseVF	PunchCnl
4¢	pink	3.25	.50	.20

1940. DOCUMENTARY ISSUE Stamps of 1917 *overprinted in black "Series 1940" and perforated 11.*

 R254

R254		UnCnl	UseFVF	CutCnl
5¢	pink	3.50	.75	.25
R255		UnCnl	UseFVF	CutCnl
8¢	pink	14.00	12.50	3.00
R256		UnCnl	UseFVF	CutCnl
10¢	pink	1.75	.40	.20
R257		UnCnl	UseFVF	CutCnl
20¢	pink	2.25	.50	.20
R258		UnCnl	UseFVF	CutCnl
25¢	pink	5.50	1.00	.20
R259		UnCnl	UseFVF	CutCnl
40¢	pink	5.50	.65	.20
R260		UnCnl	UseFVF	CutCnl
50¢	pink	6.00	.50	.20
R261		UnCnl	UseFVF	CutCnl
80¢	pink	10.00	.85	.20
R262		UnCnl	UseFVF	CutCnl
$1	yellow green	30.00	.50	.20
R263		UnCnl	UseFVF	CutCnl
$2	rose	30.00	1.00	.20
R264		UnCnl	UseFVF	CutCnl
$3	dark violet	45.00	25.00	3.25
R265		UnCnl	UseFVF	CutCnl
$4	ocher	75.00	30.00	5.00
R266		UnCnl	UseFVF	CutCnl
$5	blue	45.00	10.00	1.00
R267		UnCnl	UseFVF	CutCnl
$10	orange yellow	100.00	27.50	2.00

1940. DOCUMENTARY ISSUE Stamps of 1917 handstamped in green "Series 1940." *Perforated 12, without gum.*

R268		UnCnl	UseFVF	CutCnl
$30	vermilion		425.00	350.00
	a. larger, 2-line handstamp in black		6,000.00	
R269		UnCnl	UseFVF	CutCnl
$60	brown		625.00	450.00
	a. larger, 2-line handstamp in black		—	
R270		UnCnl	UseFVF	CutCnl
$100	green		900.00	800.00
R271		UnCnl	UseFVF	CutCnl
$500	blue		1,250.00	1,100.00
	a. larger, 2-line handstamp in black	2,750.00	2,500.00	
R272		UnCnl	UseFVF	CutCnl
$1,000	orange		600.00	375.00

No. 273 is not assigned.

1940. DOCUMENTARY ISSUE Secretaries of the Treasury from Alexander Hamilton, the first secretary, to Salmon P. Chase, who served under Lincoln, were featured on a new series of stamps. Included were portraits of Walter Forward, the first Comptroller of the Treasury, in 1841, and Roger B. Taney, who served until his appointment was rejected by Congress. The stamps were printed in three different sizes and overprinted for use in different years, their validity extending for the year on the overprint and one additional year. Stamps Nos. R274-R298 were overprinted in black "Series 1940." Stamps with a face value of $30 and above were issued without gum and are usually handstamped on documents. *They were issued with straight edges on 1 or 2 sides. Nos. R274-R285 size: 19x22mm, perforated 11.*

R274		MnHVF	UseVF	CutCnl	Perfin
1¢	carmine	3.00	2.50		.75

 R275 *Oliver Wolcott Jr.*

R278 *G.W. Campbell*

R275		MnHVF	UseVF	CutCnl	Perfin
2¢	carmine (Oliver Wolcott Jr.)	4.00	2.50	1.20	1.00
R276		MnHVF	UseVF	CutCnl	Perfin
3¢	carmine (Samuel Dexter)	15.00	7.50	1.20	3.00
R277		MnHVF	UseVF	CutCnl	Perfin
4¢	carmine (Albert Gallatin)	35.00	17.50	4.50	4.00
R278		MnHVF	UseVF	CutCnl	Perfin
5¢	carmine (G.W. Campbell)	3.00	.50	.25	.20
R279		MnHVF	UseVF	CutCnl	Perfin
8¢	carmine (Alexander Dallas)	20.00	12.00	3.00	2.00

R280
William H. Crawford

R281
Richard Rush

R282
S.D. Ingham

R280		MnHVF	UseVF	CutCnl	Perfin
10¢	carmine (William H. Crawford)	2.00	.35	.20	.20
R281		MnHVF	UseVF	CutCnl	Perfin
20¢	carmine (Richard Rush)	3.50	2.00	1.00	.50
R282		MnHVF	UseVF	CutCnl	Perfin
25¢	carmine (S.D. Ingham)	2.50	.50	.20	.20

 R283 *Louis McLane*

R284 *William J. Duane*

R283		MnHVF	UseVF	CutCnl	Perfin
40¢	carmine (Louis McLane)	35.00	15.00	4.00	3.00
R284		MnHVF	UseVF	CutCnl	Perfin
50¢	carmine (William J. Duane)	4.00	.35	.20	.20
R285		MnHVF	UseVF	CutCnl	Perfin
80¢	carmine (Roger B. Taney)	75.00	50.00	25.00	20.00

1940. DOCUMENTARY ISSUE *Nos. R286-R292 Size: 21 1/2x 36 1/4mm, perforated 11.*

 R286 *Levi Woodbury*

R286		MnHVF	UseVF	CutCnl	Perfin
$1	carmine (Levi Woodbury)	30.00	.50	.20	.20
R287		MnHVF	UseVF	CutCnl	Perfin
$2	carmine (Thomas Ewing)	35.00	.70	.20	.20
R288		MnHVF	UseVF	CutCnl	Perfin
$3	carmine (Walter Forward)	100.00	70.00	10.00	8.50

		MnHVF	UseVF	CutCnl	Perfin
R289 $4	carmine (J.C. Spencer)	60.00	30.00	6.00	2.00
R290 $5	carmine (G.M. Bibb)	35.00	1.25	.40	.25
R291 $10	carmine (R.J. Walker)	70.00	4.50	.70	.25
R292 $20	carmine (William M. Meredith)	1,250.	500.00	300.00	300.00

1940. DOCUMENTARY ISSUE *Nos. R293-R298 Size: 28 1/2x42mm, perforated 12, issued without gum.*

		MnHVF	UseVF	CutCnl	Perfin
R293 $30	carmine (Thomas Corwin)	100.00	35.00	11.00	10.00
R294 $50	carmine (James Guthrie)		1,000.	900.00	500.00
R295 $60	carmine (Howell Cobb)	200.00	40.00	30.00	20.00
R296 $100	carmine (P.F. Thomas)	150.00	50.00	20.00	10.00

R297 *J.A. Dix*

R298 *S.P. Chase*

		MnHVF	UseVF	CutCnl	Perfin
R297 $500	carmine (J.A. Dix)		800.00	450.00	250.00
R298 $1,000	carmine (S.P. Chase)		400.00	165.00	140.00

1941. DOCUMENTARY ISSUE Secretaries of the Treasury, designs as Nos. R274-R298, overprint reads "Series 1941." *Nos. R299-R317 perforated 11; Nos. R318-R323 perforated 12, without gum.*

		MnHVF	UseVF	CutCnl	Perfin
R299 1¢	carmine	2.50	1.65	.75	.60
R300 2¢	carmine	2.50	.75	.40	.30

R301 *Samuel Dexter*

R302 *Albert Gallatin*

R304 *A.J. Dallas*

		MnHVF	UseVF	CutCnl	Perfin
R301 3¢	carmine	6.00	3.00	1.25	1.00
R302 4¢	carmine	4.50	1.00	.30	.25
R303 5¢	carmine	1.00	.20	.20	.20
R304 8¢	carmine	12.50	6.50	3.00	2.75
R305 10¢	carmine	1.25	.20	.20	.20
R306 20¢	carmine	2.75	.40	.20	.20
R307 25¢	carmine	1.50	.20	.20	.20
R308 40¢	carmine	8.50	2.25	1.00	.80
R309 50¢	carmine	2.25	.20	.20	.20
R310 80¢	carmine	40.00	8.50	3.00	2.50

		MnHVF	UseVF	CutCnl	Perfin
R311 $1	carmine	8.00	.20	.20	.20

R312 *Thomas Ewing*

R315 *G.M. Bibb*

R316 *R.J. Walker*

		MnHVF	UseVF	CutCnl	Perfin
R312 $2	carmine	9.00	.30	.20	.20
R313 $3	carmine	15.00	2.00	.30	.25
R314 $4	carmine	25.00	12.50	.80	.65
R315 $5	carmine	30.00	.50	.20	.20
R316 $10	carmine	45.00	3.50	.30	.25
R317 $20	carmine	475.00	165.00	65.00	45.00
R318 $30	carmine	45.00	20.00	10.00	8.00
R319 $50	carmine	165.00	140.00	70.00	40.00
R320 $60	carmine		40.00	12.50	10.00
R321 $100	carmine	40.00	15.00	6.00	5.00
R322 $500	carmine		175.00	85.00	45.00
R323 $1,000	carmine		95.00	30.00	25.00

1942. DOCUMENTARY ISSUE Secretaries of the Treasury, designs as Nos. R274-R298, overprint reads "Series 1942." *Nos. R324-R342 perforated 11; Nos. R343-R348 perforated 12, without gum.*

		MnHVF	UseVF	CutCnl	Perfin
R324 1¢	carmine	.40	.30	.20	.20
R325 2¢	carmine	.40	.30	.20	.20
R326 3¢	carmine	.60	.50	.20	.20
R327 4¢	carmine	1.25	1.00	.40	.30
R328 5¢	carmine	.40	.20	.20	.20
R329 8¢	carmine	5.00	4.00	1.00	1.00
R330 10¢	carmine	1.00	.20	.20	.20
R331 20¢	carmine	1.00	.40	.20	.20
R332 25¢	carmine	2.00	.40	.20	.20
R333 40¢	carmine	4.50	1.00	.50	.30
R334 50¢	carmine	2.50	.20	.20	.20
R335 80¢	carmine	15.00	8.00	2.50	2.00
R336 $1	carmine	7.50	.20	.20	.20
R337 $2	carmine	8.50	.20	.20	.20
R338 $3	carmine	12.50	2.00	.25	.20
R339 $4	carmine	20.00	3.50	.30	.25

		MnHVF	UseVF	CutCnl	Perfin
R340 $5	carmine	22.50	.75	.20	.20
R341 $10	carmine	50.00	2.00	.20	.20
R342 $20	carmine	100.00	25.00	15.00	12.50
R343 $30	carmine	35.00	17.50	7.00	5.00
R344 $50	carmine	300.00	225.00	125.00	100.00
R345 $60	carmine	650.00	550.00	150.00	90.00
R346 $100	carmine	125.00	85.00	35.00	30.00
R347 $500	carmine		175.00	100.00	50.00
R348 $1,000	carmine		90.00	50.00	40.00

1943. DOCUMENTARY ISSUE Secretaries of the Treasury, designs as Nos. R274-R298, overprint reads "Series 1943." *Nos. R349-R367 perforated 11; Nos. R368-R373 perforated 12, without gum.*

		MnHVF	UseVF	CutCnl	Perfin
R349 1¢	carmine	.50	.40	.20	.20
R350 2¢	carmine	.40	.30	.20	.20
R351 3¢	carmine	2.25	2.00	.50	.40
R352 4¢	carmine	.80	.80	.30	.25
R353 5¢	carmine	.40	.25	.20	.20
R354 8¢	carmine	3.50	2.75	1.50	1.25
R355 10¢	carmine	.50	.25	.20	.20
R356 20¢	carmine	1.50	.50	.20	.20
R357 25¢	carmine	1.40	.20	.20	.20
R358 40¢	carmine	4.50	1.75	1.00	.60
R359 50¢	carmine	1.00	.20	.20	.20
R360 80¢	carmine	10.00	5.00	1.20	1.00
R361 $1	carmine	4.50	.30	.20	.20
R362 $2	carmine	8.50	.25	.20	.20
R363 $3	carmine	15.00	1.50	.30	.25
R364 $4	carmine	20.00	2.50	.40	.35
R365 $5	carmine	25.00	.40	.20	.20
R366 $10	carmine	40.00	2.50	.50	.40
R367 $20	carmine	90.00	17.50	5.00	4.50
R368 $30	carmine	30.00	17.50	4.00	3.50
R369 $50	carmine	60.00	20.00	7.50	5.00

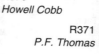

R370 *Howell Cobb*

R371 *P.F. Thomas*

		MnHVF	UseVF	CutCnl	Perfin
R370 $60	carmine		65.00	12.50	9.00
R371 $100	carmine		8.50	5.00	3.50
R372 $500	carmine		160.00	80.00	60.00
R373 $1,000	carmine		140.00	40.00	35.00

1944. DOCUMENTARY ISSUE Secretaries of the Treasury, designs as Nos. R274-R298, overprint reads "Series 1944" in type slightly larger than in 1940-43. *Nos. R374-R392 perforated 11; Nos. R393-R398 perforated 12, without gum.*

		MnHVF	UseVF	CutCnl	Perfin
R374 1¢	carmine	.40	.30	.20	.20
R375 2¢	carmine	.40	.30	.20	.20
R376 3¢	carmine	.40	.30	.20	.20
R377 4¢	carmine	.50	.40	.20	.20
R378 5¢	carmine	.40	.20	.20	.20
R379 8¢	carmine	1.50	1.00	.45	.40
R380 10¢	carmine	.40	.20	.20	.20
R381 20¢	carmine	.70	.20	.20	.20
R382 25¢	carmine	1.25	.20	.20	.20
R383 40¢	carmine	2.50	.50	.20	.20
R384 50¢	carmine	2.50	.20	.20	.20
R385 80¢	carmine	10.00	3.50	1.00	.80
R386 $1	carmine	5.00	.20	.20	.20
R387 $2	carmine	7.50	.20	.20	.20
R388 $3	carmine	10.00	1.25	.45	.30
R389 $4	carmine	15.00	9.00	1.00	.80
R390 $5	carmine	17.50	.25	.20	.20
R391 $10	carmine	35.00	1.00	.20	.20
R392 $20	carmine	75.00	12.50	3.00	2.75

Values in this catalog do not reflect the generally much lower cost of stamps acquired in mixtures, collections, bulk lots or other large-quantity purchases, not stamps sold at unusually advantageous prices to attract additional business or offered as approvals, premiums, and so forth.

R393
Thomas Corwin

R394
James Guthrie

	MnHVF	UseVF	CutCnl	Perfin
R393 $30 carmine	40.00	17.50	5.00	4.50
R394 $50 carmine	17.50	10.00	4.50	4.00
R395 $60 carmine	85.00	40.00	8.50	7.50
R396 $100 carmine		8.00	4.00	3.00
R397 $500 carmine		1,000.	800.00	500.00
R398 $1,000 carmine		155.00	50.00	40.00

1945. DOCUMENTARY ISSUE Secretaries of the Treasury, designs as Nos. R274-R298, overprint reads "Series 1945." *Nos. R399-R417 perforated 11; Nos. R418-R423 perforated 12, issued without gum.*

	MnHVF	UseVF	CutCnl	Perfin
R399 1¢ carmine	.20	.20	.20	.20
R400 2¢ carmine	.20	.20	.20	.20
R401 3¢ carmine	.50	.45	.20	.20
R402 4¢ carmine	.25	.25	.20	.20
R403 5¢ carmine	.25	.20	.20	.20
R404 8¢ carmine	4.00	1.75	.50	.30
R405 10¢ carmine	.75	.20	.20	.20
R406 20¢ carmine	4.00	.75	.40	.20
R407 25¢ carmine	1.00	.25	.20	.20
R408 40¢ carmine	4.50	.80	.40	.30
R409 50¢ carmine	2.50	.20	.20	.20
R410 80¢ carmine	15.00	7.50	3.00	1.50
R411 $1 carmine	6.50	.20	.20	.20
R412 $2 carmine	6.50	.20	.20	.20
R413 $3 carmine	12.50	2.00	.80	.60
R414 $4 carmine	17.50	3.00	.50	.30
R415 $5 carmine	17.50	.30	.20	.20
R416 $10 carmine	35.00	1.25	.20	.20
R417 $20 carmine	75.00	10.00	3.00	2.50
R418 $30 carmine	55.00	18.00	6.00	5.00
R419 $50 carmine	60.00	20.00	12.50	6.00
R420 $60 carmine	100.00	35.00	12.50	10.00
R421 $100 carmine		10.00	8.00	5.00
R422 $500 carmine	185.00	150.00	65.00	50.00
R423 $1,000 carmine	100.00	80.00	20.00	15.00

1946. DOCUMENTARY ISSUE Secretaries of the Treasury, designs as Nos. R274-R298, overprint reads "Series 1946." *Nos. R424-R442 perforated 11; Nos. R443-R448 perforated 12, issued without gum.*

	MnHVF	UseVF	CutCnl	Perfin
R424 1¢ carmine	.25	.20	.20	.20
R425 2¢ carmine	.30	.30	.20	.20
R426 3¢ carmine	.35	.25	.20	.20
R427 4¢ carmine	.50	.40	.20	.20
R428 5¢ carmine	.25	.20	.20	.20
R429 8¢ carmine	1.00	.80	.20	.20
R430 10¢ carmine	.70	.20	.20	.20
R431 20¢ carmine	1.20	.35	.20	.20
R432 25¢ carmine	3.80	.20	.20	.20
R433 40¢ carmine	2.25	.75	.20	.20
R434 50¢ carmine	2.25	.20	.20	.20
R435 80¢ carmine	8.50	3.50	.60	.50
R436 $1 carmine	7.00	.20	.20	.20
R437 $2 carmine	8.00	.20	.20	.20
R438 $3 carmine	12.50	4.50	.90	.35
R439 $4 carmine	17.50	7.50	1.50	1.00
R440 $5 carmine	17.50	.40	.20	.20
R441 $10 carmine	35.00	1.35	.20	.20
R442 $20 carmine	75.00	7.50	2.00	1.50
R443 $30 carmine	40.00	12.50	4.00	3.00
R444 $50 carmine	17.50	8.00	4.00	3.00
R445 $60 carmine	35.00	15.00	10.00	9.00
R446 $100 carmine	40.00	10.00	3.50	3.00
R447 $500 carmine		90.00	30.00	22.00
R448 $1,000 carmine		90.00	25.00	17.00

1947. DOCUMENTARY ISSUE Secretaries of the Treasury, designs as Nos. R274-R298, overprint reads "Series 1947." *Nos. R449-R467 perforated 11; Nos. R468-R473 perforated 12, issued without gum.*

	MnHVF	UseVF	CutCnl	Perfin
R449 1¢ carmine	.65	.45	.20	.20
R450 2¢ carmine	.50	.40	.20	.20
R451 3¢ carmine	.50	.45	.20	.20
R452 4¢ carmine	.65	.55	.20	.20
R453 5¢ carmine	.30	.25	.20	.20
R454 8¢ carmine	1.15	.65	.20	.20
R455 10¢ carmine	1.10	.25	.20	.20

No.	Denom	Color	MnHVF	UseVF	CutCnl	Perfin
R456	20¢	carmine	1.75	.50	.20	.20
R457	25¢	carmine	2.25	.50	.20	.20
R458	40¢	carmine	3.50	.75	.20	.20
R459	50¢	carmine	3.00	.20	.20	.20
R460	80¢	carmine	7.50	6.00	.60	.20
R461	$1	carmine	5.75	.20	.20	.20
R462	$2	carmine	8.50	.40	.20	.20
R463	$3	carmine	8.50	6.50	1.00	.60
R464	$4	carmine	10.00	4.00	.40	.35
R465	$5	carmine	15.00	.40	.20	.20
R466	$10	carmine	35.00	2.00	.50	.20
R467	$20	carmine	50.00	8.50	1.00	.70
R468	$30	carmine	55.00	15.00	3.50	2.00
R469	$50	carmine	25.00	11.00	3.50	2.00
R470	$60	carmine	65.00	30.00	13.50	7.50
R471	$100	carmine	25.00	8.50	3.50	2.00
R472	$500	carmine		140.00	40.00	35.00
R473	$1,000	carmine		75.00	30.00	20.00

1948. DOCUMENTARY ISSUE Secretaries of the Treasury, designs as Nos. R274-R298, overprint reads "Series 1948." *Nos. R474-R492 perforated 11; Nos. R493-R497 perforated 12, issued without gum.*

No.	Denom	Color	MnHVF	UseVF	CutCnl	Perfin
R474	1¢	carmine	.20	.20	.20	.20
R475	2¢	carmine	.30	.25	.20	.20
R476	3¢	carmine	.40	.35	.20	.20
R477	4¢	carmine	.40	.25	.20	.20
R478	5¢	carmine	.30	.20	.20	.20
R479	8¢	carmine	.75	.30	.20	.20
R480	10¢	carmine	.50	.20	.20	.20
R481	20¢	carmine	1.50	.30	.20	.20
R482	25¢	carmine	1.35	.20	.20	.20
R483	40¢	carmine	4.00	1.40	.30	.25
R484	50¢	carmine	2.25	.20	.20	.20
R485	80¢	carmine	6.50	4.00	1.00	.50
R486	$1	carmine	6.50	.20	.20	.20
R487	$2	carmine	9.00	.20	.20	.20
R488	$3	carmine	12.50	2.00	.40	.25
R489	$4	carmine	17.50	2.00	.75	.50
R490	$5	carmine	15.00	.40	.30	.20
R491	$10	carmine	35.00	1.00	.25	.20
R492	$20	carmine	75.00	8.50	3.00	1.50
R493	$30	carmine	40.00	17.50	4.00	2.50
R494	$50	carmine	40.00	15.00	4.00	2.00
R495	$60	carmine	55.00	20.00	8.00	4.50
R496	$100	carmine	45.00	8.00	3.25	2.00
R497	$500	carmine	110.00	100.00	40.00	25.00
R498	$1,000	carmine	75.00	60.00	25.00	18.00

1949. DOCUMENTARY ISSUE Secretaries of the Treasury, designs as Nos. R274-R298, overprint reads "Series 1949." *Nos. R499-R517 perforated 11; Nos. R518-R523 perforated 12, issued without gum.*

No.	Denom	Color	MnHVF	UseVF	CutCnl	Perfin
R499	1¢	carmine	.25	.20	.20	.20
R500	2¢	carmine	.50	.30	.20	.20
R501	3¢	carmine	.35	.30	.20	.20
R502	4¢	carmine	.50	.40	.20	.20
R503	5¢	carmine	.30	.20	.20	.20
R504	8¢	carmine	.65	.50	.20	.20
R505	10¢	carmine	.35	.25	.20	.20
R506	20¢	carmine	1.25	.60	.30	.20
R507	25¢	carmine	1.75	.65	.25	.20
R508	40¢	carmine	4.00	2.00	.40	.30
R509	50¢	carmine	3.50	.30	.20	.20
R510	80¢	carmine	8.00	4.50	1.25	.75
R511	$1	carmine	6.50	.40	.20	.20
R512	$2	carmine	8.50	2.00	.35	.25
R513	$3	carmine	13.50	5.75	1.50	1.00
R514	$4	carmine	17.00	6.00	2.50	1.25
R515	$5	carmine	17.00	2.50	.50	.40
R516	$10	carmine	35.00	2.50	1.00	.80
R517	$20	carmine	75.00	8.00	2.00	1.25
R518	$30	carmine	45.00	20.50	5.00	3.00
R519	$50	carmine	55.00	35.00	9.00	6.00
R520	$60	carmine		40.00	20.00	10.00
R521	$100	carmine	40.00	12.50	3.00	2.50
R522	$500	carmine		175.00	100.00	50.00
R523	$1,000	carmine		100.00	30.00	20.00

1950. DOCUMENTARY ISSUE Secretaries of the Treasury, designs as Nos. R274-R298, overprint reads "Series 1950." *Nos. R524-R542 perforated 11; Nos. R543-R548 perforated 12, issued without gum.*

No.	Denom	Color	MnHVF	UseVF	CutCnl	Perfin
R524	1¢	carmine	.20	.20	.20	.20
R525	2¢	carmine	.30	.20	.20	.20

Stamp	Denom	Color	MnHVF	UseVF	CutCnl	Perfin
R526	3¢	carmine	.35	.30	.20	.20
R527	4¢	carmine	.45	.35	.20	.20
R528	5¢	carmine	.30	.20	.20	.20
R529	8¢	carmine	1.20	.65	.20	.20
R530	10¢	carmine	.60	.20	.20	.20
R531	20¢	carmine	1.00	.30	.20	.20
R532	25¢	carmine	1.25	.35	.20	.25
R533	40¢	carmine	3.00	1.50	.40	.25
R534	50¢	carmine	3.50	.20	.20	.20
R535	80¢	carmine	6.50	3.50	.75	.50
R536	$1	carmine	6.50	.20	.20	.20
R537	$2	carmine	8.50	1.50	.30	.20
R538	$3	carmine	8.50	3.50	1.25	.75
R539	$4	carmine	12.50	4.50	2.00	1.00
R540	$5	carmine	17.50	.75	.30	.20
R541	$10	carmine	35.00	7.50	.75	.50
R542	$20	carmine	75.00	8.00	2.00	1.50
R543	$30	carmine	60.00	40.00	10.00	8.00
R544	$50	carmine	35.00	12.50	6.50	4.50
R545	$60	carmine		50.00	15.00	8.00
R546	$100	carmine	40.00	17.50	5.00	3.00
R547	$500	carmine		100.00	45.00	30.00
R548	$1,000	carmine		70.00	20.00	18.00

1951. DOCUMENTARY ISSUE Secretaries of the Treasury, designs as Nos. R274-R298, overprint reads "Series 1951." Nos. R549-R567 perforated 11; Nos. R568-R573 perforated 12, issued without gum.

Stamp	Denom	Color	MnHVF	UseVF	CutCnl	Perfin
R549	1¢	carmine	.20	.20	.20	.20
R550	2¢	carmine	.25	.20	.20	.20
R551	3¢	carmine	.25	.20	.20	.20
R552	4¢	carmine	.30	.20	.20	.20
R553	5¢	carmine	.30	.20	.20	.20
R554	8¢	carmine	.85	.30	.25	.20
R555	10¢	carmine	.50	.20	.20	.20
R556	20¢	carmine	1.25	.40	.20	.20
R557	25¢	carmine	1.25	.40	.20	.20
R558	40¢	carmine	3.00	1.25	.20	.30
R559	50¢	carmine	2.50	.35	.20	.20
R560	80¢	carmine	5.00	2.00	1.50	.75
R561	$1	carmine	6.50	.20	.20	.20
R562	$2	carmine	8.50	.40	.20	.20
R563	$3	carmine	12.50	3.00	1.75	1.00
R564	$4	carmine	15.00	5.00	2.00	1.00
R565	$5	carmine	12.50	.50	.25	.20
R566	$10	carmine	30.00	2.50	1.00	.75
R567	$20	carmine	70.00	8.00	3.50	3.00
R568	$30	carmine	60.00	10.00	5.00	3.50
R569	$50	carmine	45.00	12.50	5.00	4.00
R570	$60	carmine		40.00	20.00	15.00
R571	$100	carmine	40.00	12.50	6.50	5.00
R572	$500	carmine	120.00	80.00	40.00	20.00
R573	$1,000	carmine		80.00	30.00	25.00

1952. DOCUMENTARY ISSUE Secretaries of the Treasury, designs as Nos. R274-R298, and new values showing L.J. Gage (55¢, $1.10, $1.65, $2.20, $2.75, and $3.30), William Windom ($2,500), C.J. Folger ($5,000), and W.Q. Gresham ($10,000), all former secretaries of the treasury. Overprint: "Series 1952." Nos. R574-R598 perforated 12, issued without gum.

Stamp	Denom	Color	MnHVF	UseVF	CutCnl	Perfin
R574	1¢	carmine	.20	.20	.20	.20
R575	2¢	carmine	.30	.20	.20	.20
R576	3¢	carmine	.25	.20	.20	.20
R577	4¢	carmine	.25	.20	.20	.20
R578	5¢	carmine	.20	.20	.20	.20
R579	8¢	carmine	.60	.40	.20	.20
R580	10¢	carmine	.40	.20	.20	.20
R581	20¢	carmine	.90	.30	.25	.20
R582	25¢	carmine	1.25	.35	.25	.20
R583	40¢	carmine	.20	.80	.50	.40
R584	50¢	carmine	2.50	.20	.20	.20
R585	55¢	carmine	17.50	10.00	1.25	1.00
R586	80¢	carmine	8.50	2.75	.75	.70
R587	$1	carmine	4.50	1.50	—	.30
R588	$1.10	carmine	30.00	20.00	10.00	6.00
R589	$1.65	carmine	120.00	40.00	25.00	20.00
R590	$2	carmine	8.00	.30	.20	.20
R591	$2.20	carmine	75.00	50.00	30.00	15.00
R592	$2.75	carmine	100.00	55.00	25.00	15.00
R593	$3	carmine	20.00	3.50	1.25	1.00
R594	$3.30	carmine	80.00	60.00	30.00	15.00
R595	$4	carmine	17.50	3.50	2.00	1.50

Cat.	Denom.	Color	MnHVF	UseVF	CutCnl	Perfin
R596	$5	carmine	17.50	1.00	.35	.30
R597	$10	carmine	30.00	1.25	.40	.30
R598	$20	carmine	50.00	9.00	2.75	2.50
R599	$30	carmine	40.00	17.50	5.00	4.00
R600	$50	carmine	40.00	10.00	5.00	4.00
R601	$60	carmine		50.00	12.50	9.00
R602	$100	carmine	30.00	7.50	3.00	2.50
R603	$500	carmine		90.00	55.00	30.00
R604	$1,000	carmine		30.00	15.00	10.00
R605	$2,500	carmine		150.00	110.00	90.00
R606	$5,000	carmine		1,000.	800.00	700.00
R607	$10,000	carmine		650.00	400.00	300.00

1953. DOCUMENTARY ISSUE Secretaries of the Treasury, designs as Nos. R274-R298, R585, R588, R589, R591, R592, R594, and R605-R607, overprint reads "Series 1953." *Nos. R608-R632 perforated 11; Nos. R633-R640 perforated 12, issued without gum.*

Cat.	Denom.	Color	MnHVF	UseVF	CutCnl	Perfin
R608	1¢	carmine	.20	.20	.20	.20
R609	2¢	carmine	.20	.20	.20	.20
R610	3¢	carmine	.25	.20	.20	.20
R611	4¢	carmine	.30	.25	.20	.20
R612	5¢	carmine	.20	.20	.20	.20
R613	8¢	carmine	.70	.70	.20	.20
R614	10¢	carmine	.35	.25	.20	.20
R615	20¢	carmine	.70	.35	.25	.20
R616	25¢	carmine	.80	.40	.25	.20
R617	40¢	carmine	1.50	1.00	.40	.35
R618	50¢	carmine	2.25	.20	.20	.20
R619	55¢	carmine	3.25	1.75	.75	.50
R620	80¢	carmine	5.50	1.75	1.40	1.25
R621	$1	carmine	3.50	.20	.20	.20
R622	$1.10	carmine	6.50	2.25	2.00	1.50
R623	$1.65	carmine	7.50	3.50	2.75	2.00
R624	$2	carmine	6.00	.55	.25	.20
R625	$2.20	carmine	9.00	6.00	2.25	2.00
R626	$2.75	carmine	12.50	6.50	3.50	2.50
R627	$3	carmine	7.50	3.00	1.50	1.25
R628	$3.30	carmine	22.50	7.50	4.50	3.25
R629	$4	carmine	15.00	7.00	2.00	1.75
R630	$5	carmine	15.00	.90	.40	.35
R631	$10	carmine	30.00	2.00	1.00	.80
R632	$20	carmine	65.00	17.50	3.00	2.00
R633	$30	carmine	40.00	12.00	5.00	4.00
R634	$50	carmine	70.00	20.00	6.50	5.00
R635	$60	carmine	275.00	125.00	80.00	50.00
R636	$100	carmine	30.00	12.50	5.00	3.00
R637	$500	carmine	225.00	100.00	30.00	20.00
R638	$1,000	carmine	125.00	55.00	20.00	15.00
R639	$2,500	carmine	450.00	450.00	250.00	225.00
R640	$5,000	carmine		1,100.	850.00	625.00
R641	$10,000	carmine		900.00	600.00	300.00

1954. DOCUMENTARY ISSUE Secretaries of the Treasury, designs as Nos. R274-R298, R585, R588, R589, R591, R592, R594, and R605-R607. Nos. R642-R666 are without overprint. On stamps Nos. R667-R675 overprint reads: "Series 1954." *Nos. R642-R666 perforated 11; Nos. R667-R675 perforated 12, issued without gum.*

Cat.	Denom.	Color	MnHVF	UseVF	CutCnl	Perfin
R642	1¢	carmine	.20	.20	.20	.20
R643	2¢	carmine	.20	.20	.20	.20
R644	3¢	carmine	.20	.20	.20	.20
R645	4¢	carmine	.20	.20	.20	.20
R646	5¢	carmine	.20	.20	.20	.20
R647	8¢	carmine	.25	.20	.20	.20
R648	10¢	carmine	.25	.20	.20	.20
R649	20¢	carmine	.40	.30	.20	.20
R650	25¢	carmine	.60	.30	.25	.20
R651	40¢	carmine	1.25	.60	.35	.20
R652	50¢	carmine	1.60	.20	.20	.20
R653	55¢	carmine	1.50	1.25	.50	.40
R654	80¢	carmine	2.25	1.75	1.10	1.00
R655	$1	carmine	1.50	.30	.20	.20
R656	$1.10	carmine	3.25	2.50	1.50	1.00
R657	$1.65	carmine	80.00	50.00	40.00	20.00
R658	$2	carmine	1.75	.25	.25	.20
R659	$2.20	carmine	4.50	3.50	2.50	1.50
R660	$2.75	carmine	90.00	50.00	35.00	20.00
R661	$3	carmine	3.00	2.00	1.00	.75
R662	$3.30	carmine	6.50	5.00	3.00	2.00
R663	$4	carmine	4.00	3.50	2.00	1.50
R664	$5	carmine	6.00	.45	.35	.30
R665	$10	carmine	12.50	1.25	.75	.70

R666		MnHVF	UseVF	CutCnl	Perfin
$20	carmine	20.00	5.25	3.00	1.75

R667		MnHVF	UseVF	CutCnl	Perfin
$30	carmine	30.00	12.00	4.00	3.00

R668		MnHVF	UseVF	CutCnl	Perfin
$50	carmine	40.00	15.00	9.00	4.50

R669		MnHVF	UseVF	CutCnl	Perfin
$60	carmine	65.00	20.00	12.50	9.00

R670		MnHVF	UseVF	CutCnl	Perfin
$100	carmine	30.00	7.00	4.50	4.00

R671		MnHVF	UseVF	CutCnl	Perfin
$500	carmine		75.00	22.50	18.00

R672		MnHVF	UseVF	CutCnl	Perfin
$1,000	carmine	150.00	50.00	17.50	14.00

R673		MnHVF	UseVF	CutCnl	Perfin
$2,500	carmine		175.00	80.00	45.00

R674		MnHVF	UseVF	CutCnl	Perfin
$5,000	carmine		700.00	500.00	350.00

R675		MnHVF	UseVF	CutCnl	Perfin
$10,000	carmine		450.00	175.00	135.00

1955. DOCUMENTARY ISSUE Secretaries of the Treasury, designs as Nos. R293-R298 and R604-R607, overprint reads "Series 1955." *Perforated 12, issued without gum.*

R676		MnHVF	UseVF	CutCnl	Perfin
$30	carmine	35.00	10.00	5.00	3.00

R677		MnHVF	UseVF	CutCnl	Perfin
$50	carmine	35.00	12.50	8.00	6.00

R678		MnHVF	UseVF	CutCnl	Perfin
$60	carmine	65.00	20.00	10.00	4.00

R679		MnHVF	UseVF	CutCnl	Perfin
$100	carmine	30.00	6.00	4.00	3.00

R680		MnHVF	UseVF	CutCnl	Perfin
$500	carmine		120.00	25.00	18.00

R681		MnHVF	UseVF	CutCnl	Perfin
$1,000	carmine		30.00	17.50	12.50

R682		MnHVF	UseVF	CutCnl	Perfin
$2,500	carmine		125.00	75.00	45.00

R683		MnHVF	UseVF	CutCnl	Perfin
$5,000	carmine		650.00	400.00	265.00

R684		MnHVF	UseVF	CutCnl	Perfin
$10,000	carmine		450.00	175.00	90.00

1956. DOCUMENTARY ISSUE Secretaries of the Treasury, stamps Nos. R293-R298 and R605-R607, overprint reads "Series 1956." *Perforated 12.*

R685		MnHVF	UseVF	CutCnl	Perfin
$30	carmine	50.00	12.50	8.00	4.00

R686		MnHVF	UseVF	CutCnl	Perfin
$50	carmine	50.00	17.50	4.00	4.00

R687		MnHVF	UseVF	CutCnl	Perfin
$60	carmine		30.00	10.00	4.50

R688		MnHVF	UseVF	CutCnl	Perfin
$100	carmine	50.00	12.50	5.00	4.00

R689		MnHVF	UseVF	CutCnl	Perfin
$500	carmine		70.00	25.00	15.00

R690		MnHVF	UseVF	CutCnl	Perfin
$1,000	carmine		50.00	15.00	10.00

R691		MnHVF	UseVF	CutCnl	Perfin
$2,500	carmine		250.00	100.00	75.00

R692		MnHVF	UseVF	CutCnl	Perfin
$5,000	carmine		1,100.	900.00	650.00

R693		MnHVF	UseVF	CutCnl	Perfin
$10,000	carmine		400.00	125.00	100.00

1957. DOCUMENTARY ISSUE Secretaries of the Treasury, stamps Nos. R293-R298 and R605-R607, overprint reads "Series 1957." *Perforated 12.*

R694		MnHVF	UseVF	CutCnl	Perfin
$30	carmine	65.00	25.00	10.00	5.00

R695		MnHVF	UseVF	CutCnl	Perfin
$50	carmine	40.00	22.50	10.00	4.00

R696		MnHVF	UseVF	CutCnl	Perfin
$60	carmine		140.00	80.00	45.00

R697		MnHVF	UseVF	CutCnl	Perfin
$100	carmine	40.00	10.00	8.00	4.00

R698		MnHVF	UseVF	CutCnl	Perfin
$500	carmine	175.00	80.00	40.00	25.00

R699		MnHVF	UseVF	CutCnl	Perfin
$1,000	carmine		75.00	25.00	18.00

R700		MnHVF	UseVF	CutCnl	Perfin
$2,500	carmine		500.00	350.00	200.00

R701		MnHVF	UseVF	CutCnl	Perfin
$5,000	carmine		550.00	350.00	170.00

R702		MnHVF	UseVF	CutCnl	Perfin
$10,000	carmine		425.00	150.00	90.00

1958. DOCUMENTARY ISSUE Secretaries of the Treasury, stamps Nos. R293-R298 and R605-R607, overprint reads "Series 1958." *Perforated 12.*

R703		MnHVF	UseVF	CutCnl	Perfin
$30	carmine	70.00	20.00	15.00	8.00

R704		MnHVF	UseVF	CutCnl	Perfin
$50	carmine	60.00	20.00	12.50	6.50

R705		MnHVF	UseVF	CutCnl	Perfin
$60	carmine		25.00	15.00	10.00

R706		MnHVF	UseVF	CutCnl	Perfin
$100	carmine	50.00	10.00	5.00	2.00

R707		MnHVF	UseVF	CutCnl	Perfin
$500	carmine	125.00	50.00	30.00	18.00

R708		MnHVF	UseVF	CutCnl	Perfin
$1,000	carmine		65.00	30.00	20.00

R709		MnHVF	UseVF	CutCnl	Perfin
$2,500	carmine		500.00	375.00	275.00

R710		MnHVF	UseVF	CutCnl	Perfin
$5,000	carmine		1,200.	1,000.	900.00

R711		MnHVF	UseVF	CutCnl	Perfin
$10,000	carmine		600.00	500.00	300.00

1958. DOCUMENTARY NO-OVERPRINT ISSUE Secretaries of the Treasury, Nos. R293-R298 and R605-R607 without overprint. *Perforated 12.*

R711A		MnHVF	UseVF	CutCnl	Perfin
$30	carmine	37.50	7.00	5.75	4.75
	v. Vertical pair, imperforate horizontally	—			

R711B		MnHVF	UseVF	CutCnl	Perfin
$50	carmine, cut cancel, perf. initial	42.50	7.00	3.75	3.00
	v. Vertical pair, imperforate horizontally	—			

R711C		MnHVF	UseVF	CutCnl	Perfin
$60	carmine, cut cancel, perf. initial	80.00	20.00	10.00	5.00

R711D		MnHVF	UseVF	CutCnl	Perfin
$100	carmine, cut cancel, perf. initial	19.00	4.75	3.00	2.25

R711E		MnHVF	UseVF	CutCnl	Perfin
$500	carmine, cut cancel, perf. initial	85.00	25.00	10.00	7.50

R711F		MnHVF	UseVF	CutCnl	Perfin
$1,000	carmine, cut cancel, perf. initial	55.00	20.00	10.00	7.50
	v. Vertical pair, imperforate horizontally	—			

R711G		MnHVF	UseVF	CutCnl	Perfin
$2,500	carmine, cut cancel, perf. initial	—	140.00	85.00	50.00

R711H		MnHVF	UseVF	CutCnl	Perfin
$5,000	carmine, cut cancel, perf. initial	—	150.00	85.00	60.00

R711I		MnHVF	UseVF	CutCnl	Perfin
$10,000	carmine, cut cancel, perf. initial	—	125.00	50.00	25.00

1962. DOCUMENTARY ISSUE For the 100th anniversary of the Internal Revenue Service, the federal government's first commemorative documentary stamp was issued. It featured the Internal Revenue building. *Giori Press printing, watermarked, perforated 11.*

R712 *Internal Revenue building and "established 1862"*

R712		MnHVF	UseVF	CutCnl	Perfin
10¢	blue & green	1.00	.25	.20	.20
	Plate block of 4	12.00			

DECODING THE CATALOG

In 1962, to mark the centennial of the United States revenue stamps introduced to help pay the costs of the Civil War, the Internal Revenue Service issued a curiosity among U.S. revenue stamps — a design with a commemorative inscription. This 10¢ documentary revenue stamp picturing the Internal Revenue building in Washington, D.C., has "Established 1862" below "Documentary" and above the vignette. The stamp is Minkus R712.

The following year, the same 10¢ design was used without the inscription. The stamp, Minkus R713, was the final new documentary revenue stamp. Mint copies catalog about three times the value of the 1962 commemorative version. Use of the stamps was no longer required after Dec. 31, 1967.

1963. DOCUMENTARY ISSUE Date line removed.

R713 *Internal Revenue building, without commemorative inscription*

R713		MnHVF	UseVF	CutCnl	Perfin
10¢	**blue & green**	3.00	.30	.20	.20
	Plate block of 4	25.00			

Documentary stamps were no longer required after Dec. 31, 1967.

Proprietary Stamps

1862-71. THE FIRST PROPRIETARY ISSUE formed part of the first general issue of Revenue stamps. They had the same designs as the corresponding denominations and were inscribed "PROPRIETARY." Unlike other stamps in the issue, these were used only on proprietary articles, privately owned items. Prices are for used copies only. *Perforated 12.*

 RP1

RP1		Perf	Part Perf	Imperf
1¢	**red** (1862)	.50	120.00	750.00

 RP2, RP3
George Washington

RP2		Perf	Part Perf	Imperf
2¢	**blue** (1862)	.40	120.00	350.00
	v. ultramarine	60.00		
RP3		Perf	Part Perf	Imperf
2¢	**orange** (1862)	35.00		
RP4		Perf	Part Perf	Imperf
3¢	**green** (1862)	3.25	300.00	

 RP5

RP5		Perf	Part Perf	Imperf
4¢	**purple** (1862)	6.50	210.00	
RP6		Perf	Part Perf	Imperf
5¢	**red** (1864)	22.50		
RP7		Perf	Part Perf	Imperf
6¢	**orange** (1871)	1,600.00		
RP8		Perf	Part Perf	Imperf
10¢	**blue** (1864)	15.00		

1871-73. PROPRIETARY ISSUE Portrait of Washington in black in an oval. The stamps are of different sizes, and the frames vary in design according to the denominations. *Printed by Joseph R. Carpenter of Philadelphia on unwatermarked violet paper, perforated 12.*

RP9   RP10, 20   RP11, 21

RP9		UnCnl	Cnl
1¢	**green & black**		4.00
	a.imperforate		80.00
	b.inverted center	2,850.00	
RP10		UnCnl	Cnl
2¢	**green & black**		4.50
RP11		UnCnl	Cnl
3¢	**green & black**		11.00
	a.inverted center	15,000.00	
RP12		UnCnl	Cnl
4¢	**green & black**		8.00
	a.inverted center	20,000.00	

RP12, 22

RP13, 23

RP18, 28

RP14, 24

RP13
5¢   **green & black**   UnCnl   Cnl
                                125.00
      a.inverted center   75,000.00

RP14
6¢   **green & black**   UnCnl   Cnl
                                  25.00

 RP15, 25

RP15
10¢   **green & black**   UnCnl   Cnl
                                  275.00

RP16, 26

RP17, 27

RP16
50¢   **green & black**   UnCnl   Cnl
                                  550.00

RP17
$1   **green & black**   UnCnl   Cnl
                                  1,000.00

Input from stamp collectors regarding
the content of this catalog and ideas
to make it more useful is eagerly sought.
Send your comments to:
Minkus Catalog Editor
Krause Publications
700 E. State St.
Iola, WI 54990

		UnCnl	Cnl
RP18			
$5	**green & black**		3,000.00

1874. PROPRIETARY ISSUE Green paper.

		UnCnl	Cnl
RP19			
1¢	**green & black**		6.75
RP20			
2¢	**green & black**		14.00
	a.inverted center	7,500.00	
RP21			
3¢	**green & black**		45.00
RP22			
4¢	**green & black**		15.00
RP23			
5¢	**green & black**		125.00
RP24			
6¢	**green & black**		75.00
RP25			
10¢	**green & black**		50.00
RP26			
50¢	**green & black**		850.00
RP27			
$1	**green & black**		3,500.00
RP28			
$5	**green & black**		25,000.00

1875. PROPRIETARY ISSUE Portrait of Washington in various frames engraved and printed by the National Bank Note Co. *At first the stamps were printed on green silk paper and perforated 12. Later the stamps were printed on green paper with double-line USIR watermark and perforated 12. All prices are for used examples.*

 RP29, 35 *George Washington*

RP30, 36

RP34, 41, 42

		Perf	Roul
RP29			
1¢	green	1.75	
RP30			
2¢	brown	2.50	

RP31
3¢ orange — Perf 12.50 / Roul

RP32
4¢ red brown — Perf 6.00 / Roul

RP33
5¢ black — Perf 110.00 / Roul

RP34
6¢ violet blue — Perf 25.00 / Roul

1880-81. PROPRIETARY ISSUE *Green paper, watermarked USIR, perforated 12 or rouletted 6.*

RP35
1¢ green — Perf .50 / Roul 55.00

RP36
2¢ brown — Perf 1.50 / Roul 75.00

RP37
3¢ orange — Perf 4.50 / Roul 75.00

RP38
4¢ red brown — Perf 5.50 / Roul

RP39
4¢ red — Perf 4.50 / Roul 125.00

RP40 *George Washington*

RP40
5¢ black — Perf 100.00 / Roul 1,250.00

RP41
6¢ violet blue — Perf 20.00 / Roul 225.00

RP42
6¢ violet — Perf 30.00 / Roul

RP43
10¢ blue — Perf 300.00 / Roul

1898. Proprietary Issue featured a "Battleship second class," and the note over No. R147 applies here. *The stamps are watermarked double-line USIR, are rouletted 5 1/2 or hyphen-hole perforated 7.*

 RP44

 RP45

RP44

1/8¢ yellow green

	Roul 5 1/2		Hyphen-Hole	
	UnFVF	UseFVF	UnFVF	UseFVF
	.20	.20	.20	.20

RP45

1/4¢ chestnut

	Roul 5 1/2		Hyphen-Hole	
	UnFVF	UseFVF	UnFVF	UseFVF
	.20	.20	.20	.20

RP46

3/8¢ red orange

	Roul 5 1/2		Hyphen-Hole	
	UnFVF	UseFVF	UnFVF	UseFVF
	.20	.20	.20	.20

 RP47

 RP48

RP49

RP47
5/8¢ deep blue

	Roul 5 1/2		Hyphen-Hole	
	UnFVF	UseFVF	UnFVF	UseFVF
	.20	.20	.25	.20

RP48
1¢ green

	Roul 5 1/2		Hyphen-Hole	
	UnFVF	UseFVF	UnFVF	UseFVF
	1.00	.25	25.00	15.00

RP49
1 1/4¢ chocolate

	Roul 5 1/2		Hyphen-Hole	
	UnFVF	UseFVF	UnFVF	UseFVF
	.20	.20	.20	.20

RP50
1 7/8¢ slate blue

	Roul 5 1/2		Hyphen-Hole	
	UnFVF	UseFVF	UnFVF	UseFVF
	7.00	1.10	25.00	6.00

 RP51

 RP52

RP51
2¢ red brown

	Roul 5 1/2		Hyphen-Hole	
	UnFVF	UseFVF	UnFVF	UseFVF
	.80	.30	4.00	.20

RP52
2 1/2¢ carmine red

	Roul 5 1/2		Hyphen-Hole	
	UnFVF	UseFVF	UnFVF	UseFVF
	2.25	.20	2.50	.20

 RP53

 RP54

RP53
3 3/4¢ greenish black

	Roul 5 1/2		Hyphen-Hole	
	UnFVF	UseFVF	UnFVF	UseFVF
	30.00	6.00	50.00	15.00

RP54
4¢ dark red violet

	Roul 5 1/2		Hyphen-Hole	
	UnFVF	UseFVF	UnFVF	UseFVF
	7.10	1.00	50.00	15.00

 RP55

RP55
5¢ orange brown

	Roul 5 1/2		Hyphen-Hole	
	UnFVF	UseFVF	UnFVF	UseFVF
	7.10	.90	50.00	7.50

1914. WHITE NUMERAL IN CIRCLE ISSUE inscribed "Proprietary" across the top and "Series of 1914" under the numeral. *Nos. RP56-67 were offset printed on paper with single-line USPS watermark and Nos. RP68-88 double-line USIR watermark. Perforated 10.*

 RP56, 56A

RP56
1/8¢ black

UnFVF	UseFVF
.20	.15

 RP57

 RP58

 RP59

RP57
1/4¢ black

UnFVF	UseFVF
1.75	1.00

		UnFVF	UseFVF
RP58 3/8¢	black	.20	.15
RP59 5/8¢	black	3.50	1.75

RP60   RP62   RP82

		UnFVF	UseFVF
RP60 1 1/4¢	black	2.50	.80
RP61 1 7/8¢	black	35.00	15.00
RP62 2 1/2¢	black	7.50	2.50
RP63 3 1/8¢	black	80.00	50.00
RP64 3 3/4¢	black	35.00	20.00
RP65 4¢	black	50.00	27.50
RP66 4 3/8¢	black	1,250.00	—
RP67 5¢	black	110.00	70.00
RP68 1/8¢	black	.20	.20
RP69 1/4¢	black	.20	.20
RP70 3/8¢	black	.60	.30
RP71 1/2¢	black	3.00	2.75
RP72 5/8¢	black	.20	.20
RP73 1¢	black	4.00	4.00
RP74 1 1/4¢	black	.30	.25
RP75 1 1/2¢	black	3.00	2.25
RP76 1 7/8¢	black	1.00	.50
RP77 2¢	black	5.00	4.00
RP78 2 1/2¢	black	1.25	1.00
RP79 3¢	black	4.00	2.75
RP80 3 1/8¢	black	5.00	3.00
RP81 3 3/4¢	black	11.00	7.50
RP82 4¢	black	.30	.20
RP83 4 3/8¢	black	14.00	8.00
RP84 5¢	black	3.00	2.50
RP85 6¢	black	50.00	40.00
RP86 8¢	black	15.00	10.00
RP87 10¢	black	10.00	6.50
RP88 20¢	black	22.00	17.00

1919. BLUE NUMERAL IN CIRCLE ISSUE inscribed "Proprietary" and "U.S. Internal Revenue" across the top. *Offset printed, perforated 11, watermarked double-line USIR.*

 RP89   Overprint

		UnFVF	UseFVF
RP89 1¢	blue	.20	.20

RP90   RP91   RP92

		UnFVF	UseFVF
RP90 2¢	blue	.20	.20
RP91 3¢	blue	1.00	.50
RP92 4¢	blue	1.00	.50
RP93 5¢	blue	1.25	.50
RP94 8¢	blue	14.00	9.00
RP95 10¢	blue	5.00	2.00
RP96 20¢	blue	7.50	3.00
RP97 40¢	blue	45.00	10.00

Future Delivery Stamps

Issued to pay the tax on sales, agreements of sale or agreements to sell any products at an exchange or equivalent establishment for future delivery.

1918-34. FUTURE DELIVERY ISSUE Documentary stamps of 1917 overprinted in black or red as illustrated. *Double-line watermark USIR, perforated 11.* Nos. RFD1, 5, 12 Type 2: Words 2mm apart. Nos. RFD 2-4, 6-11 Type 1: Words about 8 1/2mm apart.

FUTURE   Type 2 (RFD1, 5, 12)
DELIVERY

RFD1		UnFVF	UseFVF
1¢	**rose** (2mm) Type 2	1.20	.20

RFD2

FUTURE

DELIVERY

Type 1(RFD2-11,27,28)

Type 1 (RFD2-11, 27, 28)

RFD2		UnFVF	UseFVF
2¢	**rose** Type 1	3.00	.20
RFD3		UnFVF	UseFVF
3¢	**rose** Type 1	25.00	
	Cut cancellation		12.50

RFD4

RFD6

RFD7

RFD4		UnFVF	UseFVF
4¢	**rose** Type 1	6.00	.20
RFD5		UnFVF	UseFVF
5¢	**rose** (2mm) Type 2	60.00	7.00
RFD6		UnFVF	UseFVF
10¢	**rose** Type 1	10.00	.20
	Cut cancellation		.20
RFD7		UnFVF	UseFVF
20¢	**rose** Type 1	12.50	.20
	Cut cancellation		.20
RFD8		UnFVF	UseFVF
25¢	**rose** Type 1	32.50	.75
	Cut cancellation		.20
RFD9		UnFVF	UseFVF
40¢	**rose** Type 1	35.00	1.00
	Cut cancellation		.20
RFD10		UnFVF	UseFVF
50¢	**rose** Type 1	7.50	.40
RFD11		UnFVF	UseFVF
80¢	**rose** Type 1	65.00	8.00
	Cut cancellation		.20
RFD12		UnFVF	UseFVF
80¢	**rose** (2mm) Type 2	50.00	3.00
	Cut cancellation		1.00

1918-34. FUTURE DELIVERY ISSUE *Overprint words about 2mm apart, reading up.*

RFD13		UnFVF	UseFVF
$1	**yellow green,** red overprint	25.00	.25
	Cut cancellation		.20
	a. green, black overprint		—
	Cut cancellation		125.00
	b. Overprint, reading down		275.00

RFD13-18

RFD14 *Head of Liberty*

RFD14		UnFVF	UseFVF
$2	**rose,** black overprint	30.00	.25
	Cut cancellation		.20
RFD15		UnFVF	UseFVF
$3	**violet,** red overprint	75.00	2.25
	Cut cancellation		.20
RFD16		UnFVF	UseFVF
$5	**blue,** red overprint	45.00	.50
	Cut cancellation		.20
RFD17		UnFVF	UseFVF
$10	**yellow**	75.00	1.00
	Cut cancellation		.20
RFD18		UnFVF	UseFVF
$20	**olive**	125.00	5.00
	Cut cancellation		.50

1918-34. FUTURE DELIVERY ISSUE *Words 11 1/2mm apart, perforated 12.*

FUTURE   RFD19-24

DELIVERY

RFD19		UnFVF	UseFVF
$30	**orange,** blue numerals	65.00	3.50
	Cut cancellation		1.25
RFD20		UnFVF	UseFVF
$50	**olive green**	50.00	1.00
	Cut cancellation		.35
RFD21		UnFVF	UseFVF
$60	**brown**	65.00	2.00
	Cut cancellation		.75
RFD22		UnFVF	UseFVF
$100	**pale green**	75.00	25.00
	Cut cancellation		7.00
RFD23		UnFVF	UseFVF
$500	**blue,** red numerals	65.00	12.50
	Cut cancellation		4.00
	a. orange numerals		50.00
	Cut cancellation		11.00
RFD24		UnFVF	UseFVF
$1,000	**orange yellow**	65.00	5.25
	Cut cancellation		1.50

1918-34. FUTURE DELIVERY ISSUE *Perforated 11.*

FUTURE   RFD25-26

DELIVERY

RFD25		UnFVF	UseFVF
$1	**green,** red overprint ('25)	25.00	1.00
	Cut cancellation		.20
RFD26		UnFVF	UseFVF
$10	**yellow,** black overprint	80.00	15.00
	Cut cancellation		9.00

1928-29. FUTURE DELIVERY ISSUE *Offset, overprint words about 13mm apart, perforated 10.*

FUTURE   RFD27-28

DELIVERY

RFD27		UnFVF	UseFVF
10¢	**rose**		1,000.00
RFD28		UnFVF	UseFVF
20¢	**rose**		1,000.00

Stock Transfer Stamps

These stamps were used to pay the tax due on the transfer of legal title of shares or stock certificates.

1918-29. STOCK TRANSFER ISSUE Documentary Stamps of 1917 overprinted in black or red. *Offset, double-line watermark USIR, perforated 11.*

RST1-10, 25-29

STOCK

Overprint

TRANSFER

		UnFVF	UseFVF
RST1 1¢	rose	.90	.20
RST2 2¢	rose	.30	.20
RST3 4¢	rose	.30	.20
RST4 5¢	rose	.30	.20
RST5 10¢	rose	.30	.20
RST6 20¢	rose	.60	.20
RST7 25¢	rose	1.25	.25
RST8 40¢	rose	1.25	.25
RST9 50¢	rose	.60	.20
RST10 80¢	rose	2.50	.30

STOCK TRANSFER RST11-18, 30-32

		UnFVF	UseFVF
RST11 $1	green, red overprint	60.00	20.00
	Cut cancellation		4.50
	a. Overprint reading down	125.00	20.00
	Cut cancellation		7.50
RST12 $1	green, black overprint	2.25	.25
	a. Overprint reading down		7.00
RST13 $2	rose	2.25	.20
	a. Overprint reading down		12.75
	Cut cancellation		2.25
RST14 $3	violet, red overprint	17.50	4.00
	Cut cancellation		.20
RST15 $4	yellow brown	7.50	.20
	Cut cancellation		.20
RST16 $5	blue, red overprint	5.50	.20
	a. Overprint reading down		.50
	Cut cancellation		.20
RST17 $10	yellow	14.00	.35
	Cut cancellation		.08
RST18 $20	olive bistre	70.00	20.00
	Cut cancellation		1.10

1918-29. STOCK TRANSFER ISSUE *Offset, issued without gum, perforated 12.*

STOCK RST19-24

TRANSFER

		UnFVF	UseFVF
RST19 $30	orange, green numerals (Grant)	17.50	5.00
	Cut cancellation		2.25
	a. blue numerals		55.00
RST20 $50	olive green (Cleveland)	100.00	55.00
	Cut cancellation		20.00
RST21 $60	brown (Lincoln)	100.00	22.50
	Cut cancellation		8.50
RST22 $100	pale green (Washington)	22.50	5.50
	Cut cancellation		2.25
RST23 $500	blue, red overprint (Hamilton)	300.00	120.00
	Cut cancellation		65.00
RST24 $1,000	orange yellow (Madison)	160.00	75.00
	Cut cancellation		30.00

1928-32. STOCK TRANSFER ISSUE Same as 1918-29 issue, *offset, perforated 10.*

		UnFVF	UseFVF
RST25 2¢	rose	2.25	.30
RST26 4¢	rose	2.25	.30
RST27 10¢	rose	2.00	.30
RST28 20¢	rose	2.75	.30
RST29 50¢	rose	3.50	.20
RST30 $1	yellow green	27.50	.20
RST31 $2	rose	27.50	.20
RST32 $10	yellow	30.00	.30

1920. STOCK TRANSFER ISSUE Same as 1918-29 issue, but letters of overprint with serifs. *Offset, perforated 11.*

STOCK RST33-41

TRANSFER

		UnFVF	UseFVF
RST33 2¢	rose	6.50	.75
RST34 10¢	rose	1.25	.25
RST35 20¢	rose	1.25	.25
RST36 50¢	rose	2.75	.25
RST37 $1	yellow green	37.50	9.00
	Cut cancellation		.25
RST38 $2	rose	35.00	9.00
	Cut cancellation		.25

1929. STOCK TRANSFER ISSUE Same as 1918 issue but letters of overprint with serifs. *Offset, perforated 10.*

		UnFVF	UseFVF
RST39 2¢	rose	5.00	.50
RST40 10¢	rose	1.25	.50
RST41 20¢	rose	2.00	.25

1940. STOCK TRANSFER ISSUE

Documentary Stamps of 1917-33 overprinted as illustrated, in black. *Offset, double-line USIR watermark, perforated 11. Nos. RST52-58 engraved.*

SERIES 1940   RST42

RST42-58
Overprint on white numerals in ovals

STOCK
TRANSFER

RST42		MnHVF	UseVF	CutCnl
1¢	pink	2.75	.40	.20
RST43		MnHVF	UseVF	CutCnl
2¢	pink	2.75	.40	.20
RST44		MnHVF	UseVF	CutCnl
4¢	pink	2.75	.20	.20
RST45		MnHVF	UseVF	CutCnl
5¢	pink	3.00	.20	.20
RST46		MnHVF	UseVF	CutCnl
10¢	pink	3.00	.20	.20

RST47

RST47		MnHVF	UseVF	CutCnl
20¢	pink	7.00	.20	.20
RST48		MnHVF	UseVF	CutCnl
25¢	pink	7.00	.50	.20
RST49		MnHVF	UseVF	CutCnl
40¢	pink	4.50	.50	.20
RST50		MnHVF	UseVF	CutCnl
50¢	pink	5.50	.20	.20
RST51		MnHVF	UseVF	CutCnl
80¢	pink	80.00	40.00	25.00
RST52		MnHVF	UseVF	CutCnl
$1	green	17.50	.30	.20
RST53		MnHVF	UseVF	CutCnl
$2	rose	17.50	.50	.20
RST54		MnHVF	UseVF	CutCnl
$3	violet	110.00	8.00	.20
RST55		MnHVF	UseVF	CutCnl
$4	yellow brown	35.00	.75	.20
RST56		MnHVF	UseVF	CutCnl
$5	blue	35.00	.75	.20
RST57		MnHVF	UseVF	CutCnl
$10	yellow	85.00	5.00	.40
RST58		MnHVF	UseVF	CutCnl
$20	olive bistre	200.00	70.00	15.00

Stock Transfer Stamps of 1918-29 handstamped "Series 1940" in blue. Engraved, perforated 12, issued without gum.

RST59		MnHVF	UseVF	CutCnl
$30	vermilion	700.00	400.00	250.00
RST60		MnHVF	UseVF	CutCnl
$50	olive green	700.00	650.00	175.00
RST61		MnHVF	UseVF	CutCnl
$60	brown		900.00	200.00
RST62		MnHVF	UseVF	CutCnl
$100	green		500.00	125.00
RST63		MnHVF	UseVF	CutCnl
$500	blue		1,750.00	1,100.00
RST64		MnHVF	UseVF	CutCnl
$1,000	orange		2,100.00	1,750.00

1940. STOCK TRANSFER ISSUE

New designs, with same portraits as R275-298 overprinted "Series 1940" in black. *Nos. RST65-74 perforated 11, size 19x22mm. Nos. RST75-81 size 21 1/2x36 1/4mm. Nos. RST82-87 similar designs, 28 1/2x42mm, perforated 12.*

RST65-74

RST65		MnHVF	UseVF	CutCnl
1¢	green	7.50	2.50	.40
RST66		MnHVF	UseVF	CutCnl
2¢	green	5.00	1.25	.20
RST67		MnHVF	UseVF	CutCnl
4¢	green	8.00	3.50	.50

RST68 *G.W. Campbell*

RST68		MnHVF	UseVF	CutCnl
5¢	green	6.00	1.25	.20
RST69		MnHVF	UseVF	CutCnl
10¢	green	7.50	1.50	.20
RST70		MnHVF	UseVF	CutCnl
20¢	green	25.00	7.50	.50
RST71		MnHVF	UseVF	CutCnl
25¢	green	50.00	27.50	2.00
RST72		MnHVF	UseVF	CutCnl
40¢	green	8.00	1.50	.25
RST73		MnHVF	UseVF	CutCnl
50¢	green	65.00	45.00	20.00
RST74		MnHVF	UseVF	CutCnl
80¢	green	27.50	3.50	.30

RST75-81

RST75		MnHVF	UseVF	CutCnl
$1	green	30.00	8.00	.50
RST76		MnHVF	UseVF	CutCnl
$2	green	50.00	10.00	.50
RST77		MnHVF	UseVF	CutCnl
$3	green	50.00	10.00	.50
RST78		MnHVF	UseVF	CutCnl
$4	green	225.00	175.00	60.00
RST79		MnHVF	UseVF	CutCnl
$5	green	50.00	10.00	.30
RST80		MnHVF	UseVF	CutCnl
$10	green	110.00	30.00	4.00
RST81		MnHVF	UseVF	CutCnl
$20	green	400.00	70.00	8.00
RST82		MnHVF	UseVF	CutCnl
$30	green		110.00	50.00
RST83		MnHVF	UseVF	CutCnl
$50	green	275.00	175.00	75.00
RST84		MnHVF	UseVF	CutCnl
$60	green		275.00	50.00
RST85		MnHVF	UseVF	CutCnl
$100	green		160.00	60.00
RST86		MnHVF	UseVF	CutCnl
$500	green		800.00	600.00
RST87		MnHVF	UseVF	CutCnl
$1,000	green		700.00	500.00

1941. STOCK TRANSFER ISSUE

Types of 1940 overprinted "Series 1941" in black. *Nos. RST88-104 perforated 11. Nos. RST105-110 perforated 12.*

RST88		MnHVF	UseVF	CutCnl
1¢	green	.60	.50	.20
RST89		MnHVF	UseVF	CutCnl
2¢	green	.40	.20	.20
RST90		MnHVF	UseVF	CutCnl
4¢	green	.35	.20	.20
RST91		MnHVF	UseVF	CutCnl
5¢	green	.30	.20	.20
RST92		MnHVF	UseVF	CutCnl
10¢	green	.65	.20	.20
RST93		MnHVF	UseVF	CutCnl
20¢	green	1.60	.20	.20

Cat. No.	Denom.		MnHVF	UseVF	CutCnl
RST94	25¢	green	1.60	.20	.20
RST95	40¢	green	2.00	.60	.20
RST96	50¢	green	3.50	.30	.20
RST97	80¢	green	17.50	7.00	.50
RST98	$1	green	10.00	.20	.20
RST99	$2	green	11.00	.20	.20
RST100	$3	green	17.50	1.25	.20
RST101	$4	green	30.00	7.00	.30
RST102	$5	green	30.00	.50	.20
RST103	$10	green	70.00	3.50	.50
RST104	$20	green	130.00	50.00	8.00
RST105	$30	green	135.00	120.00	25.00
RST106	$50	green	220.00	135.00	20.00
RST107	$60	green	400.00	160.00	140.00
RST108	$100	green		65.00	20.00
RST109	$500	green	850.00	700.00	550.00
RST110	$1,000	green		800.00	550.00

1942. STOCK TRANSFER ISSUE Types of 1940 overprinted "Series 1942" in black. *Nos. RST111-127 perforated 11. Nos. RST128-133 perforated 12.*

Cat. No.	Denom.		MnHVF	UseVF	CutCnl
RST111	1¢	green	.40	.25	.20
RST112	2¢	green	.40	.25	.20
RST113	4¢	green	2.75	.80	.45
RST114	5¢	green	.35	.20	.20
RST115	10¢	green	1.50	.20	.20
RST116	20¢	green	1.75	.25	.20
RST117	25¢	green	1.75	.25	.20
RST118	40¢	green	3.50	.25	.20
RST119	50¢	green	4.50	.20	.20
RST120	80¢	green	17.50	5.00	1.00
RST121	$1	green	11.00	.30	.20
RST122	$2	green	15.00	.30	.20
RST123	$3	green	22.50	1.00	.25
RST124	$4	green	30.00	20.00	.30
RST125	$5	green	27.50	.30	.20
RST126	$10	green	55.00	7.00	1.00
RST127	$20	green	130.00	30.00	4.00
RST128	$30	green	80.00	40.00	15.00
RST129	$50	green	125.00	80.00	15.00
RST130	$60	green		100.00	40.00
RST131	$100	green		75.00	20.00
RST132	$500	green		7,000.00	4,000.00
RST133	$1,000	green		350.00	175.00

1943. STOCK TRANSFER ISSUE Types of 1940 overprinted "Series 1943" in black. *Nos. RST134-150 perforated 11. Nos. RST151-156 perforated 12.*

Cat. No.	Denom.		MnHVF	UseVF	CutCnl
RST134	1¢	green	.40	.25	.20
RST135	2¢	green	.50	.35	.20
RST136	4¢	green	1.50	.20	.20
RST137	5¢	green	.40	.20	.20
RST138	10¢	green	.85	.20	.20
RST139	20¢	green	1.50	.20	.20
RST140	25¢	green	3.25	.20	.20
RST141	40¢	green	3.25	.20	.20
RST142	50¢	green	3.25	.20	.20
RST143	80¢	green	10.00	4.00	1.25
RST144	$1	green	10.00	.20	.20
RST145	$2	green	12.50	.20	.20
RST146	$3	green	15.00	.80	.20
RST147	$4	green	30.00	12.50	.75
RST148	$5	green	45.00	.25	.20
RST149	$10	green	60.00	4.00	.75
RST150	$20	green	120.00	30.00	12.50
RST151	$30	green	175.00	80.00	50.00
RST152	$50	green	250.00	120.00	22.50
RST153	$60	green		275.00	130.00
RST154	$100	green		50.00	17.50
RST155	$500	green		375.00	175.00
RST156	$1,000	green		250.00	150.00

1944. STOCK TRANSFER ISSUE Type of 1940 overprinted "Series 1944" in black. *Nos. RST157-173 perforated 11. Nos. RST174-182 perforated 12.*

Cat. No.	Denom.		MnHVF	UseVF	CutCnl
RST157	1¢	green	.60	.60	.20
RST158	2¢	green	.40	.20	.20
RST159	4¢	green	.60	.20	.20
RST160	5¢	green	.50	.20	.20
RST161	10¢	green	.65	.20	.20
RST162	20¢	green	1.20	.20	.20
RST163	25¢	green	1.75	.30	.20
RST164	40¢	green	7.50	4.50	2.00

Catalog	Denomination		MnHVF	UseVF	CutCnl
RST165	50¢	green	4.25	.20	.20
RST166	80¢	green	7.25	4.00	1.75
RST167	$1	green	7.25	.30	.20
RST168	$2	green	27.50	.50	.20
RST169	$3	green	22.50	1.20	.20
RST170	$4	green	27.50	4.50	.20
RST171	$5	green	25.00	.80	.20
RST172	$10	green	55.00	4.00	.40
RST173	$20	green	90.00	7.50	3.50
RST174	$30	green	110.00	55.00	12.50
RST175	$50	green	80.00	45.00	12.50
RST176	$60	green	135.00	90.00	60.00
RST177	$100	green	100.00	45.00	20.00
RST178	$500	green		375.00	250.00
RST179	$1,000	green			200.00
RST180	$2,500	green (William Windom)			—
RST181	$5,000	green (C.J. Folger)			—
RST182	$10,000	green (W.Q. Gresham)			1,100.00

1945. STOCK TRANSFER ISSUE
Types of 1940 overprinted "Series 1945" in black. *Nos. RST183-199 perforated 11. Nos. RST200-208 perforated 12.*

Catalog	Denomination		MnHVF	UseVF	CutCnl
RST183	1¢	green	.20	.20	.20
RST184	2¢	green	.25	.20	.20
RST185	4¢	green	.25	.20	.20
RST186	5¢	green	.25	.20	.20
RST187	10¢	green	.70	.30	.20
RST188	20¢	green	1.20	.30	.20
RST189	25¢	green	1.75	.30	.20
RST190	40¢	green	2.75	.20	.20
RST191	50¢	green	3.25	.20	.20
RST192	80¢	green	6.75	2.25	.60
RST193	$1	green	11.50	.20	.20
RST194	$2	green	15.00	.40	.20
RST195	$3	green	27.50	.50	.20
RST196	$4	green	27.50	2.25	.60
RST197	$5	green	17.50	.40	.20
RST198	$10	green	40.00	6.00	.70
RST199	$20	green	70.00	8.00	1.25
RST200	$30	green	80.00	40.00	.70
RST201	$50	green	50.00	15.00	4.00
RST202	$60	green	130.00	100.00	40.00
RST203	$100	green		20.50	12.50
RST204	$500	green		375.00	200.00
RST205	$1,000	green	1,250.00	450.00	250.00
RST206	$2,500	green			20,000.00
RST207	$5,000	green			20,000.00
RST208	$10,000	green			7,000.00

1946. STOCK TRANSFER ISSUE
Types of 1940 overprinted "Series 1946" in black. *Nos. RST209-225 perforated 11. No. RST226-234 perforated 12.*

Catalog	Denomination		MnHVF	UseVF	CutCnl
RST209	1¢	green	.20	.20	.20
RST210	2¢	green	.30	.20	.20
RST211	4¢	green	.30	.20	.20
RST212	5¢	green	.30	.20	.20
RST213	10¢	green	.75	.20	.20
RST214	20¢	green	1.30	.20	.20
RST215	25¢	green	1.30	.20	.20
RST216	40¢	green	3.00	.50	.20
RST217	50¢	green	4.00	.20	.20
RST218	80¢	green	8.50	5.50	1.75
RST219	$1	green	7.50	.50	.20
RST220	$2	green	7.50	.40	.20
RST221	$3	green	15.00	1.20	.20
RST222	$4	green	15.00	5.00	1.75
RST223	$5	green	22.50	1.00	.20
RST224	$10	green	45.00	2.25	.50
RST225	$20	green	75.00	30.00	8.50
RST226	$30	green	65.00	25.00	16.50
RST227	$50	green	50.00	30.00	10.00
RST228	$60	green	120.00	80.00	30.00
RST229	$100	green	75.00	30.00	15.00
RST230	$500	green		150.00	90.00
RST231	$1,000	green		135.00	90.00
RST232	$2,500	green			4,500.00
RST233	$5,000	green		5,000.00	
RST234	$10,000	green			1,800.00

1947. STOCK TRANSFER ISSUE
Types of 1940 overprinted "Series 1947" in black. *Nos. RST235-251 perforated 11. Nos. RST252-260 perforated 12.*

Catalog	Denomination		MnHVF	UseVF	CutCnl
RST235	1¢	green	.60	.50	.20

Cat.	Denom.	Color	MnHVF	UseVF	CutCnl
RST236	2¢	green	.50	.40	.20
RST237	4¢	green	.40	.30	.20
RST238	5¢	green	.40	.30	.20
RST239	10¢	green	.50	.40	.20
RST240	20¢	green	1.00	.40	.20
RST241	25¢	green	1.60	.40	.20
RST242	40¢	green	2.75	.60	.20
RST243	50¢	green	3.50	.25	.20
RST244	80¢	green	12.50	11.00	3.50
RST245	$1	green	7.25	.40	.20
RST246	$2	green	11.50	.60	.20
RST247	$3	green	17.50	1.25	.30
RST248	$4	green	30.00	5.00	1.00
RST249	$5	green	25.00	1.25	.25
RST250	$10	green	40.00	4.50	1.50
RST251	$20	green	80.00	25.00	5.00
RST252	$30	green	55.00	30.00	7.50
RST253	$50	green	120.00	80.00	22.50
RST254	$60	green	140.00	120.00	40.00
RST255	$100	green		25.00	12.50
RST256	$500	green		225.00	100.00
RST257	$1,000	green		80.00	40.00
RST258	$2,500	green			250.00
RST259	$5,000	green			300.00
RST260	$10,000	green			50.00

1948. STOCK TRANSFER ISSUE Types of 1940 overprinted "Series 1948" in black. *Nos. RST261-277 perforated 11. Nos. RST278-286 perforated 12.*

Cat.	Denom.	Color	MnHVF	UseVF	CutCnl
RST261	1¢	green	.25	.20	.20
RST262	2¢	green	.25	.20	.20
RST263	4¢	green	.30	.25	.20
RST264	5¢	green	.20	.20	.20
RST265	10¢	green	.30	.20	.20
RST266	20¢	green	1.20	.30	.20
RST267	25¢	green	1.20	.30	.20
RST268	40¢	green	1.65	.60	.20
RST269	50¢	green	4.00	.35	.20
RST270	80¢	green	10.00	5.00	2.25
RST271	$1	green	7.50	.40	.20
RST272	$2	green	10.00	.50	.20
RST273	$3	green	12.50	3.50	1.50
RST274	$4	green	15.00	8.00	2.25
RST275	$5	green	22.50	2.25	.20
RST276	$10	green	40.00	4.00	.65
RST277	$20	green	70.00	17.50	6.00
RST278	$30	green	80.00	35.00	20.00
RST279	$50	green	50.00	35.00	10.00
RST280	$60	green	135.00	90.00	25.00
RST281	$100	green		17.50	6.00
RST282	$500	green		200.00	100.00
RST283	$1,000	green		100.00	35.00
RST284	$2,500	green	275.00	250.00	140.00
RST285	$5,000	green		225.00	150.00
RST286	$10,000	green			50.00

1949. STOCK TRANSFER ISSUE Types of 1940 overprinted "Series 1949" in black. *Nos. RST287-303 perforated 11. Nos. RST304-312 perforated 12.*

Cat.	Denom.	Color	MnHVF	UseVF	CutCnl
RST287	1¢	green	.40	.35	.20
RST288	2¢	green	.40	.35	.20
RST289	4¢	green	.50	.40	.20
RST290	5¢	green	.50	.40	.20
RST291	10¢	green	1.25	.50	.20
RST292	20¢	green	2.00	.50	.20
RST293	25¢	green	2.50	.75	.20
RST294	40¢	green	5.00	1.25	.20
RST295	50¢	green	5.00	.20	.20
RST296	80¢	green	40.00	6.00	2.50
RST297	$1	green	9.00	.60	.20
RST298	$2	green	12.50	.75	.20
RST299	$3	green	30.00	4.00	1.00
RST300	$4	green	27.50	7.00	2.00
RST301	$5	green	35.00	2.00	.25
RST302	$10	green	40.00	4.00	1.25
RST303	$20	green	100.00	12.50	5.00
RST304	$30	green		35.00	12.50
RST305	$50	green	130.00	50.00	15.50
RST306	$60	green	150.00	130.00	40.00
RST307	$100	green		50.00	22.50

		MnHVF	UseVF	CutCnl
RST308				
$500	green		180.00	60.00
RST309				
$1,000	green		75.00	35.00
RST310				
$2,500	green			300.00
RST311				
$5,000	green			300.00
RST312				
$10,000	green		250.00	25.00

1950. STOCK TRANSFER ISSUE Types of 1940 overprinted "Series 1950" in black. *Nos. RST313-329 perforated 11. Nos. RST330-338 perforated 12.*

		MnHVF	UseVF	CutCnl
RST313				
1¢	green	.35	.30	.20
RST314				
2¢	green	.35	.25	.20
RST315				
4¢	green	.35	.30	.20
RST316				
5¢	green	.35	.20	.20
RST317				
10¢	green	1.75	.25	.20
RST318				
20¢	green	2.50	.40	.20
RST319				
25¢	green	3.50	.50	.20
RST320				
40¢	green	4.50	.80	.20
RST321				
50¢	green	7.00	.30	.20
RST322				
80¢	green	9.00	5.00	2.00
RST323				
$1	green	9.00	.35	.20
RST324				
$2	green	15.00	.60	.20
RST325				
$3	green	25.00	4.00	.50
RST326				
$4	green	30.00	6.50	2.50
RST327				
$5	green	30.00	1.50	.20
RST328				
$10	green	75.00	4.50	1.00
RST329				
$20	green	100.00	22.50	4.00
RST330				
$30	green	75.00	40.00	20.00
RST331				
$50	green	70.00	65.00	35.00
RST332				
$60	green		100.00	40.00
RST333				
$100	green		32.50	20.00
RST334				
$500	green		150.00	100.00
RST335				
$1,000	green		65.00	25.00
RST336				
$2,500	green		900.00	600.00
RST337				
$5,000	green		500.00	300.00
RST338				
$10,000	green			50.00

1951. STOCK TRANSFER ISSUE Types of 1940 overprinted "Series 1951" in black. *Nos. RST339-355 perforated 11. Nos. RST356-364 perforated 12.*

		MnHVF	UseVF	CutCnl
RST339				
1¢	green	1.00	.30	2.00
RST340				
2¢	green	1.00	.30	.20
RST341				
4¢	green	1.25	.40	.30
RST342				
5¢	green	1.00	.30	.20

		MnHVF	UseVF	CutCnl
RST343				
10¢	green	1.25	.30	.20
RST344				
20¢	green	3.50	.75	.20
RST345				
25¢	green	4.50	.80	.20
RST346				
40¢	green	11.00	7.50	1.50
RST347				
50¢	green	8.00	.75	.20
RST348				
80¢	green	12.50	8.50	3.50
RST349				
$1	green	15.00	.75	.20
RST350				
$2	green	22.50	1.00	.20
RST351				
$3	green	30.00	8.50	3.00
RST352				
$4	green	35.00	10.00	4.00
RST353				
$5	green	40.00	2.00	.20
RST354				
$10	green	75.00	8.00	.20
RST355				
$20	green	110.00	15.00	5.00
RST356				
$30	green		40.00	20.00
RST357				
$50	green		45.00	20.00
RST358				
$60	green		400.00	200.00
RST359				
$100	green		50.00	17.50
RST360				
$500	green		125.00	75.00
RST361				
$1,000	green		70.00	60.00
RST362				
$2,500	green		900.00	400.00
RST363				
$5,000	green		900.00	400.00
RST364				
$10,000	green		100.00	50.00

1952. STOCK TRANSFER ISSUE Types of 1940 overprinted "Series 1952" on black. *Perforated 11.*

		MnHVF	UseVF	CutCnl
RST365				
1¢	green	30.00	15.00	3.00
RST366				
10¢	green	30.00	15.00	3.00
RST367				
20¢	green	300.00		
RST368				
25¢	green	400.00		
RST369				
40¢	green	70.00	20.00	8.00
RST370				
$4	green	1,100.00	400.00	
RST371				
$10	green	2,000.00		
RST372				
$20	green	3,000.00		

Stock transfer stamps were discontinued in 1952.

Silver Purchase Stamps

The Silver Purchase Act of 1934 placed a 50% tax on net profits realized from the sale of silver bullion. The stamps were discontinued on June 4, 1963.

1934. SILVER PURCHASE ISSUE Documentary Stamps of 1917 overprinted. *Under $30 perforated 11; $30 and over perforated 12 and without gum.*

 RSP1

SILVER
TAX
Overprint

RSP2

		UnFVF	UseFVF	CutCnl
RSP1 1¢	rose	1.25	1.00	
RSP2 2¢	rose	1.75	.35	
RSP3 3¢	rose	1.75	1.00	
RSP4 4¢	rose	2.25	1.75	
RSP5 5¢	rose	3.50	1.75	
RSP6 8¢	rose	4.50	3.75	
RSP7 10¢	rose	5.00	2.00	
RSP8 20¢	rose	7.00	3.50	
RSP9 25¢	rose	7.50	4.00	
RSP10 40¢	rose	7.75	5.50	
RSP11 50¢	rose	7.00	6.50	
RSP12 80¢	rose	14.00	9.50	
RSP13 $1	yellow green	22.50	11.00	
RSP14 $2	rose	22.50	15.00	
RSP15 $3	violet	55.00	25.00	
RSP16 $4	ocher	45.00	18.00	
RSP17 $5	blue	45.00	18.00	
RSP18 $10	yellow	65.00	18.00	
RSP19 $30	orange	120.00	50.00	20.00
RSP20 $60	brown	125.00	70.00	30.00
RSP21 $100	pale green	120.00	30.00	
	a. 11mm spacing on overprint	165.00	65.00	
RSP22 $500	blue	375.00	225.00	100.00
RSP23 $1,000	orange yellow		110.00	60.00
	cut cancellation		32.50	
	a. 1mm spacing on overprint		500.00	

1940. DOCUMENTARY STAMPS OF 1917 OVERPRINTED "Series 1940, Silver Tax." *Double-line USIR watermark, perforated 11.*

SERIES 1940   RSP24-41

SILVER
TAX

		MnHVF	UseVF	CutCnl
RSP24 1¢	pink	15.00		
RSP25 2¢	pink	15.00		
RSP26 3¢	pink	15.00		
RSP27 4¢	pink	17.50		
RSP28 5¢	pink	9.00		
RSP29 8¢	pink	17.50		
RSP30 10¢	pink	15.00		
RSP31 20¢	pink	17.50		
RSP32 25¢	pink	17.50		
RSP33 40¢	pink	25.00		
RSP34 50¢	pink	25.00		
RSP35 80¢	pink	25.00		
RSP36 $1	yellow green	100.00		
RSP37 $2	rose	165.00		

 RSP38

		MnHVF	UseVF	CutCnl
RSP38 $3	violet	220.00		
RSP39 $4	ocher	400.00		
RSP40 $5	dark blue	525.00		
RSP41 $10	orange yellow	575.00		
RSP41a				

1940. SILVER TAX STAMPS OF 1934 HANDSTAMPED OVERPRINTED "Series of 1940" handstamped. *Perforated 12.*

		MnHVF	UseVF	CutCnl
RSP42 $30	orange		2,500.00	
RSP43 $60	brown		7,500.00	
RSP44 $100	pale green		3,000.00	

RSP45-46 are not assigned.

1941. SILVER TAX ISSUE New designs similar to Stock Transfer Stamps of 1940 but inscribed "Silver Tax." Overprinted "Series 1941" as illustrated. *Double-line USIR watermark (R139). Perforated 11.*

 RSP47-58 *Size: 19 x 22mm*

		MnHVF	UseVF	CutCnl
RSP47 1¢	gray (Alexander Hamilton)	3.50		
RSP48 2¢	gray (Oliver Wolcott Jr.)	3.50		
RSP49 3¢	gray (Samuel Dexter)	3.50		
RSP50 4¢	gray (Albert Gallatin)	5.25		

			MnHVF	UseVF	CutCnl
RSP51 5¢	**gray** (G.W. Campbell)		6.00		
RSP52 8¢	**gray** (A.J. Dallas)		7.00		
RSP53 10¢	**gray** (Wm. H. Crawford)		8.00		
RSP54 20¢	**gray** (Richard Rush)		12.50		
RSP55 25¢	**gray** (S.D. Ingham)		15.00		
RSP56 40¢	**gray** (Louis McLane)		25.00		
RSP57 50¢	**gray** (Wm. J. Duane)		30.00		
RSP58 80¢	**gray** (Roger B. Taney)		55.00		

RSP59-65 *Size: 21 1/2 x 36 1/2mm.*

			MnHVF	UseVF	CutCnl
RSP59 $1	**gray** (Levi Woodbury)		65.00	30.00	
RSP60 $2	**gray** (Thomas Ewing)		165.00	55.00	
RSP61 $3	**gray** (Walter Forward)		135.00	65.00	
RSP62 $4	**gray** (J.C. Spencer)		190.00	75.00	
RSP63 $5	**gray** (G.M. Bibb)		165.00	75.00	
RSP64 $10	**gray** (R.J. Walker)		260.00	95.00	
RSP65 $20	**gray** (Wm. M. Meredith)		450.00	300.00	

1941. SILVER TAX ISSUE *Size 28 1/2 x 42mm, perforated 12 (without gum).*

			MnHVF	UseVF	CutCnl
RSP66 $30	**gray** (Thomas Corwin)		250.00	140.00	75.00
RSP67 $50	**gray** (James Guthrie)		4,500.00	4,000.00	
RSP68 $60	**gray** (Howell Cobb)			200.00	100.00
RSP69 $100	**gray** (P.F. Thomas)			300.00	110.00
RSP70 $500	**gray** (J.A. Dix)			17,500.00	
RSP71 $1,000	**gray** (S.P. Chase)			2,500.00	1,000.00

1942. ISSUE Types of 1941 overprinted "Series 1942" in black. *Perforated 11.*

			MnHVF	UseVF	CutCnl
RSP72 1¢	**gray**		2.50		
RSP73 2¢	**gray**		2.50		
RSP74 3¢	**gray**		2.50		
RSP75 4¢	**gray**		2.50		
RSP76 5¢	**gray**		2.50		
RSP77 8¢	**gray**		5.00		
RSP78 10¢	**gray**		5.00		
RSP79 20¢	**gray**		8.00		

			MnHVF	UseVF	CutCnl
RSP80 25¢	**gray**		17.50		
RSP81 40¢	**gray**		20.00		
RSP82 50¢	**gray**		20.00		
RSP83 80¢	**gray**		55.00		
RSP84 $1	**gray**		70.00		
	a. Overprint "Series 5942"		175.00		
RSP85 $2	**gray**		70.00		
	a. Overprint "Series 5942"		175.00		
RSP86 $3	**gray**		125.00		
	a. Overprint "Series 5942"		175.00		
RSP87 $4	**gray**		125.00		
	a. Overprint "Series 5942"		175.00		
RSP88 $5	**gray**		140.00		
	a. Overprint "Series 5942"		175.00		
RSP89 $10	**gray**		350.00		
RSP90 $20	**gray**		450.00		
	a. Overprint "Series 5942"		175.00		

1942. ISSUE *Perforated 12 (no gum).*

			MnHVF	UseVF	CutCnl
RSP91 $30	**gray**		800.00	75.00	
RSP92 $50	**gray**		650.00	600.00	
RSP93 $60	**gray**			950.00	550.00
RSP94 $100	**gray**		—	495.00	325.00
RSP95 $500	**gray**		—	3,000.00	2,700.00
RSP96 $1,000	**gray**		—	3,500.00	3,000.00

1944. ISSUE Types of 1941 without overprint. *Perforated 11.*

RFD97
Alexander Hamilton

RFD98
Oliver Wolcott Jr.

RFD99
Samuel Dexter

			MnHVF	UseVF	CutCnl
RSP99 3¢	**gray**		1.25	—	

RFD100
Albert Gallatin

RFD101
G.W. Campbell

RFD102
A.J. Dallas

			MnHVF	UseVF	CutCnl
RSP102 8¢	**gray**		3.50	2.50	

RSP103 *Wm. H. Crawford*

RCT3

		MnHVF	UseVF	CutCnl
RSP103		3.50	2.50	
10¢	gray			
RSP104		MnHVF 7.00	UseVF	CutCnl
20¢	gray			
RSP105		MnHVF 9.00	UseVF	CutCnl
25¢	gray			
RSP106		MnHVF 14.00	UseVF 10.00	CutCnl
40¢	gray			
RSP107		MnHVF 14.00	UseVF 10.00	CutCnl
50¢	gray			
RSP108		MnHVF 20.00	UseVF	CutCnl
80¢	gray			
RSP109		MnHVF 40.00	UseVF 15.00	CutCnl
$1	gray			
RSP110		MnHVF 60.00	UseVF 35.00	CutCnl
$2	gray			
RSP111		MnHVF 65.00	UseVF 25.00	CutCnl
$3	gray			
RSP112		MnHVF 80.00	UseVF 60.00	CutCnl
$4	gray			
RSP113		MnHVF 90.00	UseVF 30.00	CutCnl
$5	gray			
RSP114		MnHVF 125.00	UseVF 50.00	CutCnl 15.00
$10	gray			
RSP115		MnHVF 475.00	UseVF 375.00	CutCnl 250.00
$20	gray			

1944. ISSUE *Perforated 12 (no gum).*

		MnHVF	UseVF	CutCnl
RSP116		250.00	125.00	60.00
$30	gray			
RSP117		MnHVF 550.00	UseVF 525.00	CutCnl 300.00
$50	gray			
RSP118		MnHVF	UseVF 375.00	CutCnl 175.00
$60	gray			
RSP119		MnHVF	UseVF 35.00	CutCnl 15.00
$100	gray			
RSP120		MnHVF	UseVF 425.00	CutCnl 250.00
$500	gray			
RSP121		MnHVF	UseVF 150.00	CutCnl 75.00
$1,000	gray			

Silver Tax Stamps were discontinued on June 4, 1963.

Cigarette Tube Stamps

1919. ISSUE Documentary Stamp of 1917 overprinted as "CIGTTE TUBES." *Double-line USIR watermark (R139), perforated 11.*

RCT1

Overprint

CIGTTE

TUBES

		UnFVF	UseFVF
RCT1		.75	.25
1¢	rose		

1919. ISSUE Same, *perforated 10.*

		UnFVF	UseFVF
RCT2		30.00	10.00
1¢	rose		

1933. ISSUE Large numerals in center and inscribed "Cigarette Tubes, Series of 1933." Size: 40x20 1/2mm. *Double-line USIR watermark (R139), perforated 11.*

		UnFVF	UseFVF
RCT3		2.50	1.00
1¢	rose		
RCT4		UnFVF 7.50	UseFVF 2.00
2¢	rose		

Potato Stamps

1935. ISSUE Portrait of a girl. *Unwatermarked, perforated 11.* Potato Stamps were discontinued Jan. 6, 1936, when the Agricultural Adjustment Act of Dec. 1, 1935, was discontinued.

RPS1

		UnFVF	UseFVF
RPS1		.30	
3/4¢	rose pink		
RPS2		.75	
1 1/2¢	black brown		
RPS3		.75	
2 1/4¢	yellow green		
RPS4		.75	
3¢	pale violet		
RPS5		.75	
3 3/4¢	olive		
RPS6		1.50	
7 1/2¢	orange brown		
RPS7		2.00	
11 1/4¢	deep orange		
RPS8		4.50	
18 3/4¢	violet brown		
RPS9		4.50	
37 1/2¢	orange		
RPS10		4.50	
75¢	blue		
RPS11		7.50	
93 3/4¢	lake		
RPS12		12.50	
$1.12 1/2	green		
RPS13		12.50	
$1.50	brown		

Tobacco Sale Tax Stamps

1934-35. ISSUE Documentary Stamps of 1917 overprinted "TOBACCO SALE TAX" in two horizontal lines except on $20 value where it is vertical, reading up. *Double-line USIR watermark, perforated 11.*

RTS1

		UnFVF	UseFVF
RTS1		.40	.20
1¢	rose		

		Perf	Part Perf	Imperf
RTS2		UnFVF	UseFVF	
2¢	rose	.40	.20	
RTS3		UnFVF	UseFVF	
5¢	rose	1.00	.30	
RTS4		UnFVF	UseFVF	
10¢	rose	1.35	.30	
RTS5		UnFVF	UseFVF	
25¢	rose	4.00	1.50	
RTS6		UnFVF	UseFVF	
50¢	rose	4.00	1.50	
RTS7		UnFVF	UseFVF	
$1	green	8.00	1.75	
RTS8		UnFVF	UseFVF	
$2	rose	15.00	2.00	
RTS9		UnFVF	UseFVF	
$5	blue	22.50	4.00	
RTS10		UnFVF	UseFVF	
$10	yellow	35.00	10.00	
RTS11		UnFVF	UseFVF	
$20	olive	85.00	15.00	

Playing Card Stamps

These Revenue Stamps were placed on packaged decks of playing cards, first applied during the War Between the States.

1862-63. PLAYING CARD ISSUE Designs of the first revenue issue, inscribed "PLAYING CARDS." *Unwatermarked, perforated 12.*

		Perf	Part Perf	Imperf
RPC1				
1¢	rose red	100.00	600.00	800.00

RPC2 *George Washington*

Overprint

		Perf	Part Perf	Imperf
RPC2				
2¢	light blue	3.50	140.00	
RPC3				
2¢	orange yellow	30.00		
RPC4				
3¢	dark yellow green	100.00		

RPC5 *George Washington*

		Perf	Part Perf	Imperf
RPC5				
4¢	gray brown	375.00		
RPC6				
5¢	rose red	15.00		

1894-96. PLAYING CARD ISSUE Inscribed "ON HAND," *unwatermarked, rouletted 5 1/2.*

RPC7

		UnFVF	UseFVF
RPC7			
2¢	lake	.60	.30

1894-96. PLAYING CARD ISSUE Inscribed "ACT OF" instead of "ON HAND," *unwatermarked, rouletted 5 1/2.*

RPC8

		UnFVF	UseFVF
RPC8			
2¢	ultramarine	12.50	2.00
	v. blue		3.00

1896-99. PLAYING CARD ISSUE Same design as No. RPC8, *double-line USIR watermark, rouletted 5 1/2 or 7.*

		UnFVF	UseFVF
RPC9			
2¢	pale blue	4.50	.40
	v. ultramarine	5.00	1.20

1902. PLAYING CARD ISSUE Same design as No. RPC8, *perforated 12.*

		UnFVF	UseFVF
RPC10			
2¢	dark blue		35.00

This stamp was first used in 1902, although it will sometimes be found canceled 1899 from an old canceling plate.

1917. PLAYING CARD ISSUE Stamp No. RPC9, handstamped in rose. *Rouletted 7.*

The overprint on No. RPC11 was applied at an Internal Revenue office; those on Nos. RPC12-RPC19 and on No. RPC21 were applied by the manufacturers and, together with the manufacturer's initials, dates, etc., formed a combination of overprint and cancellation.

ACT OF 1917   RPC11 *Overprint*

7 CENTS

		UnFVF	UseFVF
RPC11			
7¢ on 2¢	ultramarine	600.00	400.00

1917. PLAYING CARD ISSUE Stamp No. RPC9 with various overprints. *Rouletted 7.*

17   RPC12 *Overprinted "17" to indicate that the 7¢ tax had been paid according to the Act of 1917*

		UnFVF	UseFVF
RPC12			
7¢ on 2¢	blue		35.00
	a. Inverted overprint		35.00

7   RPC13 *Overprint*

		UnFVF	UseFVF
RPC13			
7¢ on 2¢	blue		500.00
	a. Inverted overprint	375.00	375.00

7 CTS.   RPC14 *Overprint in red, reading up*

		UnFVF	UseFVF
RPC14			
7¢ on 2¢	blue		800.00

7 CENTS   RPC15 *Overprint in black, violet, or red, reading up*

		UnFVF	UseFVF
RPC15			

| 7¢ on 2¢ blue | 7.50 |
| a. Overprint reading down | 9.00 |

There are many varieties of No. RPC15 such as "double surcharge" and "7 omitted." All command premiums.

7¢ RPC16 *Overprinted in carmine*

RPC16	UnFVF	UseFVF
7¢ on 2¢ blue		50.00
a. Inverted overprint		30.00

1918. PLAYING CARD ISSUE New design, inscribed "Playing Cards-Class A." *Double-line USIR watermark, imperforate. Size 21x40mm.*

RPC17, RPC18

RPC17	UnFVF	UseFVF
7¢ pale blue	40.00	27.50

1918-19. PLAYING CARD ISSUE Same as No. RPC17 but *private roulette 14.*

RPC18	UnFVF	UseFVF
7¢ pale blue		200.00

Both RPC17 and RPC18 served as 7¢ stamps when used before April 1, 1919, and as 8¢ stamps after that date.

RPC19 *Overprinted "7 CENTS" in violet, red, or black, private roulette 9 1/2*

7 CENTS

RPC19	UnFVF	UseFVF
7¢ pale blue		35.00
a. Inverted surcharge		30.00

1919. PLAYING CARD ISSUE Stamp No. RPC9 overprinted with various overprints. *Rouletted 7.*

REVENUE ACT OF 1918 RPC20 *Magenta or rose hand-stamp applied at an Internal Revenue office*

8 CENTS

RPC20	UnFVF	UseFVF
8¢ on 2¢ dark blue		75.00

8 RPC21 *Inverted carmine overprint*

RPC21	UnFVF	UseFVF
8¢ on 2¢ blue (inverted)		500.00

8 Cts. RPC22 *Carmine overprint*

RPC22	UnFVF	UseFVF
8¢ on 2¢ blue	100.00	.60

1922. PLAYING CARD ISSUE Inscribed "Class A." *Double-line USIR watermark, rouletted 7. Size: 19x22mm. No denomination but valued at 8¢.*

RPC23

RPC23	UnFVF	UseFVF
8¢ pale blue	15.00	1.00

1922. PLAYING CARD ISSUE Stamp No. RPC23 overprinted in carmine, blue, or black.

8¢ RPC24 *Overprint*

RPC24	UnFVF	UseFVF
8¢ pale blue		30.00
a. Inverted overprint		30.00

1924. PLAYING CARD ISSUE Flat plate printing, rouletted 7.

RPC25-RPC28 *Numeral in center of design, "CENTS" in lower ribbon. Double-line USIR watermark (R139)*

RPC25	UnFVF	UseFVF
10¢ blue	10.00	.30

1926. PLAYING CARD ISSUE *Rotary press coil stamp, perforated 10 vertically.*

RPC26	UnFVF	UseFVF
10¢ blue		.20

1927. PLAYING CARD ISSUE Flat plate printing, perforated 11.

RPC27	UnFVF	UseFVF
10¢ blue	20.00	4.50

1928. PLAYING CARD ISSUE Flat plate printing, perforated 10.

RPC28	UnFVF	UseFVF
10¢ blue	10.00	3.50

1929. PLAYING CARD ISSUE Rotary press coil stamp, perforated 10 horizontally.

RPC29 *Size 37 1/2x20mm*

RPC29	UnFVF	UseFVF
10¢ light blue		.20

1929. PLAYING CARD ISSUE Flat plate printing, perforated 10.

RPC30	UnFVF	UseFVF
10¢ blue	10.00	1.00

1929. PLAYING CARD ISSUE Flat plate printing, perforated 11.

RPC31	UnFVF	UseFVF
10¢ blue	10.00	1.00

1940. PLAYING CARD ISSUE Inscribed "PLAYING CARDS PACK," *size 20x22 1/2mm, rotary press coil stamp, perforated 10 vertically.*

RPC32

RPC32	MNHVF	UseVF
1 Pack blue		.35

1940. PLAYING CARD ISSUE *Rotary press coil stamp, perforated 10 horizontally.*

RPC33-RPC35 *Inscribed "PLAYING CARDS PACK," double-line USIR watermark (R139), size: 38x20mm*

RPC33

1 Pack	blue	MNHVF	UseVF
		2.50	.20

1940. PLAYING CARD ISSUE Flat plate printing, perforated 11.

RPC34

1 Pack	light blue	MNHVF	UseVF
		4.50	.60

1940. PLAYING CARD ISSUE Rotary press printing, perforated 10x11.

RPC35

1 Pack	light blue	MNHVF	UseVF
		160.00	75.00

The tax on playing cards was repealed effective June 22, 1965.

Wine Stamps

1914. WINE STAMP ISSUE These stamps were issued to pay the tax on cordials and wines. A large white numeral is in the center of the design. *Single-line USPS watermark, offset printed, perforated 10. Size of design: 19 1/2x22 1/4mm.*

RW1-RW14

RW1		UnFVF	UseVF
1/4¢	gray green	.50	.40
RW2		UnFVF	UseVF
1/2¢	gray green	.30	.20
RW3		UnFVF	UseVF
1¢	gray green	.40	.25
RW4		UnFVF	UseVF
1 1/2¢	gray green	2.00	1.25
RW5		UnFVF	UseVF
2¢	gray green	2.50	2.50
RW6		UnFVF	UseVF
3¢	gray green	2.50	1.00
RW7		UnFVF	UseVF
4¢	gray green	2.25	1.25
RW8		UnFVF	UseVF
5¢	gray green	.80	.40
RW9		UnFVF	UseVF
6¢	gray green	6.00	3.00
RW10		UnFVF	UseVF
8¢	gray green	3.25	1.25
RW11		UnFVF	UseVF
10¢	gray green	3.25	2.50
RW12		UnFVF	UseVF
20¢	gray green	4.00	1.50
RW13		UnFVF	UseVF
24¢	gray green	12.50	7.00
RW14		UnFVF	UseVF
40¢	gray green	2.50	.50

1914. WINE STAMP ISSUE *Imperforate, size: 47x40mm.*

RW15

RW15		UnFVF	UseFVF
$2	pale green	7.00	.20

1914-18. WINE STAMP ISSUE Same designs as 1914, *double-line USIR watermark, perforated 10.*

RW16		UnFVF	UseFVF
1/4¢	pale green	5.25	4.25
RW17		UnFVF	UseFVF
1/2¢	pale green	3.50	2.50
RW18		UnFVF	UseFVF
1¢	pale green	.25	.20
RW19		UnFVF	UseFVF
1 1/2¢	pale green	42.50	30.00
RW20		UnFVF	UseFVF
2¢	pale green	.25	.20
RW21		UnFVF	UseFVF
3¢	pale green	2.25	1.50
RW22		UnFVF	UseFVF
4¢	pale green	.75	.90
RW23		UnFVF	UseFVF
5¢	pale green	10.00	9.00
RW24		UnFVF	UseFVF
6¢	pale green	.40	.25
RW25		UnFVF	UseFVF
8¢	pale green	1.75	.40
RW26		UnFVF	UseFVF
10¢	pale green	.40	.20
RW27		UnFVF	UseFVF
20¢	pale green	.60	.30
RW28		UnFVF	UseFVF
24¢	pale green	12.50	.65
RW29		UnFVF	UseFVF
40¢	pale green	27.50	10.00

1914-18 WINE STAMP ISSUE *Imperforate.*

RW30		UnFVF	UseFVF
$2	pale green	27.50	2.75

1914-18. WINE STAMP ISSUE *Perforated 11.*

RW31		UnFVF	UseFVF
2¢	pale green	70.00	80.00

1916-18. WINE STAMP ISSUE New design, inscribed "Series of 1916," *double-line USIR watermark.*

RW32-RW52 *Size 40x47mm, offset printing, rouletted 3 1/2.*

RW32		UnFVF	UseFVF
1¢	green	.30	.30

		UnFVF	UseFVF
RW33 3¢	green	4.25	3.75
RW34 4¢	green	.25	.25
RW35 6¢	green	1.25	.65
RW36 7 1/2¢	green	7.25	3.50
RW37 10¢	green	1.00	.35
RW38 12¢	green	2.75	3.50
RW39 15¢	green	1.50	1.50
RW40 18¢	green	22.50	20.00
RW41 20¢	green	.25	.25
RW42 24¢	green	3.75	2.75
RW43 30¢	green	3.00	2.25
RW44 36¢	green	17.50	12.50
RW45 50¢	green	.50	.40
RW46 60¢	green	3.75	1.75
RW47 72¢	green	30.00	25.00
RW48 80¢	green	.60	.50
RW49 $1.20	green	6.50	5.50
RW50 $1.44	green	8.50	2.75
RW51 $1.60	green	22.50	15.00
RW52 $2	green	1.60	1.40

RW53-55 *Flat plate printing*

		UnFVF	UseFVF
RW53 $4	green	.80	.20
RW54 $4.80	green	3.00	2.75
RW55 $9.60	green	1.10	.25

RW56-59 *Size 51x81mm, perforated 12 at left, flat plate printed*

		UnFVF	UseFVF
RW56 $20	green	80.00	35.00
RW57 $40	green	165.00	45.00
RW58 $50	green	55.00	40.00
RW59 $100	green	225.00	130.00

1933-34. WINE STAMP ISSUE Designs of 1916-18, slightly smaller in size. *Offset, double-line USIR watermark (R139), rouletted 7.*

		UnFVF	UseFVF
RW60 1¢	pale green	2.75	.25
RW61 3¢	pale green	7.00	2.25
RW62 4¢	pale green	1.25	.25
RW63 6¢	pale green	10.00	4.50
RW64 7 1/2¢	pale green	2.75	.40
RW65 10¢	pale green	1.75	.20
RW66 12¢	pale green	8.00	4.00
RW67 15¢	pale green	3.75	.25
RW68 20¢	pale green	4.50	.20
RW69 24¢	pale green	4.50	.20
RW70 30¢	pale green	4.50	.20
RW71 36¢	pale green	10.00	.50
RW72 50¢	pale green	4.00	.20
RW73 60¢	pale green	7.00	.20
RW74 72¢	pale green	12.00	.25
RW75 80¢	pale green	12.00	.20
RW76 $1.20	pale green	9.00	1.25
RW77 $1.44	pale green	12.00	3.50
RW78 $1.60	pale green	300.00	150.00
RW79 $2	pale green	32.50	3.50

1933-34. WINE STAMP ISSUE *Flat plate printing.*

		UnFVF	UseFVF
RW80 $4	pale green	27.50	6.50
RW81 $4.80	pale green	27.50	12.50
RW82 $9.60	pale green	125.00	75.00

1934-40. WINE STAMP ISSUE New designs inscribed "Series of 1934," *double-line USIR watermark (R139). Size 28x25mm, offset, rouletted 7, gum.*

RW83-RW102

		UnFVF	UseFVF
RW83 1/5¢	pale green	.70	.20
RW84 1/2¢	pale green	.50	.35
RW85 1¢	pale green	.60	.20
RW86 1 1/4¢	pale green	.80	.70
RW87 1 1/2¢	pale green	5.50	5.00
RW88 2¢	pale green	1.50	.60
RW89 2 1/2¢	pale green	1.50	.40
RW90 3¢	pale green	4.50	3.75
RW91 4¢	pale green	2.25	.20
RW92 5¢	pale green	.55	.20
RW93 6¢	pale green	1.65	.45
RW94 7 1/2¢	pale green	2.00	.20

RW95			UnFVF	UseFVF
10¢	pale green		.40	.20
RW96			UnFVF	UseFVF
12¢	pale green		1.30	.20
RW97			UnFVF	UseFVF
14 2/5¢	pale green		125.00	2.75
RW98			UnFVF	UseFVF
15¢	pale green		.60	.20
RW99			UnFVF	UseFVF
18¢	pale green		1.25	.20
RW100			UnFVF	UseFVF
20¢	pale green		1.00	.20
RW101			UnFVF	UseFVF
24¢	pale green		1.75	.20
RW102			UnFVF	UseFVF
30¢	pale green		1.25	.20

RW103-RW109 inscribed "Series of 1934." Size about 39x46mm, rouletted 7, issued without gum.

RW103-113

RW103			UnFVF	UseFVF
40¢	pale green		3.00	.20
RW104			UnFVF	UseFVF
43 1/5¢	pale green		12.50	1.75
RW105			UnFVF	UseFVF
48¢	pale green		12.50	1.00
RW106			UnFVF	UseFVF
$1	pale green		15.00	10.00
RW107			UnFVF	UseFVF
$1.50	pale green		27.50	12.50

1934-40. WINE STAMP ISSUE *Intaglio, flat plate printing, size: 30x46mm. Perforated initial cancelled are worth half used price.*

RW108			UnFVF	UseFVF
$2.50	pale green		30.00	15.00
RW109			UnFVF	UseFVF
$5	pale green		25.00	7.00

1934. WINE STAMP ISSUE *Size 51x81mm, flat plate printing, perforated 12 at left.*

RW110			UnFVF	UseFVF
$20	yellow green			1,750.00
RW111			UnFVF	UseFVF
$40	yellow green			3,500.00
RW112			UnFVF	UseFVF
$50	yellow green			2,000.00
	a. Perforated 12 1/2			1,500.00
RW113			UnFVF	UseFVF
$100	yellow green		950.00	750.00
	a. Perforated 12 1/2			350.00

1941-52. WINE STAMP ISSUE New design, inscribed "Series of 1941." The values are printed in black. *Double-line USIR watermark, size 28x25mm, offset printing, rouletted 7. Issued without gum.*

RW114-RW165

RW114			MNHVF	UseVF
1/5¢	green		.50	.40
RW115			MNHVF	UseVF
1/4¢	green		1.75	1.50
RW116			MNHVF	UseVF
1/2¢	green		2.25	1.75
RW117			MNHVF	UseVF
1¢	green		1.00	.65
RW117A			MNHVF	UseVF
1 7/10¢	green			10,000.00

RW118 is not assigned.

RW119			MNHVF	UseVF
2¢	green		4.50	4.50
RW120			MNHVF	UseVF
3¢	green		4.50	4.50
RW121			MNHVF	UseVF
3 2/5¢	green		50.00	45.00
RW121A			MNHVF	UseVF
3 1/2¢	green			6,500.00
RW122			MNHVF	UseVF
3 3/4¢	green		7.50	5.50
RW123			MNHVF	UseVF
4¢	green		3.25	2.75
RW124			MNHVF	UseVF
5¢	green		2.25	2.00
RW125			MNHVF	UseVF
6¢	green		2.75	2.25

RW126 is not assigned.

RW127			MNHVF	UseVF
7¢	green		5.25	4.25
RW128			MNHVF	UseVF
7 1/2¢	green		7.50	4.50
RW129			MNHVF	UseVF
8¢	green		4.50	3.50
RW130			MNHVF	UseVF
8 1/2¢	green		27.50	17.50
RW131			MNHVF	UseVF
9¢	green		8.00	7.50
RW132			MNHVF	UseVF
10¢	green		4.25	.75

RW133 is not assigned.

RW134			MNHVF	UseVF
11 1/4¢	green		4.50	4.50
RW135			MNHVF	UseVF
12¢	green		6.50	5.50
RW136			MNHVF	UseVF
13 2/5¢	green		90.00	75.00
RW137			MNHVF	UseVF
14¢	green		22.50	20.00
RW138			MNHVF	UseVF
15¢	green		4.50	3.50
RW139			MNHVF	UseVF
16¢	green		8.50	6.50
RW140			MNHVF	UseVF
17¢	green		15.00	12.50
RW141			MNHVF	UseVF
19 1/5¢	green		125.00	6.50
RW142			MNHVF	UseVF
20¢	green		5.50	1.50
RW143			MNHVF	UseVF
20 2/5¢	green		100.00	50.00
RW144			MNHVF	UseVF
24¢	green		3.75	.20
RW145			MNHVF	UseVF
28¢	green		1,750.00	1,250.00
RW146			MNHVF	UseVF
30¢	green		1.00	.20
RW147			MNHVF	UseVF
32¢	green		125.00	7.00
RW148			MNHVF	UseVF
33 1/2¢	green		80.00	65.00
RW149			MNHVF	UseVF
36¢	green		2.75	.20
RW150			MNHVF	UseVF
38 1/4¢	green		110.00	80.00

	MNHVF	UseVF
RW151		
40¢ green	2.25	.20
RW152	MNHVF	UseVF
40 4/5¢ green	3.25	.50
RW153	MNHVF	UseVF
45¢ green	5.00	.20
RW154	MNHVF	UseVF
48¢ green	12.50	5.00
RW155	MNHVF	UseVF
50¢ green	8.00	6.50
RW156	MNHVF	UseVF
51¢ green	3.75	1.00
RW157	MNHVF	UseVF
60¢ green	3.00	.20
RW158	MNHVF	UseVF
67¢ green	10.00	3.50
RW159	MNHVF	UseVF
68¢ green	3.00	.50
RW160	MNHVF	UseVF
72¢ green	9.00	.80
RW161	MNHVF	UseVF
80¢ green	250.00	9.00
RW162	MNHVF	UseVF
80 2/5¢ green	110.00	85.00
RW163	MNHVF	UseVF
84¢ green		55.00
RW164	MNHVF	UseVF
90¢ green	15.00	.20
RW165	MNHVF	UseVF
96¢ green	10.00	.20

RW167-RW209 size 39x45 1/2mm. Engraved, rouletted 7.

	MNHVF	UseVF
RW166		
$1 green	2.00	.15
RW167	MNHVF	UseVF
$1.20 green	2.75	.15
RW168	MNHVF	UseVF
$1.44 green	1.00	.15
RW169	MNHVF	UseVF
$1.50 green	60.00	30.00
RW170	MNHVF	UseVF
$1.50 3/4 green	45.00	35.00
RW171	MNHVF	UseVF
$1.60 green	5.00	.65
RW172	MNHVF	UseVF
$1.60 4/5 green (Denomination letters 1mm high, bottom "5" is oval)	4.25	.50
Perforated, initials		7.50
v."Dolllar" design error	37.50	15.00
Bottom of "5" almost circular	350.00	150.00
RW173	MNHVF	UseVF
$1.60 4/5 green (Denomination letters 1 1/2mm high, bottom of "5" almost closes to a circle)	30.00	6.00
Bottom of "5" is oval	75.00	25.00

1941-51. WINE STAMP ISSUE *Denomination 28 1/2mm long.*

	MNHVF	UseVF
RW174		
$1.68 green	85.00	45.00
Perforated initials		32.50

 RW175

	MNHVF	UseVF
RW176	200.00	65.00
$1.88 3/10 green		
Perforated initials		30.00
RW177	MNHVF	UseVF
$1.92 green	45.00	35.00

RW178 is not assigned.

	MNHVF	UseVF
RW179		
$2.01 green	3.25	.60
RW180	MNHVF	UseVF
$2.40 green	8.00	.75
RW181	MNHVF	UseVF
$2.68 green	3.25	1.10
RW182	MNHVF	UseVF
$3 green	65.00	35.00
RW183	MNHVF	UseVF
$3.36 green	70.00	25.00
RW184	MNHVF	UseVF
$3.60 green	125.00	5.50
RW185	MNHVF	UseVF
$4 green	27.50	4.50
RW186	MNHVF	UseVF
$4.08 green	60.00	30.00
RW187	MNHVF	UseVF
$4.80 green	115.00	2.50
RW188	MNHVF	UseVF
$5 green	12.50	8.50
RW189	MNHVF	UseVF
$5.76 green	210.00	100.00

RW190-RW192 are not assigned.

	MNHVF	UseVF
RW193		
$7.20 green	18.00	.40

RW194 is not assigned.

	MNHVF	UseVF
RW195		
$8.16 green	15.00	6.00
RW195A	MNHVF	UseVF
$9.60 green		3,000.00
RW196	MNHVF	UseVF
$10 green	175.00	135.00
RW197	MNHVF	UseVF
$20 green	100.00	65.00
RW198	MNHVF	UseVF
$50 green	100.00	65.00
Perforated initials		17.50
RW199	MNHVF	UseVF
$100 green	275.00	27.50
Perforated initials		11.50
RW200	MNHVF	UseVF
$200 green	135.00	17.50
Perforated initials		7.50
RW200B	MNHVF	UseVF
$400 green		8,000.00
RW201	MNHVF	UseVF
$500 green		135.00
Perforated initials		30.00
RW202	MNHVF	UseVF
$600 green		110.00
Perforated initials		25.00
RW203	MNHVF	UseVF
$900 green		4,000.00
Perforated initials		2,500.00
RW204	MNHVF	UseVF
$1,000 green		150.00
RW205	MNHVF	UseVF
$2,000 green		1,250.00
RW206	MNHVF	UseVF
$3,000 green		180.00
RW207	MNHVF	UseVF
$4,000 green		700.00

	MNHVF	UseVF
RW175	2.75	.20
$1.80 green		

1941-51. WINE STAMP ISSUE *Denominations spelled out in one line.*

RW208

			MNHVF	UseVF
RW208				
$1	green		3.50	1.25
RW209			MNHVF	UseVF
$2	green		6.00	1.75
RW210			MNHVF	UseVF
$4	green		800.00	350.00
	Perforated initials			150.00
RW211			MNHVF	UseVF
$5	green			75.00
RW212			MNHVF	UseVF
$6	green			350.00
RW213			MNHVF	UseVF
$7	green		40.00	60.00
RW214			MNHVF	UseVF
$8	green		300.00	800.00
RW215			MNHVF	UseVF
$10	green		8.50	4.00
	Perforated initials			1.75
RW216			MNHVF	UseVF
$20	green		17.50	3.50
	Perforated initials			1.50
RW217			MNHVF	UseVF
$30	green		900.00	700.00

Wine stamps were discontinued Jan. 1, 1955.

Boating Stamps

1960. FEDERAL BOATING STAMPS To quote from the regulation: "Effective April 1, 1960, boats of more than 10 horsepower operated on waters of the United States must be numbered under the Federal Boating Act of 1958. Boating stamps available from April 1 on are available in two denominations. The $3 denomination will cover the filing of an application and will be valid for a period of three years. A $1 stamp will cover charges for the reissuance of a lost or destroyed certificate of number."

Offset, with serial number printed by letterpress; unwatermarked, rouletted.

FB1 *Motor boat in action*

		MNHVF	UseVF
FB1			
$1	carmine red, number in black	35.00	—
	Plate block of 4	150.00	
FB2		MNHVF	UseVF
$3	blue, number in red	50.00	30.00
	Plate block of 4	210.00	

Postal Notes

Fractional currency was retired in 1876. To replace it, the Post Office Department issued the first U.S. Postal Note on Sept. 3, 1883. During the next 11 years, the Post Office Department used three different contract printers to produce seven different postal note designs. Contract periods were four years. The Homer Lee Bank Note Company contract extended from 1883-1887, the American Bank Note Company contract from 1887-1891, and the Dunlap and Clarke contract from 1891-1894. In total, 70.8 million Postal Notes were issued; at least 1,200 are known to survive.

Postal notes were issued for values up to $4.99. The postal note fee was 3¢. The last day of use was June 30, 1894.

Values are for used notes from common states in fine condition without tears, creases, or stains. Territorial notes, notes from some Western and Southern states, and notes with special features, such as low serial numbers or high values, command premiums.

1883. HOMER LEE BANK NOTE CO. New York, approximately 155x85mm, date and 3¢ fee shield at left. The heavy ornate engraving often made cancels difficult to distinguish.

PN1 *(front)*

PN1 *(back)*

PN1		Fine
	black on yellow; reverse green on yellow (Sept. 3, 1883)	110.00

1884. HOMER LEE BANK NOTE CO. imprint with red serial numbers and blue places of issue. The "pay at" city notation was written in by hand. Approximately 132x87mm, as are all succeeding notes. Dollar coupons at left were detached to indicate the dollar amount of the note; 3¢ fee shield at right.

PN2
(front)

PN2
(back)

PN2   Fine
black on white; reverse blue on white   150.00

1887. HOMER LEE BANK NOTE CO. imprint. The pay at city notation was replaced with a handstamped "Any Money Order Office."

PN3

PN3   Fine
black on white; reverse blue on white   175.00

1887. HOMER LEE BANK NOTE CO. imprint "Any Money Order Office" is printed. Redesigned text on obverse and reverse caused by changes in law, dated Jan. 3, 1887.

PN4
(front)

PN4
(back)

PN4   Fine
black on white; reverse blue on white   400.00

1888. AMERICAN BANK NOTE CO. imprint. Engraved by Thomas F. Morris. Among other changes, "Any Money Order Office" line is more ornate. *"Engraved & Printed by the American Bank Note Co., N.Y."* printed at bottom obverse.

PN5

PN5   Fine
black on white; reverse blue on white   150.00
(Sept. 3, 1887)
"1890" handwritten to replace "188_"   —

1890. AMERICAN BANK NOTE CO. "189_" in date line.

PN6 (front)

Generally speaking, the more nearly equal in width all margins of a stamp are, and the farther those equal margins are from the printed design, the more desirable the stamp will be to the collector.

PN6 *(back)*

PN6

black on white; reverse blue on white

Fine
175.00

1892. DUNLAP AND CLARKE imprint, identical to American Bank Note Co. version except "Dunlap and Clarke, Philadelphia, Pa." replaces "American Bank Note" imprint at bottom obverse, and "American Bank Note Company, New York" removed from bottom reverse.

PN7 *(front)*

PN7 *(back)*

PN7

black on white; reverse blue on white
(Sept. 3, 1891)

Fine
90.00

Postal Note Stamps

1945. POSTAL NOTE ISSUE Postal Note stamps were issued Feb. 1, 1945, to supplement the Postal Money Order service. The 18 denominations of stamps, all in the same basic design, were affixed to postal note forms and canceled to indicate the amount less than a dollar. No more than two stamps were needed to show any amount from 1¢ to 99¢. Postal Notes were discontinued effective March 31, 1951. *Intaglio, perforated 11x10 1/2.*

PO1-PO18

		MNHVF	UseVF
PO1 1¢	**black**	.25	.20
	Plate block of 4	3.00	
	FDC *(Feb. 1, 1945)*		1.00
PO2 2¢	**black**	.25	.20
	Plate block of 4	3.00	
	FDC *(Feb. 1, 1945)*		1.00
PO3 3¢	**black**	.25	.20
	Plate block of 4	3.75	
	FDC *(Feb. 1, 1945)*		1.00
PO4 4¢	**black**	.30	.20
	Plate block of 4	4.50	
	FDC *(Feb. 1, 1945)*		1.00
PO5 5¢	**black**	.40	.20
	Plate block of 4	6.00	
	FDC *(Feb. 1, 1945)*		1.00
PO6 6¢	**black**	.45	.20
	Plate block of 4	6.75	
	FDC *(Feb. 1, 1945)*		1.00
PO7 7¢	**black**	.55	.20
	Plate block of 4	8.25	
	FDC *(Feb. 1, 1945)*		1.00
PO8 8¢	**black**	.70	.20
	Plate block of 4	10.00	
	FDC *(Feb. 1, 1945)*		1.00
PO9 9¢	**black**	.75	.20
	Plate block of 4	11.00	
	FDC *(Feb. 1, 1945)*		1.00
PO10 10¢	**black**	1.00	.20
	Plate block of 4	14.00	
	FDC *(Feb. 1, 1945)*		1.00
PO11 20¢	**black**	1.75	.20
	Plate block of 4	27.50	
	FDC *(Feb. 1, 1945)*		1.00
PO12 30¢	**black**	2.50	.20
	Plate block of 4	37.50	
	FDC *(Feb. 1, 1945)*		1.00
PO13 40¢	**black**	3.00	.20
	Plate block of 4	45.00	
	FDC *(Feb. 1, 1945)*		1.00
PO14 50¢	**black**	3.50	.20
	Plate block of 4	52.50	
	FDC *(Feb. 1, 1945)*		1.00
PO15 60¢	**black**	4.75	.20
	Plate block of 4	70.00	
	FDC *(Feb. 1, 1945)*		1.00
PO16 70¢	**black**	5.25	.20
	Plate block of 4	80.00	
	FDC *(Feb. 1, 1945)*		1.00
PO17 80¢	**black**	6.50	.20
	Plate block of 4	95.00	
	FDC *(Feb. 1, 1945)*		1.00
PO18 90¢	**black**	7.00	.20
	Plate block of 4	110.00	
	FDC *(Feb. 1, 1945)*		1.00

Migratory Bird Hunting Permit (Duck) Stamps

An act of Congress in March 1934 authorized the issue of receipts in the form of attractive stamps to license hunters, with the proceeds going to maintain waterfowl life in the United States. When J.N. "Ding" Darling, a newspaper editorial cartoonist and artist, also Pulitzer Prize winner, designed the first "duck" stamp, the beauty and novelty of it immediately appealed to stamp collectors.

The government was adamant that the stamp was for hunters only and had to be attached to a license. The hunter had to keep it intact for a whole year; it was not for collectors, but the pressure became too great to refuse, so 15 days before the first Duck stamp issue expired, the stamps were placed on sale for stamp collectors, and ever since philatelists have happily contributed "to the maintenance of waterfowl in the United States."

Designed by some of the finest artists, stamps of great beauty have resulted, and no page in a stamp album can be more beautiful than the Duck stamp page. All the stamps are inscribed "Migratory Bird Hunting Stamp." The first five read "Department of Agriculture," and after that "Department of the Interior." From 1946 on, all the stamps are inscribed on the back, "It is unlawful to hunt waterfowl unless you sign your name in ink on the face of the stamp."

The stamps are issued July 1 every year and expire June 30 of the following year. Each stamp reads "Void after June 30th 19--," with the hyphens being the year of expiration. Stamps are *unwatermarked*.

Note: Plate blocks must have selvage on two sides.

Issued in panes of 28.

1934. MALLARD ISSUE designed by J.N. Darling. *Intaglio, unwatermarked, perforated 11.* The design also was used on the Wetlands Preservation Issue (CM 1136) of 1984.

RH1		UnFVF	UseFVF
$1	blue	575.00	115.00
	Plate block of 6	13,000.00	
	v.Pair, imperforate	15,000.00	
	v1. Vertical pair, imperforate horizontally	—	

1935. CANVASBACK DUCK ISSUE by Frank W. Benson. *Intaglio, unwatermarked, perforated 11.*

RH2		UnFVF	UseFVF
$1	crimson	525.00	135.00
	Plate block of 6	9,000.00	

1936. CANADA GEESE ISSUE by Richard E. Bishop. *Intaglio, unwatermarked, perforated 11.*

RH3		UnFVF	UseFVF
$1	brown black	300.00	65.00
	Plate block of 6	2,500.00	

1937. SCAUP DUCKS ISSUE by J.D. Knap. *Intaglio, unwatermarked, perforated 11.*

RH4		UnFVF	UseFVF
$1	dull green	250.00	45.00
	Plate block of 6	2,250.00	

1938. PINTAIL DUCK ISSUE by Roland Clark. *Intaglio, unwatermarked, perforated 11.*

RH5		UnFVF	UseFVF
$1	violet	250.00	45.00
	Plate block of 6	2,750.00	

1939. GREEN-WINGED TEAL ISSUE by Lynn B. Hunt. *Intaglio, unwatermarked, perforated 11.*

RH6		UnFVF	UseFVF
$1	sepia	140.00	40.00
	Plate block of 6	1,500.00	

1940. BLACK MALLARD ISSUE by Francis L. Jacques. *Intaglio, unwatermarked, perforated 11.*

RH7		MNHVF	UseVF
$1	black brown	140.00	40.00
	Plate block of 6	1,200.00	

1941. RUDDY DUCKS ISSUE by E.R. Kalmbach. *Intaglio, unwatermarked, perforated 11.*

RH8		MNHVF	UseVF
$1	red brown	140.00	35.00
	Plate block of 6	1,200.00	

1942. BALDPATES ISSUE by A. Lassell Ripley. *Intaglio, unwatermarked, perforated 11.*

RH9		MNHVF	UseVF
$1	sepia	140.00	35.00
	Plate block of 6	1,200.00	

1943. WOOD DUCK ISSUE by Walter E. Bohl. *Intaglio, unwatermarked, perforated 11.*

RH10		MNHVF	UseVF
$1	carmine red	60.00	35.00
	Plate block of 6	450.00	

1944. WHITE-FRONTED GEESE ISSUE by Walter A. Weber. *Intaglio, unwatermarked, perforated 11.*

RH11		MNHVF	UseVF
$1	red orange	60.00	25.00
	Plate block of 6	450.00	

1945. SHOVELLER DUCKS ISSUE by Owen J. Gromme. *Intaglio, unwatermarked, perforated 11.*

RH12

R13

RH12		MNHVF	UseVF
$1	black	45.00	18.00
	Plate block of 6	350.00	

1946. REDHEAD DUCKS ISSUE by Robert W. Hines. *Intaglio, unwatermarked, perforated 11.*

RH13		MNHVF	UseVF
$1	chestnut brown	35.00	13.50
	Plate block of 6	300.00	
	a. rose red	—	

1947. SNOW GEESE ISSUE by Jack Murray. *Intaglio, unwatermarked, perforated 11.*

RH14

RH15

RH14		MNHVF	UseVF
$1	black	35.00	13.50
	Plate block of 6	300.00	

1948. BUFFLEHEAD DUCKS ISSUE the first by Maynard Reece, whose artwork has appeared a record five times on federal Duck stamps. *Intaglio, unwatermarked, perforated 11.*

RH15		MNHVF	UseVF
$1	light blue	45.00	13.50
	Plate block of 6	300.00	

1949. GOLDENEYE DUCKS ISSUE by "Roge" E. Preuss. *Intaglio, unwatermarked, perforated 11.*

RH16

RH17

RH16		MNHVF	UseVF
$2	emerald	50.00	13.50
	Plate block of 6	350.00	

1950. TRUMPETER SWANS ISSUE by Walter A. Weber. *Intaglio, unwatermarked, perforated 11.*

RH17		MNHVF	UseVF
$2	violet	60.00	10.00
	Plate block of 6	400.00	

1951. GADWALL DUCKS ISSUE Maynard Reece. *Intaglio, unwatermarked, perforated 11.*

RH18

RH19

RH18		MNHVF	UseVF
$2	gray black	60.00	10.00
	Plate block of 6	400.00	

1952. HARLEQUIN DUCKS ISSUE by John H. Dick. *Intaglio, unwatermarked, perforated 11.*

RH19		MNHVF	UseVF
$2	deep ultramarine	60.00	10.00
	Plate block of 6	400.00	

1953. BLUE-WINGED TEAL ISSUE by Clayton Seagears. *Intaglio, unwatermarked, perforated 11.*

RH20

RH21

RH20		MNHVF	UseVF
$2	lavender brown	60.00	12.00
	Plate block of 6	400.00	

1954. RING-NECKED DUCKS ISSUE by Harvey Sandstrom. *Intaglio, unwatermarked, perforated 11.*

RH21		MNHVF	UseVF
$2	black	60.00	8.00
	Plate block of 6	400.00	

1955. BLUE GEESE ISSUE by Stanley Searns. *Intaglio, unwatermarked, perforated 11.*

RH22

RH23

RH22		MNHVF	UseVF
$2	deep blue	60.00	8.00
	Plate block of 6	400.00	
	v. Writing inverted on reverse	—	

1956. AMERICAN MERGANSER ISSUE by Edward J. Bierly. *Intaglio, unwatermarked, perforated 11.*

RH23		MNHVF	UseVF
$2	black	60.00	8.00
	Plate block of 6	400.00	

1957. AMERICAN EIDER ISSUE by Jackson M. Abbott. *Intaglio, unwatermarked, perforated 11.*

RH24

RH25

RH24		MNHVF	UseVF
$2	yellow emerald	60.00	8.00
	Plate block of 6	400.00	
	v. Writing inverted on reverse	3,500.00	—

1958. CANADA GEESE ISSUE by Leslie C. Kouba. *Intaglio, Giori Press, unwatermarked, perforated 11.*

RH25		MNHVF	UseVF
$2	black	60.00	8.00
	Plate block of 6	400.00	

1959. RETRIEVER CARRYING MALLARD ISSUE by Maynard Reece. Inscription added to the back of the stamp: "DUCK STAMP DOLLARS BUY WETLANDS TO PERPETUATE WATERFOWL." Contest rules were changed after this year to prohibit the depiction of animals besides waterfowl. From 1959 to present stamps are printed in panes of 30. *Intaglio, unwatermarked, perforated 11.*

RH26

RH27

		MNHVF	UseVF
RH26			
$3	**blue, orange brown & black**	85.00	8.00
	Plate block of 4	375.00	
	v. Writing inverted on reverse	—	—

1960. REDHEAD DUCKS ISSUE by John A. Ruthven. *Intaglio, unwatermarked, perforated 11.*

		MNHVF	UseVF
RH27			
$3	**multicolored**	65.00	8.00
	Plate block of 4	350.00	

1961. MALLARDS ISSUE by Edward A. Morris. *Intaglio, unwatermarked, perforated 11.*

RH28

RH29

		MNHVF	UseVF
RH28			
$3	**blue, brown & yellow brown**	70.00	8.00
	Plate block of 4	375.00	

1962. PINTAILS ISSUE by Edward A. Morris. *Intaglio, unwatermarked, perforated 11.*

		MNHVF	UseVF
RH29			
$3	**multicolored**	70.00	8.00
	Plate block of 4	400.00	

1963. PACIFIC BRANT ISSUE by Edward J. Bierly. *Intaglio, unwatermarked, perforated 11.*

RH30

RH31

		MNHVF	UseVF
RH30			
$3	**multicolored**	70.00	8.00
	Plate block of 4	400.00	

1964. NENE GEESE ISSUE by Stanley Searns. *Intaglio, unwatermarked, perforated 11.*

		MNHVF	UseVF
RH31			
$3	**multicolored**	70.00	8.00
	Plate block of 6	2,000.00	

1965. CANVASBACKS ISSUE by Ron Jenkins. *Intaglio, unwatermarked, perforated 11.*

RH32

RH33

		MNHVF	UseVF
RH32			
$3	**multicolored**	70.00	8.00
	Plate block of 4	400.00	

1966. WHISTLING SWANS ISSUE by Stanley Searns. *Intaglio, unwatermarked, perforated 11.*

		MNHVF	UseVF
RH33			
$3	**deep green, black & blue**	70.00	8.00
	Plate block of 4	400.00	

1967. OLD SQUAW DUCKS ISSUE by Leslie C. Kouba. *Intaglio, unwatermarked, perforated 11.*

RH34

RH35

		MNHVF	UseVF
RH34			
$3	**multicolored**	70.00	8.00
	Plate block of 4	400.00	

1968. HOODED MERGANSERS ISSUE by C.G. Pritchard. Inscription on back of the stamp changed to "BUY DUCK STAMPS SAVE WETLANDS. SEND IN ALL BIRD BANDS. SIGN YOUR DUCK STAMP." *Intaglio, unwatermarked, perforated 11.*

		MNHVF	UseVF
RH35			
$3	**multicolored**	55.00	8.00
	Plate block of 4	280.00	

1969. WHITE-WINGED SCOTERS ISSUE by Maynard Reece. *Intaglio, unwatermarked, perforated 11.*

RH36

RH37

		MNHVF	UseVF
RH36			
$3	**multicolored**	40.00	7.00
	Plate block of 4	250.00	

1970. ROSS' GEESE ISSUE by Edward J. Bierly. *Combination of intaglio and offset, unwatermarked, perforated 11.*

		MNHVF	UseVF
RH37			
$3	**multicolored**	40.00	7.00
	Plate block of 4	250.00	

1971. CINNAMON TEAL ISSUE by Maynard Reece, his fifth Duck stamp. *Combination of intaglio and offset, unwatermarked, perforated 11.*

RH38

RH39

		MNHVF	UseVF
RH38			
$3	**multicolored**	35.00	7.00
	Plate block of 4	175.00	

1972. EMPEROR GEESE ISSUE by Arthur M. Cook. *Combination of intaglio and offset, unwatermarked, perforated 11.*

		MNHVF	UseVF
RH39			
$5	**multicolored**	22.50	7.00
	Plate block of 4	125.00	

1973. STELLER'S EIDER ISSUE by Lee LeBlanc. *Combination of intaglio and offset, unwatermarked, perforated 11.*

RH40

RH41

RH40

$5	multicolored	MNHVF	UseVF
		20.00	7.00
	Plate block of 4	100.00	

1974. WOOD DUCKS ISSUE by David A. Maass. *Combination of intaglio and offset, unwatermarked, perforated 11.*

RH41

$5	multicolored	MNHVF	UseVF
		18.00	7.00
	Plate block of 4	90.00	

1975. CANVASBACKS ISSUE by James L. Fisher. *Combination of intaglio and offset, perforated 11.*

 RH42

 RH43

RH42

$5	multicolored	MNHVF	UseVF
		14.00	7.00
	Plate block of 4	62.50	

1976. CANADA GEESE ISSUE by Alderson Magee. *Intaglio, unwatermarked, perforated 11.*

RH43

$5	green & black	MNHVF	UseVF
		14.00	7.00
	Plate block of 4	62.50	

1977. ROSS' GEESE ISSUE by Martin R. Murk. *Combination of intaglio and offset, unwatermarked, perforated 11.*

 RH44

 RH45

RH44

$5	multicolored	MNHVF	UseVF
		14.00	7.00
	Plate block of 4	62.50	

1978. HOODED MERGANSER ISSUE by Albert Earl Gilbert. *Combination of intaglio and offset, unwatermarked, perforated 11.*

RH45

$5	multicolored	MNHVF	UseVF
		14.00	7.00
	Plate block of 4	62.50	

1979. GREEN-WINGED TEAL ISSUE by Kenneth L. Michaelsen. *Combination of intaglio and offset, unwatermarked, perforated 11.*

 RH46

 RH47

RH46

$7.50	multicolored	MNHVF	UseVF
		17.50	7.00
	Plate block of 4	55.00	

1980. MALLARDS ISSUE by Richard W. Plasschaert. *Combination of intaglio and offset, unwatermarked, perforated 11.*

RH47

$7.50	multicolored	MNHVF	UseVF
		17.50	7.00
	Plate block of 4	55.00	

1981. RUDDY DUCKS ISSUE by John S. Wilson. *Combination of intaglio and offset, unwatermarked, perforated 11.*

 RH48

 RH49

RH48

$7.50	multicolored	MNHVF	UseVF
		17.50	7.00
	Plate block of 4	75.00	

1982. CANVASBACKS ISSUE by David A. Maass. *Combination of intaglio and offset, unwatermarked, perforated 11.*

RH49

$7.50	multicolored	MNHVF	UseVF
		17.50	7.00
	Plate block of 4	75.00	

1983. PINTAILS ISSUE by Phil Scholer. *Combination of intaglio and offset, unwatermarked, perforated 11.*

 RH50

 RH51

RH50

$7.50	multicolored	MNHVF	UseVF
		17.50	7.00
	Plate block of 4	75.00	

1984. WIDGEONS ISSUE by William C. Morris. *Combination of intaglio and offset, unwatermarked, perforated 11.*

RH51

$7.50	multicolored	MNHVF	UseVF
		17.50	7.00
	Plate block of 4	75.00	

After No. RH51's period of use had expired, 15 uncut sheets of 120 (four panes of 30 stamps per sheet, separated by gutters) were overprinted "1934-84" and "50th Anniversary" along the margins. These sheets were auctioned off by the U.S. Fish and Wildlife Service, beginning Sept. 1, 1985, with a minimum acceptable bid for each sheet of $2,000. Face value of the sheets, when valid for use, was $900. Fourteen sheets were sold, and one was donated to the Smithsonian Institution. Individual stamps of the sheet cannot be differentiated from normal copies of No. RH51. Various configurations were formed from the sheets and sold to collectors: horizontal and vertical pairs with a gutter between, cross-gutter blocks of four, and margin blocks. Sheets were submitted to The Philatelic Foundation for certification prior to being broken up, and each stamp from each of the sheets has a mark of the expertizer on the reverse. With such marks in place, individual stamps not attached to a margin were sold along with configurations noted above.

1984. SPECIAL COMMEMORATIVE ISSUE

RH51a

$7.50	Special Commemorative Issue	MNHVF	UseVF
	(All examples must have P.F. certificates)		
	single	325.00	
	Plate block of 6	3,500.00	
	Center gutter block	6,000.00	
	Horizontal pair w/gutter between	750.00	
	Vertical pair w/gutter between	850.00	

1985. CINNAMON TEAL ISSUE by Gerald Mobley. *Combination of intaglio and offset, unwatermarked, perforated 11.*

 RH52

 RH53

RH52

$7.50	multicolored	MNHVF	UseVF
		17.50	7.00
	Plate block of 4	75.00	

1986. FULVOUS WHISTLING DUCK ISSUE by Burton E. Moore Jr. *Combination of intaglio and offset, unwatermarked, perforated 11.*

RH53

$7.50	multicolored	MNHVF	UseVF
		17.50	7.00
	Plate block of 4	75.00	
t.	black engraved omitted	4,000.00	—

1987. REDHEAD ISSUE by Arthur G. Anderson. *Combination of intaglio and offset, unwatermarked, perforated 11 1/2x11.*

 RH54

 RH55

RH54		MNHVF	UseVF
$10	multicolored	20.00	10.00
	Plate block of 4	90.00	

1988. SNOW GOOSE ISSUE by Daniel Smith. *Combination of intaglio and offset, unwatermarked, perforated 11 1/2x11.*

RH55		MNHVF	UseVF
$10	multicolored	20.00	7.00
	Plate block of 4	100.00	

1989. LESSER SCAUP ISSUE by Neal R. Anderson. *Combination of intaglio and offset, unwatermarked, perforated 11 1/2x11.*

 RH56

 RH57

RH56		MNHVF	UseVF
$12.50	multicolored	22.50	7.00
	Plate block of 4	100.00	

1990. BLACK-BELLIED WHISTLING DUCK ISSUE by Jim Hautman. *Combination of intaglio and offset, unwatermarked, perforated 11 1/2x11.*

RH57		MNHVF	UseVF
$12.50	multicolored	22.50	7.00
	Plate block of 4	100.00	
	v. Back printing omitted	375.00	

Note: Printing on back of stamp normally is on top of gum. No. RH57v can exist only unused. Beware of copies with gum removed.

1991. KING EIDERS ISSUE by Nancy Howe. *Combination of intaglio and offset, unwatermarked, perforated 11 1/2x11.*

 RH58

 RH59

RH58		MNHVF	UseVF
$15	multicolored	27.50	12.50
	Plate block of 4	135.00	
	t. black engraved omitted	—	

1992. SPECTACLED EIDER ISSUE by Joe Hautman, brother of Jim Hautman, whose illustration was on the 1990 stamp. *Combination of intaglio and offset, unwatermarked, perforated 11 1/2x11.*

RH59		MNHVF	UseVF
$15	multicolored	27.50	12.50
	Plate block of 4	83.00	

1993. CANVASBACK ISSUE by Bruce Miller. *Combination of intaglio and offset, unwatermarked, perforated 11 1/2x11.*

 RH60

 RH61

RH60		MNHVF	UseVF
$15	multicolored	27.50	12.50
	Plate block of 4	135.00	
	a. black engraved omitted	3,000.00	

1994. RED-BREASTED MERGANSERS ISSUE by Neal Anderson. *Combination of intaglio and offset, unwatermarked, perforated 11 1/2x11.*

RH61		MNHVF	UseVF
$15	multicolored	25.00	10.00
	Plate block of 4	135.00	

1995. MALLARD ISSUE by Jim Hautman. *Combination of intaglio and offset, unwatermarked, perforated 11 1/2x11.*

 RH62

 RH63

RH62		MNHVF	UseVF
$15	multicolored	25.00	10.00
	Plate block of 4	135.00	

1996. SURF SCOTER ISSUE by Wilhelm J. Goebel. *Combination of intaglio and offset, unwatermarked, perforated 11 1/2x11.*

RH63		MNHVF	UseVF
$15	multicolored	25.00	10.00
	Plate block of 4	135.00	

1997. CANADA GOOSE ISSUE by Robert Hautman, brother of Jim and Joe Hautman, both previous winners of the U.S. Duck Stamp contest. *Combination of intaglio and offset, unwatermarked, perforated 11 1/2x11.*

 RH64

 RH65

RH64		MNHVF	UseVF
$15	multicolored	25.00	10.00
	Plate block of 4	135.00	

1998. BARROW'S GOLDENEYE ISSUE by Robert Steiner. *Combination of intaglio and offset, unwatermarked, perforated 11 1/2x11.*

RH65		MNHVF	UseVF
$15	multicolored	25.00	10.00
	Plate block of 4	135.00	

1998. BARROW'S GOLDENEYE SELF-ADHESIVE ISSUE First in a three-year test of self-adhesive hunting permit stamps. *Serpentine die cut.*

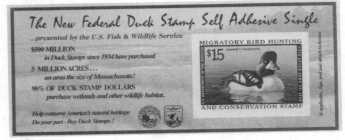 RH66

RH66		MNHVF	UseVF
$15	multicolored	30.00	15.00

1999. GREATER SCAUP ISSUE by Jim Hautman, whose illustrations were used on the 1990 and 1995 stamps. *Combination of intaglio and offset, unwatermarked, perforated 11 1/2x11.*

RH67

RH67
$15   **multicolored**
     Plate block of 4

	MNHVF	UseVF
	30.00	15.00
	135.00	

1999. GREATER SCAUP ISSUE *Serpentine die cut 10.*

RH68

RH68
$15   **multicolored**

	MNHVF	UseVF
	30.00	15.00

2000. MOTTLED DUCK ISSUE by Adam Grimm, age 21, the youngest artist to win the Federal Duck Stamp Art Competition. *Gravure by Bureau of Engraving and Printing.*

RH69 *Mottled Duck*

RH69
$15   **multicolored**
     Plate block of 4

	MNHVF	UseVF
	25.00	15.00
	100.00	

2000. MOTTLED DUCK ISSUE *Serpentine die cut.*

RH70 *Mottled Duck*

RH70
$15   **multicolored**
     FDC *(July 1, 2000)*

	MNHVF	UseVF
	25.00	15.00
		25.00

2001. NORTHERN PINTAIL ISSUE by Robert Hautman, his second win, acrylic. *Gravure by Bureau of Engraving and Printing, gummed.*

RH71 *Northern Pintail*

RH71
$15   **multicolored**
     Plate block of 4
     FDC *(June 30, 2001)*

	MNHVF	UseVF
	25.00	15.00
	100.00	
		25.00

2001. NORTHERN PINTAIL ISSUE *Gravure by Bureau of Engraving and Printing, self-adhesive, serpentine die cut.*

RH72 *Northern Pintail*

RH72
$15   **multicolored**
     FDC *(June 30, 2001)*

	MNHVF	UseVF
	25.00	15.00
		25.00

2002. BLACK SCOTER ISSUE by Joseph Hautman. *Gummed panes of 20. Perforated 11 1/4.*

RH73 *Black Scoter*

RH73
$15   **multicolored**
     Plate block of 4
     FDC *(July 1, 2002 - Washington, DC)*

	MNHVF	UseVF
	25.00	15.00
	100.00	
		25.00

2002. BLACK SCOTER ISSUE *Self-adhesive pane of 1. Serpentine die cut 11x10 3/4.*

RH74 *Black Scoter*

RH74
$15   **multicolored**
     FDC *(July 1, 2002 - Washington, DC)*

	MNHVF	UseVF
	25.00	15.00
		15.00

2003. SNOW GEESE ISSUE by Ron Louque, first time winner of the Federal Stamp Art Contest shows two Snow Geese in the skies above Chincoteaque National Wildlife Refuge. *Gummed panes of 20. Perforated 11 1/4.*

RH75 *Snow Geese*

RH75		MNHVF	UseVF
$15	multicolored	25.00	15.00
	Plate block of 4	100.00	
	FDC *(July 1, 2003 - Washington, DC)*		15.00

2003. SNOW GEESE ISSUE *Self-adhesive pane of 1. Serpentine die cut 11x10 3/4.*

RH76 *Snow Geese*

RH76		MNHVF	UseVF
$15	multicolored	25.00	
	FDC *(July 1, 2003)*		15.00

Booklets and Panes

The first postage stamp booklets issued by the United States were made more than 100 years ago, but for many years the specialty of collecting complete booklets attracted only a few collectors who had enough knowledge to build a comprehensive collection.

In 1939, Bureau Issues Association members began work on a booklet cover numbering system to replace earlier individually prepared checklists. By pooling their collections of complete booklets and reviewing the literature available, they created a system that was first published in 1955 and updated in 1975. While many collectors find the complex BIA Booklet Cover Checklist to be confusing, it remains the definitive reference required to understand the early booklets. Copies of the 1975 Booklet Cover Checklist are available for $2 from the United States Stamp Society (formerly the BIA) through David Eeles, P.O. Box 933, Columbus, OH 43216-0933.

The BIA booklet cover numbering system showed its weaknesses with the advent of folded-style booklets in 1977. While the original BIA Type Numbers worked quite well for the stapled-era booklets since the same (or similar) cover designs were often used for different booklets issued over a period of several years, the folded-style booklets all had covers with major cover differences. The old Roman numeral BIA type numbers did not work well with the frequent cover changes. So, in 1998, the BIA created a new set of cover numbers for folded-style booklets. The list, in BIA Research Paper #2, also is available for $13 from David Eeles, P.O. Box 933, Columbus, OH 43216-0933. That 100-page reference includes detailed information about all booklets issued from 1977 to date.

While collecting complete booklets was slow to catch on, interest in individual booklet panes was much greater from the start. Collectors sought out examples of panes with plate numbers in the tab or with remnants of the registration guidelines used in the manufacturing process. Early pioneers published information on them, which led to increased interest in collecting booklets as well as booklet panes.

Catalog numbers were assigned to booklet panes long before complete booklets were listed, but it wasn't until 1995 that booklets with all cover varieties were listed and priced in a major catalog. A second edition of that catalog (*The Comprehensive Catalog of United States Stamp Booklets*) was issued in 1999 by Krause Publications. And now, for the first time, a Booklet section has been added to the *Krause-Minkus Standard Catalog of U.S. Stamps.*

This booklet section is briefer than many collectors might like, but it is understandable and may be expanded as the editors receive input from collectors. It was our intent to make it as easy as possible for the average collector to use these new listings. However, with such a complex subject, it was impossible to condense all the relevant information into the listings. Collectors who want more detailed information may wish to consult the references mentioned above to increase their understanding of booklet varieties. This new section may whet your appetite.

The booklet listings are chronological in most cases. The list is a summary of all booklets and booklet panes, and, when space allows, information is included to help the reader identify the differences in the booklets and panes. Only basic information about the actual stamp (identified by Minkus number) is given since the catalog listing in the main section of this catalog goes into more detail. Throughout the booklet listings, abbreviations are used to conserve space. Most notably, "OFC" means Outside Front Cover; "IFC" means Inside Front Cover; "IBC" means Inside Back Cover; and "OBC" means Outside Back Cover. In many cases, key words or differences on a cover surface are identified in the listing, but without an actual booklet or illustration it may be hard to understand the meaning. In several cases, a number in parentheses at the end of a booklet listing indicates the number of cover varieties that exist for that booklet. Again, the reader will need to refer to the two BIA booklet cover checklists and/or the Krause *Comprehensive Catalog of United States Stamp Booklets* to fully understand all the differences.

Values of the early booklets are very difficult to establish. Precious few complete booklets survive, and they rarely trade hands. Condition of the covers (creases, stains, tears, ink notations, etc.) has a major impact on the actual value of the early booklets. Whenever possible, individual booklet panes should be collected only with the selvage tab attached. Panes without their tabs usually are regarded as space fillers and have a greatly reduced value.

There are many levels of specialization available to booklet collectors. While a beginner might feel little to offer in the way of a challenge, many people are so fascinated by the specialty that they collect booklets and booklet panes exclusively. As with all areas of stamp collecting, there really is no limit to how each of us collects stamps, but knowledge is the key to enjoying what we do collect.

1900-03. 2¢ WASHINGTON *Double-line watermark, perforated 12.*

192n

		F-VF
red or orange-red, pane of 6, horizontal double-line watermark (360 subject plates)		325.00

192n1

		F-VF
red or orange-red, pane of 6, vertical double-line watermark (180 subject plates)		325.00

B1

		F-VF
25¢ book, black on tan, no 25¢ in corners, "Puerto Rico" on OFC		6,000.00

B2

| **25¢ book, black** on tan, no 25¢ in corners, "Porto Rico" on OFC | | F-VF 6,000.00 |

B3

| **25¢ book, black** on tan, 25¢ in corners, Special Delivery on IFC, SMITH | | F-VF 5,000.00 |

B3a

| **25¢ book, black** on tan, 25¢ in corners, Special Delivery on IFC, PAYNE | | F-VF 5,000.00 |

B4

```
POST OFFICE DEPARTMENT, U. S. A.
25c. —THIS BOOK CONTAINS 12 TWO-CENT STAMPS— 25c.
            PRICE, 25 CENTS.
          DOMESTIC POSTAGE RATES.
(Apply to Guam, Hawaii, Philippines, Porto Rico, Tutuila, and
to Canada, Cuba, and Mexico.)
First-class.  Letters and sealed matter: 2 cts. for each ounce
         or fraction.  Postal cards, 1 ct. each.
Second-class. Newspapers and periodicals: 1 ct. for each four
         ounces or fraction.
Third-class.  Miscellaneous printed matter: 1 ct. for each two
         ounces or fraction.
Fourth-class. All matter not included in first three classes:
         1 ct. for each ounce or fraction
Special-delivery.  A special-delivery stamp, in addition to post-
         age, secures immediate delivery at any United
         States post office.
```

B4

| **25¢ book, black** on tan, 25¢ in corners, Special Delivery on OFC | | F-VF 5,000.00 |

B5

| **49¢ book, green** on tan, no 49¢ in corners, "Puerto Rico" on OFC | | F-VF 7,000.00 |

B6

| **49¢ book, black** on buff, no 49¢ in corners, "Porto Rico" on OFC | | F-VF 7,500.00 |

B7

| **49¢ book, black** on buff, 49¢ in corners, Special Delivery on IFC, SMITH | | F-VF 5,500.00 |

B7a

| **49¢ book, black** on buff, 49¢ in corners, Special Delivery on IFC, PAYNE | | F-VF 5,500.00 |

B8

| **49¢ book, black** on buff, 49¢ in corners, Special Delivery on OFC | | F-VF 8,500.00 |

B9

| **97¢ book, red** on tan, no 97¢ in corners, "Puerto Rico" on OFC | | F-VF 12,000.00 |

B10

| **97¢ book, black** on gray, no 97¢ in corners, "Porto Rico" on OFC | | F-VF 11,000.00 |

B11

| **97¢ book, black** on gray, 97¢ in corners, Special Delivery on IFC, SMITH | | F-VF 9,000.00 |

B11a

| **97¢ book, black** on gray, 97¢ in corners, Special Delivery on IFC, PAYNE | | F-VF 9,000.00 |

B12

| **97¢ book, black** on gray, 97¢ in corners, Special Delivery on OFC | | F-VF 9,000.00 |

1907. 1¢ FRANKLIN (PORTRAIT) *double-line watermark, perforated 12.*

211n

| **blue-green,** pane of 6 | | F-VF 425.00 |

B13

| **25¢ book, black** on green, CORTELYOU | | F-VF 6,500.00 |

B13a

| **black** on green, MEYER on OBC (5) | | F-VF 6,500.00 |

(Number in parentheses after a booklet listing indicates multiple cover varieties exist.)

1903. 2¢ WASHINGTON (FLAGS) *Double-line watermark, perforated 12.*

212n

| **carmine,** pane of 6 | | F-VF 400.00 |

B14

| **25¢ book, black** on tan, PAYNE is Postmaster General on OBC | | F-VF 3,500.00 |

B15

| **49¢ book, black** on buff, PAYNE is Postmaster General on OBC | | F-VF 6,000.00 |

B16

| **97¢ book, black** on gray, PAYNE is Postmaster General on OBC | | F-VF 12,000.00 |

1903. 2¢ WASHINGTON (SHIELD) *Double-line watermark, perforated 12.*

231n

| **carmine,** Type I pane of 6 | | F-VF 100.00 |

231n1

| **vermilion,** Type I pane of 6 | | F-VF — |

231n2

| **red,** Type I pane of 6 | | F-VF — |

231n3

| **carmine-rose,** Type I pane of 6 | | F-VF 150.00 |

231n4

| **scarlet (red-orange),** Type I pane of 6 | | F-VF 200.00 |

231n5

| **lake,** Type I pane of 6 | | F-VF 2,500.00 |

231an

| **carmine,** Type II pane of 6 | | F-VF 150.00 |

231an1

| **lake,** Type II pane of 6 | | F-VF 175.00 |

B17

| **25¢ book, black** on tan, 3-line Special Delivery on OFC, PAYNE | | F-VF 1,000.00 |

B17a

| **25¢ book, black** on tan, 4-line Special Delivery on OFC, WYNNE | | F-VF 1,000.00 |

B17a1

| **25¢ book, black** on tan, No Canal Zone on OFC, CORTELYOU (3) | | F-VF 1,500.00 |

B17b

| **25¢ book, black** on tan, Canal Zone on OFC, CORTELYOU | | F-VF 2,000.00 |

B17b1

| **25¢ book, black** on tan, 4-line Special Delivery on OFC, MEYER (5) | | F-VF 1,000.00 |

B18

| **49¢ book, black** on buff, 3-line Special Delivery on OFC, PAYNE | | F-VF 1,500.00 |

B18a

| **49¢ book, black** on buff, 4-line Special Delivery on OFC, PAYNE | | F-VF — |

B18a1

| **49¢ book, black** on buff, 4-line Special Delivery on OFC, WYNNE | | F-VF 1,500.00 |

B18a2

| **49¢ book, black** on buff, No Canal Zone on OFC, CORTELYOU (3) | | F-VF 2,000.00 |

B18b

| **49¢ book, black** on buff, Canal Zone on OFC, CORTELYOU | | F-VF 2,000.00 |

B18b1

| **49¢ book, black** on buff, 4-line Special Delivery on OFC, MEYER (5) | | F-VF 1,500.00 |

B19
	F-VF
49¢ book, **black** on pink, 4-line Special Delivery on OFC, MEYER	2,000.00

B20
	F-VF
97¢ book, **black** on gray, 3-line Special Delivery on OFC, PAYNE	3,500.00

B20a
	F-VF
97¢ book, **black** on gray, 4-line Special Delivery on OFC, WYNNE	3,500.00

B20a1
	F-VF
97¢ book, **black** on gray, No Canal Zone on OFC, CORTELYOU (3)	4,000.00

B20b
	F-VF
97¢ book, **black** on gray, Canal Zone on OFC, CORTELYOU	4,000.00

B20b1
	F-VF
97¢ book, **black** on gray, 4-line Special Delivery on OFC, MEYER (5)	3,500.00

1908. 1¢ FRANKLIN (PROFILE) *Double-line watermark, perforated 12.*

237n
	F-VF
green, pane of 6	140.00

B21
	F-VF
25¢ book, **black** on green, text on OFC (3)	2,000.00

B22
	F-VF
25¢ book, **black** on green, pictorial OFC (Post Rider insignia)	2,500.00

1908. 2¢ WASHINGTON (PROFILE) *Double-line watermark, perforated 12.*

238n
	F-VF
carmine, pane of 6, denomination shown as "TWO CENTS"	125.00

B23
	F-VF
25¢ book, **black** on tan, text on OFC (2)	1,250.00

B24
	F-VF
25¢ book, **black** on tan, pictorial OFC (Post Rider insignia)	1,250.00

B25
	F-VF
49¢ book, **black** on buff, text on OFC (2)	2,500.00

B26
	F-VF
49¢ book, **black** on pink, text on OFC	2,500.00

B27

B27
	F-VF
49¢ book, **black** on pink, pictorial OFC (Post Rider insignia)	2,000.00

B28
	F-VF
97¢ book, **black** on gray, text on OFC (3)	3,000.00

B29
	F-VF
97¢ book, **black** on gray, pictorial OFC (Post Rider insignia)	3,000.00

1910. 1¢ FRANKLIN *Single-line watermark, perforated 12.*

273n
	F-VF
green, pane of 6	125.00

B30
	F-VF
25¢ book, **black** on green, Post Rider insignia on OFC (2)	1,750.00

1910. 2¢ WASHINGTON *Single-line watermark, perforated 12.*

274n
	F-VF
carmine, pane of 6, denomination shown as "TWO CENTS"	100.00

B31
	F-VF
25¢ book, **black** on tan, Post Rider insignia on OFC (2)	975.00

B32
	F-VF
49¢ book, **black** on pink, Post Rider insignia on OFC (2)	2,000.00

B33
	F-VF
97¢ book, **black** on gray, Post Rider insignia on OFC (2)	3,500.00

1912. 1¢ WASHINGTON *Single-line watermark, perforated 12.*

297n
	F-VF
green, pane of 6	65.00

B34
	F-VF
25¢ book, **black** on green, Post Rider insignia on OFC (2)	1,250.00

B35
	F-VF
25¢ book, **green** on green, Washington Post Office on OFC (3)	1,200.00

B36
	F-VF
97¢ book, **green** on lavender, Washington Post Office on OFC	1,750.00

B43
	F-VF
73¢ combination book (4-297n & 4-298n panes), **red** on white	3,000.00

1912. 2¢ WASHINGTON *Single-line watermark, perforated 12.*

298n
	F-VF
carmine, pane of 6, denomination shown as "2 CENTS 2"	65.00

B37
	F-VF
25¢ book, **black** on tan, 33mm Post Rider insignia on OFC (2)	1,000.00

B37a
	F-VF
25¢ book, **black** on tan, patented grilled wax paper interleaves	5,000.00

B38
	F-VF
25¢ book, **red** on yellow, 27mm Post Rider insignia on OFC (3)	1,000.00

B39
	F-VF
49¢ book, **black** on pink, 33mm Post Rider insignia on OFC (2)	1,750.00

B40
	F-VF
49¢ book, **red** on pink, 27mm Post Rider insignia on OFC (3)	2,000.00

B41
	F-VF
97¢ book, **black** on gray, 33mm Post Rider insignia on OFC (2)	3,000.00

B42
	F-VF
97¢ book, **red** on blue, 27mm Post Rider insignia on OFC (3)	3,000.00

B43
	F-VF
73¢ combination book (4-297n & 4-298n panes), **red** on white	3,000.00

(Number in parentheses after a booklet listing indicates multiple cover varieties exist.)

1914. 1¢ WASHINGTON *Single-line watermark, perforated 10.*

315n
	F-VF
green, pane of 6	4.00

B44

B44

		F-VF
	25¢ **book, green** on green, Washington Post Office on OFC (3)	350.00

B45

		F-VF
	97¢ **book, green** on lavender, Washington Post Office on OFC	110.00

B49

		F-VF
	73¢ **combination book (4-315n & 4-316n panes), red** on white (3)	350.00

1914. 2¢ WASHINGTON *Single-line watermark, perforated 10.*

316n

		F-VF
	carmine, pane of 6	22.00

B46

		F-VF
	25¢ **book, red** on yellow, Post Rider insignia on OFC (3)	500.00

B47

		F-VF
	49¢ **book, red** on pink, Post Rider insignia on OFC (3)	1,000.00

B48

		F-VF
	97¢ **book, red** on blue, Post Rider insignia on OFC (3)	1,500.00

B49

		F-VF
	73¢ **combination book (4-315n & 4-316n panes), red** on white (3)	350.00

1916. 1¢ WASHINGTON *Unwatermarked, perforated 10.*

348n

		F-VF
	green, pane of 6	10.00

B50

		F-VF
	25¢ **book, green** on green, Washington Post Office on OFC	750.00

B51

		F-VF
	97¢ **book, green** on lavender, Washington Post Office on OFC	500.00

B55

		F-VF
	73¢ **combination book (4-348n & 4-349n panes), red** on white (2)	1,000.00

1916. 2¢ WASHINGTON *Unwatermarked, perforated 10.*

349n

		F-VF
	carmine, pane of 6	85.00

B52

		F-VF
	25¢ **book, red** on buff, Post Rider insignia on OFC	750.00

B53

		F-VF
	49¢ **book, red** on pink, Post Rider insignia on OFC	1,500.00

B54

		F-VF
	97¢ **book, red** on blue, Post Rider insignia on OFC	2,500.00

B55

		F-VF
	73¢ **combination book (4-348n & 4-349n panes), red** on white (2)	1,000.00

1917. 1¢ WASHINGTON *Unwatermarked, perforated 11.*

380n

		F-VF
	green, pane of 6	3.00

B56

		F-VF
	25¢ **book, green** on green, Washington Post Office on OFC (2)	500.00

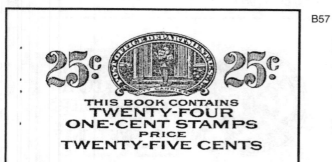

B57

B57

		F-VF
	25¢ **book, green** on green, City Mail Carrier in 32x20mm oval on OFC	150.00

B58

		F-VF
	25¢ **book, green** on green, City Mail Carrier in 29x18mm oval on OFC (4)	75.00

B59

		F-VF
	97¢ **book, green (or blue)** on lavender, Washington Post Office (4)	500.00

B66

		F-VF
	73¢ **combination book (4-380n & 4-381n panes), red** on white (4)	100.00

B76

		F-VF
	73¢ **combination book (4-380n & 4-421n panes), red** on white (3)	120.00

1917. 2¢ WASHINGTON *Unwatermarked, perforated 11.*

381n

		F-VF
	carmine, pane of 6	5.00

B60

		F-VF
	25¢ **book, red** on buff, 27mm Post Rider insignia on OFC (2)	350.00

B61

		F-VF
	25¢ **book, red** on buff, 25mm Post Rider insignia on OFC (3)	500.00

B62

		F-VF
	49¢ **book, red** on pink, 27mm Post Rider insignia on OFC (2)	750.00

B63

		F-VF
	49¢ **book, red** on pink, 25mm Post Rider insignia on OFC (2)	500.00

B64

		F-VF
	97¢ **book, red** on blue, 27mm Post Rider insignia on OFC (2)	750.00

B64a

		F-VF
	97¢ **book, red** on blue, 25mm Post Rider insignia on OFC	1,000.00

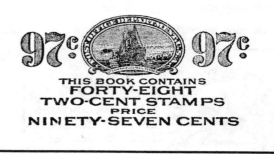

B65

B65

		F-VF
	97¢ **book, red** on blue, Steamship & Mail Tender on OFC (2)	1,500.00

B66

		F-VF
	73¢ **combination book (4-380n & 4-381n panes), red** on white (4)	100.00

1918. 1¢ WASHINGTON (AEF) *Unwatermarked, perforated 11.*

380n1

		F-VF
	green, pane of 30, tab at left or right, positions W1, 2, 3, or 4	1,000.00

380n1a

		F-VF
	green, pane of 30, tab at left or right, guideline at bottom (W5 or 6)	1,250.00

380n1b

		F-VF
	green, pane of 30, initials in tab at left or right, position W11 or 12	1,250.00

B67

		F-VF
	$3.00 **book, black** on green, "300/1 CENT POSTAGE STAMPS/$3"	15,000.00

B67x

		F-VF
	Empty $3.00 booklet, black on green, covers and interleaving only	750.00

1918. 2¢ WASHINGTON (AEF) *Unwatermarked, perforated 11.*

		F-VF
381n1	**rose,** pane of 30, tab at left or right, positions W1, 2, 3, or 4	25,000.00
381n1a	**rose,** pane of 30, tab at left or right, guideline at bottom (W5 or 6)	—
381n1b	**rose,** pane of 30, initials in tab at left or right, position W11 or 12	—
B68	**$6.00 book, black** on pink, "300/2 CENT POSTAGE STAMPS/$6"	—
B68x	**Empty $6.00 booklet, black** on pink, covers and interleaving only	2,000.00

1917-18. 3¢ WASHINGTON *Unwatermarked, perforated 11.*

		F-VF
382n	**violet,** Type I pane of 6	60.00
382An	**violet,** Type II pane of 6	50.00

B69

		F-VF
B69	**37¢ book, violet** on sage, Type I panes, (offset printed covers)	750.00
B70	**37¢ book, violet** on sage, Type II panes, (electrotype printed covers)	175.00

1923. 1¢ FRANKLIN *perforated 11 (flat plate).*

		F-VF
419n	**deep green,** pane of 6	7.00
B71	**25¢ book, green** on green, City Mail Carrier in 29x18mm oval (2)	75.00
B72	**97¢ book, green** on lavender, Washington Post Office (3)	750.00
B77	**73¢ combination book (4-419n & 4-421n panes), red** on white (3)	100.00

1923. 2¢ WASHINGTON *Perforated 11 (flat plate).*

		F-VF
421n	**carmine,** pane of 6	9.00
B73	**25¢ book, red** on buff, 25mm Post Rider insignia on OFC (4)	500.00
B74	**49¢ book, red** on pink, 25mm Post Rider insignia on OFC (4)	1,000.00
B75	**97¢ book, red** on blue, Steamship & Mail Tender on OFC (3)	1,750.00
B76	**73¢ combination book (4-380n & 4-421n panes), red** on white (3)	120.00
B77	**73¢ combination book (4-419n & 4-421n panes), red** on white (3)	100.00

1926. 2¢ WASHINGTON *Perforated 10 (rotary press).*

		F-VF
452n	**carmine,** pane of 6	75.00
B78	**25¢ book, red** on buff, Post Rider insignia on OFC (3)	500.00
B79	**49¢ book, red** on pink, Post Rider insignia on OFC	1,000.00
B80	**97¢ book, red** on blue, Steamship & Mail Tender on OFC	1,750.00

1927. 1¢ FRANKLIN *Perforated 11x10 1/2 (rotary press).*

		F-VF
474n	**green,** pane of 6	6.00
B81	**25¢ book, green** on green, Post Rider insignia on OFC (3)	65.00
B81a	**25¢ book, green** on green, Post Rider insignia, glassine interleaves	—
B82	**97¢ book, green** on lavender, Washington Post Office on OFC	500.00
B82a	**97¢ book, green** on lavender, Washington Post Office, glassine interleaves	—
B83	**97¢ book, green** on lavender, Post Rider insignia on OFC	500.00
B89	**73¢ combination book (4-474n & 4-476n panes), red** on white, Washington Post Office	500.00
B90	**73¢ combination book (4-474n & 4-476n panes), red** on white, 27mm Post Rider insignia	100.00
B90A	**73¢ combination book (4-474a & 4-476n panes), red** on white, 27mm Post Rider insignia, glassine interleaves	—
B91	**73¢ combination book (4-474n & 4-476n panes), red** on white, 24mm Post Rider insignia (2)	100.00

1927. 2¢ WASHINGTON *Perforated 11x10.5 (rotary press).*

		F-VF
476n	**carmine,** pane of 6	2.00
B84	**25¢ book, red** on buff, Post Rider insignia, wax paper interleaves (2)	7.00
B84a	**25¢ book, red** on buff, Post Rider insignia, glassine interleaves	—
B84b	**25¢ book, red** on buff, Post Rider insignia, cellophane interleaves	500.00
B85	**49¢ book, red** on pink, Post Rider insignia on OFC (2)	15.00
B86	**97¢ book, red** on blue, 25mm Post Rider insignia on OFC	175.00
B87	**97¢ book, red** on blue, 23mm Post Rider insignia on OFC (2)	30.00
B88	**97¢ book, red** on blue, Steamship & Mail Tender on OFC	750.00
B89	**73¢ combination book (4-474n & 4-476n panes), red** on white, Washington Post Office	500.00

B90

73¢ combination book (4-474n & 4-476n
panes), red on white, 27mm Post
Rider insignia

F-VF
100.00

B90a

73¢ combination book (4-474n & 4-476n
panes), red on white, 27mm Post
Rider insignia, glassine interleaves

F-VF
—

*(Number in parenthesis after a booklet listing indicates multiple cover
varieties exist).*

B91

73¢ combination book (4-474n & 4-476n
panes), red on white, 24mm Post
Rider insignia (2)

F-VF
100.00

1932. 3¢ WASHINGTON *(Stuart).*
518n

deep violet, pane of 6

F-VF
35.00

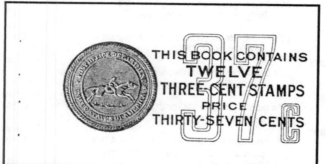

B92

B92

37¢ book, violet on buff, Post Rider wax
seal on OFC (2)

F-VF
85.00

B92a

37¢ book, violet on buff, Post Rider wax
seal on OFC, cellophane interleaves

F-VF
700.00

B93

73¢ book, violet on pink, Post Rider wax
seal on OFC (2)

F-VF
250.00

1939. 1¢ WASHINGTON *(pre-EE plates — 3mm gutter).*
525n

green, pane of 6

F-VF
3.00

B94

25¢ book, green on green, Post Rider
insignia on OFC

F-VF
45.00

B95

97¢ book, green on lavender, Post Rider
insignia on OFC

F-VF
500.00

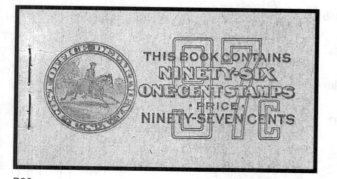

B96

B96

97¢ book, green on lavender, Washington
Post Office on OFC

F-VF
2,000.00

B98

73¢ combination book (4-525n & 4-527n
panes), red on white

F-VF
110.00

1939. 2¢ ADAMS *(pre-EE plates — 3mm gutter).*
527n

rose carmine, pane of 6

F-VF
6.00

B97

97¢ book, red on blue or blue-green, Post
Rider insignia on OFC

F-VF
30.00

B98

73¢ combination book (4-525n & 4-527n
panes), red on white

F-VF
110.00

1939. 3¢ JEFFERSON *(pre-EE plates — 3mm gutter).*
528n

deep violet, pane of 6

F-VF
10.00

B99

37¢ book, red on blue, Post Rider insignia
on OFC

F-VF
65.00

B100

73¢ book, violet on pink, Post Rider
insignia on OFC

F-VF
950.00

1942. 1¢ WASHINGTON *(EE plates — 2.5mm gutter).*
525n1

green, pane of 6

F-VF
2.00

B101

25¢ book, green on green, Post Rider wax
seal on OFC

F-VF
45.00

B102

97¢ book, green on lavender, Post Rider
wax seal on OFC

F-VF
500.00

B108

73¢ combination book (4-525n1 &
4-527n1 panes), red on white, 25mm
insignia on OFC

F-VF
65.00

B109

73¢ combination book (4-525n1 &
4-527n1 panes), red on white, 23mm
insignia on OFC

F-VF
65.00

B110

73¢ combination book (4-525n1 &
4-527n1 panes), red on white, 23mm
wax seal on OFC

F-VF
28.00

1942. 2¢ ADAMS *(EE plates — 2.5mm gutter).*
527n1

rose carmine, pane of 6

F-VF
6.00

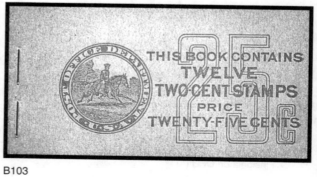

B103

B103

25¢ book, red on buff, Post Rider insignia
on OFC

F-VF
15.00

B104

25¢ book, red on buff, Post Rider wax seal
on OFC

F-VF
75.00

B105

49¢ book, red on pink, Post Rider insignia
on OFC

F-VF
15.00

B106

49¢ book, red on pink, Post Rider wax
seal on OFC

F-VF
15.00

B107

97¢ book, red on blue, Post Rider insignia on OFC   F-VF 1,000.00

B108

73¢ combination book (4-525n1 & 4-527n1 panes), red on white, 25mm insignia on OFC   F-VF 65.00

B109

73¢ combination book (4-525n1 & 4-527n1 panes), red on white, 23mm insignia on OFC   F-VF 65.00

B110

73¢ combination book (4-525n1 & 4-527n1 panes), red on white, 23mm wax seal on OFC   F-VF 28.00

1942. 3¢ JEFFERSON *(EE plates — 2.5mm gutter).*

528n1

deep violet, pane of 6   F-VF 7.00

B111

37¢ book, violet on buff, Post Rider seal on OFC, OSWEGO on IFC   F-VF 30.00

B111a

37¢ book, violet on buff, Post Rider seal on OFC, SAINT LOUIS on IFC   F-VF 15.00

B111b

37¢ book, violet on buff, Post Rider seal on OFC, blank IFC & IBC   F-VF 1,000.00

B112

73¢ book, violet on buff, Post Rider seal on OFC, OSWEGO on IFC   F-VF 50.00

B112a

73¢ book, violet on buff, Post Rider seal on OFC, SAINT LOUIS on IFC   F-VF 35.00

B112b

73¢ book, violet on buff, Post Rider seal on OFC, blank IFC & IBC   F-VF 2,000.00

1954. 3¢ STATUE OF LIBERTY *(wet printed).*

573n

deep violet, pane of 6   F-VF 4.00

B113

37¢ book, violet on buff, Post Rider wax seal on OFC   F-VF 12.00

B114

73¢ book, violet on pink, Post Rider wax seal on OFC   F-VF 17.00

1956. 3¢ STATUE OF LIBERTY *(dry printed).*

573pn

deep violet, pane of 6   F-VF 5.00

B115

37¢ book, violet on buff, Post Rider wax seal on OFC   F-VF 13.00

B116

73¢ book, violet on pink, Post Rider wax seal on OFC   F-VF 20.00

1958. 4¢ LINCOLN

574n

red violet, pane of 6   F-VF 2.00

B117

97¢ book, violet on buff, black 97¢ overprinted on 37¢ Post Rider OFC   F-VF 50.00

B118

97¢ book, violet on buff, black 97¢ overprinted on 73¢ Post Rider OFC   F-VF 25.00

B119

97¢ book, blue on yellow, Post Rider wax seal on OFC   F-VF 85.00

B120

97¢ book, blue on pink, THEIR TOWN model form of address on IBC   F-VF 25.00

B120a

97¢ book, blue on pink, experimental silicone interleaving, text on IFC   F-VF 80.00

B120b

97¢ book, blue on pink, HIS TOWN model form of address on IBC   F-VF 10.00

(Refer to BIA Booklet Cover Checklist for detailed information on cover varieties.)

1962. 5¢ WASHINGTON *(Slogan 1).*

604n1

gray blue, pane of 5 plus label ("Your Mailman"), untagged   F-VF 3.00

B121

$1.00 book (4-604n1), blue on white, Post Rider seal on OFC   F-VF 25.00

1963. 5¢ WASHINGTON *(Slogan 2).*

604n2

gray blue, pane of 5 plus label ("Use Zone Numbers"), untagged   F-VF 20.00

604n2p

Pane of 5, plus label ("Zone Numbers"), Hi-Brite paper,   F-VF 30.00

604n2z

Pane of 5, plus label ("Zone Numbers"), tagged   F-VF 80.00

B122

$1.00 book (604n2), blue on white, Post Rider seal on OFC   F-VF 100.00

B122a

$1.00 book (604n2p), blue on white, Post Rider seal on OFC   F-VF 150.00

B123

$1.00 book (604n2), blue on white, Mr. Zip on OFC   F-VF 65.00

B123a

$1.00 book (604n2p), blue on white, Mr. Zip on OFC   F-VF 100.00

B125

$1.00 book (604n2z), blue on white, Mr. Zip on OFC   F-VF 300.00

1964. 5¢ WASHINGTON *(Slogan 3).*

604n3

gray blue, pane of 5 plus label ("Use Zip Code"), untagged   F-VF 4.00

604n3p

Pane of 5, plus label ("Use Zip Code") Hi-Brite paper   F-VF 7.00

604n3z

Pane of 5, plus label ("Use Zip Code"), tagged   F-VF 2.50

B124

$1.00 book (604n3), blue on white, domestic rate chart on IFC   F-VF 12.00

B124a

$1.00 book (604n3p), blue on white, domestic rate chart on IFC   F-VF 250.00

B124b

$1.00 book (604n3), blue on white, Better Mail Services on IFC   F-VF 90.00

B124c

$1.00 book (604n3), blue on white, Minuteman IFC, 79373 OBC   F-VF 35.00

B124d

$1.00 book (604n3), blue on white, Minuteman IFC, 00000 OBC   F-VF 800.00

B126

$1.00 book (604n3z), blue on white, domestic rate chart on IFC   F-VF 15.00

B126a

$1.00 book (604n3z), blue on white, Better Mail Services on IFC   F-VF 30.00

B126b

$1.00 book (604n3z), blue on white, Minuteman IFC, 79373 OBC   F-VF 50.00

B126c

$1.00 book (604n3z), blue on white, Minuteman IFC, 00000 OBC   F-VF 8.00

1967. 6¢ ROOSEVELT *(pane of 8).*

622nz

	F-VF
black-brown, pane of 8 (320 or 400 subject plates)	1.50

B127

	F-VF
$2.00 book (4-622nz & 1-616n), brown on white, 100 dots/inch OFC	7.75

B127a

	F-VF
$2.00 book (4-622nz & 1-616n), brown on white, 130 dots/inch OFC	7.75

1968. 1¢ JEFFERSON *(pane of 8).*

616n

	F-VF
green, pane of 8 with shiny gum (320 or 400 subject plates)	1.00

616nm

	F-VF
green, pane of 8 with dull-finish gum (400 subject plates)	2.00

B127

	F-VF
$2.00 book (4-622nz & 1-616n), brown on white, 100 dots/inch OFC	7.75

B127a

	F-VF
$2.00 book (4-622nz & 1-616n), brown on white, 130 dots/inch OFC	7.75

B129

	F-VF
$2.00 book (4-652n & 1-616n), blue on white, Post Rider seal OFC	8.50

B130

	F-VF
$2.00 book (4-652n & 1-616n), blue on white, 27.5mm portrait OFC	6.00

B130a

	F-VF
$2.00 book (4-652n & 1-616n), blue on white, 29mm portrait OFC	750.00

B132

	F-VF
$2.00 book (4-652nm & 1-616nm), blue on white, experiment IFC	6.00

B132a

	F-VF
$2.00 book (4-652nm & 1-616nm), blue on white, envelope IFC	100.00

1968. 6¢ ROOSEVELT *(pane of 5).*

622n1z

	F-VF
black-brown, pane of 5 plus Slogan 4 label ("Mail Early")	1.25

622n2z

	F-VF
black-brown, pane of 5 plus Slogan 5 label ("Use Zip Code")	1.25

B128

	F-VF
$1.00 book (3-622n1z or 622n2z & 1-618n1 or 618n2), brown on white, Minuteman on IFC	7.00

B128a

	F-VF
$1.00 book (3-622n1z or 622n2z & 1-618n1 or 618n2), brown on white, envelope on IFC	7.00

1968. 2¢ FRANK LLOYD WRIGHT *(pane of 5).*

618n1

	F-VF
blue-gray, pane of 5 plus Slogan 4 label ("Mail Early"), shiny gum	1.25

618n2

	F-VF
blue-gray, pane of 5 plus Slogan 5 label ("Use Zip Code"), shiny gum	1.25

B128

	F-VF
$1.00 book (3-622n1z or 622n2z & 1-618n1 or 618n2), brown on white, Minuteman on IFC	7.00

B128a

	F-VF
$1.00 book (3-622n1z or 622n2z & 1-618n1 or 618n2), brown on white, envelope on IFC	7.00

B131

	F-VF
$1.00 book (3-652n1 or 652n2 & 1-618n1 or 618n2), blue on white	7.50

1970. 6¢ EISENHOWER *(pane of 5).*

652n1

	F-VF
blue, pane of 5 plus Slogan 4 label ("Mail Early")	1.25

652n2

	F-VF
blue, pane of 5 plus Slogan 5 label ("Use Zip Code")	1.25

B131

	F-VF
$1.00 book (3-652n1 or 652n2 & 1-618n1 or 618n2), blue on white	7.50

1970. 6¢ EISENHOWER *(pane of 8).*

652n

	F-VF
blue, pane of 8 with shiny gum	1.25

652nm

	F-VF
blue, pane of 8 with experimental dull-finish gum	1.50

B129

	F-VF
$2.00 book (4-652n & 1-616n), blue on white, Post Rider seal OFC	8.50

B130

B130

	F-VF
$2.00 book (4-652n & 1-616n), blue on white, 27.5mm portrait OFC	6.00

B130a

	F-VF
$2.00 book (4-652n & 1-616n), blue on white, 29mm portrait OFC	750.00

B132

	F-VF
$2.00 book (4-652nm & 1-616nm), blue on white, experiment IFC	6.00

B132a

	F-VF
$2.00 book (4-652nm & 1-616nm), blue on white, envelope IFC	100.00

1971. 1¢ JEFFERSON *(pane of 4).*

616n1

	F-VF
green, pane of 4 plus two labels (Slogans 5 and 4)	.75

B134

	F-VF
$1.00 book (2-663An4 & 1-616n1), claret on white, 29mm clock IBC	4.00

B134a

	F-VF
$1.00 book (2-663An4 & 1-616n1), claret on white, 27mm clock IBC	4.00

1971. 8¢ EISENHOWER *(pane of 6).*

663An4

	F-VF
reddish-brown, pane of 6, shiny gum	1.25

B134

B134

	F-VF
$1.00 book (2-663An4 & 1-616n1), claret on white, 29mm clock IBC	4.00

B134a
$1.00 book (2-663An4 & 1-616n1), claret — F-VF 4.00
on white, 27mm clock IBC

1971. 8¢ EISENHOWER (pane of 8).
663An
reddish-brown, pane of 8, shiny gum — F-VF 1.25

B133
$1.92 book (3-663An), claret on white, — F-VF 6.50
33mm clock on IBC

B133a
$1.92 book (3-663An), claret on white, — F-VF 6.50
31mm clock on IBC

1972. 8¢ EISENHOWER (pane of 7).
663An1
reddish-brown, pane of 7 plus Slogan 4 — F-VF 1.75
label ("Mail Early"), dull-finish gum

663An2
reddish-brown, pane of 7 plus Slogan 5 — F-VF 1.75
label ("Use Zip Code"), dull-finish gum

B135

B135
$2.00 book (1-663An3, 2-663An2 & — F-VF 7.00
1-663An1), claret on yellow

1972. 8¢ EISENHOWER (pane of 4).
663An3
reddish-brown, pane of 4 plus two — F-VF 1.75
double-size message labels (Slogans
6 & 7), dull-finish gum

B135
$2.00 book (1-663An3, 2-663An2 & — F-VF 7.00
1-663An1), claret on yellow

1973. 10¢ JEFFERSON MEMORIAL (pane of 8).
678n2
blue, pane of 8 — F-VF 1.75

B136
$4.00 book (5-678n2), red & blue on — F-VF 8.50
white

1973. 10¢ JEFFERSON MEMORIAL (pane of 5).
678n
blue, pane of 5 plus Slogan 8 label — F-VF 3.50
("Paying bills?")

B137
$1.00 book (2-678n), blue on white (red & — F-VF 3.50
blue print on OBC)

1974. 10¢ JEFFERSON MEMORIAL (pane of 6).
678n1
blue, pane of 6 — F-VF 5.00

B138
$1.25 combination book (1-A85n & — F-VF 7.25
1-678n1), red & blue on white

1971-75. 2¢ FRANK LLOYD WRIGHT (pane of 6).
618n
blue-gray, pane of 6 with shiny gum — F-VF 1.00
(above pane was only used as a filler in
airmail books with 11¢ stamps)

618nm
blue-gray, pane of 6 with dull-finish gum — F-VF 1.00

BA24
$1.00 book (2-A78n & 1-618n), red on — F-VF 5.00
white, 29mm clock IBC

BA24a
$1.00 book (2-A78n & 1-618n), red on — F-VF 5.00
white, 27mm clock IBC

1975. 13¢ LIBERTY BELL (pane of 6).
695n
brown, pane of 6 — F-VF 1.00

B139

B139
$.90 book (1-695n & 1-618nm), red & — F-VF 3.00
blue on white, "$10" OBC

B139a
$.90 book (1-695n & 1-618nm), red & — F-VF 100.00
blue on white, "$10.00" OBC

1975. 13¢ LIBERTY BELL (pane of 7).
695n1
brown, pane of 7 plus Slogan 8 label — F-VF 1.75
("Paying bills?")

B140
$2.99 book (1-695n1 & 2-695n2), red & — F-VF 6.00
blue on white, "$10" OBC

B140a
$2.99 book (1-695n1 & 2-695n2), red & — F-VF 15.00
blue on white, "$20" OBC

1975. 13¢ LIBERTY BELL (pane of 8).
695n2
brown, pane of 8 — F-VF 2.00

B140
$2.99 book (1-695n1 & 2-695n2), red & — F-VF 6.00
blue on white, "$10" OBC

B140a
$2.99 book (1-695n1 & 2-695n2), red & — F-VF 15.00
blue on white, "$20" OBC

1976. 13¢ LIBERTY BELL (pane of 5).
695n3
brown, pane of 5 plus Slogan 9 label (solid — F-VF 1.50
print "Collect Stamps")

695n3a
brown, pane of 5 plus Slogan 9 label — F-VF 5.00
(matrix print "Collect Stamps")

B141
$1.30 book (2-695n3), red & blue on — F-VF 3.00
white

B141a
$1.30 book (2-695n3a), red & blue on — F-VF 10.00
white

1977. 9¢ CAPITOL DOME/13¢ FLAG OVER CAPITOL Perforated
11x10 1/2.
703n
Pane of 8 (1 No. 702 - green, 7 No. 703 - — F-VF 2.75
red & blue), perforated 11x10 1/2

B142

		F-VF
B142	**$1.00 book, red & light blue** on white, screen printed cover	3.00
B142a	**$1.00 book, red & light blue** on white, solid printed cover, $10 Deposit on OBC	3.00
B142b	**$1.00 book, red & light blue** on white, solid printed cover, $20 Deposit on OBC	5.00
B142v	**$1.00 book,** red omitted on OFC	100.00

1977. 9¢ Capitol Dome/13¢ Flag over Capitol *Perforated 10.*

		F-VF
703An	Pane of 8 (1 No. 702 - green & 7 No. 703 - red & blue), perforated 10, between 2nd & 3rd rows	29.00
703An1	Pane of 8 (1 No. 702A - green & 7 No. 703A - red & blue), perforated 10, folded between 1st & 2nd rows (no selvage tab on pane)	100.00
B143	**$1.00 book, red & light blue** on white, screen printed cover	30.00
B144	**$1.00 book, red & light blue** on white, solid printed cover, $10 DEPOSIT	30.00
B144a	**$1.00 book, red & light blue** on white, solid printed cover, $20.00 DEPOSIT on OBC	30.00

1978. (15¢) Non-denominated "A"

		F-VF
719n	**orange,** pane of 8	2.25

B145

		F-VF
B145	**($3.60) book, orange** on white	7.00

1978. 15¢ Oliver Wendell Holmes

		F-VF
626Bn	**maroon,** pane of 8	2.50

		F-VF
626Bnv	**Pane of 8,** vertically imperforate	1,300.00

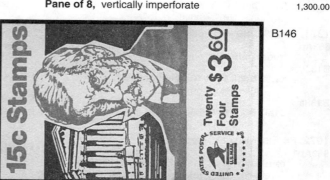

B146

		F-VF
B146	**$3.60 book, red & light blue** on white	6.50

1978. 15¢ American Flag at Ft. McHenry

		F-VF
722An	**red, blue & gray,** pane of 8	3.50
B147	**$1.20 book, red & light blue** on white	3.75

1978. 15¢ American Roses

		F-VF
724n	**orange, red & green** pane of 8	2.25
724nv	**Pane of 8,** imperforate	—
724nzo	**Pane of 8,** tagging omitted (error)	25.00

B148

		F-VF
B148	**$2.40 book, rose red & yellow green** on white	4.00
B148v	**$2.40 book, rose red & yellow green** on white, tagging omitted on both panes	75.00

1980. 15¢ Historic Windmills

		F-VF
741n	**brown** on yellow paper, pane of 10 (2 each Nos. 737-41)	3.50

B149

		F-VF
B149	**$3.00 book, light & dark blue** on blue	6.00

1981. (18¢) Non-denominated "B"

749n

    purple, pane of 8

F-VF
3.50

B150

B150

    ($4.32) booklet, dull violet on white

F-VF
7.00

1981. 6¢ Stars/18¢ America the Beautiful

756n

    Pane of 8 (2 No. 755 - blue & 6 No. 756 - multicolored)

F-VF
3.00

756nv

    Pane of 8, vertically imperforate between, perforations at outside edges

F-VF
75.00

B151

B151

    $1.20 book, blue & red on white, plate #1 over left stamp

F-VF
2.50

    Plate #1 over right stamp

50.00

B151v

    $1.20 book, blue & red on white, vertically imperforate between, perforations at outside edges

F-VF
100.00

1981. 18¢ Wildlife

767n

    brown, pane of 10 (Nos. 758-67)

F-VF
8.50

767nv

    Pane of 10, vertically imperforate

F-VF
1,500.00

767nzo

    Pane of 10, tagging omitted (error)

F-VF
750.00

B152

B152

    $3.60 book, gray & olive on white, plate #1-10 on top pane

F-VF
15.00

    plate #11-16 on top pane

35.00

B152v

    $3.60 book, gray & olive on white, both panes untagged

F-VF
—

B152v1

    $3.60 book, gray & olive on white, bottom pane untagged, plate #11

F-VF
—

1981. (20¢) Non-denominated "C"

773n

    brown, pane of 10

F-VF
5.00

B153

B153

    ($4.00) book, brown on blue

F-VF
8.00

1981. 20¢ Flag over Supreme Court *(pane of 6).*

781n

    black, dark red & blue, pane of 6

F-VF
2.50

B154

B154

    $1.20 book, blue & red on white, Wildlife Page on OBC, unscored perforations, plate #1

F-VF
3.00

B154a

    $1.20 book, blue & red on white, Wildlife Page on OBC, scored perforations, plate #1

F-VF
5.00

B154b

    $1.20 book, blue & red on white, Brooklyn Bridge on OBC, scored perforations, plate #1

F-VF
5.00

B154c

    $1.20 book, blue & red on white, Brooklyn Bridge on OBC, unscored perforations, plate #1

F-VF
5.00

1982. 20¢ Flag over Supreme Court *(pane of 10).*

781n1

    black, dark red & blue, pane of 10

F-VF
4.50

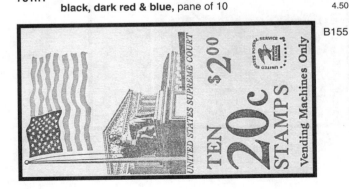

B155

B155

$2.00 book, blue & red on white, Desert
Plants on IBC & OBC, unscored
perforations, plate #1

F-VF
4.00

B155a

$2.00 book, blue & red on white, dull or
Hi-Brite, Physical Fitness on IBC,
Desert Plants on OBC, unscored
perforations, plate #1

F-VF
7.50

B155b

$2.00 book, blue & red on white, dull or
Hi-Brite, Physical Fitness on IBC,
Desert Plants on OBC, scored
perforations, plate #1

F-VF
10.00

B155c

$2.00 book, blue & red on white Hi-Brite,
Physical Fitness on IBC, 75¢ Physical
Fitness/Desert Plants on OBC,
scored perforations, plate #1

F-VF
750.00

B155d

$2.00 book, blue & red on white Hi-Brite,
Physical Fitness on IBC, 75¢ Physical
Fitness/Desert Plants on OBC,
scored perforations, plate #4

F-VF
50.00

B155e

$2.00 book, blue & red on white, Physical
Fitness on IBC, $1.00 Physical
Fitness on OBC, unscored
perforations, plate #1

F-VF
100.00

B156

$4.00 book, blue & red on white,
unscored perforations, plate #2

F-VF
8.00

B156a

$4.00 book, blue & red on white, scored
perforations, plate #2

F-VF
12.50

B156b

$4.00 book, blue & red on white Hi-Brite,
scored perforations, plate #2

F-VF
25.00

B156d

$4.00 book, blue & red on white, scored
perforations, plate #3

F-VF
25.00

B156e

$4.00 book, blue & red on white Hi-Brite,
scored perforations, plate #3

F-VF
50.00

B156f

$4.00 book, blue & red on white Hi-Brite,
scored perforations, plate #4

F-VF
500.00

B156v

$4.00 book, blue omitted on cover, albino
impression, plate #2

F-VF
750.00

1982. 20¢ Bighorn Sheep *(Type I).*
783n

blue, pane of 10, 18 3/4mm wide, overall
tagged

F-VF
5.00

783nv

Pane of 10, vertically imperforate

F-VF
—

783nzo

Pane of 10, tagging omitted (error)

F-VF
—

B157

B157

$4.00 book, blue & yellow-green on
white, plate number on top pane only,
plate #1-6, 9-10

F-VF
15.00

Plate number on top pane, plate #16-19 | 75.00
Plate number on top pane, plate #20, 22-24 | 150.00
Plate number on top pane, plate #25, 26 | 250.00
Plate number on top pane, plate #21, 29 | 500.00
Plate number on top pane, plate #28 | 400.00
Plate number on bottom pane, plate #9, 10 | 250.00
Plate number on bottom pane, plate #14, 15 | 35.00
Plate number on bottom pane, plate #16-19 | 500.00
Plate number on bottom pane, plate #20, 22-26 | 1,000.00

B157v

$4.00 book, blue & yellow-green on
white, both panes vertically
imperforate, plate #9-10

F-VF
225.00

B157v1

$4.00 book, blue & yellow-green on
white, both panes with tagging
omitted, plate #1-6

F-VF
35.00

1982. 20¢ Bighorn Sheep *(Type II).*
783An

blue, pane of 10, 18 1/2mm wide, block
tagged, plate #34

F-VF
5.00

B158

$4.00 book, blue & yellow-green on
white, plate number on top pane,
plate #34

F-VF
20.00

Plate number on bottom pane, plate #34 | 35.00

1983. $3.35 Eagle and Moon (Express Mail)
805n

multicolored, pane of 3

F-VF
60.00

B159

$28.05 book, blue & red on white, plate
#1111

F-VF
60.00

1985. (22¢) Non-denominated "D"
822n

green, pane of 10

F-VF
8.50

822nv

Pane of 10, horizontally imperforate

F-VF
—

B160

($4.40) book, green on white, plate
number on top pane, plate #1, 3, 4

F-VF
17.50

Plate number on top pane, plate #2 | 875.00
Plate number on bottom pane, plate #1 | 1,000.00
Plate number on bottom pane, plate #3 | 250.00
Plate number on bottom pane, plate #4 | 20.00

B160v

($4.40) book, green on white, both panes
horizontally imperforate

F-VF
—

1985. 22¢ Flag over Capitol
830n

black, blue & red, pane of 5

F-VF
3.00

B161

$1.10 book, blue & red on white, 5 1/4
gauge cover scoring, plate #1, 3

F-VF
5.00

B161a

$1.10 book, blue & red on white, 4 1/4
gauge cover scoring, plate #1

F-VF
5.00

B162

$2.20 book, blue & red on white, 5 1/4
gauge cover scoring, plate #1, 3

F-VF
10.00

B162a

$2.20 book, blue & red on white, 4 1/4
gauge cover scoring, plate #1

F-VF
10.00

1985. 22¢ Seashells
836n

multicolored pane of 10 (2 each Nos.
832-36)

F-VF
4.00

836nv

Pane of 10, purple omitted on No. 835

F-VF
700.00

836nv1

Pane of 10, vertically imperforate

F-VF
650.00

	F-VF
836nv2	
Pane of 10, imperforate	—
836nzo	F-VF
Pane of 10, tagging omitted (error)	—

B163

	F-VF
B163	
$4.40 book, multicolored on white, plate #1-3	10.00
Set of 7 sequential covers, plate #1, 3	65.00
Set of 7 sequential covers, plate #2	100.00

Seven sequential B163 books are necessary to show all 25 seashells.

B164

	F-VF
B164	
$4.40 book, brown & blue on white, plate #1, 3, 5, 6, 7, 10	8.00
Plate #8	10.00
B164v	F-VF
$4.40 book, brown & blue on white, purple omitted on No. 835, top pane only, plate #3	700.00
B164v1	F-VF
$4.40 book, brown & blue on white, one pane vertically imperforate, plate #7	650.00
B164v2	F-VF
$4.40 book, brown & blue on white, one pane imperforate	—
B164v3	F-VF
$4.40 book, brown & blue on white, tagging omitted	—

1985. $10.75 EAGLE AND MOON (EXPRESS MAIL) *(Type I).*

	F-VF
840n	
multicolored, pane of 3, Type I	52.00
B165	F-VF
$32.25 book, bright blue & rose red on white, plate #11111	55.00
B165a	F-VF
$32.25 book, navy blue & rose red on white Hi-Brite, plate #11111	55.00

Type I shows a grainy texture in the denomination.

1989. $10.75 EAGLE AND MOON (INTERNATIONAL EXPRESS MAIL) *(Type II).*

	F-VF
840an	
multicolored, pane of 3, Type II	52.00
B166	F-VF
$32.25 book, blue & red on white, plate #22222	55.00

Type II shows even color in the denomination.

1986. 22¢ STAMP COLLECTING

	F-VF
CM1181n	
multicolored, pane of 4 (CM1178-81)	2.00

	F-VF
CM1181nv	
Pane of 4, black omitted on CM1178 & CM1181	45.00
CM1181nv1	F-VF
Pane of 4, blue omitted on CM1178-80	2,500.00
CM1181nv2	F-VF
Pane of 4, light brown omitted	—

B167

	F-VF
B167	
$1.76 book, purple & black on white, plate #1	3.00
B167v	F-VF
$1.76 book, purple & black on white, black omitted on CM1178 & CM1181, plate #1	100.00
B167v1	F-VF
$1.76 book, purple & black on white, blue omitted on CM1178-80, plate #1	—
B167v2	F-VF
$1.76 book, purple & black on white, light brown (lithography) omitted, plate #1	—

1986. 22¢ FISH

	F-VF
CM1189n	
multicolored, pane of 5 (CM1185-89)	8.50
B168	F-VF
$2.20 book, blue, green & red on white, plate #11111, 22222	15.00

1986. 22¢ SPECIAL OCCASIONS

	F-VF
CM1223n	
multicolored, pane of 10 (2 each CM1216, CM1221 & 1 each CM1217-20, CM1222-23)	10.00

B169

	F-VF
B169	
$2.20 book, blue & red on white, plate #11111, 22222	15.00

1987. 22¢ CONSTITUTION

	F-VF
CM1289n	
multicolored, pane of 5 (CM1285-89)	4.25
CM1289nv	F-VF
Pane of 5, blue omitted	—
CM1289nv1	F-VF
Pane of 5, black omitted	—
CM1289nv2	F-VF
Pane of 5, gray & green omitted from background	7,500.00
B170	F-VF
$4.40 book, red & blue on white, plate #1111, 1112	12.50

B170v

    $4.40 book, on white, blue omitted

	F-VF
	—

B170v1

    $4.40 book, on white, black omitted

	F-VF
	—

B170v2

    $4.40 book, on white, gray & green omitted from background on one pane

	F-VF
	7,500.00

1987. 22¢ STEAM LOCOMOTIVES

CM1297n

    multicolored, pane of 5 (CM1293-97)

	F-VF
	3.75

CM1297nv

    Pane of 5, black omitted on one stamp

	F-VF
	—

CM1297nzo

    Pane of 5, tagging omitted (error)

	F-VF
	—

B171

    $4.40 book, black & yellow on white, plate #1, 2

	F-VF
	15.00

B171v

    $4.40 book, black & yellow on white, pane with black omitted on one stamp

	F-VF
	—

B171v1

    $4.40 book, black & yellow on white, all panes untagged

	F-VF
	—

1987. 22¢ FLAG WITH FIREWORKS

875n

    multicolored, pane of 20

	F-VF
	8.50

B172

    $4.40 book, multicolored on white, no plate number

	F-VF
	9.50

    plate #1111, 2222 — 15.00

    plate #2122 — 20.00

B172 was made from standard sheet stamps.

1988. (25¢) NON-DENOMINATED "E"

886n

    multicolored, pane of 10

	F-VF
	6.50

B173

    ($5.00) book, blue on white, scored perforations, plate #1111, 2122, 2222

	F-VF
	10.00

    unscored perforations, plate #2122 — 25.00

B173v

    ($5.00) book, blue on white, yellow plate # omitted, plate #111

	F-VF
	—

B173v1

    ($5.00) book, ultramarine on white, scored perforations, plate #2222

	F-VF
	25.00

1988. 25¢ PHEASANT

887n

    multicolored, pane of 10

	F-VF
	6.00

887nv

    Pane of 10, horizontally imperforate

	F-VF
	2,250.00

B174

    $5.00 book, multicolored on white, plate #A1111

	F-VF
	10.00

B174v

    $5.00 book, multicolored on white, one pane horizontally imperforate

	F-VF
	—

Fully imperforate panes were cut from printer's waste.

1988. 25¢ PHEASANT (red removed from background sky).

887an

    multicolored, pane of 10

	F-VF
	75.00

B175

    $5.00 book, multicolored on white, plate #A3111

	F-VF
	150.00

    plate #A3222 — 125.00

1988. 25¢ JACK LONDON (pane of 10).

888n

    blue, pane of 10

	F-VF
	4.50

888nzo

    Pane of 10, tagging omitted (error)

	F-VF
	—

B176

    $5.00 book, multicolored on white, plate #1, 2

	F-VF
	10.00

B176v

    $5.00 book, multicolored on white, tagging omitted

	F-VF
	—

1988. 25¢ JACK LONDON (pane of 6).

889n

    blue, pane of 6

	F-VF
	2.75

889nzo

    Pane of 6, tagging omitted (error)

	F-VF
	55.00

B177

    $1.50 book, blue & brown on white, plate #1

	F-VF
	3.00

B177v

    $1.50 book, blue & brown on white, tagging omitted

	F-VF
	75.00

B178

    $3.00 book, brown & blue on white, plate #1

	F-VF
	3.00

B178a

    $3.00 book, brown & blue on white Hi-Brite, plate #1

	F-VF
	25.00

1988. 25¢ OWL AND GROSBEAK

893n

    multicolored, pane of 10 (5 No. 892 & 5 No. No. 893)

	F-VF
	4.50

893nzo

    Pane of 10, tagging omitted (error)

	F-VF
	—

B179

    $5.00 book, red & black on white, two buds on OFC, plate #1111, 1211, 2222

	F-VF
	12.50

    Plate #2122 — 350.00

B179a

    $5.00 book, red & black on white, one bud on OFC, 5 1/4 gauge cover scoring, plate #1111, 1112, 1211, 1433, 1434, 1734, 2111, 2121, 2122, 2222, 2321, 3133, 3333, 3412, 3413, 3422, 4642, 4644, 4911, 5955

	F-VF
	12.50

    Plate #1133, 2221, 3233, 3512, 3521, 4941 — 20.00

    Plate #1414, 1634 — 75.00

    Plate #3822 — 25.00

    Plate #5453 — 250.00

B179av

    $5.00 book, red & black on white, one bud on OFC, 5 1/4 gauge cover scoring, tagging omitted

	F-VF
	—

B179b

    $5.00 book, red & black on white, one bud on OFC, 8 3/4 gauge cover scoring, plate #1133, 1433, 2121, 2221, 2321, 3133, 3333

	F-VF
	100.00

1988. 25¢ FLAG WITH CLOUDS

890An

    multicolored, pane of 6

	F-VF
	2.75

B180

    $3.00 book, red & blue on white, plate #1111

	F-VF
	5.50

1988. 25¢ CLASSIC CARS

CM1322n

    multicolored, pane of 5 (CM1318-22)

	F-VF
	10.00

B181

B181

		F-VF
	$5.00 book, black & red on white, plate #1	30.00

1988. SPECIAL OCCASIONS
CM1332n

		F-VF
	multicolored, pane of 6 (3 each CM1331-32 with gutter between)	5.00
	Unfolded pane with First Day cancel	20.00

CM1334n

		F-VF
	multicolored, pane of 6 (3 each CM1333-34 with gutter between)	5.00
	Mint unfolded pane	3,500.00
	Unfolded pane with First Day cancel	20.00

CM1334nv

		F-VF
	Pane of 6, horizontally imperforate	—

B182

B182

		F-VF
	$3.00 book (1-CM1332n & 1-CM1334n), multicolored on white, large print on IFC, plate #A1111	12.50

B182a

		F-VF
	$3.00 book (1-CM1332n & 1-CM1334n), multicolored on white, small print on IFC, plate #A1111	12.50

Unfolded panes were used by USPS for First Day Programs & Souvenir pages. They were not regularly sold to the public.

1989. 25¢ STEAMBOATS
CM1343n

		F-VF
	multicolored, pane of 5 (CM1339-43)	3.60
	Unfolded pane, plate #1	7.50
	Unfolded pane, plate #2	37.50

B183

		F-VF
	$5.00 book, blue & black on white, plate #1, 2	12.50

1989. 25¢ CHRISTMAS MADONNA
922n

		F-VF
	multicolored, pane of 10	3.00
	Unfolded pane, plate #1	10.00

922nv

		F-VF
	Pane of 10, offset red omitted	750.00

922nv1

		F-VF
	Pane of 10, imperforate	—

B184

		F-VF
	$5.00 book, multicolored on white, plate #1	10.00

1989. 25¢ SLEIGH
921n

		F-VF
	multicolored, pane of 10	3.00
	unfolded pane, plate #1111	12.50

921nv

		F-VF
	Pane of 10, red omitted	7,150.00

921nv1

		F-VF
	Pane of 10, horizontally imperforate	—

B185

		F-VF
	$5.00 book, multicolored on white, plate #1111	10.00
	Plate #2111	25.00

1990. 25¢ LOVE
CM1369n

		F-VF
	multicolored, pane of 10	5.00
	Unfolded pane, plate #1211	37.50

CM1369nv

		F-VF
	Pane of 10, pink omitted	2,000.00

B186

		F-VF
	$5.00 book, multicolored on white, plate #1211, 2222	20.00
	Plate #2111, 2211	30.00

B186v

		F-VF
	$5.00 book, multicolored on white, black plate # omitted, plate #222	—

1990. 15¢ BEACH UMBRELLA
926n

		F-VF
	multicolored, pane of 10	4.25
	Unfolded pane, plate #111111	10.00

926nv

		F-VF
	Pane of 10, blue omitted	1,650.00

B187

		F-VF
	$3.00 book, multicolored on white, plate #111111	5.75
	Plate #221111	25.00

B187v

		F-VF
	$5.00 book, multicolored on white, blue omitted on top pane only, plate #111111	1,650.00

1990. 25¢ LIGHTHOUSE
CM1382n

		F-VF
	multicolored, pane of 5 (CM1378-82)	4.00
	Unfolded pane, plate #1-3, 5	10.00
	Unfolded pane, plate #4	250.00

CM1382nv

		F-VF
	Pane of 5, white omitted	75.00

B188

		F-VF
	$5.00 book, blue & red on white, plate #1-5	15.00

B188v

		F-VF
	$5.00 book, blue & red on white, white omitted on all panes	300.00

1990. 25¢ INDIAN HEADDRESSES
CM1393n

		F-VF
	multicolored, pane of 10 (2 each CM1389-93)	5.00
	Unfolded pane, plate #1	25.00
	Unfolded pane, plate #2	35.00

CM1393nv

		F-VF
	Pane of 10, intaglio black omitted	3,850.00

B189

		F-VF
	$5.00 book, multicolored on white, plate #1, 2	12.50

1990. 25¢ CHRISTMAS TREE
934n

		F-VF
	multicolored, pane of 10	8.00
	Unfolded pane, plate #1211	10.00

B190

		F-VF
	$5.00 book, multicolored on white, plate #1211	10.00

1990. 25¢ MADONNA
936n

		F-VF
	multicolored, pane of 10	8.00
	Unfolded pane, plate #1	10.00

B191

		F-VF
	$5.00 book, multicolored on white, plate #1	10.00

1991. (29¢) NON-DENOMINATED "F" *(Bureau of Engraving and Printing).*
938n

		F-VF
	multicolored, pane of 10	6.00

B192

		F-VF
	($2.90) book, yellow & multicolored on white, plate #2222	6.00

B193

		F-VF
	($5.80) book, green, red & black on white, plate #1111, 2222	11.00
	Plate #1222	50.00
	Plate #2111, 2121, 2212	25.00

1991. (29¢) NON-DENOMINATED "F" (KCS Industries, Inc.)

939n

	F-VF
multicolored, pane of 10	25.00
Unfolded pane, plate #K1111	—
Unfolded pane with First Day cancel	10.00

(Unfolded panes were used by USPS on some souvenir pages; they were not sold to the public.)

939nv

	F-VF
Pane of 10, imperforate horizontally	—

B194

	F-VF
($2.90) book, green, red & black on white, plate #K1111	25.00

On 939n the leaf is brighter green and the background yellow is paler than on 938n.

1991. 29¢ TULIP

948n

	F-VF
multicolored, pane of 10, shiny gum	8.00
Unfolded pane, plate #K1111	10.00

948nv

	F-VF
Pane of 10, vertically imperforate	1,900.00

948nv1

	F-VF
Pane of 10, imperforate horizontally	2,800.00

B195

	F-VF
$5.80 book, green, red & black on white, plate #K1111, K2222, K3333	11.00

B195v

	F-VF
$5.80 book, green, red & black on white, top pane vertically imperforate, plate #K1111	1,900.00

1991. 29¢ TULIP *(reprint).*

948ng

	F-VF
multicolored, pane of 10, low-gloss gum	8.00

B195a

	F-VF
$5.80 book, green, red & black on white, plate #K3333	10.00

1991. 29¢ WOOD DUCK *(Bureau of Engraving and Printing — black inscription).*

950n

	F-VF
black & multicolored, pane of 10, overall tagging	8.00
Unfolded pane, plate #1111	10.00

950nv

	F-VF
Pane of 10, overall tagging, imperforate horizontally	1,000.00

950nz

	F-VF
Pane of 10, phosphored paper	8.00

B196

	F-VF
$2.90 book, black & green on white, 5 1/4 gauge cover scoring, overall tagging, plate #4444	5.75

B196a

	F-VF
$2.90 book, black & green on white, 8 3/4 gauge cover scoring, overall tagging, plate #4444	25.00

B196v

	F-VF
$2.90 book, black & green on white, 5 1/4 gauge cover scoring, phosphored paper, plate #4444	5.75

B197

	F-VF
$5.80 book, black & red on white, overall tagging, plate #1111, 2222, 4444	10.00
Plate #1211, 3331	150.00
Plate #2122, 3222, 3333	20.00
Plate #3221	75.00

B197v

	F-VF
$5.80 book, black & red on white, overall tagging, both panes horizontally imperforate between, perforated at top edge	1,200.00

1991. 29¢ WOOD DUCK *(KCS Industries, Inc. — red inscription).*

951n

	F-VF
red & multicolored, pane of 10	8.75
Unfolded pane, plate #K11111	10.00

951nv

	F-VF
Pane of 10, imperforate horizontally	1,500.00

B198

	F-VF
$5.80 book, black & multicolored on white, plate #K11111	11.00

1991. 29¢ FLAG WITH OLYMPIC RINGS

952n

	F-VF
multicolored, pane of 10	8.00
Unfolded pane, plate #K11111	10.00

952nv

	F-VF
Pane of 10, imperforate horizontally	—

B199

	F-VF
$2.90 book, black & multicolored on white, postal rate chart on OBC, plate #K11111	5.75

B200

	F-VF
$2.90 book, black & multicolored on white, Free WCSE Pass on OBC, plate #K11111	5.75

B201

	F-VF
$2.90 book, black & multicolored on white, Aviation Pioneers offer on OBC, plate #K11111	12.50

1991. 29¢ LOVE

CM1406n

	F-VF
multicolored, pane of 10	7.50
Unfolded pane, plate #1111, 1112	10.00

B202

	F-VF
$5.80 book, multicolored on white, plate #1111, 1112	11.50
Plate #1113, 1123, 2223	15.00
Plate #1212	25.00

1991. 19¢ BALLOON

953n

	F-VF
multicolored, pane of 10	4.50
Unfolded pane, plate #1111	5.00

B203

	F-VF
$3.80 book, black & blue on white, plate #1111, 2222	7.00
Plate #1222	35.00

1991. 29¢ FISHING FLIES

CM1413n

	F-VF
multicolored, pane of 5 (CM1409-13)	5.50
Unfolded pane, plate #A11111	3,000.00
Unfolded pane, plate #A22122	1,000.00
Unfolded pane, plate #A23124, A32225, A33233	75.00
Unfolded pane, plate #A23133, A23213	10.00
Unfolded pane, plate #A33213	2,000.00

CM1413v

	F-VF
Pane of 5, black omitted from CM1409-11	—

B204

	F-VF
$5.80 book, multicolored on white, 10 gauge cover scoring, plate #A22122, A22132, A22133, A23123, A23124, A23213, A31224, A32224, A32225, A33233, A33235	25.00
Plate #A11111, A23133	45.00

B204a

	F-VF
$5.80 book, multicolored on white, 5 gauge cover scoring, plate #A31224, A33233, A33235	25.00

B204b

	F-VF
$5.80 book, multicolored on white, 8 gauge cover scoring, plate #A11111, A23123, A33233, A33235	45.00
Plate #A44446, A45546, A45547	25.00

Fishing Flies booklets can contain up to four different plate number combinations on the four panes. The above prices are for the listed plate number on the top pane.

1991. 29¢ DESERT STORM

CM1416n

	F-VF
multicolored, pane of 5	4.00
Unfolded pane, plate #A11121111	10.00

	F-VF
B205	
$5.80 book, multicolored on white, plate #A11111111	25.00
Plate #A11121111	11.50

1991. 29¢ COMEDIANS

	F-VF
CM1428n	
multicolored, pane of 10 (2 each CM1424-28)	6.00
Unfolded pane, plate #1	15.00

	F-VF
CM1428nv	
Pane of 10, intaglio red & purple omitted	850.00

	F-VF
CM1428nv1	
Pane of 10, intaglio red omitted	—

	F-VF
CM1428nv2	
Pane of 10, intaglio purple omitted	—

	F-VF
B206	
$5.80 book, red, black & purple on white, plate #1, 2	15.00

	F-VF
B206v	
$5.80 book, red, black & purple on white, intaglio red & purple omitted from top pane	850.00

1991. 29¢ SPACE EXPLORATION

	F-VF
CM1441n	
multicolored, pane of 10 (CM1432-41)	8.75
Unfolded pane, plate #111111	12.50

	F-VF
B207	
$5.80 book, blue, black & red on white, plate #111111	12.50
Plate #111112	20.00

1991. (29¢) NON-DENOMINATED SANTA

	F-VF
972An	
multicolored, pane of 4 (2 each Nos. 972, 972A)	2.00
Unfolded pane, plate #A11111	15.00

	F-VF
973n	
multicolored, pane of 4	1.50
Unfolded pane, plate #A11111	3.00

	F-VF
974n	
multicolored, pane of 4	1.50
Unfolded pane, plate #A11111	3.00

	F-VF
974v	
Pane of 4, imperforate	—

	F-VF
975n	
multicolored, pane of 4	1.50
Unfolded pane, plate #A11111	3.00

	F-VF
975v	
multicolored, pane of 4, imperforate	—

	F-VF
976n	
multicolored, pane of 4	1.50
Unfolded pane, plate #A11111	3.00

	F-VF
976v	
Pane of 4, imperforate	—

	F-VF
B208	
($5.80) book (1 each Nos. 972An-976n), multicolored on white, plate #A11111, A12111	20.00

1991. (29¢) NON-DENOMINATED MADONNA

	F-VF
977n	
multicolored, pane of 10	8.00
Unfolded pane, plate #1	10.00

	F-VF
B209	
($5.80) book, multicolored on white, plate #1	11.50

1992. 29¢ HUMMINGBIRDS

	F-VF
CM1477n	
multicolored, pane of 5 (CM1473-77)	4.50
Unfolded pane, plate #A1111111, A2212222	15.00
Unfolded pane, plate #A2212112, A2212122, A2222222	7.50

	F-VF
CM1477nv	
Pane of 5, imperforate	—

	F-VF
B210	
$5.80 book, multicolored on white, plate #A1111111, A2212112, A2212222, A2222222	11.50
Plate #A2212122	25.00

Hummingbirds booklets exist with various plate number combinations on the four panes. The above prices are for the listed plate number on the top pane.

1992. 29¢ PLEDGE OF ALLEGIANCE *(Bureau of Engraving and Printing — black inscription) — perforated 10.*

	F-VF
987n	
black & multicolored, pane of 10	7.50
Unfolded pane, plate #1111	8.50

	F-VF
B211	
$2.90 book, blue & red on white, plate #1111, 2222	7.50

	F-VF
B212	
$5.80 book, blue & red on white, plate #1111, 2222	11.00
Plate #1211, 2122	250.00

1992. 29¢ PLEDGE OF ALLEGIANCE *(Bureau of Engraving and Printing — black inscription) — perforated 11x10.*

	F-VF
987an	
black & multicolored, pane of 10	12.00

	F-VF
B213	
$5.80 book, blue & red on white, plate #1111, 1211, 2122, 2222, 3333	15.00
Plate #2232	15.00
Plate #2333	500.00
Plate #4444	25.00

1993-94. 29¢ PLEDGE OF ALLEGIANCE *(KCS Industries, Inc. — red inscription).*

	F-VF
1008n	
red & multicolored, pane of 10	7.50
Unfolded pane, plate #K1111	8.50

	F-VF
B214	
$2.90 book, black, red & blue on white, 9 1/2 gauge cover scoring, plate #K1111	5.00

	F-VF
B214a	
$2.90 book, black, red & blue on white, 6 3/4 gauge cover scoring, plate #K1111	25.00

	F-VF
B215	
$5.80 book, multicolored on white, plate #K1111	11.50

1992. 29¢ WILD ANIMALS

	F-VF
CM1540n	
multicolored, pane of 5 (CM1536-40)	2.25
Unfolded pane, plate #K1111	5.00

	F-VF
CM1540nv	
Pane of 5, imperforate	2,500.00

	F-VF
B216	
$5.80 book, multicolored on white, plate #K1111	11.00

1992. 29¢ CHRISTMAS TOYS

	F-VF
1002n	
multicolored, pane of 4 (Nos. 999-1002)	3.50
Unfolded pane, plate #A111111, A222222	5.00
Unfolded pane, plate #A11211	500.00

	F-VF
1002nv	
Pane of 4, imperforate	—

	F-VF
1002nv1	
Pane of 4, imperforate horizontally	—

	F-VF
B217	
$5.80 book, multicolored on white, plate #111111, A112211, A222222	11.00

Toys booklets exist with various plate number combinations on the five panes.

1992. 29¢ MADONNA

	F-VF
1003n	
multicolored, pane of 10	8.00
Unfolded pane, plate #1	9.00

B218

	F-VF
$5.80 book, multicolored on white, plate #1	11.50

1993. 29¢ SPACE FANTASY

CM1547n

	F-VF
multicolored, pane of 5 (CM1541-45)	3.50
Unfolded pane, plate #1111, 1211	5.00
Unfolded pane, plate #2222	7.00

B219

	F-VF
$5.80 book, multicolored on white, plate #1111, 1211, 2222	11.50

1993. 29¢ SPRING GARDEN FLOWERS

CM1567n

	F-VF
multicolored, pane of 5 (CM1563-67)	5.50
Unfolded pane, plate #1	10.00

CM1567nv

	F-VF
Pane of 5, imperforate	2,750.00

CM1567nv1

	F-VF
Pane of 5, intaglio black omitted	350.00

B220

	F-VF
$5.80 book, multicolored on white, plate #1, 2	11.50

B220v

	F-VF
$5.80 book, multicolored on white, all panes with intaglio black omitted	2,000.00

B220v1

	F-VF
$5.80 book, multicolored on white, imperforate	5,000.00

1993. 29¢ ROCK 'N' ROLL

CM1583n

	F-VF
multicolored, pane of 8 (2 of CM1577, 1 each CM1578-83)	4.50
Unfolded pane, plate #A11111*, A13113	50.00
Unfolded pane, plate #A22222	8.00

Found only on panes of 7 (missing bottom Elvis stamp) from 1993 Commemorative mint set.

CM1583n1

	F-VF
multicolored, pane of 4 (CM1577, CM1581-83)	2.50
Unfolded pane, plate #A13113	75.00
Unfolded pane, plate #A22222	5.00

CM1583n1 without tab is indistinguishable from strip of the bottom 4 stamps of CM1583n.

B221

	F-VF
$5.80 book (1-CM1583n & 2-CM1583n1), multicolored on white, plate #A11111, A22222	11.00
Plate #A13113, A44444	15.00

Note: Rock 'n' Roll booklets exist with various plate number combinations on the three panes. The above prices are for the listed plate number on the top pane.

1993. 29¢ BROADWAY MUSICALS

CM1588n

	F-VF
multicolored, pane of 4 (CM1585-88)	4.95
Unfolded pane, plate #A11111, A11121, A22222	5.00

B222

	F-VF
$5.80 book, multicolored, plate #A11111, A22222, A23233	11.00
Plate #A11121, A23232	20.00

1993. 29¢ COUNTRY & WESTERN

CM1602n

	F-VF
multicolored, pane of 4 (CM1599-1602)	3.50
Unfolded pane, plate #A222222	4.00

B223

	F-VF
$5.80 book, multicolored on white, plate #A111111, A222222	11.50
Plate #A333323	1,250.00
Plate #A333333, A422222	15.00

1993. 29¢ AFRICAN VIOLETS

1018n

	F-VF
multicolored, pane of 10	5.50
Unfolded pane, plate #K1111	6.25

B224

	F-VF
$2.90 book, pink & multicolored on white, plate #K1111	6.00

B225

	F-VF
$5.80 book, multicolored on white, plate #K1111	11.50

1993. 29¢ CONTEMPORARY CHRISTMAS

1026n

	F-VF
multicolored, pane of 10 (3 each Nos. 1023-24, 2 each Nos. 1025-26)	6.50
Unfolded pane, plate #111111	7.50

1026n1

	F-VF
multicolored, pane of 10 (2 each Nos. 1023-24, 3 each Nos. 1025-26)	6.50
Unfolded pane, plate #111111	7.50

B226

	F-VF
$5.80 book (1-1026n & 1-1026n1), multicolored on white, plate #111111, 222222	15.00

1993. 29¢ MADONNA

1028n

	F-VF
multicolored, pane of 4	4.00
Unfolded pane, plate #K1-11111, K1-33333, K1-44444	5.00
Unfolded pane, plate #K2-55555	100.00

1028nv

	F-VF
Pane of 4, imperforate	—

B227

	F-VF
$5.80 book, multicolored on white, plate #K1-11111, K1-33333, K1-44444, K2-55555, K2-66666	20.00
Plate #K2-22222	11.50

1993. 29¢ AIDS AWARENESS

CM1609An

	F-VF
multicolored, pane of 5	2.50
Unfolded pane, plate #K111	3.75

B228

	F-VF
$2.90 book, black & red on white, plate #K111	5.75

1994. 29¢ LOVE - DOVE AND ROSES

CM1619n

	F-VF
multicolored, pane of 10	6.00
Unfolded pane, plate #A11111	7.00

CM1619nv

	F-VF
Pane of 10, imperforate	—

B229

	F-VF
$5.80 book, multicolored on white, plate #A11111, A21222	11.50
Plate #A12111, A12112, A12211, A22122, A22222, A22322	20.00
Plate #A11311, A12212, A21311	75.00

1994. 29¢ SUMMER GARDEN FLOWERS

CM1636n

	F-VF
multicolored, pane of 5 (CM1632-36)	4.50
Unfolded pane, plate #2	5.00

CM1636nv

	F-VF
Pane of 5, intaglio black omitted	375.00

CM1636nv1

	F-VF
Pane of 5, imperforate	500.00

B230

	F-VF
$5.80 book, multicolored on white, plate #1, 2	11.50

B230v

	F-VF
$5.80 book, multicolored on white, intaglio black omitted on all panes	1,750.00

B230v1

	F-VF
$5.80 book, multicolored on white, all panes imperforate	2,000.00

1994. 29¢ LOCOMOTIVES

CM1650n

	F-VF
multicolored, pane of 5 (CM1646-50)	4.50
Unfolded pane, plate #S11111	5.00

CM1650nv

	F-VF
Pane of 5, imperforate	—

B231

$5.80 book, multicolored, plate #S11111 · F-VF 11.50

1994. 29¢ CHRISTMAS STOCKING

1047n · F-VF

multicolored, pane of 20 · 8.50
Unfolded pane, plate #P11111, P44444 · 15.00
Unfolded pane, plate #P22222 · 50.00
Unfolded pane, plate #P33333 · 3,000.00

1047nv · F-VF

Pane of 20, horizontally imperforate · —

B232 · F-VF

$5.80 book, multicolored on white, plate #P11111, P22222, P33333, P44444 · 11.50

1994. 29¢ MADONNA

1049n · F-VF

multicolored, pane of 10 · 5.50
Unfolded pane, plate #1, 2 · 6.00

1049nv · F-VF

Pane of 10, imperforate · 5,000.00

B233 · F-VF

$5.80 book, multicolored on white, plate #1, 2 · 11.50

1994. (32¢) NON-DENOMINATED "G" *(Bureau of Engraving and Printing — black "G") — perforated 11 1/4x11.*

1054n · F-VF

black & multicolored, pane of 10 · 6.00

B234 · F-VF

($3.20) book, blue & red on shiny white, plate #1111 · 6.00

1994. (32¢) NON-DENOMINATED "G" *(Bureau of Engraving and Printing — black "G") — perforated 10.*

1056n · F-VF

black & multicolored, pane of 10 · 6.00

B235 · F-VF

($3.20) book, blue & red on dull white, plate #1111, 2222 · 6.00

B236 · F-VF

($6.40) book, blue & red on dull white, plate #1111, 2222 · 12.50

1994. (32¢) NON-DENOMINATED "G" *(American Bank Note Co. — blue "G").*

1057n · F-VF

blue & multicolored, pane of 10 · 6.00

1057nv · F-VF

Pane of 10, perforated in the tab at the top of the stamps, otherwise imperforate · —

B237 · F-VF

($6.40) book, black, red & blue on white, both panes, plate #A1111, A1211, A2222, A3333, A4444 · 12.50
Same with different plate number on bottom pane · 25.00

B237v · F-VF

($6.40) book, black, red & blue on white, one pane perforated in the tab at the top of the stamps, otherwise imperforate, plate #A2222 · —

1994. (32¢) NON-DENOMINATED "G" *(KCS Industries, Inc. — red "G").*

1058n · F-VF

red & multicolored, pane of 10 · 6.00

1058nv · F-VF

Pane of 10, imperforate · —

B238 · F-VF

($6.40) book, black, red & blue, on white, plate #K1111 · 12.50

Makeshift Vending Machine Booklets

In early 1996, the USPS contracted with Minnesota Diversified Industries (MDI) to fabricate vending machine booklets of 15 and 30 stamps in order to create $4.80 and $9.60 products. These would reduce the amount of change that would be needed to be dispensed from the vending machines. With these booklets being intended only for self-service machines, they were almost never offered from Philatelic Sales in Kansas City. These booklets all have a blue cover and window exposing up to four of the stamps. The outside back cover has a description, item number and price in varying formats.

These blue MDI books were made from stock originally intended to be made into panes of 50 and convertible booklets (self-stick sheetlets of 20). Those containing self-adhesive stamps are unique since they can not be created from the individual 20 stamp sheetlets as sold by the post office. Because of the way that they were manufactured, many different assembly varieties are found on several of the MDI booklets making it nearly impossible to collect an example of every booklet variety. It is beyond the scope of this catalog to include all of these varieties.

1996. 32¢ FLAG OVER PORCH *(MDI self-adhesive).*

1078n1 · F-VF

multicolored, pane of 15 plus label · 9.00

1078n2 · F-VF

Pane of 16 with UL or LR stamp removed, no label · 9.00

B239 · F-VF

$4.80 book (1-1078n1), blue on white (4) · 9.00

B240 · F-VF

$4.80 book (1-1078n2), blue on white (3) · 17.50

B241 · F-VF

$9.60 book (2-1078n1), blue on white (3) · 20.00

1078n2 can not be made from 1057n1 because the label is die cut and, if removed, leaves an impression of the die cutting.

The number in parentheses indicates the number of printing variations on the OBC.

1997. 32¢ LOVE CHERUB *(MDI water activated).*

B242 · F-VF

$4.80 book (15-CM1703), blue on white, plate #4222-1, 5422-1, 7633-1, 7643-1, 7644-1, 7645-1, or no plate number · 9.00

1995. 32¢ LOVE CHERUB *(water activated).*

CM1704n · F-VF

multicolored, pane of 10 · 5.50
Unfolded pane, plate #1 · 7.50

B243 · F-VF

$6.40 book, multicolored on white, plate #1 · 11.00

1997. 32¢ FLAG OVER PORCH *(MDI water activated).*

B244 · F-VF

$4.80 book (15 No. 1080), blue on white, plate #S22222 or no plate number · 9.00

1995. 32¢ FLAG OVER PORCH *(water activated).*

1081n · F-VF

multicolored, pane of 10 · 6.25
Unfolded pane, plate #11111 · 7.00

1081nv · F-VF

Pane of 10, imperforate · —

B245 · F-VF

$3.20 book, multicolored on white, plate #11111, 22222, 33332 · 6.50
Plate #23222, 44444 · —

B246 · F-VF

$6.40 book, multicolored on white, plate #11111, 22222, 23222, 33332, 44444 · 12.00

1996. 32¢ PINK ROSE *(MDI self-adhesive).*

1084n1 · F-VF

multicolored, pane of 15 plus label · 20.00

1084n2 · F-VF

multicolored, pane of 14, no label · 22.50

1084n3 · F-VF

multicolored, pane of 16, no label · 22.50

1084n4 · F-VF

multicolored, pane of 16, stamp removed from top or bottom row, no label · 22.50

B247 · F-VF

$4.80 book (1-1084n1), blue on white, with cellophane wrapper (2) · 20.00

B248

$4.80 book (1-1084n1), blue on white, no
cellophane wrapper (3)   F-VF
                                        15.00

B249

$4.80 book (1-1084n4), blue on white, no
cellophane wrapper   F-VF
                                        15.00

B250

$9.60 book (1-1084n2, 1-1084n3), blue
on white, with cellophane wrapper (3)   F-VF
                                        45.00

B251

$9.60 book (2-1084n1), blue on white, no
cellophane wrapper (3)   F-VF
                                        20.00

B252

$9.60 book (2-1084n4), blue on white, no
cellophane wrapper (3)   F-VF
                                        25.00

B252a

$9.60 book (1-1084n1, 1-1084n4), blue
on white, no cellophane wrapper   F-VF
                                        —

*1084n4 can not be made from 1084n3 because the label is die cut
and, if removed, leaves an impression of the die cutting.*

*Cellophane wrapped books have the description and item number on
a sticker and not on the booklet itself.*

1995. 20¢ BLUE JAY *(water activated).*
1087n

multicolored, pane of 10   F-VF
Unfolded pane, plate #S1111   4.25
                                        5.00

B253

$2.00 book, multicolored on white, plate
#S1111   F-VF
                                        6.50

1995. 32¢ GREAT LAKES LIGHTHOUSES
CM1719n

multicolored, pane of 5 (CM1715-19)   F-VF
Unfolded pane, plate #S11111   3.50
                                        4.00

B254

$6.40 book, multicolored on white, plate
#S11111   F-VF
                                        12.00

1995. 32¢ PEACHES AND PEAR *(water activated).*
1090n

multicolored, pane of 10 (5 No. 1090y) F-VF
Unfolded pane, plate #11111   6.25
                                        7.00

B255

$6.40 book, multicolored on white, plate
#11111   F-VF
                                        12.00

1995. 32¢ FALL GARDEN FLOWERS
CM1762n

multicolored, pane of 5 (CM1758-62)   F-VF
Unfolded pane, plate #2   4.00
                                        5.00

CM1762nv

Pane of 5, imperforate   F-VF
                                        —

B256

$6.40 book, multicolored on white, plate
#2   F-VF
                                        12.00

1995. 32¢ CONTEMPORARY CHRISTMAS *(water activated).*
1101n

multicolored, pane of 5 (3 each Nos.
1098-99, 2 each Nos. 1100-01)   F-VF
Unfolded pane, plate #P1111   6.50

                                        7.50

1101n1

multicolored, pane of 5 (2 each Nos.   F-VF
1098-99, 3 each Nos. 1100-01)   6.50
Unfolded pane, plate #P1111   7.50

B257

$6.40 book (1-1101n, 1-1101n1),   F-VF
multicolored on white, plate #P1111,   12.00
P2222, or any combination

B257v

$6.40 book (2-1101n), multicolored on   F-VF
white, plate #P1111   —

B257v1

$6.40 book (2-1101n1), multicolored on F-VF
white, plate #P1111   —

B257v2

$6.40 book (1-1101n & 1-1101n1),   F-VF
multicolored on white, bottom pane   —
shows tab at bottom, plate #P1111

B257v3

$6.40 book (1-1101n & 1-1101n1),   F-VF
multicolored on white, bottom pane   —
blank, plate #P1111

1995. 32¢ MADONNA
1113n

multicolored, pane of 10, plate number F-VF
next to LL stamp   6.50
Unfolded pane, plate #1   7.50

1113nv

Pane of 10, plate number next to UL   F-VF
stamp (miscut & misperfed)   25.00

B258

$6.40 book (2-1113n), multicolored on   F-VF
white, plate #1   12.00

B258v

$6.40 book (2-1113nv), multicolored on F-VF
white, plate #1   50.00

1996. 32¢ MIDNIGHT ANGEL *(MDI self-adhesive).*
1110n1

multicolored, pane of 15 plus label   F-VF
                                        10.00

1110n2

multicolored, pane of 16 with one stamp F-VF
removed, no label   22.50

B259

$4.80 book (1-1110n1), blue on white (2) F-VF
                                         10.00

B259A

$4.80 book (1-1110n2), blue on white   F-VF
                                        —

B260

$9.60 book (2-1110n1), blue on white (3) F-VF
                                         20.00

B261

$9.60 book (1-1110n1, 1-1110n2), blue   F-VF
on white   35.00

B262

$9.60 book (2-1110n2), blue on white (3) F-VF
                                         20.00

1996. 32¢ UTAH CENTENNIAL *(MDI water activated).*
B263

$4.80 book (15-CM1792), blue on white, F-VF
plate #P11111, P22222, or no plate   10.00
number

1996. 32¢ WINTER GARDEN FLOWERS
CM1797n

multicolored, pane of 5 (CM1793-97)   F-VF
Unfolded pane, plate #1   3.50
                                        4.00

CM1797nv

Pane of 5 (CM1793-97), imperforate   F-VF
                                        —

B264

$6.40 book, multicolored on white, plate F-VF
#1   11.00

1996. 32¢ LOVE CHERUB *(MDI self-adhesive).*
CM1798n1

multicolored, pane of 15 plus label   F-VF
                                        10.00

B265

$4.80 book, blue on white (4)   F-VF
                                        10.00

B266

$9.60 book, blue on white (3)   F-VF
                                        20.00

1996. 32¢ FULBRIGHT SCHOLARSHIPS *(MDI water activated).*
B267

$4.80 book (15-CM1806), blue on white, F-VF
plate #1-1111 or no plate number   10.00

1996. 32¢ FLAG OVER PORCH *(self-adhesive).*
1125n

multicolored, pane of 10, dated "1996" F-VF
Unfolded pane, plate #21221, 22221,   6.50
22222   7.50

B268

$6.40 book, multicolored on white, plate F-VF
#11111, 13111, 21221, 22221, 22222,   12.00

44444, 44434, 55555, 55556, 66666,
77777, 88788, 88888, 99999 (4)

1996. 32¢ GEORGIA O'KEEFFE (MDI water activated).
B269
      $4.80 book (15-CM1828), blue on white,
        plate #S1111 (2)
F-VF
10.00

1996. 32¢ TENNESSEE STATEHOOD (MDI water activated).
B270
      $4.80 book (15-CM1829), blue on white,
        plate #S11111 or no plate number (2)
F-VF
10.00

1996. 32¢ AMERICAN INDIAN DANCES (MDI water activated).
B271
      $4.80 book (3-CM1835y), blue on white,
        plate #P1111, P2222, P3333
F-VF
10.00

1996. 32¢ JAMES DEAN (MDI water activated).
B272
      $4.80 book (15-CM1841), blue on white,
        plate #S1111111 (2)
F-VF
10.00

1996. 32¢ FOLK HEROES (MDI water activated).
B273
      $4.80 book (15 from CM1842-45), blue
        on white (2)
F-VF
10.00

The contents of B273 may vary.

1996. 32¢ OLYMPIC GAMES CENTENNIAL (MDI water activated).
B274
      $4.80 book (15-CM1846), blue on white,
        plate #P1 (2)
F-VF
10.00

1996. 32¢ IOWA STATEHOOD (MDI water activated).
B275
      $4.80 book (15-CM1847), blue on white,
        plate #P1111, P2222, P3333, or no
        plate number
F-VF
10.00

1996. 20¢ BLUE JAY (self-adhesive).
1135n1
      multicolored, pane of 4
F-VF
2.00
1135n2
      multicolored, pane of 6
F-VF
3.00
B276
      $2.00 book (1-1135n1 & 1-1135n2),
        multicolored on white, 12 1/2 gauge
        cover scoring, plate #S1111, S2222
F-VF
6.50
B276a
      $2.00 book (1-1135n1 & 1-1135n2),
        multicolored on white, 8 1/2 gauge
        cover scoring, plate #S2222
F-VF
6.50

Nos. 1135n1 and 1135n2 are from B276 or B276a, the peelable strip removed and the rouletting line 2mm lower than on 1135n.

1996. 32¢ RURAL FREE DELIVERY (MDI water activated).
B277
      $9.60 book (2 panes of 15-CM1849),
        blue on white, plate #1111-2, 1112-1,
        1122-1, 1123-1, 2224-1, 2235-1,
        3235-1
F-VF
20.00

Rural Free Delivery booklets exist with various plate number combinations on the two panes.

1996. 32¢ RIVERBOATS (MDI self-adhesive).
B278
      $4.80 book (3 each CM1850-54), blue on
        white
F-VF
10.00

1996. 32¢ ENDANGERED SPECIES (MDI water activated).
B279
      $4.80 book (CM1864-78), blue on white
F-VF
10.00

1996. 32¢ MADONNA (MDI water activated).
B280
      $4.80 book (15 No. 1146), blue on white,
        plate #1111-1, 1112-1, 2222-1, or no
        plate number
F-VF
10.00

1996. 32¢ HANUKKAH (MDI self-adhesive).
B281
      $4.80 book (15-CM1880), blue on white,
        plate #V11111, or no plate number
F-VF
10.00

1996. 32¢ YELLOW ROSE
1149n1
      multicolored, pane of 4
F-VF
3.00
1149n2
      multicolored, pane of 5 plus label, plate
        #S1111 on LL stamp
F-VF
3.75
1149n3
      multicolored, pane of 6, plate #S1111 on
        LR stamp or no plate number
F-VF
4.50
B282
      $4.80 book (1-1149n1, 1-1149n2 &
        1-1149n3), multicolored on white,
        plate #S1111 on LL stamp
F-VF
10.00
B283
      $9.60 book (3-1149n3), multicolored on
        white, plate #S1111 on LR stamp
F-VF
20.00

1997. 32¢ FLAG OVER PORCH (self-adhesive).
1150n
      multicolored, pane of 5 plus label, dated
        "1997"
        Unfolded pane, plate #11111
F-VF
3.50
4.00
1150n1
      multicolored, pane of 10, dated "1997"
        Unfolded pane, plate #11111
F-VF
6.50
7.00
B284
      $4.80 book (1-1150n & 1-1150n1),
        multicolored on white, plate #11111
F-VF
10.00
B285
      $9.60 book (3-1150n1), multicolored on
        white, plate #11111
F-VF
20.00

1997. 32¢ STATUE OF LIBERTY
1154n
      multicolored, pane of 4
F-VF
2.50
1154n1
      multicolored, pane of 5 plus label, plate
        #V1111
F-VF
3.25
1154n2
      multicolored, pane of 6, die cut 11x11,
        plate #V1111 on LL stamp or no plate
        number
F-VF
4.00
1154n2v
      multicolored, pane of 6, die cut
        11 1/2x11 3/4, plate #V1111 on LL
        stamp or no plate number
F-VF
4.00
B286
      $4.80 book (1-1154n, 1-1154n1 &
        1-1154n2), multicolored on white,
        plate #V1111 on LL stamp
F-VF
10.00
B287
      $9.60 book (3-1154n2), multicolored on
        white, plate #V1111 on LL stamp
F-VF
20.00
B288
      $9.60 book (3-1154n2v), multicolored on
        white, plate #V1111 on LL stamp
F-VF
30.00

1997. 32¢ MERIAN BOTANICAL PRINTS
1159n
      multicolored, pane of 5 (1 No. 1159
        sideways, 2 each Nos. 1157-58),
        plate #S11111 or no plate number
F-VF
3.25
1160n
      multicolored, pane of 5 (1 No. 1160
        sideways, 2 each Nos. 1157-58)
F-VF
3.50
B289
      $4.80 book (2-1159n & 1-1160n),
        multicolored on white, plate
        #S11111
F-VF
10.00

1997. 32¢ Classic American Dolls *(MDI water activated).*
B290

    $4.80 book (CM1921-35), blue on white, plate #P11111, P22222, P33333, P44444 — F-VF 10.00

    Plate #23333 — 300.00

1997. 32¢ Humphrey Bogart *(MDI water activated).*
B291

    $4.80 book (15-CM1936), blue on white, plate #S11111 — F-VF 10.00

1997. 32¢ Stars and Stripes Forever *(MDI water activated).*
B292

    $4.80 book (15-CM1941), blue on white, plate #1111 or no plate number — F-VF 10.00

1997. 32¢ Classic Movie Monsters *(MDI water activated).*
B293

    $4.80 book (3 each CM1956-60), blue on white, plate #S11111 — F-VF 10.00

1997. 32¢ American Holly
1165n multicolored, pane of 4 — F-VF 2.50
1165n1 multicolored, pane of 5 plus label — F-VF 3.25
1165n2 multicolored, pane of 6 — F-VF 4.00
B294 $4.80 book (1-1165n, 1-1165n1 & 1-1165n2), multicolored on white, plate #B1111 — F-VF 10.00
B295 $9.60 book (3-1165n2), multicolored on white, plate #B1111 — F-VF 20.00

1998. 32¢ Tropical Birds *(MDI water activated).*
B296 $4.80 book (15 from CM1998-2001), blue on white, plate #B1111 — F-VF 10.00
The contents of B296 may vary.

1998. 32¢ Ballet *(MDI water activated).*
B297 $4.80 book (15-CM2032), blue on white, plate #P1111, P2222, P3333 — F-VF 10.00

1998. 32¢ Space Discovery *(MDI water activated).*
B298 $4.80 book (3-CM2036y), blue on white, plate #S11111 — F-VF 10.00

1998. 32¢ Christmas Wreaths
1190n multicolored, pane of 4 (Nos. 1187-90) — F-VF 2.50
1190n1 multicolored, pane of 5 (1 each Nos. 1187, 1189-90, 2 No. 1188) plus label — F-VF 3.25
1190n2 multicolored, pane of 6 (2 each Nos. 1187, 1189, 1 each Nos. 1188, 1190) — F-VF 4.00
B299 $4.80 book (1-1190n, 1-1190n1 & 1-1190n2), multicolored on white, plate #B111111 — F-VF 80.00

1998. (33¢) Non-denominated "H" Hat
1196n multicolored, pane of 10 — F-VF 7.00
B300 ($6.60) book, multicolored on white, plate #1111, 2222, 3333 — F-VF 14.00

1999. 33¢ Flag and Skyscrapers *(die cut 9 3/4).*
1210n multicolored, pane of 10 — F-VF 7.00
B301 $6.60 book, multicolored on white, plate #1111, 1121 — F-VF 14.00

1999. 33¢ Flag and Skyscrapers *(die cut 11).*
1211n multicolored, pane of 4 — F-VF 2.50
1211n1 multicolored, pane of 5 plus label, plate #V1111, V1112, V1121, V1122, V1212, V2212 on LL stamp — F-VF 3.25
1211n2 multicolored, pane of 6 — F-VF 4.00
B302 $4.95 book (1-1211n, 1-1211n1 & 1-1211n2), multicolored on white, plate #V1111, V1112, V1121, V1122, V1212, V2212 on LL stamp — F-VF 10.00

1999. 33¢ Fruit Berries
1221n multicolored, pane of 4 (Nos. 1218-21) — F-VF 2.50
1221n1 multicolored, pane of 5 (1 each Nos. 1218-19, 1221, 2 No. 1220) plus label — F-VF 3.25
1221n2 multicolored, pane of 6 (2 each Nos. 1218-19, 1 each Nos. 1220-21) — F-VF 4.00
B303 $4.95 book (1-1221n, 1-1221n1 & 1-1221n2), multicolored on white, plate #B1111, B1112, B2212, B2222 — F-VF 10.00
    Plate B2221 — 1,000.00

1999. 33¢ American Glass *(MDI water activated).*
B304 $4.95 book (15 from CM2072-75), blue on white — F-VF 10.00
The contents of B304 may vary.

1999. 33¢ Coral Pink Rose
1232n multicolored, pane of 4 — F-VF 2.50
1232n1 multicolored, pane of 5 plus label — F-VF 3.25
1232n2 multicolored, pane of 6, plate #S111 on reverse — F-VF 4.00
B305 $4.95 book (1-1232n, 1-1232n1 & 1-1232n2), multicolored on white, plate #S111 on reverse — F-VF 10.00

1999. 33¢ All Aboard! *(MDI water activated).*
B306 $4.95 book (3 each CM2079-83), blue on white, plate #P1111, P2222, P3333 — F-VF 10.00

1999. 33¢ Reindeer
1246n multicolored, pane of 4 — F-VF 2.50
1246n1 multicolored, pane of 5 plus label — F-VF 3.25
1246n2 multicolored, pane of 6 — F-VF 4.00
B307 $4.95 book (1-1246n, 1-1246n1 & 1-1246n2), green & gold on white, plate #B111111, B222222 — F-VF 10.00

1999. 20¢ Ring-necked Pheasant
1248n multicolored, pane of 5 (4 No. 1248, 1 No. 1248v sideways at top), plate #V1111 — F-VF 2.00
1248n1 multicolored, pane of 5 (4 No. 1248, 1 No. 1248v sideways at bottom), plate #V1111 — F-VF 2.00
B308 $2.00 book (1-1248n & 1-1248n1), multicolored on white, plate #V1111 in two places — F-VF 4.00

2000. 22¢/33¢/55¢/60¢/$3.20 U.S. Navy Submarines

		F-VF
CM2111n	multicolored, pane of 5 (CM2107-11)	10.00
B309	$9.80 prestige book, multicolored on white	F-VF 20.00

CM2111n was issued with two different descriptive texts. B309 contains one of each.

2000. (34¢) Non-denominated Statue of Liberty

		F-VF
1269n	multicolored, pane of 4, no plate number	3.00
1269n1	multicolored, pane of 6	F-VF 4.00
1269n2	multicolored, pane of 4, plate #V1111 on LR stamp	F-VF 3.00
B310	($6.80) book (1-1269n, 2-1269n1 & 1-1269n2), multicolored on white, plate #V1111 on LR stamp	F-VF 14.00

2000. (34¢) Non-denominated Flowers (*die cut 10 1/4x10 3/4*).

		F-VF
1277n	multicolored, pane of 4 (Nos. 1274-77), plate #S1111 on reverse or no plate number	3.00
1277n1	multicolored, pane of 6 (2 each Nos. 1274-75, 1 each Nos. 1276-77)	F-VF 4.00
1277n2	multicolored, pane of 6 (1 each Nos. 1274-75, 2 each Nos. 1276-77)	F-VF 4.00
B311	($6.80) book (2-1277n, 1-1277n1 & 1-1277n2), multicolored on white, plate #S1111 on reverse	F-VF 14.00

2001. 34¢ Flowers

		F-VF
1293n	multicolored, pane of 4 (Nos. 1290-93)	2.60
1293n1	multicolored, pane of 6 (2 each Nos. 1290-91, 1 each Nos. 1292-93)	F-VF 3.90
1293n2	multicolored, pane of 6 (1 each Nos. 1290-91, 2 each Nos. 1292-93)	F-VF 3.90
B312	$6.80 book (2-1293n, 1 each 1293n1, 1293n2), multicolored on white, plate #S1111 on reverse	F-VF 14.00

2001. 34¢ Statue of Liberty

		F-VF
1296n	multicolored, pane of 4, no plate number	2.60
1296n1	multicolored, pane of 6	F-VF 3.90
1296n2	multicolored, pane of 4, plate #V1111 on LR stamp	F-VF 2.60
B313	$6.80 book (1-1296n, 2-1296n1 & 1-1296n2), multicolored on white, plate #V1111 on LR stamp; other plate Nos. V1112, V1121, V1122, V2212, V2222	F-VF 14.00

2001. 34¢ Rose and Love Letter

		F-VF
CM2231n	multicolored, pane of 4, no plate number	2.80
CM2231n1	multicolored, pane of 6	F-VF 4.20
CM2231n2	multicolored, pane of 4, plate #B1111 on LL stamp	F-VF 2.80
B314	$6.80 book (1-CM2231n, 2-CM2231n1 & 1-CM2231n2), multicolored, on white, plate #B1111 on LL stamp	F-VF 14.00

2001. 20¢ George Washington (*die cut 11 1/4*).

		F-VF
1298n	dark carmine, pane of 4	1.60
1298n1	dark carmine, pane of 6	F-VF 2.40
B315	$2.00 book (1-1298n & 1-1298n1), multicolored on gray, plate #P1, P2, P3	F-VF 4.00

2001. 20¢ George Washington (*die cut 10 1/2x11 1/4*).

		F-VF
1299n	dark carmine, pane of 4, 2 of 1298 at left, 2 of 1299 at right	1.60
1299n1	dark carmine, pane of 4, 2 of 1299 at left, 2 of 1298 at right	F-VF 1.60
1299n2	dark carmine, pane of 6, 3 of 1298 at left, 3 of 1299 at right	F-VF 2.40
1299n3	dark carmine, pane of 6, 3 of 1299 at left, 3 of 1298 at right	F-VF 2.40
B316	$2.00 book (1-1299n & 1-1299n2), multicolored on gray, plate #P1, P2, P3	F-VF 4.00
B317	$2.00 book (1-1299n1 & 1-1299n3), multicolored on gray, plate #P1, P2, P3	F-VF 4.00

2001. 34¢ Apple and Orange

		F-VF
1309n	multicolored, pane of 4 (2 No. 1309y), No. 1308 upper left	2.60
1309n1	multicolored, pane of 6 (3 No. 1309y), No. 1308 upper left	F-VF 3.90
1309n2	multicolored, pane of 6 (3 No. 1309y), No. 1309 upper left	F-VF 3.90
1309n3	multicolored, pane of 4 (2 No. 1309y), No. 1308 upper left, plate number on 1309	F-VF 2.60
B318	$6.40 book (1 each 1309n, 1309n1, 1309n2, 1309n3), multicolored on white, plate #B1111 on LL stamp	F-VF 13.00

2001. 21¢ Bison (*die cut 11 1/4*).

		F-VF
1314n	dark carmine, pane of 4	1.60
1314n1	dark carmine, pane of 6	F-VF 2.40
B319	$2.00 book (1-1314n & 1-1314n1), multicolored on white, plate #P111111, P333333, P444444	F-VF 4.00

2001. 21¢ Bison (*die cut 10 1/2x11 1/4*).

		F-VF
1315n	dark carmine, pane of 4, 2 of 1314 at left, 2 of 1315 at right	1.60
1315n1	dark carmine, pane of 4, 2 of 1315 at left, 2 of 1314 at right	F-VF 1.60
1315n2	dark carmine, pane of 6, 3 of 1314 at left, 3 of 1315 at right	F-VF 2.40
1315n3	dark carmine, pane of 6, 3 of 1315 at left, 3 of 1314 at right	F-VF 2.40
B320	$2.00 book (1-1315n & 1-1315n2), multicolored on white, plate #P111111, P333333, P444444	F-VF 4.00

B321

$2.00 book (1-1315n1 & 1-1315n3), **multicolored** on white, plate #P111111, P333333, P444444

F-VF
4.00

2001. 34¢ OLD WORLD SANTAS

1330n

multicolored, pane of 4 (Nos. 1327-30)

F-VF
2.60

1330n1

multicolored, pane of 6 (2 each Nos. 1327-28, 1 each Nos. 1329-30)

F-VF
3.90

1330n2

multicolored, pane of 6 (1 each Nos. 1327-28, 2 each Nos. 1329-30)

F-VF
3.90

B322

$6.80 book (2-1326n, 1 each 1326n1, 1326n2), **multicolored** on white, plate #V1111 on reverse

F-VF
14.00

2002. 34¢ UNITED WE STAND

1336n

multicolored, pane of 4

MNHVF
2.60

1336n1

multicolored, pane of 6

MNHVF
3.90

B323

$6.80 book (2 each 1336n, 1336n1), **multicolored on white,** plate #1111

MNHVF
14.00

2002. 23¢ GEORGE WASHINGTON

1344n

green, pane of 4 (die cut 11 1/4)

MNHVF
3.00

1344n1

green, pane of 6 (die cut 11 1/4)

MNHVF
4.50

1344n3

green, pane of 4 (die cut 10 1/2x11 1/4 in left column, 11 1/4 right side of stamp)

MNHVF
6.00

1344n4

green, pane of 6 (die cut 10 1/2x11 1/4 in left column, 11 1/4 right side of stamp)

MNHVF
9.00

1344n6

green, pane of 4 (die cut 10 1/2x11 1/4 in right column, 11 1/4 left side of stamp)

MNHVF
6.00

1344n7

green, pane of 6 (die cut 10 1/2x11 1/4 in right column, 11 1/4 left side of stamp)

MNHVF
9.00

B324

$2.30 book (1-1344n & 1-1344n1) **green,** plate #P1, P2 & P4

MNHVF
7.50

B325

$2.30 book (1-1344n3 & 1-1344n4) **green,** plate #P1, P2 & P4

MNHVF
15.00

B326

$2.30 book (1-1344n6 & 1-1344n7) **green,** plate #P1, P2 & P4

MNHVF
15.00

2002. (37¢) U.S.A. FLAG

1349n

multicolored, pane of 4

MNHVF
2.80

1349n1

multicolored, pane of 6

MNHVF
4.20

B327

$7.40 book (2-1349n & 2-1349n1) **multicolored,** S11111 on cover

MNHVF
15.00

2002. (37¢) ANTIQUE TOYS

1354n

multicolored, pane of 10

MNHVF
7.50

B328

$7.40 book (2-1354n) **multicolored,** on white, no plate number

MNHVF
15.00

2002. 37¢ U.S.A. FLAG

1360An

multicolored, pane of 4

MNHVF
3.00

1360An1

multicolored, pane of 6

MNHVF
4.50

B329

$7.40 book (2-1360An & 2-1360An1) **multicolored,** #S11111 on back cover

MNHVF
15.00

2002. 37¢ ANTIQUE TOYS

1366n

multicolored, pane of 10

MNHVF
7.50

B330

$7.40 book (2-1366n) **multicolored,** on white, plate #V1111 on back cover

MNHVF
15.00

2002. HOLIDAY CRAFTS SNOWMEN

1387n

multicolored, pane of 4 (1 each Nos. 1384-87)

MNHVF
3.00

1387n1

multicolored, pane of 6 (1 each Nos. 1384-85 & 2 each Nos. 1386-87)

MNHVF
4.50

1387n2

multicolored, pane of 6 (1 each Nos. 1386-87 & 2 each Nos. 1384-85)

MNHVF
4.50

B331

$7.40 book (2-1387n, 1-1387n1 & 1-1387n2) **multicolored,** on white, plate #V1111 on back cover

MNHVF
15.00

2003. 37¢ OLD GLORY

CM2425n

multicolored, pane of 10 (2 each Nos. CM2421-25)

MNHVF
7.50

B332

$7.40 book (2-CM2425n) **multicolored,** no plate number

MNHVF
15.00

Airmail Booklets and Panes

1927. 10¢ LINDBERGH

A10n

		F-VF
	indigo, pane of 3	75.00

BA1

		F-VF
BA1	**61¢ book, blue** on white	175.00

1943. 6¢ TWIN MOTORED TRANSPORT PLANE

A25n

		F-VF
	rose red, pane of 3	3.50
BA2	**37¢ book, red** on white	F-VF 11.00
BA3	**73¢ book, red** on white	F-VF 20.00

1949. 6¢ SMALL SKYMASTER *(wet printed).*

A39n

		F-VF
	carmine, pane of 6	9.50
BA4	**73¢ book, red** on white, wingspan 68mm on OFC, printing on IFC, large print on OBC	F-VF 25.00
BA4a	**73¢ book, red** on white, wingspan 68mm on OFC, blank IFC, large print on OBC	F-VF 1,000.00
BA4b	**73¢ book, red** on white, wingspan 68mm on OFC, blank IFC, small print on OBC	F-VF 1,000.00

BA5

		F-VF
BA5	**73¢ book, red** on white, wingspan 60mm on OFC, blank IFC, small print on OBC	22.50
BA5a	**73¢ book, red** on white, wingspan 60mm on OFC, blank IFC, large print on OBC	F-VF 1,000.00

1949. 6¢ SMALL SKYMASTER *(dry printed).*

A39pn

		F-VF
	carmine, pane of 6	15.00
BA6	**73¢ book, red** on white	F-VF 30.00

1958. 7¢ JET SILHOUETTE *(blue).*

A51n

		F-VF
	blue, pane of 6	11.00
BA7	**85¢ book** (overprint on 73¢ BA4 cover), **red** on white	F-VF 30.00
BA8	**85¢ book, blue** on white	F-VF 27.50

1960. 7¢ JET SILHOUETTE *(red).*

A60n

		F-VF
	red, pane of 6	15.00
BA9	**85¢ book, blue** on white	F-VF 30.00
BA10	**85¢ book, red** on white	F-VF 30.00

1962. 8¢ AIRLINER OVER CAPITOL *(Slogan 1).*

A64n

		F-VF
	carmine, pane of 5 plus label ("Your Mailman"), untagged	6.75
A64p1n	**Pane of 5,** plus label, Hi-Brite paper	F-VF —
BA11	**80¢ book** (2-A64n), **black** on pink, wings on OFC	F-VF 15.00
BA11a	**80¢ book** (2-A64p1n), **black** on pink, wings on OFC	F-VF —
BA12	**$2.00 book** (5-A64n), **red** on pink, wings on OFC	F-VF 25.00
BA12a	**$2.00 book** (5-A64p1n), **red** on pink, wings on OFC	F-VF —

1963. 8¢ AIRLINER OVER CAPITOL *(Slogan 2).*

A64n1

		F-VF
	carmine, pane of 5 plus label ("Zone Numbers"), untagged	47.50
BA13	**$2.00 book, red** on pink, wings on OFC	F-VF 225.00
BA14	**$2.00 book, red** on pink, Mr. Zip on OFC	F-VF 225.00

1964. 8¢ AIRLINER OVER CAPITOL *(Slogan 3).*

A64n2

		F-VF
	carmine, pane of 5 plus label ("Use Zip Code"), untagged	12.50
A64zn	**carmine,** pane of 5 plus label ("Use Zip Code"), tagged	F-VF 1.65
BA15	**80¢ book** (2-A64n2), **black** on pink, wings on OFC, letter carrier on OBC	F-VF 40.00
BA15a	**80¢** (2-A64n2), **black** on pink, wings on OFC, Mr. Zip on OBC	F-VF 30.00
BA16	**$2.00 book** (5-A64n2), **red** on white, Mr. Zip on OFC	F-VF 2,500.00
BA17	**$2.00 book** (5-A64n2), **red** on pink, Mr. Zip on OFC	F-VF 75.00
BA18	**80¢ book** (2-A64zn), **black** on white, wings on OFC, "Better Mail Services" on IFC	F-VF 30.00
BA18a	**80¢ book** (2-A64zn), **black** on white, wings on OFC, Minuteman on IFC	F-VF 25.00
BA19	**80¢ book** (2-A64zn), **black** on pink, wings on OFC, Mr. Zip on OBC	F-VF 1,500.00
BA20	**$2.00 book** (5-A64zn), **red** on pink, Mr. Zip on OFC	F-VF 300.00

BA21		F-VF	
	$2.00 book (5-A64zn), **red** on white, Mr. Zip on OFC, domestic rate chart on IFC	30.00	
BA21a			
	$2.00 book (5-A64zn), **red** on white, Mr. Zip on OFC, Minuteman on IFC, 20018 on OBC	20.00	
BA21b		F-VF	
	$2.00 book (5-A64zn), **red** on white, Mr. Zip on OFC, Minuteman on IFC, 00000 on OBC	12.00	

1968. 10¢ STAR RUNWAY *(pane of 8).*

A72n2		F-VF	
	red, pane of 8, red-orange tagging	2.00	
A72n2z		F-VF	
	red, pane of 8, yellow tagging	—	
A72n2zo		F-VF	
	Pane of 8, tagging omitted (error)	—	
BA22		F-VF	
	$4.00 book (5-A72n2), **red** on white, domestic rate chart on IFC	11.00	
BA22a		F-VF	
	$4.00 book (5-A72n2), **red** on white, envelope on IFC	15.00	

1968. 10¢ STAR RUNWAY *(pane of 5).*

A72n		F-VF	
	red, pane of 5 plus Slogan 4 label ("Mail Early")	3.75	
A72nzo		F-VF	
	Pane of 5 plus Slogan 4 label, tagging omitted (error)	—	
A72n1		F-VF	
	red, pane of 5 plus Slogan 5 label ("Use Zip Code")	3.75	
A72n1zo		F-VF	
	Pane of 5 plus Slogan 5 label, tagging omitted (error)	—	
BA23		F-VF	
	$1.00 book (1-A72n & 1-A72n1), **red** on white, Minuteman on IFC	11.00	
BA23a		F-VF	
	$1.00 book (1-A72n & 1-A72n1), **red** on white, envelope on IFC	11.00	

1971. 11¢ JET SILHOUETTE

A78n		F-VF	
	red, pane of 4 plus 2 labels (Slogans 5 and 4)	1.10	
BA24		F-VF	
	$1.00 book (2-A78n & 1-618n), **red** on white, 29mm clock on IBC	5.00	
BA24a		F-VF	
	$1.00 book (2-A78n & 1-618n), **red** on white, 27mm clock on IBC	5.00	

1973. 13¢ WINGED ENVELOPE

A85n		F-VF	
	red, pane of 5 plus slogan 8 label ("Paying Bills"), red tagging	1.25	
A85nz		F-VF	
	Pane of 5, plus label, yellow-green tagging (error)	—	
B138		F-VF	
	$1.25 combination book (1-A85n & 1-678n1), **red & blue** on white	7.25	
BA25		F-VF	
	$1.30 book, **blue & red** on white	4.00	

Test Stamps

Test stamps, sometimes called familiarly "Dummy stamps," have been printed and used by the Bureau of Engraving and Printing, the U.S. Postal Service, and private companies for five purposes:

1) To develop and test stamp production and technology equipment including printing presses and stamp and booklet manufacturing equipment.

2) To develop stamp vending equipment by private companies.

3) To test and adjust stamp vending equipment at dispensing sites by the Postal Service and private companies.

4) To test stamp affixing equipment used by commercial vendors.

5) To demonstrate and promote stamp dispensing equipment.

The number of test stamps increased rapidly in the 20th century with the development and test of new stamp manufacturing equipment. Their use increased with automation of stamp manufacturing and vending, particularly with the introduction of the rotary press, coil and booklet stamps and related manufacturing equipment.

While not accountable paper, i.e. actual stamps, these stamps have generally not been made available to collectors and, in many cases, very few are known to exist. Test stamps clearly show the steps in the technological development of stamps through the years.
—Dan Undersander and Terry Scott

1860-80. WOMAN WITH PHRYGIAN HAT ISSUE Figure facing right (similar to 1861-66 essays of unknown origin with vignette facing left). The word "EXPERIMENT" appears in a straight line above vignette and "SPECIMEN" curved below; with 2s in lower corners. *Imperforate.*

 TT1-TT1D

		MNHVF
TT1	**green** on white paper	100.00
TT1A	**black** on pink paper	MNHVF —
TT1B	**black** on yellow paper	MNHVF —
TT1C	**blue** on yellow paper	MNHVF —
TT1D	**blue** on pink paper	MNHVF —
TT1E	**red** on white paper	MNHVF

1857. WASHINGTON ESSAY ISSUE Inscribed "AMERICAN BANK NOTE" above the Washington vignette and "COMPANY, NEW YORK" below. *Lathe work background and Washington vignette engraved by Bald, Cousland, & Co. Company initials added and printed by American Bank Note Co. on India paper. Imperforate.*

 TT2-TT7

		MNHVF
TT2	black	100.00
TT3	green	MNHVF 100.00
TT4	blue	MNHVF 100.00
TT5	vermilion	MNHVF 100.00
TT6	brown	MNHVF 100.00
TT7	orange	MNHVF 100.00

1861. Eagle and Stars Issue Eagle and stars with 8s in each corner and "SPECIMEN" above. *Imperforate.*

TT7A-TT7B

		MNHVF
TT7A		—
	orange on white paper	
TT7B		MNHVF
	black on stiff bond paper	—

1878-79. Blank Issue *Produced by Continental Bank Note Co. or American Bank Note Co. on gummed, soft paper, perforated 12.*

		MNHVF
TT8		—
	blank	

1879. African Woman Issue *Black geometric design and vignette engraved, blue and red coloring likely offset. The vignette has "EXPERIMENT" engraved above it and "A.B.N.C." below. Printed by American Bank Note Co., imperforate.*

TT9

		MNHVF
TT9		100.00
	multicolored	

1910s. Rembrandt Issue "SPECIMEN" appears in a straight line above the bust of Dutch artist Rembrandt with 5s in lower corners. *Printed by American Bank Note Co., perforated 12.*

TT10

		MNHVF
TT10		—
	brown on cream paper	

1890. Liberty Head Issue Facing left with "EXPERIMENT" over oval of vignette. Figure 3s in squares in lower corners. *Printed by American Bank Note Co. on stamp paper. Perforated 12. (Some examples exist with punch cancellations and overprinted "SPECIMEN.")*

TT11-TT11H

		MNHVF
TT11		100.00
	olive	
TT11A		MNHVF
	purple	100.00
TT11B		MNHVF
	blue-green	100.00
TT11C		MNHVF
	blue	100.00

		MNHVF
TT11D		100.00
	orange-red	

No. TT11E not yet assigned.

		MNHVF
TT11F		100.00
	light orange-red	
TT11G		MNHVF
	yellow	100.00
TT11H		MNHVF
	purple-black	100.00

No. TT11I not yet assigned.

1890. Burt And Tobey's Issue Inscribed "BURT & TOBEY'S" in label across top and "STAMP-BATTERY" bordering lower portion of oval containing image of stamp affixer. *Perforated 12.*

TT11J

		MNHVF
TT11J		—
	dark green	
TT11K		MNHVF
	lavender	—

1907. Blank Issue *Produced by Bureau of Engraving and Printing on gummed paper, watermark double-line USPS, perforated 12.*

		MNHVF
TT12		—
	blank	

1909. Mail-om-eter Coil Issue Inscribed, "APPLIED / AT / THE RATE / OF / 250 / PER / MINUTE."

TT13

		MNHVF
TT13		—
	red single, Shermack Type III (hyphen-hole) separations	
	Pair	—

1909. Mail-om-eter Coil Issue Inscribed, "MAIL-OM-ETER / STAMP / APPLIED AT THE / RATE OF / 250 / PER MINUTE."

TT14-TT18

		MNHVF
TT14		—
	brown single, Shermack Type III (hyphen-hole) separations	
	Pair	—
	v. On cover	—
TT15		MNHVF
	brown single, imperforate	—
	Pair	—
	v. Combination pair of TT14 and TT15	—
TT16		MNHVF
	brown single, Mail-om-eter Type I (6 large holes) separations	—
	Pair	—
TT17		MNHVF
	brown single, Mail-om-eter Type II (8 large holes) separations	—
	Pair	—

TT18 *with Mail-om-eter Type III perforations*

TT18

		MNHVF
brown single, Mail-om-eter Type III (7 small holes) separations		—
Pair		—

1909-10. SIMPLEX MFG. CO. ISSUE "AFFIXED BY" on top of eagle and shield with "THE SIMPLEX MFG. CO" in shield, "90 WEST ST. / NEW YORK" on sides, "TRADE MARK / REG. U.S. PAT. OFF" AND "MACHINE" at bottom. Solid red background. *Imperforate.*

 TT19

TT19

	MNHVF
red single	60.00

1909-10. SIMPLEX MFG. CO. ISSUE "AFFIXED BY" on top of eagle and shield with "THE SIMPLEX MFG. CO," in shield, "90 WEST ST./ NEW YORK" on sides, "TRADE MARK / REG. U.S. PAT. OFF" and "MACHINE" at bottom. Horizontal shading lines at background. *Imperforate.*

TT19A

	MNHVF
green single	60.00

1909-10. SIMPLEX STAMP AFFIXER ISSUE "SIMPLEX STAMP AFFIXER *THE DRUMMOND-LUDLOW CO.*" in oval with "POST HASTE" in inner oval and stars and stripes inside. *Imperforate.*

 TT20

TT20

	MNHVF
red single	—

1910. HAMILTON ISSUE with numbers "1, 2, 3, 4," in corners. Blank vignette, *offset by Bureau of Engraving and Printing, imperforate.*

 TT21

TT21

	MNHVF
deep red	—

1910. HAMILTON ISSUE Vignette of Alexander Hamilton, with numbers "1, 2, 3, 4," in corners. *Offset by Bureau of Engraving and Printing, perforated 11.*

 TT22-TT25

TT22

	MNHVF
deep red	—

1910. HAMILTON COIL ISSUE Hamilton vignette, with numbers "1, 2, 3, 4" in corners. *Letterpress by Bureau of Engraving and Printing, perforated 12 horizontally.*

TT23

		MNHVF
deep red single		—
Pair		—

1910. HAMILTON COIL ISSUE Hamilton vignette with numbers "1, 2, 3, 4," in corners. *Letterpress by Bureau of Engraving and Printing, perforated 12 vertically.*

TT23A

		MNHVF
deep red single		350.00
Pair		700.00

1910. HAMILTON ISSUE Hamilton vignette, with numbers "1, 2, 3, 4," in corners. *Intaglio by Bureau of Engraving and Printing, designs spaced 3.5mm horizontally, 2mm vertically, imperforate.*

TT24

	MNHVF
deep red single	—

1910. HAMILTON COIL ISSUE Hamilton vignette, with numbers "1, 2, 3, 4," in corners. *Offset by Bureau of Engraving and Printing, gummed, designs spaced 2mm apart, perforated 10 horizontally.*

TT25

		MNHVF
deep red single		—
Pair		—

1910. MINERVA HEAD ISSUE *Minerva looking right in shield design,* "HARRIS AUTOMATIC / PRESS COMPANY / SERIES 1010 / NILES, / OHIO, U.S.A." *Printed by Bureau of Engraving and Printing. Imperforate.*

 TT26

TT26

		MNHVF
red pair		1,500.00

1910. MINERVA HEAD ISSUE *in shield design* "HARRIS AUTOMATIC / PRESS COMPANY / SERIES 1010 / NILES, / OHIO, U.S.A." *with a reversed image compared to TT26. Printed by Bureau of Engraving and Printing. Imperforate.*

TT27

		MNHVF
red pair		1,500.00

1910s. COLUMBIAN BANK NOTE ISSUE George Washington with "COLUMBIAN BANK NOTE COMPANY" above and "SPECIMEN" below. *Imperforate.*

 TT27A-TT27C

TT27A

	MNHVF
black on white card	—

TT27B

	MNHVF
brown on white card	—

TT27C

	MNHVF
light blue on white card	—

1910s. STANDARD STAMP AFFIXER COIL ISSUE "STANDARD / STAMP / AFFIXER / BOSTON, MASS." *Perforated 10.5 vertically.*

 TT28

	MNHVF
TT28	
green single	—
Pair	—

1913-20S. STANDARD MAILING MACHINE CO. COIL ISSUE with "Standard" on ribbon separating "STAMP" and "AFFIXER," "STANDARD MAILING MACH" in oval above and "EVERETT / MASS" below. *Perforated 10.5 vertically.*

TT29, TT29A

	MNHVF
TT29	
red single	—
Pair	—
TT29A	MNHVF
light purple single	40.00
Pair	—

1910S. STANDARD STAMP AFFIXER COIL ISSUE inscribed "STANDARD / STAMP / AFFIXER / EVERETT" in four sections of a ribbon across the stamp and "MASS." at bottom. *Perforated 10.5 vertically.*

TT29B

	MNHVF
TT29B	
green single	—
Pair	—

1910S. STANDARD STAMP AFFIXER COIL ISSUE Inscribed "STANDARD / STAMP / AFFIXER / SOMERVILLE" in four sections of a ribbon across the stamp and "MASS." at the bottom.

TT30, TT30A, TT30B

	MNHVF
TT30	
green single, perforated vertically 8.3 / 8.5 alternating	35.00
Pair	70.00
TT30A	MNHVF
light green single perforated 8.5 vertically	—
Pair	—
TT30B	MNHVF
green single, perforated 10.5 vertically	—
Pair	—

1910S. STANDARD STAMP AFFIXER COIL ISSUE with shield and "STANDARD / STAMP / AFFIXER" in ribbon and "BOSTON, MASS." at bottom. *Perforated 10.5 vertically.*

TT31

	MNHVF
TT31	
red single	—
Pair	—

1909. AUTOMATIC VENDING CO. COIL ISSUE "UNITED STATES" above winged eagle surrounded by stars and "AUTOMATIC / VENDING CO. / 1 MADISON AVE., N.Y." below.

TT32

	MNHVF
TT32	
dark red single, imperforate	—
Pair	—
v. Vertical pair, horizontally imperforate	—
v1. U.S. Automatic Vending Co. Type I (slit) separations	—

1911-13. THE EXTENSIVE MANUFACTURING CO. COIL ISSUE "THE / EXTENSIVE / MANUFACTURING / CO. / WORLD WIDE / POSTAGE STAMP AFFIXER / 90 WEST ST NEW YORK" against a globe.

TT33, TT34, TT34A

	MNHVF
TT33	
red & blue single, perforated 8.5 vertically	—
Pair	—
TT34	MNHVF
carmine & black single, perforated 10.2 vertically	—
Pair	—
TT34A	MNHVF
carmine & black single, perforated 10.7 vertically	—
Pair	—

1910-20. MULTIPOST CO. COIL ISSUE "MULTIPOST CO. / AFFIXERS / AND / MAILING / MACHINES / ROCHESTER, N.Y."

TT35, TT36

	MNHVF
TT35	
red single, perforated 9.8 vertically, full shading lines	20.00
Pair	50.00
TT36	MNHVF
carmine single, perforated 10.2 vertically, short shading lines	20.00
Pair	40.00

1922. MAIL-O-METER COIL ISSUE Inscribed "THE / MAIL-O-METER / A CHILD CAN RUN IT / SEALS, STAMPS / AND COUNTS / 250 / ENVELOPES / PER MINUTE." *Printed by Mail-O-Meter Company.*

TT36A, TT36B, TT36C, TT36D

	MNHVF
TT36A	
red single, 9 small perforation holes	—
Pair	—

		MNHVF
TT36B		
	deep purple single, 10 small perforation holes, perforated 10.2	—
	Pair	—
TT36C		MNHVF
	deep purple single, 8 small perforation holes, perforated 12	—
	Pair	—
TT36D		MNHVF
	red single, perforated 10.2 vertically	—
	Pair	—
	On cover	—

1910-27. BLANK COIL ISSUE *gummed, rotary press. Imperforate.*

		MNHVF
TT37		
	black single	—
	Pair	—

1927-1930S. BLANK COIL ISSUE *Produced by Bureau of Engraving and Printing on cream paper with ribbed gum, rotary press, perforated 10 vertically.*

		MNHVF
TT38		
	blank single	.62
	Pair	1.25

1930-40S. BLANK COIL ISSUE *Produced by Bureau of Engraving and Printing on white paper and smooth gum, rotary press, perforated 10 vertically.*

TT39

TT39

		MNHVF
	blank single	.62
	Pair	1.25
	2 red lines 13.5mm apart, alternating wide and narrow line gaps spaced six stamps apart, pair	3.00
	either wide or narrow line gaps, pair	4.00
	Strip of 10, showing both gap widths	8.00

1910-27. BLANK COIL ISSUE *with smooth gum, rotary press.*

		MNHVF
TT40		
	blank single, perforated 10.5 vertically	—
	Pair	—

TT41

TT41

		MNHVF
	blank single, Shermack Type III (hyphen-hole) separations	—
	Paste-up pair	—

TT42

TT42

		MNHVF
	blank single, Mail-om-eter Type I (6 small holes) separations	—
	Paste-up pair	—

TT43

		MNHVF
TT43		
	blank single, Mail-om-eter Type II (8 large holes) separations	—
	Paste-up pair	—
TT44		MNHVF
	blank single, Mail-om-eter Type III (8 small holes) separations	—
	Paste-up pair	—
TT44A		MNHVF
	blank single, 7 small holes, perforated 11	—
	Pair	—

1897. BLANK COIL ISSUE *Rotary press, 25.5x25.75mm, on tan paper, rouletted 13.25, shiny gum.*

TT45

TT45

		MNHVF
	blank single	20.00
	Pair	40.00

1914-16. NEW JERSEY VENDING MACHINE COMPANY COIL ISSUE *Perforated 10.5 vertically.*

TT46

TT46

		MNHVF
	red single	—
	Pair	—

1912. WASHINGTON/FRANKLIN ISSUE *Photogravure test design for German web-fed press, six impressions across sheet, ungummed, imperforate.*

TT47

TT47

		MNHVF
	brown pair	280.00

1915. NATIONAL ENVELOPE SEALING AND STAMP MFG. COIL ISSUE *"NATIONAL" above eagle and shield with "BRATTLEBORO, VT." below. Perforated 8.5 horizontally.*

TT48

	MNHVF
TT48	
red & blue single	—
Pair	
TT48A	MNHVF
red single	—
Pair	

1920s. WIZARD LABEL AFFIXER ISSUE "MADE IN / AMERICA / U.S.A. / WIZARD LABEL AFFIXER / SOLE MANUFACTURERS / WIZARD CO. / BOSTON, MASS." *Shermack Type III separations.*

TT49

	MNHVF
TT49	
red & blue	—

1920s. WIZARD STAMP AFFIXER COIL ISSUE "MADE IN / AMERICA / U.S.A. / WIZARD STAMP AFFIXER / SOLE MANUFACTURERS / WIZARD CO. / BOSTON, MASS." *Perforated 10 vertically.*

TT50

	MNHVF
TT50	
red & blue single	—
Pair	—

1920s. POSTAGE STAMP MACHINE COIL ISSUE "POSTAGE STAMP MACHINE CO." and "33 W. 60TH ST. / NEW YORK, N.Y." in white square frame. *Perforated 8.5 vertically.*

TT51

	MNHVF
TT51	
white on red single	—
Pair	—

1920s. LICENSED SANITARY POSTAGE STATION COIL ISSUE "LICENSED / SANITARY / POSTAGE / STATION" and "OPERATED BY / SANITARY POSTAGE SERVICE CORP'N. / NEW YORK CITY."

TT52–TT53

	MNHVF
TT52	
red single, perforated 10.5 horizontally	—
Pair	—
TT53	MNHVF
red single, perforated 10.8 vertically	20.00
Pair	50.00

1920s. POSTCRAFT CO. COIL ISSUE "POSTCRAFT STAMP AFFIXER" above illustration of affixer with "POSTCRAFT CO. / 25 E. 26TH ST., N.Y." *Perforated 10 vertically.*

TT54

	MNHVF
TT54	
(color unknown) single	—
Pair	

1920s. VIDAVER MAILING MACHINE CO. INC. COIL ISSUE Name and "WEIGHS" in circle and "250 WEST 49ST / NEW YORK" below. *Perforated 10.5 vertically.*

TT55

	MNHVF
TT55	
red single	60.00
Pair	120.00

1920s. AGNEW AUTO MAILING ISSUE "AGNEW AUTO MAILING" over winged hourglass with "A PENNY SAVED / IS MONEY EARNED, *and* "MACHINE COMPANY / BOSTON, MASS USA" below.

TT56

	MNHVF
TT56	
red brown single	45.00

1920s. ROYALTY STAMP ISSUE Stamp affixer in oval surrounded by "STAMP AFFIXING MACHINE PATENTED APRIL 23, 1925" with "ROYALTY STAMP" below and "NO." in lower left corner.

TT56A

	MNHVF
TT56A	
red single	—

1920s-30s. STEARNS-DANIELS COMPANY COIL ISSUE "STAMP / AFFIXER" with "STE-DAN" in oval and "STEARNS-DANIELS CO. / BOSTON, MASS." *Perforated 10.1 vertically.*

TT57

	MNHVF
TT57	
green single	—
Pair	—

1920s-30s. EDISON DICTATING MACHINE COIL ISSUE "I PAY YOUR POSTAGE / EDISON / DICTATING MACHINE / CHANGE IN USA / SERVICE EVERYWHERE." *Perforated 10.2 vertically.*

TT58

TT58
> red single   MNHVF
> Pair   60.00
>   125.00

1920S-30S. SCHERMACK DUMMY ISSUE with "SHERMACK DUMMY STAMPS" printed parallel to perforations, 25x22mm. *Perforated 10.5 horizontally.*

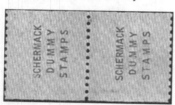 TT58A

TT58A
> red single   MNHVF
> Pair   —
>   —

1920S-30S. NATIONAL POSTAL METER COMPANY, INC. COIL ISSUE Name in circle around "NPM" and "ROCHESTER, N.Y." at bottom. *Perforated 9.8 vertically.*

 TT59

TT59
> red single   MNHVF
> Pair   —

1920S-30S. STAMPMASTERS, INC. COIL ISSUE "Postmaster / MFG. FOR STAMPMASTERS INC. / MANUFACTURERS AND DISTRIBUTORS OF PRECISION / BUILT ROLL TYPE VENDING MACHINES," with Uncle Sam and shield of stars and stripes. *Perforated 9.8 vertically.*

 TT60

TT60
> violet single   MNHVF
> Pair   15.00
>   30.00

1927. MAIL-O-METER COIL ISSUE Inscribed "THE / MAIL-O-METER COMPANY / A CHILD CAN RUN IT / SEALS, STAMPS / AND COUNTS / 10,000 / ENVELOPES / PER HOUR." *Perforated 10.5 vertically.*

 TT61

TT61
> bright red single   MNHVF
> Pair   —

1930S. CENTRAL MACHINE & SUPPLY CO. ISSUE "CENTRAL MACHINE / & SUPPLY CO." above oval containing "NU / E-Z / WA / STAMP / VENDOR" and "DAVENPORT, IA." in shield at bottom.

  TT61A

TT61A
> red single   MNHVF
> Pair   —

1930S. PURITAN MAILING MACHINE CO. ISSUE Inscribed "PURITAN / MAILING MACHINE CO." above oval containing "PEERLESS STAMP AFFIXER" and "BOSTON, MASS." in shield at bottom. *Perforated 8.5 vertically.*

TT61B
> red & black single   MNHVF
> Pair   —

1930S. ELECTRIC VENDORS INC. (ZEIGLE) COIL ISSUE No printed design, shiny smooth gum. *Perforated 10.5 vertically.*

TT62
> blue colored paper single   MNHVF
> Pair   15.00
>   35.00

TT63
> green colored paper single   MNHVF
> Pair   15.00
>   35.00

TT64
> yellow colored paper single   MNHVF
> Pair   15.00
>   35.00

TT65
> white paper single   MNHVF
> Pair   15.00
>   35.00

1930S-40S. MULTIPOST COIL ISSUE "GEO. A. CLEVELAND / MULTIPOST / MAILING SYSTEMS / & EQUIPMENT / P.O. BOX 593 / ST. PAUL 2, MINN." *Perforated 9.5 vertically.*

 TT66

TT66
> red single   MNHVF
> Pair   —

1936. BLANK ISSUE *Produced by Bureau of Engraving and Printing, gummed with gum breakers, rotary press.*

TT67
> blank, gum breaker ridges 5.5mm apart,   MNHVF
>   perforated 11x10.5   25.00
> v. vertical pair, horizontal gutter between   —

TT68
> blank, gum breaker ridges 11.0mm apart,   MNHVF
>   perforated 10   —

1943. OVERRUN COUNTRIES ISSUE Gummed pane of 50 horizontal commemorative-size blank stamps with manuscript marginal inscriptions. *Printed by American Bank Note Co., perforated 12.*

TT68A
> blank, pane of 50   MNHVF

1944-49. MULTIPOST COIL ISSUE "MULTIPOST / STAMP / AFFIXER / COMMERCIAL / CONTROLS / CORPORATION / U.S. POSTAL METER / DIVISION / ROCHESTER 2, N.Y." *Perforated 9.7 vertically.*

TT69, TT70, TT71

TT69		MNHVF
	blue single	20.00
	Pair	50.00
TT70		MNHVF
	black single	20.00
	Pair	50.00
	On cover	—
TT71		MNHVF
	blue-black single	20.00
	Pair	50.00

1944-49. MULTIPOST COIL ISSUE Cartoon character skipping over city and "COMMERCIAL / CONTROLS / MULTIPOST / mailMaster." *Perforated 9.8 vertically.*

TT72, TT73

TT72		MNHVF
	purple single	20.00
	Pair	50.00
TT73		MNHVF
	carmine single	30.00
	Pair	80.00

1944-49. MULTIPOST COIL ISSUE Cartoon character skipping over city and "FRIDEN / MULTIPOST / mailMaster." *Perforated 9.7 vertically.*

TT74

TT74		MNHVF
	carmine single	20.00
	Pair	50.00

1954. PURPLE COIL ISSUE Vertical rectangle, framed with cross-hatch design inside. *Printed by Bureau of Engraving and Printing, perforated 9.8 vertically.*

TT75-TT78

TT75		MNHVF
	purple single (large hole perforations)	1.00
	Pair	—
	Line pair	5.00
	s. Single, (small hole perforations)	1.00
	Pair	4.00
	Line pair	20.00
	v. Pair, imperforate	90.00
	Line pair, imperforate	—
	On cover and canceled "Parade of Postal Progress"	80.00

1954. CARMINE ISSUE Vertical rectangle, framed with cross-hatch design inside. *Printed by Bureau of Engraving and Printing, perforated 11x10.5.*

TT76		MNHVF
	carmine	240.00
	Block of 4, plate No. 141731 or 141732	—
	v. Block of 4, plate No. 141731 or 141732, imperforate	—
	Block of 4 with full vertical gutter, with EE bars between stamps	—

1954. CARMINE COIL ISSUE Same design as TT76 *but perforated 10 vertically, printed by Bureau of Engraving and Printing.*

TT77		MNHVF
	carmine single	200.00
	Pair	400.00
	Line pair	400.00
	v. Pair, imperforate	300.00
	Line pair, imperforate	—
	v1. Joint line block of 10 horizontally imperforate, plate Nos. 164564 or 164565	—
	v2. Joint line block of 10 imperforate, with plate Nos. 164564 or 164565	—

1958. RED VIOLET COIL ISSUE Vertical rectangle, framed with cross-hatch design inside. *Printed by Bureau of Engraving and Printing, perforated 9.8 vertically.*

TT78		MNHVF
	red violet single (large hole perforations)	1.50
	Pair	20.00
	Line pair	125.00
	s. Single (small hole perforations)	1.50
	Pair	3.00
	Line pair	12.00
	v. Pair, imperforate	300.00
	Line pair, imperforate	—
	v1. Block of 8 with joint line, sheet margin and plate Nos. 165939 and 165940, imperforate horizontally	—
	On cover and canceled "Parade of Postal Progress"	85.00
	Roll of 100 in cellophane	—

1958-59. PITNEY BOWES CO. ISSUE "POSTAGE STAMP" above circle with "FACSIMILE" below. *Imperforate.*

TT79

TT79		MNHVF
	rose carmine with overall orange tagging, Helocon paper	—
	p. black helocon paper	—
	p1. pink lumogen paper	—

1960-70. BLANK COIL ISSUE with smooth gum, rotary press, overall tagging, produced by Bureau of Engraving and Printing, perforated 10 vertically.

TT80		MNHVF
	blank single	—
	Pair	—
	joint line pair	—

1960S. STAMP-E-Z AFFIXER COIL ISSUE Plastic postage stamp affixer with "Postage Stamp Affixer" along side and "STAMP-E-Z" below. *Imperforate.*

TT80A

TT80A

	MNHVF
light purple single, imperforate	—
Pair, imperforate	—

TT80B

	MNHVF
red single, perforated 9.8 vertically	—
Pair	—

1962-80. GRAY-BLACK FTPO COIL ISSUE Inscribed "FOR / TESTING / PURPOSES / ONLY," *intaglio by Bureau of Engraving and Printing, perforated 9.8 vertically.*

TT81-TT86, TT90-TT94, TT99, TT103-TT104

TT81

	MNHVF
gray-black single, untagged, shiny gum	.50
Pair	1.00
Line pair, untagged, shiny gum	3.00
Roll of 100 in cellophane	—

TT82

	MNHVF
gray-black single, phosphorescent tagging, shiny gum	.40
Pair	.75
Line pair, phosphorescent tagging, shiny gum	3.00
p. Pair, Hi-brite, phosphorescent tagging, shiny gum	—

TT83

	MNHVF
gray-black single, phosphorescent tagging, pebble gum	1.50
Pair	3.00
Line pair, phosphorescent tagging, pebble gum	12.00
v. Pair, imperforate, phosphorescent tagging, pebble gum	50.00
Line pair, imperforate, phosphorescent tagging, pebble gum	300.00

Defacement lines:

red, (single thin line)	—
red, (one thick 1.5mm and two thin lines)	—
dark red, (three thin lines and 15 to 18mm purple band)	—
rose red, (three thin lines 10mm high and inverted "DL")	—
blue, (single thick line 4mm wide with some streaking below)	—
blue, (single thick line at least 10mm wide)	—
blue-green, (two thin lines)	—
blue, (three thin lines)	—
green, (two thin lines)	—
orange, (one thin line)	—
orange, (two diffuse lines)	—
violet, (single irregular bar from 11 to 12mm wide, color penetrating paper and affecting gum)	—
violet, (two thick lines, bottom 3mm wide and top 3.5mm wide)	—
violet, (two thick lines, bottom 3.5mm wide and top 5.5mm wide)	—
violet, (three thin lines)	—
violet, (three thick lines 1.5mm, spaced 1.5 and 0.5mm apart)	—
violet, (four lines, spaced 7mm apart)	—
violet, (four lines, spaced 4mm between top and center and 4.5mm between center and bottom)	—
violet, (five light lines)	—
violet, (six light lines, likely from same defacer as five line)	—
brown, (two thin lines)	—
brown, (one thick line)	—
black-violet, (1 line 1.5mm wide)	—
black, (one thin line)	—
black, (one thick line)	—
black, (two lines, top thicker)	—

black, (three thin lines 0.5 to 1mm)	—
black, (three lines, bottom two thick, top thin)	—
black, (three heavy lines between, greater than 2.0mm wide)	—
black, (three heavy lines, between 1.5mm and 2.0mm wide)	—
black, (five lines, 3 about 1mm wide and 2 light)	—
black, (six lines, 3 about 1mm wide and 3 light)	—
black, (six lines)	—
gray-black, (one line)	—
gray-black, (two lines, 0.5mm to 1mm)	—
gray-black, (two heavy lines greater than 1.5mm wide)	—
gray, (three lines, spaced 1.5mm between top and center lines and 2.5mm between center and bottom lines, with very irregular print)	—
gray, (three lines, spaced 2.5mm between top and center lines and 1.5mm between center and bottom lines, with very irregular print)	—
silver, (one line)	—

TT84

	MNHVF
gray-black single, phosphorescent tagging, matte gum	2.00
Pair	4.00
Line pair, phosphorescent tagging, matte gum	20.00

TT85

	MNHVF
gray-black single, untagged, matte gum, fluorescent paper	2.00
Pair	4.00
Line pair, untagged, matte gum, fluorescent paper	12.50
p. Untagged, matte gum, non-fluorescent paper	—
p1. Untagged, matte gum, Type I paper (diagonal gum striations)	—
p2. Untagged, matte gum, Type III paper (wavy, intermittent gum striations)	—

1967. TAGGING EXPERIMENT ISSUE on blank stamps identical in paper, gum and perforation, and selvage cuts to Minkus 610z-613z. *Perforated 11. Produced by Bureau of Engraving and Printing, tagging added by Pitney Bowes Co.*

TT85A

	MNHVF
blank with green tagging	—

TT85B

	MNHVF
blank with orange-red tagging	—

1970. CARMINE FTPO COIL ISSUE Inscribed "FOR / TESTING / PURPOSES / ONLY." *Intaglio by Bureau of Engraving and Printing, perforated 9.8 vertically, orange-reddish tagging. (13 of 40 known copies soiled.)*

TT86

	MNHVF
carmine single	500.00
Pair	1,000.00
Line pair	—

1970S. FLAG ISSUE Self-adhesive flag and "UNITED STATES / POSTAL SERVICE / TEST SAMPLE." *Produced by Avery Products Corp. Stamp imperforate mounted on backing which is rouletted 6.5.*

TT87

TT87

	MNHVF
blue	200.00
v. paper backing imperforate	—

1970s. Proclaim Liberty Issue Liberty Bell and Capitol with "PROCLAIM LIBERTY" and combined 6 and 7 followed by "¢ SPECIMEN-SPECIMEN." *Perforated 12x11.5.*

TT88

TT88		MNHVF
blue, red & green		

1973. Christmas Test Issue Self-adhesive dummy for Minkus No. 684 (Dove of Peace Christmas issue), *produced by Bureau of Engraving and Printing for Avery Products Corp. to add die cutting. Stamp imperforate with rounded corners on white backing paper, which is rouletted 6.6. Press sheet of 200 with horizontal and vertical gutters between panes of 50 stamps.*

TT89

TT89	MNHVF
black	6.00
Imperforate backing	—
Block of 4, matrix intact	—
Pane of 50	—

1975. Green FTPO Coil Issue Inscribed "FOR / TESTING / PURPOSES / ONLY," *intaglio by Bureau of Engraving and Printing, green tagging and shiny gum, perforated 9.8 vertically.*

TT90		MNHVF
green single		162.00
Pair		325.00
Line pair		—
v. Pair, imperforate		—

1975. Green Coil Horizontally Imperforate FTPO Issue Inscribed "FOR / TESTING / PURPOSES / ONLY." *Intaglio by Bureau of Engraving and Printing and shipped to Germany to test coil production equipment. Green tagging, shiny gum, perforated 9.8 vertically.*

TT91	MNHVF
green vertical pair, imperforate horizontally	—

1975. Green FTPO Coil Issue *Inscribed* "FOR / TESTING / PURPOSES / ONLY," *intaglio by Bureau of Engraving and Printing, untagged and matte gum, perforated 9.8 vertically.*

TT92		MNHVF
green single		225.00
Pair		450.00
Line pair		—
Block of 12 with joint line, plate Nos. 36111 and 36112		—
v. Imperforate		375.00

1980-81. Green Coil Horizontally Imperforate FTPO Issue Inscribed "FOR / TESTING / PURPOSES / ONLY." *Intaglio by Bureau of Engraving and Printing and shipped to Germany to test coil production equipment. Untagged and matte gum, perforated 9.8 vertically.*

TT93	MNHVF
green vertical pair, imperforate horizontally	400.00

1975. Orange FTPO Coil Issue Inscribed "FOR / TESTING / PURPOSES / ONLY." *Intaglio by Bureau of Engraving and Printing, on gray paper with shiny gum, tagged, perforated 9.8 vertically.*

TT94	MNHVF
orange single	750.00
Pair	1,500.00
Line pair	—

1978. Brown FTPO Coil Issue Inscribed "FOR / TESTING / PURPOSES / ONLY." *Intaglio by Bureau of Engraving and Printing, matte gum, untagged, perforated 9.8 vertically.*

TT95		MNHVF
brown single		2.00
Pair		4.00
Line pair		20.00

1980s. "Experimental" Octagon Issue "EXPERIMENTAL" *below 6 colored octagons. Printed by Bureau of Engraving and Printing, imperforate.*

TT96

TT96		MNHVF
multicolored single, imperforate		100.00
Pair		200.00
v. Block of 4, plate No. 173404		—

1989. Flag and Eagle Flying Over Trees Coil Issue *Produced by Stamp Venturers. Full rolls of each type are known.*

TT97, TT98

TT97		MNHVF
gray single, perforated 9.9		.25
Pair		.50
Perforated 9.9 with back number (from one roll of 3,000)		35.00

TT98		MNHVF
gray single, rouletted		.50
Pair		—

1990s. Martin Marietta Issue Inscribed "FOR / TESTING / PURPOSES / ONLY." *Gravure by Martin Marietta Corp. with shiny gum, untagged, imperforate.*

TT99	MNHVF
gray-black pair	150.00

1990s. Blank Coil Issue *Produced by Bureau of Engraving and Printing with shiny gum on bright white paper, no tagging, perforated 9.8 vertically.*

TT99A		MNHVF
blank single		10.00
Pair		30.00

1990s. Blank Coil Issue *Produced by Bureau of Engraving and Printing with dull gum on bright white paper, no tagging, perforated 9.8 vertically.*

TT99B		MNHVF
blank single		10.00
Pair		30.00

1992. Gray-black FTPO Coil Issue Inscribed "FOR / TESTING / PURPOSES / ONLY." *Printed on B Press by Bureau of Engraving and Printing, design 0.5mm narrower than TT81-85. Intaglio, matte gum, untagged, perforated 9.8 vertically.*

TT100		MNHVF
gray-black single		.50
Pair		1.00

1996. Blue Rectangle Coil Issue with hollow center with reversed number (every 24th stamp) etched inside square. *Printed by Bureau of Engraving and Printing, perforated 9.8 vertically, shiny gum.*

TT101

TT101

	MNHVF
blue single	50.00
Pair	100.00
Strip of 5 with number "5" crudely etched	
Strip of 5 with number "15" crudely etched	1,500.00

1996. GRAY-BLACK RECTANGLE COIL ISSUE Gray-black rectangle with hollow center. *Printed by Bureau of Engraving and Printing, perforated 10 vertically, matte gum, known in full rolls of 100.*

TT102

	MNHVF
gray-black single	100.00
Pair	275.00

1996. FTPO COIL ISSUE "FOR / TESTING / PURPOSES / ONLY." *Self-adhesive imperforate stamp on white backing paper, with 3mm gap between stamps, printed by Bureau of Engraving and Printing. Known in full rolls of 3,000 with 4-digit counting numbers on the backside of backing paper at 20-stamp intervals.*

TT103

	MNHVF
black on blue single	—
Pair	—
v1. Strip of 5 with plate number 1111	15.00
v2. Strip of 5 with back number	5.00
v3. Strip of 5 with plate number 1111 and back number on plate number stamp	25.00

1996. FTPO COIL ISSUE "FOR / TESTING / PURPOSES / ONLY." *Self-adhesive, printed by Avery Dennison. Known in rolls of 3,000 and 10,000. Stamp with simulated die cut vertical perforation, with 3mm between perforation tips. Perforated 9.8 vertically.*

TT104

	MNHVF
black single, perforations	.50
Pair	1.00
Strip of 5 with plate number V1	14.95

1996. PARROT ISSUE Parrot with "BCA PERF TEST" across bottom. *Self-adhesive, produced by Banknote Corporation of America, 22x31mm, die cut 11.7x11.5.*

TT105

BCA PERF TEST

TT105

	MNHVF
blue, red, green & black	—

1996. PARROT ISSUE Parrot with "BCA" above "00" in lower left. Stamp has hidden lettering. "c 1995 GSSC" across bottom, and "SCRAMBLED INDICIA R" vertically up right side. *Offset printed in vertical commemorative format (25x40mm) by Banknote Corporation of America, perforated 11.5.*

TT105A

BCA 00

TT105A

	MNHVF
blue, red, green & black	—

1997. PACIFIC 97 ISSUE *Blank, untagged, full pane of 40, stamps 25x40mm gummed pane, perforated 11 by Sennett Security Products at Pacific 97.*

TT106

	MNHVF
blank	

1997. STYLIZED EAGLE LINERLESS TEST COIL ISSUE with 1994 stylized eagle and black "TEST SPECIMEN" overprint. *Produced by Bureau of Engraving and Printing in rolls of 3,000. Imperforate with simulated/printed perforations, gauge 10.0, overall tagged.*

TT107

TT107

	MNHVF
red, yellow, blue & black single	25.00
Pair	60.00
Strip of 5 with plate number 1111	500.00

1998. BLUE RECTANGLE COIL ISSUE Only 25 reported, and no full coil rolls known in collectors' hands. Thin blue rectangle, hollow center. *Produced by Bureau of Engraving and Printing, perforated 9.8 vertically, self-adhesive on imperforate backing paper. Four digit counting numbers on the backside of the backing paper at 20-stamp intervals.*

TT108

TT108

	MNHVF
blue single	—
Pair	—
Strip of 3 with "3" printed horizontally	—

1999. FLAG OVER PORCH ISSUE Strip of 3 and each of 3 small mail boxes with test strip inside. Produced for Wal-Mart to sell in miniature post collection boxes. *Nine die cut perforation peaks on left, eight on right, light blue, low fluorescent paper.*

TT109, TT109A, TT109B

TT109

	MNHVF
red, blue & brown single	2.00
Strip of 3	7.00
Strip of 3 attached to original mailbox	10.00

1999. FLAG OVER PORCH ISSUE Strip of 3 and each 3 small mail boxes with test strip inside. Produced for Wal-Mart to sell in miniature post collection boxes. *Eight die cut perforation peaks on left, nine on right, dark blue, medium fluorescent paper.*

TT109A

	MNHVF
red, blue & brown single	2.00
Strip of 3	10.00
Strip of 3 attached to original mailbox	15.00

1999. FLAG OVER PORCH ISSUE Strip of 2 attached to a wooden mailbox with "ACME MAIL" logo on it. Produced for Lechter's Houseware's stores to sell in miniature post collection boxes. *Eight die cut perforations on left, nine on right, non fluorescence.*

TT109B

	MNHVF
red, dark blue & brown single	5.00
Strip of 2	15.00
v. Strip of 2 attached to original mailbox	20.00

1999. RENA COIL ISSUE "TEST" *and* "STAMP" above and below respectively, stylized eagle with letter and "RENA." *Self-adhesive imperforate stamps with rounded corners on white backing paper.*

TT110

TT110		MNHVF
blue single		10.00
Pair		25.00

2000. WORLD STAMP EXPO COIL ISSUE Flying eagle with flag and "Sennett Security Products." *Linerless self-adhesive, die cut perforations, gauge of 10.8. All known copies misperforated.*

TT111

TT111	MNHVF
multicolored single	—
Pair	—
Strip of 5	—

2000. WORLD STAMP EXPO ISSUE Flying eagle with flag over trees and "SSP." *Produced by Sennett Security Products. Perforated 11.1x11.*

TT112

TT112	MNHVF
multicolored single	10.00
Plate block No. 51111	—
Sheet of 25	—

2000. WORLD STAMP EXPO HOLOGRAM ISSUE Image of earth, 57x57mm, adhering to glossy paper. *Produced by Sennett Security Products. Imperforate.*

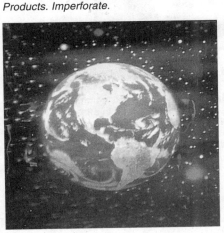
TT113

TT113	MNHVF
foil (no color)	—

2000. WORLD STAMP EXPO BCA ISSUE Eagle head, with "BCA" and "00" in black on each 38x32mm self-adhesive stamp, pane of 12 stamps in different colors/combinations on white paper with "BCA" on back and "World Stamp Expo 2000" on front. *Produced by Banknote Corporation of America. Perforations 11.5x11.*

TT114

TT114	MNHVF
Pane, multicolored	—
a. black, with cross hairs	—
b. yellow	—
c. magenta	—
d. cyan	—
e. black	—
f. 4-color process	—
g. yellow & magenta	—
h. yellow, magenta, cyan	—
i. yellow, magenta, cyan, black	—
j. yellow, magenta, cyan, black, varnish	—

2000. RED MAILBOX LINERLESS COIL ISSUE Red mailbox in vertical coil format (25 x 22mm). *Imperforate with 1 to 2mm slit mark between stamps in the right margin. Produced by Avery Dennison.*

TT115

TT115	MNHVF
red single	100.00
Pair	200.00
Pair with "xxxx" on one stamp	—

2000. FTPO COIL ISSUE Self-adhesive inscribed "FOR / TESTING / PURPOSES / ONLY." *Printed by Bureau of Engraving and Printing, vertical die cut, perforated 9.8 on white backing paper, with 2mm gap between perforation tips. Known in full rolls of 3,000 with 4-digit counting numbers on backside of backing paper at 20-stamp intervals.*

TT116	MNHVF
black on blue single	—
Pair	—
Strip of 5 with plate number 1111	—
with plate number 1111 and back numbers	—

Test Booklets

1927-30. POST RIDER SEAL ISSUE 25¢, four blank panes with waxed glassine interleaving. Covers same as K-M B81. *Blank pane of six stamps (22x25mm) perforated 11.2x10.5 with tab at top and horizontal gum breakers spaced 22.0mm apart. Produced by Bureau of Engraving and Printing.*

TTB1

TTB1n, TTB4n, TTB5n, TTB6n, TTB7n, TTB10n, TTB11n, TTB12n, TTB13n, TTB14n

Note: The illustration of this blank pane of 6 stamps is representative of all those listed, however, it is to be noted that minor variations in perforation gauge, gum type and/or gum breakers will more specifically identify the particular issue.

TTB1

    Cover, green on green, entire booklet   **MNHVF**
      n. booklet pane   —

> Every reasonable effort has been made to make the values in this catalog as accurate, realistic, and up-to-date as possible.

1930S. POST RIDER SEAL ISSUE 37¢, two horizontally uncut covers (81x86mm), two blank panes perforated 11.2x10.5 with tab at top and glassine interleaving. Covers same as K-M B92 (double size) or B99 (double size). Blank pane double width of TTB1n. Produced by Bureau of Engraving and Printing.

TTB2

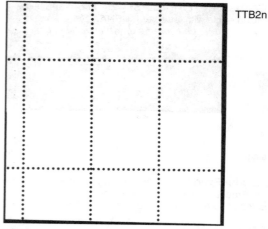

TTB2n

TTB2

    Cover, violet on buff, entire booklet   **MNHVF**
      n. booklet pane   —

1940. POST RIDER SEAL ISSUE 37¢, with 24.4mm seal on cover, two purple panes with interleaving. Covers same as K-M B92 or B99. *Purple cross-hatched rotary press printed pane, six stamps (22x25mm) perforated 11.2x10.5 with tab at top and horizontal gum breakers spaced 11.0mm apart. Intaglio printed by Bureau of Engraving and Printing.*

TTB3

TTB3n

TTB3

    Cover, purple on buff, entire booklet   **MNHVF**
      n. booklet pane   900.00

1940S. POST RIDER SEAL ISSUE 37¢, with 24.4mm seal on cover, two different blank panes with waxed glassine interleaving. Covers same as K-M B111a. *Blank pane (top), six stamps (22x25mm) perforated 11.2x10.5 with tab at top and horizontal gum breakers spaced 6.0mm apart. Blank pane (bottom), three stamps (44x25mm) perforated 11.2 x imperforate, with tab at top and horizontal gum breakers spaced 6.0mm apart. Produced by Bureau of Engraving and Printing.*

TTB4

TTB4   MNHVF
    Cover, violet on buff, entire booklet   —
    n. top pane (six stamps)   —
    n1. bottom pane (three stamps)   —

1959. POST RIDER SEAL ISSUE 97¢, four blank panes with glassine interleaving. Covers same as K-M B120. *Blank pane of six stamps (22x25mm) perforated 11.2x10.5 with tab at top. Horizontal gum breakers spaced 5.5mm apart and vertical gum breakers 21.0mm apart. Also known without gum breakers. Pane is similar to TTB1n. Produced by Bureau of Engraving and Printing.*

TTB5, 6, 8

TTB5   MNHVF
    Cover, blue on pink, entire booklet   150.00
    n. booklet pane   —

1959. POST RIDER SEAL ISSUE 97¢, four blank panes with silicone interleaving. Covers same as K-M B120. *Blank pane of six stamps (22x25mm) perforated 11.2x10.5 with tab at top. Horizontal gum breakers spaced 5.5mm apart and vertical gum breakers 21.0mm apart. Pane is similar to TTB5n. Produced by Bureau of Engraving and Printing.*

TTB6   MNHVF
    Cover, blue on pink, entire booklet   325.00
    n. booklet pane   —

1959. WINGS AND U.S. AIRMAIL ISSUE 85¢, with two blank panes with glassine interleaving. Covers same as K-M BA8. *Blank pane of six stamps (22x25mm) perforated 11.2x10.5 with tab at top and horizontal gum breakers spaced 5.5mm apart. Some booklet panes exhibit faint vertical gum breakers. Pane is similar to TTB1n. Produced by Bureau of Engraving and Printing.*

TTB7

TTB7   MNHVF
    Cover, blue on white, entire booklet   170.00
    n. booklet pane   —

1960-62. POST RIDER SEAL ISSUE 97¢, four red violet panes with glassine interleaving. Covers same as K-M B120b. *Pane red violet cross-hatched rotary press printed, six stamps (22x25mm) perforated 11.2x10.5, with staple position at top and horizontal gum breakers alternating 4.5 and 6.5mm apart and vertical gum breakers spaced 22.5mm apart with staple position at top. Panes were cut from coil sheet stock and, therefore, are mis-cut and mis-perforated. Produced by Bureau of Engraving and Printing.*

TTB8

TTB8   MNHVF
    Cover, red violet on pink, entire booklet   900.00
    n. booklet pane   —

1962-63. SMALL POST RIDER SEAL ISSUE $1.00, (violet hand-stamped "DUMMY" 29.5x4.5mm), four FTPO panes with silicone interleaving. Covers same as K-M B121 or B122. *Panes intaglio printed "FOR / TESTING / PURPOSES / ONLY" in gray-black, six stamps (22x25mm) with staple position at top, perforated 11.2x10.5, with staple position at left and horizontal gum breakers spaced 5.5mm apart. Panes were cut from FTPO coil sheet stock and, therefore, are mis-cut and mis-perforated. Produced by Bureau of Engraving and Printing.*

TTB9

TTB9   MNHVF
    Cover, blue on white, entire booklet   —
    n. booklet pane   —

1962-67. BLANK COVER ISSUE with (black press printed hollow "DUMMY" 55.0x7.5mm), two blank panes of six stamps, perforated 11.2x10.5 with tab at top and silicone interleaving. *Horizontal gum breakers are spaced 11.5mm apart and vertical breakers are spaced alternating 14.0 and 8.5mm apart. Pane is similar to TTB1n. Produced by Bureau of Engraving and Printing.*

TTB10, TTB11

TTB10   MNHVF
    Cover, black on white, entire booklet   90.00
    n. booklet pane   —

1962-67. BLANK COVER ISSUE (red press printed hollow "DUMMY" 55.0x7.5mm), two blank panes of six stamps, perforated 11.2x10.5 with tab at top and silicone interleaving. *Horizontal gum breakers are spaced 11.5mm apart and vertical breakers are spaced alternating 14.0 and 8.5mm apart tab at top. Pane is similar to TTB10n. Produced by Bureau of Engraving and Printing.*

TTB11   MNHVF
    Cover, red on white, entire booklet   200.00
    n. booklet pane   —

1963-64. MR. ZIP CARRIER ISSUE $1 "Domestic Postage Rates" on inside front cover, (violet handstamped "DUMMY" 29.5x4.5mm), four blank panes with silicone interleaving. Covers same as K-M B123, B124, B125 or B126. *Blank pane of six stamps (22x25mm), perforated 11.2x10.5, with tab at top and horizontal gum breakers spaced alternating 4.5 and 6.5mm apart horizontally and alternating 14.0 and 8.5 apart vertically. Pane is similar to TTB1n. Produced by Bureau of Engraving and Printing.*

> Condition refers to the overall appearance and quality of the stamp.

TTB12

TTB15n,
TTB16n1,
TTB17n,
TTB21n,
TTB22n

TTB12

	MNHVF
Cover, blue on white, entire booklet	125.00
n. booklet pane	—

1963-64. MR. ZIP CARRIER ISSUE $1 "Domestic Postage Rates" on inside front cover, (red press printed hollow "DUMMY" 55.0x7.5mm), four blank panes with silicone interleaving. Covers same as K-M B123, B124, B125 or B126. *Blank pane of six stamps (22x25mm), perforated 11.2x10.5, with tab at top and horizontal gum breakers spaced 11.5mm apart and alternating 14.0 and 8.5 apart vertically. Pane is similar to TTB1n. Produced by Bureau of Engraving and Printing.*

TTB13,
TTB14

TTB13

	MNHVF
Cover, blue on white, entire booklet	—
n. booklet pane	—

1963-64. MR. ZIP CARRIER ISSUE $1, "Minute Man-Buy US Savings Bonds" on inside front cover, (red press printed hollow "DUMMY" 55.0x7.5mm), four blank panes with silicone interleaving. Covers same as K-M B124c or B126b. *Blank pane of six stamps (22x25mm), perforated 11.2x10.5, with tab at top and horizontal gum breakers spaced 11.5mm apart and alternating 14.0 and 8.5 apart vertically. Pane is similar to TTB1n. Produced by Bureau of Engraving and Printing.*

TTB14

	MNHVF
Cover, blue on white, entire booklet	50.00
n. booklet pane	—

1967-68. SMALL POST RIDER SEAL ISSUE with "32 SIX CENT & 8 ONE CENT PRICE $2.00" (violet handstamped "DUMMY" 34.5x6.5mm), five FTPO panes with silicone interleaving. Covers same as K-M B127 or B127a. *Panes intaglio printed "FOR / TESTING / PURPOSES / ONLY" in gray-black. Eight stamps (22x25mm) perforated 11.2x10.5 with staple position at left, with overall green tagging, perforated 11.2x10.5, gum breakers spaced 11.0mm apart horizontally and alternating spacing of 8.5mm and 14.0mm apart vertically with staple position at left. Panes were cut from FTPO coil sheet stock and, therefore, are mis-cut and mis-perforated. Produced by Bureau of Engraving and Printing.*

TTB15

Some booklets have colored felt pen marking along the edges of the booklet for technician adjustments.

TTB15

	MNHVF
Cover, brown on white, entire booklet	150.00
n. booklet pane	50.00

1970-71. EISENHOWER PORTRAIT ISSUE with "32 SIX CENT & 8 ONE CENT PRICE $2.00" (violet handstamped "DUMMY" 29.5x4.5mm), five FTPO panes with silicone interleaving. Covers same as K-M B130. *Panes intaglio printed "FOR / TESTING / PURPOSES / ONLY" in gray-black. Eight stamps (22x25mm) perforated 11.2x10.5, with staple position at left, with overall green tagging. Panes similar to TTB15n. Panes were cut from FTPO coil sheet stock and, therefore, are mis-cut and mis-perforated. One type pane with gum breakers spaced 11.0mm horizontally and alternating 14.0 and 8.5mm apart vertically with staple position at left. Second pane type with gum breakers spaced 11.0mm apart horizontally and 22.5mm apart vertically with staple position at left. Produced by Bureau of Engraving and Printing.*

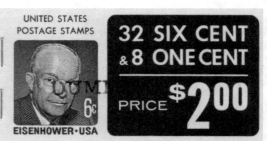

TTB16

TTB16

	MNHVF
Cover, blue on white, entire booklet with FTPO pane with gum breaker spacing 14.0mm and 8.5mm vertically	—
v. entire booklet with FTPO pane with gum breaker spacing 22.5mm vertically	—
n. TTB16 pane	—
n1. TTB16v. pane	—

1970-71. EISENHOWER PORTRAIT ISSUE with "32 SIX CENT & 8 ONE CENT PRICE $2.00" (violet handstamped "DUMMY" 34.5x6.5mm), five FTPO panes with silicone interleaving. Covers same as K-M B133a. *Panes were cut from FTPO coil sheet stock and, therefore, are mis-cut and mis-perforated. Panes, same as TTB16n. Produced by Bureau of Engraving and Printing.*

TTB17

	MNHVF
Cover, blue on white, entire booklet	—
n. TTB16 pane	—

1970-72. STAMP SILHOUETTE ISSUE "$1.00 with Twelve 8¢ and Four 1¢ Stamps" (violet handstamped "DUMMY" 29.5x4.5mm), three FTPO panes with silicone interleaving. Covers same as K-M B130. *Panes intaglio printed "FOR / TESTING / PURPOSES / ONLY" in gray-black. Six stamps (22x25mm), perforated 10.5x11.2, with staple position at left with overall green tagging and with gum breakers spaced 11.0mm apart horizontally and 22.0mm apart vertically with staple position at top. Panes were cut from FTPO coil sheet stock and, therefore, are mis-cut and mis-perforated. Produced by Bureau of Engraving and Printing.*

TTB18

TTB18   MNHVF
    Cover, claret on white, entire booklet   —
    n. booklet pane   —

1970-72. STAMP SILHOUETTE ISSUE "$1.00 with Twelve 8¢ and Four 1¢ Stamps" (violet handstamped "DUMMY" 34.5x6.5mm), three FTPO panes with silicone interleaving. Covers same as K-M B134a. *Panes were cut from FTPO coil sheet stock and, therefore, are mis-cut and mis-perforated. Pane same as TTB18n. Produced by Bureau of Engraving and Printing.*

TTB19   MNHVF
    Cover, claret on white, entire booklet   —
    n. booklet pane   —

1970-72. STAMP SILHOUETTE ISSUE "$1.00 with Twelve 8¢ and Four 1¢ Stamps" (violet handstamped hollow "DUMMY" 34.5x6.5mm), three FTPO panes with silicone interleaving. Covers same as K-M B134a. *Panes were cut from FTPO coil sheet stock and, therefore, are mis-cut and mis-perforated. Pane same as TTB18n. Produced by Bureau of Engraving and Printing.*

TTB20   MNHVF
    Cover, claret on white, entire booklet   —
    n. booklet pane   —

1971-72. EISENHOWER PORTRAIT ISSUE with "24 EIGHT CENT PRICE $1.92" (violet handstamped "DUMMY" 29.5x4.5mm), three FTPO panes with silicone interleaving. Covers same as K-M B133a. Panes intaglio printed "FOR / TESTING / PURPOSES / ONLY" in gray-black. Eight stamps (22x25mm) perforated 11.2x10.5 with staple position at left with overall green tagging, perforated 11.2x10.5, gum breakers spaced 11.0mm apart horizontally and alternating spacing of 8.5mm and 14.0mm apart vertically with staple position at left. Panes were cut from FTPO coil sheet stock and, therefore, are mis-cut and mis-perforated. Panes similar to TTB15n. Produced by Bureau of Engraving and Printing.

TTB21

TTB21   MNHVF
    Cover, claret on white, entire booklet   —
    n. booklet pane   —

1971-72. EISENHOWER PORTRAIT ISSUE with "24 EIGHT CENT PRICE $1.92" (violet handstamped "DUMMY" 34.5x6.5mm), three FTPO panes with silicone interleaving. Covers same as K-M B133a. *Panes were cut from FTPO coil sheet stock and, therefore, are mis-cut and mis-perforated. Panes same as TTB21n. Produced by Bureau of Engraving and Printing.*

TTB22   MNHVF
    Cover, claret on white, entire booklet   —
    n. booklet pane   —

1971-72. STAMP SILHOUETTE ISSUE with "$1.00 15 Six Cent & 5 Two Cent" (violet handstamped "DUMMY" 34.5x6.5mm), four FTPO panes with silicone interleaving. Covers same as K-M B128a. Panes intaglio printed "FOR / TESTING / PURPOSES / ONLY" in gray-black.

Six stamps (22x25mm), perforated 10.5x11.2, staple position at left with overall green tagging and with gum breakers spaced 11.0mm apart horizontally and 22.0mm apart vertically with staple position at top. *Panes were cut from FTPO coil sheet stock and, therefore, are mis-cut and mis-perforated. Panes similar to TTB18n. Some examples have black felt tip pen technician markings on either the front or back covers. Produced by Bureau of Engraving and Printing.*

TTB23, TTB24

TTB23   MNHVF
    Cover, brown on white, entire booklet   100.00
    n. booklet pane   50.00

1971-72. STAMP SILHOUETTE ISSUE with "$1.00 15 Six Cent & 5 Two Cent" (violet handstamped "DUMMY" 34.5x6.5mm), four FTPO panes with silicone interleaving. Covers same as K-M B131. *Panes intaglio printed "FOR / TESTING / PURPOSES / ONLY" in gray-black. Six stamps (22x25mm), perforated 10.5x11.2, with staple position at left with overall green tagging and with gum breakers spaced 11.0mm apart horizontally with staple position at top. Panes were cut from FTPO coil sheet stock and, therefore, are mis-cut and mis-perforated. Panes similar to TTB18n. Some examples have red or black felt tip pen technician markings on either the front or back covers. Produced by Bureau of Engraving and Printing.*

TTB24n

TTB24   MNHVF
    Cover, blue on white, entire booklet   90.00
    n. booklet pane   45.00

1971-72. STAMP SILHOUETTE ISSUE with "$1.00, Ten-10¢ Airmail Stamps" (violet handstamped "DUMMY" 29.5x4.5mm), two FTPO panes with silicone interleaving. Covers same as K-M BA23a. *Panes intaglio printed "FOR / TESTING / PURPOSES / ONLY" in gray-black. Six stamps (22x25mm), perforated 10.5x11.2, with staple position at left, with overall green tagging, with gum breakers spaced 11.0mm apart horizontally and alternating 14.0 and 8.5mm apart vertically with staple position at top. Panes were cut from FTPO coil sheet stock and, therefore, are mis-cut and mis-perforated. Panes similar to TTB9n. Produced by Bureau of Engraving and Printing.*

TTB25

TTB25

    Cover, red on white, entire booklet   **MNHVF**
                                        230.00
    n. booklet pane   50.00

1971-72. STAMP SILHOUETTE ISSUE with "$1.00, Ten-10¢ Airmail Stamps" (violet handstamped "DUMMY" 34.5x6.5mm), two FTPO panes with silicone interleaving. Covers same as K-M BA23a. Panes were cut from FTPO coil sheet stock and, therefore, are mis-cut and mis-perforated. Panes same as TTB25n. Produced by Bureau of Engraving and Printing.

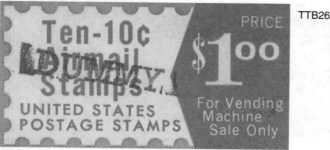

TTB26

TTB26

    Cover, red on white, entire booklet   **MNHVF**
    n. booklet pane   100.00
                                          —

Folded and Glued Booklets

BLANK COVER ISSUE Blank folded cover (43x81mm), one blank pane. *Pane blank (43x112mm), eight stamps perforated 10.9x10.6, dull gum, untagged. Tab height is about 14mm. Produced by Bureau of Engraving and Printing.*

TTB27,
TTB28,
TTB29,
TTB30,
TTB31,
TTB32,
TTB33

TTB27n

TTB27

    Cover, blank, entire booklet   **MNHVF**
    n. booklet pane   —
                                          —

FLAG OVER SUPREME COURT ISSUE Blank folded cover (43x81mm), form of Flag over Supreme Court, two blank panes. *Pane blank (43x137mm), ten stamps perforated 10.0x9.8, with shiny gum, untagged. Tab height is about 6mm, 9mm or 12mm. Produced by Bureau of Engraving and Printing.*

TTB28n Note: The illustration of this blank pane of 10 stamps is representative of all those listed, however, it is to be noted that minor variations in perforation gauge, gum type and/or gum breakers will more specifically identify the particular issue.
TTB35n, TTB36n

TTB28

    Cover, blank, entire booklet   **MNHVF**
                                         80.00
    n. booklet pane   —

$1.20 FLAG OVER SUPREME COURT ISSUE Folded cover (43x81mm), one blank pane of five stamps. Covers same as K-M B154c. Pane blank (43x133mm), five stamps (44x24mm). *Perforated 10 on long side, with dull gum, untagged. Pane is similar to TTB28An. Tab height is about 9mm high. Produced by Bureau of Engraving and Printing.*

TTB28A

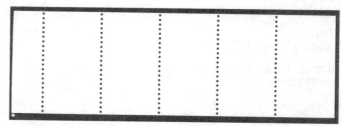

TTB28An Note: The illustration of this blank pane of 5 stamps is representative of all those listed, however, it is to be noted that minor variations in perforation gauge, gum type and/or gum breakers will more specifically identify the particular issue.

TTB28A

    Cover, Flag Over Supreme Court Issue   **MNHVF**
        entire booklet   150.00
    n. booklet pane   —

BLANK COVER ISSUE Blank fluorescent folded cover (48x81mm), form of 22¢ Flag over Capitol, one blank pane of five stamps. *Pane blank (43x137mm), five stamps (44x24mm) perforated 10 on long side, on high gloss paper with dull gum, untagged. Pane is similar to TTB28An. Tab height is about 12mm. Produced by Bureau of Engraving and Printing.*

TTB29n, TTB30n, TTB31n, TTB34n, TTB37n, TTB38n, TTB39n

TTB29

    Cover, blank, entire booklet   **MNHVF**
                                         50.00
    n. booklet pane

BLANK COVER ISSUE Blank folded cover (43x81mm), two panes of five stamps. *Pane blank (43x135mm), five stamps (44x24mm) perforated 10 on long side, on high gloss paper with dull gum, untagged. Pane is similar to TTB28An. Tab height is about 12mm. Produced by Bureau of Engraving and Printing.*

TTB30

    Cover, blank, entire booklet   **MNHVF**
    n. booklet pane   —

BLANK COVER ISSUE Blank folded cover (43x81mm), two panes of five stamps. *Pane blank (43x135mm), five stamps (44x24mm). Perforated 10 on long side, with shiny gum, untagged. Pane is similar to TTB28An. Tab height is about 12mm. Produced by Bureau of Engraving and Printing.*

TTB31

    MNHVF

    Cover, blank, entire booklet   —

    n. booklet pane

FLAG OVER CAPITOL ISSUE Blank folded cover (43x81mm), form of 22¢ Flag over Capitol, two imperforate panes. *Pane blank (43x135mm), imperforate dull gum, untagged. Produced by Bureau of Engraving and Printing or, possibly KCS Industries.*

TTB32

    MNHVF

    Cover, blank, entire booklet   65.00

    n. booklet pane   —

BLANK COVER ISSUE Blank folded cover (43x81mm), two panes with one horizontal row of gauge 10 perforations at fold. *Pane blank (43x137mm), untagged, dull gum. Produced by KCS Industries.*

TTB33n

TTB33

    MNHVF

    Cover, blank, entire booklet   —

    n. booklet pane   —

FLAG OVER CAPITOL ISSUE Folded cover (43x81mm) with one blank pane of five stamps. Covers same as K-M B133a. *Pane blank (43x130mm), five stamps (44x24mm) perforated 10 on long side, with dull gum, untagged. Pane is similar to TTB28An. Tab height is about 6mm or 9mm. Produced by Bureau of Engraving and Printing.*

TTB34

TTB34

    MNHVF

    Cover, Flag over Capitol, entire booklet   40.00

    n. booklet pane   —

1985. SEASHELLS ISSUE $4.40, folded cover (41x81mm) without black printing, two blank panes of ten stamps. Covers same as K-M B163. *Pane blank (43x137mm), 10 stamps perforated 10.0x9.8, with dull gum, untagged. Scored horizontally between stamps. Panes similar to TTB28n. Tab height is about 11mm. Produced by Bureau of Engraving and Printing.*

  TTB35

TTB35

    MNHVF

    Cover, Seashells, entire booklet   —

    n. booklet pane   —

1985. SEASHELLS ISSUE $4.40, folded cover (41x81mm), two blank panes of ten stamps. Covers same as K-M B163 without black printing. *Pane blank (43x137mm), 10 stamps perforated 10.0x9.8, with dull gum, untagged. Panes similar to TTB28n. Tab height is about 11mm. Produced by Bureau of Engraving and Printing.*

 TTB36, TTB37

TTB36

    MNHVF

    Cover, Seashells, entire booklet   —

    n. booklet pane   —

1985. SEASHELLS ISSUE $4.40, folded cover (41x81mm) two blank panes of five stamps. Covers same as K-M B163 without black printing. *Panes blank perforated 10.1 on long side. Panes similar to TTB28An. Tab height is about 11mm. Produced by Bureau of Engraving and Printing.*

TTB37

    MNHVF

    Cover, Seashells, entire booklet   —

    n. booklet pane   —

    v. Set of 7 sequential covers* *Seven sequential TTB37 books are necessary to show all 25 seashells.

Note: All known TTB37 booklets have the panes adhered to the inside back covers.

1994. HUMMINGBIRDS ISSUE $5.80, folded cover (41x84mm) with two blank panes of five stamps. Covers same as K-M B210. *Pane blank (41x137mm), five stamps (44x24mm) perforated 10.9, with glossy gum, untagged. Panes similar to TTB28An. Tab height is unknown. Produced by American Bank Note Co. All known TTB38 booklets have felt pen marks on outside front cover.*

 TTB38

TTB38

    MNHVF

    Hummingbirds, entire booklet   —

    n. booklet pane   —

1994. G (FLAG) ISSUE G Series $6.40, folded booklet cover (43x81mm) with two blank panes of five stamps similar to TTB28An. Covers same as K-M B237. Panes similar to TTB28An. Tab height is unknown. *Possibly produced by American Bank Note Co. All known TTB39 booklets have felt pen marks on outside front cover.*

   TTB39

TTB39

    MNHVF

    G (Flag), entire booklet   —

    n. booklet pane   —

1988. $5 JACK LONDON ISSUE Folded cover (43x81mm) with $5.00 Jack London exterior and unissued "The American Garden" inside back cover, with two panes of ten stamps. Covers same as K-M B176. *Pane of ten stamps with blue rectangle, perforated 10.9x9.8, untagged. The pane has an electric eye bar in the selvage over the upper left stamp, which has a number in it. Tab height is about 12mm. Produced by Bureau of Engraving and Printing.*

 TTB40

TTB40n

TTB40

    $5 Jack London, entire booklet   MNHVF
    n. booklet pane   —

1990s. Daffodil Issue Folded Daffodil cover (43x81mm) with
unissued "The American Garden" inside back cover and two panes of
ten stamps. Pane of ten stamps with blue rectangle, perforated
10.9x9.8, untagged. The pane has an electric eye bar in the selvage
over the upper left stamp. Tab height is about 12mm. Produced by
Bureau of Engraving and Printing.

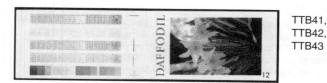

TTB41,
TTB42,
TTB43

TTB41n,
TTB43n

TTB41

    Daffodil, entire booklet   MNHVF
    n. booklet pane   —

1990s. Daffodil Issue Folded Daffodil cover (43x81mm) with
unissued "The American Garden" inside back cover and four panes of
ten stamps. *Pane of ten stamps with blue rectangle, perforated
10.9x9.8, untagged. The pane has an electric eye bar in the selvage
over the upper left stamp, which has a number in it. Tab height is
about 12mm. Produced by Bureau of Engraving and Printing.*

TTB42n, TTB43n

TTB42

    Daffodil, entire booklet   MNHVF
    n. booklet pane   —

1990s. Daffodil Issue Folded Daffodil cover (43x81mm) with
unissued "The American Garden" inside back cover and four panes of
ten stamps. Pane of ten stamps with very dark blue rectangle,
perforated 10.9x9.8, untagged. The pane has an electric eye bar in
the selvage over the upper left stamp and is the same as TTB41n
except for the very dark blue color. Tab height is about 12mm.
Produced by Bureau of Engraving and Printing.

TTB43

    Daffodil, entire booklet   MNHVF
    n. booklet pane   —

1990s. Daffodil Issue Folded Daffodil cover (43x81mm) with
no printing inside covers and four panes of ten stamps. *Pane of ten
stamps with very dark blue rectangle, perforated 10.9x9.8, untagged.
The pane has an electric eye bar in the selvage over the upper right
stamp. Tab height is about 12mm. Produced by Bureau of Engraving
and Printing.*

TTB44n

TTB44

    Daffodil, entire booklet   MNHVF
    n. booklet pane   —

1990s. Daffodil Issue Folded Daffodil cover (66x87mm) with no
printing inside covers and two panes of ten stamps. *Pane of ten large
size (29.5x21.0mm) stamps with black rectangle, perforated 10.9x9.8,
untagged. The pane has an electric eye bar in the selvage over the
upper left stamp. Tab height is about 12mm. Produced by Bureau of
Engraving and Printing.*

TTB45

TTB45n

TTB45

    Daffodil, entire booklet   MNHVF
    n. booklet pane   —

TTB46 not yet assigned.

Self-adhesive Folded and Glued Booklets

Blank Cover Issue Folded blank cover (44x81mm), *two self-
adhesive panes with one horizontal row of perforations gauge 10.9 at
fold which goes through the stamps and the backing paper. Panes
blank self-adhesive (44x132mm), untagged. Pane is similar to
TTB33n. Unknown manufacturer.*

TTB47

TTB47   MNHVF
    blank, pane   —

1999. 20¢ Ring-necked Pheasant Issue Folded blank cover
(45x83mm). Blank self-adhesive convertible booklet of ten stamps.
The top and bottom two stamps are oriented 90 degrees to the other
eight stamps in the booklet. Serpentine die cut gauge 10.5x11 for the
eight stamps in the "normal" position and 11x11 for the two stamps in
the 90 degree position. All features of this booklet closely match the
1999 Ring-necked Pheasant Booklet (K-M B308 containing 1248n
stamps). The center strip has been removed prior to folding. *Overall
tagging. Made by Avery Dennison.*

TTB48

TTB48   MNHVF
    blank, pane   —

ATM Test Sheetlets

1989. Eagle and "00" Denomination Issue *Sheetlet with 12
stamp-like labels with an eagle, "00" denomination above "USA." Back
illustrates a larger version of the eagle with "$3" above the eagle and
"Twelve 25 cent stamps" below. Copyrighted 1989 USPS. Possibly a
test booklet for the first self-adhesive (KM924n). Multicolor, self-
adhesive.*

TTB49

TTB49n

TTB49n.v.

TTB49   MNHVF
    multicolored, sheetlet   1,500.00
    v. multicolored sheetlet, darker blue   1,500.00
        paper

1990. Green Liberty Torch Issue "ATM TEST /
DEMONSTRATION SHEET," *self-adhesive sheetlet with 18 stamp-
like labels with straight-line die cut separations. Green printing on
back. Made by Avery Dennison.*

TTB50

TTB50   MNHVF
    green, pane   15.00

1990. 25¢ Stars and Stripes Issue 25¢ Stars and Stripes *self-
adhesive sheetlet with 12 multicolor stamp designs overprinted
"SPECIMEN / FOR AM TEST". Printed on polyester film with straight
line die cut separations. Black defacement line through "25 USA".
Untagged. Made by Avery International Corporation.*

TTB50A   MNHVF
    black, blue & dark red, sheetlet   —

1990. Stars and Stripes Issue 25¢ stars and stripes
*imperforate paper sheetlet with 12 multicolor stamp design. Black
diagonal line through "25¢" and "USA". Black printing on back.*

TTB50AA

TTB50AA   MNHVF
    red & blue, sheetlet   —

1992. Blank Issue *Imperforate self-adhesive ATM sheetlet with no
printing on either the front or back. Self-adhesive ATM sheetlet with
18 blank straight-line die cut labels. Manufactured by Dittler Brothers,
Inc.*

Please read the introduction to this catalog
carefully. It contains much valuable
information for all stamp collectors, and also
makes the catalog easier for you to use.

TTB50B

TTB50B
    blank, sheetlet   MNHVF
                                    —

1992. BLANK ISSUE *Imperforate self-adhesive ATM sheetlet with no printing on either the front or back. Liner with green "SELF-ADHESIVE • DO NOT WET" sloping from upper left to lower right and visible through front. Manufactured by Dittler Brothers, Inc.*

TTB50C
    blank, sheetlet   MNHVF
                                    —

1992. 29¢ EAGLE AND SHIELD ISSUE *Imperforate paper sheetlet with 17 stamp-like labels overprinted with dark blue "VOID" in the background and 1 black label with text. No printing on back.*

TTB50D

TTB50D
    brown (multicolored), sheetlet   MNHVF
                                    —

1992. MULTICOLOR LIBERTY TORCH ISSUE *Imperforate thick, slick surface, paper sheetlet with 18 stamp designs printed in black, gold and green. Black diagonal lines through "29¢". Black printing on back.*

TTB50E

TTB50E
    black, gold & green, sheetlet   MNHVF
                                    —

1992. ROSE ATM ISSUE *Imperforate gray paper sheetlet with 18 stamp-like labels of a red rose with green leaves, imprinted 29¢, with a large gray "VOID" in the background and plate No. 5111. No printing on back. Possibly made by NCR.*

TTB50F

TTB50F
    red & green, sheetlet   MNHVF
                                    —

"NCR" AND "USA" WITH FLAG ISSUE *Imperforate paper sheetlet with 12 multicolored stamp-like labels, light blue label "VOID" in the background. Blue diagonal line through "USA". Red and blue printing on back. Made by NCR.*

TTB51

TTB51
    red & blue, sheetlet   MNHVF
                                  35.00

1996. "NCR & USPS" IN WHITE STRIPES OF FLAG ISSUE *Imperforate paper sheetlet with 12 multicolor stamp-like labels. Blue diagonal line through "USA". Blue printing on back. Made by NCR.*

TTB52

TTB52
    red & blue, sheetlet   MNHVF
                                  25.00

1997. SOUVENIR ATM SHEETLET FROM PACIFIC 97 ISSUE *Self-adhesive sheetlet with 18 multicolor stamp-like labels of San Francisco scenes and Pacific 97 logo, with black obliterating lines and no die cut. Black printing on back. Made by Avery Dennison.*

TTB53

TTB53
    multicolored, sheetlet   MNHVF
                                    —

1997. SOUVENIR ATM SHEETLET FROM PACIFIC 97 ISSUE *Self-adhesive sheetlet with 18 multicolor stamp-like labels of San Francisco scenes and Pacific 97 logo, with die cuts but no black obliterating lines. Black printing on back. Made by Avery Dennison.*

TTB54
    multicolored, sheetlet   MNHVF
                                    —

1997. SOUVENIR ATM PANE FROM PACIFIC 97 ISSUE *Self-adhesive sheetlet with 18 multicolor stamp-like labels of San Francisco scenes and Pacific 97 logo, without obliterating lines or die cuts. Black printing on back. Made by Avery Dennison.*

TTB55
    multicolored, sheetlet   MNHVF
                                    —

1997. FEDERAL DUCK STAMP ISSUE *Multilayer promotional for proposed 1998 Duck Stamp Program which issued the 1998 Federal duck stamp in ATM-size self-adhesive sheetlets as well as panes of 30 gummed stamps. Back printed in color. Self-adhesive imperforate stamp design.*

TTB55A

TTB55A		MNHVF
multicolored, pane		—

1997. BUGS BUNNY SOUVENIR FROM PACIFIC 97 ISSUE *Self-adhesive sheetlet with large multicolor image of Bugs Bunny, 87x129.5mm with narrow white border, without die cuts. Image of Bugs Bunny and "32 / USA" in upper left corner replaces 32¢ Bugs Bunny stamp on issued sheetlets. Also missing Bugs signature. Black printing on back. Made by Avery Dennison.*

TTB55B

TTB55B		MNHVF
multicolored, sheetlet		10.00
v. no printing on back		—

1997. BUGS BUNNY SOUVENIR FROM PACIFIC 97 ISSUE *Self-adhesive sheetlet 81x125mm without white border with large multicolor stamp-like image of Bugs Bunny, without die cuts. Image of Bugs Bunny and "32 / USA" in upper left corner replaces 32¢ Bugs Bunny stamp on issued sheetlets. Also missing Bugs signature. Black printing on back. Made by Avery Dennison.*

TTB55C

TTB55C		MNHVF
multicolored, sheetlet		10.00

1997. "FOR ATM TESTING" AND PILLARS ISSUE *Self-adhesive sheetlet with 18 stamp-like labels inscribed "FOR ATM / TESTING" above and below a four-column building with straight line die cuts. Blue printing on back. Made by Avery Dennison for NCR.*

TTB56

TTB56		MNHVF
blue, sheetlet		375.00

1997. FTPO ISSUE *Self-adhesive sheetlet with 18 stamp-like labels with "FOR / TESTING / PURPOSES / ONLY." Straight line die cuts. Black printing on back. Made by Avery Dennison.*

TTB57, TTB58, TTB61

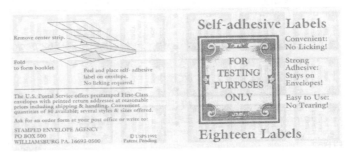

TTB57, TTB58, TTB61 *back*

TTB57		MNHVF
black, sheetlet		80.00

1998. FTPO ISSUE *Self-adhesive sheetlet with 18 stamp-like labels with "FOR / TESTING / PURPOSES / ONLY," serpentine die cuts gauge 7.8. Black printing on back. Made by Avery Dennison.*

TTB58		MNHVF
black, sheetlet		40.00

2000. SOUVENIR ATM ISSUE *Self-adhesive sheetlet with two jumbo and six definitive-size stamp-like labels from World Stamp Expo 2000, straight line die cuts. Black printing on back. Made by Avery Dennison and used as "stamps" in youth area.*

TTB59

TTB59		MNHVF
multicolored, sheetlet		5.00

TTB60 is not assigned.

2000. FTPO ISSUE *Self-adhesive sheetlet with 18 stamp-like labels with "FOR / TESTING / PURPOSES / ONLY," serpentine die cuts gauge 7.8. Blue printing on back. Made by Avery Dennison.*

TTB61 *front*

TTB61

        magenta, sheetlet   MNHVF
                                                  —

2000. NCR for ATM Testing Issue *Imperforate paper sheetlet with 18 stamp-like labels with NCR logo and "FOR / ATM / NCR / TESTING". Plate number VI. Stamp side color is black. Back printing in multicolor. Made by NCR.*

TTB62 *front*

TTB62 *back*

TTB62

        black, sheetlet   MNHVF
                                            25.00

Confederate States of America

The Confederate States of America was the government established in 1861 by the Southern states that seceded from the Union, charging that it was aggressively hostile toward their "domestic institutions."

South Carolina, the first state to secede (Dec. 20, 1860), justified its action on the grounds of continued Northern attacks on slavery, the coming to power of a sectionalist party (the Republican), and the election of a President (Abraham Lincoln) "whose opinions and purposes are hostile to slavery." It was followed, in order, by Mississippi, Florida, Alabama, Georgia, Louisiana, Texas, Virginia, Arkansas, North Carolina, and Tennessee. The attack on Ft. Sumter at Charleston, S.C., on April 12, 1861, is generally considered to mark the onset of hostilities. The war continued until spring, 1865.

Upon the outbreak of the war, the Union demonetized the postal issues that had been good for postage up to June 1, 1861, so that the Confederacy could not make use of the large quantities of stamps in its possession.

The Southern states, being primarily agrarian, had little industrial capability, including printing, and the lack of postage stamps could have hampered communications.

The provisional government of six Confederate states was formed in Montgomery, Ala., on Feb. 4, 1861. By March 6, President Jefferson Davis had made his final appointment to his cabinet, Postmaster General John H. Reagan from Texas. This appointment was one of the most difficult to fill because of the importance it would have in the newly formed government.

Shortly after taking office, Reagan instructed his postmasters to "continue the performance of their duties as such, and render all accounts and pay all moneys to the order of the government of the U.S. as they had heretofore done, until the government of the Confederate states shall be prepared to assume control of its postal affairs."

On May 13, 1861, Reagan issued his proclamation assuming control and direction of postal service within the limits of the Confederate States of America as of the first day of June. Effective June 1, 1861, new rates and regulations, including a basic 5¢ letter postage rate, would go into effect. The federal government suspended operations in the Confederate states by a proclamation issued by U.S. Postmaster General Montgomery Blair on May 27, 1861, effective May 31, 1861.

3¢ 1861 Postmasters Provisionals

From the time each Southern state joined the Confederacy until June 1, 1861, the postal system operated under the rules and rates of the U.S. government, including a basic 3¢ letter postage rate. Even though the U.S. government was technically in control of the postal system, the U.S. Post Office Department was reluctant to send supplies and stamps to the seceded states.

As the southern postmasters began to run out of stamps and envelopes, they reverted back to pre-stamp times to operate in the most efficient manner they could. A few issued their own provisional postage, even though the U.S. Post Office had made the issuance of postmaster provisionals illegal many years earlier.

By June 1, 1861, five cities are known to have issued 3¢ provisionals. Nashville prepared a sixth recorded 3¢ provisional prior to Tennessee's joining the Confederacy on July 2, 1861. The unissued 3¢ Nashville provisional was produced in a state that was in the process of seceding, while the 3¢ provisionals were used in the Confederacy before the June 1 control of the Confederate postal administration.

Hillsboro, N.C., Handstamp, Adhesive. Postmaster Calvin Parish ran short of 3¢ stamps prior to the June 1 start of the Confederate 5¢ rate. To meet the demand of his customers he applied his "paid" handstamp in black to small strips of paper and sold them for postage. Later, these would also be used to pay the 5¢ CSA rate.

CSP66-2

CSP66-1
3¢   **black,** on cover (one known)   Mint   Used
                                                      20,000.00

JACKSON, MISS., HANDSTAMP, ENVELOPE.

CSP73-1

CSP73-1   Mint   Used
3¢   **black,** entire   —

MADISON COURT HOUSE, FLA., TYPESET, ADHESIVE. The earliest postmasters' provisionals issued in the Confederacy. Earliest known use: Feb. 13, 1861. Printed for Postmaster Samuel J. Perry at a newspaper published by his eldest son.

 CSP92-1

 CSP92-1a

CSP92-1   Mint   Used
3¢   **gold,** single   17,000.00
          On cover, one known   65,000.00
CSP92-1a   Mint   Used
3¢   **gold,** "CNETS" error, one known   20,000.00

NASHVILLE, TENN., TYPESET, ADHESIVE. Strips of five of the 3¢ provisional were printed for W.D. McNish to be issued from his office. The Confederate rate was increased to 5¢, so they were never issued. It is believed some remainders were turned in to the U.S. Post Office Department in Washington, D.C. after the war's end.

CSP102-1

CSP102-1   Mint   Used
3¢   **carmine,** single, five varieties   270.00
          Strip of 5   900.00

SELMA, ALA., HANDSTAMP, ENVELOPE.

CSP128-1

CSP128-1   Mint   Used
3¢   **black,** entire   3,000.00

TUSCUMBIA, ALA., HANDSTAMP, ENVELOPE.

CSP140-1

CSP140-1   Mint   Used
3¢   **dull red** on buff, entire   18,000.00

Confederate States Postmasters Provisionals

In the interim period from June 1, 1861, until the official issuance of Confederate stamps, as well as times that the postmasters ran out of general issue stamps, many postmasters produced other provisionals. These are:

- Adhesive postage stamps printed or handstamped on paper for separation and attachment to envelopes to signify payment of postage.
- Press-printed envelopes produced in quantity and provided by the printer to the postmaster; thus there is consistency in the paper types on which these provisionals are found.
- Handstamp provisional envelopes, which have provided a challenge to the collector. To be a provisional, the envelope must have been prepared in advance of the mailing of the envelope, in most cases sold by the postmaster and carried home for later use. Handstamp provisionals are easily confused with general handstamp covers, which were not prepared in advance. Many postmasters used the same handstamp device to produce both handstamp paid and due envelopes as well as provisional envelopes. Evidence must exist that these envelopes were prepared in advance in order to classify them as provisionals. The strongest evidence is the existence of unused examples. Handstamp provisionals come in a variety of papers as they were struck on whatever paper the postmaster might have had at the time. Many were "handbacks" to the customer in order to make necessary change as little coinage existed. For this reason, we have not attempted to differentiate the handstamp paper varieties.

The listings here represent those defined by the Confederate Stamp Alliance, an association of collectors and dealers in Confederate States material. However, it should be noted that new evidence of CSA postal material continues to surface almost 150 years after the War Between the States.

By philatelic standards, all Confederate provisionals are scarce. The most common exists in only a few hundred examples. Many exist in examples of only one or two. The prices in this section are considered retail asking prices for fine examples of entire covers and examples of off-cover stamps with little or no gum. Examples of unused stamps with major amounts of original gum would be valued at considerably more.

To date, 154 different towns have been recorded as issuing provisionals. Many more surely did. We know of many other potential provisionals; however, research has yet to prove their "prepared in advance" status. As it does, they will be added to this listing.

The illustrations provided are the best available. Please note, however, they are not always to scale. Many have been reduced to fit space requirements.

ABERDEEN, MISS., HANDSTAMP, ENVELOPE.

CSP1-1

CSP1-1   Mint   Used
5¢   **black,** entire   8,000.00
CSP1-2   Mint   Used
10¢   **black,** entire, revalued 10¢ ms over 5¢   15,000.00

ABINGDON, VA., HANDSTAMP, ENVELOPE.

CSP2-3

CSP2-2

CSP2-1

		Mint	Used
2¢	**black,** entire		15,000.00

CSP2-2

		Mint	Used
5¢	**black,** entire		1,500.00
	Entire, patriotic cover		3,000.00

CSP2-3

		Mint	Used
10¢	**black,** entire, one mint known	5,000.00	7,500.00

ALBANY, GA., HANDSTAMP, ENVELOPE.

CSP3-1   CSP3-2   CSP3-3

CSP3-1

		Mint	Used
5¢	**greenish-blue,** entire		600.00
	On patriotic cover		—

CSP3-2

		Mint	Used
10¢	**greenish-blue,** entire (similar to CSP3-1)		2,000.00

CSP3-3

		Mint	Used
10¢	**greenish-blue,** entire		2,500.00

Only recorded use of this marking is on a revalued cover with CSP3-4.

CSP3-4

		Mint	Used
10¢ over 5¢	**greenish-blue,** entire (CSP3-3 over CSP3-1)		2,500.00

ANDERSON COURT HOUSE, S.C., HANDSTAMP, ENVELOPE.

CSP4-2

CSP4-1

CSP4-1

		Mint	Used
2¢	**black,** entire, no rate marking, one known		7,000.00

CSP4-2

		Mint	Used
5¢	**black,** entire	500.00	2,500.00

CSP4-3

		Mint	Used
10¢	**black,** entire, 10¢ in ms, one known		3,000.00

ATHENS, GA., WOODCUT, ADHESIVE.
Prepared for Postmaster T. Crawford and printed from a single setting of two woodcut subjects by the local newspaper, *The Banner Watchman.* Each subject is similar but has distinct differences from the other, such as the size of "PAID," normally larger on the right stamp in the pair. The size of a sheet is unknown. The largest known piece is a strip of four on cover. Notes indicate the stamps were in use only for six weeks.

CSP5-1

CSP5-1

		Mint	Used
5¢	**purple,** single	1,000.00	2,500.00
	On cover		3,500.00
	Horizontal pair	2,500.00	4,200.00
	Pair on cover		6,000.00
	Strip of 4 on cover, two known		10,000.00
	Patriotic cover		5,000.00

CSP5-1a

		Mint	Used
5¢	**purple,** vertical tete-beche pair		8,000.00
	Tete-beche pair on cover		25,000.00

ATLANTA, GA., HANDSTAMP, ENVELOPE.

CSP6-1   CSP6-2

CSP6-6   CSP6-7

CSP6-1

		Mint	Used
2¢	**black,** entire		
	On advertising cover		3,000.00

CSP6-2

		Mint	Used
5¢	**black,** entire	150.00	500.00
	On patriotic cover		3,500.00
	On advertising cover		—

CSP6-2a

		Mint	Used
10¢	**black,** entire, revalued 10¢ handstamp over 5¢		1,500.00

CSP6-3

		Mint	Used
5¢	**red,** entire (similar to CSP6-2)		3,000.00

CSP6-4

		Mint	Used
5¢	**black,** entire (similar to CSP6-1)		1,600.00

CSP6-4a

		Mint	Used
10¢	**black,** entire, revalued 10¢ handstamp over 5¢		2,500.00

CSP6-5

		Mint	Used
5¢	**black,** entire (similar to CSP6-6 with "5" sideways)		700.00

CSP6-6

		Mint	Used
10¢	**black,** entire		3,000.00

CSP6-7

		Mint	Used
10¢	**black,** entire		800.00
	On advertising cover		3,000.00

AUSTIN, MISS., TYPESET, ENVELOPE.

CSP-8

CSP8

		Mint	Used
5¢	**red** on amber, entire, canceled black "PAID," one known		75,000.00

AUSTIN, TEXAS, HANDSTAMP, ADHESIVE.

CSP9-1

CSP9-1

		Mint	Used
10¢	**black,** single		—
	Tied, one known on cover		
	On cover, uncanceled, one known		1,500.00

AUSTIN, TEXAS, HANDSTAMP, ENVELOPE.

CSP9-2

CSP9-2

		Mint	Used
10¢	**black,** entire		1,500.00

AUTAUGAVILLE, ALA., HANDSTAMP, ENVELOPE. Brass engraved handstamp used by Postmaster Albert William McNeel, similar to the woodcut used in Athens, Ga. The original brass dies used to print the 5¢ and a 10¢ stamp, as well as three paid dies, still exist and are in the hands of collectors.

 CSP10-1 CSP10-2

CSP10-1

		Mint	Used
5¢	**black,** entire		12,000.00

CSP10-2

		Mint	Used
5¢	**black,** entire		12,000.00

BALCONY FALLS, VA., HANDSTAMP, ENVELOPE.

CSP-11

CSP11

		Mint	Used
10¢	**black,** entire		1,800.00

BARNWELL COURT HOUSE, S.C., HANDSTAMP, ENVELOPE.

(Envelope)

CSP-12 'Control Mark'

CSP12

		Mint	Used
5¢	**black,** entire		3,000.00

BATON ROUGE, LA., TYPESET, ADHESIVE. Joseph McCormick was postmaster of Baton Rouge until it was occupied by Federal forces in 1862. McCormick contracted with the *Cornet and Gazette* newspaper to print stamps. They were delivered in mid-July 1861, and were used until December 1861, when regular postage arrived. Estimates indicate 1,500 copies of the 2¢, 2,500 of the 5¢, and 1,000 of the 10¢ were printed. Fewer than 200 copies remain of the 10¢ stamps. Remainders of all stamps were destroyed by the postmaster when Federal forces occupied the cities. August Dietz theorized the stamps were printed in sheets of 10 in two horizontal rows of five. The assistant postmaster at the time had indicated sometime after the war they were printed in sheets of 25.

 CSP13-1 CSP13-2

 CSP13-3 CSP13-4

CSP13-1

		Mint	Used
2¢	**green,** single, 10 varieties	5,000.00	6,000.00
	On cover, 10 varieties		30,000.00

CSP13-1a

		Mint	Used
2¢	**green,** single, "McCcrmick," 10 varieties	12,000.00	8,000.00
	On cover, "McCcrmick," error		15,000.00

CSP13-2

		Mint	Used
5¢	**green & carmine,** single, 10 varieties	1,500.00	1,500.00
	On cover, 10 varieties		7,000.00
	Pair on cover		12,500.00
	Strip of 3 on cover, 10 varieties		15,000.00
	Strip of 5 on cover, 10 varieties		25,000.00

CSP13-2a

		Mint	Used
5¢	**green & carmine,** single, "McCcrmick"	4,000.00	3,200.00
	On cover, "McCormick"		10,500.00

CSP13-3

		Mint	Used
5¢	**green & carmine,** single, 10 varieties	4,000.00	1,500.00
	On cover, 10 varieties		10,000.00

CSP13-3a

		Mint	Used
5¢	**green & carmine,** single, "McCcrmick," 10 varieties		3,000.00

CSP13-4

		Mint	Used
10¢	**blue,** single, 10 varieties		6,000.00
	On cover, one known		75,000.00

BEAUMONT, TEXAS, TYPESET, ADHESIVE. Earliest known use: *April 9, 1864.*

 CSP14-1 CSP14-3

CSP14-1

		Mint	Used
10¢	**black** on yellow, single, several varieties of each		4,500.00
	On cover, several varieties of each		75,000.00

CSP14-2

		Mint	Used
10¢	**black** on pink, single, several varieties of each		15,000.00
	On cover, several varieties of each		35,000.00

CSP14-3

		Mint	Used
10¢	**black** on yellow, single, one known		100,000.00

BLADON SPRINGS, ALA., HANDSTAMP, ENVELOPE.

 CSP15-1 CSP15-2

CSP15-1

		Mint	Used
ms 5¢	**black frame,** entire		2,000.00

CSP15-2

		Mint	Used
10¢	**black,** entire		—

BLUFFTON, S.C., HANDSTAMP, ENVELOPE.

CSP16

		Mint	Used
CSP16			
5¢	**black,** entire, one known		5,000.00

BRIDGEVILLE, ALA., HANDSTAMP, ADHESIVE.

CSP17

		Mint	Used
CSP17			
5¢	**black with red squares,** pair on cover, on pen-ruled squares		25,000.00

CAMDEN, S.C., HANDSTAMP, ENVELOPE.

CSP18-1

CSP18-2

		Mint	Used
CSP18-1			
5¢	**black,** entire		800.00
CSP18-2			
10¢	**black,** entire, used same as handstamp "PAID"	500.00	

CANTON, MISS., HANDSTAMP, ENVELOPE. Four different
envelopes were issued by W.M. Preistly, the postmaster in 1861. The first was improvised from an old canceling stamp but the other three were of different designs.

CSP19-1

		Mint	Used
CSP19-1			
5¢	**black,** entire	950.00	2,000.00
CSP19-2		Mint	Used
10¢ over 5¢	**black,** entire, revalued 10¢ ms over 5¢		3,000.00

CAROLINA CITY, N.C., HANDSTAMP, ENVELOPE.

CSP20

		Mint	Used
CSP20			
5¢	**black,** entire (two known)		6,000.00

CARTERSVILLE, GA., HANDSTAMP, ENVELOPE.

CSP21

		Mint	Used
CSP21			
(5¢)	**red,** entire		1,500.00

CHAPEL HILL, N.C., HANDSTAMP, ENVELOPE.

CSP22

		Mint	Used
CSP22			
5¢	**black,** entire		4,000.00
	On patriotic cover		6,500.00

CHARLESTON, S.C., LITHOGRAPH, ADHESIVE. Only Charleston,
Lynchburg, Va., and Memphis, Tenn., produced adhesive stamps and printed envelopes at the same time.

CSP23-1

		Mint	Used
CSP23-1			
5¢	**blue,** single	900.00	900.00
	On cover		2,500.00
	Pair	1,500.00	2,000.00
	On cover		2,000.00
	Pair on cover		5,000.00
	On patriotic cover		5,000.00
	On cover with CS7 (5¢ London Print)		6,000.00
	On cover with CSP60 (forwarded)		6,000.00

CHARLESTON, S.C., TYPOGRAPH, ENVELOPE.

CSP23-2

CSP23-7

		Mint	Used
CSP23-2		Mint	Used
5¢	**blue,** entire	1,200.00	2,500.00
CSP23-3		Mint	Used
5¢	**blue** on amber, entire	1,200.00	2,500.00
CSP23-4		Mint	Used
5¢	**blue** on orange, entire	1,200.00	2,000.00
CSP23-5		Mint	Used
5¢	**blue** on buff, entire	1,200.00	2,500.00
CSP23-6		Mint	Used
5¢	**blue** on blue, entire	3,500.00	2,500.00
CSP23-7		Mint	Used
10¢	**blue** on orange, entire, one known		80,000.00

CHARLESTON, S.C., HANDSTAMP, ENVELOPE.

CSP23-8		Mint	Used
10¢	**black,** piece, one known		5,000.00

CHARLOTTE, N.C., HANDSTAMP, ENVELOPE.

CSP23A-1

CSP23A-1

CSP23A-1		Mint	Used
5¢	**blue,** entire (two known), prepared in advance examples of handstamp "PAID"		1,800.00

CHARLOTTESVILLE, VA., HANDSTAMP, ENVELOPE.

CSP24-1   CSP24-2

CSP24-1		Mint	Used
5¢	**black,** entire, with ms initials		5,000.00

CSP24-2		Mint	Used
10¢	**black,** entire, with ms initials		5,000.00

CHATTANOOGA, TENN., HANDSTAMP, ENVELOPE.

CSP25-2

CSP25-1a		Mint	Used
5¢ over 2¢	**black,** entire	3,000.00	

CSP25-2		Mint	Used
5¢	**black,** entire		1,500.00

CHRISTIANSBURG, VA., HANDSTAMP, ENVELOPE.

CSP26-2

CSP26-1		Mint	Used
5¢	**black** on blue, entire		2,500.00

CSP26-2		Mint	Used
5¢	**blue,** entire		1,800.00

CSP26-3		Mint	Used
5¢	**black** on orange, entire		2,200.00

CSP26-4		Mint	Used
5¢	**green,** entire, with U.S. Minkus #EN29		4,000.00

CSP26-5		Mint	Used
10¢	**blue,** entire		3,500.00

CLARKSVILLE, TEXAS, HANDSTAMP, ENVELOPE.

CSP27

CSP27		Mint	Used
10¢	**black,** entire, same as handstamp "PAID" when used		

COLAPARCHEE, GA., HANDSTAMP, ENVELOPE.

  CSP28

CSP28		Mint	Used
5¢	**black,** entire with undated postmark control		3,500.00

Note: All recorded examples are used from Savannah, Ga., with a general-issue stamp on the reverse and the Colaparchee markings lined out on the front.

COLUMBIA, S.C., HANDSTAMP, ENVELOPE.

CSP29-1   CSP29-3

CSP29-4

CSP29-5

CSP29-1		Mint	Used
5¢	**blue,** entire	500.00	700.00
	blue, entire, with CS1 on cover		3,000.00
	blue, entire, used with CS8		7,500.00

CSP29-2		Mint	Used
5¢	**black,** entire	600.00	750.00

CSP29-3		Mint	Used
10¢ over 5¢	**blue,** entire		3,000.00

CSP29-4		Mint	Used
5¢	**blue,** entire, seal on back, three types of "PAID"		1,000.00
	Entire, seal on front, three types of "PAID"		2,500.00

CSP29-5		Mint	Used
10¢	**blue,** entire, seal on back, three types of "PAID"		2,000.00

CSP29-6		Mint	Used
5¢	**blue,** entire, 27mm seal on back, three types of "PAID"		4,000.00

COLUMBIA, TENN., HANDSTAMP, ENVELOPE.

CSP30

CSP30
5¢   **red**, entire

	Mint	Used
		3,500.00

COLUMBUS, GA., HANDSTAMP ENVELOPE.

CSP31-1   CSP31-2

CSP31-1
5¢   **blue**, entire
         On advertising cover

	Mint	Used
		1,000.00
		—

CSP31-2
5¢   **red**, entire

	Mint	Used
		2,000.00

COURTLAND, ALA., WOODCUT, ENVELOPE.

CSP32-1

CSP32-1
5¢   **red**, entire

	Mint	Used
		15,000.00

CUTHBERT, GA., HANDSTAMP, ENVELOPE.

PAID **10**   CSP33

CSP33
5¢   **black**, entire

	Mint	Used
	—	—

Note: Considered a provisional only when unused, used from another town or with a general-issue stamp used over it.

DALTON, GA., HANDSTAMP, ENVELOPE.

CSP34-2

CSP34-1
(5¢)   **black**, entire, rate omitted (similar to
         CSP34-2)

	Mint	Used
		750.00

CSP34-2
5¢   **black**, entire

	Mint	Used
		750.00

CSP34-2a
10¢ over 5¢ **black**, entire, revalued ms 10¢ over 5¢

	Mint	Used
		1,500.00

CSP34-2b
20¢ over 5¢ **black**, entire, revalued ms 20¢ over 5¢

	Mint	Used
		2,000.00

CSP34-3
10¢   **black**, entire (similar to CSP34-2)

	Mint	Used
		750.00

DANVILLE, VA., TYPESET, ADHESIVE. Postmaster W.D. Coleman printed these stamps some time after October 1861. He was the publisher of the local newspaper, *The "Democratic Appeal."* He estimated printing 3,000 copies of the stamp and had gum applied to the back of the paper. The stamp was assembled from borders of printing type. Coleman used this same type to produce the provisionals for Pittsylvania CH, VA., which was 20 miles from Danville.

CSP35-1

CSP35-1
5¢   **red**, single, two varieties known, laid paper
         On cover, two varieties known, cut to
             shape, laid paper
         Single, two varieties known, wove paper
         On cover, two varieties known, wove paper
         Single, two varieties known, cut to shape,
             wove paper
         On cover, two varieties known, cut to
             shape, wove paper

	Mint	Used
		6,000.00
		10,000.00
		5,500.00
		15,000.00
		4,000.00
		6,000.00

DANVILLE, VA., TYPOGRAPH, ENVELOPE Dietz suggested these envelopes were printed at the request of Postmaster W.B. Payne at the printing office of William Coleman, publisher of *The Democratic Appeal,* the local newspaper. These envelopes would have predated the Danville adhesive stamps, having been issued between June and October 1861. A letter from William Coleman indicates he does not recall printing any stamps for Postmaster Payne. He may not have considered the envelopes as stamps.

CSP35-4

CSP35-10

CSP35-2
5¢   **black**, entire, "Southern" may be straight
             or curved
         Entire, used to pay postage

	Mint	Used
		5,000.00
		7,000.00

		Mint	Used
Entire, used with other post payment evidence			4,000.00

CSP35-3
5¢   **black** on amber, entire, "Southern" may be straight or curved
Mint	Used
	5,500.00

CSP35-4
5¢   **black** on dark buff, entire, "Southern" may be straight or curved
Mint	Used
	4,000.00

DANVILLE, VA., HANDSTAMP, ENVELOPE.

CSP35-5

CSP35-6

CSP35-5
5¢   **black**, entire, ms initials "WBP"
Mint	Used
	4,000.00

CSP35-6
10¢   **black**, entire (exists in red, but not sold as provisional)
Mint	Used
	2,000.00

CSP35-7
10¢   **blue**, entire
Mint	Used
	2,500.00

CSP35-8
10¢   **black**, entire
Mint	Used
	2,500.00

CSP35-9
10¢   **black**, entire, ms initials "WBP"
Mint	Used
	2,500.00

DANVILLE, VA., TYPOGRAPH, ENVELOPE

CSP35-10
10¢   **red**, entire
Mint	Used
	—

DEMOPOLIS, ALA., HANDSTAMP, ENVELOPE. Postmaster J.Y. Hall.

CSP36-1

CSP36-1
5¢   **black**, entire, ms "J.Y. Hall"
Mint	Used
	3,500.00

CSP36-1a
5¢   **black**, entire, ms "Jno. Y. Hall"
Mint	Used
	2,000.00

CSP36-2
ms 5¢   **black**, entire, ms "J.Y. Hall"
Mint	Used
	3,500.00

EATONTON, GA., HANDSTAMP, ENVELOPE. These provisionals were found in the correspondence of Judge Nesbit. Five covers were discovered, all addressed to Capt. R.B. Nesbit. The pre-war hand-stamp was used with the "5" inserted in the date slot. The postmaster indicated an error had occurred at printing — that "paid" was to have been included in the handstamp.

CSP37

CSP37-1
5¢   **black**, entire, with handstamped "PAID" and rated postmark
Mint	Used
	3,500.00

CSP37-2
5¢ + 5¢   **black**, entire, with handstamped "PAID", double "5" and rated postmark
Mint	Used
	3,500.00

EMORY, VA., HANDSTAMP, SELVAGE.

CSP38-1

CSP38-1
5¢   **blue**, single
    blue, on cover, perforated 15 on 3 sides (exists with "5" above and below "PAID")
Mint	Used
	3,500.00
	18,000.00

EMORY, VA., HANDSTAMP, ENVELOPE.

CSP38-3

CSP38-2

CSP38-2
5¢   **blue**, entire
Mint	Used
	2,000.00

CSP38-3
10¢   **blue**, entire
Mint	Used
	4,500.00

FINCASTLE, VA., TYPESET, ENVELOPE. A letter dated 1901 exists from the postmaster of Fincastle authenticating the one known example of this cover. Postmaster Louis Housman indicates in the letter that the envelopes must have been supplied to him by the Confederate government. As we know today, this was not the case.

CSP39

CSP39
10¢   **black**, entire, one known
Mint	Used
	45,000.00

FORSYTH, GA., HANDSTAMP, ENVELOPE.

CSP40

CSP40
10¢   **black**, entire
Mint	Used
	1,500.00

FORT VALLEY, GA. HANDSTAMP, ENVELOPE.

CSP40A

CSP40A
5¢   **black**, entire
Mint	Used
	3,000.00

FRANKLIN, N.C., TYPESET, ENVELOPE. L.F. Siler was postmaster of Franklin and had these provisionals printed in the local newspaper office. The one copy known was found in family papers by Daniel H. Hamilton along with the Hillsboro, N.C. provisional.

CSP41-1

CSP41-1
5¢   **blue** on buff, entire, one known
Mint	Used
	50,000.00

FRANKLIN, N.C., HANDSTAMP, ENVELOPE.

CSP41-2

CSP41-2
5¢   **black,** entire

	Mint	Used
		500.00

FRAZIERRSVILLE, S.C., HANDSTAMP, ENVELOPE.

CSP42

CSP42
ms 5¢   **black,** entire, one known

	Mint	Used
		2,500.00

FREDERICKSBURG, VA., TYPESET, ADHESIVE.
Postmaster R.J. Thom had these stamps printed in 1866. After his death in 1868, his daughter found remainders of these stamps among her father's papers.

CSP43-3

CSP43-1

CSP43-1
5¢   **blue** on bluish, single, 10 varieties
      Block of 4, 10 varieties
      Sheet of 20, 10 varieties
      On cover, 10 varieties
      Pair on cover, 10 varieties

	Mint	Used
	250.00	600.00
	1,200.00	
	7,000.00	
		5,000.00
		15,000.00

CSP43-3
10¢   **brownish-red** on bluish, single, 10 varieties

	Mint	Used
	1,250.00	

CSP43-4
10¢   **red** on bluish, block of 4, 10 varieties

	Mint	Used
	5,000.00	

FRONT ROYAL, VA., HANDSTAMP, ENVELOPE.

CSP44-2

CSP44-1

CSP44
ms 5¢   **black,** entire, with initials

	Mint	Used
		—

CSP44-2
5¢   **black,** entire, with initials

	Mint	Used
		—

GAINESVILLE, ALA., HANDSTAMP, ENVELOPE.

CSP45-2

CSP45-1

CSP45-1
5¢   **black,** entire

	Mint	Used
		5,000.00

CSP45-2
10¢   **black,** entire, 01 instead of 10

	Mint	Used
		6,000.00

GALVESTON, TEXAS, HANDSTAMP, ENVELOPE.

CSP46-1

CSP46-2

CSP46-3

CSP46-1
5¢   **black,** entire

	Mint	Used
	500.00	1,500.00

CSP46-2
10¢   **black,** entire

	Mint	Used
		2,150.00

CSP46-3
10¢   **black,** entire

	Mint	Used
	600.00	2,500.00

CSP46-4
20¢   **black,** entire

	Mint	Used
		3,500.00

GASTON, N.C., HANDSTAMP, ENVELOPE.

CSP47

CSP47
5¢   **black,** entire, one known

	Mint	Used
		6,000.00

GEORGETOWN, S.C., HANDSTAMP, ENVELOPE.

CSP48

CSP48
5¢   **black,** entire

	Mint	Used
		1,200.00

GOLIAD, TEXAS, TYPESET, ADHESIVE.
Postmaster J.A. Clarke.

CSP49-3
Type I

CSP49-6

CSP49-6a
Type II

CSP49-1
5¢   **black,** single, ms "Clarke-P.M." in black

	Mint	Used
		6,000.00

CSP49-2
5¢   **black** on gray, single, ms "Clarke-P.M." in black

	Mint	Used
		5,000.00

CSP49-3

		Mint	Used
5¢	**black** on rose, single, ms "Clarke-P.M." in black		5,000.00

CSP49-4

		Mint	Used
10¢	**black,** single, ms "Clarke-P.M." in black	5,000.00	5,000.00

CSP49-5

		Mint	Used
10¢	**black** on rose, single, ms "Clarke-P.M." in black		5,000.00
	On patriotic cover, ms "Clarke-P.M." in black		10,000.00

CSP49-6

		Mint	Used
5¢	**black** on gray, single		7,000.00
	On cover		20,000.00

CSP49-6a

		Mint	Used
5¢	**black** on gray, single, spelled "GOILAD"		8,000.00
	Paid, one with error, spelled "GOILAD"		20,000.00

CSP49-7

		Mint	Used
10¢	**black** on gray, single		10,000.00
	On cover		35,000.00

CSP49-7a

		Mint	Used
10¢	**black** on gray, single, spelled "GOILAD"		6,000.00
	On cover, spelled "GOILAD"		30,000.00

CSP49-8

		Mint	Used
5¢	**black on** dark blue, single, four known		7,000.00

CSP49-9

		Mint	Used
10¢	**black** on dark blue, single		5,000.00
	On cover		25,000.00

GONZALES, TEXAS, LITHOGRAPH, ADHESIVE. John B. Law was postmaster of Gonzalez during the war. He was in business with Dr. Colman, and the post office was in their drugstore. They sold books and had labels printed and pasted on their books. These labels were sold and used as postage stamps during the war.

CSP50-1

CSP50-1

		Mint	Used
5¢	**gold** on dark blue, single, on glazed paper		15,000.00
	Pair on cover, on glazed paper		25,000.00

CSP50-2

		Mint	Used
10¢	**gold** on garnet, on cover, on glazed paper		15,000.00

CSP50-3

		Mint	Used
10¢	**gold** on black, on cover, on glazed paper		15,000.00

GREENSBORO, ALA., HANDSTAMP, ENVELOPE.

CSP51-2

CSP51-1

		Mint	Used
5¢	**black**, entire		2,500.00

CSP51-2

		Mint	Used
10¢	**black**, entire		3,000.00

CSP51-3

		Mint	Used
10¢	**black**, entire		4,500.00

GREENSBORO, N.C., HANDSTAMP, ENVELOPE.

CSP52-2

SP52-1

CSP52-1

		Mint	Used
10¢	**red**, entire		1,500.00

CSP52-1a

		Mint	Used
10¢	**red**, entire, due 10¢ over paid 10¢, one known		2,500.00

CSP52-2

		Mint	Used
10¢	**red**, entire, due 10¢, one known		2,500.00

GREENVILLE, ALA., TYPESET, ADHESIVE.

CSP53-1

CSP53-2

CSP53-1

		Mint	Used
5¢	**blue & red**, single, on pinkish, surface colored glazed paper	25,000.00	
	blue & red, on cover, on pinkish, surface colored glazed paper		55,000.00

CSP53-2

		Mint	Used
10¢	**blue & red**, single, on pinkish, surface colored glazed paper	—	
	blue & red, on cover, on pinkish, surface colored glazed paper		55,000.00

GREENVILLE COURT HOUSE, S.C., HANDSTAMP, ENVELOPE.

CSP55-1   CSP55-2

Control Marks

CSP55B

CSP55A

CSP55-1

		Mint	Used
5¢	**black**, entire, several types of handstamp, must have control mark on reverse		3,000.00

CSP55-2

		Mint	Used
10¢	**black**, entire, several types of handstamp, must have control mark on reverse		3,000.00

CSP55-3

		Mint	Used
20¢	**black**, entire, ms 20¢ over 10¢ handstamp, must have control mark on reverse		4,000.00

GREENWOOD DEPOT, VA., HANDSTAMP, ADHESIVE. Postmaster J. Bruce issued these primitive stamps to meet a new postal rate of 10¢, increased from 5¢, effective July 1, 1862.

CSP56

CSP56

		Mint	Used
10¢	**black** on gray-blue, entire, ms signature, laid paper		20,000.00

GRIFFIN, GA., HANDSTAMP, ENVELOPE.

CSP57

CSP57

		Mint	Used
5¢	**black**, entire		2,000.00

GROVE HILL, ALA., WOODCUT, ADHESIVE.

CSP58

CSP58

		Mint	Used
5¢	**black**, single		—
	black, on cover, two known		100,000.00

HALLETTSVILLE, TEXAS, HANDSTAMP, ADHESIVE.

CSP59

CSP59

		Mint	Used
10¢	**black** on gray-blue, on cover, on ruled paper		25,000.00

HAMBURGH, S.C., HANDSTAMP, ENVELOPE.

CSP60

PAID

CSP60A

CSP60

		Mint	Used
5¢	**black**, entire		2,500.00
	black, entire, with CSP23-1 (forwarded)		6,000.00

HARRISBURGH, TEXAS, HANDSTAMP, ENVELOPE.

CSP61-1

CSP61-1

		Mint	Used
5¢	**black**, entire, same as handstamp "PAID" when used	500.00	

HAYNESVILLE, ALA., TYPESET, ENVELOPE.

CSP62-

CSP62-1

CSP62-1

		Mint	Used
5¢	**black**, entire, same as handstamp "PAID" when used	500.00	

CSP62-2

		Mint	Used
10¢	**black**, entire, same as handstamp "PAID" when used	500.00	

HELENA, TEXAS, TYPESET, ADHESIVE.

CSP63-2

CSP63-1

CSP63-1

		Mint	Used
5¢	**black** on buff, single, upper case letters	7,500.00	6,000.00

CSP63-2

		Mint	Used
10¢	**black** on gray, single, upper & lower case letters		6,000.00

HEMPSTEAD, TEXAS, HANDSTAMP, ENVELOPE.

CSP64-2

SP64-1

CSP64-1

		Mint	Used
5¢	**blue**, entire		

CSP64-2

		Mint	Used
10¢	**blue**, entire, same as handstamp "PAID" when used		

HIGH POINT, N.C., HANDSTAMP, ENVELOPE.

CSP65

CSP65

		Mint	Used
ms 5¢	**black**, entire, same as handstamp "PAID" when used	500.00	

HILLSBORO, N.C., HANDSTAMP, ADHESIVE. Postmaster Calvin Parrish applied a bold "PAID" handstamp in black to small strips of paper and sold them as postage. One Confederate cover is known with the adhesive tied to the cover with the Hillsboro CDS and handstamp 5 in circle. The cover is dated Jan. 7, (1861).

CSP66-2

CSP66-2

		Mint	Used
5¢	**black**, on cover, one known		25,000.00

Note: See CSP66-1 among 3¢ 1861 Postmasters Provisionals.

HILLSBORO, N.C., HANDSTAMP, ENVELOPE.

CSP66-3

CSP66-3

		Mint	Used
10¢	**black**, entire, ms "Paid 10," one known		25,000.00

HOLLANDALE, TEXAS, HANDSTAMP, ENVELOPE.

CSP67

CSP67
		Mint	Used
5¢	**black,** entire		—

HOUSTON, TEXAS, HANDSTAMP, ENVELOPE.

CSP68-2

CSP68-1

CSP68-1
		Mint	Used
5¢	**red,** entire, abbreviated "Txs."	—	700.00
	red, on patriotic cover, abbreviated "Txs."		4,500.00

CSP68-2
		Mint	Used
10¢	**red,** entire, abbreviated "Tex."	—	1,500.00

CSP68-3
		Mint	Used
10¢	**black,** entire, abbreviated "Tex."		2,300.00

CSP68-4
		Mint	Used
10¢ + 5¢	**red,** entire, abbreviated "Tex."		2,500.00

CSP68-5
		Mint	Used
10¢ + 10¢	**red,** entire, abbreviated "Tex."		2,500.00

CSP68-5a
		Mint	Used
5¢ + ms 10¢	**red,** entire, abbreviated "Txs."		3,000.00

HUNTSVILLE, TEXAS, HANDSTAMP, ENVELOPE.

Control mark

CSP69-1

CSP69-2

CSP69-1
		Mint	Used
5¢	**black,** entire		2,500.00

CSP69-2
		Mint	Used
10¢	**black,** entire		—

INDEPENDENCE, TEXAS, HANDSTAMP, ADHESIVE. John McKnight was postmaster of Independence, Texas. Upon needing stamps, McKnight carved the die of a 10¢ stamp with his pen knife from a piece of oak wood. He made impressions of this die on common brown wrapping paper using homemade ink. The stamps were cut into squares and pasted to envelopes with gum arabic.

CSP70-3

CSP70-2

CSP70-1
		Mint	Used
10¢	**black** on buff, on cover		28,000.00

CSP70-2
		Mint	Used
10¢	**black** on dull rose, on cover		28,000.00

CSP70-3
		Mint	Used
10¢	**black** on buff, on cover, small 10 and ms "Paid"		35,000.00

ISABELLA, GA., HANDSTAMP, ENVELOPE.

CSP71

CSP71
		Mint	Used
ms 5¢	**black,** entire		2,000.00

IUKA, MISS., HANDSTAMP, ENVELOPE.

CSP72

CSP72
		Mint	Used
5¢	**black,** entire		2,000.00
	black, on patriotic cover		4,500.00

JACKSON, MISS., HANDSTAMP, ENVELOPE.

CSP73-2   CSP73-2a   CSP73-4

Note: See CSP73-1 among 3¢ 1861 Postmasters Provisionals.

CSP73-2
		Mint	Used
5¢	**black,** entire, two types of numeral		500.00

CSP73-2a
		Mint	Used
5¢	**black,** on patriotic cover, two types of numeral		3,000.00

CSP73-3
		Mint	Used
10¢	**black,** entire, two types of numeral		2,000.00

CSP73-3a
		Mint	Used
10¢ over 5¢	**black,** entire, two types of numeral		3,000.00

CSP73-4
		Mint	Used
10¢ over 5¢	**blue,** entire, two types of numeral		3,000.00

JACKSONVILLE, ALA., HANDSTAMP, ENVELOPE.

CSP74

CSP74
		Mint	Used
5¢	**black,** entire	—	1,500.00

JACKSONVILLE, FLA., HANDSTAMP, ENVELOPE.

CSP75

CSP75
		Mint	Used
5¢	**black,** entire, control on reverse		—

JETERSVILLE, VA., HANDSTAMP, ADHESIVE.

 CSP76

CSP76

		Mint	Used
5¢	**black,** pair on cover, laid paper, ms initials AHA for A.H. Atwood, PM		30,000.00

JONESBORO, TENN., HANDSTAMP, ENVELOPE.

 CSP77-1

CSP77-1

		Mint	Used
5¢	**black,** entire		3,500.00

CSP77-2

		Mint	Used
5¢	**dark blue,** entire		7,000.00

KINGSTON, GA., TYPOGRAPH, ENVELOPE.

CSP78-1

CSP78-2   CSP78-4   CSP78-5

CSP78-1

		Mint	Used
5¢	**black,** entire, one known		2,000.00

KINGSTON, GA., HANDSTAMP, ENVELOPE.

CSP78-2

		Mint	Used
5¢	**black,** entire	—	3,500.00

CSP78-3

		Mint	Used
5¢	**black,** entire, no "C" or "S" (similar to CSP78-2)		—

CSP78-4

		Mint	Used
5¢	**black,** entire		2,500.00

CSP78-5

		Mint	Used
5¢	**black,** entire		2,000.00

KNOXVILLE, TENN., WOODCUT, ADHESIVE. C.H. Charlton was postmaster of Knoxville when the war began and became the Confederate Postmaster. Charlton had provisional adhesive stamps, typeset envelopes, and handstamp provisionals produced. The adhesives were printed in a sheet of three horizontal rows. We do not know how large the sheet was.

 CSP79-3

CSP79-1

		Mint	Used
5¢	**brick red,** single, on grayish laid paper	1,250.00	1,000.00
	Single, ms cancel, on grayish laid paper		400.00
	Horizontal pair, on grayish laid paper	10,000.00	2,000.00
	Vertical pair, on grayish laid paper	3,000.00	
	Vertical strip of 3, on grayish laid paper	6,000.00	
	On cover, on grayish laid paper		3,500.00
	On cover, ms cancel, on grayish laid paper		2,500.00
	Pair on cover, on grayish laid paper		7,500.00

CSP79-2

		Mint	Used
5¢	**carmine,** single, on grayish laid paper	2,000.00	1,500.00
	Strip of 3, on grayish laid paper		5,000.00
	On cover, on grayish laid paper		15,000.00
	Pair on cover, on grayish laid paper		40,000.00

CSP79-3

		Mint	Used
10¢	**green,** on cover, on grayish laid paper		65,000.00

KNOXVILLE, TENN., TYPOGRAPH, ENVELOPE.

 CSP79-5

CSP79-4

		Mint	Used
5¢	**blue,** entire	750.00	1,800.00

CSP79-5

		Mint	Used
5¢	**blue** on orange, entire	750.00	2,000.00

Note: There are dangerous reprints of the envelopes. Originals have the "X" of "Knoxville" partly under the "P" of "Postage." Reprints have the "X" between the "S" of "C.S." and "P" of "Postage."

KNOXVILLE, TENN., TYPOGRAPH, PIECE.

CSP79-6

		Mint	Used
10¢	**red,** cut to shape, one known		10,000.00

CSP79-7

		Mint	Used
10¢	**red** on orange, cut to shape, one known		10,000.00

KNOXVILLE, TENN., HANDSTAMP, ENVELOPE.

CSP79-9

CSP79-8

CSP79-8

		Mint	Used
5¢	**black,** entire	750.00	1,500.00
	On patriotic cover		4,500.00

CSP79-9

		Mint	Used
10¢ over 5¢	**black,** entire (two varieties)		4,000.00

LA GRANGE, TEXAS, HANDSTAMP, ENVELOPE.

CSP80-2

CSP80-1

CSP80-1

		Mint	Used
5¢	**black,** entire	—	2,000.00

CSP80-2

		Mint	Used
10¢	**black,** entire (two varieties)		2,500.00

LAKE CITY, FLA., HANDSTAMP, ENVELOPE.

CSP81

CSP81

Mint | Used
2,000.00

10¢   **black,** entire

LAURENS COURT HOUSE, S.C., HANDSTAMP, ENVELOPE.

CSP82

CSP82A

P A I D   CSP82B

CSP82

Mint | Used
3,000.00

5¢   **black,** entire, control mark on reverse

LENOIR, N.C., WOODCUT, ADHESIVE. George W.F. Harper, the son of the postmaster of Lenoir, was responsible for looking after the post office, which was located in a small brick store building in front of the Harper residence. The die for the provisional was carved by George from a block of hollywood on Sept. 19, 1861. About 500 impressions were taken from the die which was afterwards lost. The stamps were printed on an orange-ruled fly leaf of an old account book used in the post office. The same die was used to print the handstamp envelopes as the adhesives.

CSP83-1

CSP83-1

Mint | Used
3,500.00 | 3,000.00

5¢   **blue & orange,** single, white wove paper with orange ruled lines

On cover, pen canceled, white wove paper with orange ruled lines   7,000.00

On cover, tied, white wove paper with orange ruled lines   30,000.00

On college cover (two known)   12,000.00

LENOIR, N.C., HANDSTAMP, ENVELOPE. From a pear wood handstamp prepared for Postmaster James Harpan by his son in the summer of 1861.

CSP83-2   CSP83-4

CSP83-2

Mint | Used
4,000.00

5¢   **blue,** entire

CSP83-3

Mint | Used
25,000.00

10¢   **blue,** entire, handstamp 5¢ + 5¢, one known

CSP83-4

Mint | Used
4,500.00

5¢   **blue,** entire

CSP83-5

Mint | Used
3,000.00

5¢   **black,** entire

LEXINGTON, MISS., HANDSTAMP, ENVELOPE.

CSP84-1

CSP84-1

Mint | Used
5,000.00

5¢   **black,** entire

CSP84-2

Mint | Used
5,000.00

10¢   **black,** entire

LEXINGTON, VA., HANDSTAMP, ENVELOPE.

CSP85-1   CSP85-2

CSP85-1

Mint | Used
500.00

5¢   **black,** entire, same as handstamp "PAID" cover when used

Entire, with Minkus CS7 for 10¢ rate, same as handstamp "PAID" cover when used   500.00

CSP85-2

Mint | Used
750.00 | 500.00

10¢   **black,** entire, same as handstamp "PAID" cover when used

LIBERTY & SALEM, VA., TYPESET, ADHESIVE.

CSP86

CSP86

Mint | Used
40,000.00

5¢   **black,** on cover, either postmark

LIMESTONE SPRINGS, S.C., HANDSTAMP, ADHESIVE.

CSP87

CSP87

Mint | Used
10,000.00

5¢   **black,** on cover, covers are not postmarked

Two on cover, covers are not postmarked   15,000.00

Note: The postmaster applied his 5¢ handstamp to both circular and square adhesives.

LIVINGSTON, ALA., LITHOGRAPH, ADHESIVE.

CSP88

CSP88

Mint | Used
7,000.00

5¢   **blue,** single

On cover   65,000.00

Pair on cover   140,000.00

LYNCHBURG, VA., WOODCUT, ADHESIVE. Only Lynchburg, Charleston, S.C., and Memphis, Tenn., issued provisional adhesive stamps and printed envelopes at the same time.

CSP89-1

CSP89-1

		Mint	Used
5¢	**blue,** single	1,500.00	1,000.00
	Pair		2,500.00
	On cover		3,000.00
	Pair on cover		6,000.00

LYNCHBURG, VA., TYPOGRAPH, ENVELOPE.

CSP89-2

CSP89-2

		Mint	Used
5¢	**black,** entire - (This is white envelope)		2,500.00

CSP89-3

		Mint	Used
5¢	**black** on amber, entire	1,500.00	2,000.00

CSP89-4

		Mint	Used
5¢	**black** on buff, entire		1,500.00
	On patriotic cover		4,500.00

CSP89-5

		Mint	Used
5¢	**black** on brown, entire	1,000.00	1,500.00
	On patriotic cover		10,000.00

MACON, GA., HANDSTAMP, ENVELOPE.

CSP90-1

CSP90-1

		Mint	Used
5¢	**black,** entire (one variety with "5" above "PAID" and one variety with "5" below "PAID"	200.00	500.00

MACON, GA., TYPESET, ADHESIVE.

CSP90-3

CSP90-4

CSP90-2

CSP90-5

CSP90-2

		Mint	Used
2¢	**black** on gray-green, single		7,000.00
	On cover		65,000.00

CSP90-3

		Mint	Used
5¢	**black** on light blue-green, single	850.00	600.00
	On cover		4,000.00
	On advertising cover		15,500.00
	Single comma after "OFFICE"	1,000.00	750.00
	On cover, (comma after "OFFICE")		10,000.00
	On advertising cover		15,000.00
	Pair (one of each type), on cover		

CSP90-4

		Mint	Used
5¢	**black** on yellow, single	2,500.00	800.00

	On cover		5,000.00
	On advertising cover		21,000.00
	Pair		2,000.00
	Pair on cover		8,000.00
	Pair on patriotic cover		15,000.00

CSP90-5

		Mint	Used
5¢	**black** on yellow, single	2,500.00	1,250.00
	On cover		7,000.00
	On advertising cover		—
	Pair		2,500.00
	Pair on cover		15,000.00
	On patriotic cover		25,000.00

CSP90-5a

		Mint	Used
5¢	**black** on yellow, tete-beche pair, one known		—

Note: CSP90-3, CSP90-4, and CSP90-5 exist in several minor varieties and are found on laid and wove paper.

MADISON, GA., HANDSTAMP, ENVELOPE.

CSP91-1

CSP91-1

		Mint	Used
5¢	**red,** entire	500.00	

Note: Considered a provisional only when unused, used from another town, or with a general-issue stamp used over it.

MADISON COURT HOUSE, FLA., TYPESET, ENVELOPE.

CSP92-2

CSP92-2

		Mint	Used
5¢	**black,** on cover		25,000.00

Note: See CSP92-1 among 3¢ 1861 Postmasters Provisionals.

MARIETTA, GA., HANDSTAMP, ENVELOPE.

CSP93-1

CSP93-2

CSP93-1b

Control Mark

CSP93-1

		Mint	Used
5¢	**black,** entire		300.00

CSP93-1a

		Mint	Used
10¢ over 5¢	**black,** entire, 10¢ handstamped over 5¢		2,000.00

CSP93-1b

		Mint	Used
10¢ over 5¢	**black,** entire, 10¢ handstamped "PAID" over 5¢		—

CSP93-2

		Mint	Used
5¢	**black,** entire, with undated double circle postmark control		1,800.00

MARION, VA., TYPESET, ADHESIVE. J.H. Francis was the Confederate postmaster of Marion. He had his brother, W.P. Francis, who owned the local newspaper, print these stamps for him, with the denomination handstamped within a printed border. In a letter to August Dietz, he states that he had 5¢, 10¢, 15¢, and 20¢ "check" (as they were called by him) printed to use as postage. He also states that he destroyed all but a few of the remainders when he received stamps from the post office. (It is doubtful he actually printed 15¢ and 20¢ checks as that would have been exceptionally high postage for 1861.) John W. Scott purchased the original dies from Francis and pulled impressions of 2¢, 5¢, 10¢, 15¢, and 20¢ checks. These reprints have smaller figures in the center than the issued type. These dies were sold when the Scott business was sold.

CSP94-3

CSP94-2

CSP94-1		Mint	Used
5¢	**black,** single, handstamped numerals		12,000.00
	On cover, handstamped numerals		25,000.00
CSP94-2		Mint	Used
10¢	**black,** single, handstamped numerals	25,000.00	12,000.00
	On cover, handstamped numerals		25,000.00
CSP94-3		Mint	Used
5¢	**black** on bluish, single, handstamped numerals, laid paper		—

MEMPHIS, TENN., WOODCUT, ADHESIVE. Only Memphis, Charleston, S.C., and Lynchburg, Tenn., issued provisional adhesive stamps and printed envelopes at the same time. Only Memphis entires are known with an additional 5¢ stamp to pay the 10¢ rate. The Memphis stamps were printed by Col. M.C. Gallaway, owner of the *Avalanche* newspaper and postmaster. At the close of the war, Gallaway turned over to the post office department at Washington all remainders of the stamps. There were numerous sheets of the 2¢ and large blocks but no full sheets of the 5¢. These remainders are the source of the red on chalk-white paper that sometimes have been called "reprints," but no reprints were ever made. The 2¢ was printed in panes of 50, with two panes per sheet, showing tete-beches and sideways varieties. It is believed the 5¢ stamp was also printed in sheets of 2 panes of 50 stamps each.

CSP95-2

CSP95-1

CSP95-1		Mint	Used
2¢	**blue,** single	100.00	1,500.00
	Block of 4	600.00	
	On cover positions		10,000.00
	Single, cracked plate (16, 17, 18)	150.00	1,500.00
CSP95-2		Mint	Used
5¢	**red,** single	150.00	175.00
	Pair	350.00	500.00
	Block of 4	1,100.00	
	On cover		1,750.00
	Pair on cover		4,500.00
	Strip of 4 on cover		7,000.00
	On patriotic cover		17,500.00
CSP95-2a		Mint	Used
5¢	**red,** tete-beche pair		1,500.00
	tete-beche pair on cover		4,000.00
CSP95-2b		Mint	Used
5¢	**red,** pair, one sideways	750.00	
CSP95-2c		Mint	Used
5¢	**red,** single, pelure paper	—	750.00

MEMPHIS, TENN., TYPOGRAPH, ENVELOPE.

CSP95-3

CSP95-3		Mint	Used
5¢	**red,** entire		3,000.00
CSP95-4		Mint	Used
5¢	**red** on amber, entire		4,000.00
	Entire with CS1 to make 10¢ rate		6,500.00
CSP95-5		Mint	Used
5¢	**red** on orange, entire		3,000.00
	On patriotic cover		4,000.00

MICANOPY, FLA., HANDSTAMP, ENVELOPE.

CSP96

CSP96		Mint	Used
5¢	**black,** entire		11,500.00

MILLEDGEVILLE, GA., HANDSTAMP, ENVELOPE.

Control Mark

CSP97-3

CSP97 *Examples*

CSP97-1		Mint	Used
5¢	**black,** entire with undated postmark control		250.00
CSP97-1a		Mint	Used
10¢ over 5¢	**black,** entire, 10¢ handstamp over 5¢		1,000.00
CSP97-2		Mint	Used
10¢	**black,** entire (similar to CSP97-1), with undated postmark control	225.00	1,000.00
CSP97-3		Mint	Used
10¢	**black,** entire (two types)		700.00

Note: A single Provisional exists with "PAID 10" inside control marks and with undated control marks with "PAID 5" and "PAID 10" handstamps.

MILTON, N.C., HANDSTAMP, ENVELOPE.

N.B.PATTON

PAID 5

CSP98		Mint	Used
5¢ (ms)	**black,** entire, two known		2,000.00

MOBILE, ALA., LITHOGRAPH, ADHESIVE.

CSP99-2

CSP99-1

CSP99-1

		Mint	Used
2¢	**black,** single	2,000.00	1,000.00
	Pair	—	2,100.00
	On cover		3,500.00
	Pair on cover		18,000.00
	3 singles on cover		5,500.00
	5 copies on cover		20,000.00

CSP99-2

		Mint	Used
5¢	**blue,** single	275.00	300.00
	Pair	675.00	700.00
	On cover		2,200.00
	Pair on cover		2,000.00
	Strip of 3 on cover		6,000.00
	Strip of 4 on cover		7,000.00
	Strip of 5 on cover		8,000.00

MONTGOMERY, ALA., HANDSTAMP, ENVELOPE.

CSP100-1

CSP100-3a

CSP100-7

CSP100-9

CSP100-1

		Mint	Used
5¢	**red,** entire		1,000.00

CSP100-2

		Mint	Used
5¢	**blue,** entire	400.00	900.00

CSP100-3

		Mint	Used
10¢	**red,** entire		800.00

CSP100-3a

		Mint	Used
10¢ over 5¢	**red,** entire		2,750.00

CSP100-4

		Mint	Used
10¢	**blue,** entire, Southern Express		4,500.00

CSP100-5

		Mint	Used
10¢	**black,** entire		800.00

CSP100-6

		Mint	Used
2¢	**red,** entire		2,500.00

CSP100-7

		Mint	Used
2¢	**blue,** entire		3,500.00

CSP100-8

		Mint	Used
5¢	**black,** entire		2,250.00

CSP100-9

		Mint	Used
10¢	**black,** entire		3,000.00

CSP100-10

		Mint	Used
10¢	**red,** entire		1,500.00

MONTGOMERY, ALA., HANDSTAMP, ADHESIVE.

CSP100-11

		Mint	Used
Crayon 5¢	**black,** entire, on buff, T. Welsh PM signature		13,000.00

MT. LEBANON, LA., WOODCUT, ADHESIVE. Postmaster W.F. Wells was also the publisher of the local newspaper and job shop. He was appointed postmaster in 1859 and served until 1865. There was no other printing office in town, so the postmaster would have undoubtedly printed these stamps.

CSP101

CSP101

		Mint	Used
5¢	**red-brown,** on cover, one known		400,000.00

NASHVILLE, TENN., HANDSTAMP, ENVELOPE.

CSP102-7

CSP102-7

		Mint	Used
5¢	**blue,** entire		750.00
	On patriotic envelope		1,750.00

CSP102-8

		Mint	Used
10¢ over 5¢	**blue,** on cover with CSP102-2		2,500.00

NASHVILLE, TENN., WOODCUT, ADHESIVE. Postmaster W.D. McNish.

CSP102-2

CSP102-6

CSP102-5a

CSP102-2

		Mint	Used
5¢	**carmine,** single, ribbed paper	850.00	900.00
	Pair, ribbed paper		1,800.00
	On cover, ribbed paper		2,700.00
	On patriotic cover, ribbed paper		5,000.00
	Pair on cover, ribbed paper		6,000.00
	On cover with US #27, Express Mail, ribbed paper		25,000.00

Note: See CSP102-1 among 3¢ 1861 Postmasters Provisionals.

CSP102-2a

		Mint	Used
5¢	**carmine,** vertical tete-beche pair, ribbed paper		3,000.00
	On cover/tete-beche pair, ribbed paper		30,500.00

CSP102-3

		Mint	Used
5¢	**brick red,** single, ribbed paper	850.00	500.00
	Pair, ribbed paper		1,200.00
	On cover, ribbed paper		1,000.00
	On patriotic cover, ribbed paper		6,000.00
	Pair on cover, ribbed paper		6,000.00
	On US EN29 cover with US #27, Express Mail, ribbed paper		35,000.00

CSP102-4

		Mint	Used
5¢	**gray,** single, ribbed paper	850.00	650.00
	On cover, ribbed paper		5,500.00
	Pair on cover, ribbed paper		8,500.00
	Strip of 5 on cover front, ribbed paper		15,000.00

CSP102-5

		Mint	Used
5¢	**violet brown,** single, ribbed paper	750.00	450.00
	Block of 4, ribbed paper	5,000.00	
	On cover, ribbed paper		5,000.00
	Pair on cover, ribbed paper		6,000.00
	On patriotic cover, ribbed paper		—

CSP102-5a

		Mint	Used
5¢	**violet brown,** vertical tete-beche pair, ribbed paper	3,500.00	2,500.00

CSP102-6

		Mint	Used
10¢	**green,** single, ribbed paper	3,000.00	3,000.00
	On cover, ribbed paper		15,000.00
	On cover with US 1857, Express, ribbed paper		95,000.00

On cover with CSP102-2, ribbed paper 25,000.00
On cover with 3¢ star die, Express marking 90,000.00

NEW ORLEANS, LA., WOODCUT, ADHESIVE. Postmaster John L. Riddell prepared provisional stamps in June 1861, perhaps the red stamps first, although they were not sold until the supply of blue stamps was exhausted in January 1862. Riddell, an educator and scientist, invented the binocular microscope in 1851. He was the melter and refiner for the U.S. Mint in New Orleans 1839-48 and was postmaster there from 1860.

CSP103-3

CSP103-1

			Mint	Used
CSP103-1				
2¢	**blue,** single		150.00	500.00
	Pair		500.00	1,200.00
	Block of 4		7,000.00	
	On cover			4,500.00
	Pair on cover			8,000.00
	3 singles on cover			25,000.00
	Strip of 5 on cover			35,000.00
	On patriotic cover			8,000.00
CSP103-1a			Mint	Used
2¢	**blue,** single, printed both sides		1,800.00	
	On cover, printed both sides			30,000.00
CSP103-2			Mint	Used
2¢	**red,** single		125.00	1,000.00
	Pair		300.00	
	Block of 4		1,500.00	
	On cover			35,000.00
CSP103-3			Mint	Used
5¢	**brown,** single		250.00	150.00
	Pair		525.00	325.00
	On cover			400.00
	Pair on cover			1,000.00
	Strip of 5 on cover			6,500.00
	On cover with Minkus #31			—
	On patriotic cover			3,500.00
CSP103-3a			Mint	Used
5¢	**brown,** single, printed both sides			1,750.00
	On cover, printed both sides			7,500.00
CSP103-3b			Mint	Used
5¢	**ocher,** single		700.00	700.00
	Pair			1,500.00
	On cover			2,000.00
	Pair on cover			3,000.00
	On patriotic cover			5,000.00
CSP103-4			Mint	Used
5¢	**red-brown** on bluish, single		300.00	175.00
	Pair		625.00	400.00
	Horizontal strip of 6			3,500.00
	Block of 4			2,000.00
	On cover			550.00
	Pair on cover			700.00
	Block of 4 on cover			5,000.00
	On cover with CS1 for 10¢ rate			7,500.00
	On patriotic cover			12,000.00
CSP103-4a			Mint	Used
5¢	**red-brown** on bluish, single, printed both sides			3,500.00
CSP103-5			Mint	Used
5¢	**yellow-brown** on off-white, single		125.00	200.00
	Pair		275.00	500.00
	Block of 4		650.00	
	On cover			500.00
	Pair on cover			2,000.00
	Strip of 5 on cover			—
	On patriotic cover			4,500.00
CSP103-6			Mint	Used
5¢	**red,** single		—	7,500.00
CSP103-7			Mint	Used
5¢	**red** on bluish, single			12,000.00

NEW ORLEANS, LA., HANDSTAMP, ENVELOPE.

J.L. RIDDELL P.M

CSP103-9

J.L. RIDDELL, P.M.

CSP103-10

		Mint	Used
CSP103-8			
2¢	**black,** entire, "J.L. Riddell" omitted		10,000.00
CSP103-9		Mint	Used
5¢	**black,** entire		4,500.00
CSP103-10		Mint	Used
10¢	**black,** entire		20,000.00

NEW SMYRNA, FLA., HANDSTAMP, ADHESIVE.

CSP104

		Mint	Used
CSP104			
10¢ over 5¢	**white/blue** ruled lines, on patriotic cover, one known		50,000.00

NORFOLK, VA., HANDSTAMP, ENVELOPE.

CSP105-1   CSP105-2

		Mint	Used
CSP105-1			
5¢	**blue,** entire, with initials		1,250.00
CSP105-2		Mint	Used
10¢	**blue,** entire, with initials		2,000.00

OAKWAY, S.C., HANDSTAMP, ADHESIVE.

CSP106

		Mint	Used
CSP106			
5¢	**black,** on cover		75,000.00

OXFORD, N.C., HANDSTAMP, ENVELOPE.

CSP107-2

CSP107-1

CSP107-1

		Mint	Used
5¢	**black**, entire, same as handstamp "PAID" when used	500.00	

CSP107-2

		Mint	Used
10¢	**black**, entire, same as handstamp "PAID" when used	500.00	

PATTERSON, N.C., HANDSTAMP, ENVELOPE.

CSP108-2

CSP108-1

CSP108-1

		Mint	Used
fancy 5¢	**black**, entire, same as handstamp "PAID" when used	500.00	

CSP108-2

		Mint	Used
fancy 10¢	**black**, entire, same as handstamp "PAID" when used	500.00	
ms 10¢ over 5¢	black, on patriotic cover, revalued over 5¢ handstamp		15,000.00

PENSACOLA, FLA., HANDSTAMP, ENVELOPE.

CSP109-2

CSP109-1

CSP109-1

		Mint	Used
5¢	**black**, entire		3,500.00

CSP109-2

		Mint	Used
ms 10¢ over 5¢	**black**, entire, revalued over 5¢ handstamp		4,500.00
	On patriotic cover		15,000.00

PETERSBURG, VA., TYPESET, ADHESIVE. Printed for Postmaster W.K. Bass in horizontally arranged panes of 10.

CSP110

CSP110

		Mint	Used
5¢	**red**, single	1,500.00	450.00
	Pair	2,500.00	1,500.00
	Block of 4	5,000.00	
	On cover		2,500.00
	Pair on cover		10,000.00
	With #CS1 to make 10¢ rate		55,000.00
	On patriotic cover		6,500.00
	"C" and "G," "e" missing on cover		2,100.00

PITTSYLVANIA COURT HOUSE, VA., TYPESET, ADHESIVE. Printed for Postmaster J.P. Johnson by the postmaster of Danville, Va., W.D. Coleman, using the same types and border, substituting Postmaster J.P. Johnson's name for his own.

CSP111-2

CSP111-1

		Mint	Used
5¢	**dull red**, single, wove paper	7,000.00	6,000.00
	Single, octagonally cut, wove paper		3,000.00
	On cover, wove paper		60,000.00
	On cover, octagonally cut, wove paper		25,000.00
	On patriotic cover, octagonally cut, wove paper		30,000.00

CSP111-2

		Mint	Used
5¢	**dull red**, single, laid paper		7,000.00
	Single, octagonally cut, laid paper		5,500.00
	On cover, laid paper		55,000.00
	On cover, octagonally cut, laid paper		25,000.00

PLAINS OF DURA, GA., HANDSTAMP, ENVELOPE.

CSP112-1   CSP112-2

CSP112-1

		Mint	Used
5¢	**black**, entire, with initials used as control		500.00

CSP112-2

		Mint	Used
10¢	**black**, entire, with initials used as control		500.00

PLEASANT SHADE, VA., TYPESET, ADHESIVE. R.E. Davis was appointed the first postmaster of Pleasant Shade in 1859. He served until the end of the war, at which time the post office was closed. Postmaster Davis stated he had several hundred copies of the stamps printed by A.F. Crutchfield of Petersburg, Va., who edited the *Daily Express.* Crutchfield also printed the Petersburg provisional.

CSP113

CSP113

		Mint	Used
5¢	**blue**, single	2,500.00	15,000.00
	Pair	7,000.00	
	Block of 6	25,000.00	
	On cover		30,000.00
	Pair on cover		60,000.00

PLUM CREEK, TEXAS, MANUSCRIPT, ADHESIVE.

CSP114

CSP114

		Mint	Used
10¢	**black** on blue, on cover		—

PORT GIBSON, MISS., HANDSTAMP, ENVELOPE.

CSP115

CSP115

		Mint	Used
5¢	**black**, entire, with signature		—

PORT LAVACA, TEXAS, TYPESET, ADHESIVE.

CSP116

CSP116

		Mint	Used
10¢	black, on cover		25,000.00

RALEIGH, N.C., HANDSTAMP, ENVELOPE.

CSP118-1

CSP118-1

		Mint	Used
5¢	red, entire		400.00
	red, on patriotic cover		2,500.00

CSP118-2

		Mint	Used
5¢	blue, entire (four known examples)		3,000.00

RHEATOWN, TENN., TYPESET, ADHESIVE. Printed for Postmaster D. Pence in the summer of 1861, using a form of three subjects, arranged horizontally (see Tellico Plains).

CSP119

CSP119

		Mint	Used
5¢	red, single	3,000.00	5,000.00
	Single, pen cancel		3,000.00
	Pair	5,000.00	
	On cover, four known		15,000.00

RICHMOND, TEXAS, HANDSTAMP, ENVELOPE.

CSP120-2

CSP120-1

		Mint	Used
5¢	red, entire		1,500.00

CSP120-2

		Mint	Used
10¢	red, entire		1,000.00

CSP120-2a

		Mint	Used
10¢ over 5¢	red, entire		5,000.00

CSP120-3

		Mint	Used
ms 15¢	red, entire, revalued over 10¢ handstamp		5,000.00

RINGGOLD, GA., HANDSTAMP, ENVELOPE.

CSP121

		Mint	Used
5¢	blue-black, entire		3,000.00

> Every reasonable effort has been made to make the values in this catalog as accurate, realistic, and up-to-date as possible.

RUTHERFORDTON, N.C., HANDSTAMP, ADHESIVE.

CSP122

		Mint	Used
ms 5¢	black, on cover, cut to shape, one known		55,000.00

SALEM, N.C., HANDSTAMP, ENVELOPE. Postmaster Orestes A. Keehlen had a brass die produced to print the provisional envelopes. The die exists today along with several of the office's other handstamp devices. In 1888 George Keehlen, son of the postmaster, offered 1,400 copies of a reprint from this die for sale for $125. These reprints were on Civil War period paper.

CSP123-1	CSP123-2	CSP123-3

CSP123-3a

CSP123-1

		Mint	Used
5¢	black, entire, "ms Paid 5"		2,000.00

CSP123-2

		Mint	Used
10¢	black, entire, "ms Paid 10," three known		6,000.00

CSP123-3

		Mint	Used
5¢	black, entire, handstamp "PAID 5"		2,000.00

CSP123-3a

		Mint	Used
10¢ over 5¢	black, entire, one known		3,000.00

Note: Unused reprint examples in several varieties are known. These reprints were made on wartime paper by Postmaster Keehlen's son shortly after the war to sell to Northern stamp collectors. Reprints currently sell for $125.00.

SALEM, VA. (SEE LIBERTY, VA.)

SALISBURY, N.C., TYPESET, ENVELOPE.

SALISBURY.
N. C.
POSTAGE

CSP125

·FIVE CENTS·

M.A.SMITH•P.M.

CSP125

		Mint	Used
5¢	black on greenish, entire, one known		6,000.00

San Antonio, Texas, Handstamp, Envelope.

CSP126-2

CSP126-1

CSP126-3

CSP126-1		Mint	Used
5¢	**black,** entire		—
CSP126-2		Mint	Used
10¢	**black,** entire, "PAID 10" with control mark	275.00	2,000.00
CSP126-3		Mint	Used
10¢	**black,** entire		2,500.00

Sandersville, Ga. Handstamp, Envelope.

P A I D

10   CSP126A-1

CSP126A-1		Mint	Used
10¢	**black,** entire		1,000.00

Note: Considered a provisional only when unused, used from another town, or with a general issue stamp used over it.

Savannah, Ga., Handstamp, Envelope.

CSP127-1   CSP127-1a

CSP127-2   CSP127-4

CSP127-1		Mint	Used
5¢	**black,** entire, with rosette control		300.00
	On patriotic cover		4,500.00
CSP127-1a		Mint	Used
10¢ over 5¢	**black,** entire, 10¢ handstamp over 5¢, with rosette control		1,500.00
CSP127-2		Mint	Used
5¢	**black,** entire, with rosette control		600.00
CSP127-2a		Mint	Used
20¢ over 5¢	**black,** entire, 20¢ handstamp over 5¢, with rosette control		2,000.00
CSP127-3		Mint	Used
10¢	**black,** entire, with rosette control (similar to CSP127-1)		750.00
CSP127-4		Mint	Used
10¢	**black,** entire, with rosette control (similar to CSP127-2)		750.00

Selma, Ala., Handstamp, Envelope.

CSP128-2

CSP128-3

CSP128-2		Mint	Used
5¢	**black,** entire, signature in ms		1,500.00
CSP128-3		Mint	Used
10¢	**black,** entire, signature in ms		2,500.00
CSP128-3a		Mint	Used
10¢ over 5¢	**black,** entire, signature in ms		3,000.00

Note: See CSP128-1 among 3¢ 1861 Postmasters Provisionals.

Sparta, Ga., Handstamp, Envelope.

CSP129-1

CSP129-1		Mint	Used
5¢	**red,** entire		1,000.00
CSP129-2		Mint	Used
10¢	**red,** entire (similar to CSP129-1)		2,500.00

Spartanburg, S.C., Handstamp, Adhesive.

CSP130-1b

CSP130-1

CSP130-1		Mint	Used
5¢	**black,** pair, ruled or plain wove		4,000.00
	On cover, ruled or plain wove paper		35,000.00
	Pair on cover, ruled or plain wove paper		45,000.00
CSP130-1a		Mint	Used
5¢	**black,** on cover, "5" omitted, ruled or plain wove paper		35,000.00
CSP130-1b		Mint	Used
5¢	**black,** on patriotic cover, ruled or plain wove paper		55,000.00
CSP130-2		Mint	Used
5¢	**black** on brown, single, ruled or plain wove paper		5,000.00
	On cover, ruled or plain wove paper		30,000.00
CSP130-3		Mint	Used
5¢	**black** on bluish, single, ruled or plain wove paper		5,000.00
	On cover, ruled or plain wove paper		35,000.00

Spartanburg, S.C., Handstamp, Envelope.

P A I D   CSP130-4a

CSP130-4		Mint	Used
10¢	**black,** entire, with control mark		1,500.00
CSP130-4a		Mint	Used
10¢ over 5¢	**black,** entire, with control mark		2,000.00

STATESVILLE, N.C., HANDSTAMP, ENVELOPE.

CSP131-1

CSP131-1

		Mint	Used
5¢	black, entire	500.00	1,000.00

CSP131-2

		Mint	Used
ms 10¢ over 5¢	black, revalued in ms, way marking (one known)		6,000.00

CSP131-3

		Mint	Used
10¢ over 5¢	black, entire (two known), handstamped		6,000.00

Note: Most known mint examples are forgeries. They have strong, clear strikes and complete frames. Most genuine examples have broken boxes.

SUMTER, S.C., HANDSTAMP, ENVELOPE.

CSP132-1   CSP132-2

CSP132-1

		Mint	Used
5¢	black, entire, used are same as handstamp "PAID"	400.00	

CSP132-1a

		Mint	Used
10¢ over 5¢	black, entire		1,500.00

CSP132-2

		Mint	Used
10¢	black, entire, used are same as handstamp "PAID"	400.00	

CSP132-2a

		Mint	Used
ms 2¢ on 10¢	black, entire		1,500.00

TALBOTTON, GA., HANDSTAMP, ENVELOPE.

CSP133-2   CSP133-3

CSP133-1

		Mint	Used
(5¢)	black, entire (no value similar to CSP133-2)		1,500.00

CSP133-2

		Mint	Used
5¢	black, entire		1,000.00

CSP133-2a

		Mint	Used
10¢ over 5¢	black, entire, 10¢ handstamp over 5¢		2,000.00

CSP133-3

		Mint	Used
10¢	black, entire		—

TALLADEGA, ALA., HANDSTAMP, ENVELOPE.

CSP134-1   CSP134-2

CSP134-1

		Mint	Used
5¢	black, entire, with initials		1,000.00

CSP134-2

		Mint	Used
10¢	black, entire, with initials		1,000.00

TELLICO PLAINS, TENN., TYPESET, ADHESIVE. Printed for Postmaster M.F. Johnson using a form of three subjects arranged horizontally, two valued at 5¢ and the right-most valued at 10¢. Probably printed by the same printer that did the Rheatown, Tenn., provisionals. Johnson indicated he had 250 copies of the stamps printed and then destroyed the plate.

CSP135-1   CSP135-2

CSP135-1

		Mint	Used
5¢	red, single, laid paper, settings of two 5¢ and one 10¢	1,300.00	—
	On cover, laid paper, one known	50,000.00	

CSP135-2

		Mint	Used
10¢	red, single, laid paper, settings of two 5¢ and one 10¢	2,500.00	
	Se-tenant with 5¢, laid paper, settings of two 5¢ and one 10¢	4,500.00	
	Strip of 3 (5¢+5¢+10¢), laid paper, settings of two 5¢ and one 10¢	8,000.00	

THOMASVILLE, GA., HANDSTAMP, ENVELOPE.

CSP137-1

CSP137-2

Control Mark

CSP137-1

		Mint	Used
5¢	black, entire, with dated postmark control on reverse		500.00

CSP137-2

		Mint	Used
5¢	black, entire		1,000.00
	Entire, patriotic cover		4,500.00

TULLAHOMA, TENN., HANDSTAMP, ENVELOPE.

CSP138

CSP138

		Mint	Used
10¢	black, entire		3,000.00

TUSCALOOSA, ALA., HANDSTAMP, ENVELOPE.

CSP139-1

CSP139-2

CSP139-1

		Mint	Used
5¢	black, entire, use is same as handstamp "PAID"	250.00	

CSP139-2

		Mint	Used
10¢	**black,** entire, use is same as handstamp "PAID"		250.00

TUSCUMBIA, ALA., HANDSTAMP, ENVELOPE.

CSP140-3   CSP140-4

CSP140-2

		Mint	Used
5¢	**black,** entire		2,500.00
	black, entire, patriotic see CSP140-1		4,500.00

CSP140-3

		Mint	Used
5¢	**red,** entire see CSP140-1		3,000.00

CSP140-4

		Mint	Used
10¢	**black,** entire see CSP140-1		3,500.00

Note: See CSP140-1 among 3¢ 1861 Postmasters Provisionals.

UNIONTOWN, ALA., TYPESET, ADHESIVE.

CSP142-2   CSP142-5

CSP142-1

		Mint	Used
2¢	**dark blue** on gray-blue, on cover, laid paper		—

CSP142-2

		Mint	Used
2¢	**dark blue** sheet of 4, laid paper	55,000.00	

CSP142-3

		Mint	Used
5¢	**green** on gray-blue, single, laid paper	2,500.00	4,000.00
	Pair, setting of 2x2 on laid paper		—
	On cover		6,500.00

CSP142-4

		Mint	Used
5¢	**green,** single, laid paper	2,750.00	2,000.00
	On cover, laid paper		10,000.00
	Pair on cover, setting of 2x2 on laid paper		20,000.00

CSP142-5

		Mint	Used
10¢	**red** on gray-blue, on cover, laid paper		35,000.00

UNIONVILLE, S.C., HANDSTAMP, ADHESIVE.

CSP143

CSP143

		Mint	Used
5¢	**black** on grayish, single		—
	On cover, uncancelled		18,000.00
	On cover, tied		25,000.00
	Pair on patriotic cover, one known		35,000.00

VALDOSTA, GA., HANDSTAMP, ENVELOPE.

CSP144-1   CSP144-2

Control Mark

CSP144-1

		Mint	Used
5¢ + 5¢	**black,** entire, with undated postmark control on reverse		—

CSP144-2

		Mint	Used
10¢	**black,** entire, with undated postmark control on front		2,000.00

VELASCO, TEXAS, HANDSTAMP, ENVELOPE.

CSP145

CSP145

		Mint	Used
10¢	**black,** entire, same as handstamp "PAID" when used		

VICTORIA, TEXAS, TYPESET, ADHESIVE. Printed for Postmaster J.A. Moody.

TYPE I   TYPE I   TYPE II
                Typeset

CSP146-1   CSP146-2   CSP146-3

CSP146-1

		Mint	Used
5¢	**red-brown** on green, single	20,000.00	

CSP146-2

		Mint	Used
10¢	**red-brown** on green, single	7,000.00	4,500.00
	On cover		125,000.00

CSP146-3

		Mint	Used
10¢	**red-brown** on green, single, bold "10," pelure paper	7,000.00	7,000.00

WALTERBOROUGH, S.C., HANDSTAMP, ENVELOPE.

CSP147-2

CSP147-1

		Mint	Used
10¢	**black** on buff, entire		4,500.00

CSP147-2

		Mint	Used
10¢	**carmine,** entire		5,000.00

WARRENTON, GA., HANDSTAMP, ENVELOPE.

CSP148-1

CSP148-1

		Mint	Used
5¢	**black,** entire		1,200.00

CSP148-1a

		Mint	Used
ms 10¢	**black,** entire, revalued 10¢ over 5¢		850.00

WASHINGTON, GA., HANDSTAMP, ENVELOPE.

CSP149

CSP149
		Mint	Used
10¢	black, entire, with undated postmark control on back		2,000.00

Note: Provisional covers must have the undated postmark control on the reverse. Covers with handstamped rate and paid markings and undated postmark on the front are not considered provisional uses.

WEATHERFORD, TEXAS, HANDSTAMP, ENVELOPE.

CSP150-1a

CSP150-1
		Mint	Used
5¢	black, entire		2,000.00

CSP150-1a
		Mint	Used
5¢ + 5¢	black, entire		15,000.00

WILKESBORO, N.C., HANDSTAMP, ENVELOPE.

CSP151-2

CSP151-1

CSP151-1
		Mint	Used
5¢	black, entire		6,000.00

CSP151-2
		Mint	Used
10¢ over 5¢	black, entire, 10¢ ms over 5, one known		6,000.00

WINNSBOROUGH, S.C., HANDSTAMP, ENVELOPE.

CSP152-2

CSP152-1

CSP152-1
		Mint	Used
5¢	black, entire		1,500.00

CSP152-2
		Mint	Used
10¢	black, entire		2,000.00

WYTHEVILLE, VA., HANDSTAMP, ENVELOPE.

CSP153

CSP153
		Mint	Used
5¢	black, entire		900.00

Confederate States

The Confederate States of America was the government established in 1861 by the Southern states that seceded from the Union, charging that it was aggressively hostile toward their "domestic institutions."

South Carolina, the first state to secede (Dec. 20, 1860), justified its action on the grounds of continued Northern attacks on slavery, the coming to power of a sectionalist party (the Republican), and the election of a President (Abraham Lincoln) "whose opinions and purposes are hostile to slavery." It was followed, in order, by Mississippi, Florida, Alabama, Georgia, Louisiana, Texas, Virginia, Arkansas, Tennessee and North Carolina. The attack on Ft. Sumter at Charleston, S.C., on April 12, 1861, is generally considered to mark the onset of hostilities. The war continued until spring, 1865.

The greatest romance to collecting Confederate States stamps is to have them on the envelopes on which they were used.

Confederate postal rates went into effect on June 1, 1861, when the Confederacy took over the operation of its own postal system. Up to that date the United States continued the postal service in the seceded states, and covers showing such after-secession usage are scarce. Confederate rates were 5¢ and 10¢ for single letters, the latter rate applying to those going over 500 miles; the rate was made 10¢ for all distances on July 1, 1862. A 2¢ rate for drop letters and unsealed printed matter remained in effect throughout.

The Confederate States Post Office Department prepared the following adhesive stamps to serve the seceded states. All of those issued were imperforate except two 10¢ blue engraved stamps on which experimental perforations, gauging 12 1/2, were officially applied to a limited number. Some private rouletting also was done. One stamp was never released.

Postal history plays a significant role in collecting Confederate States material. Even in off-cover stamps, an unusual or rare postal marking may greatly increase a stamp's value.

1861. THE FIRST ISSUE consisted of 5¢ and 10¢ stamps, lithographed (offset) from various stones on soft, porous paper. Earliest known dates of use are given.

Hoyer and Ludwig of Richmond, Va., printed the 5¢ green stamps from three different stones. Stone A/B produced sharp, clear impressions, almost always in the olive green shade. The first printing from Stone 1 was in olive green, and others followed in various shades of green. The impressions are clear, but not as sharp as those from Stone A/B. Stone 2 impressions come in all shades of green known except olive. They are noticeably poor and some were unofficially rouletted (Baton Rouge, La.).

CS1 *Jefferson Davis of Mississippi (1808-89), president of the Confederacy*

CS1
		UnFVF	UseFVF
5¢	**olive green,** Stone A/B *(Oct. 16, 1861)*	275.00	175.00
	Pair	600.00	400.00
	On cover (single)		250.00
	On cover (pair)		475.00
	b1. green, Stone 1 *(Oct. 23, 1861)*	200.00	150.00
	Pair	425.00	350.00
	On cover (single)		200.00
	On cover (pair)		425.00
	Sheet of 100	35,000.00	
	b2. bright green	200.00	150.00
	b3. dark green	300.00	165.00
	b4. dull green	200.00	150.00
	b5. olive green	350.00	175.00
	c. green, Stone 2 *(Dec. 2, 1861)*	200.00	150.00
	Pair	425.00	350.00
	On cover (single)		225.00
	On cover (pair)		400.00
	c1. bright green	225.00	165.00
	c2. dark green	225.00	165.00

		UnFVF	UseFVF
c3. light green		200.00	150.00

Earliest documented date of use: *Oct. 16, 1861*

The 10¢ stamps lithographed (offset) by Hoyer & Ludwig from Stone 1 (CS2), are clear and distinct and in a uniform shade of dark blue. The stamps produced by J.T. Paterson & Co. of Augusta, Ga., from Stone 2 (CS3) come in a wide range of shades, and the impressions are not as clear. They show a small colored dash below the lowest point of the upper left triangle, and a line connecting the "N" in "Confederate" with the circular frame line above.

CS2, CS6 *Thomas Jefferson, who was born and died in Virginia, was an early champion of states' rights and of an agrarian economy.*

CS2
10¢		UnFVF	UseFVF
dark blue, *(Hoyer & Ludwig)*		400.00	225.00
Pair		900.00	550.00
On cover (single)			400.00
On cover (pair)			1,250.00
Horizontal pair, gutter between		—	
v. Printed on both sides		—	
Double impression			1,000.00

Earliest documented date of use: *Nov. 8, 1861*

CS3 *Thomas Jefferson*

CS3 *Close-up*

CS3
10¢		UnFVF	UseFVF
blue *(Paterson)*		250.00	175.00
dark blue		500.00	250.00
indigo		2,500.00	1,750.00
light blue		275.00	190.00
Pair		550.00	400.00
On cover (single)			250.00
On cover (pair)			900.00
On cover (single), Stone Y			450.00
a. light milky blue, Stone Y		500.00	300.00
a1. greenish blue, Stone Y		600.00	300.00
v. Printed on both sides			2,500.00

Earliest documented date of use: *July 25, 1862*

CS4 *Andrew Jackson, a Tennesseean and "Hero of New Orleans" in the War of 1812, was in reality a foe of the principles on which the Confederacy was founded.*

CS4
2¢		UnFVF	UseFVF
green (one stone)		700.00	650.00
emerald green (very rare)		—	—
olive yellow green		750.00	700.00
light green		750.00	650.00

		UnFVF	UseFVF
dark green		750.00	650.00
On cover (single)			1,500.00
On cover (strip of 5)			10,000.00

Earliest documented date of use: *March 21, 1862*

Stone 2, which was used to produce CS1, was also used for the blue CS5. A second stone, Stone 3, was needed, and the printing from this newer stone was clearer. Only about 2% of the total 6.7 million 5¢ blue stamps were from Stone 3.

CS5 *Jefferson Davis*

CS5
5¢		UnFVF	UseFVF
blue, Stone 2 *(March 4, 1862)*		180.00	125.00
dark blue		200.00	150.00
milky blue		225.00	175.00
On cover (single)			225.00
Stone 2 on cover (pair)			425.00
a. blue, Stone 3 *(April 10, 1862)*		225.00	170.00
a1. dark blue		250.00	200.00
a2. milky blue		300.00	225.00
On cover (single)			275.00
Stone 3 on cover (pair)			500.00

Earliest documented date of use: *Feb. 28, 1862*

CS6 *Thomas Jefferson*

CS6
10¢		UnFVF	UseFVF
rose (one stone)		1,000.00	500.00
carmine		2,500.00	2,000.00
dull rose		1,000.00	500.00
dark rose		1,200.00	600.00
brown rose		1,500.00	800.00
On cover (single)			650.00

Earliest documented date of use: *March 10, 1862*

The carmine used on cover is a major Confederate variety. Its earliest known use is May 27, 1862. The brown rose color also is very scarce. Carmine and brown rose stamps on or off cover require certification.

1862. SECOND ISSUE of newly designed *letterpress* stamps was printed by Thomas De La Rue & Co. Ltd., of London, England, and by Archer & Daly of Richmond, Va., from plates made by De La Rue.

The London print (CS7) is clear and distinct on hard, medium paper with fine, evenly distributed gum.

CS7 *Jefferson Davis. Some sheets of this stamp were smuggled into the South by blockade runners early in 1862.*

CS7
5¢		UnFVF	UseFVF
light blue		24.00	30.00
On cover (single London print) before July 1, 1862			125.00

Pair	55.00	125.00
On cover (pair)		100.00

Earliest documented date of use: *April 16, 1862*

The local print (CS8) from De La Rue plates used to print CS7 but later smuggled into the South show considerably less quality and consistency. The Richmond printer used English and local paper of varying thickness, and gum ranged from light to dark and sometimes was uneven.

CS8 *Jefferson Davis*

CS8

		UnFVF	UseFVF
5¢	**blue**, normal paper (Richmond print)	13.00	20.00
	dark blue	12.00	22.50
	Pair	25.00	45.00
	Horizontal pair, gutter between	250.00	
	On cover (single) (overpaid drop)		200.00
	On cover (pair)		100.00
	p. blue, printed on thin glazed paper	25.00	35.00
	p1. dark blue, printed on thin glazed paper	25.00	35.00
	p2. blue, printed on thick paper	30.00	35.00
	p3. dark blue, printed on thin glazed paper	30.00	35.00
	v. pair, printed on both sides	2,000.00	1,000.00
	v1. "White tie"	175.00	180.00
	On cover "White tie"		400.00

Earliest documented date of use: *Aug. 15, 1862*

Private printings, erroneously called "Reprints," in both blue and black on modern paper were made for philatelic purposes.

After a boost in postage rates on July 1, 1862, the Confederate Post Office Department instructed the firm of Thomas De La Rue & Co. in London to alter the denominations of the two typographed (letterpress) stamps for which they had previously made plates. Thus the value line of "ONE CENT" was altered to read "TWO CENTS," and that of "FIVE CENTS" to "TEN CENTS." While these two new plates were duly shipped to the Confederacy and arrived safely, no official printing was ever made from them. The complete plate of 400 subjects of the 2¢ denomination was discovered many years ago, but only broken sections of the 10¢ plate were ever found. Various private printings have since been made from the 2¢ plate, and from the sections, and panes reconstructed from the 10¢ — the 2¢ usually in green and the 10¢ in various colors. None are officially printed government stamps, and as private emissions they have a value of only $3 to $5 each.

CS9 *John C. Calhoun of South Carolina, a leading defender of the Southern cause against the industrial North.*

CS9

		UnFVF	UseFVF
1¢	**orange,** (not issued)	100.00	
	deep orange	125.00	

1863-64. THIRD ISSUE *engraved and printed by Archer & Daly in Richmond, Va., unless otherwise stated. Imperforate.*

The first printing of the later Jefferson Davis issues from Archer & Daly in 1863 show uniformly clear impressions, including sharply defined shading behind the portrait, and with an even distribution of a good quality light-colored gum. In 1864 another firm, Keatinge & Ball of Columbia, S.C., printed stamps (Nos. CS16-CS17) from the same plates. They are of poorer quality, usually with filled-in impressions; and the gum is dark and unevenly applied — even at times penetrating the paper and giving it an orange hue. Copper plate intaglio on paper that varies from thin to thick.

CS10 *Jefferson Davis.* The stamp is boxed by frame lines. Usually only parts of the frame lines are seen. Value is for stamps showing at least two lines. Values of stamps showing more or less than two lines are adjusted accordingly.

CS10

		UnFVF	UseFVF
10¢	**blue** ("Frame Line")	4,000.00	1,400.00
	milky blue	4,500.00	1,400.00
	greenish blue	5,000.00	
	dark blue	5,000.00	
	Double transfer	5,000.00	1,500.00
	On cover (single)		2,000.00

Earliest documented date of use: *April 19, 1863*

Certification recommended as fakes do exist.

The stamp has vertical shading lines behind the portrait. Copper plate intaglio, imperforate.

CS11 *Jefferson Davis. The denomination is spelled out, "TEN."*

CS11

		UnFVF	UseFVF
10¢	**blue** ("T-E-N")	800.00	475.00
	milky blue	800.00	475.00
	gray blue	900.00	525.00
	On cover (single)		1,250.00
	Double transfer	900.00	800.00
	Damaged plate	900.00	800.00

Earliest documented date of use: *April 23, 1863*

Colorless vertical gash above "N" in "CENTS," clear cross-hatching. Steel plate engraved, mainly imperforate.

CS12 *Jefferson Davis*

CS12

		UnFVF	UseFVF
10¢	**blue** (Type 1)	10.00	15.00
	Pair	25.00	45.00
	milky blue	15.00	20.00
	greenish blue	15.00	20.00
	green	40.00	45.00
	Horizontal pair, gutter between	125.00	
	Sheet of 200	1,500.00	
	Pane of 100	650.00	
	On cover (single)		75.00
	On cover (pair)		175.00
	v. Perforated 12 1/2	300.00	250.00
	On cover (single) perforated		450.00

Earliest documented date of use: *April 21, 1863*

The four corner ornaments are filled in, and a thin outline encloses the entire design. Steel plate engraved. The perforated variety requires certification.

CS13 *Jefferson Davis*

CS13

		UnFVF	UseFVF
10¢	**blue** (Type 2)	10.00	20.00
	milky blue	15.00	30.00
	dark blue	10.00	20.00
	greenish blue	20.00	12.50
	green	60.00	70.00
	Pair	25.00	40.00
	On cover (single)		75.00
	On cover (pair)		175.00
	v. Perforated 12 1/2	300.00	250.00
	On cover (single) perforated		450.00

Earliest documented date of use: *May 1, 1863*

The perforated variety requires certification.

Because the portrait is similar to the 2¢ United States stamp of 1863, known as the "Black Jack," this stamp is sometimes called the "Red Jack." Steel plate engraved.

CS14 *Andrew Jackson*

CS14

		UnFVF	UseFVF
2¢	**brown red**	70.00	300.00
	pale red *("Red Jack")*	70.00	300.00
	Double transfer	100.00	300.00
	Horizontal pair, gutter between	300.00	
	Sheet of 200	6,500.00	
	On cover (single)		1,000.00
	On cover (strip of 5)		4,000.00

Earliest documented date of use: *April 21, 1863*

Beware fake cancels.

CS15 *George Washington of Virginia*

CS15

		UnFVF	UseFVF
20¢	**green**	35.00	350.00
	dark green	60.00	450.00
	yellow green	55.00	400.00
	Double transfer "Twenty"	85.00	—
	On cover (single)		1,000.00
	v. Diagonal bisect, used as 10¢ on cover		2,000.00
	v1. Horizontal bisect, used as 10¢ on cover		2,500.00

Earliest documented date of use: *June 1, 1863*

Beware of fake cancels.

Printed by Keatinge & Ball. Cross-hatch shading behind portrait is not sharp — even undistinguishable.

CS16 *Jefferson Davis*

CS16

		UnFVF	UseFVF
10¢	**deep blue** (Type I)	10.00	35.00
	Sheet of 200	1,500.00	
	Pane of 100	650.00	
	On cover (single)		125.00

Earliest documented date of use: *Sept. 4, 1864*

Printed by Keatinge & Ball. Cross-hatch shading behind portrait is not sharp — even undistinguishable — and corner ornaments are filled in.

CS17 *Jefferson Davis*

CS17

		UnFVF	UseFVF
10¢	**deep blue** (Type 2)	12.00	40.00
	Sheet of 200	1,500.00	
	Pane of 100	650.00	
	On cover (single)		125.00

Earliest documented date of use: *Sept. 4, 1864*

Canal Zone

Former U.S. Government reservation, administered by a governor appointed by the president of the United States. Area: about 553 sq. mi. Headquarters: Balboa Heights.

100 Centavos = 1 Peso; 100 Centesimos = 1 Balboa; 100 Cents = 1 Dollar.

The Canal Zone was a strip of territory across the Isthmus of Panama, extending five miles on each side of the Panama Canal but excluding the cities of Panama and Colón. It was leased from the Republic of Panama under the Hay-Banau-Varilla Treaty of 1903, under Article III of which the U.S. was granted "all the rights, power and authority within the Zone... which the United States would possess and exercise if it were the sovereign." The idea of a canal across Panama dated back almost to Balboa's discovery in 1513 that Panama was an isthmus. The Spanish conducted several surveys between 1534 and 1779 but, afraid of the threat to their monopoly of communication with Latin America, generally discouraged even the improvement of overland routes across the isthmus.

U.S. canal interest began with the California gold rush, when westbound settlers had to trek across the continent, sail around Cape Horn, or make two sea voyages separated by a journey across Panama. A U.S. postal service using the latter route was instituted in 1848 through the Pacific Mail Steamship Company.

In 1878 the French obtained a Panamanian canal concession from the government of New Granada (Colombia) and formed a canal company headed by Ferdinand de Lesseps, who had constructed the Suez Canal. The French plan, to dig a sea-level canal following essentially the line of the Panama Railroad (completed in 1855), was later changed to include locks. Because of climate, fever-breeding mosquitoes, and financial mismanagement, the French company went bankrupt in 1889 after having removed some 50 million cubic meters of rock and earth and spent $287 million. A French receiver company was equally unsuccessful.

A U.S. commission had recommended Nicaragua as the most feasible site for an American canal project, but changed its mind when the French company offered to sell its concession and works for $40 million. Congress authorized President Theodore Roosevelt to make the purchase, and a treaty was signed, but the Colombian Senate refused (August 1903) to ratify it. In November the Department of Panama declared itself independent of Colombia and leased the Canal Zone to the United States. The Canal was officially opened Aug. 15, 1914.

All stamps are engraved and recess printed unless otherwise stated.

The Canal Zone postal service was established on June 24, 1904. Its first stamps were secured from the Republic of Panama for temporary use pending the arrival of overprinted United States stamps. They were current 2, 5 and 10 centavos provisional stamps of the Republic overprinted before delivery with the words *CANAL ZONE*. The nominal values were expressed in Colombian silver, 100 centavos of which equaled 50 cents of United States gold currency. Temporary first-class postage rates for the first issue only, in Colombian silver, were: domestic post cards, 2¢; domestic letters, 5¢ per ounce or fraction; foreign letters, 10¢ per half ounce or fraction.

A treaty signed in 1977 by U.S. President Jimmy Carter and Panamanian President Omar Torrijos mandated gradual return of the Canal Zone to Panama, a process completed on Dec. 31, 1999. The Canal Zone postal service closed on Sept. 30, 1979, and Panama assumed control over the Canal Zone post offices on Oct. 1, 1979.

Regular Postal Issues

The First Government stamps were put into use early in July 1847. They superseded Postmasters' Provisionals and other stamps which were thereafter not tolerated by the Postmaster General. The 5¢ stamp paid for carrying an ordinary letter up to 300 miles, and the 10¢ value was used for letters requiring higher postage.

Rawdon, Wright, Hatch & Edson of New York engraved the stamps and printed them in sheets of 200, which were cut into panes of 100 before distribution to the post offices. *The stamps were printed on thin, bluish woven paper. They were unwatermarked and imperforate, intaglio.*

1904. Map Design Overprint Issue *on map stamps of Panama with red overprint bar and double "Panama," handstamped with blue-black "Canal Zone."*

1 *Map design PANAMA, 13 1/2mm long*

			UnFVF	UseFVF
1				
2¢		**rose carmine** *(June 24, 1904)*	520.00	500.00
	v.	PANAMA 15mm long	600.00	500.00
	v1.	PANAMA reading up & down	650.00	500.00
	v2.	P NAMA	600.00	500.00
	v3.	CANAL ZONE double overprint	2,000.00	1,500.00
	v4.	CANAL ZONE inverted overprint	850.00	600.00
	v5.	CANAL ZONE double inverted	5,000.00	

2 *Map design PANAMA, 15mm long*

3

			UnFVF	UseFVF
2				
5¢		**deep blue**	250.00	180.00
	v.	2 1/4mm between bar & A of PANAMA	500.00	500.00
	v1.	Colon between bar & P of PANAMA	500.00	500.00
	v2.	CANAL ZONE diagonally down to right	400.00	350.00
	v3.	CANAL ZONE double overprint	2,250.00	1,500.00
	v4.	CANAL ZONE inverted overprint	600.00	625.00
	v5.	Pair, 1 w/o overprint	5,000.00	5,000.00
3			UnFVF	UseFVF
10¢		**yellow orange**	425.00	275.00
	v.	2 1/4mm between bar & A of PANAMA	625.00	625.00
	v1.	Colon between bar & P of PANAMA	600.00	
	v2.	CANAL ZONE double overprint		12,500.00
	v3.	CANAL ZONE inverted overprint	625.00	625.00
	v4.	Pair, 1 w/o overprint	6,000.00	5,000.00

Counterfeit CANAL ZONE handstamps and cancellations are numerous.

Nos. 1-3 were withdrawn on July 17 and overprinted. U.S. stamps were placed on sale the following day. Beginning with this issue, rates and denominations were expressed in U.S. currency or its equivalent.

1904. Canal Zone Overprint Issue *on double-line watermarked paper, perforated 12.*

4

			UnFVF	UseFVF
4			UnFVF	UseFVF
4¢		**deep blue green**, No. 211	30.00	25.00
5			UnFVF	UseFVF
2¢		**carmine**, No. 231	30.00	21.00
	a.	scarlet	32.50	25.00
6			UnFVF	UseFVF
5¢		**deep blue**, No. 215	105.00	75.00
7			UnFVF	UseFVF
8¢		**violet black**, No. 217	160.00	110.00
8			UnFVF	UseFVF
10¢		**pale red brown**, No. 218	160.00	125.00

Dissatisfaction and concern in Panama over early United States administration led to conferences between the Panamanian authorities and William Howard Taft, U.S. Secretary of War, and a series of executive orders collectively known as the Taft Agreement.

One of the provisions required the use of Panama stamps overprinted CANAL ZONE. This automatically invalidated the current United States overprints. The new arrangements, which were to cover the construction period of the Canal, required that a stable currency be established in Panama equivalent to that of the United States. Panama stamps used in the Canal Zone were to be purchased from Panama at 40 percent of their face value. Accordingly, in succeeding issues, the Canal Zone authorities were limited to whatever Panama could supply.

1904-1906. CANAL ZONE OVERPRINT ISSUE

9, 10

Overprint

CANAL

ZONE

8 cts

9		UnFVF	UseFVF
1¢	**green**	2.80	2.00
	v. CANAL Type II	100.00	100.00
	v1. CANA L	125.00	125.00
	v2. ZONE Type II	70.00	70.00
	v3. ZONE (U-shaped)	275.00	275.00
	v4. Inverted overprint		2,250.00
	v5. Double overprint	1,250.00	1,000.00

10		UnFVF	UseFVF
2¢	**carmine red**	4.50	2.00
	v. CANA L	85.00	85.00
	v1. L sideways	2,500.00	2,000.00
	v2. ZONE (U-shaped)	275.00	275.00
	v3. Inverted overprint	250.00	275.00

1904-06. CANAL ZONE OVERPRINT ISSUE

11, 12, 13

11		UnFVF	UseFVF
2¢	**rose carmine** *(Dec. 9, 1905)*	7.00	4.00
	v. ZONE Type II	175.00	175.00
	v1. PANAMA 16mm long	45.00	45.00
	v2. PANAWA	45.00	45.00
	v3. PANAMA inverted overprint	400.00	400.00

12		UnFVF	UseFVF
5¢	**deep blue**	7.50	3.00
	v. CANAL Type II	75.00	75.00
	v1. CANA L	90.00	90.00
	v2. ZONE Type II	75.00	75.00
	v3. CANAL ZONE double overprint	600.00	600.00
	v4. PANAMA 16mm long	40.00	40.00
	v5. PANAWA	40.00	40.00
	v6. PANAM	70.00	70.00
	v7. ANAMA	80.00	80.00
	v8. PANAAM	950.00	950.00
	v9. PAN MA	75.00	75.00
	v10. PAMANA reading up	75.00	75.00
	v11. PAMANA reading down	200.00	200.00
	v12. Right P 5mm below bar	50.00	50.00
	v13. PANAMA inverted overprint, bar at bottom	800.00	1,000.00
	v14. PANAMA double overprint	1,050.00	850.00

13		UnFVF	UseFVF
10¢	**yellow orange**	20.00	10.00
	v. CANAL Type II	225.00	225.00
	v1. CANA L	200.00	200.00
	v2. ZONE Type II	175.00	175.00
	v3. red brown PANAMA overprint	29.00	29.00
	v4. PANAMA 16mm long	75.00	75.00
	v5. PANAWA	100.00	100.00
	v6. PAMANA reading down	200.00	200.00
	v7. Right P 5mm below bar	150.00	150.00
	v8. Left A touching bar	175.00	175.00
	v9. PANAMA double overprint	600.00	600.00

1904-06. CANAL ZONE OVERPRINT ISSUE

14 Large "8 cts" overprint in red — 3 varieties; "PANAMA" (15mm) reads up at left, down at right.

8 cts

14		UnFVF	UseFVF
8¢ on 50¢	**deep ocher**	30.00	18.50
	v. CANA L	175.00	175.00
	v1. ZONE Type II	1,150.00	1,150.00
	v2. CANAL ZONE inverted overprint	425.00	400.00
	v3. Right P 5mm below bar	175.00	175.00
	v4. red brown PANAMA overprint	40.00	40.00
	v5. CANAL Type II on v4	2,210.00	
	v6. ZONE Type II on v4	2,210.00	
	v7. 8¢ double overprint on v4	850.00	
	v8. Omitted 8 on v4	4,250.00	

1905-06. CANAL ZONE ISSUE

15 *Large "8 cts" overprint, both "PANAMAs" (13mm) read up.*

15		UnFVF	UseFVF
8¢ on 50¢	**deep ocher,** overprint 14	3,000.00	4,250.00
	v. CANA L	4,000.00	
	v1. PANAMA 15mm long	3,250.00	4,750.00
	v2. PANAMA reading up & down	6,500.00	6,500.00
	v3. P NAMA	3,500.00	

1905-06. CANAL ZONE ISSUE

16 *Small "8 cts." with period, both "PANAMAs" (13mm) read up.*

8 cts.

16		UnFVF	UseFVF
8¢ on 50¢	**deep ocher,** *(Nov. 1905)*	50.00	35.00
	v. ZONE Type II	200.00	200.00
	v1. PANAMA 15mm long	80.00	70.00
	v2. PANAMA reading up & down	100.00	100.00
	v3. P NAMA	85.00	

1905-06. CANAL ZONE ISSUE

17 *Small "8 cts," both "PANAMAs" (13mm) read up.*

17		UnFVF	UseFVF
8¢ on 50¢	**deep ocher,** *(April 23, 1906)*	67.50	60.00
	v. CANAL Type II	200.00	200.00
	v1. ZONE Type II	200.00	200.00
	v2. PANAMA 15mm long	80.00	70.00
	v3. PANAMA reading up & down	100.00	100.00
	v4. P NAMA	85.00	
	v5. 8¢ double overprint	1,100.00	1,100.00

Nos. 14, 15, 16, 18 without CANAL ZONE overprint were not regularly issued.

Note: The sequence for Canal Zone stamps was revised for the 2002 Minkus catalog to reflect chronological issue dates between Nos. 15 and 18.

The plate used for the CANAL ZONE overprint on Nos. 9-18 was altered five times, giving six different stages from which printings were made. A full list of the characteristic varieties and all alterations of the plate, with the approximate time they occurred and the stamps upon which the overprint is found, appears in Bartels' Check List of Canal Zone Stamps, *second edition, 1908.*

The Panama overprint was applied by a 50-subject plate to one-half of the sheet at a time and was sometimes misplaced vertically or horizontally. Such misplaced overprints exist on nearly all values. When misplaced vertically, the bar may appear at the bottom of the stamp instead of the top, and one row will be left without a bar. When misplaced horizontally the word PANAMA may appear once only, twice at either right or left, and three times on the same stamp. In some cases the overprint on two vertical rows of a sheet may overlap, giving the appearance of a double overprint. Although of interest to the specialist, such varieties are not worth appreciably more than the normal stamp.

Rejection by the Canal Zone authorities of a lot of 1¢ and 2¢ provisionals that Panama had prepared for its own postal needs resulted in alternate offer by Panama of some Department of Panama stock, that had not yet been overprinted. These were accepted and the bars obliterating COLOMBIA and the old values were applied by the Canal Zone authorities at the same time that PANAMA, CANAL ZONE and the new values were added.

1904-06. CANAL ZONE ISSUE

18 Small "8 cts." overprint in red with period; "PANAMAs" read up on left, down on right.

	UnFVF	UseFVF
18		
8¢ on 50¢ deep ocher, *(Sept. 1906)*	70.00	60.00
v. CANAL Type II	95.00	95.00
v1. ZONE Type II	200.00	200.00
v2. PAMANA reading up	120.00	120.00
v3. 8¢ omitted	750.00	750.00
v4. 8¢ double overprint	1,500.00	

1906. CANAL ZONE ISSUE

Department of Panama stamps of 1892-96 overprinted in black. Two bars of overprint obliterate "Colombia" and old values. Three printings of each denomination differ primarily in the relative position of the parts.

19 First printing

```
        CANAL
P        ZONE        P
A                    A
N                    N
A        1 ct.       A
M                    M
A                    A
```

	UnFVF	UseFVF
19		
1¢ on 20¢ slate violet *(March 1906)*	1.25	1.00

20 Second printing

21 Third printing

	UnFVF	UseFVF
20		
1¢ on 20¢ slate violet *(May 1906)*	1.25	1.00
21		
1¢ on 20¢ slate violet *(Sept. 1906)*	1.25	1.00
v. C ANAL	12.50	

22 First printing

```
        CANAL
P        ZONE        P
A                    A
N                    N
A        2 cts.      A
M                    M
A                    A
```

	UnFVF	UseFVF
22		
2¢ on 1p brown lake *(March 1906)*	2.00	1.75

23 Second printing

24 Third printing

	UnFVF	UseFVF
23	2.00	1.75
2¢ on 1p brown lake *(May 1906)*		
24	20.00	20.00
2¢ on 1p brown lake *(Sept. 1906)*		

Misplaced overprints occur with bars shifted so that both bars appear at top or bottom, or occasionally only one bar altogether.

1906-07. PORTRAIT ISSUE *printed by Hamilton Bank Note Co., perforated 11.*

25 Vasco Nuñez de Balboa (1475-1519), a Spanish explorer, was the first European to wade in the waters of the eastern shore of the Pacific Ocean (Sept. 13, 1513), after a trek through the jungles of what is now Panama. He was unofficial first governor of the city of Darién, 1510.

		UnFVF	UseFVF
25			
1¢	**deep blue green & black** *(Jan. 1907)*	2.50	1.00
	v. ANA for CANAL	70.00	70.00
	v1. CAN L	80.00	80.00
	v2. ONE for ZONE	80.00	80.00
	v3. Vertical pair, imperforate horizontally	2,250.00	1,750.00
	v4. Horizontal pair, imperforate between	1,300.00	1,300.00
	v5. Vertical pair, imperforate between	1,750.00	1,750.00
	v6. Head & overprint inverted	4,000.00	2,750.00
	v7. Overprint reading up	550.00	550.00
	v8. Pair, 1 not overprint	—	—
	v9. Double overprint	275.00	275.00
	v10. Double overprint, one inverted	1,350.00	1,350.00
26		UnFVF	UseFVF
2¢	**scarlet & black** *(Oct. 1906)*	30.00	27.50

26 Fernández de Córdoba (c1475-1526), Spanish explorer and slave trader who explored parts of Mexico and Central America, overprint reading up.

27 Francisco Fernández de Córdoba, overprint reading down.

		UnFVF	UseFVF
27			
2¢	**scarlet & black** *(Nov. 1906)*	3.50	1.20
	a. carmine & black	3.00	1.40
	v. CAN L	45.00	
	v1. Horizontal pair, imperforate between	2,000.00	1,750.00
	v2. Head & overprint inverted	—	5,000.00
	v3. Pair, 1 w/o overprint	1,750.00	1,750.00
	v4. Double overprint	500.00	500.00

28 Justo Arosemena (1817-96), a brilliant sociologist and jurist, held many high political posts, among them president of the federal state of Panama and ambassador to Chile, England and France.

		UnFVF	UseFVF
28			
5¢	**blue & black** *(Dec. 1906)*	7.00	2.50
	a. light blue & black	7.00	2.50
	b. cobalt & black	3.25	1.50
	c. dark blue & black	7.00	2.50
	v. CAN L	60.00	
	v1. CANAL only	35.00	
	v2. CANAL double overprint	500.00	350.00

29 *Manuel J. Hurtado, governor 1834-36*

30 *José de Obaldia (1845-1910)*

29

			UnFVF	UseFVF
8¢	**dark lilac & black** *(Dec. 1906)*		20.00	9.00
	v. Horizontal pair, imperforate between		2,000.00	—

30

			UnFVF	UseFVF
10¢	**dark violet & black** *(Dec. 1906)*		20.00	9.00
	v. Double overprint second inverted		3,750.00	—

Earlier printings of Nos. 25-30 are on soft and thick paper, later printings on hard, thin paper. Nos. 25 and 30 exist imperforate between stamp and sheet margin. CA of CANAL spaced 1/2mm farther apart on position 50 of the sheet on later printings of Nos. 25, 27-29.

A change of printers resulted in a new series of Panama stamps and again certain denominations were obtained for Canal Zone use. These designs were in use until 1924 and appeared with several styles of overprint.

1909. SECOND PORTRAIT ISSUE *printed by American Bank Note Co., perforated 12.*

31 *Fernández de Córdoba*

32 *Justo Arosemena*

31

			UnFVF	UseFVF
2¢	**rose red & black** *(May 29, 1909)*		12.50	6.50
	v. Horizontal pair, 1 w/o overprint		2,600.00	—
	v1. Vertical pair, 1 w/o overprint		2,750.00	—

32

			UnFVF	UseFVF
5¢	**deep blue & black** *(May 28, 1909)*		55.00	12.50

33

			UnFVF	UseFVF
8¢	**red violet & black** *(May 25, 1909)*		37.50	15.00

33 *Manuel J. Hurtado*

34 *José de Obaldia*

34

			UnFVF	UseFVF
10¢	**red violet & black** *(Jan. 19, 1909)*		40.00	15.00
	v. Horizontal pair, 1 w/o overprint		2,450.00	—
	v1. Vertical pair, 1 w/o overprint		2,600.00	—

CA of CANAL widely spaced on position 50 of the sheet of Nos. 31-34.

Inquiries developed that stamps could be obtained already overprinted by the manufacturer at no extra cost. The following overprint types I, II, IV, and V represent stamps secured in this manner until the use of overprinted Panama stamps was discontinued in 1924. Type III was local emergency issue overprinted by The Panama Canal Press. 1¢ and 2¢ stamps were supplied in booklet form beginning late in 1911.

1909-10. SECOND PORTRAIT ISSUE

CANAL ZONE   35-39 *CANAL ZONE reading up, spaced 10mm (1c) or 8 1/2mm apart; "C" serifs at top and bottom.*

35

			UnFVF	UseFVF
1¢	**deep green & black**		3.50	1.60
	v. Head & overprint inverted			15,000.00
	v1. CANAL only		500.00	
	Booklet pane of 6		750.00	

36

			UnFVF	UseFVF
2¢	**scarlet & black**		4.50	1.25
	v. Pair imperforate horizontally		1,000.00	1,000.00
	v1. CANAL double overprint		400.00	
	Booklet pane of 6		1,000.00	

37

			UnFVF	UseFVF
5¢	**deep blue & black**		19.00	3.75
	v. Double overprint		180.00	180.00

38

			UnFVF	UseFVF
8¢	**violet & black** *(March 18, 1910)*		11.00	4.75
	v. Vertical pair, 1 w/o overprint		1,500.00	

39

			UnFVF	UseFVF
10¢	**violet & black**		55.00	20.00

1912-16 PORTRAIT ISSUE

CANAL ZONE   40-43 *"C" serif at top only, "O" tilted left.*

40

			UnFVF	UseFVF
1¢	**deep green & black** *(July 1913)*		12.00	2.60
	v. Vertical pair, 1 w/o overprint		1,500.00	
	Margins imperforate		750.00	
	Perforate		1,150.00	

41

			UnFVF	UseFVF
2¢	**scarlet & black** *(Dec. 1912)*		8.00	1.40
	v. Overprint reading down		175.00	
	v1. head and overprint inverted		700.00	750.00
	v2. Horizontal pair, 1 w/o overprint		1,500.00	
	v3. CANAL only		1,100.00	
	Margins imperforate		210.00	
	Perforate		1,700.00	

42

			UnFVF	UseFVF
5¢	**deep blue & black** *(Dec. 1912)*		22.50	2.75
	t. Head of 2¢			8,000.00

43

			UnFVF	UseFVF
10¢	**red violet & black** *(Feb. 1916)*		40.00	8.00

1915-20. PORTRAIT ISSUE

CANAL ZONE   44-45 *Words spaced 9 1/2mm apart*

44

			UnFVF	UseFVF
1¢	**deep green & black** *(Dec. 1915)*		180.00	110.00
	v. Overprint reading down		315.00	
	v1. Double overprint		300.00	
	v2. ZONE double overprint		4,250.00	

45

			UnFVF	UseFVF
2¢	**scarlet & black** *(Aug. 1920)*		3,000.00	150.00

46

			UnFVF	UseFVF
5¢	**deep blue & black** *(Dec. 1915)*		725.00	200.00

1915-20. PORTRAIT ISSUE

47-49 *"C" thick at bottom, "E" with center bar same length as top and bottom bars.*

CANAL ZONE

47		UnFVF	UseFVF
1¢	**deep green & black** *(Jan. 1918)*	27.50	6.50
	v. Overprint reading down	175.00	
	Left row w/o overprint	850.00	
	Right row w/double overprint	2,500.00	

48		UnFVF	UseFVF
2¢	**scarlet & black** *(Nov. 1918)*	125.00	6.75
	v. Overprint reading down	150.00	150.00
	v1. Horizontal pair, 1 w/o overprint	2,000.00	
	Left row w/o overprint	5,000.00	

49		UnFVF	UseFVF
5¢	**deep blue & black** *(April 1920)*	180.00	30.00

1920-21. CANAL ZONE ISSUE

50-52 *"A" with flat top, small block type 1 3/4mm high.*

52 *Perfin "P"*

50		UnFVF	UseFVF
1¢	**deep green & black** *(April 1921)*	20.00	3.50
	v. Overprint reading down	2.50	
	v1. Horizontal pair, 1 w/o overprint	1,100.00	
	v2. CANAL double overprint	1,500.00	
	v3. ZONE only	2,750.00	1,400.00
	Left row w/o overprint	3,250.00	

51		UnFVF	UseFVF
2¢	**scarlet & black** *(Sept. 1920)*	10.00	2.50
	v. Horizontal pair, 1 w/o overprint	1,750.00	
	v1. Vertical pair, 1 w/o overprint	1,500.00	
	v2. Double overprint	650.00	
	v3. Double overprint second inverted	575.00	
	v4. CANAL double overprint	1,000.00	
	v5. ZONE double overprint	1,000.00	
	v6. CANAL only	2,250.00	
	Left row w/o overprint	850.00	

52		UnFVF	UseFVF
5¢	**deep blue & black** *(April 1921)*	300.00	45.00
	v. Horizontal pair, 1 w/o overprint	825.00	

Official: Nos. 40-43, 46, 47, 50, 51, and 54 with perfin "P."

From March 1915, stamps for official mail were identified by a perforated initial (perfin) letter "P." They were replaced by overprinted stamps on March 31, 1941. The use of official stamps was discontinued Dec. 31, 1951.

A special order was placed by the Canal Zone authorities for a 13¢ stamp to handle the combined registration (8¢) and foreign letter (5¢) fees. Before the arrival of the stamps, however, the registration fee was increased to 10¢ and the stamps were overprinted accordingly. This stamp was later replaced by a 10¢ denomination in the same design. The style of the CANAL ZONE overprint is different from any other issue.

1911-14. CANAL ZONE OVERPRINT ISSUE *perforated 12.*

53-54

53		UnFVF	UseFVF
10¢ on 13¢	**slate** *(Jan. 14, 1911)*	6.50	2.00
	v. 10¢ omitted	250.00	
	v1. 10¢ inverted overprint	300.00	250.00

54		UnFVF	UseFVF
10¢	**slate** *(Jan. 6, 1914)*	45.00	9.00

Official: No. 54 with perfin "P." See note after No. 52.

1914. POSTAGE DUE OVERPRINT ISSUE
Prior to 1914, regular postage stamps were used to collect amounts due on unpaid matter; some stamps were specially handstamped *Postage Due*. The first set of dues comprised overprinted U.S. stamps, notwithstanding the provisions of the Taft Agreement.

CANAL ZONE   55-57 *March 1914, Postage Due*

55		UnFVF	UseFVF
1¢	**dark carmine,** overprint on U.S. PD51	90.00	18.00

56		UnFVF	UseFVF
2¢	**dark carmine,** overprint on U.S. PD53	250.00	50.00

57		UnFVF	UseFVF
10¢	**dark carmine,** overprint on U.S. PD56	735.00	50.00

Many stamps show one or more letters of the overprint out of alignment, principally the "E" of "ZONE."

1915-19. BLUE OVERPRINT PICTORIAL ISSUE
replaced the overprinted U.S. Postage Due issues, in accordance with the Taft Agreement. *Overprint 40, perforated 12.*

58, 61 *Gate to San Geronimo Castle, Portobelo, erroneously inscribed "San Lorenzo Castle, Chagres"*

58		UnFVF	UseFVF
1¢	**black brown** *(March 1915)*	10.00	5.00
	v. Overprint 50 reading down	275.00	
	v1. Overprint 50 reading up		10.00

59, 62, 63 *Statue of Columbus. The explorer, who discovered America, anchored in Panama in 1502.*

60, 65 *Pedro J. Sosa*

59		UnFVF	UseFVF
2¢	**black brown** *(March 1915)*	200.00	15.00
	on cover		500.00

60		UnFVF	UseFVF
10¢	**black brown** *(March 1915)*	50.00	9.00

1915-19. RED OVERPRINT ISSUE *Overprint 40 or 44.*

61		UnFVF	UseFVF
1¢ on 1¢	**black brown** *(Nov. 1915)*	100.00	17.50

62, 63

Overprint

62		UnFVF	UseFVF
2¢ on 2¢	**black brown** *(Nov. 1915)*	35.00	12.50

63		UnFVF	UseFVF
2¢ on 2¢	**black brown,** overprint 44 *(Dec. 1919)*	35.00	14.00

64		UnFVF	UseFVF
4¢ on 4¢	**black brown,** overprint 44 *(Dec. 1919)*	40.00	18.00
	v. ZONE omitted	7,500.00	
	v1. 4 omitted	7,500.00	

65		UnFVF	UseFVF
10¢ on 10¢	**black brown**	24.00	5.00

Two spacings between 1 and 0 of 10 on No. 65.

1915. PANAMA NATIONAL EXPOSITION ISSUE
Honored the 400th anniversary of the European discovery of the Pacific (1513) and the completion of the canal (1914). *Perforated 12.*

66 *Relief map of Panama Canal*

67 *Balboa claims the Pacific and all its shores for Spain, Sept. 13, 1513*

66 1¢	deep blue green & black *(March 1, 1915)*	UnFVF 7.50	UseFVF 6.00
67 2¢	bright rose red & black	UnFVF 11.00	UseFVF 4.50

68 *Gatun Locks*

69 *Gaillard (Culebra) Cut*

68 5¢	deep blue & black	UnFVF 10.50	UseFVF 5.00
69 10¢	brown orange & black	UnFVF 22.50	UseFVF 10.00

1917-20. PICTORIALS OF PANAMA ISSUE

70 SS *Panama in Gaillard (Culebra) Cut*

71 SS *Panama in Gaillard (Culebra) Cut*

70 12¢	red violet & black, overprinted blue	UnFVF 20.00	UseFVF 6.00
71 15¢	turquoise blue & black, overprinted blue	UnFVF 45.00	UseFVF 24.00

72 SS *Cristobal in Gatun Locks*

73 *Drydock at Balboa*

72 24¢	yellow brown & black, overprinted blue	UnFVF 55.00	UseFVF 12.50

Official: No. 72 with perfin "P." See note after No. 52.

73 50¢	yellow orange & black *(Sept. 4, 1920)*	UnFVF 300.00	UseFVF 140.00

74 USS *Nereus in Pedro Miguel Locks*

74 1b	black purple & black *(Sept. 4, 1920)*	UnFVF 160.00	UseFVF 60.00

1921-24. CENTENARY OF INDEPENDENCE FROM SPAIN ISSUE
Stamps of Panama with black or red overprint.

75, 76 *José Vallarino (1792-1864)*

77 *Land Gate, Panama City*

75 1¢	green	UnFVF 3.75	UseFVF 1.20
	v. CANAL double inverted	2,750.00	
	Booklet pane of 6	1,000.00	
76 1¢	green, overprint 44 *(Jan. 28, 1924)*	UnFVF 525.00	UseFVF 180.00
	v. ZONE only, inverted overprint	19.00	
	v1. ZONE CANAL, inverted overprint	850.00	
77 2¢	carmine red	UnFVF 3.00	UseFVF 1.25
	v. Overprint reading down	225.00	
	v1. ZONE only	2,000.00	
	v2. Pair, 1 w/o overprint	3,500.00	
	v3. Double overprint	900.00	
	v4. CANAL double overprint	1,900.00	
	Booklet pane of 6	2,100.00	

78 *Bolivar's Praise of Independence Movement*

79 *Municipal Building 1821 and 1921, Panama City*

78 5¢	deep blue, overprinted red	UnFVF 11.00	UseFVF 3.50
	v. Overprint reading down	60.00	
	v1. red overprint 50	72.00	
	v2. black overprint 50	40.00	
79 10¢	dark red violet	UnFVF 17.50	UseFVF 6.00
	v. Overprint reading down	100.00	

Official: Nos. 75, 77-79 with perfin "P." See note after No. 52.

80 *Statue of Balboa, Panama City*

81 *Col. Tomas Herrera (1804-54), Panamanian father of American independence from Colombia, 1840*

80 15¢	light blue	UnFVF 52.50	UseFVF 14.50
81 24¢	black brown	UnFVF 57.50	UseFVF 20.00

82 *Col. Jose de Fábrega led Panama to declare independence from Spain, Nov. 28, 1821*

82 50¢	black	UnFVF 120.00	UseFVF 70.00

1924. ARMS OF PANAMA ISSUE celebrated a century of independence from Spain. *Overprinted stamps of Panama, perforated 12.*

83, 84 *Arms of Panama*

83 1¢	deep blue green	UnFVF 12.00	UseFVF 4.50
84 2¢	vermilion	UnFVF 9.00	UseFVF 2.75
84A 5¢	dark blue	UnFVF 150.00	UseFVF
84B 10¢	violet	UnFVF 150.00	UseFVF

84C		UnFVF	UseFVF
12¢	olive green	150.00	
84D		UnFVF	UseFVF
15¢	ultramarine	150.00	
84E		UnFVF	UseFVF
24¢	yellow brown	150.00	
84F		UnFVF	UseFVF
50¢	orange	150.00	
84G		UnFVF	UseFVF
$1	black	150.00	

Nos. 84A-84G were prepared for use but not issued. 600 sets exist.

1924-33. CANAL ZONE OVERPRINT ISSUE on U.S. Regular Issue Series. All Panama stamps overprinted *CANAL ZONE* were withdrawn from sale June 30, 1924 and were not valid for postage after Aug. 31, 1924. The formal opening of the Panama Canal was proclaimed by President Wilson July 20, 1920, signifying the end of the construction period of the canal. The executive order comprising the Taft Agreement was subsequently abrogated by President Coolidge, effective June 1, 1924. No change was made in operations until the end of the fiscal year, June 30, 1924. As a temporary measure to replace the overprinted Panama stamps, overprinted U.S. stamps were obtained. These were used until gradually replaced by definitive designs beginning in 1928. As in the case of the Panama issues the Canal Zone authorities were obliged to accept whatever was currently available in the U.S.

85-96 *Flat top "A"*

Overprint

```
CANAL

ZONE
```

85		UnFVF	UseFVF
1/2¢	**olive brown,** overprinted red *(April 15, 1925)*	1.25	.75

86, 112

87

86		UnFVF	UseFVF
1¢	**green**	1.40	.90
	v. CANAL only	1,750.00	
	v1. ZONE inverted overprint	450.00	450.00
	v2. ZONE CANAL	450.00	
	v3. CANAL ZONE inverted overprint	500.00	500.00
	Booklet pane of 6	44.00	
87		UnFVF	UseFVF
1 1/2¢	**yellow brown** *(April 15, 1925)*	2.00	1.40

88

89, 99, 116

88		UnFVF	UseFVF
2¢	**carmine**	9.00	1.80
	Booklet pane of 6	57.50	

89		UnFVF	UseFVF
5¢	**Prussian blue**	22.50	10.00

90, 100, 111, 117

91, 101

90		UnFVF	UseFVF
10¢	**orange yellow**	45.00	22.50
91		UnFVF	UseFVF
12¢	**maroon**	30.00	10.00
	v. ZONE, inverted overprint	37.50	30.00

92, 102, 118

93, 103

92		UnFVF	UseFVF
14¢	**blue** *(June 27, 1925)*	24.00	18.50
93		UnFVF	UseFVF
15¢	**gray black**	50.00	35.00

94, 106

95, 107

94		UnFVF	UseFVF
30¢	**olive brown**	32.50	30.00
95		UnFVF	UseFVF
50¢	**gray lilac**	80.00	45.00

96, 108

96		UnFVF	UseFVF
$1	**purple brown**	300.00	65.00

1925-28. CANAL ZONE OVERPRINT 2ND ISSUE *perforated 11.*

CANAL 97-108 *Overprint "A" with sharp-pointed top.*

ZONE

97		UnFVF	UseFVF
2¢	**carmine** *(May 26, 1926)*	32.00	9.00
	v. CANAL only	1,500.00	1,200.00
	v1. ZONE CANAL	350.00	
	v2. Horizontal pair, 1 w/o overprint	3,500.00	

98, 110, 114

98		UnFVF	UseFVF
3¢	red violet *(June 27, 1925)*	4.50	3.65
	v. ZONE ZONE	500.00	500.00

99		UnFVF	UseFVF
5¢	**Prussian blue** *(Jan. 7, 1926)*	4.50	3.65
	v. CANAL only	2,250.00	
	v1. CANAL inverted overprint	950.00	
	v2. ZONE only	2,000.00	
	v3. ZONE ZONE	1,100.00	
	v4. ZONE CANAL	325.00	
	v5. CANAL ZONE inverted overprint	500.00	
	v6. Horizontal pair, 1 w/o overprint	3,250.00	
	v7. Vertical pair, 1 w/o overprint, 1 w/overprint inverted	2,250.00	

100		UnFVF	UseFVF
10¢	**orange yellow** *(Aug. 1925)*	35.00	12.00
	v. ZONE only	3,000.00	
	v1. ZONE ZONE	3,000.00	

101		UnFVF	UseFVF
12¢	**maroon** *(Feb. 1926)*	22.50	15.00
	v. ZONE ZONE	5,000.00	

102		UnFVF	UseFVF
14¢	**blue** *(Dec. 1928)*	40.00	18.00

104

105

103		UnFVF	UseFVF
15¢	**gray black** *(Jan. 1926)*	6.50	4.50
	v. ZONE only	3,200.00	
	v1. ZONE ZONE	5,500.00	

104		UnFVF	UseFVF
17¢	**black** *(April 5, 1926)*	4.50	3.25
	v. CANAL only	1,700.00	
	v1. ZONE only	800.00	
	v2. ZONE CANAL	200.00	

105		UnFVF	UseFVF
20¢	**carmine red** *(April 5, 1926)*	7.25	3.25
	v. CANAL inverted overprint	3,500.00	
	v1. ZONE inverted overprint	3,850.00	
	v2. ZONE CANAL	3,500.00	

106		UnFVF	UseFVF
30¢	**olive brown** *(Dec. 1926)*	6.75	5.00

107		UnFVF	UseFVF
50¢	**gray lilac** *(July 1928)*	250.00	200.00

108		UnFVF	UseFVF
$1	**brown** *(April 1926)*	150.00	75.00

1927. CANAL ZONE OVERPRINT 3RD ISSUE *perforated 10.*

109 *"A" with pointed top*

109		UnFVF	UseFVF
5¢	**carmine** *(Jan. 1927)*	42.50	11.00
	CANAL only	2,000.00	
	v1. ZONE only	2,750.00	
	v2. Horizontal pair, 1 w/o overprint	3,000.00	
	Booklet pane of 6	650.00	

110		UnFVF	UseFVF
3¢	**red violet** *(May 9, 1927)*	9.00	6.00

111		UnFVF	UseFVF
10¢	**orange yellow** *(May 9, 1927)*	15.00	7.25

1927-33. CANAL ZONE OVERPRINT 4TH ISSUE *perforated 11x10 1/2.*

112 *"A" with pointed top*

112		UnFVF	UseFVF
1¢	**green** *(June 28, 1927)*	1.75	1.40
	Vertical pair, 1 w/o overprint	3,000.00	

113		UnFVF	UseFVF
2¢	**carmine red** *(June 28, 1927)*	2.50	1.00
	Booklet pane of 6	70.00	
	CANAL double on 2 bottom stamps	875.00	

114		UnFVF	UseFVF
3¢	**red violet**, No. 477 *(Feb. 1931)*	4.00	3.00
	(handmade)	925.00	

115		UnFVF	UseFVF
3¢	**red violet**, No. 518 *(Jan. 14, 1933)*	2.80	.30
	v. ZONE only	1,750.00	
	v. CANAL only	3,500.00	
	(handmade)	72.00	

116		UnFVF	UseFVF
5¢	**blue** *(Dec. 13, 1927)*	30.00	12.00

117		UnFVF	UseFVF
10¢	**orange yellow** *(July 1930)*	17.50	12.00

118		UnFVF	UseFVF
14¢	**blue** *(Jan. 14, 1933)*	6.00	3.50
	V. ZONE CANAL	1,500.00	

Official: Nos. 85, 86, 88-90, 97, 99, 100, 109, 111-114, 116, 117 with perfin "P." See note after No. 52.

1924-25. OVERPRINT POSTAGE DUE 1ST ISSUE *perforated 11.*

119 *"A" with flat top*

119		UnFVF	UseFVF
1¢	**deep rose**	115.00	25.00

120		UnFVF	UseFVF
2¢	**deep claret**	65.00	11.00

121		UnFVF	UseFVF
10¢	**deep claret**	250.00	55.00

1924-25. OVERPRINT POSTAGE DUE 2ND ISSUE *perforated 11.*

122 *"A" with pointed top*

122		UnFVF	UseFVF
1¢	**carmine**	6.75	2.25
	v. ZONE ZONE	1,350.00	
	Plate block of 6	100.00	
	On cover commercial use		300.00

123		UnFVF	UseFVF
2¢	**carmine**	12.50	3.00
	v. ZONE ZONE	1,750.00	
	Plate block of 6	180.00	
	On cover commerical use		275.00

124		UnFVF	UseFVF
10¢	**carmine**	145.00	15.00
	Plate block of 6 imprint and star	1,200.00	
	v. Vertical pair, 1 w/o overprint	2,500.00	
	v1. rose red on cover		275.00
	v2. double overprint	375.00	
	On cover		250.00

1925. Overprint Postage Due Issue

125

125		UnFVF	UseFVF
1¢	**green**	95.00	18.00

126		UnFVF	UseFVF
2¢	**carmine**, overprinted blue	27.50	7.50

127		UnFVF	UseFVF
10¢	**orange yellow**	55.00	12.00
	v. POSTAGE DUE double overprint	450.00	
	v1. POSTAG	450.00	
	v2. POSTAG double overprint	3,250.00	

1926. 150th Anniversary Declaration of Independence Issue

128 *Liberty Bell*

128		UnFVF	UseFVF
2¢	**carmine red**	4.75	3.50
	Plate block of 6	80.00	
	FDC (July 6, 1926)		45.00
	On cover		5.00

Note: Normal spacing between CANAL and ZONE of the overprint is 4.75-5mm. A few first day covers were canceled by favor on July 4, 1926, a Sunday. Price $65.00.

1928-40. First Definitive Issue

129, 257 *Maj. Gen. William C. Gorgas (1854-1920), an Army physician and sanitation expert, led the team that controlled the mosquito-borne disease yellow fever so that construction of the canal could be undertaken.*

129		UnFVF	UseFVF
1¢	**green** dry printings	.25	.20
	v. yellow green to green, wet (early) printings	.25	.20
	v1. green, dull gum (1977)	.40	.20
	Plate block of 6	.80	
	FDC (Oct. 3, 1928)		11.00
	On postcard		1.75

Coil: See No. 257.

130 *Maj. Gen. George Washington Goethals (1858-1928), a U.S. Army engineer who led the Isthmian Canal Commission that built the canal over 10 years. He also was the Canal Zone governor, 1914-16.*

130		UnFVF	UseFVF
2¢	**rose red**	.25	.20
	Plate block of 6	1.25	
	FDC (Oct. 1, 1928)		10.00

	On cover		1.00
	Booklet pane of 6	14.00	30.00

131 *Maj. Gen. George W. Goethals. Issuance coincided with the 20th anniversary of the opening of the Panama Canal, but it is not a commemorative as it was intended to pay the domestic first class letter rate for the long term.*

131		UnFVF	UseFVF
3¢	**violet** dry printings	.20	.20
	v. red violet to deep violet, wet (early) printings	.20	.20
	v1. violet, dull gum (1977)	.45	.20
	Plate block of 6	1.10	
	FDC (Aug. 15, 1934)		2.50
	On cover		.50
	Booklet pane of 6, handmade, perforated margins	165.00	
	Booklet pane of 6, machine made	35.00	30.00

Coil: See No. 230.

 132 *Gaillard Cut*

133, 258 *Maj. Gen. Harry F. Hodges*

132		UnFVF	UseFVF
5¢	**blue**	1.10	.40
	deep blue	1.10	.40
	Plate block of 6	8.25	
	FDC (June 25, 1929)		6.00
	On cover		3.50

133		UnFVF	UseFVF
10¢	**orange** dry printings	.35	.25
	v. deep orange, wet (early) printings	.35	.25
	Plate block of 6	4.75	
	FDC (Jan. 11, 1932)		60.00
	On cover		3.00

Coil: See No. 258.

134 *Lt. Col. David DuBose Gaillard*

135 *Maj. Gen. William L. Sibert*

134		UnFVF	UseFVF
12¢	**brown purple** dry printings	1.00	.75
	v. purple brown, wet (early) printings	.80	.60
	Plate block of 6	10.00	
	FDC (July 1, 1929)		65.00
	On cover		8.00

135		UnFVF	UseFVF
14¢	**dark blue**	1.10	1.15
	Plate block of 6	9.00	
	FDC (Sept. 27, 1937)		5.50
	On cover		5.00

136 *Jackson Smith*

137 *Rear Adm. Harry H. Rousseau*

136		UnFVF	UseFVF
15¢	**gray** dry printings	.75	.45
	v. dark gray, wet (early) printings	.75	.65
	Plate block of 6	7.00	
	FDC (Jan. 11, 1932)		50.00
	On cover		6.00

137		UnFVF	UseFVF
20¢	**dark brown** dry printings	.95	.30

		UnFVF	UseFVF
v.	olive brown to deep brown, wet (early) printings	1.00	.30
v1.	black brown, dull gum (1977)	1.75	.30
	Plate block of 6	6.00	
	FDC (Jan. 11, 1932)		50.00
	On cover		6.00

138 Col. Sydney B. Williamson

139 Joseph C.S. Blackburn

138

		UnFVF	UseFVF
30¢	**black** dry printings	1.40	.65
v.	brown black, wet (early) printings	1.10	.55
v1.	black, dull gum (1977)	2.25	.65
	Plate block of 6	15.00	
	FDC (April 15, 1940)		9.00
	On cover		7.00

139

		UnFVF	UseFVF
50¢	**dark lilac** dry printings	2.25	.60
v.	rose lilac, dry printings	2.25	.60
v1.	lilac, wet (early) printings	1.50	.50
v2.	rose lilac, wet (early) printings	2.00	.50
v3.	lilac, dull gum (1977)	5.00	.60
v4.	rose lilac, dull gum (1977)	3.50	.60
	Plate block of 6	17.00	
	FDC (July 1, 1929)		120.00
	On cover		16.00

Note: Used copies of the dull gum printings of this series cannot normally be distinguished from the dry printings of the same stamp issued prior to 1977.

Officials: Nos. 129-139 with perfin "P." See note after No. 52.

1929-31. CANAL ZONE OVERPRINT AIRMAIL ISSUE

AIR MAIL 140, 143

140

		UnFVF	UseFVF
10¢ on 50¢	**red lilac** (Dec. 31, 1929)	9.00	6.50

141

Flag of 5 with serif **15**

141

		UnFVF	UseFVF
15¢ on 1¢	**green,** blue overprint (April 1, 1929)	10.00	6.00

15 142 Flag of 5 curved

142

		UnFVF	UseFVF
15¢ on 1¢	**green,** blue overprint (March 1931)	125.00	100.00

143

		UnFVF	UseFVF
20¢ on 2¢	**rose red** (Dec. 31, 1929)	6.00	2.50
v.	Dropped 2 in overprint	90.00	75.00

144

144

		UnFVF	UseFVF
25¢ on 2¢	**rose red,** blue overprint (Jan. 11, 1929)	5.00	3.75

Officials: Nos. 140, 143, 143v., 144 with perfin "P." See note after No. 52.

1929-30. CANAL ZONE POSTAGE DUE OVERPRINT ISSUE

145 Postage due overprint

145

		UnFVF	UseFVF
1¢ on 5¢	**blue** (March 20, 1930)	4.50	2.75
v.	W/o POSTAGE DUE	1,250.00	

146

		UnFVF	UseFVF
2¢ on 5¢	**blue** (Oct. 18, 1930)	7.50	3.75

147

		UnFVF	UseFVF
5¢ on 5¢	**blue** (Dec. 1, 1930), horizontal bars of overprint omitted	7.50	4.00

148

		UnFVF	UseFVF
10¢ on 5¢	**blue** (Dec. 16, 1929)	7.50	4.00

1931-49. CANAL ZONE AIRMAIL ISSUE

 149 Plane over canal

154 Plane over canal

149

		MNHVF	UseVF
4¢	**rose purple**	1.15	.90
	Plate block of 6	6.00	
	FDC (Jan. 3, 1949)		1.75
	On postcard		2.25

150

		MNHVF	UseVF
5¢	**yellow green**	.65	.35
	green	.60	.30
	Plate block of 6	6.00	
	FDC (Nov. 18, 1931)		9.00
	On cover		1.10

151

		MNHVF	UseVF
6¢	**yellow brown**	.80	.35
	Plate block of 6	6.00	
	FDC (Feb. 15, 1946)		1.75
	On cover		1.00

152

		MNHVF	UseVF
10¢	**orange**	1.30	.35
	red orange	1.00	.30
	Plate block of 6	12.50	
	FDC (Nov. 18, 1931)		8.50
	On cover		.90

153

		MNHVF	UseVF
15¢	**blue**	1.25	.30
	light blue	1.25	.30
	Plate block of 6	16.00	
	FDC (Nov. 18, 1931)		18.00
	On cover		1.25

Note: Blue-green shades have been reported but are believed to be color changelings.

154

		MNHVF	UseVF
20¢	**red violet**	2.25	.30
	deep violet	2.25	.30
	Plate block of 6	24.00	
	FDC (Nov. 18, 1931)		32.00
	On cover		1.75

155			MNHVF	UseVF
30¢	**rose lake**		3.50	1.15
	dull rose		3.50	1.15
	Plate block of 6		27.00	
	FDC *(July 15, 1941)*			20.00
	On cover			7.50

156			MNHVF	UseVF
40¢	**yellow**		3.25	1.25
	lemon yellow		5.00	1.75
	Plate block of 6		36.00	
	FDC *(July 15, 1941)*			100.00
	On cover			22.00

157			MNHVF	UseVF
$1	**black**		9.00	1.50
	Plate block of 6		95.00	
	FDC *(Nov. 18, 1931)*			180.00
	On cover			75.00

Officials: Nos. 150-157 with perfin "P." See note after No. 52.

1932-41. CANAL ZONE POSTAGE DUE ISSUE

 158-162

158		UnFVF	UseFVF
1¢	**claret**	.20	.20
159		UnFVF	UseFVF
2¢	**claret**	.20	.20
160		UnFVF	UseFVF
5¢	**claret**	.50	.35
161		UnFVF	UseFVF
10¢	**claret**	2.00	1.75
162		UnFVF	UseFVF
15¢	**claret** *(April 21, 1941)*	1.50	1.50

1939 25TH ANNIVERSARY OF CANAL ISSUE *perforated 11.*

 163 *Balboa, June 1912, looking east from Sosa Hill; Administrative Building site*

 164 *Balboa, June 1936, view from Sosa, completed Administrative Building and Prado*

163		UnFVF	UseFVF
1¢	**light green**	.60	.30
	Plate block of 6	14.00	
	FDC *(Aug. 15, 1939)*		1.75
	On postcard		2.25

164		UnFVF	UseFVF
2¢	**carmine**	.65	.35
	Plate block of 6	15.00	
	FDC *(Aug. 15, 1939)*		2.50
	On cover		2.25

 165 *Gaillard (Culebra) Cut, June 1913, deepest excavation in canal*

 166 *Gaillard (Culebra) Cut, 1921, Gold and Contractor's Hills*

165		UnFVF	UseFVF
3¢	**deep violet**	.40	.20
	Plate block of 6	12.00	
	FDC *(Aug. 15, 1939)*		1.25
	On cover		1.10

166		UnFVF	UseFVF
5¢	**deep blue**	2.75	.90
	Plate block of 6	18.00	
	FDC *(Aug. 15, 1939)*		2.75
	On cover		5.00

 167 *Bas Obispo, Jan. 1910, view south from Panama Railroad relocation*

 168 *Bas Obispo, July 11, 1934, USS Houston in completed cut*

167		UnFVF	UseFVF
6¢	**red orange**	2.60	3.00
	Plate block of 6	48.00	
	FDC *(Aug. 15, 1939)*		5.00
	On cover		8.00

168		UnFVF	UseFVF
7¢	**black**	2.50	3.00
	Plate block of 6	50.00	
	FDC *(Aug. 15, 1939)*		6.00
	On cover		10.00

 169 *Gatun Lower Locks, April 15, 1911, view south from north end*

 170 *Gatun Lower Locks, June 19, 1924, view of new approach*

169		UnFVF	UseFVF
8¢	**green**	4.50	3.75
	Plate block of 6	60.00	
	FDC *(Aug. 15, 1939)*		7.00
	On cover		10.00

170		UnFVF	UseFVF
10¢	**bright blue**	3.25	2.75
	Plate block of 6	60.00	
	FDC *(Aug. 15, 1939)*		5.50
	On cover		6.00

 171 *Gaillard (Culebra) Cut, May 20, 1913, Pioneer Cut*

 172 *Gaillard (Culebra) Cut, Aug. 16, 1930, SS Santa Clara*

171		UnFVF	UseFVF
11¢	**blue green**	8.00	10.00
	Plate block of 6	130.00	
	FDC *(Aug. 15, 1939)*		11.00
	On cover		25.00

172		UnFVF	UseFVF
12¢	**lake**	10.00	11.00
	Plate block of 6	105.00	
	FDC *(Aug. 15, 1939)*		10.00
	On cover		15.00

 173 *Gamboa, July 1913, Dike, Bas Obispo Cut, Rio Chagres Bridge*

 174 *Gamboa, Dec. 7, 1922, ships at Rio Chagres crossing*

173		UnFVF	UseFVF
14¢	**dark violet**	8.50	9.50
	Plate block of 6	130.00	
	FDC *(Aug. 15, 1939)*		9.00
	On cover		20.00

174		UnFVF	UseFVF
15¢	**olive green**	11.00	4.50
	Plate block of 6	135.00	
	FDC *(Aug. 15, 1939)*		10.00
	On cover		5.00

175 *Pedro Miguel Locks, June 3, 1912, construction of gates*

176 *Pedro Miguel Locks, July 16, 1927, SS Duchesa d' Aosta, President Polk*

175		UnFVF	UseFVF
18¢	**rose carmine**	11.00	7.00
	Plate block of 6	165.00	
	FDC *(Aug. 15, 1939)*		15.00
	On cover		12.00

176		UnFVF	UseFVF
20¢	**brown**	13.00	5.50
	Plate block of 6	200.00	
	FDC *(Aug. 15, 1939)*		10.00
	On cover		8.00

177 *Gatun Spillway Dam, Feb. 5, 1913, Crest Dam construction*

178 *Gatun Spillway Dam, May 1922, Crest Dam in operation*

177		UnFVF	UseFVF
25¢	**orange**	20.00	22.00
	Plate block of 6	275.00	
	FDC *(Aug. 15, 1939)*		22.50
	On cover		45.00

178		UnFVF	UseFVF
50¢	**brown purple**	24.00	5.50
	Plate block of 6	240.00	
	FDC *(Aug. 15, 1939)*		20.00
	On cover		40.00

Note: Some of the 163-178 series, such as the 11¢, paid no specific rate and are found on cover only in combination with other stamps. Postally used copies thus sell for more than copies removed from First Day covers.

Official: Nos. 163-166, 170, 172, 174-176 with perfin "P." See note after No. 52.

1939. AIRMAIL ISSUE for the 25th anniversary of the canal opening.

179 *Douglas plane over Sosa Hill*

180 *Planes and map of Central America*

179		UnFVF	UseFVF
5¢	**greenish black** *(July 15, 1939)*	4.75	3.75
180		UnFVF	UseFVF
10¢	**red violet** *(July 15, 1939)*	4.75	3.75

181 *Sikorsky S.42 flying boat and scene near Ft. Amador*

182 *Sikorsky S.42 flying boat at Cristobal Harbor*

181		UnFVF	UseFVF
15¢	**yellow brown** *(July 15, 1939)*	4.25	1.50
182		UnFVF	UseFVF
25¢	**deep blue** *(July 15, 1939)*	15.00	10.00

183 *Sikorsky S.42 flying boat over Gaillard Cut*

184 *Sikorsky S.42 flying boat landing*

183		UnFVF	UseFVF
30¢	**carmine red** *(July 15, 1939)*	12.00	9.75

184			UnFVF	UseFVF
$1		**green** *(July 15, 1939)*	35.00	30.00

Official: Nos. 179, 180, 181, 183, 184 with perfin "P." See note below No. 52.

1939. PRESIDENTIAL SERIES OVERPRINT ISSUE *perforated 11x10 1/2.*

 185

185		UnFVF	UseFVF
1/2¢	**red orange**, U.S. No. 524, *(Sept. 1, 1939)*	.25	.20
186		UnFVF	UseFVF
1 1/2¢	**yellow brown**, U.S. No. 526, *(Sept. 1, 1939)*	.30	.25

1941. OFFICIAL OVERPRINT ISSUE Official stamps. Definitive issues overprinted in black by Panama Canal Press with OFFICIAL PANAMA CANAL. Type I: three lines on small stamps, Nos. 129/139 (PANAMA 10mm long), two lines on large horizontal stamps (PANAMA CANAL 19 1/2mm long).

 187

187P

OFFICIAL

PANAMA

CANAL

 188

189

187		MNHVF	UseVF
1¢	**green**	3.75	.40
188		MNHVF	UseVF
3¢	**red violet**	6.00	.75
189		MNHVF	UseVF
5¢	**blue**		32.50

 190

191

 193

190		MNHVF	UseVF
10¢	yellow orange	10.00	2.25
191		MNHVF	UseVF
15¢	gray black	18.00	3.00
192		MNHVF	UseVF
20¢	sepia	22.50	2.75
193		MNHVF	UseVF
50¢	red lilac	45.00	7.50
	v.PANAMA 9mm *(Sept. 22, 1941)*		800.00

1941. OFFICIAL AIRMAIL ISSUE overprint on Nos.150-175. Type II: PANAMA CANAL is 17mm long.

 194

194		MNHVF	UseVF
5¢	yellow green *(March 31, 1941)*	6.00	1.25
	green	6.00	1.25
	On cover		60.00
	v.Type II *(Sept. 22, 1941)*	—	175.00
	On cover		450.00
195		MNHVF	UseVF
6¢	yellow brown *(Nov. 1948)*	13.00	4.00
	On cover		55.00
	v.Inverted overprint		2,500.00

Note: All of No. 195v are cancelled-to-order.

196		MNHVF	UseVF
10¢	orange *(March 31, 1941)*	7.50	2.00
	red orange	7.50	2.00
	On cover		25.00
	v.Type II *(Sept. 22, 1941)*	—	295.00
	On cover		375.00
197		MNHVF	UseVF
15¢	blue *(March 31, 1941)*	9.00	1.75
	light blue	9.00	1.75
	On cover		22.00
198		MNHVF	UseVF
20¢	red violet *(March 31, 1941)*	11.00	3.50
	deep violet	11.00	3.50
	On cover		125.00
	v.Type II *(Sept. 22, 1941)*	—	185.00
	On cover		—
199		MNHVF	UseVF
30¢	rose lake *(June 1942)*	16.00	5.50
	dull sore	16.00	5.50
	On cover		45.00
	v.Type II *(Sept. 22, 1941)*	—	70.00
	On cover		150.00
200		MNHVF	UseVF
40¢	yellow *(March 31, 1941)*	18.00	6.00
	lemon yellow	20.00	8.00
	On cover		110.00
	v.Type II *(Sept. 22, 1941)*	—	200.00
	On cover		500.00
201		MNHVF	UseVF
$1	black *(March 31, 1941)*	24.00	8.00
	On cover		175.00

The use of official postage was restricted to departments and divisions of The Panama Canal, the Panama Railroad and certain other U.S. agencies in the Canal Zone. The stamps were used on official correspondence which did not enjoy the franking privilege, such as ordinary letters to foreign countries, certain official matter dispatched via parcel post and all airmail except official post office mail. Official stamps were also used to pay return receipt fees on registered official mail. First Class mail was almost always dispatched via airmail, and airmail official stamps are therefore not uncommon on cover. Ordinary official postage, however, was nearly always used on parcel post mail and covers are very rare.

Nos. 187-201 and 207 were sold to the public cancelled with Balboa Heights, Canal Zone between wavy lines until Dec. 31, 1951, when use of official stamps was discontinued. Mint stamps were available to the public at face value for three months, beginning Jan. 2, 1952. Used prices are for cancelled-to-order stamps; postally used copies are worth more. To facilitate overprinting, all sheet margins were removed and no plate numbers are known to exist.

Note: The following alignment varieties are reported on this Official Airmail Issue: "O" of "OFFICIAL" over "N" of "PANAMA" on Nos. 194 and 196-201, "O" of "OFFICIAL" over second "A" of "PANAMA" on Nos. 194-201, first "F" of "OFFICIAL" over second "A" of "PANAMA" on Nos. 194-201, and "L" of "OFFICIAL" over first "A" of "CANAL" on Nos. 195 and 201, may exist on others. None of these varieties is known to exist on Nos. 194v, 196v or 198v-200v. Price 2x-5x normal. Minor broken letters of the overprint also can be found.

Prices for CTO copies are for examples with original gum. CTO copies without gum sell for 60%-75% of normal.

1946-49. ISSUE

 202 *Maj. Gen. George W. Davis, first governor*

203 *C.E. Magoon, second governor*

202		MNHVF	UseVF
1/2¢	vermilion	.40	.25
	Plate block of 6	2.00	
	FDC *(Aug. 16, 1948)*		1.10
	On cover		1.00
203		MNHVF	UseVF
1 1/2¢	chocolate	.45	.25
	Plate block of 6	2.25	
	FDC *(Aug. 16, 1948)*		1.25
	On cover		1.50

 204 *Theodore Roosevelt*

205, 234, 263 *John F. Stevens*

204		MNHVF	UseVF
2¢	light rose carmine, dry printing	.20	.20
	v.rose carmine, wet (early) printing	.20	.20
	v1. dark rose carmine, dull gum *(1977)*	.40	.20
	v2. light rose carmine, dull gum	.25	.20
	Plate block of 6	.75	
	FDC *(Oct. 27, 1949)*		.80
	On cover		1.00
205		MNHVF	UseVF
5¢	dark blue, dry printing	.40	.20
	Prussian blue, wet (early) printing	.45	.20
	Plate block of 6	2.75	
	FDC *(April 25, 1946)*		1.00
	On cover		2.25

No. 205 may have straight edges. For coil see No. 234.

 206, 259 *John F. Wallace*

206		MNHVF	UseVF
25¢	green, dry printing	1.00	.50
	yellow green, wet (early) printing	2.50	.80
	Plate block of 6	7.50	
	FDC *(Aug. 16, 1948)*		3.75
	On cover		9.00

1947. OFFICIAL STAMP ISSUE

 207 *No. 205 with overprint 187, OFFICIAL/PANAMA/CANAL.*

207		MNHVF	UseVF
5¢	Prussian blue	10.00	4.00
	On cover		80.00

See note after No. 201.

1948. CANAL BIOLOGICAL AREA ISSUE celebrated the 25th anniversary of the establishment of the Canal Zone Biological Area. Perforated 11.

208 *Barro Colorado Island and coatimundi. The island, declared a biological area by Gov. Jay Johnson Morrow in 1923, was administered while under United States control by the Smithsonian Institution. The Island is in Gatun Lake, formed by the damming of the Chagres River during the building of the canal.*

208
10¢

	MNHVF	UseVF
black	1.10	1.00
Plate block of 6	7.50	
FDC *(April 17, 1948)*		2.75
On cover		4.00

1949. GOLD RUSH CENTENNIAL ISSUE *perforated 11.*

209 *Forty-niners arriving at Chagres*

210 *Up the Chagres River by Bungo*

209
3¢

	MNHVF	UseVF
deep blue	.40	.30
Plate block of 6	4.50	
FDC *(June 1, 1949)*		1.00
On cover		2.00

210
6¢

	MNHVF	UseVF
deep violet	.55	.35
Plate block of 6	6.00	
FDC *(June 1, 1949)*		1.00
On cover		2.50

211 *Las Cruces Trail to Panama City*

212 *Departure for San Francisco*

211
12¢

	MNHVF	UseVF
blue green	1.25	1.00
Plate block of 6	16.00	
FDC *(June 1, 1949)*		1.80
On cover		4.00

212
18¢

	MNHVF	UseVF
deep magenta	1.85	1.60
Plate block of 6	20.00	
FDC *(June 1, 1949)*		3.00
On cover		6.00

1951. WEST INDIAN CANAL WORKERS ISSUE *perforated 11.*

213 *West Indian workers in Gaillard (Culebra) Cut. During the construction period of 1904-14, 31,071 out of 45,107 workers brought to the Isthmus by the Isthmian Canal Commission were from the West Indies, and additional thousands came on their own.*

213
10¢

	MNHVF	UseVF
carmine	2.00	1.60
Plate block of 6	25.00	
FDC *(Aug. 15, 1951)*		2.75
On cover		5.00

1951-63. AIRMAIL ISSUE *perforated 11.*

214-224 *Winged emblem and globe*

214
4¢

	MNHVF	UseVF
light rose purple, dry printings	.90	.30
v.rose purple, wet (early) printings	1.00	.30
Plate block of 6 (dry)	7.00	
Plate block of 6 (wet)	8.00	
FDC *(July 16, 1951)*		1.25
On postcard		2.50

215
5¢

	MNHVF	UseVF
yellow green	.90	.50
Plate block of 4	5.50	
FDC *(Aug. 16, 1958)*		3.25
On postcard		3.00

216
6¢

	MNHVF	UseVF
light brown, dry printings	.35	.20
v.brown, wet (early) printings	.30	.20
Plate block of 6 (dry)	4.00	
Plate block of 6 (wet)	4.00	
FDC *(July 16, 1951)*		.75
On cover		.65

217
7¢

	MNHVF	UseVF
olive	.90	.40
Plate block of 4	5.00	
FDC *(Aug. 16, 1958)*		2.50
On cover		1.75

217A
8¢

	MNHVF	UseVF
carmine (perforated 10 1/2x11)	.40	.25
Plate block of 4	2.50	
FDC *(Jan. 7, 1963)*		.75
On cover		1.00

218
10¢

	MNHVF	UseVF
light red orange, dry printings	.90	.25
v.red orange, wet (early) printings	1.25	.25
Plate block of 6 (dry)	9.00	
Plate block of 6 (wet)	10.00	
FDC *(July 16, 1951)*		1.50
On cover		1.00

219
15¢

	MNHVF	UseVF
dark purple	4.00	2.50
Plate block of 4	25.00	
FDC *(Aug. 16, 1958)*		5.00
On cover		8.00

220
21¢

	MNHVF	UseVF
light blue, dry printings	6.00	2.75
v.blue, wet (early) printings	5.00	2.25
Plate block of 6 (dry)	65.00	
Plate block of 6 (wet)	65.00	
FDC *(July 16, 1951)*		4.00
On cover		15.00

221
25¢

	MNHVF	UseVF
orange yellow	8.00	4.00
Plate block of 4	75.00	
FDC *(Aug. 16, 1958)*		7.00
On cover		20.00

222
31¢

	MNHVF	UseVF
cerise	5.00	4.25
Plate block of 6	60.00	
FDC *(July 16, 1951)*		5.00
On cover		18.00
v. Horizontal pair, imperforate vertically	675.00	

223
35¢

	MNHVF	UseVF
dark blue	5.50	3.00
Plate block of 4	45.00	
FDC *(Aug. 16, 1958)*		10.00
On cover		35.00

224
80¢

	MNHVF	UseVF
light gray black, dry printings	5.75	1.75
v.gray black, wet (early) printings	8.00	1.00
Plate block of 6 (dry)	50.00	
Plate block of 6 (wet)	70.00	
FDC *(July 16, 1951)*		10.00
On cover		65.00

Beginning June 1954, Canal Zone stamps were printed by the dry process on pre-gummed paper instead of the wet intaglio method previously employed. The same plates were used, but due to the absence of paper shrinkage and other factors, the size of the sheets is slightly larger than wet process stamps.

1955. PANAMA RAILROAD CENTENNIAL ISSUE *perforated 11.*

225 *Panama Railroad. The Trans-Panama railroad was built (1848-55) with U.S. capital to support transportation of goods to the West Coast of the United States.*

225
3¢

	MNHVF	UseVF
violet	.50	.35
Plate block of 6	6.50	
FDC *(Jan. 28, 1955)*		1.25
On cover		2.00

1957. GORGAS HOSPITAL ISSUE *celebrated the 75th anniversary of the institution. Perforated 11.*

226 *Gorgas Hospital Adminstration Building with Ancon Hill in background*

226

		MNHVF	UseVF
3¢	**black** on turquoise green	.40	.50
	black on dull turquoise green	.40	.50
	Plate block of 4	3.75	
	FDC *(Nov. 17, 1957)*		1.00
	On cover		1.50

1958. SS ANCON ISSUE *perforated 11.*

227 *SS Ancon* Panama Line

227

		MNHVF	UseVF
4¢	**turquoise blue**	.40	.40
	Plate block of 4	3.00	
	FDC *(Aug. 30, 1958)*		1.00
	On cover		1.75

1958. ROOSEVELT CENTENNIAL ISSUE *perforated 11.*

228 *Theodore Roosevelt medal (reverse and obverse), map of canal*

228

		MNHVF	UseVF
4¢	**brown**	.40	.35
	Plate block of 4	2.50	
	FDC *(Nov. 15, 1958)*		1.00
	On cover		1.00

1960. BSA 50TH ANNIVERSARY ISSUE *perforated 11.*

229 *First Class Boy Scout Badge and Canal Zone Community strip*

229

		MNHVF	UseVF
4¢	**deep blue, red & deep ocher**	.55	.50
	Plate block of 4	4.00	
	FDC *(Feb. 8, 1960)*		1.00
	On cover		1.10

1960. GOETHALS COIL ISSUE *perforated 10 vertically.*

230

		MNHVF	UseVF
3¢	**deep violet**	.25	.20
	FDC *(Nov. 1, 1960)*		1.00
	On postcard		1.75
	Pair	.30	.60
	Joint line pair	.80	1.50

1960. ADMINISTRATION BUILDING ISSUE *perforated 11.*

231 *Administration building*

231

		MNHVF	UseVF
4¢	**deep rose purple**	.20	.20
	v.Dull gum	.50	.20
	Plate block of 4	.75	

		MNHVF	UseVF
	FDC *(Nov. 1, 1960)*		1.00
	On cover		.75

1960. DEFINITIVE COIL ISSUE *perforated 10 vertically.*

232

		MNHVF	UseVF
4¢	**dark rose purple**	.20	.20
	FDC *(Nov. 1, 1960)*		.80
	On cover		.75
	Pair	.35	.60
	Joint line pair	1.00	2.50

1961. US ARMY CARIBBEAN SCHOOL ISSUE Airmail, *perforated 11.*

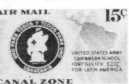

233 *Emblem*

233

		MNHVF	UseVF
15¢	**red & deep blue**	1.50	.90
	Plate block of 4	6.00	
	FDC *(Nov. 21, 1961)*		1.50
	On cover		2.50

1961. JOHN F. STEVENS COIL ISSUE *perforated 10 vertically.*

234, 263 *John F. Stevens*

234

		MNHVF	UseVF
5¢	**Prussian blue**	.20	.20
	FDC *(Feb. 10, 1962)*		1.00
	On cover		1.00
	Pair	.45	1.75
	Joint line pair	2.00	6.00

1962. GIRL SCOUTS USA 59TH ANNIVERSARY ISSUE *perforated 11.*

235 *Badge, tents on Gatun Lake*

235

		MNHVF	UseVF
4¢	**turquoise blue, dark green & ocher**	.40	.30
	Plate block of 4	1.50	
	FDC *(March 12, 1962)*		1.00
	On cover		1.25

1962. MALARIA ERADICATION ISSUE *perforated 11.*

236

236

		MNHVF	UseVF
7¢	**lemon & black**	.50	.45
	Plate block of 4	2.50	
	FDC *(Sept. 24, 1962)*		1.00
	On cover		1.00

1962. THATCHER FERRY BRIDGE ISSUE *perforated 11.*

237 *Thatcher Ferry Bridge over Panama Canal and map*

237

		MNHVF	UseVF
4¢	**black & silver**	.35	.30
	Plate block of 4	3.50	
	FDC *(Oct. 12, 1962)*		1.00
	On cover		1.25
	v.Bridge (silver) omitted	6,500.00	

Note: Some renumbering of Canal Zone stamps was put into effect for Nos. 238-54 in the 2003 Krause-Minkus catalog.

1962. ALLIANCE FOR PROGRESS ISSUE *Airmail, perforated 11.*

238 *Alliance emblem*

238		MNHVF	UseVF
15¢	**gray, blue & green**	1.00	.75
	Plate block of 4	7.00	
	FDC (Aug. 17, 1963)		1.25
	On cover		2.00

1963. PANAMA CANAL 50TH ANNIVERSARY ISSUE *perforated 11.*

239 *Cristobal*

240 *Gatun Locks*

239		MNHVF	UseVF
6¢	**green & black**	.40	.45
	Plate block of 4	2.50	
	FDC (Aug. 15, 1964)		1.75
	On postcard		3.00

240		MNHVF	UseVF
8¢	**rose red & black**	.50	.25
	Plate block of 4	1.50	
	FDC (Aug. 15, 1964)		.75
	On cover		1.10

241 *Madden Dam*

242 *Gaillard Cut*

241		MNHVF	UseVF
15¢	**blue & black**	1.25	.80
	Plate block of 4	5.50	
	FDC (Aug. 15, 1964)		1.00
	On cover		3.50

242		MNHVF	UseVF
20¢	**reddish purple & black**	1.45	.85
	Plate block of 4	8.50	
	FDC (Aug. 15, 1964)		1.50
	On cover		4.00

243 *Miraflores Locks*

244 *Balboa*

243		MNHVF	UseVF
30¢	**chocolate & black**	2.00	1.50
	Plate block of 4	12.50	
	FDC (Aug. 15, 1964)		2.50
	On cover		6.00

244		MNHVF	UseVF
80¢	**olive bistre & black**	4.25	2.75
	Plate block of 4	18.00	
	FDC (Aug. 15, 1964)		2.75
	On cover		37.50

1964-74. SEAL AND JET AIRMAIL ISSUE *perforated 11.*

245-254 *Canal Zone seal and jet plane*

245		MNHVF	UseVF
6¢	**green & black**	.35	.35
	Plate block of 4	1.75	
	FDC (July 15, 1965)		1.65
	On postcard		2.25

246		MNHVF	UseVF
8¢	**dull rose & black**	.30	.25
	Plate block of 4	1.25	
	FDC (July 15, 1965)		.80
	On cover		.50

247		MNHVF	UseVF
10¢	**dull orange & black**	.30	.25
	Plate block of 4	1.00	
	FDC (July 15, 1965)		.90
	On cover		1.00
	Booklet pane of 4	3.50	
	FDC booklet pane of 4 (Feb. 18, 1970)		3.75

Note: There were two printings of the booklet panes. The first is in light dull orange and black, the second is in dark dull orange and black. On both, three positions exist with colored bars in the tab. Price 3x normal.

248		MNHVF	UseVF
11¢	**drab & black**	.40	.30
	Plate block of 4	1.15	
	FDC (Sept. 24, 1971)		1.00
	On cover		2.00
	Booklet pane of 4	3.25	
	FDC booklet pane of 4 (Sept. 24, 1971)		4.00

Note: Three positions of the booklet panes exist with colored bars in the tab. Price 3x normal.

249		MNHVF	UseVF
13¢	**light green & black**	1.00	.30
	Plate block of 4	3.50	
	FDC (Feb. 11, 1974)		1.25
	On cover		2.25
	Booklet pane of 4	5.50	
	FDC booklet pane of 4 (Feb. 11, 1974)		4.00

Note: Three positions of the booklet panes exist with colored bars in the tab. Price 3x normal.

250		MNHVF	UseVF
15¢	**blue & black**	.55	.25
	Plate block of 4	2.00	
	FDC (July 15, 1965)		1.00
	On cover		3.00

251		MNHVF	UseVF
20¢	**purple & black**	.60	.25
	Plate block of 4	2.50	
	FDC (July 15, 1965)		1.20
	On cover		5.00

252		MNHVF	UseVF
25¢	**pale yellow green & black**	.75	1.00
	Plate block of 4	2.50	
	FDC (March 15, 1968)		1.00
	On cover		20.00

253		MNHVF	UseVF
30¢	**brown & black**	1.00	.35
	v.dull gum	1.50	
	Plate block of 4	3.50	
	Plate block of 4, dull gum	6.50	
	FDC (July 15, 1965)		1.50
	On cover		10.00

254		MNHVF	UseVF
80¢	**bistre & black**	2.25	.60
	Plate block of 4	9.00	
	FDC (July 15, 1965)		2.00
	On cover		22.00

1968. GOETHALS MEMORIAL ISSUE

255 *Goethals Memorial in Balboa, Canal Zone, honored the Army engineer who built the canal.*

255		MNHVF	UseVF
6¢	**green & blue**	.40	.20
	Plate block of 4	1.75	
	FDC (March 15, 1968)		.75
	On cover		1.00

1971. ISSUE

256 *Ruins of Ft. San Lorenzo on bluff overlooking Chagres River at its junction with the Atlantic Ocean*

256		MNHVF	UseVF
8¢	**multicolored**	.45	.35
	Plate block of 4	2.75	
	FDC *(July 14, 1971)*		.90
	On cover		1.00

1975. COIL ISSUE *perforated 10 vertically.*

257 *Maj. Gen. William Crawford Gorgas*

257		MNHVF	UseVF
1¢	**green**	.20	.20
	FDC *(Feb. 14, 1975)*		.70
	On cover		1.00
	Pair	.35	.40
	Joint line pair	.90	1.35

258 *Maj. Gen. Harry Foote Hodges*

258		MNHVF	UseVF
10¢	**orange**	.70	.45
	FDC *(Feb. 14, 1975)*		.90
	On cover		1.25
	Pair	1.50	1.35
	Joint line pair	4.25	8.00

259 *John F. Wallace*

259		MNHVF	UseVF
25¢	**dark yellow green**	2.50	2.75
	FDC *(Feb. 14, 1975)*		2.50
	On cover		7.00
	Pair	4.00	8.00
	Joint line pair	15.00	25.00

1976. REGULAR ISSUE *perforated 11.*

260 *Cascadas, 15 cubic yard dipper dredge built by Bucyrus Co. of New York, joined the digging fleet of Panama Canal on Oct. 31, 1915, established a world record for a day's work by an excavating machine in hard material Feb. 18, 1916 when she excavated and loaded into dump scows 23,305 cubic yards of rock and sand.*

260		MNHVF	UseVF
13¢	**blue, black & green**	.45	.25
	Plate block of 4	2.25	
	FDC *(Feb. 23, 1976)*		.90
	On cover		.80
	Booklet pane of 4	3.00	2.75
	FDC booklet pane of 4 *(April 19, 1976)*		4.00

All copies of the regular issue and booklet panes of #260 have dull gum as issued. Two positions of the booklet panes exist with colored bars in the tab. Price 3x normal.

1976. AIRMAIL ISSUE *paid the postcard rate to overseas (not U.S.) locations. Perforated 11.*

261

261		MNHVF	UseVF
22¢	**violet & black**	.90	2.50
	Plate block of 4	3.75	

	FDC *(May 10, 1976)*		2.65
	On postcard		9.00

All copies have dull gum as issued.

262		MNHVF	UseVF
35¢	**salmon & black**	1.25	2.50
	Plate block of 4	4.25	
	FDC *(May 10, 1976)*		2.75
	On cover		6.00

All copies have dull gum as issued.

1976. JOHN F. STEVENS ISSUE *perforated 11x10 1/2.*

263 *John F. Stevens*

263		MNHVF	UseVF
5¢	**dark blue** *(May 1976)*	.30	.45
	v.Tagged	10.00	17.00
	On cover		.75
	Plate block of 4	3.25	
	Plate block of 4, tagged	100.00	

There were 3 printings of #263. The first (1976) and third (1979) have dull gum, the second (1978) has shiny gum. Only the third printing was tagged. Exact issue dates are unknown.

1978. REGULAR ISSUE *perforated 11.*

264 *Towing locomotive ("mule") used to guide ships through the locks*

264		MNHVF	UseVF
(15¢	**deep green & blue green**	.50	.30
	Plate block of 4	2.25	
	FDC *(Oct. 25, 1978)*		.90
	On cover		1.25

All copies have dull gum as issued.

Envelopes and Wrappers

1916. BALBOA AND CORDOBA ISSUES

E1 *Vasco Nuñez de Balboa*

E2 *Fernandez de Cordoba*

E1		UnFVF	UseFVF
1¢	**green & black** *(April 24, 1916)*	15.00	11.50
	Entire *(350,000)*	110.00	50.00
	t.Head & CANAL ZONE	2,000.00	2,000.00
	t1.Frame only	1,500.00	2,500.00

E2		UnFVF	UseFVF
2¢	**carmine & black** *(April 24, 1916)*	12.50	5.50
	Entire (incl. E2a) *(1,512,000)*	100.00	35.00
	a.red & black	12.50	5.50
	Entire	85.00	45.00
	t.Head & CANAL ZONE	1,000.00	2,000.00
	t1.Frame only, red	750.00	
	t2.Frame double inverted, carmine	2,500.00	2,250.00

1918. OVERPRINTED PANAMA REGISTRATION ENVELOPE ISSUE

E3 *Vasco Nuñez de Balboa*

E3
10¢ on 5¢ black & red

		UnFVF	UseFVF
		125.00	85.00
Entire, size 6 *(25,000)*		1,500.00	2,000.00
Entire, size 8 *(10,000)*		1,100.00	2,000.00

1921. 100TH ANNIVERSARY OF INDEPENDENCE FROM SPAIN ISSUE

E4 *Procer Jose Vallarino*

E5 *Land Gate of Panama City*

E4
1¢

		UnFVF	UseFVF
	green *(Nov. 13, 1921)*	150.00	100.00
Entire *(20,681)*		700.00	400.00

E5
2¢

		UnFVF	UseFVF
	red *(Nov. 13, 1921)*	40.00	25.00
Entire *(30,000)*		275.00	140.00

1923. ARMS OF PANAMA ISSUE

E6 *Arms of Panama*

E6
2¢

		UnFVF	UseFVF
	carmine *(Dec. 15, 1923)*	60.00	40.00
Entire *(46,041)*		175.00	125.00

1924. EMBOSSED STAMPED ENVELOPES ISSUE

E7 *Benjamin Franklin*

E8 *George Washington*

E7
1¢

		UnFVF	UseFVF
	green *(July 1, 1924)*	5.00	3.00
Entire *(50,000)*		40.00	19.00

E8
2¢

		UnFVF	UseFVF
	carmine *(July 1, 1924)*	5.00	2.75
Entire *(100,000)*		40.00	19.00

1924. SEAL OF CANAL ZONE ISSUE

E9 *Seal of Panama Canal*

E9
1¢

		UnFVF	UseFVF
	green *(Oct. 24, 1924)*	2.00	1.00
Entire, size 6 *(205,000)*		28.50	18.50

E10
2¢

		UnFVF	UseFVF
	carmine *(Oct. 24, 1924)*	.75	.30
Entire, size 6 *(1,636,109)*		25.00	10.50
Entire, size 8 *(361,549)*		25.00	10.50

1928. AIRMAIL OVERPRINT ISSUE

Regular stamped envelope E10 overprinted with horizontal blue and red bars across face and box at lower left with nine lines of instructions. Additional stamps were required for airmail transmission.

E11
2¢

		UnFVF	UseFVF
	red E10, *(May 21, 1928)* entire, size 6 *(10,000)*	125.00	50.00
Entire, size 8 *(5,000)*		125.00	50.00

1929. AIRMAIL OVERPRINT ISSUE

Regular stamped envelope E10 overprinted with horizontal blue and red bars and "VIA AIR MAIL" in blue, centered; no box of instructions.

E12
2¢

		UnFVF	UseFVF
	red E10, *(Jan. 11, 1929)* entire, size 6 *(10,000)*	150.00	85.00
v. Inscription at left, entire size 6 *(Feb. 1929), (45,000)*		105.00	85.00
Entire, size 8 *(Feb. 1929), (15,200)*		150.00	65.00

1932. GORGAS AND GOETHALS ISSUES

E13 *William Crawford Gorgas*

E14 *George Washington Goethals*

E13
1¢

		UnFVF	UseFVF
	green *(April 8, 1932)*	.20	.15
Entire, size 5 *(400,000)*		1.50	.70
Entire, size 8 *(500,000)*		1.25	.70
Entire, size 13 *(400,000)*		1.10	.40

E14
2¢

		UnFVF	UseFVF
	carmine *(April 8, 1932)*	.30	.30
Entire, size 5 *(35,000)*		1.80	.70
Entire, size 7 1/2 *(4,000)*		6.75	6.25
Entire, size 8		1.00	.70
Entire, size 13		.85	.60

Note: See also E19, E21.

1932. SEAL AND GOETHALS OVERPRINT ISSUES

3   **3**   E15 *Numerals 3mm high*

E16 *Numerals 5mm high*   **3**   **3**

E15
3¢ on 2¢ carmine E10, numerals 3mm high, *(July 20, 1932)*

		UnFVF	UseFVF
		17.50	7.50
Entire, size 8 *(20,000)*		225.00	125.00

E16
3¢ on 2¢ carmine E14, numerals 5mm high, *(July 20, 1932)*

		UnFVF	UseFVF
		2.40	2.00
Entire, size 5 *(210,000)*		6.50	6.50
Entire, size 7 1/2 *(40,000)*		10.50	6.75
Entire, size 8 *(40,000)*		8.75	6.00
Entire, size 13 *(30,000)*		12.00	6.00

1934. SEAL AND GOETHALS SURCHARGE ISSUES

E17
3¢ on 2¢ carmine E10, 3 w/serifs in violet, *(Jan. 17, 1934)*

		UnFVF	UseFVF
		125.00	65.00
Entire, size 6 *(8,000)*		275.00	750.00

E18
3¢ on 2¢ carmine E14, 3 w/serifs in violet, *(Jan. 17, 1934)*

		UnFVF	UseFVF
		22.50	12.50
Entire, size 5 *(5,000)*		300.00	150.00
Entire, size 7 1/2 *(5,500)*		300.00	150.00
Entire, size 13 *(12,500)*		300.00	150.00

1934. GOETHALS ISSUE

E19
3¢

		UnFVF	UseFVF
	purple *(June 18, 1934)*	.20	.12
Entire, size 8		2.40	1.00
Entire, size 13		2.40	1.00

1949. DC-4 AIRMAIL ISSUE DC-4.

E20 *DC-4 Skymaster*

E20
6¢

		UnVF	UseVF
	blue *(Jan. 3, 1949)*	.40	.18
Entire		5.00	2.80

Note: See also E22.

1958. GOETHALS ISSUE

E21		UnVF	UseVF
4¢	blue *(Nov. 1, 1958)*	.30	.15
	Entire, size 6 3/4	1.50	1.00
	Entire, size 8	1.50	1.00

1958. DC-4 AIRMAIL ISSUE

E22		UnVF	UseVF
7¢	red *(Nov. 1, 1958)*	.35	.22
	Entire, size 6 3/4	4.50	3.25

1963. GOETHALS AIRMAIL SURCHARGE ISSUE

 E23 *Surcharge (on E19)*

E23		UnVF	UseVF
3¢ + 5¢	purple *(June 22, 1963)*	1.80	.70
	Entire, size 10	7.75	3.75

1964. JET AND TAIL ASSEMBLY AIRMAIL ISSUE

E24 *Jet liner and tail assembly*

E24		UnVF	UseVF
8¢	red *(Jan. 6, 1964)*	.50	.18
	Entire, size 6 3/4	2.25	.70

1965. GOETHALS AIRMAIL SURCHARGE ISSUE *(via Airmail under stamps)*.

E25		UnVF	UseVF
4¢ + 4¢	blue *(Oct. 15, 1965)* Design of E14.	.50	.35
	Entire	4.75	1.75

1966. JET AND TAIL ASSEMBLY REDESIGN ISSUE

E26 *Jet liner and tail assembly*

E26		UnVF	UseVF
8¢	carmine *(Feb. 25, 1966)*	.50	.35
	Entire, size 6 3/4	5.50	1.50

1968. 2¢ SURCHARGE ON E26 ISSUE

E27		UnVF	UseVF
8¢ + 2¢	carmine *(Jan. 18, 1968)*	.50	.22
	Entire, size 6 3/4	2.80	1.00

1968. 2¢ SURCHARGE ON E25 ISSUE

E28		UnVF	UseVF
4¢ + 4¢ + 2¢	blue *(Feb. 12, 1968)*	.70	.35
	Entire, size 10	2.15	.85

1969. JET AND TAIL ASSEMBLY AIRMAIL ISSUE

E29		UnVF	UseVF
10¢	ultramarine *(April 1, 1969)*	.60	.30
	Entire, size 6 3/4	3.65	3.65

1969. SURCHARGES ON E21 ISSUE

E30		UnVF	UseVF
4¢ + 1¢	blue *(Jan. 7, 1969)*	.18	.15
	Entire, size 6 3/4	2.50	.80
	Entire, size 10	2.50	.80

E31		UnVF	UseVF
4¢ + 2¢	blue *(April 28, 1969)*	.50	.30
	Entire, size 6 3/4	2.50	.85

1971. 5¢ AND 2¢ SURCHARGE ON E21 ISSUE

E32		UnVF	UseVF
4¢ + 5¢ + 2¢	blue *(May 17, 1971)*	.75	.30
	Entire, size 10	3.50	1.75

1971. 1¢ SURCHARGE ON E29 ISSUE

E33		UnVF	UseVF
10¢ + 1¢	ultramarine *(May 17, 1971)*	.45	.30
	Entire, size 6 3/4	4.00	2.25

1971. GAILLARD CUT ISSUE

 E34 *Ship in Gaillard Cut*

E34		UnVF	UseVF
8¢	green *(Nov. 17, 1971)*	.35	.15
	Entire, size 6 3/4	1.05	.75
	Entire, size 10	1.05	.75

1971. JET AND TAIL ASSEMBLY AIRMAIL ISSUE

E35		UnVF	UseVF
11¢	red *(Nov. 17, 1971)* Design of E26	.40	.22
	Entire, size 6 3/4	1.05	.75
	Entire, size 10	1.05	.75

1974. 2¢ SURCHARGE ON E34 ISSUE

E36		UnVF	UseVF
8¢ + 2¢	green *(March 2, 1974)*	.40	.22
	Entire, size 6 3/4	1.05	.75
	Entire, size 10	1.05	.75

1974. 2¢ SURCHARGE ON E35 ISSUE

E37		UnVF	UseVF
11¢ + 2¢	red *(March 2, 1974)*	.60	.30
	Entire, size 6 3/4	1.50	1.50
	Entire, size 10	1.50	1.50

1975. 3¢ SURCHARGE ON E36 ISSUE

E38		UnVF	UseVF
8¢ + 2¢ + 3¢	green *(May 3, 1975)*	.60	.30
	Entire, size 6 3/4	1.25	1.00
	Entire, size 10	1.25	1.00

1976. GAILLARD CUT ISSUE

E39		UnVF	UseVF
13¢	purple *(Feb. 23, 1976)* Design of E34	.60	.30
	Entire, size 6 3/4	.95	.40
	Entire, size 10	.95	.40

1978. 2¢ SURCHARGE ON E39 ISSUE

E40		UnVF	UseVF
13¢ + 2¢	purple *(July 5, 1978)*	.30	.20
	Entire, size 6 3/4	.85	.40
	Entire, size 10	.85	.40

Postal Cards

1907. PANAMA MAP ISSUE

 PC1 *Map of Panama; litho by American Bank Note Co., overprinted CANAL / ZONE reading up, and new value, by Isthmian Canal Commission*

PC1		UnFVF	UseFVF
1¢ on 2¢	carmine, CANAL 15mm long	40.00	25.00
	(Feb. 9, 1907) (50,000)		
	v.Double overprint	1,500.00	1,500.00
	v1.Double overprint second inverted	2,750.00	
	v2. Triple overprint one inverted	3,300.00	

PC2		UnFVF	UseFVF
1¢ on 2¢	carmine, CANAL 13mm long *(10,000)*	250.00	205.00
	(May 13, 1907)		

1908-12. BALBOA OVERPRINT ISSUE *Antique type reading down; 7mm between CANAL (13mm long) and ZONE.*

PC3-PC9 *Vasco Nuñez de Balboa; litho by Hamilton Bank Note Co., overprinted CANAL/ZONE reading down (6 types) or up (1 type), by Isthmian Canal Commission*

PC3
1¢   green & black *(165,000) (March 3, 1908)*   UnFVF 185.00   UseFVF 85.00
v.Double overprint   2,000.00

1908. TYPE 2 ISSUE *Antique type reading down; 7 1/4mm between CANAL (15mm long) and ZONE.*

PC4
1¢   green & black *(30,000) (Sept. 14, 1908)*   UnFVF 200.00   UseFVF 125.00
v.Triple overprint   1,750.00

1909. TYPE 3 ISSUE *Antique type reading down; 8mm between CANAL (12 3/4mm long) and ZONE (without period).*

PC5
1¢   green & black *(50,000) (March 1, 1909)*   UnFVF 50.00   UseFVF 32.50
Double overprint   120.00   120.00

1910. TYPE 4 ISSUE *Small Roman type reading up; 9 1/2mm between CANAL (10 1/2mm long) and ZONE.*

PC6
1¢   green & black *(40,000) (Nov. 10, 1910)*   UnFVF 200.00   UseFVF 75.00
Triple overprint   4,250.00

1908-12. TYPE 5 ISSUE *Roman type reading down; 8 1/4mm between CANAL (13mm long) and ZONE.*

PC7
1¢   green & black *(40,000) (May 10, 1911)*   UnFVF 200.00   UseFVF 70.00
v.Double overprint

1908-12. TYPE 6 ISSUE *Modified Antique type, no serifs on points of A's or N's, reading down; 8mm between CANAL (12 3/4mm long) and ZONE (with period).*

PC8
1¢   green & black *(40,000) (Dec. 20, 1911)*   UnFVF 800.00   UseFVF 70.00

1908-12. TYPE 7 ISSUE *Modified Antique type, no serifs on points of A's or N's, reading down; 6mm between CANAL (12 3/4mm long) and ZONE (without period).*

PC9
1¢   green & black *(40,000) (Sept. 19, 1912)*   UnFVF 200.00   UseFVF 70.00
v.ZONE   250.00   100.00

1913. CANAL ZONE V.N. BALBOA ISSUE *"CANAL ZONE" not overprinted but part of black printing plate.*

PC10
1¢   green & black *(634,000) (March 27, 1913)*   UnFVF 165.00   UseFVF 60.00

1921. 100TH ANNIVERSARY INDEPENDENCE FROM SPAIN ISSUE *Lithographed and overprinted by American Bank Note Co.*

PC11 *José Vallarino*

PC11
1¢   green *(Nov. 13, 1921) (50,000)*   UnFVF 1,100.00   UseFVF 400.00

1924. PANAMA COAT OF ARMS ISSUE *Offset and embossed by American Bank Note Co.*

PC12 *Arms of Panama*

PC12
1¢   green *(Jan. 1924) (60,000)*   UnFVF 700.00   UseFVF 800.00

1924. JEFFERSON CARD OVERPRINT ISSUE *US postal card, series of 1914, overprinted CANAL/ZONE by Government Printing Office, Washington, DC.*

CANAL   PC13

ZONE

PC13
1¢   green on buff *(50,000) (July 1, 1924)*   UnFVF 90.00   UseFVF 35.00

1924. SEAL OF CANAL ZONE ISSUE

PC14 *Seal of Canal Zone; typo by Panama Canal Press*

PC14
1¢   green on buff *(25,000) (Nov. 16, 1924)*   UnFVF 95.00   UseFVF 35.00

1925. JEFFERSON CARD OVERPRINT ISSUE *US postal card, series of 1914 overprinted CANAL/ZONE (block letters) by Government Printing Office, Washington, DC.*

CANAL   PC15

ZONE

PC15
1¢   green on buff *(850,000) (May, 1925)*   UnFVF 9.50   UseFVF 5.00

1936. JEFFERSON CARD OVERPRINT ISSUE *Same US card, overprinted in modified Roman type.*

CANAL   PC15

ZONE

PC16
1¢   green on buff *(2,900,000) (July 2, 1936)*   UnFVF 2.00   UseFVF 1.65
v. double overprint   1,900.00

1952. FRANKLIN CARD OVERPRINT ISSUE *Franklin; US postal card series of 1952, overprinted CANAL/ZONE by Government Printing Office, Washington DC.*

CANAL   PC17

ZONE

PC17
2¢   carmine rose on buff *(May 1, 1952)*   UnVF 2.05   UseVF 2.00

1958. PANAMA CANAL LOCK ISSUE

PC18 *Ship at Lock*

PC18
3¢   blue on buff *(Nov. 1, 1958)*   UnVF 2.00   UseVF 1.75

1958. PLANE AND MAP AIRMAIL POSTAL CARD ISSUE *plane and canal over U.S. flag as border.*

PC19 *Plane and map of Canal*

PC19
5¢   red & blue *(Nov. 1, 1953)*   UnVF 4.00   UseVF 3.75

1963. SURCHARGE ISSUE *Nos. PC18 and PC19 surcharged with scene of ship in canal in green.*

PC20 *Ship in Canal surcharge*

	UnVF	UseVF
PC20	4.25	4.00
3¢ + 1¢ **blue** on buff *(July 27, 1963)*		
PC21	UnVF	UseVF
5¢ + 1¢ **red & blue** *(July 27, 1963)*	10.00	9.50

1964. SHIP IN CANAL ISSUE

PC21A *Ship in Canal*

	UnVF	UseVF
PC21A	4.00	3.75
4¢ **violet blue** on buff *(Dec. 1, 1964)*		

1965. SHIP AT LOCK ISSUE

PC22 *Ship at Lock*

	UnVF	UseVF
PC22	1.10	1.00
4¢ **green** *(Aug. 12, 1965)*		

1965. SHIP AT LOCK AIRMAIL SURCHARGE ISSUE used PC22 with
overprint value at left, "AIR MAIL" below stamp in red.

	UnVF	UseVF
PC23	4.50	4.00
4¢ + 2¢ **red & green** *(Aug. 8, 1965)*		

1968. SHIP AT LOCK SURCHARGE ISSUE

	UnVF	UseVF
PC24	1.40	1.00
4¢ + 1¢ **green**, new value in green *(Feb. 12, 1968)*		

1968. SHIP AT LOCK AIRMAIL SURCHARGE ISSUE

	UnVF	UseVF
PC25	3.00	2.75
4¢ + 4¢ **green**, "AIR MAIL" in vermilion *(Feb. 12, 1968)*		

1969. SHIP AT LOCK ISSUE with new value.

	UnVF	UseVF
PC26	1.50	1.00
5¢ **light ultramarine** *(April 1, 1969)*		

1971. SHIP AT LOCK SURCHARGE ISSUE with new value in light
ultramarine.

	UnVF	UseVF
PC27	.45	.80
5¢ + 1¢ **light ultramarine** *(May 24, 1971)*		
PC28	UnVF	UseVF
5¢ + 4¢ **light ultrmarine**, new value in red *(May 24, 1971)*	.95	.85

Additional imprint AIR MAIL.

1974. SHIP AT LOCK ISSUE

PC29 *Ship at Lock*

	UnVF	UseVF
PC29	.95	.80
8¢ **sepia** *(Feb. 11, 1974)*		

1976. SHIP AT LOCK SURCHARGE ISSUE

	UnVF	UseVF
PC30	.80	.60
8¢ + 1¢ **sepia** *(June 1, 1976)*		

1978. SHIP AT LOCK SURCHARGE ISSUE

	UnVF	UseVF
PC31	.85	.75
8¢ + 2¢ **sepia** *(July 5, 1978)*		

Cuba

After the sinking of the *USS Maine* at Havana (February 1898) the United States intervened militarily in national unrest toward Spain, destroyed the Spanish fleet at Santiago, infested the island with land forces and acquired trusteeship of Cuba in the Treaty of Paris. After three years of U.S. military administration (marked chiefly by the eradication of yellow fever), a republic was established May 20, 1902. Rebel leader Fidel Castro took control from the corrupt dictator Fulgencio Batista in 1959 and established his own Communist dictatorship.

Regular Postal Issues

1898-1899. CUBA PUERTO PRINCIPE ISSUE

201

Thin 2   **2**   **2**

Thin 3   **3**   **3**

Thin 5   **5**   **5**

	UnFVF	UseFVF
201	45.00	30.00
1¢ on 1m chestnut		
Inverted overprint		130.00
202	UnFVF	UseFVF
2¢ on 2m chestnut	14.50	8.50
v. Inverted overprint	250.00	48.00
a. Thin "2" overprint	35.00	30.00
av1. Inverted overprint	275.00	100.00
203	UnFVF	UseFVF
3¢ on 2m chestnut		2,000.00
a. Thin "3"		3,000.00
204	UnFVF	UseFVF
3¢ on 3m chestnut	18.00	29.00
v. Inverted overprint		100.00
a. Thin "3"	48.00	40.00
av1. Inverted overprint		200.00
205	UnFVF	UseFVF
5¢ on 1m chestnut	500.00	150.00
v. Inverted overprint		600.00
a. Thin "5"	1,200.00	425.00
av1. Inverted overprint		725.00
206	UnFVF	UseFVF
5¢ on 2m chestnut	650.00	150.00
Thin "5"	1,450.00	440.00
207	UnFVF	UseFVF
5¢ on 3m chestnut	1,025.00	90.00
Inverted overprint	1,450.00	290.00
a. Thin "5"		575.00
Inverted overprint		725.00
208	UnFVF	UseFVF
5¢ on 5m chestnut	60.00	50.00
v. Inverted overprint	350.00	150.00
v1. Double overprint	—	—
a. Thin "5"	300.00	150.00
av. Inverted overprint		285.00
a2. Double overprint	—	—

Nos. 201-225 overprinted in horizontal strips of 5. Positions in 1st, 2nd and 3rd printings:

cents.	**cents.**	**cents.**	HABILITADO
Position 1	*Position 3*	*Position 4*	*Position 5*

Position 1: no serif at right of "t"

Position 2: thin numeral, except 1¢, 10¢

Position 3: broken right foot of "n"

Position 4: "t" and "l" in 10 broken

Position 5: broken "do"

1898-99. PUERTO PRINCIPE RED OVERPRINT ISSUE

 209

209
3¢ on 1¢ **purple black**

	UnFVF	UseFVF
	26.00	14.50
v. Inverted overprint		190.00
a. Thin "3"	72.00	60.00
av1. Inverted overprint		145.00

210
5¢ on 1¢ **purple black**

	UnFVF	UseFVF
	8.75	8.75
v. Inverted overprint		75.00
v1. Overprint sideways		2,600.00
v2. Double overprint	360.00	500.00
a. Thin "5"	20.00	17.50
av. Inverted overprint		285.00
av1. Overprint sideways		1,500.00
av2. Double overprint	900.00	500.00

211
10¢ on 1¢ **purple black**

	UnFVF	UseFVF
	20.00	20.00
a. Broken "1"	45.00	45.00

1898-99. PUERTO PRINCIPE BLACK OVERPRINT ISSUE

 212

212
1¢ on 1m **chestnut**

	UnFVF	UseFVF
	24.00	15.00
Inverted overprint		130.00
Broken "1"	39.00	35.00
Double overprint		225.00

213
3¢ on 1m **chestnut**

	UnFVF	UseFVF
	265.00	100.00
a2. Double overprint	1,300.00	500.00
a. Thin "3"	1,300.00	440.00
av. Double overprint	—	—

Nos. 214 and 215 are not assigned.

1898-99. PUERTO PRINCIPE BLACK OVERPRINT ISSUE

 216

216
5¢ on 1/2m **slate green**

	UnFVF	UseFVF
	230.00	60.00
v. Inverted overprint	400.00	90.00
Pair, "1" no overprint		400.00
a. Thin "5" overprint	225.00	42.50
av1. Double overprint, one diagonal		9,300.00
av2. Inverted overprint		150.00

1898-99. PUERTO PRINCIPE BLACK OVERPRINT ISSUE

217
3¢ on 1m **slate green**

	UnFVF	UseFVF
	250.00	200.00
v. Inverted overprint		225.00
a. "eents"	440.00	225.00
av. Inverted overprint		725.00
a2. Thin "3" overprint	360.00	300.00
a2v. Inverted overprint		440.00

1898-99. PUERTO PRINCIPE BLACK OVERPRINT ISSUE

218
3¢ on 2m **slate green**

	UnFVF	UseFVF
	650.00	130.00
v. Inverted overprint		725.00
a. "eents"	725.00	225.00
av1. Inverted overprint		1,300.00
a2. Thin "3" overprint	1,150.00	400.00
Inverted overprint		675.00

219
3¢ on 3m **slate green**

	UnFVF	UseFVF
	800.00	130.00
Inverted overprint		300.00
a. "eents"	1,025.00	225.00
a1. Inverted overprint		675.00
a2. Thin "3" overprint	1,200.00	300.00
Inverted overprint		625.00

220
5¢ on 1/2m **slate green**

	UnFVF	UseFVF
	250.00	60.00
a. Thin "5" overprint	360.00	

221
5¢ on 1m **slate green**

	UnFVF	UseFVF
	1,500.00	
a. "eents"		2,300.00
a2. Thin "5" overprint		2,300.00

Nos. 222-225 are not assigned.

Positions in 5th printing:

cents. *Position 1*   *Position 5*   **cents.**

Position 1: nicks in "e" and "s"
Position 3: "eents"
Position 4: thin numeral
Position 5: nick in "n"

1899. CUBA REGULAR ISSUE

 226

226
1¢ on 1¢ **yellow green**

	UnFVF	UseFVF
	4.50	.60

227
2¢ on 2¢ **carmine**, No. 191

	UnFVF	UseFVF
	4.50	.70
a. orange red, No. 192a	5.00	.60
v. "CUPA"	100.00	
v1. Inverted overprint	3,500.00	725.00
v2. "CUBA" at bottom	600.00	

228
2 1/2 ¢ on 2¢ **carmine**, No. 191

	UnFVF	UseFVF
orange red, No. 192a	3.25	.60
	3.50	3.25

229
3¢ on 3¢ **dark red violet**

	UnFVF	UseFVF
	7.50	1.50
v. CUB.A	37.50	34.25

230
5¢ on 5¢ **dark blue**

	UnFVF	UseFVF
	8.25	1.50
v. "CUPAL"	57.50	31.00

231
10¢ on 10¢ **brown**, Type I

	UnFVF	UseFVF
	21.00	8.00
v. On 10¢ Type III, special printing	6,000.00	

No. 228 was sold and used as 2¢. No. 229, Type I: 3 over P, Type II: 3 to left over P.

1899. CUBA POSTAGE DUE ISSUE

232
1¢ on 1¢ **brown carmine**

	UnFVF	UseFVF
	21.00	5.25

233
2¢ on 2¢ **brown carmine**

	UnFVF	UseFVF
	21.00	3.60
v. Inverted overprint		2,500.00

234
5¢ on 5¢ **brown carmine**

	UnFVF	UseFVF
	18.00	2.40
v. "CUPA"	150.00	140.00

235
10¢ on 10¢ **brown carmine**

	UnFVF	UseFVF
	17.50	2.00

 236

236
10¢ on 10¢ **indigo**

	UnFVF	UseFVF
	180.00	87.50
v. No period after CUBA	465.00	

1899. CUBA PICTORIALS ISSUE

237 *Columbus statue*

238 *Palm trees*

237		UnFVF	UseFVF
1¢	deep green	3.75	.25

238		UnFVF	UseFVF
2¢	rose red	3.75	.18
	Booklet pane of 6	2,000.00	

239 *Cuba*

240 *Ship*

239		UnFVF	UseFVF
3¢	slate red violet	3.75	.35

240		UnFVF	UseFVF
5¢	deep blue	5.00	.50

241 *Cane field*

241		UnFVF	UseFVF
10¢	deep yellow brown	14.00	1.10

1899. CUBA SPECIAL DELIVERY ISSUE

242 *Messenger*

242		UnFVF	UseFVF
10¢	yellow orange	42.00	10.00

1902. CUBA FOUNDING OF THE REPUBLIC ISSUE

243 *Overprint*

243		UnFVF	UseFVF
1¢ on 3¢	purple	1.50	.50
	v. Overprint sideways		
	v1. Inverted overprint	150.00	150.00
	v2. Double overprint	200.00	200.00

No. 237 overprinted.

Envelopes and Wrappers

1899. CUBA OVERPRINT ON U.S. EN 338/409

E1		UnFVF	UseFVF
1¢ on 1¢	green on buff, No. 393, overprint 1	2.00	3.00
	Entire	9.75	9.00

1c. DE PESO. *Overprint 1*

2c. DE PESO. *Overprint 2*

2c. DE PESO. *Overprint 3*

E2		UnFVF	UseFVF
1¢ on 1¢	green on light blue No. 394, overprint 1	2.25	2.50
	Entire	3.75	4.25
	v.Double overprint, entire	3,750.00	

E3		UnFVF	UseFVF
2¢ on 2¢	green on white No. 338, overprint 3	1.30	1.00
	Entire	2.50	3.00
	v.CUPA, entire	—	—
	v1.Double overprint, entire	3,750.00	3,750.00

E4		UnFVF	UseFVF
2¢ on 2¢	green on amber, No. 339, overprint 3	1.30	1.50
	Entire	3.60	3.75
	v.Double overprint	225.00	
	Entire	500.00	

E5		UnFVF	UseFVF
2¢ on 2¢	green on buff, No. 340, overprint 2	7.75	5.00
	Entire	18.00	13.50

E6		UnFVF	UseFVF
2¢ on 2¢	carmine on amber, No. 407, overprint 2	8.75	8.75
	Entire	18.00	19.50

E7		UnFVF	UseFVF
2¢ on 2¢	carmine on buff, No. 408, overprint 2	15.50	13.50
	Entire	32.50	27.50

E8		UnFVF	UseFVF
2¢ on 2¢	carmine on light blue, No. 409, overprint 2	3.00	2.00
	Entire	7.00	8.00
	v.Double overprint, entire		3,750.00

The following envelopes exist but were not regularly issued:

1¢ on 1¢ green on white
1¢ on 1¢ green on manila
2¢ on 2¢ carmine on white
2¢ on 2¢ carmine on Oriental buff
2¢ on 2¢ carmine on light blue
4¢ on 4¢ brown on white
5¢ on 5¢ blue on white

1899. CUBA COLUMBUS ISSUE

E19 *Columbus*

Watermark

E9		UnFVF	UseFVF
1¢	green on white	.75	.65
	Entire	4.00	4.00

E10		UnFVF	UseFVF
1¢	green on amber	1.00	.65
	Entire	4.00	4.00

E11		UnFVF	UseFVF
1¢	green on buff	15.00	12.00
	Entire	80.00	40.00

E12		UnFVF	UseFVF
1¢	green on blue	25.00	15.00
	Entire	80.00	40.00

E13		UnFVF	UseFVF
1¢	green on laid manila, wrapper	4.00	9.00
	Entire	10.00	45.00

E14		UnFVF	UseFVF
2¢	carmine on white	1.00	.60
	Entire	4.00	3.00

E15		UnFVF	UseFVF
2¢	carmine on amber	.70	.70
	Entire	3.50	3.00

E16		UnFVF	UseFVF
2¢	carmine on buff	10.00	8.00
	Entire	35.00	20.00

E17		UnFVF	UseFVF
2¢	carmine on blue	25.00	18.00
	Entire	60.00	50.00

E18		UnFVF	UseFVF
2¢	carmine on manila, wrapper	12.00	10.00
	Entire	25.00	50.00

E19		UnFVF	UseFVF
5¢	blue on white	3.00	2.00
	Entire	5.00	3.00

E20
5¢   blue on amber

	UnFVF	UseFVF
blue on amber	6.00	4.00
Entire	9.00	6.00

Postal Cards

1899. CUBA OVERPRINT ISSUE

CUBA.   1c. de Peso.   PC1

PC1
1¢ on 1¢ black

	UnFVF	UseFVF
1¢ on 1¢ black	11.00	12.00
v. No period after "Peso"	18.00	18.00

PC2 *Liberty*

PC2
2¢ on 2¢ black

	UnFVF	UseFVF
2¢ on 2¢ black	11.00	12.00
v. No period after "Peso"	25.00	
v1. Double overprint	135.00	

Danish West Indies (U.S. Virgin Islands)

A Territory of the United States, the group consists of the islands of St. Croix, St. Thomas, and St. John, and about 50 smaller islands, totalling 133 square miles. The islands were discovered by Columbus in 1493, and named *Las Virgenes,* in honor of St. Ursula and her companions. Spanish forces exterminated the native Caribe population by 1596. In the period from 1650 to 1917 the islands were occupied at various times by the French, the Knights of Malta, the British, and the Danes. In 1917, the Danish West Indies were purchased for $25 million dollars by the United States, following years of negotiation.

Citizenship was conferred upon the inhabitants in 1927, and in 1936 suffrage was granted to all who could read and write English. The governor and a delegate to the U.S. House of Representatives are elected.

Regular Postal Issues

1855-66. ISSUE *imperforate.*

   1 *Coat of arms*   *Watermark*   2

1
3¢   **deep carmine red** on yellowish

	UnFVF	UseFVF
deep carmine red on yellowish	185.00	185.00

2
3¢   **rose red** *(May 1865)*

	UnFVF	UseFVF
rose red (May 1865)	45.00	75.00
p. Thick paper	60.00	100.00
v. Privately rouletted 4 1/2	435.00	180.00

No. 1 had to be re-gummed after arrival in St. Croix. New gum was yellow or brown, same price. Original white gum rare.

1872-73. ISSUE *line perforated.*

   3   4

3
3¢   **brown red**

	UnFVF	UseFVF
brown red	90.00	185.00
p. Thick paper	125.00	225.00

4
4¢   **dull blue** *(Jan. 1, 1873)*

	UnFVF	UseFVF
dull blue (Jan. 1, 1873)	225.00	435.00
v. Pair imperforate	435.00	
v1. Pair, imperforate vertically	310.00	

Control marks. Nos. 1-3: 3 in left bottom square, C in right bottom square; engraver's mark B (A Buntzen) over right bottom square; No. 4: engraver's mark only.

No. 1: Many sheets destroyed when bundle with stamps fell into water while being unloaded. Remainders destroyed in 1873: No. 3 (210,000), No. 4 (200,000).

1896-1901. ISSUE *Perforated 14x13 1/2.*

   Watermark   5   *Normal frame*   *Inverted frame: Branch at right of lower arabesque is next to leaflet*

Inverted frame: Branch at right of lower arabesque is next to leaflet

5
1¢   **bright green & dull lilac,** first printing

	UnFVF	UseFVF
bright green & dull lilac, first printing	110.00	150.00

v. Frame inverted		560.00	875.00
a. apple green & dull lilac, second printing		175.00	125.00
av. Frame inverted		750.00	875.00
b. blue green & deep lilac, third printing		60.00	60.00
c. pale green & pale red lilac, thick paper, fourth printing		45.00	50.00
d. yellowish green & claret, thick paper, fifth printing		40.00	40.00
e. light green & red lilac, thick paper, sixth printing		28.00	35.00
f. green & red brown, frame inverted, thick paper, seventh printing		25.00	35.00
g. deep green & deep claret, thick paper, eighth printing		18.00	35.00
h. yellow green & brown red, frame inverted, thick paper, ninth printing		18.00	35.00
v2. Normal frame, thick paper		37.50	30.00

6   7   8   9

		UnFVF	UseFVF
6 **3¢**	**blue & rose carmine,** first printing	85.00	60.00
	v. Frame inverted	500.00	500.00
	a. sky blue & carmine rose, second printing	100.00	75.00
	av. Frame inverted	750.00	
	b. pale blue & dull rose, third printing	60.00	45.00
	bv. Frame inverted	110.00	75.00
	c. deep blue & carmine lake, thick paper, fourth printing	50.00	28.00
	cv. Frame inverted, thick paper	300.00	300.00
	cvp. Pair, normal inverted frame, thick paper	500.00	435.00
	d. gray blue & dull carmine, thick paper, fifth printing	40.00	20.00
	e. bright blue & bright carmine, thick paper, sixth printing	30.00	18.00
	f. deep gray blue & lake, frame inverted, thick paper, seventh printing	27.00	18.00
	gv. Normal frame, thick paper	275.00	275.00
	g. greenish blue & carmine red, thick paper, eighth printing	27.00	18.00
		UnFVF	UseFVF
7 **4¢**	**deep brown & deep ultramarine,** first printing	185.00	185.00
	a. bistre brown & pale blue, second printing	12.00	15.00
	v. Frame inverted	1,450.00	1,450.00
		UnFVF	UseFVF
8 **5¢**	**pale green & light gray** (1876), first printing	78.00	50.00
	a. grass green & gray, second printing	85.00	55.00
	b. pale green & brownish gray, thick paper, third printing	55.00	45.00
	c. bright green & deep gray, thick paper, fourth printing	30.00	18.00
	d. dark green & slate gray, thick paper, fifth printing	25.00	18.00
	e. deep green & dark brownish gray, thick paper, sixth printing	25.00	18.00
		UnFVF	UseFVF
9 **7¢**	**pale lilac & orange buff** (1874), first printing	100.00	95.00
	a. light violet & orange, second printing	30.00	110.00
	av. Frame inverted	60.00	185.00
		UnFVF	UseFVF
10 **10¢**	**pale ultramarine & yellow brown** (1876), first printing	95.00	40.00
	a. pale blue & brown, second printing	75.00	45.00
	b. deep ultramarine & blackish brown, thick paper, third printing	40.00	40.00
	bv. Frame inverted	435.00	435.00

c. pale ultramarine & yellowish brown, thick paper, fourth printing		45.00	37.50
d. bluish gray & pale yellow brown, thick paper, fifth printing		37.50	40.00
e. light blue & black brown, thick paper, sixth printing		25.00	25.00
f. blue & reddish brown, thick paper, seventh printing		27.00	34.00

10   11   12   13

		UnFVF	UseFVF
11 **12¢**	**pale lilac & green** (1877), first printing	185.00	185.00
	a. red lilac & yellow green, second printing	45.00	150.00
		UnFVF	UseFVF
12 **14¢**	**lilac & green,** first printing	620.00	950.00
	v. Frame inverted	2,500.00	3,750.00
		UnFVF	UseFVF
13 **50¢**	**bright purple,** first printing	155.00	250.00
	a. dull gray, violet thick paper, second printing	220.00	375.00

1898. ISSUE *perforated 13.*

14

		UnFVF	UseFVF
14 **1¢**	**pale green & claret,** frame inverted (Feb. 1898)	12.00	18.00
	v. Normal frame	225.00	370.00

1896-1901. ISSUE *Perforated 14x13 1/2.*

15   16   17   18

		UnFVF	UseFVF
15 **3¢**	**bright blue & carmine red,** frame inverted (March 1898)	9.00	12.50
	v. Normal frame	185.00	310.00
		UnFVF	UseFVF
16 **4¢**	**ocher & light gray blue** (March 1901)	11.00	11.00
	v. Frame inverted	250.00	310.00
		UnFVF	UseFVF
17 **5¢**	**green & gray,** frame inverted (June 1896)	45.00	50.00
	v. Normal frame	750.00	1,000.00
		UnFVF	UseFVF
18 **10¢**	**turquoise blue & brown ocher** (Feb. 1901)	75.00	150.00
	v. Frame inverted	925.00	1,500.00
	v1. Period between "t" & "s" of "cents"	25.00	25.00

On Nos. 19-26, Type I overprint was done locally at St. Thomas; Type II was done at Copenhagen, Denmark.

19

Overprint **I CENT**

19

		UnFVF	UseFVF
1¢ on 7¢ lilac & orange yellow, Type I overprint on No. 9 *(May 12, 1987)*		75.00	185.00
v. Frame inverted		110.00	310.00
v1. Double overprint		200.00	310.00

20   21   22   23

2

20-23 *Overprint* **CENTS**

1902

20

	UnFVF	UseFVF
2¢ on 3¢ gray blue & rose, frame inverted, Type I overprint on No. 6 *(March 1902)*	375.00	435.00
v. Normal frame	375.00	
v1. "2" w/straight tail	400.00	450.00

21

	UnFVF	UseFVF
2¢ on 3¢ bright blue & carmine red, frame inverted, Type I overprint on No. 15 *(March 1902)*	6.00	25.00
v. Normal frame	185.00	250.00
v1. "2" w/straight tail	11.00	25.00
v2. Dated ("1901")	250.00	375.00

1887-1902. ISSUE

22

	UnFVF	UseFVF
2¢ on 3¢ bright blue & carmine red, frame inverted, dark green, Type II overprint on No. 15 *(1902)*	1,950.00	
v. Normal frame	12,500.00	

23

	UnFVF	UseFVF
2¢ on 3¢ bright blue & carmine red, frame inverted, Type II overprint on No. 15 *(July 1902)*	11.00	40.00
v. Normal frame	250.00	375.00

24   25   26

8   **10**

24-25 *Overprint* **CENTS**   26 *Overprint* **CENTS**

1902   **1895**

24

	UnFVF	UseFVF
8¢ on 10¢ turquoise blue & brown ocher, Type I overprint on No. 18 *(March 1902)*	23.00	40.00
v. Frame inverted	225.00	375.00
v1. Period between "t" & "s" of "cents"	18.00	28.00
v2. "2" w/straight tail	28.00	46.50

25

	UnFVF	UseFVF
8¢ on 10¢ turquoise blue & brown ocher, Type II overprint on No. 18 *(July 1902)*	8.00	8.00
v. Frame inverted	155.00	435.00
v1. Period between "t" & "s" of "cents"	9.00	15.50

26

	UnFVF	UseFVF
10¢ on 50¢ purple, Type I overprint on No. 13 *(May 1895)*	37.50	75.00

1902-1903. ISSUE

27   28   29   30

			UnFVF	UseFVF
27	**1¢**	green	3.00	3.00
28	**2¢**	carmine *(April 1903)*	7.50	25.00
29	**5¢**	light blue	17.50	25.00
30	**8¢**	light brown *(April 1903)*	28.00	50.00

1902. POSTAGE DUE ISSUE

31   32   33   34

			UnFVF	UseFVF
31	**1¢**	deep blue	5.00	14.00
32	**4¢**	deep blue	9.00	18.00
33	**6¢**	deep blue	18.00	50.00
34	**10¢**	deep blue	15.50	50.00

Nos. 31-34: 5 types of each value.

1905. ISSUE

35   36   37

38   39   40

			UnFVF	UseFVF
35	**5b**	emerald	4.50	3.75
36	**10b**	orange	4.50	3.75
37	**20b**	light green & blue	9.00	7.50
38	**25b**	ultramarine	9.00	9.00
39	**40b**	red & brown black	9.00	7.50
40	**50b**	yellow & brown black	11.00	11.00

1905. ISSUE

5 BIT 1905
Overprint

41 42 43

41
5b on 4¢ ocher & light gray blue
v. Frame inverted overprint

	UnFVF	UseFVF
	15.00	50.00
	37.00	75.00

42
5b on 5¢ light blue

UnFVF	UseFVF
14.00	37.50

43
5b on 8¢ light brown

UnFVF	UseFVF
14.00	37.50

1905. ISSUE

44

45

46

44
1f green & blue

UnFVF	UseFVF
18.00	37.50

45
2f red orange & brown

UnFVF	UseFVF
25.00	50.00

46
5f yellow & brown

UnFVF	UseFVF
60.00	230.00

1905. POSTAGE DUE ISSUE

47 48 49 50

47
5b vermilion & drab gray

UnFVF	UseFVF
4.50	7.50

48
20b vermilion & drab gray

UnFVF	UseFVF
7.50	15.00

49
30b vermilion & drab gray

UnFVF	UseFVF
6.00	15.00

50
50b vermilion & drab gray
v. Perforated 14x14 1/2 *(1913)*
v1. Perforated 11 1/2

UnFVF	UseFVF
5.50	30.00
30.00	150.00
250.00	

1907-08. ISSUE

51 52 53 54

55 56 57 58

51
5b deep yellow green

UnFVF	UseFVF
2.50	1.85

52
10b orange red *(Jan. 1908)*

UnFVF	UseFVF
2.50	1.85

53
15b red purple & chocolate *(Sept. 1908)*

UnFVF	UseFVF
3.75	3.75

54
20b yellow, emerald & blue *(May 1908)*

UnFVF	UseFVF
28.00	25.00

55
25b Prussian blue

UnFVF	UseFVF
2.50	1.85

56
30b claret & slate *(Sept. 1908)*

UnFVF	UseFVF
45.00	45.00

57
40b vermilion & gray *(Sept. 1908)*

UnFVF	UseFVF
6.00	7.75

58
50b yellow & brown *(Sept. 1908)*

UnFVF	UseFVF
6.00	12.00

1915-16. ISSUE

59 60 61 62

63 64 65 66

59
5b pale green

UnFVF	UseFVF
5.00	4.50

60
10b orange red *(March 1915)*

UnFVF	UseFVF
5.00	4.50

61
15b red purple & red brown *(March 1915)*

UnFVF	UseFVF
4.50	45.00

62
20b yellow emerald & dark blue
(March 1915)

UnFVF	UseFVF
4.50	45.00

63
25b blue & deep blue

UnFVF	UseFVF
4.50	11.00

64
30b brown red & black *(1916)*

UnFVF	UseFVF
4.50	55.00

65
40b orange salmon & gray black *(1915)*

UnFVF	UseFVF
4.50	55.00

66
50b yellow & chocolate *(March 1915)*

UnFVF	UseFVF
4.50	55.00

Since 1917: U.S. stamps have been used.

Envelopes and Wrappers

1877-78. STAMPED ENVELOPES

E1

E2

E1		UnFVF	UseFVF
2¢	light blue *(1878)*	5.00	15.00
	Entire	20.00	75.00
	a.ultramarine	25.00	250.00
	Entire	125.00	1,000.00
E2		UnFVF	UseFVF
3¢	orange red	5.50	15.00
	Entire	20.00	75.00
	a.red orange	6.00	15.00
	Entire	20.00	75.00

Postal Cards

1877. POSTAL CARD ISSUE

PC1

PC1		UnFVF	UseFVF
6¢	violet	17.50	12.00

1878-85. POSTAL CARD

PC2

PC2		UnFVF	UseFVF
2¢	light blue	25.00	55.00

PC3

PC3		UnFVF	UseFVF
3¢	carmine rose	17.50	45.00

Nos. PC2 and 3 with added inscription in Danish and French.

1883. MESSAGE AND REPLY CARD

PC4M

PC4R

PC5M

PC5R

PC4		UnFVF	UseFVF
2¢ + 2¢	light blue, unsevered	20.00	200.00
	m.message card	10.00	30.00
	r.reply card	10.00	30.00

PC5

		UnFVF	UseFVF
3¢ + 3¢	**carmine rose,** unsevered	20.00	100.00
	m.message card	10.00	18.00
	r.reply card	10.00	18.00

1888-98. POSTAL CARD

PC6

PC7

PC6

		UnFVF	UseFVF
2¢	**light blue**	10.00	22.50

PC7

		UnFVF	UseFVF
3¢	**red**	10.00	22.50

Nos. PC6 and 7 with added inscription in French on message card: Carte postale avec réponse payée; on reply card: Carte postale-réponse.

1888-98. MESSAGE AND REPLY CARDS

PC8M

PC8R

PC9M

PC9R

PC8

		UnFVF	UseFVF
2¢ + 2¢	**light blue,** unsevered	15.00	100.00
	m.message card	5.00	20.00
	r.reply card	5.00	30.00

PC9

		UnFVF	UseFVF
3¢ + 3¢	**red,** unsevered	20.00	110.00
	m.message card	10.00	25.00
	r.reply card	10.00	30.00

1901. MESSAGE AND REPLY CARDS

PC10

1 *Overprint*

CENT

1901

PC10

		UnFVF	UseFVF
1¢ on 3¢	**red**	50.00	200.00

PC11M

PC11R

PC11

		UnFVF	UseFVF
1¢ on 3¢ +1¢ on 3¢	**carmine rose,** unsevered	45.00	275.00
	m.message card	18.00	50.00
	r.reply card	18.00	75.00

1902. MESSAGE AND REPLY CARDS

PC12

1   *Overprint*

CENT

1902

PC12
1¢ on 2¢ light blue

	UnFVF	UseFVF
	30.00	150.00

1902. MESSAGE AND REPLY CARDS

PC13

PC13
1¢ on 3¢ red

	UnFVF	UseFVF
	13.50	32.50

PC14M

PC14R

PC14
1¢ on 3¢ +1¢ on 3¢ **carmine rose,** unsevered

	UnFVF	UseFVF
	45.00	300.00
m.message card	25.00	60.00
r.reply card	25.00	75.00

1903. POSTAL CARD

PC15

PC15
1¢   **light green**

	UnFVF	UseFVF
	10.00	30.00

PC16

PC16
2¢   **carmine red**

	UnFVF	UseFVF
	20.00	75.00

1903. MESSAGE AND REPLY CARDS

PC17R

PC17
1¢ + 1¢   **light green,** unsevered

	UnFVF	UseFVF
	20.00	75.00
m.message card	10.00	20.00
r.reply card	10.00	20.00

PC18M

PC18R

PC18		**UnFVF**	**UseFVF**
2¢ + 2¢ **carmine,** unsevered		40.00	350.00
	m.message card	20.00	50.00
	r.reply card	20.00	75.00

1905. Postal Card Issue

PC19

PC19		**UnFVF**	**UseFVF**
5b	**green**	10.00	24.00

PC20

PC20		**UnFVF**	**UseFVF**
10b	**red**	13.50	32.50

1905. Message and Reply Card

PC21M

PC21R

PC21		**UnFVF**	**UseFVF**
5b + 5b **green,** unsevered		20.00	75.00
	m.message card	10.00	20.00
	r.reply card	12.00	25.00

PC22M

PC22R

PC22		**UnFVF**	**UseFVF**
10b + 10b red, unsevered		25.00	90.00
	m.message card	12.50	27.50
	r.reply card	12.50	35.00

Generally speaking, the more nearly equal in width all margins of a stamp are, and the farther those equal margins are from the printed design, the more desirable the stamp will be to the collector.

Every reasonable effort has been made to make the values in this catalog as accurate, realistic, and up-to-date as possible.

1907-08. POSTAL CARD

PC23

PC23		UnFVF	UseFVF
5b	green *(1908)*	10.00	24.00

1905. MESSAGE AND REPLY CARD

PC24

PC24		UnFVF	UseFVF
10b	red	13.50	28.50

1913. POSTAL CARD ISSUE

PC25

PC26

PC25		UnFVF	UseFVF
5b	green	100.00	200.00
PC26		**UnFVF**	**UseFVF**
10b	red	125.00	325.00

1908. MESSAGE AND REPLY CARDS

PC27M

PC27R

PC27		UnFVF	UseFVF
5b + 5b	**green,** unsevered	18.00	100.00
	m.message card	8.00	25.00
	r.reply card	8.00	25.00

PC28M

PC28R

PC28		UnFVF	UseFVF
10b + 10b	**red,** unsevered	18.00	100.00
	m.message card	7.75	25.00
	r.reply card	7.75	35.00

1913. MESSAGE AND REPLY CARDS

PC29M

PC29R

PC29		UnFVF	UseFVF
5b + 5b	**green,** unsevered	—	
	m.message card		850.00
	r.reply card		—
PC30		UnFVF	UseFVF
10b + 10b	**red,** unsevered		
	m.message card		
	r.reply card		

No. PC29: 5,000 printed. No. PC30: Authorized and possibly printed, but no example is known.

1915-16. POSTAL CARD

PC31

PC31		UnFVF	UseFVF
5b	**green**	100.00	155.00

PC32 *Christian X*

PC32		UnFVF	UseFVF
10b	**red**	125.00	240.00

Guam

At 206 square miles, Guam is the largest of the Mariana Islands, named for Maria Ana, widow of Philip IV of Spain. Discovered in 1521 by Magellan, whose crew called the group *Islas de los Ladrones* (Thieves' Islands) because of native pilfering. Spain, which conquered the islands in the late 17th century, ceded Guam to the United States in 1898 and sold the other islands to Germany. The latter were mandated to Japan after World War I. In World War II, the small Navy forces on Guam were overcome by the Japanese on Dec. 12, 1942. Recaptured in 1944, Guam was used as a base for U.S. bomber strikes at Japan. The governor, legislature, and a delegate to the U.S. House of Representatives are elected.

Regular Postal Issues

1899. OVERPRINT ISSUE United States stamps overprinted "GUAM" in black or red (13 & 14), *perforated 12.*

1

12

			UnFVF	UseFVF
1			UnFVF	UseFVF
1¢	**deep green,** U.S. No. 188		30.00	32.50
2			UnFVF	UseFVF
2¢	**carmine,** triangle III, No. 191		30.00	31.50
3			UnFVF	UseFVF
2¢	**red,** triangle III, No. 192		32.00	32.50
4			UnFVF	UseFVF
3¢	**dark red violet**		120.00	145.00
5			UnFVF	UseFVF
4¢	**chocolate**		125.00	145.00
	t. Extra frame line at top (P1 793)		—	
6			UnFVF	UseFVF
5¢	**dark blue**		40.00	37.50
7			UnFVF	UseFVF
6¢	**lake**		120.00	165.00
8			UnFVF	UseFVF
8¢	**purple brown**		150.00	165.00
9			UnFVF	UseFVF
10¢	**brown,** Type I		50.00	65.00
10			UnFVF	UseFVF
10¢	**orange brown,** Type II		3,250.00	—
11			UnFVF	UseFVF
15¢	**olive green**		175.00	165.00
12			UnFVF	UseFVF
50¢	**orange,** U.S. No. 208		350.00	300.00
	a. red orange		500.00	
13			UnFVF	UseFVF
$1	**black,** Type I, overprinted red		600.00	450.00
	a. Type II red overprint, special printing		3,250.00	

14

			UnFVF	UseFVF
14			UnFVF	UseFVF
10¢	**indigo,** U.S. No. 505 overprinted red		160.00	175.00

Hawaii

Settled by Polynesians from islands 2,000 miles to the south about 700 A.D., Hawaii was discovered in 1778 by Captain James Cook, who called the group the Sandwich Islands. He was slain there in 1779. Hawaiian chief, Kamehameha the Great, conquered and united most of the islands (1782-95), established a strong but beneficent government, and encouraged foreign trade. His son Liholiho (Kamehameha II) abolished idolatry and tabu, opened Hawaii to the American missionaries, and died on a visit to England in 1824. The reign of his brother Kauikeaouli (Kamehameha III) was a period of great prosperity and enlightenment, which gave Hawaii a liberal constitutional government, full suffrage, a high rate of literacy, and a patiently achieved recognition as an independent sovereign nation.

The benevolent but high-handed Kamehameha V revoked the liberal constitution of 1852. Revolution in 1887 forced King David Kalakaua to grant a constitution guaranteeing a responsible ministerial government. His sister, Queen Liliuokalani, intent upon restoring absolute monarchy, attempted to set this constitution aside early in 1893, but the resulting revolution forced her from the throne. The provisional government's attempt to have the country annexed by the United States was opposed by President Cleveland, and a republic was established July 4, 1894. In 1898, under President McKinley, a treaty of annexation was approved by a joint session of the U.S. Congress, and the Territory of Hawaii was established June 14, 1900. It became a state in 1959.

Until 1846 the Hawaiian government took no responsibility for the mails, which were carried free by ships and received or forwarded by merchants or other private persons. The 1846 Organic Act set up a postal system, but four years elapsed before this measure was carried out, when a treaty with the U.S. provided for the exchange of mails. At the same time, a post office was set up in Honolulu and postal rates established. In 1851 a revised law lowered rates and authorized issuance of the first Hawaiian stamps.

Regular Postal Issues

1851. HAWAIIAN POSTAGE ISSUE Numerals inscribed "Hawaiian Postage." Nos. 1-3, Type I, "P" of Postage slightly to the right of "H." Type II, "P" is directly under "H."

1-3

4

			UnFVF	UseFVF
1			UnFVF	UseFVF
2¢	**blue**		600,000.	200,000
	Pelure paper			
2			UnFVF	UseFVF
5¢	**blue**		60,000.00	35,000.00
3			UnFVF	UseFVF
13¢	**blue**		30,000.00	20,000.00

1852. H.I. & U.S. POSTAGE ISSUE Numeral inscribed. *Type I 16 1/2mm long or Type II 17 1/2mm long.*

			UnFVF	UseFVF
4			UnFVF	UseFVF
13¢	**blue**		60,000.00	37,500.00

1853-61. KAMEHAMEHA III ISSUE *intaglio, imperforate.*

No. 5, 8, 9 Kamehameha III (1813-54) was 12 when he succeeded his brother as king. His statement, "The life of the land is preserved by righteousness," is now the motto of Hawaii.

6
on 13¢

			UnFVF	UseFVF
5			UnFVF	UseFVF
5¢	**blue**		1,650.00	6,275.00
	a. Line through "HONOLULU"		3,000.00	2,500.00
	v. bright blue (reprint)		80.00	
6			UnFVF	UseFVF
5¢ on 13¢	**dull red**		8,500.00	8,000.00

7

		UnFVF	UseFVF
7			
13¢	**dull red**	725.00	800.00
	v. dull rose (reprint)	300.00	

Thick wove paper; No. 6 with pen-written overprint.

1857-61. KAMEHAMEHA III ISSUE *Thin white wove paper.*

		UnFVF	UseFVF
8			
5¢	**light blue** *(1857)*	800.00	775.00
9		UnFVF	UseFVF
5¢	**light blue** on bluish *(1861)*	300.00	210.00
	a. Line through "HONOLULU"	850.00	630.00
	b. Double impression	3,500.00	3,500.00

Reprints on ordinary white wove paper.

1863. INTER-ISLAND ISSUE *numerals inscribed at top; type set, imperforate. Thin paper.*

		UnFVF	UseFVF
10			
1¢	**blue** on bluish	7,000.00	5,000.00
11		UnFVF	UseFVF
2¢	**blue** on bluish	6,000.00	3,500.00

    12   13   17

		UnFVF	UseFVF
12			
2¢	**deep blue** on blue	8,000.00	4,500.00

1863. INTER-ISLAND REPRINT ISSUE *Color changes, thin paper.*

		UnFVF	UseFVF
13			
1¢	**black** on grayish *(1863)*	600.00	1,000.00
	Tete-beche pair	5,000.00	
14		UnFVF	UseFVF
2¢	**black** on grayish *(1863)*	900.00	750.00
	a. "2" near top of frame	3,500.00	3,000.00
	v1. "I" of INTER omitted	3,000.00	3,000.00
	v. Printed on both sides	—	20,000.00
15		UnFVF	UseFVF
2¢	**black** on greenish blue *(April 1, 1863)*	7,750.00	3,500.00
16		UnFVF	UseFVF
2¢	**black** on light blue *(1864)*	8,000.00	4,500.00

1864. INTER-ISLAND ISSUE *White wove (17, 19) or laid (18, 20) paper.*

		UnFVF	UseFVF
17			
1¢	**black**	650.00	1,200.00
18		UnFVF	UseFVF
1¢	**black,** laid paper	350.00	1,200.00
	a. "HA" in left panel	2,500.00	
	b. Tete-beche pair	8,000.00	
19		UnFVF	UseFVF
2¢	**black**	850.00	1,475.00
20		UnFVF	UseFVF
2¢	**black,** laid paper	350.00	1,200.00
	v. "I" of INTER omitted	2,250.00	
	v1. "PO" TAGE	1,000.00	

1865. INTER-ISLAND ISSUE *Numerals, inscribed INTERISLAND in left panel; type set, imperforate.*

 23

		UnFVF	UseFVF
21			
1¢	**dark blue**		350.00

		UnFVF	UseFVF
22			
2¢	**dark blue**	3,500.00	
23		UnFVF	UseFVF
5¢	**deep blue** on blue	650.00	900.00
	a. Tete-beche pair	10,000.00	

1865. INTER-ISLAND ISSUE *"HAWAIIAN POSTAGE" in both left and right panels.*

 24

		UnFVF	UseFVF
24			
5¢	**dark blue** on blue	900.00	630.00
	a. Tete-beche pair	6,000.00	

No. 10-23; 10 different types. Gutter pair, tete-beche gutter pair exists.

1861-63. KAMEHAMEHA IV ISSUE *offset.*

 25 *Kamehameha IV*

		UnFVF	UseFVF
25			
2¢	**pale rose red**	300.00	200.00
	a. deep rose red	2,000.00	2,000.00
	v. red *(1869* reprint)	60.00	90.00

A red reprint of No. 25 in 1869 was not issued for postal purposes. Sold at Honolulu Post Office with or without overprint CANCELLED.

		UnFVF	UseFVF
26			
2¢	**pale rose red**	300.00	250.00
	a. deep rose red *(1863)*	2,000.00	2,000.00
	pv. dull vermilion, *(1886,* medium, white to buff paper, reprint), vertically laid paper	300.00	350.00
	pv1. dull scarlet, *(1889,* thick, yellowish to buff paper, reprint), horizontally laid paper	2,000.00	2,750.00

Two reprints of No. 26 were made in order to have complete sets of Hawaiian stamps for sale. In 1885 the reissue 2¢ red was sent to the American Bank Note Co., and from it a new plate was engraved and 10,000 stamps printed (5,000 of these overprinted SPECIMEN in blue). Subsequently (1887) the missing plate of the reissue was found, retouched and 37,500 stamps printed from it during 1889-90. In 1892 all remaining unsold stamps were overprinted REPRINT.

1864-75. PORTRAITS ISSUE *Bureau of Engraving and Printing, intaglio, perforated 12.*

27 *Princess Victoria Kamamalu*

28 *Kamehameha IV (1834-63) reigned 1854-63, vainly sought U.S. reciprocal trade agreements, made English the school language.*

		UnFVF	UseFVF
27			
1¢	**purple** *(1871)*	12.00	10.00
28		UnFVF	UseFVF
2¢	**orange red**	20.00	12.00

29, 36, 37 *David Kalakaua (1836-91), elected king to succeed Lunalilo (No. 47) in 1874. 1877 revolution forced from him a constitution guaranteeing responsible government. He was a patron of music and dance.*

30, 39, 40 *Kamehameha V*

		UnFVF	UseFVF
29			
2¢	**deep brown** *(1875)*	10.00	4.00

No. 29 bisected and used with 5¢ stamp to make up 6¢ rate to U.S.

30
5¢   deep blue *(1866)*

	UnFVF	UseFVF
	200.00	40.00

No. 30 traces of frame lines around design.

31 *Kamehameha V*

32, 44 *Prince William Pitt Leleiohoku (1854-1877) was considered an excellent singer and composer but died of rheumatic fever at the age of 33.*

31
6¢   emerald green *(1871)*

	UnFVF	UseFVF
	32.00	12.00

32
12¢   black *(1875)*

	UnFVF	UseFVF
	72.50	37.00

33 *Mataio Kekuanaoa, father of Kamehameha IV and V*

33
18¢   dull carmine red *(1871)*

	UnFVF	UseFVF
	115.00	45.00
No gum	22.50	

1882-91. ISSUE *No. T29-32 and new designs; engraved, perforated 12.*

34, 35 *Princess Likelike (Mrs. Archibald Cleghorn) (1851-1887) sponsored many concerts and helped preserve Hawaiian music.*

34
1¢   Prussian blue *(1882)*

	UnFVF	UseFVF
	8.00	12.00

35
1¢   blue green *(1883)*, T34

	UnFVF	UseFVF
	6.00	10.00

36
2¢   lilac rose *(1882)*, T29

	UnFVF	UseFVF
	80.00	35.00

37
2¢   deep rose *(1886)*, T29

	UnFVF	UseFVF
	5.25	1.25

1890-91. LYDIA KAMEHAMEHA ISSUE *Bureau of Engraving and Printing, intaglio, perforated 12.*

38 *Lydia Kamehameha (Mrs. John O. Dominis, 1837-1917), sister of Kalakaua, reigned for two years as Queen Liliuokalani. Deposed in 1893, she swore allegiance to the republic after an abortive counter-revolution in 1895. She wrote the best-known Hawaiian song, "Aloha Oe"*

38
2¢   deep violet blue *(1890)*
v. Horizontal pair, imperforate

	UnFVF	UseFVF
	6.00	2.00
	2,500.00	

39
5¢   bright blue, T30

	UnFVF	UseFVF
	20.00	70.00

40
5¢   deep blue *(1891)*, T30

	UnFVF	UseFVF
	140.00	180.00

1882-83. KALAKAUA ISSUE

41-43 *Kalakaua*

41
10¢   black *(1882)*

	UnFVF	UseFVF
	45.00	25.00

42
10¢   vermilion *(1883)*, T41

	UnFVF	UseFVF
	42.50	16.00

43
10¢   red brown *(1884)*, T41

	UnFVF	UseFVF
	40.00	12.00

44
12¢   red purple *(1883)*, T32

	UnFVF	UseFVF
	100.00	42.50

1882. QUEEN KAPIOLANI ISSUE

45 *Queen Kapiolani*

45
15¢   red brown

	UnFVF	UseFVF
	85.00	35.00

1883. KAMEHAMEHA THE GREAT STATUE ISSUE

46 *Bronze statue, sculpted in 1880 by Thomas B. Gould (1818-81) at Kapaau, Hawaii, near Kamehameha's birthplace.*

46
25¢   black violet *(1883)*

	UnFVF	UseFVF
	165.00	75.00

1883. WILLIAM C. LUNALILO ISSUE

47 *William C. Lunalilo (1835-74), whom the legislature unanimously elected king in 1873, was liberal, pro-American and beloved, but died within 13 months.*

47
50¢   orange red *(1883)*

	UnFVF	UseFVF
	200.00	110.00

1883. QUEEN EMMA KALELEONALANI ISSUE

48 *Dowager Queen Emma Kaleleonalani, widow of Kamehameha IV, lost the 1874 election to Kalakaua, which caused a week's rioting in Honolulu.*

48
$1   rose red
Maltese cross cancellation

	UnFVF	UseFVF
	300.00	180.00
	65.00	

1893. PROVISIONAL GOVT. ISSUE *Overthrow of monarchy; Nos. 27-48 overprinted. Nos. 49-60 in red, Nos. 61-69 black.*

Provisional   49
GOVT.
1893

49
1¢   purple
v. Double overprint
v2. 189
v3. W/o period after GOVT

	UnFVF	UseFVF
	10.00	16.50
	180.00	
	525.00	
	275.00	

50
1¢   Prussian blue
v. Double overprint
v1. W/o period after GOVT
v2. Pair, one w/o overprint

	UnFVF	UseFVF
	12.00	20.00
	130.00	
	180.00	180.00
	775.00	

51
1¢   bright green
v. Double overprint
v1. Pair, one w/o overprint

	UnFVF	UseFVF
	2.00	4.00
	850.00	600.00
	7,250.00	

52
2¢   deep brown
v. Double overprint
v1. W/o period after GOVT

	UnFVF	UseFVF
	16.50	30.00
	300.00	
	350.00	

53
2¢   slate violet
v. Double overprint
v1. Inverted overprint
v2. 18 3

	UnFVF	UseFVF
	2.00	1.65
	775.00	625.00
	4,000.00	2,500.00
	600.00	500.00

54
5¢   bright blue
v. Double overprint
v1. Inverted overprint

	UnFVF	UseFVF
	8.00	3.00
	3,500.00	1,250.00
	1,250.00	

55			UnFVF	UseFVF
5¢	indigo		16.00	40.00
	v. Double overprint		650.00	
	v1. W/o period after GOVT		245.00	275.00
56			UnFVF	UseFVF
6¢	emerald green		20.00	35.00
	v. Double overprint		1,250.00	
	v1. black overprint		15,000.00	30,000.00
57			UnFVF	UseFVF
10¢	black		12.00	20.00
	v. Double overprint		700.00	300.00
58			UnFVF	UseFVF
12¢	black		12.00	25.00
	v. Double overprint		2,000.00	
59			UnFVF	UseFVF
12¢	red purple		165.00	225.00
60			UnFVF	UseFVF
25¢	black violet		37.00	60.00
	v. Double overprint		375.00	
	v1. W/o period after GOVT		350.00	350.00
61			UnFVF	UseFVF
2¢	orange red		85.00	95.00
	v. W/o period after GOVT		350.00	350.00
62			UnFVF	UseFVF
2¢	deep rose		1.65	3.00
	v. Double overprint		3,000.00	
	v1. W/o period after GOVT		65.00	80.00
62A			UnFVF	UseFVF
6¢	green		20,000.00	22,500.00
63			UnFVF	UseFVF
10¢	vermilion		20.00	40.00
	v. Double overprint		650.00	
64			UnFVF	UseFVF
10¢	red brown		10.00	16.50
	v. red overprint		20,000.00	23,500.00
65			UnFVF	UseFVF
12¢	red purple		370.00	600.00
66			UnFVF	UseFVF
15¢	red brown		25.00	40.00
	v. Double overprint		2,000.00	
67			UnFVF	UseFVF
18¢	dull carmine red		35.00	45.00
	v. Double overprint		400.00	
	v1. 18 3		500.00	500.00
	v2. W/o period after GOVT		400.00	400.00
	v3. Pair, one w/o overprint		2,500.00	
68			UnFVF	UseFVF
50¢	orange red		80.00	120.00
	v. Double overprint		325.00	
	v1. W/o period after GOVT		400.00	
69			UnFVF	UseFVF
$1	rose red		145.00	225.00
	v. W/o period after GOVT		425.00	400.00

1894-99. REPUBLIC PICTORIALS ISSUE *Bureau of Engraving and Printing, intaglio, perforated 12.*

 70, 82 *Arms*

71, 83 *Honolulu*

70		UnFVF	UseFVF
1¢	orange yellow	2.25	1.65
71		UnFVF	UseFVF
2¢	brown drab	3.00	.80

 72 *Kamehameha I statue*

73 *Hope of Statehood*

72		UnFVF	UseFVF
5¢	carmine red	5.25	2.00
73		UnFVF	UseFVF
10¢	yellow green	8.00	6.00

 74 S.S. Arawa

75 *Sanford Ballard Dole (1858-1926), justice of Hawaiian Supreme Court, led 1893 revolution, was 1st president of Hawaii, 1894-98, 1st territorial governor, 1900-03*

74		UnFVF	UseFVF
12¢	deep blue	16.50	22.50
75		UnFVF	UseFVF
25¢	deep blue	16.50	22.50

1896. OFFICIALS ISSUE *Bureau of Engraving and Printing, intaglio, perforated 12.*

 76 *Lorrin Andrews Thurston (1858-1931), a leader in revolutions of 1887 and 1893. As Reform Minister of Interior, helped draft the republic constitution and led negotiations for annexation of Hawaii by the U.S.*

76		UnFVF	UseFVF
2¢	yellow green	45.00	12.00
77		UnFVF	UseFVF
5¢	sepia	45.00	12.00
78		UnFVF	UseFVF
6¢	ultramarine	45.00	12.00
79		UnFVF	UseFVF
10¢	carmine	45.00	12.00
80		UnFVF	UseFVF
12¢	orange	45.00	12.00
81		UnFVF	UseFVF
25¢	deep violet	45.00	12.00

1899. U.S. GOVERNMENT ISSUE T70-72 changed colors; No. 84 inscribed CENTS at bottom. *Bureau of Engraving and Printing, intaglio, perforated 12.*

82		UnFVF	UseFVF
1¢	deep blue green	2.00	1.60
83		UnFVF	UseFVF
2¢	rose carmine	1.80	1.45
	a. salmon	1.80	1.45
	v. Horizontal pair, imperforate	2,250.00	
84		UnFVF	UseFVF
5¢	deep blue	8.50	4.00

Since 1899: U.S. stamps have been used in Hawaii.

Envelopes and Wrappers

1884. FIRST ISSUE Inside white.

 EN1-9 *View of Honolulu Harbor*

EN1		UnFVF	UseFVF
1¢	yellow green	4.50	4.50
	Entire	8.00	20.00
	a.green	5.00	5.00
	Entire	10.00	25.00
EN2		UnFVF	UseFVF
2¢	rose carmine	4.50	7.00
	Entire	8.00	27.50
	a.pale pink	15.00	17.50
	Entire	35.00	60.00
EN3		UnFVF	UseFVF
4¢	red	25.00	30.00
	Entire	45.00	90.00
EN4		UnFVF	UseFVF
5¢	blue	10.50	12.50
	Entire	55.00	30.00
EN5		UnFVF	UseFVF
10¢	black	35.00	40.00
	Entire	110.00	65.00

1884. SECOND ISSUE Inside blue.

			UnFVF	UseFVF
EN6				
2¢	**rose red**		250.00	250.00
	Entire		750.00	750.00
EN7			**UnFVF**	**UseFVF**
4¢	**red**		300.00	250.00
	Entire		700.00	
EN8			**UnFVF**	**UseFVF**
5¢	**deep blue**		300.00	250.00
	Entire		700.00	700.00
EN9			**UnFVF**	**UseFVF**
10¢	**black**		350.00	350.00
	Entire		800.00	

1885. SPECIAL DELIVERY ENVELOPES ISSUE (Nos. EN5 and EN9 inscribed "Special Despatch Letter" in red in upper left corner. Prices are for entires; envelopes were prepared but never issued).

		UnFVF	UseFVF
EN10			
10¢	**black,** inside white	250.00	
EN11		**UnFVF**	**UseFVF**
10¢	**black,** inside blue	250.00	

1893. PROVISIONAL GOVERNMENT OVERPRINT ISSUE *locally overprinted in black or red.*

EN12-16

		UnFVF	UseFVF
EN12			
1¢	**yellow green** red overprint	6.75	12.50
	Entire	10.00	30.00
	v.Double overprint	4,500.00	
	Entire	1,750.00	
EN13		**UnFVF**	**UseFVF**
2¢	**rose**	4.50	7.00
	Entire	6.00	18.50
	v.Double overprint	500.00	
	Entire	900.00	
	v1.Double overprint, second inverted	140.00	
	Entire	1,500.00	
	v2.Triple overprint	90.00	
	Entire	105.00	
EN14		**UnFVF**	**UseFVF**
5¢	**blue (shades)** red overprint	7.50	9.00
	Entire	15.00	22.50
	v.Double overprint	375.00	
	Entire	600.00	
	v1.Triple overprint, entire		7,500.00
EN15		**UnFVF**	**UseFVF**
10¢	**black** red overprint, E5	18.00	20.00
	Entire	32.50	120.00
	v.Double overprint, entire	1,800.00	2,000.00
	v1.Triple overprint	42.50	
	Entire	290.00	
EN16		**UnFVF**	**UseFVF**
10¢	**black** red overprint, E9	350.00	725.00
	Entire	1,100.00	

Postal Cards

1882-92. HAWAII POSTAL CARD ISSUE

PC1, 2, 5, 6, 9 *Queen Liliuokalani*

		UnFVF	UseFVF
PC1			
1¢	**red** on buff *(1882)*	40.00	80.00

		UnFVF	UseFVF
PC2			
1¢	**red** on flesh *(1889)*	40.00	50.00

1882-92. HAWAII, DIAMOND HEAD ISSUE

PC3, 3A, 7, 8, 10 *Diamond Head*

		UnFVF	UseFVF
PC3			
2¢	**black** on white	70.00	125.00
PC3A		**UnFVF**	**UseFVF**
2¢	**black** on white *(1892) (Lithographed)*	135.00	225.00

1892. HAWAII, ROYAL EMBLEM ISSUE

PC4 *Royal emblems*

		UnFVF	UseFVF
PC4			
3¢	**blue green** on white	90.00	125.00

1883-89. HAWAII, MESSAGE & REPLY CARDS

		UnFVF	UseFVF
PC5			
1¢ + 1¢	**violet** on buff, entire	240.00	400.00
	m.Message card	50.00	160.00
	r.Reply card	50.00	160.00
PC6		**UnFVF**	**UseFVF**
1¢ + 1¢	**violet** on flesh, entire *(1889)*	240.00	400.00
	m.Message card	50.00	160.00
	r.Reply card	50.00	160.00
PC7		**UnFVF**	**UseFVF**
2¢ + 2¢	**violet blue** on white, entire	350.00	500.00
	m.Message card	75.00	225.00
	r.Reply card	75.00	225.00
PC8		**UnFVF**	**UseFVF**
2¢ + 2¢	**blue** on white, entire	240.00	400.00
	m.Message card	50.00	150.00
	r.Reply card	50.00	150.00

1893. PROVISIONAL GOVERNMENT OVERPRINT ISSUE "Provisional Government/1893" *in black or red.*

		UnFVF	UseFVF
PC9			
1¢	**red** on flesh	50.00	150.00
PC10		**UnFVF**	**UseFVF**
2¢	**black** on white, red overprint	70.00	170.00
PC11		**UnFVF**	**UseFVF**
3¢	**blue green** on white, red overprint	90.00	360.00

1894. NEW DESIGN ISSUE

PC12 *Iolani Palace*

PC4. Iolani palace.

		UnFVF	UseFVF
PC12			
1¢	**red** on flesh	30.00	45.00

PC13 *Map of Pacific Ocean, Mercator projection*

		UnFVF	UseFVF
PC13			
2¢	**green** on white	60.00	100.00

Philippines

In the Spanish-American War (1898), United States forces invading the Philippines were aided by Katipunan (Revolutionary) forces. Spain ceded the islands to the U.S. (1899), and the latter decided not to relinquish control until Filipinos were ready for self-government. The Katipunans declared war on the U.S., and fighting continued until mid-1902. Despite this, U.S. civil administration began July 4, 1901. Self-rule was extended gradually until the establishment of a Commonwealth (1935). World War II brought a short period of Japanese occupation (1942-45) but following the defeat of Japan, the Philippines became a republic on July 4, 1946.

100 cents = 1 dollar. 1906: 100 centavos = 1 peso. 1962: 100 sentimos = 1 piso.

Prior to 1899: Stamps of Spanish Philippines.

Regular Postal Issues

1899. OVERPRINT ISSUE

261 *1899, April 29, 1901. U.S. #182, 188-210 (triangles in upper corners) overprinted PHILIPPINES in black or red (#274-277); perforated 12; watermark double-line USPS, #273 (U.S. #182); no watermark.*

263

		UnFVF	UseFVF
261 1¢	**deep green**	4.00	.85
	x. Overprint inverted	15,000.00	
262 2¢	**carmine** (#191)	2.25	1.20
	n. Booklet pane of 6	275.00	
263 2¢	**red** (#192)	1.65	.80
264 3¢	**dark red violet**	7.75	1.75
265 4¢	**chocolate** *(Aug. 30, 1901)*	30.00	6.00
266 5¢	**dark blue**	7.25	1.20
	x. Overprint inverted	3,725.00	3,275.00
267 6¢	**lake** *(Aug. 30, 1901)*	37.00	9.00
268 8¢	**purple** *(Aug. 30, 1901)*	37.00	10.00
269 10¢	**brown**, Type I	22.50	5.50
270 10¢	**brown**, Type II	275.00	42.50
271 15¢	**olive green** *(Aug. 30, 1899)*	40.00	10.75
	a. light olive green	42.50	12.00
272 50¢	**orange** *(Aug. 30, 1899)*	185.00	50.00

273

		UnFVF	UseFVF
273 50¢	**orange,** no watermark *(Aug. 30, 1899)*	525.00	350.00
274 $1	**black,** Type I *(Aug. 30, 1901)*	575.00	570.00
275 $1	**black,** Type II *(Aug. 30, 1901)*	3,000.00	950.00
276 $2	**dark blue** *(Aug. 30, 1901)*	1,650.00	350.00
277 $5	**dark green** *(Aug. 30, 1901)*	1,200.00	900.00

10¢: Ovals below TEN CENTS intact (#269), broken by ornaments (#270). $1: Circles enclosing $1 broken (#274), complete (#275).

Special printings: *1899,* for the Paris Exhibition, most existing copies handstamped "Special Surcharge" on the back: 1¢, 2¢ (#262), 3¢, 5¢, 10¢ (#269), 15¢, 50¢ (#271). Few copies remain. Set $3,000 ($500 ea.).

1903, for the St. Louis Exposition, most existing copies handstamped "Special Printing" on the back: 6¢, $1 (#274), $2, $5, $800, $1,050, $1,200, $2,000.

Specimen: 1¢, 2¢ (#262), 3¢, 5¢, 10¢ (#269), 15¢, 50¢ (#272), overprinted "Specimen," exist. $200 ea.

For O.B. and other official handstamps see note after #300.

1899-1901. POSTAGE DUE ISSUE

		UnFVF	UseFVF
278 1¢	**brown carmine**	8.00	1.80
	On cover, used for regular postage: *Sept. 5-19, 1902*	290.00	110.00
279 2¢	**brown carmine**	8.00	1.80
280 3¢	**brown carmine** *(1901)*	24.00	8.00

281 283 284

		UnFVF	UseFVF
281 5¢	**brown carmine**	20.00	3.00
282 10¢	**brown carmine**	25.00	6.30
283 30¢	**brown carmine** *(1901)*	300.00	125.00
284 50¢	**brown carmine**	290.00	120.00

Special Printings: *1889,* for the Paris Exhibition, most existing copies handstamped "Special Surcharge" on the back: #278, 279, 281, 282, 284 — $1,000 ea.

1907, for the Bureau of Insular Affairs on very white paper: #278-284 — $1,000 ea.

Specimen: #278, 279, 281, 282, 284, overprinted "Specimen": exist — $40.00 ea.

1901. SPECIAL DELIVERY ISSUE *Sept. 6.* U.S. #SD5 overprinted in red.

285

Overprint **PHILIPPINES**

		UnFVF	UseFVF
285 10¢	**indigo**	150.00	135.00

Special printing of 1907 for the Bureau of Insular Affairs: U.S. #SD6, 10¢ ultramarine overprinted in red, $600.

1903-04. OVERPRINT ISSUE US #211-224, 231 (2¢) with black or red (R) overprint 261; *perforated 12; watermark double-line USPS.*

		UnFVF	UseFVF
286 1¢	**deep bluish green** *(Sept. 6, 1903)*	5.25	.50
287 2¢	**carmine** *(Sept. 6, 1903)*	10.00	1.80

288   289   290

				UnFVF	UseFVF
288					
2¢	carmine, (US #231), (Nov. 1, 1904)			7.25	3.00
289				UnFVF	UseFVF
3¢	dark red violet (Nov. 1, 1904)			90.00	16.50
290				UnFVF	UseFVF
4¢	brown (Nov. 1, 1904)			100.00	30.00
	a. orange brown			100.00	27.50
291				UnFVF	UseFVF
5¢	deep blue (Jan. 4, 1904)			16.50	1.15

292   293   295

				UnFVF	UseFVF
292					
6¢	brown red (Nov. 1, 1904)			122.50	30.00
293				UnFVF	UseFVF
8¢	violet black (Nov. 1, 1904)			51.00	16.50
294				UnFVF	UseFVF
10¢	pale red brown (Nov. 1, 1904)			30.00	3.25
	x. Pair, one no overprint				1,500.00
295				UnFVF	UseFVF
13¢	black brown (Jan. 4, 1904)			43.00	22.00

296   297   298

				UnFVF	UseFVF
296					
15¢	olive green (Jan. 4, 1904)			80.00	20.00
297				UnFVF	UseFVF
50¢	orange (Sept. 6, 1903)			182.00	45.00
298				UnFVF	UseFVF
$1	black, (R), (Jan. 4, 1904)			675.00	350.00
299				UnFVF	UseFVF
$2	dark blue, (R), (Nov. 1, 1904)			1,200.00	1,075.00

300

				UnFVF	UseFVF
300					
$5	dark green, (R), (Nov. 1, 1904)			2,425.00	1,200.00

No. 288 booklet pane (6): $1,075.

Special printings: *1903,* for the St. Louis Exposition, most existing copies handstamped "Special Surcharge" on the back: 1¢, 2¢ (#288), 5¢, 13¢-$1, #286, 288, 291, 295 $1,000 ea.; #298 $2,000.

Handstamped "Special Printing" on the back: 2¢ (#287) $800.

1907, for the Bureau of Insular Affairs, on very white paper: #286, 288-297, $1,000 ea.; #298 $2,000, #299 $4,000, #300 $5,000.

On Jan. 1, 1906, all branches of the insular government began using postage stamps for official business, thus replacing the franking system in use prior to that time. Officers of these agencies were authorized, if they so desired, to overprint stamps purchased for official business with the letters O.B. This was done in various ways — manuscript, typewriter, and rubber stamp, with the latter in the majority. Most of these read "O.B.," as per the directive, but other forms such as "Official Business" or "Official Mail," and variations, are known. These overprints are found on the issues of 1899 to 1906 in various colors.

1906-31. PHILIPPINE ISSUE

T301 *2¢ José Rizal-Mercado y Alonzo (1861-96), Philippine national hero who agitated for independence from Spain. His novel,* Noli Me Tangere (Touch Me Not), *known as the Philippine* Uncle Tom's Cabin, *forced his emigration in 1886. Given permission to revisit his homeland in 1896, he was arrested, falsely accused of instigating the Katipunan rebellion, and executed by firing squad.*

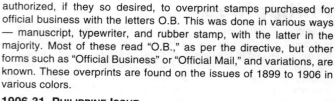

1 (1906-13): Perforated 12; watermark 301, double-line PIPS.

		UnFVF	UseFVF
301			
2¢	deep green	.35	.20
	a. yellow green (1910)	1.10	.20
	n. Booklet pane (6)	60.00	

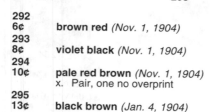

T302 *4¢ President William McKinley (1843-1901), president of the United States during the Spanish-American War, was assassinated at the Pan-American Exposition in Buffalo, N.Y.*

		UnFVF	UseFVF
302			
4¢	carmine red	.60	.20
	a. carmine lake (1910)	1.50	.20
	n. Booklet pane (6)	60.00	

T303 *6¢ Ferdinand Magellan (1480-1521) was the first to circumnavigate the globe (1519-22) but was killed in the Philippines, in April 1521, while trying to force residents of a village to give him food for his crew.*

		UnFVF	UseFVF
303			
6¢	violet	1.50	.30

T304 *8¢ Miguel Lopez de Legazpi (1510-72), led the Spanish settlement of the islands, founded Manila in 1571.*

		UnFVF	UseFVF
304			
8¢	brown	3.00	1.20

T305 *10¢ Maj. Gen. Henry Ware Lawton (1843-99), fought against Katipunan leader Aguinaldo, died in action near Manila on Dec. 19, 1899.*

		UnFVF	UseFVF
305			
10¢	blue	2.40	.25

T306 *12¢ Abraham Lincoln (1809-1865) was assassinated while president of the United States.*

		UnFVF	UseFVF
306			
12¢	**carmine lake**	6.25	2.50
307		UnFVF	UseFVF
12¢	**red orange** *(1910)*	12.00	4.50

T308 *16¢ Adam William T. Sampson (1840-1902), commanded the North American Squadron in the Spanish-American War.*

T310 *20¢ George Washington*

		UnFVF	UseFVF
308			
16¢	**black**	5.75	.60
309		UnFVF	UseFVF
16¢	**olive green** *(1911)*	4.50	1.65
310		UnFVF	UseFVF
20¢	**pale brown**	5.50	1.25
311		UnFVF	UseFVF
20¢	**olive yellow** *(1909)*	10.75	2.25

T312 *26¢ Francisco Carriedo*

T314 *30¢ Benjamin Franklin (1706-1790), patriot, first postmaster of the United States.*

		UnFVF	UseFVF
312			
26¢	**sepia**	8.00	3.75
313		UnFVF	UseFVF
26¢	**deep blue green** *(1909)*	2.80	1.30
314		UnFVF	UseFVF
30¢	**deep olive**	6.50	2.90
315		UnFVF	UseFVF
30¢	**ultramarine** *(1910)*	12.50	6.50

T316 *1p-10p Arms, City of Manila*

318

		UnFVF	UseFVF
316			
1p	**brown orange**	37.50	12.75
317		UnFVF	UseFVF
1p	**violet** *(1909)*	40.00	6.50
318		UnFVF	UseFVF
2p	**black**	45.00	1.80
319		UnFVF	UseFVF
2p	**dark chocolate** *(1913)*	115.00	4.00

320

321

		UnFVF	UseFVF
320		145.00	20.00
4p	**deep blue**		
321		UnFVF	UseFVF
10p	**green**	300.00	95.00

I P S *2 (1911-14) T301//321; perforated 12; watermark 322, single-line PIPS.*

		UnFVF	UseFVF
322		.80	.20
2¢	**green**		
	n. Booklet pane (6)	400.00	
323		UnFVF	UseFVF
4¢	**carmine lake**	3.40	.25
	n. Booklet pane (6)	500.00	
324		UnFVF	UseFVF
6¢	**deep violet**	2.40	.20
325		UnFVF	UseFVF
8¢	**brown**	11.50	.60

326

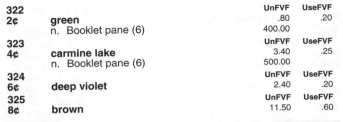

328

		UnFVF	UseFVF
326		4.30	.20
10¢	**blue**		
327		UnFVF	UseFVF
12¢	**orange**	3.25	.60
328		UnFVF	UseFVF
16¢	**olive green**	3.75	.30

329

332

		UnFVF	UseFVF
329		2.40	.20
20¢	**olive yellow**		
330		UnFVF	UseFVF
26¢	**deep blue green**	4.50	.35
331		UnFVF	UseFVF
30¢	**ultramarine**	4.50	.60
332		UnFVF	UseFVF
30¢	**gray** *(1914)*	12.00	.65
333		UnFVF	UseFVF
1p	**deep lilac**	30.00	.70
334		UnFVF	UseFVF
2p	**dark chocolate**	37.00	1.10
335		UnFVF	UseFVF
4p	**deep blue**	800.00	110.00
336		UnFVF	UseFVF
10p	**deep green**	275.00	35.00

3 (1914-23): T301//316; perforated 10; watermark 322, single-line PIPS.

		UnFVF	UseFVF
337		2.25	.18
2¢	**green**		
	n. Booklet pane (6)	350.00	
338		UnFVF	UseFVF
4¢	**carmine red**	2.25	.30
	n. Booklet pane (6)	350.00	
339		UnFVF	UseFVF
6¢	**violet**	57.00	11.00
	a. deep violet	50.00	8.00
340		UnFVF	UseFVF
8¢	**brown**	280.00	12.00
341		UnFVF	UseFVF
10¢	**blue**	35.00	.25

342

338

345

342		UnFVF	UseFVF
16¢	light yellow olive	100.00	6.00
343		UnFVF	UseFVF
20¢	orange	25.00	1.10
344		UnFVF	UseFVF
30¢	gray	75.00	3.75
345		UnFVF	UseFVF
1p	deep lilac	165.00	4.25
346		UnFVF	UseFVF
2¢	green	27.50	6.00
	n. Booklet pane (6)	500.00	
347		UnFVF	UseFVF
4¢	carmine red	38.00	3.25
	n. Booklet pane (6)	1,250.00	
348		UnFVF	UseFVF
6¢	violet	52.50	2.25
349		UnFVF	UseFVF
8¢	light brown	280.00	40.00
350		UnFVF	UseFVF
10¢	blue	75.00	1.80

351

354

351		UnFVF	UseFVF
16¢	yellow olive	125.00	9.50
352		UnFVF	UseFVF
20¢	yellow	82.50	10.50
353		UnFVF	UseFVF
30¢	gray	80.00	17.75
354		UnFVF	UseFVF
1p	deep lilac	100.00	18.75
355		UnFVF	UseFVF
2¢	light green	.25	.20
	a. green	.35	.20
	v. Horizontal pair, gutter between	3,000.00	
	v1. Vertical pair, gutter between	3,500.00	
	n. Booklet pane (6)	8.75	

356

356LP

356		UnFVF	UseFVF
2¢	green, coil (1928)	20.00	20.00
357		UnFVF	UseFVF
4¢	red carmine	.20	.20
	a. rose carmine	.40	.20
	n. Booklet pane (6)	3.60	
358		UnFVF	UseFVF
6¢	deep violet	.45	.20
	a. deep lilac	.70	.20
	b. purple	.70	.25
	n. Booklet pane (6)	60.00	
359		UnFVF	UseFVF
8¢	pale yellow brown	.30	.20
	a. deep yellow brown	.35	.20
360		UnFVF	UseFVF
10¢	deep dull blue	.30	.20
361		UnFVF	UseFVF
12¢	orange	.40	.20
362		UnFVF	UseFVF
16¢	yellow olive, T30	75.00	.25
	a. bistre	77.50	.25

363 *Adm. George Dewey (1837-1917), hero of the Battle of Manila in the Spanish-American War*

370

363		UnFVF	UseFVF
16¢	olive green (1923)	1.80	.25
	a. bistre	1.10	.25
364		UnFVF	UseFVF
20¢	yellow	.35	.20
365		UnFVF	UseFVF
26¢	deep blue green	.60	.60
	a. blue green	.65	.40
366		UnFVF	UseFVF
30¢	gray black	.70	.20
	a. black	.70	.25
367		UnFVF	UseFVF
1p	deep lilac	40.00	1.50
	a. red lilac	40.00	1.50
	b. rose lilac	40.00	2.25
368		UnFVF	UseFVF
2p	dark chocolate	37.00	1.00
369		UnFVF	UseFVF
4p	deep blue	35.00	.60
	a. dark blue	35.00	.60
370		UnFVF	UseFVF
10p	green (1926)	80.00	6.50

(1931): gutter, no watermark

371		UnFVF	UseFVF
2¢	emerald	.30	.30
372		UnFVF	UseFVF
4¢	red carmine	.35	.40
373		UnFVF	UseFVF
6¢	deep violet	1.25	2.00
374		UnFVF	UseFVF
8¢	yellow brown	1.25	2.00
375		UnFVF	UseFVF
10¢	deep dull blue	1.50	2.50
376		UnFVF	UseFVF
12¢	orange	2.25	3.75
377		UnFVF	UseFVF
16¢	bistre, T363	1.65	2.50
378		UnFVF	UseFVF
20¢	yellow	1.65	2.50
379		UnFVF	UseFVF
26¢	emerald	1.65	2.50
380		UnFVF	UseFVF
30¢	black	2.00	3.25
381		UnFVF	UseFVF
1p	violet	6.00	10.00
382		UnFVF	UseFVF
2p	purple brown	16.50	21.50
383		UnFVF	UseFVF
4p	deep blue	46.00	80.00
384		UnFVF	UseFVF
10p	deep green	120.00	200.00

Note: #371-384 originally issued in 1925 in darker shades, not sold to public.

Perforated 12; watermark 301, double-line PIPS.

1906-31. SPECIAL DELIVERY ISSUE *perforated 12; watermark 301, double-line PIPS.*

385-389 *Special delivery; messenger, engraved*

385		UnFVF	UseFVF
20¢	ultramarine	40.00	10.00
	a. pale ultramarine	40.00	12.75

Perforated 12; watermark 322, single-line PIPS.

386
20¢   **bright ultramarine** *(1911)*

	UnFVF	UseFVF
	24.50	2.25

Perforated 10; watermark 322, single-line PIPS.

387
20¢   **deep ultramarine** *(1916)*

	UnFVF	UseFVF
	225.00	65.00

Perforated 11; no watermark.

388
20¢   **ultramarine** *(1920)*

	UnFVF	UseFVF
	.70	.40
a. pale ultramarine	.70	.40
b. black violet	1.50	.70

Imperforate; no watermark.

389
20¢   **black violet** *(1931)*

	LUnFVF	UseFVF
	27.50	22.50
a. dark blue violet	40.00	37.00

1926. MADRID-MANILA FLIGHT OVERPRINT ISSUE

1926, May 13. Madrid-Manila Flight; #355/370, 345 (1p) overprinted in violet or red (R); perforated 11, #401: perforated 10. Capts. Ed Gallarza and J. Loriga, air navigators of the Spanish military school, left Madrid on April 4, 1926. Flying via Karachi and Macao, they made the first ocean crossing to Manila, landing there May 13.

390
2¢   **light green, (R)**

	UnFVF	UseFVF
	9.50	3.75

391x

398

391
4¢   **red carmine**

	UnFVF	UseFVF
	12.00	5.00
x. Overprint variety	3,700.00	

392
6¢   **deep violet, (R)**

	UnFVF	UseFVF
	57.00	16.50

393
8¢   **deep yellow brown**

	UnFVF	UseFVF
	57.00	16.75

394
10¢   **deep dull blue, (R)**

	UnFVF	UseFVF
	57.00	16.75

395
12¢   **orange**

	UnFVF	UseFVF
	57.00	30.00

396
16¢   **yellow olive, T308**

	UnFVF	UseFVF
	3,000.00	2,000.00
a. bistre, (R)	6,000.00	3,500.00

397
16¢   **olive green, T363**

	UnFVF	UseFVF
	65.00	30.00

398
20¢   **yellow**

	UnFVF	UseFVF
	65.00	30.00

399
26¢   **blue green**

	UnFVF	UseFVF
	65.00	30.00
v. Perforated 12, #330	5,300.00	

400

404

400
30¢   **gray black**

	UnFVF	UseFVF
	65.00	30.00

401
1p   **deep lilac, #345**

	UnFVF	UseFVF
	240.00	140.00

402
2p   **dark chocolate, (R)**

	UnFVF	UseFVF
	525.00	300.00

403
4p   **dark blue, (R)**

	UnFVF	UseFVF
	800.00	600.00

404
10p   **green**

	UnFVF	UseFVF
	1,275.00	800.00

1926. INAUGURATION OF LEGISLATIVE PALACE ISSUE *Frame lithographed; center typographed in black, perforated 12.*

 405

 406

405
2¢   **light green**

	UnFVF	UseFVF
	.60	.40
v. Vertical pair, imperforate between	500.00	
v1. Horizontal pair, imperforate between	275.00	
FDC		3.50

406
4¢   **scarlet**

	UnFVF	UseFVF
	.60	.40
v. Vertical pair, imperforate between	500.00	
v1. Horizontal pair, imperforate between	275.00	
FDC		3.50

 407

 408

407
16¢   **olive green**

	UnFVF	UseFVF
	1.30	1.00
v. Vertical pair, imperforate between	550.00	
v1. Horizontal pair, imperforate between	350.00	
FDC		10.00

408
18¢   **gray brown**

	UnFVF	UseFVF
	1.30	1.00
v. Vertical pair, imperforate between	550.00	
Double impression	550.00	

409
20¢   **yellow orange**

	UnFVF	UseFVF
	2.00	1.50
a. Center in brown	500.00	
v. Vertical pair, imperforate between	550.00	
v1. Pair, imperforate #409	450.00	
v2. Pair, imperforate #409a	850.00	

 410

 411

410
24¢   **gray black**

	UnFVF	UseFVF
	1.50	1.00
v. Vertical pair, imperforate between	550.00	

411
1p   **mauve**

	UnFVF	UseFVF
	60.00	45.00
v. Vertical pair, imperforate between	625.00	

405-411 *FDC (Dec. 20, 1936)*, $80.

1926. OFFICIAL OVERPRINT ISSUE *Dec. 20. Officials; #405//409 overprinted in red.*

 412

 413

Overprint   **OFFICIAL**

412
2¢   **light green & black**

	UnFVF	UseFVF
	2.40	1.25

413
4¢   **scarlet & black**

	UnFVF	UseFVF
	3.00	1.50
v. Vertical pair, gutter between	725.00	
x. FDC		10.00

414

415

414			UnFVF	UseFVF
18¢	gray brown & black		7.25	4.00
415			UnFVF	UseFVF
20¢	yellow orange & black		6.75	2.50

412-415 FDC, $50.

1928 POSTAGE DUE ISSUE *Aug. 21, engraved, perforated 11.*

416

417

418

416			UnFVF	UseFVF
4¢	brown red		.25	.25
417			UnFVF	UseFVF
6¢	brown red		.30	.30
418			UnFVF	UseFVF
8¢	brown red		.30	.30

419

420

421

419			UnFVF	UseFVF
10¢	brown red		.30	.30
420			UnFVF	UseFVF
12¢	brown red		.35	.35
421			UnFVF	UseFVF
16¢	brown red		.40	.40

422

422			UnFVF	UseFVF
20¢	brown red		.30	.25

1928. LONDON-ORIENT FLIGHT OVERPRINT ISSUE *1928, Nov. 9.*
London-Orient Flight; #355/366 and 333 (1p) overprinted in red; *perforated 11,* 1p: *perforated 12.* A flight of 4 British Southampton flying boats, commanded by Group Capt. Brown-Cave, flew from London to the Orient as a good-will gesture and an experiment toward regular airmail flights between Hong Kong and Manila.

423 *Overprint*

423			UnFVF	UseFVF
2¢	green		.60	.60
424			UnFVF	UseFVF
4¢	red carmine		.70	.70

425			UnFVF	UseFVF
6¢	deep violet		2.40	2.40
426			UnFVF	UseFVF
8¢	pale yellow brown		2.40	2.40
427			UnFVF	UseFVF
10¢	deep dull blue		2.40	2.40
428			UnFVF	UseFVF
12¢	orange		3.75	3.75
429			UnFVF	UseFVF
16¢	bistre		2.40	2.40
430			UnFVF	UseFVF
20¢	yellow		3.75	3.75
431			UnFVF	UseFVF
26¢	deep blue green		11.00	8.00
432			UnFVF	UseFVF
30¢	gray black		11.00	8.00
433			UnFVF	UseFVF
1p	deep lilac, #333		60.00	32.50

1931. OFFICIAL OVERPRINT ISSUE *May 18.* Officials. #355/366 and special delivery #388 overprinted O.B.

434

435

436

434			UnFVF	UseFVF
2¢	green		.20	.20
	x. No period after B		15.00	5.00
435			UnFVF	UseFVF
4¢	red carmine		.20	.20
	x. No period after B		14.50	6.00
436			UnFVF	UseFVF
6¢	deep violet		.20	.20

437

438

439

437			UnFVF	UseFVF
8¢	yellow brown		.20	.20
438			UnFVF	UseFVF
10¢	deep blue		.40	.20
439			UnFVF	UseFVF
12¢	orange		.35	.25
	x. No period after B		32.50	

440

441

O.B.

440			UnFVF	UseFVF
16¢	olive green, T363		.35	.20
	a. bistre		1.25	.40
441			UnFVF	UseFVF
20¢	yellow		.40	.20
	x. No period after B		25.00	

442

443

442		UnFVF	UseFVF
26¢	deep blue green	.50	.40
	a. blue green	1.50	.75
443		UnFVF	UseFVF
30¢	gray black	.45	.40

Special Delivery

444		UnFVF	UseFVF
20¢	black violet	.75	.50
	x. No period after B	20.00	15.00
	x1. Overprint double		

1932. PICTORIAL ISSUE *engraving, perforated 11.*

445 *Mayon Volcano (7,943 ft.), southern Luzon*

445		UnFVF	UseFVF
2¢	light green	.65	.40
	FDC		3.00

446 *Post Office building, Manila*

447 *Pier 7, Manila Harbor*

446		UnFVF	UseFVF
4¢	carmine	.55	.60
	FDC		4.00
447		UnFVF	UseFVF
12¢	orange	.80	1.20
	FDC		8.00

448 *Vernal Falls, Yosemite National Park, California, used in error; intended scene was Pagsanjan Falls*

448		UnFVF	UseFVF
18¢	vermilion	28.00	14.00
	FDC		20.00

449 *Rice-planting with carabao and primitive plow*

450 *Rice terraces*

449		UnFVF	UseFVF
20¢	yellow	1.00	.85
	FDC		9.00
450		UnFVF	UseFVF
24¢	light purple	1.50	1.10
	FDC		9.00

451 *Zigzag in the Kennon Road to Baguio*

451		UnFVF	UseFVF
32¢	olive brown	1.50	1.25
	FDC		9.00

1932. VON GRONAU ISSUE *Sept. 27.* #445-451 overprinted in black or green (G); *perforated 11.* Capt. Wolfgang von Gronau, head of a commercial pilots' school at Warnemunde, Germany, and 3 companions stopped at Manila during a successful round-the-world flight in a Dornier Super-Wal flying boat. They departed for Friedrichshafen on Sept. 22.

452

453

452		UnFVF	UseFVF
2¢	light green, (G)	.50	.50
	FDC		2.50
453		UnFVF	UseFVF
4¢	carmine	.50	.50
	FDC		2.50

454

455

454		UnFVF	UseFVF
12¢	orange, (G)	.80	.80
455		UnFVF	UseFVF
18¢	vermilion	4.50	4.50

456

457

456		UnFVF	UseFVF
20¢	yellow, (G)	2.50	2.50
457		UnFVF	UseFVF
24¢	light purple, (G)	2.50	2.50

458

458		UnFVF	UseFVF
32¢	olive brown, (G)	2.50	2.50

452-458 FDC, $50.

1932. #369 overprinted in orange or red (R)

459 Overprint

459

	UnFVF	UseFVF
1p on 4p deep blue	2.40	.60
a. dark blue	3.70	1.65

460

460

	UnFVF	UseFVF
2p on 4p dark blue, (R)	5.00	1.00
a. deep blue	5.00	1.00

1933. MADRID-MANILA OVERPRINT ISSUE *1933, April 11.* Madrid-Manila non-stop flight of Spanish aviator Fernando Rein y Loring; #355-366 overprinted in green.

#355-366 overprinted in green

461 Overprint

F.REIN
MADRID-MANILA
FLIGHT-1933

461

	UnFVF	UseFVF
2¢ light green	.55	.55
FDC		2.00

462   *463*   *464*

462

	UnFVF	UseFVF
4¢ red carmine	.60	.60

463

	UnFVF	UseFVF
6¢ deep violet	1.20	1.10
FDC		4.50

464

	UnFVF	UseFVF
8¢ pale yellow brown	3.50	2.50

465

	UnFVF	UseFVF
10¢ deep dull blue	3.00	1.50

466   *467*   *468*

466

	UnFVF	UseFVF
12¢ orange	2.40	1.00

467

	UnFVF	UseFVF
16¢ yellow olive, T363	2.25	1.25

468

	UnFVF	UseFVF
20¢ yellow	2.25	1.65

469

470

469

	UnFVF	UseFVF
26¢ deep blue green	3.00	2.50

470

	UnFVF	UseFVF
30¢ gray black	4.00	2.50

461-470 FDC, $48.

1933. AIRMAIL OVERPRINT ISSUE *May 26.* #355 and #445/451 overprinted in green.

471

471

	UnFVF	UseFVF
2¢ light green	.85	.70

472

	UnFVF	UseFVF
4¢ carmine	.25	.25

473

	UnFVF	UseFVF
12¢ orange	.40	.25

474   *475*

474

	UnFVF	UseFVF
20¢ yellow	.40	.25

475

	UnFVF	UseFVF
24¢ light purple	.45	.35

476

	UnFVF	UseFVF
32¢ olive brown	.65	.50

471-476 FDC, $42.50.

1934. 10TH FAR EASTERN CHAMPIONSHIP GAME ISSUE *April 14.* Typographed, perforated 11 1/2.

477 Baseball

478 Tennis

477

	UnFVF	UseFVF
2¢ yellow brown	2.00	1.00
x. T of EASTERN deformed	4.00	1.65
FDC		2.75

478

	UnFVF	UseFVF
6¢ gray blue	.35	.25
v. Vertical pair, imperforate between	2,250.00	
FDC		2.00

479 Basketball

479

	UnFVF	UseFVF
16¢ brown purple	.65	.65
v. Vertical pair, imperforate horizontally	1,200.00	
FDC		2.50

1935. PICTORIAL ISSUE *Feb. 15. Engraving, perforated 11.*

480 *2¢ José Rizal: Juan Luna painting*

480		UnFVF	UseFVF
2¢	**deep rose**	.20	.20
	FDC		1.25

481 *4¢ Allegorical figure and carabao*

482 *Philippine woman*

481		UnFVF	UseFVF
4¢	**deep yellow green**	.20	.20
	a. yellow green	.25	.20
	FDC		1.25

482		UnFVF	UseFVF
6¢	**brown**	.20	.20
	FDC		1.25

483 *Pearl fishermen*

484 *Santiago Fort in walled city of Manila*

483		UnFVF	UseFVF
8¢	**red violet**	.25	.20
	FDC		2.25

484		UnFVF	UseFVF
10¢	**rose carmine**	.35	.35
	FDC		3.00

485 *Salt spring*

485		UnFVF	UseFVF
12¢	**black**	.35	.20
	FDC		3.00

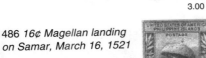

486 *16¢ Magellan landing on Samar, March 16, 1521*

487 *20¢ Juan de la Cruz, national character typifying the Filipino*

486		UnFVF	UseFVF
16¢	**deep blue**	.35	.20
	FDC		3.00

487		UnFVF	UseFVF
20¢	**bistre**	.40	.20
	FDC		4.00

488 *Rice terraces*

489 *"The Blood Compact" between Legazpi and Sikatuna, Chieftain of Bohol; Juan Luna painting*

488		UnFVF	UseFVF
26¢	**indigo**	.65	.40
	FDC		5.50

489		UnFVF	UseFVF
30¢	**deep red orange**	.55	.40
	FDC		6.00

490 *Barasoain Church*

491 *Battle of Manila Bay, May 1, 1898, in which the U.S. Navy's Asiatic Squadron under Commodore George Dewey destroyed the Spanish fleet*

490		UnFVF	UseFVF
1p	**orange & black**	3.60	2.25
	FDC		15.00

491		UnFVF	UseFVF
2p	**yellow brown & black**	5.50	2.50
	FDC		17.50

492 *Montalban Gorge*

493 *George Washington*

492		UnFVF	UseFVF
4p	**deep blue & black**	6.50	4.50
	FDC		25.00

493		UnFVF	UseFVF
5p	**deep blue green & black**	12.75	2.60
	FDC		35.00

1935. OFFICIAL OVERPRINT ISSUE *March 14. Officials; #480-489 with overprint 494.*

 494

Overprint **O.B.**

494		UnFVF	UseFVF
2¢	**deep rose**	.20	.20
	x. No period after B	15.00	5.00

 495

496

495		UnFVF	UseFVF
4¢	**deep yellow green**	.20	.20
	x. No period after B	15.00	5.00

496		UnFVF	UseFVF
6¢	**brown**	.20	.20
	x. No period after B		

497
8¢   red violet

498
10¢   rose carmine

	UnFVF	UseFVF
497		
498	.25	.20
	.25	.20

499
12¢   black

500
16¢   deep blue

	UnFVF	UseFVF
499	.25	.20
500	.35	.20

501
20¢   bistre

502
26¢   indigo

503
30¢   deep red orange

	UnFVF	UseFVF
501	.35	.25
502	.60	.40
503	.65	.55

1935. COMMONWEALTH ISSUE *Nov. 15.* Inauguration of the Commonwealth; *engraved, perforated 11.*

504-508 *The Temples of Human Progress*

504
2¢   rose red
FDC

	UnFVF	UseFVF
	.25	.15
		1.25

505
6¢   red violet
FDC

	UnFVF	UseFVF
	.30	.25
		1.50

506
16¢   dull blue
FDC

	UnFVF	UseFVF
	.40	.35
		2.00

507
36¢   light green
FDC

	UnFVF	UseFVF
	.55	.55
		2.50

508
50¢   light brown
FDC

	UnFVF	UseFVF
	.85	.85
		3.00

1935. AIRMAIL ISSUE *Dec. 2.* China Clipper flight from Manila to San Francisco.

#484, 489 overprinted in gold

Overprint

P.I.-U.S.
INITIAL FLIGHT
December-1935

509
10¢   rose carmine
FDC

	UnFVF	UseFVF
	.50	.35
		3.00

510
30¢   deep red orange
FDC

	UnFVF	UseFVF
	.85	.60
		4.50

1936. 75TH ANNIVERSARY OF RIZAL ISSUE *June 19.* Commemorated the birth of José Rizal (1861-1896) in Calamba, Laguna, June 19, 1861. *Typographed, perforated 12.*

511 *José Rizal*

512

518

519

	UnFVF	UseFVF
511	.20	.20
2¢ orange buff		
FDC		1.25

	UnFVF	UseFVF
512	.25	.25
6¢ slate blue		
v. Horizontal pair, imperforate vertically	1,000.00	
FDC		1.25

	UnFVF	UseFVF
518	.20	.20
6¢ deep yellow green		
FDC		1.25

	UnFVF	UseFVF
519	.35	.35
12¢ dark ultramarine		
FDC		3.00

513

1936-38. Commonwealth Overprint Issue

COMMON-WEALTH #480-493 with large COMMONWEALTH overprint 520 (2¢, 6¢, and 20¢) or 521 (18 1/4x2 1/4mm, other values)

	UnFVF	UseFVF
513	1.00	.85
36¢ red brown		
FDC		3.75

	UnFVF	UseFVF
520	.20	.20
2¢ deep rose		
n. Booklet pane (6)	3.00	1.00
FDC		40.00

1936. Manila-Madrid Flight Overprint Issue *Sept. 6.* Manila-Madrid flight of Philippine aviators Antonio Arnaiz and Juan Calvo. *Perforated 11.*

521

522

Overprinted in blue (B), violet (V), and black

515

COMMONWEALTH
Overprint

	UnFVF	UseFVF
521	.80	.55
4¢ deep yellow green *(1937)*		

	UnFVF	UseFVF
522	.40	.20
6¢ brown		

	UnFVF	UseFVF
514	.20	.20
2¢ on 4¢ red carmine, (B)		
FDC		1.25

	UnFVF	UseFVF
515	.20	.25
6¢ on 12¢ orange, (V)		
FDC		3.50

523

524

516

	UnFVF	UseFVF
523	.35	.35
8¢ red violet *(1937)*		

	UnFVF	UseFVF
524	.25	.20
10¢ rose carmine		
x. "COMMONWEALT"		
FDC		40.00

	UnFVF	UseFVF
516	.35	.35
16¢ on 26¢ blue green		
a. green	1.50	1.00
FDC		6.00

1936. 1st Anniversary of Commonwealth Issue *Nov. 15.* First President Manuel L. Quezon (1878-1944) ardently promoted independence as president of the Philippine senate (1916-35) and became president (1935-44) of the Commonwealth of the Philippines upon its inception. *Engraved, perforated 11.*

525

526

	UnFVF	UseFVF
525	.25	.20
12¢ black *(1937)*		

	UnFVF	UseFVF
526	.25	.20
16¢ deep blue		

	UnFVF	UseFVF
527	1.10	.60
20¢ bistre *(1937)*		

517 *President Manuel L. Quezon*

528

529

	UnFVF	UseFVF
517	.20	.20
2¢ chestnut		
FDC		1.25

			UnFVF	UseFVF
528				
26¢	indigo *(1937)*		.65	.50
529			UnFVF	UseFVF
30¢	deep red orange		.45	.20

530

531

			UnFVF	UseFVF
530				
1p	orange & black		1.00	.30
531			UnFVF	UseFVF
2p	yellow brown & black *(1937)*		6.75	4.00

532

533

			UnFVF	UseFVF
532				
4p	deep blue & black *(1937)*		25.00	4.00
533			UnFVF	UseFVF
5p	deep blue green & black *(1937)*		2.40	2.00
	FDC			50.00

Officials. #520, 527 overprinted O.B.

O. B.

O. B.

Overprint

			UnFVF	UseFVF
534				
2¢	deep rose *(1938)*		.20	.20
	x. No period after B		5.50	2.90
	FDC			50.00
535			UnFVF	UseFVF
20¢	bistre *(1938)*		1.00	.65

1937. 33RD EUCHARISTIC CONGRESS ISSUE *Feb. 3. engraved, perforated 11.*

536 *33rd Eucharistic Congress*

537   538   539

			UnFVF	UseFVF
536				
2¢	green		.20	.20
	FDC			1.00

			UnFVF	UseFVF
537				
6¢	yellow brown		.30	.20
	FDC			1.50
538			UnFVF	UseFVF
12¢	blue		.30	.20
	FDC			1.75
539			UnFVF	UseFVF
20¢	yellow orange		.45	.25
	FDC			2.00

 540

541

			UnFVF	UseFVF
540				
36¢	red violet		.85	.70
	FDC			2.25
541			UnFVF	UseFVF
50¢	carmine red		1.10	.45
	FDC			3.50

1937. CITY OF MANILA ARMS *Aug. 27. Engraved, perforated 11.*

 542 *City of Manila Arms*

543

			UnFVF	UseFVF
542				
10p	slate		6.50	3.00
543			UnFVF	UseFVF
20p	red b		3.25	2.25

542-543 FDC, $75.

1937. POSTAGE DUE ISSUE *July 29.*

 #416 overprinted

Overprint **3 CVOS. 3**

			UnFVF	UseFVF
544				
3¢ on 4¢ brown red			.25	.20
	FDC			35.00

1938-40. COMMONWEALTH OVERPRINT ISSUE #480-493 and 388 (Special delivery) with small COMMONWEALTH overprint 545 (2¢, 6¢, and 20¢) or 546 (18 1/2x1 1/4mm, other values).

 545

Overprint **COMMON-WEALTH**

			UnFVF	UseFVF
545				
2¢	deep rose *(1939)*		.20	.20
	x. Hyphen omitted		—	—
	x1. "WEALTH COMMON"		4,000.00	
	n. Booklet pane (6)		3.50	2.50

 546

Overprint **COMMONWEALTH**

546
4¢ deep yellow green *(1940)*

	UnFVF	UseFVF
	.65	.65

547

548

547
6¢ brown *(1939)*
a. deep brown
FDC *(May 12, 1939)*

	UnFVF	UseFVF
	.20	.20
	.20	.20
		35.00

548
8¢ red violet *(1939)*
x. "COMMONWEALT"

	UnFVF	UseFVF
	.20	.20
	80.00	

549

550

549
10¢ rose carmine *(1939)*
x. "COMMONWEALT"

	UnFVF	UseFVF
	.20	.20
		—

551

552

550
12¢ black *(1940)*
551
16¢ deep blue *(1938)*
552
20¢ bistre *(1939)*

	UnFVF	UseFVF
	.20	.20
	.25	.20
	.25	.20

553

554

553
26¢ indigo *(1940)*
554
30¢ deep red orange *(1939)*

	UnFVF	UseFVF
	.35	.35
	2.25	1.25

555

556

555
1p orange & black *(1938)*
FDC
556
2p yellow brown & black *(1939)*
557
4p deep blue & black *(1940)*
558
5p deep blue green & black *(1940)*

	UnFVF	UseFVF
	.65	.25
		50.00
	4.75	1.20
	120.00	100.00
	6.00	4.50

1939. SPECIAL DELIVERY ISSUE *with overprint 546, perforated 11, unwatermarked.*

559

559
20¢ violet *(April 27, 1939)*

	UnFVF	UseFVF
	.50	.50

1938-40. OFFICIAL OVERPRINT ISSUE #545-554 with overprint 560 (2¢, 6¢, and 20¢) or 561 (other values).

560

Overprint **O. B.**

560
2¢ deep rose
x. No period after B
x1. Hyphen omitted

	UnFVF	UseFVF
	.20	.20
	22.00	22.00
	20.00	20.00

561

Overprint **O. B.**

561
4¢ deep yellow green

	UnFVF	UseFVF
	.20	.20

562

562
6¢ brown

	UnFVF	UseFVF
	.20	.20

563

564

563
8¢ red violet
564
10¢ rose carmine
x. No period after O

	UnFVF	UseFVF
	.20	.20
	.20	.20
	30.00	30.00

565

566

565
12¢ black
566
16¢ deep blue

	UnFVF	UseFVF
	.20	.20
	.25	.20

567

567
20¢   bistre *(1940)*

	UnFVF	UseFVF
	.40	.40

 568

 569

568
26¢   indigo

	UnFVF	UseFVF
	.40	.40

569
30¢   deep red orange

	UnFVF	UseFVF
	.40	.40

1939. AIRMAIL OVERPRINT ISSUE *Feb. 17.* First Air Mail Exhibition.

#365a, 542 overprinted
in black or red (R)

Overprint

FIRST
AIR MAIL EXHIBITION
Feb. 17 to Feb. 9, 1939
8 CENTAVOS 8

570
8¢ on 26¢   blue green
   a. green
   FDC

	UnFVF	UseFVF
	1.00	.60
	2.25	.80
		5.00

 571

571
1p on 10p slate, (R)
FDC

	UnFVF	UseFVF
	4.00	3.00
		10.00

1939. FIRST FOREIGN TRADE ISSUE *July 5.* First Foreign Trade Week.

#481, 365a, 543 overprinted in red (R),
violet (V) or black

572
2¢ on 4¢   deep yellow green (R)
FDC

	UnFVF	UseFVF
	.20	.20
		1.50

 573

Overprint

FIRST FOREIGN
TRADE WEEK

MAY 21-27, 1939
6 CENTAVOS 6

573
6¢ on 26¢   blue green (V)
   a. green
   FDC

	UnFVF	UseFVF
	.25	.25
	.85	.40
		2.25

 574

Overprint **50 CENTAVOS 50**

FIRST FOREIGN
TRADE WEEK

MAY 21-27 1939

574
50¢ on 20p red brown
FDC

	UnFVF	UseFVF
	1.20	1.20
		6.00

1939-40. 4TH ANNIVERSARY OF THE COMMONWEALTH 1 *(Nov. 15, 1939):* T575. Engraved, perforated 11.

T575   576   577
Triumphal Arch

575
2¢   yellow green
FDC

	UnFVF	UseFVF
	.20	.20
		1.25

576
6¢   red carmine
FDC

	UnFVF	UseFVF
	.20	.20
		1.25

577
12¢   deep blue
FDC

	UnFVF	UseFVF
	.25	.20
		1.50

   T578
Malacañan Palace

579

578
2¢   green, 2 *(Nov. 15, 1939):* T578
FDC

	UnFVF	UseFVF
	.25	.20
		1.50

579
6¢   yellow orange
FDC

	UnFVF	UseFVF
	.30	.20
		1.50

   580

T581
Quezon taking oath of office

580
12¢   red carmine
FDC

	UnFVF	UseFVF
	.40	.20
		2.00

581
2¢   yellow orange, 3 *(Feb. 8, 1940):* T581
FDC

	UnFVF	UseFVF
	.25	.20
		1.25

582 583

582
6¢   green
FDC

	UnFVF	UseFVF
	.30	.20
		1.25

583		UnFVF	UseFVF
12¢	red violet	.40	.20
	FDC		2.00

1941. JOSÉ RIZAL ISSUE *April 14. Engraved; #584: rotary press, size 19x22 1/2mm, perforated 11x10 1/2; #585: flat plate, size 14 1/4x22mm, perforated 11 with 1 or 2 sides imperforate.*

584 *José Rizal*

584		UnFVF	UseFVF
2¢	deep apple green	.20	.20
	FDC		1.00

585		UnFVF	UseFVF
2¢	deep apple green, perforated 11, *(1943)*	.25	.20
	a. light apple green	.45	.40
	Booklet pane (6)	2.00	
	Booklet pane (6), #585a	4.00	

Note: #585 issued in booklet panes only.

Official: #584, overprinted 560, O.B.

586

586		UnFVF	UseFVF
2¢	deep apple green	.20	.20

1941. AIRMAIL ISSUE *June 30. Engraved, perforated 11.*

587 *Boeing 314 clipper and Moro Vinta (sailing canoe)*

588

587		UnFVF	UseFVF
8¢	scarlet	1.20	.80
	FDC		2.50

588		UnFVF	UseFVF
20¢	ultramarine	1.10	.65
	FDC		2.50

589

590

589		UnFVF	UseFVF
60¢	emerald green	2.40	1.20
	FDC		4.50

590		UnFVF	UseFVF
1p	sepia	1.00	.65
	FDC		3.00

1942-44. JAPANESE OCCUPATION ISSUE *#584 2¢, 532, 547/555 overprinted with bars obliterating UNITED STATES OF AMERICA & COMMONWEALTH. Perforated 11; #591: perforated 11x10 1/2.*

591

592

591		UnFVF	UseFVF
2¢	deep apple green *(March 4, 1942)*	.20	.20

592		UnFVF	UseFVF
5¢ on 6¢	brown *(Sept. 1, 1942)*	.20	.20
	FDC		1.50

593, 594, 595

596

593		UnFVF	UseFVF
12¢	black *(April 30, 1942)*	.30	.25

594		UnFVF	UseFVF
16¢	deep blue *(March 4, 1942)*	5.25	3.00

595		UnFVF	UseFVF
16¢ on 30¢	red orange *(Jan. 11, 1943)*	.30	.25

596		UnFVF	UseFVF
50¢ on 1p	orange & black *(April 30, 1943)*	.70	.70
	x. Double surcharge	300.00	

597

597		UnFVF	UseFVF
1p on 4p	deep blue & black *(April 30, 1943)*	145.00	135.00
	x. S inverted in PESO	125.00	

1943-44. OFFICIAL OVERPRINT ISSUE

(March 7, 1943-44): Official; #591, 592, 595 overprinted K.P. (Kagamitang Pampamahalaan = Official Business in Tagalog) and Japanese characters; #599: same overprint on #522 (large COMMONWEALTH overprint); #600: 9 1/4-10mm between bars; #601: 6mm between center bar and Japanese characters.

598		UnFVF	UseFVF
2¢	deep apple green	.20	.20

599		UnFVF	UseFVF
5¢ on 6¢	brown #522, *(June 26, 1944)*	35.00	35.00

600		UnFVF	UseFVF
5¢ on 6¢	brown	.25	.25
	x. 8-8 1/2mm between bars	.25	.25

601		UnFVF	UseFVF
16¢ on 30¢	deep red orange	.80	.80
	x. 1mm between bar and Japanese characters		

1942. CAPTURE OF BATAAN AND CORREGIDOR ISSUE *May 18. Capture of Bataan and Corregidor (May 7).*

602 *#481 overprinted*

602		UnFVF	UseFVF
2¢ on 4¢	deep yellow green	6.00	6.00
	x. RATAAN		
	FDC		4.00

1942. POSTAGE DUE ISSUE *Oct. 13.*

603 *#544 overprinted with blue bar*

603		UnFVF	UseFVF
3¢ on 4¢	brown red	35.00	35.00
	FDC		30.00

Manila post office used #544 with hand-drawn lines across United States of America from Sept. 1, 1942 until Oct. 13, when #603 arrived.

1942. AGRICULTURE AND CONSERVATION CAMPAIGN ISSUE *Nov. 12.* Agriculture and conservation campaign surtax for Red Cross; *litho by Coast and Geodetic survey office; perforated 12.*

606 *Surtax for Red Cross*

604		UnFVF	UseFVF
2¢ + 1¢	deep lilac	.25	.25
605		UnFVF	UseFVF
5¢ + 1¢	light emerald	.20	.20
606		UnFVF	UseFVF
16¢ + 2¢	orange	25.00	25.00
604-606 FDC, $40.			

1942. FIRST ANNIVERSARY GREATER EAST ASIA WAR ISSUE *Dec. 8.* First anniversary of the Greater East Asia War.

607 *#481 overprinted*

607		UnFVF	UseFVF
5¢ on 4¢	deep yellow green	.80	.55
	FDC		3.00

1943. PHILIPPINE EXECUTIVE COMMISSION ISSUE *Jan. 23.* First anniversary Philippine Executive Commission.

608 *#587 overprinted*

608		UnFVF	UseFVF
2¢ on 8¢	scarlet	.35	.35
609		UnFVF	UseFVF
5¢ on 1p	sepia	.65	.65
608-609 FDC, $3.			

1943-44. PICTORIAL ISSUE

610, 612, 618 *Nipa palm hut*

Watermark 610

610		UnFVF	UseFVF
1¢	orange *(June 7, 1943)*	.20	.20

611, 614, 620 *Planting rice seedlings*

613

611		UnFVF	UseFVF
2¢	light emerald *(April 1, 1943)*	.20	.20
	x. Broken arm		
612		UnFVF	UseFVF
4¢	deep dull green *(June 7, 1943)*	.20	.20

613		UnFVF	UseFVF
5¢	yellow brown *(April 1, 1943)*	.20	.20
614		UnFVF	UseFVF
6¢	light scarlet *(July 14, 1943)*	.20	.20
615		UnFVF	UseFVF
10¢	slate blue green *(July 14, 1943)*	.20	.20

616, 617, 622, 623 *Moro Vinta*

616		UnFVF	UseFVF
12¢	Prussian blue *(July 14, 1943)*	1.25	1.25
617		UnFVF	UseFVF
16¢	bistre brown *(July 14, 1943)*	.20	.20
618		UnFVF	UseFVF
20¢	maroon *(Aug. 16, 1943)*	1.45	1.45
619		UnFVF	UseFVF
21¢	blue violet *(Aug. 16, 1943)*	.30	.30
620		UnFVF	UseFVF
25¢	chocolate *(Aug. 16, 1943)*	.20	.20
621		UnFVF	UseFVF
1p	carmine red *(June 7, 1943)*	.75	.75
622		UnFVF	UseFVF
2p	dark purple *(Sept. 16, 1943)*	5.00	5.00
	FDC		5.50
623		UnFVF	UseFVF
5p	light bronze green *(April 16, 1944)*	10.00	8.00
	FDC		7.50

1943. CAPTURE OF BATAAN AND CORREGIDOR ISSUE *May 7.* First anniversary capture of Bataan and Corregidor; photo in Japan; *perforated 13.*

625 *Japanese soldier and map of Manila Bay*

624		UnFVF	UseFVF
2¢	deep scarlet	.20	.20
625		UnFVF	UseFVF
5¢	deep emerald	.35	.35
	x. Colorless dot after left "5"		1.50
624-625 FDC, $250.			

1943. PRINTING PRESS ISSUE *June 20.* 350th anniversary printing press (Limbagan in Tagalog).

626 *#522 overprinted*

626		UnFVF	UseFVF
12¢ on 20¢	bistre		
	x. Double surcharge	—	—
	FDC		2.50

1943. INDEPENDENCE ISSUE *Oct. 14.* Independence; Rizal monument, Philippine woman and flag; photo; *perforated 12 or imperforate; no gum.*

627 *Philippine woman and flag*

627		UnFVF	UseFVF
5¢	light blue	.20	.20
628		UnFVF	UseFVF
12¢	red orange	.25	.25

629

		UnFVF	UseFVF
17¢	carmine rose	.40	.40

627-629 FDC, $2.50.

Souvenir sheet (127 x 177mm) of 3: #627-629; gutter; marginal inscription Independence of the Philippines and excerpt from Rizal's Last Farewell; no gum.

630

		UnFVF	UseFVF
5¢ , 12¢ , 17¢	Sheet	45.00	12.00
	Sheet w/FDC cancel at Manila		3.00

1943. FLOOD RELIEF OVERPRINT ISSUE Dec. 8.

631, 633 #616, 619 overprinted BAHA (Tagalog for flood) 1943 and additional value

631

		UnFVF	UseFVF
12¢ + 21¢	Prussian blue	.25	.25

632

		UnFVF	UseFVF
20¢ + 36¢	maroon	.25	.25

633

		UnFVF	UseFVF
21¢ + 40¢	blue violet	.25	.25

631-633 FDC, $2.

1944. PORTRAIT ISSUE 5¢ Rizal. 12¢ Rev. José Burgos (1837-1872), educator and ecclesiastical reformer, who was executed, along with Fathers Mariano Gomez and Jacinto Zamora on Feb. 17, 1872, as a result of Cavite revolt; 17¢ Apolonario Mabini, the "Voice of the Revolution," a leader, with Rizal, Marcelo del Pilar, and Lopez Jaena, of Young Filipino Party. Also adviser to Aguinaldo. Litho, perforated 12.

634　　　　　　　　635　　　　　　　　636

634

		UnFVF	UseFVF
5¢	light Prussian blue	.20	.20
	v. Pair, imperforate	.40	.40

635

		UnFVF	UseFVF
12¢	light carmine red	.20	.20
	v. Pair, imperforate	.40	.40

636

		UnFVF	UseFVF
17¢	red orange	.30	.30
	v. Pair, imperforate	.40	.40

Souvenir sheet (101 x 143mm) of 3; #634-636; gutter; marginal inscription; no gum.

634-636 FDC, $2. 634v-636v FDC, $3.

637

		UnFVF	UseFVF
5¢ , 12¢ , 17¢	Sheet	5.00	3.00
	FDC		4.00

Souvenir sheet sold for 1p; surtax for care of heroes' monuments.

1944. CAPTURE OF BATAAN AND CORREGIDOR ISSUE May 7.
Second anniversary of the capture of Bataan and Corregidor.

638 #587 overprinted

638

		UnFVF	UseFVF
5¢ on 20¢	ultramarine	.85	.85

639

		UnFVF	UseFVF
12¢ on 60¢	emerald green	1.65	1.65

638-639 FDC, $3.50.

1944. OFFICIAL OVERPRINT ISSUE Aug. 10. Official; #547, 567, 590 overprinted.

640 Overprint　　　641 Overprint　　　642 Overprint

640

		UnFVF	UseFVF
5¢ on 6¢	brown	.20	.20

641

		UnFVF	UseFVF
20¢	bistre	.65	.65

642

		UnFVF	UseFVF
1p	sepia	1.65	1.65

640-642 FDC, $4.

1945. REPUBLIC ISSUE Jan. 12. First anniversary of Republic (FDC cancelled Oct. 14, 1944); lithograph; gutter; no gum.

643-645 José P. Laurel, President of Japanese-established Philippine Republic

643

		UnFVF	UseFVF
5s	light violet brown	.20	.20

644

		UnFVF	UseFVF
7s	light blue green	.20	.20

645

		UnFVF	UseFVF
20s	dull blue	.25	.25

643-645 FDC, $1.50.

1944. VICTORY OVERPRINT ISSUE First Victory issue; stamps of Philippines handstamped with large VICTORY in violet, issued by Secretary of National Defense and Communications of the island of Leyte. 1 (Nov. 8-Dec. 28): Regular postage.

VICTORY Overprint 2

646

		UnFVF	UseFVF
2¢	deep rose (Dec. 3, 1944), #520	350.00	125.00
	Booklet pane of 6	2,000.00	

647

		UnFVF	UseFVF
2¢	deep rose (Dec. 14, 1944), #545	1,600.00	

648

		UnFVF	UseFVF
2¢	deep apple green, #584	3.50	3.00

649

		UnFVF	UseFVF
4¢	deep yellow green, #481	32.50	30.00

650

		UnFVF	UseFVF
6¢	brown (Dec. 14, 1944), #482	1,800.00	1,650.00

651

		UnFVF	UseFVF
6¢	deep yellow green (Dec. 3, 1944), #518	150.00	95.00

652

		UnFVF	UseFVF
6¢	brown (Dec. 28, 1944), #522	900.00	800.00

653

		UnFVF	UseFVF
6¢	red carmine (Dec. 14, 1944), #576	180.00	150.00

654

		UnFVF	UseFVF
6¢	yellow orange (Dec. 14, 1944), #579	800.00	750.00

655

		UnFVF	UseFVF
6¢	green, #582	200.00	200.00

656

		UnFVF	UseFVF
8¢	red violet, #548	20.00	25.00

657

		UnFVF	UseFVF
10¢	rose carmine, #524	150.00	100.00

658

		UnFVF	UseFVF
10¢	rose carmine, #549	180.00	150.00

659

		UnFVF	UseFVF
12¢	dark ultramarine (Dec. 3, 1944), #519	525.00	210.00

660

		UnFVF	UseFVF
12¢	deep blue (Dec. 14, 1944), #577	3,500.00	2,400.00

661

		UnFVF	UseFVF
12¢	red violet, #583	250.00	180.00

662

		UnFVF	UseFVF
16¢	deep blue (Dec. 3, 1944), #486	925.00	

			UnFVF	UseFVF
663			UnFVF	UseFVF
16¢	deep blue, #526		600.00	430.00
664			UnFVF	UseFVF
16¢	deep blue *(Dec. 28, 1944)*, #551		180.00	120.00
665			UnFVF	UseFVF
20¢	bistre, #552		37.00	37.00
666			UnFVF	UseFVF
30¢	deep red orange *(Dec. 3, 1944)*, #529		300.00	210.00
667			UnFVF	UseFVF
30¢	deep red orange *(Dec. 3, 1944)*, #554		425.00	350.00
668			UnFVF	UseFVF
1p	orange & black *(Dec. 3, 1944)*, #555		7,500.00	5,500.00

(Dec. 3): Airmail; #472

			UnFVF	UseFVF
669			UnFVF	UseFVF
4¢	carmine		2,300.00	2,300.00

Special Delivery

			UnFVF	UseFVF
670			UnFVF	UseFVF
20¢	black violet, #388b		850.00	650.00
671			UnFVF	UseFVF
20¢	violet, #559		240.00	200.00

(Dec. 3): Postage Due; #416-422

			UnFVF	UseFVF
672			UnFVF	UseFVF
4¢	brown red		75.00	
673			UnFVF	UseFVF
6¢	brown red		110.00	
674			UnFVF	UseFVF
8¢	brown red		125.00	
675			UnFVF	UseFVF
10¢	brown red		110.00	
676			UnFVF	UseFVF
12¢	brown red		110.00	
677			UnFVF	UseFVF
16¢	brown red		115.00	
678			UnFVF	UseFVF
20¢	brown red		115.00	

Officials

			UnFVF	UseFVF
679			UnFVF	UseFVF
2¢	deep rose, #560		275.00	150.00
680			UnFVF	UseFVF
2¢	deep apple green, #586		8.75	4.50
681			UnFVF	UseFVF
4¢	deep yellow green, #495		41.00	38.00
681A			UnFVF	UseFVF
6¢	dark brown, #562		5,700.00	
682			UnFVF	UseFVF
10¢	rose carmine, #564		180.00	
683			UnFVF	UseFVF
20¢	bistre, #501		8,000.00	
684			UnFVF	UseFVF
20¢	bistre, #535		2,100.00	

1945. SECOND VICTORY OVERPRINT ISSUE *Jan. 19.* Stamps of the Philippines with overprint 685 (2¢, 6¢, 20¢), 695 (10p, 20p), 686 (other values). 1: Regular postage; #545/555, 542 (10p), 543 (20p).

685 *Overprint*

686 *Overprint*

			UnFVF	UseFVF
685			UnFVF	UseFVF
2¢	deep rose		.30	.20
	FDC			3.50
686			UnFVF	UseFVF
4¢	deep yellow green		.30	.20
	FDC			3.50

687

			UnFVF	UseFVF
687			UnFVF	UseFVF
6¢	brown		.35	.20
	FDC			3.50

688   689

			UnFVF	UseFVF
688			UnFVF	UseFVF
8¢	red violet		.35	.20
	FDC			4.50
689			UnFVF	UseFVF
10¢	rose carmine		.35	.20
	FDC			4.50

690   691

			UnFVF	UseFVF
690			UnFVF	UseFVF
12¢	black		.40	.20
	FDC			5.00
691			UnFVF	UseFVF
16¢	deep blue		.50	.20
	FDC			6.00

692   693

			UnFVF	UseFVF
692			UnFVF	UseFVF
20¢	bistre		.60	.25
	FDC			8.00
693			UnFVF	UseFVF
30¢	deep red orange *(May 1, 1945)*		.85	.70
	FDC			5.00

694

695 *Overprint*

			UnFVF	UseFVF
694			UnFVF	UseFVF
1p	orange & black		2.25	.50
	FDC			12.00
695			UnFVF	UseFVF
10p	slate		80.00	17.50
	FDC			30.00
696			UnFVF	UseFVF
20p	red brown		70.00	22.50
	FDC			37.50

697 *2: Special delivery; #559*

697		UnFVF	UseFVF
20¢	violet	1.20	.80
	v. "IC" close together		3.50
	FDC		15.00

1946. JOSÉ RIZAL ISSUE *May 28. Engraved, perforated 11x10 1/2.*

698 *José Rizal*

699

698		UnFVF	UseFVF
2¢	sepia	.30	.20

Official; #698, overprint 560, O.B.

699		UnFVF	UseFVF
2¢	sepia *(June 19, 1946)*	.15	.15

Since July 4, 1946: Stamps of Republic of Philippines.

Envelopes and Wrappers

1899-1906. U.S. ENVELOPES OVERPRINT ISSUE overprinted below stamp in same color, except when mentioned. 1: (1899-1900), #EN391-417 overprinted.

EN1-8 *1¢ Philippines*

EN9-12 *2¢ Philippines*

Prices for major numbers are for adequately margined cut squares.

EN1		UnFVF	UseFVF
1¢	green on white, #391	3.50	2.00
	Entire	8.00	9.00
EN2		UnFVF	UseFVF
1¢	green on amber, #392	20.00	15.00
	Entire	45.00	45.00
EN3		UnFVF	UseFVF
1¢	green on amber, (R) #392	25.00	20.00
	Entire	65.00	60.00
EN4		UnFVF	UseFVF
1¢	green on buff, #393	15.00	15.00
	Entire	35.00	35.00
EN5		UnFVF	UseFVF
1¢	green on buff, (R) #393	35.00	35.00
	Entire	75.00	75.00
EN6		UnFVF	UseFVF
1¢	green on blue, #394	10.00	10.00
	Entire	35.00	35.00
EN7		UnFVF	UseFVF
1¢	green on blue, (R) #394	25.00	20.00
	Entire	75.00	70.00
EN8		UnFVF	UseFVF
1¢	green on manila, wrapper #396	1.75	1.50
	Entire, wrapper	6.00	5.50
EN9		UnFVF	UseFVF
2¢	carmine on white, #401	1.50	1.50
	Entire	5.00	3.50
EN10		UnFVF	UseFVF
2¢	carmine on amber, #402	6.00	5.50
	Entire	17.50	15.00
EN11		UnFVF	UseFVF
2¢	carmine on buff, #403	6.00	6.00

	Entire	20.00	15.00
EN12		UnFVF	UseFVF
2¢	carmine on blue, #404	6.00	7.50
	Entire	15.00	12.50

 EN13, 14, 15 *4¢ Philippines*

EN16, 17 *5¢ Philippines*

EN13		UnFVF	UseFVF
4¢	brown on amber, #411	45.00	45.00
	Entire	90.00	90.00
	x.Entire with double overprint	4,000.00	
EN14		UnFVF	UseFVF
4¢	brown on white, #413	10.00	10.00
	Entire	30.00	50.00
EN15		UnFVF	UseFVF
4¢	brown on amber, #414	60.00	60.00
	Entire	175.00	125.00
EN16		UnFVF	UseFVF
5¢	blue on white, #416	6.50	6.50
	Entire	15.00	15.00
EN17		UnFVF	UseFVF
5¢	blue on amber, #417	35.00	37.50
	Entire	90.00	125.00

#13: bust pointed and undraped; inner oval with teeth. #14, 15: bust broad and draped; inner oval without teeth.

 EN18-23 *1¢ Philippines*

EN24-28 *Philippines*

(1905), #EN418-428, 430, 433 overprinted

EN18		UnFVF	UseFVF
1¢	green on white, #418	1.25	1.25
	Entire	5.00	5.00
EN19		UnFVF	UseFVF
1¢	green on amber, #419	12.00	10.00
	Entire	25.00	30.00
EN20		UnFVF	UseFVF
1¢	green on buff, #420	15.00	12.00
	Entire	30.00	25.00
EN21		UnFVF	UseFVF
1¢	green on blue, #421	12.00	10.00
	Entire	30.00	30.00
EN22		UnFVF	UseFVF
1¢	green on manila, #422	22.50	25.00
	Entire	50.00	60.00
	x.Entire, double overprint	—	—
EN23		UnFVF	UseFVF
1¢	green on manila, wrapper, #423	10.00	10.00
	Entire wrapper	25.00	20.00
EN24		UnFVF	UseFVF
2¢	carmine on white, #423	5.00	4.00
	Entire	10.00	8.00
EN25		UnFVF	UseFVF
2¢	carmine, #425	20.00	17.50
	Entire	40.00	45.00
EN26		UnFVF	UseFVF
2¢	carmine on buff, #426	20.00	30.00
	Entire	50.00	
EN27		UnFVF	UseFVF
2¢	carmine on blue, #427	20.00	20.00
	Entire	40.00	
EN28		UnFVF	UseFVF
2¢	carmine on manila, wrapper #428	12.00	12.00
	Entire	25.00	20.00
	x.Entire, double overprint	—	—

EN29

			UnFVF	UseFVF
4¢	**brown** on amber, #430		60.00	80.00
	Entire		150.00	200.00
	x.Entire, double overprint		7,000.00	

EN30

			UnFVF	UseFVF
5¢	**blue** on amber, #433		60.00	
	Entire		125.00	

(1906), #EN434, 436 overprinted

EN31

			UnFVF	UseFVF
2¢	**carmine** on white, #434		45.00	30.00
	Entire		150.00	125.00

EN32

			UnFVF	UseFVF
2¢	**carmine** on white, #436		70.00	125.00
	Entire		250.00	300.00

1908. RIZAL NEW DESIGN ISSUE

EN33-38 *2¢ Rizal*

EN33

			UnFVF	UseFVF
2¢	**green** on white		.60	.30
	Entire		1.00	.80

EN34

			UnFVF	UseFVF
2¢	**green** on amber		4.50	2.50
	Entire		10.00	8.00

EN35

			UnFVF	UseFVF
2¢	**green** on buff		6.00	4.00
	Entire		10.00	10.00

EN36

			UnFVF	UseFVF
2¢	**green** on blue		6.00	4.00
	Entire		10.00	10.00

EN37

			UnFVF	UseFVF
2¢	**green** on manila		10.00	
	Entire		15.00	25.00

EN38

			UnFVF	UseFVF
2¢	**green** on manila, wrapper		2.00	2.25
	Entire		12.00	14.00

1908. MCKINLEY NEW DESIGN ISSUE

EN39-43 *4¢ McKinley*

EN39

			UnFVF	UseFVF
4¢	**carmine** on white		.50	.30
	Entire		1.75	1.50

EN40

			UnFVF	UseFVF
4¢	**carmine** on amber		5.00	3.00
	Entire		10.00	8.00

EN41

			UnFVF	UseFVF
4¢	**carmine** on blue		5.00	4.00
	Entire		10.00	9.00

EN42

			UnFVF	UseFVF
4¢	**carmine** on buff		5.00	4.00
	Entire		10.00	20.00

EN43

			UnFVF	UseFVF
4¢	**carmine** on manila		10.00	12.00
	Entire		25.00	30.00

1927. RIZAL ISSUE

EN44 *Rizal*

EN44

			UnFVF	UseFVF
2¢	**green** on white		12.50	10.00
	Entire		35.00	30.00

1935. JUAN DE LA CRUZ ISSUE *June 19.*

EN45, 46 *Juan de la Cruz*

EN45

			UnFVF	UseFVF
2¢	**carmine** on white *(1937)*		.40	.25
	Entire		1.50	1.00

EN46

			UnFVF	UseFVF
4¢	**olive green** on white *(1937)*		.60	.40
	Entire		2.00	1.50

1944. VICTORY ISSUE #EN45, 39, 46 handstamped in violet.

VICTORY EN47

EN46A

			UnFVF	UseFVF
2¢	**green** on white		—	—

EN47

			UnFVF	UseFVF
2¢	**carmine** on white		20.00	17.50
	Entire		50.00	80.00

EN48

			UnFVF	UseFVF
4¢	**carmine** on white		—	—
	Entire		1,000.00	1,000.00

EN49

			UnFVF	UseFVF
4¢	**olive green** on white		90.00	110.00
	Entire		150.00	175.00

Postal Cards, Message & Reply Cards, Official Cards

1900. U.S. #PC13, 15 OVERPRINT BELOW STAMP *Feb.* Prices are for entires of Postal and Official cards, for unsevered or detached Message and Reply cards.

PHILIPPINES. *Overprint*

PC1

			UnFVF	UseFVF
1¢	**black** on buff		20.00	15.00
	x.No period		50.00	

PC2

			UnFVF	UseFVF
2¢	**black** on buff		42.50	42.50

1900. U.S. #MRC2 OVERPRINTED; PC1 IN BLUE *Feb.*

PC3

			UnFVF	UseFVF
2¢ + 2¢	**blue** on white, unsevered		175.00	500.00
	m.Message card		25.00	25.00
	r.Reply card		25.00	25.00

1903. U.S. #PC17, 15 OVERPRINTED *Sept. 15.*

PHILIPPINES *Overprint*

PC4

			UnFVF	UseFVF
1¢	**black** on buff		1,500.00	1,000.00

PC5

			UnFVF	UseFVF
2¢	**black** on buff		750.00	650.00

1903. U.S. #MRC1, MRC2 OVERPRINTED IN BLACK

PHILIPPINES. *Overprint*

PC6

			UnFVF	UseFVF
1¢ + 1¢	**black** on buff, unsevered		150.00	350.00
	m.Message card		25.00	25.00
	r.Reply card		25.00	25.00

PC7

			UnFVF	UseFVF
2¢ + 2¢	**blue** on white, unsevered		300.00	
	m.Message card		50.00	
	r.Reply card		50.00	

#PC7 overprinted in blue: official status doubtful.

1904. U.S. #PC17, 15 Overprinted PC6

		UnFVF	UseFVF
PC8			
1¢	**black** on buff	45.00	35.00
PC9		UnFVF	UseFVF
2¢	**black** on buff	65.00	55.00

1906. U.S. #PC17, 15 Overprinted

PHILIPPINES *Overprint*

PC11-14 *Rizal*

		UnFVF	UseFVF
PC10			
1¢	**black** on buff	300.00	300.00
PC11		UnFVF	UseFVF
2¢	**black** on buff	1,800.00	1,500.00

1907-15. Rizal 2¢ Issue

		UnFVF	UseFVF
PC12			
2¢	**black** on buff	10.00	10.00
PC13		UnFVF	UseFVF
2¢	**blue** on light blue *(1912)*	8.00	8.00
PC14		UnFVF	UseFVF
2¢	**green** on buff *(1915)*	4.00	3.50

PC15-17 *McKinley*

		UnFVF	UseFVF
PC15			
2¢	**green** on amber *(1915)*	4.00	2.00

1907-15. McKinley 4¢ Issue

		UnFVF	UseFVF
PC16			
4¢	**black** on buff	22.50	22.50
PC17		UnFVF	UseFVF
4¢	**blue** on light blue *(1912)*	25.00	25.00
PC18		UnFVF	UseFVF
4¢	**green** on buff *(1915)*	18.00	15.00

1925. Official Card #PC14 Overprinted Left of Stamp

O.B. *Overprint*

		UnFVF	UseFVF
PC19			
2¢	**green** on buff	40.00	40.00

1935. New Official Card Design

1935. New design

		UnFVF	UseFVF
PC20			
2¢	**red** on buff	3.00	2.00
	v.Official (O.B.) overprint	14.00	17.50

O.B. PC21 *Official card. #PC20 overprinted*

		UnFVF	UseFVF
PC21			
2¢	**red** on buff	15.00	15.00

1938. Postal Card #PC20 Overprinted Left of Stamp

COMMONWEALTH	COMMONWEALTH	COMMONWEALTH
PC22	PC23	PC24

		UnFVF	UseFVF
PC22			
2¢	**red** on buff	2.50	1.75
PC23		UnFVF	UseFVF
2¢	**red** on buff	50.00	50.00
PC24		UnFVF	UseFVF
2¢	**red** on buff	2.50	1.65

O.B. PC25 *Overprint*

		UnFVF	UseFVF
PC25			
2¢	**red** on buff	15.00	15.00

1941. Official Card #PC24 Overprinted Left of Stamp

O.B. PC26 *Official card. #PC24 overprinted left of stamp*

		UnFVF	UseFVF
PC26			
2¢	**red** on buff	20.00	20.00

1941. Official Card Postal card of new design overprinted below stamp.

PC27 *Rizal*

Overprint   **O.B.**

		UnFVF	UseFVF
PC27			
2¢	**green** on buff	175.00	180.00

#PC27: not issued without overprint.

1944. #PC14, 23, 24 Handstamped in Violet

VICTORY PC28 *Overprint*

		UnFVF	UseFVF
PC28			
2¢	**green** on buff	180.00	220.00
PC29		UnFVF	UseFVF
2¢	**red** on buff	650.00	
PC30		UnFVF	UseFVF
2¢	**red** on buff	300.00	500.00

1945. New Design Overprinted at Left

PC31

Overprint **VICTORY**

		UnFVF	UseFVF
PC31			
2¢	**gray brown** on buff	1.50	1.00
	FDC		3.25

Note: Not issued without overprint.

Puerto Rico

Puerto Rico, the easternmost of the Greater Antilles, was discovered by Columbus, Nov. 19, 1493. Ponce de Leon conquered it for Spain, 1509. Except for minor outbreaks, Puerto Rico remained loyal to Spain during the Spanish-American liberation movement of the early 19th century. In the Spanish-American War, however, it welcomed the American invasion of July 1898. In 1899, it was ceded to the United States by Spain.

U.S. forces landed July 25, 1898. The first military postal station opened Aug. 3 at La Playa de Ponce.

The Commonwealth of Puerto Rico is a self-governing part of the U.S. with a primary Hispanic culture. Puerto Ricans are U.S. citizens.

The commonwealth political status of Puerto Rico gives the island's citizens virtually the same control over their internal affairs as the 50 states of the United States. However, they do not vote in national elections.

Puerto Rico is represented in Congress solely by a resident commissioner who has a voice, but no vote, except in committees.

Regular Postal Issues

1898. PONCE PROVISIONAL ISSUE

 191

			UnFVF	UseFVF
191				
5¢	**violet,** handstamp on white or yellowish paper		7,500.00	

1898. COAMO PROVISIONAL ISSUE

CORREOS
5 CTS.
COAMO

192 *Coamo provisional issue; type-set in sheet of 10; 4 varieties (Type I left); imperforate; violet control mark F. Santiago (mayor of Coamo).*

5 CTS.   **5 CTS**   **5 CTS.**
Type II   Type III   Type IV

		UnFVF	UseFVF
192			
5¢	**black** Type I	600.00	975.00
	t. Type II	625.00	975.00
	t1. Type III	650.00	1,050.00
	t2. Type IV	725.00	1,125.00

1899. PORTO RICO OVERPRINT ISSUE *Overprints at 36-degree angle (first listing) or 25-degree angle.*

 193 *Nos. 193-197 overprint at 25-degree angle*

 194 *Nos. 193-197 overprint at 36-degree angle*

		UnFVF	UseFVF
193			
1¢	**deep green**	4.25	1.40
	v1. Pair, 36-degrees & 25-degrees	19.50	
	v2. PORTO RICU overprint 36-degrees	25.00	
	a. Overprint 25-degrees	6.25	2.00
194		UnFVF	UseFVF
2¢	**carmine**	3.75	1.00
	v1. Pair, 36-degree & 25-degree overprints	15.00	
	a. PORTO RICO overprint 25-degrees	4.00	2.00
	av1. PORTU RICO overprint 25-degrees	35.00	20.00
	av2. FORTO RICO overprint	—	—
	av3. PURTO RICO overprint	—	

 195 *Nos. 193-197 overprint at 36-degree angle*

		UnFVF	UseFVF
195			
5¢	**dark blue**	6.00	2.00
196		UnFVF	UseFVF
8¢	**purple brown**	18.50	10.00
	a. Overprint 25-degrees	20.00	9.00
	v1. Pair, 36-degree & 25-degree overprints	75.00	
	v2. FORTO RICO overprint	90.00	60.00
	av3. PORTO RIC overprint	125.00	110.00
197		UnFVF	UseFVF
10¢	**orange brown**	12.50	4.00
	v1. FORTO RICO	85.00	70.00

1899. POSTAGE DUE ISSUE

 198 *Overprint at 36- or 25-degree angle*

		UnFVF	UseFVF
198			
1¢	**brown carmine**	20.00	5.00
199		UnFVF	UseFVF
2¢	**brown carmine**	10.00	5.00
200		UnFVF	UseFVF
10¢	**brown carmine**	150.00	60.00

1900. PUERTO RICO ISSUE

 201

		UnFVF	UseFVF
201			
1¢	**green**	3.25	.95
202		UnFVF	UseFVF
2¢	**carmine**	3.25	1.00
203		UnFVF	UseFVF
2¢	**red**	3.50	1.00
	v. Inverted overprint		8,250.00

Envelopes and Wrappers

1899-1900. ENVELOPES OVERPRINT ISSUE

PORTO RICO.   E1

		UnFVF	UseFVF
E1			
2¢	**green** on white, No. 344	4.25	8.00
	Entire	12.50	17.50
E2		UnFVF	UseFVF
5¢	**blue** on white, No. 369	7.25	8.75
	Entire	17.50	20.00

1899-1900. WRAPPER OVERPRINT IN COLOR OF STAMP ISSUE

PORTO RICO.   E3

		UnFVF	UseFVF
E3			
1¢	**green** on manila, wrapper No. 396	1.00	1.10
	Entire	2.90	42.00

1899-1900. ENVELOPE OVERPRINTED FOR PORTO RICO ISSUE

		UnFVF	UseFVF
E4			
2¢	**carmine** on white	3.00	3.00
E5		UnFVF	UseFVF
5¢	**blue** on white	8.00	9.00

1899-1900. ENVELOPES OVERPRINT ISSUE

PORTO RICO.   E6

E6			UnFVF	UseFVF
1¢	**green** on blue, No. 394			240.00
	Entire			1,100.00
E7			UnFVF	UseFVF
2¢	**carmine** on amber, No. 402		450.00	500.00
	Entire		1,100.00	1,200.00
E8			UnFVF	UseFVF
2¢	**carmine** on buff, No. 403			500.00
	Entire			1,100.00
E9			UnFVF	UseFVF
2¢	**carmine** on buff, No. 408			600.00
	Entire			1,300.00
E10			UnFVF	UseFVF
2¢	**carmine** on blue, No. 404			—
	Entire			4,000.00
E11			UnFVF	UseFVF
4¢	**brown** on white, No. 413		200.00	500.00
	Entire		400.00	650.00

1899-1900. ENVELOPES OVERPRINT PUERTO RICO ISSUE

PUERTO RICO.   E12

E12			UnFVF	UseFVF
2¢	**carmine** on white, No. 401		4.00	3.00
	Entire red		9.00	10.00
E13			UnFVF	UseFVF
2¢	**carmine** on buff, No. 403		—	325.00
	Entire		1,200.00	1,300.00
E14			UnFVF	UseFVF
2¢	**carmine** on buff, No. 408			375.00
	Entire			1,750.00
E15			UnFVF	UseFVF
5¢	**blue** on white, No. 416		14.00	14.00
	Entire blue		45.00	49.50

1899-1900. ENVELOPES OVERPRINT ISSUE

PUERTO RICO.   E16-E19

E16			UnFVF	UseFVF
1¢	**green** on buff, No. 393		20.00	40.00
	Entire		70.00	75.00
E17			UnFVF	UseFVF
1¢	**green** on blue, No. 394		20.00	40.00
	Entire		90.00	100.00
E18			UnFVF	UseFVF
1¢	**carmine** on buff, No. 403		20.00	40.00
	Entire		90.00	125.00
E19			UnFVF	UseFVF
1¢	**carmine** on blue, No. 404		20.00	40.00
	Entire		70.00	125.00

Postal Cards

1899-1900. U.S. POSTAL CARDS ISSUE

PORTO RICO.   PC1 *21mm long*

20mm long   PORTO RICO.

PUERTO RICO.   *21 1/2mm long*

PC1		UnFVF	UseFVF
1¢	**black** on buff	150.00	160.00
	v.20mm long imprint	1,000.00	1,300.00

No. PC1: 2 settings, one lighter than other.

PC2		UnFVF	UseFVF
1¢	**black** on buff	165.00	180.00
PC3		UnFVF	UseFVF
1¢	**black** on buff	150.00	180.00

Ryukyu Islands

Government of Ryukyu (Ree-YOU-kyoo) Islands in extreme western Pacific Ocean established under U.S. Military Government after World War II.

Area: 1,003 sq. mi. (includes Okinawa, Miyako and Yaeyama groups); Population: 945,465 (1970 est.); Language: Japanese, although Ryukyuans have own unwritten language; Capital: Naha, Okinawa.

B-Yen U.S. military currency: 100 sen = 1 yen (120 yen = $1.00 U.S.). 1958, Sep U.S. currency: 100 cents = 1 dollar.

Since the first Chinese invasions in 605 AD, the Ryukyus (also known as Luchu or Luchoo) have been constantly subject to such inroads by either the Japanese or the Chinese. U.S. Commodore Matthew Perry visited the islands in 1853 and in July 1854 concluded a treaty of friendship between the islands and the United States. In 1879, the Japanese dethroned the Ryukyuan regent and converted Luchu into a prefecture despite Chinese objections. With the Japanese attack on Pearl Harbor in 1941, it was apparent that any U.S. action in the area around Japan would hinge on bases in the Ryukyus, and on March 26, 1945, the U.S. 77th Infantry Division made first landings there. On July 2, 1945, the Okinawa campaign was officially termed completed — at a cost of 12,500 American dead, 36,650 wounded.

The Army Post Office (APO) was established when U.S. forces landed on Okinawa on April 1, 1945. About May of the same year, the U.S. forces established local free mail service. Beginning in 1946, the free service was suspended and up to July 1948, all mail matter was stamped "fee paid" by the originating post office. The cancels of this period can be distinguished by the fact that the date is expressed in the international Christian form of "1946," etc. in place of the normal Japanese imperial era date of "1921 (Showa)," etc.

During this period, a provisional 7 sen stamp was created by the Kume Island postmaster with the assistance of the U.S. Navy. This was mimeographed in black and handstamped in red with the official seal of the Kume Island postmaster.

In 1947, the postal authorities secured a limited quantity of Japanese stamps. These replaced the "fee paid" hand stamps, and were of 4 types: "Ken (examined," used in Amami Oshima area); "Hirata" (name of postmaster general of Okinawa); "Tomiyama" (postmaster general of Miyaka); and "Miyara" (postmaster general of Yaeyama).

On May 26, 1947, use of both, the hand-stamped prepaid covers and the revalidated adhesives was extended to international use, and by Nov. 1, 1947, international airmail was re-established on a stampless cover basis.

Ken   Hirata   Tomiyama   Miyara

Unless otherwise stated, all stamps were postpaid by the Government Bureau of Japanese Ministry of Finance.

Regular Postal Issues

1948-49. FIRST PICTORIAL ISSUE

1, 3 *Edible cycad bush*

2, 5 *Lily*

1		MNHVF	UseVF
5s	**purple magenta** *(July 1, 1948)*	2.00	4.00

2		MNHVF	UseVF
10s	pale green	1.50	2.25
3		MNHVF	UseVF
20s	pale green	1.25	2.25

4, 6 *Trading junk*

7 *Farmer and dawn*

4		MNHVF	UseVF
30s	red	2.00	3.00
5		MNHVF	UseVF
40s	purple magenta	50.00	50.00
6		MNHVF	UseVF
50s	dull ultramarine	1.50	4.00
7		MNHVF	UseVF
1y	dull ultramarine	400.00	225.00

1949. SECOND PICTORIAL ISSUE

7a		MNHVF	UseVF
5¢	purple magenta *(July 18, 1949)*	2.75	2.50
7b		MNHVF	UseVF
10¢	pale green	3.25	3.75
7c		MNHVF	UseVF
20¢	pale green	3.25	2.75
7d		MNHVF	UseVF
30¢	red	2.75	2.75
7e		MNHVF	UseVF
40¢	purple magenta	2.75	2.25
7f		MNHVF	UseVF
50¢	dull ultramarine	3.50	3.50
7g		MNHVF	UseVF
1y	dull ultramarine	3.50	4.75

1950-58. PICTORIAL ISSUE

8 *Roof tiles*   9 *Girl*   10 *Shuri Castle*

8		MNHVF	UseVF
50¢	carmine rose	.20	.15
	p. carmine rose on white paper *(Sept. 6, 1958)*	.35	.35
9		MNHVF	UseVF
1y	blue	2.40	2.00
10		MNHVF	UseVF
2y	purple	10.00	5.00

11 *Guardian dragon*   12 *Two women*   13 *Seashells*

11		MNHVF	UseVF
3y	carmine rose	20.00	8.00
12		MNHVF	UseVF
4y	dark slate green	10.00	8.00
13		MNHVF	UseVF
5y	emerald green	10.00	6.00

1950. AIRMAIL ISSUE

14 *Dove and Ryukyus*

14		MNHVF	UseVF
8y	blue	70.00	40.00
15		MNHVF	UseVF
12y	deep emerald	40.00	17.50
16		MNHVF	UseVF
16y	carmine rose	40.00	12.50

1950. SPECIAL DELIVERY ISSUE

17 *Dragon*

17		MNHVF	UseVF
5y	bright blue	30.00	12.50

1951. RYUKYU UNIVERSITY ISSUE

18 *Ryukyu University*

18		MNHVF	UseVF
3y	chocolate *(Feb. 12, 1951)*	50.00	20.00

1951. ARBOR WEEK ISSUE

19 *Pine tree*

19		MNHVF	UseVF
3y	emerald green *(Feb. 19, 1951)*	25.00	15.00

1951-54. AIRMAIL ISSUE

20 *Heavenly maiden*

20		MNHVF	UseVF
13y	Prussian blue *(Oct.1, 1951)*	1.75	1.00
21		MNHVF	UseVF
18y	light green *(Oct. 1, 1951)*	3.25	3.00
22		MNHVF	UseVF
30y	bright magenta *(Oct. 1, 1951)*	4.00	1.50
23		MNHVF	UseVF
40y	purple *(Aug. 16, 1954)*	6.00	4.00
24		MNHVF	UseVF
50y	yellow orange *(Aug. 16, 1954)*	8.00	5.00

1952. OVERPRINT ISSUE Nos. 25, 26 overprinted in sheets of 100 (10 x 10).

No. 25, types 1-6: 1st printing: narrow bar spacing, top characters small (1), large (2). 2nd printing: wide bar spacing, top characters small (3), large (4), or mixed (5). 3rd printing: wide bar spacing, top characters thin, 10 yen about 7.8mm long (instead of 7mm).

No. 26, types 3-5: top characters small (3), large (4), or mixed (5).

 25

		MNHVF	UseVF
25			
10y on 50s T1, 2 *(Jan. 1, 1952)*		10.00	8.00
v. T3, 4 *(June 5, 1952)*		30.00	20.00
v1. T5 *(June 5, 1952)*, T6 *(Dec. 8, 1952)*		37.50	37.50
26		MNHVF	UseVF
100y on 2y purple, T4 *(June 16, 1952)*		1,200.00	900.00
v. T3			
v1. T5			

1952. ESTABLISHMENT OF RYUKYU ISLAND GOVERNMENT ISSUE

27 *Dove, bean sprout, and Ryukyus*

		MNHVF	UseVF
27			
3y	**deep claret** *(April 1, 1952)*	100.00	30.00

1952-53. HISTORICAL SITES ISSUE

28 *Madanbashi Bridge*

29 *Main hall, Shuri Castle*

		MNHVF	UseVF
28			
1y	**rose red**	.20	.20
29		MNHVF	UseVF
2y	**deep emerald**	.25	.30

30 *Shuri Gate*

31 *Stone gate, Soenji Temple*

		MNHVF	UseVF
30			
3y	**turquoise**	.50	.30
31		MNHVF	UseVF
6y	**blue** *(Jan. 20, 1953)*	4.00	2.50

32 *Benzaiten-do Temple*

33 *Sonohan Utaki, Shuri Castle*

		MNHVF	UseVF
32			
10y	**bright rose red** *(Jan. 20, 1953)*	1.75	.70
33		MNHVF	UseVF
30y	**olive green** *(Jan. 20, 1953)*	8.00	5.00
	a. light olive green	25.00	

34 *Tamaudun, Shuri*

35 *Stone bridge, Hosho Pond, Enkaku Temple*

		MNHVF	UseVF
34			
50y	**rose purple** *(Jan. 20, 1953)*	12.00	5.00
35		MNHVF	UseVF
100y	**brown claret** *(Jan. 20, 1953)*	15.00	3.00

1953. MATTHEW PERRY ISSUE

36 *Reception at Shuri Castle*

37 *Perry and the American fleet*

		MNHVF	UseVF
36			
3y	**purple magenta**	12.00	5.00
37		MNHVF	UseVF
6y	**dark cobalt**	1.50	1.50

1953. NEWSPAPER WEEK ISSUE

38 *Chofu Ota*

		MNHVF	UseVF
38			
4y	**yellow brown** *(Oct. 1, 1953)*	12.00	4.00

1954-55. INDUSTRIAL ARTS ISSUE

39 *Pottery*

40 *Lacquerware*

41 *Textiles*

		MNHVF	UseVF
39			
4y	**brown** *(June 25, 1954)*	.75	.50
40		MNHVF	UseVF
15y	**light scarlet** *(June 20, 1955)*	2.75	1.00
41		MNHVF	UseVF
20y	**yellow orange** *(June 20, 1955)*	3.50	2.00

1954. NEWSPAPER WEEK ISSUE

42 *Shigo Toma*

42
4y   blue *(Oct. 1, 1954)*   MNHVF 12.00   UseVF 4.00

1955. SWEET POTATO ISSUE Celebrated the 350th anniversary of the introduction of the sweet potato to the Ryukyu Islands.

43 *Noguni Shrine*

43
4y   blue *(Nov. 26, 1955)*   MNHVF 10.00   UseVF 6.00

1956. ARBOR WEEK ISSUE

44 *Trees*

44
4y   blue green *(Feb. 18, 1956)*   MNHVF 10.00   UseVF 4.00

1956. CEREMONIAL DANCERS ISSUE

45 *Willow dance*   46 *Straw hat dance*   47 *Warrior costume*

45
5y   rose purple *(May 1, 1956)*   MNHVF 1.25   UseVF .50
46
8y   blue violet   MNHVF 1.50   UseVF 1.50
47
14y   dark red brown *(June 8, 1956)*   MNHVF 2.75   UseVF 1.75

1956. TELEPHONE ISSUE

48 *Telephone*

48
4y   blue violet   MNHVF 15.00   UseVF 6.00

1956. NEW YEAR'S ISSUE

49 *Pine, bamboo, and plum*

49
2y   multicolored *(Dec. 1, 1956)*   MNHVF 2.50   UseVF 1.00

1957. AIRMAIL ISSUE

50 *Heavenly maiden with flute*

50
15y   blue green *(Aug. 1, 1957)*   MNHVF 5.00   UseVF 2.00
51
20y   deep carmine   MNHVF 7.50   UseVF 5.00
52
35y   light green   MNHVF 12.50   UseVF 6.00
53
45y   light red brown   MNHVF 15.00   UseVF 7.50
54
60y   violet black   MNHVF 20.00   UseVF 9.00

1957. NEWSPAPER WEEK ISSUE

55 *Map of Okinawa*

55
4y   deep violet blue *(Oct. 1, 1957)*   MNHVF 1.00   UseVF .75

1957. NEW YEAR ISSUE

56 *Phoenix*

56
2y   multicolored *(Dec. 1, 1957)*   MNHVF .40   UseVF .20

1958. POSTAGE STAMP ISSUE celebrated the 10th anniversary of Ryukyu stamps.

57 *Ryukyu stamps*

57
4y   multicolored   MNHVF .75   UseVF .60

1958-61. CHANGE TO U.S. CURRENCY ISSUE

58 *Yen symbol and potter sign*

58			MNHVF	UseVF
1/2¢	yellow orange		1.00	.15
	v. Pair, imperforate		750.00	.15

59			MNHVF	UseVF
1¢	pale green		1.20	.15

60			MNHVF	UseVF
2¢	dark blue		1.35	.15

61			MNHVF	UseVF
3¢	dark rose red		1.25	.15

62			MNHVF	UseVF
4¢	light emerald		1.75	.20

63			MNHVF	UseVF
5¢	brown salmon		4.00	.20

64			MNHVF	UseVF
10¢	turquoise green		5.00	.25

65			MNHVF	UseVF
25¢	blue violet		7.00	.50
	p. Gummed paper (April 20, 1961)		8.00	.60

66			MNHVF	UseVF
50¢	gray black		15.00	.75
	p. Gummed paper (April 20, 1961)		10.00	1.25

67			MNHVF	UseVF
$1	light red violet		10.00	1.50

1958. RESTORATION OF SHURI MON ISSUE The Gate of Courtesy is on the road to Shuri City.

68 *Gate of Courtesy*

68			MNHVF	UseVF
3¢	multicolored (Oct. 15, 1958)		1.50	1.00

1958. NEW YEAR'S ISSUE

69 *Lion dance*

69			MNHVF	UseVF
1 1/2¢	multicolored (Dec. 10, 1958)		.35	.20

1959. ARBOR WEEK ISSUE

70 *Landscape*

70			MNHVF	UseVF
3¢	emerald green, blue & red (April 30, 1959)		.80	.75
	v. red omitted		—	

1959. JAPANESE BIOLOGICAL EDUCATION SOCIETY ISSUE

71 *Yonaguni moth*

71			MNHVF	UseVF
3¢	multicolored (July 23, 1959)		1.50	1.00

1959. NATIVE FLORA AND FAUNA ISSUE

72 *Hibiscus*   73 *Moorish Idol*   74 *Seashell*

72			MNHVF	UseVF
1/2¢	multicolored (Aug. 10, 1959)		.30	.15

73			MNHVF	UseVF
3¢	multicolored		1.25	.25

74			MNHVF	UseVF
8¢	multicolored		8.00	3.75

75 *Butterfly*

76 *Jellyfish*

75			MNHVF	UseVF
13¢	multicolored		2.50	1.25

76			MNHVF	UseVF
17¢	deep violet blue, chestnut & yellow		17.50	7.50

1959. NEW YEAR'S ISSUE

77			MNHVF	UseVF
1 1/2¢	multicolored & gold (Dec. 1, 1959)		.60	.30

1959. AIRMAIL OVERPRINT ISSUE

78

78			MNHVF	UseVF
9¢ on 15y blue green (Dec. 20, 1959)			5.00	2.00
	v. Inverted overprint		700.00	

79			MNHVF	UseVF
14¢ on 20y deep carmine			8.00	4.00

80			MNHVF	UseVF
19¢ on 35y light green			9.00	5.00

81			MNHVF	UseVF
27¢ on 45y light red brown			10.00	6.00

82			MNHVF	UseVF
35¢ on 60y violet black			12.50	4.00

Several varieties of overprints exist.

1960. RYUKYU UNIVERSITY ISSUE celebrates its 10th anniversary.

83 *University badge*

83			MNHVF	UseVF
3¢	multicolored		1.00	.60

1960-61. FLORA AND FAUNA REDRAWN ISSUE with Japanese inscription.

		83A		83B		84

		MNHVF	UseVF
83A			
1/2¢	**multicolored** *(Oct. 1961)*	.30	.30
83B		MNHVF	UseVF
3¢	**multicolored** *(Aug. 23, 1961)*	1.00	.25
84		MNHVF	UseVF
8¢	**multicolored** *(1961)*	1.00	.75

85

86

		MNHVF	UseVF
85			
13¢	**multicolored** *(1961)*	1.50	.75
86		MNHVF	UseVF
17¢	**multicolored** *(1961)*	10.00	3.50

1960. AIRMAIL OVERPRINT ON REGULAR ISSUE

	87		88		89

		MNHVF	UseVF
87			
9¢ on 4y brown #39 *(Aug. 3, 1961)*		4.00	1.00
v.	Inverted overprint	3,500.00	
88		MNHVF	UseVF
14¢ on 5y rose purple, overprinted brown #45		3.00	1.25
89		MNHVF	UseVF
19¢ on 15y light claret, overprinted red #40		3.00	1.75

90

91

		MNHVF	UseVF
90			
27¢ on 14y dark red brown, overprinted blue #47		5.00	3.00
91		MNHVF	UseVF
35¢ on 20y yellow orange, overprinted green #41		6.00	3.00

1960. DANCES ISSUE showed traditional Ryukyu dances.

92 *Munjuru*

93 *Inoha*

		MNHVF	UseVF
92			
1¢	**multicolored** *(Nov. 1, 1962)*	1.00	.75

		MNHVF	UseVF
93		2.25	1.00
2 1/2¢	**multicolored**		

94 *Batoma*

95 *Banafu*

		MNHVF	UseVF
94		1.00	.50
5¢	**multicolored**		
95		MNHVF	UseVF
10¢	**multicolored**	1.00	.50

1960. ATHLETIC ISSUE

96 *Torch and Nago Bay*   97 *Runners*

		MNHVF	UseVF
96		4.00	1.75
3¢	**light blue, deep blue green & orange red** *(Nov. 8, 1960)*		
97		MNHVF	UseVF
8¢	**orange yellow & blue green**	1.00	1.00

1960. NEW YEAR'S ISSUE

98 *Bulls fighting*

		MNHVF	UseVF
98		2.00	1.50
1 1/2¢	**bistre, blue & brown red** *(Dec. 10, 1960)*		

1960. SECOND NATIONAL CENSUS ISSUE

99 *Egret in flight*

		MNHVF	UseVF
99		6.00	2.00
3¢	**brown**		

1961. ARBOR WEEK ISSUE

100 *Pine tree*

		MNHVF	UseVF
100		1.75	1.25
3¢	**yellow green, red & blue green** *(May 1, 1961)*		

1961. NAHA CITY ISSUE

101 *City, ship, and boat*

101			MNHVF	UseVF
3¢	turquoise blue *(May 20, 1961)*		2.00	1.00

1961-71. DANCERS ISSUE Country name added in English.

102 *Munjuru*

102A *Inoba*

102			MNHVF	UseVF
1¢	multicolored *(Dec. 5, 1961)*		.20	.20
102A			MNHVF	UseVF
2 1/2¢	multicolored *(June 20, 1962)*		.20	.20

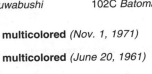

102B *Nuwabushi*   102C *Batoma*   102D *Banafu*

102B			MNHVF	UseVF
4¢	multicolored *(Nov. 1, 1971)*		.20	.20
102C			MNHVF	UseVF
5¢	multicolored *(June 20, 1961)*		.25	.20
102D			MNHVF	UseVF
10¢	multicolored *(June 20, 1962)*		.50	.30

103 *Shundun*

104 *Baidori*

103			MNHVF	UseVF
20¢	multicolored *(Jan. 20, 1964)*		2.25	1.25
104			MNHVF	UseVF
25¢	multicolored *(Feb. 1, 1962)*		1.25	1.00

105 *Nobori-kuduchi*

106 *Koteibushi*

105			MNHVF	UseVF
50¢	multicolored *(Sept. 1, 1961)*		2.50	1.00
106			MNHVF	UseVF
$1	multicolored *(Sept. 1, 1961)*		5.00	.50

1961. AIRMAIL ISSUE

107 *Heavenly maiden*

108 *Heavenly maiden*

107			MNHVF	UseVF
9¢	multicolored *(Sept. 21, 1961)*		.50	.20

108			MNHVF	UseVF
14¢	multicolored		.75	.40

109 *Wind god*

110 *Wind god*

109			MNHVF	UseVF
19¢	multicolored		.80	.60
110			MNHVF	UseVF
27¢	multicolored		2.50	.75

111 *Heavenly maiden and hillside*

111			MNHVF	UseVF
35¢	multicolored		2.00	1.00

1961. MERGER OF TOWNSHIPS ISSUE Takamine, Kanegushiku, and Miwa merged into Itoman.

112 *White Silver Temple*

112			MNHVF	UseVF
3¢	red brown *(Oct. 1, 1961)*		2.00	1.00
	v. Horizontal pair, imperforate between		300.00	
	v1. Vertical pair, imperforate between		500.00	

1961. BOOK WEEK ISSUE

113 *Books*

113			MNHVF	UseVF
3¢	multicolored *(Nov. 12, 1961)*		1.25	1.00

1961. NEW YEAR'S ISSUE

114 *Eagles and sun*

114			MNHVF	UseVF
1 1/2¢	gold, vermilion & black *(Dec. 10, 1961)*		2.50	1.00

Nos. 115-118 are not assigned.

1962. RYUKYU ISLANDS GOVERNMENT ISSUE

119 *Government buildings*

119
1 1/2¢   **multicolored** *(April 1, 1962)*

	MNHVF	UseVF
	.70	.50

120
3¢   **blue green, red & greenish gray**

	MNHVF	UseVF
	1.00	.75

1962. MALARIA ISSUE draws attention to the World Health Organization drive to eradicate malaria.

121 *Anopheles mosquito*

122 *Malaria-eradication symbol*

121
3¢   **multicolored** *(April 7, 1962)*

	MNHVF	UseVF
	.75	.50

122
8¢   **deep blue, yellow & red**

	MNHVF	UseVF
	1.00	.85

1962. CHILDREN'S DAY ISSUE

123 *Dolls and toys*

123
3¢   **multicolored** *(May 5, 1962)*

	MNHVF	UseVF
	1.25	.80

1962. FLOWER ISSUE

124 *Hibiscus tiliacus*

125 *Eythrila varieta orientalis*

126 *Schima superba*

124
1/2¢   **multicolored** *(June 1, 1962)*

	MNHVF	UseVF
	.20	.20

125
3¢   **multicolored**

	MNHVF	UseVF
	.30	.20

126
8¢   **multicolored**

	MNHVF	UseVF
	.35	.35

127 *Impatiens balsamina*

128 *Alpinia speciosa*

127
13¢   **multicolored**

	MNHVF	UseVF
	.50	.50

128
17¢   **multicolored**

	MNHVF	UseVF
	.75	.75

See also Nos. 142, 244, 244A.

1962. STAMP WEEK ISSUE

129 *Bowl*

129
3¢   **multicolored** *(July 5, 1962)*

	MNHVF	UseVF
	3.50	2.00

1962. JAPAN KENDO MEETING ISSUE

130 *Kendo practitioner*

130
3¢   **multicolored**

	MNHVF	UseVF
	3.75	2.00

1962. NEW YEAR'S ISSUE

131 *Rabbit near water, textile design*

131
1 1/2¢   **multicolored** *(Dec. 10, 1962)*

	MNHVF	UseVF
	1.25	.75

1963. ADULT DAY ISSUE

132 *Stone relief of man and woman*

132
3¢   **gold, black & blue** *(Jan. 15, 1963)*

	MNHVF	UseVF
	1.00	.75

1963. REFORESTATION ISSUE

133 *Trees*

133
3¢   **multicolored** *(March 25, 1963)*

	MNHVF	UseVF
	1.00	.75

1963. DEFINITIVE ISSUE

134 *Gooseneck cactus*

134
1 1/2¢   multicolored *(April 5, 1963)*   MNHVF .20   UseVF .20
1963. OPENING OF ROUND ROAD ISSUE

135 *Okinawa*

135
3¢   multicolored *(April 30, 1963)*   MNHVF 1.50   UseVF .75
1963. BIRD WEEK ISSUE

136 *Hawks*

136
3¢   multicolored *(May 10, 1963)*   MNHVF 1.25   UseVF .75
1963. SHIOYA BRIDGE ISSUE Commemorates opening of bridge over Shioya Bay.

137 *Shioya Bridge*

137
3¢   multicolored *(June 5, 1963)*   MNHVF 1.25   UseVF .75
1963. STAMP WEEK ISSUE

138 *Tsuikin-wan lacquerware*

138
3¢   multicolored *(July 1, 1963)*   MNHVF 3.75   UseVF 2.00
1963. AIRMAIL ISSUE

139 *Plane over gate*

140 *Airliner*

139
5 1/2¢   multicolored *(Aug. 28, 1963)*   MNHVF .35   UseVF .20
140
7¢   multicolored   MNHVF .40   UseVF .20

1963. JUNIOR CHAMBER OF COMMERCE ISSUE meeting of the International organization held at Naha, Okinawa.

141 *Map and JCI emblem*

141
3¢   multicolored *(Sept. 16, 1963)*   MNHVF .85   UseVF .60
1963. DEFINITIVE ISSUE

142 *Mamaomoto*

142
15¢   Mamaomoto *(Oct. 15, 1963)*   MNHVF 1.00   UseVF .60
1963. NATIONAL CULTURAL TREASURES ISSUE

143 *Nakagusuku Castle*

143
3¢   multicolored *(Nov. 1, 1963)*   MNHVF .85   UseVF .50
1963. HUMAN RIGHTS ISSUE celebrated the 15th anniversary of the Universal Declaration of Human Rights.

144 *Stylized flame*

144
3¢   multicolored *(Dec. 10, 1963)*   MNHVF .85   UseVF .50
1963. NEW YEAR'S ISSUE

145 *Dragon*

145
1 1/2¢   multicolored *(Dec. 10, 1963)*   MNHVF .65   UseVF .20
No. 146 is not assigned.

The minimum stamp value in this catalog (20¢) represents the cost to a retail stamp dealer to maintain in inventory and supply to a collector on demand a single copy of even the most common stamp in fault-free condition and a grade of fine-to-very-fine.

1964. MOTHER'S DAY ISSUE

147 *Carnation*

147
3¢   **multicolored** *(May 10, 1964)*   MNHVF .50   UseVF .35

1964. AGRICULTURAL CENSUS ISSUE

148 *Pineapples*

148
3¢   **multicolored** *(June 1, 1964)*   MNHVF .50   UseVF .35

1964. PHILATELIC WEEK ISSUE

149 *Minsah obi (sash woven of kapok)*

149
3¢   **multicolored, rose**   MNHVF .60   UseVF .35
    a. deep carmine   .85   .50

1964. GIRL SCOUT ISSUE 10th anniversary.

150 *Girl Scout*

150
3¢   **multicolored** *(Aug. 31, 1964)*   MNHVF .50   UseVF .35

1964. RYUKYU-JAPAN MICROWAVE SYSTEM ISSUE

151 *Shuri relay tower*

152 *Parabolic antenna*

151
3¢   **green** *(Sept. 1, 1964)*   MNHVF 1.25   UseVF .75
    v. Overprint "1" inverted overprint in date   25.00   20.00
      (pos 8)

152
8¢   **ultramarine**   MNHVF 2.00   UseVF 1.50

Broken type and inking varieties exist. Shifted overprints are fairly common.

1964. OLYMPIC TORCH FLIGHT ISSUE The Olympic torch reached Okinawa enroute to Tokyo.

153 *Gate of Courtesy*

153
3¢   **multicolored** *(Sept. 7, 1964)*   MNHVF .30   UseVF .20

1964-65. KARATE ISSUE

154 *Naihanchi stance*

155 *Makiwara*

154
3¢   **multicolored** *(Oct. 5, 1964)*   MNHVF .60   UseVF .25
155
3¢   **multicolored** *(Feb. 5, 1965)*   MNHVF .45   UseVF .25

156 *Kumite*

156
3¢   **multicolored** *(June 5, 1965)*   MNHVF .45   UseVF .25

1964. NATIONAL CULTURAL TREASURES ISSUE

157 *Miyara Dunchi, 1819*

157
3¢   **multicolored** *(Nov. 1, 1964)*   MNHVF .30   UseVF .25

1964. NEW YEAR'S ISSUE

158 *Snake and iris*

158
1 1/2¢   **multicolored** *(Dec. 10, 1964)*   MNHVF .30   UseVF .20

1965. Boy Scout Issue 10th anniversary Ryukyuan Boy Scouts.

159 *Scouts*

159		MNHVF	UseVF
3¢	multicolored (Feb. 6, 1965)	.50	.25

1965. Kin Power Plant Issue

160 *Kin Power Plant*

160		MNHVF	UseVF
3¢	multicolored (July 1, 1965)	.30	.25

1965. Onoyama Athletic Facility Issue

161 *Main stadium*

161		MNHVF	UseVF
3¢	multicolored (July 1, 1965)	.30	.25

1965. Philatelic Week Issue

162 *Samisen*

162		MNHVF	UseVF
3¢	multicolored (July 1, 1965)	.50	.25

1965. International Cooperation Year Issue

163		MNHVF	UseVF
3¢	multicolored (July 1, 1965)	.30	.20

1965. Naha City Hall Issue

164 *Naha City Hall*

164		MNHVF	UseVF
3¢	multicolored (Sept. 18, 1965)	.30	.20

1965. Turtle Issue

165 *Box turtle*

166 *Hawksbill turtle*

165		MNHVF	UseVF
3¢	brown (Oct. 20, 1965)	.40	.25
166		MNHVF	UseVF
3¢	white (Jan. 20, 1966)	.40	.25

167 *Asian terrapin*

167		MNHVF	UseVF
3¢	multicolored (April 20, 1966)	.35	.25

1965. New Year's Issue

168 *Horse*

168		MNHVF	UseVF
1 1/2¢	multicolored (Dec. 10, 1965)	.20	.15
	v. gold omitted	500.00	

1966. Wildlife Conservation Issue

169 *Okinawa woodpecker*   170 *Sika deer*   171 *Dugong*

169		MNHVF	UseVF
3¢	multicolored (Feb. 15, 1966)	.30	.25
170		MNHVF	UseVF
3¢	multicolored (March 15, 1966)	.30	.25
171		MNHVF	UseVF
3¢	multicolored (April 20, 1966)	.30	.25

1966. Bird Week Issue

172 *Bungalow swallow*

172		MNHVF	UseVF
3¢	multicolored (May 10, 1966)	.20	.20

1966. Memorial Day Issue End of the Battle of Okinawa 1945.

173 *Lilies and ruins of city*

173		MNHVF	UseVF
3¢	multicolored (June 23, 1966)	.20	.20

1966. UNIVERSITY OF RYUKYUS ISSUE

174 *University of Ryukyus*

174
3¢ **multicolored** *(July 1, 1966)*

	MNHVF	UseVF
	.20	.20

1966. PHILATELIC WEEK ISSUE

175 *18th century lacquerware*

175
3¢ **multicolored** *(August 1966)*

	MNHVF	UseVF
	.20	.20

1966. 20TH ANNIVERSARY UNESCO ISSUE

176 *Tile-roofed house*

176
3¢ **multicolored** *(Sept. 20, 1966)*

	MNHVF	UseVF
	.20	.20

1966. MUSEUM ISSUE

177 *Museum building*

177
3¢ **multicolored** *(Oct. 6, 1966)*

	MNHVF	UseVF
	.20	.20

1966. NATIONAL CULTURAL TREASURES ISSUE

178 *Tomb of Nakasone-Tuimya Genga*

178
3¢ **multicolored** *(Nov. 1, 1966)*

	MNHVF	UseVF
	.20	.20

1966. NEW YEAR'S ISSUE

179 *Ram in iris wreath*

179
1 1/2¢ **multicolored** *(Dec. 10, 1966)*

	MNHVF	UseVF
	.20	.15

1966-67. TROPICAL FISH ISSUE

180 *Amphipron frenatus*

181 *Ostracion tuberculotus*

180
3¢ **multicolored** *(Dec. 20, 1966)*

	MNHVF	UseVF
	.30	.20

181
3¢ **multicolored** *(Jan. 10, 1967)*

	MNHVF	UseVF
	.30	.20

182 *Forcipiger longirostris*

183 *Balistoides (niger) conspicilum*

182
3¢ **multicolored** *(April 10, 1967)*

	MNHVF	UseVF
	.30	.20

183
3¢ **multicolored** *(May 25, 1967)*

	MNHVF	UseVF
	.30	.20

184 *Chaetodon ephippium*

184
3¢ **multicolored** *(June 10, 1967)*

	MNHVF	UseVF
	.30	.20

No. 185 is not assigned.

1967. PHILATELIC WEEK ISSUE

186 *Tsuboya Urn*

186
3¢ **multicolored** *(April 20, 1967)*

	MNHVF	UseVF
	.25	.20

1967-68. SEASHELL ISSUE

187 *Mitra mitra*

188 *Murex Aranea triremis*

189 *Lambis Harpago chiragra*

			MNHVF	UseVF
187 3¢	**multicolored** *(July 20, 1967)*		.25	.20
188 3¢	**multicolored** *(Aug. 30, 1967)*		.25	.20
189 3¢	**multicolored** *(Jan. 18, 1968)*		.30	.20

190 *Turba Olearia mamoratus*

191 *Euprotomus bulla*

			MNHVF	UseVF
190 3¢	**multicolored** *(Feb. 20, 1968)*		.30	.20
191 3¢	**multicolored** *(June 5, 1968)*		.60	.30

1967. INTERNATIONAL TOURIST YEAR ISSUE

192 *Red-tiled roofs*

			MNHVF	UseVF
192 3¢	**multicolored** *(Sept. 11, 1967)*		.25	.20

1967. ANTI-TUBERCULOSIS ISSUE

193 *Mobile TB unit*

			MNHVF	UseVF
193 3¢	**multicolored** *(Oct. 13, 1967)*		.25	.20

1967. NATIONAL CULTURAL TREASURES ISSUE

194 *Hojo Bridge, Enkaku Temple*

			MNHVF	UseVF
194 3¢	**multicolored**		.25	.20

1967. NEW YEAR'S ISSUE

195 *Monkey*

			MNHVF	UseVF
195 1 1/2¢	**multicolored** *(Dec. 11, 1967)*		.25	.20

1967. TV STATION ISSUE

196 *Tower & map*

			MNHVF	UseVF
196 3¢	**multicolored** *(Dec. 22, 1967)*		.20	.20

1968. VACCINATION ISSUE honored 120th anniversary of first vaccinations in Ryukyu.

197 *Dr. Kijin Nakachi and assistant*

			MNHVF	UseVF
197 3¢	**multicolored** *(March 15, 1968)*		.20	.20

1968. PHILATELIC WEEK ISSUE

198 *Pill box*

			MNHVF	UseVF
198 3¢	**multicolored** *(April 18, 1968)*		.50	.40

1968. LIBRARY WEEK ISSUE

199 *Youth running toward library*

			MNHVF	UseVF
199 3¢	**multicolored** *(May 13, 1968)*		.30	.20

1968. RYUKYUAN POSTAGE ISSUE celebrates 20th anniversary of Ryukyuan postage stamps.

200 *Mail carriers and early stamp*

			MNHVF	UseVF
200 3¢	**multicolored** *(May 13, 1968)*		.30	.20

1968. ENKAKU TEMPLE RECONSTRUCTION ISSUE

201 *Main gate*

201			MNHVF	UseVF
3¢	multicolored (July 15, 1968)		.30	.20

1968. ELDERLY PEOPLE'S DAY ISSUE

202 *Old man's dance*

202			MNHVF	UseVF
3¢	multicolored (Sept. 15, 1968)		.30	.20

1968-69. CRAB ISSUE

203 *Mictyris longicarpus*

204 *Uca dubia*

203			MNHVF	UseVF
3¢	multicolored (Oct. 10, 1968)		.40	.20
204			MNHVF	UseVF
3¢	multicolored (Feb. 5, 1969)		.40	.20

205 *Baptozius vinosus*

206 *Cardisoma carnifex*

205			MNHVF	UseVF
3¢	multicolored (March 5, 1969)		.40	.25
206			MNHVF	UseVF
3¢	multicolored (May 15, 1969)		.50	.25

207 *Ocypode Ceratophthalma*

207			MNHVF	UseVF
3¢	multicolored (June 2, 1969)		.50	.25

1968. NATIONAL CULTURAL TREASURES ISSUE

208 *Saraswati Pavilion*

208			MNHVF	UseVF
3¢	multicolored (Nov. 1, 1968)		.30	.20

1968. ALL-JAPAN SOFTBALL TENNIS TOURNAMENT ISSUE

209 *Tennis player*

209			MNHVF	UseVF
3¢	multicolored (Nov. 3, 1968)		.50	.20

1968. NEW YEAR'S ISSUE

210 *Cock and iris*

210			MNHVF	UseVF
1 1/2¢	multicolored (Dec. 10, 1968)		.20	.20

1969. BOXING ISSUE 20th anniversary all-Japan amateur boxing championships.

211 *Boxer*

211			MNHVF	UseVF
3¢	multicolored (Jan. 3, 1969)		.30	.20

1969. PHILATELIC WEEK ISSUE

212 *Ink slab screen*

212			MNHVF	UseVF
3¢	multicolored (April 17, 1969)		.30	.20

1969. UHF Circuit System Issue

213 *Box antenna*

213		MNHVF	UseVF
3¢	multicolored *(July 1, 1969)*	.30	.20

1969. Formative Education Conference Issue

214 *Gate of Courtesy*

214		MNHVF	UseVF
3¢	multicolored *(Aug. 1, 1969)*	.30	.20

1969. Folklore & Festival Issue

215 *Tug of war festival*

216 *Hari boat race*

215		MNHVF	UseVF
3¢	multicolored *(Aug. 1, 1969)*	.35	.20
216		MNHVF	UseVF
3¢	multicolored *(Sept. 5, 1969)*	.45	.20

217 *Izaiho ceremony*

218 *Ushideiku*

217		MNHVF	UseVF
3¢	multicolored *(Oct. 3, 1969)*	.45	.20
218		MNHVF	UseVF
3¢	multicolored *(Jan. 20, 1970)*	.55	.20

219 *Unjiyami*

219		MNHVF	UseVF
3¢	multicolored *(Feb. 27, 1970)*	.55	.20

1969. Provisional Issue overprint on No. 125.

220

220		MNHVF	UseVF
1/2¢ on 3¢ multicolored		.40	.30

1969. National Cultural Treasures Issue

221 *Nakamura-ke farm house*

221		MNHVF	UseVF
3¢	multicolored *(Nov. 1, 1969)*	.20	.20

1969. New Year's Issue

222 *Dog and flowers*

222		MNHVF	UseVF
1 1/2¢	multicolored *(Dec. 10, 1969)*	.25	.15

1969. Emigration to Hawaii Issue

223 *Kyuzo Toyama statue*

223		MNHVF	UseVF
3¢	multicolored *(Dec. 5, 1969)*	.35	.20
	v. Overprint "1969" omitted	2,000.00	
	v1. Wide-spread bars	650.00	

1970. Philatelic Week Issue

224 *Sake flask*

224		MNHVF	UseVF
3¢	multicolored *(April 15, 1970)*	.30	.20

1970. CLASSIC OPERA ISSUE

225 *The Bell*

226 *Child and kidnapper*

		MNHVF	UseVF
225			
3¢	multicolored (April 28, 1970)	.50	.25
225A		MNHVF	UseVF
3¢	Sheet (4) #225	4.00	3.75
226		MNHVF	UseVF
3¢	multicolored (May 29, 1970)	.50	.25
226A		MNHVF	UseVF
3¢	Sheet (4) #226	4.00	3.75

227 *Robe of Feathers*

228 *Vengeance of Two Young Sons*

		MNHVF	UseVF
227			
3¢	multicolored (June 30, 1970)	.50	.25
227A		MNHVF	UseVF
3¢	Sheet (4) #227	4.00	3.75
228		MNHVF	UseVF
3¢	multicolored (July 30, 1970)	.50	.25
228A		MNHVF	UseVF
3¢	Sheet (4) #228	4.00	3.75

229 *Virgin and the Dragon*

		MNHVF	UseVF
229			
3¢	multicolored (Aug. 25, 1970)	.50	.25
229A		MNHVF	UseVF
3¢	Sheet (4) #229	4.00	3.75

1970. UNDERWATER OBSERVATORY ISSUE

230 *Underwater observatory*

		MNHVF	UseVF
230			
3¢	multicolored (May 22, 1970)	.30	.20

Users of this Catalog are invited
to write to us if they have information
which they feel will supplement or correct
any material contained herein. All such
communications will be answered.

1970-71. GREAT MEN ISSUE

231 *Noboru Jahana (1865-1908)*   232 *Saion Gushichan Bunjaku (1682-1761)*   233 *Choho Giwan (1823-1876)*

		MNHVF	UseVF
231			
3¢	deep carmine (Sept. 25, 1970)	.60	.30
232		MNHVF	UseVF
3¢	multicolored (Dec. 22, 1970)	.90	.50
233		MNHVF	UseVF
3¢	gray (Jan. 22, 1971)	.60	.30

1970. CENSUS ISSUE

234 *People*

		MNHVF	UseVF
234			
3¢	multicolored (Oct. 1, 1970)	.30	.20

1970. NATIONAL CULTURAL TREASURES ISSUE

235 *Great Cycad of Une*

		MNHVF	UseVF
235			
3¢	multicolored	.30	.20

1970. NATIONAL ELECTIONS ISSUE

236 *Government buildings*

		MNHVF	UseVF
236			
3¢	multicolored (Nov. 15, 1970)	1.00	.25

1970. NEW YEAR'S ISSUE

237 *Wild boar and cherry blossoms*

		MNHVF	UseVF
237			
1 1/2¢	multicolored (Dec. 10, 1970)	.20	.10

1971. FOLK CRAFT ISSUE

238 *Hand loom*

239 *Filature*

238		MNHVF	UseVF
3¢	multicolored (Feb. 16, 1971)	.40	.20
239		MNHVF	UseVF
3¢	multicolored (March 16, 1971)	.40	.20
240		MNHVF	UseVF
3¢	multicolored (April 30, 1971)	.40	.20
241		MNHVF	UseVF
3¢	multicolored (May 20, 1971)	.40	.20

242 *Fisherman*

242		MNHVF	UseVF
3¢	multicolored (June 15, 1971)	.40	.20

1971. PHILATELIC WEEK ISSUE

243 *Taku water carrier*

243		MNHVF	UseVF
3¢	multicolored (April 15, 1971)	.40	.20

1971. DEFINITIVE ISSUE

244 *Sandanka flower*

244A *Ohgocho flower*

244		MNHVF	UseVF
2¢	multicolored (Sept. 30, 1971)	.20	.20
244A		MNHVF	UseVF
3¢	multicolored (May 10, 1971)	.20	.20

1971. NAHA CITY ISSUE 50th anniversary as a municipality.

245 *Old and new city with emblem*

245		MNHVF	UseVF
3¢	multicolored (May 20, 1971)	.30	.20

1971-72. GOVERNMENT PARK ISSUE

246 *Mabuni Hill*

247 *Mt. Arashi*

246		MNHVF	UseVF
3¢	green & multicolored (July 30, 1971)	.30	.20
247		MNHVF	UseVF
3¢	blue & multicolored (Aug. 30, 1971)	.30	.20

248 *Yabuchi Island*

248		MNHVF	UseVF
4¢	multicolored (Jan. 20, 1972)	.30	.20

1971. NATIONAL CULTURAL ISSUE

249 *Deva King, Torinji Temple*

249		MNHVF	UseVF
4¢	multicolored (Dec. 1, 1971)	.30	.20

1971. NEW YEAR'S ISSUE

250 *Rat and chrysanthemums*

250		MNHVF	UseVF
2¢	multicolored (Dec. 10, 1971)	.10	.10

1971. NURSES ISSUE 25th anniversary of nurses' training.

251 *Student nurse*

251		MNHVF	UseVF
4¢	multicolored (Dec. 24, 1971)	.30	.20

No. 252 not assigned.

1972. SEASCAPES ISSUE

255 *Coral Reef*

253 *Islands*   254 *Seashore*

253		MNHVF	UseVF
5¢	**multicolored** *(March 21, 1972)*	.35	.25
254		MNHVF	UseVF
5¢	**multicolored** *(March 30, 1972)*	.35	.25
255		MNHVF	UseVF
5¢	**multicolored** *(April 14, 1972)*	.35	.25

1972. PHILATELIC WEEK ISSUE

256 *Sake pot*

256		MNHVF	UseVF
5¢	**multicolored** *(April 20, 1972)*	.35	.25

1972. REVERSION OF RYUKYU ISLAND TO JAPAN ISSUE

257 *U.S. & Japanese flags, dove*

257		MNHVF	UseVF
5¢	**multicolored** *(April 17, 1972)*	.50	.40

Ryukyu stamps were discontinued and replaced with those of Japan on May 15, 1972, as the Ryukyu Islands reverted to Japanese control.

Documentary Stamps

1952-54. FIRST REVENUE ISSUE *horizontally oriented numerals, offset, perforated 13 x 13 1/2.*

R1   R2   R3

R1		MNHVF	UseVF
1y	**brown** *(July 15, 1952)*	16.00	12.00
R2		MNHVF	UseVF
3y	**red** *(July 15, 1952)*	20.00	15.00
R3		MNHVF	UseVF
5y	**green** *(July 15, 1952)*	25.00	17.50
R4		MNHVF	UseVF

R4   R5   R6

R4			
10y	**blue** *(July 15, 1952)*	32.50	22.50
R5		MNHVF	UseVF
50y	**purple** *(July 15, 1952)*	40.00	27.50
R6		MNHVF	UseVF
100y	**yellow brown** *(July 15, 1952)*	62.50	35.00
R7		MNHVF	UseVF
500y	**deep green** *(April 16, 1954)*	250.00	150.00
R8		MNHVF	UseVF
1000y	**carmine** *(April 16, 1954)*	300.00	185.00

1958. SECOND REVENUE ISSUE *vertically oriented numerals, offset, no gum, perforated 10, 10 1/2, 11, and combinations.*

R9   R10   R11

R9		MNHVF	UseVF
1¢	**red brown** *(Sept. 16, 1958)*	32.00	32.00
R10		MNHVF	UseVF
3¢	**red orange** *(Sept. 16, 1958)*	40.00	40.00
R11		MNHVF	UseVF
5¢	**blue green** *(Sept. 16, 1958)*	50.00	50.00

R12   R13   R14

R12		MNHVF	UseVF
10¢	**blue** *(Sept. 16, 1958)*	75.00	75.00
R13		MNHVF	UseVF
50¢	**purple** *(Sept. 16, 1958)*	130.00	130.00
R14		MNHVF	UseVF
$1	**yellow brown** *(Sept. 16, 1958)*	200.00	200.00
R15		MNHVF	UseVF
$5	**deep green** *(Sept. 16, 1958)*	335.00	335.00
R16		MNHVF	UseVF
$10	**carmine** *(Sept. 16, 1958)*	450.00	450.00

1959-69. THIRD REVENUE ISSUE Office building. *Offset (1¢-50¢ values) and intaglio ($1-$50 values), perforated 13 x 13 1/2.*

R17   R18   R19

R17
1¢ **brown** *(1959)*
MNHVF	UseVF
4.00	2.00

R18
3¢ **red** *(1959)*
MNHVF	UseVF
4.00	1.50

R19
5¢ **purple** *(1959)*
MNHVF	UseVF
6.00	4.00

R20   R21   R22

R20
10¢ **green** *(1959)*
MNHVF	UseVF
12.50	8.00

R21
20¢ **yellow brown** *(1969)*
MNHVF	UseVF
85.00	60.00

R22
30¢ **olive** *(1969)*
MNHVF	UseVF
92.50	75.00

R23   R24   R25

R23
50¢ **blue** *(1959)*
MNHVF	UseVF
40.00	17.50

R24
$1 **yellow olive** *(1959)*
MNHVF	UseVF
55.00	17.50

R25
$2 **orange vermilion** *(1969)*
MNHVF	UseVF
235.00	70.00

R26
$3 **purple** *(1969)*
MNHVF	UseVF
400.00	95.00

 R27   R28

R27
$5 **vermilion orange** *(1959)*
MNHVF	UseVF
125.00	65.00

R28
$10 **dull blue green** *(1959)*
MNHVF	UseVF
200.00	85.00

R29
$20 **red carmine** *(1969)*
MNHVF	UseVF
1,100.00	245.00

R30
$30 **blue** *(1969)*
MNHVF	UseVF
1,150.00	400.00

R31
$50 **violet black** (1969)
MNHVF	UseVF
1,750.00	800.00

Unemployment Insurance Stamps

1961. FIRST UNEMPLOYMENT ISSUE certified, offer cancellation in an official booklet, a one-day contact for a day laborer. *Offset, unwatermarked, without gum, rouletted.*

 RUI1, 3 *Dove*

RUI2 *Shield*

RUI1
2¢ **violet pink** *(Jan. 10, 1961)*
MNHVF	UseVF
800.00	800.00

RUI2
4¢ **violet** *(Jan. 10, 1961)*
MNHVF	UseVF
55.00	55.00

1966. SECOND UNEMPLOYMENT ISSUE *Offset, unwatermarked, perforated 13 x 13 1/2.*

RUI3
2¢ **red pink** *(Feb. 1, 1966)*
MNHVF	UseVF
800.00	800.00

 RUI4 *Shield, bolder denomination*

RUI4
4¢ **deep violet** *(Feb. 1, 1966)*
MNHVF	UseVF
32.50	32.50

1968. THIRD UNEMPLOYMENT ISSUE *Offset, unwatermarked, perforated 13 x 13 1/2.*

 RUI5 *Cycad*

RUI5
8¢ **brown** *(April 19, 1968)*
MNHVF	UseVF
42.50	42.50

1967-72. SURCHARGED UNEMPLOYMENT ISSUE *Perforated 13 x 13 1/2.*

RUI6 *Dove overprinted 8¢*

RUI7 *Shield, overprinted 8¢*

RUI8 *Shield, overprinted 12¢*

RUI6
8¢ on 2¢ **reddish pink** *(1967)*
MNHVF	UseVF
80.00	80.00

RUI7
8¢ on 4¢ **deep violet** *(1972)*
MNHVF	UseVF
42.50	42.50

RUI8
12¢ on 4¢ **deep violet** (1971)
MNHVF	UseVF
32.50	32.50

Allied Military Government

The rejuvenation of the postal systems of war-torn Europe was of prime importance after World War II. As part of this effort, postage stamps were produced by the United States for use in areas where American Troops were involved as part of the Allied Military Government (AMG) in Italy, France, Germany, and Austria.

The U.S. War Department ordered postage stamps (and currency) designed and produced for each of these areas by the Bureau of Engraving and Printing in Washington, D.C.

To augment the efforts of the BEP, additional quantities of stamps were produced locally in some of the countries by reproducing or overprinting stamps of the BEP design or by overprinting stamps available locally.

AMG — Italy

Although printed for use in all of occupied Italy by the U.S. Bureau of Engraving and Printing (BEP), only a minute quantity was ever used in Italy proper. Practically the entire printing was put on sale and used in Sicily. Therefore it acquired the name "Sicily Issue."

1943. SICILY & SOUTHERN ITALY *Sept. 17, 1943. Lithographed by Bureau of Engraving and Printing, Washington, D.C. Italy and denomination in black, perforated 11, no watermark.*

IYA1   IYA2   IYA3

		FVFNH	UseFVF
IYA1 15c	pale orange *(Aug. 24, 1943)*	1.00	.80
IYA2 25c	pale yellow olive	1.00	.80
IYA3 30c	drab gray	1.00	.80

IYA4   IYA5   IYA6

		FVFNH	UseFVF
IYA4 50c	light red violet	1.00	.80
IYA5 60c	dull yellow, *(Oct. 15, 1943)*	1.00	.75
IYA6 1L	pale emerald	1.00	.80

IYA7   IYA8   IYA9

		FVFNH	UseFVF
IYA7 2L	rose red *(Oct. 14, 1943)*	1.00	1.00
IYA8 5L	pale turquoise blue *(Oct. 20, 1943)*	11.00	2.00
IYA9 10L	pale yellow brown *(Oct. 20, 1943)*	1.00	3.00

1943. ITALY OVERPRINT ISSUE *Dec. 10, 1943. Italy No. 350//354 overprinted in red (shades) or blue (B).*

IYA10   IYA11   IYA11A

		FVFNH	UseFVF
IYA10 20c	bright rose red (B)	1.50	3.00
IYA11 35c	deep blue	15.00	17.00
IYA11A 35c	deep blue, vermilion overprint	15.00	17.00

 IYA12   IYA12A

		FVFNH	UseFVF
IYA12 50c	light violet	.75	1.00
IYA12A 50c	light violet, orange overprint	.75	1.00

1945. VENEZIA GIULIA ISSUE *Sept. 22, 1945-47. Contemporary Italian stamps with overprint size 16 x 12mm or 14 x 10mm (No. 23) or 27 x 14mm (No. 33, 35-43), by R. Fortuna, Trieste.*

1: Postage, on Empire issue, watermark 9 No. 348//364.

IYA13   IYA14   IYA17

		FVFNH	UseFVF
IYA13 10c	deep bistre brown (No. 348)	.30	.35
	x. Overprint inverted	3.50	3.75
IYA14 20c	bright rose (No. 350)	.40	.50
IYA15 20L	green *(July 10, 1946)* (No. 364)	2.25	3.50

Note: Due to the urgent need for postage stamps, some issues were overprinted AMG-VG even though they contained the fascist symbol of the Roman ax. Values containing this symbol were the 10c brown, 20c red, and the 60c green. Because a few sheets of the 20c value with the fasces were inadvertently overprinted, a larger printing was permitted in December 1946 to prevent speculation in this issue.

No watermark, No. 733//739.

		FVFNH	UseFVF
IYA16 10c	sepia *(Nov. 30, 1945)* (No. 733)	.30	.20
IYA17 20c	rose red *(Dec. 6, 1946)* (No. 737)	.25	.50
	x. Overprint inverted	13.00	13.50
IYA18 60c	light orange red *(Nov. 30, 1945)* (No. 739)	.25	.25

Watermark 743, winged wheel, No. 743//749.

		FVFNH	UseFVF
IYA19 20c	rose red (No. 743)	.30	.50
	x. Overprint inverted	60.00	66.00
	x1. Overprint doubled	120.00	120.00
IYA20 60c	dark blue green (No. 744)	.45	.30
	x. Overprint inverted	50.00	55.00
	x1. Overprint doubled	90.00	60.00

IYA19   IYA20   IYA21

IYA21
1L   dark violet (No. 745)

	FVFNH	UseFVF
	.30	.30
x. Overprint inverted	45.00	46.00

IYA22   IYA23   IYA24

IYA22
2L   bright rose red (No. 747)

	FVFNH	UseFVF
	.35	.35
x. Overprint inverted	45.00	46.00
x1. Overprint doubled	45.00	46.00

IYA23
5L   rose red (Oct. 16, 1945) (No. 748)

	FVFNH	UseFVF
	.65	.50
x. Overprint inverted	240.00	250.00

IYA24
10L   deep violet (No. 749)

	FVFNH	UseFVF
	.90	1.25
x. Overprint inverted	18.00	

On Peace issue, No. 798//818.

IYA25   IYA26

IYA25
25c   deep turquoise green (Jan. 8, 1947) (No. 798)

	FVFNH	UseFVF
	.25	.30

x. Overprint inverted

IYA26
2L   dark chocolate (July 17, 1947) (No. 805)

	FVFNH	UseFVF
	.60	.75

 IYA27   IYA28

IYA27
3L   scarlet (Jan. 8, 1947) (No. 806)

	FVFNH	UseFVF
	.45	.30

IYA28
4L   light orange red (Jan. 2, 1947) (No. 807)

	FVFNH	UseFVF
	.70	.40

 IYA29   IYA30

IYA29
6L   blue violet (July 17, 1947) (No. 809)

	FVFNH	UseFVF
	1.75	2.25

IYA30
20L   deep red lilac (July 23, 1947) (No. 814)

	FVFNH	UseFVF
	26.00	1.50

 IYA31   IYA32

IYA31
25L   dark blue green (July 10, 1946) (No. 815)

FVFNH	UseFVF
4.25	6.00

IYA32
50L   deep chocolate (July 10, 1946) (No. 817)

FVFNH	UseFVF
4.75	7.50

 IYA33

IYA33
100L   carmine rose (Sept. 13, 1946) (No. 818)

FVFNH	UseFVF
17.50	25.00

Note: The 20L denomination was used extensively, resulting in one of the scarcest mint AMG-VG stamps.
2: Airmail, on No. 379, 819//826.

 IYA34

IYA34
50c   dark brown (No. 379)

	FVFNH	UseFVF
	.25	.50
x. Overprint inverted	40.00	45.00
x1. Overprint doubled	120.00	120.00

 IYA35

IYA35
1L   dark slate blue (July 23, 1947) (No. 819)

FVFNH	UseFVF
.25	.50

 IYA36   IYA37

IYA36
2L   deep blue (Jan. 16, 1947) (No. 820)

FVFNH	UseFVF
.25	.50

IYA37
5L   bright green (Jan. 23, 1947) (No. 822)

FVFNH	UseFVF
1.75	2.50

IYA38   IYA39

IYA38		FVFNH	UseFVF
10L	rose carmine *(Jan. 23, 1947)* (No. 823)	1.75	2.50

IYA39		FVFNH	UseFVF
25L	deep blue *(Sept. 13, 1946)* (No. 824)	1.75	2.50
	x. Overprint inverted	90.00	160.00
	x1. Overprint doubled	330.00	350.00

IYA40   IYA41

IYA40		FVFNH	UseFVF
25L	ocher brown *(July 23, 1947)* (No. 825)	15.00	20.00

IYA41		FVFNH	UseFVF
50L	dark green *(Sept. 13, 1946)* (No. 826)	3.25	5.00
	x. Overprint inverted	210.00	240.00

3: On special delivery, Nos. 829, 832.

IYA42   IYA43

IYA42		FVFNH	UseFVF
10L	deep blue *(Sept. 3, 1946)*	3.50	4.50

IYA43		FVFNH	UseFVF
30L	deep violet *(Sept. 3, 1946)*	8.50	12.25
	x. Overprint inverted	220.00	240.00

Note: On Oct. 1, 1947, Italian stamps overprinted AMG-VG, for use in and around the Territory of Trieste, ceased being issued. They were superseded by similar Italian stamps overprinted AMG-FTT. This was in conformity with the establishment of the Free Territory of Trieste.

AMG — France

The first issue of AMG postage stamps produced for France, titled Supplemental French Postage Stamps, because of the touchy political situation in France, was printed by the United States Bureau of Engraving and Printing (BEP) in its surface printing division. The issue was made available by the Treasury Department through the Allied Military Government authorities to the provisional French Government of Gen. Charles DeGaulle for general use throughout liberated France. Initially, these stamps replaced the existing stocks of stamps used during the occupation by the German-controlled Vichy Government. The subject for the design of this series of stamps was taken from a photograph of the *Arc de Triomphe* in Paris, furnished by the Washington Public Library.

1944. FRANCE I ISSUE Oct. 5, 1944. Arch of Triumph, typographed by Bureau of Engraving and Printing, Washington, perforated 11.
1: Numerals in colors of stamps.

FLA773   FLA774   FLA775

FLA773			
5c	rose purple		

FLA774			
10c	pearl gray		

		FVFNH	UseFVF
		.35	.35

		FVFNH	UseFVF
		.35	.35

FLA775		FVFNH	UseFVF
25c	gray brown	.35	.35

FLA776   FLA777   FLA778

FLA776		FVFNH	UseFVF
50c	olive bistre	.50	.70

FLA777		FVFNH	UseFVF
1f	light blue green	.90	.90

FLA778		FVFNH	UseFVF
1.50f	rose	1.90	.90

FLA779   FLA780

FLA781   FLA782

FLA779		FVFNH	UseFVF
2.50f	light red violet	.90	.90

FLA780		FVFNH	UseFVF
4f	ultramarine	1.90	1.90

FLA781		FVFNH	UseFVF
5f	gray black	1.90	1.90

FLA782		FVFNH	UseFVF
10f	light orange	37.50	35.00

Note: The design of the 1.50 Franc stamp was in error as the value was listed as FRANCS instead of the correct one franc fifty centimes. This was remedied on the France II issue. The FRANCE 10 Fr. value is one of the scarcest AMG stamps. Only 720,000 were printed.

1945. FRANCE II ISSUE The second issue, called the Committee French Postage Stamps, Series 1944, was distributed in the same manner as the first issue. No data has been found to ascertain the first date of issue of this series of stamps. The same basic design of the first issue was utilized. However, the numerals and denominational wording were not incorporated into the design but were added by overprinting the numerals and either CENTIMES, FRANC, or FRANCS in black.

2: (Feb. 12, 1945): Additional values, figures in black.

FLA783   FLA784   FLA785

FLA783		FVFNH	UseFVF
30c	orange	.30	.30

FLA784		FVFNH	UseFVF
40c	pearl gray	.30	.30

FLA785		FVFNH	UseFVF
50c	olive bistre	.30	.30

FLA786

FLA787

FLA788

GDA1102

GDA1103

GDA1104

		FVFNH	UseFVF
FLA786		.30	.30
60c	light violet		
FLA787		.30	.30
80c	light emerald		
FLA788		.30	.30
1.20f	gray brown		

		FVFNH	UseFVF
GDA1102		.20	.20
4p	drab gray *(July 1, 1945)*		
	p. Early printing	.25	.25
GDA1103		.20	.20
5p	light yellow emerald		
	p. Early printing	.25	.25
	pl. Thin white paper	.35	
GDA1104		.20	.20
6p	yellow		
	p. Early printing	.20	.25
	pl. Thin white paper	.35	.25

FLA789

FLA790

FLA791

GDA1105

GDA1106

GDA1107

		FVFNH	UseFVF
FLA789		.30	.30
1.50f	light vermilion		
FLA790		.30	.30
2f	yellow		
FLA791		.30	.30
2.40f	carmine rose		

		FVFNH	UseFVF
GDA1105		.20	.20
8p	orange		
	p. Early printing	.20	.25
GDA1106		.20	.20
10p	gray brown *(July 1, 1945)*		
	p. Early printing	.20	.20
GDA1107		.20	.20
12p	bright purple		
	p. Early printing	.20	.30

 FLA792

GDA1108

GDA1109

		FVFNH	UseFVF
FLA792		.30	.30
3f	rose purple		

		FVFNH	UseFVF
GDA1108		.20	.20
15p	carmine red *(July 1, 1945)*		
	p. Early printing	.20	.25
GDA1109		.20	.20
25p	deep ultramarine *(July 1, 1945)*		
	p. Early printing	.25	.25

AMG — Germany

After World War II, Germany (and Berlin separately) was divided into four occupation zones with joint overall administration, except for territory east of the Oder and Neisse rivers, which was divided between USSR (Kaliningrad Oblast formerly Konigsberg) and Poland (provinces of Olsztyn, Kozcalin, Szeczecin, Zielona Gora, Wroclaw and Opole, formerly known as Allenstein, Koslin, Stettin, Grunberg, Breslau, and Oppeln respectively). In many cases, newly created districts of Germany did not follow historical boundaries. The Saar, in French zone, was made autonomous. Failure of negotiations for unification of Germany led to creation of two republics: *Democratic* (East Germany — from USSR zone) and *Federal* (West Germany — British, U.S., and French zones).

100 pfennig = 1 reichsmark.

1945. U.S. AND BRITISH ZONES ISSUE *March 19-July 1945. AM POST (Allied Military), Washington printing, no white patches in spandrel, offset by Bureau of Engraving and Printing, Washington, D.C., perforated 11, thick cloudy white to tan paper; p: (early printing) thick, smooth, clear white paper, shades.*

GDA1101 *Washington printing spandrel, Brunswick printing spandrel*

		FVFNH	UseFVF
GDA1101		.20	.20
3p	bright lilac *(July 1, 1945)*		
	p. Early printing	.25	.25

Note: The 5 pfennig value on thin paper was used mostly in the Hamburg Postal District. The 6 pfennig on thin paper was used only in the Kiel Postal District, and it is the scarcest value of the set.

Note: 6p, 8p, and 12p sold and used in West sector of Berlin until middle September 1945.

Stamps overprinted "Military / Permit / Office / Fiscal Stamp" and value: revenue.

Forgeries: 3p-25p overprinted "German" and "8p" with blue overprint "6."

AMG — Austria

Designed, prepared, and printed by the United States Bureau of Engraving and Printing (BEP), this was the final issue of the Allied Military Government produced by the BEP in Washington, D.C. All subsequent postal items needed for use in occupied or policed territory were produced in proximity to the site.

1945. AMERICAN, BRITISH & FRENCH ZONES ISSUE *June 28-Nov. 1945. Posthorn, offset by U.S. Bureau of Engraving and Printing, Washington, D.C., perforated 11, thick paper, unwatermarked.*

AXA991

AXA992

AXA993

AXA994

AXA995

AXA996

AXA991		FVFNH	UseFVF
1g	turquoise blue *(Nov. 20, 1945)*	.20	.25
AXA992		FVFNH	UseFVF
3g	orange	.20	.25
AXA993		FVFNH	UseFVF
4g	dull brown orange *(July 15, 1945)*	.20	.25
AXA994		FVFNH	UseFVF
5g	emerald	.20	.25

AXA995		FVFNH	UseFVF
6g	bright purple	.20	.25
AXA996		FVFNH	UseFVF
8g	rose carmine	.20	.25
AXA997		FVFNH	UseFVF
10g	drab gray	.20	.25
AXA998		FVFNH	UseFVF
12g	brown drab	.20	.25
AXA999		FVFNH	UseFVF
15g	bright rose red *(July 15, 1945)*	.25	.25

HOW TO DIFFERENTIATE AMONG THE THREE GERMAN PRINTINGS.

Entirely new plates, using the same design as that of the Washington Printing, first delivered Sept. 19, 1944, were prepared and used by Harrison & Sons, Ltd., for a British Printing, beginning in August 1945; and new plates were made by the Georg Westermann Co. of Brunswick, Germany, for a Brunswick Printing, also beginning in August 1945.

Minute variations as well as paper and gum differences permit easy identification of each of the printings.

Washington Printing

No white triangles in the corners of the arabesques.

End of right leg of the "M" in the oval has a slight curve, but is not concentric with the curve of the oval.

Because of paper shortages during World War II, the Bureau of Engraving and Printing used whatever paper stock was available; smooth, white paper at first. The porous paper used for the subsequent printings can vary from tan to white. In addition, the gums also vary from white to tan.

British Printing

This printing is the easiest to detect. The perforations are much smaller and finer than on the other two printings. In addition, the British Printing was produced by photogravure and has a different appearance from the other two printings, which were offset lithographed.

Brunswick Printing

White triangles are found adjacent to the arabesques in the four corners, but most apparent in the upper right.

End of right leg of the "M" curves concentric with the oval.

AXA997

AXA998

AXA999

AXA1000

AXA1001

AXA1002

	FVFNH	UseFVF
	.25	.25

AXA1000
20g   chestnut

	FVFNH	UseFVF
	.20	.25

AXA1001
25g   bright blue

	FVFNH	UseFVF
	.20	.25

AXA1002
30g   red violet

AXA1003

AXA1004

AXA1005

AXA1003
40g   light blue

	FVFNH	UseFVF
	.20	.25

AXA1004
60g   apple green

	FVFNH	UseFVF
	.25	.25

AXA1005
1s   red lilac *(Aug. 13, 1945)*

	FVFNH	UseFVF
	.30	.40

AXA1006

AXA1007

AXA1006
2s   yellow *(Aug. 13, 1945)*

	FVFNH	UseFVF
	.35	.55

AXA1007
5s   deep blue violet *(Aug. 13, 1945)*

	FVFNH	UseFVF
	.55	.75

1946. POSTAGE DUE ISSUE All remaining stocks of the AMG Austria Issue, with the exception of the 1 and 4 groschen values, were turned over to the newly established Renner Government, operating under the sanction of the Allied authorities. As this government already had issued definitive stamps by April and May 1946, they had the AMG issue overprinted PORTO for temporary use as postage due stamps until their own definitive postage due stamps were released.

April 23-May, 1946. No. 992//1007 overprinted.

AXA1042

AXA1043

AXA1044

AXA1042
3g   orange

	FVFNH	UseFVF
	.35	.30

AXA1043
5g   emerald

	FVFNH	UseFVF
	.35	.30

AXA1044
6g   bright purple

	FVFNH	UseFVF
	.35	.30

AXA1045

AXA1046

AXA1047

AXA1045
8g   rose carmine
  x. Overprint inverted

	FVFNH	UseFVF
	.35	.30
	20.00	20.00

AXA1046
10g   drab gray

	FVFNH	UseFVF
	.35	.30

AXA1047
12g   brown drab

	FVFNH	UseFVF
	.40	.30

AXA1048

AXA1049

AXA1050

AXA1048
15g   bright rose red

	FVFNH	UseFVF
	.40	.30

AXA1049
20g   chestnut

	FVFNH	UseFVF
	.40	.30

AXA1050
25g   bright blue

	FVFNH	UseFVF
	.40	.30

AXA1051

AXA1052

AXA1053

AXA1051
30g   red violet

	FVFNH	UseFVF
	.40	.30

AXA1052
40g   light blue

	FVFNH	UseFVF
	.40	.30

AXA1053
60g   apple green

	FVFNH	UseFVF
	.40	.30

AXA1054

AXA1055

AXA1056

AXA1054
1s   red lilac *(May 20, 1946)*

	FVFNH	UseFVF
	.50	.40

AXA1055
2s   yellow *(May 20, 1946)*

	FVFNH	UseFVF
	.50	.40

AXA1056
5s   deep blue violet *(May 20, 1946)*

	FVFNH	UseFVF
	.70	.50

Note: Inverted overprint: 3g, 8g-12g, 20g, 30g, 60g, 1s exist.

Stamps used as money

Stamps became legal tender during the American Civil War and after, 1862-1875, first by custom and then by law. These specialized uses of postage stamps are collectible today as Postage Stamp Envelopes, Encased Postage Stamps and Postage Currency.

Paper money in denominations of less than the dollar unit was required in commerce because during the Civil War the gold, silver and copper coins in circulation largely disappeared. This was due to several factors.

There was no pervading fear in the North that the armed forces of the Confederacy would prevail and shatter the Union. Rather, it would appear that a hoarding of hard money was caused by an ingrained distrust of paper money. The Yankee worker simply felt more secure when his paper wages had been converted to gold and silver. Consequently, he gave a cool reception to "greenbacks," which could not be redeemed for either gold or silver and were suspiciously regarded as "faith paper." This practically expressed preference for coins inevitably depreciated the paper money in terms of the gold standard. Gold coins commanded a premium of 3% over U.S. and state paper money in January 1862, the month following the general suspension of specie payment by banks and the Federal Treasury, and 32% by the end of 1862. At one point in 1864 it required $285 in paper to purchase $100 in gold. The distrust of the government's fiat paper was further heightened by a snowballing national debt, which reached $2.8 billion in 1865.

A monetary situation in which gold commanded a substantial premium over a like face value of paper dollars swiftly drove gold coins from commercial channels, effectively removing the United States from a gold standard. It also created a favorable condition for the exporting of silver coins, which disappeared from the marketplace, but at a less precipitous pace than gold.

Plenty of customers for gold coins existed. In 1858 Canada had adopted a decimal system of coinage with a dollar unit similar to that of the United States. In lieu of a sufficient coins of British origin, Canada unofficially adopted the coinage of the United States and used it widely in domestic trade. The West Indies and many Latin American countries also used large quantities of U.S. silver coinage.

Disappearance of gold from American trade channels and the willingness of foreign users of U.S. silver coins to pay for them with gold combined to produce a legal and highly profitable bullion trade, which speculators and bankers found irresistible: Greenbacks were exchanged for silver coins, which were then exchanged for gold in Canada, the West Indies or Latin America. The gold was then returned to the United States, where it was used to purchase more greenbacks at the metal's high premium rate. A safer round-robin route to riches can hardly be imagined.

During the last week of June and the first week of July, 1862, more than $25 million in subsidiary coins vanished from circulation in the North. Illogically, the Philadelphia Mint continued a small but steady production of silver coins during the 1860s. Bullion dealers obtained them directly from the mint and sped them abroad. In 1863, the entire production of silver coins was exported.

The withdrawal of subsidiary silver coins in the summer of 1862 all but paralyzed the institutions and practice of everyday commerce. The smallest denominations of official money available were discounted $5 Legal Tender Notes and the copper-nickel cents that had been fed into circulation in great quantities. When first forced upon the public in 1857, the copper-nickel cent, which was intrinsically worth about 60% of face value, had been considered a nuisance; it was regularly discounted 3% and more in large transactions. But with the disappearance of silver coins, the ugly duckling became the belle of the ball. It became the only alternative to walking, or going without a newspaper, or buying a pound of pomegranates and receiving change in kumquats and quince. Cents were bundled in bags of 25, 50 and 100 in a hopeless attempt to bridge the gap between the 1¢ piece and the $5 bill. By March 1863, the lowly cent commanded a premium of 20%, but few could be found.

The disappearance of nearly all official coinage from trade channels resulted in an outpouring of private emergency monies. State bank notes of $1 and $2 denominations were cut into fractional parts. Other banks issued notes in denominations of $1.25, $1.50 and $1.75. Eastern cities issued their own fractional notes. Merchants, reviving a practice prevalent during the coin shortages of 1837 and 1857, made change in their own promissory notes or "shinplasters," redeemable in merchandise at the issuer's place of business. Private issues of Civil War tokens began.

Postage Stamp Envelopes

Among the emergency monies called into use was the common postage stamp. The use of stamps as a low-denomination medium of exchange led directly to the issuing of the highly successful Postage Currency and Fractional Currency series.

By the time the Civil War began, the adhesive postage stamp had become a well-established part of the public routine. Inasmuch as they were of official origin, had a constant value throughout the country and were easily obtained, consideration of postage stamps as a medium of exchange for coin-deprived people was inevitable. In early July 1862, Horace Greeley, publisher of the politically influential *New York Tribune*, suggested that stamps pasted on a half sheet of paper, with the other half folded over the stamps to afford them protection from wear, would make an excellent coin substitute. The coin-starved public agreed.

But fragile, gummed stamps could not be carried loose.

Methods of protecting the stamps were quickly devised. They were pasted on sheets of light vellum

A postage stamp envelope and typical contents.

paper — with or without a protective flap — which also bore an advertising message and a large numeral indicating the total face value of the stamps. Stamps were also encased in small envelopes, approximately 70 by 35 mm in size, on the outside of which was printed the value of the contents and an advertising message.

Both methods of using stamps as emergency money had drawbacks. Pasting the stamps on sheets of paper did not provide them sufficient protection from wear. Envelopes offered better protection but provided an opportunity for petty larceny. Few recipients had the time to check the contents of each envelope to determine if it contained the proper denominational total of stamps, or if the stamps were unused, or if rectangles of colored paper had been substituted for the stamps.

Existing pieces are extremely rare. Prices given in these listings reflect the rarity of the individual envelopes and the desirability of their imprints. If any stamps are included with the envelopes there is no way of telling whether they are original.

Postage Stamp Envelopes

KL#	Name, address and notations	Value
1-25	H. Armstrong, Hosiery, Laces, etc. 140 6th Ave, (NYC)	700.
3-?	Arthur, Gregory & Co., Stationer 39 Nassau St. NYC	650.
5-25	Bergen & Tripp, Stationer 114 Nassau St, (NYC)	650.
7-25	Berlin & Jones, Stationer 134 William St, NYC	650.

KL#	Name, address and notations	Value
9-15	Joseph Bryan, Clothing 214 Fulton St, Brooklyn	725.
9-50	Same	650.
11-25	P.D. Braisted, Jr. Billiards 14-16 4th Ave, NYC	650.
13-50	G.C. Brown, Tobacco 669 Broadway, NYC	650.
15-25	John M. Burnett, Stationer 51 William St, NYC	650.
15-25hw50		650.

KL#	Name, address and notations	Value
15-50	Same	650.
17-25	Chas. T. Chickhaus, Tobacco 176 Broadway, NYC	725.
19-?	Clarry & Reilley, Stationer 12-14 Spruce St, NYC	725.

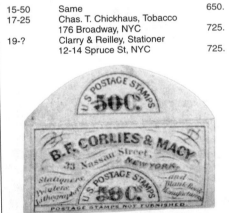

KL#	Name, address and notations	Value
21-50hw25	B.F. Corlies & Macy, Stationer 33 Nassau St, NYC	725.
23-30	Crook & Duff, Bar-Lunch-Dining 39-40 Park Row, (NYC)	800.
25-?	Cutter Tower & Co, Stationer 128 Nassau St, NYC	650.
27-25	Dawley, Stationer & Printer 28, 30 & 32 Center St., (NYC)	650.
28-50	T.R. Dawley, Printer Cor, Reade & Center Streets, NYC	650.
29-0hw25	Mad (Ame) A. Doubet, Importer 697 & 951 Broadway, (NYC)	725.
31-25	Francis Duffy, Oysters & Dining 239-241 8th Ave, (NYC)	725.
33-25	Embree, Stationer 130 Grand St, (NYC)	650.
34-50	Jno. C. Force Brooklyn	800.
35-25	Fox's Old Bowery Theatre (NYC)	800.

KL#	Name, address and notations	Value
37-?	German Opera 485 Broadway, NYC	400.

KL#	Name, address and notations	Value
39-75	Gould's Dining Rooms 35 Nassau St, NYC	650.
40-50	Arthur Gregory NYC	800.
41-25	Harlem & NY Navigation Co Sylvan Shore & Sylvan Grove, (NYC) "LEGAL CURRENCY"	850.
43-5	Harpel, Printers Cincinnati	725.
45-10	Irving House, Hotel Broadway & 12th St, NYC	650.
47-25	James, Hatter 525 broadway, (NYC)	650.
49-0	Hamilton Johnston, Stationer 545 Broadway, (NYC) with Washington portrait	825.
51-25	C.O. Jones, Stationer 76 Cedar St, NYC	650.
53-?	Kaiser & Waters, Stationer 104 Fulton St, NYC	650.
55-60	Kavanagh & Freeman, Billiards 10th & Broadway, NYC	725.
57-25	Lansingh's Gent's Furnishings 57-50 Albany	650.
59-10	J. Leach, Stationer 86 Nassau St, NYC Type I, Value in central diamond, most common type (vars.)	575.
59-15		650.
59-20		575.

KL#		Value
59-25		575.
59-30		650.
59-50		575.
59-75		700.

KL#	Name, address and notations	Value
60-15	As Above	700.
60-25	As Above	
	Type II, Eagle between "U" and "S" (vars) 575.	
60-50		575.
61-25	As above	
	Type III, Large central oval with denomination (vars.)	575.
61-50	As Above	
	Type V, Denomination in oval, flag left, shield right, similar to H. Smith design	575.

KL#	Name, address and notations	Value
62-25	As above	
	Type IV, deonomination between flags	575.
63-50	As above	575.
71-75	D.W. Lee, Stationer	
	82 Nassau St, NYC	575.
72-0	R. Letson, Mercantile	
	Dining Room, 256 Broadway, NYC	575.
73-25	J.W. Lingard	
	New Bowery Theatre, (NYC)	650.
74-25	Macoy & Herwig, Stationers	
	112-114 Broadway, (NYC)	650.
75-20	Hy Maillards, Confectionery	
	621 Broadway, (NYC)	650.
75-25	Same	650.
75-25	Frank McElroy, Stationers	
	113 Nassau St, (NYC)	650.
81-10	Metropolitan Hotel NYC	650.
83-25	Miller & Grant, Importers, Laces	
	73 Broadway, NYC	725.

KL#	Name, address and notations	Value
85-50	W.H. Murphy (by D. Murphy's Sons)	
	Stationers, 372 Pearl St, NYC	650.
87-?	Wm. Murphy, Stationer	
	438 Canal St, NYC	650.
89-25	National Express Co.	
	74 Broadway, NYC	800.
93-20	New York Central Railroad (N.Y.C.R.R.)	
	NYC	725.
95-50	N.Y. Consolidated Stage Co.	
	(NYC)	725.

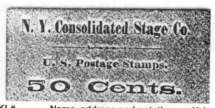

KL#	Name, address and notations	Value
97-25	Niblos Garden - Wm Wheatley	
	(Edwin Forrest) (NYC)	725.
97-50	Same except Ravel Troupe	
	(NYC)	725.
101-10	Nixon's Cremorne Garden, Palace of	
	Music 14th and 6th Ave, (NYC)	975.
101-25hw10		725.

NIXON'S CREMORNE GARDEN.
PALACE OF MUSIC. } 14th STREET AND 6th AVENUE { EQUESTRIAN SCHOOL.

Postage 25 CTS. Stamps.

OPERA, BALLET,   PROMENADE, EQUESTRIANISM.

ADMISSION TWENTY-FIVE CENTS.

KL#	Name, address and notations	Value
101-25	Postal type hand stamp appears to read "CREMORNE (GARD)EN"	725.

KL#	Name, address and notations	Value
103-25	Chris O'Neills, Liquors	
	Hudson Ave, Brooklyn	
	"UNCLE SAM'S CHANGE"	800.
105-?	Oyster Bay House	
	553 Broadway, NYC	650.
107-25	The Oyster House	
	604 Broadway, NYC	650.
109-0	Pettit & Crook's Dining Rooms	
	136 Water St, NYC	
	"UNCLE SAM'S CHANGE"	800.

KL#	Name, address and notations	Value
111-50	Pomroy's	
	699 Broadway, NYC	650.
113-50	Power, Bogardus & Co., Steamship Line	
	Pier 34, No. River, NYC	700.
115-50	S. Raynor, Envelope Manuf'r	
	118 William St, NYC	650.

CAPT. TOM REEVES' BILLIARD SALOON, No. 214 BROADWAY, One door below the Museum,   NEW-YORK. U. S. POSTAGE STAMPS. 25 Cents.

KL#	Name, address and notations	Value
117-25	Capt. Tom Reeves, Billiards	
	214 Broadway, NYC	800.

REVERE HOUSE, Nos. 604, 606 & 608 Broadway, COR. HOUSTON-ST.,   NEW YORK. ON THE EUROPEAN PLAN. SMITH & GREEN. U. S. POSTAGE STAMPS. 25 CENTS.

KL#	Name, address and notations	Value
119-25	Revere House	
	604-608 Broadway, NYC	650.
121-?	Thomas Richardson,	
	Chop Steak & Oyster House	
	66 Maiden Lane, NYC	650.
122-50	E.M. Riggin, Sanford House	
	336 Delaware Ave., Pine St. Wharf,	
	Philadelphia	650.
123-25	Wm Robins, Excelsion Envelope	
	Manufactory 51 Ann St, NYC	575.
125-25	R. Scovel, Stationer	
	26 Nassau St, (NYC)	650.
126-25	Reuben Scovel	
	"GOVERNMENT CURRENCY"	
	26 Nassau St, (NYC)	650.
126-50	Same	650.

KL#	Name, address and notations	Value
127-25	C.C. Shelley, Stationer	
	68 Barclay St, NYC	650.

KL#	Name, address and notations	Value
127-50	Same (one known)	700.
128-10	H. Smith, Stationer	
	137 Williams St, NYC	
	Type I, denomination in	
	oval, flag left, shield right (vars.)	575.
128-13	Same	575.
128-25	Same	575.
128-50	Same	575.
129-15hw50	As above	
	Type II, fancy border, no flag,	
	denomination below postage stamps	575.
129-50	Same	575.
130-25	Snow & Hapgood	
	22 Court St., Boston	650.
131-25	Sonneborn, Stationer	
	130 Nassau St., NYC (vars.)	650.
133-25	Taylor's Hotel	
	Exchange Place, Jersey City (vars.)	725.
133-50	Same	725.

135-?   Dion Thomas, Stationer
       142 Nassau St, NYC   725.

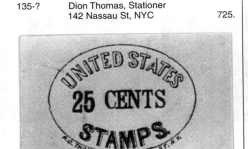

KL#	Name, address and notations	Value
137-25	R.D. Thompson, Stationer 104 Fulton St, NYC (vars.)	650.
139-25	G.W. & S. Turney 77 Chatham St, NYC	650.
140-?	S.C. Upham 403 Chestnut St., Phil.	650.
141-25	James Wiley, Wines & Liquors 307 Broadway, NYC	650.
141-50	Same	650.

PIECES WITH NO COMPANY NAME

KL#	Name, address and notations	Value
151-25	Blank - marked by hand Envelope perhaps hand made	500.
152-10	U.S. POSTAGE STAMPS 10 CENTS	—
153-20	U.S. POSTAGE STAMPS 20 CENTS	500.

KL#	Name, address and notations	Value
155-25	U.S. POSTAGE STAMPS 25 CENTS (vars.)	500.

KL#	Name, address and notations	Value
156-25	POSTAGE STAMPS 25 CENTS Does not say U.S. postage as others do.	500.
157-25	"UNITED STATES POSTAGE STAMPS" in oval	500.

KL#	Name, address and notations	Value
157-30	U.S. POSTAGE STAMPS 30 CENTS	500.

KL#	Name, address and notations	Value
159-50	U.S. POSTAGE STAMPS 50 CENTS (vars.)	500.
161-75	U.S. POSTAGE STAMPS 75 CENTS	500.

KL#	Name, address and notations	Value
163-7590	U.S. POSTAGE STAMPS 90 CENTS Hand changed from 75 cents.	650.

Envelopes come with various color ink and paper color combinations. Much of this new information became available through the sale of the Moreau hoard by Bowers & Merena. Photos on this page courtesy of Bowers & Merena.

A single hoard of these pieces consisting of a "cigar box full" is known to exist but it has not been seen or cataloged. A small group is known to have been lost in a fire some years ago. The author is indebted to Jackson Storm and to the Chase Bank Collection for some of the illustrations, and to Gene Hessler for some of the photography.

Encased Postage Stamps

The method of stamp packaging that best satisfied the dual requirements of visibility and protection was patented on Aug. 12, 1862, by a New England inventor, John Gault, who encased a single postage stamp in a round brass frame (25mm in diameter) with a clear mica frontpiece through which the stamp could be viewed.

The reverse of this case bore the advertising message of the participating merchant who purchased a quantity of Gault's "encased postage stamps" as a means of giving his customers the precise change required by their purchases.

Stamps encased by Gault were the 1¢, 3¢, 5¢, 10¢, 12¢, 24¢, 30¢, and 90¢ denominations of the Series of 1861-1869. That series also contains a 2¢ and a 15¢ stamp, but the 2¢ stamp wasn't issued until July 6, 1863, and the 15¢ value came along in 1866.

But for the eventual authorization of Postage and Fractional Currency, Gault's encased postage stamps probably would have become the chief means of "spending" postage stamps, although they, too, had their disadvantages:

The protective mica shield was easily cracked, and the encased stamps cost the distributing merchant the face value of the stamps, plus about 2¢ per holder. In view of the 20% premium existing on official coins, the additional 2¢ was of little consequence in the instance of the higher-denomination stamps, but in the case of the popular 1¢ stamp, it meant an expenditure of 3¢ for every 1¢ encased postage stamp obtained from Gault for monetary use.

The timing of the initiation of Gault's encased stamps also worked against their quantity distribution. At the time of their appearance in midsummer of 1862, the Postmaster General, Montgomery Blair, was still not reconciled to the idea of using postage stamps for money and was doing his utmost to prevent quantity sales of stamps to anyone desiring them for coinage purposes.

Three factors must be considered in concert in the grading of encased postage stamps: the stamp, the case, and the protective mica. The relative condition of each of these factors affects the overall grade.

Aerated Bread Co., New York

KL#	Denom.	Fine	VF	XF
EPS1	1¢	800.	1250.	1500.

Ayer's Cathartic Pills
(Long arrows variety)

KL#	Denom.	Fine	VF	XF
EPS2	3¢	100.	175.	250.
EPS3	5¢	125.	275.	350.
EPS4	10¢	250.	500.	650.

(Short arrows variety)

KL#	Denom.	Fine	VF	XF
EPS5	1¢	150.	225.	300.
EPS6	3¢	100.	175.	250.
EPS7	5¢	125.	275.	350.
EPS8	10¢	200.	350.	500.
EPS9	12¢	300.	550.	1000.
EPS10	24¢	1200.	2000.	3000.
EPS11	30¢	1500.	3000.	4000.

Take Ayer's Pills

KL#	Denom.	Fine	VF	XF
EPS12	1¢	150.	250.	325.
EPS13	3¢	100.	150.	225.
EPS14	5¢	100.	200.	300.
EPS15	10¢	175.	375.	500.
EPS16	12¢	300.	550.	1000.
EPS17	90¢	Two known are both suspect as being counterfeit or altered.		

Ayer's Sarsaparilla
(Small Ayer's)

KL#	Denom.	Fine	VF	XF
EPS18	1¢	300.	625.	925.
EPS19	3¢	350.	550.	750.
EPS20	10¢	300.	625.	925.
EPS21	12¢	700.	1400.	2000.

(Medium Ayer's)

KL#	Denom.	Fine	VF	XF
EPS22	1¢	150.	225.	300.
EPS23	3¢	100.	175.	225.
EPS24	5¢	150.	225.	300.
EPS25	10¢	175.	300.	450.
EPS26	12¢	300.	550.	1000.
EPS27	24¢	1200.	2000.	3000.
EPS28	30¢	1500.	3000.	4000.
EPS29	90¢	2500.	5000.	9000.

(Large Ayer's)

KL#	Denom.	Fine	VF	XF
EPS30	3¢	275.	400.	750.
EPS31	10¢	450.	700.	1000.

Bailey & Co., Philadelphia

KL#	Denom.	Fine	VF	XF
EPS32	1¢	375.	550.	1000.
EPS33	3¢	375.	550.	1000.
EPS34	5¢	400.	650.	1300.
EPS35	10¢	400.	600.	1250.
EPS36	12¢	1000.	1500.	2500.

Joseph L. Bates "Fancy Goods," Boston Fancygoods One Word

KL#	Denom.	Fine	VF	XF
EPS41	1¢	150.	225.	300.
EPS42	3¢	300.	450.	650.
EPS43	10¢	200.	375.	600.

Joseph L. Bates Fancy Goods Two Words

KL#	Denom.	Fine	VF	XF
EPS37	1¢	150.	225.	300.
EPS38	3¢	350.	675.	850.
EPS39	10¢	200.	375.	600.
EPS40	12¢	300.	550.	1000.

Brown's Bronchial Troches

KL#	Denom.	Fine	VF	XF
EPS44	1¢	225.	375.	550.
EPS45	3¢	175.	300.	400.
EPS46	5¢	175.	300.	400.
EPS47	10¢	250.	375.	500.
EPS48	12¢	600.	1000.	1400.

F. Buhl & Co., Detroit

KL#	Denom.	Fine	VF	XF
EPS49	1¢	400.	650.	1100.
EPS50	3¢	400.	700.	1250.
EPS51	5¢	400.	650.	1100.
EPS52	10¢	750.	1000.	2000.
EPS53	12¢	750.	1500.	2000.

Burnett's Cocoaine Kalliston

KL#	Denom.	Fine	VF	XF
EPS54	1¢	150.	250.	375.
EPS55	3¢	125.	175.	275.
EPS56	5¢	150.	300.	425.
EPS57	10¢	200.	550.	800.
EPS58	12¢	300.	550.	1000.
EPS59	24¢	1500.	2000.	3000.
EPS60	30¢	1750.	3000.	4000.
EPS61	90¢	2500.	5000.	9000.

Burnett's Cooking Extracts
(Plain frame)

KL#	Denom.	Fine	VF	XF
EPS62	1¢	150.	250.	375.
EPS63	3¢	150.	275.	425.
EPS64	5¢	150.	250.	375.
EPS65	10¢	200.	375.	550.
EPS66	12¢	300.	550.	1000.
EPS67	24¢	1500.	2000.	3000.
EPS68	30¢	1750.	3000.	4000.
EPS69	90¢	2500.	5000.	9000.

(Ribbed frame)

KL#	Denom.	Fine	VF	XF
EPS70	10¢	350.	650.	800.

A.M. Claflin, Hopkinton, R.I.

KL#	Denom.	Fine	VF	XF
EPS71	1¢	3000.	6250.	12,750.
EPS72	3¢	3000.	4000.	6000.
EPS73	5¢	3000.	4000.	6000.
EPS74	12¢	3000.	5000.	7500.

H.A. Cook, Evansville, Ind.

KL#	Denom.	Fine	VF	XF
EPS75	5¢	350.	650.	1300.
EPS76	10¢	600.	1200.	2500.

Dougan, New York

KL#	Denom.	Fine	VF	XF
EPS77	1¢	800.	1500.	2500.
EPS78	3¢	800.	1500.	2500.
EPS79	5¢	600.	1000.	2000.
EPS80	10¢	1000.	2000.	3000.

Drake's Plantation Bitters, New York

KL#	Denom.	Fine	VF	XF
EPS81	1¢	175.	225.	300.
EPS82	3¢	125.	275.	400.
EPS83	5¢	200.	300.	400.
EPS84	10¢	225.	375.	550.
EPS85	12¢	300.	550.	1000.
EPS86	24¢	1500.	2500.	3000.
EPS87	30¢	2000.	3000.	4000.
EPS88	90¢	2750.	5500.	9000.

Ellis, McAlpin & Co., Cincinnati

KL#	Denom.	Fine	VF	XF
EPS89	1¢	600.	1250.	1850.

EPS90	3¢	600.	1250.	1750.
EPS91	5¢	800.	1650.	2300.
EPS92	10¢	600	1250.	1750.
EPS93	12¢	800.	1500.	2250.
EPS94	24¢	1200.	2000.	3000

G.G. Evans, Philadelphia

KL#	Denom.	Fine	VF	XF
EPS95	1¢	300.	600.	900.
EPS96	3¢	400.	700.	1000.
EPS97	5¢	450.	750.	1250.
EPS98	10¢	450.	750.	1250.

J. Gault
(Plain frame)

KL#	Denom.	Fine	VF	XF
EPS99	1¢	150.	225.	300.
EPS100	2¢	—	12,000.	—
	(Three known)			
EPS101	3¢	150.	250.	350.
EPS102	5¢	150.	250.	375.
EPS103	10¢	200.	300.	500.
EPS104	12¢	300.	550.	1000.
EPS105	24¢	1250.	2000.	3000.
EPS106	30¢	1500.	3000.	4000.
EPS107	90¢	2500.	5000.	9000.

(Ribbed frame)

KL#	Denom.	Fine	VF	XF
EPS108	1¢	400.	700.	1000
EPS109	3¢	400.	700.	1000
EPS110	5¢	275.	1450.	600.
EPS111	10¢	300.	550.	700.
EPS112	12¢	500.	800.	1500.
EPS113	24¢	1500.	2750.	3500.
EPS114	30¢	1750.	3000.	4000.

L.C. Hopkins & Co., Cincinnati

KL#	Denom.	Fine	VF	XF
EPS115	1¢	700.	1250.	1750.
EPS116	3¢	600.	1150.	1500.
EPS117	5¢	800.	1500.	2250.
EPS118	10¢	700.	1250.	1750.

Irving House, N.Y. (Hunt & Nash)
(Plain frame)

KL#	Denom.	Fine	VF	XF
EPS119	1¢	150.	250.	350.
EPS120	3¢	150.	250.	350.
EPS121	5¢	400.	700.	1000.
EPS122	10¢	200.	300.	450
EPS123	12¢	300.	550.	1000.
EPS124	24¢	1250.	2000.	3000.
EPS125	30¢	1500.	3000.	4000.

(Ribbed frame)

KL#	Denom.	Fine	VF	XF
EPS126	1¢	400.	700.	1000.
EPS127	3¢	400.	700.	1000
EPS128	5¢	450.	750.	1500.
EPS129	10¢	350.	550.	750.
EPS130	12¢	500.	800.	1500.
EPS131	24¢	1500.	2750.	3500.

Kirkpatrick & Gault, New York

KL#	Denom.	Fine	VF	XF
EPS132	1¢	150.	225.	300.
EPS133	3¢	125.	200.	275.
EPS134	5¢	175.	350.	500.
EPS135	10¢	200.	300.	500.
EPS136	12¢	300.	550.	1000.
EPS137	24¢	1250.	2000.	3000.
EPS138	30¢	1500.	3000.	4000.
EPS139	90¢	2500.	5000.	9000.

Lord & Taylor, New York

KL#	Denom.	Fine	VF	XF
EPS140	1¢	400.	650.	1250.
EPS141	3¢	400.	650.	1250.
EPS142	5¢	400.	650.	1250.
EPS143	10¢	400.	700.	1500.
EPS144	12¢	800.	1500.	2000.
EPS145	24¢	1500.	2500.	3500.
EPS146	30¢	2000.	4000.	5000.
EPS147	90¢	4000.	7500.	9000.

Medum's Family Wine Emporium, New York
(Plain frame)

KL#	Denom.	Fine	VF	XF
EPS148	1¢	250.	350.	500.
EPS149	3¢	350.	500.	800.
EPS150	5¢	300.	450.	600.
EPS151	10¢	300.	450.	700.
EPS152	12¢	650.	1250.	1750.

(Ribbed frame)

KL#	Denom.	Fine	VF	XF
EPS153	10¢	400.	700.	1000.

B.F. Miles, Peoria

KL#	Denom.	Fine	VF	XF
EPS154	5¢	3500.	7000.	9000.

John W. Norris, Chicago

KL#	Denom.	Fine	VF	XF
EPS155	1¢	750.	1000.	1700.
EPS156	3¢	1000.	1750.	3000.
EPS157	5¢	1000.	1750.	3000.
EPS158	10¢	1000.	1750.	3000.

North America Life Insurance Co., New York
(Straight "Insurance")

KL#	Denom.	Fine	VF	XF
EPS159	1¢	175.	250.	350.
EPS160	3¢	175.	250.	350.
EPS161	10¢	200.	375.	600.
EPS162	12¢	450.	1000.	1500.

(Curved "Insurance") (Trial Piece)

KL#	Denom.	Fine	VF	XF
EPS163	1¢	225.	500.	1000.
EPS164	10¢	300.	500.	750.

Pearce, Tolle & Holton, Cincinnati

KL#	Denom.	Fine	VF	XF
EPS165	1¢	1000.	1750.	3000.
EPS166	3¢	800.	1500.	2500.
EPS167	5¢	1000.	1750.	3000.
EPS168	10¢	1100.	2000.	3500.

Sands' Ale

KL#	Denom.	Fine	VF	XF
EPS169	5¢	800.	1500.	2500.
EPS170	10¢	1000.	1750.	2750.
EPS171	30¢	2000.	3500.	5000.

Schapker & Bussing, Evansville, Ind.

KL#	Denom.	Fine	VF	XF
EPS172	1¢	400.	700.	1000.
EPS173	3¢	225.	350.	600.
EPS174	5¢	450.	750.	1250.
EPS175	10¢	450.	800.	1250.
EPS176	12¢	500.	1250.	1750.

John Shillisto & Co., Cincinnati

KL#	Denom.	Fine	VF	XF
EPS177	1¢	400.	700.	1000.
EPS178	3¢	250.	350.	600.
EPS179	5¢	250.	450.	900.
EPS180	10¢	275.	425.	750.
EPS181	12¢	500.	1250.	1750.

S. Steinfeld, New York

KL#	Denom.	Fine	VF	XF
EPS182	1¢	1000.	1700.	2500.
EPS183	10¢	1000.	1600.	2500.
EPS184	12¢	1000.	1750.	2750.

N.G. Taylor & Co., Philadelphia

KL#	Denom.	Fine	VF	XF
EPS185	1¢	800.	1250.	1900.

EPS186	3¢	800.	1250.	1750.
EPS187	5¢	800.	1500.	2000.
EPS188	10¢	800.	1250.	1750.

Tremont House (Gage Brothers & Drake), Chicago

KL#	Denom.	Fine	VF	XF
EPS189	1¢	150.	225.	300.
EPS190	5¢	150.	300.	375.
EPS191	10¢	200.	325.	450.
EPS192	12¢	350.	600.	1250.

Weir & Larminie, Montreal

KL#	Denom.	Fine	VF	XF
EPS193	1¢	450.	750.	1250.
EPS194	3¢	400.	700.	1000.
EPS195	5¢	500.	800.	1500.
EPS196	10¢	600.	900.	1700.

White the Hatter, New York

KL#	Denom.	Fine	VF	XF
EPS197	1¢	750.	1000.	1900.
EPS198	3¢	800.	1500.	2500.
EPS199	5¢	900.	1750.	3000.
EPS200	10¢	800.	1500.	2500.

Postage Currency

All methods of using stamps for money that had been employed prior to July 17, 1862, suffered the ultimate disadvantage of being illegal, with the consequence that the holder of the stamps could neither redeem them at the post office nor exchange them for Treasury notes.

On that date, however, President Lincoln signed into law a measure proposed in self-defense by Treasury Secretary Salmon P. Chase, providing that "postage and other stamps of the United States" were to be receivable for all dues to the U.S. and were to be redeemable at any "designated depository" in sums less than $5. The law also prohibited the issue by "any private corporation, banking association, firm, or individual" of any note or token for a sum less than $5 — a provision that was widely ignored as the private sector continued its efforts to overcome a coin shortage in the face of which the government seemed helpless.

The new law was not without its problems of practicality, either. The post office, already facing a stamp shortage before the gummed bits of paper had been declared legal tender, faced the almost impossible task of providing sufficient stamps for postal use as well as "coinage" use.

There was also the problem of which office would redeem nearly exhausted specimens of stamps that had been circulating for some time. Blair refused to take them in trade for new stamps, and Chase would not exchange them for paper money because the Treasury hadn't issued them in the first place.

Blair's obstinacy ultimately melted before the heat of public pressure, and he agreed to redeem the masses of soiled and stuck-together stamps, but he continued to insist that the actual intent of the poorly written law had been for the Treasury Department to print and distribute special stamps that would bear a general resemblance to postage stamps but would be of a different design. A compromise was finally worked out whereby the Treasury Department would sell and redeem specially marked stamps that the post office would also accept for postage. Blair agreed to print the special stamps for the Treasury.

Before the stamps could be printed, a further decision was made to issue them in a larger, more convenient size, and to print them on a heavier, ungummed paper. Credit for the final form in which Postage Currency appeared is given to Gen. F.E. Spinner, treasurer of the United States. Spinner pasted unused postage stamps on small sheets of Treasury security paper of uniform size, signed his name to some of them and passed them out to his friends as samples of currency. Congress responded to Spinner's suggestion by authorizing the printing of reproductions of postage stamps on Treasury paper in arrangements patterned after Spinner's models. In this form, the "stamps" ceased to be stamps; they became, in effect, fractional government promissory notes, a development not authorized by the initial enabling legislation of July 17, 1862. Nonetheless, the notes would be issued without legal authorization until passage of the Act of March 3, 1863, which provided for the issuing of fractional notes by the federal government.

Five issues of Postage and Fractional Currency in the total amount of $369 million were printed and released to circulation between Aug. 21, 1862, and Feb. 15, 1876. Then a flood of silver from the Comstock Lode drove down silver bullion prices, reducing the intrinsic value of silver coins to a point below face value, thereby insuring that they would remain in circulation. The silver price drop further augmented the supply of circulating silver by triggering a flow back to the United States — where they could be exchanged for their greater face value — of the hundreds of millions of silver coins that had been exported since 1862.

Congressional Acts of Jan. 14, 1875, and April 17, 1876, provided for the redemption of Postage and Fractional Currency in silver coins, and all but about $1.8 million worth was returned to the Treasury for redemption. The outstanding notes remain legal tender and can purchase their face value equivalent in goods and services today.

First Issue "Postage Currency"

August 21, 1862 - May 27, 1863

Denominations: 5¢, 10¢, 25¢, 50¢

The First Issue of U.S. government stamp money is the only one of the five issues to be identified by name as Postage Currency. The initial printing of the First Issue was released through Army paymasters on Aug. 1, 1862, and was provided for general circulation a few weeks later.

Although it is a moot point, Postage Currency probably constitutes an illegal issue of fractional notes. Rather than being strictly "postage and other stamps of the United States," and despite being "receivable for postage stamps at any U.S. post office," Postage Currency took the form of reproductions of postage stamps printed on paper that carried the promise of the United States to exchange the currency for United States Notes, which gave Postage Currency the attributes of a promissory note, a development beyond the intent of the enabling Act of July 17, 1862.

The stamps reproduced on Postage Currency are the brown or buff 5¢ stamp of the Series of 1861, bearing the portrait of Thomas Jefferson, and the green 10c stamp of the same series, with George Washington's portrait. The 25¢ and 50¢ denominations bear multiple reproductions of the appropriate stamp. Various colors of paper were used in printing the four notes of the First Issue, but the color does not influence the collector value of the individual note. Faces of the notes are printed in a color approximating the color of the genuine postage stamp, backs are all printed in black.

An interesting feature of the First Issue is the existence of notes with both perforated and straight edges. Apparently, the idea of perforated Postage Currency was a carry-over from the postage stamp printing process and was discarded when the demand for Postage Currency exceeded the capacity of the perforating machines.

Inasmuch as the Bureau of Engraving and Printing had not yet been established, contracts for printing of the First Issue were awarded to private bank note printing companies. The National Bank Note Co. printed the face, and the American Bank Note Co. printed the back. The ABNC monogram appears on the backs of some notes.

Total value of Postage Currency issued was more than $20 million.

5 CENTS

KL#	Fr#	Date	Description	VG	VF	Unc
3209	1228	17.7.1862.	Brown. One 5 cent Jefferson stamp at center. Perf. edges; ANBC's monogram on back.	14.00	16.00	155.
3210	1229		Perf. edges; back w/o ANBC's monogram.	15.00	22.00	180.
3211	1230		Straight edges; ANBC's monogram on back.	14.50	16.00	50.00
3212	1231		Straight edges; back w/o ANBC's monogram.	15.00	21.00	150.

10 CENTS

KL#	Fr#	Date	Description	VG	VF	Unc
3213	1240	17.7.1862.	Green. One 10 cent Washington stamp at center. Perf. edges; ANBC's monogram on back.	15.00	18.50	115.
3214	1241		Perf. edges; back w/o ABNC's monogram	15.50	30.00	130.
3215	1242		Straight edges; ABNC's monogram on back.	11.50	13.00	40.00
3216	1243		Straight edges; back w/o ABNC's monogram	12.50	40.00	150.

25 CENTS

KL#	Fr#	Date	Description	VG	VF	Unc
3217	1279	17.71862.	Brown. Horizontal row of five 5 cent Jefferson stamps. Perf. edges; ABNC's monogram on back.	16.00	25.00	170.

3218	1280	Perf. edges; back w/o ABNC's monogram	25.00	60.00	275.
3219	1281	Straight edges; ABNC's monogram on back.	11.50	15.00	75.00
3220	1282	Straight edged; back w/o ABNC's monogram.	13.00	60.00	300.

50 CENTS

KL#	Fr#	Date	Description	VG	VF	Unc
3221	1310	17.7.1862.	Green. Horizontal row of five 10 cent Washington stamps. #12 perf. edges; ABNC's monogram on back.	24.00	30.00	290.00
3222	1310-A		#14 perf. edges; ABNC's monogram on back	—	Rare	—
3223	1311		Perf. edges; back w/o ABNC's monogram.	30.00	70.00	300.
3224	1312		Straight edges: ABNC's monogram on back.	17.00	18.50	120.00
3225	1313		Straight edges; back w/o ABNC's monogram.	20.00	75.00	300.

Postage and Fractional Currency Shield

The Postage and Fractional Currency Shield was one of the measures by which the Treasury Department sought to overcome and prevent the widespread counterfeiting of Fractional Currency notes.

The shields consisted of a type set of the first three issues of Postage and Fractional Currency mounted on a heavy cardboard shield surmounted by an eagle and 13 stars. Size of the framed unit was 24 by 28 inches. The shields were made available to banks and other commercial institutions in 1866-67 to provide them with a file of genuine notes to use as a reference when checking suspect notes. Those qualified to receive the shield paid face value for the notes ($4.66), plus a presumed transportation charge, for a total cost believed to be $7.50.

The 39 closely trimmed notes (20 faces and 19 backs) mounted on the shield are specimen notes printed on one side only. They include the scarce 15¢ Sherman/Grant essays and the two faces of the 3¢ note, which are distinguished by dark and light backgrounds to Washington's portrait. The shields upon which the notes were pasted are known in gray, pink and green, with gray being the most common.

Although the shields were produced in a quantity believed to be in excess of 4,500, it is presumed that fewer than 200 remain intact, with many of those folded, faded or water-stained. Apparently demand for the shields was less than the Treasury Department had anticipated, and the surplus shields were carelessly stored -- by common account in an old shed behind the Treasury Building. The number of intact shields was further reduced by early collectors who obtained them solely to secure the scarcer notes, which they removed from the shield.

SUBJECT INDEX

C

O

P

U

V

W